TWENTIETH-CEN
BRITISH POLITICAI
1900–2000

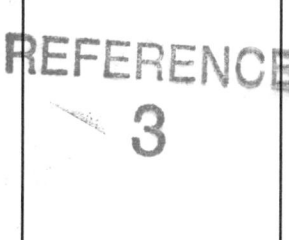
This book is due for return not later than the
last date stamped below, unless recalled sooner.

Also by David Butler

THE BRITISH GENERAL ELECTION OF 1951
THE ELECTORAL SYSTEM IN BRITAIN 1918–1951
THE BRITISH GENERAL ELECTION OF 1955
THE STUDY OF POLITICAL BEHAVIOUR
ELECTIONS ABROAD (*editor*)
THE BRITISH GENERAL ELECTION OF 1959 (*with Richard Rose*)
THE BRITISH GENERAL ELECTION OF 1964 (*with Anthony King*)
THE BRITISH GENERAL ELECTION OF 1966 (*with Anthony King*)
POLITICAL CHANGE IN BRITAIN (*with Donald Stokes*)
THE BRITISH GENERAL ELECTION OF 1970 (*with Michael Pinto-Duschinsky*)
THE CANBERRA MODEL
THE BRITISH GENERAL ELECTION OF FEBRUARY 1974 (*with Dennis Kavanagh*)
THE BRITISH GENERAL ELECTION OF OCTOBER 1974 (*with Dennis Kavanagh*)
THE 1975 REFERENDUM (*with Uwe Kitzinger*)
COALITIONS IN BRITISH POLITICS (*editor*)
POLICY AND POLITICS (*with A. H. Halsey*)
THE BRITISH GENERAL ELECTION OF 1979 (*with Dennis Kavanagh*)
REFERENDUMS (*with A. Ranney*)
EUROPEAN ELECTIONS AND BRITISH POLITICS (*with David Marquand*)
DEMOCRACY AT THE POLLS (*with H. Penniman and A. Ranney*)
THE BRITISH GENERAL ELECTION OF 1983 (*with Dennis Kavanagh*)
DEMOCRACY AND ELECTIONS (*with V. Bognador*)
PARTY STRATEGIES IN BRITAIN (*with Paul Jowett*)
GOVERNING WITHOUT A MAJORITY
INDIA DECIDES (*with Ashok Lahiri and Prannoy Roy*)
THE BRITISH GENERAL ELECTION OF 1987 (*with Dennis Kavanagh*)
THE BRITISH GENERAL ELECTION OF 1992 (*with Dennis Kavanagh*)
ELECTIONEERING (*with A. Ranney*)
FAILURE IN BRITISH GOVERNMENT (*with A. Adonis and T. Travers*)
BRITISH ELECTIONS SINCE 1945
CONGRESSIONAL REDISTRICTING (*with B. Cain*)
THE BRITISH GENERAL ELECTION OF 1997 (*with Dennis Kavanagh*)
BRITISH POLITICS AND EUROPEAN ELECTIONS 1999 (*with Martin Westlake*)

TWENTIETH-CENTURY BRITISH POLITICAL FACTS 1900–2000

BY

DAVID BUTLER

AND

GARETH BUTLER

EIGHTH EDITION

Published in Great Britain 2000

First edition 1963   Fifth edition 1980
Reprinted with corrections 1964   Sixth edition 1986
Second edition 1968   Reprinted 1987
Third edition 1969   Seventh edition 1994
Fourth edition 1975   Eighth edition 2000

MACMILLAN PRESS LTD
Houndmills, Basingstoke, Hampshire RG21 6XS
and London
Companies and representatives throughout the world

A catalogue record for this book is available from the British Library

ISBN: 0–333–77221–0 hardcover
       0–333–77222–9 paperback

First published in the United States of America 2000 by

ST. MARTINS PRESS, INC.,
Scholarly and Reference Division,
175 Fifth Avenue,
New York, N.Y. 10010

ISBN: 0–312–22947–X

Library of Congress Cataloging-in-Publication Data

Butler, David, 1924–
     Twentieth-century British political facts, 1900–2000 / by David Butler and Gareth
Butler.— 8th ed.
       p. cm.
     Rev. ed. of: British political facts, 1900–1994. 7th ed. 1994
     Includes bibliographical references and index.
     ISBN 0–312–22947–X (cloth)
       1. Great Britain—Politics and government—20th century—Handbooks, manuals, etc. 2.
Great Britain—Economic conditions—20th century—Handbooks, manuals, etc. 3. Great
Britain—Social conditions—20th century—Handbooks, manuals, etc. I. Butler, Gareth. II.
Butler, David, 1924– British political facts, 1900–1994. III. Title.

JN231 .B8 2000
941.082—dc21   00–020047

Printed and bound in Great Britain by Antony Rowe Ltd, Chippenham

CONTENTS

IV. ELECTIONS

V. POLITICAL ALLUSIONS

XI. THE ECONOMY

XII. THE PUBLIC SECTOR

XIII. ROYALTY

XIV. BRITISH ISLES

INTRODUCTION TO THE EIGHTH EDITION

THE table of contents offers the simplest justification for this book – but inevitably it is a book that must justify itself in different ways to different readers. The scholar, the journalist, the politician and the everyday pedant were each in the authors' minds at some point during its compilation. Some of those who look at this book will, we hope, be delighted to find in compact and reliable form data that might still have eluded them after searching through a dozen standard works of reference; others will at least discover from our pages where the information they seek may be found; a few, we fear, will be infuriated by our omissions and, despite all our efforts at checking, by our errors.

The idea of writing this book grew gradually in the mind of one of its authors as, in the course of his years as a student and a teacher at Nuffield College (which is devoted to research in contemporary subjects), he noticed the amount of time that he and others wasted in searching for seemingly obvious facts about twentieth-century Britain. If, therefore, any reader has been especially in our minds, he is the graduate student writing a thesis on any domestic theme in the last century. We hope he will find here not only an expeditious way of checking basic facts but also, if he finds time to browse through our lists and tables, a stimulating reminder of people and considerations that must have played a part, perhaps only as background in the situations he is analysing.

But we are not concerned solely with academic needs. Experience of checking facts in newspaper offices and broadcasting studios, and the anecdotes of friends in Whitehall and Westminster, have made plain to us how much elementary political data is annoyingly elusive. Many admirable works of reference exist but the right one is not always to hand; most of them, moreover, are compiled on an annual basis – which can be very frustrating for those who are trying to trace an office or a statistic over a number of years.

The compiler of any work of reference is limited by space and time. How much data shall be included? How far shall other works be duplicated? How many hours is it worth devoting to any particular entry? In this book we have had to exclude interesting information either because it would fill a disproportionate number of pages or because it could not be obtained without more labour than we thought justified. We have consoled ourselves for setting out data in abbreviated form by giving references to more exhaustive sources.

Indeed, since the compilation of reference books is, even more than other research, systematised plagiarism, perhaps the most valuable part of these pages lies in these citations. We have not attempted an exhaustive bibliography – except for a compilation of bibliographies and general reference books – but we have throughout tried to list all major authorities.

The title, *British Political Facts 1900–2000,* provides a reasonably close delimitation of the scope of this book. *British* indicates that we have been concerned with the domestic history of the United Kingdom. But it is not possible to set precise boundaries to the term 'domestic' and we have perhaps strayed beyond them by listing Colonies, Governors-General, and some Ambassadors, as well as including a chapter on Britain's relations with Europe.

Political is potentially ambiguous, but we have used it to stress that our interest is in the power of the state. We have tried to list the principal people who were involved in the government of Britain at any moment in this century; we have recorded election results – as providing the basis for political authority – and major legislation – as representing its use; we have assembled, in summary form, statistical data which show some of the social and economic background to all political action.

Facts indicates that we have tried to eschew political judgements as far as possible. Some value judgements may be implicit in our selection of material, but we believe that virtually everything here would be acceptable as non-controversial evidence in debates over the nature of twentieth-century British history. It is a waste of time to argue about verifiable questions of fact. But it is also a waste of time to assemble facts except as a basis for argument. Because in this book we have stuck rigidly to facts, it does not mean that we overrate them. Analysis of our past and present situation is far more important than mere fact-gathering. Unlike Martha we are fully aware which is the better part

1900–2000 is a somewhat arbitrary period – but any historical period must be arbitrary. However, our terminal date in this edition has the finality of the millennium. Our opening date was a numerological accident – but it would be hard to find a better watershed without going back at least to 1885, which because of space, and still more because of the availability of the data, was impracticable. We have endeavoured to treat every one of our hundred years equally, providing as full and exact data about 1901 as about 1995. With some statistics this has proved impossible and some time-series are regrettably discontinuous. But in general it will be found that we have resisted the temptation to make a special favourite of the more recent past; it is not our fault that there was no Gallup polling before 1938 and that local election results cannot usefully be pursued very far back.

In compiling this book we have become very conscious of the strengths and weaknesses of other reference books – and particularly of the importance of pedantic accuracy and clear presentation. We have certainly not avoided all the pitfalls into which we have observed others falling; therefore, by way both of excuse and of warning, it may be worth describing a few of the difficulties we have faced. The general problems of finding exact data on British politics were best exemplified in the gathering of complete lists of ministries over the last century – the most time-consuming of all our operations. There are a number of publications which purport to list all ministerial appointments – the most useful of these are the two Parliamentary handbooks, *Dod* and *Vacher*. There is also the Stationery Office publication *H.M. Ministers and Heads of Public Departments* which used to appear four to five times a year. Lists of ministers are also printed in *Hansard* once a fortnight during sessions. But all these sources have the same disadvantage – no indication is given of the date when a minister was appointed or left office. A man may indeed be appointed and leave office between the publication of these lists, so that there is no record whatever of his elevation. Since 1931 *Keesing's Contemporary Archives* and, from 1988 to 1997, *Keesing's UK Record*, have recorded most government appointments – but they depend on newspaper sources and are not altogether infallible. The Indexes to *The Times* are the best means of checking on ministerial changes, though here too there are problems. *Palmer's Index to The Times* which was not superseded by the *Official Index* until 1906 is far from satisfactory; under the heading 'Official Appointments' is the depressing injunction 'See every issue'. From 1906 the *Official Index* is much more thorough, although misprints and references to different editions of the paper do occur. Even *The Times*, moreover, has occasionally missed a minor government change. An additional complication lies in the range of possible days which might be considered the date of appointment: there is the announcement from Downing Street, the press report the following day, the official gazetting a week or more later, the exchange of seals and the kissing of hands. None of these may represent the precise date on which the new minister took over his duties, but, wherever possible, we have used the earliest and most public announcement. Until 1960 this was usually the date of *The Times* report, but more recently most resignations or reshuffles have been widely publicised by the broadcast media on the day they actually take place, and this is the date we have used. Peerages sometimes cause further confusion, since weeks usually elapse before a newly elevated minister's title is announced. Care has also to be taken when a familiar minister disappears behind a new name – the fact that Mr Ivor Guest, Lord Ashby St Ledgers, and Viscount Wimborne were one and the same person is not immediately apparent. Another snag arises, particularly in wartime and since the late 1960s, when the titles and functions of departments changed kaleidoscopically.

In many other fields the sources of confusion were almost equally numerous. The search for reliable and consistent evidence about newspaper circulations, religious affiliations and trade disputes caused us particular trouble. But it would be tedious to quote all the gaps in existing works of reference which we have – with very varying success – tried to fill. We must, however, mention the complications which arise from the structure of the United Kingdom. The changes in Ireland in 1922 inevitably cause a break in all national statistical time-series and since then many tables have, perforce, to exclude Northern Ireland as well as Eire; but the administrative separation of Scotland causes almost as many difficulties. Statistics are compiled independently north and south of the Border, quite often on different bases. Sometimes this arises from the different legal or administrative systems – as with education; but in the case of population and vital statistics the Registrars-General seem unnecessarily perverse in presenting their census findings in differing forms. A new contributor to this edition is the Internet, which now provides much up-to-date material on web-sites recorded in our Bibliographical Note.

This book was first compiled at the beginning of the 1960s. It has been checked, updated and modified through successive editions in response to the reactions of its readers. It is the people who have used the book most – academics, civil servants, librarians, journalists, party officials and officers of the Houses of Parliament – who have been its keenest and most constructive critics.

The preparation and revision of this book has indeed depended on a vast amount of help from many quarters, ranging from scholars and friends who have spent many hours assisting us to check on obscure details, to unidentified voices at the end of official telephones. We must thank above all, Jenny Freeman, who in 1961 bore so much of the brunt of preparing the first edition, and Anne Sloman who co-authored the fourth and fifth editions, introducing valuable new features. After them come the Warden, Fellows and Students of Nuffield College, who have made so many contributions over the years. But we owe a deep debt of gratitude to officials in Parliament, in party headquarters, in government departments and newspaper offices, to many colleagues in the academic world and in the B.B.C., especially to those in news information and the reference library, to complete strangers who have sent us corrections and suggestions, and to our publisher. We must also acknowledge what we owe to anonymous compilers of the many works of reference from which we have so freely drawn. We give here an incomplete list of those who have supplied information or emendations in the preparation of one or more of the successive editions of this book and, although many have given unstinted help, we must draw special attention to the encyclopaedic precision of Mr S. M. Lees and Mr P. C. Thompson who have saved us from so many errors.

P. Addison	Sir F. Berman	R. Butt
K. Alderman	H.B. Berrington	P. Campbell
R. F. Allen	N. Birnbaum	T.J.M. Cartwright
L. Anderson	N. Blewett	A.N. Cass
J.M. Austen	G.D.M. Block	J. Chesshire
G.S. Bain	V. Bogdanor	Sir N. Chester
Priscilla Baines	J. M. Bouen	D.M. Clark
C. Ballinger	D. Brack	H.A. Clegg
F. M. Barlow	K. Britto	R. Clements
C. J. Bartlett	P. Brierley	P.C. Collison
L. Baston	M. G. Brock	Sara Conwill
E. Batstone	P.A. Bromhead	D. Cowling
F. Beamish	B. Bush	F.W.S. Craig
Lord. Beloff	E. Butler	M. Crick
M. Berlins	Lord Butler	B. Criddle

J.A. Cross
D.F. Crossley
S. Cursley
J. K. Curtice
P. Davies
P. Dawson
N. Deakin
A. Devermond
C. Dobson
Margaret Douglas
Monica Dowley
G. Drewry
C. Driver
B. Dye
Dorothy Edmunds
N.D. Ellis
Sir T. Evans
H.R.M. Farmer
Sir E. Fellowes
A. Flanders
A. Fox
Lord Fraser of Kilmorack
Oonagh Gay
Yash Ghai
Sir M. Gilbert
S. Gordon
B. Gosschalk
A.H. Halsey
T. Harris
B.H. Harrison
M. Harrison
A.J. Hastings
S.C. Hawtrey
C.G. Hazlehurst
D. Heald
J. Hemingway
A. Hetherington
A E. Holmans
C.C. Hood
A. Hunt
Helen Irwin
R.J. Jackson
D. Jeffcock
Jenny Jeger
Lord Jenkins

Chandrike Kaul
A.L. Keillor
B. Keith-Lucas
Christine Kennedy
A.S. King
U.W. Kitzinger
A. L. Lamaison
F. Lawson
S. M. Lees
J. Legg
T.O. Lloyd
A.B. Lyons
Lord MacCarthy
J.C. McCrudden
B. MacDonald
K. MacDonald
Sir D. MacDougall
A. MacIntyre
R. McKibbin
D. McKie
A.F. Madden
G. Marshall
J. Maule
Elizabeth Meehan
J.S. Milner
B.R. Mitchell
Janet Morgan
J. Morland Craig
J. Muellbauer
D.L. Munby
R. Neuss
H.G. Nicholas
P. Norton
C. O'Leary
R. O'Leary
P. Oppenheimer
J. Palmer
Lord Pannell
J. Paxton
H. Pelling
Dame M. Perham
M. Pinto-Duschinsky
A.M. Potter
D. Prysor-Jones
G. Pyatt

C. Rallings
C. Raphael
R.A. Rempel
N. Rees
Anne Rhodes
Catherine Rimmer
P.G. Richards
Mrs P. Ryan
M. Ryle
J.C. Sainty
I. St John
S. Sargent
Kerry Schott
Olivia Seligman
C. Seymour-Ure
D.M. Shapiro
L.J. Sharpe
Audrey Skeats
Lord Skidelsky
M.G.M. Sloman
M. Steed
D. Stephen
S. Symes
Anne Taylor
A.J.P. Taylor
A. Teasdale
M. Thrasher
T. Travers
Mrs R. Wagner
R. Watford
N.D. Walker
W. Wallace
A.H. Warren
Nita Watts
P. Way
Jo Webb
Louise Welby Everard
Jane Wigan
D. Wilkinson
P.M. Williams
Barbara Williamson
T. Wilson
B. Winetrobe
R. Worcester
R. Wybrow

While we could not have completed this book without these far-flung helpers (not to mention the indefatigable assistance of our secretaries) we should stress our sole responsibility for its inevitable errors. Our readers are earnestly invited to let us know of any that they may detect.

MINISTRIES

The following list contains the names of all those who have held paid and political ministerial office since 1900. It leaves out some office-holders, since from time to time various offices in the Royal Household have ceased to be political appointments. The list also omits some politicians with government posts, since various other offices, such as the Second Church Estates Commissioner, are not regarded as part of the Ministry. Assistant Government Whips were unpaid until 1964 and are not listed before that date but see J. Sainty, 'Assistant Whips 1922–64' *Parliamentary History*, pp. 201–4, 1985, for a listing of unpaid Whips. Parliamentary Private Secretaries are also unlisted.

The problems of compiling this list are discussed in the introduction. As far as possible the date cited is the one on which the announcement of the appointment appeared in *The Times*, except where it is plain that the news received wide publicity the previous day. Where more than one person holds the same title the starting and finishing dates are given. In almost all other cases it may be assumed that the starting date of the new appointment represents the vacating of the office.

Ministers in the Cabinet are printed in **BOLD TYPE CAPITALS** throughout this section. Ministers outside the Cabinet and Ministers of State are printed in CAPITALS. Junior ministers are in ordinary print. The seven leading offices are placed first in each Ministry; the remainder are arranged alphabetically, except for the Law Officers and the political appointments to the Royal Household which are placed at the end together with the Treasury appointments reserved for whips.

In these lists – and throughout the book – titles are placed in brackets if acquired during the tenure of office or on transfer to the next office. U-S. denotes Under-Secretary; F.S. Financial Secretary; P.S. Parliamentary Secretary.

This section has been sub-divided chronologically at changes of Prime Minister, except when few other offices changed hands as in 1902, 1923, 1937, 1955, 1963 and 1976; further divisions are made for the drastic reconstructions of 1915, 1931 and May 1945.

CONSERVATIVE GOVERNMENT 1900–1905

P.M.	**M of SALISBURY** (3rd)	1900–11 Jul 02	*Foreign O.*	**M of SALISBURY** *(3rd) (P.M.)*	1900	
	A. BALFOUR	12 Jul 02–4 Dec 05		**M of LANSDOWNE**	1 Nov 00	
1st Ld of	**A. BALFOUR**	1900	*U-S.*	St J. Brodrick	1900	
Treasury	*(office combined with P.M. when*			Vt Cranborne*	7 Nov 00	
	Balfour succeeded Salisbury)			*(4th M of Salisbury)*		
Ld Pres.	**D of DEVONSHIRE**	1900		Earl Percy*	9 Oct 03	
	M of LONDONDERRY	13 Oct 03	*Home O.*	**Sir M. WHITE-RIDLEY**	1900	
Ld Chanc.	**E of HALSBURY**	1900		**C. RITCHIE**	1 Nov 00	
Privy Seal	**Vt CROSS**	1900		**A. AKERS-DOUGLAS**	8 Aug 02	
	M of SALISBURY *(3rd) (P.M.)*		*U-S.*	J. Collings	1900	
		Nov 00		T. Cochrane	8 Aug 02	
	A. BALFOUR *(P.M.)*	12 Jul 02	*Admiralty*	**G. GOSCHEN**	1900	
	M of SALISBURY *(4th)*	11 Oct 03		**E of SELBORNE**	1 Nov 00	
Exchequer	**Sir M. HICKS-BEACH**	1900		**Earl CAWDOR**	5 Mar 05	
	C. RITCHIE	8 Aug 02	*P.& F.S.*	Sir W. Macartney	1900	
	A. CHAMBERLAIN	6 Oct 03		H. Arnold-Forster	7 Nov 00	
F.S.	R. Hanbury	1900		E. Pretyman	11 Oct 03	
	A. Chamberlain	7 Nov 00	*Civil Ld*	A. Chamberlain	1900	
	W. Hayes Fisher	8 Aug 02		E. Pretyman	7 Nov 00	
	A. Elliot	10 Apr 03		A. Lee	11 Oct 03	
	V. Cavendish	9 Oct 03	*B.Ag.&Fish.*	**W. LONG**	1900	

*MP. Not a member of the House of Lords.

1

CONSERVATIVE GOVERNMENT 1900–1905 (contd.)

Office	Name	Date
B.Ag.&Fish. (contd.)	R. HANBURY	14 Nov 00
	E of ONSLOW	19 May 03
	A. FELLOWES	12 Mar 05
Colonies	J. CHAMBERLAIN	1900
	A. LYTTELTON	11 Oct 03
U-S.	E of Selborne	1900
	E of Onslow	12 Nov 00
	D of Marlborough	23 Jul 03
B.Educ.	(office not established)	
	D of DEVONSHIRE	1 Apr 00
	M of LONDONDERRY	8 Aug 02
V.-Pres.of Com.of Council on Education	Sir J. Gorst	1900
	(office abolished 8 Aug 02)	
P.S.	Sir W. Anson	8 Aug 02
India	Ld G. HAMILTON*	1900
	St J. BRODRICK	6 Oct 03
U-S.	E of Onslow	1900
	E of Hardwicke	12 Nov 00
	Earl Percy*	8 Aug 02
	E of Hardwicke	15 Oct 03
	M of Bath	19 Jan 05
Ld Lieut. Ireland	Earl CADOGAN	1900
	(office not ministerial 8 Aug 02)	
Chief Sec. Ireland	G. BALFOUR	1900
	G. WYNDHAM	7 Nov 00
	(office in cabinet)	
	G. WYNDHAM	8 Aug 02
	W. LONG	12 Mar 05
V.-Pres. Dept. Agric. for Ireland	(Sir) H. Plunkett	1900
Ld Chanc. Ireland	Ld ASHBOURNE	1900
D.Lanc.	Ld JAMES of HEREFORD	1900
	(office not in cabinet)	
	Sir W. WALROND	8 Aug 02
Loc.Govt.B.	H. CHAPLIN	1900
	W. LONG	7 Nov 00
	G. BALFOUR	12 Mar 05
P.S.	T. Russell	1900
	(Sir) J. Lawson	11 Nov 00
	A. Jeffreys	27 Jun 05
Paym.-Gen.	D of MARLBOROUGH	1900
	SIR S. CROSSLEY	11 Mar 02
Postm.-Gen.		
	D of NORFOLK	1900
	M of LONDONDERRY	2 Apr 00
	(office in cabinet)	
	M of LONDONDERRY	7 Nov 00
	A. CHAMBERLAIN	8 Aug 02
	Ld STANLEY*	6 Oct 03
Scotland	Ld BALFOUR of BURLEIGH	1900
	A. MURRAY	6 Oct 03
	M of LINLITHGOW	2 Feb 05
B. Trade	C. RITCHIE	1900
	G. BALFOUR	7 Nov 00
	M of SALISBURY (4th)	12 Mar 05
P.S.	E of Dudley	1900
	A. Bonar Law	8 Aug 02
War	M of LANSDOWNE	1900
	St J. BRODRICK	1 Nov 00
	H. ARNOLD-FORSTER	6 Oct 03
F.S.	J. Powell Williams	1900
	Ld Stanley*	7 Nov 00
	W. Bromley-Davenport	11 Oct 03
U-S.	G. Wyndham	1900
	Ld Raglan	12 Nov 00
	E of Hardwicke	8 Aug 02
	E of Donoughmore	15 Oct 03
Works	A. AKERS-DOUGLAS	1900
	(office not in cabinet)	
	Ld WINDSOR	8 Aug 02

Law Officers

Att.-Gen.	Sir R. WEBSTER	1900
	Sir R. FINLAY	7 May 00
Sol.-Gen.	Sir R. FINLAY	1900
	Sir E. CARSON	7 May 00
Ld Advoc.	A. MURRAY	1900
	S. DICKSON	18 Oct 03
Sol.-Gen. Scotland	S. DICKSON	1900
	D. DUNDAS	18 Oct 03
	E. SALVESEN	30 Jan 05
	J. CLYDE	16 Oct 05
Att.-Gen. Ireland	J. ATKINSON	1900
	J. CAMPBELL	4 Dec 05
Sol.-Gen. Ireland	D. BARTON	1900
	G. WRIGHT	30 Jan 00
	J. CAMPBELL	8 Jul 03

Whips

P.S.to Treasury	Sir W. WALROND	1900
	Sir A. Acland Hood	8 Aug 02
Lds of Treasury	W. Hayes Fisher	1900–8 Aug 02
	H. Anstruther	1900–11 Oct 03
	Ld Stanley*	1900–7 Nov 00
	A. Fellowes	7 Nov 00–15 Mar 05
	H. Forster	8 Aug 02–4 Dec 05
	Ld Balcarres*	11 Oct 03–4 Dec 05
	G. Loder	29 Mar 05–8 Apr 05
	Ld E. Talbot*	16 Jun 05–4 Dec 05

H.M. Household

Treasurer	Vt CURZON* (Earl Howe)	1900
	V. CAVENDISH	3 Dec 00
	M of HAMILTON*	11 Oct 03
Compt.	Vt VALENTIA*	1900
V.Chamb.	A. FELLOWES	1900
	Sir A. ACLAND HOOD	3 Dec 00
	Ld WOLVERTON	17 Nov 02
Ld Chamb.	E of HOPETOUN	1900
	E of CLARENDON	12 Nov 00
Ld Steward	E of PEMBROKE	1900
Cap. Gents at Arms	Ld BELPER	1900
Cap. Yeo. of Guard	Earl WALDEGRAVE	1900
Master of Horse	D of PORTLAND	1900

*MP. Not a member of the House of Lords.

CONSERVATIVE GOVERNMENT 1900–1905 (*contd.*)

Master of	E of COVENTRY	1900		Ld Bagot	1900–2 Jul 01
Buckhounds	Ld CHESHAM	2 Nov 00		E of Kintore	1900–4 Dec 05
	(office abolished 1901)			E of Denbigh	1900–4 Dec 05
Lds in	E of Clarendon	1900–30 Oct 00		Earl Howe	30 Oct 00–1 Oct 03
Waiting	Ld Harris	1900–4 Dec 00		Ld Kenyon	4 Dec 00–4 Dec 05
	Ld Churchill *(Vt)*	1900–4 Dec 05		E of Erroll	19 Oct 03–4 Dec 05
	Ld Lawrence	1900–4 Dec 05			

LIBERAL GOVERNMENT 1905–1908

P.M.	**Sir H. CAMPBELL-BANNERMAN**	
		5 Dec 05–5 Apr 08
Ld Pres.	**E of CREWE**	10 Dec 05
Ld Chanc.	**Ld LOREBURN**	10 Dec 05
Privy S.	**M of RIPON**	10 Dec 05
Exchequer	**H. ASQUITH**	10 Dec 05
F.S.	R. McKenna	12 Dec 05
	W. Runciman	29 Jan 07
Foreign 0.	**Sir E. GREY**	10 Dec 05
U-S.	Ld E. Fitzmaurice* *(Ld)*	18 Dec 05
Home 0.	**H. GLADSTONE**	10 Dec 05
U-S.	H. Samuel	12 Dec 05
Admiralty	**Ld TWEEDMOUTH**	10 Dec 05
P.& F.S.	E. Robertson	12 Dec 05
Civil Ld	G. Lambert	18 Dec 05
B. Ag.&	**Earl CARRINGTON**	10 Dec 05
Fish.		
Colonies	**E of ELGIN**	10 Dec 05
U-S.	W. Churchill	12 Dec 05
B. Educ.	**A. BIRRELL**	10 Dec 05
	R. MCKENNA	23 Jan 07
P.S.	T. Lough	18 Dec 05
India	**J. MORLEY**	10 Dec 05
U-S.	J. Ellis	12 Dec 05
	C. Hobhouse	29 Jan 07
Chief Sec.	**J. BRYCE**	10 Dec 05
Ireland	**A. BIRRELL**	23 Jan 07
V.-Pres.	Sir H. Plunkett	12 Dec 05
Dept. Agric.	T. Russell	21 May 07
for Ireland		
D. Lanc.	**Sir H. FOWLER**	10 Dec 05
Loc.Govt.B.	**J. BURNS**	10 Dec 05
P.S.	W. Runciman	18 Dec 05
	T. Macnamara	29 Jan 07
Paym.-Gen.	R. CAUSTON	12 Dec 05
Postm.-Gen.	**S. BUXTON**	10 Dec 05
Scotland	**J. SINCLAIR**	10 Dec 05
B. Trade	**D. LLOYD GEORGE**	10 Dec 05
P.S.	H. Kearley	18 Dec 05
War	**R. HALDANE**	10 Dec 05
U-S.	E of Portsmouth	12 Dec 05
F.S.	T. Buchanan	14 Dec 05
Works	L. HARCOURT	10 Dec 05
	(office in cabinet)	
	L. HARCOURT	27 Mar 07

Law Officers

Att.-Gen.	SIR J. WALTON	12 Dec 05

Law Officers (*cont.*)

Att.-Gen.	SIR W. ROBSON	28 Jan 08
Sol.-Gen.	SIR W. ROBSON	12 Dec 05
	SIR S. EVANS	28 Jan 08
Ld Advoc.	T. SHAW	12 Dec 05
Sol.-Gen.	A. URE	18 Dec 05
Scotland		
Att.-Gen.	R. CHERRY	20 Dec 05
Ireland		
Sol.-Gen.	R. BARRY	20 Dec 05
Ireland		

Whips

P.S. to	G. WHITELEY	12 Dec 05
Treasury		
Lds of	H. Lewis	18 Dec 05–5 Apr 08
Treasury	J. Pease	18 Dec 05–5 Apr 08
	F. Freeman-Thomas	
		21 Dec 05–2 Feb 06
	C. Norton	21 Dec 05–5 Apr 08
	J. Fuller	2 Feb 06–27 Feb 07
	J. Whitley	27 Feb 07–5 Apr 08

H.M. Household

Treasurer	SIR E. STRACHEY	18 Dec 05
Compt.	Master of ELIBANK*	18 Dec 05
V. Chamb.	W. BEAUMONT	
	(Ld Allendale)	18 Dec 05
	J. FULLER	27 Feb 07
Ld Chamb.	Vt ALTHORP	18 Dec 05
Ld Steward	Ld HAWKESBURY	
	(1st E of Liverpool)	18 Dec 05
	Earl BEAUCHAMP	31 Jul 07
Master	E of SEFTON	18 Dec 05
of Horse	E of GRANARD	6 Sep 07
Cap.Gents	Earl BEAUCHAMP	18 Dec 05
at Arms	Ld DENMAN	31 Jul 07
Cap.Yeo.	D of MANCHESTER	18 Dec 05
of Guard	Ld ALLENDALE	29 Apr 07
Lds in	Ld Denman	18 Dec 05–31 Jul 07
Waiting	E of Granard	18 Dec 05–21 Aug 07
	Ld Acton	18 Dec 05–5 Apr 08
	Earl Granville	18 Dec O5–5 Apr 08
	Ld Hamilton of Dalzell	
		18 Dec 05–5 Apr 08
	Ld Colebrooke	21 Feb 06–5 Apr 08
	Ld Herschell	31 Jul 07–5 Apr 08
	Ld O'Hagan	1 Nov 07–5 Apr 08

*MP. Not a member of the House of Lords.

LIBERAL GOVERNMENT 1908–1915

P.M.	H. ASQUITH	5 Apr 08–25 May 15
Ld Pres.	Ld TWEEDMOUTH	12 Apr 08
	Vt WOLVERHAMPTON	13 Oct 08
	Earl BEAUCHAMP	16 Jun 10
	Vt MORLEY	3 Nov 10
	Earl BEAUCHAMP	5 Aug 14
Ld Chanc.	Ld LOREBURN (Earl)	12 Apr 08
	Vt HALDANE	10 Jun 12
Privy Seal	M of RIPON	12 Apr 08
	E of CREWE	9 Oct 08
	Earl CARRINGTON	23 Oct 11
	M of CREWE	13 Feb 12
Exchequer	D. LLOYD GEORGE	12 Apr 08
F.S.	C. Hobhouse	12 Apr 08
	T. McKinnon Wood	23 Oct 11
	C. Masterman	13 Feb 12
	E. Montagu	11 Feb 14
	F. Acland	3 Feb 15
Foreign O.	Sir E. GREY	12 Apr 08
U-S.	Ld Fitzmaurice	12 Apr 08
	T. McKinnon Wood	19 Oct 08
	F. Acland	23 Oct 11
	N. Primrose	4 Feb 15
Home O.	H. GLADSTONE	12 Apr 08
	W. CHURCHILL	14 Feb 10
	R. MCKENNA	23 Oct 11
U-S.	H. Samuel	12 Apr 08
	C. Masterman	7 Jul 09
	E. Griffith	19 Feb 12
	C. Harmsworth	4 Feb 15
Admiralty	R. MCKENNA	12 Apr 08
	W. CHURCHILL	23 Oct 11
P. & F.S.	T. Macnamara	13 Apr 08
Civil Ld	G. Lambert	12 Apr 08
B.Ag. &	Earl CARRINGTON	12 Apr 08
Fish.	W. RUNCIMAN	23 Oct 11
	Ld LUCAS	6 Aug 14
P.S.	(post not established)	
	Sir E. Strachey (Ld Strachie)	20 Dec 09
	Ld Lucas	23 Oct 11
	Sir H. Verney	10 Aug 14
Colonies	E of CREWE	12 Apr 08
	L. HARCOURT	3 Nov 10
U-S.	J. Seely	12 Apr 08
	Ld Lucas	23 Mar 11
	Ld Emmott	23 Oct 11
	Ld Islington	10 Aug 14
B.Educ.	W. RUNCIMAN	12 Apr 08
	J. PEASE	23 Oct 11
P.S.	T. McKinnon Wood	13 Apr 08
	C. Trevelyan	19 Oct 08
	C. Addison	10 Aug 14
India	J. MORLEY (Vt)	12 Apr 08
	E of CREWE	3 Nov 10
	Vt MORLEY	7 Mar 11
	E of CREWE (M of)	25 May 11
U-S.	T. Buchanan	12 Apr 08
	Master of Elibank*	5 Jun 09
	E. Montagu	20 Feb 10
	C. Roberts	17 Feb 14

Chief Sec. Ireland	A. BIRRELL	12 Apr 08
V. Pres. Dept. Agric. Ireland	T. Russell	12 Apr 08
D.Lanc.	Sir H. FOWLER (Vt Wolverhampton)	12 Apr 08
	Ld FITZMAURICE	13 Oct 08
	H. SAMUEL	25 Jun 09
	J. PEASE	14 Feb 10
	C. HOBHOUSE	23 Oct 11
	C. MASTERMAN	11 Feb 14
	E. MONTAGU	3 Feb 15
Loc.Govt B.	J. BURNS	12 Apr 08
	H. SAMUEL	11 Feb 14
P.S.	C. Masterman	12 Apr 08
	H. Lewis	7 Jul 09
Paym.-Gen.	R. CAUSTON(Ld Southwark)	12 Apr 08
	I. GUEST (Ld Ashby St Ledgers)	23 Feb 10
	Ld STRACHIE	23 May 12
Post.-Gen.	S. BUXTON	12 Apr 08
	H. SAMUEL	14 Feb 10
	C. HOBHOUSE	11 Feb 14
Ass.	(post not established)	
	Sir H. Norman	3 Jan 10
	C. Norton	20 Feb 10
Scotland	J. SINCLAIR (Ld Pentland)	12 Apr 08
	T. MCKINNON WOOD	13 Feb 12
B.Trade	W. CHURCHILL	12 Apr 08
	S. BUXTON	14 Feb 10
	J. BURNS	11 Feb 14
	W. RUNCIMAN	5 Aug 14
P.S.	(Sir) H. Kearley	12 Apr 08
	H. Tennant	10 Jan 09
	J. Robertson	25 Oct 11
War	R. HALDANE (Vt)	12 Apr 08
	J. SEELY	12 Jun 12
	H. ASQUITH (P.M.)	30 Mar 14
	Earl KITCHENER	5 Aug 14
F.S.	F. Acland	12 Apr 08
	C. Mallet	4 Mar 10
	F. Acland	31 Jan 11
	H. Tennant	25 Oct 11
	H. Baker	14 Jun 12
U-S.	Ld Lucas	12 Apr 08
	J. Seely	23 Mar 11
	H. Tennant	14 Jun 12
Works	L. HARCOURT	12 Apr 08
	Earl BEAUCHAMP	3 Nov 10
	Ld EMMOTT	6 Aug 14
Law Officers		
Att.-Gen.	Sir W. ROBSON	12 Apr 08
	Sir R. ISAACS	7 Oct 10
	(office in cabinet) Sir R. ISAACS	4 Jun 12
	Sir J. SIMON	19 Oct 13
Sol.-Gen.	Sir S. EVANS	12 Apr 08
	Sir R. ISAACS	6 Mar 10
	Sir J. SIMON	7 Oct 10

*MP. Not a member of the House of Lords.

LIBERAL GOVERNMENT 1908–1915 (contd.)

Sol.-Gen.	Sir S. BUCKMASTER	19 Oct 13		F. Guest	16 Apr 11–21 Feb 12
Ld Advoc.	T. SHAW	12 Apr 08		Sir A. Haworth	23 Feb 12–16 Apr 12
	A. URE	14 Feb 09		H. Webb	16 Apr 12–25 May 15
	R. MUNRO	30 Oct 13		C. Beck	3 Feb15–25 May 15
Sol.-Gen.	A. URE	12 Apr 08		W. Rea	3 Feb 15–25 May 15
Scotland	A. DEWAR	18 Feb 09	**H.M.Household**		
	W. HUNTER	18 Apr 10	Treasurer	Sir E. STRACHEY	12 Apr 08
	A. ANDERSON	3 Dec 11		W. DUDLEY WARD	20 Dec 09
	T. MORISON	30 Oct 13		F. GUEST	21 Feb 12
Att.-Gen.	R. CHERRY	12 Apr 08	Compt.	Master of ELIBANK*	12 Apr 08
Ireland	R. BARRY	2 Dec 09		E of LIVERPOOL (2nd)	12 Jul 09
	C. O'CONNOR	26 Sep 11		Ld SAYE & SELE	1 Nov 12
	I. O'BRIEN	24 Jun 12	V. Chamb.	(Sir) J. FULLER	12 Apr 08
	T. MOLONY	10 Apr 13		G. Howard	6 Feb 11
	J. MORIARTY	20 Jun 13	Ld Chamb.	Vt ALTHORP*	
	J. PIM	1 Jul 14		(Earl Spencer)	12 Apr 08
Sol.-Gen.	R. BARRY	12 Apr 08		Ld SANDHURST	14 Feb 12
Ireland	C. O'CONNOR	2 Dec 09	Ld Steward	Earl BEAUCHAMP	12 Apr 08
	I. O'BRIEN	19 Oct 11		E of CHESTERFIELD	22 Jun 10
	T. MOLONY	24 Jun 12	M.of Horse	E of GRANARD	12 Apr 08
	J. MORIARTY	25 Apr 13	Cap. Gents	Ld DENMAN	12 Apr 08
	J. PIM	20 Jun 13	at Arms	Ld COLEBROOKE	26 Jun 11
	J. O'CONNOR	1 Jul 14	Cap. Yeo.	Ld ALLENDALE	12 Apr 08
Whips			of Guard	E of CRAVEN	2 Oct 11
P.S. to	G. WHITELEY	12 Apr 08	Lds in	Ld O'Hagan	12 Apr 08–15 Apr 10
Treasury	J. PEASE	3 Jun 08	Waiting	Ld Hamilton of Dalzell	
	Master of ELIBANK*	14 Feb 10			12 Apr 08–2 Oct 11
	P. ILLINGWORTH	7 Aug 12		Ld Colebrooke	12 Apr 08–26 Jun 11
	J. GULLAND	24 Jan 15		Ld Herschell	12 Apr 08–25 May15
Lds of	J. Pease	12 Apr 08–3 Jun 08		Ld Acton	12 Apr 08–25 May 15
Treasury	H. Lewis	12 Apr 08–7 Jul 09		Earl Granville	12 Apr 08–25 May 15
	C. Norton	12 Apr 08–7 Jul 09		Ld Tweedmouth	15 Apr 10–4 Dec 11
	J. Whitley	12 Apr 08–20 Feb 10		Ld Willingdon	19 Jul 11- 31 Jan 13
	O. Partington	6 Jul 09–19 Jan 11		Vt Allendale	2 Oct 11–25 May 15
	J. Gulland	7 Jul 09–24 Jan 15		Ld Loch	4 Dec 11–1 May14
	W. Benn	20 Feb 10–25 May 15		Ld Ashby St Ledgers	
	E. Soares	20 Feb 10–16 Apr 11		(Ld Wimborne)	31 Jan 13–8 Feb 15
	P. Illingworth	28 Feb 10–7 Aug 12		Ld Stanmore	1 May 14–25 May 15
	W. Jones	19 Jan 11–25 May 15		Ld Ranksborough	8 Feb 15–25 May 15

COALITION GOVERNMENT 1915–1916

P.M.	**H. ASQUITH** (Lib)		U-S. Ass.	Ld Newton (C)	18 Aug 16
		25 May 15–5 Dec 16	Home O.	**Sir J. SIMON** (Lib)	25 May 15
Ld Pres.	**M of CREWE** (Lib)	25 May 15		**Sir H. SAMUEL** (Lib)	10 Jan 16
Ld Chanc.	**Ld BUCKMASTER** (Lib)	25 May 15	U-S.	W. Brace (Lab)	30 May 15
Privy Seal	**Earl CURZON** (C)	25 May 15	Admiralty	**A. BALFOUR** (C)	25 May 15
Exchequer	**R. MCKENNA** (Lib)	25 May 15	P.& F.S.	T. Macnamara (Lib)	30 May 15
F.S.	E. Montagu (Lib)	26 May 15	Civil Ld	D of Devonshire (C)	9 Jun 15
	(also D. Lanc.)			E of Lytton (C)	26 Jul 16
	(office in cabinet)		B.Ag.&	**E of SELBORNE** (C)	25 May 15
	E. MONTAGU (Lib)	16 Jan 16	Fish.	**E of CRAWFORD** (C)	11 Jul 16
	T. MCKINNON WOOD		P.S.	F. Acland (Lib)	30 May 15
	(Lib)	9 Jul 16	Blockade	Ld R. CECIL*(C)	23 Feb 16
Foreign O.	**Sir E. GREY** (Vt) (Lib)	25 May 15		(also U-S. at F.O.)	
U-S.	Ld R. Cecil* (C)	30 May 15	Colonies	**A. BONAR LAW** (C)	25 May 15
	(also Blockade)		U-S.	A. Steel-Maitland (C)	30 May 15
	(office in cabinet)		B.Educ.	**A. HENDERSON** (Lab)	25 May 15
	Ld R. CECIL*(C)	23 Feb 16		**M of CREWE** (Lib)	18 Aug 16

*MP. Not a member of the House of Lords.

COALITION GOVERNMENT 1915–1916 *(contd.)*

P.S.	H. Lewis (Lib)	30 May 15	*Works*	**L. HARCOURT** *(Vt)* (Lib)		25 May 15
Health &	**W. LONG** (C)	25 May 15	*Law Officers*			
L.Govt.B.			*Att.-Gen.*	Sir E.CARSON (C)		25 May 15
P.S.	W. Hayes Fisher (C)	30 May 15		Sir F. SMITH (C)		3 Nov 15
India	**A. CHAMBERLAIN** (C)	25 May 15	*Sol.-Gen.*	Sir F. SMITH (C)		2 Jun 15
U-S.	Ld Islington (Lib)	30 May 15		(Sir) G. CAVE (C)		8 Nov 15
Chief Sec.	**A. BIRRELL** (Lib)	25 May 15	*Ld Advoc.*	R. MUNRO (Lib)		8 Jun 15
Ireland	*(office vacant 3 May 16)*		*Sol.-Gen.*	T. MORISON (Lib)		8 Jun 15
	H. DUKE (C)	31 Jul 16	*Scotland*			
V. Pres.	T. Russell (Lib)	30 May 15	*Att.-Gen.*	J. GORDON (C)		8 Jun 15
Dept. Agric.			*Ireland*	J. CAMPBELL (C)		9 Apr 16
for Ireland			*Sol.-Gen.*	J. O'CONNOR (Nat)		8 Jun 15
D.Lanc.	**W. CHURCHILL** (Lib)	25 May 15	*Ireland*			
	H. SAMUEL (Lib)	25 Nov 15	*Whips*			
	E. MONTAGU (Lib)	11 Jan 16	*P.S. to*	J. GULLAND (Lib)30 May 15–5 Dec 16		
	(also F.S. at Treasury)		*Treasury*	Ld E. TALBOT* (C)		
	T. MCKINNON WOOD (Lib) 9 Jul 16				30 May 15–5 Dec 16	
	(also F.S. at Treasury)		*Lds of*	G. Howard (Lib)	27 May 15–5 Dec 16	
Munitions	**D. LLOYD GEORGE** (Lib) 25 May 15		*Treasury*	G. Roberts (Lab)	27 May 15–5 Dec 16	
	E. MONTAGU (Lib)	9 Jul 16		W. Bridgeman (C) 27 May 15–5 Dec 16		
P.S.	C. Addison (Lib) 30 May 15–8 Dec 16			W. Rea (Lib)	27 May 15–5 Dec 16	
	A. Lee(C) 11 Nov 15–9 Jul 16		*H. M. Household*			
Paym.-Gen.	Ld NEWTON (C)	9 Jun 15	*Treasurer*	J. HOPE (C)		30 May 15
	(office in cabinet)		*Compt.*	C. ROBERTS (Lib)		30 May 15
	A. HENDERSON (Lab)	18 Aug 16	*V.Chamb.*	C. BECK (Lib)		30 May 15
Min.without	**M of LANSDOWNE** (C)	25 May 15	*Ld Chamb.*	Ld SANDHURST (Lib)		9 Jun 15
Portfolio			*Ld Steward*	Ld FARQUHAR (C)		9 Jun 15
Postm.-Gen.	H. SAMUEL (Lib)	26 May 15	*Master*	E of CHESTERFIELD (Lib)		
	J. PEASE (Lib)	18 Jan 16	*of Horse*			9 Jun 15
Ass.	H. Pike Pease (C)	30 May 15	*Cap.Gents*	Ld COLEBROOKE (Lib)		9 Jun 15
Scotland	**T. MCKINNON WOOD**		*at Arms*			
	(Lib)	25 May 15	*Cap.Yeo.*	Ld SUFFIELD (C)		9 Jun 15
	H. TENNANT (Lib)	9 Jul 16	*of Guard*			
B. Trade	**W. RUNCIMAN** (Lib)	25 May 15	*Lds in*	Ld Herschell (Lib)	9 Jun 15–5 Dec 16	
P.S.	E. Pretyman (C)	30 May 15	*Waiting*	Vt Allendale(Lib)	9 Jun 15–5 Dec 16	
War	**Earl KITCHENER**	25 May 15		Ld Stanmore (Lib)	9 Jun 15–5 Dec 16	
	D. LLOYD GEORGE (Lib)	6 Jul 16		Ld Ranksborough		
U-S.	H. Tennant (Lib)	30 May 15		(Lib)	9 Jun 15–5 Dec 16	
	E of Derby (C)	6 Jul 16		Vt Valentia* (C)	9 Jun 15–5 Dec 16	
F.S.	H. Forster (C)	30 May 15		Ld Hylton (C)	9 Jun 15–5 Dec 16	

COALITION GOVERNMENT 1916–1922

From 6 Dec 1916 to 31 Oct 1919 there was an inner war cabinet of 5–7 ministers.

Three were members throughout:
  D. LLOYD GEORGE
  Earl CURZON
  A. BONAR LAW
The other members were:

A. HENDERSON (Lab)	10 Dec 16–12 Aug 17	
Vt MILNER (C)	10 Dec 16–18 Apr 18	
J. SMUTS+	22 Jun 17–10 Jan 19	
G. BARNES (Lab)	29 May 17–3 Aug 17	
	13 Aug 17–10 Jan 19	
A. CHAMBERLAIN (C)	18 Apr 18–31 Oct 19	
SIR E. GEDDES (C)	10 Jan 19–31 Oct 19	

P.M.	**D. LLOYD GEORGE** (Lib)	
		6 Dec 16–19 Oct 22
Ld Pres.	**Earl CURZON** (C)	10 Dec 16
	A. BALFOUR (C)	23 Oct 19
Ld Chanc.	**Ld FINLAY** (C)	10 Dec 16
	Ld BIRKENHEAD *(Vt)* (C)	10 Jan 19
Privy Seal	**E of CRAWFORD** (C)	15 Dec 16
	A. BONAR LAW (C)	10 Jan 19
	A. CHAMBERLAIN (C)	23 Mar 21
Exchequer	**A. BONAR LAW** (C)	10 Dec 16
	A. CHAMBERLAIN (C)	10 Jan 19
	Sir R. HORNE (C)	1 Apr 21
F.S.	Sir H. Lever (Lib)	
		15 Dec 16–19 May 19
	S. Baldwin (C)	18 Jun 17–1 Apr 21

*MP. Not a member of the House of Lords.   +Not a member of the House of Commons.

COALITION GOVERNMENT 1916–1922 (contd.)

F.S. (contd.)	E. Young (Lib)	1 Apr 21–19 Oct 22
Foreign O.	**A. BALFOUR** (C)	10 Dec 16
	Earl CURZON (Marq.) (C)	23 Oct 19
U.-S.	Ld R. Cecil* (C)	10 Dec 16
	C. Harmsworth (Lib)	10 Jan 19
Ass.U.-S.	Ld Newton (C)	10 Dec 16
	(post abolished 10 Jan 19)	
Home O.	**Sir G. CAVE** (Vt) (C)	10 Dec 16
	E. SHORTT (Lib)	10 Jan 19
U.-S.	W. Brace (Lab)	10 Dec 16
	Sir H. Greenwood (Lib)	10 Jan 19
	(Sir) J. Baird (C)	29 Apr 19
Admiralty	**Sir E. CARSON** (C)	10 Dec 16
	Sir E. GEDDES (C)	17 Jul 17
	W. LONG (C)	10 Jan 19
	Ld LEE (C)	13 Feb 21
P.& F.S.	T. Macnamara (Lib)	10 Dec 16
	Sir J. Craig (C)	2 Apr 20
	L. Amery (C)	1 Apr 21
Add.P.S.	E of Lytton (C)	7 Feb 17
	(post abolished 27 Jan 19)	
Civil Ld	E. Pretyman (C)	14 Dec 16
	E of Lytton (C)	27 Jan 19
	E of Onslow (C)	26 Oct 20
	B. Eyres-Monsell (C)	1 Apr 21
2nd.Civil Ld	A. Pease (C)	10 Dec 16
	(post abolished 10 Jan 19)	
Ag.& Fish.	**R. PROTHERO**	
	(Ld Ernle) (C)	10 Dec 16
	Ld LEE (C)	15 Aug 19
	(Board renamed Min. 15 Aug 19)	
	Sir A. GRIFFITH-BOSCAWEN (C)	
		13 Feb 21
P.S.	Sir R. Winfrey (Lib)	
		14 Dec 16–10 Jan 19
	D of Marlborough (C)	
		18 Feb 17–21 Mar 18
	Vt Goschen (C)	26 Mar 18–18 Jun 18
	Ld Clinton (C)	18 Jun 18–10 Jan 19
	Sir A. Griffith-Boscawen (C)	
		10 Jan 19–13 Feb 21
(& Dep. Min. Fisheries 18 Nov 19)		
	E of Onslow (C)	5 Apr 21–7 Apr 21
	E of Ancaster (C)	7 Apr 21–19 Oct 22
(& Dep. Min. Fisheries 28 Oct 21)Air		
	Ld COWDRAY (Lib)	3 Jan 17
	Ld ROTHERMERE (Lib)	26 Nov 17
	Ld WEIR (Lib)	26 Apr 18
(War & Air combined 10 Jan 19–		
13 Feb 21 & office in cabinet)		
	W. CHURCHILL (Lib)	10 Jan 19
	(office not in cabinet)	
	F. GUEST (Lib)	1 Apr 21
P.S. Air Council	J. Baird (C)	14 Dec 16
	(post abolished 10 Jan 19)	
U.-S.	J. Seely (Lib)	10 Jan 19
	G. Tryon (C)	22 Dec 19
	M of Londonderry (C)	2 Apr 20
	Ld Gorell (Lib)	18 Jul 21
Blockade	Ld R. CECIL* (C)	10 Dec 16
	(also U.-S. at Foreign O.)	
	Sir L. WORTHINGTON-EVANS (C)	
		18 Jul 19
	(office abolished 10 Jan 19)	
P.S.	F. Leverton Harris(C)	22 Dec 16
	(post abolished 10 Jan 19)	
Colonies	**W. LONG** (C)	10 Dec 16
	Vt MILNER (C)	10 Jan 19
	W. CHURCHILL (Lib)	13 Feb 21
U.-S.	(Sir) A. Steel-Maitland (C)	10 Dec 16
	W. Hewins (C)	26 Sep 17
	L. Amery (C)	10 Jan 19
	E. Wood (C)	1 Apr 21
B.Educ.	**H. FISHER** (Lib)	10 Dec 16
P.S.	(Sir) H. Lewis (Lib)	10 Dec 16
Food	Vt DEVONPORT (Lib)	10 Dec 16
Control	Ld RHONDDA (Vt) (Lib)	19 Jun 17
	J. CLYNES (Lab)	9 Jul 18
	G. ROBERTS (Lab)	10 Jan 19
	C. McCURDY (Lib)	19 Mar 20
	(office abolished 31 Mar 21)	
P.S.	(Sir) C. Bathurst (C)	12 Dec 16
	J. Clynes (Lab)	2 Jul 17
	W. Astor (C)	18 Jul 18
	C. McCurdy (Lib)	27 Jan 19
	Sir W. Mitchell-Thomson (C)	
		19 Apr 20
Health	(Dept under Loc. Govt Bd)	
	C. ADDISON (Lib)	24 Jun 19
	Sir A. MOND (Lib)	1 Apr 21
P.S. (Loc.	W. Hayes Fisher (C)	10 Dec 16
Govt Bd.)	S. Walsh (Lab)	28 Jun 17
	W. Astor (Vt) (C)	27 Jan 19
	E of Onslow (C)	7 Apr 21
India	**A. CHAMBERLAIN** (C)	10 Dec 16
	E. MONTAGU (Lib)	17 Jul 17
	Vt PEEL (C)	19 Mar 22
U.-S.	Ld Islington (Lib)	10 Dec 16
	Ld Sinha (Lib)	10 Jan 19
	E of Lytton (C)	22 Sep 20
	Earl Winterton (C)*	20 Mar 22
Ld Lieut.	(not usually min. office)	
Ireland	Vt FRENCH	6 May 18
	(office in cabinet)	
	Vt FRENCH (E of Ypres)	28 Oct 18
	(office not in cabinet 2 Apr 21)	
Chief Sec.	**(Sir) H. DUKE** (C)	10 Dec 16
Ireland	**E. SHORTT** (Lib)	5 May 18
	I. MACPHERSON (Lib)	10 Jan 19
	Sir H. GREENWOOD (Lib)	
		2 Apr 20
V. Pres.	(Sir) T. Russell (Lib)	10 Dec 16
Dept.	H. Barrie (C)	15 Jan 19
Agric.		
Ireland		
Labour	**J. HODGE** (Lab)	10 Dec 16
	G. ROBERTS (Lab)	17 Aug 17
	Sir R. HORNE (C)	10 Jan 19
	T. MACNAMARA (Lib)	19 Mar 20

*MP. Not a member of the House of Lords.

COALITION GOVERNMENT 1916–1922 *(contd.)*

P.S.	W. Bridgeman (C)	22 Dec 16
	G. Wardle (Lab)	10 Jan 19
	Sir A. Montague-Barlow (C)	2 Apr 20
D.Lanc.	**Sir F. CAWLEY** (Lib)	10 Dec 16
	Ld BEAVERBROOK (C)	10 Feb 18
	(& Min. of Propaganda/Information)	
	Ld DOWNHAM (C)	4 Nov 18
	(office not in cabinet)	
	E of CRAWFORD (C)	10 Jan 19
	Vt PEEL (C)	1 Apr 21
	Sir W. SUTHERLAND (Lib)	
		7 Apr 22
Loc.Govt B.	**Ld RHONDDA**(Lib)	10 Dec 16
	W. HAYES FISHER	
	(Ld Downham) (C)	28 Jun 19
	Sir A.GEDDES (C)	4 Nov 18
	C. ADDISON (Lib)	10 Jan 19
	(24 Jun 19 became Min. of Health)	
Munitions	**C. ADDISON** (Lib)	10 Dec 16
(Supply)	**W. CHURCHILL** (Lib)	17 Jul 17
	(office not in cabinet)	
	Ld INVERFORTH (C)	10 Jan 19
P.S.	Sir L. Worthington-Evans (C)	
		14 Dec 16–30 Jan 18
	F. Kellaway (Lib)	14 Dec 16–1 Apr 20
	J. Seely (Lib)	10 Jul 18–10 Jan 19
	J. Baird (C)	10 Jan 19–29 Apr 19
P.& F.S.	Sir L. Worthington-Evans (C)	
		30 Jan 18–18 Jul 18
	J. Hope (C)	27 Jan 19–31 Mar 21
National	N. CHAMBERLAIN+ (C)	15 Dec 16
Service	Sir A. GEDDES (C)	17 Aug 17
	(office held jointly with	
	Reconstruction Jan-May 19 &	
	with Trade May–Aug 19;	
	formally abolished 19 Dec 19)	
P.S.	S. Walsh (Lab)	17 Mar 17–28 Jun 17
	C. Beck (Lib)	28 Jun 17–19 Dec 19
	Vt Peel (C)	15 Apr 18–10 Jan 19
	(post abolished 19 Dec 19)	
Paym.-Gen.	Sir J. COMPTON-RICKETT (Lib)	
		15 Dec 16
	Sir T. WALTERS (Lib)	26 Oct 19
Pensions	G. BARNES (Lab)	10 Dec 16
	J. HODGE (Lab)	17 Aug 17
	Sir L. WORTHINGTON-EVANS (C)	
		10 Jan 19
	I. MACPHERSON (Lib)	2 Apr 20
P.S.	Sir A. Griffith-Boscawen (C)	
		22 Dec 16
	Sir J. Craig (C)	10 Jan 19
	G. Tryon (C)	2 Apr 20
Postm.-Gen.	A. ILLINGWORTH (Lib)	10 Dec 16
	F. KELLAWAY (Lib)	1 Apr 21
Ass.	H. Pike Pease (C)	10 Dec 16
Min.	**A. HENDERSON** (Lab)	
without		10 Dec 16–12 Aug 17
Portfolio	**Vt MILNER** (C)	10 Dec 16–18 Apr 18
	J. SMUTS[1]	22 Jun 17–10 Jan 19
	Sir E. CARSON (C)	
		17 Jul 17–21 Jan 18
	G. BARNES[1] (Lab)	
		13 Aug 17–27 Jan 20
	A. CHAMBERLAIN[1] (C)	
		18 Apr 18–10 Jan 19
	Sir E. GEDDES (C)	
		10 Jan 19–19 May 19
	Sir L. WORTHINGTON-EVANS (C)	
		2 Apr 20–13 Feb 21
	C. ADDISON (Lib)	1 Apr 21–14 Jul 21
Reconstruc.	C. ADDISON(Lib)	17 Jul 17
	(office combined with Nat.Service	
	10 Jan 19; for junior Ministers see	
	National Service & Reconstruction)	
Scotland	**R. MUNRO** (Lib)	10 Dec 16
P.S. Min. of	(Sir) J. Pratt (Lib)	8 Aug 19
Health for		
Scotland		
Shipping	SIR J. MACLAY (Ld) (Lib)	10 Dec 16
	(office abolished 31 Mar 21)	
P.S.	Sir L. Chiozza Money (Lib)	22 Dec 16
	L. Wilson (C)	10 Jan 19
Supply	Ld INVERFORTH (C)	10 Jan 19
	(office abolished 31 Mar 21)	
B.Trade	**Sir A. STANLEY** (Lib)	10 Dec 16
	Sir A. GEDDES (C)	26 May 19
	Sir R. HORNE (C)	19 Mar 20
	S. BALDWIN (C)	1 Apr 21
P.S.	G. Roberts (Lab)	14 Dec 16
	G. Wardle (Lab)	17 Aug 17
	W. Bridgeman (C)	10 Jan 19
	Sir P. Lloyd-Greame (C)	22 Aug 20
	Sir W. Mitchell-Thomson (C)	1 Apr 21
Sec.	Sir A. Steel-Maitland (C)	14 Sep 17
Overseas	Sir H. Greenwood (Lib)	29 Apr 19
Trade	F. Kellaway (Lib)	2 Apr 20
	Sir P. Lloyd-Greame (C)	1 Apr 21
	(Director Overseas Trade)	
P.S. Mines	W. Bridgeman (C)	22 Aug 20
Transport	*(office not established)*	
	Sir E. GEDDES (C)	19 May 19
	(office not in cabinet)	
	Vt Peel (C)	7 Nov 21
	(office in cabinet)	
	E of CRAWFORD (C)	12 Apr 22
P.S.	Sir R. Williams (Lib)	23 Sep 19
	A. Neal (Lib)	28 Nov 19
War	**E of DERBY** (C)	10 Dec 16
	Vt MILNER (C)	18 Apr 18
	(10 Jan 19 War O.& Air Min.combined)	
	W. CHURCHILL (Lib)	10 Jan 19
	(13 Feb 21 War only)	
	Sir L. WORTHINGTON-EVANS (C)	
		13 Feb 21
U-S.	I. Macpherson (Lib)	14 Dec 16
	Vt Peel (C)	10 Jan 19
	Sir R. Sanders (C)	1 Apr 21
F.S.	H. Forster (Ld) (C)	10 Dec 16

[1]A member of the War Cabinet.

COALITION GOVERNMENT 1916–1922 (contd.)

F.S.	Sir A. Williamson (Lib)	18 Dec 19	Lds of	J. Hope (C)	14 Dec 16–27 Jan 19
(contd.)	G. Stanley (C)	1 Apr 21	Treasury	J. Pratt (Lib)	14 Dec 16–8 Aug 19
P.S.	Earl Stanhope (C)	14 Dec 16		S. Baldwin (C)	29 Jan 17–18 Jun 17
	(post abolished 10 Jan 19)			J. Parker (Lab)	29 Jan 17–19 Oct 22
Works	Sir A. MOND (Lib)	10 Dec 16		J. Towyn Jones (Lib)	
	E of CRAWFORD (C)	1 Apr 21			29 Jan 17–4 Jul 22
	(office in cabinet)			(Sir) R. Sanders (C) 5 Feb 19–1 Apr 21	
	E of CRAWFORD (C)	7 Apr 22		Sir G. Collins (Lib)	
Law Officers					8 Aug 19–10 Feb 20
Att.-Gen.	Sir F. SMITH (C)(Ld Birkenhead)			W. Edge (Lib) 18 Aug 19–1 Aug 22	
		10 Dec16		Sir W. Sutherland (Lib)	
	Sir G. HEWART (Lib)	10 Jan 19			15 Feb 20–7 Apr 22
	(office in cabinet)			Sir J. Gilmour (C) 1 Apr 21–19 Oct 22	
	Sir G. HEWART (Lib)	7 Nov 21		T. Lewis (Lib) 4 Jul 22–26 Jul 22	
	(office not in cabinet)				
	Sir E. POLLOCK (C)	6 Mar 22	***H.M Household***		
Sol.-Gen.	Sir G. HEWART (Lib)	10 Dec 16	Treasurer	(Sir) J. CRAIG (C)	14 Dec 16
	Sir E. POLLOCK (C)	10 Jan 19		(office vacant 22 Jan 18)	
	(Sir) L. SCOTT (C)	6 Mar 22		R. SANDERS (C)	11 Jun 18
Ld Advoc.	J. CLYDE (C)	10 Dec 16		B. EYRES-MONSELL (C)	5 Feb 19
	T. MORISON (Lib)	25 Mar 20		G. GIBBS (C)	1 Apr 21
	C. MURRAY (C)	5 Mar 22	Compt.	Sir E. CORNWALL (Lib)	14 Dec 16
Sol.-Gen.	T. MORISON (Lib)	10 Dec 16		G. STANLEY (C)	28 Feb 19
Scotland	C. MURRAY (C)	25 Mar 20		H. BARNSTON (C)	7 Apr 21
	A. BRIGGS CONSTABLE (C)		V.Chamb.	C. BECK (Lib)	14 Dec 16
		16 Mar 22		W. DUDLEY WARD (Lib)	9 Dec 17
	W. WATSON (C)	24 Jul 22	Ld Chamb.	Ld SANDHURST (Vt) (Lib)	14 Dec 16
Ld Chanc.	Sir J. O'BRIEN (Lib)	10 Dec 16		D of ATHOLL (C)	20 Nov 21
Ireland	Sir J. CAMPBELL (C)	4 Jun 18	Ld Steward	Ld FARQUHAR (Vt) (C)	14 Dec 16
	Sir J. ROSS (C)	27 Jun 21	Master	E of CHESTERFIELD (Lib)	14 Dec 16
Att.-Gen.	J. O'CONNOR (Nat)	8 Jan 17	of Horse		
Ireland	A. SAMUELS (C)	7 Apr 18	Cap.Gents	Ld COLEBROOKE (Lib)	14 Dec 16
	D. HENRY (C)	6 Jul 19	at Arms		
	T. BROWN (C)	5 Aug 21	Cap.Yeo.	Ld SUFFIELD (C)	14 Dec 16
	(office vacant from 16 Nov 21)		of Guard	Ld HYLTON (C)	21 May 18
Sol.-Gen.	J. CHAMBERS (C)	19 Mar 17	Lds in	Ld Herschell (Lib)	
Ireland	A. SAMUELS (C)	12 Sep 17	Waiting		14 Dec 16–11 Feb 19
	J. POWELL+(C)	7 Apr 18		Ld Stanmore (Lib)	
	D. HENRY (C)	27 Nov 18			14 Dec 16–19 Oct 22
	D. WILSON (C)	6 Jul 19		Ld Ranksborough (Lib)	
	T. BROWN (C)	12 Jun 21			14 Dec 16–4 Apr 21
	(office vacant from 5 Aug 21)			Vt Valentia (C) 14 Dec 16–19 Oct 22	
Whips				Ld Hylton (C) 14 Dec 16–18 May 18	
P.S. to	Ld E. TALBOT*(C)			Ld Kenyon (C) 14 Dec 16–11 Sep 18	
Treasury		14 Dec 16–1 Apr 21		Ld Somerleyton (C)	
	N. PRIMROSE (Lib)				18 May 18–19 Oct 22
		14 Dec 16–2 Mar 17		E of Jersey (C) 11 Jan 19–17 Aug 19	
	F. GUEST (Lib) 2 Mar 17–1 Apr 21			E of Bradford (C) 11 Feb 19–19 Oct 22	
	C. MCCURDY (Lib)			E of Onslow (C) 17 Aug 19–21 Nov 20	
		1 Apr 21–19 Oct 22		E of Lucan (C) 12 Nov 20–19 Oct 22	
	L. WILSON (C) 1 Apr 21–19 Oct 22			E of Clarendon (C) 4 Apr 21–19 Oct 22	

CONSERVATIVE GOVERNMENT 1922–1924

P.M.	**A. BONAR LAW**		Privy Seal	(office vacant)	
		23 Oct 22–20 May 23		**Ld R. CECIL***	25 May 23
	S. BALDWIN	22 May 23–22 Jan 24	Exchequer	**S. BALDWIN**	27 Oct 22
Ld Pres.	**M of SALISBURY**	24 Oct 22		(& P.M. from 22 May)	
Ld Chanc.	**Vt CAVE**	24 Oct 22		**N. CHAMBERLAIN**	27 Aug 23

*MP. Not a member of the House of Lords. +Not a member of the House of Commons.

CONSERVATIVE GOVERNMENT 1922–1924 *(contd.)*

F.S.	J. Hills	6 Nov 22
	A. Boyd-Carpenter	12 Mar 23
	(office in cabinet)	
	Sir W. JOYNSON-HICKS	
		25 May 23
	(office not in cabinet)	
	W. Guinness	5 Oct 23
Foreign O.	Marquess CURZON	24 Oct 22
U-S.	R. McNeill	31 Oct 22
Home O.	**W. BRIDGEMAN**	24 Oct 22
U-S.	G. Stanley	31 Oct 22
	G. Locker-Lampson	12 Mar 23
Admiralty	**L. AMERY**	24 Oct 22
P.& F.S.	B. Eyres-Monsell	31 Oct 22
	A. Boyd-Carpenter	25 May 23
Civil Ld	M of Linlithgow	31 Oct 22
Ag.& Fish.	**Sir R. SANDERS**	24 Oct 22
P.S. Ag. &	E of Ancaster	31 Oct 22
Deputy Min.		
Fisheries		
Air	Sir S. Hoare	31 Oct 22
	(office in cabinet)	
	Sir S. HOARE	25 May 23
U-S.	D of Sutherland	31 Oct 22
Colonies	**D of DEVONSHIRE**	24 Oct 22
U-S.	W. Ormsby-Gore	31 Oct 22
B.Educ.	**E. WOOD**	24 Oct 22
P.S.	Ld E. Percy*	21 Mar 23
	E of Onslow	25 May 23
Health	**Sir A. GRIFFITH-BOSCAWEN**	24 Oct 22
	N. CHAMBERLAIN	7 Mar 23
	Sir W. JOYNSON-HICKS	27 Aug 23
P.S.	E of Onslow	31 Oct 22
	Ld E. Percy*	25 May 23
India	**Vt PEEL**	24 Oct 22
U-S.	Earl Winterton*	31 Oct 22
Labour	**Sir A. MONTAGUE-BARLOW**	31 Oct 22
P.S.	A. Boyd-Carpenter	6 Nov 22
	H. Betterton	12 Mar 23
D. Lanc.	**M of SALISBURY**	24 Oct 22
	(office not in cabinet)	
	J. DAVIDSON	25 May 23
Paym.-Gen.	*(office vacant)*	
	N. CHAMBERLAIN	5 Feb 23
	Sir W. JOYNSON-HICKS	15 Mar 23
	A. BOYD-CARPENTER	25 May 23
Pensions	G. TRYON	31 Oct 22
P.S.	C. Craig	13 Feb 23
Postm.-		
Gen.	N. CHAMBERLAIN	31 Oct 22
	Sir W. JOYNSON-HICKS	7 Mar 23
	(office in cabinet)	
	Sir L. WORTHINGTON-EVANS	
		28 May 23
Scotland	**Vt NOVAR**	24 Oct 22

P.S. Min. of	J. Kidd	31 Oct 22
Health for	W. Elliot	15 Jan 23
Scotland		
B. Trade	**Sir P. LLOYD-GREAME**	24 Oct 22
P.S.	Vt Wolmer*	31 Oct 22
Sec.	Sir W. Joynson-Hicks	
Overseas		31 Oct 22–12 Mar 23
Trade	A. Buckley	12 Mar 23–18 Nov 23
Sec.Mines	G. Lane Fox	6 Nov 22
Transport	Sir J. BAIRD	31 Oct 22
P.S.Off. of	W. Ashley	31 Oct 22
Works &	J. Moore-Brabazon	8 Oct 23
Min.of	*(Trans.only)*	
Transport		
War	**E of DERBY**	24 Oct 22
U-S.	W. Guinness	31 Oct 22
	W. Ashley	8 Oct 23
F.S.	S. Jackson	31 Oct 22
	R. Gwynne	15 Mar 23
Works	Sir J. BAIRD	31 Oct 22

Law Officers

Att.-Gen.	Sir D. HOGG	24 Oct 22
Sol.-Gen.	Sir T. INSKIP	31 Oct 22
Ld Advoc.	W. WATSON	24 Oct 22
Sol.-Gen.	D. FLEMING+	6 Nov 22
Scotland	F. THOMSON	5 Apr 23

Whips

P.S. to	L. WILSON	31 Oct 22
Treasury	B. EYRES-MONSELL	25 Jul 23
Lds of	D. King	31 Oct 22–22 Jan 24
Treasury	A. Buckley	31 Oct 22–12 Mar 23
	G. Hennessy	11 Dec 22–22 Jan 24
	F. Thomson	7 Feb 23–10 Apr 23
	W. Cope	20 Mar 23–22 Jan 24
	P. Ford	10 Apr 23–20 Dec 23
	Sir J. Gilmour	20 Dec 23–22 Jan 24

H. M. Household

Treasurer	G. GIBBS	6 Nov 22
Compt.	H. BARNSTON	31 Oct 22
V. Chamb.	D. HACKING	20 Nov 22
Ld Chamb.	E of CROMER	20 Nov 22
Ld Steward	E of SHAFTESBURY	20 Nov 22
Master	M of BATH	20 Nov 22
of Horse		
Cap.Gents	E of CLARENDON	20 Nov 22
at Arms		
Cap.Yeo.	Ld HYLTON	20 Nov 22
of Guard		
Lds in	Vt Valentia	20 Nov 22–22 Jan 24
Waiting	Ld Somerleyton	20 Nov 22–22 Jan 24
	E of Bradford	20 Nov 22–22 Jan 24
	E of Lucan	20 Nov 22–22 Jan 24
	E of Malmesbury	
		20 Nov 22–22 Jan 24
	E of Albemarle	20 Nov 22–22 Jan 24

*MP. Not a member of the House of Lords. +Not a member of the House of Commons.

LABOUR GOVERNMENT 1924

P.M.	**R. MACDONALD**		Scotland	**W. ADAMSON**	22 Jan 24
		22 Jan 24–3 Nov 24	P.S. Health	J. Stewart	23 Jan 24
Ld Pres.	**Ld PARMOOR**	22 Jan 24	for Scotland		
Ld Chanc.	**Vt HALDANE**	22 Jan 24	B.Trade	**S. WEBB**	22 Jan 24
Privy Seal	**J. CLYNES**	22 Jan 24	P.S.	A. Alexander	23 Jan 24
Exchequer	**P. SNOWDEN**	22 Jan 24	Sec.	W. Lunn	23 Jan 24
F.S.	W. Graham	23 Jan 24	Overseas		
Foreign O.	**R. MACDONALD** (P.M.)	22 Jan 24	Trade		
U-S.	A. Ponsonby	23 Jan 24	Sec.Mines	E. Shinwell	23 Jan 24
Home O.	**A. HENDERSON**	22 Jan 24	Transport	H. GOSLING	24 Jan 24
U-S.	R. Davies	23 Jan 24	War	**S. WALSH**	22 Jan 24
Admiralty	**Vt CHELMSFORD**	22 Jan 24	U-S.	C. Attlee	23 Jan 24
P.& F.S.	C. Ammon	23 Jan 24	F.S.	J. Lawson	23 Jan 24
Civil Ld	F. Hodges	24 Jan 24	Works	**F. JOWETT**	22 Jan 24
Ag.& Fish.	**N. BUXTON**	22 Jan 24	***Law Officers***		
P.S.	W. Smith	23 Jan 24	Att.-Gen.	Sir P. HASTINGS	23 Jan 24
Air	**Ld THOMSON**	22 Jan 24	Sol.-Gen.	Sir H. SLESSER	23 Jan 24
U-S.	W. Leach	23 Jan 24	Ld Advoc.	H. MACMILLAN+	8 Feb 24
Colonies	**J. THOMAS**	22 Jan 24	Sol.-Gen.	J. FENTON+	18 Feb 24
U-S.	Ld Arnold	23 Jan 24	Scotland		
B Educ.	**C. TREVELYAN**	22 Jan 24	***Whips***		
P.S.	M. Jones	23 Jan 24	P.S. to	B. SPOOR	23 Jan 24
Health	**J. WHEATLEY**	22 Jan 24	Treasury		
P.S.	A. Greenwood	23 Jan 24	Lds of	F. Hall	2 Feb 24
India	**Ld OLIVIER**	22 Jan 24	Treasury	T. Kennedy	2 Feb 24
U-S.	R. Richards	23 Jan 24		J. Robertson	2 Feb 24
Labour	**T. SHAW**	22 Jan 24		G. Warne	24 Feb 24
P.S.	Margaret Bondfield	23 Jan 24	***H.M. Household***		
D.Lanc.	**J. WEDGWOOD**	22 Jan 24	Treasurer	T. GRIFFITHS	2 Feb 24
Paym.-Gen.	H. GOSLING	6 May 24	Compt.	J. PARKINSON	2 Feb 24
P.S.	J. Muir	28 Jan 24	V. Chamb.	J. DAVISON	2 Feb 24
Pensions	F. ROBERTS	23 Jan 24	Lds in	Earl De La Warr	8 Feb 24
P.S.	(office vacant)		Waiting	Ld Muir-Mackenzie	8 Feb 24
Postm.-Gen.	**V. HARTSHORN**	22 Jan 24			

CONSERVATIVE GOVERNMENT 1924–1929

P.M.	**S. BALDWIN**	4 Nov 24 –4 Jun 29	P.& F.S.	C. Headlam	16 Dec 26
Ld Pres.	**Marquess CURZON**	6 Nov 24	(Contd.)		
	E of BALFOUR	27 Apr 25	Civil Ld	Earl Stanhope	11 Nov 24
Ld Chanc.	**Vt CAVE**	6 Nov 24	Ag.& Fish.	**E. WOOD**	6 Nov 24
	Ld HAILSHAM (Vt)	28 Mar 28		**W. GUINNESS**	4 Nov 25
Privy Seal	**M of SALISBURY**	6 Nov 24	P.S.	Ld Bledisloe	11 Nov 24
Exchequer	**W. CHURCHILL**	6 Nov 24		E of Stradbroke	5 Feb 28
F.S.	W. Guinness	11 Nov 24	Air	**Sir S. HOARE**	6 Nov 24
	R. McNeill		U-S.	Sir P. Sassoon	11 Nov 24
	(Ld Cushendun)	5 Nov 25	Colonies	**L. AMERY**	6 Nov 24
	A. Samuel	1 Nov 27	U-S.	W. Ormsby-Gore	12 Nov 24
Foreign O.	**(Sir) A. CHAMBERLAIN**	6 Nov 24	Dom.O.	**L. AMERY**	11 Jun 25
U-S.	R. McNeill	11 Nov 24	U-S.	E of Clarendon	5 Aug 25
	G. Locker-Lampson	7 Dec 25		Ld Lovat	5 May 27
Home O.	**Sir W. JOYNSON-HICKS**	6 Nov 24		E of Plymouth	1 Jan 29
U-S.	G. Locker-Lampson	11 Nov 24	B Educ.	**Ld E. PERCY***	6 Nov 24
	D. Hacking	8 Dec 25	P.S.	Duchess of Atholl	11 Nov 24
	Sir V. Henderson	9 Nov 27	Health	**N. CHAMBERLAIN**	6 Nov 24
Admiralty	**W. BRIDGEMAN**	6 Nov 24	P.S.	Sir K. Wood	11 Nov 24
P.& F.S.	J. Davidson	11 Nov 24	India	**E of BIRKENHEAD**	6 Nov 24

*MP. Not a member of the House of Lords.   +Not a member of the House of Commons.

CONSERVATIVE GOVERNMENT 1924–1929 *(contd.)*

India	**Vt PEEL**	18 Oct 28
(contd.)		
U-S.	Earl Winterton*	11 Nov 24
Labour	**Sir A. STEEL-MAITLAND**	
		6 Nov 24
P.S.	H. Betterton	11 Nov 24
D. Lanc.	**Vt CECIL of CHELWOOD**	
		10 Nov 24
	Ld CUSHENDUN	19 Oct 27
Paym.-Gen.	*(office vacant)*	
	D of SUTHERLAND	28 Jan 25
	E of ONSLOW	2 Dec 28
Pensions	G. TRYON	11 Nov 24
P.S.	G. Stanley	11 Nov 24
Postm.-		
Gen.	Sir W. MITCHELL-THOMSON	
		11 Nov 24
Ass.	Vt Wolmer*	11 Nov 24
Scotland	**Sir J. GILMOUR**	6 Nov 24
	(S. of State for Scotland 15 Jul 26)	
U-S.	W. Elliot	26 Jul 26
P.S. Health for		
Scotland	W. Elliot	11 Nov 24
	(post abolished 26 Jul 26)	
B.Trade	**Sir P. LLOYD-GREAME**	6 Nov 24
	(changed name to Sir P. Cunliffe-Lister 27 Nov 24)	
P.S.	Sir B. Chadwick	11 Nov 24
	H. Williams	13 Jan 28
Sec.		
Overseas	A. Samuel	11 Nov 24
Trade	D. Hacking	9 Nov 27
Sec.Mines	G. Lane-Fox	11 Nov 24
	D. King	13 Jan 28
Transport	W. ASHLEY	11 Nov 24
P.S.	J. Moore-Brabazon	11 Nov 24
	(post vacant from 14 Jan 27)	
War	**Sir L. WORTHINGTON-EVANS**	
		6 Nov 24
U-S.	E of Onslow	11 Nov 24
	D of Sutherland	2 Dec 28
F.S.	D. King	11 Nov 24
	A. Duff Cooper	13 Jan 28
Works	**Vt PEEL**	10 Nov 24
	M of LONDONDERRY	18 Oct 28

Law Officers		
Att.-Gen.	**Sir D. HOGG**	6 Nov 24
	(Ld Hailsham)	
	(office not in cabinet)	
	Sir T. INSKIP	28 Mar 28
Sol.-Gen.	Sir T. INSKIP	11 Nov 24
	Sir F. MERRIMAN	28 Mar 28
Ld Advoc.	W. WATSON	11 Nov 24
	A. MACROBERT	23 Apr 29
Sol.-Gen.	D. FLEMING	11 Nov 24
Scotland	A. MACROBERT	30 Dec 25
	W. NORMAND	23 Apr 29
Whips		
P.S.to	B. EYRES-MONSELL	7 Nov 24
Treasury		
Lds of	G. Hennessy	13 Nov 24–10 Dec 25
Treasury	Ld Stanley*	13 Nov 24–9 Nov 27
	F. Thomson	13 Nov 24–14 Jan 28
	(Sir) W. Cope	13 Nov 24–14 Jan 28
	Vt Curzon*	13 Nov 24–15 Jan 29
	D. Margesson	28 Aug 26–4 Jun 29
	G. Bowyer	28 Dec 27–4 Jun 29
	F. Penny	13 Jan 28–4 Jun 29
	M of Titchfield*	13 Jan 28–4 Jun 29
	E. Wallace	1 Jan 29–4 Jun 29
H.M. Household		
Treasurer	G. GIBBS	13 Nov 24
	SIR G. HENNESSY	13 Jan 28
Compt.	SIR H. BARNSTON	13 Nov 24
	SIR W. COPE	13 Jan 28
V.Chamb.	D. HACKING	13 Nov 24
	(Sir) G. HENNESSY	10 Dec 25
	(Sir) F. THOMSON	13 Jan 28
Cap.Gents	E of CLARENDON	1 Dec 24
at Arms	E of PLYMOUTH	26 Jun 25
	E of LUCAN	1 Jan 29
Cap.Yeo.	Ld DESBOROUGH	1 Dec 24
of Guard		
Lds in	Vt Gage	1 Dec 24–4 Jun 29
Waiting	Ld Somers	1 Dec 24–23 Mar 26
	E of Lucan	1 Dec 24–1 Jan 29
	E of Airlie	1 Apr 26–4 Jun 29
	Ld Templemore	1 Jan 29–4 Jun 29

LABOUR GOVERNMENT 1929–1931

P.M.	**R. MACDONALD**	
		5 Jun 29–24 Aug 31
Ld Pres.	**Ld PARMOOR**	7 Jun 29
Ld Chanc.	**Ld SANKEY**	7 Jun 29
Privy Seal	**J. THOMAS**	7 Jun 29
	V. HARTSHORN	5 Jun 30
	T. JOHNSTON	24 Mar 31
Exchequer	**P. SNOWDEN**	7 Jun 29
F.S.	F. Pethick-Lawrence	11 Jun 29
Foreign O.	**A. HENDERSON**	7 Jun 29
U-S.	H. Dalton	11 Jun 29

Home O.	**J. CLYNES**	7 Jun 29
U-S.	A. Short	11 Jun 29
Admiralty	**A. ALEXANDER**	7 Jun 29
P.& F.S.	C. Ammon	11 Jun 29
Civil Ld	G. Hall	11 Jun 29
Ag.& Fish.	**N. BUXTON**	7 Jun 29
	C. ADDISON	5 Jun 30
P.S.	C. Addison	11 Jun 29
	Earl De La Warr	5 Jun 30
Air	**Ld THOMSON**	7 Jun 29
	Ld AMULREE	14 Oct 30

*MP. Not a member of the House of Lords.

LABOUR GOVERNMENT 1929–1931 (contd.)

U-S.	F. Montague	11 Jun 29	Transport	H MORRISON		7 Jun 29
Colonies	**Ld PASSFIELD**	7 Jun 29		(office in cabinet)		
U-S.	W. Lunn	11 Jun 29		**H. MORRISON**		19 Mar 31
	D. Shiels	1 Dec 29	P.S.	Earl Russell		11 Jun 29
Dom.O.	**Ld PASSFIELD**	7 Jun 29		A. Ponsonby (Ld)		1 Dec 29
	J. THOMAS	5 Jun 30		J. Parkinson		1 Mar 31
U-S.	A. Ponsonby	11 Jun 29	War	**T. SHAW**		7 Jun 29
	W. Lunn	1 Dec 29	U-S.	Earl De La Warr		11 Jun 29
B Educ.	**Sir C. TREVELYAN**	7 Jun 29		Ld Marley		5 Jun 30
	H. LEES-WOOD	2 Mar 31	F.S.	E. Shinwell		11 Jun 29
P.S.	M. Jones	11 Jun 29		W. Sanders		5 Jun 30
Health	**A. GREENWOOD**	7 Jun 29	Works	**G. LANSBURY**		7 Jun 29
P.S.	Susan Lawrence	11 Jun 29				

Law Officers

India	**W. BENN**	7 Jun 29
U-S.	D. Shiels	11 Jun 29

Att.-Gen.	Sir W. JOWITT		7 Jun 29
Sol.-Gen.	Sir J. MELVILLE		7 Jun 29
	Sir S. CRIPPS		22 Oct 30

	Earl Russell	1 Dec 29
	Ld Snell	13 Mar 31
Labour	**MARGARET BONDFIELD**	7 Jun 29
P.S.	J. Lawson .	11 Jun 29
D. Lanc.	SIR O. MOSLEY	7 Jun 29

Ld Advoc.	C. AITCHISON		17 Jun 29
Sol.-Gen. Scotland	J. WATSON[+]		17 Jun 29

	C. ATTLEE	23 May 30
	Ld PONSONBY	13 Mar 31
Paym.-Gen.	Ld ARNOLD	7 Jun 29
	(office vacant 6 Mar 31)	

Whips

P.S. to Treasury	T. KENNEDY		14 Jun 29
Lds of Treasury	C. Edwards	11 Jun 29–13 Mar 31	
	J. Parkinson	11 Jun 29–1 Mar 31	
	A. Barnes	11 Jun 29–23 Oct 30	
	W. Whiteley	27 Jun 29–24 Aug 31	
	W. Paling	27 Jun 29–24 Aug 31	
	E. Thurtle	23 Oct 30–24 Aug 31	
	H. Charleton	13 Mar 31–23 Aug 31	

Pensions	F. ROBERTS	7 Jun 29
P.S.	(post vacant)	
Postm.-Gen.	H. LEES-SMITH	7 Jun 29
	C. ATTLEE	2 Mar 31
Ass.	S. Viant	7 Jul 29
Scotland	**W. ADAMSON**	7 Jun 29
U-S.	T. Johnston	7 Jun 29
	J. Westwood	25 Mar 31

H.M. Household

Treasurer	B. SMITH		24 Jun 29
Compt.	T. HENDERSON		24 Jun 29
V.Chamb.	J. HAYES		24 Jun 29
Lds in	Earl De La Warr	18 Jul 29–24 Aug 31	
Waiting	Ld Muir-Mackenzie		
		18 Jul 29–22 May 30	

B. Trade	**W. GRAHAM**	7 Jun 29
P.S.	W. Smith	11 Jun 29
Sec. Over- seas Trade	G. Gillett	7 Jul 29
Sec. Mines	B. Turner	1 Jun 29
	E. Shinwell	5 Jun 30

NATIONAL GOVERNMENT 1931–1935

P.M.	**R. MACDONALD** (N.Lab)		U-S.	A. Eden (C)		3 Sep 31
	24 Aug 31–7 Jun 35			Earl Stanhope (C)		18 Jan 34
Ld Pres.	**S. BALDWIN** (C)	25 Aug 31	Home O.	**Sir H. SAMUEL** (Lib)		25 Aug 31
Ld Chanc.	**Ld SANKEY** (Vt) (N.Lab)	25 Aug 31		**Sir J. GILMOUR** (C)		28 Sep 32
Privy Seal	Earl PEEL(C)	3 Sep 31	U-S.	O. Stanley (C)		3 Sep 31
	(office in cabinet)			D. Hacking (C)		22 Feb 33
	Vt SNOWDEN (N. Lab)	5 Nov 31		H. Crookshank (C)		29 Jun 34
	S. BALDWIN (C)	29 Sep 32	Admiralty	Sir A. CHAMBERLAIN (C)		
	(office not in cabinet)					25 Aug 31
	A. EDEN (C)	31 Dec 33		(office in cabinet)		
Exchequer	**P. SNOWDEN** (Vt) (N.Lab)	25 Aug 31		**Sir B. EYRES-MONSELL** (C)		
	N. CHAMBERLAIN (C)	5 Nov 31				5 Nov 31
F.S.	W. Elliot (C)	3 Sep 31	P.& F.S.	Earl Stanhope (C)		3 Sep 31
	L. Hore-Belisha (L.Nat)	29 Sep 32		Ld Stanley*(C)		10 Nov 31
	A. Duff Cooper (C)	29 Jun 34	Civil Ld	E. Wallace (C)		10 Nov 31
Foreign O.	**M of READING** (Lib)	25 Aug 31	Ag.& Fish.	Sir J. GILMOUR (C)		25 Aug 31
	Sir J. SIMON (L.Nat)	5 Nov 31		(office in cabinet)		

*MP. Not a member of the House of Lords. [+]Not a member of the House of Commons.

NATIONAL GOVERNMENT 1931–1935 *(contd.)*

Ag.& Fish.	**Sir J. GILMOUR**(C)	5 Nov 31
(contd.)	**W. ELLIOTT** (C)	28 Sep 32
P.S.	*(office vacant)*	
	Earl De La Warr (N.Lab)	10 Nov 31
Air	Ld AMULREE (N.Lab)	25 Aug 31
	(office in cabinet)	
	M of LONDONDERRY (C)	5 Nov 31
U-S.	Sir P. Sassoon (C)	3 Sep 31
Colonies	**J. THOMAS** (N.Lab)	25 Aug 31
	Sir P. CUNLIFFE-LISTER (C)	5 Nov 31
U-S.	Sir R. Hamilton (Lib)	3 Sep 31
	E of Plymouth (C)	29 Sep 32
Dom.O.	**J. THOMAS** (N.Lab)	25 Aug 31
U-S.	M. MacDonald (N.Lab)	3 Sep 31
B.Educ.	Sir D. MACLEAN (Lib)	25 Aug 31
	(office in cabinet)	
	Sir D. MACLEAN (Lib)	5 Nov 31
	Ld IRWIN *(Vt Halifax)* (C)	15 Jun 32
P.S.	Sir K. Wood (C)	3 Sep 31
	H. Ramsbotham (C)	10 Nov 31
Health	**N. CHAMBERLAIN** (C)	25 Aug 31
	Sir E. YOUNG (C)	5 Nov 31
P.S.	E. Simon (Lib)	22 Sep 31
	E. Brown (L.Nat.)	10 Nov 31
	G. Shakespeare (L.Nat)	30 Sep 32
India	**Sir S. HOARE** (C)	25 Aug 31
U-S.	*(office vacant)*	
	M of Lothian (Lib)	10 Nov 31
	R. Butler (C)	29 Sep 32
Labour	Sir H. BETTERTON (C)	25 Aug 31
	(office in cabinet)	
	Sir H. BETTERTON (C)	5 Nov 31
	O. STANLEY (C)	29 Jun 34
P.S.	M. Gray (Lib)	3 Sep 31
	R. Hudson (C)	10 Nov 31
D.Lanc.	M of LOTHIAN (Lib)	25 Aug 31
	(Sir) J. DAVIDSON (C)	10 Nov 31
Paym.-Gen.	Sir T. WALTERS (Lib)	4 Sep 31
	Ld ROCHESTER (N.Lab)	23 Nov 31
Pensions	G. TRYON (C)	3 Sep 31
P.S.	*(office vacant)*	
	C. Headlam (C)	10 Nov 31
	(vacant from 29 Sep 32)	
Post.-Gen.	W. ORMSBY-GORE (C)	3 Sep 31
	Sir K. WOOD (C)	10 Nov 31
	(office in cabinet)	
	Sir K. WOOD (C)	20 Dec 33
Ass.	G. White (Lib)	3 Sep 31
	Sir E. Bennett (N.Lab)	21 Oct 32
Scotland	Sir A. SINCLAIR (Lib)	25 Aug 31
	(office in cabinet)	
	Sir A. SINCLAIR (Lib)	5 Nov 31
	Sir G. COLLINS (L.Nat)	28 Sep 32
U-S.	N. Skelton (C)	3 Sep 31
B. Trade	**Sir P. CUNLIFFE-LISTER** (C)	25 Aug 31
	W. RUNCIMAN (L.Nat)	5 Nov 31

P.S.	G. Lloyd-George (Lib)	3 Sep 31
	L. Hore-Belisha (L.Nat)	10 Nov 31
	L. Burgin (L.Nat)	29 Sep 32
Sec.	Sir E. Young (C)	3 Sep 31
Overseas Trade	J. Colville (C)	10 Nov 31
Sec.Mines	I. Foot (Lib)	3 Sep 31
	E. Brown (L.Nat)	30 Sep 32
Transport	J. PYBUS (L.Nat)	3 Sep 31
	O. STANLEY (C)	22 Feb 33
	L. HORE-BELISHA (L.Nat)	29 Jun 34
P.S.	(Sir) G. Gillett (N. Lab)	4 Sep 31
	E of Plymouth (C)	25 Nov 31
	C. Headlam (C)	29 Sep 32
	(office vacant 5 Jul 34)	
	A. Hudson (C)	12 Apr 35
War	M of CREWE (Lib)	26 Aug 31
	(office in cabinet)	
	Vt HAILSHAM (C)	5 Nov 31
U-S.	*(office vacant)*	
	Earl Stanhope (C)	10 Nov 31
	Ld Strathcona (C)	24 Jan 34
F.S.	A. Duff Cooper (C)	3 Sep 31
	D. Hacking (C)	29 Jun 34
Works	M of LONDONDERRY (C)	25 Aug 31
	(office in cabinet)	
	W. ORMSBY-GORE (C)	5 Nov 31

Law Officers

Att.-Gen.	Sir W. JOWITT (N.Lab)	3 Sep 31
	Sir T. INSKIP (C)	26 Jan 32
Sol.-Gen.	Sir T. INSKIP (C)	3 Sep 31
	Sir F. MERRIMAN (C)	26 Jan 32
	Sir D. SOMERVELL (C)	29 Sep 33
Ld Advoc.	C. AITCHISON (N Lab)	3 Sep 31
	W.NORMAND (C)	2 Oct 33
	D. JAMIESON (C)	28 Mar 35
Sol.-Gen. Scotland	J. WATSON+ (N.Lab)	4 Sep 31
	W. NORMAND (C)	10 Nov 31
	D. JAMIESON (C)	2 Oct 33
	T. COOPER (C)	15 May 35

Whips

P.S. to Treasury	Sir B. EYRES-MONSELL (C)	3 Sep 31
	D. Margesson (C)	10 Nov 31
Lds of Treasury	D. Margesson (C)	26 Aug 31–10 Nov 31
	Sir F. Penny (C)	3 Sep 31–12 Nov 31
	A. Glassey (Lib)	14 Sep 31–12 Nov 31
	M of Titchfield* (C)	3 Sep 31–12 Nov 31
	E. Wallace (C)	3 Sep 31–12 Nov 31
	(Sir) W. Womersley (C)	12 Nov 31–7 Jun 35
	Sir V. Warrender (C)	12 Nov 31–30 Sep 32
	G. Shakespeare (L.Nat)	12 Nov 31–30 Sep 32
	A. Hudson (C)	12 Nov 31–12 Apr 35
	Sir L. Ward (C)	12 Nov 31–1 May 35

*MP. Not a member of the House of Lords.   +Not a member of the House of Commons.

NATIONAL GOVERNMENT 1931–1935 *(contd.)*

Treasury	G. Davies (C)	11 Oct 32–7 Jun 35	*V.Chamb.*	Sir F. PENNY (C)	12 Nov 31
(contd.)	J. Blindell (L.Nat)	30 Sep 32–7 Jun 35	*(contd.)*	Sir V. WARRENDER (C)	30 Sep 32
	J. Stuart (C)	1 May 35–7 Jun 35		Sir L.WARD (C)	1 May 35
	A. Southby (C)	23 Apr 35–7 Jun 35	*Cap.Gents*	E of LUCAN (C)	12 Nov 31
			at Arms		
H.M. Household			*Cap.Yeo.*	Ld STRATHCONA (C)	12 Nov 31
Treasurer	Sir G. HENNESSY (C)	3 Sep 31	*of Guard*	Ld TEMPLEMORE (C)	24 Jan 34
	Sir F. THOMSON (C)	12 Nov 31	*Lds in*	Ld Templemore (C)	
	Sir F. PENNY (C)	1 May 35	*Waiting*		12 Nov 31–24 Jan 34
Compt.	G. OWEN (Lib)	14 Sep 31		Vt Gage (C)	12 Nov 31–7 Jun 35
	W.REA (Lib)	12 Nov 31		Vt Allendale (Lib)	
	Sir F. PENNY (C)	30 Sep 32			12 Nov 31–28 Sep 32
	Sir V. WARRENDER (C)	1 May 35		E of Munster (C)	24 Jan 34–7 Jun 35
V.Chamb.	Sir F. THOMSON (C)	3 Sep 31		E of Feversham (C)	24 Jan 34–7 Jun 35

NATIONAL GOVERNMENT 1935–1940

P.M.	**S. BALDWIN**	7 Jun 35–28 May 37	*Admiralty*	**Sir B. EYRES-MONSELL**	7 Jun 35
	N. CHAMBERLAIN[1]			*(Vt Monsell)*	
		28 May 37–10 May 40		**Sir S. HOARE**	5 Jun 36
Ld Pres.	**R. MACDONALD**	7 Jun 35		**A. DUFF COOPER**	28 May 37
	Vt HALIFAX	28 May 37		**Earl STANHOPE**	27 Oct 38
	Vt HAILSHAM	9 Mar 38		**W. CHURCHILL**[1]	3 Sep 39
	Vt RUNCIMAN	31 Oct 38	*P.& F.S.*	Sir V. Warrender	18 Jun 35
	Earl STANHOPE	3 Sep 39		Ld Stanley*	28 Nov 35
Ld Chanc.	**Vt HAILSHAM**	7 Jun 35		G. Shakespeare	28 May 37
	Ld MAUGHAM	9 Mar 38		Sir V. Warrender	3 Apr 40
	Vt CALDECOTE	3 Sep 39	*Civil Ld*	K. Lindsay	18 Jun 35
Privy Seal	**M of LONDONDERRY**	7 Jun 35		J. Llewellin	28 May 37
	Vt HALIFAX	22 Nov 35		A. Hudson	14 Jul 39
	Earl De La WARR	28 May 37	*Ag.& Fish.*	**W. ELLIOT**	7 Jun 35
	Sir J. ANDERSON	31 Oct 38		**W. MORRISON**	29 Oct 36
	Sir S. HOARE[1]	3 Sep 39		**Sir R. DORMAN-SMITH**	29 Jan 39
	Sir K. WOOD	3 Apr 40	*P.S.*	Earl De La Warr	18 Jun 35
Exchequer	**N. CHAMBERLAIN**	7 Jun 35		H. Ramsbotham	28 Nov 35
	Sir J. SIMON[1]	28 May 37		E of Feversham	30 Jul 36
F.S.	A. Duff Cooper	18 Jun 35		Ld Denham	19 Sep 39
	W. Morrison	22 Nov 35	*Air*	**Sir P. CUNLIFFE-LISTER**	
	J. Colville	29 Oct 36		*(Vt Swinton)*	7 Jun 35
	E. Wallace	16 May 38		**Sir K. WOOD**[1]	16 May 38
	H. Crookshank	21 Apr 39		**Sir S. HOARE**	3 Apr 40
Foreign O.	**Sir S. HOARE**	7 Jun 35	*U-S.*	Sir P. Sassoon	18 Jun 35
	A. EDEN	22 Dec 35		A. Muirhead	28 May 37
	Vt HALIFAX[1]	21 Feb 38		H. Balfour	16 May 38
U-S.	Earl Stanhope	18 Jun 35–16 Jun 36	*Colonies*	**M. MACDONALD**	7 Jun 35
	Vt Cranborne*	6 Aug 35–20 Feb 38		**J. THOMAS**	22 Nov 35
	E of Plymouth	30 Jul 36–12 May 39		**W. ORMSBY-GORE**	28 May 36
	R. Butler	25 Feb 38–10 May 40		**M. MACDONALD**	16 May 38
Home O.	**Sir J. SIMON**	7 Jun 35	*U-S.*	E of Plymouth	18 Jun 35
	Sir S. HOARE	28 May 37		Earl De La Warr	30 Jul 36
	Sir J. ANDERSON	3 Sep 39		M of Dufferin & Ava	28 May 37
U-S.	E. Wallace	18 Jun 35	*Min. for*	*(office not established)*	
	G. Lloyd	28 Nov 35	*Co-ord.*	**Sir T. INSKIP**	13 Mar 36
	O. Peake	21 Apr 39	*of Def.*	**Ld CHATFIELD**[1]	29 Jan 39
P.S. Min.	A. Lennox-Boyd	6 Sep 39		*(office abolished 3 Apr 40)*	
Home	W. Mabane	24 Oct 39	*Dom.O.*	**J. THOMAS**	7 Jun 35
Security				**M. MACDONALD**	22 Nov 35

---

*MP. Not a member of the House of Lords.   [1] Member of War Cabinet 1939–40.

NATIONAL GOVERNMENT 1935–1940 (contd.)

Dom.O.	**Ld STANLEY***	16 May 38	*Pensions*	R. HUDSON		18 Jun 35
(contd.)	**M. MACDONALD**	31 Oct 38		H. RAMSBOTHAM		30 Jul 36
	Sir T. INSKIP *(Vt. Caldecote)*	29 Jan 39		Sir W. WOMERSLEY		7 Jun 39
	A. EDEN	3 Sep 39	*Min.*	**A. EDEN**	7 Jun 35–22 Dec 35	
U-S.	Ld Stanley*	18 Jun 35	*without*			
	D. Hacking	28 Nov 35	*Portfolio for*			
	M of Hartington* *(D of*	4 Mar 36	*League of*			
	Devonshire)		*Nations Affairs*			
Ec. Warfare	R. CROSS	3 Sep 39	*Min.*	**Ld E. PERCY***	7 Jun 35–31 Mar 36	
B.Educ.	**O. STANLEY**	7 Jun 35	*without*	**L. BURGIN**	21 Apr 39–14 Jul 39	
	Earl STANHOPE	28 May 37	*Portfolio*	**Ld HANKEY**[1]	3 Sep 39–10 May 40	
	Earl De La WARR	27 Oct 38	*Postm.-Gen.*	G. TRYON		7 Jun 35
	H. RAMSBOTTOM	3 Apr 40		W. MORRISON		3 Apr 40
P.S.	H. Ramsbotham	18 Jun 35	*Ass.*	Sir E. Bennett		18 Jun 35
	Earl De La Warr	28 Nov 35		Sir W. Womersley		6 Dec 35
	G. Shakespeare	30 Jul 36		W. Mabane		7 Jun 39
	K. Lindsay	28 May 37		C. Waterhouse		24 Oct 39
Food	**W. MORRISON**		*Scotland*	**Sir G. COLLINS**		7 Jun 35
	(combined with D. Lanc. 4 Sep 39)			**W. ELLIOT**		29 Oct 36
	Ld WOOLTON	3 Apr 40		**J. COLVILLE**		16 May 38
P.S.	A. Lennox-Boyd	11 Oct 39	*U-S.*	N. Skelton		18 Jun 35
Health	**Sir K. WOOD**	7 Jun 35		J. Colville		28 Nov 35
	W. ELLIOT	16 May 38		H. Wedderburn		29 Oct 36
P.S.	G. Shakespeare	18 Jun 35		J. McEwen		6 Sep 39
	R. Hudson	30 Jul 36	*Shipping*	*(office not established)*		
	R. Bernays	28 May 37		**Sir J. GILMOUR**		13 Oct 39
	Florence Horsbrugh	14 Jul 39		**R. HUDSON**		3 Apr 40
India (&	**M of ZETLAND**	7 Jun 35	*P.S.*	Sir A. Salter		13 Nov 39
Burma 1937-)			*Supply*	*(office not established)*		
U-S.	R. Butler	18 Jun 35		**L. BURGIN**		14 Jul 39
	Ld Stanley*	28 May 37	*P.S.*	J. Llewellin		14 Jul 39
	A. Muirhead	16 May 38	*B.Trade*	**W. RUNCIMAN**		7 Jun 35
	Sir H. O'Neill	11 Sep 39		**O. STANLEY**		28 May 37
Information	*(office not established)*			**Sir A. DUNCAN**		5 Jan 40
	Ld MACMILLAN	4 Sep 39	*P.S.*	L. Burgin		18 Jun 35
	Sir J. REITH	5 Jan 40		E. Wallace		28 May 37
P.S.	Sir E. Grigg	19 Sep 39		R. Cross		16 May 38
	(office vacant 3 Apr 40)			G. Lloyd-George		6 Sep 39
Labour	**E. BROWN**	7 Jun 35	*Sec.*	J. Colville		18 Jun 35
	(3 Sep 39 Lab. & Nat S.)		*Overseas*	E. Wallace		28 Nov 35
P.S.	A. Muirhead	18 Jun 35	*Trade*	R. Hudson		28 May 37
	R. Butler	28 May 37		G. Shakespeare		3 Apr 40
	A. Lennox-Boyd	25 Feb 38	*Sec.Mines*	H. Crookshank		18 Jun 35
	R. Assheton	6 Sep 39		G. Lloyd		21 Apr 39
D.Lanc.	Sir J. DAVIDSON	18 Jun 35	*Transp.*	L. HORE-BELISHA		18 Jun 35
	Earl WINTERTON*	28 May 37		*(office in cabinet)*		
	(office in cabinet)			**L. HORE-BELISHA**		29 Oct 36
	Earl WINTERTON*	11 Mar 38		**L. BURGIN**		28 May 37
	W. MORRISON	29 Jan 39		**E. WALLACE**		21 Apr 39
	(4 Sep 39–3 Apr 40 combined		*P.S.*	A. Hudson		18 Jun 35
	with Min. of Food)			R. Bernays		14 Jul 39
	(office not in cabinet)		*War*	**Vt HALIFAX**		7 Jun 35
	G. (Ld) TRYON	3 Apr 40		**A. DUFF COOPER**		22 Nov 35
Paym.-Gen.	Ld ROCHESTER	18 Jun 35		**L. HORE-BELISHA**[1]		28 May 37
	Ld HUTCHISON	6 Dec 35		**O. STANLEY**[1]		5 Jan 40
	E of MUNSTER	2 Jun 38	*U-S.*	Ld Strathcona		18 Jun 35
	Earl WINTERTON*	29 Jan 39		E of Munster		29 Jan 39
	(office vacant from Nov 39)			Vt Cobham		19 Sep 39

*MP. Not a member of the House of Lords.   [1] Member of War Cabinet 1939–40.

NATIONAL GOVERNMENT 1935–1940 *(contd.)*

F.S	D. Hacking	18 Jun 35	*Lds of*	S. Furness	20 May 38–10 May 40
	Sir V. Warrender	28 Nov 35	*Treasury*	Sir J. Edmondson	4 Apr 39–13 Nov 39
	Sir E. Grigg	3 Apr 40	*(contd.)*	P. Buchan-Hepburn	
Works	**W. ORMSBY-GORE**	7 Jun 35			13 Nov 39–10 May 40
	Earl STANHOPE	16 Jun 36		W. Boulton	12 Feb 40–10 May 40
	(office not in cabinet)				
	Sir P. SASSOON	28 May 37	**H.M. Household**		
	H. RAMSBOTHAM	7 Jun 39	*Treasurer*	Sir F. PENNY	18 Jun 35
	Earl DE LA WARR	3 Apr 40		Sir L. WARD	28 May 37
				A. HOPE	18 Oct 37
Law Officers				C. WATERHOUSE	4 Apr 39
Att.-Gen.	Sir T. INSKIP	18 Jun 35		R. GRIMSTON	12 Nov 39
	Sir D. SOMERVELL	18 Mar 36	*Compt.*	Sir G. BOWYER	21 Jun 35
Sol.-Gen.	Sir D. SOMERVELL	18 Jun 35		Sir L. WARD	6 Dec 35
	Sir T. O'CONNOR	19 Mar 36		Sir G. DAVIES	28 May 37
Ld Advoc.	D. JAMIESON	18 Jun 35		C. WATERHOUSE	18 Oct 37
	T. COOPER	25 Oct 35		C. KERR	4 Apr 39
Sol.-Gen.	T. COOPER	18 Jun 35	*V.Chamb.*	Sir L. WARD	18 Jun 35
Scotland	A. RUSSELL+	29 Nov 35		(Sir) G. DAVIES	6 Dec 35
	J. REID	25 Jun 36		A. HOPE	28 May 37
				R. CROSS	18 Oct 37
Whips				R. GRIMSTON	18 May 38
P.S. to	D. MARGESSON	18 Jun 35		Sir J. EDMONDSON	12 Nov 39
Treasury					
Lds of	J. Stuart	18 Jun 35–10 May 40	*Cap.Gents*	E of LUCAN	18 Jun 35
Treasury	(Sir) A. Southby	18 Jun 35–28 May 37	*at Arms*		
	Sir W. Womersley	18 Jun 35–6 Dec 35	*Cap.Yeo.*	Ld TEMPLEMORE	18 Jun 35
	G. Davies	18 Jun 35–6 Dec 35	*of Guard*		
	(Sir) J. Blindell	18 Jun 35–28 May 37	*Lds in*	Vt Gage	18 Jun 35–11 Apr 39
	A. Hope	6 Dec 35–28 May 37	*Waiting*	E of Munster	18 Jun 35–2 Jun 38
	(Sir) H. Morris-Jones			E of Feversham	18 Jun 35–30 Jul 36
		6 Dec 35–28 May 37		M of Dufferin & Ava	
	C. Kerr	28 May 37–4 Apr 39			29 Oct 36–28 May 37
	T. Dugdale	28 May 37–12 Feb 40		E of Erne	29 Oct 36–25 Jul 39
	C. Waterhouse	28 May 37–18 Oct 37		Earl Fortescue	26 Aug 37–10 May 40
	R. Cross	28 May 37–18 Oct 37		E of Birkenhead	12 Jul 38–10 May 40
	P. Munro	18 Oct 37–10 May 40		Vt Bridport	11 Apr 39–10 May 40
	R. Grimston	18 Oct 37–18 May 38		Ld Ebury	25 Jul 39–10 May 40

COALITION GOVERNMENT 1940–1945

P.M. and	**W. CHURCHILL**[1] (C)		*Exchequer*	**Sir J. ANDERSON**[1] (Nat)	24 Sep 43
Defence		10 May 40–23 May 45	*(contd.)*		
Ld Pres.	**N. CHAMBERLAIN**[1](Nat)	3 Oct 40	*F.S.*	H. Crookshank (C)	15 May 40
	C. ATTLEE[1] (Lab)	24 Sep 43		R. Assheton (C)	7 Feb 43
Ld Chanc.	Vt SIMON (L.Nat)	12 May 40		O. Peake (C)	29 Oct 44
Privy Seal	**C. ATTLEE**[1](Lab)	11 May 40	*Foreign O.*	**Vt HALIFAX**[1] (C)	11 May 40
	Sir S. CRIPPS[1] (Lab)	19 Feb 42		**A. EDEN**[1] (C)	22 Dec 40
	(office not in war cabinet)		*U-S.*	R. Butler (C)	15 May 40
	Vt CRANBORNE (C)	22 Nov 42		R. Law (C)	20 Jul 41
	(office in war cabinet)			G. Hall (Lab)	25 Sep 43
	Ld BEAVERBROOK[1] (C)	24 Sep 43	*Home O.*	Sir J. ANDERSON (Nat)	
Exchequer	Sir K. WOOD (C)	12 May 40	*& Home*		12 May 40
	(office in war cabinet)		*Security*	H. MORRISON (Lab)	2 Oct 40
	Sir K. WOOD[1] (C)	3 Oct 40		*(office in war cabinet)*	
	(office not in war cabinet)			**H. MORRISON**[1] (Lab)	22 Nov 42
	Sir K. WOOD (C)	19 Feb 42	*U-S.*	O. Peake (C)	15 May 40
	(office in war cabinet)			E of Munster (C)	31 Oct 44

+Not a member of the House of Commons.   [1] Member of War Cabinet.

COALITION GOVERNMENT 1940–1945 *(contd.)*

P.S. Home	W. Mabane (L.Nat)	
		15 May 40–3 Jun 42
Security	Ellen Wilkinson (Lab)	
		8 Oct 40–23 May 45
Admiralty	A. ALEXANDER (Lab)	11 May 40
P.&F.S.	Sir V. Warrender (C)	17 May 40
	(Ld Bruntisfield)	
Civil Ld	A. Hudson (C)	15 May 40
	R. Pilkington (C)	4 Mar 42
F.S.	G. Hall (Lab)	4 Feb 42
	J. Thomas (C)	25 Sep 43
Ag.& Fish.	R. HUDSON (C)	14 May 40
P.S.	Ld Moyne (C) 15 May 40–8 Feb 41	
	T. Williams (Lab)	
		15 May 40–23 May 45
	D of Norfolk (C) 8 Feb 41–23 May 45	
Air	Sir A. SINCLAIR (Lib)	11 May 40
P.S.	H. Balfour (C) 15 May 40–21 Nov 44	
	Ld Sherwood (Lib)	
		20 Jul 41–23 May 45
	R. Brabner (C) 21 Nov 44–27 Mar 45	
	Q. Hogg (C) 12 Apr 45–23 May 45	
Aircraft	Ld BEAVERBROOK (C)	14 May 40
Production	*(office in war cabinet)*	
	Ld BEAVERBROOK[1] (C)	2 Aug 40
	(office not in war cabinet)	
	J. MOORE-BRABAZON (C) 1 May 41	
	J. LLEWELLIN (C)	22 Feb 42
	Sir S. CRIPPS (Lab)	22 Nov 42
P.S.	J. Llewellin (C)	15 May 40
	F. Montague (Lab)	1 May 41
	B. Smith (Lab)	4 Mar 42
	A. Lennox-Boyd (C)	11 Nov 43
Civil Av.	*(office not established)*	
	Vt SWINTON(C)	8 Oct 44
P.S.	R. Perkins (C)	22 Mar 45
Colonies	Ld LLOYD (C)	12 May 40
	Ld MOYNE (C)	8 Feb 41
	Vt CRANBORNE (C)	22 Feb 42
	O. STANLEY (C)	22 Nov 42
U-S.	G. Hall (Lab)	15 May 40
	H. Macmillan (C)	4 Feb 42
	D of Devonshire (C)	1 Jan 43
Dom. O.	Vt CALDECOTE (C)	14 May 40
	Vt CRANBORNE* (C)	3 Oct 40
	(office in war cabinet)	
	C. ATTLEE[1](Lab)	19 Feb 42
	(office not in war cabinet)	
	Vt CRANBORNE (C)	24 Sep 43
U-S.	G. Shakespeare (L.Nat)	15 May 40
	P. Emrys-Evans (C)	4 Mar 42
Economic	H. DALTON (Lab)	15 May 40
Warfare	Vt WOLMER (C)	22 Feb 42
	(E of Selborne)	
P.S.	D. Foot (Lib)	17 May 40

B.Educ.	H. RAMSBOTHAM (C)	14 May 40
	R. BUTLER (C)	20 Jul 41
	(3 Aug 44 becomes Min. of Education)	
P.S.	C. Ede (Lab)	15 May 40
Food	Ld WOOLTON (C)	13 May 40
	J. LLEWELLIN (C)	11 Nov 43
P.S.	R. Boothby (C)	15 May 40
	G. Lloyd-George (Ind.L)	22 Oct 40
	W. Mabane (L.Nat)	3 Jun 42
Fuel, Light	*(office not established)*	
& Power	G. LLOYD-GEORGE (Ind.L) 3 Jun 42	
P.S.	G. Lloyd (C) 3 Jun 42–23 May 45	
	T. Smith (Lab) 3 Jun 42–23 May 45	
Health	M. MACDONALD (N.Lab) 13 May 40	
	E. BROWN (L.Nat)	8 Feb 41
	H. WILLINK (C)	11 Nov 43
P.S.	Florence Horsbrugh (C)	15 May 40
India &	L. AMERY (C)	13 May 40
Burma		
P.S.	D of Devonshire (C)	17 May 40
	E of Munster (C)	1 Jan 43
	E of Listowel (Lab)	31 Oct 44
Information	A. DUFF COOPER (C)	12 May 40
	(attended war cabinet from 28 May 40)	
	B. BRACKEN (C)	20 Jul 41
P.S.	H. Nicolson (N. Lab)	17 May 40
	E. Thurtle (Lab)	20 Jul 41
Labour &	E. BEVIN (Lab)	13 May 40
Nat. S.	*(office in war cabinet)*	
	E. BEVIN[1] (Lab)	3 Oct 40
P.S.	R. Assheton (C) 15 May 40–4 Feb 42	
	G. Tomlinson (Lab)	
		8 Feb 41–23 May 45
	M. McCorquodale (C)	
		4 Feb 42–23 May 45
D Lanc.	Ld HANKEY (Ind)	14 May 40
	A. DUFF COOPER (C)	20 Jul 41
	E. BROWN (L.Nat)	11 Nov 43
Min.	H. MACMILLAN (C)	30 Dec 42
resident		
N.W.Africa		
Min.	**O. LYTTELTON**[1] (C)	19 Feb 42
resident	**R. CASEY**[+1](Ind)	19 Mar 42
Mid.East	*(office not in war cabinet 23 Dec 43)*	
	Ld MOYNE (C)	28 Jan 44
	Sir E. GRIGG (C)	21 Nov 44
Deputy	Ld Moyne (C) 27 Aug 42–28 Jan 44	
Min.of State		
Min.	J. LLEWELLIN (C)	22 Nov 42
resident	B. SMITH (Lab)	11 Nov 43
Washington		
for Supply		
Min.	Vt SWINTON (C)	8 Jun 42
resident	H. BALFOUR (C)	21 Nov 44
W. Africa		

*MP. Not a member of the House of Lords.   +Not a member of the House of Commons.
[1] Member of War Cabinet.

COALITION GOVERNMENT 1940–1945 (contd.)

Min. without. Portfolio	**A. GREENWOOD**¹ (Lab)	11 May 40–22 Feb 42		T. & C.	(office not established)	
	(not in war cabinet)			Planning	W. MORRISON (C)	30 Dec 42
	Sir W. JOWITT (Lab)	30 Dec 42–8 Oct 44			(Minister designate until 7 Feb 43)	
Paym.-Gen.	Vt CRANBORNE* (C)	15 May 40		P.S.	H. Strauss (C)	30 Dec 42
	(office vacant 3 Oct 40)				A. Jenkins (Lab)	22 Mar 45
	Ld HANKEY (Ind)	20 Jul 41		B. Trade	Sir A. DUNCAN (C)	12 May 40
	Sir W. JOWITT (Lab)	4 Mar 42			O. LYTTELTON (C)	3 Oct 40
	Ld CHERWELL (C)	30 Dec 42			Sir A. DUNCAN (C)	29 Jun 41
Pensions	Sir W. WOMERSLEY (C)	15 May 40			J. LLEWELLIN (C)	4 Feb 42
P.S.	Ellen Wilkinson (Lab)	17 May 40			H. DALTON (Lab)	22 Feb 42
	Ld Tryon (C)	8 Oct 40		P.S.	G. Lloyd-George (Lib)	
	W. Paling (Lab)	8 Feb 41			(& P.S. Food 22 Oct 40)	15 May 40
Post.-Gen.	W. MORRISON (C)	15 May 40			C. Waterhouse (C)	8 Feb 41
	H. CROOKSHANK (C)	7 Feb 43		Sec.	H. Johnstone (Lib)	15 May 40
Ass.	C. Waterhouse (C)	17 May 40		Overseas	S. Summers (C)	22 Mar 45
	A. Chapman (C)	1 Mar 41		Trade		
	R. Grimston (C)	4 Mar 42		Sec.Mines	D. Grenfell (Lab)	15 May 40
Reconstruc.	(office not established)			Sec. Petrol	G. Lloyd (C)	15 May 40–3 Jun 42
	Ld WOOLTON¹ (C)	11 Nov 43			(3 Jun 42 combined in	
Scotland	E. BROWN (L. Nat)	14 May 40			Min. of Fuel, Light & Power)	
	T. JOHNSTON (Lab)	8 Feb 41		Transport	Sir J. REITH (Nat)	14 May 40
P.S.	J. Westwood (Lab)				J. MOORE-BRABAZON (C)	3 Oct 40
		17 May 40–23 May 45			(1 May 41 became	
	H. Wedderburn (C)	8 Feb 41–4 Mar 42			Min. of War Transport)	
	A. Chapman (C)	4 Mar 42–23 May 45		(War)	**Ld BEAVERBROOK**¹ (C)	4 Feb 42
Shipping	R. CROSS (C)	14 May 40		Production	(office vacant 19 Feb 42)	
	(1 May 41 combined with				**O. LYTTELTON**¹ (C)	12 Mar 42
	Min. of Transport as				(Minister of Production)	
	Min. of War Transport)			P.S.	G. Garro-Jones (Lab)	10 Sep 42
P.S.	Sir A. Salter (Ind)	15 May 40		War	A. EDEN (C)	11 May 40
Soc.	(office not established)				D. MARGESSON (C)	22 Dec 40
Insurance	Sir W. JOWITT (Lab)	8 Oct 44			Sir J. GRIGG (Nat)	22 Feb 42
	(renamed Nat.Insurance			U-S.	Sir H. Page Croft (C)	
	17 Nov 44)				(Ld Croft)	17 May 40–23 May 45
P.S.	C. Peat (C)	22 Mar 45			Sir E. Grigg (C)	17 May 40–4 Mar 42
State	**Ld BEAVERBROOK**¹ (C)	1 May 41			A. Henderson (Lab)	4 Mar 42–7 Feb 43
(Min.of)	**O. LYTTELTON**¹ (C)	29 Jun 41		F.S.	R. Law (C)	17 May 40
	(office vacant 12 Mar 42)				D. Sandys (C)	20 Jul 41
	R. Law (C)	24 Sep 43			A. Henderson (Lab)	7 Feb 43
Supply	H. MORRISON (Lab)	12 May 40		War Transp.	Ld LEATHERS (C)	1 May 41
	Sir A. DUNCAN (C)	3 Oct 40		P.S.	F. Montague (Lab)	
	(office in war cabinet)					18 May 40–1 May 41
	Ld BEAVERBROOK¹	29 Jun 41			(renamed War Transport	
	(office not in war cabinet)				1 May 41)	
	Sir A. DUNCAN (C)	4 Feb 42			J. Llewellin (C)	1 May 41–4 Feb 42
P.S.	H. Macmillan (C)	15 May 40–4 Feb 42			Sir A. Salter (Ind)	29 Jun 41–4 Feb 42
	Ld Portal (C)	4 Sep 40–22 Feb 42			P. Noel-Baker (Lab)	4 Feb 42–23 May 45
	R. Assheton (C)	4 Feb 42–7 Feb 43		Works	Ld TRYON (C)	18 May 40
	C. Peat (C)	4 Mar 42–22 Mar 45			Sir J. REITH (Ld) (Nat)	3 Oct 40
	D. Sandys (C)	7 Feb 43–21 Nov 44			(Min. of Works & Buildings	
	J. Wilmot (Lab)	21 Nov 44–23 May 45			& 1st Com. Works 3 Oct 40)	
	J. de Rothschild (Lib)				Ld PORTAL (C)	22 Feb 42
		22 Mar 45–23 May 45			(Min. of Works and Planning	
					11 Feb 42	
					Min. of Works Feb 43)	

*MP. Not a member of the House of Lords.   ¹ Member of War Cabinet.

COALITION GOVERNMENT 1940–1945 *(contd.)*

Works	D. SANDYS (C)	21 Nov 44
(contd.)		
P.S.	G. Hicks (Lab) 19 Nov 40–23 May 45	
	H. Strauss (C) 4 Mar 42–30 Dec 42	
Law Officers		
Att.-Gen.	Sir D. SOMERVELL (C)	15 May 40
Sol.-Gen.	Sir W. JOWITT (Lab)	15 May 40
	Sir D. MAXWELL FYFE(C)	4 Mar 42
Ld Advoc.	T. COOPER (C)	15 May 40
	J. REID (C)	5 Jun 41
Sol.-Gen.	J. REID (C)	15 May 40
Scotland	(Sir) D. MURRAY (C)	5 Jun 41
Whips		
P.S. to	D. MARGESSON (C)	
Treasury		17 May 40–22 Dec 40
	Sir C. EDWARDS (Lab)	
		17 May 40–12 Mar 42
	J. STUART (C) 14 Jan 41–23 May 45	
	W. WHITELEY (Lab)	
		12 Mar 42–23 May 45
Lds of	S. Furness (L.Nat)	
Treasury		12 May 40–18 May 40
	J. Stuart (C)	12 May 40–14 Jan 41
	P. Munro (C)	12 May 40–13 Mar 42
	P. Buchan-Hepburn (C)	
		12 May 40–26 Jun 40
	W. Boulton (C)	12 May 40–13 Mar 42
	W. Paling (Lab)	18 May 40–8 Feb 41
	J. Thomas (C)	26 Jun 40–25 Sep 43
	T. Dugdale (C)	8 Feb 41–23 Feb 42

Lds of	W. Adamson (Lab) 1 Mar 41–2 Oct 44	
Treasury	A. Young (C)	23 Feb 42–3 Jul 44
(contd.)	J. McEwen (C)	13 Mar 42–6 Dec 44
	L. Pym (C)	13 Mar 42–23 May 45
	A. Beechman (L. Nat)	
		25 Sep 43–23 May 45
	C. Drewe (C)	3 Jul 44–23 May 45
	W. John (Lab)	2 Oct 44–23 May 45
	P. Buchan-Hepburn (C)	
		6 Dec 44–23 May 45
H.M. Household		
Treasurer	R. GRIMSTON (C)	17 May 40
	Sir J. EDMONDSON (C)	12 Mar 42
Compt.	W. WHITELEY (Lab)	17 May 40
	W. JOHN (Lab)	12 Mar 42
	G. MATHERS (Lab)	2 Oct 44
V.Chamb.	Sir J. EDMONDSON (C)	17 May 40
	W. BOULTON (C)	12 Mar 42
	A. YOUNG (C)	13 Jul 44
Cap.Gents	Ld SNELL (Lab) 31 May 40–21 Apr 44	
at Arms	Earl FORTESCUE (C)	22 Mar 45
Cap. Yeo.	Ld TEMPLEMORE (C)	31 May 40
of Guard		
Lds in	Earl Fortescue (C)	
Waiting		31 May 40–22 Mar 45
	Vt Clifden (Lib) 31 May 40–22 Mar 45	
	Ld Alness (L.Nat)	
		31 May 40–23 May 45
	M of Normanby (C)	
		22 Mar 45–23 May 45

CARETAKER GOVERNMENT 1945

P.M. and	**W. CHURCHILL**		*Air U-S.*	Earl Beatty	26 May 45
Min.of		23 May 45–26 Jul 45	*Aircraft*	E. BROWN	25 May 45
Defence			*Production*		
Ld Pres.	**Ld WOOLTON**	25 May 45	*P.S.*	A. Lennox-Boyd	26 May 45
Ld Chanc.	**Vt SIMON**	25 May 45	*Civil Av.*	Vt SWINTON	25 May 45
Privy S.	**Ld BEAVERBROOK**	25 May 45	*P.S.*	R. Perkins	26 May 45
Exchequer	**Sir J. ANDERSON**	25 May 45	*Colonies*	**O. STANLEY**	25 May 45
F.S.	O. Peake	26 May 45	*U-S.*	D of Devonshire	26 May 45
Foreign O.	**A. EDEN**	25 May 45	*Dom.O.*	**Vt CRANBORNE**	25 May 45
Min.of State	W. Mabane	25 May 45	*U-S.*	P. Emrys-Evans	26 May 45
U-S.	Ld Dunglass*	26 May 45–26 Jul 45	*Educ.*	**R. LAW**	25 May 45
	Ld Lovat	26 May 45–13 Jul 45	*P.S.*	Thelma Cazalet-Keir	26 May 45
Home O.	**Sir D. SOMERVELL**	25 May 45	*Food*	J. LLEWELLIN	25 May 45
U-S.	E of Munster	26 May 45	*P.S.*	Florence Horsbrugh	26 May 45
Admiralty	**B. BRACKEN**	25 May 45	*Fuel &*	G. LLOYD-GEORGE	25 May 45
P.& F.S.	Ld Bruntisfield	26 May 45	*Power*		
Civil Ld	R. Pilkington	26 May 45	*P.S.*	Sir A. Hudson	26 May 45
F.S.	J. Thomas	26 May 45	*Health*	H. WILLINK	25 May 45
Ag. & Fish.	**R. HUDSON**	25 May 45	*P.S.*	H. Kerr	26 May 45
P.S.	D of Norfolk	26 May 45	*India &*	**L. AMERY**	25 May 45
	D. Scott	26 May 45	*Burma*		
Air	**H. MACMILLAN**	25 May 45	*P.S.*	E of Scarbrough	26 May 45
U-S.	Q. Hogg	26 May 45			

*MP. Not a member of the House of Lords.

CARETAKER GOVERNMENT 1945 (contd.)

Information	G. LLOYD	25 May 45	*War*	**Sir J. GRIGG**	25 May 45
Labour &	**R. BUTLER**	25 May 45	*U.-S.*	Ld Croft	26 May 45
National S.			*F.S.*	M. Petherick	26 May 45
P.S.	M. McCorquodale	26 May 45	*War*	Ld LEATHERS	25 May 45
D. Lanc.	Sir A. SALTER	25 May 45	*Transp.*		
Min.	Sir E. GRIGG	25 May 45	*P.S*	P. Thorneycroft	26 May 45
resident			*Works*	D. SANDYS	25 May 45
Mid. East			*P.S.*	R. Manningham-Buller	26 May 45
Min.	H. BALFOUR	25 May 45			
resident			***Law Officers***		
W. Africa			*Att.-Gen.*	Sir D. MAXWELL FYFE	25 May 45
Nat.	L. HORE-BELISHA	25 May 45	*Sol.-Gen.*	Sir W. MONCKTON+	25 May 45
Insurance			*Ld Advoc.*	J. REID	25 May 45
P.S.	C. Peat	26 May 45	*Sol.-Gen.*	Sir D. MURRAY	25 May 45
Paym.-Gen.	Ld CHERWELL	25 May 45	*Scotland*		
Pensions	Sir W. WOMERSLEY	25 May 45			
P.S.	W. Sidney (*Ld De L'Isle*)	26 May 45	***Whips***		
Postm.-Gen.	H. CROOKSHANK	25 May 45	*P.S. to*	J. STUART	26 May 45
Ass.	W. Anstruther-Gray	26 May 45	*Treasury*		
Production	**O. LYTTELTON**	25 May 45	*Lds of*	A. Beechman	28 May 45
	(*& Pres. B Trade*)		*Treasury*	C. Drewe	25 May 45
P.S.	J. Maclay	28 May 45		P. Buchan-Hepburn	25 May 45
Scotland	**E of ROSEBERY**	25 May 45		R. Cary	28 May 45
P.S.	A. Chapman	26 May 45		C. Mott-Radclyffe	28 May 45
	T. Galbraith	26 May 45			
Supply	Sir A. DUNCAN	25 May 45	***H.M. Household***		
P.S.	R. Grimston	26 May 45	*Treasurer*	Sir J. EDMONDSON	28 May 45
Town &	W. MORRISON	25 May 45	*Compt.*	L. PYM	28 May 45
Country			*V. Chamb.*	A. YOUNG	28 May 45
Planning			*Cap.Gents*	Earl FORTESCUE	28 May 45
P.S.	R. Tree	26 May 45	*at Arms*		
B.Trade	**O. LYTTELTON**	25 May 45	*Cap.Yeo.*	Ld TEMPLEMORE	28 May 45
	(*& Min. of Production*)		*of Guard*		
P.S.	C. Waterhouse	26 May 45	*Lds in*	Ld Alness	28 May 45
Sec. Over-	S. Summers	26 May 45	*Waiting*	M of Normanby	28 May 45
seas Trade				D of Northumberland	28 May 45

LABOUR GOVERNMENT 1945–1951

P.M.	**C. ATTLEE**	26 Jul 45–26 Oct 51	*Econ S.*	D. Jay	5 Dec 47
Ld Pres.	**H. MORRISON**	27 Jul 45		(*office vacant 2 Mar 50*)	
	Vt ADDISON	9 Mar 51		J. Edwards	19 Oct 50
Ld Chanc.	**Ld JOWITT** (*Vt*)	27 Jul 45	*Foreign O.*	**E. BEVIN**	27 Jul 45
Privy Seal	**A. GREENWOOD**	27 Jul 45		**H. MORRISON**	9 Mar 51
	Ld INMAN	17 Apr 47	*Min.of*	P. NOEL-BAKER	3 Aug 45
	Vt ADDISON	7 Oct 47	*State*	H. McNEIL	4 Oct 46
	E. BEVIN	9 Mar 51		K. YOUNGER	28 Feb 50
	R. STOKES	26 Apr 51	*U.-S.*	H. McNeil	4 Aug 45–4 Oct 46
	(*also Min. of Materials 6 Jul 51*)			C. Mayhew	4 Oct 46–2 Mar 50
Exchequer	**H. DALTON**	27 Jul 45		Ld Henderson	7 Jun 48–26 Oct 51
	Sir S. CRIPPS	13 Nov 47		E. Davies	2 Mar 50–26 Oct 51
	H. GAITSKELL	19 Oct 50	*Home O.*	C. EDE	3 Aug 45
Min. Econ.	(*office not established*)		*U.-S.*	G. Oliver	4 Aug 45
Affairs	**Sir S. CRIPPS**	29 Sep 47		K. Younger	7 Oct 47
	(*office combined with Exch.13 Nov 47*)			G. de Freitas	2 Mar 50
	H. GAITSKELL	28 Feb 50–19 Oct 50	*Admiralty*	**A. ALEXANDER**	3 Aug 45
F.S.	W. Glenvil Hall	4 Aug 45		(*office not in cabinet*)	
	D. Jay	2 Mar 50		Vt HALL	4 Oct 46

+Not a member of the House of Commons.

LABOUR GOVERNMENT 1945–1951 (contd.)

Admiralty (contd.)	Ld PAKENHAM	24 May 51
P. & F.S.	J. Dugdale	4 Aug 45
	J. Callaghan	2 Mar 50
Civil Ld	W. Edwards	4 Aug 45
Ag.& Fish.	T. WILLIAMS	3 Aug 45
P.S.	E of Huntingdon	4 Aug 45–22 Nov 50
	P. Collick	5 Sep 45–7 Oct 47
	G. Brown	7 Oct 47–26 Apr 51
	E of Listowel	22 Nov 50–26 Oct 51
	A. Champion	26 Apr 51–26 Oct 51
Air	Vt STANSGATE	3 Aug 45
	(office not in cabinet)	
	P.NOEL-BAKER	4 Oct 46
	A. HENDERSON	7 Oct 47
U-S.	J. Strachey	4 Aug 45
	G. de Freitas	27 May 46
	A. Crawley	2 Mar 50
Aircraft	J. WILMOT	4 Aug 45
Production	(office abolished 1 Apr 46)	
P.S.	A. Woodburn	4 Aug 45
Civil	Ld WINSTER	4 Aug 45
Aviation	Ld NATHAN	4 Oct 46
	(office in cabinet)	
	Ld PAKENHAM	31 May 48
	(office not in cabinet)	
	Ld PAKENHAM	28 Feb 50
	Ld OGMORE	1 Jun 51
P.S.	I. Thomas	10 Aug 45
	G. Lindgren	4 Oct 46
	F. Beswick	2 Mar 50
Colonies	G. HALL	3 Aug 45
	A. CREECH-JONES	4 Oct 46
	J. GRIFFITHS	28 Feb 50
Min.	E of LISTOWEL	4 Jan 48
	J. DUGDALE	28 Feb 50
U-S.	A. Creech Jones	4 Aug 45
	I. Thomas	40 Oct 46
	D. Rees-Williams	7 Oct 47
	T. Cook	2 Mar 50
C.R.O.	(office not established)	
	Vt ADDISON	7 Jul 47
	P. NOEL-BAKER	7 Oct 47
	P. GORDON-WALKER	28 Feb 50
Min.	A. HENDERSON 14 Aug 47–7 Oct 47	
U-S.	A. Bottomley	7 Jul 47
	P. Gordon-Walker	7 Oct 47
	Ld Holden	2 Mar 50
	D. Rees-Williams (Ld Ogmore) 4 Jul 50	
	E of Lucan	1 Jun 51
Defence	C. ATTLEE (P.M.)	27 Jul 45
	A. ALEXANDER (Vt)	20 Dec 46
	E. SHINWELL	28 Feb 50
Dom. O.	Vt ADDISON	3 Aug 45
	(became C.R.O. 7 Jul 47)	
U-S.	J. Parker	4 Aug 45
	A. Bottomley	10 May 46
Educ.	Ellen WILKINSON	3 Aug 45
	G. TOMLINSON	10 Feb 47
P.S.	A. Jenkins	4 Aug 45
	D. Hardman	30 Oct 45
Food	Sir B. SMITH	3 Aug 45
	J. STRACHEY	27 May 46
	M. WEBB	28 Feb 50
P.S.	Edith Summerskill	4 Aug 45
	S. Evans	2 Mar 50
	F. Willey	18 Apr 50
Fuel &	E. SHINWELL	3 Aug 45
Power	(office not in cabinet)	
	H. GAITSKELL	7 Oct 47
	P. NOEL-BAKER	28 Feb 50
P.S.	W. Foster	4 Aug 45
	H. Gaitskell	10 May 46
	A. Robens	7 Oct 47
	H. Neal	26 Apr 51
Health	A. BEVAN	3 Aug 45
	(office not in cabinet)	
	H. MARQUAND	17 Jan 51
P.S.	C. Key	4 Aug 45
	J. Edwards	12 Feb 47
	A. Blenkinsop	1 Feb 49
India &	Ld PETHICK-LAWRENCE	3 Aug 45
Burma	E of LISTOWEL	17 Apr 47
	(14 Aug 47 & 4 Jan 48	
	offices abolished)	
U-S.	A. Henderson	4 Aug 45–14 Aug 47
Information	E. WILLIAMS	4 Aug 45
	E of LISTOWEL	26 Feb 46
	(office wound up 31 Mar 46)	
Lab. &	G. ISAACS	3 Aug 45
Nat.S.	A. BEVAN	17 Jan 51
	A. ROBENS	24 Apr 51
P.S.	N. Edwards	4 Aug 45
	F. Lee	2 Mar 50
D.Lanc.	J. HYND	4 Aug 45
	Ld PAKENHAM	17 Apr 47
	(office in cabinet)	
	H. DALTON	31 May 48
	Vt ALEXANDER	28 Feb 50
Nat.	J. GRIFFITHS	4 Aug 45
Insurance	Edith SUMMERSKILL	28 Feb 50
P.S.	G. Lindgren	4 Aug 45
	T. Steele	4 Oct 46
	H. Taylor	2 Mar 50
Paym.-Gen.	(office vacant)	
	A. GREENWOOD	9 Jul 46
	(office not in cabinet)	
	H. Marquand	5 Mar 47
	(office in cabinet)	
	Vt ADDISON	2 Jul 48
	(office not in cabinet)	
	Ld MACDONALD	
	of GWAENYSGOR	1 Apr 49
Min.	A. ALEXANDER 4 Oct 46–20 Dec 46	
without	A. GREENWOOD	
Portfolio		17 Apr 47–29 Sep 47
Pensions	W. PALING	3 Aug 45
	J. HYND	17 Apr 47
	G. BUCHANAN	7 Oct 47
	H. MARQUAND	2 Jul 48
	G. ISAACS	17 Jan 51
P.S.	Jennie Adamson	4 Aug 45

LABOUR GOVERNMENT 1945–1951 (contd.)

P.S.	A. Blenkinsop	10 May 46
(Pensions)	C. Simmons	1 Feb 49
Postm.-Gen.	E of LISTOWEL	4 Aug 45
	W. PALING	17 Apr 47
	N. EDWARDS	28 Feb 50
Ass.	W. Burke	10 Aug 45
	C. Hobson	7 Oct 47
Scotland	**J. WESTWOOD**	3 Aug 45
	A. WOODBURN	7 Oct 47
	H. MCNEIL	28 Feb 50
U-S.	G. Buchanan	4 Aug 45–7 Oct 47
	T. Fraser	4 Aug 45–26 Oct 51
	J. Robertson	7 Oct 47–2 Mar 50
	Margaret Herbison	2 Mar 50–26 Oct 5
Supply	J. WILMOT	3 Aug 45
	G. STRAUSS	7 Oct 47
P.S.	W. Leonard	4 Aug 45–7 Oct 47
	A. Woodburn	1 Apr 46–7 Oct 47
	J. Freeman	7 Oct 47–23 Apr 51
	J. Jones	7 Oct 47–2 Mar 50
	M. Stewart	2 May 51–26 Oct 51
T.& C.	L. SILKIN	4 Aug 45
Planning	(office in cabinet)	
	H. DALTON	28 Feb 50
	(recast as Local Government	
	& Planning 31 Jan 51)	
P.S.	F. Marshall	10 Aug 45
	E. King	7 Oct 47
	G. Lindgren	2 Mar 50
B.Trade	**Sir S. CRIPPS**	27 Jul 45
	H. WILSON	29 Sep 47
	Sir H. SHAWCROSS	24 Apr 51
P.S.	E. Smith	4 Aug 45
	J. Belcher	12 Jan 46
	J. Edwards	1 Feb 49
	H. Rhodes	2 Mar 50
Sec.	H. Marquand	4 Aug 45
Overseas	H. Wilson	5 Mar 47
Trade	A. Bottomley	7 Oct 47
Transp.	A. BARNES	3 Aug 45
P.S.	G. Strauss	4 Aug 45
	J. Callaghan	7 Oct 47
	Ld Lucas of Chilworth	2 Mar 50
War	**J. LAWSON**	3 Aug 45
	(office not in cabinet)	
	F. BELLENGER	4 Oct 46
	E. SHINWELL	7 Oct 47
	J. STRACHEY	28 Feb 50
U-S.	Ld Nathan	4 Aug 45
	Ld Pakenham	4 Oct 46–17 Apr 47
F.S.	F. Bellenger	4 Aug 45
	J. Freeman	4 Oct 46–17 Apr 47
U-& F.S.	J. Freeman	17 Apr 47
	M. Stewart	7 Oct 47
	W. Wyatt	2 May 51
Works	G. TOMLINSON	4 Aug 45
	C. KEY	10 Feb 47
	R. STOKES	28 Feb 50
	G. BROWN	26 Apr 51

P.S.	H. Wilson	4 Aug 45
	E. Durbin	5 Mar 47
	Ld Morrison	26 Sep 48

Law Officers

Att.-Gen.	Sir H. SHAWCROSS	4 Aug 45
	Sir F. SOSKICE	24 Apr 51
Sol.-Gen.	Sir F. SOSKICE	4 Aug 45
	Sir L. UNGOED-THOMAS	24 Apr 51
Ld Advoc.	G. THOMSON	10 Aug 45
	J. WHEATLEY	7 Oct 47
Sol.-Gen.	D. BLADES[+]	10 Sep 45
Scotland	J. WHEATLEY	19 Mar 47
	D. JOHNSTON	24 Oct 47

Whips

P.S .to	W. WHITELEY	3 Aug 45
Treasury		
Lds of	R. Taylor	4 Aug 45–26 Oct 51
Treasury	J. Henderson	4 Aug 45–1 Jan 50
	M. Stewart	10 Aug 45–30 Mar 46
	A. Blenkinsop	10 Aug 45–10 May 46
	F. Collindridge	10 Aug 45–9 Dec 46
	C. Simmons	30 Mar 46–1 Feb 49
	W. Hannan	10 May 46–26 Oct 51
	J. Snow	9 Dec 46–3 Mar 50
	R. Adams	1 Feb 49–23 Apr 50
	W. Wilkins	1 Jan 50–26 Oct 51
	H. Bowden	3 Mar 50–26 Oct 51
	C. Royle	23 Apr 50–26 Oct 51

H.M. Household

Treasurer	G. MATHERS	4 Aug 45
	A. PEARSON	30 Mar 46
Compt.	A. PEARSON	4 Aug 45
	M. STEWART	30 Mar 46
	F. COLLINDRIDGE	9 Dec 46
V.Chamb.	J. SNOW	10 Aug 45
	M. STEWART	9 Dec 46
	E. POPPLEWELL	16 Oct 47
Cap.Gents	Ld AMMON	4 Aug 45
at Arms	Ld SHEPHERD	18 Oct 49
Cap.Yeo.	Ld WALKDEN	4 Aug 45
of Guard	Ld SHEPHERD	6 Jul 49
	Ld LUCAS of CHILWORTH	
		18 Oct 49
	E of LUCAN	5 Mar 50
	Ld ARCHIBALD	8 Jun 51
Lds in	Ld Westwood	10 Sep 45–17 Jan 47
Waiting	Ld Pakenham	14 Oct 45–4 Oct 46
	Ld Henderson	21 Oct 45–7 Jun 48
	Ld Chorley	11 Oct 46–31 Mar 50
	Ld Morrison	17 Jan 47–26 Sep 48
	Ld Lucas of Chilworth	
		9 Jul 48–18 Oct 49
	Ld Shepherd	14 Oct 48–6 Jul 49
	Ld Kershaw	6 Jul 49–26 Oct 51
	Ld Darwen	18 Oct 49–26 Dec 50
	Ld Burden	31 Mar 50–26 Oct 51
	Ld Haden-Guest	13 Feb 51–26 Oct 51

[+]Not a member of the House of Commons.

CONSERVATIVE GOVERNMENT 1951–1957

P.M.	**(Sir) W. CHURCHILL**	
		26 Oct 51–5 Apr 55
	Sir A. EDEN	6 Apr 55–9 Jan 57
Ld Pres.	**Ld WOOLTON**	28 Oct 51
	M of SALISBURY	24 Nov 52
Ld Chanc.	**Ld SIMONDS**	30 Oct 51
	Vt KILMUIR	18 Oct 54
Privy Seal	**M of SALISBURY**	28 Oct 51
	H. CROOKSHANK	7 May 52
	R. BUTLER	20 Dec 55
Exchequer	**R. BUTLER**	28 Oct 51
	H. MACMILLAN	20 Dec 55
Min.Econ.	Sir A. SALTER	31 Oct 51
Affs	*(24 Nov 52 office abolished)*	
F.S.	J. Boyd-Carpenter	31 Oct 51
	H. Brooke	28 Jul 54
Econ.S.	R. Maudling	24 Nov 52
	Sir E. Boyle	7 Apr 55
	D. Walker-Smith	11 Nov 56
Foreign O.	**(Sir) A. EDEN**	28 Oct 51
	H. MACMILLAN	7 Apr 55
	S. LLOYD	20 Dec 55
Min.of	S. LLOYD	30 Oct 51–18 Oct 54
State	M of READING	11 Nov 53–9 Jan 57
	A. NUTTING	18 Oct 54–3 Nov 56
	A. NOBLE	9 Nov 56–9 Jan 57
U-S.	M of Reading	31 Oct 51–11 Nov 53
	A. Nutting	31 Oct 51–18 Oct 54
	D. Dodds-Parker	11 Nov 53–18 Oct 54
	R. Turton	18 Oct 54–20 Dec 55
	D. Dodds-Parker	20 Dec 55–9 Jan 57
	Ld J. Hope*	18 Oct 54–9 Nov 56
	D. Ormsby-Gore	9 Nov 56–9 Jan 57
Home O.&	**Sir D. MAXWELL FYFE**	
Welsh Affs.	*(Vt Kilmuir)*	28 Oct 51
	G. LLOYD-GEORGE	18 Oct 54
U-S.	D. Llewellyn	5 Nov 51–14 Oct 52
	Sir H. Lucas-Tooth	3 Feb 52–20 Dec 55
	Ld Lloyd	24 Nov 52–18 Oct 54
	Ld Mancroft	18 Oct 54–9 Jan 57
Admiralty	J. THOMAS *(Vt Cilcennin)*	31 Oct 51
	Vt HAILSHAM	2 Sep 56
P.& F.S.	A. Noble	5 Nov 51
	G. Ward	20 Dec 55
Civil Ld	S. Wingfield Digby	5 Nov 51
Ag.& Fish.	Sir T. DUGDALE	31 Oct 51
	(office in cabinet)	
	Sir T. DUGDALE	3 Sep 53
	D. HEATHCOAT AMORY	28 Jul 54
	(18 Oct 54 Min. of Ag. & Fish.	
	combined with Min. of Food)	
P.S.	W. Deedes	20 Dec 55–9 Jan 57
	Ld Carrington	5 Nov 51–18 Oct 54
	R. Nugent	5 Nov 51–9Jan 57
	Earl St Aldwyn	18 Oct 54–9 Jan 57
	H. Nicholls	7 Apr 55–9 Jan 57
Air	Ld DE L'ISLE & DUDLEY	31 Oct 51
	N. BIRCH	20 Dec 55
U-S.	N. Birch	3 Nov 51
	G. Ward	29 Feb 52
	C. Soames	20 Dec 55
Colonies	**O. LYTTELTON**	28 Oct 51
	A. LENNOX-BOYD	28 Jul 54
Min.	A. LENNOX-BOYD	2 Nov 51
	H. HOPKINSON	7 May 52
	J. HARE	20 Dec 55
	J. MACLAY	18 Oct 56
U-S.	E of Munster	5 Nov 51
	Ld Lloyd	18 Oct 54
C.R.O.	**Ld ISMAY**	28 Oct 51
	M of SALISBURY	12 Mar 52
	Vt SWINTON	24 Nov 52
	E of HOME	7 Apr 55
U-S.	J. Foster	3 Nov 51
	D. Dodds-Parker	18 Oct 54
	A. Noble	20 Dec 55
	Ld J. Hope*	9 Nov 56
Co-ord. of	**Ld LEATHERS**	30 Oct 51
Transport	*(3 Sep 53 office abolished)*	
Fuel & Power		
Defence	**W. CHURCHILL** *(P.M.)*	28 Oct 51
	Earl ALEXANDER of TUNIS	
		1 Mar 52
	H. MACMILLAN	18 Oct 54
	S. LLOYD	7 Apr 55
	Sir W. MONCKTON	20 Dec 55
	A. HEAD	18 Oct 56
P.S.	N. Birch	28 Feb 52
	Ld Carrington	18 Oct 54
	E of Gosford	26 May 56
Education	Florence HORSBRUGH	2 Nov 51
	(office in cabinet)	
	Florence HORSBRUGH	3 Sep 53
	Sir D. ECCLES	18 Oct 54
P.S.	K. Pickthorn	5 Nov 51
	D. Vosper	18 Oct 54
Food	G. LLOYD-GEORGE	31 Oct 51
	(office in cabinet)	
	G. LLOYD-GEORGE	3 Sep 53
	D. HEATHCOAT AMORY	18 Oct 54
	(& combined with Min. of Ag. & Fish.)	
P.S.	C. Hill	31 Oct 51
Fuel &	G. LLOYD	31 Oct 51
Power	A. JONES	20 Dec 55
P.S.	L. Joynson-Hicks	5 Nov 51
	D. Renton	20 Dec 55
Health	**H. CROOKSHANK**	30 Oct 51
	(office not in cabinet)	
	I. MACLEOD	7 May 52
	R. TURTON	20 Dec 55
P.S.	Patricia Hornsby-Smith	3 Nov 51
Housing &	**H. MACMILLAN**	30 Oct 51
Loc.Govt	**D. SANDYS**	18 Oct 54
P.S.	E. Marples	3 Nov 51
	W. Deedes	18 Oct 54
	E. Powell	20 Dec 55

*MP. Not a member of the House of Lords.

CONSERVATIVE GOVERNMENT 1951–1957 (contd.)

Lab. &	**Sir W. MONCKTON**	28 Oct 51
Nat.S.	**I. MACLEOD**	20 Dec 55
P.S.	Sir P. Bennett	31 Oct 51
	H. Watkinson	28 May 52
	R. Carr	20 Dec 55
D.Lanc.	Vt SWINTON	31 Oct 51–24 Nov 52
	(also Min. of Materials)	
	(office in cabinet 24 Nov 52)	
	Ld WOOLTON *(Vt)*	24 Nov 52
	(1 Sep 53–16 Aug 54	
	also Min. of Materials)	
	E of SELKIRK	20 Dec 55
Materials	Vt SWINTON	31 Oct 51–24 Nov 52
	(also D. Lancaster)	
	Sir A. SALTER	24 Nov 52–1 Sep 53
	(1 Sep 53–16 Aug 54 Ld Woolton	
	combined Materials with D. Lanc.	
	in cabinet.	
	16 Aug 54 Min. of Materials wound up)	
Min.without	E of MUNSTER	18 Oct 54–8 Jan 57
Portfolio		
Nat.Ins.	O. PEAKE	31 Oct 51
	(3 Sep 53 combined	
	with Min. of Pensions)	
Paym.-Gen.	**Ld CHERWELL**	30 Oct 51
	(office not in cabinet)	
	E of SELKIRK	11 Nov 53
	(20 Dec 55 office vacant)	
	(office in cabinet)	
	Sir W. MONCKTON	18 Oct 56
Pensions	D. HEATHCOAT AMORY	5 Nov 51
(& Nat.Ins.)	*(1 Sep 53 Mins combined)*	
	O. PEAKE	3 Sep 53
	(office in cabinet)	
	O. PEAKE	18 Oct 54
	(office not in cabinet)	
	J. BOYD-CARPENTER	20 Dec 55
P.S.	J. Smyth	5 Nov 51–20 Dec 55
	R. Turton	5 Nov 51–18 Oct 54
	E. Marples	18 Oct 54–20 Dec 55
	Edith Pitt	20 Dec 55–9 Jan 57
	R. Wood	20 Dec 55–9 Jan 57
Post.-Gen.	Earl DE LA WARR	5 Nov 51
	C. HILL	7 Apr 55
Ass.	D. Gammans	5 Nov 51
	C. Alport	20 Dec 55
Power	*(see Fuel & Power)*	
Scotland	**J. STUART**	30 Oct 51
Min.	E of HOME	2 Nov 51
	T. GALBRAITH	7 Apr 55
	(Ld Strathclyde)	
U-S.	T. Galbraith	2 Nov 51–5 Apr 55
	W. Snadden	2 Nov 51–3 Jun 55
	J. Henderson Stewart	4 Feb 52–9 Jan 57
	J. Browne	7 Apr 55–9 Jan 57
	N. Macpherson	13 Jun 55–9 Jan 57
Supply	D. SANDYS	31 Oct 51
	S. LLOYD	18 Oct 54
	R. MAUDLING	7 Apr 55

P.S.	T. Low	3 Nov 51
	Sir E. Boyle	28 Jul 54
	F. Erroll	7 Apr 55
	I. Harvey	11 Nov 56
B.Trade	**P. THORNEYCROFT**	30 Oct 51
Min.	D. HEATHCOAT AMORY	3 Sep 53
	T. LOW	28 Jul 54
P.S.	H. Strauss	3 Nov 51
	D. Kaberry	7 Apr 55
	D. Walker-Smith	19 Oct 55
	F. Erroll	11 Nov 56
Sec.	H. Hopkinson	3 Nov 51
Overseas	H. Mackeson	28 May 52
Trade	*(3 Sep 53 office abolished,*	
	Min. of State took over)	
Transport	J. MACLAY	31 Oct 51
(& Civil	A. LENNOX-BOYD	7 May 52
Av.)	*(Ministries of Transport & Civil*	
	Aviation merged 1 Oct 53)	
	J. BOYD-CARPENTER	28 Jul 54
	H. WATKINSON	20 Dec 55
P.S.	J. Braithwaite	5 Nov 51–1 Nov 53
	R. Maudling	18 Apr 52–24 Nov 52
	J. Profumo	24 Nov 52–9 Jan 57
	H. Molson	11 Nov 53–9 Jan 57
War	A. HEAD	31 Oct 51
	J. HARE	18 Oct 56
U-S.& F.S.	J. Hutchison	5 Nov 51
	F. Maclean	18 Oct 54
Works	(Sir) D. ECCLES	1 Nov 51
	N. BIRCH	18 Oct 54
	(office in cabinet)	
	P. BUCHAN-HEPBURN	20 Dec 55
P.S.	H. Molson	3 Nov 51
	R. Bevins	11 Nov 53

Law Officers

Att.-Gen.	Sir L. HEALD	3 Nov 51
	Sir R. MANNINGHAM-BULLER	18 Oct 54
Sol.-Gen.	Sir R. MANNINGHAM-BULLER	3 Nov 51
	Sir H. HYLTON-FOSTER	18 Oct 54
Ld Advoc.	J. CLYDE	2 Nov 51
	W. MILLIGAN	30 Dec 54
Sol.-Gen.	W. MILLIGAN+	3 Nov 51
Scotland	W. GRANT	10 Jan 55

Whips

P.S. to	P. BUCHAN-HEPBURN	30 Oct 51
Treasury	E. HEATH	30 Dec 55
Lds of	H. Mackeson	7 Nov 51–28 May 52
Treasury	(Sir) H. Butcher	7 Nov 51–3 Jul 53
	E. Heath	7 Nov 51–20 Dec 55
	T. Galbraith *(Jnr)*	7 Nov 51–4 Jun 54
	D. Vosper	7 Nov 51–18 Oct 54
	H. Oakshott	28 May 52–13 Jun 55
	M. Redmayne	3 Jul 53–9 Jan 57
	R. Thompson	28 Jul 54–8 Apr 56
	G. Wills	26 Oct 54–9 Jan 57

+Not a member of the House of Commons.

CONSERVATIVE GOVERNMENT 1951–1957 (contd.)

Lds of	P. Legh	13 Jun 55–9 Jan 57	*Capt.Gents*	Earl FORTESCUE	5 Nov 51
Treasury	E. Wakefield	24 Jan 56–9 Jan 57	*at Arms*		
(contd.)	H. Harrison	8 Apr 56–9 Jan 57	*Capt.Yeo.*	E of ONSLOW	5 Nov 51
H.M. Household			*of Guard*		
Treasurer	(Sir) C. DREWE	7 Nov 51	*Lds in*	E of Birkenhead	5 Nov 51–28 Jan 55
	T. GALBRAITH *(Jnr)*	13 Jun 55	*Waiting*	E of Selkirk	5 Nov 51–11 Nov 53
Compt.	R. CONANT	7 Nov 51		Ld Lloyd	7 Nov 51–24 Nov 52
	T. GALBRAITH *(Jnr)*	7 Jun 54		Ld Mancroft	15 Dec 52–18 Oct 54
	H. OAKSHOTT	13 Jun 55		Ld Hawke	11 Nov 53–9 Jan 57
V. Chamb.	H. STUDHOLME	7 Nov 51		Ld Fairfax	18 Oct 54–9 Jan 57
	R. THOMPSON	8 Apr 56		Ld Chesham	28 Jan 55–9 Jan 57

CONSERVATIVE GOVERNMENT 1957–1964

P.M.	**H. MACMILLAN**		*Min. of*	P.THOMAS	27 Jun 63–16 Oct 64
		10 Jan 57–13 Oct 63	*State*	E of Gosford	18 Jan 57–23 Oct 58
	Sir A. DOUGLAS-HOME		*U-S.*	I. Harvey	18 Jan 57–24 Nov 58
	(formerly E of Home)			M of Lansdowne	23 Oct 58–20 Apr 62
		18 Oct 63–16 Oct 64		J. Profumo	28 Nov 58–16 Jan 59
1st.Sec.	**R. BUTLER**	13 Jul 62		R. Allan	16 Jan 59–7 Oct 60
of State	*(office wound up 18 Oct 63)*			J. Godber	28 Oct 60–27 Jun 61
Ld Pres.	**M of SALISBURY**	13 Jan 57		P. Thomas	27 Jun 61–27 Jun 63
	E of HOME	29 Mar 57		P. Smithers	16 Jul 62–29 Jan 64
	Vt HAILSHAM	17 Sep 57		R. Mathew	30 Jan 64–16 Oct 64
	E of HOME	14 Oct 59	*Home O.*	**R. BUTLER**	13 Jan 57
	Vt HAILSHAM *(Q. Hogg)*	27 Jul 60		**H. BROOKE**	13 Jul 62
	(also Min. for Science)		*Min.Home*	D. VOSPER	28 Oct 60
Ld Chanc.	**Vt KILMUIR**	14 Jan 57	*Affs*	D. RENTON	27 Jun 61
	Ld DILHORNE	13 Jul 62		Earl JELLICOE	17 Jul 62
Privy Seal	**R. BUTLER**	13 Jan 57		Ld DERWENT	21 Oct 63
	(also Home Sec.)		*U-S.*	Patricia Hornsby-Smith	
	Vt HAILSHAM	14 Oct 59			18 Jan 57–22 Oct 59
	(also Min. for Science)			J. Simon	18 Jan 57–6 Jan 58
	E. HEATH	27 Jul 60		D. Renton	17 Jan 58–27 Jun 61
	S. LLOYD	20 Oct 63		D. Vosper	22 Oct 59–28 Oct 60
Exchequer	**P. THORNEYCROFT**	13 Jan 57		Earl Bathurst	8 Feb 61–16 Jul 62
	D. HEATHCOAT AMORY	6 Jan 58		C. Fletcher-Cooke	27 Jun 61–27 Feb 63
	S. LLOYD	27 Jul 60		C. Woodhouse	16 Jul 62–16 Oct 64
	R. MAUDLING	13 Jul 62		Mervyn Pike	1 Mar 63–16 Oct 64
	(see also Paymaster-General)		*Admiralty*	E of SELKIRK	16 Jan 57
F.S.	E. Powell	16 Jan 57		Ld CARRINGTON	16 Oct 59
	J. Simon	6 Jan 58		Earl JELLICOE	22 Oct 63
	Sir E. Boyle	22 Oct 59		*(1 Apr 64, reorganised*	
	A. Barber	16 Jul 62		*under Min. of Defence)*	
	A. Green	23 Oct 63	*P.& F.S.*	C. Soames	18 Jan 57
Econ.S.	N. Birch	16 Jan 57		R. Allan	17 Jan 58
	(office vacant 6 Jan 58)			C. Orr Ewing	16 Jan 59
	F. Erroll	23 Oct 58		*(16 Oct 59 office vacant)*	
	A. Barber	22 Oct 59	*Civil Ld*	T. Galbraith	18 Jan 57
	E. du Cann	16 Jul 62		C. Orr Ewing	16 Oct 59
	M. Macmillan	21 Oct 63		J. Hay	3 May 63
Foreign O.	**S. LLOYD**	14 Jan 57	*Ag.Fish*	D. HEATHCOAT AMORY	14 Jan 57
	E of HOME	27 Jul 60	*& Food*	J. HARE	6 Jan 58
	R. BUTLER	20 Oct 63		C. SOAMES	27 Jul 60
Min. of	A. NOBLE	16 Jan 57–16 Jan 59	*P.S.*	Earl St Aldwyn	18 Jan 57–27Jun 58
State	D. ORMSBY-GORE			J. Godber	18 Jan 57–28 Oct 60
		16 Jan 57–27 Jun 61		Earl Waldegrave	27 Jun 58–16 Jul 62
	J. PROFUMO	16 Jan 59–27 Jul 60		W. Vane	28 Oct 60–16 Jul 62
	J. GODBER	27 Jun 61–27 Jun 63		Ld St.Oswald	16 Jul 62–16 Oct 64
	E of DUNDEE	9 Oct 61–16 Oct 64		J. Scott-Hopkins	16 Jul 62–16 Oct 64

CONSERVATIVE GOVERNMENT 1957–1964 *(contd.)*

Air	G. WARD	16 Jan 57
	J. AMERY	28 Oct 60
	H. FRASER	16 Jul 62
	(1 Apr 64, reorganised under	
	Min. of Defence)	
U-S.	C. Orr Ewing	18 Jan 57
	A. Neave	16 Jan 59
	W. Taylor	16 Oct 59
	J. Ridsdale	16 Jul 62
Aviation	*(see Transport & Civil Aviation)*	
	D. SANDYS	14 Oct 59
	P. THORNEYCROFT	27 Jul 60
	(office not in cabinet)	
	J. AMERY	16 Jul 62
	(for Junior Ministers see	
	Transport & Civil Aviation)	
P.S.	G. Rippon	22 Oct 59
	C. Woodhouse	9 Oct 61
	B. de Ferranti	16 Jul 62
	N. Marten	3 Dec 62
Colonies	**A. LENNOX-BOYD**	14 Jan 57
	I. MACLEOD	14 Oct 59
	R. MAUDLING	9 Oct 61
	(joint minister with C.R.O. 13 Jul 62)	
	D. SANDYS	13 Jul 62
Min.	E of PERTH	16 Jan 57
	M of LANSDOWNE	20 Apr 62
	(joint with C.R.O. 21 Oct 63)	
U-S.	J. Profumo	18 Jan 57
	J. Amery	28 Nov 58
	H. Fraser	28 Oct 60
	N. Fisher	16 Jul 62–16 Oct 64
	R. Hornby	24 Oct 63–16 Oct 64
	(joint with C.R.O 21 Oct 63)	
C.R.O.	**E of HOME**	14 Jan 57
	D. SANDYS	27 Jul 60
	(joint with Col. O. 13 Jul 62)	
Min.	C. ALPORT	22 Oct 59–8 Feb 61
	D of DEVONSHIRE	6 Sep 62–16 Oct 64
	(joint with Col. O. 21 Oct 63)	
U-S.	C. Alport	18 Jan 57
	R. Thompson	22 Oct 59
	D of Devonshire	28 Oct 60–6 Sep 62
	B. Braine	8 Feb 61–16 Jul 62
	J. Tilney	16 Jul 62–16 Oct 64
	(joint with Col. O. 21 Oct 63)	
Defence	**D. SANDYS**	13 Jan 57
	H. WATKINSON	14 Oct 59
	P. THORNEYCROFT	13 Jul 62
P.S.	Ld Mancroft	18 Jan 57
	(11 Jun 57 office vacant)	
	(Defence Dept. reorganised 1 Apr 64)	
Min.of State		1 Apr 64
Air	H. FRASER	
Army	J. RAMSDEN	1 Apr 64
Navy	Earl JELLICOE	1 Apr 64
U-S. Air Force	J. Ridsdale	1 Apr 64
U-S.Army	P. Kirk	1 Apr 64
U-S.Navy	J. Hay	1 Apr 64

Education	**Vt HAILSHAM**	13 Jan 57
	G. LLOYD	17 Sep 57
	Sir D. ECCLES	14 Oct 59
	Sir E. BOYLE	13 Jul 62
	(Education & Science 1 Apr 64)	
	Q. HOGG *(Vt Hailsham)*	1 Apr 64
Min.of State	**Sir E. BOYLE**	1 Apr 64
	(office not in cabinet)	
	Ld NEWTON	1 Apr 64
P.S.	Sir E. Boyle	18 Jan 57
	K. Thompson	22 Oct 59
	C. Chataway	16 Jul 62
	(reorganisation 1 Apr 64)	
U-S.	E of Bessborough	1 Apr 64
	C. Chataway	1 Apr 64
Health	D. VOSPER	16 Jan 57
	D. WALKER-SMITH	17 Sep 57
	E. POWELL	27 Jul 60
	(office in cabinet)	
	E. POWELL	13 Jul 62
	A. BARBER	20 Oct 63
P.S.	J. Vaughan-Morgan	18 Jan 57
	R. Thompson	17 Sep 57
	Edith Pitt	22 Oct 59
	B. Braine	16 Jul 62–16 Oct 64
	Ld Newton	6 Sep 62–1 Apr 64
	M of Lothian	24 Mar 64–16 Oct 64
Housing,	**H. BROOKE**	13 Jan 57
Loc. Govt	**C. HILL**	9 Oct 61
Welsh Affs	**Sir K. JOSEPH**	13 Jul 62
Min. of State for Welsh Affs	Ld BRECON	12 Dec 57
P.S.	R. Bevins	18 Jan 57
	Sir K. Joseph	22 Oct 59–9 Oct 61
	Earl Jellicoe	27 Jun 61–16 Jul 62
	G. Rippon	9 Oct 61–16 Jul 62
	F. Corfield	16 Jul 62–16 Oct 64
	Ld Hastings	3 Dec 62–16 Oct 64
Labour &	**I. MACLEOD**	14 Jan 57
Nat. S.	**E. HEATH**	14 Oct 59
	(12 Nov 59 Min. of Labour)	
	J. HARE	27 Jul 60
	J. GODBER	20 Oct 63
P.S.	R.Carr	19 Jan 57
	R. Wood	14 Apr 58
	P. Thomas	22 Oct 59
	A. Green	27 Jun 61
	W. Whitelaw	16 Jul 62
D.Lanc.	**C. HILL**	13 Jan 57
	I. MACLEOD	9 Oct 61
	Ld BLAKENHAM	20 Oct 63
	(J. Hare)	
Paym.-Gen.	R. MAUDLING	16 Jan 57
	(office in cabinet)	
	R. MAUDLING	17 Sep 57
	Ld MILLS	14 Oct 59
	(after 9 Oct 61 Chief Sec. to	
	Treasury & Paym.-Gen.)	
	H. BROOKE	9 Oct 61
	J. BOYD-CARPENTER	13 Jul 62

CONSERVATIVE GOVERNMENT 1957–1964 *(contd.)*

Pensions	J. BOYD-CARPENTER	16 Jan 57
& Nat.Ins.	N. MACPHERSON	16 Jul 62
	R. WOOD	21 Oct 63
P.S.	Edith Pitt	19 Jan 57–22 Oct 59
	R. Wood	19 Jan 57–14 Apr 58
	W. Vane	14 Apr 58–28 Oct 60
	Patricia Hornsby-Smith	
		22 Oct 59–31 Aug 61
	B. Braine	28 Oct 60–8 Feb 61
	R. Sharples	8 Feb 61–16 Jul 62
	Margaret Thatcher	9 Oct 61–16 Oct 64
	S. Maydon	16 Jul 62–16 Oct 64
Min.without	E of MUNSTER	16 Jan 57
Portfolio	Ld MANCROFT	11 Jun 57
	E of DUNDEE	23 Oct 58
	(office in cabinet)	
	Ld MILLS	9 Oct 61–14 Jul 62
	W. DEEDES	13 Jul 62–16 Oct 64
	Ld CARRINGTON	
		20 Oct 63–16 Oct 64
Post.-Gen.	E. MARPLES	16 Jan 57
	R. BEVINS	22 Oct 59
Ass.	K. Thompson	18 Jan 57
	Mervyn. Pike	22 Oct 59
	R. Mawby	1 Mar 63
Power	**Ld MILLS**	13 Jan 57
	(office not in cabinet)	
	R. WOOD	14 Oct 59
	(office in cabinet)	
	F. ERROLL	20 Oct 63
P.S.	D. Renton	18 Jan 57
	Sir I. Horobin	17 Jan 58
	J. George	22 Oct 59
	J. Peyton	25 Jun 62
Science	**Vt HAILSHAM**	14 Oct 59
	(Q. Hogg)	
	(1 Apr 64 Educ. & Science)	
P.S.	D. Freeth	8 Feb 61
	E of Bessborough	24 Oct 63
	(1 Apr 64. Educ. & Science)	
Scotland	J. Maclay	13 Jan 57
	M. NOBLE	13 Jul 62
Min.of State	Ld STRATHCLYDE	17 Jan 57
	Ld FORBES	23 Oct 58
	J. BROWNE	22 Oct 59
	(Ld Craigton)	
U-S.	J. Browne	18 Jan 57–22 Oct 59
	N. Macpherson	19 Jan 57–28 Oct 60
	Ld J. Hope*	18 Jan 57–22 Oct 59
	T. Galbraith	22 Oct 59–8 Nov 62
	G. Leburn	22 Oct 59–15 Aug 63
	R. Brooman-White	
		28 Oct 60–12 Dec 63
	Lady Tweedsmuir*	3 Dec 62–16 Oct 64
	A. Stodart	19 Aug 63–16 Oct 64
	G. Campbell	12 Dec 63–16 Oct 64
Supply	A. JONES	16 Jan 57
	(office wound up 22 Oct 59)	
P.S.	W. Taylor	18 Jan 57
	(office wound up 22 Oct 59)	

Technical	*(office not established)*	
Co-op.	D. VOSPER	27 Jun 61
	R. CARR	9 May 63
B.Trade	**Sir D. ECCLES**	13 Jan 57
	R. MAUDLING	14 Oct 59
	F. ERROLL	9 Oct 61
	E. HEATH	20 Oct 63
	(also Sec. of State for Industry Trade	
	& Regional Development)	
Min.of State	D. WALKER-SMITH	16 Jan 57
	J. VAUGHAN-MORGAN	17 Sep 57
	F. ERROLL	22 Oct 59
	Sir K. JOSEPH	9 Oct 61
	A. GREEN	16 Jul 62–23 Oct 63
	Ld DERWENT	6 Sep 62–23 Oct 63
	Ld DRUMALBYN	
		23 Oct 63–16 Oct 64
	(formerly N. Macpherson)	
	E. DU CANN	21 Oct 63–16 Oct 64
P.S.	F. Erroll	18 Jan 57
	J. Rodgers	24 Oct 58
	N. Macpherson	28 Oct 60
	D. Price	17 Jul 62
Transport	**H. WATKINSON**	13 Jan 57
& Civil Av.	*(14 Oct 59 Min.of Transport only)*	
	E. MARPLES	14 Oct 59
	(see above, Min. of Aviation)	
P.S.	R. Nugent	18 Jan 57–22 Oct 59
	A. Neave	18 Jan 57–16 Jan 59
	J. Hay	16 Jan 59–3 May 63
	Ld Chesham	22 Oct 59–16 Oct 64
	J. Hughes-Hallett	26 Apr 61–16 Oct 64
	T. Galbraith	3 May 63–16 Oct 64
War	J. HARE	16 Jan 57
	C. SOAMES	6 Jan 58
	J. PROFUMO	27 Jul 60
	J. GODBER	27 Jun 63
	J. RAMSDEN	21 Oct 63
	(1 Apr 64 reorganised	
	under Min. of Defence)	
U-S.& F.S.	J. Amery	18 Jan 57
	H. Fraser	28 Nov 58
	J. Ramsden	28 Oct 60
	P. Kirk	24 Oct 63
Works	H. MOLSON	16 Jan 57
	Ld J. HOPE*	22 Oct 59
	(16 Jul 62 Min. of Public	
	Building & Works)	
	G. RIPPON	16 Jul 62
	(office in cabinet)	
	G. RIPPON	20 Oct 63
	(Min. of Public Building & Works)	
P.S.	H. Nicholls	18 Jan 57
	R. Thompson	28 Oct 60
	R. Sharples	16 Jul 62

Law Officers

Att.-Gen.	Sir R. MANNINGHAM-BULLER	
		17 Jan 57
	Sir J. HOBSON	16 Jul 62

*MP. Not a member of the House of Lords.

CONSERVATIVE GOVERNMENT 1957–1964 *(contd.)*

Sol.-Gen.	Sir H. HYLTON-FOSTER	17 Jan 57
	Sir J. SIMON	22 Oct 59
	Sir J. HOBSON	8 Feb 62
	Sir P. RAWLINSON	19 Jul 62
Ld Advoc.	W. MILLIGAN	17 Jan 57
	W. GRANT	5 Apr 60
	I. SHEARER+	12 Oct 62
Sol.-Gen.	W. GRANT	17 Jan 57
Scotland	D. ANDERSON	11 May 60
	N. WYLIE	27 Apr 64

Whips

P.S. to	E. HEATH	17 Jan 57
Treasury	M. REDMAYNE	14 Oct 59
Lds of	M. Redmayne	21 Jan 57–14 Oct 59
Treasury	P. Legh	21 Jan 57–17 Sep 57
	E. Wakefield	21 Jan 57–23 Oct 58
	H. Harrison	21 Jan 57–16 Jan 59
	A. Barber	9 Apr 57–19 Feb 58
	R. Brooman-White	28 Oct 57–21 Jun 60
	P. Bryan	19 Feb 58–9 Feb 61
	M. Hughes-Young	23 Oct 58–6 Mar 62
	G. Finlay	16 Jan 59–28 Oct 60
	D. Gibson-Watt	22 Oct 59–29 Nov 61
	R. Chichester-Clark	21 Jun 60–29 Nov 61
	J. Hill	28 Oct 60–16 Oct 64
	W. Whitelaw	6 Mar 61–16 Jul 62
	J. Peel	29 Nov 61–16 Oct 64
	M. Noble	29 Nov 61–13 Jul 62
	F. Pearson	6 Mar 62–19 Oct 63
	G. Campbell	6 Sep 62–12 Dec 63
	M. Hamilton	6 Sep 62–16 Oct 64

	M. McLaren	21 Nov 63–16 Oct 64
	I. MacArthur	12 Dec 63–16 Oct 64

H.M. Household

Treasurer	H. OAKSHOTT	19 Jan 57
	P. LEGH (*Ld Newton*)	16 Jan 59
	E. WAKEFIELD	21 Jun 60
	M. HUGHES-YOUNG	6 Mar 62
Compt.	(Sir) G. WILLS	19 Jan 57
	E. WAKEFIELD	23 Oct 58
	H. HARRISON	16 Jan 59
	R. CHICHESTER-CLARK	29 Nov 61
V. Chamb.	R. THOMPSON	21 Jan 57
	P. LEGH	17 Sep 57
	F. WAKEFIELD	16 Jan 59
	R. BROOMAN-WHITE	21 Jun 60
	G. FINLAY	28 Oct 60
Cap.Gents	Earl FORTESCUE	21 Jan 57
at Arms	Earl ST ALDWYN	27 Jun 58
Cap.Yeo.	E of ONSLOW	21 Jan 57
of Guard	Ld NEWTON	28 Oct 60
	Vt GOSCHEN	6 Sep 62
Lds in	Ld Hawke	21 Jan 57–11 Jun 57
Waiting	Ld Fairfax	21 Jan 57–21 Jun 57
	Ld Chesham	21 Jan 57–22 Oct 59
	M of Lansdowne	11 Jun 57–23 Oct 58
	Earl Bathurst	17 Sep 57–8 Feb 61
	E of Gosford	23 Oct 58–22 Oct 59
	Ld St Oswald	22 Oct 59–16 Jul 62
	Earl Jellicoe	8 Feb 61–27 Jun 61
	Ld Hastings	6 Mar 61–3 Dec 62
	Ld Denham	27 Jun 61–16 Oct 64
	M of Lothian	6 Sep 62–3 Mar 64
	Earl Ferrers	3 Dec 62–10 Oct 64

LABOUR GOVERNMENT 1964–1970

P.M.	**H. WILSON**	16 Oct 64–19 Jun 70
1st.Sec.	**G. BROWN**	16 Oct 64
of State	**M. STEWART**	11 Aug 66–18 Mar 68
	(office linked to Dept. of Econ.Affairs 16 Oct 64–29 Aug 67)	
	BARBARA CASTLE	6 Apr 68
	(office linked to Min. of Employment)	
Ld Pres.	**H. BOWDEN**	16 Oct 64
	R. CROSSMAN	11 Aug 66
	F. PEART	18 Oct 68
Ld Chanc.	**Ld GARDINER**	16 Oct 64
Privy Seal	**E of LONGFORD**	18 Oct 64
	Sir F. SOSKICE	23 Dec 65
	E of LONGFORD	6 Apr 66
	Ld SHACKLETON	16 Jan 68
	F. PEART	6 Apr 68
	Ld SHACKLETON	18 Oct 68
Exchequer	**J. CALLAGHAN**	16 Oct 64
	R. JENKINS	30 Nov 67
Chief Sec.	**J. DIAMOND**	20 Oct 64
	(office in cabinet)	
	J. DIAMOND	1 Nov 68

Min.of State	D. TAVERNE	6 Apr 68
	W. RODGERS	13 Oct 69
F.S.	N. MacDermot	21 Oct 64
	H. Lever	29 Aug 67
	D.TAVERNE	13 Oct 69
Econ.S.	A. Crosland	19 Oct 64
	(de facto Min. of State, Econ. Affs; office abolished 22 Dec 64)	
Economic	**G. BROWN**	16 Oct 64
Affs	**M. STEWART**	11 Aug 66
	P. SHORE	29 Aug 67
	(office abolished 6 Oct 69)	
Min.of	A. CROSLAND	20 Oct 64
State	*(until 22 Dec 64 nominally Econ. Sec. to Treasury)*	
	A. ALBU	27 Jan 65–7 Jan 67
	T. URWIN	6 Apr 68–6 Oct 69
U-S.	M. Foley	21 Oct 64–6 Apr 66
	W. Rodgers	21 Oct 64–7 Jan 67
	H. Lever	7 Jan 67–29 Aug 67
	P. Shore	7 Jan 67–29 Aug 67
	A. Williams	29 Aug 67–6 Oct 69

+Not a member of the House of Commons.

LABOUR GOVERNMENT 1964–1970 (contd.)

U-S. (contd.)	E. Dell	29 Aug 67–6 Apr 68
Foreign O. (& C.R.O.)	**P. GORDON-WALKER***	16 Oct 64
	M. STEWART	22 Jan 65
	G. BROWN	11 Aug 66
	M. STEWART	16 Mar 68
	(merged with Comm.O. 17 Oct 68)	
Min.of State	Ld CARADON	16 Oct 64–19 Jun 70
	G. THOMSON	19 Oct 64–6 Apr 66 & 7 Jan 67–29 Aug 67
	W. PADLEY	19 Oct 64–7 Jan 67
	Ld CHALFONT	23 Oct 64–19 Jun 70
	Eirene WHITE	11 Apr 66–7 Jan 67
	F. MULLEY	7 Jan 67–6 Oct 69
	G. ROBERTS	29 Aug 67–13 Oct 69
	Ld SHEPHERD	17 Oct 68–19 Jun 70
U-S.	Ld Walston	20 Oct 64–7 Jan 67
	W. Rodgers	7 Jan 67–3 Jul 68
	M. Foley	3 Jul 68–19 Jun 70
	W. Whitlock	17 Oct 68–13 Oct 69
	E. Luard	13 Oct 69–19 Jun 70
Home O.	**Sir F. SOSKICE**	18 Oct 64
	R. JENKINS	23 Dec 65
	J. CALLAGHAN	30 Nov 67
Min.of State	Alice BACON	19 Oct 64
	Ld STONHAM	29 Aug 67
	Shirley WILLIAMS	13 Oct 69
U-S.	Ld Stonham	20 Oct 64–29 Aug 67
	G. Thomas	20 Oct 64–6 Apr 66
	M. Foley	6 Apr 66–7 Jan 67
	D. Taverne	6 Apr 66–6 Apr 68
	D. Ennals	7 Jan 67–1 Nov 68
	E. Morgan	6 Apr 68–19 Jun 70
	M. Rees	1 Nov 68–19 Jun 70
Ag.Fish. & Food	**F. PEART**	18 Oct 64
	C. HUGHES	6 Apr 68
P.S.	J. Mackie	20 Oct 64–19 Jun 70
	J. Hoy	21 Oct 64–19 Jun 70
Aviation	R. JENKINS	18 Oct 64
	F. MULLEY	23 Dec 65
	J. STONEHOUSE	7 Jan 67
	(office abolished 15 Feb 67)	
P.S.	J. Stonehouse	20 Oct 64–6 Apr 66
	J. Snow	6 Apr 66–7 Jan 67
Colonies	**A. GREENWOOD**	18 Oct 64
	E of LONGFORD	23 Dec 65
	F. LEE	6 Apr 66
	(came under Dept. of Comm. Affs 1 Aug 66 office abolished 7 Jan 67)	
U-S.	Eirene White	20 Oct 64–11 Oct 65
	Ld Taylor	20 Oct 64–11 Apr 66
	Ld Beswick	11 Oct 65–1 Aug 66
	(Ld Taylor & Ld Beswick were also U-S. at C.R.O.)	
	J. Stonehouse	6 Apr 66–7 Jan 67
C.R.O.	**A. BOTTOMLEY**	18 Oct 64
	(re-named Commonwealth Affs 1 Aug 66)	
	H. BOWDEN	11 Aug 66
	G. THOMSON	29 Aug 67
	(merged with Foreign O. 17 Oct 68)	
Min.of State	C. HUGHES	19 Oct 64–6 Apr 66
	Judith HART	6 Apr 66–26 Jul 67
	G. THOMAS	7 Jan 67–6 Apr 68
	Ld SHEPHERD	26 Jul 67
U-S.	Ld Taylor	20 Oct 64
	Ld Beswick	11 Oct 65
	(held jointly with U-S. at Colonies until 1 Aug 66)	
	W. Whitlock	26 Jul 67
Defence	**D. HEALEY**	16 Oct 64
Min.Army & Dep.Sec. of State	F. MULLEY	19 Oct 64
	G. REYNOLDS	24 Dec 65
	(no Dep. Sec. of State after 24 Dec 65 office abolished 7 Jan 67)	
U-S.Army	G. Reynolds	20 Oct 64
	M. Rees	24 Dec 65
	D. Ennals	6 Apr 66
	J. Boyden	7 Jan 67
	I. Richard	13 Oct 69
Min.Navy	C. MAYHEW	19 Oct 64
	J. MALLALIEU	19 Feb 66
	(office abolished 7 Jan 67)	
U-S.Navy	J. Mallalieu	21 Oct 64
	Ld Winterbottom	6 Apr 66
	M. Foley	7 Jan 67
	D. Owen	3 Jul 68
Min. Air Force	Ld SHACKLETON	19 Oct 64
	(office abolished 7 Jan 67)	
U-S.Air Force	B. Millan	20 Oct 64
	M. Rees	16 Apr 66
	Ld Winterbottom	1 Nov 68
Min. of Defence for Admin.	G. REYNOLDS	7 Jan 67
	R. HATTERSLEY	15 Jul 69
Min. of Defence for Equipment	R. MASON	7 Jan 67
	J. MORRIS	16 Apr 68
Educ. & Science	**M. STEWART**	18 Oct 64
	A. CROSLAND	22 Jan 65
	P. GORDON-WALKER	29 Aug 67
	E. SHORT	6 Apr 68
Min.of State	Ld BOWDEN	19 Oct 64–11 Oct 65
	R. PRENTICE	20 Oct 64–6 Apr 66
	E. REDHEAD	11 Oct 65–7 Jan 67
	G. ROBERTS	6 Apr 66–29 Aug 67
	Shirley WILLIAMS	7 Jan 67–13 Oct 69
	Alice BACON	29 Aug 67–19 Jun 70
	G. FOWLER	13 Oct 69–19 Jun 70
Min. of State (Arts)	Jennie LEE	17 Feb 67–19 Jun 70
U-S.	J. Boyden	20 Oct 64–24 Feb 65
	D. Howell	20 Oct 64–13 Oct 69
	Jennie Lee *(Arts)*	24 Feb 65–17 Feb 67
	Joan Lestor	13 Oct 69–19 Jun 70

*MP. Not a member of the House of Lords.

LABOUR GOVERNMENT 1964–1970 (contd.)

Employment	**Barbara CASTLE**	6 Apr 68
& Productivity		
Min.of State	E. DELL	13 Oct 69
U-S.	E. Fernyhough	6 Apr 68–13 Oct 69
	R. Hattersley	6 Apr 68–15 Jul 69
	H. Walker	6 Apr 68–19 Jun 70
Health	K. ROBINSON	18 Oct 64
	(office abolished 1 Nov 68)	
P.S.	Sir B. Stross	20 Oct 64
	C. Loughlin	24 Feb 65
	J. Snow	7 Jan 67
Health	(known as S. of S. for Social Services)	
& Soc.Sec.		
	R. CROSSMAN	1 Nov 68
Min.of	S. SWINGLER	1 Nov 68–19 Feb 69
State	D. ENNALS	1 Nov 68–19 Jun 70
	Lady SEROTA	25 Feb 69–19 Jun 70
U-S.	N. Pentland	1 Nov 68–13 Oct 69
	C. Loughlin	1 Nov 68–20 Nov 68
	J. Snow	1 Nov 68–13 Oct 69
	B. O'Malley	13 Oct 69–19 Jun 70
	J. Dunwoody	13 Oct 69–19 Jun 70
Housing	**R. CROSSMAN**	18 Oct 64
& Loc.	**A. GREENWOOD**	11 Aug 66
Govt	(office not in cabinet)	
	A. GREENWOOD	6 Oct 69
	R. MELLISH	31 May 70
Min.of	F. WILLEY	17 Feb 67
State	N. MACDERMOT	
		29 Aug 67–28 Sep 68
	D. HOWELL	13 Oct 69
Min.for	K. ROBINSON	1 Nov 68
Planning	(office abolished 6 Oct 69)	
and Land		
P.S.	R. Mellish	18 Oct 64–29 Aug 67
	J. MacColl	20 Oct 64–13 Oct 69
	Ld Kennet	6 Apr 66–19 Jun 70
	A. Skeffington	17 Feb 67–19 Jun 70
	R. Freeson	13 Oct 69–19 Jun 70
P.S.	R. Marsh	20 Oct 64–11 Oct 65
	E. Thornton	21 Oct 64–6 Apr 66
	Shirley Williams	6 Apr 66–7 Jan 67
	E. Fernyhough	7 Jan 67–6 Apr 68
	R. Hattersley	7 Jan 67–6 Apr 68
Labour	R. GUNTER	18 Oct 64
	(6 Apr 68 reorganised as Min.of	
	Employment & Productivity)	
D.Lanc.	**D. HOUGHTON**	18 Oct 64
	(office not in cabinet)	
	G. THOMSON	6 Apr 66
	F. LEE	7 Jan 67
	(office in cabinet)	
	G. THOMSON	6 Oct 69
Local Govt & Regional Planning		
	(office created 6 Oct 69)	
	A. CROSLAND	6 Oct 69
Min.of State	T. URWIN	6 Oct 69
Land &	F. WILLEY	18 Oct 64
Nat.Res.	(office wound up 17 Feb 67)	

P.S.	Ld Mitchison	64–6 Apr 66
	A. Skeffington	21 Oct 64–17 Feb 67
Overseas	**Barbara CASTLE**	18 Oct 64
Dev.	**A. GREENWOOD**	23 Dec 65
	A. BOTTOMLEY	11 Aug 66
	(office not in cabinet)	
	R. PRENTICE	29 Aug 67
	Judith HART	6 Oct 69
P.S.	A. Oram	21 Oct 64
	B. Whitaker	13 Oct 69
Paym.-Gen.	G. WIGG	19 Oct 64–12 Nov 67
	(office vacant 12 Nov 67)	
	(office in cabinet)	
	Ld SHACKLETON	6 Apr 68
	Judith HART	1 Nov 68
	H. LEVER	6 Oct 69
Pensions	Margaret HERBISON	18 Oct 64
& Nat.Ins.	(6 Aug 66 became Min.	
	of Social Security)	
P.S.	H. Davies	20 Oct 64–6 Aug 66
	N. Pentland	21 Oct 64–6 Aug 66
Min.	Sir E. FLETCHER	
without		19 Oct 64–6 Apr 66
Portfolio	Ld CHAMPION	21 Oct 64–7 Jan 67
	(office in cabinet)	
	D. HOUGHTON	6 Apr 66–7 Jan 67
	Ld SHACKLETON	
		7 Jan 67–16 Jan 68
	P. GORDON-WALKER	
		7 Jan 67–21 Aug 67
	G. THOMSON	17 Oct 68–6 Oct 69
	P. SHORE	6 Oct 69–19 Jun 70
Post.-Gen.	A. BENN	19 Oct 64
	E. SHORT	4 Jul 66
	R. MASON	6 Apr 68
	J. STONEHOUSE	1 Jul 68
	(1 Oct 69 Post Office	
	became a Public Corporation)	
Ass.	J. Slater	20 Oct 64
Posts & Tel.	J. STONEHOUSE	1 Oct 69
P.S.	J. Slater	1 Oct 69
	N. Pentland	13 Oct 69
Power	F. LEE	18 Oct 64
	R. MARSH	6 Apr 66
	R. GUNTER	6 Apr 68
	R. MASON	1 Jul 68
	(office abolished 6 Oct 69)	
P.S.	J. Morris	21 Oct 64
	Ld Lindgren	10 Jan 66
	J. Bray	6 Apr 66
	R. Freeson	7 Jan 67–6 Oct 69
Public	C. PANNELL	19 Oct 64
Building	R. PRENTICE	6 Apr 66
& Works	R. MELLISH	29 Aug 67
	J. SILKIN	30 Apr 69
P.S.	Jennie Lee (Arts)	20 Oct 64
	J. Boyden	24 Feb 65
	Ld Winterbottom	7 Jan 67
	C. Loughlin	20 Nov 68

LABOUR GOVERNMENT 1964–70 *(contd.)*

Scotland	**W. ROSS**	18 Oct 64
Min.of State	G. WILLIS	20 Oct 64–7 Jan 67
	D. MABON	7 Jan 67–19 Jun 70
	Ld HUGHES	13 Oct 69–19 Jun 70
U-S.	Ld Hughes	21 Oct 64–13 Oct 69
	Judith Hart	20 Oct 64–6 Apr 66
	D. Mabon	21 Oct 64–7 Jan 67
	B. Millan	6 Apr 66–19 Jun 70
	N. Buchan	7 Jan 67–19 Jun 70
Social Security	Margaret HERBISON	6 Aug 66
	Judith HART	26 Jul 67
	(office abolished 1 Nov 68, see Health & Soc. Security)	
P.S.	H. Davies	6 Aug 66–7 Jan 67
	N. Pentland	6 Aug 66–1 Nov 68
	C. Loughlin	7 Jan 67–1 Nov 68
Tech.	**F. COUSINS**	18 Oct 64
	A. BENN	4 Jul 66
Min.of State	J. STONEHOUSE	15 Feb 67–1 Jul 68
	J. MALLALIEU	1 Jul 68–13 Oct 69
	R. PRENTICE	6 Oct 69–10 Oct 69
	Ld DELACOURT-SMITH	13 Oct 69–19 Jun 70
	E. VARLEY	13 Oct 69–19 Jun 70
P.S.	Ld Snow	19 Oct 64–6 Apr 66
	R. Marsh	11 Oct 65–6 Apr 66
	P. Shore	6 Apr 66–7 Jan 67
	E. Dell	6 Apr 66–29 Aug 67
	J. Bray	7 Jan 67–24 Sep 69
	G. Fowler	29 Aug 67–13 Oct 69
	A. Williams	6 Oct 69–19 Jun 70
	N. Carmichael	13 Oct 69–19 Jun 70
	E. Davies	13 Oct 69–19 Jun 70
B.Trade	**D. JAY**	18 Oct 64
	A. CROSLAND	29 Aug 67
	R. MASON	6 Oct 69
Min.of State	G. DARLING	20 Oct 64–6 Apr 68
	E. REDHEAD	20 Oct 64–11 Oct 65
	R. MASON	20 Oct 64–7 Jan 67
	Ld BROWN	11 Oct 65–19 Jun 70
	J. MALLALIEU	7 Jan 67–1 Jul 68
	E. DELL	6 Apr 68–13 Oct 69
	W. RODGERS	1 Jul 68–13 Oct 69
	G. ROBERTS	13 Oct 69–19 Jun 70
P.S.	Ld Rhodes	20 Oct 64
	Ld Walston	7 Jan 67
	Gwyneth Dunwoody	29 Aug 67
Transport	**T. FRASER**	18 Oct 64
	BARBARA CASTLE	23 Dec 65
	R. MARSH	6 Apr 68
	(office not in cabinet)	
	F. MULLEY	6 Oct 69
Min.of State	S. SWINGLER	29 Aug 67
	(office vacant)	1 Nov 68
P.S.	Ld Lindgren	20 Oct 64–10 Jan 66
	S. Swingler	20 Oct 64–29 Aug 67
	J. Morris	10 Jan 66–6 Apr 68
	N. Carmichael	29 Aug 67–13 Oct 69
	R. C. Brown	6 Apr 68–19 Jun 70
P.S. *(contd.)*	A. Murray	13 Oct 69–19 Jun 70
Wales	**J. GRIFFITHS**	18 Oct 64
	C. HUGHES	6 Apr 66
	G. THOMAS	6 Apr 68
Min.of State	G. ROBERTS	20 Oct 64
	G. THOMAS	6 Apr 66
	Eirene WHITE	7 Jan 67
U-S.	H. Finch	21 Oct 64
	I. Davies	6 Apr 66
	E. Rowlands	13 Oct 69

Law Officers

Att.-Gen.	Sir E. JONES	18 Oct 64
Sol.-Gen.	Sir D. FOOT	18 Oct 64
	Sir A. IRVINE	24 Aug 67
Ld Advoc.	G. STOTT+	20 Oct 64
	H. S. WILSON (Ld)+	26 Oct 67
Sol.-Gen. Scotland	J. LEECHMAN+	20 Oct 64
	H. S. WILSON+	11 Oct 65
	E. STEWART+	26 Oct 67

Whips

P.S. to Treasury	E. SHORT	18 Oct 64
	J. SILKIN	4 Jul 66
	R. MELLISH	30 Apr 69
	(office vacant)	31 May 70
Lds of Treasury	G. Rogers	21 Oct 64–11 Jan 66
	G. Lawson	21 Oct 64–1 Apr 67
	J. McCann	21 Oct 64–11 Apr 66
		29 Jul 67–13 Oct 69
	I. Davies	21 Oct 64–6 Apr 66
	Harriet Slater	21 Oct 64–6 Apr 66
	J. Silkin	11 Jan 66–11 Apr 66
	A. Fitch	16 Apr 66–13 Oct 69
	J. Harper	16 Apr 66–19 Jun 70
	W. Whitlock	11 Apr 66–7 Jul 66
		1 Apr 67–28 Jul 67
	W. Howie	16 Apr 66–1 Apr 67
	H. Gourlay	7 Jul 66–29 Oct 68
	B. O'Malley	1 Apr 67–13 Oct 69
	W. Harrison	29 Oct 68–19 Jun 70
	N. McBride	13 Oct 69–19 Jun 70
	E. Perry	13 Oct 69–19 Jun 70
	E. Armstrong	13 Oct 69–19 Jun 70
Ass.Whips	A. Fitch	22 Oct 64–16 Apr 66
	H. Gourlay	22 Oct 64–7 Jul 66
	J. Harper	22 Oct 64–16 Apr 66
	W. Howie	22 Oct 64–16 Apr 66
	B. O'Malley	22 Oct 64–1 Apr 67
	J. Silkin	22 Oct 64–11 Jan 66
	C. Morris	25 Jan 66–29 Jul 67
	E. Bishop	16 Apr 66–1 Apr 67
	R. W. Brown	16 Apr 66–20 Jan 67
	W. Harrison	16 Apr 66–28 Oct 68
	N. McBride	16 Apr 66–13 Oct 69
	I. Evans	7 Jul 66–6 Feb 68
	E. Armstrong	20 Jan 67–13 Oct 69
	H. Walker	1 Apr 67–5 Apr 68
	E. Varley	29 Jul 67–30 Nov 68
	E. Perry	6 Feb 68–13 Oct 69

+Not a member of the House of Commons.

LABOUR GOVERNMENT 1964–1970 *(contd.)*

Ass. Whips	D. Concannon	11 Apr 68–19 Jun 70	*V. Chamb.*	W. WHITLOCK	21 Oct 64
(contd.)	M. Miller	29 Oct 68–13 Oct 69		J. McCANN	11 Apr 66
	T. Boston	13 Oct 69–19 Jun 70		C. MORRIS	29 Jul 67
	J. Hamilton	13 Oct 69–19 Jun 70		A. FITCH	13 Oct 69
	R. Dobson	13 Oct 69–19 Jun 70	*Cap.Gents*	Ld SHEPHERD	21 Oct 64
	W. Hamling	13 Oct 69–19 Jun 70	*at Arms*	Ld BESWICK	29 Jul 67
			Cap.Yeo.	Ld BOWLES	28 Dec 64
H.M. Household			*of Guard*		
Treasurer	S. IRVING	21 Oct 64	*Lds in*	Ld Hobson	21 Oct 64–17 Feb 66
	J. SILKIN	11 Apr 66	*Waiting*	Ld Beswick	28 Dec 64–11 Oct 65
	C. GREY	7 Jul 66		Ld Sorensen	28 Dec 64–20 Apr 68
	C. MORRIS	13 Oct 69		Lady Phillips	10 Dec 65–19 Jun 70
Compt.	C. GREY	21 Oct 64		Ld Hilton	6 Apr 66–19 Jun 70
	W. WHITLOCK	7 Jul 66		Lady Serota	23 Apr 68–25 Feb 69
	W. HOWIE	1 Apr 67		Lady Llewelyn-Davies	
	I. EVANS	6 Feb 68			13 Mar 69–19 Jun 70

CONSERVATIVE GOVERNMENT 1970–1974

P.M.	**E. HEATH**	19 Jun 70–4 Mar 74	*Min.of*	R. SHARPLES	23 Jun 70–7 Apr 72
P.S. Civil	D. Howell[1]	23 Jun 70–26 Mar 72	*State*	Ld WINDLESHAM	
Service	K. Baker	7 Apr 72–4 Mar 74			23 Jun 70–26 Mar 72
Dept	G. Johnson-Smith	5 Nov 72–4 Mar 74		M. CARLISLE	7 Apr 72–4 Mar 74
Ld Pres.	**W. WHITELAW**	20 Jun 70		Vt COLVILLE	21 Apr 72–4 Mar 74
	R. CARR	7 Apr 72	*U-S.*	M. Carlisle	24 Jun 70
	J. PRIOR	5 Nov 72		D. Lane	7 Apr 72
Ld.Chanc.	**Q. HOGG**	20 Jun 70	*Ag. Fish.*	**J. PRIOR**	20 Jun 70
	(Ld Hailsham)		*& Food*	**J. GODBER**	5 Nov 72
Privy Seal	**Earl JELLICOE**	20 Jun 70	*Min.of State*	A. STODART	7 Apr 72
	Ld WINDLESHAM	5 Jun 73	*P.S.*	A. Stodart	24 Jun 70–7 Apr 72
Exchequer	**I. MACLEOD**	20 Jun 70		P. Mills	7 Apr 72–5 Nov 72
	A. BARBER	25 Jul 70		Peggy Fenner	5 Nov 72–4 Mar 74
Chief Sec.	**M. MACMILLAN**	23 Jun 70		Earl Ferrers	8 Jan 74–4 Mar 74
	P. JENKIN	7 Apr 72	*Aviation*	F. CORFIELD	15 Oct 70
	T. BOARDMAN	8 Jan 74	*Supply*	D. Price	15 Oct 70
Min.of	T. HIGGINS	23 Jun 70	*P.S.*	*(abolished 1 May 71; functions*	
State	J. NOTT	7 Apr 72		*transferred to Procurement*	
F.S.	P. JENKIN	23 Jun 70		*Executive, Min. of Defence)*	
	T. HIGGINS	7 Apr 72	*Defence*	**Ld CARRINGTON**	20 Jun 70
For.&	**Sir A. DOUGLAS-HOME**	20 Jun 70		**I. GILMOUR**	8 Jan 74
Comm. O			*Min.of*	Ld BALNIEL*	23 Jun 70
Min.of	J. GODBER	23 Jun 70–5 Nov 72	*State*	I. GILMOUR	5 Nov 72
State	Lady TWEEDSMUIR			G. YOUNGER	8 Jan 74
		7 Apr 72–4 Mar 74	*Min. of*	I. GILMOUR	7 Apr 71
	J. AMERY	5 Nov 72–4 Mar 74	*State for*	*(office abolished 5 Nov 72)*	
	Ld BALNIEL*	5 Nov 72–4 Mar 74	*Procurement*		
U-S.	M of Lothian	24 Jun 70–7 Apr 72	*U-S.*	P. Kirk	24 Jun 70
	A. Royle	24 Jun 70–8 Jan 74	*Navy*	A. Buck	5 Nov 72
	A. Kershaw	15 Oct 70–5 Jun 73	*U-S. Air*	Ld Lambton	24 Jun 70
	P. Blaker	8 Jan 74–4 Mar 74		A. Kershaw	5 Jun 73
Min. for	R. WOOD	15 Oct 70		Ld Strathcona	8 Jan 74
Overseas			*U-S. Army*	I. Gilmour	24 Jun 70
Development[2]				G. Johnson-Smith	7 Apr 71
Home O.	**R. MAUDLING**	20 Jun 70		P. Blaker	5 Nov 72
	R. CARR	18 Jul 72		D. Smith	8 Jan 74

*MP. Not a Member of the House of Lords.

[1] Also Junior Lord of Treasury 24 Jun 70–6 Jan 71; P.S. Dept Employment 5 Jan 71–Mar 72.

[2] The Ministry of Overseas Development formally came under the Foreign Office 12 Nov 70.

CONSERVATIVE GOVERNMENT 1970–1974 (contd.)

Educ. & **MARGARET THATCHER** 20 Jun 70
Science
Min.of N. ST. JOHN-STEVAS (Arts) 2 Dec 73
State W. VAN STRAUBENZEE
24 Jun 70–5 Nov 72
U.-S. Ld Belstead 24 Jun 70–5 Jun 73
N. St. John-Stevas 5 Nov 72–2 Dec 73
Ld Sandford 5 Jun 73–4 Mar 74
T. Raison 2 Dec 73–4 Mar 74
Emp. (& Productivity to 12 Nov 70)
R. CARR 20 Jun 70
M. MACMILLAN 7 Apr 72
W. WHITELAW 2 Dec 73
Min.of P. BRYAN 23 Jun 70
State R. CHICHESTER-CLARK 7 Apr 72
U.-S. D. Smith 24 Jun 70–8 Jan 74
D. Howell 5 Jan 71–26 Mar 72
N. Scott 8 Jan 74–4 Mar 74
Energy **Ld CARRINGTON** (S.of S.) 8 Jan 74
Min. **P. JENKIN** (Minister) 8 Jan 74
Min.of D. HOWELL 8 Jan 74
State
U.-S. P. Emery 8 Jan 74
Env. **P. WALKER** 15 Oct 70
G. RIPPON 5 Nov 72
Min. for G. PAGE 15 Oct 70
Loc. Govt &
Development
Min. for J. AMERY 15 Oct 70
Housing & P. CHANNON 5 Nov 72
Construction
Min. for J. PEYTON 15 Oct 70
Transport
Industries
U.-S. E. Griffiths 15 Oct 70–4 Mar 74
P. Channon 15 Oct 70–26 Mar 72
M. Heseltine 15 Oct 70–7 Apr 72
Ld Sandford 15 Oct 70–5 Jun 73
K. Speed 7 Apr 72–4 Mar 74
R. Eyre 7 Apr 72–4 Mar 74
Lady Young 5 Jun 73–4 Mar 74
H. Rossi 8 Jan 74–4 Mar 74
Health & **Sir K. JOSEPH** 20 Jun 70
Soc. Security
Min.of State Ld ABERDARE 23 Jun 70–8 Jan 74
P.S. P. Dean 24 Jun 70–4 Mar 74
M. Alison 24 Jun 70–4 Mar 74
Housing & **P. WALKER** 24 Jun 70–15 Oct 70
Local Govt (15 Oct 70 office reorganised
under Environment)
Min.of State G. PAGE 23 Jun 70–15 Oct 70
P.S. P. Channon 24 Jun 70–15 Oct 70
E. Griffiths 24 Jun 70–15 Oct 70
Ld Sandford 24 Jun 70–15 Oct 70
D.Lanc. (with special responsibility
for Europe)
A. BARBER 20 Jun 70
G. RIPPON 28 Jul 70
J. DAVIES 5 Nov 72
Northern **W. WHITELAW** 24 Mar 72
Ireland **F. PYM** 2 Dec 73

Min.of P. CHANNON 26 Mar 72–5 Nov 72
State Ld WINDLESHAM
26 Mar 72–5 Jun 73
W. VAN STRAUBENZEE
5 Nov 72–4 Mar 74
D. HOWELL 5 Nov 72–8 Jan 74
U.-S. D. Howell 26 Mar 72–5 Nov 72
P. Mills 5 Nov 72–4 Mar 74
Ld Belstead 5 Jun 73–4 Mar 74
Overseas R. WOOD 23 Jun 70–15 Oct 70
Dev. (under Foreign Office 15 Oct 70)
Paym.-Gen. Vt ECCLES (Min. for Arts) 23 Jun 70
(office in cabinet)
M. MACMILLAN 2 Dec 73
Min. Ld DRUMALBYN 15 Oct 70
without Ld ABERDARE 8 Jan 74
Portfolio
Posts & C. CHATAWAY 24 Jun 70
Tel. Sir J. EDEN 7 Apr 72
Public J. AMERY 23 Jun 70–15 Oct 70
Buildings (15 Oct 70 office reorganised
& Works under Dept of Environment)
P.S. A. Kershaw 24 Jun 70–15 Oct 70
Scotland **G. CAMPBELL** 20 Jun 70
Min.of Lady TWEEDSMUIR 23 Jun 70
State Ld POLWARTH 7 Apr 72
U.-S. A. Buchanan-Smith
24 Jun 70–4 Mar 74
G. Younger 24 Jun 70–8 Jan 74
E. Taylor 24 Jun 70–28 Jul 71
H. Monro 28 Jul 71–4 Mar 74
E. Taylor 8 Jan 74–4 Mar 74
Tech. **G. RIPPON** 20 Jun 70
J. DAVIES 28 Jul 70–15 Oct 70
(15 Oct 70 office reorganised
under Trade and Industry)
Min.of Sir J.EDEN 23 Jun 70–15 Oct 70
State E of BESSBOROUGH
24 Jun 70–15 Oct 70
P.S. D. Price 24 Jun 70–15 Oct 70
N. Ridley 24 Jun 70–15 Oct 70
Trade **M. NOBLE** 20 Jun 70–15 Oct 70
Trade & **J. DAVIES** 15 Oct 70
Industry **P. WALKER** 5 Nov 72
Trade & **Sir G. HOWE** 5 Nov 72
Consumer
Affairs
Min.of State F. CORFIELD 24 Jun 70–15 Oct 70
P.S. A. Grant 24 Jun 70–15 Oct 70
Min.for M. NOBLE 15 Oct 70
Trade (**Sir G. HOWE** & in cabinet 5 Nov 72)
U.-S. A. Grant 15 Oct 70
E of Limerick 7 Apr 72
Min.for Sir J. EDEN 15 Oct 70
Industry T. BOARDMAN 7 Apr 72–8 Jan 74
U.-S. N. Ridley 15 Oct 70
P. Emery 7 Apr 72–8 Jan 74
Min. for Aerospace
(& Shipping 5 Nov 72)
F. CORFIELD 1 May 71
M. HESELTINE 7 Apr 72

CONSERVATIVE GOVERNMENT 1970–1974 *(contd.)*

U-S.	D. Price	1 May 71	*Ass.Whips*	K. Speed	29 Jun 70–8 Nov 71	
	C. Onslow	7 Apr 72	*(contd.)*	H. Rossi	21 Oct 70–7 Apr 72	
Min. for	C. CHATAWAY	7 Apr 72		H. Gray	8 Nov 71–30 Oct 73	
Ind.Dev.				J. Thomas	8 Nov 71–30 Oct 73	
U-S.	A. Grant	7 Apr 72		M. Jopling	8 Nov 71–30 Oct 73	
Transport	**J. PEYTON**	23 Jun 70–15 Oct 70		O. Murton	8 Nov 71–7 Apr 72	
P.S.	M. Heseltine	24 Jun 70–15 Oct 70		M. Fox	13 Apr 72–2 Dec 73	
	(Transport merged with			K. Clarke	13 Apr 72–8 Jan 74	
	Environment 15 Oct 70)			D. Walder	30 Oct 73–4 Mar 74	
Wales	**P. THOMAS**	20 Jun 70		A. Hall-Davis	30 Oct 73–4 Mar 74	
Min.of State	D. GIBSON-WATT	23 Jun 70		R. Hicks	30 Oct 73–4 Mar 74	
				A. Butler	8 Jan 74–4 Mar 74	
Law Officers				C. Parkinson	8 Jan 74–4 Mar 74	
Att.-Gen.	Sir P. RAWLINSON	23 Jun 70				
Sol.-Gen.	Sir G. HOWE	23 Jun 70	***H.M. Household***			
	Sir M. HAVERS	5 Nov 72	*Treasurer*	H. ATKINS	24 Jun 70	
Ld Advoc.	N. WYLIE	23 Jun 70		B. WEATHERILL	2 Dec 73	
Sol.-Gen.	D. BRAND	23 Jun 70	*Compt.*	W. ELLIOTT	24 Jun 70	
Scotland	I. STEWART[+]	5 Nov 72		R. EYRE	24 Sep 70	
				B. WEATHERILL	7 Apr 72	
Whips				W. CLEGG	2 Dec 73	
P.S. to	F. PYM	20 Jun 70	*V. Chamb.*	J. MORE	24 Jun 70	
Treasury	H. ATKINS	2 Dec 73		B. WEATHERILL	17 Oct 71	
Lds of	R. Eyre	24 Jun 70–23 Sep 70		W. CLEGG	7 Apr 72	
Treasury	D. Howell[1]	24 Jun 70–6 Jan 71		P. HAWKINS	2 Dec 73	
	H. Monro	24 Jun 70–28 Jul 71	*Cap.Gents*	Earl ST ALDWYN	24 Jun 70	
	B. Weatherill	24 Jun 70–17 Oct 71	*at Arms*			
	W. Clegg	24 Jun 70–7 Apr 72	*Cap.Yeo.*	Vt GOSCHEN	24 Jun 70	
	V. Goodhew	21 Oct 70–9 Oct 73	*of Guard*	Ld DENHAM	20 Nov 71	
	P. Hawkins	5 Jan 71–2 Dec 73	*Lds in*	Ld Mowbray	24 Jun 70–4 Mar 74	
	T. Fortescue	8 Nov 71–21 Sep 73	*Waiting*	Ld Denham	24 Jun 70–20 Nov 71	
	K. Speed	8 Nov 71–7 Apr 72		Ld Bethell	24 Jun 70–5 Jan 71	
	H. Rossi	7 Apr 72–8 Jan 74		Earl Ferrers	5 Jan 71–8 Jan 74	
	O. Murton	7 Apr 72–30 Oct 73		M of Lothian	7 Apr 72–27 Jul 73	
	M. Jopling	30 Oct 73–4 Mar 74		E of Gowrie	7 Apr 72–4 Mar 74	
	H. Gray	30 Oct 73–4 Mar 74		Lady Young	21 Apr 72–5 Jun 73	
	J. Thomas	30 Oct 73–4 Mar 74		Ld Strathcona	27 Jun 73–8 Jan 74	
	M. Fox	2 Dec 73–4 Mar 74		Ld Sandys	8 Jan 74–4 Mar 74	
	K. Clarke	8 Jan 74–4 Mar 74		Earl Cowley	8 Jan 74–4 Mar 74	
Ass.Whips	V. Goodhew	29 Jun 70–21 Oct 70		Earl Alexander of Tunis		
	P. Hawkins	29 Jun 70–5 Jan 71			8 Jan 74–4 Mar 74	
	T. Fortescue	29 Jun 70–8 Nov 71				

LABOUR GOVERNMENT 1974–79

P.M.	**H. WILSON**	4 Mar 74–5 Apr 76	*Paym.-Gen.*	E. DELL	7 Mar 74
	J. CALLAGHAN			*(Shirley Williams and office*	
		5 Apr 76–4 May 79		*combined with Prices &*	
Civil Service	R. SHELDON	7 Mar 74		*Consumer Protection 8 Apr 76*	
Dept Min.	C. MORRIS	18 Oct 74		*and then with Education 10 Sep 76)*	
of State			*Ld Chanc.*	**Ld ELWYN-JONES**	5 Mar 74
P.S.	J. Grant	7 Mar 74–18 Oct 74	*Privy Seal*	**Ld SHEPHERD**	7 Mar 74
Ld Pres.	**E. SHORT**	5 Mar 74		**Ld PEART**	10 Sep 76
	M. FOOT	8 Apr 76	*Exchequer*	**D. HEALEY**	5 Mar 74
Min.Privy	G. FOWLER	18 Oct 74	*Chief Sec.*	J. BARNETT	7 Mar 74
Council Off.	Ld CROWTHER-HUNT	23 Jan 76		*(office in cabinet)*	
	J. SMITH	8 Apr 76		**J. BARNETT**	21 Feb 77
Min.of State	Lady BIRK	3 Jan 79	*F.S.*	J. GILBERT	7 Mar 74
P.S.	W. Price	18 Oct 74		R. SHELDON	17 Jun 75

[+]Not a member of the House of Commons.
[1]Also P.S. Civil Service Dept. 23 Jun 70–26 Mar 72.

LABOUR GOVERNMENT 1974–1979 (contd.)

Min.of	R. SHELDON	18 Oct 74
State	D. DAVIES	17 Jun 75
For. &	**J. CALLAGHAN**	5 Mar 74
Comm. O.	**A. CROSLAND**	8 Apr 76
	D. OWEN	21 Feb 77
Min.of	D. ENNALS	7 Mar 74–8 Apr 76
State	R. HATTERSLEY	7 Mar 74–10 Sep 76
	Ld GORONWY-ROBERTS	4 Dec 75–4 May 79
	E. ROWLANDS	14 Apr 76–4 May 79
	D. OWEN	10 Sep 76–21 Feb 77
	F. JUDD	21 Feb 77–4 May 79
U-S.	Joan Lestor	8 Mar 74–12 Jun 75
	Ld Goronwy-Roberts	8 Mar 74–4 Dec 75
	E.Rowlands	12 Jun 75–14 Apr 76
	J. Tomlinson	17 Mar 76–4 May 79
	(see also Overseas Development)	
	E. Luard	14 Apr 76–4 May 79
Home O.	**R. JENKINS**	5 Mar 74
	M. REES	10 Sep 76
Min. of	Ld HARRIS	8 Mar 74–3 Jan 79
State	A. LYON	8 Mar 74–14 Apr 76
	B. JOHN	14 Apr 76–4 May 79
	Ld BOSTON	3 Jan 79–4 May 79
U-S.	Shirley Summerskill	8 Mar 74
Ag. Fish.	**F. PEART**	5 Mar 74
& Food	**J. SILKIN**	10 Sep 76
Min.of	N. BUCHAN	8 Mar 74
State	E. BISHOP	18 Oct 74
P.S.	R. Moyle	11 Mar 74
	E. Bishop	28 Jun 74
	G. Strang	18 Oct 74
Defence	**R. MASON**	5 Mar 74
	F. MULLEY	10 Sep 76
Min. of	W. RODGERS	8 Mar 74
State	J. GILBERT	10 Sep 76
U-S. Navy	F. Judd	8 Mar 74
	P. Duffy	14 Apr 76
U-S. Army	Ld Brayley	8 Mar 74
	R. C. Brown	18 Oct 74
U-S. Air	B. John	8 Mar 74
	J. Wellbeloved	14 Apr 76
Educ. &	**R. PRENTICE**	5 Mar 74
Science	**F. MULLEY**	10 Jun 75
	SHIRLEY WILLIAMS	10 Sep 76
Min.of	G. FOWLER	8 Mar 74
State	Ld CROWTHER-HUNT	18 Oct 74
	G. FOWLER	23 Jan 76
	G. OAKES	10 Sep 76
Min.of State	Ld DONALDSON (Arts)	14 Apr 76
U.S.	E. Armstrong	7 Mar 74–12 Jun 75
	H. Jenkins (Arts)	8 Mar 74–14 Apr 76
	Joan Lestor	12 Jun 75–21 Feb 76
	Margaret Jackson	12 Mar 76–4 May 79
Emp.	**M. FOOT**	5 Mar 74
	A. BOOTH	8 Apr 76
Min. of	A. BOOTH	8 Mar 74
State	H. WALKER	14 Apr 76
U-S.	J. Fraser	8 Mar 74–14 Apr 76
	H. Walker	11 Mar 74–14 Apr 76
U.S.	J. Grant	14 Apr 76–4 May 79
(contd.)	J. Golding	14 Apr 76–4 May 79
Energy	**E. VARLEY**	5 Mar 74
	A. BENN	10 Jun 75
Min.of	Ld BALOGH	7 Mar 74
State	J. SMITH	4 Dec 75
	D. MABON	14 Apr 76
U-S.	G. Strang	7 Mar 74–18 Oct 74
	A. Eadie	7 Mar 74–4 May 79
	J. Smith	18 Oct 74–4 Dec 75
	Ld Lovell-Davis	4 Dec 75–14 Apr 76
	G. Oakes	14 Apr 76–10 Sep 76
	J. Cunningham	10 Sep 76–4 May 79
Env.	**A. CROSLAND**	5 Mar 74
	P. SHORE	8 Apr 76
Min.for	J. SILKIN	7 Mar 74
Planning &	*(office in cabinet & in*	
Loc. Govt	*Dept of Environment)*	
	J. SILKIN	18 Oct 74
	(office abolished 10 Sep 76)	
Min.for	F. MULLEY	7 Mar 74
Transport	J. GILBERT	12 Jun 75
	(separate Department and	
	office in cabinet 10 Sep 76)	
Min. for	R. FREESON	7 Mar 74
Housing &		
Construction		
Min. of	C. MORRIS	7 Mar 74
State (Urban Affs)		
	(post abolished 18 Oct 74)	
Min.of	*(Sport, Recreation and Water*	
State	*Resources 24 Aug 76)*	
	D. HOWELL	7 Mar 74
U-S.	N. Carmichael	8 Mar 74–4 Dec 75
	G. Kaufman	8 Mar 74–12 Jun 75
	G. Oakes	8 Mar 74–14 Apr 76
	Lady Birk	18 Oct 74–3 Jan 79
	E.Armstrong	12 Jun 75–4 May 79
Health &	**Barbara CASTLE**	5 Mar 74
Soc.	**D. ENNALS**	8 Apr 76
Security		
(Soc. Serv.)		
Min.of	B. O'MALLEY	8 Mar 74–6 Apr 76
State	D. OWEN	26 Jul 74–10 Sep 76
	S. ORME	8 Apr 76–10 Sep 76
	S. ORME	10 Sep 76–4 May 79
	(in cabinet as Min. for Soc. Security)	
	R. MOYLE	10 Sep 76–4 May 79
U-S.	D. Owen	8 Mar 74–26 Jul 74
	R. C. Brown	8 Mar 74–18 Oct 74
	A. Jones	18 Oct 74–12 Jun 75
	M. Meacher	12 Jun 75–14 Apr 76
	E. Deakins	14 Apr 76–4 May 79
	Ld Wells-Pestell	3 Jan 79–4 May 79
U-S.	A. Morris	11 Mar 74–4 May 79
(Disabled)		
Industry	**A. BENN**	5 Mar 74
	(also 7 Mar 74–29 Mar 74	
	Min. for Posts and	
	Telecommunications)	
	E. VARLEY	10 Jun 75

LABOUR GOVERNMENT 1974–1979 (contd.)

Min.of	E. HEFFER	7 Mar 74–9 Apr 75
State	Ld BESWICK	11 Mar 74–4 Dec 75
	G. MACKENZIE	10 Jun 75–14 Apr 76
	G. KAUFMAN	4 Dec 75–4 May 79
	A. WILLIAMS	14 Apr 76–4 May 79
U-S.	G. Mackenzie	7 Mar 74–10 Jun 75
	M. Meacher	7 Mar 74–12 Jun 75
	G. Kaufman	12 Jun 75–4 Dec 75
	Ld Melchett	4 Dec 75–10 Sep 76
	N. Carmichael	4 Dec 75–14 Apr 76
	L. Huckfield	4 Apr 76–4 May 79
	R. Cryer	10 Sep 76–20 Nov 78
D. Lanc.	**H. LEVER**	5 Mar 74
Northern	**M. REES**	5 Mar 74
Ireland	**R. MASON**	10 Sep 76
Min.of	S. ORME	7 Mar 74–8 Apr 76
State	R. MOYLE	27 Jun 74–10 Sep 76
	D. CONCANNON	
		14 Apr 76–4 May 79
	Ld MELCHETT	10 Sep 76–4 May 79
U-S.	Ld Donaldson	11 Mar 74–14 Apr 76
	D.Concannon	27 Jun 74–14 Apr 76
	J. Dunn	14 Apr 76–4 May 79
	R.Carter	14 Apr 76–4 May 79
	T. Pendry	11 Nov 78–4 May 79
Overseas	Judith HART	7 Mar 74
Dev.	*(office in cabinet)*	
	R. PRENTICE	10 Jun.75
	(office not in cabinet)	
	F. JUDD	21 Dec 76
	Judith HART	21 Feb 77
P.S.	W. Price	11 Mar 74
	J. Grant	18 Oct 74
	F. Judd	14 Apr 76
	J. Tomlinson *(also at For.O.)*	3 Jan 77
Prices &	**SHIRLEY WILLIAMS**	5 Mar 74
Consumer	**R. HATTERSLEY**	10 Sep 76
Protection		
Min.of	A. WILLIAMS	8 Mar 74
State	J. FRASER	14 Apr 76
U-S.	R. Maclennan	11 Mar 74
Scot. O.	**W. ROSS**	5 Mar 74
	B. MILLAN	8 Apr 76
Min.of	B. MILLAN	8 Mar 74–8 Apr 76
State	Ld HUGHES	8 Mar 74–8 Aug 75
	Ld KIRKHILL	8 Aug 75–15 Dec 78
	G. MACKENZIE	14 Apr 76–4 May 79
U-S.	R. Hughes	11 Mar 74–22 Jul 75
	H. Brown	28 Jun 74–4 May 79
	H. Ewing	18 Oct 74–4 May 79
	F. McElhone	12 Sep 75–4 May 79
Soc.	*(office not in cabinet)*	
Security	**S. ORME**	10 Sep 76
	(in Dept. of Health & Soc.Security)	
U-S.	K. Marks	5 Dec 75–4 May 79
	G. Barnett	14 Apr 76–4 May 79
	Lady Stedman	3 Jan 79–4 May 79
Trade	**P. SHORE**	5 Mar 74

Trade	**E. DELL**	8 Apr 76
(contd.)	**J. SMITH**	11 Nov 78
U-S.	E. Deakins	8 Mar 74–14 Apr 76
	S. Clinton Davis	8 Mar 74–4 May 79
	M. Meacher	14 Apr 76–4 May 79
Transport	**W. RODGERS**	10 Sep 76
U-S.	J. Horam	12 Sep 76
Wales	**J. MORRIS**	5 Mar 74
U-S.	E. Rowlands	7 Mar 74–12 Jun 75
	B. Jones	7 Mar 74–4 May 79
	A. Jones	12 Jun 75–4 May 79

Law Officers

Att.-Gen.	S. SILKIN	7 Mar 74
U-S.	A. Davidson	26 Jul 74
Sol.-Gen.	P. ARCHER	7 Mar 74
Ld Advoc.	R. KING-MURRAY	8 Mar 74
Sol.-Gen.	J. McCLUSKEY+(Ld)	14 Mar 74
Scotland		

Whips

P.S. to	R.MELLISH	5 Mar 74
Treasury	**R. MELLISH**	26 Jul 76
	(office in cabinet 26 Jul 74–8 Apr 76)	
	M. COCKS	8 Apr 76
Lds of	D. Coleman	8 Mar 74–6 Jul 78
Treasury	J. Dunn	8 Mar 74–14 Apr 76
	J. Golding	8 Mar 74–18 Oct 74
	T. Pendry	8 Mar 74–18 Jan 77
	J. Hamilton	8 Mar74–28 Jun 74
	M. Cocks	28 Jun 74–8 Apr 76
	J. Dormand	18 Oct 74–4 May 79
	D. Stoddart	4 Apr 76–18 Nov 77
	E. Graham	14 Apr 76–4 May 79
	T. Cox	19 Jan 77–4 May 79
	P. Snape	23 Nov 77–4 May 79
	A. Stallard	5 Jul 78–17 Jan 79
	A. Bates	17 Jan 79–4 May 79
Ass. Whips	M. Cocks	8 Mar 74–24 Jun 74
	T. Cox	8 Mar 74–19 Jan 77
	E. Perry	8 Mar 74–24 Oct 74
	J. Dormand	14 Mar 74–18 Oct 74
	L. Pavitt	14 Mar 74–5 Feb 76
	W. Johnson	22 Jun 74–23 Jan 75
	Betty Boothroyd	24 Oct 74–4 Nov 75
	J. Ellis	24 Oct 74–8 Nov 76
	Margaret Jackson	27 Jan 75–12 Mar 76
	D. Stoddart	27 Jan 75–14 Apr 76
	P. Snape	20 Nov 75–23 Nov 77
	A. Stallard	5 Feb 76–5 Jul 78
	A. Bates	12 Mar 76–17 Jan 79
	F. White	14 Apr 76–31 Oct 78
	J. Tinn	16 Jun 76–4 May 79
	J. Ashton	8 Nov 76–9 Nov 77
	Ann Taylor	19 Jan 77–4 May 79
	J. Marshall	23 Nov 77–4 May 79
	J. Dean	6 Jul 78–4 May 79
	J. Evans	31 Oct 78–4 May 79
	B. Davies	17 Jan 79–4 May 79

+Not a member of the House of Commons.

LABOUR GOVERNMENT 1974–1979 (contd.)

H.M. Household			*Lds in*	Lady Birk	14 Mar 74–18 Oct 74
Treasurer	W. HARRISON	7 Mar 74	*Waiting*	Ld Wells-Pestell	14 Mar 74–3 Jan 79
Compt.	J. HARPER	8 Mar 74	*(contd.)*	Ld Winterbottom	
	J. HAMILTON	5 Jul 78			29 Oct 74–27 Oct 78
V. Chamb.	D. CONCANNON	8 Mar 74		Ld Lovell-Davis	29 Oct 74–4 Dec 75
	J. HAMILTON	28 Jun 74		Ld Melchett	29 Oct 74–4 Dec 75
	D.COLEMAN	5 Jul 78		Lady Stedman	4 Dec 75–3 Jan 79
Cap.Gents	Lady LLEWELYN-DAVIES			Ld Oram	23 Jan 76–23 Mar 78
at Arms		11 Mar 74		Ld Wallace of Coslany	
Cap.Yeo.	Ld STRABOLGI	11 Mar 74			28 Feb 77–4 May 79
of Guard				Lady David	27 Oct 78–4 May 79
Lds in	Ld Jacques	14 Mar 74–19 Jan 77		Ld Leonard	27 Oct 78–4 May 79
Waiting	Ld Garnsworthy	14 Mar 74–4 Sep 74		Ld Jacques	11 Jan 79–4 May 79

CONSERVATIVE GOVERNMENT 1979–1990

P.M.	**Margaret THATCHER**		*Econ.Sec.*	P. LILLEY	13 Jun 87
		4 May 79–28 Nov 90	*(contd.)*	R. Ryder	24 Jul 89
Min.of State	P. CHANNON	7 May 79		J. Maples	24 Jul 90
Civil Service	B. HAYHOE	5 Jan 81	*Min.of*	P. REES	6 May 79–14 Sep 81
Dept	*(Department abolished 12 Nov 81)*		*State*	Ld COCKFIELD	
Ld Pres.	**Ld SOAMES**	5 May 79			6 May 79–6 Apr 82
	F. PYM	14 Sep 81		J. BRUCE-GARDYNE	
	J. BIFFEN	7 Apr 82			15 Sep 81–11 Nov 81
	Vt WHITELAW	11 Jun 83		B. HAYHOE	11 Nov 81–2 Sep 85
	J. WAKEHAM	10 Jan 88		J. WAKEHAM	6 Apr 82–13 Jun 83
	Sir G. HOWE	24 Jul 89		I. GOW	2 Sep 85–19 Nov 85
	J. MACGREGOR	2 Nov 90		P. BROOKE	19 Nov 85–13 Jun 87
Min. of	E of GOWRIE	11 Jun 83		*(office vacant)*	
State, Privy	*(office vacant 11 Sept 84)*		*For.&*	**Ld CARRINGTON**	5 May 79
Council	R. LUCE	2 Sep 85	*Comm.O.*	**F. PYM**	6 Apr 82
Office	D. MELLOR	24 Jul 90		**Sir G. HOWE**	11 Jun 83
Ld Chanc.	**Ld HAILSHAM**	5 May 79		**J. MAJOR**	24 Jul 89
	Ld HAVERS	13 Jun 87		**D. HURD**	26 Oct 89
	Ld MACKAY	26 Oct 87	*Min.of*	D. HURD	6 May 79–11 Jun 83
Privy Seal	**Sir I. GILMOUR**	5 May 79	*State*	N. RIDLEY	6 May 79–29 Sep 81
	H. ATKINS	14 Sep 81		P. BLAKER	6 May 79–29 May 81
	Lady YOUNG	6 Apr 82		R. LUCE	30 Sep 81–5 Apr 82
	J. BIFFEN	11 Jun 83		Ld BELSTEAD	5 Apr 82–13 Jun 83
	J. WAKEHAM	13 Jun 87		C. ONSLOW	5 Apr 82–13 Jun 83
	Ld BELSTEAD	10 Jan 88		R. LUCE	11 Jun 83–2 Sep 85
Exchequer	**Sir G. HOWE**	5 May 79		Lady YOUNG	13 Jun 83–13 Jun 87
	N. LAWSON	11 Jun 83		M. RIFKIND	13 Jun 83–11 Jan 86
	J. MAJOR	26 Oct 89		T. RENTON	2 Sep 85–13 Jun 87
Chief Sec.	**J. BIFFEN**	5 May 79		Lynda CHALKER	
	L. BRITTAN	5 Jan 81			11 Jan 86–24 Jul 89
	P. REES	11 Jun 83		Ld GLENARTHUR	
	J. MACGREGOR	2 Sep 85			13 Jun 87–24 Jul 89
	J. MAJOR	13 Jun 87		D. MELLOR	13 Jun 87–26 Jul 88
	N. LAMONT	24 Jul 89		W.WALDEGRAVE	
F.S.	N. LAWSON	6 May 79			26 Jul 88–2 Nov 90
	N. RIDLEY	30 Sep 81		Ld BRABAZON of TARA	
	J. MOORE	18 Oct 83			24 Jul 89–24 Jul 90
	N. LAMONT	21 May 86		F. MAUDE	24 Jul 89–14 Jul 90
	P. LILLEY	24 Jul 89		T. GAREL-JONES	
	F. MAUDE	14 Jul 90			14 Jul 90–28 Nov 90
Econ.Sec.	J. BRUCE-GARDYNE	11 Nov 81		E of CAITHNESS	
	J. MOORE	13 Jun 83			14 Jul 90–28 Nov 90
	I. STEWART	18 Oct 83		D. HOGG	2 Nov 90–28 Nov 90

CONSERVATIVE GOVERNMENT 1979–1990 *(contd.)*

Min. of State (Overseas Dev.)	N. MARTEN	8 Oct 79
	T. RAISON	6 Jan 83
	C. PATTEN	10 Sep 86
	Lynda CHALKER	24 Jul 89
U-S.	R. Luce	6 May 79
	Ld Trefgarne	14 Sep 81
	M. Rifkind	6 Apr 82
	R. Whitney	13 Jun 83
	T. Renton	11 Sep 84
	T. Eggar	2 Sep 85
	T. Sainsbury	24 Jul 89
	M. Lennox-Boyd	24 Jul 90
Home O.	W. WHITELAW	5 May 79
	L. BRITTAN	11 Jun 83
	D. HURD	3 Sep 85
	D. WADDINGTON	26 Oct 89
Min.of State	T. RAISON	6 May 79–6 Jan 83
	L. BRITTAN	6 May 79–5 Jan 81
	P. MAYHEW	5 Jan 81–13 Jun 83
	D. WADDINGTON	6 Jan 83–13 Jun 87
	D. HURD	13 Jun 83–11 Sep 84
	Ld ELTON	11 Sep 84–25 Mar 85
	G. SHAW	11 Sep 84–10 Sep 86
	E of CAITHNESS	10 Sep 86–10 Jan 88
	D. MELLOR	10 Sep 86–13 Jun 87
	J. PATTEN	13 Jun 87–28 Nov 90
	T. RENTON	13 Jun 87–28 Oct 89
	Earl FERRERS	10 Jan 88–28 Nov 90
	D. MELLOR	27 Oct 89–22 Jul 90
	Angela RUMBOLD	23 Jul 90–28 Nov 90
U-S.	Ld Belstead	7 May 79–6 Apr 82
	Ld Elton	6 Apr 82–11 Sep 84
	D. Mellor	6 Jan 83–10 Sep 86
	Ld Glenarthur	27 Mar 85–10 Sep 86
	D. Hogg	10 Sep 86–26 Jul 89
	P. Lloyd	25 Jul 89–28 Nov 90
Ag. Fish. &Food	P. WALKER	5 May 79
	M. JOPLING	11 Jun 83
	J. MACGREGOR	13 Jun 87
	J. S. GUMMER	24 Jul 89
Min.of State	Earl FERRERS	7 May 79–13 Jun 83
	A. BUCHANAN-SMITH	7 May 79–13 Jun 83
	J. MACGREGOR	13 Jun 83–2 Sep 85
	J. S. GUMMER	2 Sep 85–26 Jul 88
	Ld BELSTEAD	13 Jun 83–13 Jun 87
	Lady TRUMPINGTON	28 Sep 89–28 Nov 90
U-S.	J. Wiggin	7 May 79–29 Sep 81
	Peggy Fenner	14 Sep 81–10 Sep 86
	D. Thompson	10 Sep 86–24 Jul 89
	Lady Trumpington	13 Jun 87–28 Sep 89
	R. Ryder	25 Jul 88–24 Jul 89
	D. Curry	26 Jul 89–28 Nov 90
	D. Maclean	26 Jul 89–28 Nov 90

Office	Name	Date
Min.for the Arts	N. ST JOHN-STEVAS	5 May 79
	(office out of cabinet)	
	P. CHANNON	5 Jan 81
	E of GOWRIE	13 Jun 83
	(D.Lanc. & office in cabinet 11 Sep 84)	
	E of GOWRIE	11 Sep 84
	(office out of cabinet)	
	R. LUCE	2 Sep 85
	D. MELLOR	23 Jul 90
Defence	F. PYM	5 May 79
	J. NOTT	5 Jan 81
	M. HESELTINE	6 Jan 83
	G. YOUNGER	9 Jan 86
	T. KING	24 Jul 89
Min.of State	Ld STRATHCONA	6 May 79
	Vt TRENCHARD	5 Jan 81–29 May 81
Min. of State (Armed Forces)	P. BLAKER	29 May 81
	J. STANLEY	13 Jun 83
	I. STEWART	13 Jun 87
	A. HAMILTON	25 Jul 88
Min.of State (Defence Procurement)	Vt TRENCHARD	29 May 81
	G. PATTIE	6 Jan 83
	A. BUTLER	11 Sep 84
	N. LAMONT	2 Sep 85
	Ld TREFGARNE	21 May 86
	A. CLARK	24 Jul 89
Min.of State (Defence Support)	Ld TREFGARNE	2 Sep 85–21 May 86
U-S.Army	B. Hayhoe	6 May 79
	P. Goodhart	5 Jan 81–29 May 81
U-S.Navy	K. Speed	6 May 79–18 May 81
U-S.Air	G. Pattie	6 May 79–29 May 81
	(Defence Dept reorganised May 81)	
U-S. (Armed Forces)	P. Goodhart	29 May 81–30 Sep 81
	J. Wiggin	15 Sep 81–11 Jun 83
	Ld Trefgarne	13 Jun 83–1 Sep 85
	R. Freeman	21 May 86–15 Dec 88
	M. Neubert	19 Dec 88–23 Jul 90
U-S.(Def. Procure.)	G. Pattie	29 May 81
	I. Stewart	6 Jan 83
	J. Lee	18 Oct 83
	A. Hamilton	10 Sep 86
	T. Sainsbury	13 Jun 87
	E of Arran	25 Jul 89
	K. Carlisle	26 Jul 90
Educ.& Science	M. CARLISLE	5 May 79
	Sir K. JOSEPH	14 Sep 81
	K. BAKER	21 May 86
	J. MACGREGOR	24 Jul 89
	K. CLARKE	2 Nov 90
Min.of State	Lady YOUNG	7 May 79–14 Sep 81
	P. CHANNON	5 Jan 81–13 Jun 83
	C. PATTEN	5 Sep 85–10 Sep 86
	Angela RUMBOLD	10 Sep 86–24 Jul 90
	T. EGGAR	24 Jul 90–28 Nov 90

CONSERVATIVE GOVERNMENT 1979–1990 (contd.)

U-S.	R. Boyson	7 May 79–13 Jun 83
	N. Macfarlane	7 May 79–15 Sep 81
	W. Shelton	15 Sep 81–13 Jun 83
	W. Waldegrave	15 Sep 81–13 Jun 83
	P. Brooke	13 Jun 83–19 Nov 85
	R. Dunn	13 Jun 83–26 Jul 88
	G. Walden	19 Nov 85–13 Jun 87
	Lady Hooper	13 Jun 87–26 Jul 88
	R. Jackson	13 Jun 87–24 Jul 90
	J. Butcher	26 Jul 88–24 Jul 89
	A. Howarth	24 Jul 89–28 Nov 90
	M. Fallon	24 Jul 90–28 Nov 90
Emp.	**J. PRIOR**	5 May 79
	N. TEBBIT	14 Sep 81
	T. KING	16 Oct 83
	Ld YOUNG of GRAFFHAM	
		2 Sep 85
	N. FOWLER	13 Jun 87
	M. HOWARD	3 Jan 90
Min. of	E of GOWRIE	7 May 79–15 Sep 81
State	M. ALISON	15 Sep 81–13 Jun 83
	P. MORRISON	13 Jun 83–2 Sep 85
	J. S. GUMMER	18 Oct 83–11 Sep 84
	K. CLARKE	2 Sep 85–13 Jun 87
	(Paym.-Gen. and in cabinet)	
	J. COPE	13 Jun 87–25 Jul 89
	T. EGGAR	25 Jul 89–23 Jul 90
	(office vacant)	
U-S.	J. Lester	7 May 79–5 Jan 81
	P. Mayhew	7 May 79–5 Jan 81
	D. Waddington	5 Jan 81–6 Jan 83
	P. Morrison	5 Jan 81–13 Jun 83
	J. S. Gummer	6 Jan 83–18 Oct 83
	A. Clark	13 Jun 83–24 Jan 86
	P. Bottomley	11 Sep 84–23 Jan 86
	D. Trippier	2 Sep 85–13 Jun 87
	I. Lang	31 Jan 86–10 Sep 86
	J. Lee	10 Sep 86–26 Jul 89
	P. Nicholls	13 Jun 87–28 Jul 90
	Ld Strathclyde	26 Jul 89–24 Jul 90
	R. Jackson	24 Jul 90–28 Nov 90
	Vt Ullswater	24 Jul 90–28 Nov 90
	E. Forth	24 Jul 90- 28 Nov 90
Energy	**D. HOWELL**	5 May 79
	N. LAWSON	14 Sep 81
	P. WALKER	11 Jun 83
	C. PARKINSON	13 Jun 87
	J. WAKEHAM	24 Jul 89
Min. of	H. GRAY	7 May 79
State	A. BUCHANAN-SMITH	13 Jun 83
	P. MORRISON	13 Jun 87
	(office vacant 26 Jul 90)	
U-S.	N. Lamont	7 May 79–5 Sep 81
	J. Moore	7 May 79–13 Jun 83
	D. Mellor	15 Sep 81–6 Jan 83
	E of Avon	6 Jan 83–11 Sep 84
	G. Shaw	13 Jun 83–11 Sep 84
	A. Goodlad	11 Sep 84–13 Jun 87
	D. Hunt	11 Sep 84–13 Jun 87
	M. Spicer	13 Jun 87–3 Jan 90
	Lady Hooper	26 Jul 88–28 Jul 89

U-S.	T. Baldry	3 Jan 90–28 Nov 90
(contd.)	C. Moynihan	24 Jul 90–28 Nov 90
Env.	**M. HESELTINE**	5 May 79
	T. KING	6 Jan 83
	P. JENKIN	11 Jun 83
	K. BAKER	2 Sep 85
	N. RIDLEY	21 May 86
	C. PATTEN	24 Jul 89
Min. of	T. KING	6 May 79
State	LD BELLWIN	6 Jan 83
(Loc. Govt)	K. BAKER	11 Sep 84
	W. WALDEGRAVE	2 Sep 85
	R. BOYSON	10 Sep 86
	M. HOWARD	13 Jun 87
	J. S. GUMMER	25 Jul 88
	D. HUNT	25 Jul 89
	M. PORTILLO	4 May 90
Min. of	J. STANLEY	7 May 79
State	I. GOW	13 Jun 83
(Housing)	J. PATTEN	2 Sep 85
	W. WALDEGRAVE	13 Jun 87
	E of CAITHNESS	25 Jul 88
	M. HOWARD	25 Jul 89
	M. SPICER	3 Jan 90
Min.of	Ld ELTON	27 Mar 85
State	W. WALDEGRAVE	10 Sep 86
	Ld BELSTEAD	13 Jun 87
	E of CAITHNESS	10 Jan 88
	M. HOWARD	25 Jul 88
	D. TRIPPIER	24 Jul 89
U-S.(Sport)	H. Monro	7 May 79–30 Sep 81
	N. MacFarlane	15 Sep 81–2 Sep 85
	R. Tracy	7 Sep 85–13 Jun 87
	C. Moynihan	22 Jun 87–26 Jul 90
	R. Atkins	26 Jul 90–28 Nov 90
U-S.	M. Fox	7 May 79–5 Jan 81
	G. Finsberg	7 May 79–15 Sep 81
	Ld Bellwin	7 May 79–6 Jan 83
	G. Shaw	5 Jan 81–13 Jun 83
	Sir G. Young	15 Sep 81–10 Sep 86
	W. Waldegrave	13 Jun 83–2 Sep 85
	E of Avon	11 Sep 84–27 Mar 85
	Angela Rumbold	2 Sep 85–10 Sep 86
	Ld Skelmersdale	10 Sep 86–13 Jun 87
	C. Chope	10 Sep 86–22 Jul 89
	Marion Roe	13 Jun 87–26 Jul 88
	D. Trippier	13 Jun 87–23 Jul 89
	Virginia Bottomley	25 Jul 88–28 Oct 89
	Ld Hesketh	31 Jan 89–2 Nov 90
	D. Heathcoat-Amory	
		28 Oct 89–28 Nov 90
	P. Nicholls	26 Jul 90–12 Oct 90
	Ld Strathclyde	26 Jul 90–7 Sep 90
	Lady Blatch	7 Sep 90–28 Nov 90
	R. Key	12 Oct 90–28 Nov 90
Health &	**P. JENKIN**	5 May 79
Soc.	**N. FOWLER**	14 Sep 81
Security		
(Social	**J. MOORE**	13 Jun 87
Services)	*(Social Security a separate*	
	Dept 25 Jul 88)	

CONSERVATIVE GOVERNMENT 1979–1990 (contd.)

Health	**K. CLARKE**	25 Jul 88			**K. BAKER**	24 Jul 89
	W. WALDEGRAVE	2 Nov 90		*Northern*	**H. ATKINS**	5 May 79
Min. of	G. VAUGHAN	7 May 79		*Ireland*	**J. PRIOR**	14 Sep 81
State	K. CLARKE	5 Mar 82			**D. HURD**	11 Sep 84
(Health)	B. HAYHOE	2 Sep 85			**T. KING**	3 Sep 85
	A. NEWTON	10 Sep 86			**P. BROOKE**	24 Jul 89
	D. MELLOR	25 Jul 88		*Min.of*	M. ALISON	7 May 79–15 Sep 81
	Ld TRAFFORD	25 Jul 89		*State*	H. ROSSI	7 May 79–5 Jan 81
	Virginia BOTTOMLEY	28 Oct 89			A. BUTLER	5 Jan 81–11 Sep 84
Min. of	R. PRENTICE	7 May 79			E of GOWRIE	15 Sep 81–10 Jun 83
State	H. ROSSI	5 Jan 81			E of MANSFIELD	13 Jun 83–12 Apr 84
(Social	R. BOYSON	12 Jun 83			R. BOYSON	11 Sep 84–10 Sep 86
Security)	A. NEWTON	11 Sep 84			N. SCOTT	10 Sep 86–13 Jun 87
	J. MAJOR	10 Sep 86			J. STANLEY	13 Jun 87–25 Jul 88
	N. SCOTT	13 Jun 87			I. STEWART	25 Jul 88–25 Jul 89
U-S.	Sir G. Young	7 May 79–15 Sep 81			J. COPE	25 Jul 89–28 Nov 90
	Lynda Chalker	7 May 79–5 Mar 82		*U-S.*	Ld Elton	7 May 79–15 Sep 81
	G. Finsberg	15 Sep 81–14 Jun 83			P. Goodhart	7 May 79–5 Jan 81
	Ld Elton	15 Sep 81–6 Apr 82			G. Shaw	7 May 79–5 Jan 81
	A. Newton	5 Mar 82–11 Sep 84			D. Mitchell	5 Jan 81–13 Jun 83
	Ld Trefgarne	6 Apr 82–14 Jun 83			J. Patten	5 Jan 81–13 Jun 83
	J. Patten	14 Jun 83–2 Sep 85			N. Scott	15 Sep 81–11 Sep 86
	Ld Glenarthur	14 Jun 83–26 Mar 85			C. Patten	14 Jun 83–2 Sep 85
	R. Whitney	11 Sep 84–10 Sep 86			Ld Lyell	12 Apr 84–25 Jul 89
	Lady Trumpington	30 Mar 85–13 Jun 87			R. Needham	3 Sep 85–28 Nov 90
	J. Major	2 Sep 85–10 Sep 86			P. Viggers	10 Sep 86–26 Jul 89
	N. Lyell	10 Sep 86–13 Jun 87			B. Mawhinney	10 Sep 86–28 Nov 90
	Edwina Currie	10 Sep 86–16 Dec 88			P. Bottomley	4 Jul 89–28 Jul 90
	M. Portillo	13 Jun 87–25 Jul 88			Ld Skelmersdale	24 Jul 89–28 Nov 90
	Ld Skelmersdale	13 Jun 87–25 Jul 89		*Paym.-Gen.*	**A. MAUDE**	5 May 79
	R.Freeman	16 Dec 88–4 May 90			**F. PYM**	5 Jan 81
	Lady Hooper	29 Sep 89–28 Nov 90			**C. PARKINSON**	14 Sep 81
	S. Dorrell	4 May 90–28 Nov 90			*(office vacant 11 Jun 83)*	
Industry	**Sir K. JOSEPH**	7 May 79			*(office not in cabinet)*	
	P. JENKIN	14 Sep 81			J. GUMMER	11 Sep 84
	(12 Jun 83 office reorganised as Trade				*(office in cabinet)*	
	and Industry)				**K. CLARKE** *(also Min.Emp.)*	2 Sep 85
Min.of State	A. BUTLER	6 May 79–5 Jan 81			*(office not in cabinet)*	
	Vt TRENCHARD	6 May 79–5 Jan 81			P. BROOKE	13 Jun 87
	N. TEBBIT	5 Jan 81–14 Sep 81			E of CAITHNESS	24 Jul 89
	N. LAMONT	14 Sep 81–12 Jun 83			R. RYDER	14 Jul 90
Min. of	K. BAKER	5 Jan 81–12 Jun 83		*Min.without*	**Ld YOUNG OF GRAFFHAM**	
State	*(Industry & Info. Tech.)*			*Portfolio*		11 Sep 84–3 Sep 85
U-S.	D. Mitchell	6 May 79–5 Jan 81		*Scot.O.*	**G. YOUNGER**	5 May 79
	M. Marshall	6 May 79–15 Sep 81			**M. RIFKIND**	11 Jan 86
	J. MacGregor	5 Jan 81–14 Jun 83		*Min.of State*	E of MANSFIELD	7 May 79–13 Jun 83
	J. Wakeham	15 Sep 81–6 Apr 82			Ld GRAY of CONTIN	
	J. Butcher	6 Apr 82–14 Jun 83				13 Jun 83–11 Sep 86
D.Lanc.	**N. ST JOHN STEVAS** *(Arts)*				Ld GLENARTHUR	
		5 May 79				10 Sep 86–13 Jun 87
	F. PYM	5 Jan 81			I. LANG	13 Jun 87–28Nov 90
	Lady YOUNG	27 Oct 81			Ld SANDERSON	13 Jun 87–7 Sep 90
	C. PARKINSON	6 Apr 82			M. FORSYTH	7 Sep 90–28 Nov 90
	Ld COCKFIELD	11 Jun 83		*U-S.*	A. Fletcher	7 May 79–14 Jun 83
	E of GOWRIE *(Arts)*	11 Sep 84			R. Fairgrieve	7 May 79–15 Sep 81
	N. TEBBIT	3 Sep 85			M. Rifkind	7 May 79–6 Apr 82
	K. CLARKE	13 Jun 87			A. Stewart	15 Sep 81–10 Sep 86
	(also Min.Trade)				J. Mackay	6 Apr 82–14 Jun 87
	A. NEWTON	25 Jul 88			M. Ancram	13 June 83–14 Jun 87
					I. Lang	10 Sep 86–13 Jun 87

CONSERVATIVE GOVERNMENT 1979–1990 *(contd.)*

Scot. O.	Ld J. Douglas-Hamilton*	
(contd.)		13 Jun 87–28 Nov 90
	M. Forsyth	13 Jun 87–7 Sep 90
	Ld Strathclyde	7 Sep 90–28 Nov 90
Soc.	**J. MOORE**	25 Jul 88
Security	**A. NEWTON**	23 Jul 89
Min.of	N. SCOTT	25 Jul 88
State	Ld Skelmersdale	24 Jul 88–26 Jul 89
U-S.	P. Lloyd	25Jul 88–28 Jul 89
	Ld Henley	25 Jul 89–28 Nov 90
	Gillian Shephard	25 Jul 89–28 Nov 90
Trade	**J. NOTT**	5 May 79
	J. BIFFEN	5 Jan 81
	Ld COCKFIELD	6 Apr 82
	(office reorganised as Trade & Industry)	
	C. PARKINSON	12 Jun 83
	N. TEBBIT	16 Oct 83
	L. BRITTAN	2 Sep 85
	P. CHANNON	24 Jan 86
	Ld YOUNG of GRAFFHAM	
		13 Jun 87
	N. RIDLEY	24 Jul 89
	P. LILLEY	14 Jul 90
Min. for	Sally OPPENHEIM	6 May 79
Consumer	G. VAUGHAN	5 Mar 82
Affairs	*(office abolished 13 Jun 83)*	
Min.of	N. LAMONT	13 Jun 83–2 Sep 85
State	G. SHAW	10 Sep 86–13 Jun 87
Min.for	C. PARKINSON	7 May 79
Trade	P. REES	14 Sep 81
	P. CHANNON	13 Jun 83
	A. CLARK	24 Jan 86
	Ld TREFGARNE	25 Jul 89
	T. SAINSBURY	23 Jul 90
Min. for	K. BAKER	13 Jun 83
Industry &	G. PATTIE	11 Sep 84
Info. Tech.	*(office vacant 13 Jun 87)*	
Min.for	D. HOGG	24 Jul 89
Industry	Ld HESKETH	2 Nov 90
Min. for	J. REDWOOD	2 Nov 90
Corporate		
Affairs		
U-S.	N. Tebbit	7 May 79–5 Jan 81
	R. Eyre	7 May 79–5 Mar 82
	Ld Trefgarne	5 Jan 81–15 Sep 81
	I. Sproat	15 Sep 81–12 Jun 83
	J. Butcher	14 Jun 83–26 Jul 88
	A. Fletcher	14 Jun 83–2 Sep 85
	D. Trippier	14 Jun 83–2 Sep 85
	Ld Lucas of Chilworth	
		11 Sep 84–13 Jun 87
	M. Howard	2 Sep 85–13 Jun 87
	R. Atkins	13 Jun 87–26 Jul 89
	F. Maude	13 Jun 87–26 Jul 89
	E. Forth	26 Jul 88–24 Jul 90
	J. Redwood	26 Jul 89–2 Nov 90
	E. Leigh	2 Nov 90–28 Nov 90

Transport	N. FOWLER *(Minister)*	11 May 79
	(office in cabinet 5 Jan 81)	
	N. FOWLER *(Sec. of S)*	5 Jan 81
	D. HOWELL	14 Sep 81
	T. KING	11 Jun 83
	N. RIDLEY	16 Oct 83
	J. MOORE	21 May 86
	P. CHANNON	13 Jun 87
	C. PARKINSON	24 Jul 89
Min.of	Lynda CHALKER	18 Oct 83–10 Jan 86
State	D. MITCHELL	23 Jan 86–25 Jul 88
	M. PORTILLO	25 Jul 88–4 May 90
	R. FREEMAN	4 May 90–28 Nov 90
	Ld BRABAZON of TARA	
		23 Jul 90–28 Nov 90
P.S.	K. Clarke	7 May 79–5 Jan 81
U-S.	K. Clarke	5 Jan 81–5 Mar 82
	Lynda Chalker	5 Mar 82–18 Oct 83
	R. Eyre	5 Mar 82–11 Jun 83
	D. Mitchell	11 Jun 83–23 Jan 86
	M. Spicer	11 Sep 84–13 Jun 87
	E of Caithness	2 Sep 85–10 Sep 86
	P. Bottomley	23 Jan 86–24 Jul 89
	Ld Brabazon of Tara	
		10 Sep 86–23 Jul 89
	R. Atkins	25 Jul 89–22 Jul 90
	P. McLoughlin	25 Jul 89–28 Nov 90
	C. Chope	23 Jul 90–28 Nov 90
Wales	**N. EDWARDS**	5 May 79
	P. WALKER	13 Jun 87
	D. HUNT	4 May 90
Min.of State	J. S. THOMAS	17 Feb 83
	W. ROBERTS	15 Jun 87
U-S.	M. Roberts	7 May 79–6 Jan 83
	W. Roberts	7 May 79–13 Jun 87
	M. Robinson	3 Oct 85–15 Jun 87
	I. Grist	15 Jun 87–28 Nov 90

Law Officers

Att.-Gen.	Sir M. HAVERS	6 May 79
	Sir P. MAYHEW	13 Jun 87
Sol.-Gen.	Sir I. PERCIVAL	6 May 79
	Sir P. MAYHEW	11 Jun 83
	Sir N. LYELL	15 Jun 87
Ld Advoc.	J. MACKAY⁺*(Ld)*	7 May 79
	Ld CAMERON of LOCHBROOM	
		16 May 84
	P. FRASER (Ld)	4 Jan 89
Sol.-Gen.	N. FAIRBAIRN	7 May 79
Scotland	P. FRASER	28 Jan 82
	A. RODGER⁺	4 Jan 89

Whips

P.S.to	M. JOPLING	5 May 79
Treasury	J. WAKEHAM	11 Jun 83
	D. WADDINGTON	13 Jun 87
	T. RENTON	28 Oct 89
Lds of	C. Mather	7 May 79–1 Oct 81
Treasury	P. Morrison	7 May 79–5 Jan 81

*MP. Not a member of the House of Lords.   ⁺Not a member of the House of Commons.

CONSERVATIVE GOVERNMENT 1979–1990 *(contd.)*

Lds of *Treasury*	Ld J. Douglas-Hamilton*	
		7 May 79–1 Oct 81
	J. MacGregor	7 May 79–5 Jan 81
	D. Waddington	16 May 79–5 Jan 81
	R. Boscawen	9 Jan 81–17 Feb 83
	J. Wakeham	9 Jan 81–15 Sep 81
	J. Cope	9 Jan 81–13 Jun 83
	A. Newton	1 Oct 81–5 Mar 82
	P. Brooke	1 Oct 81–13 Jun 83
	J. S. Gummer	1 Oct 81–6 Jan 83
	A. Goodlad	16 Feb 82–10 Sep 84
	D. Thompson	14 Jan 83–10 Sep 86
	D. Hunt	23 Feb 83–10 Sep 84
	I. Lang	11 Jun 83–1 Feb 86
	T. Garel-Jones	11 Jun 83–16 Oct 86
	J. Major	3 Oct 84–1 Nov 85
	A. Hamilton	3 Oct 84–10 Sep 86
	T. Sainsbury	7 Oct 85–23 Jun 87
	M. Neubert	10 Feb 86–26 Jul 88
	T. Durant	16 Oct 86–19 Dec 88
	M. Lennox-Boyd	16 Oct 86–25 Jul 88
	P. Lloyd	16 Oct 86–24 Jul 88
	D. Lightbown	26 Jun 87–24 Jul 90
	K. Carlisle	27 Jul 88–22 Jul 90
	A. Howarth	27 Jul 88–24 Jul 89
	D. Maclean	27 Jul 88–24 Jul 89
	S. Dorrell	20 Dec 88–3 May 90
	J. Taylor	26 Jul 89–28 Nov 90
	D. Heathcoat-Amory	
		26 Jul 89–28 Oct 89
	T. Sackville	30 Oct 89–28 Nov 90
	M. Fallon	10 May 90–22 Jul 90
	S. Chapman	25 Jul 90–28 Nov 90
	G. Knight	25 Jul 90–28 Nov 90
	I. Patnick	25 Jul 90–28 Nov 90
Ass. Whips	R. Boscawen	16 May 79–9 Jan 81
	J. Cope	16 May 79–9 Jan 81
	A. Newton	16 May 79–30 Sep 81
	J. Wakeham	16 May 79–9 Jan 81
	P. Brooke	16 May 79–30 Sep 81
	J. S. Gummer	9 Jan 81–30 Sep 81
	A. Goodlad	9 Jan 81–5 Feb 82
	D. Thompson	9 Jan 81–14 Jan 83
	N. Budgen	30 Sep 81–8 May 82
	D. Hunt	30 Sep 81–22 Feb 83
	I. Lang	30 Sep 81–10 Jun 83
	T. Garel-Jones	16 Mar 82–10 Jun 83
	A. Hamilton	11 May 82–3 Oct 84
	J. Major	14 Jan 83–2 Oct 84
	D. Hogg	22 Feb 83–10 Oct 84
	M. Neubert	15 Jun 83–9 Feb 86
	T. Sainsbury	15 Jun 83–7 Oct 85
	T. Durant	3 Oct 84–16 Oct 86
	P. Lloyd	3 Oct 84–16 Oct 86
	M. Lennox-Boyd	3 Oct 84–16 Oct 86
	F. Maude	7 Oct 85–15 Jun 87
	G. Malone	10 Feb 86–15 Jun 87
	M. Portillo	16 Oct 86–15 Jun 87
	D. Lightbown	16 Oct 86–25 Jun 87

Ass. Whips *(contd.)*	R. Ryder	16 Oct 86–24 Jul 88
	K. Carlisle	18 Jun 87–25 Jul 88
	A. Howarth	18 Jun 87–25 Jul 88
	D. Maclean	18 Jun 87–25 Jul 88
	S. Dorrell	26 Jun 87–19 Dec 88
	J. Taylor	26 Jul 88–25 Jul 89
	D. Heathcoat-Amory	
		26 Jul 88–25 Jul 89
	T. Sackville	26 Jul 88–29 Oct 89
	M. Fallon	26 Jul 88–10 May 90
	S. Chapman	20 Dec 88–25 Jul 90
	G. Knight	28 Jul 89–25 Jul 90
	I. Patnick	28 Jul 89–25 Jul 90
	N. Baker	2 Nov 89–28 Nov 90
	T. Wood	10 May 90–28 Nov 90
	T. Boswell	25 Jul 90–28 Nov 90
	N. Hamilton	25 Jul 90–28 Nov 90
	T. Kirkhope	25 Jul 90–28 Nov 90
H.M. Household		
Treasurer	J. S. THOMAS	6 May 79
	A. BERRY	17 Feb 83
	J. COPE	11 Jun 83
	D. HUNT	15 Jun 87
	T. GAREL-JONES	25 Jul 89
	A. GOODLAD	22 Jul 90
Compt.	S. LE MARCHANT	7 May 79
	A. BERRY	30 Sep 81
	C. MATHER	17 Feb 83
	R. BOSCAWEN	16 Oct 86
	T. GAREL-JONES	26 Jul 88
	A. GOODLAD	25 Jul 89
	Sir G. YOUNG	23 Jul 90
V. Chamb.	A. BERRY	7 May 79
	C. MATHER	30 Sep 81
	R. BOSCAWEN	17 Feb 83
	T. GAREL-JONES	16 Oct 86
	M. NEUBERT	26 Jul 88
	T. DURANT	20 Dec 88
	D. LIGHTBOWN	25 Jul 90
Cap.Gents *at Arms*	Ld DENHAM	6 May 79
Cap.Yeo. *of Guard*	Ld SANDYS	6 May 79
	E of SWINTON	20 Oct 82
	Vt DAVIDSON	10 Sep 86
Lds in *Waiting*	Vt Long	9 May 79–28 Nov 90
	Ld Mowbray and Stourton	
		9 May 79–22 Sep 80
	Ld Lyell	9 May 79–12 Apr 84
	Ld Cullen of Ashbourne	
		9 May 79–27 May 82
	Ld Trefgarne	9 May 79–5 Jan 81
	E of Avon	22 Sep 80–6 Jan 83
	Ld Skelmersdale	9 Jan 81–10 Sep 86
	Ld Glenarthur	27 May 82–10 Jun 83
	Ld Lucas of Chilworth	
		6 Jan 83–9 Sep 84
	Lady Trumpington	
		11 Jun 83–25 Mar 85
	E of Caithness	8 May 84–2 Sep 85

*MP. Not a member of the House of Lords.

CONSERVATIVE GOVERNMENT 1979–1990 *(contd.)*

Lds in	Ld Brabazon of Tara		*Lds in*	Ld Strathclyde	12 Aug 88–24 Jul 89
Waiting		19 Sep 84–10 Sep 86	*Waiting*	Ld Henley	13 Feb 89–24 Jul 90
(contd.)	Lady Cox	3 Apr 85–2Aug 85	*(contd.)*	Vt Ullswater	26 Jul 89–22 Jul 90
	Vt Davidson	17 Sep 85–10 Sep 86		Ld Reay	2 Aug 89–28 Nov 90
	Lady Hooper	17 Sep 85–14 Jun 87		E of Strathmore	2 Aug 89–28 Nov 90
	Ld Hesketh	10 Sep 86–31 Jan 89		Lady Blatch	15 Jan 90–7 sep 90
	Ld Beaverbrook	10 Sep 86–28 Jul 89		Ld Cavendish	14 Sep 90–28 Nov90
	E of Dundee	3 Oct 86–26 Jul 89		Vt Astor	11 Oct 90–28 Nov 90
	E of Arran	18 Jun 87–24 Jul 89			

CONSERVATIVE GOVERNMENT 1990–1997

P.M.	**J. MAJOR**	28 Nov 90–2 May 97
First S.of State and Deputy P.M.		
	M. HESELTINE	5 Jul 95
Ld Pres.	**J. MACGREGOR**	28 Nov 90
	A. NEWTON	10 Apr 92
U-S.	R. Jackson	28 Nov 90
	(office under Min for Civil Service	
	11 Apr 92)	
Ld Chanc.	**Ld MACKAY of CLASHFERN**	
		28 Nov 90
U-S.	J. Taylor	14 Apr 92
	J. Evans	29 Nov 95
	G. Streeter	2 Jun 96
Privy Seal	**Ld WADDINGTON**	28 Nov 90
	Ld WAKEHAM	10 Apr 92
	Vt CRANBORNE	20 Jul 94
Exchequer	**N. LAMONT**	28 Nov 90
	K. CLARKE	27 May 93
Chief Sec.	**D. MELLOR**	28 Nov 90
	M. PORTILLO	10 Apr 92
	J. AITKEN	20 Jul 94
	W. WALDEGRAVE	5 Jul 95
F.S.	F. MAUDE	28 Nov 90
	S. DORRELL	14 Apr 92
	Sir G. YOUNG	20 Jul 94
	M. JACK	6 Jul 95
E.S.	J. Maples	28 Nov 90
	A. Nelson	14 Apr 92
	(Min.of State 20 Jul 94–6 Jul 95)	
	Angela KNIGHT	6 Jul 95
	P. Oppenheim	23 Jul 96–2 May 97
Min.	Gillian SHEPHARD	
		28 Nov 90–10 Apr 92
	Sir J. COPE *(also Paym.-Gen.)*	
		14 Apr 92–20 Jul 94
	A. NELSON	20 Jul 94–6 Jul 95
	D. HEATHCOAT-AMORY	
	(also Paym.-Gen.)	20 Jul 94–20 Jul 96
Foreign &	**D. HURD**	28 Nov 90
Comm.O.	**M. RIFKIND**	5 Jul 95
Min.of	E of CAITHNESS	
State		28 Nov 90–15 Apr 92
	D. HOGG	28 Nov 90–5 Jul 95
	T. GAREL-JONES	
		28 Nov 90–6 Jun 93
	A. GOODLAD	14 Apr 92–5 Jul 95
	D. HEATHCOAT-AMORY	
		7 Jun 93–20 Jul 94

Foreign O.	D. DAVIS	20 Jul 94–2 May 97
(contd.)	J. HANLEY	5 Jul 95–2 May 97
	Sir N. BONSOR	6 Jul 95–2 May 97
Min.of	*(Overseas Development)*	
State	Lynda (Lady) CHALKER	28 Nov 90
U-S.	M. Lennox-Boyd	28 Nov 90
	A. Baldry	20 Jul 94
	(office vacant 6 Jul 95)	
	L. Fox	23 Jul 96
Home O.	**K. BAKER**	28 Nov 90
	K. CLARKE	10 Apr 90
	M. HOWARD	27 May 93
Min.of	J. PATTEN	28 Nov 90–14 Apr 92
State	Earl FERRERS	
		28 Nov 90–20 Jul 94
	Angela RUMBOLD	
		28 Nov 90–14 Apr 92
	P. LLOYD	15 Apr 92–20 Jul 94
	M. JACK	15 Apr 92–27 May 93
	D. MACLEAN	27 May 93–2 May 97
	M. FORSYTH	20 Jul 94–5 Jul 95
	Lady BLATCH	20 Jul 94–2 May 97
	Ann WIDDECOMBE	
		6 Jul 95–2 May 97
U-S.	P. Lloyd	28 Nov 90–15 Apr 92
	C. Wardle	15 Apr 92–20 Jul 94
	N. Baker	20 Jul 94–18 Oct 95
	T. Kirkhope	18 Oct 95–2 May 97
	T. Sackville	29 Nov 95- 2 May 97
Ag.Fish.	**J. S. GUMMER**	28 Nov 90
& Food	**Gillian SHEPHARD**	27 May 93
	W. WALDEGRAVE	20 Jul 94
	D. HOGG	5 Jul 95
Min.of	Lady TRUMPINGTON	28 Nov 90
State	D. CURRY	14 Apr 92
	M. JACK	27 May 93
	A. BALDRY	6 Jul 95
P.S.	D. Curry	28 Nov 90–14 Apr 92
	D. Maclean	28 Nov 90–15 Apr 92
	Earl Howe	14 Apr 92–6 Jul 95
	N. Soames	14 Apr 92–20 Jul 94
	Angela Browning	20 Jul 94–2 May 97
	T. Boswell	6 Jul 95–2 May 97
Min.for	T. RENTON	28 Nov 90–11 Apr 92
the Arts	*(11 Apr 92 See National Heritage)*	
Defence	**T. KING**	28 Nov 90
	M. RIFKIND	10 Apr 92
	M. PORTILLO	5 Jul 95

CONSERVATIVE GOVERNMENT 1990–1997 *(contd.)*

Min.of State (Defence Procure-ment)	A. CLARK	28 Nov 90
	J. AITKEN	14 Apr 92
	R. FREEMAN	20 Jul 94
	J. ARBUTHNOT	6 Jul 95
Min.of State (Armed Services)	A. HAMILTON	28 Nov 90
	J. HANLEY	27 May 93
	N. SOAMES	20 Jul 94
U-S.	K. Carlisle	28 Nov 90–15 Apr 92
	E of Arran	28 Nov 90–15 Apr 92
	Vt Cranborne	22 Apr 92–20 Jul 94
	Ld Henley	20 Jul 94–6 Jul 95
	Earl Howe	6 Jul 95–2 May 97
Educ.& Science	**K. CLARKE**	28 Nov 90
	(became Dept for Education 10 Apr 1992)	
	J. PATTEN	10 Apr 92
	Gillian SHEPHARD	20 Jul 94
	(became Dept of Education and Employment 5 Jul 95)	
Min.of State	T. EGGAR	28 Nov 90
	Lady BLATCH	14 Apr 92
	E. FORTH	20 Jul 94–6 Jul 95
	Ld HENLEY	6 Jul 95–2 May 97
U-S.	A. Howarth	28 Nov 90–14 Apr 92
	M. Fallon	28 Nov 90–14 Apr 92
	R. Atkins *(Sport)*	28 Nov 90–14 Apr 92
	E. Forth	14 Apr 92–20 Jul 94
	N. Forman	14 Apr 92–11 Dec 92
	T. Boswell	19 Dec 92–6 Jul 95
	R. Squire	27 May 93–2 May 97
	J. Paice	7 Jul 95–2 May 97
	Cheryl Gillan	6 Jul 95–2 May 97
Employ-ment	**M. HOWARD**	28 Nov 90
	GILLIAN SHEPHARD	11 Apr 92
	D. HUNT	27 May 93
	M. PORTILLO	20 Jul 94
	(office abolished 5 Jul 95)	
Min.of State	M. FORSYTH	14 Apr 92
	Ann WIDDECOMBE	20 Jul 94
U-S.	R. Jackson	28 Nov 90–14 Apr 92
	E. Forth	28 Nov 90–14 Apr 92
	Vt Ullswater	28 Nov 90–16 Sep 93
	P. McLoughlin	14 Apr 92–27 May 93
	Ann Widdecombe	27 May 93–20 Jul 94
	Ld Henley	16 Sep 93–20 Jul 94
	J. Paice	20 Jul 94–5 Jul 95
	P. Oppenheim	20 Jul 94–5 Jul 95
Energy	**J. WAKEHAM**	28 Nov 90
	(office abolished 11 Apr 92)	
U-S.	D. Heathcoat-Amory	28 Nov 90–11 Apr 92
	C. Moynihan	28 Nov 90–11 Apr 92
Environ-ment	**M. HESELTINE**	28 Nov 90
	M. HOWARD	11 Apr 92
	J. S. GUMMER	27 May 93
Min.for Local Goverment *(and Inner Cities 94)*	M. PORTILLO	28 Nov 90
	J. REDWOOD	15 Apr 92
	D. CURRY	27 May 93

Min.for Environment *(& Countryside)*		
	D. TRIPPIER	28 Nov 90
	D. MACLEAN	14 Apr 92
	T. YEO	27 May 93
	R. ATKINS	7 Jan 94
	Earl FERRERS	6 Jul 95
Min.for Housing *(Construction 6 Jul 95)*		
	Sir G. YOUNG	28 Nov 90
	Vt ULLSWATER	20 Jul 94
	(Construction and Planning)	
	R. JONES	6 Jul 95
	Lady BLATCH	21 May 91–13 Apr 92
U-S.	Lady Blatch	28 Nov 90–21 May 91
	R. Key	28 Nov 90–15 Apr 92
	T. Yeo	28 Nov 90–15 Apr 92
	T. Baldry	28 Nov 90–20 Jul 94
	Ld Strathclyde	15 Apr 92–16 Sep 93
	R. Squire	15 Apr 92–27 May 93
	Lady Denton	16 Sep 93–11 Jan 94
	E of Arran	11 Jan 94–20 Jul 94
	Sir P. Beresford	20 Jul 94–2 May 97
	R. Jones	20 Jul 94–6 Jul 95
	J. Clappison	6 Jul 95–2 May 97
Health	**W. WALDEGRAVE**	28 Nov 90
	Virginia BOTTOMLEY	10 Apr 92
	S. DORRELL	5 Jul 95
Min.of State	Virginia BOTTOMLEY	28 Nov 90
	B. MAWHINNEY	14 Apr 92
	G. MALONE	20 Jul 94
U-S.	Lady Hooper	28 Nov 90–14 Apr 92
	S. Dorrell	28 Nov 90–14 Apr 92
	T. Sackville	14 Apr 92–29 Nov 95
	T. Yeo	15 Apr 92–27 May 93
	Lady Cumberlege	14 Apr 92–2 May 97
	J. Bowis	27 May 93–23 Jul 96
	S. Burns	23 Jul 96–2 May 97
D.Lanc.	**C. PATTEN**	28 Nov 90
	W. WALDEGRAVE	10 Apr 92
	(from 12 Apr 92 also Min.for Public Service)	
	D. HUNT	20 Jul 94
	R. FREEMAN	5 Jul 95
P.S.	R. Jackson	15 Apr 92
	D. Davis	27 May 93
	R. Hughes	20 Jul 94
	J. Horam	6 Mar 95
	D.Willetts	28 Nov 95
	M. Bates	16 Dec 96
Min.without Portfolio	**J. HANLEY**	20 Jul 94
	B. MAWHINNEY	5 Jul 95
Nat. Heritage	**D. MELLOR**	11 Apr 90
	P. BROOKE	25 Sep 92
	S. DORRELL	20 Jul 94
	Virginia BOTTOMLEY	5 Jul 95
Min. of State U-S.	I. SPROAT	6 Jul 95
	R. Key	14 Apr 92–27 May 93
	I. Sproat	27 May 93–6 Jul 95
	Vt Astor	20 Jul 94–6 Jul 95
	Ld Inglewood	6 Jul 95–2 May 97

CONSERVATIVE GOVERNMENT 1990–1997 *(contd.)*

Northern	**P. BROOKE**	28 Nov 90
Ireland	**Sir P. MAYHEW**	10 Apr 92
Min.of	B. MAWHINNEY	
State		28 Nov 90–14 Apr 92
	Ld BELSTEAD *(also Paym.-Gen.)*	
		28 Nov 90–14 Apr 92
	M. MATES	15 Apr 92–24 Jun 93
	R. ATKINS	14 Apr 92–11 Jan 94
	Sir J. WHEELER	25 Jun 93–2 May 97
	M. ANCRAM	11 Jan 94–2 May 97
U-S.	R. Needham	28 Nov 90–15 Apr 92
	J. Hanley	3 Dec 90–27 May 93
	E of Arran	22 Apr 92–11 Jan 94
	M. Ancram	27 May 93–5 Jan 94
	Lady Denton	20 Jul 94–2 May 97
	T. Smith	6 Jan 94–20 Oct 94
	M. Moss	25 Oct 94–2 May 97
Paym-	Ld BELSTEAD	28 Nov 90
Gen.	*(see N.Ireland)*	
	Sir J. COPE	14 Apr 92
	(see Treasury)	
	D. HEATHCOAT-AMORY	
	(see Treasury)	20 Jul 94–20 Jul 96
	D. WILLETTS	20 Jul 96
	M. BATES	16 Dec 96
Scot.O.	**I. LANG**	28 Nov 90
	M. FORSYTH	5 Jul 95
Min.of	M. FORSYTH	28 Nov 90
State	Ld FRASER of CARMYLLIE	
		14 Apr 92
	Ld J. DOUGLAS-HAMILTON*	
		6 Jul 95
U-S.	Ld J. Douglas-Hamilton*	
		28 Nov 90–6 Jul 95
	A. Stewart	28 Nov 90–8 Feb 95
	G. Kynoch	8 Feb 95–2 May 97
	Ld Strathclyde	28 Nov 90–14 Apr 92
	Sir H. Munro	14 Apr 92–6 Jul 95
	E of Lindsay	6 Jul 95–2 May 97
	R. Robertson	6 Jul 95–2 May 97
Soc.Sec.	**A. NEWTON**	28 Nov 90
	P. LILLEY	10 Apr 92
Min.of	N. SCOTT	28 Nov 90–20 Jul 94
State	W. HAGUE	20 Jul 94–5 Jul 95
	Ld MACKAY of ARDBRECKNISH	
		20 Jul 94–2 May 97
	A. BURT	6 Jul 95–2 May 97
U-S.	Ld Henley	28 Nov 90–16 Sep 93
	M. Jack	28 Nov 90–14 Apr 92
	Ann Widdecombe	
		30 Nov 90–27 May 93
	A. Burt	14 Apr 92–6 Jul 95
	W. Hague	27 May 93–20 Jul 94
	Vt Astor	16 Sep 93–20 Jul 94
	J. Arbuthnot	20 Jul 94–6 Jul 95
	R. Evans	20 Jul 94–2 May 97
	A. Mitchell	6 Jul 95–2 May 97
	O. Heald	6 Jul 95–2 May 97

Trade	**P. LILLEY**	28 Nov 90
	M. HESELTINE	10 Apr 92
	I. LANG	5 Jul 95
Min.for	T. SAINSBURY	28 Nov 90
Trade	R. NEEDHAM	14 Apr 92
	A. NELSON	6 Jul 95
Min.for	Ld HESKETH	28 Nov 90–21 May 91
Industry	*(office vacant 23 May 91–15 Apr 92)*	
	T. SAINSBURY	15 Apr 92
	(office vacant 20 Jul 94)	
Min.for Corporate Affairs		
	J. REDWOOD	28 Nov 90–13 Apr 92
	(office vacant)	
Min.for Energy (and Industry 20 Jul 94)		
	T. EGGAR	15 Apr 92
	G. KNIGHT	5 Jul 95
Min.for Consumer Affairs		
	Earl FERRERS	20 Jul 94–6 Jul 95
	(office vacant 6 Jul 95)	
Min.of	Ld STRATHCLYDE	
State		11 Jan 94–20 Jul 94
	Ld FRASER of CARMYLLIE	
		6 Jul 95–2 May 97
U-S.	Ld Reay	22 May 91–14 Apr 92
	E. Leigh	28 Nov 90–27 May 93
	N. Hamilton	14 Apr 92–25 Oct 94
	J. Evans	27 Oct 94–2 May 97
	Lady Denton	14 Apr 92–16 Sep 93
	P. McLoughlin	27 May 93–20 Jul 94
	C. Wardle	20 Jul 94–11 Feb 95
	I. Taylor	20 Jul 94–2 May 97
	R. Page	14 Feb 95–2 May 97
	P. Oppenheim	7 Jul 95–23 Jul 96
Transport	**M. RIFKIND**	28 Nov 90
	J. MACGREGOR	10 Apr 92
	B. MAWHINNEY	20 Jul 94
	Sir G. YOUNG	5 Jul 95
Min.of	Ld BRABAZON of TARA	
State		28 Nov 90–14 Apr 92
(Min. for Public Transport)		
	R. FREEMAN	28 Nov 90–20 Jul 94
(Min. for Railways and Roads)		
	E of CAITHNESS	14 Apr 92–11 Jan 94
	J. WATTS	20 Jul 94–2 May 97
U-S.	C. Chope	28 Nov 90–14 Apr 92
	P. McLoughlin	28 Nov 90–14 Apr 92
	S. Norris	14 Apr 92–23 Jul 96
	K. Carlisle	14 Apr 92–27 May 93
	R. Key	27 May 93–20 Jul 94
	Ld Mackay of Ardbrecknish	
		11 Jan 94–20 Jul 94
	Vt Goschen	20 Jul 94–2 May 97
	J. Bowis	23 Jul 96–2 May 97
Wales	**D. HUNT**	28 Nov 90
	J. REDWOOD	20 Jul 94
	W. HAGUE	5 Jul 95
Min. of	Sir W.ROBERTS	
State U-S.		28 Nov 90–20 Jul 94

*MP. Not a member of the House of Lords.

CONSERVATIVE GOVERNMENT 1990–1997 *(contd.)*

Min. of	N. Bennett	3 Dec 90–20 Jul 94		*Ass. Whips*	D. Willetts	20 Jul 94–7 Jul 95
State U-S.	G. Jones	14 Apr 92–2 May 97		*(contd.)*	L. Fox	20 Jul 94–28 Nov 95
(contd.)	R. Richards	20 Jul 94–2 Jun 96			P. McLoughlin	7 Jul 95–23 Jul 96
	J. Evans	2 Jun 96–2 May 97			R. Knapman	7 Jul 95–23 Jul 96
					G. Streeter	7 Jul 95–28 Nov 95

Law Officers

				R. Ottaway	18 Oct 95–23 Jul 96
Att.Gen.	Sir P. MAYHEW	28 Nov 90		G. Brandreth	25 Nov 95–12 Dec 96
	Sir N. LYELL	10 Apr 92		S. Coe	2 Jun 96–2 May 97
Sol.Gen.	Sir N. LYELL	28 Nov 90		A. Coombs	23 Jul 96–2 May 97
	Sir D. SPENCER	14 Apr 92		Jacqui Lait	23 Jul 96–2 May 97
Ld Adv.	Ld FRASER of CARMYLLIE			P. Ainsworth	23 Jul 96–2 May 97
		28 Nov 90		M. Carrington	12 Dec 96–2 May 97
	Ld RODGER	14 Apr 92			

Ld MACKAY of DRUMADOON

H.M.Household

		7 Nov 95		*Treasurer*	A. GOODLAD	28 Nov 90
Sol.Gen.	A. RODGER+	28 Nov 90			D. HEATHCOAT-AMORY	15 Apr 92
Scotland	T. DAWSON+	14 Apr 92			G. KNIGHT	7 Jun 93
	D. MACKAY+	4 May 95			A. MACKAY	23 Jul 96
	P. CULLEN+	7 Nov 95		*Compt.*	D. LIGHTBOWN	28 Nov 90
					T. WOOD	7 Jul 95

Whips

				Vice-	J. TAYLOR	28 Nov 90
P.S.to	R. RYDER	28 Nov 90		*Chamb.*	S. CHAPMAN	15 Apr 92
Treasury	A. GOODLAD	5 Jul 95			T. KIRKHOPE	7 Jul 95
Lds of	T. Sackville	28 Nov 90–14 Apr 92			A. MACKAY	18 Oct 96
Treasury	S. Chapman	28 Nov 90–14 Apr 92			D. CONWAY	23 Jul 96
	G. Knight	28 Nov 90–27 May 93		*Cap.Gents*	Ld DENHAM	28 Nov 90
	I. Patnick	28 Nov 90–20 Jul 94		*at Arms*	Ld HESKETH	22 May 91
	N. Baker	3 Dec 90–20 Jul 94			Vt ULLSWATER	16 Sep 93
	T. Wood	15 Apr 92–6 Jul 95			Ld STRATHCLYDE	20 Jul 94
	T. Boswell	15 Apr 92–10 Dec 92		*Cap.Yeo.*	Vt DAVIDSON	28 Nov 90
	T. Kirkhope	16 Dec 92–7 Jul 95		*of Guard*	E of STRATHMORE	30 Dec 91
	A. Mackay	27 May 93–18 Oct 95			E of ARRAN	20 Jul 94
	A. Mitchell	20 Jul 94–6 Jul 95			Ld CHESHAM	8 Jul 95
	D. Conway	20 Jul 94–23 Jul 96		*Lords in*	Vt Long	28 Nov 90–2 May 97
	B. Wells	8 Jul 95–2 May 97		*Waiting*	Ld Reay	28 Nov 90–21 May 91
	D. Willetts	8 Jul 95–22 Jul 96			E of Strathmore	28 Nov 90–30 Dec 91
	S. Burns	8 Jul 95–23 Jul 96			Ld Cavendish	28 Nov 90–22 Apr 92
	P. McLoughlin	23 Jul 96–2 May 97			Vt Astor	28 Nov 90–16 Sep 93
	R. Knapman	23 Jul 96–2 May 97			Earl Howe	30 May 91–15 Apr 92
	R. Ottaway	23 Jul 96–2 May 97			Lady Denton	30 Dec 91–15 Apr 92
	G. Brandreth	12 Dec 96- 2 May 97			Vt St.Davids	22 Apr 92–20 Jul 94
Ass. Whips	T. Wood	28 Nov 90–14 Apr 92			Vt Goschen	22 Apr 92–20 Jul 94
	T. Boswell	28 Nov 90–14 Apr 92			Lady Trumpington	
	N. Hamilton	28 Nov 90–14 Apr 92				22 Apr 92–2 May 97
	T. Kirkhope	28 Nov 90–11 Jan 93			Ld Mackay of Ardbrecknish	
	D. Davis	3 Dec 90–27 May 93				15 Oct 93–11 Jan 94
	R. Hughes	15 Apr 92–20 Jul 94			Ld Annaly	18 Mar 94–20 Jul 94
	J. Arbuthnot	15 Apr 92–20 Jul 94			Ld Lucas of Crudwell	
	A. Mackay	15 Apr 92–27 May 93				21 Jul 94–2 May 97
	A. Mitchell	11 Jan 93–20 Jul 94			Lady Miller of Hendon	
	M. Brown	27 May 93- 7 May 94				21 Jul 94–2 May 97
	D. Conway	27 May 93–20 Jul 94			Ld Inglewood	21 Jul 94–6 Jul 95
	B. Wells	10 May 94–7 Jul 95			E of Lindsay	12 Jan 94–6 Jul 95
	M. Bates	20 Jul 94–12 Dec 96			E of Courtown	8 Jul 95–2 May 97
	S. Burns	20 Jul 94–7 Jul 95				

+Not a member of the House of Commons.

LABOUR GOVERNMENT 1997–

P.M.	**T. BLAIR**	2 May 97
Deputy P.M.	**J. PRESCOTT**	2 May 97
	(Also Sec.of State for the Environment)	
Ld Pres.	**Ann TAYLOR**	3 May 97
	Margaret BECKETT	27 Jul 98
P.S.	P. Tipping	16 Dec 99
Ld Chanc.	**Ld IRVINE**	2 May 97
Min. of State	G. HOON	28 Jul 98–17 May 99
U-S.	G. Hoon	6 May 97–28 Jul 98
	K. Vaz	17 May 99–28 Jul 99
	D. Lock	29 Jul 99–
	Jane Kennedy	11 Oct 99–
Privy Seal	**Ld RICHARD**	3 May 97
	Lady JAY	27 Jul 98
Exchequer	**G. BROWN**	2 May 97
Chief Sec.	**A. DARLING**	3 May 97
	S. BYERS	27 Jul 98
	A. MILBURN	23 Dec 98
	A. SMITH	11 Oct 99
F.S.	Dawn PRIMAROLO	6 May 97
	Barbara ROCHE	4 Jan 99
	S. TIMMS	29 Jul 99
E.S.	Helen Liddell	6 May 97
	Patricia HEWITT	28 Jul 98
	Melanie JOHNSON	29 Jul 99
Paym.-Gen.	G. ROBINSON	3 May 97
	Dawn PRIMAROLO	4 Jan 99
Foreign & Comm.O.		
	R. COOK	2 May 97
Min.of State	D. HENDERSON	3 May 97–27 Jul 98
	D. FATCHETT	6 May 97–10 May 99
	T. LLOYD	6 May 97–29 Jul 99
	Joyce QUIN	28 Jul 98–29 Jul 99
	G. HOON	17 May 99–11 Oct 99
	J. BATTLE	29 Jul 99–
	P. HAIN	29 Jul 99–
	K. VAZ	11 Oct 99
U-S.	Lady Symons	6 May 97
	Lady Scotland	29 Jul 99
Home O.	**J. STRAW**	2 May 97
Min.of State	A. MICHAEL	6 May 97–27 Oct 98
	Joyce QUIN	6 May 97–28 Jul 98
	Ld WILLIAMS OF MOSTYN	28 Jul 98–29 Jul 99
	P. BOATENG	28 Oct 98–
	C. CLARKE	29 Jul 99–
	Barbara ROCHE	29 Jul 99–
U-S.	Ld Williams of Mostyn	6 May 97–28 Jul 98
	G. Howarth	6 May 97–29 Jul 99
	M. O'Brien	6 May 97–
	Kate Hoey	28 Jul 98–29 Jul 99
	Ld Bassam	29 Jul 99–
Ag.Fish. & Food	**J. CUNNNINGHAM**	3 May 97
	N. BROWN	27 Jul 98
Min.of State	J. ROOKER	6 May 97–29 Jul 99
	Joyce QUIN	29 Jul 99–
	Lady HAYMAN	29 Jul 99–

P.S.	E. Morley	6 May 97–
	Ld Donoughue	6 May 97–29 Jul 99
Defence	**G. ROBERTSON** (Ld)	3 May 97
	G. HOON	11 Oct 99
Min.of State	J. REID	6 May 97
(Armed Forces)	D. HENDERSON	28 Jul 98
	J. SPELLAR	29 Jul 99
State	Ld GILBERT	6 May 97
(Def. Proc.)	Lady SYMONS	29 Jul 99
U-S.	J. Spellar	6 May 97
	P. Kilfoyle	29 Jul 99
Educ. & Employment		
	D. BLUNKETT	2 May 97
Min.of State	A. SMITH.	3 May 97–11 Oct 99
	S. BYERS	6 May 97–27 Jul 98
	Lady BLACKSTONE	6 May 97–
	Estelle MORRIS	28 Jul 98–
	Tessa JOWELL	11 Oct 99
U-S.	A. Howarth	6 May 97–28 Jul 98
	Estelle Morris	6 May 97–28 Jul 98
	K. Howells	6 May 97–28 Jul 98
	Margaret Hodge	28 Jul 98–
	G. Mudie	28 Jul 98–29 Jul 99
	C. Clarke	28 Jul 98–29 Jul 99
	Jacqui Smith	29 Jul 99–
	M. Wicks	29 Jul 99–
	M. Wills	29 Jul 99–
Environment		
	J. PRESCOTT	2 May 97
	(also Deputy P.M.)	
Min.for Transport	**G. STRANG**	3 May 97
	(office not in Cabinet)	
	J. REID	27 Jul 98
	Helen LIDDELL	17 May 99
	Ld MACDONALD	29 Jul 99
Min.for Environment	M. MEACHER	3 May 97
Min.for Local Govt.	Hilary ARMSTRONG	6 May 97
Min.for Regions	R. CABORN	6 May 97
	N. RAYNSFORD	29 Jul 99
U-S.	N. Raynsford	6 May 97–29 Jul 99
	Glenda Jackson	6 May 97–29 Jul 99
	Angela Eagle	6 May 97–28 Jul 98
	Lady Hayman	6 May 97–28 Jul 98
	A. Meale	28 Jul 98–29 Jul 99
	Ld Whitty	28 Jul 98–
	Beverley Hughes	29 Jul 99–
	K. Hill	29 Jul 99–
	C. Mullin	29 Jul 99–
Health	**F. DOBSON**	3 May 97
	A. MILBURN	11 Oct 99
Min.of State	Tessa JOWELL	6 May 97–11 Oct 99
	A. MILBURN	6 May 97–23 Dec 98
	Lady JAY	6 May 97–27 Jul 98
	J. DENHAM	30 Dec 98–
U-S.	P. Boateng	6 May 97–28 Oct 98
	Lady Hayman	28 Jul 98–29 Jul 99
	J. Hutton	29 Oct 98–11 Oct 99

LABOUR GOVERNMENT 1997– *(contd.)*

U-S.	Ld Hunt of King's Heath	29 Jul 99–		*U-S.*	Angela Eagle	28 Jul 98–
(contd.)	Gisella Stuart	29 Jul 99–		*(contd.)*	S. Timms	28 Jul 98–4 Jan 99
	Yvette Cooper	11 Oct 99–			H. Bayley	4 Jan 99–
Internat. Dev.				*U-S. (Women)*		
	Clare SHORT	3 May 97			Joan Ruddock	11 Jun 97–28 Jul 98
U-S.	G. Foulkes	6 May 97		*Trade*	**Margaret BECKETT**	2 May 97
D.Lanc.	**D. CLARK**	3 May 97			**P. MANDELSON**	27 Jul 98
	J. CUNNINGHAM	27 Jul 98			**S. BYERS**	23 Dec 98
	Mo MOWLAM	11 Oct 99		*Min.for*	Ld CLINTON-DAVIS	6 May 97
Min.of	D. FOSTER	3 May 97–6 May 97		*Trade*	B. WILSON	28 Jul 98
State	Ld FALCONER	28 Jul 98–			R. CABORN	29 Jul 99
	I. MCCARTNEY	29 Jul 99–		*Min. for Competitiveness*		
P.S. Cabinet O.					I. MCCARTNEY	6 May 97–29 Jul 99
	P. Kilfoyle	6 May 97–29 Jul 99		*Min. for Energy & Competitiveness*		
	G. Stringer	9 Nov 99–			Helen LIDDELL	29 Jul 99–
Min.without Portfolio				*Min. for Industry*		
	P. MANDELSON	5 May 97			J. BATTLE	6 May 97–29 Jul 99
	(office vacant 27 Jul 98)			*Min. for Small Business*		
Nat.Heritage (Jul 97 Culture,Media and Sport)					Patricia HEWITT	29 Jul 99–
	C. SMITH	3 May 97		*Min. for Eur. (also in Treasury)*		
Min.of State	T. CLARKE	6 May 97–28 Jul 98			Ld SIMON	8 May 97–29 Jul 99
U-S.(Arts)	M. Fisher	6 May 97		*U-S.*	N. Griffiths	6 May 97–28 Jul 98
	A. Howarth	28 Jul 98			Barbara Roche	6 May 97–4 Jan 99
U-S.(Tourism)					K. Howells	28 Jul 98–
	Janet Anderson	28 Jul 98			Ld Sainsbury	28 Jul 98–
U-S.(Sport)	T. Banks	8 May 97			M. Wills	4 Jan 99–29 Jul 99
	Kate Hoey	29 Jul 99			A. Johnson	29 Jul 99–
Northern Ireland				*Wales*	**R. DAVIES**	3 May 97
	Mo MOWLAM	3 May 97			**A. MICHAEL**	27 Oct 98
	P. MANDELSON	11 Oct 99			**P. MURPHY**	29 Jul 99
Min.of	A. INGRAM	6 May 97–		*U-S.*	W. Griffiths	6 May 97–28 Jul 98
State	P. MURPHY	6 May 97–28 Jul 99			P. Hain	6 May 97–29 Jul 99
U-S.	T. Worthington	6 May 97–28 Jul 98			J. O. Jones	28 Jul 98–29 Jul 99
	Ld Dubs	6 May 97–			D. Hanson	29 Jul 99
	J. McFall	28 Jul 98–		*Law Officers*		
	G. Howarth	29 Jul 99–		*Att.Gen.*	J. MORRIS	6 May 97
Paym.-Gen. (see Treasury)					Ld WILLIAMS OF MOSTYN	29 Jul 99
Scot.O.	**D. DEWAR**	3 May 97		*Sol.Gen.*	Ld FALCONER	6 May 97
	J. REID	17 May 99			R. CRANSTON	28 Jul 98
Min.of	H. MCLEISH	6 May 97–29 Jul 99		*Ld. Adv.*	Ld HARDIE	7 May 97
State	B. WILSON	6 May 97–28 Jul 98		*Sol.Gen.*	C. BOYD+	7 May 97
	Helen LIDDELL	28 Jul 98–17 May 99		*Scotland*		
	B. WILSON	29 Jul 99–			*(Scottish Law Officers ceased*	
Advocate	Linda CLARK	17 May 99			*to be UK Ministers 17 May 99)*	
Gen.				*Whips*		
U-S.	S. Galbraith	6 May 97–29 Jul 99		*P.S.to Treasury*		
	M. Chisholm	6 May 97–10 Dec 97			N. BROWN	3 May 97
	C. Macdonald	11 Dec 97–29 Jul 99			*(office in Cabinet)*	
	Ld Sewel	6 May 97–29 Jul 99			**Ann TAYLOR**	27 Jul 98
	Ld Macdonald of Tradeston			*Lds of Treasury*		
		3 Aug 98–29 Jul 99			R. Ainsworth	8 May 97–
Soc.Sec.	**Harriet HARMAN**	3 May 97			G. Allen	8 May 97–28 Jul 98
	A. DARLING	27 Jul 98			J. Dowd	8 May 97–
Min.of	F. FIELD	3 May 97–28 Jul 98			J. McFall	8 May 97–28 Jul 98
State	*(office vacant)*				J. O. Jones	8 May 97–28 Jul 98
	S. TIMMS	4 Jan 99–29 Jul 99			C. Betts	28 Jul 98–
	J. ROOKER	29 Jul 99–			D. Jamieson	28 Jul 98–
U-S.	K. Bradley	6 May 97–28 Jul 98			Jane Kennedy	28 Jul 98–11 Oct 99
	Lady Hollis	6 May 97–			G. Pope	18 Nov 99–

+Not a member of the House of Commons.

LABOUR GOVERNMENT 1997– (*contd.*)

Ass.Whips	C. Betts	8 May 97–28 Jul 98	*Compt.*	T. MCAVOY	8 May 97
	D. Clelland	8 May 97–	*Vice-*	Janet ANDERSON	8 May 97
	K. Hughes	8 May 97–	*Chamb.*	G. ALLEN	28 Jul 98
	D. Jamieson	8 May 97–28 Jul 98	*Cap.Gents at Arms*		
	Jane Kennedy	8 May 97–28 Jul 98		Ld CARTER	6 May 97
	G. Pope	8 May 97–	*Cap.Yeo. of Guard*		
	Bridget Prentice	8 May 97–28 Jul 98		Ld MCINTOSH	3 May 97
	M. Hall	28 Jul 98–	*Lords in*	Ld Haskel	8 May 97–28 Jul 98
	D. Hanson	28 Jul 98–29 Jul 99	*Waiting*	Lady Farrington	8 May 97–
	K. Hill	28 Jul 98–29 Jul 99		Ld Whitty	8 May 97–28 Jul 98
	Anne McGuire	28 Jul 99–		Lady Gould	8 May 97–18 Dec 98
	M. Sutcliffe	29 Jul 99–		Ld Hoyle	8 May 97–9 Apr 99
	T. McNulty	18 Oct 99–		Lady Ramsay	18 Dec 98–
	D. Touhig	17 Nov 99–		Lady Amos	28 Jul 98–
				Ld Hunt of King's Heath	
H.M.Household					28 Jul 98–29 Jul 99
Treasurer	G. MUDIE	8 May 97		Ld Burlison	9 Apr 99–
	K. BRADLEY	28 Jul 98		Ld Bach	29 Jul 99–

Ministerial Salaries

	Prime Minister*	Secretaries of State*	Other Dept. Ministers*	Reduced Parl. Salary
1831	£5,000	£5,000	£2,000	–
1937	£10,000	£5,000	£5,000	–
1965	£14,000	£8,500	£8,500	–
1972	£20,000	£13,000	£7,500	–
1978	£22,000	£14,300	£8,250	–
1979	£23,500	£19,650	£12,625	–
1980	£34,650+	£23,500	£16,250	–
1981	£36,725+	£23,500	£19,775	£6,930
1982	£38,200+	£28,950	£20,575	£8,130
1983	£38,200+	£28,950	£20,575	£8,460
1984	£38,987+	£29,367	£20,867	£11,443
1985	£40,808+	£30,188	£20,708	£12,792
1986	£42,745+	£31,625	£21,795	£13,375
1987	£44,775+	£33,145	£22,875	£13,875
1988	£45,787+	£34,157	£23,887	£16,911
1989	£46,109+	£34,479	£24,209	£18,148
1990	£46,750+	£35,120	£24,850	£20,101
1991	£50,724	£38,105	£26,962	£21,809
1992	£53,007	£39,820	£28,175	£23,227
1994	£54,438	£40,895	£28,936	£23,854
1995	£55,900	£41,994	£29,713	£24,495
1996	£58,557	£43,991	£31,125	£25,660
1997	£100,000	£60,000	£31,125	£43,000
1998	£102,750	£61,650	£31,981	£45,066

*Not including the salary Ministers receive as members of Parliament.
+Throughout her period as Prime Minister Mrs Thatcher opted to receive only the same salary as other Cabinet Ministers. Mr Blair also refused to take part of his salary.

Opposition Salaries

		Chief Opposition Whip	
	Leader of the Opposition*	House of Commons*	House of Lords
1937	£2,000	–	–
1957	£3,000	–	–
1965	£4,500	£3,750	£1,500
1972	£9,500	£7,500	£2,500
1978	£10,450	£8,250	£3,248
1979	£16,225	£12,625	£7,124
1980	£20,950	£16,250	£9,950
1981	£20,950	$16,250	£9,950
1982	£24,100	£18,650	£6,925
1983	£26,575	£20,575	£17,840
1984	£26,947	£20,867	£18,770
1985	£27,518	£20,798	£19,710
1986	£28,825	£21,795	£20,645
1987	£30,225	£22,875	£21,570
1988	£31,237	£23,887	£25,618
1989	£31,559	£24,209	£27,377
1990	£32,200	£24,850	£29,971
1991	£34,937	£26,962	£32,519
1992	£36,509	£28,175	£33,982
1994	£37,495	£28,936	£35,099
1995	£38,502	£29,713	£36,239
1996	£40,332	£31,125	£38,313
1997	£55,612	£31,125	£39,462
1998	£56,513	£31,981	£40,547

*Not including the Parliamentary salary – see above.
Since 1975 the opposition parties have received financial assistance ('Short money') which in 1999 amounted to just under £4000 per seat.

Ministerial Offices, 1900–2000

This list includes almost all specifically named ministerial offices held by Ministers or Ministers of State, apart from appointments in the Royal Household or, after 1950, Ministers of State without a functional title. It does not include offices held by junior ministers. In the 1980s it became increasingly common to give specific titles to Ministers of State in the larger departments, especially in Defence, Environment, Trade and Transport. Minor variations in these labels were frequent and are not listed here.

Admiralty. First Lord of, 1900–64

Agriculture. President of the Board of Agriculture, 1900–2; President of the Board of Agriculture and Fisheries, 1903–19; Minister of Agriculture and Fisheries, 1919–1955; Minister of Agriculture, Fisheries and Food, 1955–

Aerospace. Min. for, 1971–74

Air. President of the Air Board, 1917; President of the Air Council, 1917–1918; Secretary of State, 1918–64

Aircraft Production. Minister. 1940–1946

Armed Forces. Minister for, 1981–

Arts. Under Secretary of State, 1965–67; Minister of State, 1967–70; Secretary of State, 1974–76; Minister of State, 1976–79: Minister for Arts, 1979–92; Secretary of State for the National Heritage, 1992–7; Secretary of State for Culture, Media and Sport, 1997–

Attorney-General, 1900–

Attorney-General for Ireland, 1900–22

Aviation. Minister, 1959–67 *(under Transport) (see Civil Aviation),* Minister of State for Aviation and Shipping 1990–1994

Aviation Supply. Minister, 1970–71

Blockade. Minister, 1916–19

Burma. Secretary of State for India and Burma, 1937–47; Secretary of State for Burma, 1947–48

Cabinet Office. Minister for the, 1998–

Civil Aviation. Minister, 1944–53: Minister of Transport and Civil Aviation, 1953–59; Minister of Aviation, 1959–67; Minister of State for Aviation 1990–

Civil Service. Minister for the, 1968–

Colonies. Secretary of State, 1900–67

Commonwealth. Secretary of State for Dominions, 1925–47; Secretary of State for Commonwealth Relations, 1947–66; Secretary of State for Commonwealth Affairs, 1966–68

Construction. (see Environment)

Consumer Affairs. Minister for, 1979–1983 *(under Trade)*

Co-ordination of Defence. Minister, 1936–40

Co-ordination of Transport, Fuel and Power; Secretary of State, 1951–53

Corporate Affairs. Minister for 1990– *(under Trade)*

Culture, Media and Sport. Secretary of State 1997–

Defence. Minister, 1940–64; Secretary of State, 1964–

Defence. Minister for the Armed Forces, 1981–

Defence Support. Minister, 1985–86

Defence Procurement. Minister for, 1971–72, 1981–

Defence for Administration. Minister of, 1967–70

Defence for Air Force. Minister of, 1964–67

Defence for Army. Minister of, 1964–67

Defence for Equipment. Minister of, 1967–70

Defence for Navy. Minister of, 1964–67

Deputy Prime Minister, 1942–45, 1945–51, 1951–55, 1962–63, 1979–88, 1989–90, 1995–

Dominions. Secretary of State, 1925–47

Duchy of Lancaster. Chancellor, 1900–

Economic Affairs. Minister, Sep–Nov 1947, Feb–Oct 1950, 1951–52; Secretary of State, 1964–69. Minister of State for Economic Affairs, 1957–64

Economic Warfare. Minister, 1939–45

Education. President of the Board of Education, 1900–44; Minister of Education, 1944–64; Secretary of State for Education and Science, 1964–92; Secretary of State for Education, 1992–4; Secretary of State for Education and Employment, 1994–

Employment and Productivity. Secretary of State, 1968–70

Employment. Secretary of State, 1970–

Energy. Secretary of State, 1974–92; Minister for, Jan–Mar 1974,1992–94 *(see also under Trade)*

Environment, (Transport and the Regions 1997–). Secretary of State, 1970–; Minister for Local Government, 1970–; Minister for Environment (and Countryside), 1979– (*From 1985 onwards the titles attached to the 2 to 4 Ministers in the Environment Department changed constantly; Construction, Housing, Local Government, Water, Inner Cities, Countryside, Planning, Regions and Regeneration were variously combined, often for short periods and without any change in the ministerial team). (See also Transport)*

First Secretary of State, 1962–63, 1964–70, 1995–97

Food. Minister, 1916–21, and 1939–54 *(see Agriculture)*

Foreign Affairs. Secretary of State, 1900–68

Foreign and Commonwealth Affairs. Secretary of State, 1968–

Fuel and Power. Minister, 1944–57 *(see Power)*

Fuel, Light and Power. Minister, 1942–44 *(see Fuel and Power)*

Health. Minister, 1919–68; Minister of State, 1968–70; also Minister for, 1979–; Secretary of State, 1988–,

Health and Social Security. 1968–1988. *(See Social Services)*

Heritage. Minister for, 1991–92. Secretary of State, 1992–97 *(see Culture)*

Home Affairs. Secretary of State, 1900–

Home Security. Minister, 1939–45

Housing and Local Government. Minister of Town and Country Planning, 1943–51; Minister of Local Government and Planning, 1951; Minister of Housing and Local Government, 1951–70 *(see Local Government; see also Environment)*

India. Secretary of State for India, 1900–37; Secretary of State for India and Burma, 1937–47

Industrial Development. Minister, 1972–74

Industry. Secretary of State for Industry, Trade and Regional Development, 1963–64; Minister for, 1970–74, 1983–; Secretary of State, 1974–83 *(see Trade)*

Information. Minister, Mar–Nov 1918 and 1939–46

Information Technology. Minister for Industry and Information Technology, 1981–83; Minister for Information Technology, 1983–87

Ireland. Lord Lieutenant 1900–2, 1919–21

Ireland. Chief Secretary to the Lord Lieutenant of Ireland, 1900–22 *(Irish Office wound up 1924)*

International Development. Secretary of State, 1997–

Labour. Minister of Labour, 1916–39; Minister of Labour and National Service, 1939–59; Minister of Labour, 1959–68

Land and Natural Resources. Minister, 1964–67

Local Government. President of the Local Government Board, 1900–19 *(see Housing and Local Government)*

Local Government.Minister,1970– *(under Environment)*

Local Government and Planning. Minister, 1951 *(see Housing and Local Government)*

Local Government and Regional Planning. Secretary of State, 1969–70 *(see Planning and Local Government)*

Lord Advocate, 1900–

Lord Chancellor, 1900–

Lord Chancellor of Ireland, 1900–22

Lord President of the Council, 1900–97

Lord Privy Seal, 1900–

Materials. Minister, 1951–54

Mines. Secretary for Mines Department, 1920–42

Ministers Resident Overseas. Allied H.Q., North Africa, 1942–5; Washington for Supply, 1942–5; West Africa, 1942–5; Middle East, 1942–3, 1944–5

Munitions. Minister, 1915–19 *(see Supply)*

National Heritage. Sec.of State for 1992–7 *(see Culture)*

National Insurance. Minister, 1944–53; Minister of Pensions and National Insurance, 1953–66

National Service. Minister, 1917–19; Minister of Labour and National Service, 1939–59

Northern Ireland. Secretary of State, 1972–

Overseas Development. Minister, 1964–9 *(see International Development)*

Overseas Trade. Secretary for Overseas Trade, 1917–53

Paymaster-General.,1900–

Pensions. Minister of Pensions, 1916–53; Minister of Pensions and National Insurance, 1953–66

Petroleum. Secretary for Petroleum Department, 1940–42

Planning and Land. Minister, 1968–69

Planning and Local Government. Minister for Planning and Local Government, 1974–76 *(under Environment)*

Portfolio. Minister without Portfolio, 1915–21, 1935–36, 1939–42, 1942–44, 1946, 1947, 1954–68, 1968–74, 1984–85, 1994–98

Postmaster-General, 1900–69

Post and Telecommunications. Minister, 1969–74 *(under Technology)*

Power. Minister, 1957–69 *(see Fuel and Power)*

President of the Council, 1997–

Prices and Consumer Protection. Secretary of State, 1974–79

Prime Minister, 1900–

Privy Council Office. Minister of State, 1974–79, 1983–4, 1985–90

Production. Minister, 1942–45

Public Building and Works. Minister, 1962–70 *(see Housing and Construction)*

Public Transport, Minister for, 1988– *(under Transport)*

Reconstruction. Minister, 1917–19 and 1944–45

Railways and Roads. (see Transport)

Science. Minister, 1959–64

Scotland. Secretary, 1900–26; Secretary of State, 1926–

Shipping. Minister, 1916–21 and 1939–41 *(see War Transport)*

Social Insurance. Minister, Oct–Nov 1944 *(see National Insurance)*

Social Security. Minister, 1966–68 *(see Health and Social Security)*; Secretary of State, 1988–; also Minister for Social Security, 1976– (and Disabled People 1987–)

Social Services. Secretary of State, 1968–88

Solicitor-General, 1900–

Solicitor-General for Ireland, 1900–22

Solicitor-General for Scotland, 1900–

Sport (and Recreation). Minister of State, 1974–79

State. Minister of *(at Foreign Office)*, 1941–42, 1943–50

State, First Secretary of, 1962–63, 1964–70, 1995–7

Supply. Minister, 1919–21 and 1939–59

Technical Cooperation. Secretary for, 1961–64

Technology. Minister, 1964–70

Town and Country Planning. Minister of Town and Country Planning, 1943–51 *(see Local Government and Planning)*

Trade. President of the Board of Trade, 1900–70, 1992–98; Secretary of State of Trade and Industry, 1970–74, 1983–92, 1998–; Secretary of State for Trade, 1974–83; also Minister for Trade, 1970–72, 1983–; Minister for Trade and Consumer Affairs, 1972–74; Minister for Industry and Information Technology, 1983–87; Minister for Industry and Enterprise, 1989–90; Minister for Corporate Affairs, 1990–92; Minister for Energy and Industry, 1994–7; Minister for Consumer Affairs, 1994–97; Minister for Science Energy and Industry, 1997–; Minister for Trade and Competitiveness in Europe, 1997–; *(see Industry)*

Transport. Minister of Transport, 1919–41; Minister of War Transport, 1941–46; Minister of Transport, 1946–53; Minister of Transport and Civil Aviation, 1953–59; Minister of Transport, 1959–70; Minister for Transport Industries, 1970–74; Minister for Transport, 1974–76, 1997–; Secretary of State, 1976–79, 1981–97; Minister of Transport, 1979–81; Minister of State for Public Transport, 1990–94; Minister of State for Aviation and Shipping, 1990–94; Minister for Railways and Roads (and Public Transport 1996–97), 1994–97

Treasury. Chancellor of the Exchequer,1900–; Chief Secretary, 1961–; Financial Secretary, 1900–; Economic Secretary, 1947–50, 1950–51, 1952–58, 1958–64, 1981–; Minister of State, 1964–9, 1970–87, 1990–92

Urban Affairs. Minister of State, 1974–74

Wales. Minister for Welsh Affairs, 1951–57; Secretary of State for Wales, 1964–; also Minister of State for Welsh Affairs, 1957–64

War. Secretary of State, 1900–64

War Transport. Minister, 1941–46 *(see Shipping and Transport)*

Women. Minister, 1997–

Works. First Commissioner of Works, 1900–40; Minister of Works and Buildings, 1940–42; Minister of Works and Planning, 1942–43; Minister of Works, 1943–62; Minister of Public Building and Works, 1962–70

Holders of Ministerial Offices

Prime Minister

1900 M of Salisbury (3rd)
12 Jul 02 A. Balfour
5 Dec 05 Sir H. Campbell-
Bannerman
5 Apr 08 H. Asquith
6 Dec 16 D. Lloyd George
23 Oct 22 A. Bonar Law
22 May 23 S. Baldwin
22 Jan 24 R. MacDonald
4 Nov 24 S. Baldwin
5 Jun 29 R. MacDonald
7 Jun 35 S. Baldwin
28 May 37 N. Chamberlain
10 May 40 W. Churchill
26 Jul 45 C. Attlee
26 Oct 51 (Sir) W.Churchill
6 Apr 55 Sir A. Eden
10 Jan 57 H. Macmillan
18 Oct 63 Sir A. Douglas-Home
16 Oct 64 H. Wilson
19 Jun 70 E. Heath
4 Mar 74 H. Wilson
5 Apr 76 J. Callaghan
4 May 79 Margaret Thatcher
28 Nov 90 J. Major
2 May 97 T. Blair

Deputy Prime Minister

19 Feb 42–23 May 45
C. Attlee
26 Jul 45–24 Feb 51
H. Morrison
26 Oct 51– 6 Apr 55
(Sir) A. Eden
13 Jul 62–18 Oct 63
R. Butler
4 May 79–10 Jan 88
W. Whitelaw
24 Jul 89– 1 Nov 90
Sir G. Howe
20 Jul 95– 2 May 97
M. Heseltine
2 May 97–
J.Prescott

Lord President of the Council

1900 D of Devonshire
13 Oct 03 M of Londonderry
10 Dec 05 E of Crewe
12 Apr 08 Ld Tweedmouth
13 Oct 08 Vt Wolverhampton
16 Jun 10 Earl Beauchamp
3 Nov 10 Vt Morley
5 Aug 14 Earl Beauchamp
25 May 15 M of Crewe
10 Dec 16 Earl Curzon
23 Oct 19 (Sir) A. Balfour (E of Balfour)
24 Oct 22 M of Salisbury (4th)

22 Jan 24 Ld Parmoor
6 Nov 24 Marquess Curzon
27 Apr 25 E of Balfour
7 Jun 29 Ld Parmoor
25 Aug 31 S. Baldwin
7 Jun 35 R. MacDonald
28 May 37 Vt Halifax[1]
9 Mar 38 Vt Hailsham (1st)
31 Oct 38 Vt Runciman
3 Sep 39 Earl Stanhope
11 May 40 N. Chamberlain
3 Oct 40 Sir J. Anderson
24 Sep 43 C. Attlee
25 May 45 Ld Woolton
27 Jul 45 H. Morrison
9 Mar 51 Vt Addison
28 Oct 51 Ld Woolton[1]
24 Nov 52 M of Salisbury (5th)
29 Mar 57 E of Home
17 Sep 57 Vt Hailsham (2nd)[1]
14 Oct 59 E of Home
27 Jul 60 Vt Hailsham (2nd) (Q. Hogg)
16 Oct 64 H. Bowden
11 Aug 66 R. Crossman
18 Oct 68 F. Peart
20 Jun 70 W. Whitelaw
7 Apr 72 R. Carr
5 Nov 72 J. Prior
5 Mar 74 E. Short
8 Apr 76 M. Foot
5 May 79 Ld Soames
14 Sep 81 F. Pym
5 Apr 82 J. Biffen
11 Jun 83 Vt Whitelaw
13 Jun 87 J. Wakeham
10 Jan 88 J. MacGregor
11 Apr 92 A. Newton

(President of the Council)

2 May 97 Ann Taylor
27 Jul 98 Margaret Beckett

Lord Chancellor

1900 E of Halsbury
10 Dec 05 Ld Loreburn (E)
10 Jun 12 Vt Haldane
25 May 15 Ld Buckmaster
10 Dec 16 Ld Finlay
10 Jan 19 Ld Birkenhead (Vt)
24 Oct 22 Vt Cave
22 Jan 24 Vt Haldane
6 Nov 24 Vt Cave
28 Mar 28 Ld Hailsham (Vt)
7 Jun 29 Ld Sankey (Vt)
7 Jun 35 Vt Hailsham
9 Mar 38 Ld Maugham (Vt)
3 Sep 39 Vt Caldecote
12 May 40 Vt Simon
27 Jul 45 Ld Jowitt

30 Oct 51 Ld Simonds
18 Oct 54 Vt Kilmuir
13 Jul 62 Ld Dilhorne
16 Oct 64 Ld Gardiner
20 Jun 70 Ld Hailsham
5 Mar 74 Ld Elwyn-Jones
5 May 79 Ld Hailsham
13 Jun 87 Ld Havers
26 Oct 87 Ld Mackay
2 May 97 Ld Irvine

Lord Privy Seal

1900 Vt Cross
1 Nov 00 M of Salisbury (3rd)
12 Jul 02 A. Balfour
11 Oct 03 M of Salisbury (4th)
10 Dec 05 M of Ripon
9 Oct 08 E of Crewe
23 Oct 11 Earl Carrington
13 Feb 12 M of Crewe
25 May 15 Earl Curzon
15 Dec 16 E of Crawford
10 Jan 19 A. Bonar Law
23 Mar 21 A. Chamberlain
24 Oct 22 (office vacant)
25 May 23 Ld R. Cecil
22 Jan 24 J. Clynes
6 Nov 24 M of Salisbury (4th)
7 Jun 29 J. Thomas
5 Jun 30 V. Hartshorn
24 Mar 31 T. Johnston
3 Sep 31 Earl Peel
5 Nov 31 Vt Snowden
29 Sep 32 S. Baldwin
31 Dec 33 A. Eden
7 Jun 35 M of Londonderry
22 Nov 35 Vt Halifax
28 May 37 Earl De La Warr
31 Oct 38 Sir J. Anderson
3 Sep 39 Sir S. Hoare
3 Apr 40 Sir K. Wood
11 May 40 C. Attlee
19 Feb 42 Sir S. Cripps
22 Nov 42 Vt Cranborne (5th M of Salisbury)
24 Sep 43 Ld Beaverbrook
27 Jul 45 A. Greenwood
17 Apr 47 Ld Inman
7 Oct 47 Vt Addison
9 Mar 51 E. Bevin
26 Apr 51 R. Stokes
28 Oct 51 M of Salisbury (5th)
7 May 52 H. Crookshank
20 Dec 55 R. Butler
14 Oct 59 Vt Hailsham (2nd)
27 Jul 60 E. Heath
20 Oct 63 S. Lloyd
18 Oct 64 E of Longford
23 Dec 65 Sir F. Soskice
6 Apr 66 E of Longford

[1]Also Party Chairman

16 Jan 68 Ld Shackleton
6 Apr 68 F. Peart
18 Oct 68 Ld Shackleton
20 Jun 70 Earl Jellicoe
5 Jun 73 Ld Windlesham
7 Mar 74 Ld Shepherd
10 Sep 76 Ld Peart
5 May 79 Sir I. Gilmour
14 Sep 81 H. Atkins
6 Apr 82 Lady Young
11 Jun 83 J. Biffen
13 Jun 87 J. Wakeham
10 Jan 88 Ld Belstead
28 Nov 90 Ld Waddington
11 Apr 92 J. Wakeham
20 Jul 94 Vt Cranborne
2 May 97 Ld Richard
27 Jul 98 Lady Jay

Secretary of State for Economic Affairs

16 Oct 64 G. Brown
11 Aug 66 M. Stewart
29 Aug 67 P. Shore
(office wound up 8 Oct 69)

Chancellor of the Exchequer

1900 Sir M. Hicks-Beach
8 Aug 02 C. Ritchie
6 Oct 03 A. Chamberlain
10 Dec 05 H. Asquith
12 Apr 08 D. Lloyd-George
25 May 15 R. McKenna
10 Dec 16 A. Bonar Law
10 Jan 19 A. Chamberlain
1 Apr 21 Sir R. Horne
24 Oct 22 S. Baldwin
27 Aug 23 N. Chamberlain
22 Jan 24 P. Snowden
6 Nov 24 W. Churchill
7 Jun 29 P. Snowden
5 Nov 31 N. Chamberlain
28 May 37 Sir J. Simon
12 May 40 Sir K. Wood
24 Sep 43 Sir J. Anderson
27 Jul 45 H. Dalton
13 Nov 47 Sir S. Cripps
19 Oct 50 H. Gaitskell
28 Oct 51 R. Butler
20 Dec 55 H. Macmillan
13 Jan 57 P. Thorneycroft
6 Jan 58 D. Heathcoat-Amory
27 Jul 60 S. Lloyd
13 Jul 62 R. Maudling
16 Oct 64 J. Callaghan
30 Nov 67 R. Jenkins
20 Jun 70 I. Macleod
25 Jul 70 A. Barber
25 Mar 74 D. Healey
5 May 79 Sir G. Howe
11 Jun 83 N. Lawson
26 Oct 89 J. Major

28 Nov 90 N. Lamont
27 May 93 K. Clarke
2 May 97 G. Brown

Secretary of State for Foreign Affairs

1900 M of Salisbury (3rd)
1 Nov 00 M of Lansdowne[1]
10 Dec 05 Sir E. Grey*(Vt)*
10 Dec 16 A. Balfour
23 Oct 19 Earl Curzon*(M)*[1]
22 Jan 24 R. MacDonald
6 Nov 24 (Sir) A. Chamberlain
7 Jun 29 A. Henderson
25 Aug 31 M of Reading
5 Nov 31 Sir J. Simon
7 Jun 35 Sir S. Hoare
22 Dec 35 A. Eden
21 Feb 38 Vt Halifax
22 Dec 40 A. Eden
27 Jul 45 E. Bevin
9 Mar 51 H. Morrison
28 Oct 51 (Sir) A. Eden
7 Apr 55 H. Macmillan
20 Dec 55 S. Lloyd
27 Jul 60 E of Home
20 Oct 63 R. Butler
16 Oct 64 P. Gordon-Walker
22 Jan 65 M. Stewart
11 Aug 66 G. Brown
16 Mar 68 M. Stewart

(Secretary of State for Foreign and Commonwealth Affairs)

17 Oct 68 M. Stewart
20 Jun 70 Sir A. Douglas-Home
5 Mar 74 J. Callaghan
8 Apr 76 A. Crosland
21 Feb 77 D. Owen
5 May 79 Ld Carrington
5 Apr 82 F. Pym
11 Jun 83 Sir G. Howe
14 Jun 89 J. Major
26 Oct 89 D. Hurd
5 Jul 95 M. Rifkind
2 May 97 R.Cook

Secretary of State for the Home Department

1900 Sir M. White-Ridley
1 Nov 00 C. Ritchie
8 Aug 02 A. Akers-Douglas
10 Dec 05 H. Gladstone
14 Feb 10 W. Churchill
23 Oct 11 R. McKenna
25 May 15 Sir J. Simon
10 Jan 16 H. Samuel
10 Dec 16 Sir G. Cave *(Vt)*
10 Jan 19 E. Shortt
24 Oct 22 W. Bridgeman
22 Jan 24 A. Henderson
6 Nov 24 Sir W. Joynson-Hicks

7 Jun 29 J. Clynes
25 Aug 31 Sir H. Samuel
28 Sep 32 Sir J. Gilmour
7 Jun 35 Sir J. Simon
28 May 37 Sir S. Hoare
3 Sep 39 Sir J. Anderson
3 Oct 40 H. Morrison
25 May 45 Sir D. Somervell
3 Aug 45 C. Ede
28 Oct 51 Sir D. Maxwell-Fyfe
18 Oct 54 G. Lloyd-George
13 Jan 57 R. Butler[1]
13 Jul 62 H. Brooke
18 Oct 64 Sir F. Soskice
23 Dec 65 R. Jenkins
30 Nov 67 J. Callaghan
20 Jun 70 R. Maudling
19 Jul 72 R. Carr
5 Mar 74 R. Jenkins
10 Sep 76 M. Rees
5 May 79 W. Whitelaw
11 Jun 83 L. Brittan
2 Sep 85 D. Hurd
26 Oct 89 D. Waddington
28 Nov 90 K. Baker
11 Apr 92 K. Clarke
27 May 93 M. Howard
2 May 97 J. Straw

First Lord of the Admiralty

1900 G. Goschen
1 Nov 00 E of Selborne
5 Mar 05 Earl Cawdor
10 Dec 05 Ld Tweedmouth
12 Apr 08 R. McKenna
23 Oct 11 W. Churchill
25 May 15 A. Balfour
10 Dec 16 Sir E. Carson
17 Jul 17 Sir E. Geddes
10 Jan 19 W. Long
13 Feb 21 Ld Lee
24 Oct 22 L. Amery
22 Jan 24 Vt Chelmsford
6 Nov 24 W. Bridgeman
7 Jun 29 A. Alexander
25 Aug 31 Sir A. Chamberlain
5 Nov 31 Sir B. Eyres-Monsell
         (Vt Monsell)
5 Jun 36 Sir S. Hoare
28 May 37 A. Duff Cooper
27 Oct 38 Earl Stanhope
3 Sep 39 W. Churchill
11 May 40 A. Alexander
25 May 45 B. Bracken
3 Aug 45 A. Alexander
4 Oct 46 Vt Hall
24 May 51 Ld Pakenham
31 Oct 51 J. Thomas
         (Vt Cilcennin)
2 Sep 56 Vt Hailsham
16 Jan 57 E of Selkirk
16 Oct 59 Ld Carrington

[1]*Also Party Chairman*

22 Oct 63 Earl Jellicoe
(office wound up 1 Apr 64)

Minister for Aerospace (and Shipping)

1 May 71 F. Corfield
7 Apr 72 M. Heseltine
(office wound up 5 Mar 74)

President of the Board of Agriculture (and Fisheries 1903)

1900 W. Long
14 Nov 00 R. Hanbury
19 May 03 E of Onslow
12 Mar 05 A. Fellowes
10 Dec 05 Earl Carrington
23 Oct 11 W. Runciman
6 Aug 14 Ld Lucas
25 May 15 E of Selborne
11 Jul 16 E of Crawford
10 Dec 16 R. Prothero *(Ld Ernle)*

(Minister of Agriculture and Fisheries) (and Food, 18 Oct 54)

15 Aug 19 Ld Lee
13 Feb 21 Sir A. Griffith-Boscawen
24 Oct 22 Sir R. Sanders
22 Jan 24 N. Buxton
6 Nov 24 E. Wood
4 Nov 25 W. Guinness
7 Jun 29 N. Buxton
5 Jun 30 C. Addison
25 Aug 31 Sir J. Gilmour
28 Sep 32 W. Elliot
29 Oct 36 W. Morrison
29 Jan 39 Sir R. Dorman-Smith
14 May 40 R. Hudson
3 Aug 45 T. Williams
31 Oct 51 Sir T. Dugdale
28 Jul 54 D. Heathcoat Amory
6 Jan 58 J. Hare
27 Jul 60 C. Soames
18 Oct 64 F. Peart
6 Apr 68 C. Hughes
20 Jun 70 J. Prior
5 Nov 72 J. Godber
5 Mar 74 F. Peart
10 Sep 76 J. Silkin
5 May 79 P. Walker
11 Jun 83 M. Jopling
13 Jun 87 J. MacGregor
24 Jul 89 J. S. Gummer
27 May 93 Gillian Shephard
20 Jul 94 W. Waldegrave
5 Jul 95 D. Hogg
3 May 97 J.Cunningham
27 Jul 98 N.Brown

President of the Air Board

3 Jan 17 Ld Cowdray

(President of the Air Council)

26 Nov 17 Ld Rothermere
26 Apr 18 Ld Weir

(Secretary of State for Air)

10 Jan 19 W. Churchill
1 Apr 21 F. Guest
31 Oct 22 Sir S. Hoare
22 Jan 24 Ld Thomson
6 Nov 24 Sir S. Hoare
7 Jun 29 Ld Thomson
14 Oct 30 Ld Amulree
5 Nov 31 M of Londonderry
7 Jun 35 Sir P. Cunliffe-Lister *(Vt Swinton)*
16 May 38 Sir K. Wood
3 Apr 40 Sir S. Hoare
11 May 40 Sir A. Sinclair
25 May 45 H. Macmillan
3 Aug 45 Vt Stansgate
4 Oct 46 P. Noel-Baker
7 Oct 47 A. Henderson
31 Oct 51 Ld De L'Isle
20 Dec 55 N. Birch
16 Jan 57 G. Ward
28 Oct 60 J. Amery
16 Jul 62 H. Fraser
(office wound up 1 Apr 64)

Minister of Aircraft Production

14 May 40 Ld Beaverbrook
1 May 41 J. Moore-Brabazon
22 Feb 42 J. Llewellin
22 Nov 42 Sir S. Cripps
25 May 45 E. Brown
4 Aug 45 J. Wilmot
(office wound up 1 Apr 46)

Minister of State for the Armed Forces

29 May 81 P. Blaker
13 Jun 83 J. Stanley
13 Jun 87 A. Clark
25 Jul 88 A. Hamilton
27 May 93 J. Hanley
20 Jul 94 N. Soames
6 May 97 J. Reid
28 Jul 98 D. Henderson
27 Jul 99 J. Spellar

Minister for the Arts

20 Oct 64 Jennie Lee *(U-S)*
17 Feb 67 Jennie Lee *(Min)*
23 Jun 70 Vt Eccles
2 Dec 73 N. St John-Stevas
8 Mar 74 H. Jenkins
14 Apr 76 Ld Donaldson
5 May 79 N. St John-Stevas

5 Jun 81 P. Channon
13 Jun 83 E of Gowrie
2 Sep 85 R. Luce
26 Jul 90 D. Mellor
28 Nov 90 T. Renton
(11 Apr 92 under National Heritage)

Attorney-General

1900 Sir R. Webster
7 May 00 Sir R. Finlay
12 Dec 05 Sir J. Walton
28 Jan 08 Sir W. Robson
7 Oct 10 Sir R. Isaacs
19 Oct 13 Sir J. Simon
25 May 15 Sir E. Carson
3 Nov 15 Sir F. Smith
10 Jan 19 Sir G. Hewart
6 Mar 22 Sir E. Pollock
24 Oct 22 Sir D. Hogg
23 Jan 24 Sir P. Hastings
6 Nov 24 Sir D. Hogg
28 Mar 28 Sir T. Inskip
7 Jun 29 Sir W. Jowitt
26 Jan 32 Sir T. Inskip
18 Mar 36 Sir D. Somervell
25 May 45 Sir D. Maxwell-Fyfe
4 Aug 45 Sir H. Shawcross
24 Apr 51 Sir F. Soskice
3 Nov 51 Sir L. Heald
18 Oct 54 Sir R. Manningham-Buller
16 Jul 62 Sir J. Hobson
1 Oct 64 Sir E. Jones
23 Jun 70 Sir P. Rawlinson
7 Mar 74 S. Silkin
5 May 79 Sir M. Havers
13 Jun 87 Sir P. Mayhew
15 Apr 92 Sir N. Lyell
3 May 97 J. Morris
27 Jul 99 Ld Williams of Mostyn

Minister of Blockade

10 Dec 16 Ld R. Cecil
18 Jul 18 Sir L. Worthington-Evans
(office wound up 10 Jan 19)

Church Estates Commissioner

(see p. 70)

Minister of Civil Aviation

8 Oct 44 Vt Swinton
4 Aug 45 Ld Winster
4 Oct 46 Ld Nathan
31 May 48 Ld Pakenham
1 Jun 51 Ld Ogmore
31 Oct 51 J. Maclay
7 May 52 A. Lennox-Boyd

(Minister of Transport and Civil Aviation)

1 Oct 53 A. Lennox-Boyd
28 Jul 54 J. Boyd-Carpenter
20 Dec 55 H. Watkinson

(Minister of Aviation)

14 Oct 59 D. Sandys
27 Jul 60 P. Thorneycroft
16 Jul 62 J. Amery
18 Oct 64 R. Jenkins
23 Dec 65 F. Mulley
7 Jan 67 J. Stonehouse
(office absorbed into Min. of Technology 15 Feb 67)

Minister for Aviation (under Transport)

23 Jul 90 Ld Brabazon
15 Apr 92 E of Caithness
(12 Jan 94 office reduced to U-S level)

Minister of Aviation Supply

15 Oct 70 F. Corfield
(office absorbed into Min. of Defence 1 May 71)

Minister for the Civil Service

1 Nov 68 H. Wilson
19 Jun 70 E. Heath
4 Mar 74 H. Wilson
5 Apr 76 J. Callaghan
4 May 79 Margaret Thatcher
28 Nov 90 J. Major
2 May 97 T. Blair

(Minister for the Public Service)

10 Apr 92 W. Waldegrave
20 Jul 94 D. Hunt
5 Jul 95 R. Freeman
(office wound up May 2 1997)

Secretary of State for the Colonies

1900 J. Chamberlain
6 Oct 03 A. Lyttelton
10 Dec 05 E of Elgin
12 Apr 08 E of Crewe
3 Nov 10 L. Harcourt
25 May 15 A. Bonar Law
10 Dec 16 W. Long
10 Jan 19 Vt Milner
13 Feb 21 W. Churchill
24 Oct 22 D of Devonshire
22 Jan 24 J. Thomas
6 Nov 24 L. Amery
7 Jun 29 Ld Passfield
25 Aug 31 J. Thomas
5 Nov 31 Sir P. Cunliffe-Lister

7 Jun 35 M. MacDonald
22 Nov 35 J. Thomas
28 May 36 W. Ormsby-Gore
16 May 38 M. MacDonald
12 May 40 Ld Lloyd
8 Feb 41 Ld Moyne
22 Feb 42 Vt Cranborne
22 Nov 42 O. Stanley
3 Aug 45 G. Hall
4 Oct 46 A. Creech Jones
28 Feb 50 J. Griffiths
28 Oct 51 O. Lyttelton
28 Jul 54 A. Lennox-Boyd
14 Oct 59 I. Macleod
9 Oct 61 R. Maudling
13 Jul 62 D. Sandys
18 Oct 64 A. Greenwood
23 Dec 65 E of Longford
6 Apr 66 F. Lee
(office came under Commonwealth Affairs 1 Aug 66 and abolished 6 Jan 67)

Minister for Consumer Affairs (under Trade)

8 May 79 Sally Oppenheim
5 Mar 82 G. Vaughan
(office wound up 13 Jun 83)
20 Jul 94 Earl Ferrers
(office wound up 6 Jul 95)

Minister for Corporate Affairs (under Trade)

24 Jul 89 J. Redwood
(office vacant 15 Apr 92)

Minister for Co-ordination of Defence

13 Mar 36 Sir T. Inskip
29 Jan 39 Ld Chatfield

(Minister of Defence)

10 May 40 W. Churchill
27 Jul 45 C. Attlee
20 Dec 46 A. Alexander
28 Feb 50 E. Shinwell
28 Oct 51 W. Churchill
1 Mar 52 Earl Alexander of Tunis
18 Oct 54 H. Macmillan
7 Apr 55 S. Lloyd
20 Dec 55 Sir W. Monckton
18 Oct 56 A. Head
13 Jan 57 D. Sandys
14 Oct 59 H. Watkinson
13 Jul 62 P. Thorneycroft

(Secretary of State)

1 Apr 64 P. Thorneycroft
16 Oct 64 D. Healey
20 Jun 70 Ld Carrington[1]
8 Jan 74 I. Gilmour

5 Mar 74 R. Mason
10 Sep 76 F. Mulley
5 May 79 F. Pym
5 Jan 81 J. Nott
8 Jan 83 M. Heseltine
9 Jan 86 G. Younger
24 Jul 89 T. King
15 Apr 92 M. Rifkind
5 Jul 95 M. Portillo
2 May 97 G. Robertson (Ld)
11 Oct 99 G. Hoon

Minister of Defence for Administration

7 Jan 67 G. Reynolds
15 Jul 69 R. Hattersley
(office wound up 19 Jun 70)

Minister of State (Armed Forces)

29 May 81 P. Blaker
13 Jun 83 J. Stanley
13 Jun 87 A. Clark
25 Jul 88 A. Hamilton
27 May 92 J. Hanley
20 Jan 94 N. Soames
6 May 97 J. Reid
27 Jul 98 D. Henderson
29 Jul 99 J. Spellar

Minister of State for Defence Procurement

7 Apr 71 I. Gilmour
(office vacant 5 Nov 72)
29 May 81 Vt Trenchard
6 Jan 83 G. Pattie
11 Sep 84 A. Butler
2 Sep 85 N. Lamont
21 May 86 Ld Trefgarne
13 Jun 87 I. Stewart
24 Jul 89 A. Clark
15 Apr 92 J. Aitken
20 Jul 94 R. Freeman
5 Jul 95 J. Arbuthnot
6 May 97 Ld Gilbert
29 Jul 99 Lady Symons

Minister for Defence Support

2 Sep 85 Ld Trefgarne
(office wound up 10 Sep 86)

Minister of Defence for Air Force

1 Apr 64 H. Fraser
19 Oct 64 Ld Shackleton
(office wound up 7 Jan 67)

Minister of Defence for Army

1 Apr 64 J. Ramsden
19 Oct 64 F. Mulley
24 Dec 65 G. Reynolds
(office wound up 7 Jan 67)

[1] *Also Party Chairman*

Minister of Defence for Navy

1 Apr 64 Earl Jellicoe
19 Oct 64 C. Mayhew
19 Feb 66 J. Mallalieu
(office wound up 7 Jan 67)

Minister of Defence for Equipment

7 Jan 67 R. Mason
6 Apr 68 J. Morris
(office wound up 19 Jun 70)

Secretary of State for Dominion Affairs

11 Jun 25 L. Amery
7 Jun 29 Ld Passfield
5 Jun 30 J. Thomas
22 Nov 35 M. MacDonald
16 May 38 Ld Stanley
31 Oct 38 M. MacDonald
29 Jan 39 Sir T. Inskip
        (Vt Caldecote)
3 Sep 39 A. Eden
14 May 40 Vt Caldecote
3 Oct 40 Vt Cranborne
19 Feb 42 C. Attlee
24 Sep 43 Vt Cranborne
3 Aug 45 Vt Addison

(Secretary of State for Commonwealth Relations)

7 Jul 47 Vt Addison
7 Oct 47 P. Noel-Baker
28 Feb 50 P. Gordon-Walker
28 Oct 51 Ld Ismay
12 Mar 52 M of Salisbury
24 Nov 52 Vt Swinton
7 Apr 55 E of Home
27 Jul 60 D. Sandys
18 Oct 64 A. Bottomley

(Secretary of State for Commonwealth Affairs)

1 Aug 66 A. Bottomley
11 Aug 66 H. Bowden
29 Aug 67 G. Thomson
(17 Oct 68 office merged
with Foreign Office)

Minister of Economic Warfare

3 Sep 39 R. Cross
15 May 40 H. Dalton
22 Feb 42 Vt Wolmer (E of
        Selborne)
(office wound up 23 May 45)

President of the Board of Education

1 Jan 00 D of Devonshire
8 Aug 02 M of Londonderry
10 Dec 05 A. Birrell
23 Jan 07 R. McKenna

12 Apr 08 W. Runciman
23 Oct 11 J. Pease
25 May 15 A. Henderson
18 Aug 16 M of Crewe
10 Dec 16 H. Fisher
24 Oct 22 E. Wood
22 Jan 24 C. Trevelyan
6 Nov 24 Ld E. Percy
7 Jun 29 Sir C. Trevelyan
2 Mar 31 H. Lees-Smith
25 Aug 31 Sir D. Maclean
15 Jun 32 Ld Irwin
        (Vt Halifax)
7 Jun 35 O. Stanley
28 May 37 Earl Stanhope
27 Oct 38 Earl De La Warr
3 Apr 40 H. Ramsbotham
20 Jul 41 R. Butler

(Minister of Education)

3 Aug 44 R. Butler
25 May 45 R. Law
3 Aug 45 Ellen Wilkinson
10 Feb 47 G. Tomlinson
2 Nov 51 Florence Horsbrugh
18 Oct 54 Sir D. Eccles
13 Jan 57 Vt Hailsham (2nd)
17 Sep 57 G. Lloyd
14 Oct 59 Sir D. Eccles
13 Jul 62 Sir E. Boyle

(Secretary of State for Education and Science)

1 Apr 64 Q. Hogg
18 Oct 64 M. Stewart
22 Jan 65 A. Crosland
29 Aug 67 P. Gordon-Walker
6 Apr 68 E. Short
20 Jun 70 Margaret Thatcher
5 Mar 74 R. Prentice
10 Jun 75 F. Mulley
10 Sep 76 Shirley Williams
5 May 79 M. Carlisle
14 Sep 81 Sir K. Joseph
21 May 86 K. Baker
24 Jul 89 J. MacGregor
2 Nov 90 K. Clarke

(Secretary of State for Education)

15 Apr 92 J. Patten

(Secretary of State for Education and Employment)

20 Jul 94 Gillian Shephard
2 May 97 D. Blunkett

Secretary of State for Employment and Productivity

6 Apr 68 Barbara Castle
20 Jun 70 R. Carr

(Secretary of State for Employment)

12 Nov 70 R. Carr
7 Apr 72 M. Macmillan
2 Dec 73 W. Whitelaw
5 Mar 74 M. Foot
8 Apr 76 A. Booth
5 May 79 J. Prior
14 Sep 81 N. Tebbit
16 Oct 83 T. King
2 Sep 85 Ld Young of
        Graffham
13 Jun 87 N. Fowler
3 Jan 90 M. Howard
12 Apr 92 Gillian Shephard
27 May 93 D. Hunt
(office merged with Education
20 Jul 94)

Secretary of State for Energy

8 Jan 74 Ld Carrington
5 Mar 74 E. Varley
10 Jun 75 A. Benn
5 May 79 D. Howell
14 Sep 81 N. Lawson
11 Jun 83 P. Walker
13 Jun 87 C. Parkinson
24 Jul 89 J. Wakeham
(office merged with Trade
15 Apr 92)

Minister for Energy (under Trade)

15 Apr 92 T. Eggar
(Industry and Energy 20 Jul 94)

Secretary of State for the Environment

15 Oct 70 P. Walker
5 Nov 72 G. Rippon
5 Mar 74 A. Crosland
8 Apr 76 P. Shore
5 May 79 M. Heseltine
6 Jan 83 T. King
11 Jun 83 P. Jenkin
2 Sep 85 K. Baker
21 May 86 N. Ridley
24 Jul 89 C. Patten
28 Nov 90 M. Heseltine
11 Apr 92 M. Howard
27 May 93 J. S. Gummer

(Environment, Transport and the Regions)

2 May 97 J. Prescott

Minister for Environment (under Environment)

27 Mar 85 Ld Elton
10 Sep 86 W. Waldegrave
13 Jun 87 Ld Belstead
25 Jul 88 M. Howard

24 Jul 89   D. Trippier
14 Apr 92   D. Maclean
27 May 93   T. Yeo
8 Jan 94   R. Atkins
6 Juk 95   Earl Ferrers
3 May 97   M. Meacher

Minister of Food Control

10 Dec 16   Vt Devonport
19 Jun 17   Ld Rhondda *(Vt)*
9 Jul 18   J. Clynes
10 Jan 19   G. Roberts
19 Mar 20   C. McCurdy
(office wound up 31 Mar 21)

Minister of Food

4 Sep 39   W. Morrison
3 Apr 40   Ld Woolton
11 Nov 43   J. Llewellin
3 Aug 45   Sir B. Smith
27 May 46   J. Strachey
28 Feb 50   M. Webb
31 Oct 51   G. Lloyd-George
18 Oct 54   D. Heathcoat-Amory
*(and combined with Agriculture
and Fisheries)*

Foreign Affairs

(See p.56)

Minister of Fuel, Light and Power

3 Jun 42   G. Lloyd-George

(Minister of Fuel and Power)

25 May 45   G. Lloyd-George
3 Aug 45   E. Shinwell
7 Oct 47   H. Gaitskell
28 Feb 50   P. Noel-Baker
31 Oct 51   G. Lloyd
20 Dec 55   A. Jones

(Minister of Power)

13 Jan 57   Ld Mills
14 Oct 59   R. Wood
20 Oct 63   F. Erroll
18 Oct 64   F. Lee
6 Apr 66   R. Marsh
6 Apr 68   R. Gunter
6 Jul 68   R. Mason
*(office absorbed into
Technology 6 Oct 69)*

Minister of Health

24 Jun 19   C. Addison
1 Apr 21   Sir A. Mond
24 Oct 22   Sir A. Griffith-
            Boscawen
7 Mar 23   N. Chamberlain
27 Aug 23   Sir W. Joynson-Hicks
22 Jan 24   J. Wheatley
6 Nov 24   N. Chamberlain

7 Jun 29   A. Greenwood
25 Aug 31   N. Chamberlain
5 Nov 31   Sir E. Young
7 Jun 35   Sir K. Wood
16 May 38   W. Elliot
13 May 40   M. MacDonald
8 Feb 41   E. Brown
11 Nov 43   H. Willink
3 Aug 45   A. Bevan
17 Jan 51   H. Marquand
30 Oct 51   H. Crookshank
7 May 52   I. Macleod
20 Dec 55   R. Turton
16 Jan 57   D. Vosper
17 Sep 57   D. Walker-Smith
27 Jul 60   E. Powell
20 Oct 63   A. Barber
18 Oct 64   K. Robinson
*(combined with Ministry of Social
Security 1 Nov 68–25 Jul 88. See
Social Services and Health) (See
below, under Local Government
and under Social Services)*

Secretary of State for Health

5 Jul 88   K. Clarke
2 Nov 90   W. Waldegrave
10 Apr 92   Virginia Bottomley
5 Jul 95   S. Dorrell
2 May 97   F. Dobson
11 Oct 99   A. Milburn

Minister for Health (under Social Services)

7 May 79   G. Vaughan
5 Mar 82   K. Clarke
2 Sep 85   B. Hayhoe
11 Sep 84   A. Newton
10 Sep 86   D. Mellor

(under Health)

25 Jul 89   Ld Trafford
28 Oct 89   Virginia Bottomley
15 Apr 92   B. Mawhinney
20 Jul 94   G. Malone
6 May 97   Lady Jay
28 Jul 98   Lady Hayman
29 Jul 99   Tessa Jowell

Home Office

(See p. 56)

Minister of Housing (under Local Government and under Environment)

7 May 79   J. Stanley
13 Jun 83   I. Gow
2 Sep 85   J. Patten
13 Jun 87   W. Waldegrave
25 Jul 88   E of Caithness
25 Jul 89   M. Howard
3 Jan 90   M. Spicer
28 Nov 90   Sir G. Young

Secretary of State for India (and Burma 1937–48)

1900   Ld G. Hamilton
6 Oct 03   St J. Brodrick
10 Dec 05   J. Morley *(Vt)*
3 Nov 10   E of Crewe
7 Mar 11   J. Morley
25 May 11   E of Crewe *(M)*
25 May 15   A. Chamberlain
17 Jul 17   E. Montagu
19 Mar 22   Vt Peel
22 Jan 24   Ld Olivier
6 Nov 24   E of Birkenhead
18 Oct 28   Vt Peel
7 Jun 29   W. Benn
25 Aug 31   Sir S. Hoare
7 Jun 35   M of Zetland
13 May 40   L. Amery
3 Aug 45   Ld Pethick-Lawrence
17 Apr 47   E of Listowel
*(4 Jan 1948 India & Burma
Offices wound up)*

Minister for Industrial Development

7 Apr 72   C. Chataway
(office abolished 5 Mar 74)

Minister for Industry (under Trade & Industry)

15 Oct 70   Sir J. Eden
7 Apr 72   T. Boardman
(office abolished 8 Jan 74)

Secretary of State for Industry, Trade and Regional Development

20 Oct 63   E. Heath
(office abolished 16 Oct 64)

Secretary of State for Industry

5 Mar 74   A. Benn
10 Jun 75   E. Varley
5 May 79   Sir K. Joseph
14 Sep 81   P. Jenkin
*(11 Jun 83 office merged with
Trade)*

Minister for Industry and Information Technology

13 Jun 83   K. Baker
11 Sep 84   G. Pattie
(office wound up 13 Jun 87)

Minister for Industry (under Trade and Industry)

13 Jun 83   N. Lamont
2 Sep 85   P. Morrison
13 Jun 87   K. Clarke
24 Jul 88   A. Newton
25 Jul 89   D. Hogg
2 Nov 90   Ld Hesketh

(office vacant 23 May 91)
15 Apr 92 T. Sainsbury

Minister for Industry and Energy

20 Jul 94 T. Eggar
5 Jul 95 G. Knight
6 May 97 J. Battle

Minister of Information

10 Feb 18 Ld Beaverbrook
4 Nov 18 Ld Downham
(office wound up 10 Jan 19)
4 Sep 39 Ld Macmillan
5 Jan 40 Sir J. Reith
12 May 40 A. Duff Cooper
20 Jul 41 B. Bracken
25 May 45 G. Lloyd
4 Aug 45 E. Williams
24 Feb 46 E of Listowel
(office wound up 31 Mar 46)

International Development

2 May 97 Clare Short

Chief Secretary for Ireland

1900 G. Balfour
7 Nov 00 G. Wyndham
12 Mar 05 W. Long
10 Dec 05 J. Bryce
23 Jan 07 A. Birrell
31 Jul 16 (Sir) H. Duke
5 May 18 E. Shortt
10 Jan 19 I. Macpherson
2 Apr 20 Sir H. Greenwood
(post vacant 19 Oct 22,
office abolished 6 Dec 22)

Lord Chancellor of Ireland

1900 Ld Ashbourne
12 Dec 05 Sir S. Walker
26 Sep 11 K. Barry
10 Apr 13 (Sir) I. O'Brien
4 Jun 18 Sir J. Campbell
27 Jun 21 Sir J. Ross
(ceased to be executive
office 27 Jun 21)

Lord Lieutenant of Ireland

(office in Cabinet only Jun 95–
8 Aug 02 and 8 Oct 19–2 Apr 21.
See p.461)

Attorney-General for Ireland

1900 J. Atkinson
4 Dec 05 J. Campbell
20 Dec 05 R. Cherry
2 Dec 09 R. Barry
26 Sep 11 C. O'Connor
24 Jun 12 I. O'Brien
10 Apr 13 T. Molony

20 Jun 13 J. Moriarty
1 Jul 14 J. Pim
8 Jun 15 J. Gordon
9 Apr 16 J. Campbell
8 Jan 17 J. O'Connor
7 Apr 18 A. Samuels
6 Jul 19 D. Henry
5 Aug 21 T. Brown
(post vacant 16 Nov 21)

Solicitor-General for Ireland

1900 D. Barton
30 Jan 00 G. Wright
8 Jan 03 J. Campbell
20 Dec 05 R. Barry
2 Dec 09 C. O'Connor
19 Oct 11 I. O'Brien
24 Jun 12 T. Molony
25 Apr 13 J. Moriarty
20 Jun 13 J. Pim
1 Jul 14 J. O'Connor
19 Mar 17 J. Chambers
12 Sep 17 A. Samuels
7 Apr 18 J. Powell
27 Nov 18 D. Henry
6 Jul 19 D. Wilson
2 Jun 21 T. Brown
(post vacant 5 Aug 21)

Minister of Labour

10 Dec 16 J. Hodge
17 Aug 17 G. Roberts
10 Jan 19 Sir R. Horne
19 Mar 20 T. Macnamara
31 Oct 22 Sir A. Montague-
Barlow
22 Jan 24 T. Shaw
6 Nov 24 Sir A. Steel-
Maitland
7 Jun 29 Margaret Bondfield
25 Aug 31 Sir H. Betterton
29 Jun 34 O. Stanley
7 Jun 35 E. Brown

(Minister of Labour and National Service)

3 Sep 39 E. Brown
13 May 40 E. Bevin
25 May 45 R. Butler
3 Aug 45 G. Isaacs
17 Jan 51 A. Bevan
24 Apr 51 A. Robens
28 Oct 51 Sir W. Monckton
20 Dec 55 I. Macleod
14 Oct 59 E. Heath

(Minister of Labour)

12 Nov 59 E. Heath
27 Jul 60 J. Hare
20 Oct 63 J. Godber
18 Oct 64 R. Gunter

(6 Apr 68 office reorganised
as Ministry of Employment
and Productivity)

Chancellor of the Duchy of Lancaster

1900 Ld James of Hereford
8 Aug 02 Sir W. Walrond
10 Dec 05 Sir H. Fowler
(Vt Wolverhampton)
13 Oct 08 Ld Fitzmaurice
15 Jun 09 H. Samuel
14 Feb 10 J. Pease
23 Oct 11 C. Hobhouse
11 Feb 14 C. Masterman
3 Feb 15 E. Montagu
25 May 15 W. Churchill
25 Nov 15 H. Samuel
11 Jan 16 E. Montagu
9 Jul 16 T. McKinnon Wood
10 Dec 16 Sir F. Cawley
10 Feb 18 Ld Beaverbrook
4 Nov 18 Ld Downham
10 Jan 19 E of Crawford
1 Apr 21 Vt Peel
7 Apr 22 Sir W. Sutherland
24 Oct 22 M of Salisbury
25 May 23 J. Davidson
22 Jan 24 J. Wedgwood
10 Nov 24 Vt Cecil
19 Oct 27 Ld Cushendun
7 Jun 29 Sir O. Mosley
23 May 30 C. Attlee
13 May 31 Ld Ponsonby
25 Aug 31 M of Lothian
10 Nov 31 (Sir) J. Davidson
28 May 37 Earl Winterton
29 Jan 39 W. Morrison
3 Apr 40 G. Tryon
14 May 40 Ld Hankey
20 Jul 41 A. Duff Cooper
11 Nov 43 E. Brown
25 May 45 Sir A. Salter
4 Aug 45 J. Hynd
27 Apr 47 Ld Pakenham
11 May 48 H. Dalton
28 Feb 50 Vt Alexander
31 Oct 51 Vt Swinton
24 Nov 52 Ld Woolton[1]
20 Dec 55 E of Selkirk
13 Jan 57 C. Hill
9 Oct 61 I. Macleod[1]
20 Oct 63 Ld Blakenham[1]
18 Oct 64 D. Houghton
6 Apr 66 G. Thomson
7 Jan 67 F. Lee
6 Oct 69 G. Thomson
20 Jun 70 A. Barber
28 Jul 70 G. Rippon
5 Nov 72 J. Davies
5 Mar 74 H. Lever

[1]*Also Party Chairman*

5 May 79 N. St John-Stevas
5 Jan 81 F. Pym
14 Sep 81 Lady Young
6 Apr 82 C. Parkinson[1]
11 Jun 83 Ld Cockfield
11 Sep 84 E of Gowrie
3 Sep 85 N. Tebbit[1]
13 Jun 87 K. Clarke
25 Jul 88 A. Newton
24 Jul 89 K. Baker[1]
28 Nov 90 C. Patten[1]
11 Apr 92 W. Waldegrave
20 Jul 94 D. Hunt
5 Jul 95 R. Freeman
3 May 97 D. Clark
(and Min. for Public Service)
27 Jul 98 J. Cunningham
(and Min. for Cabinet Office)
11 Oct 99 Mo Mowlam

President of the Local Government Board

1900 H. Chaplin
7 Nov 00 W. Long
12 Mar 05 G. Balfour
10 Dec 05 J. Burns
11 Feb 14 H. Samuel
25 May 15 W. Long
10 Dec 16 Ld Rhondda
28 Jun 17 W. Hayes Fisher
4 Nov 18 Sir A.Geddes
10 Jan 19 C. Addison
(24 Jun 19 the Local Government Board became the Ministry of Health)

Secretary of State for Health and Social Security

5 May 79 P. Jenkin
14 Sep 81 N. Fowler
13 Jun 87 J. Moore

Secretary of State for Health

25 Jul 88 K. Clarke
2 Nov 90 W. Waldegrave
11 Apr 92 Virginia Bottomley
5 Jul 95 S. Dorrell
2 May 97 F. Dobson

Minister of Land and Natural Resources

17 Oct 64 F. Willey
(17 Feb 67 office wound up)

Minister for Planning and Land

1 Nov 68 K. Robinson
(6 Oct 69 office wound up)

Minister of Local Government and Planning

1 Jan 51 H. Dalton
(30 Oct 51 office wound up)

(Minister of Housing and Local Government)

30 Oct 51 H. Macmillan
18 Oct 54 D. Sandys
13 Jan 57 H. Brooke
9 Oct 61 C. Hill
13 Jul 62 Sir K. Joseph
18 Oct 64 R. Crossman
11 Aug 66 A. Greenwood
31 May 70 R. Mellish
20 Jun 70 P. Walker
(15 Oct 70 reorganised as Local Government and Development under Dept. of Environment)

Minister for Local Government and Development

15 Oct 70 G. Page
(office wound up 5 Mar 74)

Minister for Planning and Local Government

7 Mar 74 J. Silkin
(office wound up 10 Sep 76)

Minister for Housing and Construction

15 Oct 70 J. Amery
5 Nov 72 P. Channon
7 Mar 74 R. Freeson
7 May 79 J. Stanley
13 Jun 83 I. Gow
2 Sep 85 J. Patten
13 Jun 87 W. Waldegrave
13 Jul 88 E of Caithness
25 Jul 89 M. Spicer
28 Nov 90 Sir G. Young

Minister for Local Government (under Environment)

6 May 79 T. King
6 Jan 83 Ld Bellwin
11 Sep 84 K. Baker
2 Sep 85 W. Waldegrave
10 Sep 86 R. Boyson
13 Jun 87 M. Howard
25 Jul 88 J. S. Gummer[1]
25 Jul 89 D. Hunt
4 May 90 M. Portillo
15 Apr 92 J. Redwood
27 May 93 D. Curry
6 May 97 Hilary Armstrong

Lord Advocate

(see below, Scotland)

Minister of Materials

6 Jul 51 R. Stokes
31 Oct 51 Vt Swinton
24 Nov 52 Sir A. Salter

1 Sep 53 Ld Woolton
(16 Aug 54 office wound up)

Minister of Munitions

25 May 15 D. Lloyd George
9 Jul 16 E. Montagu
10 Dec 16 C. Addison
17 Jul 17 W. Churchill
10 Jan 19 Ld Inverforth
(and Minister designate for Ministry of Supply. Office abolished 21 Mar 21)

Secretary of State for National Heritage

11 Apr 92 D. Mellor
24 Sep 92 P. Brooke
20 Jul 94 S. Dorrell
5 Jul 95 Virginia Bottomley
3 May 97 C. Smith
(Changed to Min. of Culture, Sport and the Arts Jul 97)

Minister of National Service

19 Aug 16 N. Chamberlain
17 Aug 17 Sir A. Geddes
(office abolished Aug 19)

Secretary of State for Northern Ireland

24 Apr 72 W. Whitelaw
2 Dec 73 F. Pym
5 Mar 74 M. Rees
10 Sep 76 R. Mason
5 May 79 H. Atkins
14 Sep 81 J. Prior
11 Sep 84 D. Hurd
3 Sep 85 T. King
24 Jul 89 P. Brooke
15 Apr 92 Sir P. Mayhew
3 May 97 Mo Mowlam
11 Oct 99 P. Mandelson

Minister of (for) Overseas Development

18 Oct 64 Barbara Castle
23 Dec 65 A. Greenwood
11 Aug 66 A. Bottomley
29 Aug 67 R. Prentice
6 Oct 69 Judith Hart
23 Jun 70 R. Wood
7 Mar 74 Judith Hart
10 Jun 75 R. Prentice
21 Dec 76 F. Judd
21 Feb 77 Judith Hart
6 May 79 N. Marten
6 Jan 83 T. Raison
10 Sep 86 C. Patten
24 Jul 89– Lynda (Lady)
2 May 97 Chalker
(from 10 Jun 75 the Foreign

[1]*Also Party Chairman*

Secretary became technically Minister of Overseas Development while the Minister for Overseas Development took day-to-day charge of the Department. It ceased to be a separate Department from 5 May 79 to 3 May 97 when it was reconstituted; see International Development)

Paymaster-General

1900	D of Marlborough
11 Mar 02	Sir S. Crossley
12 Dec 05	R. Causton *(Ld Southwark)*
23 Feb 10	I. Guest *(Ld Ashby St Ledgers)*
23 May 12	Ld Strachie
9 Jun 15	Ld Newton
18 Aug 16	A. Henderson
15 Dec 16	Sir J. Compton-Rickett
26 Oct 19	Sir T. Walters
24 Oct 22	*(office vacant)*
5 Feb 23	N. Chamberlain
15 Mar 23	Sir W. Joynson-Hicks
25 May 23	A. Boyd-Carpenter
22 Jan 24	*(office vacant)*
6 May 24	H. Gosling
6 Nov 24	*(office vacant)*
28 Jul 25	D of Sutherland
2 Dec 28	E of Onslow
7 Jun 29	Ld Arnold
6 Mar 31	*(office vacant)*
4 Sep 31	Sir T.Walters
23 Nov 31	Ld Rochester
6 Dec 35	Ld Hutchison
2 Jun 38	E of Munster
29 Jan 39	Earl Winterton
Nov 39	*(office vacant)*
15 May 40	Vt Cranborne
3 Oct 40	*(office vacant)*
20 Jul 41	Ld Hankey
4 Mar 42	Sir W. Jowitt
30 Dec 42	Ld Cherwell
3 Aug 45	*(office vacant)*
9 Jul 46	A. Greenwood
5 Mar 47	H. Marquand
2 Jul 48	Vt Addison
1 Apr 49	Ld Macdonald
30 Oct 51	Ld Cherwell
11 Nov 53	E of Selkirk
20 Dec 55	*(office vacant)*
18 Oct 56	Sir W. Monckton
16 Jan 57	R Maudling
14 Oct 59	Ld Mills
9 Oct 61	H. Brooke
13 Jul 62	J. Boyd-Carpenter
19 Oct 64	G. Wigg
12 Nov 67	*(office vacant)*
6 Apr 68	Ld Shackleton

1 Nov 68	Judith Hart
6 Oct 69	H. Lever
23 Jun 70	Vt Eccles
2 Dec 73	M. Macmillan
7 Mar 74	E. Dell
8 Apr 76	Shirley Williams
5 May 79	A. Maude
5 Jan 81	F. Pym
14 Sep 81	C. Parkinson[1]
11 Jun 83	*(office vacant)*
11 Sep 84	J. S. Gummer
2 Sep 85	K. Clarke
13 Jun 87	P. Brooke[1]
24 Jul 89	E of Caithness
24 Jul 90	R. Ryder
28 Nov 90	Ld Belstead
15 Apr 92	Sir J. Cope
20 Jul 94	D. Heathcoat-Amory
20 Jul 96	D. Willetts
16 Dec 96	M. Bates
3 May 97	G. Robinson
4 Jan 99	Dawn Primarolo

Minister of Pensions

10 Sep 16	G. Barnes
17 Aug 17	J. Hodge
10 Jan 19	Sir L. Worthington-Evans
2 Apr 20	I. Macpherson
31 Oct 22	G. Tryon
23 Jan 24	F. Roberts
11 Nov 24	G. Tryon
7 Jun 29	F. Roberts
3 Sep 31	G. Tryon
18 Jun 35	R. Hudson
30 Jul 36	H. Ramsbotham
7 Jun 39	Sir W.Womersley
3 Aug 45	W. Paling
17 Apr 47	J. Hynd
7 Oct 47	G. Buchanan
2 Jul 48	H. Marquand
17 Jan 51	G. Isaacs
5 Nov 51	D. Heathcoat-Amory

(Minister of Pensions and National Insurance)

3 Sep 53	O. Peake
20 Dec 55	J. Boyd-Carpenter
16 Jul 62	N. Macpherson
21 Oct 63	R. Wood
18 Oct 64	Margaret Herbison

(6 Aug 66 recast as Social Security)

Minister of Social Insurance

8 Oct 44	Sir W. Jowitt

(Minister of National Insurance)

17 Nov 44	Sir W. Jowitt
25 May 45	L. Hore-Belisha
4 Aug 45	J. Griffiths
28 Feb 50	Edith Summerskill

31 Oct 51	O. Peake

(3 Sep 53 combined with Ministry of Pensions)

Minister without Portfolio

25 May 15–5 Dec 16	M of Lansdowne
10 Dec 16–12 Aug 17	A. Henderson
10 Dec 16–18 Apr 18	Vt Milner
22 Jun 17–10 Jan 19	J. Smuts
17 Jul 17–21 Jan 18	Sir E. Carson
13 Aug 17–27 Jan 20	G. Barnes
28 Apr 18–10 Jan 19	A. Chamberlain
10 Jan 19–19 May 19	Sir E. Geddes
2 Apr 20–13 Feb 21	Sir L. Worthington-Evans
1 April 21–14 Jul 21	C. Addison
7 Jun 35–22 Dec 35	A. Eden
7 Jun 35–31 Mar 36	Ld E. Percy
21 Apr 39–14 Jul 39	L. Burgin
3 Sep 39–10 May 40	Ld Hankey
11 May 40–22 Feb 42	A. Greenwood
30 Dec 42–8 Oct 44	Sir W. Jowitt
4 Oct 46–20 Dec 46	A. Alexander
17 Apr 47–29 Sep 47	A. Greenwood
18 Oct 54–11 Jun 57	E of Munster
11 Jun 57–23 Oct 58	Ld Mancroft
23 Oct 58–9 Oct 61	E of Dundee
9 Oct 61–14 Jul 62	Ld Mills
13 Jul 62–16 Oct 64	W. Deedes
20 Oct 63–16 Oct 64	Ld Carrington
19 Oct 64–6 Apr 66	E. Fletcher
21 Oct 64–7 Jan 67	Ld Champion
6 Apr 66–7 Jan 67	D. Houghton
7 Jan 67–29 Aug 67	P. Gordon Walker

[1] *Also Party Chairman*

7 Jan 67–16 Jan 68
    Ld Shackleton
17 Oct 68–6 Oct 69
    G. Thomson
6 Oct 69–19 Jun 70
    P. Shore
15 Oct 70–8 Jan 74
    Ld Drumalbyn
8 Jan 74–4 Mar 74
    Ld Aberdare
11 Sep 84–5 Sep 85
    Ld Young
20 Jul 94–5 Jul 95
    J. Hanley[1]
5 Jul 95–2 May 97
    B. Mawhinney[1]
3 May 97–27 Jul 98
    P. Mandelson

Secretary of State for Prices and Consumer Protection

5 Mar 74 Shirley Williams
10 Sep 76 R. Hattersley
(office wound up 5 May 79)

Minister for Consumer Affairs (under Trade)

6 May 79 Sally Oppenheim
5 Mar 82 G. Vaughan
(13 Jun 83 office wound up)

Postmaster-General

1900 D of Norfolk
2 Apr 00 M of Londonderry
8 Aug 02 A. Chamberlain
6 Oct 03 Ld Stanley
10 Dec 05 S. Buxton
14 Feb 10 H. Samuel
11 Feb 14 C. Hobhouse
26 May 15 H. Samuel
18 Jan 16 J. Pease
10 Dec 16 A. Illingworth
1 Apr 21 F. Kellaway
31 Oct 22 N. Chamberlain
7 Mar 23 Sir W. Joynson-Hicks
28 May 23 Sir L. Worthington-Evans
22 Jan 24 V. Hartshorn
11 Nov 24 Sir W. Mitchell-Thomson
7 Jun 29 H. Lees-Smith
2 Mar 31 C. Attlee
3 Sep 31 W. Ormsby-Gore
10 Nov 31 Sir K. Wood
7 Jun 35 G. Tryon
3 Apr 40 W. Morrison
30 Dec 42 H. Crookshank
4 Aug 45 E of Listowel
17 Apr 47 W. Paling
28 Feb 50 N. Edwards
5 Nov 51 Earl De La Warr

7 Apr 55 C. Hill
16 Jan 57 E. Marples
22 Oct 59 R. Bevins
19 Oct 64 A. Wedgwood Benn
4 Jul 66 E. Short
6 Apr 68 R. Mason
1 Jul 68 J. Stonehouse
(Post Office became a Public Corporation 1 Oct 69)

(Minister of Posts and Telecommunications)

1 Oct 69 J. Stonehouse
24 Jun 70 C. Chataway
7 Apr 72 Sir J. Eden
9 Mar 74 T. Benn
(29 Mar 74 office abolished)

Minister of Public Building and Works

16 Jul 62 G. Rippon
18 Oct 64 C. Pannell
6 Apr 66 R. Prentice
29 Aug 67 R. Mellish
30 Apr 69 J. Silkin
23 Jun 70 J. Amery
(15 Oct 70 reorganised as Housing and Construction under Environment. See Local Government)

Minister of Public Transport (under Transport)

23 Jul 88 M. Portillo
4 May 90 R. Freeman

Minister Resident in Middle East

19 Feb 42 O. Lyttelton
19 Mar 42 R. Casey

(Minister of State in Middle East)

28 Jan 44 Ld Moyne
21 Nov 44 Sir E. Grigg
(office abolished 27 Jul 45)

Minister Resident at Allied H.Q. in N.W. Africa

30 Dec 42 H. Macmillan
(office abolished 23 May 45)

Minister Resident in W. Africa

8 Jun 42 Vt Swinton
21 Nov 44 H. Balfour
(office abolished 27 Jul 45)

Minister Resident in Washington for Supply

22 Nov 42 J. Llewellin
11 Nov 43 B. Smith
(office abolished 23 May 45)

Minister of Reconstruction

17 Jul 17–10 Jan 19
    C. Addison
10 Jan 19–Aug 19
    Sir A. Geddes
11 Nov 43–23 May 45
    Ld Woolton

Minister for Science

14 Oct 59 Vt Hailsham
(1 Apr 64 combined with Dept. of Education)

Secretary for Scotland

1900 Ld Balfour
6 Oct 03 A. Murray
2 Feb 05 M of Linlithgow
10 Dec 05 J. Sinclair *(Ld Pentland)*
13 Feb 12 T. McKinnon Wood
9 Jul 16 H. Tennant
10 Dec 16 R. Munro
24 Oct 22 Vt Novar
22 Jan 24 W. Adamson
6 Nov 24 Sir J. Gilmour

(Secretary of State for Scotland)

15 Jul 26 Sir J. Gilmour
7 Jun 29 W. Adamson
25 Aug 31 Sir A. Sinclair
28 Sep 32 Sir G. Collins
29 Oct 36 W. Elliot
16 May 38 J. Colville
14 May 40 E. Brown
8 Feb 41 T. Johnston
25 May 45 E of Rosebery
3 Aug 45 J. Westwood
7 Oct 47 A. Woodburn
28 Feb 50 H. McNeil
30 Oct 51 J. Stuart
13 Jan 57 J. Maclay
13 Jul 62 M. Noble
18 Oct 64 W. Ross
19 Jun 70 G. Campbell
5 Mar 74 W. Ross
8 Apr 76 B. Millan
5 May 79 G. Younger
11 Jan 86 M. Rifkind
28 Nov 90 I. Lang
5 Jul 95 M. Forsyth
2 May 97 D. Dewar
17 May 99 J. Reid

Lord Advocate

1900 A. Murray
18 Oct 03 S. Dickson
12 Dec 05 T. Shaw
14 Feb 09 A. Ure
30 Oct 13 R. Munro
10 Dec 16 J. Clyde
25 Mar 20 T. Morison
5 Mar 22 C. Murray

[1] *Also Party Chairman*

24 Oct 22 W. Watson
8 Feb 24 H. Macmillan
11 Nov 24 W. Watson
23 Apr 29 A. MacRobert
17 Jun 29 C. Aitchison
2 Oct 33 W. Normand
28 Mar 35 D. Jamieson
25 Oct 35 T. Cooper
5 Jun 41 J. Reid
10 Aug 45 G. Thomson
7 Oct 47 J. Wheatley
2 Nov 51 J. Clyde
30 Dec 54 W. Milligan
5 Apr 60 W. Grant
12 Oct 62 I. Shearer
20 Oct 64 G. Stott
26 Oct 67 H. S. Wilson *(Ld)*
23 Jun 70 N. Wylie
8 Mar 74 R. King Murray
7 May 79 J. Mackay *(Ld)*
16 May 84 Ld Cameron of
        Lochbroom
4 Jan 89 Ld Fraser of
        Carmyllie
15 Apr 92 A. Rodger *(Ld)*
4 May 95 Ld Mackay of
        Drumadoon
7 May 97 Ld Hardie
(no longer a UK office 17 May 99)

Solicitor-General for Scotland

1900 S. Dickson
18 Oct 03 D. Dundas
30 Jan 05 E. Salvesen
16 Oct 05 J. Clyde
18 Dec 05 A. Ure
18 Feb 08 A. Dewar
18 Apr 10 W. Hunter
3 Dec 11 A. Anderson
30 Oct 13 T. Morison
25 Mar 20 C. Murray
16 Mar 22 A. Briggs Constable
24 Jul 22 W. Watson
6 Nov 22 D. Fleming
5 Apr 23 F. Thomson
18 Feb 24 J. Fenton
11 Nov 24 D. Fleming
30 Dec 25 A. MacRobert
23 Apr 29 W. Normand
17 Jun 29 J. Watson
10 Nov 31 W. Normand
2 Oct 33 D. Jamieson
15 May 35 T. Cooper
29 Nov 35 A. Russell
25 Jun 36 J. Reid
5 Jun 41 (Sir) D. Murray
10 Sep 45 D. Blades
19 Mar 47 J. Wheatley
24 Oct 47 D. Johnston
3 Nov 51 W. Milligan
10 Jan 55 W. Grant
11 May 60 D. Anderson
27 Apr 64 N. Wylie

20 Oct 64 J. Leechman
11 Oct 65 H.S. Wilson
26 Oct 67 E. Stewart
23 Jun 70 D. Brand
5 Nov 72 I. Stewart
14 Mar 74 J. McCluskey *(Ld)*
7 May 79 N. Fairbairn
28 Jan 82 P. Fraser
4 Jan 89 A. Rodger
15 Apr 92 T. Dawson
4 May 95 D. Mackay
7 May 97 C. Boyd
29 Jul 99 Lynda Clark
(no longer a UK office 17 May 99)

Minister of Shipping

10 Dec 16 Sir J. Maclay*(Ld)*
(office wound up 31 Mar 21)
13 Oct 39 Sir J. Gilmour
3 Apr 40 R. Hudson
14 May 40 R. Cross
(1 May 41 combined with
Ministry of Transport to form
Ministry of War Transport)

Minister of Social Security

6 Aug 66 Margaret Herbison
26 Jul 67 Judith Hart

(Secretary of State for Social Services) (& Head of the Department of Health and Social Security)

17 Oct 68 R. Crossman
20 Jun 70 Sir K. Joseph
5 Mar 74 Barbara Castle
8 Apr 76 D. Ennals
5 May 79 P. Jenkin
14 Sep 81 N. Fowler
13 Jun 87 J. Moore
(office recast 25 Jul 88)
(see Health)

Secretary of State for Social Security

25 Jul 88 J. Moore
23 Jul 89 A. Newton
11 Apr 92 P. Lilley
2 May 97 Harriet Harman
27 Jul 98 A. Darling

Minister for Social Security (under Social Services)

10 Sep 76 S. Orme
7 May 79 R. Prentice
8 Jan 81 H. Rossi
13 Jun 83 R. Boyson
11 Sep 84 A. Newton
10 Sep 86 J. Major
13 Jun 87 N. Scott
20 Jul 94 W. Hague
5 Jul 95 A. Burt
3 May 97 F. Field

27 Jul 98 *(office vacant)*
4 Jan 99 S. Timms
29 Jul 99 J. Rooker

Solicitor-General

1900 Sir R. Finlay
7 May 00 Sir E. Carson
12 Dec 05 Sir W. Robson
28 Jan 08 Sir S. Evans
6 Mar 10 Sir R. Isaacs
7 Oct 10 Sir J. Simon
19 Oct 13 Sir S. Buckmaster
2 Jun 15 Sir F. Smith
8 Nov 15 Sir G. Cave
10 Dec 16 Sir G. Hewart
10 Jan 19 Sir E. Pollock
6 Mar 22 Sir L. Scott
31 Oct 22 Sir T. Inskip
23 Jan 24 Sir H. Slesser
11 Nov 24 Sir T. Inskip
28 Mar 28 Sir F. Merriman
7 Jun 29 Sir J. Melville
22 Oct 30 Sir S. Cripps
3 Sep 31 Sir T. Inskip
26 Jan 32 Sir F. Merriman
29 Sep 33 Sir D. Somervell
19 Mar 36 Sir T. O'Connor
15 May 40 Sir W. Jowitt
4 Mar 42 Sir D. Maxwell-Fyfe
25 May 45 Sir W. Monckton
4 Aug 45 Sir F. Soskice
24 Apr 51 Sir L. Ungoed-
        Thomas
3 Nov 51 Sir R. Manningham-
        Buller
18 Oct 54 Sir H. Hylton-Foster
22 Oct 59 Sir J. Simon
8 Feb 62 Sir J. Hobson
19 Jul 62 Sir P. Rawlinson
18 Oct 64 Sir D. Foot
24 Aug 67 Sir A. Irvine
23 Jun 70 Sir G. Howe
5 Nov 72 Sir M. Havers
7 Mar 74 P. Archer
5 May 79 Sir I. Percival
13 Jun 83 Sir P. Mayhew
13 Jun 87 Sir N. Lyell
15 Apr 92 Sir D. Spencer
6 May 97 Ld Falconer
28 Jul 98 R. Cranston

Minister with Responsibility for Sport

(U-S., Educ. & Sci.)
20 Oct 64 D. Howell
(M. of S., Housing & Local Govt.)
13 Oct 69 D. Howell
(U-S., Housing & Local Govt.)
24 Jun 70 E. Griffiths
(U-S., Environment)
15 Oct 70 E. Griffiths
(M. of S., Environment)
7 Mar 74 D. Howell

(U-S., Environment)
7 May 79   H. Monro
15 Sep 81   N. MacFarlane
7 Sep 85   R. Tracy
22 Jun 87   C. Moynihan
26 Jul 90   R. Atkins
(U-S., Educ. & Sci.)
28 Nov 90   R. Atkins
(U-S., Nat. Heritage)
14 Apr 92   R. Key
27 May 93   I. Sproat
(U-S.,Environment)
8 May 97   T. Banks
(Min., Culture Media and Sport
29 Jul 99   Kate Hoey

Minister of State

1 May 41   Ld Beaverbrook
29 Jun 41   O. Lyttelton
(office abolished 12 Mar 42)
24 Sep 43   R. Law
25 May 45   W. Mabane
3 Aug 45   P. Noel Baker
4 Oct 46   H. McNeil
28 Feb 50   K. Younger
*(office came formally under
Foreign Office May 50)*

First Secretary of State

13 Jul 62   R. Butler
18 Oct 63   *(office vacant)*
16 Oct 64   G. Brown
11 Aug 66   M. Stewart
6 Apr 68   Barbara Castle
19 Jun 70   *(office vacant)*
20 Jul 95   M. Heseltine
2 May 97   *(office vacant)*

Minister of Supply

14 Jul 39   L. Burgin
12 May 40   H. Morrison
3 Oct 40   Sir A. Duncan
29 Jun 41   Ld Beaverbrook
4 Feb 42   Sir A. Duncan
3 Aug 45   J. Wilmot
7 Oct 47   G. Strauss
31 Oct 51   D. Sandys
18 Oct 54   S. Lloyd
7 Apr 55   R. Maudling
16 Jan 57   A. Jones
(office wound up 22 Oct 59)

Secretary for Technical Cooperation

27 Jun 61   D. Vosper
9 May 63   R. Carr
(office abolished 16 Oct 64)

Ministry of Technology

18 Oct 64   F. Cousins
4 Jul 66   A. Benn
20 Jun 70   G. Rippon

28 Jul 70   J. Davies
*(15 Oct 70 office reorganised
under Trade and Industry)*

Minister of Town and Country Planning

30 Dec 42   W. Morrison
4 Aug 45   L. Silkin
28 Feb 50   H. Dalton
*(recast as Local Government
and Planning 31 Jan 51)*

President of the Board of Trade

1900   C. Ritchie
7 Nov 00   G. Balfour
12 Mar 05   M of Salisbury
10 Dec 05   D. Lloyd George
12 Apr 08   W. Churchill
14 Feb 10   S. Buxton
11 Feb 14   J. Burns
5 Aug 14   W. Runciman
10 Dec 16   Sir A. Stanley
26 May 19   Sir A. Geddes
19 Mar 20   Sir R. Horne
1 Apr 21   S. Baldwin
24 Oct 22   Sir P. Lloyd-Greame
22 Jan 24   S. Webb
6 Nov 24   Sir P. Lloyd-Greame
*(changed name to Cunliffe-Lister
27 Nov 24)*
7 Jun 29   W. Graham
25 Aug 31   Sir P. Cunliffe-Lister
5 Nov 31   W. Runciman
28 May 37   O. Stanley
5 Jan 40   Sir A. Duncan
3 Oct 40   O. Lyttelton
29 Jun 41   Sir A. Duncan
4 Feb 42   J. Llewellin
22 Feb 42   H. Dalton
25 May 45   O. Lyttelton
27 Jul 45   Sir S. Cripps
29 Sep 47   H. Wilson
24 Apr 51   Sir H. Shawcross
30 Oct 51   P. Thorneycroft
13 Jan 57   Sir D. Eccles
14 Oct 59   R. Maudling
9 Oct 61   F. Erroll
20 Oct 63   E. Heath
18 Oct 64   D. Jay
29 Aug 67   A. Crosland
6 Oct 69   R. Mason
20 Jun 70   M. Noble

(Secretary of State for Trade and Industry)

15 Oct 70   J. Davies
5 Nov 72   P. Walker

(Secretary of State for Trade)
(see also Industry)

5 Mar 74   P. Shore
8 Apr 76   E. Dell

12 Nov 78   J. Smith
5 May 79   J. Nott
14 Sep 81   J. Biffen
5 Apr 82   Ld Cockfield

(Secretary of State for Trade and Industry)

11 Jun 83   C. Parkinson
16 Oct 83   N. Tebbit
2 Sep 85   L. Brittan
24 Jan 86   P. Channon
13 Jun 87   Ld Young of Graffham
24 Jul 89   N. Ridley
14 Jul 90   P. Lilley

(President of the Board of Trade)

11 Apr 92   M. Heseltine
2 May 97   Margaret Beckett

(Secretary of State for Trade)

27 Jul 98   P. Mandelson
23 Dec 98   S. Byers

Minister for Trade (under Trade and Industry)

15 Oct 70   M. Noble

(Minister for Trade and Consumer Affairs)

Nov 72   Sir G. Howe
(office wound up 5 Mar 74)

Minister for Trade

7 May 79   C. Parkinson
14 Sep 81   P. Rees
13 Jun 83   P. Channon
24 Jan 86   A. Clark
25 Jul 89   Ld Trefgarne
23 Jul 90   T. Sainsbury
15 Apr 92   R. Needham
6 Jul 95   A.Nelson
6 May 97   Ld Clinton-Davis
28 Jul 98   B. Wilson

Minister of Transport

19 May 19   Sir E. Geddes
7 Nov 21   Vt Peel
12 Apr 22   E of Crawford
31 Oct 22   Sir J. Baird
24 Jan 24   H. Gosling
11 Nov 24   W. Ashley
7 Jun 29   H. Morrison
3 Sep 31   J. Pybus
22 Feb 33   O. Stanley
29 Jun 34   L. Hore-Belisha
28 May 37   L. Burgin
21 Apr 39   E. Wallace
14 May 40   Sir J. Reith
3 Oct 40   J. Moore-Brabazon

(Minister of War Transport)

1 May 41 Ld Leathers
3 Aug 45 A. Barnes

(Minister of Transport)

6 Mar 46 A. Barnes
31 Oct 51 J. Maclay
7 May 52 A. Lennox-Boyd

(Minister of Transport and Civil Aviation)

1 Oct 53 A. Lennox-Boyd
28 Jul 54 J. Boyd-Carpenter
20 Dec 55 H. Watkinson

(Minister of Transport)

14 Oct 59 E. Marples
18 Oct 64 T. Fraser
23 Dec 65 Barbara Castle
6 Apr 68 R. Marsh
6 Oct 69 F. Mulley
23 Jun 70 J. Peyton

(Minister for Transport Industries)

15 Oct 70 J. Peyton

(Minister for Transport)

7 Mar 74 F. Mulley
12 Jun 75 J. Gilbert

(Secretary of State for Transport)

10 Sep 76 W. Rodgers

(Minister of Transport)

5 May 79 N. Fowler

(Secretary of State for Transport)

5 Jan 81 N. Fowler
14 Sep 81 D. Howell
11 Jun 83 T. King
16 Oct 83 N. Ridley
21 May 86 J. Moore
13 Jun 87 P. Channon
24 Jul 89 C. Parkinson
28 Nov 90 M. Rifkind
15 Apr 92 J. MacGregor
20 Jul 94 B. Mawhinney
5 Jul 95 Sir G. Young

(Minister for Transport)

3 May 97 G. Strang
27 Jul 98 J. Reid
17 May 99 Helen Liddell
29 Jul 99 Ld Macdonald of Tradeston

Treasury

(see p. 56 for Chancellor of the Exchequer)

Chief Secretary

9 Oct 61 H. Brooke
13 Jul 62 J. Boyd-Carpenter
20 Oct 64 J. Diamond
23 Jun 70 M. Macmillan
7 Apr 72 P. Jenkin
8 Jan 74 T. Boardman
7 Mar 74 J. Barnett
5 May 79 J. Biffen
5 Jan 81 L. Brittan
11 Jun 83 P. Rees
2 Sep 85 J. MacGregor
13 Jun 87 J. Major
24 Jul 89 N. Lamont
28 Nov 90 D. Mellor
10 Apr 92 M. Portillo
20 Jul 94 J. Aitken
5 Jul 95 W. Waldegrave
3 May 97 A. Darling
27 Jul 98 S. Byers
23 Dec 98 A. Milburn
11 Oct 99 A. Smith

Secretary of State for War

1900 M of Lansdowne
1 Nov 00 St J. Brodrick
6 Oct 03 H. Arnold-Forster
10 Dec 05 R. Haldane *(Vt)*
12 Jun 12 J. Seely
30 Mar 14 H. Asquith
5 Aug 14 Earl Kitchener
6 Jul 16 D. Lloyd George
10 Dec 16 E of Derby
18 Apr 18 Vt Milner
10 Jan 19 W. Churchill
13 Feb 21 Sir L. Worthington-Evans
24 Oct 22 E of Derby
22 Jan 24 S. Walsh
6 Nov 24 Sir L. Worthington-Evans
7 Jun 29 T. Shaw
26 Aug 31 M of Crewe
5 Nov 31 Vt Hailsham
7 Jun 35 Vt Halifax
22 Nov 35 A. Duff Cooper
28 May 37 L. Hore-Belisha
5 Jan 40 O. Stanley
11 May 40 A. Eden
22 Dec 40 D. Margesson
22 Feb 42 Sir J. Grigg
3 Aug 45 J. Lawson
4 Oct 46 F. Bellenger
7 Oct 47 E. Shinwell

28 Feb 50 J. Strachey
31 Oct 51 A. Head
18 Oct 56 J. Hare
6 Jan 58 C. Soames
27 Jul 60 J. Profumo
27 Jun 63 J. Godber
21 Oct 63 J. Ramsden
(office abolished 1 Apr 64)

Minister for Welsh Affairs

28 Oct 51 Sir D. Maxwell-Fyfe
18 Oct 54 G. Lloyd-George
13 Jan 57 H. Brooke
9 Oct 61 C. Hill
13 Jul 62 Sir K. Joseph

(Secretary of State for Wales)

18 Oct 64 J. Griffiths
6 Apr 66 C. Hughes
6 Apr 68 G. Thomas
20 Jun 70 P. Thomas[1]
5 Mar 74 J. Morris
5 May 79 N. Edwards
3 Jun 87 P. Walker
4 May 90 D. Hunt
27 May 93 J. Redwood
5 Jul 95 W. Hague
3 May 97 R. Davies
27 Oct 98 A. Michael
28 Jul 99 P. Murphy

Minister for Women

11 Jun 97 Joan Ruddock[2]
28 Jun 98 Lady Jay[3]

First Commissioner of Works

1900 A. Akers-Douglas
8 Aug 02 Ld Windsor
10 Dec 05 L. Harcourt
3 Nov 10 Earl Beauchamp
6 Aug 14 Ld Emmott
25 May 15 L. Harcourt *(Vt)*
10 Dec 16 Sir A. Mond
1 Apr 21 E of Crawford
31 Oct 22 Sir J. Baird
22 Jan 24 F. Jowett
10 Nov 24 Vt Peel
18 Oct 28 M of Londonderry
7 Jun 29 G. Lansbury
25 Aug 31 M of Londonderry
5 Nov 31 W. Ormsby-Gore
16 Jun 36 Earl Stanhope
28 May 37 Sir P. Sassoon
7 Jun 39 H. Ramsbotham
3 Apr 40 Earl De La Warr
18 May 40 Ld Tryon
3 Oct 40 Sir J. Reith *(Ld)*

[1] *Also Party Chairman*
[2] *U-S. Social Security*
[3] *Ld Privy Seal*

(Minister of Works & Buildings and First Commissioner of Works)

23 Oct 40 Ld Reith

(Minister of Works and Planning)

11 Feb 42 Ld Reith
21 Feb 42 Ld Portal

(Minister of Works)

Feb 43 Ld Portal
21 Nov 44 D. Sandys
4 Aug 45 G. Tomlinson
10 Feb 47 C. Key
28 Feb 50 R. Stokes
26 Apr 51 G. Brown
18 Nov 51 (Sir) D. Eccles
1 Oct 54 N. Birch

20 Dec 55 P. Buchan-Hepburn
16 Jan 57 H. Molson
22 Oct 59 Ld J. Hope
(16 Jul 62 recast as Public Building and Works)

Leaders of the House of Commons

1900	A. Balfour
5 Dec 05	Sir H. Campbell-Bannerman
5 Apr 08	H. Asquith
10 Dec 16	A. Bonar Law
23 Mar 21	A. Chamberlain
23 Oct 22	A. Bonar Law
22 May 23	S. Baldwin
22 Jan 24	R. MacDonald
4 Nov 24	S. Baldwin
5 Jun 29	R. MacDonald
7 Jun 35	S. Baldwin
28 May 37	N. Chamberlain
11 May 40	C. Attlee*
19 Feb 42	Sir S. Cripps
22 Nov 42	A. Eden
27 Jul 45	H. Morrison
9 Mar 51	C. Ede
30 Oct 51	H. Crookshank
7 Apr 55	R. Butler
9 Oct 61	I. Macleod
20 Oct 63	S. Lloyd
16 Oct 64	H. Bowden
11 Aug 66	R. Crossman
6 Apr 68	F. Peart
20 Jun 70	W. Whitelaw
7 Apr 72	R. Carr
5 Nov 72	J. Prior
5 Mar 74	E. Short
8 Apr 76	M. Foot
5 May 79	N. St John-Stevas
5 Jan 81	F. Pym
5 Apr 82	J. Biffen
13 Jun 87	J. Wakeham
24 Jul 89	Sir G. Howe
3 Nov 90	J. MacGregor
11 Apr 92	A. Newton
2 May 97	Ann Taylor
27 Jul 98	Margaret Beckett

Leaders of the House of Lords

1900	3rd M of Salisbury
12 Jul 02	D of Devonshire
13 Oct 03	M of Lansdowne
10 Dec 05	M of Ripon
14 Apr 08	E of Crewe (M)+
10 Dec 16	Earl Curzon (M)
22 Jan 24	Vt Haldane
6 Nov 24	Marquess Curzon
27 Apr 25	4th M of Salisbury
7 Jun 29	Ld Parmoor
25 Aug 31	M of Reading
5 Nov 31	1st Vt Hailsham
7 Jun 35	M of Londonderry
22 Nov 35	Vt Halifax
27 Oct 38	Earl Stanhope
14 May 40	Vt Caldecote
3 Oct 40	Vt Halifax
22 Dec 40	Ld Lloyd
8 Feb 41	Ld Moyne
21 Feb 42	Vt Cranborne (5th M of Salisbury)
3 Aug 45	Vt Addison
28 Oct 51	5th M of Salisbury
29 Mar 57	E of Home
27 Jul 60	2nd Vt Hailsham
20 Oct 63	Ld Carrington
18 Oct 64	E of Longford
16 Jan 68	Ld Shackleton
20 Jun 70	Earl Jellicoe
5 Jun 73	Ld Windlesham
7 Mar 74	Ld Shepherd
10 Sep 76	Ld Peart
5 May 79	Ld Soames
14 Sep 81	Lady Young
11 Jun 83	Vt Whitelaw
10 Jan 88	Ld Belstead
28 Nov 90	Ld Waddington
11 Apr 92	Ld Wakeham
20 Jul 94	Vt Cranborne
2 May 97	Ld Richard
27 Jul 98	Lady Jay

Government Chief Whip

(Parliamentary Secretary to the Treasury)

1900	Sir W. Walrond
8 Aug 02	Sir A. Acland Hood
12 Dec 05	G. Whiteley
3 Jun 08	J. Pease
14 Feb 10	Master of Elibank
7 Aug 12	P. Illingworth
24 Jan 15	J. Gulland
30 May 15	J. Gulland
30 May 15	Ld E. Talbot
14 Dec 16	Ld E. Talbot
14 Dec 16	N. Primrose
2 Mar 17	Ld E. Talbot
2 Mar 17	F. Guest
1 Apr 21	C. McCurdy
1 Apr 21	L. Wilson
31 Oct 22	L. Wilson
25 Jul 23	B. Eyres-Monsell
23 Jan 24	B. Spoor
7 Nov 24	B. Eyres-Monsell
14 Jun 29	T. Kennedy
3 Sep 31	Sir B. Eyres-Monsell
10 Nov 31	D. Margesson
17 May 40	D. Margesson
17 May 40	Sir C. Edwards
14 Jan 41	Sir C. Edwards
14 Jan 41	J. Stuart
12 Mar 42	J. Stuart
12 Mar 42	W. Whiteley
26 May 45	J. Stuart
3 Aug 45	W. Whiteley
30 Oct 51	P. Buchan-Hepburn
30 Dec 55	E. Heath
14 Oct 59	M. Redmayne
18 Oct 64	E. Short
4 Jul 66	J. Silkin
30 Apr 69	R. Mellish
20 Jun 70	F. Pym
2 Dec 73	H. Atkins
5 Mar 74	R. Mellish
8 Apr 76	M. Cocks
5 May 79	M. Jopling
11 Jun 83	J. Wakeham
13 Jun 87	D. Waddington
28 Oct 89	T. Renton
28 Nov 90	R. Ryder
5 Jul 95	A. Goodlad
3 May 96	N. Brown
27 Jul 98	Ann Taylor

Government Chief Whip in the House of Lords

(usually Captain of the Gentlemen at Arms—see footnotes for exceptions)

1900	Earl Waldegrave[1]
18 Dec 05	Ld Ribblesdale[2]
29 May 07	Ld Denman[3]
15 Mar 11	Ld Colebrooke[4]
9 Jun 15	Ld Colebrooke[4]
9 Jun 15	D of Devonshire[5]
26 Jul 16	Ld Colebrooke[4]
26 Jul 16	Ld Hylton[6]
20 Nov 22	E of Clarendon
22 Jan 24	Ld Muir-Mackenzie[7]
1 Dec 24	E of Clarendon
26 Jun 25	E of Plymouth
1 Jan 29	E of Lucan
18 Jul 29	Earl De La Warr[7]
17 Jan 30	Ld Marley[7]
12 Nov 31	E of Lucan
31 May 40	Ld Templemore[1]

*Although Mr Attlee fulfilled the role of Leader of the House of Commons during this period he was technically only Deputy Leader to Mr Churchill

+During the summer of 1911 Vt Morley was temporarily Leader of the House of Lords

[1] Captain of the Yeomen of the Guard.
[2] Without office.
[3] Lord in Waiting 1907; Captain of Gentlemen at Arms 1907–11.
[4] Lord in Waiting 1911; Captain of Gentlemen at Arms 1911–22.
[5] Civil Lord of the Admiralty.
[6] Lord in Waiting 1916–18; Captain of Yeomen of Guard 1918–22.
[7] Lord in Waiting.

4 Aug 45	Ld Ammon
18 Oct 49	1st Ld Shepherd
5 Nov 51	Earl Fortescue
27 Jun 58	Earl St Aldwyn
21 Oct 64	2nd Ld Shepherd
29 Jul 67	Ld Beswick
24 Jun 70	Earl St Aldwyn
11 Mar 74	Lady Llewelyn-Davies
6 May 79	Ld Denham
23 May 91	Ld Hesketh
16 Sep 93	Vt Ullswater
20 Jul 94	Ld Strathclyde
6 May 97	Ld Carter

Second Church Estates Commissioner

(not a Minister but always an MP from the governing party)

1895	(Sir) L. Knowles
1906	C. Hobhouse
1906	F. Stevenson
1907	J. Tomkinson
1910	(Sir) C. Nicholson
1919	(Sir) W. Mount
1923	J. Birchall
1924	G. Middleton
1924	J. Birchall
1929	G. Middleton

1931	R. Denman
1943	J. Mills
1945	T. Burden
1950	Sir R. Acland
1951	(Sir) J. Crowder
1957	(Sir) H. Ashton
1962	(Sir) J. Arbuthnot
1964	L. Mallalieu
1970	(Sir) M. Worsley
1974	E. Bishop
1974	T. Walker
1979	(Sir) W. van Straubenzee
1987	M. Alison
1997	S. Bell

Size of Cabinets and Governments 1900–2000
(at 1 Jan)

	1900	1910	1917	1920	1930	1940	1950	1960	1970	1980	1990	1999
Cabinet Mins.	19	19	5	19	19	9	18	19	21	22	22	22
Non-Cab. Mins	10	7	33	15	9	25	20	20	33	38	33	34
Junior Mins	31	36	47	47	30	40	43	43	48	47	48	49
No.of M.P.s in paid Govt. posts	33	43	60	58	50	58	68	65	85	86	80	82
No. of Peers in paid Govt. posts	27	19	25	23	8	16	13	17	17	21	22	24
Total paid Govt posts	60	62	85	81	58	74	81	82	102	107	103	106
Parliamentary Private Secs in Commons	9	16	12	13	26	25	27	36	30	37	47	47
Total no.of MPs involved in Government	42	59	72	71	76	83	95	101	115	123	127	129

Social and Educational Composition of British Cabinets 1895–1997[1]

				No.	Class			PS	Education		
					Ar.	Mid.	Work		Eton	Univ	O&C
Aug	1895	Con.	Salisbury	19	8	11	–	16	7	15	14
Jul	1902	Con.	Balfour	19	9	10	–	16	9	14	13
Dec	1905	Lib.	Campbell-Bannerman	19	7	11	1	11	3	14	12
Jul	1914	Lib.	Asquith	19	6	12	1	11	3	15	13
Jan	1919	Coal.	Ll.George	21	3	17	1	12	2	13	8
Nov	1922	Con.	Bonar Law	16	8	8	–	14	8	13	13
Jan	1924	Lab.	MacDonald	19	3	5	11	8	-	6	6
Nov	1924	Con.	Baldwin	21	9	12	–	21	7	16	16
Jan	1929	Lab.	MacDonald	18	2	4	12	5	-	6	3
Aug	1931	Nat.	MacDonald	20	8	10	2	13	6	11	10
Jun	1935	Con.	Baldwin	22	9	11	2	14	9	11	10
May	1937	Con.	Chamberlain	21	8	13	–	17	8	16	13
May	1945	Con.	Churchill	16	6	9	1	14	7	11	9
Aug	1945	Lab.	Attlee	20	–	8	12	5	2	10	5
Oct	1951	Con.	Churchill	16	5	11	–	14	7	11	9
Apr	1955	Con.	Eden	18	5	13	–	18	10	16	14
Jan	1957	Con.	Macmillan	18	4	14	–	17	8	16	15
Oct	1963	Con.	Home	24	5	19	–	21	11	17	17
Oct	1964	Lab.	Wilson	23	1	14	8	8	1	13	11
Jun	1970	Con.	Heath	18	4	14	–	15	4	15	15
Mar	1974	Lab.	Wilson	21	1	16	4	7	–	16	11
Apr	1976	Lab.	Callaghan	22	1	13	7	7	–	15	10
May	1979	Con.	Thatcher	22	3	19	–	20	6	18	17
Nov	1990	Con.	Major	22	3	17	2	14	2	20	17
May	1997	Lab.	Blair	22	–	15	7	8	–	21	3
Average 25 Cabinets				20	5	13	3	13	5	14	12
		14 Con. Cabinets		19	7	13	–	17	7	14	13
		7 Lab. Cabinets		20	0.5	15	9	7	0.5	14	6
		2 Lib. Cabinets		19	6	11.5	1	11	3	14.5	12.5

[1]This table is largely based on W.L. Guttsman, *The British Political Elite* (1963). *Aristocrats* are those who had among their grandparents the holder of a hereditary title. *Working class* are those whose fathers appear to have had a manual occupation when they were growing up. *Schools* are classified as public schools if members of the Headmasters' Conference.

Women Cabinet Ministers

1929–31	Margaret Bondfield	1992–97	Virginia Bottomley
1945–47	Ellen Wilkinson	1992–97	Gillian Shephard
1953–54	Florence Horsbrugh	1997–	Margaret Beckett
1964–70	Barbara Castle	1997–	Ann Taylor
& 1974–76		1997–	Mo Mowlam
1968–69	Judith Hart	1997–98	Harriet Harman
1970–74	Margaret Thatcher	1997–	Clare Short
& 1979–90		1998–	Lady Jay
1982–83	Lady Young		

Durability of Prime Ministers 1900–2000

	Years as PM	No.of Times PM	Age	Pre-PM Years in HC	Post-PM Years in HC	Years Lived after PM
M of Salisbury	13.9	3	55	15[1]	0	1
Margaret Thatcher	11.6	1	53	20	2	–
H. Asquith	8.8	1	55	22	6	11
(Sir) W. Churchill	8.8	2	65	38	9	10
H. Wilson	7.9	2	48	19	7	19
J. Major	7.6	1	47	11	–	–
S. Baldwin	7.2	3	56	15	0	11
J. R. MacDonald	6.9	2	58	14	2	2
H. Macmillan	6.9	1	62	29	1	22
C. Attlee	6.3	1	62	23	4	16
D. Lloyd George	5.10	1	53	26	22	22
E. Heath	3.8	1	53	20	–	–
A. Balfour	3.5	1	53	28	17	24
J. Callaghan	3.1	1	64	31	8	–
N. Chamberlain	2.11	1	68	19	0.5	0.5
Sir H. Campbell-Bannerman	2.4	1	69	37	0	0
Sir A. Eden	1.9	1	58	32	0	20
Sir A. Douglas-Home	1.0	1	60	15[2]	10	31
A. Bonar Law	0.7	1	63	22	0	0
T. Blair	–	–	43	14	–	–

[1] Plus 17 years in the House of Lords
[2] Plus 13 years in the House of Lords

Long Tenure of Ministerial Office

The following are the only twentieth century British politicians to have served more than 20 years in ministerial office:

Years		First Office	Last Office	Years		First Office	Last Office
29	Sir W. Churchill	1905	1955	22	Sir A. Chamberlain	1895	1931
28	E of Balfour	1885	1929	21	Vt Swinton	1920	1957
25	R. Butler	1932	1964	21	M of Salisbury	1866	1902
24	D of Devonshire	1863	1903	21	Sir M. Hicks-Beach	1868	1902
22	E of Halsbury	1875	1905	20	Ld Ashbourne	1877	1905
22	W. Long	1886	1921	20	Vt Hailsham	1945	1987
20	Ld G. Hamilton	1874	1903	20	K. Clarke	1972	1997

Long Tenure in One Department

18	Vt Long	Ld in Waiting	1979–97
17	E of Halsbury	Ld Chancellor	1885–6,66–92,95–05
17	Ld Ashbourne	Ld Chanc. Ireland	1885–6,86–92.95–05
15	W. Roberts	U-S, then Min. Welsh O.	1979–94
15	M of Salisbury	Prime Minister	1885–6,86–92,95–02
15	M of Salisbury	Foreign Sec.	1878–80,85–86,87–92,95–00
13	Ld Gage	Ld in Waiting	1924–29,31–39
12	(Sir) A. Eden	Foreign Sec.	1935–38,40–45,51–55
		(also U-S For.O. 31–33)	
12	G. (Ld)Tryon	Min. Pensions	1922–23,24–29,31–35
		(also P.S. Pensions 20–22,40–41)	
12	Ld Hailsham	Ld Chancellor	1970–74,79–87
12	Ld Denham	Cap.Gent.at Arms	1979–91
		(also a Whip 1961–64,70–74)	
11	E of Kintore	Ld in Waiting	1885–86,95–05
		(also a Whip 86–89)	
11	Margaret Thatcher	Prime Minister	1979–90
11	Sir E. Grey	Foreign Sec.	1905–16
		(also U-S For.O. 92–95)	
10	Ld Mackay	Ld Chancellor	1987–97
10	J. Atkinson	Att.-Gen.Ireland	1892–92,95–05
10	Earl St Aldwyn	Cap.Gent.at Arms	1958–64,70–74

Oldest and Youngest Ministers

The oldest M.P. to hold Cabinet office was Sir W. Churchill (80 in 1955); the oldest peers were Vt Halsbury (82 in 1905) and Vt Addison (82 in 1951) and the only other octogenarians were M of Ripon (80 in 1908) and Earl Balfour (80 in 1929). The oldest holder of any ministerial office was Ld Muir-Mackenzie (85 in 1930). The youngest Cabinet minister was H. Wilson (31 in 1947). The youngest M.P. to hold any office was H. Wilson (29 in 1945). R. Butler (1932), E. Rowlands (1969), and Ann Taylor (1977) also held office at 29; the youngest peer was Earl De La Warr (23 in 1924).

Cabinet Members Dying in Office[1]

5 Jun 1916	Earl Kitchener	30 Mar 1940	Sir J. Gilmour
20 Mar 1925	Marquess Curzon	21 Sep 1943	Sir K. Wood[2]
5 Oct 1930	Lord Thomson	6 Feb 1947	Ellen Wilkinson
13 Mar 1931	V. Hartshorn	14 Apr 1951	E. Bevin
15 Jun 1932	Sir D. Maclean	30 Jul 1970	I. Macleod
13 Oct 1936	Sir G. Collins	19 Feb 1977	A. Crosland

[1]H. Gaitskell, the Leader of the Opposition, died on 18 Jan 63.
J. Smith, the Leader of the Opposition, died on 14 May 94.
[2]Chancellor of the Exchequer but not actually in the War Cabinet.

Cabinet Members Suffering Electoral Defeat while Holding Office

Apr 1908	W. Churchill[1]	Nov 1935	R. MacDonald[1]
Feb 1914	C. Masterman[1]		M. MacDonald[1]
May 1914	C. Masterman[2]	Jul 1945	L. Amery
Mar 1921	Sir A. Griffith-Boscawen[1]		B. Bracken
Nov 1922	Sir A. Griffith-Boscawen		Sir J. Grigg
Mar 1923	Sir A. Griffith-Boscawen[2]		H. Macmillan
Dec 1923	Sir A. Montague-Barlow		Sir D. Somervell
Oct 1924	F. Jowett	Feb 1950	A. Creech Jones
May 1929	Sir A. Steel-Maitland	Oct 1964	A. Barber

[1] Sought another seat and continued in office   [2] By-election defeat followed by resignation

Jan 1965	P. Gordon-Walker[2]	May 1997	M. Forsyth
Jun 1970	J. Diamond		R. Freeman
Feb 1974	G. Campbell		I. Lang
May 1979	Shirley Williams		A. Newton
Apr 1992	C. Patten		M. Portillo
			M. Rifkind
			W. Waldegrave

[1] Sought another seat and continued in office
[2] By-election defeat followed by resignation

Some leaders of major parties, though not in office, have suffered electoral defeat: A. Balfour (1906), H. Asquith (1918,1924), A. Henderson (1931), Sir H. Samuel (1935), Sir A. Sinclair (1945)

In Jan 1906 8 members of the Conservative Cabinet who left office in Dec 1905 were defeated, including A. Balfour who had been Prime Minister.

In Dec 1918 10 Asquithian Liberals who had left office in Dec 1916 were defeated including H. Asquith.

In Nov 1922 2 National Liberal members of the Coalition Cabinet who left office in Oct 1922 were defeated.

In Oct 1931 13 members of the Labour Cabinet who left office in Aug 1931 were defeated, including A. Henderson, the Party Leader.

On two occasions the Government Chief Whip was defeated (J. Pease in Jan 1910 and L. Wilson in Nov 1922). On both occasions a new seat was very speedily found.

These Ministers of Cabinet rank were found seats in by-elections:- 1916: H. Fisher, Sir A. Stanley; 1917: Sir A. Geddes, Sir E. Geddes 1924: A. Henderson; 1940: E. Bevin, O. Lyttelton, Sir J. Reith, Sir A. Duncan; 1942: Sir J. Grigg; 1963: Sir A. Douglas-Home, Q. Hogg; 1965: F. Cousins.

(See also p.257 for defeated Ministers' attempts at re-election.)

Ministerial Resignations

Resignations from ministerial office are not easy to classify. A retirement on the ground of ill-health may always conceal a protest or a dismissal. However, there are some cases where ministers have unquestionably left office because they were not willing to continue to accept collective responsibility for some part of Government policy and some cases where the individual actions of ministers have been thought impolitic or unworthy. The following list does not include resignations made necessary because of private scandals, except when the resignation became the subject of public comment. Nor does it include even the most publicised 'refusals to serve' (e.g. I. Macleod and E. Powell in 1963).

16 Sep 03	J. Chamberlain (Imperial preference)
4–15 Sep 03	C. Ritchie, Ld Balfour of Burleigh, Ld G. Hamilton, D of Devonshire, A. Elliot (free trade)
6 Mar 05	G. Wyndham (Ireland)
30 Mar 14	J. Seely (Curragh mutiny)
2 Aug 14	Vt Morley, J. Burns (entry into war)
5 Aug 14	C. Trevelyan (entry into war)
19 Oct 15	Sir E. Carson (conduct of war in the Balkans)
31 Dec 15	Sir J. Simon (compulsory National Service)
3 May 16	A. Birrell (Irish rebellion)
25 Jun 16	E of Selborne (Irish policy)
12 Jul 17	A. Chamberlain (campaign in Mesopotamia)
8 Aug 17	N. Chamberlain (Ministry of National Service)
17 Nov 17	Ld Cowdray (conduct of the Air Ministry)
21 Jan 18	Sir E. Carson (Ireland)
25 Apr 18	Ld Rothermere (Air Force)
22 Nov 18	Ld R. Cecil (Welsh disestablishment)
12 Nov 19	J. Seely (role of Air Ministry)
14 Jul 21	C. Addison (housing)
9 Mar 22	E. Montagu (Turkey)
18 Nov 23	A. Buckley (abandonment of free trade)
28 Aug 27	Vt Cecil (disarmament)
19 May 30	Sir O. Mosley (unemployment)
2 Mar 31	Sir C. Trevelyan (education)

6 Mar 31	Ld Arnold (free trade)
9 Oct 31	G. Lloyd-George, G. Owen (calling of election)
28 Sep 32	Sir H. Samuel, Sir A. Sinclair, Vt Snowden, M of Lothian, I. Foot, Sir R. Hamilton, G. White, W. Rea, Vt Allendale (free frade)
18 Dec 35	Sir S. Hoare (Laval Pact)
22 May 36	J. Thomas (Budget leak)
20 Feb 38	A. Eden, Vt Cranborne (negotiations with Mussolini)
12–16 May 38	Earl Winterton, Vt Swinton (Air Force strength)
16 May 38	Ld Harlech (partition of Palestine)
1 Oct 38	A. Duff Cooper (Munich)
21 Jan 41	R. Boothby (blocked Czechoslovakian assets)
1 Mar 45	H. Strauss (treatment of Poles by Yalta Conference)
16 Jul 45	Ld Lovat (reluctance to be a minister)
26 May 46	Sir B. Smith (overwork and criticism)
13 Nov 47	H. Dalton (Budget leak)
13 Dec 48	J. Belcher (Lynskey tribunal)
16 Apr 50	S. Evans (agricultural subsidies)
23 Apr 51	A. Bevan, H. Wilson, J. Freeman (Budget proposals)
20 Jul 54	Sir T. Dugdale (Crichel Down)
31 Oct 56	A. Nutting (Suez)
5 Nov 56	Sir E. Boyle (Suez)
29 Mar 57	M of Salisbury (release of Archbishop Makarios)
6 Jan 58	P. Thorneycroft, E. Powell, N. Birch (econ. policy)
24 Nov 58	I. Harvey (private scandal)
8 Nov 62	T. Galbraith (Security) *(exonerated and given new office 5 May 63)*
5 Jun 63	J. Profumo (lying to the House of Commons)
19 Feb 66	C. Mayhew (defence estimates)
3 Jul 66	F. Cousins (incomes policy)
26 Jul 67	Margaret Herbison (Social Services policy)
16 Jan 68	E of Longford (delay in raising of school age)
5 Feb 68	W. Howie (enforcement of Party discipline)
16 Mar 68	G. Brown (conduct of Government business)
1 Jul 68	R. Gunter (general dissatisfaction)
24 Sep 69	J. Bray (permission to publish)
28 Jul 71	E. Taylor (entry into the E.E.C.)
17 Oct 71	J. More (entry into the E.E.C.)
18 Jul 72	R. Maudling (Poulson Inquiry)
22 May 73	Ld Lambton (private scandal)
23 May 73	Earl Jellicoe (private scandal)
25 Sep 74	Ld Brayley (former business interests)
17 Oct 74	N. Buchan (agricultural policy)
9 Apr 75	E. Heffer (opposing EEC membership in Commons)[1]
10 Jun 75	Dame J. Hart (dissatisfaction with PM)
21 Jul 75	R. Hughes (incomes policy)
21 Feb 76	Joan Lestor (education cuts)
21 Dec 76	R. Prentice (disenchantment with Government)
9 Nov 77	J. Ashton (Government's handling of power dispute)
20 Nov 78	R. Cryer (failure to support Kirkby Coop.)
17 Jan 79	A. Stallard (extra seats for Northern Ireland)
18 May 81	K. Speed (defence estimates)[1]
21 Jan 82	N. Fairbairn (handling of a Scottish prosecution)
5 Apr 82	Ld Carrington, H. Atkins, R. Luce (Falklands)
8 May 82	N. Budgen (Northern Ireland policy)
11 Oct 83	C. Parkinson (private scandal)
16 Nov 85	I. Gow (Anglo-Irish Accord)
7 Jan 86	M. Heseltine (Westland affair)
22 Jan 86	L. Brittan (Westland affair)
16 Dec 88	Edwina Currie (remarks on salmonella scare)
29 Oct 89	N. Lawson (P.M.'s economic advice)
13 Jul 90	N. Ridley (remarks about Germany)
1 Nov 90	Sir G. Howe (P.M.'s attitude to Europe)
22 Sep 92	D. Mellor (private scandal)

24 Jun 93	M. Mates (links with Asil Nadir)
5 Jan 94	T. Yeo (private scandal)
11 Jan 94	E of Caithness (private scandal)
20 Oct 94	T. Smith (payment for questions)
25 Oct 94	N. Hamilton (payment for questions)
8 Feb 95	A. Stewart (threatening behaviour)
11 Feb 95	C. Wardle (immigration policy)
6 Mar 95	R. Hughes (private scandal)
26 Jun 95	J. Redwood (to contest leadership)
5 Jul 95	J. Aitken (to fight libel action)
2 Jun 96	R. Richards (private scandal)
22 Jul 96	D. Heathcoat-Amory (European policy)
11 Dec 96	D. Willetts (conduct as whip)
4 May 97	D. Foster (ministerial appointment)
10 Dec 97	M. Chisholm (single parent policy)
27 Jul 98	F. Field (ministerial appointment)
27 Oct 98	R. Davies (private scandal)
23 Dec 98	P. Mandelson (private financial arrangements)
23 Dec 98	G. Robinson (private financial arrangements)

[1]Technically a dismissal, not a resignation.

Parliamentary Private Secretaries to Prime Ministers

1900–02	E. Cecil	1952–55	C. Soames
1906–08	H. Carr-Gomm	1955–55	R. Carr
1908–10	G. Howard	1955–58	R. Allan
1910–15	C. Lyell	1958–59	A. Barber
1915–16	Sir J. Barran	1959–63	K. Cunningham
1916–17	D. Davies	1963–64	F. Pearson
1918–18	W. Astor	1964–66 ⎰	P. Shore
1918–20	(Sir) W. Sutherland	1964–67 ⎱	E. Fernyhough
1920–22	Sir P. Sassoon	1967–68	H. Davies
1922–23	J. Davidson	1968–69 ⎰	H. Davies
1923–24	S. Herbert	1969–69 ⎱	E. Varley
1924–24	L. MacNeil Weir	1969–70	H. Davies
1924–27	S. Herbert	1970–74	T. Kitson
1927–29	C. Rhys	1974–75	W. Hamling
1929–31 ⎰	L. MacNeil Weir	1975–75	K. Marks
1929–31 ⎱	R. Morrison	1975–76	J. Tomlinson
1931–32 ⎰	R. Glyn	1976–76	J. Cunningham
1931–32 ⎱	F. Markham	1976–79	R. Stott
1932–35 ⎰	(Sir) R. Glyn	1979–83	I. Gow
1932–35 ⎱	J. Worthington	1983–87	M. Alison
1935–35	G. Lloyd	1987–88	A. Hamilton
1935–37	T. Dugdale	1988–90	M. Lennox-Boyd
1937–40	Ld Dunglass	1990–90	P. Morrison
1940–41	B. Bracken	1990–94	G. Bright
1941–45	G. Harvie-Watt	1994–97	J. Ward
1945–46	G. de Freitas	1997– ⎰	B. Grocott
1946–51	A. Moyle	1997–98 ⎱	Anne Coffey

Biographical Notes

Prime Ministers, Deputy Prime Ministers, Chancellors of the Exchequer, Foreign Secretaries, and Leaders of the Opposition.

(Virtually all the most eminent politicians of this century have held one of these four positions, but, common sense being more important than consistency, two of the most outstanding exceptions have been added to the list – Joseph Chamberlain and Aneurin Bevan).

Adamson, William
  b.1863. *Educ*. Elementary. Miner. Union official. M.P. (Lab.) for West Fife, 1910–35. Leader of Opposition, 1918–21. Sec. for Scotland, 1924, Sec. of State for Scotland, 1929–31. d.1945.

Anderson, John (Sir). 1st Vt Waverley (1952)
  b. 1882.*Educ*. George Watson's Coll., Edin., Edinburgh and Leipzig Univs. Entered Col.O.,1905. Sec. to Min. of Shipping, 1917–19. K.C.B., 1919. Addit. Sec. to Loc. Govt. Bd, 1919. 2nd Sec. to Min. of Health, 1919. Ch. of Bd of Inland Revenue, 1919–22. Joint U-S. to Ld Lieut. of Ireland, 1920–22. P.U-S. Home O., 1922–32. Gov. of Bengal, 1932–37. M.P. (Nat.) for Scottish Univs., 1938–50. Ld Privy S., 1938–39. Home Sec. and Min. of Home Security, 1939–40. Ld Pres. of Council, 1940–43. Chanc. of Exch., 1943–45. d. 1958.

Asquith, Herbert Henry. 1st E of Oxford and Asquith (1925)
  b. 1852. *Educ*. City of London School; Oxford. Barrister, 1876. M.P. (Lib.) for E. Fife, 1886–1918. M.P. for Paisley, 1920–24. Home Sec., 1892–95. Chanc. of Exch., 1905–8. P.M. 1908–16. Leader of Lib. party, 1908–1926. Sec. for War, 1914. Formed Coalition Govt., 1915. Resigned as P.M., became Leader of Opposition, 1916. Resigned Leadership of Lib. party, 1926. d. 1928.

Attlee, Clement Richard. 1st Earl Attlee (1955)
  b. 1883. *Educ*. Haileybury; Oxford. Barrister, 1906; practised, 1906–9. Lecturer at L.S.E., 1913–23. M.P. (Lab.) for Limehouse, Stepney, 1922–50. M.P. for W. Walthamstow, 1950–55. P.P.S. to J. R. MacDonald, 1922–24. U-S. for War, 1924. Chanc. of D. of Lanc., 1930–31. Postm.-Gen., 1931. Dep. Leader of Lab. party in Commons, 1931–35. Leader of Lab. party, 1935–55. Leader of Opposition, 1935–40. Ld Privy S., 1940–42. Sec. for Dominions, 1942–43. Ld Pres. of Council, 1943–45. Dep.P.M., 1942–45. Leader of Opposition, 1945. P.M., 1945–51. Min. of Def., 1945–46. Leader of Opposition, 1951–1955. d. 1967.

Baldwin, Stanley. 1st Earl Baldwin of Bewdley (1937)
  b. 1867. *Educ*. Harrow; Cambridge. Family business. M.P. (Con.) for Bewdley div. of Worcs., 1908–37. Joint F.S. to Treas., 1917–21; Pres. of Bd.of Trade, 1921–22; Chanc. of Exch., 1922–23. Leader of Con. party, 1923–37. P.M., 1923–24, 1924–29 and 1935–37. Leader of Opposition, 1924, 1929–31. Ld Pres. of Council, 1931–35. Ld Privy S., 1932–33. d.1947.

Balfour, Arthur James (Sir). 1st Earl of Balfour (1922)
  b. 1848. *Educ*. Eton; Cambridge. M.P. (Con.) for Hertford, 1874–85. M.P. for E. Manchester, 1885–1906. M.P. for City of London, 1906–22. P.P.S. to Ld Salisbury, 1878–80. Pres.of Loc. Govt. Bd., 1885. Sec. for Scotland, 1886. (Member of Cabinet, Nov 1886.) Ch.Sec. for Ireland, 1887–91. Leader of Commons and 1st Ld of Treas., 1891–92 and 1895–1905. P.M., 1902–5. Leader of Con. party, 1902–11. Member of Committee of Imperial Defence, 1914. Attended war cabinet meetings, 1914–15. 1st Ld of Admir., 1915–16. For. Sec., 1916–19. Ld Pres. of Council, 1919–22 and 1925–29. K.G., 1922. d. 1930.

Barber, Anthony Perrinott Lysberg. Ld Barber (Life Peer 1974)
  b. 1920. *Educ*. Retford G.S.; Oxford. Barrister, 1948. M.P. (Con.) for Doncaster, 1951–64. M.P. for Altrincham and Sale, 1965–74. Con. Whip, 1955–58; P.P.S. to P.M., 1958–59. Econ. S. to Treasury, 1959–62. F.S., 1962–63. Min. of Health, 1963–64. Ch. of Con. Party Organisation, 1967–70. Chanc. of D. of Lanc., 1970. Chanc. of Exch., 1970–74.

Bevan, Aneurin
  b. 1897. *Educ*. Elem.; Central Labour College. Miner. M.P. (Lab.) for Ebbw Vale, 1929–60. Deputy Leader of Lab. party, 1959–60. Min. of Health, 1945–51. Min. of Lab. and Nat.Service, 1951. Resigned, 1951. Treasurer of Lab. party, 1956–60. d. 1960.

Bevin, Ernest
  b. 1881. *Educ*. Elem. National Organiser of Dockers' Union, 1910–21. Gen. Sec. of T. & G.W.U., 1921–40. Member of General Council for T.U.C., 1925–40. M.P. (Lab.) for Cent. Wandsworth, 1940–50. M.P. for E. Woolwich, 1950–51. Min. of Lab. and Nat. Service, 1940–45. For. Sec., 1945–51. Ld Privy S., Mar–Apr 1951. d. 1951.

Blair, Anthony Charles Linton
  b. 1953. *Educ*. Fettes; Oxford. Barrister. M.P. (Lab.) for Sedgefield, 1983–; Leader of the Opposition 1994–97; P.M. 1997–.

Bonar Law, Andrew
> b. 1858. *Educ.* Canada and Glasgow H.S. Family business. M.P. (Con.) for Blackfriars, Glasgow, 1900–6. M.P. for Dulwich, 1906–10. M.P. for Bootle, 1911–18. M.P. for C. Glasgow, 1918–23. P.S. to Bd. of Trade, 1902–5. Leader of Con. party in Commons, 1911–21. Col. Sec., 1915–16. Chanc. of Exch., 1916–19. Ld Privy S. and Leader of Commons, 1919–21. Resigned, 1921. P.M. and Leader of Con. party, 1922–23. Resigned, 1923. d. 1923.

Brown, George Alfred. Ld George-Brown (Life Peer 1970)
> b. 1914. *Educ.* Secondary. M.P. (Lab.) for Belper, 1945–70. P.P.S. to Min. of Lab. and Nat. Service, 1945–47, and to C. of Exchequer, 1947. Joint Parliamentary Secretary, Min. of Ag. and Fish., 1947–51. Min. of Works, Apr–Oct 1951. First Sec. of State and Sec. of State for Econ. Affairs, 1964–66. For. Sec., 1966–68. Resigned, 1968. Deputy Leader of the Labour Party, 1960–70. d. 1985.

Brown, (James) Gordon
> b.1951. *Educ.* Kirkcaldy H.S.; Glasgow Univ. Lecturer, journalist. M.P. (Lab.) for Dunfermline E., 1983–. Chanc. of the Exch., 1997–.

Butler, Richard Austen. Ld Butler of Saffron Walden (Life Peer 1965)
> b. 1902. *Educ.* Marlborough; Cambridge. M.P. (Con.) for Saffron Walden, 1929–65. U.-S. India O., 1932–37. P.S. Min. of Lab., 1937–38. U-S. For. O., 1938–41. Pres. Bd. of Educ.,1941–44. Min. of Educ., 1944–45. Min. of Lab., 1945. Chanc. of Exch., 1951–55. Leader of Commons, 1955–61. Ld Privy S., 1955–59. Home Sec., 1957–62. First Sec. of State and Min. in charge of C. African O., 1962–63. For. Sec., 1963–64. Ch. of Con. party organisation,1959–61. Master of Trinity College, Cambridge, 1965–78. d. 1982.

Callaghan, (Leonard) James. Ld Callaghan of Cardiff (Life Peer 1987)
> b. 1912. *Educ.* Elem. and Portsmouth Northern Secondary Schools. M.P. (Lab.) for S. Cardiff, 1945–50. M.P. for S.E. Cardiff, 1950–83. M.P. for S. Cardiff and Penarth, 1983–7. P.S. Min. of Transport, 1947–50. P.S. and F.S. Admiralty, 1950–51. Chanc. of the Exch., 1964–67. Home Sec., 1967–70. For. Sec., 1974–76. P.M., 1976–79. Leader of Opposition, 1979–80. K.G. 1985.

Campbell-Bannerman, Henry (Sir)
> b. 1836. *Educ.* Glasgow H.S.; Glasgow Univ. and Cambridge. Family business. M.P. (Lib.) for Stirling Burghs, 1868–1908. F.S. to War O., 1871–74 and 1880–82. Sec. to Admir., 1882–84. Ch. Sec. for Ireland (without seat in cabinet), 1884–85. Sec. for War, 1886 and 1892–95. G.C.B., 1895. Leader of Lib. party in Commons, 1899–1908. P.M., 1905–8. Resigned, 1908. d. 1908.

Carrington, 6th Ld (1938), Peter Alexander Rupert Carington
> b. 1919. *Educ.* Eton; Sandhurst. Army 1939–45. Banker. P.S. Min. of Ag. and Fish., 1951–54. P.S. Min. of Defence, 1954–56. High Commissioner to Australia, 1956–59. 1st Ld of Admiralty, 1959–63. Leader of House of Lords, 1963–64. Sec. of State for Defence, 1970–74. Sec. of State for Energy, 1974. Ch. of Con. Party Organisation, 1972–74. For. Sec.,1979–82. Secretary-General of N.A.T.O., 1984–9. European peace negotiator in former Yugoslavia, 1991–2.

Chamberlain, (Arthur) Neville
> b. 1869. *Educ.* Rugby; Mason Science College, Birmingham. Business career. Ld Mayor of Birmingham, 1915–16. Dir.-Gen. of Nat. Service, 1916–17. M.P. (Con.) for Ladywood, Birmingham, 1918–29. M.P. for Edgbaston, Birmingham, 1929–40. Postm.-Gen., 1922–23. Paym.-Gen., 1923. Min. of Health, 1923. Chanc. of Exch., 1923–24. Min. of Health, 1924–29 and 1931. Ch. of Con. party organisation, 1930–31. Chanc.of Exch., 1931–37. P.M. and Leader of Con. party, 1937–40. Ld Pres. of Council, 1940. Resigned, 1940. d. 1940.

Chamberlain, Joseph
> b. 1836. *Educ.* University College School. Family business. Mayor of Birmingham, 1873–75. M.P. (Lib.) for Birmingham, 1876–85. M.P. for W. Birmingham, 1885–86, M.P. (Lib.U.) for W. Birmingham, 1886–1914. Pres. of Bd of Trade, 1880–85. Pres. of Loc. Govt. Bd., 1886. Col. Sec., 1895–1903. d. 1914.

Chamberlain, (Joseph) Austen (Sir)
> b. 1863. *Educ.* Rugby; Cambridge. M.P. (Lib.U.) for E. Worcs., 1892–1914. M.P. (Un.) for W. Birmingham, 1914–37. Lib. U. Whip, 1892. Civil Ld of Admir., 1895–1900. F.S. to Treas.,1900–2. Postm.-Gen., 1902–3. Chanc. of Exch., 1903–5. Sec. for India, 1915–17. Resigned, 1917. Min. without Portfolio in war cabinet, 1918–19. Chanc. of Exch., 1919–21. Ld Privy S. and Leader of Con. party in Commons, 1921–22. For. Sec., 1924–29. K.G., 1925. 1st Ld of Admir., 1931. d. 1937.

Churchill, Winston Leonard Spencer (Sir)
> b. 1874. *Educ.* Harrow; Sandhurst. Army, 1895–1900. M.P. (Con.) for Oldham, 1900–4. M.P. (Lib.) for Oldham, 1904–6. M.P. (Lib.) for N.W. Manchester, 1906–8. M.P. (Lib.) for Dundee, 1908–22. M.P. (Const. then Con.) for Epping, 1924–45; M.P. (Con.) for Woodford, 1945–64. U-S. for Col. O., 1905–8. Pres. of Bd. of Trade, 1908–10. Home Sec., 1910–11. 1st Ld of Admiralty, 1911–15. Chanc. of D. of Lanc., 1915. Min. of Munitions, 1917–19. Sec. for War and Air, 1919–21. Sec. for Air and Col., 1921. Col. Sec., 1921–22. Chanc. of Exch., 1924–29. 1st Ld of Admir., 1939–40. P.M. and Min. of Def., 1940–45. Leader of Con. party, 1940–55. Leader of Opposition, 1945–51. Min. of Def., 1951–52. P.M., 1951–55. K.G., 1953. d. 1965.

Clarke, Kenneth

b. 1940. *Educ.* Nottingham H.S.; Cambridge. Barrister. M.P.(Con.) Rushcliffe, 1970–. Asst.Whip, 1972–4. Ld Com., 1974, P.S.Transport, 1979–82. Min.Health, 1982–5. Paym.-Gen. and Emp.Min., 1985–7. Chanc. of D. of Lanc. and Min.Trade, 1987–8. Sec.of State Health, 1988–90, Sec.of State Educ., 1990–2. Home Sec., 1992–3. Chanc. of Exch., 1993–97.

Clynes, John Richard

b. 1869. *Educ.* Elementary. Cotton worker; union official. M.P. (Lab) for N.E. Manchester, 1906–18. M.P. for Manchester, Platting, 1918–31, 1935–45. Food controller, 1918. Leader of Opposition, 1921–2. Lord Privy Seal, 1924. Home Sec., 1929–31. d.1949.

Cook, Robin (Robert) Finlayson,

b.1946. *Educ.* Aberdeen G.S.; Edinburgh Univ. Adult educator. M.P. (Lab.) for Edinburgh Cent., 1974–83, M.P. for Livingston, 1983–. For. Sec., 1997–.

Cripps, (Richard) Stafford (Sir)

b. 1889. *Educ.* Winchester; London. Barrister. M.P. (Lab.) for E. Bristol, 1931–50. M.P. for S.E. Bristol, 1950. Kt., 1930. Sol.-Gen., 1930–31. Brit. Amb. to U.S.S.R., 1940–42. Ld Privy S. and Leader of Commons, 1942. Min. of Aircraft Prod., 1942–45. Pres. of Bd. of Trade, 1945–47. Min. for Econ. Affairs, 1947. Chanc. of Exch., 1947–50. d. 1952.

Crosland, (Charles) Anthony Raven

b. 1918. *Educ.* Highgate; Oxford. M.P. (Lab.) for South Glos., 1950–55; M.P. for Grimsby, 1959–77. Min. of State, Econ. Affairs, 1964–65. Sec. of State Educ. and Science, 1965–67. President of the Bd. of Trade, 1967–69. Sec. of State for Local Govt and Regional Planning, 1969–70. Sec. of State for the Environment, 1974–76. For. Sec., 1976–77. d. 1977.

Curzon, George Nathaniel. Ld Curzon (1898), 1st Earl (1911), 1st Marquess Curzon of Kedleston (1921)

b. 1859. *Educ.* Eton; Oxford. M.P. (Con.) for Southport, 1886–98. U-S. India O., 1891–92. U-S. For. 0., 1895–98. Viceroy of India, 1899–1905. Entered H. of Lords as Irish Representative Peer, 1908. Ld Privy Seal, 1915–16. Ld Pres. of Council, 1916–19. Member of war cabinet, Leader of Lords, 1916–24. For. Sec., 1919–24. Ld Pres. of Council, 1924–25. Leader of Con. Party, Lords, 1916–25. d. 1925

Dalton, (Edward) Hugh John Neale. Ld Dalton (Life Peer 1960)

b. 1887. Eton; Cambridge, L.S.E. Barrister, 1914. Univ. Lecturer, London, 1919–36. M.P. (Lab.) for Peckham, 1924–29. M.P. Bishop Auckland, 1929–31 and 1935–59. U-S. For. O., 1929–31. Min. of Econ. Warfare, 1940–42. Pres. of Bd. of Trade, 1942–45. Chanc. of Exch., 1945–47. Chanc. of D. of Lanc., 1948–50. Min. of Town and Country Planning, 1950–51. Min. of Loc. Govt and Planning, 1951. d. 1962.

Douglas-Home, Sir Alec (Alexander Frederick). Ld Dunglass (1918–51). 14th E of Home (1951–63). Ld Home of the Hirsel (Life Peer 1974)

b. 1903. *Educ.* Eton; Oxford. M.P. (Con.) for S. Lanark, 1931–45. M.P. for Lanark, 1950–51. M.P. for Kinross and W. Perthshire, 1963–74. P.P.S. to N. Chamberlain, 1937–40. Joint U-S. For. O., 1945. (Succ. to Earldom 1951) Min. of State Scottish O., 1951–55. Sec. Commonwealth Relations, 1955–60. Dep. Leader of Lords, 1956–57. Ld Pres. of Council, 1957 and 1959–60. Leader of Lords, 1957–60. For. Sec., 1960–63. K.T., 1962. P.M., 1963–64 (Renounced peerage 1963). Leader of Con. Party, 1963–65. For. Sec., 1970–74. d. 1995.

Eden, (Robert) Anthony (Sir). 1st E of Avon (1961)

b. 1897. *Educ.* Eton; Oxford. M.P. (Con.) for Warwick and Leamington, 1923–57. P.P.S. to Sir A. Chamberlain (For. Sec.), 1926–29. U-S. For. O., 1931–33. Ld Privy S., 1933–35. Min. without Portfolio for League of Nations Affairs, 1935. For. Sec., 1935–38. Resigned, 1938. Sec. for Dominions, 1939–40. Sec. for War, 1940. For. Sec., 1940–45. Leader of Commons, 1942–45. Dep. Leader of Opposition, 1945–51. For. Sec., 1951–55. K.G., 1954. P.M. and Leader of Con. party, 1955–57. d. 1977.

Foot, Michael Mackintosh

b. 1913. *Educ.* Leighton Park Sch., Reading; Oxford. Journalist. M.P. (Lab) for Plymouth Devonport, 1945–55. M.P. for Ebbw Vale, 1960–83. M.P. for Blaenau Gwent, 1983–92. Sec. for Employment 1974–76; Lord Pres. of Council and Leader of House of Commons, 1976–79. Leader of Opposition, 1980–83. Dep. Leader of Labour Party, 1976–80. Leader of Labour Party, 1980–83.

Gaitskell, Hugh Todd Naylor

b. 1906. *Educ.* Winchester; Oxford. M.P. (Lab.) for S. Leeds, 1945–63. Princ. Private Sec. to Min. of Econ. Warfare, 1940–42. Princ. Asst. Sec. Bd. of Trade, 1942–45. P.S. Min. of Fuel and Power, 1946–47. Min. of Fuel and Power, 1947–50. Min. of State for Econ.Affairs, 1950. Chanc. of Exch., 1950–51. Leader of Lab. party, 1955–63. d. 1963.

Gordon Walker, Patrick Chrestien. Ld Gordon-Walker (Life Peer 1974)

b. 1907. *Educ.* Wellington; Oxford. University Teacher. M.P. (Lab.) for Smethwick, 1945–64. M.P. (Lab.) Leyton, 1966–74. P.P.S. to H. Morrison, 1946. Parl. U.-S., Commonwealth Relations O., 1947–50. Sec. of State for Commonwealth Relations, 1950–51. For. Sec., 1964–65. Min. without Portfolio, 1967. Sec. for Educ. and Science, 1967–68. d. 1980.

Grey, Edward (Sir). 1st Vt Grey of Fallodon (1916)

b. 1862. *Educ.* Winchester; Oxford. Succ. to Btcy., 1882. M.P. (Lib.) for Berwick-on-Tweed, 1885–1916. U-S. For. O., 1892–95. For. Sec., 1905–16. (For. Sec. in Lords, 1916). Leader of Lib. party, Lords, 1923–24. d. 1933.

Hague, William Jefferson

b. 1961. *Educ.* Wath-on-Dearne Comp.; Oxford. Management consultant. M.P. (Con.) for Richmond (Yorks), 1989–. U-S. Soc. Sec.1993–94. Min.of State, Soc. Sec. 1994–5. Sec of State for Wales, 1995–7. Leader of the Opposition 1997–.

Halifax, 3rd Vt (1934). Edward Frederick Lindley Wood. 1st Ld Irwin (1925), 1st E of (1944)

b. 1881. *Educ.* Eton; Oxford. M.P. (Con.) for Ripon, 1910–25. U-S. Col. O., 1921–22. Pres. of Bd. of Educ., 1922–24. Min. of Agric., 1924–25. Viceroy of India, 1926–31. Pres. of Bd. of Educ., 1932–35. Sec. for War, 1935. Ld Privy S., 1935–37. Leader of Lords, 1935–38. Ld Pres. of Council, 1937–38. For. Sec., 1938–40. Leader of Lords, 1940. Brit. Amb. to U.S.A., 1941–46. d. 1959.

Healey, Denis Winston. Lord Healey (Life Peer 1992)

b. 1917. *Educ.* Bradford G.S.; Oxford. M.P. (Lab.) for Leeds South-East, 1952–55. M.P. for Leeds East, 1955–92. Sec. for Defence, 1964–70. Chanc. of Exch., 1974–79. Dep. Leader of Lab. Party, 1980–83.

Heath, Edward Richard George (Sir)

b. 1916. *Educ.* Chatham House School, Ramsgate; Oxford. M.P. (Con.) for Bexley, 1950–74. M.P. for Sidcup, 1974–83. M.P. for Old Bexley and Sidcup, 1983–. Con. Whip, 1951–55. Chief Whip, 1955–59. Min. of Labour, 1959–60. Lord Privy Seal, 1960–63. Sec. for Trade & Industry, 1963–64. Leader of the Con. Party, 1965–75. Leader of the Opposition, 1965–70. P.M., 1970–74. Leader of the Opposition, 1974–75. K.G., 1992.

Heathcoat Amory, Derick. 1st Vt Amory (1960)

b. 1899. *Educ.* Eton; Oxford. M.P. (Con.) for Tiverton, 1945–60. Min. of Pensions, 1951–53. Min. of State for Bd. of Trade, 1953–54. Min. of Ag., Fish. and Food, 1954–58. Chanc.of Exch., 1958–60. High Commissioner for the U.K. in Canada, 1961–63. d. 1981.

Henderson, Arthur

b. 1863. *Educ.* Elem. M.P. (Lab.) for Barnard Castle, 1903–18. M.P. for Widnes, 1919–22. M.P. for Newcastle E., 1923. M.P. for Burnley, 1924–31. M.P. for Clay Cross, 1933–35. Sec. of Lab. party, 1911–34. Treasurer of Lab. party, 1930–35. Leader of Lab. party in Commons, 1908–10 and 1914–17. Chief Whip, 1914. Pres. Bd. of Educ., 1915–16. Paym.-Gen., 1916. Min. without portfolio and member of war cabinet, 1916–17. Resigned from cabinet, 1917. Chief Lab. party Whip, 1920–24 and 1925–27. Home Sec., 1924. For.Sec., 1929–31. Leader of Lab. Opposition, 1931–32. d. 1935.

Heseltine, Michael Ray Dibdin

b. 1933. *Educ.* Shrewsbury; Oxford. Publisher. M.P. (Con.) for Tiverton, 1966–74, M.P. for Henley, 1974–. U-S. Transport, 1970–72. Min. for Aerospace and Shipping, 1972–4. Sec. of State for Environment, 1979–83. Sec. of State for Defence, 1983–6. Sec. of State for Environment, 1990–92. Pres. of B. of Trade, 1992–5. First Sec. of State and Deputy P.M., 1995–97.

Hicks Beach, Michael Edward (Sir). 1st Vt St Aldwyn (1906), 1st Earl (1915)

b. 1837. *Educ.* Eton; Oxford. Succ. to Btcy., 1854. M.P. (Con.) for E. Gloucs., 1864–85. M.P. for W. Bristol, 1885–1906. Sec. of Poor Law Bd., 1868. U-S. Home O., 1868. Ch. Sec. for Ireland, 1874–78. (Seat in cabinet, 1876.) Sec. for Col., 1878–80. Chanc. of Exch. and Leader of Commons, 1885–86. Leader of Opposition in Commons, 1886. Ch. Sec. for Ireland, 1886–87. Resigned, 1887, but remained in cabinet without portfolio. Pres. of Bd. of Trade, 1888–92. Chanc. of Exch., 1895–1902. Resigned 1902. d. 1916.

Hoare, Samuel John Gurney (Sir). 1st Vt Templewood (1944)

b. 1880. *Educ.* Harrow; Oxford. M.P. (Con.) for Chelsea, 1910–44. Succ. to Btcy., 1915. Sec. for Air, 1922–24 and 1924–29. Sec. for India, 1931–35. For. Sec., 1935. 1st Ld of Admir., 1936–37. Home Sec., 1937–39. Ld Privy S., 1939–40. Sec. for Air, 1940. Brit. Amb. to Spain, 1940–44. d. 1959.

Horne, Robert Stevenson (Sir). 1st Vt Horne of Slamannan (1937)

b. 1871. *Educ.* George Watson's Coll., Edin.; Glasgow Univ. Member of Faculty of Advocates, 1896. K.B.E., 1918. M.P. (Con.) for Hillhead, Glasgow, 1918–37. Min. of Lab., 1919–20. Pres. of Bd. of Trade, 1920–21. Chanc. of Exch., 1921–22. d. 1940.

Howe, (Richard Edward) Geoffrey (Sir). Ld Howe of Aberavon (Life Peer 1992)

b. 1926. *Educ.* Winchester; Cambridge. Barrister. M.P. (Con.) for Bebington, 1964–66. M.P. for Reigate, 1970–74. M.P. for Surrey East, 1974–92. Sol.-Gen., 1970–72. Min. for Trade and Consumer Affairs, 1972–74. Chanc. of Exch., 1979–83. For. Sec., 1983–9. Ld Pres. and Deputy P.M. 1989–90. Resigned 1990.

Hurd, Douglas Richard. Lord Hurd of Westwell (Life Peer 1997)

b.1930. *Educ.* Eton; Cambridge. Diplomat. Pol. Sec. to E. Heath, 1968–73. M.P. (Con.) for Mid-Oxon, 1974–83. M.P. for Witney, 1983–97. Min. of State Foreign Office, 1979–83. Home Office, 1983–4. Sec. of State for N.Ireland, 1984–5. Home Sec., 1985–9. For.Sec., 1989–95.

Jenkins, Roy Harris. Ld Jenkins of Hillhead (Life Peer 1987)

b. 1920. *Educ*. Abersychan G.S.; Oxford. Army, 1939–45. M.P. (Lab.) for Central Southwark, 1948–50. M.P. (Lab.) for Stechford, Birmingham, 1950–76. M.P. (S.D.P.) for Glasgow Hillhead, 1982–87. P.P.S. Commonwealth Relations O., 1949–50. Min. of Aviation, 1964–65. Home Sec., 1965–67. Chanc. of Exch., 1967–70. Deputy Leader of Lab. party, 1970–72. Home Sec., 1974–76. President of European Economic Commission, 1977–81. Leader of SDP, 1982–83. Leader of (Social and) Liberal Democrat Peers 1987–97.

Kinnock, Neil Gordon

b. 1942 *Educ*. Lewis Sch., Pengam; U.of Wales (Cardiff). M.P. (Lab.) for Bedwellty, 1970–83. M.P. for Islwyn, 1983–94. P.P.S. to Sec. of State for Employment, 1974–75. Chief Opposition Spokesman on Education, 1979–83. Leader of the Opposition, and Leader of Labour Party, 1983–92. European Commissioner 1994–.

Lamont, Norman Stewart Hughson. Ld Lamont (Life Peer 1998)

b.1942. *Educ*. Loretto; Cambridge. Merchant banker. M.P. (Con.) for Kingston-on-Thames, 1972–97. U-S. Energy, 1979–81. Min.of State for Industry, 1981–5. Min.of State (Defence Procurement), 1985–6; Fin.Sec. Treasury, 1986–9. Chief Sec., 1989–90. Chanc. of Exch., 1990–93.

Lansbury, George

b. 1859. *Educ*. Elem. M.P. (Lab.) for Bow and Bromley, 1910–12 and 1922–35. First Comm. of Works, 1929–31. Leader of the Opposition, 1931–35. Leader of the Labour Party, 1932–35. d. 1940.

Lansdowne, 5th M of (1866). Henry Charles Keith Petty-Fitzmaurice, Vt Clanmaurice (1845–63), E of Kerry (1863–66)

b. 1845. *Educ*. Eton; Oxford. Succ. to M. 1866. Junior Ld of Treas. (Lib.), 1869–72. U-S. for War, 1872–74. U-S. India O., 1880. Resigned and opposed Lib. Govt. in Lords, 1880. Gov.-Gen. of Canada, 1883–88. Viceroy of India, 1888–94. Sec. for War (Con.), 1895–1900. For. Sec., 1900–5. Leader of Con. party in Lords, 1903–16. Min. without portfolio, member of war cabinet, 1915–16. Left Con. party, 1917. d. 1927.

Lawson, Nigel. Ld Lawson (Life Peer 1992)

b. 1932. *Educ*. Westminster; Oxford. Journalist. M.P. (Con.) for Blaby, Feb. 1974–1992. Opposition Spokesman on Treasury and Economic Affairs, 1977–79. F.S. to Treasury, 1979–81. Sec. for Energy, 1981–83; Chanc. of Exch., 1983–89. Resigned 1989.

Lloyd, (John) Selwyn Brooke. Ld Selwyn-Lloyd (Life Peer 1976)

b. 1904. *Educ*. Fettes; Cambridge. Barrister, 1930. M.P. (Con.) for Wirral, 1945–76. Min. of State For. O., 1951–54. Min. of Supply, 1954–55. Min. of Def., 1955. For. Sec., 1955–60. Chanc. of Exch., 1960–62. Lord Privy Seal and Leader of the House of Commons, 1963–64. Speaker of the House of Commons, 1971–76. d.1978.

Lloyd George, David. 1st Earl Lloyd George of Dwyfor (1945)

b. 1863. *Educ*. Church School. Solicitor, 1884. M.P. (Lib.) for Caernarvon Boroughs, 1890–1945 (Ind. L., 1931–35). Pres. of Bd. of Trade, 1905–8. Chanc. of Exch., 1908–15. Min. of Munitions, 1915–16. Sec. for War, 1916. P.M., 1916–22. Leader of Lib. party, 1926–31. d. 1945.

MacDonald, James Ramsay

b. 1866. *Educ*. Drainie School. M.P. (Lab.) for Leicester, 1906–18. M.P. for Aberavon, Glamorganshire, 1922–29. M.P. for Seaham, 1929–35. (Nat. Lab., 1931–35.) M.P. (Nat. Lab.) for Scottish Univs., 1936–37. Sec. of L.R.C. and Lab. party, 1900–12. Treas. of Lab. party, 1912–29. Chairman of I.L.P., 1906–9. Ch. of Lab. party, 1911–14. Resigned Chairmanship, 1914. Ch. of P.L.P. and Leader of official Opposition, 1922. Leader of Lab. party, 1922–31. P.M.and For. Sec., 1924. P.M., 1929–31. P.M. of National Govt., 1931–35. Ld Pres. of Council, 1935–37. d. 1937.

McKenna, Reginald

b. 1863. *Educ*. St. Malo, Ebersdorf and King's Coll. School; Cambridge. Barrister, 1887. M.P. (Lib.) for N. Monmouthshire, 1895–1918. F.S. to Treas., 1905–7. Pres. Bd. of Educ., 1907–8. 1st Ld of Admir., 1908–11. Home Sec., 1911–15. Chanc. of Exch., 1915–16. Ch. of Midland Bank, 1919–43. d. 1943.

Macleod, Iain Norman

b. 1913. *Educ*. Fettes; Cambridge. Journalist. M.P. (Con.) for Enfield West, 1950–70. Min. of Health, 1952–55. Min. of Labour, 1955–59. Sec. of State for Colonies, 1959–61. Chanc. of D. of Lanc. and Leader of House of Commons, 1961–63. Ch. of Con. party organisation, 1961–63. Editor of Spectator, 1963–65. Chanc. of Exch., 1970. d. 1970.

Macmillan, (Maurice) Harold. 1st E of Stockton (1984)

b. 1894. *Educ*. Eton; Oxford. M.P. (Con.) for Stockton-on-Tees, 1924–29 and 1931–45. M.P. (Con.) for Bromley, 1945–64. P.S. Min. of Supply, 1940–42. U-S. Col. O., 1942. Min. Resident at Allied H.Q. in N.W. Africa, 1942–45. Sec. for Air, 1945. Min. of Housing and Loc. Govt., 1951–54. Min. of Def., 1954–55. For. Sec., 1955. Chanc. of Exch., 1955–57. P.M. and Leader of Con. party, 1957–63. d.1986.

Major, John

b. 1943. *Educ*. Rutlish G.S. Banker. M.P.(Con.) for Huntingdon 1979–. Whip, 1983–5. U-S. Soc.Sec., 1985–6. Min. of State D.H.S.S., 1986–7. Chief Sec. Treasury, 1987–89. For. Sec., 1989. Ch.of Exch., 1989–90. P.M. and Leader of the Conservative Party, 1990–97.

Maudling, Reginald
  b. 1917. *Educ.* Merchant Taylors'; Oxford. Barrister, 1940. M.P. (Con.) for Barnet, 1950–74. M.P. for Chipping Barnet, 1974–79. P.S. Min. of Civil Aviation, 1952. Econ. Sec. to Treasury, 1952–55. Min. of Supply, 1955–57. Paym.-Gen., 1957–59. Pres. Bd. of Trade, 1959–61. Sec. of State for Colonies, 1961–62. Chanc. of Exch., 1962–64. Deputy Leader of Con. party, 1965–72. Home Sec., 1970–72. Resigned, 1972. d. 1979.

Morrison, Herbert Stanley. Ld Morrison of Lambeth (Life Peer 1959)
  b. 1888. *Educ.* Elem. Member of L.C.C., 1922–45. Leader of Council, 1934–40. M.P. (Lab.) for S. Hackney, 1923–34, 1929–31, 1935–45. M.P. for E. Lewisham, 1945–50. M.P. for S. Lewisham, 1950–59. Min. of Transport, 1929–31. Min. of Supply, 1940. Home Sec. and Min. of Home Security, 1940–45. Member of war cabinet, 1942–45. Dep. P.M., 1945–51. Ld Pres. of Council and Leader of Commons, 1945–51. For. Sec., 1951. Dep. Leader of Opposition, 1951–55. d. 1965.

Owen, David Anthony Llewellyn. Lord Owen (Life Peer 1992)
  b. 1938. *Educ.* Bradfield; Cambridge. Doctor, 1962. M.P. (Lab.) for Plymouth Sutton, 1966–74. M.P. for Plymouth Devonport, 1974–92. U-S. for Navy, 1968–70. U-S. Health and Social Security, 1974. Min. of State Health and Social Security, 1974–76. Min. of State For. O., 1976–77. For. Sec., 1977–79. Leader of SDP, 1983–89.

Prescott, John Leslie
  b.1938. *Educ.* Grange Sch. Mod., Ellesmere Port. Hull. Seaman. M.P. (Lab.) for Hull E., 1970. Dep. Leader of Lab. Party, 1994–. Deputy P.M. and Sec. of State for Environment, Transport and Regions, 1997–.

Pym, Francis Leslie. Ld Pym (Life Peer 1987)
  b. 1922. *Educ.* Eton; Cambridge. M.P. (Con.) for Cambridgeshire, 1961–83. M.P. for Cambridgeshire S.E., 1983–87. Parl. Sec. to the Treasury and Government Chief Whip, 1970–73. Sec. for Northern Ireland, 1973–74. Sec. for Defence, 1979–81. Chanc. of D. of Lancaster, Paym.-Gen. and Leader of House of Commons, 1981. Lord Pres. of Council and Leader of House of Commons, 1981–82. For. Sec., 1982–83.

Reading, 1st M of (1926). Rufus Daniel Isaacs (Sir), 1st Ld (1914), 1st Vt (1916) 1st E of (1917)
  b. 1860. *Educ.* Brussels, Anglo-Jewish Acad., London, University College Sch. Family business. Barrister, 1887. M.P. (Lib.) for Reading, 1904–13. Kt., 1910. Sol.-Gen, 1910. Att. Gen., 1910–13 (seat in cabinet, 1912). Ld Chief Justice, 1913–21. Brit Amb. to U.S.A., 1918–19. Viceroy of India, 1921–26. For. Sec., 1931. Leader of Lords, 1931; Leader of Lib. party, Lords, 1930–35. d. 1935.

Rifkind, Malcolm Leslie, Sir
  b. 1946. *Educ.* Geo. Watson's; Edinburgh Univ. Advocate. M.P. (Con.) for Edinburgh Pentlands, 1974–97. U-S. Scotland, 1979–82; U-S. For. O., 1982–3. Min.of State. For.O, 1983–6. Sec of S. Scotland, 1986–90, Sec. of S. Transport, 1990–92. Sec. of State Def., 1992–95. For. Sec., 1995–97. K.C.M.G. 1997.

Ritchie, Charles Thomson. 1st Ld Ritchie of Dundee (1905)
  b. 1838. *Educ.* City of London School. M.P. (Con.) for Tower Hamlets, 1874–85. M.P. for St. George's in the East, 1885–92. M.P for Croydon, 1895–1903. F.S. to Admir., 1885–86. Pres. of Loc. Govt. Bd., 1886–92. Pres. of Bd. of Trade, 1895–1900. Home Sec., 1900–2. Chanc. of Exch., 1902–3. Resigned, 1903. d. 1906.

Salisbury, 3rd M of (1868). Robert Arthur Talbot Gascoyne-Cecil, Vt Cranborne (1865–68)
  b. 1830. *Educ.* Eton; Oxford. M.P (Con.) for Stamford, 1853–68. Sec. for India, 1866. Resigned, 1867. Succ. to M. 1868. Sec. for India, 1874–76. For. Sec., 1878–80. Leader of Opposition in Lords, 1881–85. Leader of the Con. party, 1885–1902. P.M. and For. Sec., 1885–86. P.M., 1886–87. P.M. and For. Sec., 1887–92 and 1895–1900. P.M. and Ld Privy S., 1900–2. d.1903.

Simon, John Allsebrook (Sir), 1st Vt Simon (1940)
  b. 1873. *Educ.* Fettes; Oxford. Barrister. M.P. (Lib.) for Walthamstow. 1906–18. M.P. for Spen Valley, 1922–31. M.P. (L. Nat.) for Spen Valley, 1931–40. Kt., 1910. Sol.-Gen., 1910–13. Att.-Gen. (with seat in cabinet), 1913–15. Home Sec., 1915–16. For. Sec., 1931–35. Leader of L. Nat. party, 1931–40. Home Sec. and Dep. Leader of Commons, 1935–37. Chanc. of Exch., 1937–40. Ld. Chanc., 1940–45. d.1954.

Smith, John
  b. 1938. *Educ.* Dunoon G.S.; Edinburgh Univ. Barrister. M.P. (Lab.) for N.Lanarkshire, 1970–83. M.P. for Monklands E., 1983–94. U-S. for Energy, 1974–5. Min.of State Energy, 1975–76. Min.Privy Council Off., 1976–78. Sec. of State Trade, 1978–79. Leader of Opposition, 1992–4. d.1994.

Snowden, Philip. 1st Vt Snowden (1931)
  b. 1864. *Educ.* Bd. School. M.P. (Lab.) for Blackburn, 1906–18. M.P. for Colne Valley, 1922–31. Ch. of I.L.P., 1903–6 and 1917–20. Chanc. of Exch., 1924, 1929–31 and 1931. Ld Privy S., 1931–32. Resigned, 1932. d.1937.

Stewart, (Robert) Michael Maitland. Ld Stewart of Fulham (Life Peer 1979)
  b. 1906. *Educ.* Christ's Hospital; Oxford. Teacher. M.P. (Lab.) Fulham East, 1945–55 and for Fulham, 1955–79. Vice-Chamberlain, H.M. Household, 1946. Comptroller, H.M. Household, 1946–47. U-S. for War, 1947–51. P.S. Min. of Supply, 1951. Sec. for Educ. and Science, 1964–65. For. Sec., 1965–66. Sec. of State for Econ. Affairs, 1966–67. First Sec. of State, 1966–68. For. (and Commonwealth) Sec., 1968–70. d.1990.

Thatcher, Mrs Margaret Hilda (nee Roberts), Lady Thatcher (Life Peer 1992)
    b. 1925. *Educ.* Grantham Girls' School; Oxford. Research Chemist. Barrister. M.P. (Con.) for Finchley, 1959–92. P.S. to Min. of Pensions and Nat. Insurance, 1961–64. Sec. of State for Education and Science, 1970–74. Leader of the Conservative Party, 1975–90. Leader of the Opposition, 1975–79. P.M., 1979–90.

Thorneycroft, (George Edward) Peter. Ld Thorneycroft of Dunston (Life Peer 1967)
    b. 1909. *Educ.* Eton; Woolwich. Barrister, 1935. M.P. (Con.) for Stafford, 1938–45. M.P. (Con.) for Monmouth, 1945–66. P.S. Min. of War Transport, 1945. Pres. of Bd. of Trade, 1951–57. Chanc. of Exch., 1957–58. Resigned, 1958. Min. of Aviation, 1960–62. Min. of Defence, 1962–64. Sec. of State for Defence, 1964. Ch. of Con. party organisation 1975–81. d.1994.

Whitelaw, William Stephen Ian, 1st Viscount Whitelaw of Penrith (1983)
    b.1918. *Educ.* Winchester; Oxford. Landowner. M.P. (Con.) for Penrith and the Border, 1955–83. Whip 1959–62. P.S. Min. of Labour, 1962–4. Opposition Chief Whip, 1964–70. Ld. Pres., 1970–72. Sec. of State N.Ireland, 1972–73. Sec. of State Employment, 1973–4. Dep. Leader of Opposition, 1975–9. Deputy P.M., 1979–86. Home Sec., 1979–83. Ld Pres. and Leader of House of Lords, 1983–86. d.1999.

Wilson, (James) Harold (Sir). Ld Wilson of Rievaulx. (Life Peer 1983)
    b. 1916. *Educ.* Wirral G.S.; Oxford. University teacher, Director of Economics and Statistics, Min. of Fuel and Power, 1943–44. M.P. (Lab.) for Ormskirk, 1945–50. M.P. (Lab.) for Huyton, 1950–83. P.S. Min. of Works, 1945–47. Sec. for Overseas Trade, 1947. Pres. Bd. of Trade, 1947–51. Resigned, 1951. Leader, Lab. party, 1963–76. Leader of the Opposition, 1963–64. P.M., 1964–70. Leader of the Opposition, 1970–74. P.M., 1974–76. K.G., 1976. d.1995.

Wood, (Howard) Kingsley (Sir)
    b. 1881. *Educ.* Central Foundation Boys School. Solicitor, 1903. Kt., 1918. M.P. (Con.) for W. Woolwich, 1918–43. P.P.S. to Min. of Health, 1919–22. P.S. Min. of Health, 1924–29. P.S. Bd. of Educ., 1931. Postm.-Gen., 1931–35 (seat in cabinet, 1933). Min. of Health, 1935–38. Sec. for Air, 1938–40. Ld Privy S., 1940. Chanc. of Exch., 1940–43. d.1943.

Index of Ministers

The educational information is necessarily incomplete. It is not always possible to trace the name or status of an elementary or secondary school. When several schools are recorded, the last is normally named here. All schools that are unstarred are 'public schools' or, more precisely, were in the 1970s members of the Headmasters' Conference. However this can be misleading, particularly for Ministers educated in the 19th century. RNC Dartmouth is also unstarred. By courtesy, we have listed the Royal Military College (Sandhurst) and the Royal Military Academy (Woolwich) in the University column.

In this index, promotion from a knighthood to a higher order of chivalry or to a baronetcy is not recorded.

+ denotes a Privy Councillor.

When an individual appears more than once on a page, the number is indicated. Double entries are given when an individual held office under different names, and where a title was acquired after office had been held.

		Born	Died	School	University	Page reference
	Abercorn, 3rd D of (1913). J. Hamilton, M of Hamilton (1885)	1869	1953	Eton		2
+	Aberdare, 4th Ld (1957). M. G. L. Bruce	1919	–	Winchester	Oxford	34
	Acland, Sir F. D. (14th Bt 1926)	1874	1939	Rugby	Oxford	4^4, 5
+	Acland Hood, Sir A. F. (4th Bt 1892), 1st Ld St Audries (1911)	1853	1917	Eton	Oxford	3^2
	Acton, 2nd Ld (1902) R. M. Dalberg-Acton	1870	1924	Privately	Oxford	3, 5
	Adams, (H.) R.	1912	1978	Emanuel	London	23
	Adamson, Jessie	1882	1962	Elementary		22
+	Adamson, W.	1863	1936	Elementary		11, 13
	Adamson, W. M.	1881	1945	Elementary		20
+	Addison, 1st Vt (1945) 1st Ld (1937). C. Addison	1869	1951	Trinity Coll., Harrogate*	London	4, 6, 7, 8^4, 12^2, 21, 22^3
+	Ailwyn, 1st Ld (1921). Sir A. E. Fellowes (KCVO 1911)	1855	1924	Eton	Cambridge	23
	Ainsworth, P. M.	1956	–	Bradfield	Oxford	47
	Ainsworth, R. W.	1952	–	Foxford Comp.*		49
	Airlie, 12th E of (1900). D. L. G. W. Ogilvy	1893	1968	Eton		12
	Aitchison, Ld (Scot, Judge 1933). C. M. Aitchison	1882	1941	Falkirk H.S.*	Edinburgh	13, 14
(+)	Aitken, J.	1942	–	Eton	Oxford	44^2, 45
+	Akers-Douglas, A., 1st Vt Chilston (1911)	1851	1926	Eton	Oxford	1, 2
	Albemarle, 8th E of (1884). A. A. C. Keppel	1858	1942	Eton		10
	Albu, A. H.	1903	1994	Tonbridge	London	29
+	Aldington, 1st Ld (1962). Sir T. A. R. W. Low (KCMG 1957) (Life Peer 1999)	1914	–	Winchester	Oxford	25^2
+	Alexander of Hillsborough, 1st E (1963). A. V. Alexander 1st Vt (1950)	1885	1965	Elementary		11, 12, 18, 21, 22^3
+	Alexander of Tunis, 1st E (1952). H. R. L. G. Alexander, 1st Vt (1946)	1891	1969	Harrow	Sandhurst	24
+	Alexander of Tunis, 2nd E (1969). S. W. D. Alexander, Ld Rideau (1952)	1935	–	Harrow		35
+	Alison, M. J. H.	1926	–	Eton	Oxford	34, 40, 41
	Allan, of Kilmahew, Ld (Life Peer 1973). R. A. Allan	1914	1979	Harrow	Cambridge	26^2

+ Erroll of Hale, 1st Ld (1964). F.J. Erroll (Life Peer 1999)	1914	–	Oundle	Cambridge	25^2, 26, 28^4
Evans, I. L.	1927	1984	Llanelli G.S.*	Swansea	32
Evans of Parkside, Ld (Life Peer 1998). J. Evans	1930	–	Jarrow Cent.S.*		37
Evans, J.	1950	–	Hawarden H.S.*	London	44, 46^2, 47
Evans, S. N.	1898	1970	Elementary		22
+ Evans, Sir S. T. (GCB 1916)	1859	1929	Secondary	London	3, 4
Ewing, Lord (Life Peer 1992). H. Ewing	1931	–	Beith H. S.*		37
Eyre, Sir R. E. (Kt 1983)	1924	–	K.Edward VI Birmingham	Cambridge	34, 35^2, 42^2
+ Eyres-Monsell, Sir B. M. (GBE 1929), 1st Vt Monsell (1935)	1881	1969	H.M.S. Britannia*		7, 9, 10^2, 12, 13, 14, 15
Fairbairn, Sir N. (Kt 1988)	1933	1995	Loretto	Edinburgh	42
Fairfax, 13th Ld (1939). T. B. M. Fairfax	1923	1964	Eton		26, 29
Fairgrieve, Sir (T.) R. (Kt 1981)	1924	1999	Sedbergh		41
Falconer of Thornton, Ld (Life Peer 1997). C. L. Falconer	1951	–	Glenalmond	Cambridge	49
Fallon, M.	1952	–	Epsom	St.Andrews	40, 43^2, 44, 45
Fanshawe, Ld (Life Peer 1983). Sir A. H. F. Royle (KCMG 1974)	1927	–	Harrow	Sandhurst	33
+ Farquhar, 1st E (1922). Sir H. B. Farquhar (1st Bt 1892), 1st Ld (1898), 1st Vt (1917)	1844	1922	Privately		6, 9
Farrington, Lady (Life Peer 1997). Josephine Farrington	1940	–	Secondary		49
Fatchett, D.	1945	1999	Lincoln	Birmingham	48
+ Fellowes, Sir A. E. (KCVO 1911), 1st Ld Ailwyn (1921)	1855	1924	Eton	Cambridge	23
Fenner, Dame P. E.	1922	–	Ide Hill S.*		33, 39
Fenton, Sir J. C. (Kt 1945)	1880	1951	George Watson's Edinburgh	Edinburgh & Sorbonne	11
+ Fernyhough, E.	1908	1993	Elementary		31^2
+ Ferrers, 13th E (1954). R. W. S. Ferrers	1929	–	Winchester	Cambridge	29, 33, 35^2, 39^2, 44, 45, 46
Feversham, 3rd E of (1916). C. W. S. Duncombe	1906	1964	Eton		15^2, 17
+ Field, F.	1942	–	St.Clemt Danes G.S.*	Hull	49
Finch, Sir H. J. (Kt 1945)	1898	1979	Elementary		32
+ Finlay, 1st Vt (1919). Sir R. Finlay (Kt 1895), 1st Ld (1916)	1842	1929	Edinburgh Acad.	Edinburgh	2^2, 6
Finlay, Sir G. B. (1st Bt 1964)	1917	–	Marlborough		29^2
Finsberg, Ld (Life Peer 1992). Sir G. Finsberg (Kt 1984)	1926	1996	C.of London		40, 41
+ Fisher, H. A. L.	1865	1940	Winchester	Oxford,Paris & Gottingen	7
Fisher, M.	1944	–	Eton	Cambridge	49
Fisher, Sir N. T. L. (Kt 1974)	1913	1996	Eton	Cambridge	27
Fitch, (E.) A.	1915	1985	Kingswood		32^2, 33
+ Fitzalan, 1st Vt (1921). E. B. Fitzalan-Howard.(Assumed name of Talbot 1876). Ld E. Talbot	1855	1947	Oratory Sch.		2, 6, 9
+ Fitzmaurice, 1st Ld (1906). Ld E. G. Fitzmaurice	1846	1935	Eton	Cambridge	3, 4^2
Fleming, Ld (Scot. Judge 1926). D. Fleming	1877	1944	Glasgow H.S.*	Edinburgh & Glasgow	10, 12
Fletcher, Sir A. M. (Kt 1986)	1929	1989	Greenock H. S.*		41, 42
+ Fletcher, Ld (Life Peer 1970). Sir E. G. M. Fletcher (Kt 1964)	1903	1990	Radley	London	31
Fletcher-Cooke, Sir C. (Kt 1981)	1914	–	Malvern	Cambridge	26

	Name			School	University	Pages
+	Ismay, 1st Ld (1947). H. L. Ismay	1887	1965	Charterhouse	Sandhurst	24
+	Jack, J. M.	1946	–	Bradford G.S.	Leicester	44^3, 46
	Jackson, Glenda	1936	–	West Kirby*	R.A.D.A.	48
	Jackson, Sir (F.) S. (GCIE 1927)	1870	1947	Harrow	Cambridge	10
+	Jackson, Margaret (Mrs M. M. Beckett)	1943	–	Notre Dame H. S. Norwich*	Manchester	36, 37
	Jackson, R. V.	1946	–	Falcon Coll. Rhodesia	Oxford	40^2, 44, 45^2
	Jacques, Ld (Life Peer 1968). J. H. Jacques	1905	1995	Secondary	Manchester	38^2
+	James of Hereford, 1st Ld (1895). H.James	1828	1911	Cheltenham		2
+	Jamieson, Ld (Scot. Judge 1935). D. Jamieson	1880	1952	Fettes	Glasgow & Edinburgh	14^2, 17
	Jamieson, D. G.	1947	–	St.Peter's C.	Open Univ. Birmingham*	49^2
+	Jay, Lady (Life Peer 1992). Margaret Jay	1939	–	Blackheath H.S.*	Oxford	48^2
+	Jay, Ld (Life Peer 1987). D. P. T. Jay	1907	1996	Winchester	Oxford	21^2, 32
+	Jeffreys, A. F.	1848	1906	Privately	Oxford	2
+	Jellicoe, 2nd E (1935). G. P. J. R. Jellicoe (Life Peer 1999)	1918	–	Winchester	Cambridge	26^2, 27, 29, 33
+	Jenkin, Ld (Life Peer 1987). (C.) P. F. Jenkin	1926	–	Clifton	Cambridge	33^2, 34, 40^2, 41
	Jenkins, A.	1884	1946	Elementary		19, 22
	Jenkins of Putney, Ld (Life Peer 1981). H. G. Jenkins	1908	–	Enfield G.S.*		36
+	Jenkins of Hillhead (Life Peer 1987). R. H. Jenkins	1920	–	Abersychan G.S.*	Oxford	29, 30^2, 36
	Jersey 8th E of (1915). G. H. R. C. Villiers, Vt Grandison (1873)	1873	1923	Eton	Oxford	9
	John, B. T.	1934	1988	Pontypridd Boys' G.S.*	London	36^2
	John, W.	1878	1955	Elementary		20^2
	John-Mackie, Ld (Life Peer 1981). J. Mackie	1916	1994	Aberdeen G.S.*		30
	Johnson, A. A.	1950	–	Sloane G.S. Chelsea*		49
	Johnson, Melanie	1955	–	Clifton H.S.*	London & Cambridge	48
	Johnson, W.	1917	–	Devon Ho. Margate*		37
	Johnson-Smith, Sir G. (Kt 1981)	1924	–	Charterhouse	Oxford	33^2
+	Johnston, Ld (Scot.Judge 1961). D. H. Johnston	1907	1985	Aberdeen G.S.*	Oxford & Edinburgh	23
+	Johnston, T.	1882	1965	Lenzie Academy*	Glasgow	12, 13, 19
+	Johnstone, H.	1895	1945	Eton	Oxford	19
+	Jones, (T.) A.	1911	1983	Cyfarthfa S.S.*	London	24, 28
+	Jones, A. Creech	1891	1964	Elementary		22^2
+	Jones, Sir F. E. (Kt 1964). Ld Elwyn-Jones (Life Peer 1974)	1909	–	Llanelli G.S.*	Aberystwyth & Cambridge	32, 35
	Jones, G. H.	1947	–	Secondary		47
	Jones, J. H.	1894	1962	Rotherham*		23
	Jones, J. O.	1954	–	Rhydfelin*	Cardiff	49^2
	Jones, J. T.	1858	1925	Elementary		9
	Jones, M.	1885	1939	Elementary	Reading	11, 13
+	Jones, (S.) B.	1938	–	Hawarden G.S.*		37
	Jones, R. B.	1950	–	Merchant Taylors'	St. Andrews	45^2
+	Jones, (T.) A.	1924	1983	Porth Cty G.S.*		36, 37
	Jones, W.	1860	1915	Bangor Normal Coll.*	Aberystwyth & Oxford	5
+	Jopling, Ld. (Life Peer 1997). (T.) M. Jopling	1930	–	Cheltenham	Newcastle	35^2, 39, 42

II

PARTIES

Conservative Party

Party Leaders

1900	M of Salisbury	21 Apr 55	Sir A. Eden
14 Jul 02	A. Balfour	22 Jan 57	H. Macmillan
13 Nov 11	A. Bonar Law[1]	11 Nov 63	Sir A. Douglas-Home
21 Mar 21	A. Chamberlain[1]	2 Aug 65	E. Heath
23 Oct 22	A. Bonar Law[1]	11 Feb 75	Margaret Thatcher
28 May 23	S. Baldwin	28 Nov 90	J. Major
31 May 37	N. Chamberlain[2]	19 Jun 97	W. Hague
9 Oct 40	(Sir) W. Churchill[2]		

[1] A. Bonar Law (1911–21) and A. Chamberlain (1921–22) were Leaders of the Conservative Party in the House Commons. Formerly when the party was in Opposition there were separate Leaders in the Commons and the Lords and the title 'Leader of the Conservative and Unionist Party' did not officially exist. It was conferred in Oct 1922 on A. Bonar Law when he was selected for his second term of office.

[2] N. Chamberlain remained the Leader of the Conservative Party until 4 Oct 40, although he was succeeded as Prime Minister by W. Churchill on 10 May 40 and resigned from the Government on 30 Sep 40.

Conservative Party Leadership Elections

In 1965 the Conservative Party introduced a procedure for the leader to be elected by a ballot of M.P.s. If there was no clear winner on the first ballot (defined by having over 50% of the votes, and being 15% clear of the second placed candidate), the rules stated that the election should go to a second ballot; if there was still no winner with over 50%, it should go to a run-off between the best-placed candidates. This procedure has been used six times.

1965	*1st ballot*				
28 Jul 65	E. Heath[1]	150			
	R. Maudling	133			
	E. Powell	15			

1975	*1st ballot*			*2nd ballot*	
4 Feb 75	Margaret Thatcher	130	11 Feb 75	Margaret Thatcher	140
	E. Heath	119		W. Whitelaw	79
	H. Fraser	16		Sir G. Howe	19
				J. Prior	19
				J. Peyton	11

1989	*1st ballot*[2]				
5 Dec 89	Margaret Thatcher	314			
	Sir A. Meyer	33			

1990	*1st ballot*			*2nd ballot*	
20 Nov 90	Margaret Thatcher	204	27 Nov 90	J. Major	185[3]
	M. Heseltine	152		M. Heseltine	131
				D. Hurd	56

[1] Although the rules required a larger majority, R. Maudling immediately withdrew in favour of E. Heath.
[2] There were 27 abstentions.
[3] Although the rules required a larger majority, both M. Heseltine and D. Hurd withdrew in favour of J. Major when the results of the second ballot were known.

1995　　*1st ballot*[4]
4 Jul 95　　J. Major　　　218
　　　　　　J. Redwood　　89

1997	*1st ballot*			*2nd ballot*			*3rd ballot*	
10 Jun 97	K. Clarke	49	17 Jun 97	K. Clarke	64	19 Jun 97	W. Hague	92
	W. Hague	41		W. Hague	62		K. Clarke	70
	J. Redwood	27		J. Redwood	38			
	P. Lilley	24						
	M. Howard	23						

[4] There were 22 abstentions.

Deputy Leader

4 Aug 65–18 Jul 72	R. Maudling
12 Feb 75– 4 Aug 91	W. Whitelaw *(Vt)*
1 Jun 98–15 Jun 99	P. Lilley

Leader in the House of Lords

1900	3rd M of Salisbury		1957	E of Home
1902	D of Devonshire		1960	2nd Vt Hailsham
1903	M of Lansdowne		1963	Ld Carrington
1916	Earl Curzon *(M)*		1970	Earl Jellicoe
1925	4th M of Salisbury		1973	Ld Windlesham
1930	1st Vt Hailsham		1973	Ld Carrington
1935	M of Londonderry		1979	Ld Soames
1935	Vt Halifax		1981	Lady Young
1938	Earl Stanhope		1983	Vt Whitelaw
1940	Vt Caldecote		1988	Ld Belstead
1940	Vt Halifax		1990	Ld Waddington
1941	Ld Lloyd		1992	Ld Wakeham
1941	Ld Moyne		1994	Vt Cranborne
1942	Vt Cranborne *(5th M of Salisbury)*		1998	Ld Strathclyde

Principal Party Officials

Chairman of the Party Organisation

Jun 11–Dec 16	A. Steel-Maitland	Jan 65–Sep 67	E. du Cann
Dec 16–Mar 23	Sir G. Younger	Sep 67–Jul 70	A. Barber
Mar 23–Nov 26	S. Jackson	Jul 70–Apr 72	P. Thomas
Nov 26–May 30	J. Davidson	Apr 72–Jun 74	Ld Carrington
Jun 30–Apr 31	N. Chamberlain	Jun 74–Feb 75	W. Whitelaw
Apr 31–Mar 36	Ld Stonehaven	Feb 75–Sep 81	Ld Thorneycroft
Mar 36–Mar 42	(Sir) D. Hacking	Sep 81–Sep 83	C. Parkinson
Mar 42–Sep 44	T. Dugdale	Oct 83–Sep 85	J. S. Gummer
Oct 44–Jul 46	R. Assheton	Sep 85–Jun 87	N. Tebbit
Oct 46–Jul 55	Ld Woolton *(Vt)*	Jun 87–Jul 89	P. Brooke
Jul 55–Sep 57	O. Poole	Jul 89–Nov 90	K. Baker
Sep 57–Oct 59	Vt Hailsham	Nov 90–Apr 92	C. Patten
Oct 59–Oct 61	R. Butler	Apr 92–Jul 94	Sir N. Fowler
Oct 61–Apr 63	I. Macleod	Jul 94–Jul 95	J. Hanley
Apr 63–Oct 63	I. Macleod *(joint)*	Jul 95–Jun 97	B. Mawhinney
Apr 63–Oct 63	Ld Poole *(joint)*	Jun 97–Oct 98	Ld Parkinson
Oct 63–Jan 65	Vt Blakenham	Oct 98–	M. Ancram

Deputy Chairman

May 24–Jan 26	M of Linlithgow	Jul 89–May 90	Ld Young of Graffham
Sep 57–Oct 59	O. Poole *(Ld)*	May 90–Nov 90	D. Trippier
Oct 59–Oct 63	Sir T. Low *(Ld Aldington)*	Nov 90–Apr 92	Sir J. Cope
Oct 64–Oct 75	Sir M. Fraser *(Ld)*	Apr 92–Jul 95	Dame A. Rumbold
Apr 72–Jun 74	J. Prior	May 92–Jul 94	G. Malone
Mar 75–Nov 77	W. Clark	Jul 94–Jul 95	M. Dobbs
Mar 75–May 79	A. Maude	Jul 94–Jul 95	J. Maples
Nov 77–May 79	Lady Young	Jul 95–Jun 98	M. Trend
May 79–Jun 83	A. McAlpine*(Ld)*	Mar 98–	R. Hodgson
Jun 83–Sep 84	M. Spicer	Jun 98–Oct 98	M. Ancram
Sep 85–Oct 86	J. Archer	Oct 98–Jun 99	A. Norman
Sep 85–Jul 89	P. Morrison	Jun 99–	D. Prior

Treasurers[1]

Aug 11–Mar 23	Earl Farquhar	Apr 74–Jul 77	Sir A. Silverstone *(Ld Ashdown)*
Mar 23–Apr 29	Vt Younger	Apr 74–Mar 75	W. Clark
Jan 30–Jul 31	Sir S. Hoare	Aug 75–Nov 90	A. McAlpine *(Ld)*
Jul 31–Nov 33	Ld Ebbisham	May 79–Jun 83	Ld Boardman
Nov 33–Jun 38	Vt Greenwood	Apr 82–Apr 90	Sir O. Wade
Jun 38–Feb 47	Vt Marchwood	Dec 84–Jan 88	Sir C. Johnston *(Ld)*
Feb 47–Apr 60	C. Holland-Martin	Jan 88–Mar 93	Ld Laing
Feb 48–Mar 52	Ld De L'Isle	Apr 90–Jul 92	Vt Beaverbrook
Mar 52–Oct 55	O. Poole	Apr 91–Apr 92	Sir J. Cope
Oct 55–Jan 62	Sir H. Studholme	Jul 92–Feb 93	T. Smith
Oct 60–Nov 65	R. Allan	Mar 93–Jun 97	C. Hambro*(Ld)*
Jan 62–Aug 66	R. Stanley	Mar 93–Jun 97	Ld Harris of Peckham
Nov 65–Apr 77	Ld Chelmer	Jun 97–Jun 98	Sir G. Kirkham
Aug 66–Apr 74	Sir T. Brinton	Jun 98–	M. Ashcroft

Chairman of Executive Committee of the Party 1930–98

Oct 30	Sir H. Kingsley Wood	Sep 65	Sir C. Hewlett
Mar 32	G. Herbert	Jul 71	(Sir) J. Taylor
Apr 37	Sir G. Stanley	Jul 76	Sir C. Johnston
Apr 38	Sir E. Ramsden	Jul 81	Sir R. Sanderson*(Ld)*
Apr 43	R. Proby	Jul 86	Sir P. Lane*(Ld)*
Apr 46	N. Colman	Jul 91	Sir B. Feldman*(Ld)*
Apr 51	A. Nutting	Mar 96	R. Hodgson
Apr 52	Sir E. Errington	*(post abolished Mar 98)*	
Feb 57	Sir E. Edwards *(Ld Chelmer)*		

Chairman of National Convention

Mar 98   R. Hodgson

Principal Agent

1885–Jul 03	R. Middleton	Mar 23–Feb 24	Sir R. Hall
Jul 03–Nov 05	L. Wells	Mar 24–Jan 27	(Sir) H. Blain
Nov 05–Dec 06	A. Haig	Jan 27–Feb 28	Sir L. Maclachlan
Dec 06–Jan 12	P. Hughes	Feb 28–Feb 31	R. Topping
May 12–Jun 15	J. Boraston		
Jun 15–Apr 20	{ (Sir) J. Boraston		
Jun 15–Apr 20	{ W. Jenkins		
Apr 20–Dec 20	W. Jenkins		
Dec 20–Mar 23	(Sir) M. Fraser		

General Director

Feb 31–Sep 45	(Sir) R. Topping
Oct 45–Aug 57	(Sir) S. Pierssene
Aug 57–Jun 66	(Sir) W. Urton

[1]From Feb 1948 to Jul 1977 and from May 1979 to Mar 1993 the office of Treasurer was held jointly.

Director of Organisation
Jun 66–Jan 76   (Sir) R. Webster
Feb 76–Jun 88   (Sir) A. Garner

Director of Organisation and Campaigning
Jun 88–May 92   (Sir) J. Lacy

Director of Campaigning
Jun 92–Jul 98   (Sir) T. Garrett

Director of Field Operations
Jul 98–   S. Gilbert

Director of Strategy
1999   A. Cooper

Director of Policy
1999   D. Finkelstein

Director-General
Apr 74–Mar 75   M. Wolff
Nov 92–Feb 95   P. Judge

Chief Executive
Jul 98   A. Norman
Jun 99   D. Prior

Director of Publicity & Communications

1945	E. O'Brien	1978	G. Reece
1946	M. Chapman Walker	1980	Sir H. Boyne
1955	G. Schofield	1982	A. Shrimsley
1956	R. Sims	1985	H. Thomas
1961	G. Hutchinson	1986	M. Dobbs
1964	J. Pemberton	1989	B. Bruce
1965	*(office vacant)*	1990	S. Woodward
1966	T. Rathbone	1991	T. Collins
1968	G. Tucker	1994	H. Colver
1969	R. Lewis	1995	T. Collins *(acting)*
1970	D. Harker	1996	C. Lewington
1975	A. Todd	1997	*(post vacant)*
1976	T. Hooson		

Director of Political Operations and Communications
1997–99   A. Cooper

Director of Media
1998   G. Mackay
1999   Amanda Platell

Director of Presentation
1999   C. Evans

Conservative Research Department
Chairman

1930	N. Chamberlain[1]	1974	I. Gilmour
1940	Sir K. Wood	1975	A. Maude
1943	Sir J. Ball *(acting)*	1979	*(post vacant)*
1945	R. Butler	1997	D. Willetts
1964	*(post vacant)*	1997	*(post vacant)*
1971	Sir M. (Ld) Fraser		

[1]The Conservative Research Department was organised by Lord E. Percy in 1929 but there was no Chairman until Feb 1930.

Director

1930–39	(Sir) J. Ball	1974–79	C. Patten
1939–45	*(post vacant)*	1979–82	A. Howarth
1945–51	D. Clarke *(joint from 48)*	1982–84	P. Cropper
1948–51	H. Hopkinson *(joint)*	1984–85	*(post vacant)*
1948–59	P. Cohen *(joint)*	1985–89	R. Harris
1951–64	M. Fraser *(joint to 59)*	1989–95	A. Lansley
1964–70	B. Sewill	1995–99	D. Finkelstein
1970–74	J. Douglas	1999–	R. Nye

SOURCES:- Annual Conference Reports of the National Union of Conservative and Unionist Associations, and information from the Conservative Research Department.

Chief Whip in the House of Commons

1900	Sir W. Walrond	1964	W. Whitelaw
1902	Sir A. Acland Hood	1970	F. Pym
1911	Ld Balcarres	1973	H. Atkins
1913	Ld E. Talbot	1979	M. Jopling
1921	L. Wilson	1983	J. Wakeham
1923	(Sir) B. Eyres-Monsell	1987	D. Waddington
1931	D. Margesson	1989	T. Renton
1941	J. Stuart	1990	R. Ryder
1948	P. Buchan-Hepburn	1994	A. Goodlad
1951	E. Heath	1997	J. Arbuthnot
1959	M. Redmayne		

Chief Whip in the House of Lords

1900	Earl Waldegrave	1945	Earl Fortescue
1911	D of Devonshire	1958	Earl St Aldwyn
1916	Ld Hylton	1977	Ld Denham
1922	E of Clarendon	1991	Ld Hesketh
1925	E of Plymouth	1993	Vt Ullswater
1929	E of Lucan (5th)	1994	Ld Strathclyde
1940	Ld Templemore	1998	Ld Henley

SOURCES:- *Dod's Parliamentary Companion,* 1900–. For a full list of whips see F.M.G. Wilson, 'Some Career Patterns in British Politics; Whips in the House of Commons, 1906–66', *Parliamentary Affairs,* 24 (Winter 1970–1) pp. 33–42.

Chairman of 1922 Committee[1]

Jan 23–Nov 32	(Sir) G. Rentoul	Nov 55–Nov 64	J. Morrison
Dec 32–Dec 35	W. Morrison	Nov 64–Mar 66	Sir W Anstruther-Gray
Dec 35–Jul 39	Sir H. O'Neill	May 66–Jul 70	Sir A. Harvey
Sep 39–Nov 39	Sir A. Somerville	Jul 70–Nov 72	Sir H. Legge-Bourke
Dec 39–Dec 40	W. Spens	Nov 72–Nov 84	E. du Cann
Dec 40–Dec 44	A. Erskine Hill	Nov 84–Apr 92	C. Onslow
Dec 44–Jun 45	J. McEwen	Apr 92–May 97	Sir M. Fox
Aug 45–Nov 51	Sir A. Gridley	May 97–	Sir A. Hamilton
Nov 51–Nov 55	D. Walker-Smith		

[1] Or the Conservative (Private) Members' Committee. This is an organisation of the entire membership of the Conservative Party in the Commons. It acts as a sounding board of Conservative opinion in the House, but has no official role in formulating policy for the party.

SOURCES:- *The Times Index,* 1923–, information from the 1922 Committee, R. T. Mackenzie, *British Political Parties* (1955) pp.57–61, P. Goodhart, *The 1922* (1973) and Conservative Research Department.

Conservative Shadow Cabinets

Little has been published about the Conservative arrangements when in opposition. The situation appears to have been as follows:–

1906–14 After the 1906 defeat, Conservative ex-ministers met regularly in what was known as a 'Shadow' Cabinet. Only after 1910 was new blood brought in, e.g. F. E. Smith and Sir A. Steel-Maitland.

1924 S. Baldwin summoned a formal Shadow Cabinet of all ex-ministers which met weekly during the Session and which had a secretariat.

1929–31 There was a Consultative Committee which met regularly and was serviced by the Research Department.

1945–51 The Chief Whip sent out notices to a regular Shadow Cabinet meeting, formally known as the Consultative Committee. Names were added but never subtracted and W. Churchill allowed the numbers to grow to about 24. No formal minutes were kept. The following seem to have attended regularly.

W. Churchill (1945–51)	H. Crookshank	M of Salisbury
—	A. Eden	O. Stanley
Sir J. Anderson	W. Elliot	J. Stuart
R. Assheton	R. Law	H. Willink
B. Bracken	O. Lyttelton	Vt Woolton
P. Buchan-Hepburn	H. Macmillan	*Secretary*
R. Butler	D. Maxwell Fyfe	H. Hopkinson (1945–50)
Ld Cherwell	W. Morrison	D. Clarke (1950–51)

1964–70 A Leader's Consultative Committee met regularly as soon as the party went into opposition and formal minutes were kept.

Sir A. Douglas-Home (1964–65)	C. Soames	Q. Hogg (1965–70)
	P. Thorneycroft	Earl Jellicoe (1967–70)
—	*Secretary*	Sir K. Joseph (1965–70)
Lord Blakenham	Sir M. Fraser	S. Lloyd (1965–66)
J. Boyd-Carpenter		I. Macleod (1965–70)
Sir E. Boyle	E. Heath (1965–70)	E. Marples (1965–66)
R. Butler		R. Maudling (1965–70)
Ld Carrington	Ld Balniel (1967–70)	M. Noble (1965–69)
Vt Dilhorne	A. Barber (1966–70)	Mervyn Pike (1966–67)
E. Heath	J. Boyd-Carpenter	E. Powell (1965–68)
J. Godber	(1965–66)	M. Redmayne (1965–66)
Q. Hogg	Sir E. Boyle (1965–70)	G. Rippon (1966–70)
Sir K. Joseph	G. Campbell (1969–70)	D. Sandys (1965–70)
S. Lloyd	R. Carr (1967–70)	C. Soames (1965–66)
I. Macleod	Ld Carrington (1965–70)	Margaret Thatcher
E. Marples	Vt Dilhorne (1965–66)	(1967–70)
R. Maudling	Sir A. Douglas-Home	P. Thorneycroft (1965–66)
M. Noble	(1965–70)	P. Walker (1966–70)
E. Powell	E. du Cann (1965–67)	(W. Whitelaw, *Chief Whip*)
M. Redmayne	J. Godber (1965–70)	*Secretary*
D. Sandys	Ld Harlech (1966–67)	Sir M. Fraser

1974–79   Procedures followed the general pattern of 1964–70

E. Heath (1974–5)

—

A. Barber (–74)
A. Buchanan-Smith
R. Carr
Ld Carrington
P. Channon
Sir A. Douglas-Home (–74)
I. Gilmour
Ld Hailsham
M. Heseltine
Sir G. Howe
P. Jenkin
Sir K. Joseph
M. Macmillan (–74)
J. Peyton
J. Prior
F. Pym
T. Raison
G. Rippon
N. St John-Stevas
N. Scott
Margaret Thatcher
P. Thomas

W. Van Straubenzee
P. Walker
W. Whitelaw
Ld Windlesham (–74)
(H. Atkins, *Chief Whip*)
Secretary
Sir M. Fraser*(Ld)*

Margaret Thatcher
(1975–79)

—

J. Biffen (1975–6,1977–79)
A. Buchanan-Smith
(1975–76)
M. Carlisle (1978–79)
Ld Carrington (1975–79)
J. Davies (1976–78)
N.Edwards (1975–79)
N. Fowler (1975–76
(Sir)I. Gilmour (1975–79)
Ld Hailsham (1975–79)
M. Heseltine (1975–79)
Sir G. Howe (1975–79)

P. Jenkin (1975–79)
Sir K. Joseph (1975–79)
T. King (1976–79)
A. Maude (1975–79)
R. Maudling (1975–76)
A. Neave (1975–79)
J. Nott (1976–79)
Sally Oppenheim
(1975–79)
J Peyton (1975–79)
J. Prior (1975–79)
F. Pym (1975–79)
T. Raison (1975–79)
N. St John-Stevas
(1975–79)
E. Taylor (1976–79)
Ld Thorneycroft (1975–79)
W. Whitelaw (1975–79)
G. Younger (1975–79)
(H. Atkins *Chief Whip*)
Secretary
Ld Fraser (1975–76)
C. Patten (1975–79)
D. Wolfson (1979–79)

1997–   W. Hague (1997–)

—

P. Ainsworth (1998–)
M. Ancram (1997–)
Angela Browning (1999–)
Vt Cranborne (1997–98)
D. Curry (1997–98)
S. Dorrell (1997–98)
I. Duncan-Smith (1997–)
Sir N. Fowler (1997–99)
L. Fox (1998–)
Sir A. Goodlad (1997–98)
D. Heathcoat-Amory
(1999–)

Ld Henley (1999–)
M. Howard (1997–99)
B. Jenkin (1999–)
A. Lansley (1999–)
P. Lilley (1997–99)
A. Mackay (1997–)
J. Maples (1997–)
F. Maude (1997–)
Sir B. Mawhinney
(1997–98)
Theresa May (1999–)
Ld Parkinson (1997–98)
J. Redwood (1997–)
Gillian Shephard (1997–99)

Ld Strathclyde (1998–)
G. Streeter (1999–)
Ann Widdecombe (1997–)
D. Willetts (1998–)
T. Yeo (1999–)
Sir G. Young (1997–)
(J. Arbuthnot *Chief Whip*)
(Secretary
D. Finkelstein (1997–98)
D. Finkelstein (1998–)
(joint)
G. Osborne (1998–)*(joint)*

SOURCE:-M. Punnett, *Front Bench Opposition* (1973); *The Times.*

Party Membership

The Conservative Party has seldom published figures of its total membership. Membership is a loose term, usually associated with the payment of an annual subscription, but exact records are not always kept locally, let alone nationally. In 1953 it was claimed that the party had reached an all-time record membership of 2,805,832, but this was a temporary peak. One estimate for 1969–70 suggests that the party's membership in Great Britain was then 1.12 to 1.34 million. The Houghton Committee estimated that in 1975 the Conservatives had an average membership of 2,400 per constituency, which is equal to about 1.12 million. Membership of the Young Conservatives fell from a peak of 157,000 in 1949 to 80,000 in 1959 and to 50,000 in 1968. In 1982 an internal study suggested that the membership was just under 1.2m. and a similar figure was found in 1984. Estimates in the press in 1993 suggested that previous suggested membership totals had been greatly exaggerated, and that the figure had in any case fallen sharply, so that in 1997 there were probably only a quarter of a million members.

SOURCES:- Nuffield Election Studies; *Committee on Financial Aid to Political Parties* (Cmnd 6601/1976 p.31); M. Pinto-Duschinsky, *British Political Finance 1830–1980* (1980). P. Whiteley and P. Seyd, *True Blues* (1994)

Party Finance

The Conservative Party did not publish its central accounts until 1968. In 1912 Sir A. Steel-Maitland, the Party Chairman, put the party's annual income centrally at £80,000 and suggested that the extra expenses of a general election, centrally, were £80,000 to £120,000. In 1929 J. Davidson, then Chairman, put the cost of the general election at £290,000 (although this included some grants to local campaigns).

The Houghton Committee estimated that in 1975–76 the Conservative party raised £1.8m. at the centre and £4.5m. in the constituencies, a total of £6.3m.

In the year ending March 1983, the Conservative Party raised £4.8m.centrally and about £8.0m. locally. In the year ending March 1984 (containing a general election), central income totalled almost £10m.

The routine expenditure annually reported since 1968 has been:

1967–68	£1,071,000	1978–79	£4,800,000	1989–90	£10,800,000
1968–69	£1,054,000	1979–80	£5,200,000	1990–91	£14,900,000
1969–70	£1,052,000	1980–81	£5,500,000	1991–92	£23,400,000
1970–71	£1,668,000	1981–82	£4,200,000	1992–93	£11,500,000
1971–72	£1,249,000	1982–83	£4,700,000	1993–94	£14,100,000
1972–73	£1,481,000	1983–84	£8,600,000	1994–95	£15,300,000
1973–74	£2,134,000	1984–85	£5,600,000	1995–96	£21,400,000
1974–75	£2,867,000	1985–86	£5,500,000	1996–97	£42,500,000
1975–76	£1,874,000	1986–87	£7,500,000	1997–98	£13,200,000
1976–77	£2,177,000	1987–88	£15,600,000		
1977–78	£2,754,000	1988–89	£10,200,000		

SOURCES:- Annual Conference Reports of the National Union of Conservative and Unionist Associations; N. Blewett, *The Peers, the Parties and the People: The General Elections of 1910* (1972), p 291; R. Rhodes James, *Memoirs of a Conservative* (1969); M. Harrison, in R. Rose and A. Heidenhammer (eds.), *Comparative Political Finance* (1963); R. Rose, Influencing Voters (1967) pp. 260–8; M. Pinto-Duschinsky, *The British General Election of 1970* (1971), pp. 282–3, and 'Central Office and "Power" in the Conservative Party', *Political Studies*, 20 (Mar 72) pp. 1–16; *Committee on Financial Aid to Political Parties* (Cmnd 6601/1976 p. 31); M. Pinto-Duschinsky, *British Political Finance, 1830–1980* (1981); Conservative Party Headquarters; M. Linton, *Money and Votes* (Institute for Public Policy Research 1994). *The Funding of Political Parties* (Cmnd 4057/1998).

Party Structure

Until 1998 the Conservative Central Office (answerable to the Leader of the Party) and the National Union of Conservative Associations had a had a separate but symbiotic relationship. Formally the Leader alone promulgated party policy and appointed the chief party officials. In 1998 the party organisation and the National Union merged under a fifteen person Board of Management, a minority of whom were appointed by the Leader. The Provision was made for a National Convention to meet twice a year.

National Union of Conservative and Unionist Associations

Annual Conferences, 1900–[1]

Date	Place	President	Chairman
19 Dec 00	London	M of Zetland	Ld Windsor
26–27 Nov 01	Wolverhampton	Ld Llangattock	Sir A. Hickman
14–15 Oct 02	Manchester	E of Dartmouth	Sir C. Cave
1–2 Oct 03	Sheffield	E of Derby	F. Lowe
28–29 Oct 04	Southampton	D of Norfolk	H. Bowles
14–15 Nov 05	Newcastle	Ld Montagu	Sir W. Plummer
27 Jul 06	London	D of Northumberland	H. Imbert-Terry
14–15 Nov 07	Birmingham	D of Northumberland	D of Rutland
19–20 Nov 08	Cardiff	E of Plymouth	Sir R. Hodge
17–18 Nov 09	Manchester	Earl Cawdor	Sir T. Wrightson
17 Nov 10	Nottingham	E of Derby	H. Chaplin
16–17 Nov 11	Leeds	D of Portland	Ld Kenyon
14–15 Nov 12	London	Ld Faber	Sir W. Crump
12–14 Nov 13	Norwich	Ld Farquhar	A. Salvidge
1914–16	*No conference held*	Sir A. Fellowes	Sir H. Samuel
1917	London	Sir A. Fellowes	Sir H. Samuel
1918–19	*No conference held*	Sir A. Fellowes	Sir H. Samuel
10–11 Jun 20	Birmingham	Sir A. Fellowes	J. Williams
17–18 Nov 21	Liverpool	A. Chamberlain	Sir A. Benn
15–16 Dec 22	London	E of Derby	Sir A. Leith
25–26 Oct 23	Plymouth	Ld Mildmay	Sir H. Nield
2–3 Oct 24	Newcastle	D of Northumberland	E of Selborne
8–9 Oct 25	Brighton	G. Loder	Sir P. Woodhouse
7–8 Oct 26	Scarborough	G. Lane-Fox	Dame C.Bridgeman
6–7 Oct 27	Cardiff	Vt Tredegar	Sir R. Sanders
27–28 Sep 28	Gt Yarmouth	Ld Queenborough	J. Gretton
21–22 Nov 29	London	Ld Faringdon	G. Rowlands
1 Jul 30	London	N. Chamberlain	C'tess of Iveagh
1931	*No conference held*	N. Chamberlain	G. Herbert
6–7 Oct 32	Blackpool	Ld Stanley	Earl Howe
5–6 Oct 33	Birmingham	E of Plymouth	Sir G. Ellis
4–5 Oct 34	Bristol	Ld Bayford	Regina Evans
3–4 Oct 35	Bournemouth	G. Herbert	Sir W. Cope
1–2 Oct 36	Margate	Ld Ebbisham	Sir L. Brassey
7–8 Oct 37	Scarborough	Ld Bingley	Clara Fyfe
1938	*No conference held*	M of Londonderry	Sir E. Ramsden
1939	*No conference held*	M of Londonderry	N. Colman
1940	*No conference held*	Ld Queenborough	Lady Hillingdon
1941	*No conference held*	Ld Queenborough	Sir C. Headlam
1942	*No conference held*	M of Salisbury	R. Catterall
20–21 May 43	London	M of Salisbury	R. Catterall
1944	*No conference held*	M of Salisbury	Mary Whitehead
14–15 Mar 45	London	Ld Courthope	R. Butler
3–5 Oct 46	Blackpool	O. Stanley	R. Proby
2–4 Oct 47	Brighton	H. Macmillan	Mrs Hornyold-Strickland
7–9 Oct 48	Llandudno	G. Summers	Sir H. Williams
12–14 Oct 49	London	Vt Swinton	D. Graham
12–14 Oct 50	Blackpool	Sir D. Maxwell-Fyfe	A. Nutting
1951	*No conference held*	Ld Ramsden	Lucille Sayers
9–11 Oct 52	Scarborough	Sir T. Dugdale	C. Waterhouse
8–10 Oct 53	Margate	M of Salisbury	Anne Warde
7–9 Oct 54	Blackpool	A. Eden	Sir G. Llewellyn
6–8 Oct 55	Bournemouth	Lucille Sayers	Evelyn Emmet
11–13 Oct 56	Llandudno	R. Butler	Sir E. Edwards
10–12 Oct 57	Brighton	E of Woolton	Katherine Elliot
8–11 Oct 58	Blackpool	Sir R. Proby	Sir S. Bell
1959	*No conference held*	H. Brooke	E. Brown
12–15 Oct 60	Scarborough	H. Brooke	E. Brown

Date	Place	President	Chairman
11–14 Oct 61	Brighton	Vt Hailsham	Sir D. Glover
10–13 Oct 62	Llandudno	Sir G. Llewellyn	Sir J. Howard
8–11 Oct 63	Blackpool	E of Home	Margaret Shepherd
1964	*No conference held*	Vtess Davidson	Sir M. Bemrose
12–15 Oct 65	Brighton	Vtess Davidson	Sir M. Bemrose
13–16 Oct 66	Blackpool	S. Lloyd	Sir D. Mason
18–21 Oct 67	Brighton	Ld Chelmer	Adelaide Doughty
9–12 Oct 68	Blackpool	R. Maudling	Sir T.Constantine
8–11 Oct 69	Brighton	Lady Brooke	D. Crossman
7–10 Oct 70	Blackpool	(I. Macleod)	Sir E. Leather
13–16 Oct 71	Brighton	W. Whitelaw	Unity Lister
11–14 Oct 72	Blackpool	Dame M. Shepherd	W. Harris
10–13 Oct 73	Blackpool	A. Barber	Margot Smith
1974	*No conference held*	P. Thomas	Sir A. Graesser
7–10 Oct 75	Blackpool	P. Thomas	Sir A. Graesser
5–8 Oct 76	Brighton	Ld Hewlett	Shelagh Roberts
11–14 Oct 77	Blackpool	Ld Carrington	D. Sells
10–14 Oct 78	Brighton	Dame A. Doughty	Sir H. Redfearn
9–12 Oct 79	Blackpool	F. Pym	D. D-Handley
11–15 Oct 80	Brighton	Sir T. Constantine	Dame A. Springman
13–16 Oct 81	Blackpool	E. du Cann	F. Hardman
12–15 Oct 82	Brighton	Sir J. Taylor	D. Walters
11–14 Oct 83	Blackpool	Sir G. Howe	P. Lane
9–12 Oct 84	Brighton	Sir A. Graesser	Dame P. Hunter
8–11 Oct 85	Blackpool	Sir H. Atkins	Sir B. Feldman
7–10 Oct 86	Bournemouth	P. Lawrence	
6–9 Oct 87	Blackpool	G. Younger	Dame J. Seccombe
11–14 Oct 88	Brighton	Dame S. Roberts	Sir I. McLeod
10–13 Oct 89	Blackpool	Vt Whitelaw	Sir S. Odell
9–12 Oct 90	Bournemouth	Sir D. D-Handley	Dame M.Fry
7–10 Oct 91	Blackpool	J. Wakeham	Sir J. Barnard
6–9 Oct 92	Brighton	Sir D. Walters	J. Mason
5–8 Oct 93	Blackpool	Dame W. Mitchell	Sir B. Feldman
9–12 Oct 94	Bournemouth	B. Stuttaford	Sir B. Feldman
8–11 Oct 95	Blackpool	D. Kelly	R. Hodgson
6–9 Oct 96	Bournemouth	Dame H. Byford	R. Hodgson
7–10 Oct 97	Blackpool	J. Taylor	R. Hodgson
5–9 Oct 98	Bournemouth	G. Park	R. Hodgson
4–7 Oct 99	Blackpool	B. Hanson	R. Hodgson

[1] 1900–12, National Union of Conservative and Constitutional Associations; 1912–17 National Unionist Association of Conservative and Liberal-Unionist Associations; 1917–24 National Unionist Association; 1924–98 National Union of Conservative and Unionist Associations. 1998– National Convention.

SOURCES:- *National Union Gleanings* 1900–12, *Gleanings and Memoranda* 1912–33, *Politics in Review* 1934–39, all published by the National Union of Conservative Associations; National Union of Conservative and Unionist Associations, Annual Conference Reports, 1958– ; for Conservative Party Manifestos and major reports, pamphlets etc. from 1950s and early 60s, see G.D.M.Block, *A Source Book of Conservatism* (1964). See also I. Bulmer-Thomas, *The Growth of the British Party System* (1965).

Labour Party

Party Leaders and Deputy Leaders

Chairman of the Parliamentary Party

1906	K. Hardie
1908	A. Henderson
1910	G. Barnes
1911	R. MacDonald
1914	A. Henderson
1917	W. Adamson
1921	J. Clynes

Vice-Chairman

1906	D. Shackleton
1908	G. Barnes
1910	J. Clynes
1911	W. Brace
1912	J. Parker
1912	A. Gill
1915	{ J. Hodge *Acting*
1916	{ G. Wardle *Chairmen*
1918	J. Clynes
1921	{ J. Thomas *(Joint)*
1921	{ S. Walsh *(Joint)*

Chairman and Leader of the Parliamentary Party

1922	R. MacDonald[1]
1931	A. Henderson[2]
1932	G. Lansbury
1935	C. Attlee[1]
1955	H. Gaitskell
1963	H. Wilson

Leader of the Parliamentary Party[1]

1970	H. Wilson
1976	J. Callaghan

Leader of the Labour Party

1980	M. Foot
1983	N. Kinnock
1992	J. Smith
1994	T. Blair

Deputy Leader

1922	{ S. Walsh *(Joint)*
1922	{ J. Wedgwood *(Joint)*
1923	J. Clynes
1931	{ J. Clynes *(Joint)*
1931	{ W. Graham *(Joint)*
1931	C. Attlee
1935	A. Greenwood
1945	H. Morrison
1956	J. Griffiths
1959	A. Bevan
1960	G. Brown
1970	R. Jenkins
1972	E. Short
1976	M. Foot
1980	D. Healey
1983	R. Hattersley
1992	Margaret Beckett
1994	J. Prescott

[1] When the Labour Party was in power in 1924,1929–31,1940–45,1945–51 and 1964–70 a Liaison Committee was set up. After 1970 the Labour Party elected a separate Chairman (see p.156)

[2] A. Henderson lost his seat in the 1931 election. The acting leader of the Parliamentary Labour Party was G. Lansbury.

Leadership Elections

From 1922 to 1981 the Parliamentary Labour Party, when in opposition, elected its Leader and Deputy Leader at the beginning of each session. Most elections were uncontested, but there were these exceptions. (The figures in brackets show the result of the first ballot. The date is for the final ballot).

Leader

1922 *1st ballot*
21 Nov 22 R. MacDonald 61
           J. Clynes   56

1935 *1st ballot*
26 Nov 35 C. Attlee   58
           H. Morrison   44
           A. Greenwood   33

2nd ballot
3 Dec 35 C. Attlee   88
          H. Morrison   48

1955	*1st ballot*						
14 Dec 55	H. Gaitskell	157					
	A. Bevan	70					
	H. Morrison	40					

1960	*1st ballot*	
3 Nov 60	H. Gaitskell	148
	H. Wilson	81

1961	*1st ballot*	
2 Nov 61	H. Gaitskell	171
	A. Greenwood	59

1963	*1st ballot*			*2nd ballot*	
7 Feb 63	H. Wilson	115	14 Feb 63	H. Wilson	144
	G. Brown	88		G. Brown	103
	J. Callaghan	41			

1976	*1st ballot*			*2nd ballot*			*3rd ballot*	
25 Mar 76	M. Foot	90	30 Mar 76	J. Callaghan	141	5 Apr 76	J. Callaghan	176
	J. Callaghan	84		M.Foot	133		M. Foot	137
	R. Jenkins	56		D. Healey	38			
	A. Benn	37						
	D. Healey	30						
	A. Crosland	17						

1980	*1st ballot*			*2nd ballot*	
4 Nov 80	D. Healey	112	10 Nov 80	M. Foot	139
	M. Foot	83		D. Healey	129
	J. Silkin	38			
	P. Shore	32			

Deputy Leader

1952	1*st ballot*	
11 Nov 52	H. Morrison	194
	A. Bevan	82

1953	*1st ballot*	
29 Oct 53	H. Morrison	181
	A. Bevan	76

1956	*1st ballot*	
2 Feb 56	J. Griffiths	141
	A. Bevan	111
	H. Morrison	40

1960	*1st ballot*			*2nd ballot*	
10 Nov 60	G. Brown	118	10 Nov 60	G. Brown	146
	F. Lee	73		F. Lee	83
	J. Callaghan	55			

1961	*1st ballot*	
12 Nov 61	G. Brown	169
	Barbara Castle	56

1970	*1st ballot*	
8 Jul 70	R. Jenkins	133
	M. Foot	67
	F. Peart	48

1971	*1st ballot*				**2nd ballot**	
10 Nov 71	R. Jenkins	140		17 Nov 71	R. Jenkins	140
	M. Foot	96			M. Foot	126
	A. Benn	46				

1972	*1st ballot*				**2nd ballot**	
15 Apr 72	E. Short	111		25 Apr 72	E. Short	145
	M. Foot	89			M. Foot	116
	A. Crosland	61				

1976	*1st ballot*	
21 Oct 76	M. Foot	166
	Shirley Williams	128

1980

13 Nov 80   D.Healey   *unop.*

At a special conference at Wembley, 24 Jan 1981, the Labour Party endorsed a procedure by which the Party's Leader and Deputy Leader should be re-elected each year by the Party Conference with 40% of the vote allocated to the Trade Unions, 30% to the Parliamentary Party and 30% to the constituency parties.

The system was first used on 1 Oct 1981 when D. Healey defeated A. Benn for the Deputy Leadership.

Deputy Leader

1 Oct 1981	*1st ballot*					*2nd ballot*			
	TU	CLP	MP	Total		TU	CLP	MP	Total
A. Benn	6.410	23.483	6.734	36.627	D. Healey	24.994	5.673	19.759	50.426
D. Healey	24.696	5.367	15.306	45.369	A. Benn	15.006	24.327	10.241	49.574
J. Silkin	8.894	1.150	7.959	18.004					

The first time the procedure was used for electing both Leader and Deputy Leader was on 2 Oct 1983.

Leader

2 Oct 1983	*1st ballot*			
	TU	CLP	MP	Total
N. Kinnock	29.042	27.452	14.778	71.272
R. Hattersley	10.878	0.577	7.833	19.288
E. Heffer	0.046	1.971	4.286	6.303
P. Shore	0.033	0.000	3.103	3.137

Deputy Leader

2 Oct 1983	*1st ballot*			
	TU	CLP	MP	Total
R. Hattersley	35.237	15.313	16.716	67.266
M. Meacher	4.730	14.350	8.806	27.886
D. Davies	0.000	0.241	3.284	3.525
Gwyneth Dunwoody	0.033	0.096	1.194	1.323

There was another leadership election on 2 Oct 1988, when A. Benn challenged N. Kinnock for the leadership and E. Heffer and J. Prescott challenged R. Hattersley for the deputy leadership.

Leader

2 Oct 1988	*1st ballot*			
	TU	CLP	MP	Total
N. Kinnock	39.660	24.128	24.842	88.630
A. Benn	0.340	5.872	5.158	11.370

Deputy Leader

2 Oct 1988	*1st ballot*			
	TU	CLP	MP	Total
R. Hattersley	31.339	18.109	17.376	66.823
J. Prescott	8.654	7.845	7.195	23.694
E. Heffer	0.007	4.046	5.430	9.483

After the 1992 election N. Kinnock and R. Hattersley stood down as Leader and Deputy Leader. An election was held on 18 Jul 92, at a special conference in London.

Leader

18 Jul 1992	*1st ballot*			
	TU	CLP	MP	Total
J. Smith	38.518	29.311	23.187	91.016
B. Gould	1.482	0.689	6.813	8.984

Deputy Leader

18 Jul 1992	*1st ballot*			
	TU	CLP	MP	Total
Margaret Beckett	25.394	19.038	12.871	57.303
J. Prescott	11.627	7.096	9.406	28.129
B. Gould	2.979	3.866	7.723	14.568

At the 1993 Party Conference the Party approved a change in the rules under which trade unions and constituency parties were obliged to ballot members individually in leadership elections and divide their votes accordingly (One Member One Vote). In addition the proportions in the electoral college were adjusted to three equal thirds for each of the constituent elements. This new procedure was used for the first time in July 1994 following the death of J. Smith. The results were declared on 21 July 1994.

Leader

21 Jul 1994	*1st ballot*			
	TU	CLP	MP	Total
T. Blair	52.3	58.2	60.5	57.0
J. Prescott	28.4	24.4	19.6	24.1
Margaret Beckett	19.3	17.4	19.9	18.9

Deputy Leader

21 Jul 1994	*1st ballot*			
	TU	CLP	MP	Total
J. Prescott	55.6	59.4	53.7	56.5
Margaret Beckett	44.4	40.6	46.3	43.5

SOURCES:- 1988 Party Annual Conference Reports, Labour Year Books; H. Pelling, *A Short History of the Labour Party* (4th Ed.,1972), p. 130. *Keesing's Contemporary Archive, Keesing's U.K. Record 1988–97.*

Leader in the House of Lords

1924	Vt Haldane	1952	Earl Jowitt	1976	Ld Peart
1928	Ld Parmoor	1955	Vt (Earl) Alexander	1982	Ld Cledwyn
1931	Ld Ponsonby	1964	E of Longford	1992	Ld Richard
1935	Ld Snell	1968	Ld Shackleton	1998	Lady Jay
1940	Ld Addison	1974	Ld Shepherd		

Chief Whip in the House of Commons

1906	D. Shackleton	1920	A. Henderson	1966	J. Silkin
1906	A. Henderson	1924	B. Spoor	1969	R. Mellish
1907	G. Roberts	1925	A Henderson	1976	M. Cocks
1914	A. Henderson	1927	T. Kennedy	1985	D. Foster
1914	F. Goldstone	1931	(Sir) C. Edwards	1995	D. Dewar
1916	G. Roberts	1942	W. Whiteley	1997	N. Brown
1916	J. Parker	1955	H. Bowden	1998	Ann Taylor
1919	W. Tyson Wilson	1964	E. Short		

SOURCE:– For a full list of whips see F.M.G. Wilson, 'Some Career Patterns in British Politics; Whips in the House of Commons, 1906–66', *Parliamentary Affairs*, 24 (Winter 1970–1) pp. 33–42.

Chief Whip in the House of Lords

1924	Ld Muir-Mackenzie	1944	Ld Southwood	1967	Ld Beswick
1924	E De La Warr	1945	Ld Ammon	1973	Lady Llewelyn-Davies
1930	Ld Marley	1949	Ld Shepherd (1st)	1982	Ld Ponsonby
1937	Ld Strabolgi	1954	E of Lucan (6th)	1990	Ld Graham of Edmonton
1941	E of Listowel	1964	Ld Shepherd (2nd)	1997	Ld Carter

SOURCES:- *Dod's Parliamentary Companion*, 1900– ; Labour Party Annual Conference Reports.

Labour Representation Committee – National Executive Officers

Chairman		Treasurer		Secretary	
1900	F. Rogers	1902	F. Rogers	1900	R. MacDonald
1902	R. Bell	1903	A. Gee		
1904	D. Shackleton	1904	A. Henderson		

Labour Party – National Executive Committee
The Chairman is listed as Chairman of Annual Conference at end of year in office; (see pp.156–7)

Secretary

		(General Secretary)		*Deputy General Secretary*	
1906	R. MacDonald	1959	M. Phillips	1997	Margaret McDonagh
1912	A. Henderson	1962	A. Williams	1998	*(office abolished)*
1935	J. Middleton	1968	(Sir) H. Nicholas		
1944	M. Phillips	1972	R. Hayward		
		1982	J. Mortimer		
		1985	L. Whitty		
		1995	T. (Ld) Sawyer		
		1998	Margaret McDonagh		

Treasurer

1906	A. Henderson	1956	A. Bevan	1981	E. Varley
1912	R. MacDonald	1960	H. Nicholas	1984	A. Booth
1929	A. Henderson	1964	D. Davies *(acting)*	1984	S. McCluskie
1936	G. Lathan	1965	D. Davies	1992	T. Burlison
1943	A. Greenwood	1967	J. Callaghan	1996	Margaret Prosser
1954	H. Gaitskell	1976	N. Atkinson		

National Agent

1908	A. Peters	1951	A. Williams	1979	D. Hughes
1919	E. Wake	1962	Sara Barker	1985	Joyce Gould
1929	E. Shepherd	1969	R. Hayward		
1946	R. Windle	1972	R. (Ld) Underhill		

(Director, Organisation and Development)

1990	Joyce Gould	1993	P. Coleman	1996	D. Gardner

Assistant Gen. Sec. (Elections and Local Recruitment)

1998	D. Gardner
1999	D. Evans

Director of Campaigns and Elections

1994	Joy Johnson	1995	Sally Morgan	1996	*(post vacant)*

Research Secretary[1]

1942	M. Phillips	1952	D. Ginsburg	1974	G. Bish
1945	M. Young	1960	P. Shore	1993	R. Wales
1950	W. Fienburgh	1965	T. Pitt	1996–97	M. Taylor

(Assistant Gen Sec. Policy and Campaigns)

1997	M. Taylor	1998	*(post vacant)*	1999	N. Peccorelli

Director of Publicity (Communications)

1921	W. Henderson	1979	M. Madden	1990	J. Underwood
1945	A. Bax	1982	N. Grant	1990	D. Hill[2]
1962	J. Harris	1983	*(post vacant)*	1993	Joy Johnson
1964	P. Clark	1985	P. Mandelson		

Chief Party Spokesperson

1994	D. Hill	1998	*(post vacant)*

Assistant Gen. Secretary (Media and Communications)

1999	P. Murphy

---

[1] From 1922 to 1942 A. Greenwood acted as Secretary to the Research Department which was established in 1922 (at first as Joint Research and Information Department).
[2] In 1993 D. Hill took the title 'Chief Spokesperson'.

SOURCES:– Labour Representation Committee Annual Conference Reports, 1900–5, and Labour Party Annual Conference Reports, 1906–.

Parliamentary Labour Party – Parliamentary Committee

This committee was originally known as the Executive Committee of the Parliamentary Labour Party. Its name was changed in 1951 to avoid confusion with the N.E.C. The committee was first elected in 1923 to take the place of the Policy Committee of the P.L.P. It consists of 18 Commons members (12 until 1981, 15 from 1981 to 1988), elected at the opening of every session of Parliament by members of the P.L.P. with seats in the House of Commons. There are six ex officio members: the Leader and Deputy Leader of the Party, the Chief Whip in the House of Commons, the Leader of the Labour Peers, the Chief Whip of the Labour Peers and their elected representative. The elected Commons members of the Parliamentary Committee sit on the Front Bench with the Party's Leader, Deputy Leader, Chief Whip and the Assistant Whips. Ex-Labour Ministers have the right, by custom of the House, to sit on the Front Bench, but usually prefer a place on the Back Benches. The officers and the elected 18 are joined on the Front Benches by a number of other members who have been allotted the responsibility of looking after particular subjects. After 1955 it became the practice of the Leader of the P.L.P. to invite members to take charge of particular subjects, and these members included some who are not members of the Parliamentary Committee. In 1924 and 1929 when the Labour Party was in office a Consultative Committee of twelve was appointed representative of both Front and Back Benches. During the wartime coalition the P.L.P. elected an Administrative Committee of twelve, with Peers' representation, all of whom were non-Ministers. When the Labour Party was in office from 1945 to 1951, and from 1964 to 1970, the P. L.P. set up a small Liaison Committee of three elected backbench M.P.s, the Leader of the House, the Government Chief Whip, and an elected backbench Labour Peer. Until 1964 the Leader acted as Chairman at P.L.P. meetings when the party was in Opposition. Since 1970 the P.L.P. has elected a separate chairman.

Parliamentary Labour Party – Executive Committee

The figures denote the order of successful candidates in the ballot.

1923–29

(number indicates position in the ballot)

	Feb 1923	Dec 1924	Dec 1925	Dec 1926	Dec 1927[a]
W. Adamson	9	–	11	11	8
H. Dalton	–	–	–	3	7
R. Davies	12	–	–	–	–
W. Graham	–	8	2	2	3
A. Henderson	10	–	1		2
T. Johnston	3	–	–	4	4
F. Jowett	6	–	–	–	–
G. Lansbury	2	1	10	9	10
H. Lees-Smith	–	11	4	6	6
J. Maxton	–	6	–	–	–
E. Morel	5	–	–	–	–
F. Roberts	–	12	–	–	–
T. Shaw	11	–	7	–	12
E. Shinwell	7	–	–	–	–
R. Smillie	–	2	5	7	–
P. Snowden	1	3	1	1	1
J. Thomas	4	4	3	5	5
C. Trevelyan	–	7	6	8	11
S. Walsh	–	–	8	–	–
S. Webb	10	–	9	10	9
J. Wedgwood	–	9	–	–	–
J. Wheatley	8	5	–	–	–

[a] There is no record of an Executive Committee election in 1928.

1931

On 28 Aug 31 officers were elected to the P.L.P.:

A. Henderson *(Leader)*
J. Clynes *(Deputy Leader)*,
W. Graham *(2nd Deputy Leader)*
T. Kennedy *(Chief Whip)*

On 8 Sep 31 the following were elected to the P.L.P. Committee:

C. Addison	Mary Hamilton
A. Alexander	T. Johnston
J. Barr	G. Lansbury
H. Dalton	H. Lees-Smith
E. Edwards	F. Pethick-Lawrence
A. Greenwood	E. Shinwell
D. Grenfell	

All but G. Lansbury and D. Grenfell were defeated in the Oct 31 election.

1931–35

(number indicates position in the ballot)

	Nov 1931	Nov 1932	Nov 1933	Nov 1934
Sir S. Cripps	1	1	2	1
D. Grenfell	2	2	1	2
G. Hicks	4	3	3	5
M. Jones	7	7	4	6
W. Lunn	5	4	6	4
N. Maclean	6	6	7	7
T. Williams	3	5	5	3

1935–40

	Nov 1935	Nov 1936	Nov 1937	Nov 1938	Nov 1939
A. Alexander	6	5	2	2	1
W. Wedgwood Benn	–	–	7	5	2
J. Clynes	1	6	–	–	–
H. Dalton	2	3	5	3	10
D. Grenfell	5	4	4	4	4
G. Hall	–	–	–	–	7
T. Johnston	3	2	3	6	–
M. Jones	10	8	11	12	–
J. Lawson	–	–	–	–	12
H. Lees-Smith	9	11	8	8	5
W. Lunn	11	–	–	–	–
N. Maclean	12	–	–	–	–
H. Morrison	4	1	1	1	8
P. Noel-Baker	–	10	12	10	11
F. P-Lawrence	8	9	9	9	6
D. Pritt	–	12	–	–	–
E. Shinwell	–	–	10	11	9
T. Williams	7	7	6	7	3

Parliamentary Labour Party (Parliamentary Committee)

1951–63

(number indicates position in ballot)

	Nov 1951	Nov 1952	Nov 1953	Nov 1954	Jun 1955	Nov 1956	Nov 1957	Nov 1958	Nov 1959	Nov 1960	Nov 1961	Nov 1962	Nov 1963
A. Bevan	12	9[a]	–	7	3	3	1	–	–	–	–	–	–
A. Bottomley	–	–	–	–	–	–	12	9	–	–	–	–	–
G. Brown	–	–	–	1	8	10	9	–	8	–	–	–	–
J. Callaghan	7	6	4	10	3	5	5	5	2	1	7	1	2
R. Crossman	–	–	–	–	–	–	–	–	13[d]	–	–	–	–
H. Dalton	8	5	5	4	–	–	–	–	–	–	–	–	–
J. Chuter Ede	5	2	6	9	–	–	–	–	–	–	–	–	–
T. Fraser	–	–	–	–	14[c]	12	8	12	7	6	9	5	6
H. Gaitskell	3	3	2	1[b]	2[c]	–	–	–	–	–	–	–	
P. G-Walker	–	–	–	–	–	11	6	9[d]	8	11	6	5	–
A. Greenwood	12	–	–	–	10	6	7	8	6[d]	–	–	–	–
J. Griffiths	1	1	1	1[b]	1[c]	–	–	–	–	–	–	–	–
R. Gunter	–	–	–	–	–	–	–	–	–	7	6	10	8
W. G. Hall	2	9	12	11	–	–	–	–	–	–	–	–	–
D. Healey	–	–	–	–	–	–	–	–	12	5	4	9	7
D. Houghton	–	–	–	–	–	–	–	–	–	10	3	4	3
D. Jay	–	–	–	–	–	–	–	–	–	–	–	13[e]	11
F. Lee	–	–	–	–	–	–	–	–	5	12	12	12	10
G. Mitchison	–	–	–	–	12	4	2	3	10	3	8	7	12
P. Noel-Baker	9	8	10	8	9	8	10	10	–	–	–	–	–
A. Robens	4	4	7	6	4	2	6	7	4	–	–	–	–
E. Shinwell	11	11	11	7	–	–	–	–	–	–	–	–	–
Sir F. Soskice	–	7	3	3	–	7	4	4	3	2	2	2	4
M. Stewart	–	–	–	–	–	–	–	–	–	4	5	8	1
R. Stokes	6	–	–	–	11	–	–	–	–	–	–	–	–
E. Summerskill	10	10	8	5	6	9	–	11	–	–	–	–	–
F. Willey	–	–	–	–	–	–	–	–	11	11	10	11	9
H. Wilson	–	–	13[a]	12	5	1	1	2	1	9	1	3	–
K. Younger	–	–	–	–	13[c]	11	–	–	–	–	–	–	–

[a] A. Bevan resigned from the Parliamentary Committee on 14 Apr 54; H. Wilson, who was 13th in order of votes obtained, took his place on the Committee on 28 Apr 54.
[b] H. Gaitskell and J. Griffiths both obtained 170 votes and tied for first place.
[c] H. Gaitskell and J. Griffiths were elected Leader and Deputy Leader of the Labour Party on 14 Dec 55 and 2 Feb 56, K. Younger and T. Fraser as runners-up filled the vacant places on the Parliamentary Committee.
[d] A. Greenwood resigned from the Parliamentary Committee on 13 Oct 60. R. Crossman, who was 13th in order of votes obtained, took his place on the Committee for a few weeks until the 1960–61 sessional elections in November.
[e] D. Jay joined the Committee when H. Wilson was elected Leader.

1970–73

	Jul 1970	Nov 1971	Nov 1972	Nov 1973
A. Benn	5	10	11	8
J. Callaghan	1	4	5	1
Barbara Castle	2	15[a]	–	–
A. Crosland	3	8	3	4
M. Foot	6	2	4	2
D. Healey	2	12	6	7
D. Houghton	4	–	–	–
R. Jenkins	–	–	–	5
H. Lever	8	7[a]	9	8
F. Peart	10	6	8	–
R. Prentice	–	13[a]	1	3

1970–73 *(cont ...)*

	Jul 1970	Nov 1971	Nov 1972	Nov 1973
M. Rees	–	–	10	10
W. Ross	–[c]	5	7	12
P. Shore	–	11	12[b]	11
E. Short	9	1	–	–
J. Silkin	–	14[a]	(12[b])	(13)
G. Thomson	11	9[a]	–	–
Shirley Williams	7	3	1	6

[a] H. Lever and G. Thomson resigned on 10 Apr 72. They were replaced by R. Prentice and J. Silkin, who had 13th and 14th place respectively in the original ballot. When E. Short became Deputy Leader, Mrs B. Castle beat E. Heffer 111–89, to take his place on the Committee on 3 May 72.

[b] J. Silkin, who tied with P. Shore for 12th place, withdrew, making a second ballot unnecessary.

[c] W. Ross joined the committee in Nov 70 when D. Houghton became Chairman of the P.L.P.

1979–88[b]

	Jun 1979	Nov 1990	Nov 1981[b]	Nov 1982	Nov 1983	Oct 1984	Oct 1985	Oct 1986	Jun 1987	Nov 1988
P. Archer	–	–	14	9	8	7	10	9	–	–
A. W. Benn	–	(13)[a]	–	–	–	–	–	–	–	–
A. Booth	7	8	8	6	–	–	–	–	–	–
G. Brown	–	–	–	–	–	–	–	–	11	1
D. Clark	–	–	–	–	–	–	–	11	14	4
R. Cook	–	–	–	–	10	15	5	–	8	5
J. Cunningham	–	–	–	–	5	3	9	8	11	14
D. Davies	–	–	–	–	–	12	13	3	6	–
F. Dobson	–	–	–	–	–	–	–	–	10	7
Gwyneth Dunwoody	–	–	15	13	12	10	–	–	–	–
B. Gould	–	–	–	–	–	–	–	14	1	7
R. Hattersley	4	1	3	4	–	–	–	–	–	–
D. Healey	1	–	–	–	1	2	3	4	–	–
E. Heffer	–	–	13	15	11	–	–	–	–	–
R. Hughes	–	–	–	–	–	–	15	–	7	–
B. John	–	–	10	12	–	–	–	–	–	–
B. Jones	–	–	–	–	9	8	11	6	–	12
G. Kaufman	–	3	2	1	2	1	1	1	4	3
N. Kinnock	–	12	7	2	–	–	–	–	–	–
R. Mason	11	10	–	–	–	–	–	–	–	–
M. Meacher	–	–	–	–	13	11	12	15	3	10
B. Millan	–	–	12	14	–	–	–	–	–	–
S. Orme	6	6	11	10	15	4	2	5	–	–
D. Owen	10	–	–	–	–	–	–	–	–	–
J. Prescott	–	–	–	–	6	8	4	12	2	13
G. Radice	–	–	–	–	14	13	8	10	–	–
M. Rees	9	4	6	11	–	–	–	–	–	–
Jo Richardson	–	–	–	–	–	–	–	–	11	15
W. Rodgers	8	9	–	–	–	–	–	–	–	–
P. Shore	3	5	1	3	3	6	–	–	–	–
J. Silkin	2	7	4	7	7	–	–	–	–	–
J. Smith	12	11	9	8	4	5	7	2	5	2
J. Straw	–	–	–	–	–	–	–	–	15	11
E. Varley	5	2	5	5	–	–	–	–	–	–

[a] A. Benn took over the place vacated by W. Rodgers when he joined the SDP.

[b] The PLP Committee was enlarged from 12 to 15 elected members in 1981.

1989–97

In 1989 the rules for the election of the Parliamentary Committee were changed in favour of women M.P.s; the total size was increased to 18, at least three of whom had to be women. In 1993 the rules were further amended so that M.P.s had to vote for at least four women candidates.

	Nov 1989	Nov 1990	Nov 1991	Jul 1992	Oct 1993	Nov 1994	Nov 1995	Jul 1996
Margaret Beckett	17	3	6	–	–	2	1	1
A. Blair	4	8	8	2	6	–	–	–
D. Blunkett	–	–	–	15	17	15	11	17
G. Brown	1	2	1	1	4	3	3	14
D. Clark	1	7	10	18	7	13	9	9
T. Clarke	–	–	–	17	13	–	19	18
Ann Clwyd	14	11	4	10	–	–	–	–
R. Cook	3	4	2	3	1	1	2	5
J. Cunningham	8	13	12	12	18	10	–	12
R. Davies	–	–	(19)[a]	11	12	4	11	11
D. Dewar	15	8	10	14	11	4	5	6
F. Dobson	10	16	6	4	2	6	8	7
B. Gould	9	17	5	6	–	–	–	–
Harriet Harman	–	–	–	6	–	5	18	19
B. Jones	16	13	17	–	–	–	–	–
G. Kaufman	5	5	12	–	–	–	–	–
Joan Lestor	6	–	–	–	15	16	14	–
M. Meacher	12	10	15	13	10	11	15	10
Mo Mowlam	–	–	–	6	5	8	6	8
J. Prescott	11	18	15	5	2	–	–	–
G. Robertson	–	–	–	–	16	7	17	16
Jo Richardson	7	15	18	–	–	–	–	–
Clare Short	–	–	–	–	–	–	16	3
C. Smith	–	–	–	6	9	9	7	15
J. Smith	2	1	3	–	–	–	–	–
G. Strang	–	–	–	–	–	17	12	4
J. Straw	18	6	14	16	8	14	13	13
Ann Taylor	–	12	9	11	14	18	10	2

[a] R. Davies was elected to the Shadow Cabinet as a result of a by-election in Nov 92 following the resignation of B.Gould.

Chairmen of Parliamentary Committee 1924–70

(with Labour in power)

1924   Parliamentary Executive Committee
1924   R. Smillie

1929–31   Consultative Committee
1929   H. Snell   1930   J. Barr

1940–5   Administrative Committee
1940   H. Lees-Smith *(acting)*[1]   1942   F. Pethick-Lawrence
1943   A. Greenwood *(acting)*[1]

1945–51   Liaison Committee
1945   N. Maclean   1946   M. Webb
1950   W. Glenvil Hall

1964–70   Liaison Committee
1964   E. Shinwell   1967   D. Houghton

[1] During C. Attlee's membership of the war-time Coalition, the Labour Party appointed an acting Chairman each session.

Chairman of Parliamentary Labour Party, 1970–

Nov 1970	D. Houghton	Nov 1983	J. Dormand
Mar 1974	I. Mikardo	Jul 1987	S. Orme
Nov 1974	C. Hughes	Jul 1992	D. Hoyle
Jun 1979	F. Willey	May 1997	C. Soley

Secretary, Parliamentary Labour Party 1943–

1943	C. Johnson	1979	B. Davies
1959	(Sir) G. Barlow	1992	A. Haworth

SOURCES:- 1923–29, *Daily Herald* and *Directory* for National Council of Labour, TUC General Council, Labour Party and the Parliamentary Labour Party (published annually by the Labour Party); 1931–, Labour Party Annual Conference Reports; *The Times*; and *Labour Party Directory*.

Labour Representation Committee – Annual Conferences, 1900–1905

Date	Place	Chairman
27–28 Feb 00	London	W. Steadman
1 Feb 01	Manchester	J. Hodge
20–22 Feb 02	Birmingham	W. Davies
19–21 Feb 03	Newcastle	J. Bell
4–5 Feb 04	Bradford	J. Hodge
26–29 Jan 05	Liverpool	A. Henderson

Labour Party–Annual Conferences, 1906–1999

Date	Place	Chairman
15–17 Feb 06	London	A. Henderson
24–26 Jan 07	Belfast	J. Stephenson
20–22 Jan 08	Hull	W. Hudson
27–29 Jan 09	Portsmouth	J. Clynes
9–11 Feb 10	Newport	J. Keir Hardie
1–3 Feb 11	Leicester	W. Robinson
24–26 Jan 12	Birmingham	B. Turner
29–31 Jan 13	London	G. Roberts
27–30 Jan 14	Glasgow	T. Fox
1915	*No conference held*	
26–28 Jan 16	Bristol	W. Anderson
23–26 Jan 17	Manchester	G. Wardle
23–25 Jan 18[1]	Nottingham	W. Purdy
26–28 Jun 18	London	W. Purdy
25–27 Jun 19	Southport	J. McGurk
22–25 Jun 20	Scarborough	W. Hutchinson
26–29 Jun 23	London	S. Webb
7–10 Oct 24	London	R. MacDonald
29 Sep–2 Oct 25	Liverpool	C. Cramp
11–15 Oct 26	Margate	R. Williams
3–7 Oct 27	Blackpool	F. Roberts
1–5 Oct 28	Birmingham	G. Lansbury
30 Sep–4 Oct 29	Brighton	H. Morrison
6–10 Oct 30	Llandudno	Susan Lawrence
5–8 Oct 31	Scarborough	S. Hirst
3–7 Oct 32	Leicester	G. Lathan
2–6 Oct 33	Hastings	J. Compton
1–5 Oct 34	Southport	W. Smith
30 Sep–4 Oct 35	Brighton	W. Robinson
5–9 Oct 36	Edinburgh	Jennie Adamson
4–8 Oct 37	Bournemouth	H. Dalton
1938	*No conference held*	
29 May–2 Jun 39	Southport	G. Dallas
13–16 May 40	Bournemouth	Barbara Gould
2–4 Jun 41	London	J. Walker
25–28 May 42	London	W. Green
14–18 Jun 43	London	A. Dobbs
11–15 Dec 44	London	G. Ridley

21–25 May 45	Blackpool	Ellen Wilkinson
10–14 Jun 46	Bournemouth	H. Laski
26–30 May 47	Margate	P. Noel-Baker
17–21 May 48	Scarborough	E. Shinwell
6–10 Jun 49	Blackpool	J. Griffiths
2–6 Oct 50	Margate	S. Watson
1–3 Oct 51	Scarborough	Alice Bacon
29 Sep–3 Oct 52	Morecambe	H. Earnshaw
28 Sep–2 Oct 53	Margate	Arthur Greenwood
27 Sep–1 Oct 54	Scarborough	W. Burke
10–14 Oct 55	Margate	Edith Summerskill
1–5 Oct 56	Blackpool	E. Gooch
30 Sep–4 Oct 57	Brighton	Margaret Herbison
29 Sep–3 Oct 58	Scarborough	T. Driberg
28–29 Nov 59	Blackpool	Barbara Castle
3–7 Oct 60	Scarborough	G. Brinham
2–6 Oct 61	Blackpool	R. Crossman
2–5 Oct 62	Brighton	H. Wilson
30 Sep–4 Oct 63	Scarborough	D. Davies
12–13 Dec 64	Brighton	Anthony Greenwood
27 Sep–Oct 65	Blackpool	R. Gunter
3–7 Oct 66	Brighton	W. Padley
2–6 Oct 67	Scarborough	J. Boyd
30 Sep–4 Oct 68	Blackpool	Jennie Lee
29 Sep–3 Oct 69	Brighton	Eirene White
28 Sep–2 Oct 70	Blackpool	A. Skeffington
4–8 Oct 71	Brighton	I. Mikardo
2–6 Oct 72	Blackpool	A. Benn
1–5 Oct 73	Blackpool	W. Simpson
27–30 Nov 74	London	J. Callaghan
26 Apr 75[2]	London	F. Mulley
29 Sep–Oct 75	Blackpool	F. Mulley
27 Sep–1 Oct 76	Blackpool	T. Bradley
3–7 Oct 77	Brighton	Joan Lestor
2–6 Oct 78	Blackpool	Joan Lestor
1–5 Oct 79	Brighton	F. Allaun
29 Sep–3 Oct 80	Blackpool	Lady Jeger
27 Sep–2 Oct 81	Brighton	A. Kitson
27 Sep–1 Oct 82	Blackpool	Dame J. Hart
3–8 Oct 83	Brighton	S. McCluskey
1–5 Oct 84	Blackpool	E. Heffer
29 Sep–4 Oct 85	Bournemouth	A. Hadden
28 Sep–3 Oct 86	Blackpool	N. Hough
27 Sep–2 Oct 87	Brighton	S. Tierney
2–7 Oct 88	Blackpool	N. Kinnock
1–6 Oct 89	Brighton	D. Skinner
30 Sep–5 Oct 90	Blackpool	Jo Richardson
29 Sep–4 Oct 91	Brighton	J. Evans
27 Sep–2 Oct 92	Blackpool	T. Clarke
26 Sep–1 Oct 93	Brighton	D. Blunkett
3–7 Oct 94	Blackpool	D. Blunkett
29 Apr 95[3]	London	G.Colling
2–6 Oct 95	Brighton	G. Colling
30 Sep–4 Oct 96	Blackpool	Diana Jeuda
29 Sep–3 Oct 97	Brighton	R. Cook
28 Sep–2 Oct 98	Blackpool	R. Rosser
27 Sep–1 Oct 99	Blackpool	Brenda Etchells

[1] Adjourned for one month. Resumed 26 Feb 18 in London.

[2] Special Conference on thhe Common Market.

[3] Special Conference on the Party Constitution.

SOURCES:- 1900–5 Reports of the Labour Representation Committee Annual Conferences, Labour Party Annual Conference Reports 1906–; L. Minkin, *The Labour Party Conference* (1978)

Party Membership

Year	Constit. & Central Parties	Total Indiv. Members (000s)	T.U.s No.	T.U.s Members (000s)	Soc.&Co-op Socs. No.	Soc.&Co-op Socs. Members (000s)	Total Membership (000s)
1900–1	7	–	41	353	3	23	376
1901–2	21	–	65	455	2	14	469
1902–3	49	–	127	847	2	14	861
1903–4	76	–	165	956	2	14	970
1904–5	73	–	158	855	2	15	900
1905–6	73	–	158	904	2	17	921
1906–7	83	–	176	975	2	21	998
1907	92	–	181	1,050	2	22	1,072
1908	133	–	176	1,127	2	27	1,159
1909	155	–	172	1,451	2	31	1,486
1910	148	–	151	1,394	2	31	1,431
1911	149	–	141	1,502	2	31	1,539
1912	146	–	130	1,858	2	31	1,895
1913	158	–	a	a	2	33	a
1914	179	–	101	1,572	2	33	1,612
1915	177	–	111	2,054	2	33	2,093
1916	199	–	119	2,171	3	42	2,220
1917	239	–	123	2,415	3	47	2,465
1918	389	b	131	2,960	4	53	3,013
1919	418	–	126	3,464	7	47	3,511
1920	492	–	122	4,318	5	42	4,360
1921	456	–	116	3,974	5	37	4,010
1922	482	–	102	3,279	5	32	3,311
1923	503	–	106	3,120	6	36	3,156
1924	529	–	108	3,158	7	36	3,194
1925	549	–	106	3,338	8	36	3,374
1926	551	–	104	3,352	8	36	3,388
1927	532	–	97	3,239	6	55c	3,294
1928	535	215	91	2,025d	7	52	2,292d
1929	578	228	91	2,044	6	59	2,331
1930	607	277	89	2,011	7	58	2,347
1931	608	297	80	2,024	7	37	2,358
1932	608	372	75	1,960	9	40	2,372
1933	612	366	75	1,899	9	40	2,305
1934	614	381	72	1,858	8	40	2,278
1935	614	419	72	1,913	9	45	2,378
1936	614	431	73	1,969	9	45	2,444
1937	614	447	70	2,037	8	43	2,528
1938	614	429	70	2,158	9	43	2,630
1939	614	409	72	2,214	6	40	2,663
1940	614	304	73	2,227	6	40	2,571
1941	585	227	68	2,231	6	28	2,485
1942	581	219	69	2,206	6	29	2,454
1943	586	236	69	2,237	6	30	2,503
1944	598	266	68	2,375	6	32	2,673
1945	649	487	69	2,510	6	41	3,039
1946	649	645	70	2,635d	6	42	3,322d

a Owing to the operation of the Osborne Judgement, it was made impossible to compile membership statistics for 1913.

b Individual membership statistics were not compiled 1918–27.

c The Royal Arsenal Co-operative Society, through its Political Purposes Committee, continued its affiliation with the Labour Party; its membership is included in the 1927–60 totals.

d From 1928 to 1946 inclusive, trade unionist members of the Labour Party had to 'contract in' to payment to party political funds.

Year	Constit. & Central Parties	Total Indiv. Members (000s)	T.U.s No.	T.U.s Members (000s)	Soc.&Co-op Socs. No.	Soc.&Co-op Socs. Members (000s)	Total Membership (000s)
1947	649	608	73	4,386	6	46	5,040
1948	656	629	80	4,751	6	42	5,422
1949	660	730	80	4,946	5	41	5,717
1950	661	908	83	4,972	5	40	5,920
1951	667	876	82	4,937	5	35	5,849
1952	667	1,015	84	5,072	5	21	6,108
1953	667	1,005	84	5,057	5	34	6,096
1954	667	934	84	5,530	5	35	6,498
1955	667	843	87	5,606	5	35	6,484
1956	667	845	88	5,658	5	34	6,537
1957	667	913	87	5,644	5	26	6,583
1958	667	889	87	5,628	5	26	6,542
1959	667	845	87	5,564	5	25	6,437
1960	667	790	86	5,513	5	25	6,328
1961	667	751	86	5,550	5	25	6,326
1962	667	767	86	5,503	5	25	6,296
1963	667	830	83	5,507	6	21	6,358
1964	667	830	83	5,502	6	21	6,353
1965	659	817	79	5,602	6	21	6,440
1966	658	776	79	5,539	6	21	6,336
1967	657	734	75	5,540	6	21	6,295
1968	656	701	68	5,364	6	21	6,087
1969	656	681	68	5,462	6	22	6,164
1970	656	680	67	5,519	6	24	6,223
1971	659	700	67	5,559	6	25	6,284
1972	659	703	62	5,425	9	40	6,169
1973	651	665	60	5,365	9	42	6,073
1974	623	692	63	5,787	9	39	6,518
1975	623	675	61	5,750	9	44	6,469
1976	623	659	59	5,800	9	48	6,459
1977	623	660	59	5,913	9	43	6,616
1978	623	676	59	6,260	9	55	6,990
1979	623	666	59	6,511	9	58	7,236
1980	623	348	54	6,407	0	56	6,811
1981	623	277	54	6,273	0	58	6,608
1982	623	274	50	6,185	0	57	6,516
1983	633	295	47	6,101	0	59	6,456
1984	633	323	46	5,844	9	60	6,227
1985	633	313	44	5,827	9	60	6,200
1986	633	297	44	5,778	9	58	6,133
1987	633	289	44	5,564	9	55	5,908
1988	633	266	44	5,481	9	56	5,804
1989	633	294	44	5,335	9	53	5,682
1990	633	311	44	4,922	9	54	5,287
1991	634	261	34	4,811	13	54	5,126
1992	634	280	38	4,634	14	51	4,965
1993	634	266					
1994	634	305					
1995	641	365					
1996	641	400					
1997	641	401					
1998	641	392					

SOURCES:- Labour Party Annual Conference *Reports*. But see P. Seyd, *Labour's Grassroots* (1992)

The Labour Party – Organisation and Constitutions

The Labour Representation Committee was formed on 27 Feb 1900 to promote a distinct Labour group in Parliament, representing the affiliated trade unions and socialist societies. After the General Election of 1906 the L.R.C. group of M.P.s decided to assume the title of 'Labour Party' and elected their first officers and whips. Policy was determined by the Labour Party through the annual conference and its executive authority, the National Executive Committee. There was no official party leader, but an annually elected chairman of the parliamentary party. There were scarcely any official Labour Party constituency organisations (except for those provided by local trades councils, groups of miners' lodges, and local branches of the I.L.P.). In 1914 there were only two constituency associations with individual members, Woolwich and Barnard Castle, which Will Crooks and Arthur Henderson had built up on their own.

The Reorganisation of the Labour Party, 1918

The reorganisation of the Labour Party was projected by Arthur Henderson in collaboration with Sidney Webb. Their main aims were to provide local Labour Parties in every constituency or group of constituencies. These local Labour Parties were to be based fundamentally on individual subscribing membership, though representation was provided for Trades Councils, trade union branches, and socialist societies. The members of the N.E.C. were to be elected by the annual conference as a whole (though eleven were to be elected from candidates nominated by the trade unions and socialist societies as a single group, five were to represent the Local Labour Parties, and four were to be women). The scheme also involved an increase in affiliation fees.

The original plan was amended, so that the N.E.C. was increased to a membership of 23 (adding two to the number specified for affiliated organisations). It was agreed that the election programme should be produced by the N.E.C. and P.L.P. jointly, subject to the aims of the Party and the decisions of the annual conferences. The object of the pre-war Party had been to 'organise and maintain in Parliament and in the country a political Labour Party'. In 1918 this was changed to a new formula: 'to secure for the producers by hand and by brain the full fruits of their industry, and the most equitable distribution thereof that may be possible, upon the basis of the common ownership of the means of production and the best obtainable system of popular administration and control of each industry and service'.[1]

Modifications since 1918

The 1918 constitution was modified in 1937 in favour of the local constituency Labour Parties, which had repeatedly demanded a greater share in the control of party affairs. Representation of the constituency parties on the N.E.C. was increased from five to seven. The seven were to be elected by the vote of the constituency delegates alone. The twelve trade union representatives and one representative of the socialist societies were to be elected separately by their respective conference delegations. The five women members may be nominated by any affiliated organisation and are elected by a vote of the whole party conference. The Leader (since 1929) and the Deputy Leader (since 1953) are ex officio members of the N.E.C. The Treasurer of the Party may be nominated by any affil-

[1] The 1914 and 1918 Labour Party Constitutions are set out and compared in G.D.H.Cole, *A History of the Labour Party from 1914* (1948), pp. 71–81.

iated organisation, and is elected by the vote of the whole party conference. In 1972 a Young Socialist elected by the National Conference of Labour Party Young Socialists was added to the N.E.C. In 1981 the procedure for the election of Leader and Deputy Leader was changed (see p. 147).

In 1990 the party Conference agreed in principle to a changed pattern of policy-making with the establishment of a Policy Forum and the production of a rolling programme of party policy. The National Policy Forum met first in May 1993. In 1997, some drastic changes were made following an N.E.C. document *Partnership in Power*. The National Conference remained supreme in policy making, considering reports from a 175 member National Policy Forum, elected for a two-year term. It would divide into eight Commissions charged with reviewing all programmes within the life of a Parliament. The National Executive was again restructured. It became composed of the Leader and the Deputy Leader, the Leader of the European Parliamentary Labour Party, the Treasurer, 3 Front-bench M.P.s, 1 Youth member, 1 Black Socialist, 12 Trade Unionists, 1 from the Socialist and Co-operative Societies, 6 Constituency Labour Party representatives, 2 local government representatives and 3 back-bench M.P.s; the women's section was abolished but half the representatives from the T.U. Section, the Constituency Labour Parties, the new Local Government section and the Parliamentary Labour Party were to be women. M.P.s were barred from most sections.

SOURCES:- H. Pelling, *The Origins of the Labour Party, 1880–1900* (1954); F. Bealey and H. Pelling, *Labour and Politics, 1900–1906* (1958); P. Poirier, *The Advent of the Labour Party* (1958); G.D.H. Cole, *A History of the Labour Party from 1914* (1948); R.T. McKenzie, *British Political Parties* (1955); L.Minkin, *The Labour Party Conference* (1978). Since 1918 complete lists of Labour Party publications have been given in the Labour Party Annual Conference Reports. See also I. Bulmer-Thomas, *The Growth of the British Party System* (1965); P. Whiteley and P. Seyd, *Labour's Grass Roots* (1992)

Sponsored M.P.s

The tables on p. 162 summarise information on the number of Labour M.P.s. with Trade Union or Co-operative financial sponsorship. Such sponsorship was discontinued in 1995.

M.P.s have also been sponsored by organisations which are not affiliated to the Labour Party. The two major instances of this are the National Union of Teachers and the National Farmers' Union.

National Union of Teachers

The N.U.T. sponsored and assisted parliamentary candidates from 1895 to 1974. The number of sponsored candidates varied, but a strict parity between the parties was always attempted. The practice ceased after 1974.

Sponsored M.P.s (Labour) 1918–92

	1918	1922	1923	1924	1929	1931	1935	1945	1950	1951	1955	1959	1964	1966	1970	Feb 1974	Oct 1974	1979	1983	1987	1992
NUM	25	41	43	40	42	26	32	34	37	36	34	31	29	26	20	18	18	16	14	13	14
TGW	3	7	10	10	13	1	7	17	16	14	14	14	21	27	19	23	22	22	25	33	38
NUR	1	3	4	3	8	–	5	12	10	9	8	5	6	7	5	6	6	12	10	8	12
TSSA	–	–	–	–	7	–	6	9	7	7	5	5	7	5	4	3	3	3	2	2	2
GMW	4	5	5	4	6	2	6	10	6	6	4	4	9	10	12	13	13	14	11	11	17
ASW	1	1	3	2	6	1	2	3	3	3	2	1	–	–	–	2	3	1	1	–	–
USDAW	–	1	4	4	4	1	6	8	8	9	9	9	10	10	9	6	5	5	2	8	3
I&S	–	2	1	3	4	1	1	2	2	2	2	2	1	1	2	2	1	2	1	1	–
UTFWA	4	3	3	2	4	–	–	3	2	1	1	1	1	1	–	–	–	–	–	–	–
AEU	1	7	4	4	3	2	3	4	8	8	6	8	19	17	16	17	16	21	17	12	13
ASSET	–	–	–	–	–	–	–	–	–	–	–	–	–	2	3	9	12	10	8	10	13
ETU	–	–	–	–	–	–	–	–	1	1	1	1	1	1	3	3	3	3	4	3	3
APEX	–	–	–	–	–	–	–	–	1	1	1	3	3	4	3	6	6	6	5	3	–
NUPE	–	–	–	–	–	–	–	–	–	1	1	2	1	2	5	6	6	6	7	4	12
Others	10	16	25	16	17	1	10	15	9	9	6	10	11	17	11	13	13	11	8	22	16
TU Sponsored	49	86	102	88	114	35	78	120	111	108	95	93	120	132	112	127	129	132	115	130	143
Co-op Sponsored	1	4	6	5	9	1	9	23	18	16	18	16	20	18	17	16	16	17	8	10	14
Unsponsored	7	52	83	58	164	10	67	250	186	171	164	149	177	213	158	158	172	120	86	139	114
Total MPs	57	142	191	151	287	46	154	393	315	295	277	258	317	363	287	301	319	269	209	229	271

SOURCES:- 1918–24 *Labour Party Annual Conference Reports*; 1929–59 M.Harrison, *Trade Unions and the Labour Party* (1960); J.Bailey, *The British Co-operative Movement* (1955); W. Muller, *The Kept Men* (1977): Nuffield College Election Studies.

N.U.T. adopted and supported M.P.s, 1900–1974

	Total	Con.	Lab.	Lib.
1900	3	1	–	2
1906	2	–	–	2
1910 (Jan)	1	–	–	1
1910 (Dec)	2	–	–	2
1918	1	1	–	–
1922	3	1	2	–
1923	3	–	3	–
1924	4	1	3	–
1929	5	–	5	–
1931	3	1	2	–
1935	5	1	4	–
1945	2	–	2	–
1950	4	–	4	–
1951	4	–	4	–
1955	6	2	4	–
1959	6	2	4	–
1964	5	1	4	–
1966	4	1	3	–
1970	5	2	3	–
1974 (Feb)	5	1	4	–
1974 (Oct)	4	1	3	–

SOURCES:- Information received from the National Union of Teachers; J.D.Stewart, *British Pressure Groups* (1958).

National Farmers' Union

In 1909 the N.F.U. set up a Parliamentary Fund with the object of sending two sponsored M.P.s to Parliament from each side of the House. Although sometimes 'independent on agricultural questions' all N.F.U. M.P.s have been Conservatives. Since 1945 the N.F.U. has not sponsored any candidates and has adopted a position of strict neutrality between the political parties.

N.F.U.-sponsored M.P.s 1921–1935

Election	M.P.s
1922	4
1923	3
1924	2
1929	No candidates
1931	No candidates
1935	2

SOURCES:- National Farmers' Union Yearbooks, 1900–60; P. Self and H. Storing, *The State and the Farmer* (1962), pp.42–7, 204; J.D. Stewart, *British Pressure Groups* (1958), pp.173–4.

Party Finance

Labour Party Central Annual Income (excluding special General Election Funds):

1910*	£12,000
1920	£55,000
1930	£44,000
1940	£51,000
1950*	£197,000
1960	£225,000
1970*	£1,034,000
1980	£2,801,000
1990	£6,274,000
1997	£24,100,000

*Asterisks denote general election years. For details of the Party's Constituency expenditure in general elections see p. 260. In 1912, the annual affiliation fee for constituency parties and trade unions was set at 1d per member. It was raised by stages: 1918 – 2d; 1920 – 3d; 1931 – 4d; 1937 – 4d; 1940 – 5d; 1948 – 6d; 1957 – 9d; 1963 – 1/-; 1970 – 7p, and thereafter almost every year: the affiliation fee was 32p in 1980, by 1992 it was £1.60 and by 1999 £17.50. In 1990 Trade Union affiliation fees provided 67% of the Labour Party's routine annual income; in 1998 the figure had fallen to 32%.

SOURCES:-The Labour Party has always published Accounts in its Annual Conference Reports. M. Harrison, *Trade Unions and the Labour Party* (1960); R. Rose, *Influencing Voters* (1967); M. Harrison's chapter in R. Rose and A. Heidenheimer, *'Comparative Political Finance'*, *Journal of Politics* (1963); Committee on Financial Aid to Political Parties (Cmnd 6601/1976); M. Pinto-Duschinsky, *British Political Finance 1830–1980* (1981); Labour Party Annual Reports; M. Linton, *Money and Votes* (Institute for Public Policy Research 1994); *The Funding of Political Parties* (Cmnd 4057/1998), p. 30.

Liberal Party

The Liberal Party split, following D. Lloyd George's supplantation of H. Asquith as Prime Minister in 1916. The two wings merged again on the eve of the 1923 election. In 1931 the party split once more between the National Liberals (who gradually merged with the Conservatives), the Liberals, and the Independent Liberals (a Lloyd George family group); the Independent Liberals rejoined the Liberals in the mid-1930s.

The Alliance and the Merger

From 1981 to 1987 the Liberal party was linked in the Alliance with the newly formed Social Democratic Party (see p. 181). On 14 Jun 1987 the Liberal leader D. Steel proposed merging the two parties. On 17 Sep 1987 the Liberal Conference in Harrogate voted to start negotiations. On 23 Jan 1988 a special Liberal Assembly convened in Blackpool voted to proceed with the merger. This took place on 3 Mar 1988 following an affirmative ballot by the membership of both parties (see below for Social and Liberal Democrats).

Leader[1]

1900	Sir H. Campbell-Bannerman	26 Nov 35	Sir A. Sinclair
30 Apr 08	H. Asquith[2] (E of Oxford and Asquith)	2 Aug 45	C. Davies
		5 Nov 56	J. Grimond
14 Oct 26	D. Lloyd George[3]	18 Jan 67	J. Thorpe
4 Nov 31	Sir H. Samuel[4]	7 Jul 76	D. Steel[5]

Deputy Leader

1929–31	H. Samuel	1962–64	D. Wade
1949–51	Lady M. Lloyd George	1985–88	A. Beith

Leader in the House of Lords

1900	E of Kimberley	1923	Vt Grey	1944	Vt Samuel
1902	Earl Spencer	1924	Earl Beauchamp	1955	Ld Rea
1905	M of Ripon	1931	M of Reading	1967	Ld Byers
1908	E (M) of Crewe	1936	M of Crewe	1984–88	Lady Sear

National Liberal Federation, 1900–1936

Chairman of Committee		Treasurer		Secretary	
1900	(Sir) E. Evans	1901	W. Hart	1893	(Sir) R. Hudson
1902	Sir G. Lunn	1903	J. Massie	1922	F. Barter
1905	A. Brampton	1907	R. Bird	1925	H. Oldman
1930	R. Muir	1910	F. Wright	1930	H. Oldman & W. Davies
1933	R. Walker	1923	Sir R. Hudson	1931	W. Davies
1934	M. Gray	1927	Sir F. Layland-Barratt		
		1934	P. Heffer		

[1] All were Liberal 'Leaders in the House of Commons'. Sir H. Campbell-Bannerman from 1905 to 1908 and H. Asquith from 1908 to 1926 were formally the only 'Leaders of the Liberal Party' from 1900 until the 1969 Constitution came into force.
[2] After H. Asquith's defeat at the 1918 General Election, Sir D. Maclean was elected chairman of the Parliamentary Party but relinquished the post on H. Asquith's return to the Commons in Mar 1920.
[3] D. Lloyd George was the Chairman of the Parliamentary Liberal party from Dec 1924.
[4] After the general election in 1931 there were three Liberal groups in the House of Commons. Sir H. Samuel led the main group of Liberal M.P.s, D. Lloyd George led a small family group of Independent Liberals and Sir J. Simon led the Liberal National group (see Minor Parties). On 25 Nov 1935 D. Lloyd George and the other Independent Liberals rejoined the Liberal Party in the House of Commons.
[5] An electoral college representing all constituency associations voted: D. Steel 12,541; J. Pardoe 7,032. J. Grimond was acting Leader 12 May 1976–7 Jul 1976.

Liberal Party Organisation, 1936–88

Head

1936	W. Davies *(Secretary)*
1952	H. Harris *(General Director)*
1960	D. Robinson *(Directing Secretary)*
1961	P. Kemmis *(Secretary)*
1965	T. Beaumont *(Head of Liberal Party Organisation)*
1966	P. Chitnis *(Head of Liberal Party Organisation)*[1]
1970	E. Wheeler *(Head of Liberal Party Organisation)*[2]
1977	H. Jones *(Sec.-General)*[3]
1983	J. Spiller *(Sec.-General)*
1985	A. Ellis *(Sec.-General)*

Chairman of Executive Committee 1938–69   *Chairman of Party 1966–*

1936	M. Gray		1966	Ld Byers
1946	P. Fothergill		1967	T. Beaumont (Ld)
1949	Ld Moynihan		1968	Ld Henley
1950	F. Byers		1969	D. Banks
1952	P. Fothergill		1970	R. Wainwright
1954	G. Acland		1972	C. Carr
1957	D. Abel		1973	K. Vaus
1959	L. Behrens		1976	G. Tordoff
1961	D. Banks		1980	R. Pincham
1963	B. Wigoder		1983	Joyce Rose
1965	G. Evans		1984	P. Tyler
1968	J. Baker		1986	T. Clement-Jones

Treasurer[4]

1937–50	Sir A. McFadyean		1962–65	Sir A. Murray
1937–40	P. Heffer		1963–65	T. Beaumont
1941–47	Ld Rea		1966–67	J. Thorpe
1942–47	H. Worsley		1967–68	L. Smith
1947–53	Ld Moynihan		1968–69	J. Pardoe
1950–58	W. Grey		1969–72	Sir F. Medlicott
1950–52	Vt Wimborne		1972–77	P. Watkins
1953–62	Sir A. Suenson-Taylor *(Ld Grantchester)*		1977–83	Ld Lloyd of Kilgerran
1955–59	P. Fothergill		1977–83	M. Palmer
1959–62	Heather Harvey		1983–86	A. Jacobs
1959–60	P. Lort-Phillips		1986–88	C. Fox
1961–62	J. McLaughlin		1986–88	T. Razzall
1962–66	R. Gardner-Thorpe			

SOURCES:- *Liberal Magazine* 1900–1950; *Liberal Year Book* 1900–1939; *Dod's Parliamentary Companion* 1950–; *Annual Reports* of the Liberal Party 1956–.

---

[1] P. Chitnis resigned in 1969. From Oct 1969 to Nov 1970 E. Wheeler was Director of Organisation. From Dec 1969 to Jun 1970 Mrs D. Gorsky was General Election Campaign Editor.
[2] In 1969 the post of Chairman of the Executive Committee was combined with the Chairmanship of the Party.
[3] E. Wheeler left in 1976. From Aug 1976 until Mar 1977 Mrs M. Wingfield was acting head of the Liberal Party Organisation.
[4] Until 1965 the post of Treasurer was held jointly by two or three officers. This practice was reverted to in 1977.

Chief Whips in House of Commons

				Coalition Liberal Chief Whip	
1900	H. Gladstone	1935	Sir P. Harris		
1905	G. Whiteley	1945	T. Horabin	1916	N. Primrose
1908	J. Pease	1946	F. Byers	1916	F. Guest
1910	Master of Elibank	1950	J. Grimond	1921	C. McCurdy
1912	P. Illingworth	1956	D. Wade	1922	E. Hilton Young
1915	J. Gulland	1962	A. Holt		
1919	*(office vacant)*[1]	1963	E. Lubbock		
1923	V. Phillipps	1970	D. Steel		
1924	Sir G. Collins	1976	C. Smith		
1926	R. Hutchinson	1977	A. Beith		
1930	Sir A. Sinclair	1985	D. Alton		
1931	G. Owen	1987–8	J. Wallace		
1932	W. Rea				

Chief Whips in House of Lords

1896	Ld Ribblesdale	1949	M of Willingdon
1907	Ld Denman	1950	Ld Moynihan
1911–22	Ld Colebrooke	1950	Ld Rea
1919–24	Ld Denman *(Ind. Lib.)*	1955	Ld Amulree
1924	Ld Stanmore	1977	Ld Wigoder
1944	Vt Mersey	1984	Ld Tordoff

SOURCE:- *Dod's Parliamentary Companion* 1900–.

National Liberal Federation – Annual Conferences, 1900–1935

Date	*Place*	*President*
27–28 Mar 00	Nottingham	R. Spence Watson
14–15 May 01	Bradford	R. Spence Watson
13–14 May 02	Bristol	A. Birrell
14–15 May 03	Scarborough	A. Birrell
12–13 May 04	Manchester	A. Birrell
18–19 May 05	Newcastle	A. Birrell
23–24 May 06	Liverpool	A. Acland
6–7 Jun 07	Plymouth	A. Acland
18–19 Jun 08	Birmingham	Sir W. Angus
1–2 Jul 09	Southport	Sir W. Angus
25 Nov 10	Hull	Sir W. Angus
23–24 Nov 11	Bath	Sir J. Brunner
21–22 Nov 12	Nottingham	Sir J. Brunner
26–27 Nov 13	Leeds	Sir J. Brunner
1914–1918	*No conference held*	
27–28 Nov 19	Birmingham	Sir G. Lunn
25–26 Nov 20	Bradford	J. Robertson
24–25 Nov 21	Newcastle	J. Robertson
17–18 May 22	Blackpool	J. Robertson
30 May–1 Jun 23	Buxton	Sir D. Maclean
22–23 May 24	Brighton	Sir D. Maclean
14–15 May 25	Scarborough	Sir D. Maclean
17–18 Jun 26	Weston-s-Mare	J. Spender
26–27 May 27	Margate	Sir C. Hobhouse
11–12 Oct 28	Gt.Yarmouth	Sir C. Hobhouse
3–4 Oct 29	Nottingham	Sir C. Hobhouse
16–17 Oct 30	Torquay	A. Brampton
14–15 May 31	Buxton	A. Brampton
28–29 Apr 32	Clacton	A. Brampton
18–19 May 33	Scarborough	R. Muir
2–5 May 34	Bournemouth	R. Muir
23–25 May 35	Blackpool	R. Muir

[1] J. Hogge and G. Thorne were elected joint whips, not chief whip, in Feb 1919.

Liberal Party Assemblies[1] 1936–1988

Date	Place	President
18–19 Jun 36	London	Ld Meston
27–31 May 37	Buxton	Ld Meston
19–20 May 38	Bath	Ld Meston
11–12 May 39	Scarborough	Ld Meston
1940	*No assembly held*	
18–19 Jul 41	London	Ld Meston
4–5 Sep 42	London	Ld Meston
15–16 Jul 43	London	Ld Meston
1944	*No assembly held*	
1–3 Feb 45	London	Lady V. Bonham-Carter
9–11 May 46	London	Lady V. Bonham-Carter
24–26 Apr 47	Bournemouth	I. Foot
22–24 Apr 48	Blackpool	E. Dodds
24–26 Mar 49	Hastings	Sir A. MacFadyean
27–28 Jan 50	London	Sir A. MacFadyean
29–30 Sep 50	Scarborough	P. Fothergill
1951	*No assembly held*	
15–17 May 52	Hastings	R. Walker
9–10 Apr 53	Ilfracombe	L. Robson
22–24 Apr 54	Buxton	H. G. White
14–16 Apr 55	Llandudno	Ld Rea
27–29 Sep 56	Folkestone	L. Behrens
19–21 Sep 57	Southport	N. Micklem
18–21 Sep 58	Torquay	Sir A. Comyns Carr
1959	*No assembly held*	H. Glanville
29 Sep–1 Oct 60	Eastbourne	Sir A. Murray
21–23 Sep 61	Edinburgh	E. Malindine
19–22 Sep 62	Llandudno	Sir F. Brunner
10–14 Sep 63	Brighton	Ld Ogmore
4–5 Sep 64	London	R. Fulford
22–25 Sep 65	Scarborough	Nancy Seear
21–24 Sep 66	Brighton	Ld Henley
20–23 Sep 67	Blackpool	Ld Wade
18–21 Sep 68	Edinburgh	D. Banks
17–20 Sep 69	Brighton	Ld Beaumont of Witley
23–26 Sep 70	Eastbourne	Ld Beaumont of Witley
15–18 Sep 71	Scarborough	Stena Robson
19–23 Sep 72	Margate	S. Terrell
18–22 Sep 73	Southport	T. Jones
17–21 Sep 74	Brighton	Ld Lloyd of Kilgerran
16–20 Sep 75	Scarborough	A. Holt
12 Jun 76	Manchester *(Special Assembly)*	Margaret Wingfield
14–18 Sep 76	Llandudno	Margaret Wingfield
26 Sep–1 Oct 77	Brighton	B. Goldstone
21 Jan 78	Blackpool *(Special Assembly)*	G. Evans
12–16 Sep 78	Southport	Ld Evans of Claughton
28–29 Sep 79	Margate	M. Steed
8–13 Sep 80	Blackpool	Joyce Rose
14–19 Sep 81	Llandudno	R. Holme
20–25 Sep 82	Bournemouth	V. Bingham
19–24 Sep 83	Harrogate	J. Griffiths
17–22 Sep 84	Bournemouth	Ld Tordoff
16–21 Sep 85	Dundee	A. Watson
21–26 Sep 86	Eastbourne	D. Penhaligon
13–18 Sep 87	Harrogate	D. Wilson
22–23 Jan 88	Blackpool *(Special Assembly)*	A. Slade

[1] Liberal Presidents normally held office from Annual Assembly to Annual Assembly. Until 1970 they were instituted at the beginning of the Assembly which marked the start of their term, and performed the President's duties at that Assembly. From 1970 on they have been instituted at the end of the Assembly and no longer actually presided over debates. Presidents are listed on that basis here.
SOURCES:- *Liberal Year Book* 1902–1939; *The Liberal Magazine* 1900–1950; National Liberal Federation, *Annual Reports* 1900–1936; *Keesing's Contemporary Archives* 1931–.

The Liberal Publication Department published miscellaneous collections of Pamphlets and Leaflets, 1908–30. The *Liberal Magazine* was published from 1893 to 1950. J. S. Rasmussen, *The Liberal Party, A Study of Retrenchment and Revival* (1965); A. Watkins, *The Liberal Dilemma* (1966); T. Wilson, *The Downfall of the Liberal Party 1914–35* (1966); C. Cook, *A Short History of the Liberal Party* (1976); A. Cyr, *Liberal Party Politics in Britain* (1977).

(Social and) Liberal Democrats

On 2 Mar 1988 the result of a ballot was published in which Liberal Party members voted by 46,376 to 6,365 to merge with the Social Democratic Party (which voted by 18,722 to 9,929 to do the same). The new party was officially launched the following day (3 Mar 1988). Its full title was the Social and Liberal Democrats (SLD), with the short title 'the Democrats'. On 16 Oct 1989, following a membership ballot, the party announced that it was henceforth to be known as the Liberal Democrats (although for formal, legal purposes, it retained its full title).

Leader
28 Jul 1988   P. Ashdown[1]
9 Aug 1999   C. Kennedy[2]

Deputy Leader of Parliamentary Party
1988   A. Beith

Leader in the House of Lords
1988   Ld Jenkins
1997   Ld Rodgers

President

1988–90	I. Wrigglesworth	1994–98	R. Maclennan
1990–94	C. Kennedy	1998–	Lady Maddock

Treasurer
1988   T. Razzall *(Ld)*

General Secretary 1988–97
1988   A. Ellis
1989   G. Elson

Chief Executive 1997–
1997   Elizabeth Pamplin

Director of (Media) Communications

1989	Olly Grender	1997	Jane Bonham-Carter
1995	*(office vacant)*	1998	D. Walter

Party Conferences

25–29 Sep 88	Blackpool	18–22 Sep 94	Brighton
3–5 Mar 89	Bournemouth	11–12 Mar 95	Scarborough
9–15 Sep 89	Brighton	17–21 Sep 95	Glasgow
10–11 Mar 90	Cardiff	15–17 Mar 96	Nottingham
15–20 Sep 90	Blackpool	22–26 Sep 96	Brighton
15–17 Mar 91	Nottingham	8–9 Mar 97	Cardiff
9–12 Sep 91	Bournemouth	21–25 Sep 97	Eastbourne
7–8 Mar 92	Glasgow	14–15 Mar 98	Southport
13–17 Sep 92	Harrogate	20–24 Sep 98	Brighton
29–31 May 93	Nottingham	5–7 Mar 99	Edinburgh
19–23 Sep 93	Torquay	19–23 Sep 99	Harrogate
12–13 Mar 94	Cardiff		

Party Finance
Total net central income

1988–89	£1.2m	1993	£1.8m
1989–90	£1.4m	1994	£2.4m
1990–91	£1.6m	1995	£2.3m
1991–92	£1.9m	1996	£2.7m
1992–93	£3.0m	1997	£3.8m

Source:– *The Funding of Political Parties* (Cmnd 4057/1998), p. 31.
[1] In a postal ballot of party members P. Ashdown was elected Leader by 41,401 votes to 16,202 for A. Beith.
[2] In a postal ballot C. Kennedy received 22,724 votes; S. Hughes 16,233; M. Bruce 4,643; Jackie Ballard 3,978; D. Rendel 3,428. After preferences had been distributed C. Kennedy defeated S. Hughes by 28,425 (57%) to 21,833 (43%).

Minor Parties

Minor parties contesting Parliamentary Elections (England, Scotland and Wales)

(for parties that split from major parties see pp.172–182)

Name	Date of Founding	Principal Founder or key policy	MPs elected	Candidates First	Last	Lost No.	Deposits
Action Party	1953 (1948)	Mosley's Union Movement renamed (see p.178)		1959	1972	8	8
Agricultural	1931	Formed as Norfolk Farmers		1933	1933	1	0
All-Party Alliance	1967	J. Creasey		1967	1968	3	3
Anti-Federalist League	1991	A. Sked		1992	1997	19	19
Anti-Partition League	1948			1950	1951	5	5
Anti Waste League	1921	Ld Rothermere	(1)	1921	1921	4	0
Br. Empire Party	1951			1951	1951	1	1
British Movement	1968	C. Jordan		1969	1974	3	3
British National Party (1)	1961	Merger of Whites Defence League and Nat.Lab. Party		1964	1966	4	4
British National) Party (2)	1982	New National Front and other groups led by J. Tyndall		1983	1997	120	118
Br.People's Party	1939	D of Bedford		1939	1946	2	2
Br.Socialist Pty	1911	H. Hyndman		1913	1918	19	2
Br.Un. of Fascists	1932	Sir O. Mosley (see p.178)		1940	1941	3	3
Campaign for SocialDemocracy	1973	D. Taverne	(1)	1974	1974	6	4
Common Wealth	1942	Sir R. Acland (see p.172)	(4)	1943	1945	35	16
C'wealth Land Pty	1919	J. Peace		1931	1931	2	2
Communist Pty of England (Marxist Leninist)	1972			1973	1974	16	16
Communist Party of GB	1920	(see p.172)	(5)	1922	1997	573	5364
Cooperative Party	1917	Allied with Labour after 1918		1918	1918	11	0
Cornish Nationalist Pty	1975	J. Whetter		1979	1983	2	2
Democratic Pty (1)	1942	N. Leith-Hay-Clark		1945	1945	5	5
Democratic Pty (2)	1969	D. Donnelly		1969	1970	7	6
Ecology Party	1975	Successor to People		1976	1984	170	170
Empire Free Trade Crusade	1929	Ld Beaverbrook	(1)	1930	1931	2	0
English National Party	1974	F. Hansford-Miller		1974	1976	4	4
Fellowship Party	1955			1959	1979	8	8
Fife Socialist League	1953			1959	1959	1	1
Green Party	1985	Successor to Ecology		1986	1999	510	509
Highland Land League	1909			1918	1918	4	3
Ind. Democratic Alliance	1973	Succeeds All-Party Alliance		1974	1974	6	6
Independent Labour Pty	1893	Broke with Lab.Party1931 (see p.173)	(11)	1930	1970	82	35
Ind.Nuclear Disarmament Election Committee	1962	Patricia Arrowsmith		1964	1964	2	2
Ind. P'mentary Group	1920	H. Bottomley	(5)	1920	1921	7	3
Internat.Marxist Group	1966			1974	1977	4	4
Irish Civil Rights Ass	1972			1974	1974	7	7
Irish National Movement	1882		(9)[1]	1900	1929	12	0
Islamic Party	1989			1990	1992	5	5
Labour Ind.Group	1949	Expelled Lab. MPs		1950	1950	5	2
League of Empire Loyalists	1954	A. Chesterton, Merged with Nat. Front 1967		1957	1964	4	4
Liberal Party	1988	M. Meadowcroft		1988	1992	188	187
Liverpool Protestant P.	1903			1931	1945	3	0
Mebyon Kernow	1951	Cornish Independence		1970	1997	12	12
Monster Raving Loony	1983	Screaming Lord Sutch		1983	1999		

[1]All of these victories were by T.P. O'Connor in Liverpool (Scotland).

Name	Date of Founding	Principal Founder or key policy	MPs elected	Candidates First	Candidates Last	Lost No.	Lost Deposits
Mudiad Gweriniaethol Ÿ Cymru	1950	Welsh Republican Movement		1950	1950	1	1
National Democratic And Labour Party	1915	To support war and later the Coalition (see p.177)	(10)	1918	1920	29	6
Nat.Democratic Party	1963	D. Brown		1964	1974	8	7
Nat. Farmers Union	1908	(see p. 163)	(8)	1918	1922	10	3
Nat. Federation of Discharged and Demobilised Sailors and Soldiers	1917			1917	1918	6	3
National Fellowship	1962	E. Martell		1963	1967	1	0
National Front	1967	Merger of British Nat.Party and League of Empire Loyalists (see p.177)		1968	1997	571	566
Nat.Independence P.	1972	Nat.Front breakaway		1972	1974	3	3
National Labour Party	1958	J. Bean merged 1960 with White Defence League		1959	1959	1	1
National Party	1917	H. Page Croft	(2)	1917	1920	29	13
National Party	1966	E. Martell		1967	1967	1	1
National Prohibition P.	1887			1923	1923	1	1
National Socialist P.	1916	Breakaway from Br. Socialist Party		1918	1918	4	4
National Union of Small Shopkeepers	1943			1959	1968	3	3
Natural Law Party	1992	Transcendental meditation		1992	1999	519	519
New Conservative Party	1960	J. Dayton		1960	1961	4	4
New Party	1931	Sir O. Mosley (see p.178)		1931	1931	25	3
Patriotic Party	1962	R. Hilton		1964	1966	3	3
People	1973			1974	1974	11	11
People's League for Defence of Freedom	1956	E. Martell		1957	1957	1	1
Plaid Cymru	1925	(see p.179)					
Pro-Life	1996	Anti-Abortion		1997	1997	53	53
Radical Alliance	1965	From supporters of C.N.D.		1966	1966	2	2
Red Front	1987	Alliance of left groups		1987	1987	14	14
Referendum Party	1995	Sir J. Goldsmith	(1)	1997	1997	547	505
Revolutionary Communist Party (1)	1944			1945	1945	1	1
Revolutionary Communist Party (2)	1981			1983	1992	15	15
Scottish Lab.Party(1)	1900			1900	1908	10	0
Scottish Lab.Party(2)	1975	J. Sillars (see p.180)		1978	1979	4	3
Scottish Militant Lab.	1992	Militant tendency		1992	1992	1	0
Scottish Nat. Party	1928	(see p. 180)					
Scottish Party	1932	From supporters of S.N.P.		1933	1933	1	0
Sc.Prohibition Party	1901	E. Scrymgeour	(4)	1908	1931	10	0
Scottish Socialist Alliance	1996			1997	1997	18	17
Social Credit	1935	J. Hargrave		1935	1950	2	2
Social Democratic Federation	1881	H. Hyndman		1900	1910	37	0
Soc.Democratic Party	1988	D. Owen, opponents of Lib./SDP merger		1988	1991	9	5
Socialist Labour P.(1)	1903			1918	1918	3	1
Socialist Labour P.(2)	1996	A. Scargill		1997	1999	70	68
Socialist Party of GB	1904			1945	1997	20	20
Socialist Workers Pty	1976	Formerly Internat. Socialist Group		1976	1978	8	8
Union Movement	1948	(see Action Party p. 178)					
United Country Party	1979	P. Moore		1979	1979	2	2
United Democratic Party	1974			1974	1974	13	13
United Empire Party	1930	Ld Beaverbrook. Merged with Empire Free Trade Crusade		1930	1930	3	1

Name	Date of Founding	Principal Founder or key policy	MPs elected	Candidates First	Candidates Last	Lost No.	Lost Deposits
United Kingdom Indep. P.	1993	A. Sked, M. Holmes		1993	1999	206	205
Vectis National Party	1969			1970	1970	1	1
Wessex Regional Party	1979	A. Thynne		1979	1983	16	16
Women's Party	1917	Emmeline Pankhurst		1918	1918	1	0
Workers' Pty of Scot.	1966			1969	1969	1	1
Workers' Revolutionary Party	1959			1974	1997	123	123

SOURCES:- F.W.S. Craig, *Minor Parties at British Parliamentary Elections 1885–1974* (1975). BBC Political Research Unit.

Notes on the Principal Minor Parties

Common Wealth

This party was founded in 1942 by Sir Richard Acland (Liberal M.P. for Barnstaple) during the war-time electoral truce. Its immediate aim was to contest all by-elections where a 'reactionary' candidate was in the field, and was not opposed by a Labour or other 'progressive' candidate. Seats were won at Eddisbury (J. Loverseed, 1943), Skipton (H. Lawson, 1944), and Chelmsford (E. Millington, 1945). In 1943 membership of Common Wealth was proscribed by the Labour Party. In the 1945 General Election, Common Wealth put up twenty-three candidates but were only successful in Chelmsford, where no Labour candidate stood: the victor there, E. Millington, joined the Labour Party. Sir R. Acland joined the Labour Party as soon as the 1945 results were known. Common Wealth survived as an organisation but contested no further parliamentary elections.

Communist Party

The Communist Party of Great Britain was founded in July 1920. In its early years it sought to affiliate to the Labour Party but was rebuffed. In 1922 J.T.W. Newbold (Motherwell) was elected to Parliament; S. Saklatvala (N. Battersea) was also elected in 1922 as a Labour M.P. (although a member of the Communist Party). After defeat in 1923, he was elected again in 1924 as a Communist. Since 1924 the Labour Party has ruled that no member of the Communist Party could be an individual member of the Labour Party and in 1935, 1943, and 1946 the Labour Party turned down further Communist requests for affiliation. In 1935 and again in 1945 W. Gallacher was elected as a Communist for W. Fife; and in 1945 P. Piratin was elected for the Mile End division of Stepney. In 1991 the party voted narrowly to change its name to Democratic Left and concentrate on political debate rather than contesting elections, although four candidates using the former party's full title did contest the 1992 General Election.

Secretaries of the Communist Party: 1920–29 A. Inkpin, 1929–56 H. Pollitt, 1956–75 J. Gollan, 1975–90 G. McLennan, 1990–91 Nina Temple.

Candidates

1922	5	1935	2	1959	18	1974 (Oct)	29
1923	5	1945	21	1964	36	1979	38
1924	8	1950	100	1966	57	1983	35
1929	25	1951	10	1970	58	1987	19
1931	26	1955	17	1974 (Feb)	44		

SOURCES:- H. Pelling, *The British Communist Party* (1975); F. Beckett, *The Rise and Fall of the British Communist Party* (1998)

Co-operative Party

In 1917 the Co-operative Congress agreed to organise as a political party. In the 1918 General Election one Co-operative M.P. was elected; he joined with the Labour Party in the House of Commons. Labour and Co-operative candidates never opposed each other at elections but it was not till 1926 that a formal understanding was reached and Co-operative Parties were made eligible for affiliation to divisional Labour Parties. In 1938 the Co-operative Party adopted a written constitution and in 1941 its representatives were invited to attend meetings of the National Council of Labour on equal terms with the Labour Party and the T.U.C. In 1946, the 1926 agreement with the Labour Party was replaced; Co-operative candidates were to run formally as Co-operative and Labour Candidates, and after the General Election of 1959 it was agreed that the number of Co-operative candidates should be limited to 32. In 1951 the Co-operative Party adopted a new constitution to prevent its members from joining organisations proscribed by the Labour Party.

Co-operative M.P.s and Candidates

	M.P.s	Candidates		M.P.s	Candidates		M.P.s	Candidates
1918	1	10	1950	18	33	1974 (Oct)	16	22
1922	4	11	1951	16	37	1979	17	25
1923	6	10	1955	18	38	1983	8	17
1924	5	10	1959	16	30	1987	10	20
1929	9	12	1964	19	27	1992	14	26
1931	1	18	1966	18	24	1997	26	26
1935	9	21	1970	17	27			
1945	23	33	1974 (Feb)	6	25			

SOURCES:- J. Bailey, *The British Co-operative Movement* (1955); Reports of the Annual Co-operative Congress 1900–. *The People's Year Book* 1932.

Green Party

The Green Party was founded in 1985 as the successor to the Ecology Party (founded in 1975). It describes itself as the only party committed to ecological sustainability and social justice. It has never had one 'Leader' but has nominated two or more 'main speakers' from its executive. The party made its mark in the 1989 European Elections when it secured 15 per cent of the national vote and pushed the Liberal Democrats into third place in every constituency but one. But it suffered from internal disagreements and, despite some success in local elections, it made negligible impact in Westminster elections. In the 1999 European Parliament elections it secured two seats and 6.8 per cent of the vote.

Ecology/Green Vote

	Candidates	% of UK vote	% per candidate
1979	53	0.1	1.5
1983	108	0.1	1.0
1987	133	0.2	1.4
1992	254	0.5	1.3
1997	95	0.2	1.4

Independent Labour Party

The Independent Labour Party, formed in 1893, was one of the founding bodies of the Labour Representation Committee in 1900. The I.L.P. was affiliated to the Labour Party but it held its own conferences, sponsored its own parliamentary candidates, and maintained its own policies, even after the 1918 revision of the Labour Party constitution. Differences with the Labour Party grew in the late 1920s and the 37 I.L.P. Members among the 288 Labour M.P.s elected in 1929 provided some of the second Labour Government's strongest critics. At the 1930 conference of the I.L.P., it was agreed that I.L.P. members should vote against the Labour Government when its actions conflicted with I.L.P. policy. The I.L.P. was disaffiliated by the 1932 Labour Party Conference. In 1935 17 I.L.P. candidates stood, all against Labour candidates, and four (all in Glasgow) were successful. In 1945 three of the five I.L.P. candidates won but, after the death of the party's leader James Maxton in 1946, the I.L.P. M.P.s one by one rejoined the Labour Party. In the elections of 1950 and 1951 there were three I.L.P. candidates and in 1955 and 1959 two candidates. All lost their deposits. There were no candidates after 1959.

M.P.s (since 1931)

1932–46	J. Maxton	1932–33	R. Wallhead
1932–39	J. McGovern	1935–47	C. Stephen
1932–39	G. Buchanan	1946–47	J. Carmichael
1932–33	D. Kirkwood		

SOURCES:- R. Dowse, *Left in the Centre* (1966); D. Howell, *British Workers and the I.L.P.* (1984).

Irish Parliamentary Parties up to 1922

From the days of Parnell until the First World War between 80 and 86 Irish Nationalists sat in the House of Commons, at times divided by internal frictions but with a safe control of more than three-quarters of the seats in Ireland. Divisions over support for the war and the Easter Rebellion broke the party's hold and in 1918 only 7 of its 58 candidates were elected (while Sinn Fein candidates won 73 seats). T.P. O'Connor, from 1885 the solitary Irish Nationalist Member representing an English constituency, continued to be returned unopposed for the Scotland Division of Liverpool until his death in 1929.

Chairmen of the Irish Parliamentary Party

| 1900 | J. Redmond |
| 1917 | J. Dillon |

SOURCE:- F.S.L. Lyons, *The Irish Parliamentary Party 1890–1910* (1951).

Irish Parties since 1922

Since 1922 candidates under the label 'Irish Nationalist' have fought only two or three of the Northern Ireland seats, but from 1922 to 1924 they held one of the two Fermanagh and Tyrone Seats (the other was held by Sinn Fein) and from 1929 to 1955 they held both. T. P. O'Connor continued to represent the Scotland division of Liverpool until 1929 and the Exchange division of Liverpool was fought by Nationalists on three occasions. Sinn Fein reappeared as a political force in 1955 and 1959, contesting all 12 Northern Ireland seats. In 1955 Sinn Fein candidates won Mid-Ulster and Fermanagh and South Tyrone but they were disqualified as felons. From 1943 to 1950, from 1951 to 1955 and from 1966 onwards Belfast West was held by candidates using the label 'Eire Labour', 'Republican Labour', and then 'Social Democratic and Labour'. The S.D.L.P., founded in 1970, became the main party representing the Republican or Nationalist aspirations of the Roman Catholic minority.

Nationalist M.P.s

1918–29	T. P. O'Connor	1929–34	J. Devlin
1922–24	T. Harbison	1934–35	J. Stewart
1924–29	C. Healy	1935–50	P. Cunningham
1931–35	C. Healy	1935–51	A. Mulvey
1950–55	C. Healy	1951–55	M. O'Neill

Sinn Fein M.P.s
1955–55 P. Clarke
1955–56 T. Mitchell
1983–92 G. Adams
1997–   G. Adams
1997–   M. McGuinness

Eire Labour M.P.s
1943–50 J. Beattie
1951–55 J. Beattie

Republican Labour M.P.
1966–70 G. Fitt

Independent Socialist M.P.
1979–83 G. Fitt

S.D.L.P. M.P.s
1970–79 G. Fitt
1983–   J. Hume
1986–   S. Mallon
1987–   E. McGrady
1992–97 J. Hendron

Independent Republican M.P.s
1969–Feb 74   Bernadette Devlin (Bernadette McAliskey) (Independent Unity)
1970–Feb 74   F. McManus (Independent Unity)
Oct 74–81   F. Maguire (Independent Unity)
1981–81   R. Sands (Anti H-Block)
1981–83   O. Carron (Anti H-Block)

After 1969 increasing fissures developed in the Ulster Unionist Party which had dominated Northern Ireland's representation at Westminster. In 1970, I. Paisley standing as a Protestant Unionist defeated the Official Unionist Candidate in North Antrim. In 1971 he formed the Democratic Unionist Party. In 1970 W. Craig formed the Vanguard Movement and in January 1974 the Unionists split further. In the February 1974 election, 11 of the 12 Ulster seats were won by candidates standing under the banner of a new United Ulster Unionist Council in opposition to those Unionists who supported Mr Faulkner's Executive Council and the Sunningdale proposals for a Council of Ireland. Of the 11, 8 were members of the Unionist party under H. West, 2 carried the Vanguard label and I.Paisley was successful as a Democratic Unionist. In October 1974 H. West who had acted as Unionist Leader was the only one of the 11 to be defeated. J. Molyneaux succeeded him as parliamentary leader. Vanguard was wound up in September 1977. In 1979 3 Paisleyites, 1 Independent Unionist (J. Kilfedder), 1 U.U.U.P. and 5 official Unionists were successful. In 1983 3 Paisleyites, 11 Official Unionists and J. Kilfedder were successful. In 1986 all 15 Unionists resigned their seats to force by-elections in protest at the Anglo-Irish agreement; one, the Official Unionist, M. Robinson, in Newry and Armagh, lost his seat to the S.D.L.P. At the 1987 election 9 Official Unionists, 3 Democratic Unionists and J. Kilfedder were elected; all these seats were retained in 1992, despite a strong challenge in North Down from the Conservative Party, which had been organising in the area since 1987 and received official blessing at the 1991 Conservative Party Conference.

After the death in 1995 of Sir J. Kilfedder, R. McCartney was elected in North Down as a United Kingdom Unionist. He retained his seat in 1997 along with two D.U.P. M.P.s (I. Paisley and P. Robinson) and 10 Official Unionists.

Alliance Party of Northern Ireland

The non-Sectarian Alliance Party, founded in 1970, was joined by S.Mills, a Unionist M.P., in 1972. He did not stand in February 1974. The Alliance Party Leader 1973–84 was O. Napier, followed by J. Cushnahan (1984–87), J. (Ld) Alderdice (1987–98) and S. Neeson (1998–).

Election	Candidates	Lost Deposits	% of N.I. vote
1974 (Feb)	3	2	n.a.
1974 (Oct)	5	1	6.4
1979	12	7	11.9
1983	11	7	8.0
1987	16	4	9.9
1992	16	5	8.7
1997	17	6	8.0

Liberal National Party (National Liberal Party after 1948)

In October 1931 23 Liberal Members broke with the party and formed the Liberal National Group. The subsequent electoral history of the Liberal National Party falls into three periods: at the 1931 General Election some of the Liberal National candidates were opposed by Conservatives but none of them by Liberals. After 1931, a Conservative only once opposed a Liberal National (Scottish Universities 1946) but they were not opposed by Liberals (except in Denbigh 1935 and St. Ives 1937) until 1945. Of 41 candidates in 1931, 35 were returned as Members of Parliament and when the 'Samuelite' Liberals left the government over the Ottawa Agreements in 1932, the 'Simonite' Liberal Nationals remained. In 1935, 33 of 44 candidates were returned, and in 1945, 13 of 51 candidates. E. Brown, however, who had succeeded Sir J. Simon as leader on 4 December 1940, was defeated. In May 1947 the Woolton-Teviot agreement was signed, which urged the combination of Conservative and Liberal National Constituency Associations, and in 1948 the party was renamed the National Liberal Party. After the 1966 General Election only two M.P.s styled themselves Conservative and National Liberal. Two other members of the Group were elected as Conservatives by Joint Associations. In 1966 these four M.P.s relinquished the room assigned to them in the House of Commons to the Liberal Party. The group became an integral part of the Conservative Party.

Chairmen of the Parliamentary Party		Chief Whips	
1931	Sir J. Simon	1931	A. Glassey
1940	E. Brown	1931	G. Shakespeare
1945	(Sir) J. Henderson-Stewart	1932	(Sir) J. Blindell
1946	Sir S. Holmes	1937	C. Kerr
1947	J. Maclay	1940	H. Holdsworth
1956	(Sir) J. Duncan	1945–66	(Sir) H. Butcher
1959	Sir J. Henderson-Stewart		
1961–4	Sir C. Thornton Kemsley		

SOURCES:-Information from the National Liberal Party, and *Dod's Parliamentary Companion*, 1931–66.

Liberal Unionist Party

The Liberal Unionist Party was based upon those Liberals who, under J. Chamberlain and the M of Hartington, broke with the party over Irish Home Rule in 1886. After they accepted office in Ld Salisbury's 1895 government, they became increasingly fused with the Conservative Party and, although they had preserved a separate organisation with separate funds, the final merger in 1912 was to some extent a recognition of a *fait accompli*. The President between 1886 and 1904 was M of Hartington (D of Devonshire) and between 1904 and 1912 J. Chamberlain. The Organising Secretary between 1895 and 1912 was J. Boraston.

Liberal Unionist M.P.s

| 1900 | 68 | 1910 (Jan) | 31 |
| 1906 | 23 | 1910 (Dec) | 35 |

Militant

Militant, known internally as the Revolutionary Socialist League, secretly infiltrated the Labour Party for almost forty years, using the Trotskyist tactic of 'entryism'. The R.S.L. was established in 1955, a democratic centralist Marxist-Leninist Party with its own central committee and annual conference. The Militant newspaper was founded in 1964. Leading figures were its General Secretary, P. Taaffe, and T. Grant. At its peak in the mid-1980s, Militant had more than 8,000 members, and achieved prominence in leading Liverpool City Council's resistance to Government spending controls. Two Militant members, D. Nellist and T. Fields, were elected as Labour M.P.s in 1983, and a third, P. Wall, in 1987. Both Taaffe and Grant were expelled from the Labour Party in 1983, the first of around 200 expulsions over the next decade culminating in the two surviving M.P.s in 1991 (both lost their seats to official Labour candidates at the 1992 election). In 1992 Grant and several of his followers were expelled from Militant itself for opposing its decision to abandon 'entryism' and work mainly outside the Labour Party under the name Militant Labour. In 1997 under the label the Socialist Party, it fielded 19 candidates. In Scotland it has since had several local councillors elected, and, in 1999 fighting under the name Scottish Socialist Party, its leader, T. Sheridan, was elected to the Scottish Parliament.

SOURCE:- M. Crick, *The March of Militant* (1986).

National Democratic Party

The National Democratic Party was formed in 1915 to unite support amongst the Labour Movement for the Lloyd George Government. The N.D.P. had its origins in the dispute within the Labour Movement during the war and its greatest strength in the jingoist trade unions, the Liverpool Dockers, the Musicians' Union, some of the Textile Workers, and parts of the Miners' Federation. It was also, in part, the successor to the projected anti-socialist Trade Union Labour Party and included among its members the Labour Ministers who refused to resign from the Government in 1918. G. Barnes, Labour member of the War Cabinet, was its accepted leader. In the 1918 Election the Party put up 28 candidates, all for working-class constituencies, and returned 15 to Parliament. Before the 1922 Election the surviving N.D.P. M.P.s joined the National Liberal Party, but only one (G. Roberts) was re-elected. The Party ceased to exist in 1923.

SOURCES:- G.D.H. Cole, *A History of the British Labour Party from 1914* (1945); G. N. Barnes, *From Workshop to War Cabinet* (1924); Labour Party Annual Conference Reports, 1916–18; Trades Union Congress Reports, 1916–18.

The National Front and British National Party

The National Front was formed by a merger of the League of Empire Loyalists and the British National Party in 1966. The Greater Britain Movement joined in 1967. The leader of the League of Empire Loyalists, A. K. Chesterton, President of the British National Party, became Executive Director. In 1970 A. K. Chesterton was succeeded by J. O'Brien, who was succeeded in 1972 by J. Tyndall (previously leader of the Greater Britain Movement). In 1974 J. Read ousted J. Tyndall but the courts ruled the ouster illegal. J. Read formed the National Party and J. Tyndall resumed as leader with M. Webster as National Activities Organiser. In 1982 a breakaway faction under J. Tyndall, the New National Front, merged with other groups to form the British National Party.

National Front Candidates

	No.	Av. % vote	Highest % vote
1970	10	3.6	5.6
1974 (Feb)	54	3.3	7.8
1974 (Oct)	90	3.1	9.5
1979	303	1.3	7.6
1983	60	1.1	2.4
1987	–	–	–
1992	14	0.8	1.2
1997	6	0.9	1.2

British National Party Candidates

	No.	Av. % vote	Highest % vote
1983	54	0.5	1.2
1987	2	0.6	0.8
1992	13	1.2	3.6
1997	57	1.3	7.5

SOURCE: M. Walker, *The National Front* (1977); C.Husbands, *Racial Exclusionism in the Cities: Support for the National Front* (1983)

National Party

A small group of dissident Conservatives led by H. Page Croft, formed this party in September 1917, with a programme described by one historian as of 'xenophobic imperialism'. Most of its members drifted back to the Conservative fold and fought under the Conservative label in 1918: only Sir H. Page Croft and Sir R. Cooper survived the election (when they made a special point of attacking the sale of honours) and in 1921 it was decided not to maintain a separate parliamentary party.

National Labour Party

The party was formed in 1931 from the small group of Labour M.P.s who supported the National Government under Ramsay MacDonald. In the 1931 General Election 13 of its 20 candidates were elected. In 1935 8 of its 20 candidates were elected. In 1945 of the remaining National Labour members 3 retired, 2 stood unsuccessfully as National candidates, and 2 as Independents (one, K. Lindsay, stood successfully–but in a new constituency, English Universities).

Natural Law Party

The British branch of the world wide Natural Law Party was formed in 1992. It is dedicated to finding solutions to problems through Natural Law, following the teachings of Maharashi Mahesh Yogi and through yogic flying. The party has fought elections extensively but with no success.

Chair: 1992 G. Clements

	Candidates	% of UK vote	% per candidate
1992	309	0.2	0.4
1997	193	0.1	0.3

New Party, British Union of Fascists, Union Movement

Sir Oswald Mosley (Conservative, then Independent M.P. 1918–24, Labour M.P. 1926–31) resigned from the Labour Government in May 1930 after his Memorandum for dealing with unemployment had been rejected by the Cabinet. In October 1930 a resolution calling upon the National Executive to consider the Memorandum was narrowly defeated at the Labour Party Conference. On 6 December 1930 the Mosley Manifesto summarising the main proposals in the Memorandum was published, signed by 17 Labour M.P.s. Six of the 17 signatories of the Manifesto resigned from the Labour Party to form the new Party in February 1931 (Sir Oswald and Lady Cynthia Mosley, O. Baldwin, W. J. Brown, R. Forgan, and J. Strachey), but Baldwin and Brown remained members for only one day and Strachey resigned in June. The New Party received two further recruits before the 1931 General Election, W. E. D. Allen (Conservative) and R. Dudgeon (Liberal). In the Election the New Party contested 24 seats but failed to win a single one, the New Party M.P.s all losing their seats, and, apart from Sir Oswald Mosley, their deposits.

In 1932 the New Party was renamed the British Union of Fascists after Mosley had been to Italy to study the 'modern movements'. The Director of Organisation and Deputy Leader was R. Forgan. In the 1935 General Election, the B.U.F. put up no candidates and, with the slogan 'Fascism next Time', advised their supporters not to vote. The B.U.F. fought a number of by-elections in 1939 and 1940, before it was proscribed by the Government on 30 May 1940.

In 1948, Sir Oswald Mosley formed the Union Movement. Its first Parliamentary contest was in the 1959 General Election, when he fought North Kensington, losing his deposit. The Union Movement fought two by-elections in the 1959 Parliament and in the 1966 General Election Sir Oswald Mosley and 3 other candidates stood; they gained on average 3.7% of the vote. In 1999 Plaid Cymru made great advances in the Welsh Assembly elections (see p.468) and the European Parliament elections (see p.514).

SOURCES:- C. Cross, *The Fascists in Britain* (1961); R. Skidelsky, *Oswald Mosley* (1975).

Plaid Cymru

The party was founded in 1925 and has fought elections consistently since then, but without any success at the Parliamentary level until a by-election victory in Carmarthen in 1966. The seat was lost in 1970 but in the February 1974 election, two seats, Caernarvon and Merioneth were won. Carmarthen was recaptured in October 1974 but lost in 1979. In 1987 Plaid Cymru gained Ynys Mon (Anglesey), and in 1992 Ceredigion and Pembroke North. In 1999 Plaid Cymru made great advances in the Welsh Assembly elections (see p.468) and the European Parliament elections (see p.514).

	Plaid Cymru Candidates		
	Candidates	Seats Won	% of Welsh vote
1929	1	–	0.0
1931	2	–	0.1
1935	1	–	0.3
1945	6	–	1.1
1950	7	–	1.2
1951	4	–	0.7
1955	11	–	3.1
1959	20	–	5.2
1964	23	–	4.8
1966	20	–	4.3
1970	36	–	11.5
1974 (Feb)	36	2	10.7
1974 (Oct)	36	3	10.8
1979	36	2	8.1
1983	38	2	7.8
1987	38	3	7.3
1992	38	4	8.8
1997	40	4	9.9

Plaid Cymru M.P.s

1966–70	G. Evans
(Feb) 1974–79	G. Evans
(Oct) 1974	D. Wigley
(Feb) 1974–92	D. Thomas
1987–	I. Jones
1992–	E. Llwyd
1992–	C. Dafis

SOURCE:- A. Butt-Philip, *The Welsh Question* (1975)

Referendum Party

The Referendum Party was founded by Sir J. Goldsmith in October 1995 with the sole object of forcing a Referendum on British membership of the European Union. Sir J. Goldsmith devoted £20m. to the enterprise. The party attracted considerable attention during the 1997 election. In June 1997 Sir J. Goldsmith died and the party announced that it would devote its efforts to propaganda rather than to parliamentary candidacies. In January 1999 P. Sykes and the Goldsmith family announced the formation of the Democracy Movement as a non-party successor.

	Candidates	Lost Deposits	% of UK vote	% per candidate
1997	547	505	2.6	3.1

Scottish Labour Party

The Scottish Labour Party was formed in January 1976 by Scots, mostly members of the Labour Party, who were dissatisfied with the Government's proposals for devolution to Scotland. Two Labour M.P.s, J. Sillars (Ayrshire South) and J. Robertson (Paisley), became members of the S.L.P., but did not resign the Labour Whip until 26 July 1976. They then indicated that the S.L.P. would act as an independent party within Parliament. At the S.L.P.'s first Congress at Stirling in October 1976, the leadership suspended the credentials of one delegation and expelled four others for being under the influence of the extreme Left, mainly the International Marxist Group. This led to a walk-out by one third of the delegates. The S.L.P. won three district council seats in May 1977. It fought 3 seats in the 1979 General Election. Only J. Sillars saved his deposit but he narrowly lost his seat. In 1981 the party was wound up and J. Sillars joined the Scottish National Party.

SOURCE.- H. Drucker, *Breakaway: the Scottish Labour Party* (1978).

Scottish National Party

The party was formed in 1928 as the National Party of Scotland. In 1934 it merged with a body called the Scottish Party (founded 1932) and the name was then changed to the Scottish National Party. Its first success was in the Motherwell by-election of April 1945; but the victor, R. McIntyre, was defeated in the General Election three months later. In 1967 a seat was won in the Hamilton by-election but lost in 1970. In 1970, however, a Scottish Nationalist won Western Isles. In November 1973 the Govan, Glasgow, seat was won in a by-election but lost four months later. In the General Elections of 1974 the Scottish Nationalists made great advances in votes and seats, but fell back sharply in 1979. (See p.458 for the S.N.P.s performance in the 1999 Scottish Parliament elections and p.514 for the European elections.)

Scottish National Party Candidates

	Candidates		Candidates	Seats	% of Scottish Vote
1929	2	1970	65	1	11.4
1931	3	1974 (Feb)	70	7	21.9
1935	6	1974 (Oct)	71	11	30.4
1945	8	1979	71	2	17.3
1950	3	1983	72	2	11.8
1951	2	1987	71	3	14.0
1955	2	1992	72	3	21.5
1959	5	1997	72	6	22.1
1964	15				
1966	23				

Scottish National Party M.P.s

1945–45	R. McIntyre
1967–70, 1974 (Feb)–79	Winifred Ewing
1970–87	D. Stewart
1973–1974 (Feb)	Margo Macdonald
1974 (Feb)–79	D. Henderson
1974 (Feb)–79	I. MacCormick
1974 (Feb)–79	G. Reid
1974 (Feb)–79	H. Watt
1974 (Feb)–87	G. Wilson
1974 (Oct)–79, 87–	Margaret Bain (Margaret Ewing)
1974 (Oct)–79	G. Crawford
1974 (Oct)–79	G. Thompson
1974 (Oct)–79, 87–	A. Welsh
1987–	A. Salmond
1988–92	J. Sillars
1990–92	D. Douglas
1995–	Roseanna Cunningham
1997–	J. Swinney
1997–	A. Morgan

Social Democratic Party

The Social Democratic Party was launched by four former Labour Cabinet Ministers in protest, following the Labour Party Special Conference on 24 Jan 81. In its first year it recruited a total of 25 sitting Labour M.P.s and one Conservative M.P. and two of its founders (Shirley Williams and R. Jenkins) won parliamentary by-elections. It formed an Alliance with the Liberal party and shared out constituencies with them in the 1983 general election, when the two parties jointly won 26% of the votes and 23 seats (6 S.D.P). The S.D.P won two further seats in by-elections in 1984 and early 1987 but in the General Election of 1987 only 6 S.D.P M.P.s survived. The party was seriously split over the Liberal Party's proposal in June 1987 that the two parties should merge. On 6 Aug 1987 the membership voted narrowly to proceed with merger negotiations, whereupon D. Owen resigned as leader. R. Maclennan (one of only two S.D.P M.P.s to support merger) was elected leader unopposed on 29 Aug 1988. A draft constitution for a new merged party was published on 11 Dec 1987, and an amended version on 18 Jan 1988; both were rejected by D. Owen and his supporters. The Council for Social Democracy voted to put the merger proposals to the party membership on 31 Jan 1988 and a vote in favour of merger was announced on 2 Mar 1988. The Social Democratic Party was formally subsumed into the Social and Liberal Democrats on 3 Mar 1988.

Three of the five S.D.P M.P.s (D. Owen, J. Cartwright and Rosie Barnes) refused to be involved in the merged party and relaunched a continuing S.D.P on 8 Mar 1988. The party had limited success in by-elections and after disappointing results in local elections in May 1989 the party wound down its operations, conceding it could no longer operate as a national party. It formally suspended operations in Jun 1990. Although attempts were later made to revive it, from Jun 1990 on the three M.P.s sat as independent Social Democrats. D. Owen did not contest his seat in the 1992 General Election. J. Cartwright and Rosie Barnes fought the 1992 election as Independent Social Democrats but lost.

Leader
1982   R. Jenkins
1983   D. Owen

SOURCE:- I. Crewe and A. King, *SDP* (1996)

United Kingdom Independence Party (UKIP)

The United Kingdom Independence Party was founded in August 1993 to campaign against British membership of the European Union. It secured 3.3 per cent of the vote in the 24 constituencies it fought in the 1994 Euro-Elections. In 1997 it lost out to the more publicised Referendum Party.

	Candidates	*% of UK vote*	*% per candidate*
1997	194	0.3	1.2

In the 1999 Euro-elections it secured 7.0 per cent of the UK vote and three seats.

Independent M.P.s

The number of Independent M.P.s has been small and, even among those few elected without the label of one of the parties already listed, a substantial proportion were in fact elected with the tacit support of a major party or in default of its candidate. All but one of the M.P.s elected as Independents fall within six broad categories.

Independents in University Seats

1922	J. Butler	1945	Eleanor Rathbone
1923	G. Davies	1937	(Sir) A. Herbert
1924	(Sir) E. Graham-Little	1945	Sir A. Herbert
1929	(Sir) E. Graham-Little	1937	Sir A. Salter
1931	(Sir) E. Graham-Little	1937	Sir A. Salter
1935	(Sir) E. Graham-Little	1937	T. Harvey
1945	(Sir) E. Graham-Little	1945	W. Harris
1929	Eleanor Rathbone	1945	K. Lindsay
1931	Eleanor Rathbone	1945	Sir J. Boyd-Orr
1935	Eleanor Rathbone		

Independents emerging from war-time situations

1917	N. Billing	1942	W. Brown
1918	N. Billing	1945	W. Brown
1918	H. Bottomley	1942	G. Reakes
1918	R. Barker	1942	T. Driberg[1]
1941	W. Kendall	1944	C. White[1]
1945	W. Kendall		

Dissident Conservatives

1902	T. Sloan	1922	G. Hall Caine[2]
1906	T. Sloan	1923	O. Mosley
1903	E. Mitchell	1929	Sir R. Newman
1910	F. Bennett-Goldney[2]	1930	E. Taylor[2]
1920	Sir C. Townshend	1937	D. Lipson
1920	C. Palmer	1945	D. Lipson[3]
1921	Sir T. Polson	1940	Sir C. Headlam[2]
1922	J. Erskine[2]	1945	J. McKie[3]
1922	J. Erskine	1945	J. Little
1922	H. Becker[2]	1959	Sir D. Robertson

[1] Later accepted Labour Whip.
[2] Later accepted Conservative Whip.
[3] These candidacies might be put into a different category.

Dissident Liberal

1900	Sir J. Austin		1924	A. Hopkinson[3]
1902	J. Wason		1931	A. Hopkinson[3]
1922	G. Roberts[3]		1935	A. Hopkinson[3]
1922	A. Hopkinson		1929	Sir T. Robinson
1923	A. Hopkinson			

[3]These candidacies might be put into a different category.

Dissident Labour

1915	C. Stanton		1970	S. Davies
1922	Sir O. Thomas		1972	D. Taverne
1929	N. Maclean		1974 (Feb)	D. Taverne
1945	D. Pritt		1974 (Feb)	E. Milne

Supported by the Left

1922	E. Scrymgeour		1929	E. Scrymgeour
1923	E. Scrymgeour		1938	V. Bartlett
1924	E. Scrymgeour		1945	V. Bartlett

Independent

1997   M. Bell

Minor Parties – Representation in the House of Commons

Year	Total	Ir.N.	S.N.P	P.C	U.U.	Comm.	I.L.P	I.C.	I.Lab	Other
1900	82	82	–	–	–	–	–	–	–	–
1906	83	83	–	–	–	–	–	–	–	–
1910 (Jan)	84	82	–	–	–	–	–	–	–	2
1910 (Dec)	84	84	–	–	–	–	–	–	–	–
1918	83	80[1]	–	–	–	–	–	–	–	3
1922	12	3	–	–	–	–	1	4	1	3
1923	7	3	–	–	–	–	–	–	–	4
1924	5	1	–	–	–	–	1	–	–	3
1929	8	3	–	–	–	–	–	–	–	4
1931	5	2	–	–	–	–	–	–	–	3
1935	9	2	–	–	–	1	4	–	–	2
1945	22	3	–	–	1	2	3	4	1	8
1950	3	2	–	–	–	–	–	–	–	1
1951	3	3	–	–	–	–	–	–	–	–
1955	2	2	–	–	–	–	–	–	–	–
1959	1	–	–	–	–	–	–	–	–	1
1964	–	–	–	–	–	–	–	–	–	–
1966	1	1	–	–	–	–	–	–	–	–
1970	6	3	1	–	1	–	–	–	1	–
1974 (Feb)	24	1	7	2	11	–	–	2	1	–
1974 (Oct)	26	2	11	3	10	–	–	–	–	–
1979	16	2	2	2	10	–	–	–	–	–
1983	21	2	2	2	15	–	–	–	–	–
1987	23	3	3	3	14	–	–	–	–	–
1992	24	4	3	4	13	–	–	–	–	–
1997	28	5	6	4	12	–	–	–	–	1

[1] There were 73 Sinn Fein candidates elected in Ireland in 1918 who never took their seats. There were also 7 Irish Nationalists who did not sit.

SOURCES:- *The Constitutional Year Book*, 1919; D. Butler, *The Electoral System in Britain since 1918* (1963); G. Thayer, *The British Political Fringe* (1965); F.W.S. Craig, *British Parliamentary Election Statistics, 1918–87* (1988); F.W.S. Craig, *Minor Parties at British Parliamentary Elections, 1885–1974* (1975).

Registration of Political Parties

Under the *Registration of Political Parties Act, 1998*, all parties wishing to put forward candidates for election were required to record their title and responsible officials with the Registrar of Companies. Initially 77 parties registered. The Registrar's function was to be taken over by the Electoral Commission proposed in the *Political Parties, Elections and Referendums Bill* of 2000.

Political Pressure Groups and 'Think-tanks'

Specialist pressure goups are listed at a number of other points in the book. (See p. 367, p.409, p.503, and p.519). The following is a selection of pressure groups with a more generalised remit:

Centre for Policy Studies 1974–
Fabian Society 1884–
Institute for Public Policy Research 1989–
P.E.P. (Political and Economic Planning) 1931–
P.S.I. (Policy Studies Institute) 1978–
Adam Smith Institute 1977–
Social Market Foundation 1989–
Politeia 1995–
Charter 88 1988–
Demos 1993–
Constitution Unit 1995–

III

PARLIAMENT

House of Commons

Speaker of the House of Commons

1895	W. Gully (Vt Selby)	Lib.		21 Oct 59	Sir H. Hylton-Foster[1]	Con.
20 Jun 05	J. Lowther (Vt Ullswater)	Con.		26 Oct 65	H. King (Ld Maybray-King)	Lab.
28 Apr 21	J. Whitley	Co.Lib.		12 Jan 71	S. Lloyd (Ld Selwyn-Lloyd)	Con.
21 Jun 28	E. Fitzroy[1]	Con.		3 Feb 76	G. Thomas (Vt Tonypandy)	Lab.
9 Mar 43	D. Clifton Brown (Vt Ruffside)	Con.		15 Jun 83	B. Weatherill (Ld Weatherill)	Con.
1 Nov 51	W. Morrison (Vt Dunrossil)	Con.		17 Apr 92	Betty Boothroyd	Lab.

Chairman of Ways and Means

1900	J. Lowther	Con.	1959	Sir G. Touche	Con.
1905	G. Lawson	Con.	1962	Sir W. Anstruther-Gray	Con.
1906	A. Emmott	Lib.	1964	H. King	Lab.
1911	J. Whitley	Lib.	1965	Sir S Storey	Con.
1921	J. Hope	Con.	1966	Sir E. Fletcher	Lab.
1924	R. Young	Lab.	1968	S. Irving	Lab.
1924	J. Hope	Con.	1970	Sir R. Grant-Ferris	Con.
1929	R. Young	Lab.	1974	G. Thomas	Lab.
1931	Sir D. Herbert	Con.	1976	O. Murton	Con.
1943	D. Clifton Brown	Con.	1979	B. Weatherill	Con.
1943	J. Milner	Lab.	1983	(Sir) H. Walker	Lab.
1945	C. Williams	Con.	1992	M. Morris	Con.
1945	J. Milner	Lab.	1997	Sir A. Haselhurst	Con.
1951	Sir C. MacAndrew	Con.			

Deputy Chairman of Ways and Means
(office created 1902)

1902	A. Jeffreys	Con.	1950	Sir C. MacAndrew	Con.
1905	L. Hardy	Con.	1951	Sir R. Hopkin Morris[1]	Lib.
1906	J. Caldwell	Lib.	1956	Sir G. Touche	Con.
1910	J. Whitley	Lib.	1959	Sir W. Anstruther-Gray	Con.
1911	D. Maclean	Lib.	1962	Sir R. Grimston	Con.
1919	Sir E. Cornwall	Lib.	1964	Sir S. Storey	Con.
1922	E. Fitzroy	Con.	1965	R. Bowen	Lib.
1924	C. Entwistle	Lib.	1966	S. Irving	Lab.
1924	E. Fitzroy	Con.	1968	H. Gourlay	Lab.
1928	D. Herbert	Con.	1970	Betty Harvie Anderson	Con.
1929	H. Dunnico	Lab.	1973	E. Mallalieu	Lab.
1931	R. Bourne[1]	Con.	1974	O. Murton	Con.
1938	D. Clifton Brown	Con.	1976	Sir M. Galpern	Lab.
1943	J. Milner	Lab.	1979	G. Irvine	Con.
1943	C. Williams	Con.	1982	E. Armstrong	Lab.
1945	Sir C. MacAndrew	Con.	1987	Sir P. Dean	Con.
1945	H. Beaumont	Lab.	1992	G. Lofthouse	Lab.
1948	F. Bowles	Lab.	1997	M. Martin	Lab.

Second Deputy Chairman of Ways and Means
(office created 1971)

1971	E. Mallalieu	Lab.	1981	E. Armstrong	Lab.
1973	O. Murton	Con.	1982	(Sir) P. Dean	Con.
1974	*(office vacant)*		1987	Betty Boothroyd	Lab.
1974	Sir M. Galpern	Lab.	1993	Dame J. Fookes	Con.
1976	G. Irvine	Con.	1997	M. Lord	Con.
1979	R. Crawshaw	Lab.			

[1] Died in office.

Officers of the House of Commons

Clerk		Librarian	
1900	(Sir) A. Milman	1887	R. Walpole
1902	Sir C. Ilbert	1908	A. Smyth
1920	(Sir) T. Webster	1937	V. Kitto
1930	(Sir) H. Dawkins	1946	H. Saunders
1937	(Sir) G. Campion	1950	S. Gordon
1948	(Sir) F. Metcalfe	1968	D. Holland
1954	(Sir) E. Fellowes	1976	D. Menhennet
1962	(Sir) B. Cocks	1991	D. Englefield
1974	(Sir) D. Lidderdale	1993	Jennifer Tanfield
1976	(Sir) R. Barlas	2000	Priscilla Baines
1979	(Sir) C. Gordon		
1983	(Sir) K. Bradshaw		
1987	(Sir) C. Boulton		
1994	(Sir) D. Limon		
1998	W. McKay		

Parliamentary Sessions

Around 1900, sessions of Parliament lasted from February to July or August. Occasionally Parliament sat through the summer. In 1930 both Houses agreed that they should adjourn between July and October, and that the session should last from September or October to the September or October of the following year. During the adjournments the Speaker or the Lord Chancellor has the power to give notice of an earlier meeting of his House if it is in the national interest.

Since 1945 there has normally been a Christmas Recess of about three weeks and Recesses of one week at Easter and in late May. The Summer Recess has usually lasted from late July to mid-October.

Parliamentary Hours of Sitting

In 1902 the House of Commons met from 2 p.m. until 11.30 p.m., but this was altered in 1906 to 2.45 p.m. until 11.30 p.m., to allow more time for lunch. During the 1939–45 war the time for rising in the evening was changed to 10.30 p.m. From 1945 the normal hours for sitting became 2.30 p.m. until 10.30 p.m. on every weekday except Friday although the House often sits later than this. From 1900 to 1939 the House met on Fridays from noon to 5.30 p.m. From 1939 the House met on Fridays at 11 a.m. and normally adjourned for the weekend at 4.30 p.m. In 1967 as an experiment, the House also met from 10 a.m. to 1 p.m. on Mondays and Wednesdays but these morning sittings were discontinued from October 1967. From 1980 the House normally met at 9.30 a.m. on Friday and adjourned at 3 p.m.

Since 1995 it has not met on some Fridays (12 in 1997–8). From 1997–9, it has also met on Wednesdays at 9.30 a.m., and since 1999 on Thursdays at 11.30 a.m.

In 1999, as an experiment, normal sitting hours on Thursdays were changed to 11.30 a.m. to 7.30 p.m.

On 30 November 1999 experimental sittings began in Westminster Hall on Tuesday and Wednesday mornings and on Thursday afternoons. They were intended to provide extra time for adjournment debates and for the discussion of Select Committee Reports.

Cancelled Sittings

If the House sits for more than 24 hours (or 19 hours on a Thursday) the next day's business is lost. This has happened on these occasions since 1900:

19 Jul 04	Finance Bill
20 Mar 07	Consolidated Fund Bill
22 Jul 36	Unemployment Assistance Regulations
11 Jun 51	Finance Bill
13 Jul 67	Abortion Bill
12 Jun 69	Divorce Reform Bill
24 Jul 75	Remuneration Bill
21 Jun 77	Price Commission Bill
28 Jul 77	Consolidated Fund Bill
4 Aug 80	Consolidated Fund Bill
1 Apr 81	British Telecommunications Bill
22 May 84	Local Government Bill
5 Mar 85	Water (Fluoridation) Bill
10 Dec 86	Teachers' Pay Bill
10 Nov 87	Felixstowe Dock and Railway Bill
14 Jun 88	Housing Bill

Emergency Recalls of the House of Commons

Under Standing Order No 12, which dates from 1948, the Speaker may give notice that the House of Commons will sit earlier than the date agreed on adjournment if the public interest requires it, following representations from Ministers. This Standing Order has been used sixteen times:

27–29 Sep 49	Devaluation
12–19 Sep 50	Korean War
4 Oct 51	Prorogation and dissolution
12–14 Sep 56	Suez crisis
18 Sep 59	Prorogation and dissolution
17–23 Oct 61	Berlin crisis
16 Jan 68	Government expenditure cuts
26–27 Aug 68	Czechoslovakia, Nigeria
26–29 May 70	Prorogation and dissolution
22–23 Sep 71	Northern Ireland
9–10 Jan 74	Fuel
3–4 Jun 74	Northern Ireland
3 Apr 82	Falkland Islands
14 Apr 82	Falkland Islands
6–7 Sep 90	Kuwait
24–25 Sep 92	Exchange rate policy, UN operations
31 May 95	Bosnia
2–3 Sep 98	Passage of Anti-Terrorism legislation

Government and Private Members' Time

Until 1939 Government business had precedence at every sitting of the House of Commons except certain Wednesdays and Fridays and Tuesday evenings after 8.15 p.m. until Easter. This generally gave Private Members about eight Wednesdays and thirteen Fridays on which they had precedence. This was always subject to the possibility that the House, or Government, might direct that the time was needed for Government business. Between 1914 and 1918 and between 1939 and 1948 Private Members' time was abolished completely. When Private Members' time was restored, the Government retained precedence on all days except for twenty Fridays. Private Members' motions were also allowed on some Mondays. In the nine sessions 1950–51 to 1958–59 an average of ten days was allotted to Private Members' Bills and nine days to Private Members' motions.

In 1960 four extra half-days (two Mondays and two Wednesdays) were allotted for consideration of Private Members' motions in addition to the twenty Fridays. From 1967 to 1970 sixteen of the twenty Fridays were given to Bills and four to motions. Since 1970 the number of Fridays for Bills has been between ten and twelve. Since 1995 Private Members' motions have been debated on Wednesday mornings, and, since November 1999, in the new Westminster Hall meetings.

Broadcasting of Parliament

Television cameras were first allowed into Parliament for the opening of the session and the Queen's Speech on 28 Oct 58. On 11 Dec 67 the Commons approved without a division a proposal for a closed-circuit experiment with radio only. This was carried out in Apr and May 68. In Feb 68 the House of Lords engaged in a three-day radio and television closed-circuit experiment. But the House of Commons on a free vote rejected the idea of broadcasting Parliament on 24 Nov 66 (131–130), on 19 Oct 72 (191–165) and on 30 Jan 74 (189–164). On 24 Feb 75 the House of Commons approved (354–152) a four-week experiment with the live radio broadcasting of its proceedings and this took place from 9 Jun to 4 Jul 75. On 16 Mar 76 the House approved (299–124) the idea of permanent sound broadcasting. A select committee of six M.P.s (*Chairmen*: 1978: R. Mellish; 1979: Sir A. Royle; 1983: Sir P. Goodhart) was set up on 6 Feb 78 to supervise the arrangements to be made with the broadcasting authorities. A similar Lords Committee was also set up (*Chairman*: 1978: Ld Aberdare). Amendments proposing the appointment of a manager of broadcasting operations and a House of Commons broadcasting unit to control the scheme were defeated (64–53) and (68–49). Regular sound broadcasting began on 3 Apr 1978. Private members subsequently introduced Ten Minute Rule Bills to test opinion on televising proceedings, as follows:

4 Jul 1978	defeated (181–161).
30 Jan 1980	first reading carried (202–201) on deputy speaker's casting vote.
15 Dec 1981	defeated (176–158).
13 Apr 1983	(select committees only): first reading carried (153–138).
2 Nov 1983	first reading carried (164–159).

On 8 Dec 1983, the Lords voted (74–24) for the public televising of some of its proceedings for an experimental period, and the select committee recommended a six-month experiment which began on 23 Jan 1985. On 22 Jul 1985 the House of Lords extended the experiment and on 12 May 1986 agreed to make television a permanent feature.

There were regular attempts by supporters of the televising of the House of Commons to air the issue, using Ten Minute Rule bills. On 20 Nov 1985 a motion moved by Dame J. Fookes to allow the televising of proceedings was narrowly defeated (275–263). On 9 Feb 1988 the House voted, 318–264, to allow a limited experiment in televising proceedings under strict conditions, laid down by a newly appointed select committee on televising the proceedings of the House. Televising began on 21 Nov 1989. The Select Committee reviewed the first six months of the experiment, and when the House approved their report (19 Jul 1990) it effectively ended the debate on whether televising was desirable; it was formally made permanent on 1 May 1991. Under the permanent arrangements put in place in 1991, integrated coverage of both Houses of Parliament was undertaken by the Parliamentary Broadcasting Unit Limited (PARBUL), financed by the broadcasting companies. Although the strict conditions laid down by the House of Commons when it first approved the televising experiment were subsequently relaxed slightly, television directors are still not allowed to show reaction shots during question time or ministerial statements, or to show any scenes of disturbances. In 1992 the cable television industry established the Parliamentary Channel, to provide 'gavel to gavel' live coverage of the House of Commons and recorded coverage of the House of Lords and committees. The BBC took over the channel in Sep 1998 and it is now carried on cable, digital satellite and digital terrestrial television (sound only).

Broadcasting Committee 1989–
(11 members)

| 1989 | Sir G. Howe | 1992 | A. Newton |
| 1991 | J. McGregor | 1997 | E. Clarke |

Source: Broadcasting Select Committee Report (H.C.11/1990–1); House of Commons Factsheet no. 40, May 1992.

Main Occupations of Members of Parliament 1918–1951 (percentages)

| | Conservative | | | | Labour | | | |
	Average 1918–45	1945	1950	1951	Average 1918–35	1945	1950	1951
Professional	52	61	62	58	24	49	47	46
Business	32	33	31	33	4	10	10	9
Unoccupied	12	3	5	6	–	–	–	–
Workers	4	3	3	5	72	41	43	45
	100	100	100	100	100	100	100	100

Source: to 1950 J. Ross *Electors and Elected* (1955)

Main Occupations of Members of Parliament 1951– (percentages)

Conservative

	51	55	59	64	66	70	Feb 74	Oct 74	79	83	87	92	97
Professional	41	46	46	48	46	45	44	46	45	45	42	39	37
Business	37	30	30	26	29	30	32	33	34	36	37	38	39
Misc.	22	24	23	25	23	24	23	20	20	19	20	22	23
Workers		–	–	1	1	1	1	1	1	1	1	1	1
	100	100	100	100	100	100	100	100	100	100	100	100	100

Labour

	51	55	59	64	66	70	Feb 74	Oct 74	79	83	87	92	97
Professional	35	36	38	41	43	48	46	49	43	42	40	42	45
Business	9	12	10	11	9	10	9	8	7	9	10	8	9
Misc.	19	17	17	16	18	16	15	15	14	16	21	28	33
Workers	37	35	35	32	30	26	30	28	36	33	29	22	13
	100	100	100	100	100	100	100	100	100	100	100	100	100

Source: Nuffield General Election Studies

Education of Conservative and Labour M.P.s 1906–1997 (percentages)

	Conservative		Labour	
	Public School	University Educated	Public School	University Educated
1906	67	57	0	0
1910 (Jan)	74	58	0	0
1910 (Dec)	76	59	0	0
1918	81	49	3	5
1922	78	48	9	15
1923	79	50	8	14
1924	78	53	7	14
1929	79	54	12	19
1931	77	55	8	17
1935	81	57	10	19
1945	85	58	23	32
1950	85	62	22	41
1951	75	65	23	41
1955	76	64	22	40
1959	72	60	18	39
1964	75	63	18	46
1966	80	67	18	51
1970	74	64	17	53
1974 (Feb)	74	68	17	56
1974 (Oct)	75	69	18	57
1979	77	73	17	57
1983	70	71	14	53
1987	68	70	14	56
1992	62	73	14	61
1997	61	81	16	66

Source: To 1950 J. Ross *Electors and Elected* (1955); since 1950 Nuffield Studies

House of Commons Business

Sessions		Allocation of Time		Bills			Questions		
				Private			Daily Av.		
Date of	Date	Sitting	Length	MPs'	Total	Royal		Starred	
Meeting	Prorogued	Days	of Day	Days	Introduced	Assent	Yes	No	Total
3 Dec 00	15 Dec 00	11	5h 38m	3	–	–	–	–	314
23 Jan 01	17 Aug 01*	121	9h 5m	14	303	127	69	–	6,448*
16 Jan 02	18 Dec 02	181	8h 51m	17	300	121	–	–	7,168
17 Feb 03	14 Aug 03	115	9h 8m	14	311	131	28	18	4,536
2 Feb 04	15 Aug 04	124	9h 19m	13	308	121	38	18	5,933
14 Feb 05	11 Aug 05	114	9h 12m	12	309	86	47	19	6,244

Dissolution 8 Jan 06. Duration 5 years, 2 months, 7 days

13 Feb 06	21 Dec 06	156	8h 32m	16	346	121	70	22	11,865
12 Feb 07	28 Aug 07	131	8h 28m	13	294	116	72	21	10,147
29 Jan 08	21 Dec 08	171	7h 39m	18	364	129	75	21	13,811
16 Feb 09	3 Dec 09	179	8h 38m	14	325	110	62	19	12,251

Dissolution 10 Jan 10. Duration 3 years, 10 months, 28days

15 Feb 10	28 Nov 10	103	6h 36m	9	289	101	81	24	8,201

Dissolution 28 Nov 10. Duration 9 months, 13 days

* Although the session of 1901 was not due to begin until 14 Feb, Parliament sat for three days between 23 and 25 Jan to discuss business arising out of the death of Queen Victoria.

Sessions		Allocation of Time		Bills			Questions Daily Av. Starred		
Date of Meeting	Date Prorogued	Sitting Days	Length of Day	Private MPs' Days	Total Introduced	Royal Assent	Yes	No	Total
31 Jan 11	16 Dec 11	172	7h 49m	11	373	134	87	21	15,439
14 Feb 12	7 Mar 13	206	8h 1m	14	343	101	97	19	19,913
10 Mar 13	15 Aug 13	102	7h 55m	10	315	108	88	18	18,936
10 Feb 14	18 Sep 14	130	7h 14m	16	391	168	55	16	7,705
11 Nov 14	27 Jan 16	155	6h 40m	–	162	152	72	16	12,976
15 Feb 16	22 Dec 16	127	7h 11m	–	112	105	108	20	15,743
7 Feb 17	6 Feb 18	181	7h 21m	–	102	91	92	16	19,146
12 Feb 18	21 Nov 18	119	7h 16m	–	99	86	89	15	12,025

Dissolution 25 Nov 18. Duration 7 years, 9 months, 25 days

4 Feb 19	23 Dec 19	163	7h 16m	16	203	152	126	27	20,523
10 Feb 20	23 Dec 20	167	8h 20m	17	215	138	110	22	18,652
15 Feb 21	10 Nov 21	141	8h 0m	11	202	125	101[d]	19[d]	14,133[d]
14 Dec 21	19 Dec 21	4	6h 5m	–	–	–			
7 Feb 22	4 Aug 22	113	8h 3m	11	196	105			

Dissolution 26 Oct 22. Duration 3 years, 8 months, 22 days

20 Nov 22	15 Dec 22	20	7h 54m	10	–	10	103[e]	18[e]	12,860[e]
13 Feb 23	16 Nov 23	114	8h 34m	17	181	78	107	21	12,370

Dissolution 16 Nov 23. Duration 11 months, 27 days

8 Jan 24	9 Oct 24	129	7h 50m	21	248	79	101	25	13,092

Dissolution 9 Oct 24. Duration 9 months, 1 day

2 Dec 24	22 Dec 25	148	8h 17m	22	247	145	91	23	14,035
2 Feb 26	15 Dec 26	151	7h 55m	21	180	105	71	17	10,713
8 Feb 27	22 Dec 27	144	7h 53m	19	195	91	74	14	10,536
7 Feb 28	3 Aug 28	115	7h 34m	24	168	79	67	13	7,559
6 Nov 28	10 May 29	100	7h 0m	–	115	64	68	17	7,074

Dissolution 10 May 29. Duration 4 years, 5 months, 8 days

25 Jun 29	1 Aug 30	189	7h 57m	31	237	132	93	24	18,327
28 Oct 30	7 Oct 31	187	7h 47m	21	212	106	78	15	14,373

Dissolution 8 Oct 31. Duration 2 years, 4 months, 12 days

3 Nov 31	17 Nov 32	155	7h 32m	1	125	103	69	10	9,667
22 Nov 32	17 Nov 33	143	7h 33m	26	147	92	58	8	7,559
21 Nov 33	16 Nov 34	156	7h 49m	22	173	111	58	9	8,768
20 Nov 34	25 Oct 35	151	7h 36m	–	116	98	59	9	8,449

Dissolution 25 Oct 35. Duration 3 years, 11 months, 21 days

26 Nov 35	30 Oct 36	137	7h 55m	19	149	111	82	13	10,215
3 Nov 36	22 Oct 37	157	7h 47m	24	170	126	79	11	11,769
26 Oct 37	4 Nov 38	168	7h 42m	26	179	113	85	14	13,787
8 Nov 38	23 Nov 39	200	7h 34m	14	227	171	92	17	18,460
28 Nov 39	20 Nov 40	127	6h 53m	–	80	73	84	27	13,536
21 Nov 40	11 Nov 41	113	5h 50m	–	55	54	77	23	10,825
12 Nov 41	10 Nov 42	116	6h 23m	–	46	46	80	23	11,592
11 Nov 42	23 Nov 43	122	7h 1m	–	59	58	83	22	11,911
24 Nov 43	28 Nov 44	153	7h 14m	–	55	52	77	17	11,498
29 Nov 44	15 Jun 45	95	6h 51m	–	57	48	91	18	7,856

Dissolution 15 Jun 45. Duration 9 years, 5 months, 2 days

[c] The figures for questions in the first 1922 session are included in those for the second 1922 session.
[d] For both sessions in 1921.
[e] For both sessions in 1922.

| Sessions | | Allocation of Time | | | Bills | | Questions Daily Av. Starred | | |
Date of Meeting	Date Prorogued	Sitting Days	Length of Day	Private MPs' Days	Total Introduced	Royal Assent	Yes	No	Total
1 Aug 45	6 Nov 46	212	7h 45m	–	106	104	128	30	7,313
12 Nov 46	20 Oct 47	164	8h 38m	–	73	71	108	22	17,310
21 Oct 47	13 Sep 48	171	8h 13m	–	92	89	97	21	16,303
14 Sep 48	25 Oct 48	10	7h 2m	–	–	–	132	41	853
26 Oct 48	16 Dec 49	208	7h 48m	10	146	125	86	18	17,334

Dissolution 3 Feb 50. Duration 4 years, 4 months, 15 days

1 Mar 50	26 Oct 50	105	7h 50m	5	58	57	105	19	9,861
31 Oct 50	4 Oct 51	153	8h 20m	19	107	81	108	18	15,720

Dissolution 5 Oct 51. Duration 1 year, 7 months, 4 days

31 Oct 51	30 Oct 52	157	8h 48m	18	113	88	99	17	14,192
4 Nov 52	29 Oct 53	162	8h 12m	20	78	62	91	16	13,878
3 Nov 53	25 Nov 54	187	8h 11m	19	113	95	89	15	15,990
30 Nov 54	6 May 55	84	7h 58m	10	72	33	90	17	7,262

Dissolution 6 May 55. Duration 3 years, 6 months, 6 days

7 Jun 55	5 Nov 56	219	7h 57m	25	126	101	86	16	18,285
6 Nov 56	1 Nov 57	159	7h 40m	20	93	75	90	20	14,259
5 Nov 57	23 Oct 58	156	7h 54m	20	112	89	84	18	12,734
28 Oct 58	18 Sep 59	159	7h 48m	20	113	89	89	21	14,518

Dissolution 18 Sep 59. Duration 4 years, 3 months, 11 days

20 Oct 59	27 Oct 60	160	8h 2m	22	103	80	81	21	13,471
1 Nov 60	24 Oct 61	168	8h 30m	22	117	79	73	22	13,778
31 Oct 61	25 Oct 62	160	8h 23m	22	108	75	65	23	12,226
30 Oct 62	8 Nov 63	162	8h 15m	22	105	72	67	31	13,948
12 Nov 63	25 Sep 64	155	8h 14m	22	155	102	66	37	14,291

Dissolution 25 Sep 64. Duration 4 years, 11 months, 5 days

27 Oct 64	10 Mar 66	177	9h 0m	22	158	94	74	46	19,148
9 Nov 65	8 Nov 65	65	8h 15m	22	74	21	67	56	7,978

Dissolution 10 Mar 66. Duration 1 year, 5 months, 13 days

18 Apr 66	27 Oct 67	246	9h 50m	25	210	127	69	69	33,965
31 Oct 67	25 Oct 68	176	9h 2m	22	142	76	64	77	24,910
30 Oct 68	22 Oct 69	164	9h 26m	24	158	73	81	78	23,464
28 Oct 69	29 May 70	122	8h 16m	24	152	60	81	78	17,461

Dissolution 29 May 70. Duration 4 years, 1 month, 11 days

29 Jun 70	28 Oct 71	206	8h 16m	24	164	110	83	99	33,946
2 Nov 71	26 Oct 72	180	9h 17m	24	149	84	77	97	28,946
31 Oct 72	25 Oct 73	164	8h 53m	24	153	83	47	109	25,788
30 Oct 73	8 Feb 74	60	8h 21m	6	77	17	41	104	8,690

Dissolution 8 Feb 74. Duration 3 years, 7 months, 10 days

6 Mar 74	20 Sep 74	87	8h 28m	10	86	50	48	133	15,738

Dissolution 20 Sep 74. Duration 6 months, 14 days

Sessions		Allocation of Time		Bills			Questions		
				Private				Daily Av.	
Date of Meeting	Date Prorogued	Sitting Days	Length of Day	MPs' Days	Total Introduced	Royal Assent	Yes	Starred No	Total
22 Oct 74	12 Nov 75	198	9h 20m	22	183	99	47	137	36,652
19 Nov 75	22 Nov 76	191	9h 13m	22	174	100	49	167	41,460
24 Nov 76	26 Oct 77	149	9h 10m	22	141	56	46	163	31,269
3 Nov 77	24 Oct 78	169	9h 24m	24	136	60	49	175	37,775
31 Oct 78	7 Apr 79	86	8h 17m	15	115	50	54	153	17,851

Dissolution 7 Apr 79. Duration 4 years, 5 months, 16 days

9 May 79	13 Nov 80	244	8h 55m	25	217	102	51	164	52,635
20 Nov 80	30 Oct 81	163	9h 7m	22	145	78	50	139	30,863
4 Nov 81	28 Oct 82	174	8h 8m	22	143	59	52	135	32,430
3 Nov 82	13 May 83	115	8h 34m	17	134	56	53	149	23,220

Dissolution 13 May 1983. Duration 4 years, 4 days

15 Jun 83	31 Oct 84	213	8h 59m	24	181	76	65	188	53,995
6 Nov 84	30 Oct 85	172	9h 06m	25	153	75	86	183	46,314
5 Nov 85	7 Nov 86	172	8h 56m	25	162	69	101	185	49,140
12 Nov 86	18 May 87	109	8h 32m	19	124	51	12	196	34,537

Dissolution 18 May 87. Duration 3 years, 11 months, 4 days

17 Jun 87	15 Nov 88	159	11h 31m	26	168	62	110	219	72,666
22 Nov 88	16 Nov 89	136	11h 38m	25	179	46	136	225	63,472
21 Nov 89	1 Nov 90	127	11h 32m	25	162	45	148	248	66,045
7 Nov 90	22 Oct 91	125	10h 50m	24	171	69	173[c]	205	37,664
31 Nov 91	16 Mar 92	63	11h 2m.	12	97	47	97	193	18,433

Dissolution 16 Mar 1992. Duration 4 years, 8 months, 30 days

27 Apr 92	22 Nov 93	240	8h 16m	25	220	68	30	236	63,684
18 Nov 93	3 Nov 94	154	8h 10m	25	142	41	30	267	45,610
16 Nov 94	8 Nov 95	159	8h 16m	20	102	54	31	283	49,897
15 Nov 95	17 Oct 96	146	8h 45m	13[d]	147	60	31	246	40,307
23 Oct 96	21 Mar 97	86	8h 21m	7[d]	121	59	30	214	21,061

Dissolution 8 Apr 97. Duration 4 years, 11 months, 11 days

7 May 97	19 Nov 98	241	8h 47m	13	202	62	34	219	60,765
24 Nov 98	11 Nov 99	149	9h 15m	13	135	35	34	216	37,157
17 Nov 99									

SOURCES:– Information from the *'Black Book'*, a compilation of Parliamentary statistics at the House of Commons, and the *Sessional Returns of the House of Commons*. Questions to Ministers taken from D. N. Chester and N. Bowring, *Questions in Parliament* (1962), pp. 87–8, and 316; and information from the Journal Office, House of Commons.

[c] From Nov 90 only the highest-placed questions for oral answer appeared on the order paper
[d] Does not include Wednesday morning sittings introduced in 1995

Fathers of the House of Commons

	M.P. until	Length of service			
		as M.P.		as Father	
		y.	m.	y.	m.
(Sir) W. Bramston Beach	Aug 1901	44	4	2	4
Sir M. Hicks Beach	Jan 1906	41	6	4	5
G. Finch	May 1907	39	6	1	4
Sir H. Campbell-Bannerman	Apr 1908	39	6	11	
Sir J. Kennaway	Jan 1910	39	9	1	9
T. Burt	Nov 1918	44	10	8	11
T. P. O'Connor	Nov 1929	49	7	10	11
D. Lloyd George	Dec 1944	54	8	15	1
Earl Winterton	Oct 1951	46	11	6	10
Sir H. O'Neill	Oct 1952	37	8	1	0
D. Grenfell	Sep 1959	37	2	6	11
Sir W. Churchill	Sep 1964	62	0[a]	5	0
R. Butler	Jan 1965	35	8		4
(Sir) R. Turton	Feb 1974	44	8	9	1
G. Strauss	Apr 1979	46	11[a]	5	0
J. Parker	May 1983	46	7	4	1
J. Callaghan	May 1987	41	10	4	0
Sir B. Braine	Mar 1992	42	1	3	10
Sir E. Heath	(*elected February 1950*)				

[a]By tradition the title of Father of the House goes to the member with the longest continuous service. Sir W. Churchill's service (1900–08, 1908–22 & 1924–19 was broken in 1908 and again in 1922–4. His continuous service was therefore exactly 40 years. G. Strauss sat 1929–31 and then 1934–79.

Long-service M.P.s

Apart from the Fathers of the House (all but three of whom served over 38 years) the following M.P.s served 38 years or more:

Years		
49	G. Lambert	91–24, 29–45
48	A. Balfour	74–06, 06–22
47	J. Gretton	95–06, 07–43
47	H. Chaplin	68–06, 07–16
45	Sir A. Chamberlain	92–14, 14–37
42	J. Talbot	68–78, 78–10
42	M. Foot	45–55, 60–92
41	Sir W. Hart Dyke	65–06
40	Sir W. Lawson	59–65, 68–85, 86–00, 03–06
40	E. Shinwell	22–24, 28–31, 35–70
40	W. Long	80–92, 93–21
40	D. Healey	52–92
39	Sir G. Courthope	06–45
39	W. Thorne	06–45
39	Sir T. Moore	25–64
39	Sir C. Taylor	35–74
39	Sir L. Ropner	23–29, 31–64
39	Sir H. Fraser	45–84
39	J. Amery	50–66, 69–92
38	Sir J. Pease	65–03
38	J. Round	68–06

Years		
38	Sir J. Agg-Gardner	74–80, 85–95, 00–06, 11–28
38	J. Chamberlain	76–14
38	J. Collings	80–86, 86–18
38	J. Lowther	83–21
38	Ld H. Cecil	95–06, 10–37
38	W. Nicholson	97–35
38	E. Fitzroy	00–06, 10–43
38	W. Elliott	18–23, 24–45, 46–58
38	G. Oliver	22–31, 35–64
38	H. Macmillan	24–29, 31–45, 45–64
38	Dame I. Ward	31–45, 50–74
38	G. Lloyd	31–45, 50–74
38	Sir J. Langford-Holt	45–83
38	A. Lewis	45–83
38	G. Thomas	45–83
38	J. Silverman	45–83
38	F. Willey	45–83
38	Sir H. Wilson	45–83
38	Sir D. Walker-Smith	45–83
38	Sir J. Ridsdale	54–92
38	P. Channon	59–97

In 2000 Sir E. Heath (50–), T. Benn (50–60, 63–83, 84–), Sir J. Morris (59–), T. Dalyell (62–), Sir R. Body (55–59, 66–), Sir G. Johnson Smith (59–64 ,65–), Sir P. Emery (59–66, 67–),and Sir P. Tapsell (59–64, 66–) were the only MPs to have sat for over 38 years.

Sir J. Fergusson (55–57, 59–68, 85–06), Sir F. Powell 57–59, 63–68, 72–74, 80–81, 85–10), and Lord C. Hamilton (65–8, 69–88, 10–18) with substantially interrupted service can be listed with Sir W. Churchill, D. Lloyd George, G. Lambert, Sir J. Agg-Gardner and G. Strauss as the only members to leave the House fifty years after entering it.

Oldest and Youngest M.P.s

The oldest M.P.s have been S. Young (96 in 1918); D. Logan (92 in 1964); Sir W. Churchill (89 in 1964); W. Thorne (88 in 1945); R. Cameron (87 in 1913); J. Collings (86 in 1918); Sir S. Chapman (86 in 1945); E. Shinwell (85 in 1970); and S. O. Davies (85 in 1972).

The youngest M.P.s have been Vt Turnour (Earl Winterton) (21 in 1904); J. Esmonde (21 in 1915); P. Whitty (21 in 1916); J. Sweeney (21 in 1918); E. Harmsworth (21 in 1919); Sir H. Lucas-Tooth (21 in 1924); and Bernadette Devlin (21 in 1969).

M.P.s of Ethnic Minority Origin

1892–95	D. Naoraji	1991–92	A. Kumar
1895–05	Sir M. Bhownagree	1997–	A. Kumar
1922–23	S. Saklatvala	1992–97	N. Deva
1924–29	S. Saklatvala	1992–	P. Khabra
1987–	B. Grant	1997–	Oona King
1987–	Diane Abbott	1997–	M. Singh
1987–	P. Boateng	1997–	M. Sarwar
1987–	K. Vaz		

Family Connections of M.P.s

Many M.P.s have had extended family connections with other present or past M.P.s. Often, when through the female line, these are difficult to check. However, the following include the most outstanding examples of parliamentary families.

Acland	Sir R. Acland (1935–45, 1947–55); s. of Sir F. Acland (1906–22,1923–4,1932–39); s. of Sir A. Acland (1885–99); s. of Sir T. Acland (1837–47, 1865–85).
Aitken	J. Aitken (1974–97), s. of Sir W. Aitken, (1950–64) and nephew of Sir M. Aitken (1910–16) who was father of M. Aitken (1945–50).
Astor	W. W. Astor (1935–45, 1951–52) and his brothers J. J. Astor (1951–59) and M. Astor (1945–51) were sons of Vtess Astor (1919–45) and W. Astor (1910–19). W. Astor's brother J. J. Astor (1922–45) and his son J. Astor (1964–74) also sat.
Baldwin	(E Baldwin of Bewdley). O. Baldwin (1929–31, 1945–57); s. of S. Baldwin (1908–37); s. of A. Baldwin (1892–1908).
Benn	(Vt Stansgate) H. Benn (1999–); s. of A. Wedgwood Benn (1950–60,1963–83, 1984–); s. of W. Benn (1906–27, 1928–31, 1937–41); s. of Sir J. Benn (1892–95, 1904–10).
Butler	Sir A. Butler (1970–92); s. of R. A. Butler (1929–65); nephew of Sir G. Butler (1923–29).
Cavendish	(D of Devonshire) M. of Hartington (1923–38); s. of V. Cavendish (1865–68, 1880–91); s. of Ld E. Cavendish (1865–74, 1880–91) b. of M of Hartington (1857–68, 1869–91) and of Ld G. Cavendish (1859–80) and of Ld F. Cavendish (1865–82); sons of W. Cavendish (1829–34). Four of the sisters of the M of Hartington (1923–38) were married to M.P.s – H. Macmillan (1924–9, 1931–45, 1945–64); J. Stuart (1923–59); H. Hunloke (1938–44); F. Holland-Martin (1951–60) and then Vt Hinchingbrooke (1941–62).

Cecil (M of Salisbury) Vt Cranborne (1979–87); s. of Vt Cranborne (1950–54); s. of Vt Cranborne (1929–41); s. of Vt Cranborne (1885–92, 1893–1903); s. of Vt Cranborne (1853–68); s. of Vt Cranborne (1813–23); s. of Vt Cranborne (1774–80).

Chamberlain N. Chamberlain (1918–40); b. of Sir A. Chamberlain (1892–1937); s. of J. Chamberlain (1876–1914).

Channon P. Channon (1959–97); s. of Sir H. Channon (1935–58) and g.s. of Countess of Iveagh (1927–35) and Vt Elveden (1908–10, 1912–27). This is the only example of a seat, Southend, being held successively by four members of one family.

Churchill (D of Marlborough) W. Churchill (1970–97); s. of R. Churchill (1940–5); s. of Sir W. Churchill (1900–22, 1924–64); s. of Ld R. Churchill (1874–94); s. of M of Blandford (1844–45, 1847–57); s. of M of Blandford (1818–20, 1826–30, 1832–35, 1838–40); s. of M of Blandford (1790–96, 1802–04). N. Soames is g.s. of Sir W. Churchill.

Clifton Brown G. Clifton Brown (1992–); grandson of G. Clifton Brown (1945–50); nephew of H. Clifton Brown (1922–23, 1924–45); and D. Clifton Brown (1918–23.1924–51); sons of J. Clifton Brown (1876–80); grandson of Sir W. Brown (1846–59).

Cryer J. Cryer(1997–), s. of Anne Cryer (1997–) and of R. Cryer (1974–83, 1987–94).

Douglas-Hamilton (D of Hamilton) Ld J. Douglas-Hamilton (1974–97); son of M. of Clydesdale (1930–40); brother of Ld M. Douglas-Hamilton (1950–54).

Foot M. Foot (1945–55, 1960–92); b. of (Sir) D. Foot (1931–45, 1957–70) and s. of I. Foot (1922–4, 1929–35).

Guest (Vt Wimborne) I. Guest (1935–45); s. of I. Guest (Vt Wimborne) (1906–10) who was b. of F. Guest (1910–22, 1923–9, 1931–37), O. Guest (1918–22, 1935–45) and C. Guest (1910–18, 1922–3, 1937–45).

Henderson A. Henderson (1903–18, 1919–22, 1923, 1924–31, 1933–5), sat in the House with two sons, Arthur (1923–4, 1929–31, 1935–66) and William (1923–4, 1929–31).

Hogg (Vt Hailsham) D. Hogg (1979–); s. of Q. Hogg (1938–50, 1963–70); s. of Sir D. Hogg (1922–8); nephew of Sir J. Hogg (1865–8, 1871–87), and grandson of Sir. J. Hogg (1835–57).

Hurd D. Hurd (1974–97); s. of Sir A. Hurd (1945–64); s. of (Sir) P. Hurd (1918–23, 1924–45).

Jeger Lena Jeger (1957– 1970); widow of S. Jeger (1945–57); b. of G. Jeger (1945–71).

Lindsay (E of Crawford and Balcarres) Ld Balniel (1955–74); s. of Ld Balniel (1924–40) and nephew of J. Lindsay (1955–59); sons of Ld Balcarres (1895–1913); s. of Ld Balcarres (1874–80).

Lloyd George D. Lloyd George (1890–1944) sat in the House with his son Gwilym (1924–50, 1951–7) and his daughter Megan (1929–51, 1957–66).

Mallalieu Sir J. Mallalieu (1945–79) and Sir (E.) L. Mallalieu (1931–35, 1947–74); sons of Sir F. Mallalieu (1916–22).

Montagu-
Douglas-Scott (D of Buccleuch) E of Dalkeith (1960–73); s. of E of Dalkeith (1923–35) and nephew of Ld W. Scott (1935–50); s. of E of Dalkeith (1895–1906); s. of E of Dalkeith (1853–60, 1874–80).

Morris Estelle Morris (1992–) d. of C. Morris (1963–83) and niece of J. Morris (1964–97).

Morrison Sir C. Morrison (1963–92); b. of Sir P. Morrison (1974–92); s.of J. Morrison (1942–64); s. of H. Morrison (1918–23, 1924–31); b. of J. Morrison (1900–06, 1910–12).

Nicholson Emma Nicholson (1987–97); d. of Sir G. Nicholson (1931–5, 1937–66); nephew of J. Nicholson (1921–4) and O. Nicholson (1924–31); sons of W. Nicholson (1897–1935); s. of W. Nicholson (1866–74, 1880–85).

Ormsby-Gore (Ld Harlech). D. Ormsby-Gore (1950–61); s. of W. Ormsby-Gore (1910–38); s. of G. Ormsby Gore (1901–4); s. of W. Ormsby-Gore (1847–52, 1858–76) and nephew of J. Ormsby-Gore (1837–41, 1859–76); sons of W. Ormsby-Gore (1806–7, 1830–1, 1835–7).

Rathbone T. Rathbone (1974–97); s. of J. Rathbone (1935–41) and Beatrice Rathbone (Wright) (1941–5).

Ridley N. Ridley (1959–92); grandson of M. Ridley (1900–05); s. of Sir M. Ridley (1868–00); s. of Sir M. Ridley (1859–68) and b. of G. Ridley(1856–60) and of E. Ridley (1878–80); s. of Sir M. Ridley (1812–1836); s. of Sir M. Ridley (1768–1812); s. of M. Ridley (1747–74).

Silkin J.Silkin, (1963–83) and S.Silkin (1964–83); sons of L. Silkin (1936–50).

Stanley (E of Derby) R. Stanley (1950–66); s. of Ld Stanley (1917–18, 1922–38) and nephew of O. Stanley (1924–50); sons of Ld Stanley (1892–1906) and nephews of A. Stanley (1898–1918); sons of Ld Stanley (1848–69) and nephews of F. Stanley (1865–86); sons of Ld Stanley (1824–44) and nephews of H. Stanley (1832–37); s. of Ld Stanley (1796–1832); s. of E. Stanley (1774–76); s. of J. Stanley 1741–71; s. of E. Stanley (1727–36); s. of Sir T. Stanley (1695–98).

Wood R.Wood (1950–79) and Ld Irwin (1937–45), sons of Ld Irwin (1910–1925); grandson of Sir C. Wood (1826–66).

Spouse's Succession

In the following cases a wife took over at a by-election the seat being left vacant by her husband's death, elevation to the peerage, disqualification, or resignation.

1919	Lady Astor (Plymouth, Sutton)
1921	Margaret Wintringham (Louth)
1923	Mabel Philipson (Berwick-on-Tweed)
1927	Countess of Iveagh (Southend)
1930	Lady Noel-Buxton (Norfolk North)
1937	Agnes Hardie (Glasgow, Springburn)
1937	Lady Davidson (Hemel Hempstead)
1941	Beatrice Rathbone (Bodmin)
1943	Lady Apsley (Bristol Central)
1953	Lena Jeger (Holborn & St. Pancras, S.)
1957	Lady Gammans (Hornsey)
1982	Helen McElhone (Glasgow, Queen's Park)
1986	Llin Golding (Newcastle-under-Lyme)
1990	Irene Adams (Paisley North)

In 1931 Sir O. Mosley failed to take over his wife's seat at Stoke. In 1958 Katherine Elliot was defeated at Glasgow, Kelvingrove, when seeking to succeed her husband. In 1969 Ann Forrest was defeated in Mid-Ulster when seeking to succeed her husband.

In 1929 H. Dalton took over the seat, Bishop Auckland, which his wife had won in a 1929 by-election. In 1929 W. Runciman took over the seat, St Ives, which his wife had won in a 1928 by-election.

The Duchess of Atholl (1923–38) sat for the West Perthshire seat which her husband (M of Tullibardine) had occupied (1910–17).

In 1997 Ann Cryer won the Keighley seat for which her husband sat 1974–83.

In 1984 Caroline Jackson succeeded R. Jackson as MEP for Wiltshire.

The only cases of husband and wife sitting together in the House of Commons have been

W. and Hilda Runciman	1928–29
H. and Ruth Dalton	1929–29
Sir O. and Lady C. Mosley	1929–31
A. Bevan and Jennie Lee	1929–31
(married in 1934)	1945–60
W. and Jennie Adamson	1938–45
J. and Florence Paton	1945–50
R. and Anne Kerr	1966–70
J. and Gwyneth Dunwoody	1966–70
N. and Anne Winterton	1983–
P. and Virginia Bottomley	1984–
G. and Bridget Prentice*	1992–
R. and Julie Morgan	1997–
A. and Ann Keen	1997–
A. Mackay and Julie Kirkbride	1997–

* Separated

A. Lyon (1966–83) and Clare Short (1983–), though married, did not sit in the same House. Some M.P.s have married after one had left the House: N. Fisher (1950–83) and Patricia Ford (1953–55); J. Sillars (1970–79, 1988–92) and Margo Macdonald (1973–74); C. Stephen (1935–47) and Dorothy Jewson (1923–24).

Shirley Summerskill (1964–83) sat with her ex-husband J. Ryman (1974–87).

Filial Succession

In the following cases a son or daughter was nominated to fill a vacancy left by a parent.

1908	S. Baldwin *Con.* (Bewdley)
1909	T. Lundon *I.Nat* (Limerick E.)
1913	R. McCalmont *U.U.* (Antrim E.)
1913	P. Meehan *I.Nat.* (Queens Co., Leix)
1914	A. Chamberlain *Con.* (Birmingham)
1940	N. Grattan-Doyle *Con.* (Newcastle N.) (defeated)
1945	G. Lambert *Con.* (South Molton)
1946	J. Little *U.U.* (Down) (defeated)
1953	Patricia Ford *U.U.* (Sir W. Smiles) (Down N.)
1959	P. Channon *Con.* (Southend W.)
1970	G. Janner *Lab.* (Leicester N.W.)
1983	Susan Palmer *Lab.* (Bristol N.W.) (defeated)
1987	Hilary Armstrong *Lab.* (Durham N.W.)

Dual Mandates

From 1973 to 1979 all the UK members of the European Assembly were nominated from the House of Commons or the House of Lords. In the first direct elections, 10 M.P.s were elected as MEPs as well as 4 Peers. Since then the following M.P.s have served simultaneously at Westminster and Strasbourg.

1979–	I. Paisley (Dem.U.)		1983–84	R. Boyes (Lab)
1979–	J. Hume (SDLP)		1983–84	Ann Clwyd (Lab)
1979–89	J. Taylor (U.U.)		1983–84	R. Caborn (Lab)
1979–84	Sir B. Rhys-Williams (Con)		1983–84	A. Rogers (Lab)
1979–87	T. Normanton (Con)		1987–89	W. Griffiths (Lab)
1979–84	Elaine Kellett-Bowman (Con)		1987–89	Joyce Quin (Lab)
1983–84	R. Jackson (Con)		1992–94	G. Hoon (Lab)
1983–84	D. Harris (Con)		1992–94	L. Smith (Lab)
1983–84	D. Curry (Con)		1992–94	G. Stevenson (Lab)
1983–84	J. Taylor (Con)		1997–99	Anne McIntosh (Con)
1983–84	E. Forth (Con)			

In 1999 16 M.P.s were elected as Members of the Scottish Parliament and 6 M.P.s were elected to the Welsh Assembly.

Critical Votes in the House of Commons since 1900

Votes in the House of Commons have only rarely disturbed or threatened to disturb a government or to prevent its implementing its programme. Moreover prudent governments have retreated rather than face the risk of defeat (e.g. over In Place of Strife, 1969). The following occasions do not constitute an exhaustive list (e.g. only 5 of the 9 minor defeats inflicted on the Labour Government of 1924 are included) but they probably include all that caused any serious stir.

15 Feb 1904	327–276	Government majority (on Liberal Free Trade motion) cut by desertion of 26 Unionist Free Traders.
20 Jul 1905	199–196	Government defeated on Estimates for Irish Land Commission.
11 Nov 1912	227–206	Government defeated on Amendment to financial resolution of the Government of Ireland Bill.
7 Jul 1914	269–246	Government won guillotine on Budget despite 22 Lib. abstentions, one Lib. No; setback leads to abandonment of Revenue Bill.
8 Nov 1916	213–117	Government survived challenge on sale of German property in Nigeria but 65 Cons rebelled, provoking Bonar Law to think of Cabinet reconstruction.

9 May 1918	293–106	Lloyd George victory over Maurice affair. Coupons in Dec 1918 election issued largely on basis of how Libs voted in this division.
23 Oct 1919	185–113	Amendment to Alien Restriction Bill carried on report stage against Government.
25 Feb 1920	123–57	Motion for increased police pensions carried against Government.
19 Jul 1921	137–135	Amendment to Finance Bill exempting Provident Societies from Corporation Profits Tax carried against Government.
10 Apr 1923	145–138	Government defeated on procedural motion over ex-Servicemen's salaries.
21 Jan 1924	328–256	Baldwin Government, meeting new parliament, defeated by Lib. and Lab. votes.
7 Apr 1924	221–212	Government defeated on second reading of Rent Restriction Bill.
16 Jun 1924	189–126	New Clause to London Traffic Bill carried against Government.
18 Jul 1924	171–149	Government defeated on amendment to Unemployment Insurance Bill.
8 Oct 1924	364–198	MacDonald Government defeated on Lib. amendment for enquiry into Campbell case. Dissolution follows at once.
27 Feb 1930	280–271	Government defeats key Amendment to Coal Bill, saved by support of 4 Libs and abstention of 8 Libs.
21 Jan 1931	282–249	Government defeat on Report Stage over subsidy to Catholic schools (41 Lab. Noes).
14 Mar 1931	173–168	Government survives challenge over appointment of Sir E. Gowers to chair Mines Reorganisation Commission.
16 Mar 1931	277–273	Government defeated over abolition of University M.P.s (2 Lab. M.P.s voted with Opposition and 20 abstained).
8 Sep 1931	309–250	National Government wins first vote (on procedural motion); Ayes 243: Con., 53 Lib., 12 Lab., 3 Ind.; Noes: 242 Lab., 9 Ind.
11 Feb 1935	404–133	Government wins Second Reading for Government of India Bill (with 80 Con. Noes).
1 Apr 1936	156–148	Government defeated on adjournment motion over equal pay for civil servants (vote reversed 6 Apr 1936).
8 May 1940	281–200	Chamberlain wins confidence motion but Con. Noes (33) and abstentions (about 65) force his resignation.
18 Mar 1943	335–119	Government wins motion on Beveridge Report but 97 Lab. M.P.s out of 99 non-ministers voting defy Whip.
28 Mar 1944	117–116	Government defeated on equal pay for women (vote reversed 30 May 1944, 429–23).
13 Dec 1945	345–98	Government obtains approval for the American Loan. Cons officially abstained, but 74 Con. and 23 Lab. M.P.s voted No; 8 Cons also voted Aye.
1 Apr 1947	386–85	Government obtains Second Reading for National Service Bill (72 Lab. and 1 Con. Noes).
9 Mar 1950	310–296	First division in new parliament (on Steel Nationalisation) showed Government with nominal majority of five could carry on.
29 Mar 1950	283–257	Government defeated on adjournment motion following debate on Fuel and Power.
9 Apr 1951	237–219	Motion to annul a Rationing Order carried against the Government.
5 Jul 1951	157–141	Motion to annul a Prices Order carried against the Government.
16 Jul 1951	232–229	Government defeated on amendment to the Forestry Bill.
6 Dec 1956	313–260	Government wins confidence vote on Suez action (15 Con. abstentions).
17 Jun 1963	321–252	Government survives adjournment debate on Profumo Affair (27 Con. abstentions).
10 Mar 1964	287–20	Government secures Second Reading of Resale Prices Bill with Labour abstaining (20 Con. Noes and about 20 abstentions).
24 Mar 1964	204–203	Government defeats Amendment excluding medicines from Resale Prices Bill (31 Con. voting against Government and over 20 abstaining).
6 May 1965	310–306	Approval for White Paper on Steel Nationalisation.
6 Jul 1965	180–167	New Clause to Finance Bill carried against Government.
21 Dec 1965	276–48	Rhodesia oil embargo order approved. Cons officially abstained but 48 Cons voted No and 31 Aye.
30 May 1968	129–52	Reintroduction of prescription charges approved but 49 Lab. Noes and over 150 Lab. abstentions.
3 Mar 1969	224–62	Motion approving In Place of Strife White Paper carried but 55 Lab. Noes and 40 Lab. abstentions.
28 Oct 1971	356–244	Approval for negotiated terms on European entry. 69 Lab. M.P.s voted for and 20 abstained. 39 Con. M.P.s voted against and 2 abstained.
17 Feb 1972	309–301	Government secures Second Reading of European Communities Bill (15 Con. Noes and 4 Con. abstentions; there were 4 Lab. abstentions; Libs divided 5–1 Aye).
13 Jul 1972	301–284	Government secures Third Reading of European Communities Bill (16 Con. Noes; 4 Con. and 13 Lab. abstentions).
22 Nov 1972	275–240	Government defeated on immigration rules (7 Con. Noes and 49 Con. abstentions).
13 Jun 1973	267–250	Government defeated on new Clause to Maplin Development Bill (17 Con. Ayes and 10 Con. abstentions).

13 Jun 1973	255–246	Government secures Third Reading of Maplin Development Bill.
12 Jul 1973	285–264	Government defeated on export of live animals for slaughter (23 Cons voted Aye).
20 Jun 1974	311–290	Government defeated in debate on industrial policy.
27 Jun 1974	298–289	Opposition motion on Rates carried against Government.
		[The above were only two of the seventeen government defeats during the short Parliament of 1974.]
29 Jan 1975	280–265	Government defeated on amendment to the Social Security Benefits Bill (9 Lab. Ayes).
17 Jul 1975	108–106	Government defeated on Opposition amendment to Finance Bill reducing V.A.T. on TV sets.
4 Aug 1975	268–261	Government defeated on clause to the Housing Finance (Special Provisions) Bill.
10 Mar 1976	284–256	Government defeated on motion approving public expenditure plans. (Next day Government won confidence motion 297–280.)
27 May 1976	304–303	In disputed vote Government set aside Standing Order rule on hybridity of Aircraft and Shipbuilding Nationalisation Bill. (Government won retaken vote on 29 Jun 311–297 with 14 Nationalists abstaining.)
28 Jun 1976	259–0	Government defeated on motion for adjournment (through failing to contest it) following debate on its child benefits scheme.
8 Nov 1976	311–310	Government secures guillotine on Lords amendments on Aircraft and Shipbuilding Acts.
10 Nov 1976	310–308	Key clause in Dock Labour Bill defeated through two Lab. abstentions (J. Mackintosh and B. Walden).
7 Feb 1977	130–129	Government lost Second Reading of the Redundancy Rebates Bill by one vote, due to unpaired absence of the P.M. (Subsequently reintroduced in modified form.)
22 Feb 1977	312–283	Government defeated over guillotine on Scotland and Wales Bill (with 22 Lab. Noes and 21 abstentions).
17 Mar 1977	293–0	Government defeated on adjournment motion to discuss public expenditure plans (all Lab. M.P.s abstained).
23 Mar 1977	322–298	Government survives Con. motion of censure with Lib. votes, following Lib-Lab. Pact.
5 Apr 1977	203–185	Government defeated on adjournment motion following debate on training colleges in Scotland, through Lab. abstentions.
22 Nov 1977	199–184	Government loses first clause of the Scotland Devolution Bill.
5 Dec 1977	158–126	Government defeated on adjournment motion on Crown Agents' affair by M.P.s demanding public inquiry.
7 Dec 1977	161–160	Government defeated over Scotland Devolution Bill provision for Secretary of State to have regard to national pay policy (2 Lab. Noes).
13 Dec 1977	319–222	Government recommendation of proportional representation for European Parliament elections rejected on Free Vote (Lab. 147 for, 115 against; Con. 61 for, 198 against).
23 Jan 1978	291–281	Motion to devalue Green Pound by 7.5%, not 5%, carried against Government.
25 Jan 1978	166–151	Amendment to Scotland Devolution Bill, making 40% of electorate voting 'Yes' in referendum a precondition for the Bill taking effect carried against Government (34 Lab. in majority).
25 Jan 1978	204–118	Amendment to Scotland Devolution Bill, excluding Orkney and Shetland, carried against Government.
14 Feb 1978	298–243	Referendum decision of 25 Jan 77 confirmed on Report Stage (40 Lab. in majority).
8 May 1978	312–304	Amendment to reduce standard rate of Income Tax from 34p. to 33p. carried against Government.
10 May 1978	288–286	Amendment to raise threshold for higher tax rates from £7,000 to £8,000 carried against Government.
19 Jul 1978	293–260	Amendment to Wales Bill barring M.P.s from standing for Welsh Assembly carried against Government.
24 Jul 1978	291–281	Government defeated on clause in Dock Labour Bill giving dock workers local priority in jobs.
26 Jul 1978	276–275	Lords Amendment to Scotland Bill concerning non-Scottish legislation decided by Scottish M.P.s votes upheld against Government. (Lords amendment on Forestry powers also carried 288–266.)
13 Dec 1978	285–283	Government defeated on retention of powers to use sanctions against firms breaching pay policy.
28 Mar 1979	311–310	Government defeated on Conservative vote of No Confidence.
23 Apr 1980	477–49	Government faces rebellion on closed shop.

15 Dec 1982	290–272	Government defeated on amendment to immigration rules (51 Cons voting with Opposition or abstaining).
19 Jul 1983	322–218	Government advice on delaying M.P.s' pay increase rejected.
2 Apr 1984	472–57	Government wins on union right to contract in to political levy (42 Cons vote against).
14 Apr 1986	296–282	Government defeated on Second Reading of Shops Bill (Sunday trading).
4 Nov 1992	319–316	Government wins paving motion on Maastricht Treaty.
8 Mar 1993	314–292	Government defeated on Committee of Regions in Maastricht Bill (26 Cons vote against).
22 Jul 1993	324–316	Defeat of Government motion on Social Policy Protocol of Maastricht Treaty. (On the next day the decision was reversed 339–301 on a confidence motion).
6 Dec 1994	319–311	Government defeated on extension of V.A.T. on fuel and power for charities (7 Conservatives vote against).
6 Nov 1995	322–271	One of four Government defeats in 'free' votes on Nolan proposals on M.P.s' ethics.
19 Dec 1995	299–297	Government defeated on EU fisheries 'take note' motion (3 Con. Noes and 7 abstentions).
26 Feb 1996	320–319	Government wins by one vote over Scott Report on Arms-for-Iraq (3 Cons vote against).
10 Jun 1996	302–123	One of three Government defeats in 'free' votes on M.P.s' pay.
10 Dec 1997	457–107	Government wins vote on lone parent benefit (47 Lab. vote against).
20 May 1999	310–270	Government wins vote on disability cuts but 67 Lab. vote against.
3 Nov 1999	320–262	One of three government victories on the Welfare Reform Bill (up to 55 Lab. vote against).

SOURCE: Philip Norton and Mark Stuart

Government Defeats 1970–1999 on the floor of the House of Commons

1970–74	6	1983–87	2
1974	17	1987–92	1
1974–79	42	1992–97	9
1979–83	1	1997–99	–

Confidence Motions since 1945

Many motions before the House of Commons are implicitly treated as questions of confidence. Between 1900 and 1945 only two such motions were carried against the Government.

	Voting		
	For Government	Against Government	Issue
21 Jan 24	151	328	General confidence
8 Oct 24	198	359	Campbell case

Since 1945 the question of confidence has only been put explicitly to the House on the following occasions. On 14 Dec 1978, 24 Sep 92 and 23 Jul 1993 the motion expressed confidence. All the other motions expressed no confidence. The only one carried against the Government was on 28 Mar 1979.

	Voting		
	For Government	Against Government	Issue
5 Dec 45	381	197	Nationalisation
4 Dec 52	304	280	Handling of parliamentary business
1 Nov 56	323	255	Suez intervention
6 Dec 56	312	260	Suez intervention
5 Feb 62	326	228	Attitude to United Nations

	Voting		
	For Government	Against Government	Issue
26 Jul 62	351	256	Government reshuffle
10 Nov 64	315	294	General confidence
2 Feb 65	306	289	General confidence
2 Aug 65	303	290	General confidence
26 Jul 66	325	246	Economic management
1 Dec 66	329	246	Economic management
24 Jul 67	333	200	Economic management
17 Feb 72	309	301	European Communities Bill
6 Mar 72	317	270	European Communities Bill
19 Nov 73	304	286	Economic management
11 Mar 76	297	280	General confidence
9 Jun 76	309	290	Economic management
23 Mar 77	322	298	General confidence
20 Jul 77	312	282	Economic management
14 Dec 78	300	290	Economic management
28 Mar 79	310	311	General confidence
28 Feb 80	327	268	Economic management
27 Jul 81	334	262	Economic management
28 Oct 81	312	250	Economic management
31 Jan 85	395	222	Economic management
22 Nov 90	367	247	General confidence
27 Mar 91	358	238	Poll tax
24 Sep 92	322	296	Economic management
23 Jul 93	339	299	Maastricht treaty
1 Dec 93	*282*	*95*	*(HL) General Confidence**
28 Nov 94	329	44	European Communities Bill

* This is the only example of a no confidence motion being moved in the House of Lords.

Guillotine Motions since 1945

From 1945 to 1993 the average number of guillotine motions was between two and three per year. All were carried except one (the Scotland and Wales Bill 22 Feb 1977). The session numbers are:

Session	Guillotine motions	Session	Guillotine motions	Session	Guillotine motions
1946–47	2	1965–66	–	1982–83	3
1947–48	–	1966–67	1	1983–84	3
1948–49	1	1967–68	2	1984–85	2
1950–51	–	1968–69	1	1985–86	3
1951–52	2	1969–70	1	1986–87	3
1952–53	2	1970–71	2	1987–88	9
1953–54	2	1971–72	5	1988–89	13
1954–55	–	1972–73	1	1989–90	6
1955–56	–	1973–74	–	1990–91	3
1956–57	1	1974–75	–	1991–92	6
1957–58	1	1975–76	10	1992–93	5
1958–59	–	1976–77	1	1993–94	6
1959–60	–	1977–78	4	1994–95	–
1960–61	2	1978–79	–	1995–96	1
1960–62	5	1979–80	7	1996–97	4
1962–63	2	1980–81	4	1997–98	16
1963–64	–	1981–82	5	1998–99	10
1964–65	–				

M.P.s' Suspension

Members acting in sustained defiance of the chair can be named and suspended from the service of the House of Commons for five sitting days. The following list includes all that have occurred since 1945:

18 Jul 49	E. Smith	18 Feb 88	H. Cohen
27 Nov 51	S. Silverman	15 Mar 88	A. Salmond
26 Mar 52	Bessie Braddock	13 Apr 88	D. Nellist
23 May 68	Dame I. Ward	20 Apr 88	R. Brown
13 Mar 72	C. Loughlin	25 Jul 88	T. Dalyell
12 Feb 81	I. Paisley	14 Mar 89	J. Sillars
8 Apr 81	R. Brown	24 Jul 89	T. Dalyell
15 Jul 81	R. Brown	7 Mar 90	J. Browne
16 Nov 81	J. McQuade, P. Robinson, I. Paisley	23 Jul 90	D. Douglas
26 May 82	A. Faulds	2 Jul 92	D. Skinner[1]
2 May 84	T. Dalyell	29 Nov 93	I. Paisley[1]
17 Jul 84	D. Skinner	26 Jan 95	D Campbell-Savours[1]
31 Jul 84	M. Flannery	20 Apr 95	D. Tredinnick[2], G. Riddick[3]
11 Nov 85	B. Sedgemore	6 May 95	D. Skinner[1]
20 Jan 86	D. Wigley	29 Jul 97	R. Wareing[4]
12 Nov 87	T. Dalyell	12 Jul 99	E. Ross[5]
24 Nov 87	D. Wigley	21 Oct 99	D. Touhig[6]
11 Jan 88	J. Hughes	21 Oct 99	M. Kali Mountford[7]
25 Jan 88	K. Livingstone		

[1] Suspended only for rest of day
[2] Suspended for 20 days (Cash for Questions)
[3] Suspended for 10 days (Cash for Questions)
[4] Suspended for 5 days (non-disclosure of directorship.)
[5] Suspended for 10 days (disclosure of Select Committee draft report)
[6] Suspended for 3 days (receiving a leaked Select Committee report)
[7] Suspended for 5 days (disclosure of a Select Committee report)

Regnal Years

Until 1962 the dates of Acts of Parliament were recorded in terms of the regnal years during the session in which they were passed. Regnal years date from the accession of the sovereign. Thus the act listed as 11 & 12 Geo. VI, c. 65 was passed in the parliamentary session during the eleventh and twelfth regnal year of George VI (1948). The parliamentary session of 1948–49 covered three regnal years, and its acts appear under the style 12, 13 & 14 Geo. VI. Since 1963 Acts of Parliament have been recorded by the calendar year and the chapter number, e.g. *Finance Act* 1963, c. 25.

Sovereign	Regnal Year	Date
Victoria	63	20 Jun 1899–19 Jun 1900
	64	20 Jun 00–22 Jan 01
Edward VII	1	22 Jan 01–21 Jan 02
	10	22 Jan 10– 6 May 10
George V	1	6 May 10–5 May 11
	26	6 May 35–20 Jan 36
Edward VIII	1	20 Jan 36–11 Dec 36
George VI	1	11 Dec 36–10 Dec 37
	16	11 Dec 51–6 Feb 52
Elizabeth II	1	6 Feb 52–5 Feb 53
	10	6 Feb 61– 5 Feb 62

Select Committees

Select Committees have been appointed for many purposes and have a long history in both Houses. In the Commons, Select Committees have long been used in connection with public expenditure, parliamentary procedure, legislation, and for ad hoc enquiries, sometimes of a quasi-judicial character. In the nineteenth century and up to 1914 Select Committees were also used for a wide range of specific enquiries, many of which would now be undertaken by a Government Inquiry or even a Royal Commission. Between the wars Select Committees were also occasionally used to examine Empire matters. Select Committees may be set up for a session or part of a session to consider a specific matter e.g. the Select Committee on Patent Medicines in 1914, the Select Committee on Tax-Credit in 1972–73, or the Select Committee on Conduct of Members in 1975–76 and 1976–77. Others are set up more regularly by custom.[1]

The Public Accounts Committee has existed continuously since 1862.

An Estimates Committee later subsumed in the Expenditure Committee, was set up in one form or another in most sessions from 1912 to 1979.

The Nationalised Industries Committee existed from 1956 to 1979. Other 'specialist Committees' to consider either a subject area, e.g. Race Relations and Immigration, or a Department, e.g. Education and Science, were appointed after the 'Crossman Reforms' in 1966; they were appointed for each session, for the duration of a Parliament from 1979. In 1979 a new structure of Select Committees was established to cover the work of each major Government Department.

Powers: In their order of reference, and under Standing Orders, Commons Select Committees have had powers of varying extent given to them by the House.

Except for Select Committees on Bills or procedure committees, Select Committees are now usually given powers to send for persons, papers and records (although only the House can act to punish contempt of such summons), to sit at times when the House is adjourned, to meet outside the Palace of Westminster ('to adjourn from place to place'), to report from time to time ('to report to the House and publish as many reports as they wish'), to appoint sub-committees from among their own members, and to appoint expert advisers.

Duration: Some Select Committees are more permanent than others. All share a degree of impermanence in that their membership needs to be reappointed every Parliament. In March 1974 for the first time the membership of a Select Committee (the Expenditure Committee) was appointed for the duration of a Parliament and all Select Committees are now appointed on this basis.

Chairmen: Apart from the Public Accounts Committee, the Committee on Statutory Instruments, the Committee on the Parliamentary Commissioner and latterly the Select Committee on European Scrutiny, the Chairmen of the Select Committees used until 1979 normally to be from the Government Party. This no longer applies nor did it ever apply necessarily to sub-committees.

Chairmen's Liaison Committee: In recent decades the practice grew up for Chairmen of Select Committees to meet in an informal Committee from time to time to discuss subjects of common interest such as the allocation of funds available for overseas visits. The Committee was not a Select Committee of the House until 1980.

---

[1] Since 1968–69 Select Committee returns showing membership attendance etc have been published regularly as House of Commons Papers.

Committee of Selection, 1840–

Chairman (since 1945)

1945	T. Smith	1964	C. Kenyon	1979	(Sir) P. Holland
1947	G. Mathers	1969	G. Rogers	1984	(Sir) M. Fox
1951	Sir G. Touche	1970	H. Gurden	1992	Sir F. Montgomery
1956	Sir R. Conant	1974	H. Delargy	1997	J. McWilliam
1960	Sir P. Agnew	1976	F. Willey		

Although the task of the Committee of Selection has for many years been predominantly the selection of Members to serve on Standing Committees on Bills, the Committee was originally set up to appoint Committees on Private Bills and is still appointed under Private Business S.O. 109. It has 11 Members. It also proposes Select Committee members for appointment by the House.

The Committee of Selection nominates:

Public Business

(1)   Members of Standing Committees;
(2)   Some or all members of Select Committees on hybrid Bills (if the House orders);
(3)   The Commons members of Joint Committees on hybrid Bills (if the House orders);
(4)   The two members whom the Speaker is to consult, if practicable, before giving his certificate to a money bill;
(5)   Since 1979 all members of Select Committees

Private Business

(1)   The panel of members to serve on committees on unopposed bills;
(2)   Committees on unopposed bills;
(3)   Members of committees on opposed bills;
(4)   Eight members to serve on the Standing Orders Committee under S.O. 103;
(5)   The panel of members to act as commissioners under the Private Legislation Procedure (Scotland) Act 1936;
(6)   Commons Members on Joint Committees on special procedure petitions.

Terms of Reference: The Committee would appear to interpret its instructions in S.O. 62 to have 'regard ... to the composition of the House' by choosing Standing Committees as far as possible in direct ratio to the size of the parties in the House, except that since the 1930s the Liberal Party has usually been given a higher representation than its size would merit on this basis – a Liberal member being appointed to all Committees of five members and above. In the four Parliaments since 1945 in which the size of the Government majority has been small the Committee of Selection has usually selected Members so as to give the Government a majority of one. In the 1974 Parliament, with a minority Government, no party had a majority on any standing Committee. The Committee tends to appoint those Members who spoke on the second reading of the Bill. In recent times of heavy legislation and expanding parliamentary activity it would appear that the role of the whips in offering advice as to which members are anxious, willing, or available to serve on a particular Committee has been strengthened.

Although no Government whip is appointed to the Committee a senior opposition whip was always appointed until 1974.

Committee of Public Accounts, 1862–

Chairman

1896	A. O'Connor	1931	M. Jones	1959	H. Wilson
1901	Sir A. Hayter	1938	F. Pethick-Lawrence	1962	D. Houghton
1906	V. Cavendish	1941	W. Elliot	1964	J. Boyd-Carpenter
1908	(Sir) R. Williams	1943	Sir A. Pownall	1970	H. Lever
1919	F. Acland	1945	O. Peake	1973	E. Dell
1921	A. Williams	1948	R. Assheton	1976	E. Du Cann
1923	F. Jowett	1950	Sir R. Cross	1979	J. Barnett
1924	W. Guiness	1950	C. Waterhouse	1983	R. Sheldon
1924	W. Graham	1951	J. Edwards	1997	D. Davis
1929	A. Samuel	1952	(Sir) G. Benson		

The Committee is made up of no more than 15 members, including the Chairman, and meets on about 30 days each session. The Chairman is usually a member of the Opposition.

Usual Terms of Reference: 'for the examination of the accounts showing the appropriation of the sums granted by parliament to meet the public expenditure', 'and of such other accounts laid before parliament as the committee may think fit' (added 15 Nov 34). 'The Committee shall have power to send for persons, papers and records, and to report from time to time' (added 14 Nov 33). The Committee is aided in its work by the Comptroller and Auditor General whose staff audit the accounts of government departments. These audits and the Comptroller's subsequent report to the House of Commons provide the basic materials for the Committee's enquiries. In 1978 the Committee began to hear evidence in public. Since 1983 (when the National Audit Office was set up) most of the Committee's work has been on that Office's 'value for money' reports on government activities.

See also Public Accounts Commission (p.219).

Comptroller and Auditor-General

1896	R. Mills	1921	(Sir) G. Upcott	1976	Sir D. Henley
1900	D. Richmond	1946	Sir F. Tribe	1981	(Sir) G. Downey
1904	(Sir) J. Kempe	1958	Sir E. Compton	1989	(Sir) J. Bourn
1911	(Sir) H. Gibson	1966	Sir B. Fraser		
1921	Sir M. Ramsay	1971	Sir D. Pitblado		

Estimates Committee, 1912–1970

Chairman

1912	Sir F. Banbury	1927	A. Bennett	1945	B. Kirby
1914	(suspended)	1929	H. Charleton	1950	A. Anderson
1917	*(see National*	1930	H. Romeril	1951	Sir R. Glyn
	Expenditure Committee)	1931	Sir V. Henderson	1953	C. Waterhouse
1920	Sir F. Banbury	1935	Sir I. Salmon	1957	R. Turton
1924	Sir J. Marriott	1939	*(see National*	1961	Sir G. Nicholson
1926	(Sir) V. Henderson		*Expenditure Committee)*	1964	W. Hamilton

The Committee originally consisted of 15 members. In 1921 this was increased to 24, and in 1924 to 28. From 1948 to 1960 it had 36 members and from 1960 to 1970, 43 members. The Chairman was usually a Government supporter.

Terms of Reference: 'to examine and report upon such of the Estimates presented to the Committee as may seem fit to the Committee' (7 Apr 12 original terms), 'and to suggest the form in which the estimates shall be presented for examination, and to report what if any economies consistent with the policy implied in those estimates may be effected therein' (added in 1921). Until 1939 the Estimates Committee seldom appointed sub-committees, although power to do so had been given in 1924; after 1945, however, following the example set by the Select Committee on National Expenditure, it invariably did so. In 1956 the wording of the terms of reference was rearranged but the substance remained unchanged.

In 1960 the terms were altered to read: 'to examine such of the estimates presented to this House as may seem fit to the committee and report how, if at all, the policy implied in those estimates may be carried out more economically and, if the committee think fit, to consider the principal variations between the estimates and those relating to the previous financial year, and the form in which the estimates are presented to the House'. The committee had power to send for persons, papers, and records, and sit notwithstanding any adjournment of the House, to adjourn from place to place, and to report from time to time: to appoint sub-committees and to refer to such sub-committees any of the matters referred to the committee [each sub-committee has the same powers of sending for persons, etc., sitting and adjourning as the main committee], and to report from time to time the minutes of evidence taken before sub-committees and reported by them to the committee.

In Sessions 1965 and 1966 the House gave the Estimates Committee the power 'to appoint persons with technical or scientific knowledge for the purpose of particular enquiries, either to supply information which is not readily available or to elucidate matters of complexity within the Committee's order of reference'. From 1965–70 the practice was to appoint sub-committees specialising in particular fields. The Select Committee was replaced by the Expenditure Committee in 1971.

Committee on National Expenditure, 1917–1920 and 1939–1945

Chairman

1917	H. Samuel	1919–20 Sir F. Banbury	1939–45 Sir J. Wardlaw-Milne

No Estimates were presented to Parliament during the two wars, and the Committee on Estimates lapsed. A Committee on National Expenditure was established each year. It consisted of 26 members 1917–20, and 32 members 1939–45. It met about 13 days a session between 1917–20, and about 19 days a session between 1939–45.

1939–45 *Terms of Reference:* 'to examine the current expenditure defrayed out of moneys provided by Parliament for the Defence Services, for Civil Defence, and for other services directly connected with the war, and to report what, if any, economies, consistent with the execution of the policy decided by the Government, may be effected therein'.

Expenditure Committee, 1971–1979

Chairman

1970	E. du Cann	1973 Sir H. D'Avigdor-Goldsmid	1974 J. Boyden

The Committee consisted of 49 members with a quorum of 9.

Terms of Reference: 'to consider how, if at all, the policies implied in the figures of expenditure and in the estimates may be carried out more economically, and to examine the form of the paper and of the estimates presented to this House'. The Committee's work was carried out through six largely autonomous sub-committees (General; Defence and External Affairs; Employment and Social Services; Trade and Industry; Environment; Education; Arts and Home Affairs).

Nationalised Industries Committee, 1956–1979

Chairman

1956	Sir P. Spens	1964	E. Popplewell	1972	(Sir) J. Hall
1957	Sir T. Low	1966	I. Mikardo	1974	R. Kerr
1961	Sir R. Nugent	1970	Sir H. D'Avigdor-Goldsmid		

The Committee was appointed on a sessional basis; it had 13 members (1956–66), 18 members (1966–70), 14 members (1970–74), 13 members (1974–5) and 15 members (1974–9). The Chairman was always a Government supporter.

Terms of Reference: 'to examine the reports and accounts of the nationalised industries established by statute, whose controlling boards are wholly appointed by Ministers of the Crown and whose annual receipts are not wholly or mainly derived from moneys provided by Parliament or advanced by the Exchequer'. In the 1965–66 and 1966–67 Sessions the Committee's terms of reference were amended to enable them to enquire into the Post Office. From 1968–69 the Committee's terms of reference were extended to include the Independent Television Authority, Cable and Wireless Ltd, the Horserace Totalisator Board and certain activities of the Bank of England.

Committee on Agriculture, 1966–1969

Chairman

1966   T. Watkins

Terms of Reference: 'To consider the activities in England and Wales of the Ministry of Agriculture, Fisheries and Food.' The Committee had power to send for persons, papers, and records, to sit notwithstanding any adjournment of the House, to adjourn from place to place, and to admit strangers during the examination of witnesses unless they otherwise order. The Committee ceased to exist in Feb 1970.

Committee on Science and Technology, 1966–79

Chairman

1966	A. Palmer	1970	A. Neave	1974	A. Palmer

Terms of Reference: 'To consider Science and Technology.' The Committee had power to send for persons, and papers.

Committee on Education and Science, 1968–1970

Chairman

1968   F. Willey

Terms of Reference: 'To consider the activities of the Department of Education and Science and the Scottish Education Department.' The Committee ceased to exist in 1970.

Committee on Race Relations and Immigration, 1968–79

Chairman

1968	A. Bottomley	1970	W. Deedes	1974	F. Willey

The Committee had 12 Members, and a quorum of 4.

Terms of Reference: 'To review policies, but not individual cases, in relation to: (a) the operation of the Race Relations Act 1968 with particular reference to the work of the Race Relations Board and the Community Relations Commission, and (b) the admission into the United Kingdom of Commonwealth citizens and foreign nationals for settlement.'

Committee on Overseas Aid,1968–71
(Overseas Development, 1973–79)

Chairman

1968	Margaret Herbison	1973	Sir B. Braine	1978	K. McNamara
1970–71	B. Braine	1974	Sir G. de Freitas		

The first Committee had between 10 and 18 Members, with a quorum of between 4 and 9. After 1973 it had 9 Members.

Terms of Reference: 'To consider the activities of the Ministry of Overseas Development.' The Committee ceased to exist in 1971. It was re-established under a new title in 1973, 'to consider United Kingdom assistance for overseas development'.

Committee on Scottish Affairs, 1969–1972

Chairman

1969	T. Steele	1970	Sir J. Gilmour	1971	J. Brewis

The Committee had 16 Members and a quorum of 8.

Terms of Reference: 'To consider Scottish Affairs.'

Committee on European Secondary Legislation, 1974–76; European Legislation etc., 1976–

Chairman

1974	J. Davies	1979	J. Silverman	1992	J. Hood
1976	Sir J. Eden	1983	N. Spearing		

The Committee's membership since 1974 has been 16. There are currently three subcommittees.

Terms of Reference: To consider draft proposals of EC secondary legislation and to 'report their opinion as to whether such proposals or other documents raise questions of legal and political importance ... and to what extent they may affect the law of the United Kingdom'. Expanded in 1976 to cover documents submitted to the Council of Ministers 'whether or not such documents originate from the Commission'. The Committee has powers to send for persons, papers and records, to sit during the Adjournment, and to adjourn from place to place.

Procedure, 1961–76; Procedure (Sessional) Committee, 1976–

Chairman

1961	I. Macleod	1966	D. Chapman	1979	T. Higgins
1963	S. Lloyd	1970	(Sir) R. Turton	1983	Sir P. Emery
1964	A. Irvine	1974	S. Irving	1997	N. Winterton
1965	A. Blenkinsop				

The Committee has 15 Members and a quorum of 4.

It was long the practice of the House to set up Committees from time to time to make recommendations on its procedure. But since 1961 a Select Committee on Procedure has been appointed every Session to report on matters which the House refers to it. It came to be referred to as the 'Sessional Committee' to distinguish it from a Procedure Committee set up for the lifetime of the 1974 Parliament which reported in Aug 1978. It has powers to send for persons, papers and records and to report from time to time. It lapsed between Feb 74 and Nov 74 and in the 1978–79 Session. In the 1979–83 Parliament the full committee did not meet, although T. Higgins chaired Committees on Procedure (Supply) and Procedure (Finance).

House of Commons Services Committee, 1965–1992

Chairman

1965	H. Bowden	1972	J. Prior	1982	J. Biffen
1966	R. Crossman	1974	A. Bottomley	1987	J. Wakeham
1968	F. Peart	1976	M. Foot	1989	Sir G. Howe
1970	W. Whitelaw	1979	N. St John-Stevas	1990	J. MacGregor
1972	R. Carr	1981	F. Pym		

Terms of Reference: 'To advise Mr Speaker on the control of the accommodation and services in that part of the Palace of Westminster and its precincts occupied by or on behalf of the House of Commons and to report thereon to this House.' This Committee was set up as a result of a recommendation of the Select Committee on the Palace of Westminster of Session 1964–65, whose main task had been to consider the arrangements to be made by the Commons following the transfer on 26 Apr 1965 of control of the Palace from the Lord Great Chamberlain on behalf of the Crown to the two Houses.

The Committee consisted of 19 members appointed by the House. It had power to send for persons, papers, and records, to sit notwithstanding the adjournment of the House, to report from time to time, and to appoint Sub-Committees, each of which consists of three members. Each Sub-Committee has similar powers to the main Committee (except of course power to nominate Sub-Committees). The Committee usually appointed four main Sub-Committees: the Accommodation and Administration Sub-Committee, the Catering Sub-Committee, the Library Sub-Committee and the Computer Sub-Committee. The Catering Sub-Committee replaced the 'Select Committee on Kitchen and Refreshment Rooms' appointed every session since the late nineteenth century.

The Leader of the House was always appointed Chairman of the Committee (except in 1974–76).

See also House of Commons Commission (below), and Domestic Committees.

House of Commons Commission 1978–

Under the House of Commons (Administration) Act of 1978, a House of Commons Commission was appointed to control the internal finances of the House. Independent of Government, it comprises the Speaker, the Leader of the House, one M.P. nominated by the Leader of the Opposition, and three other non-ministerial M.P.s (including one, in practice, nominated by the minority parties).

Following a report by Sir R. Ibbs (H.C. 38/1990–1), the services Committee was abolished. It was replaced by four Domestic Committees plus a Financial and Services Committee to advise the House of Commons Commissions.

Domestic Committees 1992–

Accommodation (and Works) Committee 1992– (9)

Chairman

1992   (Sir) R. Powell
1997   Sir S. Chapman

Administration Committee 1992– (9)

Chairman

1992   J. Hood
1997   Marion Roe

Catering Committee 1992– (9)

Chairman

1992   Sir C. Shepherd
1997   D. Turner

Information Committee 1992– (9)

Chairman

1992   G. Waller
1997   J. O. Jones
1998   R. Allan

Other Committees

Finance and Services Committee 1992– (9)

Chairman

1992   P. Channon
1997   L. Moonie

Modernisation 1997– (15)

Chairman

1997   Ann Taylor
1998   Margaret Beckett

Deregulation 1995– (18)

Chairman

1995   B. Field
1997   P. Pike

Environmental Audit 1998– (16)

Chairman

1998   J. Horam

Committee on Members' Interests, 1975–95 (13)

This Committee was established following a 1974 report (H.C. 108/1974–5) to scrutinise a new Register of Members' outside interests. It also looked at Members' staff and lobbyists. In 1995 its functions were taken over by the Committee on Standards and Privileges.

Chairman

1975   F. Willey
1980   (Sir) G. Johnson-Smith

Committee of Privileges, c.1630–95

The Committee of Privileges only met when prima facie breaches of privileges were referred to it by the House. Unlike other committees it included senior members from both the Front Benches. It was ordered to be appointed by long-standing tradition on the first day of every session. Until 1940 it was chaired by the Prime Minister. From 1940 to 1945 C. Attlee, as Deputy Prime Minister, took the chair. Since 1945 the Chairman was usually, but not always, the Leader of the House.

In 1995 it was reconstituted as the Committee on Standards and Privileges (see p. 215), with a Parliamentary Commissioner for Standards reporting to it.

Chairman

1940	C. Attlee	1965	H. Bowden	1979	N. St John Stevas
1945	H. Morrison	1967	R. Crossman	1981	F. Pym
1946	A. Greenwood	1968	F. Peart	1982	J. Biffen
1947	H. Morrison	1971	W. Whitelaw	1987	J. Wakeham
1948	C. Ede	1972	R. Carr	1989	Sir G. Howe
1952	H. Crookshank	1973	J. Prior	1990	J. MacGregor
1956	R. Butler	1974	G. Strauss	1992	A. Newton
1964	S. Lloyd				

The Committee had 17 members in 1994.

The following include all Reports of the Select Committee of Privileges and a few from ad hoc Committees.

1902	Imprisonment of a Member: C. O'Kelly.
1902	Imprisonment of a Member: P. McHugh.
1909	D of Norfolk: alleged interference in an election.
1911	E of Aberdeen and E of Roden: alleged interference in an election.
1924	*Daily Herald*: reflection on the impartiality of the Chairman of Committees.
1926	*Daily Mail*: allegations of corrupt motives against M.P.s.
1929–30	E. Sandham: allegations of drunkenness and acceptance of bribes against M.P.s.
1932–33	H. Bowles and E. Huntsman: reflections on a Private Bill Committee's impartiality.
1933–34	Sir S. Hoare and E of Derby: alleged improper pressure on witnesses to a Committee.
1937–38	D. Sandys: summons to Military Court of Inquiry.
1937–38	Official Secrets Act.
1938–39	Official Secrets Act.
1939–40	Detention of A. Ramsay under Section 18B of Defence of the Realm Act.
1939–40	Conduct of R. Boothby.
1940–41	Conduct of R. Boothby.
1940–41	*Observer* publication of Secret Session debate.
1940–41	Grampian electricity supply bill: Highland Development League circular to M.P.s alleging irregularities in bill procedure.
1941–42	Disclosure of Secret Session proceedings by J. McGovern.
1942–43	H. Metcalf and J. Reid: payment of expense cheque to M.P. to attend prosecution by Board of Trade.
1943–44	N.U.D.A.W.: withdrawal of Trade Union financial support from W. Robinson on ground of refusal to resign seat.
1944–45	G. Reakes and D. Henderson. Offer to make donation to constituency association in return for M.P.s' help.
1945–46	Writ of Summons served on officer of House within precincts.
1945–46	Disclosure in conversation of Secret Session information by E. Granville.
1945–46	Posters threatening publication of names of M.P.s voting for bread rationing.
1946–47	Assault on P. Piratin in precincts of the House.
1946–47	Action by Civil Service Clerical Association calculated to influence W. Brown.
1946–47	G. Schofield and S. Dobson (Editor and Political Correspondent of *Evening News*): refusal to reveal source of information to Committee.
1946–47	Article by G. Allighan alleging disclosure to newspapers of information from party meetings.
1946–47	Disclosure of party meeting information by E. Walkden in return for payment.
1947–48	H. Dalton: Budget disclosure.
1947–48	The Chairman of Ways and Means (J. Milner): personal explanation that he acted professionally as a solicitor against a Member.
1947–48	Broadcast and interview in *Daily Mail* by C. Brogan alleging that Secret Session information would be given to Russia.
1948–49	Alleged misrepresentation by *Daily Worker* of Member's speech (R. Blackburn).
1950	J. MacManaway: election of a Member, being a clergyman of the Church of Ireland.
1951	Abuse of members not related to transactions in House (S. Silverman, I. Mikardo). Comment on B.B.C. 'Any Questions' programme on matter referred to Committee.
1951	Report in *Sutton Coldfield News* of speech by Lady Mellor criticising ruling by the Chair.
1951	Obstruction of J. Lewis by the police.
1952–53	Amendment of the law relating to the disability of some clergy from sitting and voting in the House of Commons.
1953	Article by Mrs P. Ford in *Sunday Express* (Mrs Braddock).
1953	*Daily Worker* article (M.P.s vote money into their own pockets).
1955	Action by Bishop against chaplain after communication with M.P.
1956	*Sunday Graphic* advocates telephone campaign against A. Lewis.
1956	*Sunday Express* article on M.P.s' petrol rationing allowances.
1956	*Evening News* cartoon on petrol rationing.
1956–57	G. Strauss: threat of libel action by the London Electricity Board, following letter from the Member to the Paymaster-General.
1957	Comment on B.B.C. 'Any Questions' programme on matter referred to Committee: report of speech in *Romford Recorder* on petrol rationing.
1957–58	Order in Council directing that the Report of the Judicial Committee on a Question of Law concerning the *Parliamentary Privilege Act 1770* be communicated to the House of Commons.
1957–58	G. Strauss: recommendations of the Committee arising out of the case involving the London Electricity Board.

1958–59	Report of an Inquiry into the methods adopted by the London Electricity Board for the disposal of scrap cable.
1959–60	C. Pannell: allegation of threat in a letter from C. Jordan.
1960–61	A. Wedgwood Benn: petition for redress of grievances regarding the disqualification of peers.
1963–64	Q. Hogg: complaint by G. Wigg concerning a speech at the Town Hall, Chatham, on 19 Mar 64.
1964–65	P. Duffy: complaint concerning speech at Saddleworth on 12 Feb 65 alleging drunkenness among Conservative Members.
1964–65	F. Allaun: complaint concerning letter addressed to Members and advocating racial and anti-semitic views.
1964–65	The Chancellor of the Exchequer: complaint by Sir R. Cary concerning passages of speech reported in the *Daily Telegraph* 5 Jul 65, on Members' business interests.
1966–67	G. Fitt: complaint concerning allegations of treachery in *Protestant Telegraph*.
1967–68	E. Hooson: complaint concerning allegations of treachery in interview published in *Town* magazine.
1967–68	W. Hannan: complaint concerning letter in the *Scotsman* by Mrs W. Ewing, M.P., reflecting on the conduct of members.
1967–68	A. Palmer: complaint concerning article about biological warfare published in the *Observer* from information allegedly supplied by T. Dalyell, M.P.
1968–69	Mrs R. Short: report in *Wolverhampton Press and Star* of a speech by Alderman Peter Farmer imputing partial conduct to a Member.
1968–69	Sir D. Glover: certain events attending to a visit of a Sub-Committee of the Select Committee on Education and Science to the University of Essex.
1968–69	R. Maxwell: article published in the *Sunday Times* reflecting on the conduct of a Member as Chairman of the Catering Sub-Committee of the Select Committee on House of Commons Services and as a member of that Committee.
1969–70	J. Mackintosh: matter reported in *The Times* which disclosed a breach of privilege.
1970–71	D. Steel: report in the *Sun* of alleged attempt by a trade union to influence actions of certain Members. (Report made in following Session.)
1970–71	A. Lewis: assault upon a servant of the House.
1970–71	W. Hamilton: publication by the *Daily Mail* of an article purporting to give an account of proceedings in a Select Committee not yet reported to the House. (Report made in following Session.)
1970–71	On a Motion moved by the Leader of the House. Rights of Members detained in prison.
1971–72	On a Motion moved by a member of the Government. Matter of the style and title of the Member for Berwick-upon-Tweed.
1972–73	R. Carter: serving of writ within the precincts of the House of Commons.
1973–74	A. Wedgwood Benn: alleged intimidation by Aims of Industry.
1973–74	J. Ashton: allegations about Members' financial interests.
1974–75	Eric Ogden: allegations made in Liverpool and West Derby on conduct of a member.
1974–75	G. Cunningham: words alleged to have been spoken by A. Scargill and other matters relating to N.U.M. conditions to be placed on M.P.s sponsored by them.
1974–75	J. Rooker: disclosure of evidence in *The Economist* from Select Committee on a Wealth Tax, before evidence reported to House.
1975–76	Sir B. Braine: reported accusation of bias in a Select Committee by National Abortion Campaign Steering Committee and threatened refusal to give evidence.
1975–76	J. Harper: possible contempt by National Coal Board in dismissing W. Grimshaw, a witness before the Select Committee on Nationalised Industries.
1976–77	M. Lipton: newspaper report alleging interference of the Totalisation Board on members.
1976–77	R. Adley: Press Association report of threat by the National Union of Public Employees to withdraw sponsorship from 6 members if they did not take certain action.
1977–78	F. Willey: *Daily Mail* and *Guardian* reports of proceedings of the Select Committee on Race Relations and Immigration.
1977–78	M. Foot: Publication of proceedings of the House and application of the sub judice rule (Colonel B.).
1978–79	C. Price: Court citation of Hansard without permission of House.
1980–81	D. Campbell-Savours: conversation about British Steel policy towards Workington.
1980–81	R. Parry: important letter from solicitors to M.P.
1982–83	T. Davis: behaviour of witnesses before Select Committee on Abortion (Amendment) Bill.
1982–83	R. Brown: comments by K. Livingstone and other GLC members.
1982–83	Sir A. Kershaw: leak of Foreign Affairs Committee report on Falklands.
1983–84	T. Jessel: threat by GLC Chairman to penalise constituencies of London members voting in a particular way.
1984–85	Sir E. Gardner: publication by *The Times* of Home Affairs Committee draft Report on police special powers.
1985–86	Environment Committee: Leak of draft Report of Environment Committee on radio-active waste.
1986–87	Mr Speaker: showing of Zircon film within the Palace of Westminster.

1988–89	Clare Short: Alleged misconduct of a Parliamentary Agent.
1989–90	Education Committee: Premature disclosure of proceedings of Education Committee.
1989–90	Public Accounts Committee: Premature disclosure of proceedings of Public Accounts Committee.
1990–91	K. Barron: Guidelines issued by Yorkshire N.U.M.
1994–95	T. Benn: Publication of Committee proceedings.
1994–95	D. Tredinnick and G. Riddick: Payment for putting Questions.

Committee on Standards and Privileges 1995–

Following a Report from the Committee on Standards in Public Life under Ld Nolan, the House voted to replace the Committee of Privileges and the Select Committee on Members' Interests with a Committee on Standards and Privileges and appointed a Parliamentary Commissioner for Standards to report to it. The following matters have been reported on.

1995–96	The Code of Conduct and the Guide to the Rules relating to the conduct of Members
1995–96	J. Aitken: Failure to register a directorship
1995–96	R. Thomason: Failure to declare an interest
1995–96	Mo Mowlam: Failure to register a payment
1995–96	W. Cash: Alleged breach of advocacy rules
1995–96	C. Goodson-Wickes: Failure to declare an interest
1995–96	P. Nicholls: Alleged breach of advocacy rules
1996–97	D. Atkinson: Failure to register an interest
1996–97	A. Mitchell: Alleged improper pressure on Select Committee members
1996–97	M. Howard: Alleged conflict of interest
1996–97	D. Willetts: Alleged improper pressure on Select Committee members
1997–98	N. Hamilton and other M.P.s: Payments by Mr Al Fayed for parliamentary activities
1997–98	G. Robinson: Failure to register a directorship
1997–98	H. Flight: Alleged breach of advocacy rules
1997–98	Ld Steel: Failure to declare an interest and failure to deposit an employment agreement
1997–98	G. Robinson: Failure to register a directorship
1997–98	G. Galloway: Failure to declare an interest
1997–98	R. Wareing: Failure to register a directorship
1997–98	K. Clarke: Failure to record a paid-for journey
1997–98	T. Blair: Failure to register hospitality
1997–98	J. Prescott: Alleged failure to register a donation
1997–98	S. Dorrell: Failure to declare an interest
1997–98	G. Robinson: Failure to register a directorship
1997–98	Public Access to Registers of Interests
1997–98	Appeal Procedures
1997–98	Retirement of the Parliamentary Commissioner
1998–99	F. Maude: Failure to register an interest
1998–99	Sir E. Heath: Failure to register an interest
1998–99	G. Robinson: Failure to register a shareholding
1998–99	E. Leigh; Failure to register support from an outside body
1998–99	Teresa Gorman: Failure to register a directorship
1998–99	P. Mandelson: Non-registration of free flights; failure to register a loan from another M.P.
1998–99	D. Touhig: Premature disclosure of a Select Committee Report
1998–99	Kali Mountford: Unauthorised receipt of a draft Select Committee Report
1998–99	Mo Mowlam: Failure to register a financial contribution
1998–99	J. Cunningham: Failure to register a financial contribution
1999–00	B. George: Failure to account for expenses
1999–00	B. Wells: Failure to declare an interest
1999–00	W. Hague: Failure to record use of Lord Archer's gym

Committee on Standards and Privileges (11)

Chairman

1994	A. Newton
1997	R. Sheldon

Parliamentary Commissioner for Standards

1994   Sir G. Downey
1999   Elizabeth Filkin

Statutory Instruments, 1947 (Statutory Rules and Orders, 1944–47)
(since 1972 a Joint Committee of both Houses)

Chairman

1944	Sir C. MacAndrew	1970	A. Booth	1987	R. Cryer
1950	G. Nicholson	1974	G. Page	1994	A. Bennett
1951	E. Fletcher	1979	R. Cryer	1997	D. Tredinnick
1964	G. Page	1983	A. Bennett		

The Committee had between 7 and 11 members, meeting fortnightly. Since 1972 it has had 14 members, 7 from each House, meeting weekly when the House is sitting. The Chairman has always been an opposition member from the House of Commons.

Terms of Reference: The original terms of 21 Jun 44 have been considerably enlarged by additional powers conferred in subsequent years.

In 1972 the procedure for considering Statutory Instruments was changed. The vast majority of instruments are now considered by a Joint Committee of Members of both Houses. However, the Statutory Instruments Select Committee still exists to consider instruments on which proceedings are subject to proceedings in the House of Commons only. The Joint Committee has power to consider every instrument which is laid before each House of Parliament and upon which proceedings may be or might have been taken in either House of Parliament in pursuance of an Act of Parliament. It also has power to draw the attention of the House of Commons to other Statutory Instruments on any of the following grounds:

(i) that they involve public money; (ii) that they are immune from challenge in the courts; (iii) that they have effect retrospectively; (iv) that there seems to have been an unjustifiable delay in publication of the S.I. or in laying it before Parliament; (v) that there seems to have been an unjustifiable delay in sending notification to the Speaker; (vi) that it appears to make unusual or unexpected use of the powers conferred by the Statute under which it is made; (vii) if elucidation is considered necessary; (viii) that the drafting appears to be defective– or on any other ground that does not impinge on its merits or the merits of the policy behind it.

The Committee has powers to sit when it wishes, to report from time to time, to call for witnesses and to appoint sub-committees. It is obliged to give any government department an opportunity to explain an S.I. or other document before drawing it to the attention of the House.

Since 1890 the Statutory Rules and Orders, and since 1948 the S.I.s, have been published in annual volumes.

The distinction between 'General' and 'Local' follows that adopted between public Acts and local and personal Acts of Parliament. The documents registered as Statutory Instruments do not include rules of an executive character, or rules made by other bodies, e.g. local authorities, unless confirmed by a government department. Statutory Instruments also include some rules made by statutory authorities which are not government departments, e.g. the Law Society, General Dental Council, Rule Committee of Church Assembly.

Statutory Instruments

Year	Total	Annual General	Local
1900	995	174	821
1910	1,368	218	1,150
1920	2,475	916	1,559
1929	1,262	391	871
1940	2,222	1,626	596
1950	2,144	1,211	933
1960	2,495	733	1,762
1970	2,044	1,040	1,004
1980	2,051	1,197	854
1990	2,664	1,408	1,256
1997	3,114	1,663	1,451

Committee on Public Petitions, 1842–1974

Chairman (1945–1974)

1945	S. Viant	1966	D. Griffiths
1951	C. Lancaster	1970	J. Jennings
1964	G. Pargiter		

The Committee was appointed during most sessions since April 1842. It had 10 members, and a quorum of 3. It had power to send for persons, papers and records. It was abolished in 1974.

Terms of Reference: To clarify and prepare abstracts of Petitions 'in such form and manner as shall appear to them best suited to convey to the House all requisite information respecting their contents'. 'All Petitions presented to the House, with the exception of such as are deposited in the Private Bill Office' are referred to the Committee. The Committee was required in its reports to state the number of signatures to each petition. It had no power to consider the merits of the petitions.

Committee on Parliamentary Commissioner for Administration, 1967–1997

Chairman

1967	Sir H. Munro-Lucas-Tooth	1992	J. Pawsey
1970	M. Stewart	1997	*(See Select Committee on*
1974	C. Fletcher-Cooke		*Public Administration*
1974	(Sir) A. Buck		*below)*

The Committee had 11 members and a quorum of 3.

Terms of Reference: 'To examine the reports laid before this House by the Parliamentary Commissioner for Administration and Matters in Connection therewith.' The Committee has power to send for persons and papers.

Parliamentary Commissioner for Administration (Ombudsman)

The Parliamentary Commissioner for Administration is appointed by Letters Patent under the provisions of the *Parliamentary Commissioner Act, 1967*, which came into force on 7 Apr 67. His function is to investigate complaints referred to him by Members of the House of Commons from members of the public who claim to have sustained injustice in consequence of maladministration in connection with actions taken by or on behalf of Government Departments. (Other public bodies such as the nationalised industries and local government are outside his jurisdiction.) Under the Act the Commissioner is required to report the results of each investigation to the Member who referred the complaint to him and also to make an annual report to each House of Parliament on the performance of his functions. In addition he may make other reports to Parliament with respect to those functions if he thinks fit; and he may make a special report to Parliament if he considers that injustice caused to the complainant by maladministration has not been or will not be remedied. The Commissioner may be removed from office only upon an Address from both Houses of Parliament.

Since 1972 there have been separate Health Commissioners for England, Scotland and Wales. These posts have at times been combined with that of the Parliamentary Commissioner for Administration. Under the *Health Services Commissioners Act 1992*, they are answerable to the Committee of the Parliamentary Commissioner for Administration.

There is a separate Parliamentary Commissioner for Administration for Northern Ireland.

Parliamentary Commissioner For Administration 1967–

1 Apr 67	Sir E. Compton	1 Jan 85	(Sir) A. Barrowclough
1 Apr 71	Sir A. Marre	1 Jan 90	(Sir) W. Reid
1 Apr 76	Sir I. Pugh	1 Jan 97	M. Buckley
3 Jan 79	(Sir) C. Clothier		

Commissioner for Public Appointments 1995–

18 Dec 95	Sir L. Peach
1 Mar 99	Dame R. Fritchie

Ombudsman Cases

Year	No. of cases disposed of during the year	Member informed case outside jurisdiction	Member informed case is discontinued	Investigation completed and result reported to Member
1967	849	561	100	188
1968	1,181	72	780	374
1969	790	44	543	302
1970	651	36	230	259
1971	516	29	539	182
1972	596	31	817	261
1973	536	28	512	239
1974	653	37	427	252
1975	916	57	619	321
1976	863	50	529	329
1977	846	528		318

Year	No. of cases disposed of during the year	Member informed case outside jurisdiction	Member informed case is discontinued	Investigation completed and result reported to Member
1978	1,305	927	35	343
1979	801	541	22	238
1980	927	686	16	225
1981	929	694	7	228
1982	784	574	8	202
1983	809	605	6	198
1984	850	658	9	183
1985	788	606	5	177
1986	719	549	2	168
1987	656	509	2	145
1988	657	529	8	120
1989	639	502	11	126
1990	245	35	12	177
1991	769	580	6	183
1992	857	661	6	190
1993	926	715	3	208
1994	1105	870	9	226
1995	1474	1226	3	245
1996	1679	1413	6	260
1997	1679	1303	4	376
1998	1134	762	–	372

Source: Annual Reports of the Parliamentary Commissioner for Administration.

Public Accounts Commission 1984–

The Public Accounts Commission was set up by *National Audit Act 1983*. It is composed of nine members of the House of Commons of whom two – the Chairman of the Public Accounts Committee and the Leader of the House – are ex-officio. The remaining seven, none of whom may be Ministers of the Crown, are appointed by the House. The Commission was appointed to take office on 1 Jan 1984. The Act gave the Commission three main functions: to appoint an accounting officer for the National Audit Office; to appoint an auditor for the National Audit Office; and to examine the National Audit Office Estimates and lay them before the House, with such modifications as it thinks fit. In this last capacity, the Commission can examine all the expenses of the Office, including such things as accommodation, salaries of staff and superannuation provision.

Chairman

1984	(Sir) E. du Cann
1987	Sir P. Hordern
1996	Sir T. Higgins
1997	R. Sheldon

Select Committees since 1979

Following the Report of the Williams/Renton Committee (H.C. 588/1977–78), fourteen Select Committees were appointed in 1979 'to examine the expenditure, administration and policy of the principal government departments ... and associated public bodies'. In Jan 1980 a Liaison Select Committee, comprising the chairmen of the Committees (and some additional members) was appointed. Their membership varied between 9 and 11 until 1983 when all Committees except Scottish Affairs (13) were allotted 11 members. Only the Foreign Affairs, Home Affairs and Treasury Committees were empowered to appoint a sub-committee, but, after departmental mergers, this was later allowed for the Environment and the Education & Employment Committees.

Source: G. Drewry, *The New Select Committees* (1988)

Agriculture (9) (11)

1979	Sir W. Elliott
1983	J. Spence
1986	Sir R. Body
1987	(Sir) J. Wiggin
1997	P. Luff

Culture, Media and Sport 1997–(11)
(successor to National Heritage)

1997	G. Kaufman

Defence (10) (11)

1979	Sir J. Langford-Holt
1981	C. Onslow
1982	Sir T. Kitson
1983	Sir H. Atkins
1987	M. Mates
1992	Sir N. Bonsor
1996	M. Colvin
1997	B. George

Education, Science and Arts (9) (11)
(Education, 1992–1996)
(Education & Employment 1996–)

1979	C. Price
1983	Sir W. Van Straubenzee
1987	T. Raison
1989	(Sir) M. Thornton
1997–8	Margaret Hodge *(joint)*
1997–	D. Foster *(joint)*
1998–9	M. Wicks *(joint)*

Education & Employment Sub-Committee 1996–7 (8)

1996	E. Ross

Employment Sub-Committee 1997– (8)

1997	D. Foster

Education Sub-Committee 1997– (11)

1997	Margaret Hodge
1998	M. Wicks
1999	B. Sheerman

Employment 1980–1996 (9) (11)

1979	J. Golding
1982	J. Craigen
1983	R. Leighton
1992	G. Janner

Energy (10) (11) 1981–92

1979	(Sir) I. Lloyd
1989	M. Clark

Environment 1980–1997 (10) (11)

1979	B. Douglas-Mann
1981	R. Freeson
1983	Sir H. Rossi
1992	R. Jones
1995	A. Bennett

Environment, Transport and Regional Affairs 1997– (17)

1997	A. Bennett *(joint)*
1997	Gwyneth Dunwoody *(joint)*

Environment Sub-Committee 1997– (11)

1997	A. Bennett

Transport Sub-Committee 1997–

1997	Gwyneth Dunwoody

Foreign Affairs (11) (12)

1979	Sir A. Kershaw
1987	D. Howell
1997	D. Anderson

Foreign Affairs Overseas Development Sub-committee (5)

1979	K. McNamara
1982	F. Hooley
1983	*(not reconstituted)*

Health (11)

1991	N. Winterton
1992	Marion Roe
1997	D. Hinchcliffe

Home Affairs (11)

1979	Sir G. Page
1981	Sir J. Eden
1983	Sir E. Gardner
1987	Sir J. Wheeler
1992	Sir I. Lawrence
1997	C. Mullin
1999	R. Corbett

Home Affairs Sub-committee on Race Relations and Immigration 1980–7 (5)

1980	J. Wheeler
1987	*(not reconstituted)*

Home Affairs Sub-Committee 1992–3 (5)

1992	J. Greenway

(not continued 1993)

International Development 1997–(11)

1997	B. Wells

National Heritage 1992–97 (11)

1992	G. Kaufman

(See Culture, Media & Sport)

Northern Ireland (13)

1994	Sir J. Kilfedder
1995	C. Soley
1997	P. Brooke

Public Service 1995–7 (11)

1995	G. Radice

Public Administration 1997– (11)

1997	R. Morgan
1999	T. Wright

Science and Technology (11)

1992	Sir G. Shaw
1997	M. Clark

Scottish Affairs (13)

1979	D. Dewar
1981	R. Hughes
1982	D. Lambie

(In abeyance 1987–92)

1992	W. McKelvey
1997	D. Marshall

Social Services (9) (11)
(Social Security and Health 1988–91)
Social Security 1991–)

1979	Renee Short
1987	F. Field
1997	A. Kirkwood

Trade and Industry (11)
(Industry and Trade 1979–83)

1979	Sir D. Kaberry
1983	K. Warren
1992	R. Caborn
1997	M. O'Neill

Transport (10) (11) 1979–97

1979	T. Bradley
1983	H. Cowans
1985	G. Bagier
1987	D. Marshall
1992	R. Adley
1993	P. Channon

(see Environment)

Treasury and Civil Service 1979–95 (11)

1979	E. du Cann
1983	T. Higgins
1992	J. Watts
1994	Sir T. Arnold

Treasury 1995–

1996	M. Carrington
1997	G. Radice

Treasury and Civil Service Sub-committee 1979–95 (5)

1979	R. Sheldon
1981	J. Bray
1982	M. Meacher
1983	A. Mitchell
1987	G. Radice

(1995 *see* Public Service Committee)

Treasury Sub-committee 1998–

1998	Sir P. Lloyd
1998	Sir M. Spicer

Welsh Affairs (11)

1979	L. Abse
1981	D. Anderson
1983	G. Wardell
1997	M. Jones

Payment of M.P.s

1912	M.P.s receive first salary; £400 per year paid to all members not receiving salaries as Ministers or officers of the House.
1913	£100 of M.P.s' salaries made tax-exempt in respect of parliamentary expenses. This remained in force until 1954.
1924	M.P.s allowed free rail travel between London and their constituencies.
1931	Salary cut to £360 as an economy measure.
1934	Salary restored to £380 and then to £400.
1937	Salary increased to £600.
1946	Salary increased to £1,000 and salaries of £500 authorised for M.P.s who, as Ministers or Leaders of the Opposition, had an official salary of less than £5,000. Free travel was granted between M.P.s' homes and Westminster as well as to their constituencies.

1953   A sessional allowance of £2 per day introduced for every day (except Friday) on which the House sat: this was payable to all M.P.s including Ministers.

1957   The sessional allowance (usually amounting to about £280 p.a.) was replaced by an annual £750 to cover parliamentary expenses. The whole £1,750 drawn by ordinary M.P.s was subject to tax but M.P.s could claim as tax free any expenses up to £1,750 incurred in respect of parliamentary duties.

1964   Salary increased to £3,250 per year, following Lawrence Committee Report.

1965   Members' Pensions Act. First comprehensive pensions scheme introduced for M.P.s and dependants. Members contribute £150 per year and the Exchequer an amount equal to the aggregate of the Members' contributions. Members receive pensions from the age of 65 or on ceasing to be an M.P. if later, provided they have served for 10 years or more. The pension of £600 per year for 10 years' service increases to £900 after 15 years' service and by £24 for each further year thereafter.

1969   Secretarial allowance of up to £500 introduced. Members to have free telephone calls within the U.K.

1972   M.P.s' pay increased to £3,500 following Boyle Committee recommendations. Secretarial allowance increased to up to £1,000. An allowance of up to £750 for additional cost of living away from main residence and London members to receive a London supplement of £175 p.a. Travel allowances extended and a terminal grant equivalent to 3 months' salary established for M.P.s who lose their seats at a General Election.

1972   Parliamentary and Other Pensions Act. Existing pensions scheme revised. Minimum qualifying period reduced from 10 years to 4. M.P.s' benefits based on 1/60th of final salary for each year of reckonable service. Contributions to be 5% of salary. Early retirement option available from 60 onwards on an actuarially reduced pension.

1976   Pension scheme amended to provide for pensions to be based on a notional pensionable salary of £8,000.

1977   M.P.s' pay increased to £6,270. Secretarial allowance (also research assistance and general office expenses) increased to up to £3,687. London supplement increased to £385 p.a. Travel allowances further extended and allowance introduced for overnight stays away from home of up to £1,814.

1983   M.P.s' pay linked to Civil Service rates. Secretarial allowance raised to £12,000 and other allowances increased.

1992   Following a Top Salaries Review Board enquiry into office costs, the House voted for a substantial increase in the allowance for office, research and secretarial Costs. MPs with constituencies in Inner London are entitled to a payment of £1,222 a year; MPs with constituencies outside London are entitled to claim up to £10,958 a year for staying overnight away from home.

	M.P.s' basic pay	Office costs		M.P.s' basic pay	Office costs
1911	£400		1983	£15,308	£11,364
1931	£360		1984	$16,106	£12,437
1934	£380		1985	£16,904	£13,211
1935	£400		1986	£17,702	£20,140
1937	£600		1987	£18,500	£21,302
1954	£1,250		1988	£22,548	£22,588
1964	£3,250		1989	£24,107	£24,903
1969	£3,250	£500	1990	£26,701	£27,166
1972	£4,500	£1,000	1991	£28,970	£28,986
1974	£4,500	£1,750	1992	£30,854	£39,960
1975	£5,750	£3,200	1993	£30,854	£40,380
1976	£5,750	£3,512	1994	£31,687	£41,308
1977	£6,270	£3,687	1995	£33,189	£42,754
1978	£6,897	£4,200	1996	£34,085	£43,908
1979	£9,450	£4,600	1997	£43,000	£46,364
1980	£11,750	£8,000	1998	£43,860	£47,568
1981	£13,950	£8,480	1999	£45,066	£49,232
1982	£14,510	£8,820			

See p. 52 for Ministers' pay, and reduced parliamentary salaries payable to Ministers and other paid office-holders.

Seats Forfeited

These members left or were expelled from the House before or after their conviction and imprisonment on criminal charges.

2 Mar 03	A. Lynch	Nat.	Galway
1 Aug 22	H. Bottomley	Ind.	Hackney South
31 Jul 41	Sir P. Latham	Con.	Scarborough & Whitby
6 Dec 54	P. Baker	Con.	S. Norfolk
27 Aug 76	J. Stonehouse	Lab.(Ind)	Walsall South

These members forfeited their seats as a result of being adjudged bankrupt.

17 Sep 03	P. McHugh	Nat.	N. Leitrim (re-elected)
15 Jul 09	N. Murphy	Nat.	S. Kilkenny
1 Oct 28	C. Homan	Con.	Ashton under Lyne

In addition, H. Bottomley resigned his seat 16 May 12 after filing his bankruptcy petition.

These members forfeited their seats when it transpired that they held a government contract. All but one were re-elected in the ensuing by-election.

2 Feb 04	A. Gibbs	City of London	(re-elected)
2 Feb 04	V. Gibbs	St Albans	(defeated)
21 Apr 12	Sir S. Samuel	Whitechapel	(re-elected)
10 Feb 25	W. Preston	Walsall	(re-elected)

In Nov 1924, J. Astor (Dover) forfeited his seat for inadvertently voting before taking the oath. He was re-elected unopposed in the ensuing by-election.

These members gave up their seats when under censure for some aspect of their parliamentary conduct.

26 Feb 31	T. Mardy Jones	Lab.	Pontypridd (abuse of travel voucher)
11 Jun 36	J. Thomas	N.Lab.	Derby (Budget leak)
11 Jun 36	Sir A. Butt	Con.	Balham & Tooting (Budget leak)
30 Oct 47	G. Allighan	Lab.	Gravesend (expelled by a vote of 187–75 for breach of privilege)
3 Feb 49	J. Belcher	Lab.	Sowerby (following Lynskey Tribunal)
5 Jun 63	J. Profumo	Con.	Stratford-on-Avon (lying to the House)
25 Jul 77	J. Cordle	Con.	Bournemouth E. (Poulson affair)

On 16 Aug 1916 C. Leach (Colne Valley) was deprived of his seat under the Lunacy (Vacating of Seats) Act 1886.

A. Ramsay, Con. Peebles and Southern, remained an M.P. from 1940 to 1945 although, being detained under Regulation 18B of the Defence of the Realm Act until Dec 1944, he was unable to sit from May 40 to Dec 44.

Various other members have resigned their seats while under the shadow of some minor private or public scandal but in almost every case it seems that they could well have remained as members had they chosen to do so. For a list of successful election petitions, which led to the original result being disallowed by the courts see p.262.

House of Lords

Lord Chairman of Committees
(A Deputy Speaker of the House of Lords. The Lord Chancellor (see p.55) acts as Speaker)

1889	E of Morley	1957	Ld Merthyr
1905	4th E of Onslow	1965	E of Listowel
1911	E of Donoughmore	1977	Ld Aberdare
1931	5th E of Onslow	1992	Ld Ampthill
1944	Ld Stanmore	1994	Ld Boston of Faversham
1946	E of Drogheda		

Principal Deputy Chairman of Committees
(Salaried Chairman of Select Committee on European Communities)

1974	Ld Diamond	1983	Lady Llewelyn-Davies of Hastoe
1974	Lady Tweedsmuir of Belhelvie	1986	Lady Serota
1977	Ld Greenwood of Rossendale	1992	Ld Boston of Faversham
1980	Lady White	1994	Ld Tordoff

Officers of the House of Lords
Clerk of the Parliaments

1885	(Sir) H. Graham	1959	(Sir) V. Goodman
1917	Sir A. Thring	1963	(Sir) D. Stephens
1930	Sir E. Alderson	1974	(Sir) P. Henderson
1934	(Sir) H. Badeley	1983	(Sir) J. Sainty
1949	(Sir) R. Overbury	1990	(Sir) M. Wheeler-Booth
1953	(Sir) F. Lascelles	1996	(J.) M. Davies

Librarian

1897	A. Strong	1956	C. Dobson
1904	E. Gosse	1977	R. Morgan
1914	A. Butler	1991	D. Jones
1922	C. Clay		

Sources: *Hansard; Dod's Parliamentary Companion; Whitaker's Almanack.*

Composition of the House of Lords
(including minors)

Year	Duke[a]	Marq	Earl	Vt	Baron	Life Peer[b]	Law Lords[c]	Rep.Peers Scot[d]	Ir	Bishops	Total
1901	26	22	123	32	314	–	4	16	28	26	591
1910	25	23	124	42	334	–	4	16	28	26	662
1920	26	29	130	64	393	–	6	16	27	26	716
1930	24	26	134	73	428	–	7	16	18	26	753
1939	24	28	139	84	456	–	7	16	13	26	785
1950	23	30	137	95	503	–	11	16	6	26	847
1960	25	30	132	111	531	31	8	16	1	26	908
1970	29	30	163	110	530	163	11	–	–	26	1,057
1980	28	30	157	105	477	330	19	–	–	26	1,171
1990	27	29	156	102	471	358	19	–	–	26	1,186
1 Nov 1999	29	34	173	103	420	478	27	–	–	26	1,290
1 Dec 1999	2	1	22	14	52	525	27	–	–	26	670

[a]Including Peers of the Blood Royal.
[b]Created by the Life Peerages Act, 1958.
[c]Life Peers created under the Appellate Jurisdiction Act 1876.
[d]Scottish and Irish peers sitting by virtue of UK title are listed under the latter. In 1963 all Scottish peers became entitled to sit and are listed under their senior title.

Sources: *Constitutional Year Book*, 1900–39; *Dod's Parliamentary Companion*, 1940–.

Creation of Peerages

Administration[a]		New Hereditary Creations[a]	Life Peers		Advanced in Rank	Ministry		Average Annual Creations[b]
			Law	Other		Total	Yrs	
Salisbury	1895–02	42	2	–	n.a.	44	7	6
Balfour	1902–05	17	1	–	5	23	3.5	5
C-Bannerman	1905–08	20	1	–	–	21	2.5	9
Asquith	1908–15	61	6	–	13	80	7	9
Asquith	1915–16	17	–	–	2	19	1.5	11
Lloyd George	1916–22	90	1	–	25	116	5.5	16
Bonar Law	1922–23	3	–	–	–	3	0.5	6
Baldwin	1923–24	7	1	–	1	9	0.5	10
MacDonald	1924	4	–	–	1	5	0.5	5
Baldwin	1924–29	37	5	–	10	52	4.5	18
MacDonald	1929–31	18	2	–	–	20	2.5	8
MacDonald	1931–35	43	1	–	6	50	3.5	12
Baldwin	1935–37	27	2	–	5	34	2	14
Chamberlain	1937–40	18	2	–	4	24	3	36
Churchill	1940–45	60	2	–	9	71	5.5	11
Attlee	1945–51	75	11	–	8	94	6.5	10
Churchill	1951–55	31	2	–	6	39	3.5	9
Eden	1955–57	19	–	–	3	22	2	11
Macmillan	1957–63	42	9	47	6	104	6	7
Douglas-Home	1963–64	14	1	16	1	32	1	30
Wilson	1964–70	6	2	152	1	161	5.5	29
Heath	1970–74	–	4	30	–	34	3.5	9
Wilson	1974–76	–	3	81	–	84	2	40
Callaghan	1976–79	–	2	58	–	60	3	20
Thatcher	1979–90	4	11	193	–	208	11.5	18
Major	1990–97	–	11	161	–	172	6.5	26
Blair[c]	1997–99	1	4	149	–	154	2	62

[a] These figures can be misleading as dissolution honours created by an outgoing ministry fall, in fact, into the following ministry, e.g., of H. Wilson's new creations 6 were those of Sir A. Douglas-Home.
[b] Excluding the creation of Law Lords and advancements in rank.
[c] Up to end of 1999, not including New Year honours 2000 or Life Peerages given to existing hereditary peers.

See p.327 for Political Honours Scrutiny Committee.

House of Lords Sittings and Business

	Sessions and Sittings		Membership and Attendance				Work of the House					
Session[a]	Sittings	Average sitting	Total membership[b]	Without writ of summons[bc]	On leave of absence[b]	Average attendance	Public bills first in Lords	Gov. bills first in Lords[d]	Divisions	Starred questions	Written questions	Unstarred (debatable) questions
L1955–56	136	3hrs 34m.	876	78	n.a.	104	20	9	26	203	82	11
1956–57	103	3hrs 54m.	871	73	n.a.	112	20	7	32	209	55	9
1957–58	103	3hrs 50m.	885	70	n.a.	124	22	8	19	184	28	6
1958–59	109	4hrs 15m.	e	e	232	134	25	9	26	244	32	11
1959–60	113	3hrs 59m.	907	76	192	136	17	9	16	264	48	12
1960–61	125	4hrs 48m.	918	57	193	142	11	7	48	290	73	12
1961–62	115	4hrs 44m.	932	74	203	143	17	8	47	275	72	12
1962–63	127	5hrs 30m.	965	100	202	140	19	5	158	297	84	9
1963–64	110	4hrs 51m.	976	85	207	151	23	11	25	340	77	23
1964–65	124	4hrs 47m.	1,018	91	186	194	34	6	34	370	73	37
S1965–66	50	5hrs 16m.	1,020	94	195	191	13	7	16	151	33	12
L1966–67	191	5hrs 17m.	1,045	99	182	241	48	18	85	660	96	61
1967–68	139	5hrs 47m.	1,061	83	190	225	44	14	72	437	92	28
1968–69	109	5hrs 03m.	1,064	91	193	235	28	9	47	363	92	35
S1969–70	83	4hrs 47m.	1,062	93	199	225	28	12	18	287	108	33
L1970–71	153	6hrs 19m.	1,078	101	171	264	37	11	196	511	283	37
1971–72	141	5hrs 46m.	1,073	98	169	249	40	15	171	494	315	26
1972–73	128	5hrs 38m.	1,080	101	173	240	32	13	73	460	281	31
S1973–74	45	5hrs 51m.	1,079	105	193	245	22	7	19	139	92	5
S1974	64	5hrs 28m.	1,108	100	171	246	31	13	21	192	171	23
1974–75	162	5hrs 44m.	1,121	110	170	262	49	20	119	560	350	35
1975–76	155	6hrs 15m.	1,139	95	143	275	51	27	146	553	517	41
1976–77	105	5hrs 41m.	1,140	90	135	281	40	11	45	385	380	36
1977–78	126	5hrs 51m.	1,154	88	128	282	30	22	96	439	544	46
1978–79	59	5hrs 51m.	1,155	88	130	292	38	27	21	217	432	23
1979–80	206	6hrs 9m.	1,171	85	172	290	50	11	303	765	1277	68
1980–81	143	6hrs 43m.	1,179	87	160	296	48	12	184	537	857	31
1981–82	147	6hrs 20m.	1,174	97	150	284	42	10	146	531	1098	36
S1982–83	94	6hrs 35m.	1,181	97	143	294	40	11	89	357	619	36
L1983–84	178	7hrs 13m.	1,183	99	153	321	48	14	237	691	1350	60
1984–85	151	6hrs 47m.	1,174	95	142	320	40	12	145	573	1142	45

1985–86	165	7hrs 21m.	1,171	89	135	317	34	16	250	631	1182	44
S1986–87	84	6hrs 38m.	1,185	89	133	325	26	14	80	317	622	24
L1987–88	192	7hrs 6m.	1,185	84	169	333	21	9	279	742	1405	51
1988–89	153	7hrs 2m.	1,183	93	149	316	24	11	12	572	1202	35
1989–90	147	7hrs 18m.	1,186	86	139	318	23	8	186	551	1204	31
1990–91	137	6hrs 28m.	1,196	78	136	324	26	10	104	531	1304	42
S1991–92	74	7hrs 1m.	1,196	80	133	337	28	5	83	276	664	22
L1992–93	194	6hrs 52m.	1,208	85	82	379	39	12	165	739	2567	90
1993–94	142	6hrs 51m.	1,204	84	77	378	24	6	136	540	1974	56
1994–95	142	6hrs 22m.	1,190	85	68	376	43	11	106	515	2172	42
1995–96	136	6hrs 53m.	1,207	80	66	372	38	13	110	498	2471	26
S1996–97	79	6hrs 40m.	1,204	74	63	381	36	7	67	262	1349	27
L1997–98	228	7hrs 2m.	1,297	68	63	417	44	18	179	832	5729	129
1998–99	154	7hrs 36m.	1,290	63	52	446	29	9	99	539	4322	83

a S beside the date of a session indicates a shortened session drawn to an early conclusion by a General Election. L shows a prolonged session usually following an election.
b Figures at the end of the session in question.
c Includes minors and bankrupts.
d Excludes Consolidation Bills, on average an extra 7 per session.
e Records not kept.

SOURCE: House of Lords Information Office.

Party Organisation in the House of Lords

From the early 1920s Conservative peers met weekly in an Association of Independent Unionist Peers, much on the lines of the 1922 Committee. In 1982 it was renamed the Association of Conservative Peers. From 1945 to 1974 Liberal peers held their weekly meetings jointly with Liberal M.P.s. After 1974 they held their own weekly meetings, but Liberal Peers who were members of the Liberal 'shadow administration' formed in 1977 met Liberal M.P.s on a regular basis. Labour peers are entitled to attend the meetings of the Parliamentary Labour Party, but since the 1930s they have also had their own weekly meetings.

Party Strengths in the House of Lords 1900–38

Year	Con.	Lib.U.	Lib.	Lab.	Irish Nat.	Not stated	Minors	Total
1 Dec 00	354	111	69	–	1	9	15	589
31 Mar 16	360	107	93	–	1	51	11	623
10 Feb 20	491	–	130	1	1	67	26	716
31 Dec 30	489	–	79	17	–	140	27	752
31 Oct 38	519	23	55	13	–	141	24	775

Source: *Constitutional Year Book.*

Party Strengths in the House of Lords 1945–99

Year	Con.	Lab.	Lib (D)	X-bench	Other	Total
1945	400	16	63	–	280	769
1955	507	55	42	–	241	855
1975	292	149	30	281	387	1139
1985	376	122	76	245	360	1179
1990	425	110	74	234	353	1186
1 Nov 99	483	194	73	354	107	1211
1 Dec 99	233	183	54	163	33	656

Sources: 1955 & 1990; *Dod's Parliamentary Companion*: 1975 & 1985; D. Shell *The House of Lords* (1989): 1999 Parliamentary Information Service.

Attendance at the House of Lords by Party
(for the period 31 Oct 67 to 1 Aug 68)

	Peers who attended more than 33% ('working House')			Peers who attended more than 5% but less than 33%			Peers who attended up to 5%			Peers who did not attend			Total		
	C	S	Total	C	S	Total	C	S	Total	C	S	Total	C	S	Total
Lab.	81	14	95	8	5	13	4	1	5	2	1	3	95	21	116
Con.	38	87	125	24	86	110	9	70	79	6	31	37	77	274	351
Lib.	8	11	19	2	6	8	2	8	10	1	3	4	13	28	41
Other	26	26	52	61	24	85	22	56	78	32	307	339	141	413	554
Total	163	138	291	95	121	216	37	135	172	41	342	383	326	736	1062

C = created peers. S = peers by succession. Attendance at Committees of the House (other than the Appellate Committee) has been taken into account.

Source: *House of Lords Reform* (Cmnd. 3799/1968).

Critical votes in the House of Lords since 1900

The following represent outstanding occasions when the House of Lords has set itself against the House of Commons. In cases of repeated defiance on the same issue the final vote alone is normally recorded. Two notable instances of the Lords yielding, de facto, to the Commons (10 Aug 11 and 15 Dec 98) are also included.

27 Nov 08	272–96	2nd Reading refused for Licensing Bill.
30 Nov 09	350–75	2nd Reading refused for Finance Bill.
10 Aug 11	131–114	3rd Reading for Parliament Bill.
30 Jan 13	326–69	2nd Reading refused for government of Ireland Bill (refusal repeated 15 Jul 13 by 302–64).
13 Feb 13	251–51	2nd Reading refused for Established Church (Wales) Bill (refusal repeated 22 Jul 13 by 243–48).
24 Jul 13	166–42	2nd Reading refused for Plural Voting Bill (refusal repeated 15 Jul 14 by 119–49).
22 Jan 18	131–42	P.R. Amendment to Representation of the People Bill carried.
3 Feb 30	156–42	Insistence on one year limit to Unemployment Act.
24 Jun 30	208–13	Insistence on 'quota' amendment to Coal Mines Bill.
15 Jul 30	168–36	Insistence on 'spreadover' amendment to Coal Mines Bill.
18 Feb 31	168–22	2nd Reading refused for Education (School Attendance) Bill.
2 Jul 31	80–29	Amendment restricting Alt. Vote in Representation of the People Bill carried.
2 Jun 48	181–28	Capital punishment amendment to Criminal Justice Bill rejected.
8 Jun 48	177–81	2nd Reading refused for Parliament Bill (refusal repeated 23 Sep 48 by 204–34 and 29 Nov 49 by 110–37).
8 Jun 49	103–29	Insistence on amendment delaying Vesting Day under Iron and Steel Act (compromise later reached and Royal Assent to Act 16 Dec 49).
10 Jul 56	238–95	2nd Reading refused for Death Penalty (Abolition) Bill.
18 Jun 68	193–184	Rhodesia Sanctions Order rejected (but passed without division 18 Jul 68).
16 Oct 69	229–78	Insistence on Amendments to Bill delaying redistribution of seats.
11 Nov 75	186–86	Insistence on Amendments to Trade Union and Labour Relations Bill that barred Closed Shop in Journalism.
22 Oct 76	147–71	3rd Reading refused for British Transport Docks (Felixstowe) Bill, a Private Bill designed to bring Felixstowe Harbour into public ownership.
22 Nov 76	197–90	Insistence on Amendments to Aircraft and Shipbuilding Bill that excluded ship-repairing.
13 Mar 80	216–112	Clause of the Education (No. 2) Bill to give local authorities power to charge for home-to-school transport rejected.
9 Apr 84	235–15	Amendment to 2nd Reading of Rates Bill (stating that it would 'result in damaging constitutional changes in the relationship between central and local government', etc.) rejected.
11 Jun 84	238–217	Amendment to 2nd Reading of Local Government (Interim Provisions) Bill (stating that the Bill was a 'dangerous precedent', etc.) rejected.
28 Jun 84	191–143	Amendment carried to insert a clause postponing the coming into force of the Local Government (Interim Provisions) Bill until the passing of the main Act to abolish the GLC and Metropolitan County Councils.
7 May 85	152–135	Amendment to Local Government Bill preserving some environmental powers of GLC. This was the first of four amendments to the Bill carried against the Government.
23 May 88	317–184	Amendment on poll tax.
4 Jun 90	207–74	Amendment to War Crimes Bill. (Technically on a Free Vote against Government proposals for the continued trial of Nazi Criminals).
18 Apr 91	177–79	Amendment to Criminal Justice Bill on mandatory life sentence for murder.
20 Oct 92	125–100	Motion for enquiry into pit closures.
14 Mar 95	191–145	Amendment on remarried war widows' pension rights.
26 Jun 95	142–126	Amendment giving right of appeal against mandatory life sentence.
5 Feb 96	223–105	Motion to ensure the public broadcasting of 'listed' sporting events.
21 Jan 97	158–135	One of four Government defeats on the Firearms Bill.
21 Jul 97	149–132	Amendment to limit revenue-varying powers of the Scottish Parliament.
27 Jan 98	207–97	Motion to revoke the ban on selling beef on the bone.
7 Jul 98	319–108	Amendment to curtail charging of tuition fees in Scottish Universities.
20 Oct 98	165–140	First of six Government defeats over the European Parliamentary Elections Bill.
15 Dec 98	167–73	European Parliamentary Elections Bill rejected at 2nd Reading.
27 Jul 99	353–203	Motion to refer House of Lords Bill to Committee of Privileges.
26 Oct 99	221–81	Passage of House of Lords Act.

Government Defeats in House of Lords 1979–99

1979–80	15	1989–90	20
1980–81	18	1990–91	17
1981–82	7	1991–92	6
1982–83	5	1992–93	19
1983–84	20	1993–94	16
1984–85	17	1994–95	8
1985–86	22	1995–96	10
1986–87	3	1996–97	10
1987–88	17	1997–98	18
1988–89	12	1998–99	31

Source: House of Lords Library

Main Landmarks in the Reform of the House of Lords, 1900–

In 1900 the legislative powers of the two Houses were in theory equal, with the exception of the privileges of the House of Commons in relation to financial measures.

1908 Rosebery Committee's Report. The House approved the following principal recommendations:
(1) That a strong and efficient second Chamber was necessary for the balance of Parliament;
(2) That this objective should be achieved by the reform and reconstitution of the House of Lords;
(3) That, as a necessary preliminary to reform, it should be accepted that the possession of a peerage should no longer of itself entail the right to sit and vote in the House.
No action was taken to implement these recommendations.

1911 Parliament Act. Provided that-
(1) Bills certified by the Speaker of the House of Commons as Money Bills were to receive the Royal Assent one month after being sent to the House of Lords, even without the consent of the latter House; and
(2) any other Public Bill (except one for extending the life of a Parliament) passed by the House of Commons in three successive Sessions and rejected by the House of Lords was nevertheless to receive the Royal Assent, provided that 2 years had elapsed between the second reading in the first session and the third reading in the third session of the House of Commons.

1918 Bryce Report. Recommended that the differences between the 2 Houses should be settled by some means of joint consultation. Proposed that the House should consist of two elements. (i) 246 members elected by members of the House of Commons arranged in geographical areas and voting by Proportional Representation with a single transferable vote. (ii) 80 peers to be elected for a period of 12 years by a Joint Committee of both Houses of Parliament on which all parties should be represented. No action was taken to implement this Report.

1922 Government proposed House of Lords of 350 members consisting of some 'elected either directly or indirectly from the outside', hereditary peers elected by their order, and members nominated by the Crown. Resolutions criticised for vagueness, debate adjourned and not renewed.

1927 Further proposals introduced by government but later dropped.

1929 Vt Elibank's Life Peers Bill withdrawn before Second Reading.

1934 M of Salisbury's Parliament (Reform) Bill read a second time but not proceeded with in committee.

1935 Ld Rockley's Life Peers Bill read a second time but not proceeded with in committee.

1946 Travelling Expenses. Agreed that regular attenders at the House of Lords should be reimbursed for their travelling expenses. In practice made to apply to peers attending at least one-third of the sittings of the House.

1948 Agreed Statement of Party Leaders. A statement of nine principles agreed to but not acted upon. The most important of these were:
(1) The second Chamber should be complementary to and not a rival to the lower House, and
(2) The revised constitution of the House of Lords should be such as to secure as far as practicable that a permanent majority was not assured for any one political party.

1948 Criminal Justice Act. Privileges of Peers in Criminal Proceedings abolished.

1949 Parliament Act. Reduced the delaying powers of the House to two sessions and one year.

1956 Swinton Committee Report. Recommended provision of official Leave of Absence. This was put into effect in 1958. There were normally about 200 members of the House who have Leave of Absence at any one time.

1957 Expenses. Provision made for Peers to claim a maximum of three guineas a day for expenses incurred in attendance at the House. This was in addition to travelling expenses and claims were not subject to any minimum number of attendances.

1958 Life Peerages Act. Provided for the creation by the Sovereign, on the advice of the Prime Minister, of Life Peers and Peeresses. Women were thus for the first time enabled to become Members of the House of Lords. One of the objectives of this Act was to provide more balance of parliamentary representation in the House of Lords. This is achieved by the convention enabling recommendations for Life Peerages made by Opposition party leaders to be conveyed to the Queen through the agency of the Prime Minister.

1963 Peerage Act. Provided for–
    (1) the option for Peers to disclaim within one year (one month in the case of Members of the House of Commons) their peerages for life without such a disclaimer affecting the subsequent devolution of the peerage;[1]
    (2) the abolition of elections for Scottish Representative Peers and the admission of all Scottish Peers to membership of the House;
    (3) the removal from Irish Peers of certain disabilities relating to their voting and candidature at parliamentary elections;
    (4) the admission of all female holders of hereditary peerages to membership of the House of Lords.

1964 Expenses. Provision made for increasing the maximum expenses to which Peers were entitled from three guineas to four-and-a-half guineas per day (increased to £6 10s. in 1969, to £8.50 in 1972, and to £13.50 in 1977).

1967 The Government announced their intention of introducing legislation to reform the House of Lords and an all-party committee was established.

1968 Formal discussions were broken off after the Lords' rejection of the Southern Rhodesia Sanctions Order in June and the government introduced their own Parliament (No. 2) Bill dealing with both powers and composition.

1969 The Bill was dropped in April. Though the Peers themselves approved of the proposals, it met with strong opposition in the House of Commons from sections of both the Labour and Conservative parties.

1977 At the Labour Party Conference a motion was carried by 6,248,000 votes to 91,000 for the 'total abolition of the House of Lords and the reform of Parliament into an efficient single-chamber legislating body without delay'.

1997– The Labour Government acted on its election promise to reform the House of Lords. A Bill was introduced in November 1998 to end the voting rights of hereditary peers. It was amended to allow 92 hereditary peers (2 ex officio and the rest elected by their party colleagues) to sit until the Second stage of reform was completed. Following a White Paper (Cm 4183) a Royal Commission was set up under Lord Wakeham to produce a comprehensive report on the role and functions of the House. The House of Lords Act became law in Nov 99.

[1]These peers have disclaimed their titles:

1963   Vt Stansgate (A.Wedgwood Benn)
        Ld Altrincham (J. Grigg)
        Ld Hailsham (Q. Hogg) (Life Peerage 1970)
        E of Home (Sir A. Douglas-Home (Life Peerage 1974) (d.1994) His son resumed the title)
1964   Ld Southampton (E. Fitzroy (d. 1989) His son resumed the title)
        Ld Monkswell (W. Collier (d.1980) His son resumed the title)
        Ld Beaverbrook (M. Aitken (d.1985) His son resumed the title)
        E of Sandwich (V. Montagu (d.1995) His son resumed the title)
1966   Ld Fraser of Allander (Sir H. Fraser (d.1987)
1970   E of Durham (A. Lambton)
1971   Ld Sanderson of Ayot (A.Sanderson)
1972   Ld Reith (C. Reith)
1973   Ld Silkin (A. Silkin)
1975   Ld Archibald (G. Archibald (d.1997))
1977   Ld Merthyr (T. Lewis)
1994   E of Selkirk (since 1997 sits as Life Peer, Ld Selkirk)
1995   Vt Camrose (M. Berry, sits as Life Peer, Ld Hartwell))

Sources: 1908 (H.L. 234), Select Committee Report on the House of Lords; Cd. 9038/1918, *The Reform of the Second Chamber* (Conference: Vt Bryce); Cmd. 7380/1948, *Report of the Inter Party Conference on the Parliament Bill*; H.M.S.O. (24 Jan 56), Report of the Select Committee on the Power of the House in Relation to the Attendance of its Members; Cmnd.3779/1968, House of Lords Reform; P.A. Bromhead, *The House of Lords and Contemporary Politics, 1911–1957* (1958); Sir I. Jennings, Parliament (2nd ed., 1957); 10th Report of the House of Lords Select Committee on Procedure (Aug 1971); J. Morgan, *The House of Lords and the Labour Government, 1964–70* (1975); D. Shell, *The House of Lords*, (2nd ed. 1992); J. Griffith and M. Ryle, *Parliament* (1989); Wakeham Committee Report (2000); Parliamentary Website: www.parliament.uk

IV

ELECTIONS

General Election Statistics

It is impossible to present election statistics in any finally authoritative way. Until 1998 British statutes made no acknowledgement of the existence of political parties, and in most general elections the precise allegiance of at least a few of the candidates has been in doubt. This, far more than arithmetic error, explains the discrepancies between the figures provided in various works of reference. Such discrepancies, however, are seldom on a serious scale (except, perhaps, for 1918). Election figures suffer much more from being inherently confusing than from being inaccurately reported. The complications that arise from unopposed returns, from plural voting, from two-member seats, and, above all, from variations in the number of candidates put up by each party are the really serious hazards in psephological interpretation.

In the figures which follow an attempt is made to allow for these factors by a column which shows the average vote won by each opposed candidate (with the vote in two-member seats halved, and with University seats excluded). This still gives a distorted picture, especially when, as in 1900 or 1931, there were many unopposed candidates or when, as in 1929, 1931, or 1950, there was a sharp change in the number of Liberals standing; in 1918 the situation was so complicated that any such statistics are omitted, as they are likely to confuse more than to clarify; for other elections they should be regarded as corrective supplements to the cruder percentages in the previous column rather than as substitutes for them. The turn-out percentages are modified to allow for the distorting effect of the two-member seats which existed up to 1950.

To simplify classification, some arbitrary decisions have been made. Before 1918 candidates have been classified as Conservative, Liberal, or Irish Nationalist, even if their designation had a prefix such as Tariff Reform or Independent, but only officially sponsored candidates are classed as Labour. From 1918 onwards candidates who were not offi-cially recognised by their party have been classified with 'Others' (except that in 1935 Independent Liberals are placed with Liberals). Liberal Unionists have been listed as Conservatives throughout. Liberal National, National Labour, and National candidates are listed with Conservatives except in 1931. From 1974 onwards all Northern Ireland candi-dates are classed as 'Other', and the votes for the few Conservative candidates are left in that category. The speaker is listed with his or her former party.

General Election Results, 1900–1997

	Total Votes	MPs Elected	Candidates	Unopposed Returns	% Share of Total Vote	Vote per Opposed Candidate
1900. 28 Sep–24 Oct						
Conservative	1,797,444	402	579	163	51.1	52.5
Liberal	1,568,141	184	406	22	44.6	48.2
Labour	63,304	2	15	–	1.8	26.6
Irish Party	90,076	82	100	58	2.5	80.0
Others	544	–	2	–	0.0	2.2
Elec. 6,730,935 Turnout 74.6%	3,519,509	670	1,102	243	100.0	–

	Total Votes	MPs Elected	Candidates	Unopposed Returns	% Share of Total Vote	Vote per Opposed Candidate
1906. 12 Jan–7 Feb						
Conservative	2,451,454	157	574	13	43.6	44.1
Liberal	2,757,883	400	539	27	49.0	52.6
Labour	329,748	30	51	–	5.9	39.9
Irish Party	35,031	83	87	74	0.6	63.1
Others	52,387	–	22	–	0.9	18.8
Elec. 7,264,608	5,626,503	670	1,273	114	100.0	–
Turnout 82.6%						
1910. 14 Jan–9 Feb						
Conservative	3,127,887	273	600	19	46.9	47.5
Liberal	2,880,581	275	516	1	43.2	49.2
Labour	505,657	40	78	–	7.6	38.4
Irish Party	124,586	82	104	55	1.9	77.7
Others	28,693	–	17	–	0.4	15.4
Elec. 7,694,741	6,667,404	670	1,315	75	100.0	–
Turnout 86.6%						
1910. 2–19 Dec						
Conservative	2,420,566	272	550	72	46.3	47.9
Liberal	2,295,888	272	467	35	43.9	49.5
Labour	371,772	42	56	3	7.1	42.8
Irish Party	131,375	84	106	53	2.5	81.9
Others	8,768	–	11	–	0.2	9.1
Elec. 7,709,981	5,228,369	670	1,190	163	100.0	–
Turnout 81.1%						
1918. Sat., 14 Dec *(The results were declared on 28 Dec 1918)*						
Coalition Unionist	3,504,198	335	374	42	32.6	
Coalition Lib.	1,455,640	133	158	27	13.5	
Coalition Lab.	161,521	10	18	–	1.5	
(Coalition)	(5,121,359)	(478)	(550)	(69)	(47.6)	
Conservative	370,375	23	37	–	3.4	
Irish Unionist	292,722	25	38	–	2.7	
Liberal	1,298,808	28	253	–	12.1	
Labour	2,385,472	63	388	12	22.2	
Irish Nat.	238,477	7	60	1	2.2	
Sinn Fein	486,867	73	102	25	4.5	
Others	72,503	10	197	–	5.3	
Elec. 21,392,322	10,766,583	707	1,625	107	100.0	
Turnout 58.9%						
1922. Wed., 15 Nov						
Conservative	5,500,382	345	483	42	38.2	48.6
National Lib.	1,673,240	62	162	5	11.6	39.3
Liberal	2,516,287	54	328	5	17.5	30.9
Labour	4,241,383	142	411	4	29.5	40.0
Others	462,340	12	59	1	3.2	28.3
Elec. 21,127,663	14,393,632	615	1,443	57	100.0	–
Turnout 71.3%						

	Total Votes	MPs Elected	Candidates	Unopposed Returns	% Share of Total Vote	Vote per Opposed Candidate
1923. Thu., 6 Dec						
Conservative	5,538,824	258	540	35	38.1	42.6
Liberal	4,311,147	159	453	11	29.6	37.8
Labour	4,438,508	191	422	3	30.5	41.0
Others	260,042	7	31	1	1.8	27.6
Elec. 21,281,232 Turnout 70.8%	14,548,521	615	1,446	50	100.0	–
1924. Wed., 29 Oct						
Conservative	8,039,598	419	552	16	48.3	51.9
Liberal	2,928,747	40	340	6	17.6	30.9
Labour	5,489,077	151	512	9	33.0	38.2
Communist	55,346	1	8	–	0.3	25.0
Others	126,511	4	16	1	0.8	29.1
Elec. 21,731,320 Turnout 76.6%	16,639,279	615	1,428	32	100.0	–
1929. Thu., 30 May						
Conservative	8,656,473	260	590	4	38.2	39.4
Liberal	5,308,510	59	513	–	23.4	27.7
Labour	8,389,512	288	571	–	37.1	39.3
Communist	50,614	–	25	–	0.3	5.3
Others	243,266	8	31	3	1.0	21.2
Elec. 28,850,870 Turnout 76.1 %	22,648,375	615	1,730	7	100.0	–
1931. Tue., 27 Oct						
Conservative	11,978,745	473	523	56	55.2}	
Nat. Labour	341,370	13	20	–	1.6}	62.9
Liberal Nat.	809,302	35	41	–	3.7}	
Liberal	1,403,102	33	112	5	6.5}	28.8
(Nat.Govt.)	(14,532,519)	(554)	(696)	(61)	(67.0)	–
Ind.Liberal	106,106	4	7	–	0.5	35.8
Labour	6,649,630	52	515	6	30.6	33.0
Communist	74,824	–	26	–	0.3	7.5
New Party	36,377	–	24	–	0.2	3.9
Others	256,917	5	24	–	1.2	21.9
Elec. 29,960,071 Turnout 76.3%	21,656,373	615	1,292	67	100.0	–
1935. Thu., 14 Nov						
Conservative	11,810,158	432	585	26	53.7	54.8
Liberal	1,422,116	20	161	–	6.4	23.9
Labour	8,325,491	154	552	13	37.9	40.3
Ind.Lab.Party	139,577	4	17	–	0.7	22.2
Communist	27,117	1	2	–	0.1	38.0
Others	272,595	4	31	1	1.2	21.3
Elec. 31,379,050 Turnout 71.2%	21,997,054	615	1,348	40	100.0	–

	Total Votes	MPs Elected	Candidates	Unopposed Returns	% Share of Total Vote	Vote per Opposed Candidate
1945. Thu., 5 Jul *(The results were declared on 26 July 1945)*						
Conservative	9,988,306	213	624	1	39.8	40.1
Liberal	2,248,226	12	306	–	9.0	18.6
Labour	11,995,152	393	604	2	47.8	50.4
Communist	102,780	2	21	–	0.4	12.7
Common Wealth	110,634	1	23	–	0.4	12.6
Others	640,880	19	104	–	2.0	15.4
Elec. 33,240,391 Turnout 72.7%	25,085,978	640	1,682	3	100.0	–
1950. Thu., 23 Feb						
Conservative	12,502,567	298	620	2	43.5	43.7
Liberal	2,621,548	9	475	–	9.1	11.8
Labour	13,266,592	315	617	–	46.1	45.7
Communist	91,746	–	100	–	0.3	2.0
Others	290,218	3	56	–	1.0	12.6
Elec. 33,269,770 Turnout 84.0%	28,772,671	625	1,868	2	100.0	–
1951. Thu., 25 Oct						
Conservative	13,717,538	321	617	4	48.0	48.6
Liberal	730,556	6	109	–	2.5	14.7
Labour	13,948,605	295	617	–	48.8	49.2
Communist	21,640	–	10	–	0.1	4.4
Others	177,329	3	23	–	0.6	16.8
Elec. 34,645,573 Turnout 82.5%	28,595,668	625	1,376	4	100.0	–
1955. Thu., 26 May						
Conservative	13,286,569	344	623	–	49.7	50.2
Liberal	722,405	6	110	–	2.7	15.1
Labour	12,404,970	277	620	–	46.4	47.3
Communist	33,144	–	17	–	0.1	4.2
Others	313,410	3	39	–	1.1	20.8
Elec. 34,858,263 Turnout 76.7%	26,760,498	630	1,409	–	100.0	–
1959. Thu., 8 Oct						
Conservative	13,749,830	365	625	–	49.4	49.6
Liberal	1,638,571	6	216	–	5.9	16.9
Labour	12,215,538	258	621	–	43.8	44.5
Communist	30,897	–	18	–	0.1	4.1
Plaid Cymru	77,571	–	20	–	0.3	9.0
Scot. Nat. P.	21,738	–	5	–	0.1	11.4
Others	12,464	1	31	–	0.4	11.0
Elec. 35,397,080 Turnout 78.8%	27,859,241	630	1,536	–	100.0	–

	Total Votes	MPs Elected	Candidates	Unopposed Returns	% Share of Total Vote	Vote per Opposed Candidate
1964. Thu., 15 Oct						
Conservative	12,001,396	304	630	–	43.4	43.4
Liberal	3,092,878	9	365	–	11.2	18.5
Labour	12,205,814	317	628	–	44.1	44.1
Communist	45,932	–	36	–	0.2	3.4
Plaid Cymru	69,507	–	23	–	0.3	8.4
Scot. Nat. P.	64,044	–	15	–	0.2	10.7
Others	168,422	–	60	–	0.6	6.4
Elec. 35,892,572 Turnout 77.1%	27,655,374	630	1,757	–	100.0	–
1966. Thu., 31 Mar						
Conservative	11,418,433	253	629	–	41.9	41.8
Liberal	2,327,533	12	311	–	8.5	16.1
Labour	13,064,951	363	621	–	47.9	48.7
Communist	62,112	–	57	–	0.1	3.0
Plaid Cymru	61,071	–	20	–	0.2	8.7
Scot. Nat. P.	128,474	–	20	–	0.5	14.1
Others	201,302	2	49	–	0.6	8.6
Elec. 35,964,684 Turnout 75.8%	27,263,606	630	1,707	–	100.0	–
1970. Thu., 18 Jun						
Conservative	13,145,123	330	628	–	46.4	46.5
Liberal	2,117,035	6	332	–	7.5	13.5
Labour	12,179,341	287	624	–	43.0	43.5
Communist	37,970	–	58	–	0.1	1.1
Plaid Cymru	175,016	–	36	–	0.6	11.5
Scot. Nat. P.	306,802	1	65	–	1.1	12.2
Others	383,511	6	94	–	1.4	9.1
Elec. 39,342,013 Turnout 72.0%	28,344,798	630	1,837	–	100.0	–
1974. Thu., 28 Feb						
Conservative	11,868,906	297	623	–	37.9	38.8
Liberal	6,063,470	14	517	–	19.3	23.6
Labour	11,639,243	301	623	–	37.1	38.0
Communist	32,741	–	44	–	0.1	1.7
Plaid Cymru	171,364	2	36	–	0.6	10.7
Scot. Nat. P.	632,032	7	70	–	2.0	21.9
National Front	76,865	–	54	–	0.3	3.2
Others (G.B.)	131,059	2	120	–	0.4	2.2
Others (N.I.)*	717,986	12	48	–	2.3	25.0
Elec. 39,798,899 Turnout 78.7%	31,333,226	635	2,135	–	100.0	–

	Total Votes	MPs Elected	Candidates	Unopposed Returns	% Share of Total Vote	Vote per Opposed Candidate
1974. Thu., 10 Oct						
Conservative	10,464,817	277	623	–	35.8	36.7
Liberal	5,346,754	13	619	–	18.3	18.9
Labour	11,457,079	319	623	–	39.2	40.2
Communist	17,426	–	29	–	0.1	1.5
Plaid Cymru	166,321	3	36	–	0.6	10.8
Scot. Nat. P.	839,617	11	71	–	2.9	30.4
National Front	113,843	–	90	–	0.4	2.9
Others(G.B.)	81,227	–	118	–	0.3	1.5
Others (N.I.)	702,094	12	43	–	2.4	27.9
Elec. 40,072,971	29,189,178	635	2,252	–	100.0	–
Turnout 72.8%						
1979. Thu., 3 May						
Conservative	13,697,690	339	622	–	43.9	44.9
Liberal	4,313,811	11	577	–	13.8	14.9
Labour	11,532,148	269	623	–	36.9	37.8
Communist	15,938	–	38	–	0.1	0.9
Plaid Cymru	132,544	2	36	–	0.4	8.1
Scot. Nat. P.	504,259	2	71	–	1.6	17.3
National Front	190,747	–	303	–	0.6	1.6
Ecology	38,116	–	53	–	0.1	2.0
Workers Rev. P.	13,535	–	60	–	0.1	0.5
Others (G.B.)	85,338	–	129	–	0.3	1.3
Others (N.I.)*	695,889	12	64	–	2.2	18.8
Elec. 41,093,264	31,220,010	635	2,576	–	100.0	–
Turnout 76.0%						
1983. Thu., 9 Jun						
Conservative	13,012,315	397	633	–	42.4	43.5
Liberal	4,210,115	17	322	–	13.7	27.7
Social Democrat	3,570,834	6	311	–	11.6	24.3
(Alliance)	(7,780,949)	(23)	(633)	–	(25.4)	(26.0)
Labour	8,456,934	209	633	–	27.6	28.3
Communist	11,606	–	35	–	0.04	0.8
Plaid Cymru	125,309	2	36	–	0.4	7.8
Scot. Nat. P.	331,975	2	72	–	1.1	11.8
National Front	27,065	–	60	–	0.1	1.0
Others (G.B.)	193,383	–	282	–	0.6	1.4
Others (N.I.)*	764,925	17	95	–	3.1	17.9
Elec. 42,197,344	30,671,136	650	2,579	–	100.0	–
Turnout 72.7%						

*From 1974 onwards, no candidates in Northern Ireland are included in the major party totals although it might be argued that some independent Unionists should be classed with the Conservatives and that Northern Ireland Labour candidates should be classed with Labour.

	Total Votes	MPs Elected	Candidates	Unopposed Returns	% Share of Total Vote	Vote per Opposed Candidate
1987. Thu., 11 Jun						
Conservative	13,763,066	376	633	–	42.3	43.4
Liberal	4,173,450	17	327	–	12.8	25.5
Social Democrat	3,168,183	5	306	–	9.7	20.6
(Alliance)	(7,341,633)	(22)	(633)	–	(22.5)	(23.2)
Labour	10,029,778	229	633	–	30.8	31.2
Plaid Cymru	123,599	3	38	–	0.3	7.3
Scot. Nat. P.	416,473	3	71	–	1.3	14.0
Others (G.B.)	151,519	–	241	–	0.5	1.2
Others (N.I.)*	730,152	17	77	–	2.2	22.1
Elec. 43,181,321	32,529,568	650	2,325	–	100.0	–
Turnout 75.3%						
1992. Thu., 8 Apr						
Conservative	14,0482,283	336	634	–	41.9	42.3
Liberal Democrat	5,999,384	20	632	–	17.8	18.3
Labour	11,559,735	271	634	–	34.4	35.2
Plaid Cymru	154,439	4	38	–	0.5	8.8
Scot. Nat. P.	629,552	3	72	–	1.9	21.5
Others (G.B.)	436,207	–	838	–	1.0	1.3
Others (N.I.)*	740,485	17	100	–	2.2	17.2
Elec. 43,249,721	33,612,693	651	2325	–	100.0	–
Turnout 77.7%						
1997. Thu., 1 May						
Conservative	9,600,940	165	640	–	30.7	31.0
Liberal Democrat	5,243,440	46	639	–	16.8	17.3
Labour	13,517,911	419	639	–	43.2	44.5
Plaid Cymru	161,030	4	40	–	0.5	12.4
Scot. Nat. P.	622,260	6	72	–	2.0	22.1
Referendum	811,827	–	547	–	2.6	3.1
Others (G.B.)	549,874	1	1139	–	1.7	1.0
Others (N.I.)*	790,778	18	117	–	2.5	15.3
Elec. 43,784,559	31,287,702	659	3724	–	100.0	–
Turnout 71.5%						

For European Parliament election results see p. 514. For Scottish Parliament and Welsh Assembly results see pp. 459, 461.

*From 1974 onwards, no candidates in Northern Ireland are included in the major party totals although it might be argued that some independent Unionists should be classed with the Conservatives and that Northern Ireland Labour candidates should be classed with Labour. In 1987 and 1992 some explicitly Conservative candidates in Northern Ireland are still excluded from the UK party totals.

General Election Results by Regions[a]

	1900	1906	Jan 1910	Dec 1910	1918	1922	1923	1924	1929	1931	1935	1945	1950
County of London													
Con	51	19	3	30	Coal.	43	29	39	24	53	39	12	12
Lib	8	38	25	26	53	9	11	3	2	4	1	–	–
Lab	–	2	1	3	Op.	9	22	19	36	5	22	48	31
Others	–	–	–	–	9	1	–	1	–	–	–	–	–
Rest of S. England													
Con	123	45	107	104	Coal.	130	89	150	111	156	147	88	144
Lib	32	107	46	49	149	23	48	5	18	4	3	3	1
Lab	–	3	2	2	Op.	9	27	10	35	5	15	91	54
Others	–	–	–	–	16	3	1	–	1	–	–	3	–
Midlands													
Con	60	27	49	50	Coal.	53	45	64	35	80	67	24	35
Lib	27	59	31	30	67	17	17	2	5	3	1	–	1
Lab	1	2	8	8	Op.	17	25	21	47	4	19	64	59
Others	–	–	–	–	16	–	–	–	–	–	–	2	–
North of England													
Con	98	31	45	50	Coal.	82	57	101	51	146	106	43	61
Lib	55	102	86	82	121	27	48	9	10	9	5	2	1
Lab	–	20	22	21	Op.	60	64	59	108	15	60	128	107
Others	1	1	1	1	50	2	2	2	2	1	–	–	1
Wales													
Con	6	–	2	3	Coal.	6	4	9	1	11	11	4	4
Lib	27	33	27	26	20	10	12	10	9	8	6	6	5
Lab	1	1	5	5	Op.	18	19	16	25	16	18	25	27
Others	–	–	–	–	15	1	–	–	–	–	–	–	–
Scotland													
Con	36	10	9	9	Coal.	13	14	36	20	57	43	29	32
Lib	34	58	59	58	54	27	22	8	13	7	3	–	1
Lab	–	2	2	3	Op.	29	34	26	37	7	20	37	37
Others	–	–	–	–	17	2	12	1	1	–	5	5	–
(Northern) Ireland[a]													
Con	19	16	19	17	Coal.	10	10	12	10	10	10	9	10
Lib	1	3	1	1	–	–	–	–	–	–	–	–	–
Lab	–	–	–	–	Op.	–	–	–	–	–	–	–	–
Others	81	82	81	83	101	2	2	–	2	2	2	3	2
University													
Con	9	9	9	9	Coal.	8	9	8	8	8	9	4	–
Lib	–	–	–	–	13	3	2	3	2	2	1	1	–
Lab	–	–	–	–	Op.	–	–	–	–	–	–	–	–
Others	–	–	–	–	1	1	1	1	2	2	2	7	–
Totals													
Con	402	157	273	272	Coal.	345	258	419	260	521	432	213	298
Lib	184	400	275	272	478	116	159	40	59	37	20	12	9
Lab	2	30	40	42	Op.	142	191	151	288	52	154	393	315
Others	82	83	82	84	229	12	7	5	8	5	9	22	3
Total	670	670	670	670	707	615	615	615	615	615	615	640	625

[a]In 1918 all Coalition and all non-Coalition candidates are listed together. In fact a substantial number of the 48 Conservatives who were elected without the Coupon worked with the Government. Virtually no Coupons were issued to Irish candidates but 23 out of the 101 non-University seats in Ireland went to Unionists.
The vertical lines indicate redistributions of seats.
Northern England includes Cheshire, Lancashire, Yorkshire, and all counties to their north.
Midlands includes Hereford, Worcs., Warwickshire, Northants., Lincs., Notts., Leics., Staffs., Shropshire, Derbyshire.
Southern England includes the rest of England, except for the County of London (the old L.C.C. area), but from 1974 the seats in the outer areas of the Greater London Council are classed with the County of London and not with the rest of Southern England.

General Election Results by Regions[a]

	1951	1955	1959	1964	1966	1970	Feb 1974	Oct 1974	1979	1983	1987	1992	1997
London (GLC'74)													
Con	14	15	18	10	6	9	42	41	50	56	58	48	11
Lib	–	–	–	–	–	–	–	–	–	2	3	1	6
Lab	29	27	24	32	36	33	50	51	42	26	23	35	58
Others	–	–	–	–	–	–	–	–	–	–	–	–	–
Rest of S. England													
Con	153	163	171	156	134	169	136	128	146	168	170	161	95
Lib	–	–	1	3	4	2	5	5	3	5	3	6	22
Lab	46	42	34	46	67	34	21	29	13	3	3	10	48
Others	–	1	–	–	1	1	–	–	–	–	–	–	–
Midlands													
Con	35	39	49	42	35	51	43	40	57	70	67	57	28
Lib	–	–	–	–	–	–	–	–	–	–	–	–	1
Lab	59	57	47	54	61	45	54	58	41	30	33	43	74
Others	–	–	–	–	–	–	1	–	–	–	–	–	–
North of England													
Con	69	75	77	53	44	63	47	44	53	68	63	53	13
Lib	2	2	2	–	2	–	4	3	4	6	4	3	5
Lab	99	90	88	114	121	104	112	117	107	89	96	107	139
Others	–	–	–	–	–	–	1	–	–	–	–	–	1
Wales													
Con	6	6	7	6	3	7	8	8	11	14	8	6	–
Lib	3	3	2	2	1	1	2	2	1	2	3	1	2
Lab	27	27	27	28	32	27	24	23	22	20	24	27	34
Others	–	–	–	–	–	1	2	3	22	2	3	4	4
Scotland													
Con	35	36	31	24	20	23	21	16	22	21	10	11	–
Lib	1	1	1	4	5	3	3	3	3	8	9	9	10
Lab	35	34	38	43	46	44	40	41	44	41	50	49	56
Others	–	–	1	–	–	1	7	11	2	2	3	3	6
Northern Ireland													
Con	9	10	12	12	11	8	–	–	–	–	–	–	
Lib	–	–	–	–	–	–	–	–	–	–	–	–	–
Lab	–	–	–	–	–	–	–	–	–	–	–	–	–
Others	3	2	–	–	1	4	12	12	12	17	17	17	18
University													
Con	–	–	–	–	–	–	–	–	–	–	–	–	–
Lib	–	–	–	–	–	–	–	–	–	–	–	–	–
Lab	–	–	–	–	–	–	–	–	–	–	–	–	–
Others	–	–	–	–	–	–	–	–	–	–	–	–	–
Total													
Con	321	344	365	304	253	330	297	277	339	397	376	336	165
Lib	6	6	6	9	12	6	14	13	11	23	22	20	46
Lab	295	277	258	317	363	286	301	319	269	209	229	271	419
Others	3	3	1	2	2	8	23	26	16	21	23	26	29
Total	625	630	630	630	630	630	635	635	635	650	650	651	659

The vertical lines indicate redistributions of seats.

Northern England includes Cheshire, Lancashire, Yorkshire, and all counties to their north.

Midlands includes Hereford, Worcs., Warwickshire, Northants., Lincs., Notts., Leics., Staffs., Shropshire, Derbyshire.

Southern England includes the rest of England, except for the County of London (the old L.C.C. area), but from 1974 the seats in the outer areas of the Greater London Council are classed with the County of London and not with the rest of Southern England.

Referendum on E.E.C. Membership
(Thursday 5 June 1975)

'Do you think that the United Kingdom should stay in the European Community (the Common Market)?'

	Total electorate[1]	Total votes[2]	% turnout[1]	%[2] 'yes'	Highest 'yes'	Lowest 'yes'
England	33,339,959	21,722,222	64.6	68.7	76.3	62.9
Wales	2,015,766	1,345,545	66.7	64.8	74.3	56.9
Scotland	3,698,462	2,286,676	61.7	58.4	72.3	29.5
N. Ireland[2]	1,032,490	498,751	47.4	52.1	52.1	52.1
U.K.[1]	40,086,677	29,453,194	64.5	64.5	76.3	29.5

[1] The electorate figures are for the civilian electorate only. The 370,000 service votes are included only in the total votes and the 'Yes' percentages.
[2] The votes were counted on a county basis except in Northern Ireland which was treated as a single unit. In 66 of the 68 counties there was a 'Yes' majority (Shetland voted 56.3% 'No' and Western Isles 70.5% 'No').
(For the 1979 and 1997 referendums in Scotland and Wales see pp.458 and 460).

Party Changes between Elections

The party composition of the House of Commons changes continuously partly owing to Members changing their allegiance and partly owing to by-election results. The following table shows the net change due to both causes during the life of each Parliament. (Seats vacant at dissolution are included under the last incumbent's party.)

		Con.	Lib.	Lab.	Others
1895–1900	Dissolution	399	189	–	82
1900–05	Election	402	184	2	82
	Dissolution	369	215	4	82
1906–09	Election	157	400	30	83
	Dissolution	168	373	46	83
1910	Election	273	275	40	82
	Dissolution	274	274	40	82
1910–18	Election	272	271	42	85
	Dissolution	281	260	39	90
1918–22[a]	Election	383	161	73	90
	Dissolution	378	155	87	87
1922–23	Election	345	116	142	12
	Dissolution	344	117	144	10
1923–24	Election	258	159	191	7
	Dissolution	259	158	193	5
1924–29	Election	419	40	151	5
	Dissolution	400	46	162	7

[a]In this form the 1918–22 figures are highly misleading. This amplification may help.

	Co.U.	Con.	Co.Lib.	Lib.	Co.Lab.	Lab.	O.
Election	355	48	133	28	10	63	90
Dissolution	313	65	120	35	11	76	87

		Con.	Lib.	Lab.	Others
1929–31	Election	260	59	288	8
	Dissolution	263	57	281[b]	14
1931–35	Election	521	37	52	5
	Dissolution	512	34	59	10
1935–45	Election	432	20	154	9
	Dissolution	398	18	166	33
1945–50	Election	213	12	393	22
	Dissolution	218	10	391	21
1950–51	Election	298	9	315	3
	Dissolution	298	9	314	4
1951–55	Election	321	6	295	3
	Dissolution	322	6	294	3
1955–59	Election	344	6	277	3
	Dissolution	340	6	281	3
1959–64	Election	365	6	258	1
	Dissolution	360	7	262	2
1964–66	Election	304	9	317	–
	Dissolution	304	10	316	–
1966–70	Election	253	12	363	2
	Dissolution	264	13	346	7
1970–74	Election	330	6	287	7
	Dissolution	323	11	287	9
1974	Election	297	14	301	23
	Dissolution	297	15	300	23
1974–79	Election	277	13	319	26
	Dissolution	284	14	309	28
1979–83	Election	339	11	269	16
	Dissolution	336	(42)[c]	240	17
1983–87	Election	397	(23)[c]	209	21
	Dissolution	393	(27)[c]	208	22
1987–92	Election	376	23	229	23
	Dissolution	369	23	231	28
1992–97	Election	336	20	271	24
	Dissolution	324	26	275	26
1997–	Election	165	46	419	29

[b]This figure includes 15 National Labour M.P.s.
[c]Liberal/SDP Alliance.

M.P.s' Changes of Allegiance

The difficulties in compiling an exact and comprehensive list of all floor-crossings, Whip withdrawals, Whip resignations, and Whip restorations are enormous. The list which follows is probably fairly complete as far as floor-crossings go (except for 1918–22) but it certainly omits a number of Members who relinquished the Whip for a time. It also omits cases of M.P.s who stood without official party support in their constituencies but who remained in good standing with the Whips and, in some cases, of M.P.s taking the Whip immediately before a General Election (as happened with several Members in 1918 and a few in 1945) or immediately after a General Election (as happened with the Lloyd George Group in 1935). No attempt has been made to record shifts between the various factions of Irish Nationalism. Throughout this list the test, in so far as it can be applied, is whether the M.P. was officially in receipt of the weekly documentary Whip.

Parliament of 1900–05

			from	*to*	
Nov 02	*J. Wason	Orkney & Shetland	L.U.	Ind.	Won by-el Nov 02; took Lib Whip by 05
Apr 03	*J. W. Wilson	N. Worcs.	L.U.	Lib.	
Apr 03	Sir M. Foster	London Univ	L.U.	Lib.	
Jan 04	+W. Churchill	Oldham	Con.	Ind.	Con. Whip restored after 2 weeks; Lib. Whip taken Apr 04
Jan 04	*Sir J. Dickson-Poynder	Chippenham	Con.	Ind.	Con. Whip restored after 2 weeks; Lib.Whip taken Apr 04
Feb 04	*T. Russell	S. Tyrone	L.U.	Lib.	
Feb 04	J. Wilson	Falkirk	L.U.	Lib.	
Mar 04	+J. Seely	I. of Wight	Con.	Ind.	Won by-el Apr 04 unop.; took Lib. Whip May 04
Apr 04	+I. Guest	Plymouth	Con.	Lib.	
Aug 04	E. Hain	St Ives	L.U.	Lib.	
Aug 04	G. Kemp	Heywood	L.U.	Lib.	
Jul 04	J. Jameson	W. Clare	I.Nat.	Con.	
Nov 04	R. Rigg	Appleby	Lib.	Ind.	Resigned seat Dec 04
Mar 05	E. Mitchell	N. Fermanagh	Ind.C.	Lib.	
Mar 05	J. Wood	E. Down	L.U.	Lib.	
Mar 05	E. Hatch	Gorton	Con.	Ind.	
Mar 05	Sir E. Reed	Cardiff D.	Lib.	L.U.	

Parliament of 1906–09

Feb 06	*J. W. Taylor	Chester-le-S.	Lib.	Lab.	
Feb 06	A. Taylor	E. Toxteth	Con.	Lib.	
Feb 07	*R. Hunt	Ludlow	Con.	–	Whip withdrawn. Whip restored Mar 07
Nov 07	L. Renton	Gainsboro'	Lib.	Con.	
Aug 08	*A. Corbett	Tradeston	L.U.	Ind.Lib.	
Mar 09	T. Kincaid Smith	Stratford-on-Avon	Lib.	Ind.	Lost by-el May 09
May 09	A. Cross	Camlachie	L.U.	Lib.	
Oct 09	C. Bellairs	King's Lynn	Lib.	L.U.	

Parliament of 1910

Nov 10	Sir J. Rees	Montgomery	Lib.	L.U.	

Parliament of 1911–18

Jan 14	D. Mason	Coventry	Lib.	Ind.	
Feb 14	*B. Kenyon	Chesterfield	Lab.	Lib.	Introduced as new M.P. by Lab. but resigned Whip after 2 weeks

*Re-elected for same seat at next General Election.
+Elected for different seat at next General Election.

Apr 14	W. Johnson	Nuneaton	Lab.	Lib.	Lab. Whip withdrawn
Apr 15	*J. Hancock	Mid-Derbys.	Lab.	Lib.	Lab. Whip withdrawn
Sep 17	*H. Page Croft	Christchurch	Con.	Nat.P.	
Sep 17	*Sir R. Cooper	Walsall	Con.	Nat.P.	
Jul 18	E. John	E. Denbigh	Lib.	Lab.	
Jul 18	J. Martin	St.Pancras E.	Lib.	Lab.	

In Nov 18 a number of Liberals became Independent or Labour and some Labour members accepted the label Coalition Labour or Coalition National Democratic Party shortly before the dissolution of Parliament.

Parliament of 1919–22

Throughout this parliament the confusion of party labels and the movements within and between the Coalition and non-Coalition wings of each party make it impossible to attempt any comprehensive listing of all switches. The following changes were, however, more clear cut.

Apr 19	*J. Wedgwood	Newcastle-under-Lyme	Co.Lib.	Lab.	Lab. Whip granted May 19
Oct 19	E. Hallas	Duddeston	Co.NDP	Lab.	
Nov 19	C. Malone	Leyton E.	Co.Lib.	Ind.	Joined Communist Party Jul 20
Oct 20	*O. Mosley	Harrow	Co.Con.	Ind.	
Oct 20	*Sir O. Thomas	Anglesey	Lab.	Ind.	
Feb 22	*A. Hopkinson	Mossley	Co.Lib.	Ind.	

Parliament of 1922–23

Jan 23	*J. Erskine	Westminster St.George's	I.Con.	Con.	
Jan 23	*H. Becker	Richmond	I.Con.	Con.	
Jan 23	*G. Hall Caine	Dorset E.	I.Con.	Con.	
Jul 23	A. Evans	Leicester E.	Lib.	Con.	
Oct 23	G. Roberts	Norwich	Ind.	Con.	

Parliament of 1923–24

Feb 24	G. Davies	Welsh Univ.	Ind.	Lab.	
May 24	O. Mosley	Harrow	Ind.	Lab.	

Parliament of 1924–29

Jan 26	Sir A. Mond	Carmarthen	Lib.	Con.	Made peer Jun 28
Feb 26	E. Hilton Young	Norwich	Lib.	Ind.	Took Con. Whip May 26
Oct 26	*J. Kenworthy	Hull C.	Lib.	Lab.	Won by-el Nov 26
Nov 26	D. Davies	Montgomery	Lib.	Ind.	
Feb 27	G. Spencer	Broxtowe	Lab.	Ind.	Expelled from party
Feb 27	+W. Benn	Leith	Lib.	Ind	Resigned seat Feb 27
Feb 27	L. Haden Guest	Southwark N.	Lab.	Ind.	Lost by-el Mar 27
Oct 27	*Sir R. Newman	Exeter	Con.	Ind.	
Jul 28	*Sir B. Peto	Barnstaple	Con.	–	Whip withdrawn; restored Nov 28

Parliament of 1929–31

Jun 29	Sir W. Jowitt	Preston	Lib.	Lab.	Won by-el Jul 29
Feb 30	*N. Maclean	Govan	I.Lab.	Lab.	
Feb 31	Sir O. Mosley	Smethwick	Lab.	N.P.	
Feb 31	Lady C. Mosley	Stoke	Lab.	N.P.	
Feb 31	R. Forgan	W. Renfrew	Lab.	N.P.	
Feb 31	W. Allen	Belfast W.	Con.	N.P.	Became Ind. Jun 31
Feb 31	C. R. Dudgeon	Galloway	Lib.	N.P.	Became Ind. Jun 31
Feb 31	J. Strachey	Aston	Lab.	N.P.	Became Ind. Jun 31
Feb 31	O. Baldwin	Dudley	Lab.	Ind.	
Feb 31	W. Brown	Wolverh'ton W.	Lab.	Ind.	
Mar 31	*Sir W. Wayland	Canterbury	Con.	–	Whip withdrawn; restored Apr 31

*Re-elected for same seat at next General Election.
+Elected for different seat at next General Election.

Jun 31	*E. Brown	Leith	Lib.	Ind.	Became L.Nat. Oct 31
Jun 31	*Sir R. Hutchison	Montrose	Lib.	Ind.	Became L.Nat. Oct 31
Jun 31	*Sir J. Simon	Spen Valley	Lib.	Ind.	Became L.Nat. Oct 31
Sep 31	*E. Taylor	Paddington S.	Ind.	Con.	

In Oct 31, 23 Liberal Members broke with the party to form the Liberal National Group. A further 6 Liberals, most notably the Lloyd George family, became Independent Liberals. 15 Labour members under R.MacDonald formed the National Labour Group.

Parliament of 1931–35

Nov 31	*G. Buchanan	Gorbals	Lab.	ILP	
Nov 31	*J. McGovern	Shettleston	Lab.	ILP	
Nov 31	J. Maxton	Bridgeton	Lab.	ILP	
Nov 31	*D. Kirkwood	Dumbarton	Lab.	ILP	Returned to Lab. Aug 33
Nov 31	R. Wallhead	Merthyr	Lab.	ILP.	Returned to Lab. Sep 33
Nov 32	*J. Leckie	Walsall	Lib.	L.Nat.	
Dec 32	A. Curry	Bp Auckland	L.Nat.	Lib.	
Dec 32	F. Llewellyn Jones	Flint	L.Nat.	Lib.	
Feb 33	H. Nathan	Beth' Gn N.E.	I.L.	Ind.	Took Lab. Whip Jun 34
Jun 34	W. McKeag	Durham	Lib.	L.Nat.	
Jun 34	J. Hunter	Dumfries	Lib.	L.Nat.	
Jun 34	J. Lockwood	Shipley	Con.	Ind.	
May 35	F. Astbury	Salford W.	Con.	Ind.	
May 35	L. Thorp	Nelson & C.	Con.	Ind.	
May 35	A. Todd	Berwick	Con.	Ind.	
May 35	*D'ess of Atholl	Kinross&W.P.	Con.	Ind.	Whip restored Sep 35
May 35	*Sir J. Nall	Hulme	Con.	Ind.	Whip restored Nov 35
Jul 35	*G. Morrison	Scottish Un.	Lib.	L.Nat.	

Parliament of 1935–45

Jun 36	H. Macmillan	Stockton	Con	Ind.	Whip restored Jul 37
Oct 36	R. Bernays	Bristol N.	Lib.	L.Nat.	
Apr 38	D'ess of Atholl	Kinross&W.P	Con.	Ind.	Lost by-el Dec 38
Oct 38	H. Holdsworth	Bradford S	Lib.	L.Nat.	
Nov 38	A. Hopkinson	Mossley	Nat.	Ind.	
Jan 39	*Sir S. Cripps	Bristol E.	Lab.	–	Expelled from party; Whip restored Feb 45
Mar 39	*A. Bevan	Ebbw Vale	Lab.	–	Expelled from party;Whip restored Dec 39
Mar 39	*G. Strauss	Lambeth N.	Lab.	–	Expelled from party;Whip restored Feb 40
May 39	*G. Buchanan	Gorbals	ILP	Lab.	
Dec 39	*C. Davies	Montgomery	L.Nat	Ind.	Took Lib. Whip Aug 42
Mar 40	*D. Pritt	Ham'smith N.	Lab.	–	Expelled from party
May 40	A. Ramsay	Peebles	Con.	Ind.	Detained until Dec 44
Feb 42	*E. Granville	Eye	L.Nat.	Ind.	Took Lib.Whip Apr 45
Feb 42	*Sir M. Macdonald	Inverness	L.Nat.	Ind.	Whip restored by 45
Feb 42	L. Hore-Belisha	Devonport	L.Nat.	Ind.	
Feb 42	S. King-Hall	Ormskirk	N.Lab.	Ind.	
Feb 42	*Sir H. Morris-Jones	Denbigh	L.Nat.	Ind.	Whip restored May 43
Feb 42	+K. Lindsay	Kilmarnock	N.Lab.	Ind.	
May 42	C. Cunningham-Reid	St M'lebone	Con.	–	Whip withdrawn
Sep 42	Sir R. Acland	Barnstaple	Lib.	C.W.	
Mar 43	A. Maclaren	Burslem	Lab.	Ind.	
Nov 44	J. Loverseed	Eddisbury	C.W.	Ind.	Took Lab.Whip May 45
Jan 45	*T. Driberg	Maldon	Ind.	Lab.	
May 45	*J. Little	Down	U.U.	Ind.	
May 45	*C. White	W.Derbyshire	Ind.	Lab.	

*Re-elected for same seat at next General Election.
+Elected for different seat at next General Election.

Parliament of 1945–50

Apr 46	E. Millington	Chelmsford	C.W.	Lab.	
Oct 46	T. Horabin	N. Cornwall	Lib.	Ind.	Took Lab.Whip Nov 47
Mar 47	*J. McGovern	Shettleston	ILP	Lab.	
Jul 47	C. Stephen	Camlachie	ILP	Ind.	Took Lab.Whip Oct 47
Oct 47	*J. Carmichael	Bridgeton	ILP.	Ind.	Took Lab.Whip Nov 47
Nov 47	E. Walkden	Doncaster	Lab.	Ind.	
Mar 48	*J. McKie	Galloway	Ind.C.	Con.	
Apr 48	J. Platts-Mills	Finsbury	Lab.	–	Expelled from party
May 48	A. Edwards	Middlesbro'	Lab.	–	Expelled from party, took Con.Whip Aug 49
Oct 48	I. Bulmer-Thomas	Keighley	Lab.	Ind.	Took Con.Whip Jan 49
Nov 48	E. Gander Dower	Caithness & Sutherland	Con.	Ind.	
May 49	L. Solley	Thurrock	Lab.	–	Expelled from party
May 49	K. Zilliacus	Gateshead	Lab.	–	Expelled from party
Jul 49	L. Hutchinson	Rusholme	Lab.	–	Expelled from party

Parliament of 1950–51

Aug 50	R. Blackburn	Northfield	Lab.	Ind.	

Parliament of 1951–55

Jun 54	Sir J. Mellor	Sutton Cold	Con.	Ind.	Whip restored Jul 54
Jul 54	*H. Legge-Bourke	Isle of Ely	Con.	Ind.	Whip restored Oct 54
Nov 54	*G. Craddock	Bradford S.	Lab.	–	⎫
Nov 54	*S. Davies	Merthyr	Lab.	–	⎪
Nov 54	*E. Fernyhough	Jarrow	Lab.	–	⎬ Whip withdrawn; restored
Nov 54	*E. Hughes	S. Ayrshire	Lab.	–	⎪ Feb 55
Nov 54	*S. Silverman	Nelson & C.	Lab.	–	⎪
Nov 54	*V. Yates	Ladywood	Lab.	–	⎭
Nov 54	*J. McGovern	Shettleston	Lab.	–	Whip withdrawn; restored Mar 55
Mar 55	*A. Bevan	Ebbw Vale	Lab.	–	Whip withdrawn; restored Apr 55
Mar 55	Sir R. Acland	Gravesend	Lab.	Ind.	Resigned seat to fight by-el; expelled from party

Parliament of 1955–59

Nov 56	C. Banks	Pudsey	Con.	Ind.	Whip restored Dec 58
May 57	P. Maitland	Lanark	Con.	Ind.	Whip restored Dec 57
May 57	Sir V. Raikes	Garston	Con.	Ind.	Resigned seat Oct 57
May 57	A. Maude	Ealing S.	Con.	Ind.	Resigned seat Apr 58
May 57	*J. Biggs-Davison	Chigwell	Con.	Ind.	Whip restored Jul 58
May 57	*A. Fell	Yarmouth	Con.	Ind.	Whip restored Jul 58
May 57	*Vt Hinchingbrooke	S.Dorset	Con.	Ind.	Whip restored Jul 58
May 57	L. Turner	Oxford	Con.	Ind.	Whip restored Jul 58
May 57	P. Williams	Sunderl'd S	Con.	Ind.	Whip restored Jul 58
Nov 57	Sir F. Medlicott	C.Norfolk	Con.	Ind.	Whip restored Nov 58
Jan 59	*Sir D. Robertson	Caithness & Sutherland	Con.	Ind.	

Parliament of 1959–64

Mar 61	A. Brown	Tottenham	Lab.	Ind.	Took Con. Whip May 62
Mar 61	*W. Baxter	W. Stirling	Lab.	–	⎫
Mar 61	*S. Davies	Merthyr	Lab.	–	⎪
Mar 61	*M. Foot	Ebbw Vale	Lab.	–	⎬ Whip withdrawn; restored
Mar 61	*E. Hughes	S. Ayrshire	Lab.	–	⎪ May 63
Mar 61	*S. Silverman	Nelson & C.	Lab.	–	⎭
Mar 61	*K. Zilliacus	Gorton	Lab.	–	Whip suspended; restored Jan 62
Oct 61	Sir W. Duthie	Banff	Con.	Ind.	Whip restored Nov 63
Jan 64	D. Johnson	Carlisle	Con.	Ind.	

*Re-elected for same seat at next General Election.

Parliament of 1964–66
    [None]

Parliament of 1966–70

Jul 66	G. Hirst	Shipley	Con.	Ind.	
Aug 66	*G. Fitt	Belfast W.	R.Lab.	SDLP	Expelled by Rep.Lab.
Dec 66	*R. Paget	Northampton	Lab.	Ind.	Whip restored Jun 67
Jan 68	D. Donnelly	Pembroke	Lab.	Ind.	Expelled from party Mar 68
Feb 68	24 M.P.s		Lab.	–	Whip suspended for month

Parliament of 1970–74

Oct 71	*I. Paisley	N. Antrim	Pr.U.	Dem.U.	
Feb 72	R. Gunter	Southwark	Lab.	Ind.	
Oct 72	*D. Taverne	Lincoln	Lab.	Dem.L.	Won by-el Mar 73
Dec 72	S. Mills	Belfast N.	U.U.	Con.	Joined Alliance Party Apr 73

Parliament of 1974

Jul 74	C. Mayhew	Woolwich E.	Lab.	Lib.	

Parliament of 1974–79

Oct 75	W. Craig	Belfast E.	UUUC	Vanguard	Wound up Vanguard and rejoined UUUC Feb 78
Oct 75	*J. Kilfedder	N. Down	UUUC	Ind. U.	
Apr 76	J. Stonehouse	Walsall N.	Lab.	Ind.	
Jul 76	J. Sillars	S. Ayrshire	Lab.	Sc.Lab	Formed Sc.Lab.P. Apr 76
Jul 76	J. Robertson	Paisley	Lab.	Sc.Lab.	
May 77	*I. Paisley	N. Antrim	UUUC	Dem.U.	
May 77	J. Dunlop	Mid-Ulster	UUUC	Ind.	
Oct 77	+R. Prentice	Newham N. E.	Lab.	Con.	

Parliament of 1979–83

Nov 79	G. Fitt	Belfast W.	SDLP	Ind. Soc.	
Feb 81	T. Ellis	Wrexham	Lab.	SDP	
Feb 81	R. Crawshaw	Liv.Toxteth	Lab.	SDP	
Mar 81	T. Bradley	Leicester E.	Lab.	SDP	
Mar 81	*J. Cartwright	Woolwich E.	Lab.	SDP	
Mar 81	J. Horam	Gateshead W.	Lab.	SDP	
Mar 81	*R. Maclennan	Caithness & Sutherland	Lab.	SDP	
Mar 81	J. Roper	Farnworth	Lab.	SDP	
Mar 81	*D. Owen	Devonport	Lab.	SDP	
Mar 81	W. Rodgers	Stockton	Lab.	SDP	
Mar 81	N. Sandelson	Hayes & H.	Lab.	SDP	
Mar 81	M. Thomas	Newcastle E.	Lab.	SDP	
Mar 81	*I. Wrigglesworth	Thornaby	Lab.	SDP	
Mar 81	E. Lyons	Bradford W.	Lab.	SDP	
Mar 81	C. B-Fowler	Norfolk N.W.	Con.	SDP	
Jul 81	J. Wellbeloved	Erith & C.	Lab.	SDP	
Sep 81	M. O'Halloran	Islington N.	Lab.	SDP	Became I.Lab. Mar 83
Oct 81	D. Mabon	Greenock	Lab.	SDP	
Oct 81	R. Mitchell	Soton, Itchen	Lab.	SDP	
Oct 81	D. Ginsburg	Dewsbury	Lab.	SDP	
Oct 81	J. Dunn	Liv.Kirkdale	Lab.	SDP	
Oct 81	T. McNally	Stockport S	Lab.	SDP	
Oct 81	E. Ogden	Liv. W. Derby	Lab.	SDP	
Nov 81	J. Grant	Islington C.	Lab.	SDP	
Nov 81	G. Cunningham	Islington S.	Lab.	I.Lab	Became SDP Jun 82
Dec 81	R. Brown	Hackney S.	Lab.	SDP	
Dec 81	J. Thomas	Abertillery	Lab.	SDP	
Dec 81	E. Hudson-Davies	Caerphilly	Lab.	SDP	

*Re-elected for same seat at next General Election.
+Elected for different seat at next General Election.

Dec 81	B. Douglas-Mann	Mitcham	Lab.	Ind.SDP	Lost by-elec.Jun 82
Jan 82	B. Magee	Leyton	Lab.	Ind.Lab.	Became SDP Mar 82
Aug 82	R. Mellish	Bermondsey	Lab.	Ind.Lab.	Resigned seat Jan 83

Parliament of 1983–87
[None]

Parliament of 1987–92

Mar 88	*R. Maclennan	Caithness & Sutherland	SDP	(Lib)Dem	
Mar 88	*C. Kennedy	Ross, Cromarty & Skye	SDP	(Lib)Dem	
May 88	R. Brown	Leith	Lab.	–	Whip withdrawn for 3 months
Mar 90	R. Douglas	Dunf'line W.	Lab.	I.Lab.	Joined SNP Oct 90
Dec 91	D. Nellist	Cov'try S.E	Lab	–	Expelled from Party
Dec 91	T. Fields	Broad Green	Lab.	–	Expelled from Party
Mar 92	J. Browne	Winchester	Con.	–	Whip withdrawn

Parliament of 1992–97

Jul 93	R. Allason	Torbay	Con.	–	Whip withdrawn; restored Jul 94
Nov 94	*Teresa Gorman	Billericay	Con	–	
Nov 94	N. Budgen	Wolv'ton SW	Con	–	
Nov 94	M. Cartiss	Gt.Yarmouth	Con.	–	Whip withdrawn; restored
Nov 94	*C. Gill	Ludlow	Con.	–	Apr 95
Nov 94	*R. Shepherd	Aldridge-B.	Con.	–	
Nov 94	A. Marlow	North'ton N.	Con.	–	
Nov 94	*J.Wilkinson	Ruislip-Nd	Con.	–	
Nov 94	*Sir R. Body	Holland-w-B.	Con.	–	Resigned whip; whip restored Apr 96
Oct 95	+A. Howarth	Stratford/Avon	Con	Lab.	
Dec 95	Emma Nicholson	Devon W.& T.	Con	Lib.D.	
Feb 96	P. Thurnham	Bolton N.E.	Con.	Ind.	Joined Lib.D.Oct 96
Nov 96	Sir J. Gorst	Hendon N.	Con.	–	Said 'Free from Whip'
Mar 97	Sir G. Gardiner	Reigate	Con.	Ref.	

Parliament of 1997–

Nov 97	P. Temple-Morris	Leominster	Con.	Ind.	Took Lab. Whip Jun 98
Jun 97	R. Wareing	Liv.W.Derby	Lab.	–	Suspended till Nov 97
Aug 98	T. Graham	Renfrewshire W.	Lab.	–	Whip withdrawn
Jun 97	M. Sarwar	Glasgow,Govan	Lab.	–	Whip withdrawn; restored Mar 99
Apr 97	D. Canavan	Falkirk W.	Lab.	–	Whip withdrawn
Dec 99	S. Woodward	Witney	Con.	Lab.	

*Re-elected for the same seat at the next general Election
+Elected for a different seat at the next General Election

M.P.s elected under New Label

In addition to the floor crossings recorded above there are the following instances of ex-M.P.s, after an interval out of Parliament, returning to the House under a designation basically different from the ones under which they had previously sat.

(Sir) R. Acland	Lib. 35–42	C.W. 42–45	Lab. 47–55
C. Addison	Lib. 10–22	Lab. 29–31, 34–35	
P. Alden	Lib. 06–18	Lab. 23–24	
W. Allen	Lib. 92–00	Nat. 31–35	
C. Bellairs	Lib. 06–10	Con. 15–31	
(Sir) A. Bennett	Lib. 22–23	Con. 24–30	

Name				
W.W. Benn	Lib. 06–27	Lab. 28–31, 37–41		
(Sir) E. Bennett	Lib. 06–10	Lab. 29–31	N.Lab. 31–45	
H. Bottomley	Lib. 06–12	Ind. 18–22		
T. Bowles	Con. 92–06	Lib. 10–10		
J. Bright	L.U. 89–95	Lib. 06–10		
W. Brown	Lab. 29–31	Ind. 42–50		
C. Buxton	Lib. 10–10	Lab. 22–31		
N. Buxton	Lib. 05–06, 10–18	Lab. 22–24, 29–30		
(Sir) W. Churchill	Con. 00–04	Lib. 04–22	Con. 24–64	
(Sir) H. Cowan	Lib. 06–22	Con. 23–29		
A. Crawley	Lab. 45–51	Con. 62–67		
R. Denman	Lib. 10–18	Lab. 29–31	N.Lab. 31–45	
(Sir) C. Entwistle	Lib. 18–24	Con. 31–45		
R. Fletcher	Lib. 23–24	Lab. 35–42		
(Sir) D. Foot	Lib. 31–45	Lab. 57–70		
G. Garro-Jones	Lib. 24–29	Lab. 35–47		
W. Grenfell	Lib. 80–82, 85–86, 92–93	Con. 00–06		
Sir E. Grigg	Lib. 22–25	Con. 33–45		
C. Guest	Lib. 10–18, 22–23	Con. 37–45		
F. Guest	Lib. 10–22, 23–29	Con. 31–37		
O. Guest	Co.Lib. 18–22	Con. 35–45		
T. Harvey	Lib. 10–18, 23–24	Ind. 37–45		
E. Hemmerde	Lib. 06–10, 12–18	Lab. 22–24		
J. Horam	Lab. 70–81	SDP 81–83	Con. 92–	
(Sir) B. Janner	Lib. 31–35	Lab. 45–70		
R. Jenkins	Lab. 48–77	SDP 82–87		
(Sir) W. Jowitt	Lib. 29–29	Lab. 29–31	Ind. 31–31	Lab. 39–45
E. King	Lab. 45–50	Con. 64–79		
H. Lawson	Lib. 85–92, 93–95	Lib.U. 05–06, 10–16		
H. Lees-Smith	Lib. 10–18	Lab. 22–23, 24–31, 35–42		
G. Lloyd-George	Lib. 22–24, 29–50	Con. 51–57		
(Lady) M. Lloyd-George	Lib. 29–51	Lab. 57–66		
F. Maddison	Lib. 97–00	Lab. 06–10		
E. Mallalieu	Lib. 31–35	Lab. 48–74		
C. Malone	Co.Lib. 18–19	Ind. 19–22	Comm. 22	Lab. 28–31
(Sir) F. Markham	Lab. 29–31	N.Lab. 35–45	Con. 51–64	
H. Mond	Lib. 23–24	Con. 29–30		
(Sir) O. Philipps	Lib. 06–10	Con. 16–22		
A. Ponsonby	Lib. 08–18	Lab. 22–30		
E. Powell	Con. 50–74	U.U. 74–87		
S. Saklatvala	Lab. 22–23	Comm. 24–29		
Sir A. Salter	Ind. 37–50	Con. 52–54		
J. Seddon	Lab. 06–10	Co.N.D.P. 18–22		
(Sir) C. Seely	L.U. 95–06	Lib. 16–18		
J. Sillars	Lab. 70–76	Sc.Lab. 76–79	S.N.P. 88–92	
(Sir) E. Spears	Lib. 22–24	Con. 31–45		
G. Spero	Lib. 23–24	Lab. 29–31		
C. Stephen	Lab. 22–31	I.L.P. 35–47	Lab.47–47	
J. Strachey	Lab. 29–30	N.P.30–31	Ind.31–31	Lab. 45–63
(Sir) C. Trevelyan	Lib. 99–18	Lab. 22–31		
P. Tyler	Lib. 74–74	Lib.Dem 92–		
Mrs S.Williams	Lab. 64–79	SDP 81–83		
J. (Havelock) Wilson	Lib. 92–00	Lab. 06–10	Co.N.D.P. 18–22	

M.P.s Denied Party Renomination since 1922

When a sitting M.P. does not stand again, it is often unclear whether the retirement is entirely voluntary. Irreparable conflicts with the local party may lie behind formal statements about reasons of health or age or business. At least in the following cases, there is little doubt that the local party failed to renominate a sitting and willing M.P. who was still in receipt of the party whip at Westminster. Up to 1983 this list does not include M.P.s whose seats were substantially changed by redistribution and who failed to secure renomination for any part of their old seat, e.g. in Feb 1974 Sir R. Russell and E. Bullus, Con. members for Wembley N. and Wembley S., were spurned for the successor seats, Brent North and Brent South, while W. Wells, Lab. member for Walsall N., was denied renomination in the redistribution seat of the same name. It is plain that in the overwhelming majority of cases the disagreement could be ascribed to personal rather than ideological considerations. In several of the 1983 and 1997 cases, the M.P.s were seeking renomination in a substantially redrawn constituency, often against another sitting M.P.

Conservative

1923	Sir C. Warner (Lichfield)	1974	Sir C. Taylor (Eastbourne)
1929	Sir R. Newman (Exeter)[a]	1979	B. Drayson (Skipton)
1935	J. Lockwood (Shipley)	1979	R. Cooke (Bristol W.)
1935	H. Moss (Rutherglen)	1983	T. Benyon (Wantage)
1938	Duchess of Atholl (Perth & Kinross)[b]	1983	M. Brotherton (Louth)
1945	J. McKie (Galloway)	1983	J. Bruce-Gardyne (Knutsford)
1945	C. Cunningham-Reid (St.Marylebone)[b]	1983	R. Mawby (Totnes)
1945	H. Clifton Brown (Newbury)	1983	G. Morgan (Clwyd N.W.)
1950	N. Bower (Harrow, West)	1983	W. Rees-Davies (Thanet North)
1950	C. Challen (Hampstead)	1983	K. Stainton (Sudbury)
1950	A. Marsden (Chertsey)	1987	C. Murphy (Welwyn & Hatfield)
1950	Sir G. Fox (Henley)	1992	Sir A. Meyer (Clwyd N.W.)
1951	E. Gates (Middleton & Prestwich)	1992	J. Browne (Winchester)[b]
1954	Lord M. Douglas Hamilton (Inverness)	1997	H. Booth (Finchley)
1959	N. Nicolson (Bournemouth E.)	1997	W.Churchill (Davyhulme)
1959	Sir F. Medlicott (C. Norfolk)	1997	Dame J. Fookes (Plymouth, Drake)
1959	L. Turner (Oxford)	1997	M. Stephen (Shoreham)
1959	C. Banks (Pudsey)	1997	Sir C. Townsend (Bexleyheath)
1964	M. Lindsay (Solihull)	1997	Sir J. Wheeler (Westminster N.)
1964	O. Prior-Palmer (Worthing)	1997	D. Ashby (Leics.N.W.)
1964	D. Johnson (Carlisle)[b]	1997	Sir N. Scott (Kensington & C.)
1964	J. Henderson (Glasgow, Cathcart)	1997	Sir G. Gardiner (Reigate)[b]
1964	R. Harris (Heston & Isleworth)		

Ulster Unionist

1945	D. Little (Down)[a]	1970	G. Currie (Down, North)
1959	M. Hyde (Belfast N.)		

Labour

1929	N. Maclean (Glasgow,Govan)[a]	1955	J. Glanville (Consett)
1929	E. Davies (Ebbw Vale)	1959	E. Davies (Enfield E.)
1945	T. Groves (West Ham, Stratford)[b]	1964	J. Baird (Wolverhampton N.E.)
1945	H. Charleton (Leeds S.)	1964	W. Warbey (Ashfield)
1950	N. Maclean (Glasgow, Govan)	1970	Margaret McKay (Clapham)
1950	R. Adams (C. Wandsworth)	1970	S. O. Davies (Merthyr)[a]
1951	J. Mack (Newcastle-under-Lyme)	1973	D. Taverne (Lincoln)[a]
1955	J. Kinley (Bootle)	1974	E. Milne (Blyth)[a]

[a] Stood as an Independent and won.
[b] Stood as an Independent and lost.

1974	E. Griffiths (Sheffield, Brightside)[b]
1974	W. Baxter (W. Stirlingshire)
1979	Sir A. Irvine (Liverpool, Edge Hill)[c]
1983	F. Tomney (Hammersmith N.)
1983	J. Barnett (Heywood & Royton)
1983	S. Cohen (Leeds S.E.)
1983	S. C. Davies (Hackney C.)
1983	M. English (Nottingham W.)
1983	B. Ford (Bradford N.)[b]
1983	R. Fletcher (Ilkeston)
1983	F. Hooley (Sheffield, Heeley)
1983	A. Lewis (Newham N.W.)
1983	Helen McElhone (Glasgow, Queens Park)
1983	A. McMahon (Glasgow, Govan)
1983	C. Morris (Manchester Openshaw)
1983	F. Mulley (Sheffield Park)
1983	E. Ogden (Liverpool W. Derby)
1983	R. Race (Tottenham)
1983	J. Sever (Birmingham Ladywood)
1983	A. Stallard (St Pancras N.)
1983	J. Tilley (Lambeth & Vauxhall)
1987	R. Freeson (Brent E.)
1987	M. Maguire (Makerfield)
1987	N. Atkinson (Tottenham)
1987	M. Cocks (Bristol S.)
1987	A. Woodall (Hemsworth)
1987	E. Roberts (Hackney N.)
1987	J. Forrester (Stoke N.)
1992	D. Nellist (Coventry S.E.)[b]
1992	R. Brown (Edinburgh, Leith)[b]
1992	T. Fields (Liverpool Broad Green)[b]
1992	J. Hughes (Coventry N.E.)[b]
1992	S. Bidwell (Southall)
1997	R. Hughes (Aberdeen C.)
1997	M. Madden (Bradford W.)
1997	B. Davies (Oldham C. & Royton)
1997	Mildred Gordon (Bow & Poplar)
1997	N. Spearing (Newham S.)
1997	M. Watson (Glasgow, C.)
1997	J. Dunnachie (Glasgow, Pollok)
1997	J. Fraser (Norwood)
1997	D. Young (Bolton S.E.)

[a] Stood as an Independent and won.
[b] Stood as an Independent and lost.
[c] Died before the next election.

Sources: R.J. Jackson, *Whips and Rebels* (1968); J. Pentney, 'Worms that Turned', *Parliamentary Affairs* (Autumn 1977), pp. 363–73.

By-elections

	Total* By-elections	Changes	Con. +	Con. –	Lib +	Lib –	Lab +	Lab –	Oth. +	Oth. –	No.per Year	%with Change
1900–05	113	30	2	26	20	4	3	–	5	–	22	27
1906–09	101	20	12	–	–	18	5	–	3	2	25	20
1910	20	–	–	–	–	–	–	–	–	–	20	–
1911–18	245	31	16	4	4	16	2	4	10	8	31	13
1918–22	108	27	4	13	5*	11*	14	1	4	2	27	25
1922–23	16	6	1	4	3	1	2	–	–	1	16	38
1923–24	10	3	2	1	–	1	1	1	–	–	10	30
1924–29	63	20	1	16	6	3	13	1	–	–	14	32
1929–31	36	7	4	1	–	1	2	4	1	1	15	19
1931–35	62	10	–	9	–	1	10	–	–	–	15	16
1935–45	219	30	–	29	–	–	13	1	17	–	23	14
1945–50	52	3	3	–	–	–	–	–	–	3	11	6
1950–51	16	–	–	–	–	–	–	–	–	–	10	–
1951–55	48	1	1	–	–	–	–	1	–	–	13	2
1955–59	52	6	1	4	1	1	4	–	–	1	12	12
1959–64	62	9	2	7	1	–	6	2	–	–	15	14
1964–66	13	2	1	1	1	–	–	1	–	–	9	15
1966–70	38	16	12	1	1	–	–	15	3	–	9	42
1970–74	30	9	–	5	5	–	2	3	2	1	9	30
1974	1	–	–	–	–	–	–	–	–	–	1	–
1974–79	30	7	6	–	1	–	–	7	–	–	6	23
1979–83	20	7	1	4	4	–	1	1	1	2	5	35
1983–87	31[a]	6	–	4	4	–	1	1	1	1	8	19
1987–92	23	8	–	7	3	–	4	1	1	–	4	35
1992–97	17	8	–	8	4	–	3	–	1	–	3	47

*Up to 1918, and to a lesser extent to 1926, the number of by-elections is inflated by the necessity for Ministers to stand for re-election on appointment. In 53 such cases the returns were unopposed.

[a] 15 of the 31 by-elections were in N. Ireland. In mainland G.B. there were 16 by-elections – an annual incidence of 4 with a turnover rate of 31%.

Seats Changing Hands at By-elections
* Denotes seats regained at the subsequent General Election

Date	Constituency	General Election	By-election

General Election 28 Sep–24 Oct 1900

Date	Constituency	General Election	By-election
26 Sep 01	N.E. Lanark.	Lib.	Con.
21 Nov 01	Galway	Con.	Nat.
10 May 02	Bury	Con.	Lib.
29 Jul 02	Leeds N.	Con.	Lib.
1 Aug 02	Clitheroe	Lib.	Lab.
18 Aug 02	S. Belfast	Con.	Ind.U.
22 Oct 02	*Devonport	Lib.	Con.
19 Nov 02	Orkney & Shetland	Con.	I.Lib.
2 Jan 03	E. Cambs.	Con.	Lib.
1 Mar 03	Woolwich	Con.	Lab.
17 Mar 03	*E. Sussex	Con.	Lib.
20 Mar 03	*N.Fermanagh	Con.	I.Con.
24 Jul 03	Barnard C.	Lib.	Lab.
26 Aug 03	Argyll	Con.	Lib.
17 Sep 03	St.Andrews	Con.	Lib.
15 Jan 04	Norwich	Con.	Lib.
30 Jan 04	*Ayr	Con.	Lib.
12 Feb 04	*Mid-Herts.	Con.	Lib.
17 Mar 04	E. Dorset	Con.	Lib.
6 Apr 04	I. of Wight	Con.	I.Con.
20 Jun 04	Devonport	{ Con.02 Lib.00	Lib.
26 Jul 04	*W. Salop	Con.	Lib.
10 Aug 04	N.E. Lanark	{ Con.01 Lib.00	Lib.
7 Jan 05	Stalybridge	Con.	Lib.
26 Jan 05	N. Dorset	Con.	Lib.
3 Mar 05	Bute	Con.	Lib.
5 Apr 05	Brighton	Con.	Lib.
1 Jun 05	*Whitby	Con.	Lib.
29 Jun 05	Finsbury E.	Con.	Lib.
13 Oct 05	*Barkston Ash	Con.	Lib.

General Election 12 Jan–7 Feb 06

Date	Constituency	General Election	By-election
3 Aug 06	Cockermouth	Lib.	Con.
31 Dec 06	Mid-Cork	Nat.	I.Nat.
30 Jan 07	N.E.Derbys+	Lib.	Lab.
26 Feb 07	*Brigg	Lib.	Con.
4 Jul 07	*Jarrow	Lib.	Lab.
18 Jul 07	*Colne V.	Lib.	I.Lab.
31 Jul 07	N.W. Staffs+	Lib.	Lab.
17 Jan 08	*Mid-Devon	Lib.	Con.
31 Jan 08	S. Hereford	Lib.	Con.
24 Mar 08	Peckham	Lib.	Con.
24 Apr 08	*Manchester N.W.	Lib.	Con.
20 Jun 08	*Pudsey	Lib.	Con.
1 Aug 08	*Haggerston	Lib.	Con.
24 Sep 08	*Newcastle-on-Tyne	Lib.	Con.
2 Mar 09	Glasgow C.	Lib.	Con.
1 May 09	Cork City	Nat.	I.Nat.
4 May 09	Attercliffe	Lib	Lab.
4 May 09	Stratford-on-Avon	Lib.	Con.
15 Jul 09	Mid-Derbys.	Lib.	Lab.
28 Oct 09	*Bermondsey	Lib.	Con.

General Election 14 Jan–9 Feb 10

Date	Constituency	General Election	By-election
1910	no change		

General Election 2–19 Dec 10

Date	Constituency	General Election	By-election
28 Apr 11	Cheltenham	Lib.	Con.
13 Nov 11	Oldham	Lib.	Con.
21 Nov 11	S. Somerset	Lib.	Con.
20 Dec 11	N. Ayrshire	Lib.	Con.
5 Mar 12	Manchester S.	Lib.	Con.
13 Jul 12	Hanley	Lab.	Lib.
26 Jul 12	Crewe	Lib.	Con.
8 Aug 12	Manchester N.W.	Lib.	Con.
10 Sep 12	Edinburghshire	Lib.	Con.
26 Nov 12	Bow & Bromley	Lab.	Con.
30 Jan 13	Londonderry	Con.	Lib.
18 Mar 13	S. Westmorland	Con.	I.Con.
16 May 13	E. Cambs.	Lib.	Con.
20 Aug 13	Chesterfield	Lab.	Lib.
8 Nov 13	Reading	Lib.	Con.
12 Dec 13	S. Lanarks.	Lib.	Con.
19 Feb 14	Bethnal G.S.W.	Lib.	Con.
26 Feb 14	Leith	Lib.	Con.
20 May 14	N.E. Derbys.	Lab.	Con.
23 May 14	Ipswich	Lib.	Con.
9 Dec 14	Tullamore	Nat.	I.Nat.
25 Nov 15	Merthyr Tydfil	Lab.	Ind.
9 Mar 16	E. Herts	Con.	Ind.
15 Nov 16	W. Cork	I.Nat.	Nat.
23 Dec 16	*Ashton-u-Lyne	Con.	Lib. (Unop.)
23 Dec 16	Sheffield, Attercliffe	Con.	Lib.
3 Feb 17	N. Roscommon	Nat.	S.F.
10 May 17	S. Longford	Nat.	S.F.
10 Jul 17	E. Clare	Nat.	S.F.
10 Aug 17	Kilkenny	Nat.	S.F.
2 Nov 17	Salford N.	Lib.	Lab.
19 Apr 18	Tullamore	{ I.Nat 14 Nat. 10	S.F.
20 Jun 18	E. Cavan	Nat.	S.F.

General Election 14 Dec 18

Date	Constituency	General Election	By-election
1 Mar 19	*Leyton W.	Co.U.	Lib.
29 Mar 19	Hull C.	Co.U.	Lib.
16 Apr 19	C. Aberdeen & Kincardine	Co.U.	Lib.
27 May 19	E. Antrim	Con.	Ind.U.
16 Jul 19	Bothwell	Co.U.	Lab.
30 Aug 19	*Widnes	Co.U.	Lab.
20 Dec 19	Spen Valley	Co.Lib	Lab.
7 Feb 20	Wrekin	Co.Lib	Ind.
27 Mar 20	*Dartford	Co.Lib	Lab.
27 Mar 20	Stockport	Co.Lab	Co.U.
6 Jun 20	Louth	Co.U.	Lib.
27 Jul 20	S. Norfolk	Lib.	Lab.
12 Jan 21	*Dover	Co.U.	Ind.

+ Miners candidates standing as Lib-Lab who only joined the Labour Party in 1909.

Date	Constituency	General Election	By-election
2 Mar 21	*Woolwich E.	Lab.	Co.U.
3 Mar 21	*Dudley	Co.U.	Lab.
4 Mar 21	*Kirkcaldy	Co.Lib	Lab.
5 Mar 21	Penistone	Lib.	Lab.
7 Jun 21	Westminster St George's	Co.U.	Ind.
16 Jun 21	Hertford	Ind.	Ind.
8 Jun 21	*Heywood & Radcliffe	Co.Lib	Lab.
14 Dec 21	*Southwark S.E.	Co.Lib	Lab.
18 Feb 22	*Manchester Clayton	Con.	Lab.
20 Feb 22	Camberwell N.	Co.U.	Lab.
24 Feb 22	Bodmin	Co.U.	Lib.
30 Mar 22	*Leicester E.	Co.Lib	Lab.
25 Jul 22	Pontypridd	Co.Lib	Lab.
18 Aug 22	Hackney S.	Ind.	Co.U.
18 Oct 22	Newport	Co.Lib	Con.

General Election 15 Nov 22

Date	Constituency	General Election	By-election
3 Mar 23	*Mitcham	Con.	Lab.
3 Mar 23	Willesden E.	Con.	Lib.
6 Mar 23	Liverpool, Edge Hill	Con.	Lab.
7 Apr 23	Anglesey	Ind.	Lib.
31 May 23	Berwick on Tweed	Nat.L.	Con.
21 Jun 23	Tiverton	Con.	Lib.

General Election 6 Dec 23

Date	Constituency	General Election	By-election
22 May 24	Liverpool W. Toxteth	Con.	Lab.
5 Jun 24	Oxford	Lib.	Con.
31 Jul 24	Holland w. Boston	Lab.	Con.

General Election 29 Oct 24

Date	Constituency	General Election	By-election
17 Sep 25	Stockport	Con.	Lab.
17 Feb 26	Darlington	Con.	Lab.
12 Mar 26	English U.	Lib.	Con.
29 Apr 26	East Ham N.	Con.	Lab.
28 May 26	Hammersmith N.	Con.	Lab.
29 Nov 26	Hull C.	Lib.	Lab.
23 Feb 27	Stourbridge	Con.	Lab.
28 Mar 27	*Southwark N.	Lab.	Lib.
31 May 27	Bosworth	Con.	Lib.
9 Jan 28	Northampton	Con.	Lab.
9 Feb 28	*Lancaster	Con.	Lib.
6 Mar 28	St Ives	Con.	Lib.
4 Apr 28	Linlithgow	Con.	Lab.
13 Jul 28	Halifax	Lib.	Lab.
29 Oct 28	Ashton-u-Lyne	Con.	Lab.
29 Jan 29	*N.Midlothian	Con.	Lab.
7 Feb 29	Battersea S.	Con.	Lab.
20 Mar 29	Eddisbury	Con.	Lib.
21 Mar 29	*N. Lanark	Con.	Lab.
21 Mar 29	Holland	Con.	Lib.

General Election 30 May 29

Date	Constituency	General Election	By-election
31 Jul 29	Preston	Lib.	Lab.
14 Dec 29	Liverpool, Scotland	I.Nat. (Unop.)	Lab.
6 May 30	Fulham W.	Lab.	Con.
30 Oct 30	Paddington S.	Con.	Ind.
6 Nov 30	Shipley	Lab.	Con.
26 Mar 31	Sunderland	Lab.	Con.
30 Apr 31	Ashton-u-Lyne	Lab.	Con.

General Election 27 Oct 31

Date	Constituency	General Election	By-election
21 Apr 32	Wakefield	Con.	Lab.
26 Jul 32	Wednesbury	Con.	Lab.
27 Feb 33	Rotherham	Con.	Lab.
25 Oct 33	*Fulham E.	Con.	Lab.
24 Apr 34	Hammersmith N	Con.	Lab.
14 May 34	West Ham, Upton	Con.	Lab.
23 Oct 34	Lambeth N.	Lib.	Lab.
25 Oct 34	*Swindon	Con.	Lab.
6 Feb 35	*Liverpool, Wavertree	Con.	Lab.
16 Jul 35	Liverpool, W. Toxteth	Con.	Lab.

General Election 14 Nov 35

Date	Constituency	General Election	By-election
18 Mar 36	Dunbartonshire	Con.	Lab.
6 May 36	Camberwell, Peckham	Con.	Lab.
9 Jul 36	Derby	Con.	Lab.
26 Nov 36	Greenock	Con.	Lab.
27 Feb 37	Oxford Univ.	Con.	I.Con.
19 Mar 37	English Univs.	Con.	Ind.
29 Apr 37	Wandsworth C.	Con.	Lab.
22 Jun 37	Cheltenham	Con.	I.Con.
13 Oct 37	Islington N.	Con.	Lab.
16 Feb 38	Ipswich	Con.	Lab.
6 Apr 38	Fulham W.	Con.	Lab.
5 May 38	Lichfield	Con.	Lab.
7 Nov 38	Dartford	Con.	Lab.
17 Nov 38	Bridgwater	Con.	Ind.
21 Dec 38	Kinross & W. Perth	Con. (Ind.)	Con.
17 May 39	Southwark N.	Con.	Lab.
24 May 39	Lambeth, Kennington	Con.	Lab.
1 Aug 39	Brecon & Radnor	Con.	Lab.
24 Feb 40	Cambridge Univ.	Con.	I.Con.
8 Jun 40	*Newcastle N.	Con.	I.Con.
25 Mar 42	Grantham	Con.	Ind.
29 Apr 42	Rugby	Con.	Ind.
29 Apr 42	*Wallasey	Con.	Ind.
25 Jun 42	Maldon	Con.	Ind.
9 Feb 43	Belfast W.	Un.	Eire Lab.
7 Apr 43	*Eddisbury	Con.	C.W.
7 Jan 44	*Skipton	Con.	C.W.
17 Feb 44	W. Derbyshire	Con.	Ind.
12 Apr 45	*Motherwell	Lab.	S.Nat.

Date	Constituency	General Election	By-election	Date	Constituency	General Election	By-election
13 Apr 45	Scottish Univs.	Con.	Ind.	28 Mar 68	Meriden	Lab.	Con.
26 Apr 45	Chelmsford	Con.	C.W.	28 Mar 68	*Dudley	Lab.	Con.
				13 Jun 68	*Oldham W.	Lab.	Con.
	General Election 5 Jul 45			27 Jun 68	Nelson& Colne	Lab.	Con.
18 Mar 46	English Univs.	Ind.	Con.	27 Mar 69	Walthamstow E	Lab.	Con.
6 Jun 46	Down	Ind.U.	Un.	17 Apr 69	Mid-Ulster	U.U.	Ind.
29 Nov 46	Scottish Univs.	Ind.	Con.	26 Jun 69	*Birmingham	Lab.	Lib.
28 Jan 48	*Glasgow,	I.L.P.	Con.		Ladywood		
	Camlachie			30 Oct 69	*Swindon	Lab.	Con.
				4 Dec 69	Wellingborough	Lab.	Con.
	General Election 23 Feb 50						
					General Election 18 Jun 70		
1950–51	*no change*			27 May 71	*Bromsgrove	Con.	Lab.
				13 Apr 72	Merthyr Tydfil	I.Lab.	Lab.
	General Election 25 Oct 51			26 Oct 72	Rochdale	Lab.	Lib.
13 May 53	Sunderland S.	Lab.	Con.	7 Dec 72	*Sutton & Cheam	Con.	Lib.
				1 Mar 73	Lincoln	Lab.	Dem.Lab.
	General Election 26 May 55			26 Jul 73	Isle of Ely	Con.	Lib.
11 Aug 55	Mid-Ulster	S.F.	Un.	26 Jul 73	*Ripon	Con.	Lib.
8 May 56	Mid-Ulster	S.F.55	I.Un.	8 Nov 73	*Glasgow Govan	Lab.	SNP
		Un.55		8 Nov 73	Berwick on Tweed	Con.	Lib.
14 Feb 57	*Lewisham N.	Con.	Lab.				
28 Feb 57	Carmarthen	Lib.	Lab.		*General Election 28 Feb 74*		
12 Feb 58	Rochdale	Con.	Lab.				
13 Mar 58	*Glasgow,	Con.	Lab.	1974	*no change*		
	Kelvingrove						
27 Mar 58	*Torrington	Con.	Lib.		*General Election 10 Oct 74*		
				26 Jun 75	Woolwich W.	Lab.	Con.
	General Election 8 Oct 59			4 Nov 76	*Walsall N.	Lab.	Con.
17 Mar 60	*Brighouse &	Lab.	Con.	14 Nov 76	*Workington	Lab.	Con.
	Spenborough			31 Mar 77	*Birmingham	Lab.	Con.
4 May 61	*Bristol S.E.[a]	Lab.	Con.		Stechford		
14 Mar 62	Orpington	Con.	Lib.	28 Apr 77	*Ashfield	Lab.	Con.
6 Jun 62	Middlesbrough			2 Mar 78	Ilford N.	Lab.	Con.
	West	Con.	Lab.	29 Mar 79	Liverpool,	Lab.	Lib.
22 Nov 62	Glasgow,	Con.	Lab.		Edge Hill		
	Woodside						
22 Nov 62	*S. Dorset	Con.	Lab.		*General Election 3 May 79*		
23 Aug 63	Bristol S.E.	Lab. 59	Lab.	9 Apr 81	Fermanagh &	Ind.	Anti-H
		Con. 61[a]			S. Tyrone		Block
7 Nov 63	Luton	Con.	Lab.	22 Oct 81	*Croydon N.W.	Con.	Lib.
14 May 64	Rutherglen	Con.	Lab.	26 Nov 81	*Crosby	Con.	SDP
				25 Mar 82	Glasgow, Hillhead	Con.	SDP
	General Election 15 Oct 64			3 Jun 82	Mitcham &	SDP	Con.
21 Jan 65	*Leyton	Lab.	Con.		Morden		
24 Mar 65	Roxburgh Sel.	Con.	Lib.	8 Oct 82	*Birmingham,	Con.	Lab.
	& Peebles				Northfield		
				24 Feb 83	Bermondsey	Lab.	Lib.
	General Election 31 Mar 66						
					General Election 9 June 83		
14 Jul 66	*Carmarthen	Lab.	P.C.	14 Jun 84	*Portsmouth S.	Con.	SDP
9 Mar 67	*Glasgow Pollok	Lab.	Con.	4 Jul 85	Brecon & Radnor	Con.	Lib.
21 Sep 67	*Walthamstow W.	Lab.	Con.	26 Jan 86	Newry & Armagh	U.U.	SDLP
21 Sep 67	Cambridge	Lab.	Con.	4 Apr 86	*Fulham	Con.	Lab.
2 Nov 67	*Hamilton	Lab.	SNP	8 May 86	*Ryedale	Con.	Lib.
2 Nov 67	Leicester S.W.	Lab.	Con.	26 Feb 87	Greenwich	Lab.	SDP
28 Mar 68	*Acton	Lab.	Con.				

[a] Seat awarded to Con. on petition.

Date	Constituency	General Election	By-election	Date	Constituency	General Election	By-election
General Election 11 Jun 87				9 Jun 94	Eastleigh	Con.	Lib.D.
10 Nov 88	*Glasgow, Govan	Lab.	SNP	15 Dec 94	Dudley	Con.	Lab
4 Apr 89	*Vale of Glamorgan	Con.	Lab.	25 May 95	Perth	Con.	S.Nat.
				15 Jun 95	N.Down	UPUP	UKU
22 Mar 90	*Mid Staffs	Con.	Lab.	27 Jul 95	†Littleborough		
16 Mar 91	*Monmouth	Con.	Lab.		& Saddleworth	Con.	Lib.D.
8 Oct 90	*Eastbourne	Con.	Lib.D.	11 Apr 96	Staffs S.E.	Con.	Lab.
7 Mar 91	*Ribble Valley	Con.	Lib.D.	28 Feb 97	Wirral S.	Con.	Lab.
7 Nov 91	*Langbaurgh	Con.	Lab.				
7 Nov 91	*Kincardine & Deeside	Con.	Lib.D.		*General Election 1 May 1997*		
General Election 9 Apr 92							
6 May 93	Newbury	Con.	Lib.D.				
29 Jul 93	*Christchurch	Con.	Lib.D.	†Seat won by Labour in 1997.			

Notable Retention of Seats in By-elections

In addition, there have over the years been a number of by-elections where the seat did not change hands, but which were seen as having great significance at the time. These are outstanding examples:

19 Mar 24	Westminster (Abbey)	The official Conservative defeated the independent (W. Churchill) by 43 votes.
19 Mar 31	Westminster (St George's)	The official Conservative defeated an independent candidate supported by owners of popular newspapers.
27 Oct 38	Oxford	The official Conservative (Q. Hogg) defeated the independent anti-appeasement candidate.
24 Feb 49	Hammersmith South	Labour held on to a marginal seat – the Conservatives' best hope of a win during the post-war Labour government (1945–51).
27 Jan 66	Hull North	Swing of 4.5% to Lab. encouraged govt. to call a general election.
28 Apr 77	Grimsby	Lab. held seat unexpectedly when it was losing safer seats elsewhere.
16 Jul 82	Warrington	Lab. held seat despite enormous swing to newly founded SDP (R. Jenkins).
8 Mar 83	Darlington	Lab. held seat in three-cornered race when defeat could have ended M. Foot's leadership.

M.P.s Resigning to Fight By-elections

The following M.P.s on changing their party, or for other reasons, voluntarily resigned their seats to test public opinion in a by-election:

Date of by-election	M.P.	Constituency	Former label	New label	Whether successful
18 Nov 02	J. Wason	Orkney & Shetland	L.U.	Ind.L.	Yes
6 Apr 04	J. Seely	I. of Wight	Con.	Ind.	Yes (unop.)
19 Aug 04	W. O'Brien	Cork City	Nat.	Nat.	Yes
31 Dec 06	D. Sheehan	Mid-Cork	Nat.	Ind.Nat.	Yes (unop.)
21 Dec 08	C. Dolan	N. Leitrim	Nat.	Ind.Nat.	No
4 May 09	T. Kincaid-Smith	Stratford	Lib.	Ind.	No
26 Nov 12	G. Lansbury	Bow & Bromley	Lab.	Ind.	No

Date of by-election	M.P.	Constituency	Former label	New label	Whether successful
18 Feb 14	W. O'Brien	Cork City	Ind.Nat.	Ind.Nat.	Yes (unop.)
21 Jul 14	R. Hazleton	N. Galway	Nat.	Nat.	Yes (unop.)
29 Nov 26	J. Kenworthy	Hull Central	Lib.	Lab.	Yes
28 Mar 27	L. Guest	Southwark N.	Lab.	Const.	No
31 Jul 29	Sir W. Jowitt	Preston	Lib.	Lab.	Yes
21 Dec 38	D'ss of Atholl	Kinross & W. Perth	Con.	Ind.	No
[a]26 May 55	Sir R. Acland	Gravesend	Lab.	Ind.	No
1 Mar 73	D. Taverne	Lincoln	Lab.	D. Lab.	Yes
3 Jun 82	B. Douglas-Mann	Mitcham & Morden	Lab.	Ind.SDP	No
23 Jan 86	15 M.P.s	N. Ireland	Un.	Un.	14 Yes

[a] Date of General Election which overtook the by-election.

Some members have been compelled to seek re-election because they inadvertently held a government contract or appointment, or because they voted before taking the oath. This last happened in 1925.

Until the *Re-election of Ministers Acts of 1919 and 1926* there were many cases of members having to seek re-election on appointment to ministerial office. In eight instances they were unsuccessful:

5 Apr 05	G. Loder	Brighton
24 Apr 08	W. Churchill	Manchester N.W.
20 Dec 11	A. Anderson	N. Ayrshire
5 Mar 12	Sir A. Haworth	Manchester S.
19 Feb 14	C. Masterman	Bethnal Green S.W.
23 May 14	C. Masterman	Ipswich
3 Mar 21	Sir A. Griffith-Boscawen	Dudley
25 Jul 22	T. Lewis	Pontypridd

The following ministers, defeated in a general election, stayed in office until a subsequent by-election.

Successful in by-election and continued in office		*Defeated in by-election and resigned office*	
Jan 1910	J. Seely	1922	Sir A. Griffith-Boscawen
Jan 1910	J. Pease	1922	J. Hills
Dec 1910	C. Masterman[a]	1922	G. Stanley
1935	R. Macdonald	1965	P. Gordon Walker
1935	M. Macdonald		
1950	Sir F. Soskice		

[a] Unseated on petition Jun 1911 but won by-election Jul 1911.

In 1959 J. Browne, a Scottish Office minister, was defeated in the general election but was given a peerage (Ld Craigton) and stayed in office. In 1983 H. Gray, an energy minister, was defeated in the general election but was given a peerage (Ld Gray of Contin) and stayed in office. In 1992 Lynda Chalker was defeated but was given a peerage and stayed in office.

See also pp.73–4 for Cabinet Ministers defeated while holding office.

Electoral Administration

From 1900 to 1918 electoral arrangements were governed primarily by the *Representation of the People Act, 1867*, as modifed by the *Ballot Act, 1872*, the *Corrupt Practices Act, 1883*, the *Franchise Act, 1884*, the *Registration Act, 1885*, and the *Redistribution of Seats Act, 1885*. The *Representation of the People Act, 1918*, the *Equal Franchise Act, 1928*, the *Representation of the People Act, 1948* (consolidated in 1949), and the *Representation of the People Act, 1969*, constitute the only major legislation in the century.

There have been seven major inquiries into electoral questions:

1908–10	Royal Commission on Electoral Systems
1917	Speaker's Conference on Electoral Reform
1930	Ullswater Conference on Electoral Reform
1943–44	Speaker's Conference on Electoral Reform
1965–68	Speaker's Conference on Electoral Law
1972–74	Speaker's Conference on Electoral Law
1977–78	Speaker's Conference on Electoral Law
1998	Commission on alternative voting systems (Lord Jenkins)

The Franchise. From 1885 the United Kingdom had a system of fairly widespread male franchise, limited however by a year's residence qualification and some other restrictions. Voting in more than one constituency was permitted to owners of land, to occupiers of business premises, and to university graduates. The *Representation of the People Act, 1918*, reduced the residence qualification to six months and enfranchised some categories of men who had not previously had the vote. It also enfranchised women over 30. In 1928 the *Equal Franchise Act* lowered the voting age for women to 21. In 1948 the *Representation of the People Act* abolished the business and university votes for parliamentary elections; it also abolished the six months residence qualification.

In 1969 the *Representation of the People Act* provided votes for everyone as soon as they reached the age of 18.

Electorate

Year	Population	Population over 21	Electorate	Electorate as % of Adult Population[a] Male	Total
1900	41,155,000	22,675,000	6,730,935	58	27
1910	44,915,000	26,134,000	7,694,741	58	28
1919	44,599,000	27,364,000	21,755,583	–	78
1929	46,679,000	31,711,000	28,850,870	–	90
1939	47,762,000	32,855,000	32,403,559	–	97
1949	50,363,000	35,042,000	34,269,770	–	98
1959	52,157,000	35,911,000	35,397,080	–	99
1970	55,700,000	40,784,000[b]	39,153,000	–	96
1979	55,822,000	42,100,000[b]	41,769,000	–	99
1990	57,801,000	45,512,000[b]	43,719,000	–	96
1997	59,000,000	46,428,000[b]	44,204,000	–	95

[a] This percentages makes allowance for plural voting. In the period before 1914 this amounted to about 500,000. After 1918 the business vote reached its peak in 1929 at 370,000. The university electorate rose from 39,101 in 1900 to 217,363 in 1945. See J. Todd and P. Butcher, *Electoral Registration 1981* (1982) and S. Smith, *The Electoral Register, 1991* (1993) for estimates of the efficiency of the registration process.
[b] Population over 18.

Source: For 1990 and 1997, Home Office.

Redistribution. The *Redistribution of Seats Act, 1885*, left the House of Commons with 670 members. The 1885 Act, while removing the worst of the anomalies, specifically rejected the principle that constituencies should be approximately equal in size. This principle was, however, substantially accepted in the *Representation of the People Act, 1918*, on the recommendation of the Speaker's conference of 1917, although Wales, Scotland and Ireland were allowed to retain disproportionate numbers of seats. The 1918 Act increased the size of the House of Commons to 707 but this fell to 615 in 1922 on the creation of the Irish Free State. Population movements produced sustantial anomalies in representation and the *Redistribution of Seats Act, 1944*, authorised the immediate subdivision of constituencies with more than 100,000 electors, which led to 25 new seats being created for the 1945 election and raised the size of Parliament to 640. It also provided for the estabishment of Permanent Boundary Commissioners to report every three to seven years. The Boundary Commissioners' first recommendations were enacted in the *Representation of the People Act, 1948* (with the controversial addition by the Government of 17 extra seats as well as the abolition of the 12 University seats), and the 1950 Parliament had 625 members. The next reports of the Boundary Commissioners, given effect by resolutions of the House in December 1954 and January 1955, increased the number of constituencies to 630. The controversy caused by these changes led to the *Redistribution of Seats Act, 1958*, which modified the rules governing the Boundary Commissioners' decisions and asked them to report only every 10 to 15 years. The Boundary Commissioners started their revision in 1965; they reported in 1969, but the Labour Government secured the temporary rejection of their proposals. In November 1970 the Conservative Government gave effect to the 1969 proposals. The House of Commons elected in 1974 therefore had 635 constituencies. In 1977 the Boundary Commissioners began work on a fresh general revision of boundaries and in February 1978 a Speaker's Conference recommended that the representation of Northern Ireland should be increased from 12 to 17 seats. An Act authorising the Boundary Commissioners to proceed on this basis was passed in March 1979. In 1983 the general revision resulted in a House of Commons of 650. The laws on redistribution were consolidated in the *Parliamentary Constituencies Act, 1986*. In 1992 the number of seats rose to 651 because of an extra seat created to cope with the over-large constituencies around Milton Keynes. In 1991 the Boundary Commissions initiated a further redrawing of boundaries to be completed in 1995; but in 1992 a new *Redistribution Act* required them to report by the end of 1994; it also reduced the maximum interval between reviews from 15 to 12 years. The redistribution of seats, completed in 1996, increased the size of the House to 659.

Election Expenses

Candidates' expenses were restricted by the *Corrupt Practices Act, 1883*, on a formula based on the number of electors. Candidates still had to bear the administrative costs of the election. The *Representation of the People Act, 1918*, removed from the candidates responsibility for the Returning Officers' fees and lowered the maximum limits on expenditure. This limit was further reduced by the *Representation of the People Act, 1948*, and only slightly increased by the *Representation of the People Act, 1969*; in February 1974 the *Representation of the People Act, 1974*, provided a further increase. Since the *Representation of the People Act, 1985*, it has been increased by Orders in Council to keep pace with inflation. In the following table the effect of variations in the number of unopposed candidates should be borne in mind (unopposed candidates seldom spent as much as £200). It is notable how the modifications in the law have kept electioneering costs stable despite a fivefold depreciation in the value of money and a fivefold increase in the size of the electorate.

Candidates' Election Expenses

Year	Total Expenditure	Candidates	Average per Candidate	Con.	Lib.	Lab.
1900	777,429	1,002	776	731	831	419
1906	1,166,858	1,273	917	–	–	–
1910 (Jan)	1,295,782	1,315	985	1,109	1,075	881
1910 (Dec)	978,312	1,191	821	918	882	736
1918	No returns	1,625	–	–	–	–
1922	1,018,196	1,443	706	–	–	540
1923	982,340	1,446	679	845	789	464
1924	921,165	1,428	645	–	–	436
1929	1,213,507	1,730	701	905	782	452
1931	654,105	1,292	506	–	–	–
1935	722,093	1,348	536	777	495	365
1945	1,073,216	1,682	638	780	532	595
1950	1,170,124	1,868	626	777	459	694
1951	946,018	1,376	688	773	488	658
1955	904,677	1,409	642	692	423	611
1959	1,051,219	1,536	684	761	532	705
1964	1,229,205	1,757	699	790	579	751
1966	1,130,882	1,707	667	766	501	726
1970	1,392,796	1,786	761	949	828	667
1974 (Feb)	1,780,542	2,135	951	1,197	745	1,127
1974 (Oct)	2,168,514	2,252	963	1,275	725	1,163
1979	3,557,441	2,576	1,381	2,190	1,013	1,897
1983	6,145,264	2,579	2,383	3,320	2,520	2,927
1987	8,305,721	2,325	3,572	4,400	3,400	3,900
1992	10,443,407	2,948	3,542	5,840	3,169	5,090
1997	12,929,207	3,724	3,471	6,211	3,144	6,011

These figures are based on the official returns from the candidates. What constitutes an election expense is a matter of judgment, particularly since there have been no petitions to test the law on expenses since 1929, although the unsuccessful prosecution of the victorious candidate in Newark (see p.262) threw some light on the subject. Party headquarters have provided separate estimates of the amount spent centrally in general elections. (See also pp.142, 164 and 169.) The whole question of party and election finance came under review by the Neill Committee on Standards in Public Life which reported in October 1998 (Cd.4057/1998).

European Referendum Expenses

In the 1975 Referendum each side was awarded £125,000 from public funds on condition that they published their accounts from 27 Mar 1975 onwards. Britain in Europe, the pro-Market 'umbrella organisation', reported an outlay of £1,481,583. On the other side the National Referendum Campaign reported £131,354. It has been estimated that Britain in Europe actually spent £1,850,000 in all.

Lost Deposits

The *Representation of the People Act, 1918* provided that any parliamentary candidate would have to deposit, on nomination, £150 in cash with the returning officer. This money would be forfeit to the state unless the candidate received one-eighth of the valid votes cast. In 1985 the deposit was raised from £150 to £500 but the condition of forfeiture was lowered from one-eighth to one-twentieth (5%).

	Con.	Lab.	Lib. (Alln.)	Comm.	Other	Total	% of all Candidates
1918	3	6	44	–	108	161	9.9
1922	1	7	31	1	12	52	3.6
1923	–	17	8	–	2	27	1.9
1924	1	28	30	1	8	68	4.7
1929	18	35	5	21	14	113	6.5
1931	–	21	6	21	37	85	6.6
1935	1	16	40	–	24	81	6.0
1945	5	2	76	12	87	182	10.8
1950	5	–	319	97	40	461	24.6
1951	3	1	66	10	16	96	7.0
1955	3	1	60	15	21	100	7.1
1959	2	1	55	17	41	116	7.6
1964	5	8	52	36	85	186	10.6
1966	9	3	104	57	64	237	13.9
1970	10	6	184	58	150	408	22.2
1974 (Feb)	8	25	23	43	222	321	15.0
1974 (Oct)	28	13	125	29	247	442	19.6
1979	3	22	303	38	635	1,001	38.1
1983	5	119	10	35	570	739	28.7
1987	–	–	1	19	288	289	12.4
1992	3[1]	1	11	–	888	903	30.6
1997	7[1]	–	10	–	1576	1593	42.8
Deposits lost in General Elections							
1918–83	110	331	1,561	491	2,383	4,876	14.7
1987–97	10	1	22	19	1,176	2,768	29.9
1918–97	120	332	1,583	510	3,559	7,646	19.9
Deposits lost in By-elections							
1918–85	23	19	94	37	439	612	22.5
1986–97	4	2	11	–	231	248	51.4
All lost deposits							
1918–97	138	353	1,675	547	4,138	8,521	22.0

[1] All in N.Ireland

Women candidates and MPs 1918–1997

	Conservative		Labour		Liberal (Alln.)		Other		Total	
	Cands.	M.P.s	Cands.	M.P.s	Cands.	M.P.s	Cands.	M.P.s	Cands.	M.P.s
1918	1	–	4	–	4	–	8	1	17	1
1922	5	1	10	–	16	1	2	–	33	2
1923	7	3	14	3	12	2	1	–	34	8
1924	12	3	22	1	6	–	1	–	41	4
1929	10	3	30	9	25	1	4	1	69	14
1931	16	13	36	–	6	1	4	1	62	15
1935	19	6	35	1	11	1	2	1	67	9
1945	14	1	45	21	20	1	8	1	87	24
1950	28	6	42	14	45	1	11	–	126	21
1951	29	6	39	11	11	–	–	–	74	17
1955	32	10	43	14	12	–	2	–	89	24
1959	28	12	36	13	16	–	1	–	81	25
1964	24	11	33	18	25	–	8	–	90	29
1966	21	7	30	19	20	–	9	–	80	26
1970	26	15	29	10	23	–	21	1	99	26
1974 (Feb)	33	9	40	13	40	–	30	1	143	23
1974 (Oct)	30	7	50	18	49	–	32	2	161	27
1979	31	8	52	11	51	–	76	–	210	19
1983	40	13	78	10	115	–	87	–	280	23
1987	46	17	92	21	106	2	85	1	329	41
1992	59	20	138	37	144	2	227	1	568	60
1997	66	13	156	102	139	3	311	2	672	120

Election Petitions

There have been 17 instances of election petitions leading to the original result being disallowed by the courts.

Jul 00	Maidstone (bribery by agent)
Jul 00	Monmouth (false expense statement)
Jan 06	Worcester (bribery)
Jan 06	Bodmin (treating by candidate)
Jan 10	E. Dorset (undue influence)
Jan 10	Kerry (intimidation)
Jan 10	Hartlepool (undue influence)
Dec 10	Cheltenham (irregular accounts) (candidate a felon)
Dec 10	E. Cork (treating)
Dec 10	Exeter (disallowed votes)
Dec 10	Hull C. (treating)
Dec 10	N. Louth (irregular accounts)
Dec 10	W. Ham N. (irregular accounts)
Nov 22	Berwick-on-Tweed (false expense return)
Dec 23	Oxford (false expense return)
May 55	Fermanagh and S. Tyrone (candidate a felon)
Aug 55	Mid-Ulster (candidate a felon)
May 61	Bristol S.E. (candidate a peer)

On 19 Oct 50 the House of Commons decided that the seat at West Belfast stood vacant because the successful candidate was ineligible as a minister of the Church of Ireland.

On 20 Jul 55 the House of Commons declared the Mid-Ulster seat vacant because the successful candidate was a felon; the same candidate was re-elected in the ensuing by-election; the defeated Unionist successfully petitioned for the seat as the only eligible candidate. However on 6 Feb 56 the seat was again declared vacant, as the Unionist too was found ineligible through holding an office of profit under the Crown.

Since 1918 there have been only four unsuccessful election petitions: in 1929 by the defeated Conservative candidate in Plymouth, Drake; in 1959 by Sir O. Mosley in Kensington North; in 1992 by Sinn Fein in West Belfast; and in 1997 by the Conservative in Winchester who had lost by two votes.

On 19 Mar 1999 Fiona Jones, MP for Newark, automatically lost her seat on being convicted of presenting fraudulent expense accounts for the 1997 election. On 15 Apr 1999 the conviction was reversed on appeal and on Apr 29 1999 she was reinstated as an M.P.

Sources on Electoral Matters

Official returns, listing candidates' votes and expenses, have been published as Parliamentary Papers about one year after every General Election, except 1918: 1901 (352) lix, 145; 1906 (302) xcvi, 19; 1910 (259) lxxiii, 705; 1911 (272) lxii, 701; 1924 (2) xviii, 681; 1924–5 (151) xviii, 775; 1926 (1) xxii, 523, 1929–30 (114) xxiv, 755; 1931–2 (109) xx, 1; 1935–6 (1 50) xx, 217; 1945–6 (128) xix, 539; 1950 (146) xviii, 311; 1951–2 (210) xxi, 841; 1955 (141) xxxii, 91 3; 1959–60 (173) xxiv, 1031; 1964–5 (220) xxv, 587; 1966–7 (162) liv, 1; 1970–1 (305) xxii, 41; 1974–5 (69); 1974–5 (478) ; 1979–80 (374), 1983–4 (130); 1987–8(426); 1992–3(408);1998–9(260)

More usable returns, identifying candidates by party and supplying supplementary data, are to be found in the following works:

Dod's Parliamentary Companion, Vacher's Parliamentary Companion, and *Whitaker's Almanack,* all issued annually (or more often).

Parliamentary Poll Book, by F. H. McCalmont (7th ed. 1910). This gives all returns from 1832 to 1910 (Jan). In 1971 it was reprinted and updated to 1918.

Pall Mall Gazette House of Commons, issued in paperback form after each election from 1892 to 1910 (Dec).

The Times House of Commons, issued after every election since 1880 except for 1918, 1922, 1923 and 1924.

The Constitutional Year Book, issued annually from 1885 to 1939. Up to 1920 it gives all results from 1885. Up to 1930 it gives the results for all post-1918 contests. Thereafter it records the latest four elections.

The most convenient and reliable source of constituency results, giving percentages as well as absolute figures, is provided by F. W. S. Craig in *British Parliamentary Election Results 1885–1918* (1973), *British Parliamentary Election Results 1918–1949* (1969), *British Parliamentary Election Results 1950–1970* (1971), *Britain Votes III* (1984) and *Europe Votes II* (1985). All by-election results are listed in C. Cook and J. Ramsden (eds.), *By-elections in British Politics* (2nd ed.1997), and in P. Norris, *British By-elections* (1990).

The 1975 Referendum results are set out in Cmnd 6105/1975.

From 1945, the results of each election have been analysed in statistical appendices to the Nuffield College series of studies, R. B. McCallum and Alison Readman, *The British General Election of 1945* (1947), H. G. Nicholas, *The British General Election of 1950* (1951), D. Butler and others, *The British General Election of 1951* (1952), *The British General Election of 1955* (1955), *The British General Election of 1959* (1960), *The British General Election of 1964* (1965), *The British General Election of 1966* (1966), *The British General Election of 1970* (1971), *The British General Election of February 1974* (1974), *The British General Election of October 1974* (1975), *The British General Election of 1979* (1980), *The British General Election of 1983*(1984),*The British General Election of 1987* (1988), *The British General Election of 1992* (1992), *The British General Election of 1997* (1997) and *The 1975 Referendum* (1975). See also A. K. Russell, *Liberal Landslide: The General Election of 1906* (1973) and N. Blewett, *The Peers, the Parties and the People; the General Elections of 1910* (1972). For 1983, 1987 and 1992 see also R. Waller, *The Almanack of British Politics* (6th ed. 1999); I. Crewe and A. Fox, *British Parliamentary Constituencies: A Statistical Compendium* (1984); C. Rallings and M. Thrasher, *Media Studies in the New Parliamentary Constituencies* (1995).

Further data is to be found in D. Butler, *The Electoral System in Britain since 1918* (2nd ed. 1963); J. F. S. Ross *Parliamentary Representation* (2nd ed. 1948) and J. F. S. Ross, *Elections and Electors* (1955); R. Leonard, *Elections in Britain* (2nd ed. 1992); F. W. S. Craig, *British Electoral Facts 1832–1987* (1988); M. Kinnear, *The British Voter 1885–1966* (1968); and H. Pelling, *Social Geography of British Elections 1885–1910* (1967). See also the *Report* of the Royal Commission on Electoral Systems (Cd. 5163/1910; evidence Cd.5352/1910) and the *Report* of the Independent Commission on the Voting System (Cm.4090/98).

Census data arranged on a constituency basis is available in *Census 1966: General and Parliamentary Constituency Tables* (1969), in *Census 1971: General and Parliamentary Constituency Tables* (1974), in *Census 1981: General and Parliamentary Constituency Tables* (1983) and in *Census 1991: General and Parliamentary Constituency Tables* (1994).

The problems of electoral administration are also dealt with in the reports of the Speaker's Conferences on Electoral Reform of 1917, 1944, 1966, 1972–4 and 1977–8 and the Ullswater Conference of 1930 (Cmnd. 8463/1917, Cmnd. 3636/1930, Cmnd. 6534 and 6543/1944, Cmnd. 2917 and 2932/1966, Cmnd. 3202 and 3275/1967, Cmnd. 3550/1968, Cmnd.5363/1973, Cmnd. 5547/1974, (minutes of evidence are available for the 1972–3 and 1977–8 Speaker's Conferences), Cmnd. 7110/1978 and in the reports of the Boundary Commissioners (Cmnd. 7260, 7274, 7270, 7231 of 1947, Cmnd. 9311–4 of 1954 and Cmnd. 4084–7 of 1969). See also H. L. Morris, *Parliamentary Franchise Reform in England from 1885 to 1918* (New York 1921), D. E. Butler, 'The Redistribution of Seats', *Public Administration*, Summer 1955, pp. 125–47, and F. W. S. Craig, *Boundaries of Parliamentary Constituencies 1885–1972* (1972). See also I. McLean and D. Butler, *Fixing the Boundaries* (1995) and D. Rossiter et al., *The Boundary Commissions: Redrawing the UK's Map of Parliamentary Constituencies* (1999).

Public Opinion Polls

Gallup Poll

The British Institute of Public Opinion was established in 1937. Its name was changed in 1952 to Social Surveys (Gallup Poll) Ltd. Since 1995 it has been known as the Gallup Organisation. Its poll findings were published exclusively in the *News Chronicle* until October 1960. Since 1961 its findings have been published regularly in the *Daily Telegraph* and the *Sunday Telegraph*. As the years advanced, its questions on politics became increasingly systematic and detailed. Some of its early findings are collected in *Public Opinion, 1935–1946*, edited by H. Cantril (1951). Others may be found in the *News Chronicle*, in occasional pamphlets, in *The Gallup International Public Opinion Polls: Great Britain 1937–75*, and in the monthly *Gallup Political Index* available since 1960 from Social Surveys (Gallup Poll) Ltd. It is now based at Drapers Court, Kingston Hill Rd, Kingston, Surrey KT1 2BG.

National Opinion Polls (NOP)

National Opinion Polls were established in 1957 as an affiliate of Associated Newspapers Ltd. and political findings were published in the *Daily Mail* intermittently until 1961 and then regularly until 1979. In 1979 Associated Newspapers sold NOP to MAI; MAI merged NOP with another research company under the name MAI Research. Political polls continue to be published under the NOP name, published intermittently by the *Daily Mail* and the *Mail on Sunday* and later by the *Independent* and the BBC. In 1998 they polled for the *Sunday Times*. Findings from the regular political surveys and from other ad hoc political opinion polls were published in the bi-monthly *N.O.P. Social Political and Economic Review* until 1992. NOP is now based at Ludgate House, 245 Blackfriars Road, London SE1 9UL (www.nop.co.uk).

Marplan Ltd/ICM Research

Marplan (present address 5–13 Great Suffolk Street, London S.E.1) was founded in 1959 as a subsidiary of Interpublic and later of Research International. It published opinion polls for various newspapers from 1962 onwards. Since 1980 its polls have been reported regularly in the *Guardian*. In 1989 its principal political researchers left to form ICM Research. ICM Research is now based at Knighton House, 56 Mortimer St, London W1N 7DG (www.icmresearch.co.uk).

Opinion Research Centre (ORC)

The Opinion Research Centre was founded in 1965. It has conducted private polls for the Conservative Party ever since. It published a regular monthly poll in the *Evening Standard* and other newspapers from 1967 to 1976. It merged with Louis Harris in 1983 to form the Harris Research Centre.

Louis Harris Research Ltd./Harris Research Centre

In 1969 the *Daily Express* abandoned the poll which, since the 1940s, it had run from within its own office and joined with the Opinion Research Centre and the American expert Louis Harris in setting up an independent new polling organisation, Louis Harris Research Ltd. In 1972 the *Daily Express* sold its shares. Louis Harris Research Ltd and the Opinion Research Centre share a single Managing Director, and merged with Opinion Research Centre in 1983 to form the Harris Research Centre. In 1994 it was bought by the French research company SOFRES, now merged with Taylor Nelson AGB. In addition to continuing to carry out private polling for the Conservative Party, it also published polls in the *Observer* and for London Weekend Television's current affairs programmes. In 1997 it polled for the *Independent*. The Harris Research Centre is now based at Holbrooke House, 34–38 Hill Rise, Richmond, Surrey.

Market & Opinion Research International (MORI)

MORI, under the chairmanship of Robert Worcester, conducted extensive political surveys from 1969, including private studies for the Labour Party. From 1978 it published regular polls in the *(Evening) Standard* and the *Sunday Times,* as well as occasional polls for *The Times, Daily Express* and *Daily Star,* the *Scotsman, The Economist* and the B.B.C. Since 1993, it has published regular polls for *The Times.*

MORI is now based at 32 Old Queen Street, London SW1H 9HP (www.mori.com.)

Voting Intentions

In the 1990s there were three regularly published monthly series of poll findings on voting intention; Gallup in the *Daily Telegraph,* ICM in the *Guardian* and MORI in *The Times.*

The Gallup series is much the oldest (although it did switch to telephone polling in 1997). The following tables show in summary form the answers to the Gallup Poll question 'If there were a General Election tomorrow, how would you vote?' and to questions about approval of the government's record, approval of the Prime Minister and of the Leader of the Opposition, as well as answers to the Party fortunes question, 'Regardless of how you are going to vote yourself, which party do you think is most likely to win?'

Voting Intentions (Gallup Poll)

	Government %	Opposition %	Don't Know %
1939 Feb	54	30	16
1940 Feb	51	27	22

Gallup Poll Findings

		Voting Intention				Approve Govt Record %	Approve P.M. %	Approve Opposition Leader %	Party thought likely to win	
		Con. %	Lab. %	Lib. %	Other %				Con. %	Lab. %
1945	Jan	–	–	–	–	–	–	–	–	–
	Feb	27	47	12	12	–	–	–	22	33
	Mar	–	–	–	–	–	–	–	–	–
	Apr	28	47	14	11	–	–	–	–	–
	May	–	–	–	–	–	–	–	–	–
	Jun	32	45	15	8	–	–	–	–	–
	Jul	–	–	–	–	–	–	–	–	–
	Aug	–	–	–	–	–	66	–	–	–
	Sep	–	–	–	–	–	–	–	–	–
	Oct	–	–	–	–	57	–	–	–	–
	Nov	–	–	–	–	–	–	–	–	–
	Dec	–	–	–	–	–	–	–	–	–

OPINION POLLS

Gallup Poll Findings

		Voting Intention				Approve Govt Record %	Approve P.M. %	Approve Opposition Leader %	Party thought likely to win	
		Con. %	Lab. %	Lib. %	Other %				Con. %	Lab. %
1946	Jan	32	52	11	4	–	–	–	–	–
	Feb	–	–	–	–	–	–	–	–	–
	Mar	–	–	–	–	–	–	–	–	–
	Apr	–	–	–	–	–	–	–	–	–
	May	40	43	13	3	–	–	–	–	–
	Jun	–	–	–	–	42	–	–	–	–
	Jul	–	–	–	–	42	–	–	–	–
	Aug	–	–	–	–	46	–	–	–	–
	Sep	–	–	–	–	–	–	–	–	–
	Oct	–	–	–	44	53	–	–	–	–
	Nov	–	–	–	–	–	–	–	–	–
	Dec	–	–	–	–	43	52	–	–	–
1947	Jan	41	44	12	2	–	–	–	–	–
	Feb	–	–	–	–	–	–	–	–	–
	Mar	43	43	10	2	39	46	–	–	–
	Apr	–	–	–	–	–	–	–	–	–
	May	–	–	–	–	–	51	–	–	–
	Jun	42	42	12	2	42	–	–	–	–
	Jul	42	42	12	2	38	51	–	32	46
	Aug	44	41	11	3	–	–	–	–	–
	Sep	44	39	11	4	–	–	–	–	–
	Oct	–	–	–	–	36	41	–	–	–
	Nov	50.5	38	9	2	–	–	–	–	–
	Dec	–	–	–	–	41	44	–	–	–
1948	Jan	44	43	10	1	44	45	–	–	–
	Feb	46	42	8	3	–	–	–	–	–
	Mar	46	43	8	2	35	39	–	–	–
	Apr	42	41	10	6	–	–	–	–	–
	May	45	41	11	2	–	–	–	–	–
	Jun	–	–	–	–	–	–	–	–	–
	Jul	48	39	9	3	36	40	–	36	42
	Aug	48	41	8	2	–	–	–	–	–
	Sep	47	41	10	1	37	37	–	–	–
	Oct	46	41	9	2	–	–	–	–	–
	Nov	46	43	8	2	43	45	–	–	–
	Dec	–	–	–	–	–	–	–	–	–
1949	Jan	44	40	13	2	44	45	–	–	–
	Feb	44	43	9	2	–	–	–	–	–
	Mar	41	43	13	2	46	47	–	–	–
	Apr	42	43	13	1	–	–	–	–	–
	May	46	40	11	3	37	44	–	–	–
	Jun	46	41	10	2	–	–	–	–	–
	Jul	44	40	12	2	39	46	–	–	–
	Aug	46	40	11	1	–	–	–	–	–
	Sep	46	40	12	2	36	45	–	30	46
	Oct	45	39	12	2	–	–	–	–	–
	Nov	43	40	14	2	39	43	–	–	–
	Dec	45	41	12	1	–	–	–	–	–

Gallup Poll Findings

		Voting Intention			Approve Govt Record	Approve P.M.	Approve Opposition Leader	Party thought likely to win	
		Con. %	Lab. %	Lib. %	Other %	%	%	%	Con. %	Lab. %
1950	Jan	44	41	12	2	41	44	–	–	–
	Feb	43	44	12	–	–	–	–	20	40
	Mar	43	45	8	2	–	–	–	–	–
	Apr	45	47	7	–	–	–	–	–	–
	May	43	46	9	–	41	50	–	–	–
	Jun	43	46	9	1	–	–	–	–	–
	Jul	42	43	11	3	–	–	–	–	–
	Aug	44	46	8	1	44	49	–	–	–
	Sep	43	45	10	1	–	–	–	–	–
	Oct	42	45	10	2	45	47	–	–	–
	Nov	–	–	–	–	–	–	–	–	–
	Dec	43	44	11	1	38	49	–	–	–
1951	Jan	51	38	10	1	–	–	–	–	–
	Feb	51	37	9	1	31	44	–	–	–
	Mar	51	36	10	2	–	–	–	–	–
	Apr	50	38	9	2	32	49	–	–	–
	May	49	40	9	1	35	57	–	–	–
	Jun	48	41	10	1	–	–	–	–	–
	Jul	49	39	10	–	31	43	–	–	–
	Aug	50	38	10	1	–	–	–	45	32
	Sep	52	41	6	–	35	44	–	44	30
	Oct	50	44	4	1	–	–	–	45	29
	Nov	–	–	–	–	–	–	–	–	–
	Dec	47	45	6	1	44	55	–	–	–
1952	Jan	44	48	6	1	–	–	–	–	–
	Feb	41	47	10	1	44	53	–	–	–
	Mar	41	48	9	1	–	–	–	–	–
	Apr	–	–	–	–	–	–	–	–	–
	May	43	49	7	–	40	51	–	–	–
	Jun	40	49	9	1	–	–	–	16	63
	Jul	40	50	8	1	–	–	–	–	–
	Aug	40	48	6	5	–	–	–	–	–
	Sep	41	48	9	1	44	48	–	25	55
	Oct	41	48	9	1	–	–	–	–	–
	Nov	43	46	9	1	47	51	–	–	–
	Dec	44	45	9	1	51	–	–	–	–
1953	Jan	42	46	10	1	46	51	–	–	–
	Feb	42	46	10	1	–	–	–	–	–
	Mar	46	44	8	1	–	–	–	–	–
	Apr	47	45	7	–	60	–	–	–	–
	May	47	45	7	–	–	–	–	38	40
	Jun	46	46	7	1	–	–	–	–	–
	Jul	–	–	–	–	–	–	–	–	–
	Aug	45	46	8	1	49	–	–	–	–
	Sep	44	47	7	1	–	–	–	43	35
	Oct	45	45	7	–	54	56	–	–	–
	Nov	–	–	–	–	–	–	–	–	–
	Dec	45	47	7	1	–	–	–	–	–

OPINION POLLS

Gallup Poll Findings

		Voting Intention				Approve Govt Record %	Approve P.M. %	Approve Opposition Leader %	Party thought likely to win	
		Con. %	Lab. %	Lib. %	Other %				Con. %	Lab. %
1954	Jan	45	46	7	1	50	–	–	–	–
	Feb	45	47	7	–	50	–	–	36	34
	Mar	46	45	7	1	–	–	–	–	–
	Apr	46	46	7	–	–	48	–	–	–
	May	45	47	6	–	–	–	–	–	–
	Jun	45	47	7	–	47	–	–	–	–
	Jul	–	–	–	–	–	–	–	–	–
	Aug	42	48	8	1	–	–	–	–	–
	Sep	43	48	8	1	–	–	–	33	39
	Oct	45	45	8	1	–	–	–	–	–
	Nov	46	47	6	1	–	–	–	34	26
	Dec	49	49	2	–	–	–	–	–	–
1955	Jan	46	45	7	1	53	52	–	–	–
	Feb	46	44	8	1	–	–	–	–	–
	Mar	46	44	8	1	–	–	–	–	–
	Apr	48	44	7	1	–	73	–	52	22
	May	51	47	2	–	57	71	–	54	18
	Jun	–	–	–	–	–	–	–	–	–
	Jul	47	43	9	1	–	68	–	–	–
	Aug	44	47	7	1	–	–	–	–	–
	Sep	48	44	7	1	–	70	–	–	–
	Oct	46	44	8	1	–	63	–	–	–
	Nov	44	45	9	1	–	61	–	–	–
	Dec	45	46	7	–	44	60	–	–	–
1956	Jan	45	46	7	–	–	–	–	–	–
	Feb	44	46	9	1	–	50	–	–	–
	Mar	44	47	7	1	34	45	–	–	–
	Apr	43	48	8	1	–	41	–	–	–
	May	43	47	9	1	40	54	42	–	–
	Jun	–	–	–	–	–	–	–	–	–
	Jul	42	49	8	1	36	50	46	–	–
	Aug	43	49	6	1	–	–	–	–	–
	Sep	43	46	10	–	–	51	53	–	–
	Oct	42	47	9	1	–	47	–	–	–
	Nov	45	46	8	–	–	52	44	–	–
	Dec	45	46	8	1	–	56	–	–	–
1957	Jan	43	48	7	1	–	50	–	–	–
	Feb	42	48	8	1	–	–	–	–	–
	Mar	40	51	7	1	–	45	–	–	–
	Apr	41	51	7	1	–	44	–	–	–
	May	41	50	7	1	–	54	41	–	–
	Jun	–	–	–	–	–	–	–	–	–
	Jul	41	49	8	1	–	–	–	–	–
	Aug	40	48	10	1	–	–	–	–	–
	Sep	33	52	14	–	–	44	39	24	51
	Oct	37	49	13	1	37	30	–	–	–
	Nov	38	49	12	–	–	39	–	–	–
	Dec	41	47	9	1	–	–	–	26	46

Gallup Poll Findings

		Voting Intention				Approve Govt Record	Approve P.M.	Approve Opposition Leader	Party thought likely to win	
		Con. %	Lab. %	Lib. %	Other %	%	%	%	Con. %	Lab. %
1958	Jan	40	47	12	–	38	46	40	–	–
	Feb	36	44	18	1	–	35	–	–	–
	Mar	–	–	–	–	–	–	–	–	–
	Apr	38	46	15	–	30	37	–	–	–
	May	34	47	19	–	30	37	–	–	–
	Jun	39	43	17	–	40	50	–	–	–
	Jul	–	–	–	–	41	–	37	–	–
	Aug	42	42	15	–	41	53	–	40	31
	Sep	44	43	13	–	43	55	32	–	–
	Oct	45	41	12	1	47	57	41	44	29
	Nov	46	42	10	1	48	55	42	–	–
	Dec	47	42	9	1	50	55	45	43	28
1959	Jan	45	45	8	1	48	53	47	39	28
	Feb	43	47	8	1	41	54	43	–	–
	Mar	45	47	6	1	44	57	46	–	–
	Apr	44	44	10	1	46	60	48	–	–
	May	45	44	10	1	47	62	47	–	–
	Jun	45	43	11	–	49	58	44	–	–
	Jul	45	41	12	–	53	62	42	–	–
	Aug	47	41	10	1	56	67	46	–	–
	Sep	50	43	5	–	–	–	–	56	20
	Oct	48	46	5	1	–	–	–	51	21
	Nov	48	44	7	1	–	–	–	–	–
	Dec	47	44	7	1	–	–	–	–	–
1960	Jan	47	43	8	1	–	–	–	–	–
	Feb	47	43	9	–	–	64	43	–	–
	Mar	47	42	10	1	–	57	40	–	–
	Apr	45	42	11	1	–	56	46	–	–
	May	45	42	11	1	–	79	47	–	–
	Jun	45	43	10	1	–	70	56	–	–
	Jul	47	43	9	1	–	65	43	–	–
	Aug	47	42	10	–	59	72	48	–	–
	Sep	47	40	11	1	59	74	43	–	–
	Oct	50	37	12	–	59	72	48	–	–
	Nov	46	40	13	–	56	69	44	–	–
	Dec	47	37	14	1	–	–	–	–	–
1961	Jan	45	41	12	1	59	72	35	–	–
	Feb	44	42	13	1	48	64	45	–	–
	Mar	44	40	15	1	51	63	45	–	–
	Apr	43	40	15	1	50	64	43	–	–
	May	44	40	14	1	49	58	45	–	–
	Jun	43	40	15	1	52	58	45	–	–
	Jul	44	41	14	–	49	54	51	–	–
	Aug	38	43	17	2	38	45	47	–	–
	Sep	40	45	13	1	39	43	46	–	–
	Oct	43	43	12	1	47	55	57	–	–
	Nov	41	43	14	1	43	54	42	–	–
	Dec	38	43	17	1	–	–	–	–	–

OPINION POLLS

Gallup Poll Findings

		Voting Intention				Approve Govt Record	Approve P.M.	Approve Opposition Leader	Party thought likely to win	
		Con. %	Lab. %	Lib. %	Other %	%	%	%	Con. %	Lab. %
1962	Jan	42	42	15	1	43	53	50	–	–
	Feb	40	42	17	–	41	48	45	51	23
	Mar	39	44	16	–	41	50	50	41	17
	Apr	33	41	25	1	37	46	48	–	–
	May	34	39	25	–	38	47	48	36	36
	Jun	35	39	25	–	37	46	48	31	42
	Jul	35	41	22	1	41	47	47	28	42
	Aug	34	43	22	1	37	42	47	–	–
	Sep	34	45	20	1	38	42	51	30	39
	Oct	34	43	20	2	36	43	54	37	37
	Nov	39	47	13	1	41	47	51	29	42
	Dec	37	46	16	1	36	41	52	–	–
1963	Jan	35	48	16	–	34	42	49	–	–
	Feb	32	48	18	1	34	40	–	–	–
	Mar	33	50	15	1	30	35	44	26	52
	Apr	34	49	16	–	33	35	52	24	55
	May	36	47	16	1	38	41	53	25	57
	Jun	31	51	16	1	31	35	54	17	58
	Jul	33	51	14	1	32	37	57	16	68
	Aug	34	50	15	1	39	42	59	22	55
	Sep	33	49	16	1	38	40	56	23	55
	Oct	36	48	14	1	36	41	60	23	55
	Nov	37	49	12	1	44	42	67	30	53
	Dec	39	47	13	–	46	48	65	28	48
1964	Jan	39	47	13	–	41	43	63	29	45
	Feb	39	48	12	1	42	42	62	27	57
	Mar	39	48	12	–	41	44	64	31	47
	Apr	38	50	10	–	46	44	61	23	58
	May	39	50	10	–	41	44	62	21	65
	Jun	41	50	8	–	45	44	62	22	61
	Jul	40	49	9	–	43	46	56	26	56
	Aug	43	49	7	–	48	46	61	32	48
	Sep	44	47	8	–	42	47	58	41	38
	Oct	44	46	8	3	–	–	35	39	–
	Nov	38	50	11	–	49	60	39	–	–
	Dec	40	50	9	–	48	64	41	–	–
1965	Jan	42	46	10	–	39	56	38	27	46
	Feb	45	45	9	–	43	60	37	49	28
	Mar	43	46	9	1	47	58	38	41	34
	Apr	39	47	12	–	45	63	34	41	38
	May	44	43	12	–	39	56	36	40	34
	Jun	47	42	9	1	35	48	36	52	23
	Jul	46	45	8	–	36	51	32	44	30
	Aug	49	41	8	1	39	50	51	57	24
	Sep	42	48	8	1	42	54	49	56	24
	Oct	41	49	9	–	49	61	47	39	39
	Nov	42	48	8	1	50	65	48	35	44
	Dec	40	48	10	1	55	66	43	35	46

Gallup Poll Findings

		Voting Intention			Approve Govt Record	Approve P.M.	Approve Opposition Leader	Party thought likely to win	
		Con. %	Lab. %	Lib. %	Other %	%	%	%	Con. %	Lab. %
1966	Jan	42	47	9	1	51	65	48	32	42
	Feb	42	50	7	–	48	60	40	20	62
	Mar	40	51	8	1	–	–	–	11	69
	Apr	–	–	–	–	53	63	39	–	–
	May	35	53	10	1	54	69	44	–	–
	Jun	39	52	7	1	44	58	33	27	48
	Jul	41	48	8	2	42	61	33	25	55
	Aug	44	44	10	1	35	52	32	39	41
	Sep	42	45	11	1	34	49	37	37	37
	Oct	43	44	11	1	32	43	46	37	35
	Nov	44	42	12	1	33	46	32	41	34
	Dec	42	46	10	1	40	51	35	–	–
1967	Jan	42	45	10	1	40	51	29	–	–
	Feb	37	48	13	1	44	57	24	–	–
	Mar	42	42	12	2	40	53	26	–	–
	Apr	45	41	11	2	44	42	33	–	–
	May	46	40	12	1	38	43	35	–	–
	Jun	48	41	9	1	36	46	37	–	–
	Jul	43	41	13	2	35	48	32	–	–
	Aug	43	42	13	2	33	45	28	–	–
	Sep	45	41	10	3	29	40	31	–	–
	Oct	45	38	14	3	–	38	39	56	19
	Nov	46	36	11	6	28	41	44	62	13
	Dec	49	32	12	6	21	34	37	–	–
1968	Jan	45	39	11	4	23	33	32	–	–
	Feb	52	30	12	5	22	36	31	–	–
	Mar	50	31	15	4	18	35	29	–	–
	Apr	54	30	12	3	17	31	28	78	7
	May	56	28	11	5	19	27	31	73	11
	Jun	51	28	14	6	19	28	28	–	–
	Jul	50	30	13	7	18	30	28	76	13
	Aug	49	34	11	4	21	30	27	–	–
	Sep	47	37	11	4	24	33	27	–	–
	Oct	47	39	9	4	29	38	27	55	25
	Nov	50	32	14	3	20	31	37	–	–
	Dec	55	29	11	4	17	28	30	–	–
1969	Jan	53	31	11	4	23	34	31	–	–
	Feb	54	32	11	2	22	32	34	–	–
	Mar	52	34	10	3	22	35	31	–	–
	Apr	51	30	13	5	21	30	29	–	–
	May	52	30	13	4	19	29	28	76	9
	Jun	51	35	12	2	24	35	29	–	–
	Jul	55	31	11	2	23	30	40	–	–
	Aug	47	34	15	3	25	26	29	–	–
	Sep	46	37	13	3	29	39	29	–	–
	Oct	46	44	7	2	34	43	33	46	33
	Nov	45	41	10	3	35	41	33	48	31
	Dec	50	39	9	1	31	38	32	54	26

OPINION POLLS

Gallup Poll Findings

		Voting Intention				Approve Govt Record %	Approve P.M. %	Approve Opposition Leader %	Party thought likely to win	
		Con. %	Lab. %	Lib. %	Other %				Con. %	Lab. %
1970	Jan	48	41	7	3	32	42	38	54	25
	Feb	48	41	9	2	31	42	41	53	24
	Mar	46	41	9	3	35	42	39	54	27
	Apr	47	42	7	3	40	45	34	47	31
	May	42	49	7	1	42	49	28	26	56
	Jun	42	49	7	1	40	51	28	13	68
	Jul	–	–	–	–	–	–	–	–	–
	Aug	47	43	7	2	–	–	–	–	–
	Sep	46	44	8	1	21	35	59	–	–
	Oct	46	46	6	–	29	42	62	–	–
	Nov	43	48	6	2	31	39	66	–	–
	Dec	46	44	6	3	37	45	59	–	–
1971	Jan	42	47	8	2	35	41	61	–	–
	Feb	41	49	8	1	31	37	61	–	–
	Mar	38	50	8	3	33	38	59	–	–
	Apr	44	48	6	1	40	43	57	–	–
	May	38	50	9	2	31	35	61	–	–
	Jun	36	54	8	2	22	31	58	–	–
	Jul	33	55	8	3	36	32	58	–	–
	Aug	42	46	7	2	35	37	51	–	–
	Sep	35	54	8	2	30	32	57	–	–
	Oct	40	50	8	2	32	35	54	–	–
	Nov	42	48	7	2	35	38	52	–	–
	Dec	42	48	7	2	34	39	54	–	–
1972	Jan	40	48	9	2	37	39	54	–	–
	Feb	40	49	8	2	34	37	53	23	57
	Mar	39	48	9	2	35	36	51	–	–
	Apr	43	44	10	2	43	41	39	–	–
	May	40	46	11	2	36	39	45	35	40
	Jun	41	47	10	2	36	40	44	–	–
	Jul	39	49	9	2	31	35	45	–	–
	Aug	40	49	7	3	32	35	47	25	56
	Sep	38	49	9	2	30	33	43	23	57
	Oct	40	48	8	3	33	34	53	28	53
	Nov	37	45	15	2	32	37	50	28	52
	Dec	38	46	12	3	36	39	44	32	42
1973	Jan	38	44	15	2	33	38	40	31	46
	Feb	38	47	12	2	33	37	45	46	–
	Mar	39	43	16	2	38	41	41	–	–
	Apr	38	41	17	3	32	37	41	26	50
	May	38	43	14	4	35	38	40	26	51
	Jun	41	42	14	2	37	43	41	34	47
	Jul	35	45	17	2	31	37	45	22	55
	Aug	31	38	28	2	29	34	39	26	47
	Sep	33	43	22	1	29	36	42	23	51
	Oct	33	39	25	2	30	36	46	29	47
	Nov	36	38	22	2	31	39	37	35	36
	Dec	36	42	18	3	34	37	31	43	–

Gallup Poll Findings

		Voting Intention				Approve Govt Record	Approve P.M.	Approve Opposition Leader	Party thought likely to win	
		Con. %	Lab. %	Lib. %	Other %	%	%	%	Con. %	Lab. %
1974	Jan	40	38	19	3	36	39	38	40	35
	Feb	39	37	20	2	32	38	38	60	20
	Mar	35	43	19	3	–	–	–	–	–
	Apr	33	49	15	2	48	53	38	19	52
	May	33	46	17	3	40	50	35	26	48
	Jun	35	44	17	3	41	49	36	25	51
	Jul	35	38	21	6	32	41	33	32	36
	Aug	35	30	21	4	37	44	35	27	44
	Sep	37	40	18	4	28	41	29	18	55
	Oct	36	41	19	3	37	45	32	18	55
	Nov	35	46	14	4	40	50	32	–	–
	Dec	33	47	16	3	42	51	31	–	–
1975	Jan	34	48	13	4	37	49	29	–	–
	Feb	45	41	11	3	32	47	64	–	–
	Mar	42	44	11	3	37	51	60	–	–
	Apr	43	45	10	2	32	44	45	–	–
	May	45	39	11	4	26	40	41	45	29
	Jun	44	40	13	2	31	46	35	44	29
	Jul	43	40	12	4	27	46	37	46	28
	Aug	40	42	14	3	32	45	37	46	30
	Sep	38	41	16	3	30	45	39	44	29
	Oct	42	40	13	3	30	46	45	45	32
	Nov	39	44	12	4	31	45	42	43	35
	Dec	40	41	14	4	27	40	40	45	29
1976	Jan	40	42	14	3	29	42	42	45	32
	Feb	45	40	10	3	32	45	49	46	30
	Mar	44	41	9	5	30	46	43	49	30
	Apr	41	46	9	3	39	57	40	44	37
	May	44	41	10	4	32	43	36	51	28
	Jun	44	40	11	4	28	36	31	48	29
	Jul	41	41	13	5	32	46	33	44	32
	Aug	44	41	10	5	29	44	33	45	33
	Sep	42	42	11	4	29	46	40	44	34
	Oct	48	36	11	4	20	36	40	57	20
	Nov	55	30	11	3	19	33	41	66	18
	Dec	49	34	11	5	18	35	34	62	17
1977	Jan	47	34	14	4	21	37	39	57	21
	Feb	46	33	14	6	21	36	35	62	18
	Mar	49	33	13	4	22	37	35	62	20
	Apr	49	33	11	6	23	38	40	67	16
	May	53	33	8	5	23	43	45	74	12
	Jun	47	37	10	5	28	44	44	69	15
	Jul	49	34	10	6	24	45	42	71	13
	Aug	48	37	9	5	33	43	45	64	19
	Sep	45	41	8	5	32	49	47	54	28
	Oct	45	45	8	2	41	59	49	49	31
	Nov	45	42	8	4	41	55	47	46	35
	Dec	44	44	8	3	41	53	44	48	32

OPINION POLLS

Gallup Poll Findings

		Voting Intention				Approve Govt Record	Approve P.M.	Approve Opposition Leader	Party thought likely to win	
		Con. %	Lab. %	Lib.* %	Other %	%	%	%	Con. %	Lab. %
1978	Jan	43	43	8	4	43	57	42	46	38
	Feb	48	39	9	4	43	54	41	40	40
	Mar	48	41	8	3	41	51	45	52	30
	Apr	45	43	7	3	44	51	39	45	38
	May	43	43	8	4	41	54	40	48	33
	Jun	45	45	6	3	40	50	38	39	43
	Jul	45	43	8	3	40	52	38	40	42
	Aug	43	47	6	3	30	55	35	42	36
	Sep	49	42	6	2	39	51	40	42	36
	Oct	42	47	7	3	44	56	39	47	35
	Nov	43	48	6	3	44	54	33	36	41
	Dec	48	42	6	3	37	53	39	41	40
1979	Jan	49	41	6	3	34	48	38	44	35
	Feb	53	33	11	3	23	33	48	65	20
	Mar	51	37	8	3	27	39	47	61	23
	Apr	50	40	8	2	33	43	43	59	23
	May	43	41	13	2	–	–	–	–	–
	Jun	42	43	12	2	34	41	63	–	–
	Jul	41	46	11	1	34	41	61	–	–
	Aug	41	44	12	2	38	45	57	–	–
	Sep	40	45	12	2	36	45	53	–	–
	Oct	40	45	12	2	34	46	57	–	–
	Nov	39	43	15	2	38	44	55	–	–
	Dec	38	42	18	2	34	40	53	28	44
1980	Jan	36	45	16	3	33	39	53	29	45
	Feb	37	42	18	2	30	37	50	29	45
	Mar	37	49	11	2	30	38	53	27	55
	Apr	36	45	15	3	36	41	55	25	52
	May	39	43	15	2	37	44	51	24	57
	Jun	40	45	11	3	35	43	48	28	54
	Jul	40	43	14	2	33	41	46	28	55
	Aug	38	44	14	3	35	41	53	28	50
	Sep	35	45	16	3	29	37	48	22	58
	Oct	40	43	13	3	30	38	48	30	53
	Nov	36	47	15	1	29	34	38	22	60
	Dec	35	47	14	3	29	35	30	18	67
1981	Jan	33	46	18	2	26	31	26	17	65
	Feb	36	35	20	8	29	34	22	25	42
	Mar	30	34	32*	4	23	30	23	17	50
	Apr	30	34	33	2	24	30	21	20	44
	May	32	35	29	3	29	35	26	18	56
	Jun	29	37	30	2	26	33	28	18	60
	Jul	30	40	26	3	23	30	25	13	63
	Aug	28	38	32	1	23	28	23	18	52
	Sep	32	36	29	2	26	32	28	19	46
	Oct	29	28	40	2	24	33	27	14	39
	Nov	26	29	42	2	23	28	16	17	31
	Dec	23	23	50	3	18	25	19	12	23

*Includes SDP 1981–89.

Gallup Poll Findings

		Voting Intention				Approve Govt Record %	Approve P.M. %	Approve Opposition Leader %	Party thought likely to win	
		Con. %	Lab. %	Lib.* %	Other %				Con. %	Lab. %
1982	Jan	27	29	39	3	24	32	18	16	27
	Feb	27	34	36	2	24	29	19	21	35
	Mar	31	33	33	2	29	34	21	32	33
	Apr	31	29	37	2	32	35	23	23	27
	May	41	28	29	1	42	44	18	43	21
	Jun	45	25	28	1	48	51	14	63	13
	Jul	46	27	24	2	47	52	16	66	12
	Aug	44	26	27	1	42	49	15	58	17
	Sep	44	30	23	2	40	48	16	58	19
	Oct	40	29	27	3	40	46	20	58	20
	Nov	42	34	21	2	39	44	22	55	22
	Dec	41	34	22	2	37	44	20	54	25
1983	Jan	44	31	22	2	43	49	17	61	19
	Feb	43	32	22	2	39	45	17	62	19
	Mar	39	28	29	3	41	47	19	66	11
	Apr	40	35	22	2	38	44	21	59	21
	May	49	31	17	2	45	50	18	76	11
	Jun	45	26	26	2	44	48	17	87	5
	Jul	44	28	26	1	46	52	11	49	16
	Aug	44	25	29	1	44	51	10	56	10
	Sep	45	24	29	1	47	53	9	64	12
	Oct	42	35	20	2	41	48	58	48	28
	Nov	43	36	19	1	40	49	48	53	26
	Dec	42	36	19	2	38	47	40	49	27
1984	Jan	41	38	19	1	42	49	43	58	22
	Feb	43	33	21	2	41	48	45	59	23
	Mar	41	38	19	1	41	46	47	50	35
	Apr	41	36	20	2	42	46	42	52	28
	May	38	36	23	2	37	41	42	50	30
	Jun	37	38	23	1	36	41	43	49	31
	Jul	37	38	22	2	36	41	43	43	37
	Aug	36	39	22	2	34	39	37	49	29
	Sep	37	36	25	1	34	40	43	54	28
	Oct	44	32	21	2	43	50	35	64	19
	Nov	44.5	30	23.5	1	41	48	59	67	17
	Dec	39.5	31	27.5	2	34	43	36	67	16
1985	Jan	39	33	25.5	2	33	40	36	65	16
	Feb	35	32	31.5	1	31	37	31	63	19
	Mar	33	39.5	25.5	2	30	37	37	53	28
	Apr	34	34.5	26.5	2	32	38	36	54	28
	May	30.5	34	33.5	2	28	36	38	46	26
	Jun	34.5	34.5	30	1	31	38	37	44	31
	Jul	27.5	38	32.5	2	28	34	38	37	27
	Aug	24	40	34	2	23	30	34	34	33
	Sep	29	29.5	39	2.5	29	35	29	41	25
	Oct	32	38	28	2	29	33	50	39	28
	Nov	35	34	29.5	1.5	29	36	46	47	25
	Dec	33	32.5	32.5	2.5	34	39	47	47	24

*Includes SDP 1981–89.

OPINION POLLS

Gallup Poll Findings

		Voting Intention				Approve Govt Record %	Approve P.M. %	Approve Opposition Leader %	Party thought likely to win	
		Con. %	Lab. %	Lib.* %	Other %				Con. %	Lab. %
1986	Jan	29.5	34	35	1.5	27	31	44	40	27
	Feb	29.5	35.5	33.5	1.5	25	29	40	35	30
	Mar	29.5	34	34.5	2	29	33	39	45	27
	Apr	28	38.5	31.5	2	23	28	40	36	40
	May	27.5	37	32.5	3	27	31	47	28	49
	Jun	34	39	24.5	2.5	27	30	41	35	43
	Jul	33	38	27	2	30	34	43	43	38
	Aug	30	36.5	30	3.5	25	28	38	38	39
	Sep	32.5	38	27.5	2	30	35	46	43	38
	Oct	37.5	37.5	22	2.5	33	36	47	49	32
	Nov	36	39.5	22	2.5	36	36	44	55	28
	Dec	41	32.5	22.5	3	34	38	36	65	18
1987	Jan	34.5	39.5	23.5	2.5	30	35	39	63	19
	Feb	36	34.5	27.5	2	32	35	37	65	19
	Mar	37.5	29.5	31.5	1.5	35	39	34	69	10
	Apr	40.5	28	29	2.5	41	43	26	74	6
	May	39	28	30	3	38	44	30	87	8
	Jun	41	34	23.5	1.5	36	41	45	77	11
	Jul	44.5	33	20.5	2	44	46	35	–	–
	Aug	45.5	35.5	17.5	1.5	42	46	36	–	–
	Sep	44	33	20	3	40	48	40	–	–
	Oct	52	31.5	13.5	3	46	52	39	–	–
	Nov	46.5	33	17	3.5	43	47	39	–	–
	Dec	46.5	34.5	16	3	42	47	40	69	15
1988	Jan	45.5	37	15	2.5	42	48	35	74	12
	Feb	46	36	15	3	40	45	36	71	14
	Mar	42	36.5	19.5	2	40	42	32	70	14
	Apr	40.5	41.5	15	3	35	40	39	74	16
	May	45	36	14.5	4.5	40	43	39	68	17
	Jun	42	43	11	4	39	42	38	71	17
	Jul	41.5	39	16	3.5	39	42	32	78	11
	Aug	45.5	33.5	17	4	41	45	27	79	9
	Sep	43	36.5	17.5	3	42	45	30	80	11
	Oct	45.5	34	17.5	3	43	48	33	83	8
	Nov	42.5	36	17	4.5	38	45	29	–	–
	Dec	43	32	19.5	5.5	38	44	26	78	13
1989	Jan	42.6	35.5	16.7	5.3	36.6	43.8	28.1	79	9
	Feb	41.0	36.4	17.9	4.7	34.2	41.6	28.7	74	10
	Mar	38.9	37.7	17.9	5.4	33.1	39.7	29.2	68	15
	Apr	39.2	38.4	17.0	5.5	34.6	40.6	31.7	70	17
	May	40.9	40.8	12.8	4.4	35.8	40.9	35.0	64	22
	Jun	38.2	41.3	11.0	9.4	32.8	37.7	37.5	47	40
	Jul	35.5	42.3	10.0	11.1	29.9	34.8	37.9	52	34
	Aug	36.8	42.3	9.3	11.3	31.8	35.6	36.2	56	22
	Sep	36.4	41.2	11.5	10.8	31.1	35.8	37.2	59	22
	Oct	36.2	47.0	8.3	8.6	29.0	33.1	45.1	45	42
	Nov	36.3	46.5	9.3	8.1	28.1	29.6	40.9	–	–
	Dec	37.3	46.2	9.4	7.1	30.1	32.2	42.7	52	36

*Includes SDP 1981–89.

Gallup Poll Findings

		Voting Intention				Approve Govt Record	Approve P.M.	Approve Opposition Leader	Party thought likely to win	
		Con. %	Lab. %	Lib.Dem. %	Other %	%	%	%	Con. %	Lab. %
1990	Jan	36.1	45.0	10.7	8.4	28.8	32.6	40.6	50	36
	Feb	32.7	47.3	11.6	8.5	24.9	29.2	39.6	38	48
	Mar	28.5	52.0	10.9	8.6	21.6	24.3	40.4	26	62
	Apr	28.1	51.8	11.6	8.4	22.2	23.2	40.1	33	56
	May	32.7	47.5	12.3	7.5	25.6	26.1	37.9	38	52
	Jun	33.7	49.5	8.8	8.1	26.1	27.7	38.2	48	41
	Jul	34.4	47.9	9.9	7.8	27.5	30.1	39.4	45	42
	Aug	35.1	47.6	9.3	7.9	28.8	31.8	38.8	48	40
	Sep	34.6	46.6	11.1	7.6	29.1	32.5	42.4	47	41
	Oct	34.3	46.4	13.0	6.3	28.1	31.5	44.1	43	40
	Nov	37.9	42.1	13.7	6.6	29.8	25.9	38.8	–	–
	Dec	44.6	39.1	10.5	5.8	34.3	49.3	33.5	60	27
1991	Jan	44.3	39.2	10.8	5.7	36.6	50.1	37.1	53	33
	Feb	44.3	39.3	11.0	5.4	37.0	59.3	38.3	62	27
	Mar	41.2	36.2	17.3	5.2	33.0	56.9	37.4	65	24
	Apr	40.9	37.1	16.5	5.6	33.2	53.9	34.8	53	42
	May	37.2	38.3	19.4	5.1	29.7	49.7	39.4	38	46
	Jun	36.5	39.5	18.7	5.0	29.8	47.8	34.9	42	25
	Jul	38.3	39.1	17.6	4.8	30.4	50.2	36.9	48	36
	Aug	38.5	38.8	17.1	5.5	31.4	52.1	35.8	52	31
	Sep	40.5	36.9	17.1	5.5	33.9	54.1	33.9	58	25
	Oct	41.0	40.4	13.8	4.8	33.2	52.0	39.3	47	37
	Nov	39.5	38.9	16.6	5.0	32.3	50.0	36.0	45	37
	Dec	40.6	38.9	15.0	5.6	33.2	49.6	33.4	45	35
1992	Jan	39.0	39.2	16.8	5.0	30.2	48.4	33.0	47	36
	Feb	38.9	37.6	18.3	5.2	29.7	48.5	33.6	56	26
	Mar	37.4	37.8	19.7	5.1	29.4	46.4	35.4	39	35
	Apr	38.5	38.0	20.0	3.5	33.8	48.5	40.0	55	22
	May	40.6	39.3	16.1	3.9	36.7	54.3	48.6	63	15
	Jun	39.8	40.4	15.2	4.5	34.0	51.7	47.0	62	16
	Jul	39.1	41.4	14.8	4.6	30.4	49.2	48.5	62	16
	Aug	38.4	42.6	14.1	4.9	26.2	45.2	38.8	56	23
	Sep	36.9	44.5	14.2	4.5	22.4	38.7	33.6	56	26
	Oct	32.0	48.4	14.4	5.3	14.0	25.6	45.1	43	37
	Nov	30.2	51.5	13.5	4.8	13.9	23.3	48.9	34	44
	Dec	32.2	48.1	14.6	5.1	15.9	27.0	46.3	33	46
1993	Jan	33.0	47.9	13.9	5.2	17.4	31.2	43.0	45	37
	Feb	31.9	47.4	15.4	5.4	16.0	27.9	45.1	39	43
	Mar	30.0	48.3	15.8	6.0	14.4	24.9	47.2	–	–
	Apr	30.9	47.4	16.0	5.8	16.0	26.0	47.0	45	37
	May	26.8	44.2	23.6	5.5	13.8	23.1	44.4	52	32
	Jun	24.2	45.8	24.5	5.6	11.0	18.4	43.0	35	42
	Jul	25.4	44.7	24.7	5.2	12.2	19.5	45.0	40	39
	Aug	23.7	42.9	28.3	5.1	12.0	19.5	43.7	36	37
	Sep	24.3	45.0	24.7	6.0	11.9	19.4	44.2	38	36
	Oct	26.2	45.6	22.6	5.5	13.1	22.6	53.1	41	34
	Nov	25.4	46.2	22.4	6.0	12.3	20.2	49.6	40	39
	Dec	26.8	46.4	21.3	5.4	14.0	22.9	50.1	41	38

OPINION POLLS

Gallup Poll Findings

		Voting Intention				Approve Govt Record %	Approve P.M. %	Approve Opposition Leader %	Party thought likely to win	
		Con. %	Lab. %	Lib.Dem. %	Other %				Con. %	Lab. %
1994	Jan	25.5	48.2	20.8	5.5	13.8	21.6	50.5	46	38
	Feb	26.3	47.6	21.0	5.1	14.0	23.2	52.5	34	43
	Mar	25.9	47.7	20.4	5.6	13.9	22.5	50.3	–	–
	Apr	24.4	48.3	22.4	4.9	12.0	19.3	48.5	–	–
	May	22.8	49.2	23.1	4.9	11.1	18.6	–	–	–
	Jun	21.6	51.8	20.3	6.3	10.7	18.8	–	–	–
	Jul	22.0	54.7	17.4	5.9	11.3	19.8	50.0	–	–
	Aug	23.0	55.5	16.6	4.4	11.9	19.7	58.3	–	–
	Sep	22.8	55.5	16.7	5.0	12.4	21.2	46.3	–	–
	Oct	22.8	56.7	15.5	5.1	12.7	21.9	50.6	–	–
	Nov	23.24	57.4	15.0	4.3	11.2	21.3	49.3	–	–
	Dec	20.4	60.9	14.3	4.4	9.7	18.1	55.3	–	–
1995	Jan	22.7	59.0	13.7	4.6	10.5	18.4	56.2	–	–
	Feb	21.8	59.5	13.7	4.9	10.5	19.1	58.5	–	–
	Mar	23.8	58.0	13.9	4.7	11.2	20.8	58.5	–	–
	Apr	22.5	57.2	15.3	5.1	11.5	20.6	60.6		
	May	21.3	57.4	16.6	4.7	10.2	20.5	64.7	–	–
	Jun	22.6	58.2	14.8	4.5	11.9	21.8	65.8	–	–
	Jul	25.5	57.2	12.9	4.5	13.9	26.4	62.4	–	–
	Aug	24.7	55.5	15.0	4.8	13.8	25.6	58.8	–	–
	Sep	26.2	54.4	14.6	4.7	13.2	25.7	55.5	–	–
	Oct	24.3	58.9	13.0	3.9	14.7	25.3	63.1	–	–
	Nov	24.3	59.5	12.3	4.0	13.5	25.1	62.2	–	–
	Dec	24.7	58.0	13.0	4.3	14.7	26.6	63.5	–	–
1996	Jan	23.1	55.6	16.8	4.4	13.8	24.4	60.5	–	–
	Feb	25.4	55.4	14.9	4.4	14.4	24.2	58.5	–	–
	Mar	23.9	57.3	15.1	3.7	13.3	25.2	61.5	–	–
	Apr	23.8	57.2	14.3	4.6	14.0	24.1	62.2	–	–
	May	24.3	54.8	16.0	5.0	13.8	24.2	60.2	–	–
	Jun	26.1	54.9	14.5	4.4	15.0	25.1	59.6	–	–
	Jul	27.0	54.1	14.0	4.9	15.0	26.1	56.8	–	–
	Aug	26.9	53.3	13.8	6.0	16.3	26.5	53.4	–	–
	Sep	27.0	54.1	13.9	5.0	17.4	27.8	56.3	–	–
	Oct	25.8	54.7	15.0	4.6	16.8	27.5	59.4	–	–
	Nov	25.8	55.8	12.6	5.8	18.2	28.4	60.5	–	–
	Dec	26.0	56.0	12.5	5.4	17.2	26.9	57.6	–	–
1997	Jan	33.0	50.5	11.3	5.1	24.0	34.1	61.7	–	–
	Feb	32.8	50.9	10.8	5.7	25.5	34.9	64.1	–	–
	Mar	29.8	53.7	10.8	5.8	25.3	33.3	68.3	–	–
	Apr	–	–	–	–	–	–	–	–	–
	May	23.3	56.9	14.7	5.0	76.0	–	–	–	–
	Jun	24.2	60.4	11.5	3.9	71.7	–	–	–	–
	Jul	25.3	58.5	12.0	4.2	67.6	–	–	–	–
	Aug	26.8	57.6	11.4	4.3	63.4	–	–	–	–
	Sep	23.1	62.0	11.0	3.9	71.7	–	–	–	–
	Oct	23.2	63.2	9.7	4.0	69.6	–	–	–	–
	Nov	23.6	58.6	13.0	4.9	61.0	–	–	–	–
	Dec	24.6	56.6	13.8	5.0	54.3	–	–	–	–

Gallup Poll Findings

		Voting Intention				Approve Govt Record %	Approve P.M. %	Approve Opposition Leader %	Party thought likely to win	
		Con. %	Lab. %	Lib.Dem. %	Other %				Con. %	Lab. %
1998	Jan	26.8	54.9	13.1	5.2	52.5	–	–	–	–
	Feb	28.1	54.4	12.9	4.8	52.4	–	–	–	–
	Mar	29.3	51.1	14.4	5.6	46.8	–	–	–	–
	Apr	26.5	53.8	15.3	4.5	54.9	–	–	–	–
	May	25.9	55.2	13.8	5.1	61.2	–	–	–	–
	Jun	27.1	54.1	12.8	6.0	54.8	–	–	–	–
	Jul	27.8	53.9	12.7	5.5	55.0	–	–	–	–
	Aug	28.0	54.9	12.0	5.1	54.4	–	–	–	–
	Sep	28.0	54.1	12.6	5.2	53.3	–	–	–	–
	Oct	25.3	56.5	13.0	5.3	55.6	–	–	–	–
	Nov	27.2	54.3	13.1	5.5	54.7	–	–	–	–
	Dec	27.1	55.5	12.3	5.0	53.2	–	–	–	–
1999	Jan	27.8	53.7	13.1	5.4	51.8	–	–	–	–
	Feb	27.5	53.9	13.6	5.0	50.3	–	–	–	–
	Mar	28.5	53.3	12.8	5.4	50.3	–	–	–	–
	Apr	26.1	55.4	12.9	5.6	56.5	–	–	–	–
	May	26.7	53.6	13.8	6.0	56.5	–	–	–	–
	Jun	26.7	50.2	15.2	8.0	51.6	–	–	–	–
	Jul	27.6	51.5	14.0	7.0	52.9	–	–	–	–
	Aug	27.7	51.6	14.4	6.4	53.0	–	–	–	–
	Sep	27.6	52.8	13.3	6.4	51.8	–	–	–	–
	Oct	27.6	53.2	12.7	6.5	51.3	–	–	–	–
	Nov	27.4	52.8	14.3	5.5	51.5	–	–	–	–
	Dec	27.0	54.2	13.3	5.5	52.1	–	–	–	–

Opinion Poll Accuracy in General Elections

The following is a list of all major poll predictions of general election results.

	Actual Result (G.B.)	Gallup Poll	NOP	Daily Express
1945				
Con.	39.5	+1.5		
Lab.	49.0	–2.0		
Lib.	9.2	+1.3		
1950				
Con.	43.1	+0.4	+1.4	
Lab.	46.8	–1.8	–2.8	
Lib.	9.3	+1.2	+1.7	
1951				
Con.	47.8	+1.7	+2.2	+2.2
Lab.	49.3	–2.3	–3.3	–6.3
Lib.	2.6	+0.4	+0.9	(+4.1)[a]
1955				
Con.	49.3	+1.7	+1.9	
Lab.	47.3	+0.2	–0.1	
Lib.	2.8	–1.3	–0.6	

	Actual Result (G.B.)	Gallup Poll	NOP	Daily Express		
1959						
Con	48.8	−0.3	−0.8	+0.3		
Lab	44.6	+1.9	+0.5	+0.8		
Lib	6.1	−1.6	(+2.4)[a]	−1.1		
					Research Services	
1964						
Con	42.9	+1.6	+1.4	+1.6	+2.1	
Lab	44.8	+1.2	+2.6	+1.1	+1.2	
Lib	11.4	+2.9	−3.5	−0.3	−2.4	
1966						
Con	41.4	−1.4	+0.2	−4.0	+0.2	
Lab	48.7	+2.3	−1.9	+5.9	+1.0	
Lib	8.6	−0.6	−1.2	−0.9	−0.3	
				Louis Harris	ORC	
1970						
Con	46.2	−4.2	−2.2	−0.2	+0.3	
Lab	43.8	+5.2	+4.3	+4.2	+1.7	
Lib	7.6	−0.1	−1.2	−2.6	−1.1	
1974 Feb						
Con	38.6	+0.9	+O.9	+1.6	+1.1	
Lab	38.0	−0.5	−2.5	−2.8	−1.3	
Lib	19.8	+0.7	+2.2	+1.4	+1.4	
Other	3.6	−1.1	−0.6	−0.9	−1.2	
1974 Oct						
Con	36.7	−0.7	−5.7	−2.1	−2.3	
Lab	40.2	+1.3	+5.3	+2.8	+1.6	
Lib	18.8	+0.2	+0.7	+0.5	+0.6	
Other	4.3	−0.8	−0.3	−1.2	+0.1	
				MORI	Marplan	
1979						
Con	44.9	−1.9	+1.1	−0.5	+0.1	
Lab	37.8	+3.2	+1.2	+1.0	+0.8	
Lib	14.1	−0.6	−1.6	−0.6	−0.6	
Other	3.2	−0.7	−0.7	+0.1	−0.3	
						Harris
1983						
Con	43.5	+2.0	+3.5	+0.3	+2.5	+3.5
Lab	28.3	−1.8	−3.3	−0.3	−2.3	−3.3
Alln	26.0	0.0	0.0	0.0	0.0	0.0
Other	2.2	−0.2	−0.2	−0.2	+2.0	+2.0
1987						
Con	43.3	−2.3	−1.3	+0.7	−1.3	−1.3
Lab	31.5	+2.5	+3.5	+0.5	+3.5	+3.5
Alln	23.1	+0.4	−2.1	−1.1	−2.1	−2.1
Other	2.1	−0.6	−0.1	−0.1	−0.1	−0.1
1992						
Con	42.8	−4.3	−3.8	−4.0	−4.0	
Lab	35.2	+2.8	+6.8	+3.8	+2.8	
Lib.D.	18.3	+1.7	−1.3	−1.7	−1.7	
Other	3.7	−0.2	−1.7	−1.7	+0.3	

	Actual Result (G.B.)	Gallup Poll	NOP	MORI	ICM	Harris
1997						
Con	31.4	+1.6	−3.4	−1.4	+1.6	−0.4
Lab	44.4	+2.6	−5.6	+2.6	−1.4	+3.6
Lib.D.	17.2	−3.2	−3.2	+1.8	+0.8	−2.2
Other	7.0	−1.0	+1.0	−2.0	−1.0	−1.0

[a] Error in Liberal and Other vote combined.

In 1970 Marplan (on a U.K. not a G.B. basis) produced a forecast for *The Times* that overestimated Labour's lead by 9.6%.

In Oct 74 a Marplan poll in the *Sun* underestimated the Conservative lead by 1.1%. A Research Services poll in the *Observer* overestimated the Conservative lead by 4.4%. A separate MORI poll in the *Evening Standard* overestimated the Conservative lead by 0.9%.

The Common Market Referendum on 5 Jun 75 yielded a 67.2% 'yes' vote see p.513. On that morning the opinion poll forecasts of a 'yes' vote were: Gallup 68%; ORC 73.7%; Louis Harris 72%; Marplan (decided voted) 58% 'yes', 27% 'no'.

Sources: For a comprehensive description of British opinion polling see F. Teer and J. D. Spence, *Political Opinion Polls* (1973); see also R. Hodder Williams, *Public Opinion Polls and British Politics* (1970). P. Rose, *The Polls and the 1970 Election* (1970) gives full documentation about the 1970 findings. Each of the Nuffield *British General Election* series includes analyses of the polls. But R. Worcester *British Public Opinion* (1991) provides the fullest record of political polling since 1945; see also Market Research Society's report on the 1992 performance of the polls (1994).

V

POLITICAL ALLUSIONS

The student of political history becomes familiar with allusive references to places, events, scandals, phrases and quotations. This chapter attempts to collect the most outstanding of these allusions.

Political Place-Names

At one time or another in the twentieth century the following place-names were sufficiently famous to be alluded to without further explanation. Any such list must necessarily be very selective. No foreign names are included here even though that means omitting Agadir, Chanak, Munich, Suez, the Falklands, the Gulf, Bosnia and Kosovo. No venues of party conferences are included, even though that means omitting Scarborough (Labour, 1960), Blackpool (Conservative, 1963) and Brighton (Conservative, 1984). No constituency names are included as such, even though that means omitting some, like Bewdley or Ebbw Vale, which are indelibly associated with individuals and others where sensational elections had a lasting national impact, like Colne Valley (1907), St George's Westminster (1931), East Fulham (1933), Orpington (1962), Smethwick (1964), Lincoln (1973), and Crosby (1981).

Abbey House, Victoria St, SW1. Conservative Party Headquarters 1946–58.

Abingdon St, SW1. Site of Liberal Party Headquarters 1910–34.

Admiralty House, SW1. Apartments of First Lord of Admiralty until 1960. Residence of H. Macmillan during Downing St repairs 1960–63 and since 1965 of Secretary of State for Defence and other ministers.

Aldermaston, Berkshire. Site of Atomic Weapons Research Establishment. Starting or finishing-point of the Campaign for Nuclear Disarmament's Easter Marches 1958–63, 1967 and 1988.

Ashridge, Herts. Site of Conservative Party College, 1929–39.

Astley Hall. Worcestershire home of S. (Earl) Baldwin 1902–47.

Bachelor's Walk, Dublin. Scene (26 Jul 1914) of disturbance in which soldiers killed three rioters.

Balmoral Castle, Aberdeenshire. Summer home of the Sovereign since 1852.

Birch Grove, Sussex. Home of H. Macmillan 1906–86.

Blenheim Palace, Oxfordshire. Home of Dukes of Marlborough. Birthplace of (Sir) W. Churchill.

Bowood, Wiltshire. Home of Marquesses of Lansdowne.

Brixton, London, SW2. Scene of anti-police riots in April and July 1981.

Broadstairs, Kent. Birthplace and home of Edward Heath.

Buckingham Palace. Bought by George III in 1761. Official residence of the Sovereign since 1837.

Cable Street, Whitechapel, London. Scene of confrontations with the British Union of Fascists, 1935–36.

Carlton Club. London meeting place of Conservatives. Scene (19 Oct 1922) of gathering which brought down the Lloyd George Coalition.

Carmelite House, E.C.4. Long the Headquarters of the *Daily Mail* and *Evening News*.

Catherine Place. London home of T. Garel-Jones, and meeting place of ministers on 20 Nov 90.

Chartwell, Kent. Home of (Sir) W. Churchill 1923–65.

Chatsworth, Derbyshire. Home of Dukes of Devonshire.

Chequers, Buckinghamshire. Country house given to the nation by Lord Lee of Fareham in 1917 and used as country residence for Prime Ministers from 1921.

Cherry Cottage, Buckinghamshire. Home of C. (Earl) Attlee 1951–61.

Cherkley Court, Surrey. Home of Ld Beaverbrook 1916–64.

Chevening, Kent. Country House bequeathed to the nation by Earl Stanhope. Now allocated by the Prime Minister to a Cabinet colleague. Site of Budget preparations in the 1980s and 1990s.

Church House, SW1. Meeting place of the Church Assembly 1920–28 and of the Synod 1928–; and of both Houses of Parliament, Nov–Dec 1940, May–Jun 1941, Jun–Aug 1944. Scene of United Nations preparatory meeting 1945 and of many Conservative gatherings.

Churt, Surrey. Home of D. Lloyd George (E) 1921–45.

Clay Cross, Derbyshire. Urban District Council which refused to implement 1972 *Housing Act.*

Cliveden, Buckinghamshire. Home of 2nd and 3rd Vt Astor. Alleged centre of 'Cliveden Set' in 1930s. Scene (1962) of events in the Profumo affair.

Coldharbour Lane, Brixton, London. Childhood home of J. Major, featured in 1991 Party conference speech and in party election broadcast in 1992.

Congress House, Gt. Russell St, WC1. Headquarters of Trades Union Congress 1960–.

Cowley St, London, SW1. Headquarters of the Social Democratic Party, 1981–88, and of the (Social and) Liberal Democrats 1988–.

Criccieth, Caernarvonshire. Welsh home of D. Lloyd George (E) 1880–1945.

Crichel Down, Dorset. The refusal to derequisition some land here led, ultimately, to the resignation of the Minister of Agriculture in Jul 1954.

Cross St, Manchester. Headquarters of the *(Manchester) Guardian* until 1970.

Curragh, The, Co. Kildare. Military camp; scene of 'mutiny' 20 Mar 1914.

Dalmeny, Midlothian. Home of Earls of Rosebery.

Dorneywood, Buckinghamshire. Country house bequeathed to the nation in 1954 by Ld Courtauld-Thomson as an official residence for any Minister designated by the Prime Minister.

Downing St, SW1. No. 10 is the Prime Minister's official residence. No. 11 is the official residence of the Chancellor of the Exchequer. No. 12 houses the offices of the Government Whips.

Dublin Castle. Offices of the Irish Administration until 1922.

Durdans, The, Epsom. Home of 5th E of Rosebery 1872–1929.

Eccleston Square, SW1. Site of Headquarters of the Labour Party and of the Trades Union Congress 1918–29.

Ettrick Bridge, Roxburgh. Constituency home of Sir D. Steel since 1966. Scene of meeting of Alliance leaders, 29 May 1983.

Euston Lodge, Phoenix Park, Dublin. Residence of the Ld-Lieutenant of Ireland.

Falloden, Northumberland. Home of Sir E. (Vt) Grey 1862–1933.

Fleet St, EC4. Location of *Daily Telegraph* and *Daily Express* until the late 1980s. Generic name for the London press.

Fort Belvedere, Berkshire. Country home of Edward VIII 1930–36.

Grand Hotel, Brighton. Scene of bombing on 11 Oct 1984 at Conservative Conference.

Great George St, SW1. Site of the Treasury and, 1964–69, of the Department of Economic Affairs.

Greenham Common, Berkshire. Air base at which Cruise missiles were first sited (Nov 83). Women protesters camped outside it from Sep 81 until 1991.

Hampstead. London suburb which, during H. Gaitskell's leadership of the Labour Party, provided a generic name for the set of intellectuals associated with him.

Hatfield House, Hertfordshire. Home of Marquesses of Salisbury.

Highbury, Birmingham. Home of J. Chamberlain 1868–1914.

Hirsel, The, Berwickshire. Home of Earls of Home.

Holy Loch, Argyll. Site of U.S. atomic submarine base 1962–92.

Howth, Co. Dublin. Scene of gun-running 26 Jul 1914.

Invergordon, Ross and Cromarty. Site of naval protest in Sep 1931 over proposed pay reductions.

Islington. London borough where T. Blair and other New Labour figures lived 1994–1997.

Jarrow, Durham. Shipbuilding town where unemployment reached 73% in 1935. Start of Jarrow to London protest march, Oct 1936.

Kilmainham Jail, Dublin. Scene of execution of the leaders of the 1916 rising.

King St, WC2. Site of Communist Party Headquarters since early 1920s.

Knowsley, Lancashire. Home of Earls of Derby.

Larne, Co. Antrim. Scene of gun-running 24 Apr 1914.

Limehouse, E14. Scene of speech by D. Lloyd George 30 Jul 1909; became generic name for political vituperation. Also home of D. Owen 1965– and scene of meeting on 25 Jan 81, which produced 'The Limehouse Declaration' which anticipated the formation of the Social Democratic Party.

Londonderry House, W1. London home of Marquesses of Londonderry until 1946.

Lord North St, SW1. Home of H. Wilson 1971–76.

Lossiemouth, Morayshire. Home of R. MacDonald, 1906–1937.

Maze, The, County Antrim (formerly Long Kesh). Prison where many convicted terrorists were held from 1968 onwards. Scene of hunger strike in which 10 Republican prisoners died in 1981.

Millbank, SW1. BBC moved their Westminster operations to No.4 Millbank in 1990, and were soon followed by ITN and Sky News. The Labour Party's media and electioneering operation moved to the Millbank Tower in 1995.

Molesworth, Cambridgeshire. Air base. Scene of demonstrations against Cruise missiles 1985–93.

Notting Hill, W11. Scene of racial disturbances in Aug 1958.

Old Queen St, SW1. Site of Conservative Party Headquarters 1941–46. Site of Conservative Research Department 1930–1981.

Olympia, W14. Exhibition Hall; scene (7 Jun 1934) of Mosley meeting which provoked violence.

Palace Chambers, SW1. Headquarters of Conservative Party 1922–41.

Pembroke Lodge, W8. Home of A. Bonar Law 1909–16.

Poplar. London borough whose Poor Law Guardians (including G. Lansbury) were imprisoned in 1921 for paying more than national rates of relief.

Portland Place, W1. Headquarters of the British Broadcasting Corporation 1932–.

Printing House Square, EC4. Headquarters of *The Times* 1785–1974.

Relugas, Morayshire. Fishing lodge of Sir E. Grey; scene of 'Relugas Compact' with H. Asquith and R. Haldane Sep 1905.

St James Palace, W1. Royal Palace. Foreign Ambassadors continue to be accredited to the Court of St James.

St Paul's, Bristol. Scene of anti-police riot, Apr 1980.

St Stephen's Chambers, SW1. Site of Conservative Headquarters 1900–18.

Sandringham House, Norfolk. Royal residence since 1861.

Scapa Flow, Orkney. Naval anchorage where German Fleet was scuttled 21 Jun 1919. Scene of trouble at the time of the Invergordon 'mutiny' Sep 1931.

Scilly Isles, Cornwall. Location of H. Wilson's country cottage 1959–1985.

Selsdon Park. Hotel in Croydon. Scene of Conservative Shadow Cabinet's weekend meeting, 30 Jan–1 Feb 1970.

Shanklin, Isle of Wight. Scene (Feb 1949) of meeting of Labour Party leaders.

Sidney St, E1. Scene of police siege of anarchists 3 Jan 1911.

Smith Square, SW1. Location of the Labour Party Headquarters (Transport House) 1928–1980; of the Conservative Party Headquarters since 1958; and of the Liberal Party Headquarters 1965–68.

Southall. West London suburb with large population of Asian origin. Scene of violent disturbances in anti-National Front riot, 23 Apr 1979.

Stormont, Belfast. Site of Parliament and Government of Northern Ireland.

Stornaway House, W. Home of Ld Beaverbrook 1920–40. Scene of Stornoway Pact with Baldwin 31 Mar 1931.

Sunningdale, Surrey. Location of Civil Service College where a Conference on Northern Ireland 6–9 Dec 73 produced the Sunningdale Agreement on power-sharing and a Council of Ireland.

Swinton, Yorkshire. Home of E of Swinton. Conservative Party College 1948–1971.

Taff Vale, Glamorgan. In 1901 the Taff Vale Railway Company successfully sued a trade union for loss due to a strike.

Threadneedle St, EC2. Site of the Bank of England.

Tonypandy, Glamorgan. Scene of violent miners' strike to which W. Churchill sent troops in Nov 1910.

Toxteth, Liverpool 8. Scene of rioting, Jul 1981.

Transport House, SW1. Headquarters of the Transport and General Workers' Union and of the Labour Party 1928–80 and of the Trades Union Congress 1928–60.

Walworth Rd, London, SE17. 150 Walworth Rd was the headquarters of the Labour Party 1980–1997.

Wapping, East London. Site of headquarters of News International, where *The Times*, the *Sunday Times*, the *Sun* and the *News of the World* have been produced and printed since 1986.

Westbourne, Birmingham. Home of N. Chamberlain 1911–40.

Westminster, London. Parliament meets in the Palace of Westminster and Westminster has become a generic name for parliamentary activity.

Wharf, The, Sutton Courtenay, Berkshire. Home of H. Asquith 1912–28.

Whitehall, London. Many government departments are situated in Whitehall and it has become a generic name for civil service activity.

Whittingehame, East Lothian. Home of A. Balfour 1848–1930.

Windsor Castle, Berkshire. Official royal residence since 11th century.

Political Quotations

From time to time an isolated phrase becomes an established part of the language of political debate. Such phrases are frequently misquoted and their origins are often obscure. Here are a few which seem to have had an especial resonance. The list is far from comprehensive; it merely attempts to record the original source for some well-used quotations.

When was a war not a war? When it was carried on by *methods of barbarism* in South Africa?

SIR H. CAMPBELL-BANNERMAN, in a speech to the National Reform Union, 14 Jun 01

For the present, at any rate, I must proceed alone. *I must plough my furrow alone*, but before I get to the end of that furrow it is possible that I may not find myself alone.

E of ROSEBERY, in a speech at the City Liberal Club, 19 Jul 01

To the distinguished representatives of the commercial interests of the Empire ... I venture to allude to the impression which seemed generally to prevail among their brethren across the seas, that the old country must *wake up* if she [England] intends to maintain her old position of preeminence in her colonial trade against foreign competitors.

PRINCE of WALES (later GEORGE V) at a lunch at Guildhall on the completion of his tour of the Empire, 5 Dec 01

What is the advice I have to offer you? You have to *clear your slate*. It is six years since you were in office ... The primary duty of the Liberal Party is to wipe its slate clean.

E. of ROSEBERY, speaking to a Liberal audience at Chesterfield, 16 Dec 01. Sir H. CAMPBELL-BANNERMAN replied at Leicester 'I am no believer in *the doctrine of the clean slate.*'

I should consider that I was but ill-performing my duty if we were to profess a settled conviction when *no settled conviction* exists.

A. BALFOUR, House of Commons, 10 Jun 03

If I believed that there was the smallest reasonable chance of success, I would have no hesitation in advising my fellow-countrymen to endeavour to end the present system by *armed revolt*.

J. REDMOND, House of Commons, 12 Apr 05

It [the Chinese Labour Contract] cannot in the opinion of his Majesty's Government, be classified as slavery in the extreme acceptance of the word without some risk of *terminological inexactitude*.

W. CHURCHILL, House of Commons, 22 Feb 06

You mean it is *Mr Balfour's poodle!* It fetches and carries for him. It barks for him. It bites anybody that he sets it on to.

D. LLOYD GEORGE, replying to H. Chaplin, M.P., who had claimed in a House of Commons debate on the *House of Lords (Restoration of Powers) Bill*, that the Lords was the watchdog of the Constitution, 26 Jun 07

If we believe a thing to be bad, and if we have a right to prevent it, it is our duty to try to prevent it and to *damn the consequences*.

LORD MILNER, in a speech at Glasgow in opposition to Lloyd George's 1909 Finance Bill, 26 Nov 09

Wait and see.

H. ASQUITH, repeated four times to Opposition members pressing for a statement when speaking on the *Parliament Act Procedure Bill*, House of Commons, 4 Apr 10

We were beaten by *the Bishops and the rats.*

G. WYNDHAM, on the passing of the *Parliament Bill* by the House of Lords, 10 Aug 11

La Grande Illusion.

Title of a book by N. ANGELL, first published in 1909 as *Europe's Optical Illusion* and republished as *The Great Illusion* in 1910

The lamps are going out all over Europe. We shall not see them lit again in our lifetime.

SIR E. GREY, 3 Aug 14, talking in his room at the Foreign Office, quoted in his autobiography *Twenty five Years*, vol. II, p. 20

Your King and Country Need YOU

Advertisement in *Daily Mail* and other papers 5 Aug 14. Basis for drawing on the cover of *London Opinion*, 5 Sep 14, designed by A. LEETE, depicting LORD KITCHENER with arresting eyes and pointing finger above the caption 'Your Country needs you'; reproduced by Parliamentary Recruiting Committee for use as recruiting poster and issued Sep 14

The maxim of the British people is *'business as usual'*.

W. CHURCHILL in a speech at the Guildhall, 9 Nov 14

To secure for the producers by hand or by brain the full fruits of their industry and the most equitable distribution thereof that may be possible upon the basis of *the common ownership of the means of production (distribution and exchange)*.

Listed under party objects in the Constitution of the Labour Party adopted at the Annual Conference in London 26 Feb 18 (words in brackets added at the 1928 Conference). Clause abandoned 1996

What is our task? To make Britain *a fit country for heroes to live in*.

D. LLOYD GEORGE, speech at Wolver-hampton, 24 Nov 18

We will get everything out of her [Germany] that you can squeeze out of a lemon and a bit more ... *I will squeeze until you can hear the pips squeak*.

SIR E. GEDDES, in a speech at the Drill Hall, Cambridge, 9 Dec 18

They are a lot of *hard-faced men* .... who look as if they had done very well out of the war.

A Conservative politician (often said to be Baldwin), quoted by J.M. Keynes *in Economic Consequences of the Peace* (Macmillan, 1919), p. 133

First let me insist on what our opponents habitually ignore, indeed what they seem intellectually incapable of under-standing, namely the *inevitable gradualness* of our scheme of change.

S. WEBB, in his Presidential Address to the Labour Party Conference Queen's Hall, Langham Place, 26 June 23

Until our educated and politically minded democracy has become predominantly *a property-owning democracy*, neither the national equilibrium nor the balance of the life of the indi-vidual will be restored.

A. SKELTON, in *Constructive Conservatism* (Blackwood, 1924), p. 17; subsequently used by A. EDEN at Conservative Conference, Blackpool, 3 Oct 46, and by W. CHURCH-ILL, 5 Oct 46

Although I know that there are those who work for different ends from most of us in this House, yet there are many in all ranks and all parties who will re-echo my prayer *'give peace in our time, O Lord'*.

S. BALDWIN speaking in House of Commons on Trade Unions (Political Fund) Bill, 6 Mar 25

Not a penny off the pay, not a second on the day.

Slogan coined by A.J. COOK, Secretary of the National Union of Mineworkers, and used frequently in the run-up to the miners' strike of 1926

We can conquer unemployment.

Title of a pamphlet which was a potted version of the Liberal Yellow Book (1929)

Safety first Stanley Baldwin, the man you can trust.

Slogan on election posters used by the Conservative Party in 1929; the slogan 'Safety First' was previously used by the Conservatives in the 1922 Election

I remember when I was a child being taken to the celebrated Barnum's Circus ... the exhibit which I most desired to see was the one described as 'the Boneless Wonder'. My parents judged that the spectacle would be too revolting for my youthful eyes, and I have waited fifty years to see the *Boneless Wonder* sitting on the Treasury Bench.

W. CHURCHILL, referring to R. Mac-Donald during a debate on Amendment Bill, 28 Jan 31

What the proprietorship of these papers is aiming at is power, and *power without responsibility, the prerogative of the harlot throughout the ages*.

S. BALDWIN, attacking the Press Lords in a speech at Queen's Hall, London, during Westminster St George's by-election campaign, 18 Mar 31. The phrase was suggested by his cousin, Rudyard Kipling

I hope you have read the Election programme of the Labour Party. It is the most fantastic and impracticable programme ever put before the electors ... This is not Socialism. *It is Bolshevism run mad.*

P. SNOWDEN, election broadcast, 17 Oct 31

I think it is well also for the man in the street to realise that there is no power on earth that can protect him from being bombed. Whatever people may tell him, *the bomber will always get through.*

S. BALDWIN, in the House of Commons, 10 Nov 32

That this House will in no circumstances *fight for its King and Country.*

Oxford Union motion, 9 Feb 33

[You are] placing ... the Movement in an absolutely wrong position to be *hawking your conscience round from body to body asking to be told what you ought to do with it.*

E. BEVIN, attacking G. Lansbury at the Labour Party Conference, Brighton, 1 Oct 35

My lips are not yet unsealed.

S. BALDWIN, speaking in the House of Commons, on the Abyssinian crisis, 10 Dec 35, later quoted as 'My lips are sealed'

A Corridor for Camels.

Heading of a first leader in *The Times*, on the Hoare Laval Pact, written by G. DAWSON, 16 Dec 35

I put before the whole House my own views with *appalling frankness....* supposing I had gone to the country and.... said that we must rearm, does anybody think that this pacific democracy would have rallied to the cry? I cannot think of anything that would have made the loss of the election from my point of view more certain.

S. BALDWIN, speaking in the House of Commons, 12 Nov 36 (See W. Churchill in 1948)

Something ought to be done to find these people employment ... *Something will be done.*

EDWARD VIII, on a visit to South Wales, 18 Nov 36

How horrible, fantastic, incredible it is that we should be digging trenches and trying on gas-masks here because of *a quarrel in a faraway country between people of whom we know nothing.*

N. CHAMBERLAIN, referring to Czechoslovakia in a Broadcast 27 Sep 38

Britain will not be involved in a European war this year, or next year either.

Daily Express headline, 30 Sep 38 inspired by LD BEAVERBROOK. Cited as basis for 'There will be no war' campaign in the *Daily Express*

This is the second time in history that there has come back from Germany to Downing Street, peace with honour. I believe that it is *peace for our time.*

N. CHAMBERLAIN, referring back to Disraeli's comment on the Congress of Berlin (1878), in a speech from a window of 10 Downing Street on return from Munich, 30 Sep 38

Speak for England, Arthur.

L. AMERY, R. BOOTHBY; shouted out as Arthur Greenwood rose to speak in the House of Commons, 2 Sep 39

Whatever may be the reason, whether it was that *Hitler* thought he might get away with what he had got without fighting for it, or whether it was that, after all, the preparations are not sufficiently complete, one thing is certain; he *has missed the bus.*

N. CHAMBERLAIN, speaking at Conservative Central Council, 4 Apr 40

You have sat too long here for any good you have been doing. Depart, I say, and let us have done with you. *In the name of God, go!*

L. AMERY, quoting Cromwell (1653) to N. Chamberlain in the House of Commons, 7 May 40

I have nothing to offer but *blood, toil, tears and sweat.*

W. CHURCHILL, House of Commons, 13 May 40

We shall fight on the beaches, we shall fight on the landing grounds, we shall fight in the fields and in the streets.

W. CHURCHILL, House of Commons, 4 Jun 40

If the British Empire and its Commonwealth last for a thousand years, men will still say, *'This was their finest hour'.*

W. CHURCHILL, broadcast to the nation when the fall of France was imminent, 18 Jun 40

Guilty Men

Political tract written by Michael FOOT, Frank OWEN and Peter HOWARD, using pseudonym Cato, published Jul 40

Never in the field of human conflict was *so much owed by so many to so few.*

W. CHURCHILL, House of Commons, 20 Aug 40

Give us the tools and we will finish the job.

W. CHURCHILL, broadcast to the nation, 9 Feb 41

When I warned them [the French] that Britain would fight on alone ... their General told their Prime Minister ... in three weeks England will have her neck wrung like a chicken. *Some chicken, some neck.*

W. CHURCHILL, speaking to the Canadian Parliament, 30 Dec 41

I have not become the King's first Minister in order *to preside over the liquidation of the British Empire.*

W. CHURCHILL, speech at the Mansion House, 10 Nov 42

Pounds, shillings and pence have become quite *meaningless symbols.*

A. GREENWOOD, in the House of Commons, 16 Feb 43

Let us face the future.

Title of Labour Party Manifesto, May 1945

No *Socialist* system can be established without a political police ... They would have to fall back on some form of *Gestapo.*

W. CHURCHILL, election broadcast, 4 Jun 45

You have no right whatever to speak on behalf of the Government. Foreign Affairs are in the capable hands of Ernest Bevin. His task is quite sufficiently difficult without the embarrassment of irresponsible statements of the kind which you are making ... *a period of silence on your part would be welcome.*

C. ATTLEE in a letter to H. Laski, Chairman of the Labour Party NEC 20 Aug 45

From Stettin in the Baltic to Trieste in the Adriatic, *an iron curtain* has descended across the Continent.

W. CHURCHILL, at Westminster College, Fulton, U.S.A., 5 Mar 46. The phrase can be traced back to Mrs Snowden's visit to Russia in 1920 or even to Queen Elisabeth of Belgium in 1914 referring to the barrier between her and her native Bavaria.

We are the masters at the moment and not only for the moment, but for a very long time to come.

SIR H. SHAWCROSS, in the House of Commons during third reading of the *Trade Disputes and Trade Union Bill,* 2 Apr 46

We know that you, the organised workers of the country, are our friends ... As for the rest, they do not matter *a tinker's curse.*

E. SHINWELL, speaking at ETU Conference, Margate, 7 May 47

For in the case of nutrition and health, just as in the case of education, *the gentleman in Whitehall really does know better* what is good for people than the people know themselves.

D. JAY, from *The Socialist Case* (1947) p. 258

No attempt at ethical or social education can eradicate from my heart a deep burning hatred for the Tory Party ... So far as I am concerned, they are *lower than vermin.*

A. BEVAN, at Manchester, 4 Jul 48

I have authorised the relaxation of controls affecting more than 60 commodities for which the Board of Trade is responsible.

H. WILSON, House of Commons, 4 Nov 48

The Hon. Member asked two other questions. One of them was how many licences and permits are to be issued after the removal of the 200,000 Board of Trade licences and the 5,000 or 6,000 others which were as the result of yesterday's little *bonfire....*

H. WILSON, as President of the Board of Trade, House Commons, 5 Nov 48

Baldwin ... confesses *putting party before country.*

W. CHURCHILL, entry in index to *The Gathering Storm*, Vol.I of *The Second World War* (1948) (see S. Baldwin 12 Nov 36)

The Right Road for Britain

Conservative Party policy statement, 1949

The language of priorities is the religion of socialism.

A. BEVAN, Labour Party Conference, Blackpool, 8 Jun 49

Whose finger on the trigger?

Daily Mirror, front-page headline on eve of the election, 24 Oct 51

We think it is a good thing *to set the people free*, as much as is possible in our complicated modern society, from the trammels of state control and bureaucratic management.

W. CHURCHILL, in a BBC broadcast, 3 May 52

The right technique of economic opposition at the moment can be summed up in a slogan. The slogan is that the Opposition should keep itself on the constructive and sunny side of Mr Butskell's dilemma. Mr *Butskell[ism]* ... is a composite of the present Chancellor and the previous one.

Article in *The Economist* refering to R. Butler and H. Gaitskell, 13 Feb 54

I know that the right kind of political leader for the Labour Party is *a desiccated calculating machine.*

A. BEVAN, taken as referring to H. Gaitskell, though Bevan subsequently denied this, at the Tribune meeting during Labour Party Conference at Scarborough, 29 Sep 54

There ain't gonna be no war.

H. MACMILLAN, at press conference, on return from Summit, 24 Jul 55

Reporter: Mr Butler, would you say that this is *the best Prime Minister we have*? R. Butler: Yes.

R. BUTLER, interviewed by the Press Association at London Airport, Dec 55

Most Conservatives, and almost certainly some of the wiser Trade Union Leaders, are waiting to feel *the smack of firm government.*

Daily Telegraph editorial written by the Deputy Editor D. MCLACHLAN, 3 Jan 56

And all these financiers, all the little *gnomes of Zurich* and the other financial centres about whom we keep on hearing, started to make their dispositions in regard to sterling.

H. WILSON, in the House of Commons Debate on the Address, 12 Nov 56

During the past few weeks I have felt sometimes that *the Suez Canal was flowing through my drawing-room.*

LADY EDEN, opening Gateshead Conservative Association Headquarters, 20 Nov 56

Let us be frank about it, most of our people have *never had it so good*.

H. MACMILLAN, speaking at Bedford to a Conservative Party rally, 21 Jul 57

If you carry this resolution ... you'll send the British Foreign Secretary, whoever he was, *naked into the Conference Chamber*.

A. BEVAN, Labour Party Conference, Brighton, 3 Oct 57

And you call that statesmanship. I call it *an emotional spasm*.

A. BEVAN, speaking on unilateral disarmament, Labour Party Conference, Brighton, 3 Oct 57

I thought the best thing to do was to settle up *these little local difficulties*, and then turn to the wider vision of the Commonwealth.

H. MACMILLAN, referring to the resignation of Treasury Ministers in a statement at London Airport before leaving for Commonwealth tour, 7 Jan 58

Jaw-jaw is better than war-war.

H. MACMILLAN, Canberra, 30 Jan 58; echoing CHURCHILL, 'Talking jaw to jaw is better than going to war', White House lunch, 26 Jun 54

Introducing *Super-Mac.*

VICKY, caption of cartoon depicting H. Macmillan in a Superman outfit; first appeared in *Evening Standard*, 6 Nov 58

Life's better with the Conservatives. Don't let Labour ruin it.

Slogan on Conservative posters in the 1959 General Election

What matters is that Mr Macmillan has let Mr Lloyd know that at the Foreign Office, in these troubled times, *enough is enough*.

Article by David WOOD, *The Times* Political Correspondent, 1 Jun 59

Britain belongs to you.

Title of Labour Party election manifesto, published 18 Sep 59

The wind of change is blowing through this Continent, and, whether we like it or not, this growth of national consciousness is a political fact.

H. MACMILLAN, address to Joint Assembly of Union Parliament, Cape Town, 3 Feb 60

We have developed instead an affluent, open and democratic society, in which the class escalators are continually moving and in which *people are divided not so much between 'haves' and 'have-nots' as between 'haves' and 'have-mores'*.

R. BUTLER, at a Conservative Political Centre Summer School, 8 Jul 60

There are some of us, Mr Chairman, who will *fight and fight and fight again* to save the party we love.

H. GAITSKELL, Labour Party Conference, Scarborough, 3 Oct 60

The present Colonial Secretary ... has been *too clever by half* ... I believe that the Colonial Secretary is a very fine bridge player ... It is not considered immoral, or even bad form to outwit one's opponents at bridge ... It almost seems to me as if the Colonial Secretary, when he abandoned the sphere of bridge for the sphere of politics, brought his bridge technique with him.

M OF SALISBURY, referring to I. MACLEOD and his policies for Africa, House of Lords, 7 May 61

SCOTT: Do you think the Unions are going to respond to what amounts in effect to a 'wage freeze' in the public sector?
LLOYD: Well, I said that I wasn't going to deal with every possible circumstance. This is a pause rather than a *wage freeze*.

S. LLOYD interviewed on B.B.C. *Radio Newsreel* by Hardiman Scott about the 'July measures'

It does mean, if this is the idea, the end of Britain as an independent European state ... it means the end of *a thousand years of history*.

H. GAITSKELL, Labour Party Conference, Brighton, 3 Oct 62

It is a moral issue.

Heading of *The Times* leader on the Profumo Affair, 11 Jun 63

A great party is not to be brought down because of a *squalid affair between a woman of easy virtue and a proven liar.*

LORD HAILSHAM, in a B.B.C. interview with R. McKenzie about the Profumo Affair, 13 Jun 63

He would, wouldn't he?

Mandy RICE-DAVIES in a Magistrates Court on 28 Jun 63, referring to a peer denying knowing her

And in bygone days, commanders were taught that, when in doubt, they should march their troops towards the sound of gunfire. I intend to *march my troops towards the sound of gunfire.*

J. GRIMOND, in a speech to the Liberal Assembly at Brighton, 15 Sep 63

We are re-defining and we are re-stating our socialism in terms of the *scientific revolution* ... the Britain that is going to be forged in *the white heat* of this revolution will be no place for restrictive practices or out-dated methods on either side of industry.

H. WILSON, Labour Party Conference, Scarborough, 1 Oct 63

I hope that it will soon be possible for *the customary processes of consultation* to be carried on within the Party about its future leadership.

H. MACMILLAN, in the letter in which he announced his resignation as P.M.; read out to the Conservative Party Conference at Blackpool by the Earl of Home, 10 Oct 63

After half a century of democratic advance, the whole process has ground to a halt with *a 14th Earl.*

H. WILSON, in a speech at Belle Vue, Manchester, 19 Oct 63

When you come to think of it, he is *the 14th Mr Wilson.*

Lord HOME in a television interview by Kenneth Harris on ITV, 21 Oct 63

Let's go with Labour.

Labour Party slogan used 1964

If the British public falls for this [Labour policies] it will be *stark staring bonkers.*

Q. HOGG, press conference at Conservative Central Office during the election campaign, 12 Oct 64

I have been given *the bed of nails.*

R. GUNTER, on his appointment as Minister of Labour, 18 Oct 64

Smethwick Conservatives can have the satisfaction of having topped the poll, of having sent a Member who, until another election returns him to oblivion, will serve his time here as *a Parliamentary leper.*

H. WILSON, referring Peter Griffiths, M.P., who defeated Patrick Gordon Walker in an allegedly racist election campaign at Smethwick, House of Commons, 4 Nov 64

A week is a long time in politics.

Attributed to H. WILSON, probably first used in a lobby briefing late in 1964

In this connection [use of military force in Rhodesia] the Prime Ministers noted the statement by the British Prime Minister that on the expert advice available to him, the cumulative effects of the economic and financial sanctions might well bring the rebellion to an end within *a matter of weeks rather than months.*

Final communique of Commonwealth Prime Ministers' Conference at Lagos, released 12 Jan 66; referring back to unreported speech by H. WILSON also on 12 Jan 66

Action not words.

Title of Conservative manifesto, published 6 Mar 66

You KNOW Labour Government works.

Labour Party slogan used in 1966 election

Now one encouraging gesture from the French Government, which I welcome, and the Conservative leader *rolls on his back like a spaniel.*

H. WILSON, Bristol, 18 Mar 66

It is difficult for us to appreciate the pressures which are put on men ... in the highly organised strike committees in the individual ports by this *tightly knit group of politically motivated men* ... who are now determined to exercise back-stage pressures ... endangering the security of the industry and the economic welfare of the nation.

H. WILSON, House of Commons, 20 Jun 66

Sterling has been under pressure for the past two and a half weeks. After an improvement in the early weeks of May, we were *blown off course* by the seven weeks seamen's strike.

H. WILSON, House of Commons, 20 Jul 66

Every dog is allowed one bite, but a different view is taken of *a dog* that goes on biting all the time. He may *not get his licence returned* when it falls due.

H. WILSON, speech to Parliamentary Labour Party, 2 Mar 67

It does not mean, of course, that *the pound* here in Britain *in your pocket* or purse or in your bank *has been devalued.*

H. WILSON, television and radio broadcast announcing devaluation of the pound, 20 Nov 67

As I look ahead, I am filled with foreboding. Like the Roman, I seem to see *'the River Tiber foaming with much blood'*

E. POWELL, speech to a Conservative Political Centre Meeting in Birmingham, 20 Apr 68, referring to the Aeneid *'Thybrim multo spumantem sanguine cerno'.*

In place of strife.

Title of Government White Paper on industrial relations legislation, 19 Jan 69

I will never consent to preside over a Government which is not allowed to govern ... I have no intention of being a MacDonald. Nor do I intend to be another Dubcek. *Get your tanks off my lawn,* Hughie!

Remark attributed to H. WILSON, addressing H. SCANLON, at a private dinner at Chequers to discuss *In Place of Strife*, 1 Jun 69

Selsdon Man is designing a system of society for the ruthless and the pushing, the uncaring ... His message to the rest is: you're out on your own.

H. WILSON, at a Rally of the Greater London Party in Camden Town Hall, 21 Feb 70; referring to the Conservative policy-forming meeting at Selsdon Park, Croydon, 31 Jan 70

Nor would it be in the interests of the Community that its enlargement should take place except with the *full-hearted consent* of Parliament and people of the new member countries.

E. HEATH in a speech to the Franco-British Chamber of Commerce in Paris, 5 May 70

I am determined, therefore, that a Conservative Government shall introduce *a new style of government.*

E. HEATH, in foreword to Conservative manifesto, published May 70

This would, *at a stroke,* reduce the rise in prices, increase productivity and reduce unemployment.

Wrongly reported in *The Times* as having been said by E. HEATH at a press conference at Central Office, 16 Jun 70; actually taken from a Conservative Press Release (No. G.E.228) distributed at the press conference

We believe that the essential need of the country is to gear its policies to the great majority of the people, who are not *lame ducks.*

J. DAVIES, speaking in a debate on public expenditure and taxation, House of Commons, 4 Nov 70; echoing a speech by A. BENN in the House of Commons ['the next question is what safeguards are there against the support of lame ducks'] on 1 Feb 68

Yesterday's Men.

Slogan on Labour poster caricaturing Conservative leaders, May 70; subsequently title of B.B.C. television programme about Labour leaders in opposition, transmitted 17 Jun 71

We say that what Britain needs is a new *Social Contract*. That is what this document [Labour's Programme 1972] is all about.

J. CALLAGHAN, Labour Party Conference, 2 Oct Blackpool, 72; but A. BENN had used the phrase in a 1970 Fabian pamphlet *The New Politics*. J.-J. Rousseau's *Le Contrat Social* was published in 1762

It is the unpleasant and *unacceptable face of capitalism*, but one should not suggest that the whole of British industry consists of practices of this kind.

E. HEATH, replying to a question from J. Grimond about the Lonrho affair, House of Commons, 15 May 73

From 31 December, they [most industrial and commercial premises] will be limited [in the use of electricity] to *three* specified *days* each *week*.

E. HEATH, House of Commons, 13 Dec 73

Looking around the House, one realises that *we are all minorities now* – indeed, some more than others.

J. THORPE, House of Commons, after the election of the Speaker, 6 Mar 74

We believe that the only way in which the maximum degree of national cooperation can be achieved is for *a government of national unity* to be formed.

J. THORPE in a letter to E. Heath, 4 Mar 74. Later in the year the phrase became a central theme in the Conservatives' October campaign

With its [the local government world's] usual spirit of patriotism and its tradition of service to the community's needs, it is coming to realize that, for the time being at least, *the party is over.*

A. CROSLAND, at a civic luncheon at Manchester 9 May 1975

Ladies and Gentlemen, I stand before you tonight in my green chiffon evening gown, my face softly made up, my fair hair gently waved ... The *Iron Lady* of the Western World. Me? A cold war warrior? Well, yes if that is how they wish to interpret my defence of values and freedoms fundamental to our way of life.

Margaret THATCHER, speaking in her Finchley constituency, 31 Jan 76, referring to a report in the Soviet *Red Star*, 23 Jan 76

That part of his speech was rather like being *savaged by a dead sheep.*

D. HEALEY, 14 Jun 78, replying to a Commons attack by Sir G. Howe

Labour isn't working.

Slogan on Conservative poster designed by Saatchi and Saatchi, showing dole queue in Aug 1978 and widely used in the 1979 election

Crisis? What Crisis? (Journalist: 'What .... of the mounting chaos in the country at the moment?'
Callaghan: 'I don't think that other people in the world would share the view that there is mounting chaos.')

Sun headline, 11 Jan 79, referring to J. CALLAGHAN at London airport on return home from Guadaloupe summit during widespread strikes, 10 Jan 1979

The Labour Way is the Better Way.

Title of Labour election manifesto published Apr 1979

I don't see how we can talk with Mrs Thatcher ... I will say to the lads, come on, get your *snouts in the trough.*

S. WEIGHELL, speaking in London, 10 Apr 79, echoing his speech at the Labour Party Conference, Blackpool, 6 Oct 78, 'If you want it to go out ... that you now believe in the philosophy of the pig trough those with the biggest snouts get the largest share, I reject it.'

There is no alternative.

A phrase widely attributed to Margaret THATCHER in 1979 and 1980

We are fed up with *fudging and mudging*, with mush and slush.

D. OWEN, at Labour Party Conference, Blackpool, 2 Oct 80

The Lady's not for turning.

Margaret THATCHER, Conservative Party Conference, Brighton, 10 Oct 80

Breaking the mould of British politics.

Phrase widely used after 1981 about the goals of the Alliance. Its origin seems to lie in R. JENKINS, *What Matters Now* (1972), quoting Andrew Marvell on Cromwell 'Casting Kingdoms of Old/Into another mould.'

Go back to your constituencies and *prepare for Government.*

D. STEEL addressing Liberal Party Conference in Llandudno, 18 Sep 81

He [his unemployed father in the 1930s] didn't riot. *He got on his bike* and looked for work.

N. TEBBIT, Conservative Party Conference, Blackpool, 15 Oct 81

'GOTCHA'

Sun headline on 4 May 82 on the sinking of the Argentine cruiser Belgrano

Let me make one thing absolutely clear. *The NHS is safe with us.*

Margaret THATCHER, addressing Conservative Party Conference, Brighton, 8 Oct 82

Heckler: 'At least Mrs Thatcher has got *guts.*'
Kinnock: 'And it's a pity that people had to leave theirs on the ground at *Goose Green* in order to prove it.'

N. KINNOCK during TV South's election programme *'The South Decides'*, 5 Jun 83

The enemy within is just as dangerous to our liberty ... It is a battle that we must win.

Margaret THATCHER referring to A. Scargill and the Miners' Strike, article in *Daily Express*, 20 Jul 84

We must try to starve the terrorist and the hijacker of *the oxygen of publicity* on which they depend.

Margaret THATCHER, quoted in *Financial Times*, 16 Jul 85

I'll tell you what happens with impossible promises. You start with implausible resolutions, which are then pickled into a rigid dogma or code. And you end up with the *grotesque chaos of a Labour Council* – a Labour Council – *hiring taxis to scuttle round a city handing out redundancy notices* to its own workers.

N. KINNOCK, addressing Labour Party Conference in Bournemouth, 1 Oct 85 (these words are from the advance text)

As one person said, it is perhaps being *economical with the truth.*

Sir R. ARMSTRONG, Permanent Secretary to the Cabinet, under cross examination in an Australian Court over the British Government's attempt to prevent publication of the book *Spycatcher*, 18 Nov 86. The phrase can be traced back to Mark Twain and Edmund Burke.

I think we've been through a period where too many people have been given to understand that if they have a problem, it's the government's job to cope with it ... They're casting their problem on society. And, you know, *there is no such thing as society.* There are individual men and women, and there are families, and no government can do anything except through people, and people must look to themselves first.

Margaret THATCHER, article in *Woman's Own*, 31 Oct 87

Nigel was Chancellor. Nigel's position was *unassailable,* unassailable.

Margaret THATCHER, in an interview with B.Walden on ITV three days after N. Lawson's resignation, 29 Oct 89

I have a young family and for the next few years I should like to *devote more time* to them while they are still so young.

N. FOWLER in his letter of resignation to the Prime Minister, 3 Jan 90 and

I am naturally very sorry to see you go, but understand your reasons for doing so, particularly your wish to be able to *spend more time with your family.*

Margaret THATCHER replying to N. FOWLER's resignation letter, 3 Jan 90.

The President of the Commission, M. Delors, said at this conference the other day that he wanted the European Parliament to be the democratic body of the Community, he wanted the Commission to be the Executive, and he wanted the Council of Ministers to be the Senate. *No. No. No.*

Margaret THATCHER speaking in the House of Commons on her return from the Rome summit, 30 Oct 90

The time has come for others to consider their own response to the *tragic conflict of loyalties* with which I have myself wrestled for perhaps too long.

Sir G. HOWE in his resignation speech, House of Commons, 13 Nov 90

Britain has done itself no good by the distinction drawn between the skill of blue collar and white collar workers ... In the next ten years we will have to continue to make changes which will make the whole of this country a *genuinely classless society.*

J. MAJOR writing in *Today,* 24 Nov 90

I want to see us build *a country that is at ease with itself,* a country that is confident and a country that is able and willing to build a better quality of life for all its citizens.

J. MAJOR speaking in Downing Street on becoming Prime Minister, 28 Nov 90

Rising unemployment and the recession have been the price we've had to pay to get inflation down. But that is *a price well worth paying.*

N. LAMONT, House of Commons, 16 May 91

The *green shoots of economic spring* are appearing once again.

N. LAMONT speaking at the Conservative Party Conference, 9 Oct 91

Labour's Double Whammy.

Slogan attacking Labour tax plans coined by Conservative Central Office and used on pre-election publicity material, Feb 92

I think what is important is if we can get the government to understand the notion of *tough on crime, tough on the causes of crime.* If we can get them to agree to that then we've got a chance.

T. BLAIR, in an interview on *The World This Weekend,* BBC Radio, 21 Feb 93

Je ne regrette rien.

N. LAMONT speaking at a press conference during the Newbury by-election campaign, 12 May 93

Fifty years from now Britain will still be the country of long shadows on county grounds, *warm beer,* invincible green suburbs, dog lovers and pools fillers and – as George Orwell said – 'old maids bicycling to holy communion through the morning mist' and – if we get our way – Shakespeare will still be read even in school.

J. MAJOR, Speech to Conservative Group for Europe, 22 April 1993

I can bring other people into the Cabinet, that is right, but where do you think most of the poison has come from? It is coming from the dispossessed and the never-possessed. You and I can both think of ex-ministers who are going around causing all sorts of trouble. Would you like three more of the *bastards* out there?

J. MAJOR, referring to Eurosceptic critics in Cabinet in off-the-record remarks to M. Brunson of ITN, 23 Jul 93

The old values – neighbourliness, decency, courtesy – they're still alive, they're still the best of Britain ... It is time to return to those core values, time to get *back to basics*, to self-discipline and respect for the law, to consideration for others, to accepting responsibility for yourself and your family and not shuffling off on other people and the State.

J. MAJOR, Conservative Party Conference, Blackpool, 8 Oct 93

Under my leadership, I will *never* allow this country to *be isolated* or left behind *in Europe*.

T. BLAIR, Labour Party Conference, Blackpool, 4 Oct 94

Our party: New Labour. Our mission: New Britain. *New Labour New Britain.*

T. BLAIR, Labour Party Conference, Blackpool, 4 Oct 94

On message

Phrase attributed by journalists to Labour Party media officials at the Party Conference in Brighton, Oct 95

If it falls to me to cut out the cancer of bent and twisted journalism in our country with the simple *sword of truth* and the trusty shield of British fair play, so be it. I am ready for the fight.

J. AITKEN on resigning office to fight a libel action, 10 Apr 95. (He was jailed for perjury, 7 Jun 99)

Ask me my three main priorities for government and I will tell you; *education, education and education.*

T. BLAIR, Conference Speech, Blackpool, 1 Oct 96

Tell the kids to *get their scooters off my lawn.*

Words attributed to K. CLARKE at lunch with BBC Political Correspondents, 4 Dec 96, referring to press officials at Conservative Central Office allegedly trying to control his public statements. It was an echo of H. WILSON'S remark to H. Scanlon, 1 Jun 69.

The powers are like those of any local authority. Powers that are constitutionally there can be used, but the Scottish Labour Party has no plans to raise income tax. And once the power is given, it's like any parish council, it's got the right to exercise it.

T. BLAIR in an interview published in the *Scotsman*, 4 Apr 97

There is *something of the night* in his personality.

Remark attributed to ANNE WIDDECOMBE referring to M. HOWARD, first quoted in *The Sunday Times*, 11 May 97

Our task today is not to fight old battles but to show that there is a *third way,* a way of marrying together an open competitive and successful economy with a just and decent human society.

T. BLAIR in a speech at Malmo, Sweden, 6 Jun 97

Kitchen Table Politics.

A phrase about party strategy, used in Conservative Central Office (but echoing Congressman R. Gephardt), first publicised in *The Times*, 8 Mar 99

In Europe, not run by Europe.

Slogan used by the Conservatives in the 1999 European Elections, drawn from the 1997 Manifesto, allegedly first suggested by W. HAGUE

Political Scandals

The following list is not comprehensive but indicates most of the more celebrated examples. A few others are implicit in the list of ministerial resignations on pp.74–75. See also Seats Forfeited (p.223) and Election Petitions (p.262).

1904	Wyndham (Ministerial involvement with Irish Home Rule Schemes)
1912	Marconi (Ministers dealing in shares)
1918	Pemberton Billing (Libel action involving many public figures)
1918	Maurice (Army Council's disciplining of a General)
1921	Bottomley (M.P. and financial practice)
1922ff.	Maundy Gregory (Sale of honours)
1936	Budget leak (Minister telling M.P. of budget plans)
1940	Boothby (Minister influencing handling of blocked Czech assets)
1947	Allighan (M.P. leaking Parliamentary Labour Party meetings)
1948	Belcher/Stanley (Influence peddling at the Board of Trade)
1951	Burgess/Maclean (Spies fleeing to Moscow)
1954	Crichel Down (Minister's handling of sequestrated land)
1957	Bank Rate (Alleged leak)
1962	Vassall (Spy scandal)
1963	Profumo (Minister lying to the House)
1972	Poulson (Influence peddling in building)
1973	Jellicoe/Lambton (Sex scandal)
1976	Stonehouse (M.P.'s simulated drowning)
1976–9	Thorpe (Liberal Leader ultimately acquitted of conspiracy to murder)
1979	Blunt (Spy scandal)
1983	Parkinson (Sex scandal)
1986	Westland (Helicopter takeover)
1992	Mellor (Ministerial indiscretion)
1992	Matrix-Churchill (Arms for Iraq)
1993	Mates (Involvement with Asil Nadir scandal)
1994	'Back to Basics' (A succession of six private scandals affecting Ministers and Conservative M.P.s)
1995–7	Cash for Questions (Allegations that a number of Conservative M.P.s had accepted improper payment)
1995–9	Aitken (Payment of a hotel bill leading to a Cabinet resignation and a jail sentence for perjury)
1998	Mandelson (Unreported house-puchase loan)

Major Civil Disturbances and Demonstrations (in Great Britain)

8 Nov 1910	Tonypandy
16 Aug 1911	Liverpool ('Bloody Sunday' clash between police and strikers)
1915–16	Anti-German riots in the East End
11 Nov 1918	Armistice Day
31 Jul 1919	Glasgow ('Bloody Friday' confrontation between police and strikers)
3–10 May 1926	General Strike
Sep 1932	Unemployed demonstrations provoke violence in Birkenhead, Belfast and London
7 Jun 1934	Olympia (violence at Mosley rally)
4 Oct 1936	Cable Street (confrontation between police and anti-fascists)
Nov 1936	Jarrow Hunger March
8 May 1945	VE-Day
15 Aug 1945	VJ-Day
24 Aug 1958	Nottingham (race riot)
Apr 1958	First Aldermaston March
31 Aug 1958	Notting Hill Gate (race riot)
17 Mar 1968	Grosvenor Square (Demonstration against Vietnam War)
15 Jun 1968	Red Lion Square (confrontation between Nat.Front and opponents)
Jan–Mar 1972	Saltley (mass picketing of the coke depot)
Jul–Sep 1977	Grunwick, Dollis Hill (mass picketing of photographic factory)
23 Apr 1979	Southall (confrontation between police and anti-National Front demonstrators)
2 Apr 1980	St Paul's, Bristol (anti-police riots)

11–13 Apr 1981	Brixton (anti-police riot with racial overtones; more trouble Jul 81)
5–6 Jul 1981	Toxteth (major riot)
1981–91	Greenham Common (women's protests against nuclear weapons)
Mar 1984–Mar 85	Miners' Strike (many confrontations between police and pickets)
6 Oct 1985	Broadwater Farm, North London (riot)
Jan 1986–Feb 87	Wapping (confrontation between police and pickets)
31 Mar 1990	London and many other places (anti-poll tax demonstrations and riots)
Apr 1990	Strangeways Prison, Manchester (prisoners' riot)
Oct 1992	Anti-Pit Closure demonstrations
Jul-Aug 1991	Series of Youth riots in Leeds, Telford, Cardiff, Oxford and Newcastle
1993–4	Twyford Down (Winchester Bypass)
1995	Newhaven and other ports and airports. Export of live animals
1995–7	Newbury Bypass
1 Mar 1998	Countryside March to Hyde Park

Political Assassinations
(Members of the House of Lords or House of Commons)

22 Jun 1922	Field-Marshal Sir H. Wilson (shot in London by Sinn Fein)
5 Apr 1979	A. Neave (IRA bomb in his car at the House of Commons)
27 Aug 1979	Earl Mountbatten (killed by bomb on holiday in the Irish Republic)
10 Oct 1984	Sir A. Berry (IRA bomb at Conservative Conference)
30 Jul 1990	I. Gow (IRA bomb at his Sussex home)

VI

CIVIL SERVICE

Heads of Departments and Public Offices

The Permanent Secretary is the official head and usually the accounting officer of the Department and is responsible to the Minister for all the Department's activities. In some Departments, e.g. Defence since 1964, there are also Second Permanent Secretaries who are official heads and usually accounting officers for large blocks of work. Except where stated otherwise, all the following had the title of Permanent Secretary or Permanent Under-Secretary. The name is that by which they were known while in office; if a title was acquired while in office it is placed in brackets.

Admiralty

1884	Sir E. MacGregor
1907	Sir I. Thomas
1911	Sir G. Greene
1917	Sir O. Murray
1936	Sir R. Carter
1940	Sir H. Markham
1947	(Sir) J. Lang
1961	Sir C. Jarrett
1964	*(see Defence)*

Agriculture & Fisheries

1892	(Sir) T. Elliott
1913	Sir S. Olivier
1917	(Sir) D. Hall
1920	Sir F. Floud
1927	Sir C. Thomas
1936	(Sir) D. Fergusson
1945	Sir D. Vandepeer
1952	Sir A. Hitchman

(Agriculture, Fisheries & Food)

1955	Sir A. Hitchman
1959	Sir J. Winnifrith
1968	Sir B. Engholm
1973	Sir A. Neale
1978	(Sir) B. Hayes
1983	(Sir) M. Franklin
1987	(Sir) D. Andrews
1993	(Sir) R. Packer

Air

1917	Sir A. Robinson
1920	(Sir) W. Nicholson
1931	(Sir) C. Bullock
1936	Sir D. Banks
1939	Sir A. Street
1945	Sir W. Brown
1947	Sir J. Barnes
1955	Sir M. Dean
1963	(Sir) M. Flett
1964	*(see Defence)*

Aircraft Production

(Director-General)

1940	Sir A. Rowlands
1943	Sir H. Scott
1945–45	Sir F. Tribe

Aviation

(see Transport & Civil Aviation)

1959	Sir W. Strath
1960	(Sir) H. Hardman
1963	Sir R. Way
1966	Sir R. Clarke
1966–67	Sir R. Melville

Burma

(see India & Burma)

Cabinet

(Secretary to the Cabinet)

1916	(Sir) M. Hankey
1938	Sir E. Bridges
1947	Sir N. Brook
1963	Sir B. Trend
1973	Sir J. Hunt
1979	Sir R. Armstrong
1988	Sir R. Butler
1998	Sir R. Wilson

(Permanent Secretary to the Cabinet Office)

1998	R. Mountfield
1999	B. Bender

(Chief Scientific Adviser)

1964	Sir S. Zuckerman (Ld)
1971	Sir A. Cottrell
1974	*(post vacant)*
1986	(Sir) J. Fairclough
1990	Sir W. Stewart
1995	Sir R. May

(Head of Government Statistical Service)

1968	(Sir) C. Moser
1978	(Sir) A. Boreham
1986	(Sir) J. Hibbert
1992	W. McLennan
1995	T. Holt

(see Office for National Satistics)

Central Policy Review Staff

(Director-General)

1970	Ld Rothschild
1974	Sir K. Berrill
1980	R. Ibbs
1982	J. Sparrow
1983	*(post vacant)*

(see p. 307 for Economic Advisers)

Civil Aviation

(Director-General)

1941	Sir W. Hildred
1946	Sir H. Self
1947	Sir A. Overton
1953	*(see Transport & Civil Aviation)*

Civil Service Commission

(First Commissioner)

1892	W. Courthope
1907	Ld F. Hervey
1910	(Sir) S. Leathers
1928	(Sir) R. Meiklejohn
1939	(Sir) P. Waterfield
1951	P. Sinker
1954	(Sir) L. Helsby
1959	Sir G. Mallaby
1965	Sir G. Abell
1968	J. Hunt
1971	K.Clucas
1974	F. Allen

Civil Service Commission

(First Commissioner) (cont.)

1981	A. Fraser
1983	D. Trevelyan
1989	J. Holroyd
1994	Anne Bowtell
1995	Sir M. Bett

Head of the Home Civil Service

1919	Sir W. Fisher
1939	Sir H. Wilson
1942	Sir R. Hopkins
1945	Sir E. Bridges
1956	Sir N. Brook
1963	Sir L. Helsby
1968	Sir W. Armstrong
1974	Sir D. Allen
1978	Sir I. Bancroft
1981 ⎰	Sir R. Armstrong
1981 ⎱	Sir D. Wass
1983	Sir R. Armstrong
1988	Sir R. Butler
1998	Sir R. Wilson

Civil Service Department

1968	Sir W. Armstrong
1974	Sir D. Allen
1978	Sir I. Bancroft
1981	*(post vacant)*

Colonial Office

1897	(Sir) E. Wingfield
1900	(Sir) M. Ommaney
1907	Sir F. Hopwood
1911	Sir J. Anderson
1916	Sir G. Fiddes
1921	Sir J. Masterton-Smith
1925	Sir S. Wilson
1933	Sir J. Maffey
1937	Sir C. Parkinson
1940	Sir G. Gater
1940	Sir C. Parkinson
1942	Sir G. Gater
1947	Sir T. Lloyd
1956	Sir J. Macpherson
1959	Sir H. Poynton
1966	*(see Commonwealth Affairs)*

Commonwealth Relations Office

1947	Sir E. Machtig
1947	Sir A. Carter
1949	Sir P. Liesching
1955	Sir G. Laithwaite
1959	Sir A. Clutterbuck
1962–66	Sir S. Garner

(Commonwealth Affairs)

1966	Sir S. Garner
1968–68	Sir M. James

Culture, Media & Sport

(see National Heritage)

1997	(Sir) H. Phillips
1998	R. Young

Customs Establishment

(Chairman)

1900	(Sir) G. Ryder
1903	(Sir) T. Pittar

(Board of Customs and Excise)

1909	(Sir) L. Guillemard
1919	Sir H. Hamilton
1927	Sir F. Floud
1930	J. Grigg
1930	(Sir) E. Forber
1934	Sir E. Murray
1941	Sir W. Eady
1942	Sir A. Carter
1947	Sir W. Croft
1955	Sir J. Crombie
1963	Sir J. Anderson
1965	Sir W. Morton
1969	Sir L. Petch
1973	(Sir) R. Radford
1978	(Sir) D. Lovelock
1983	(Sir) A. Fraser
1987	(Sir) B. Unwin
1993	(Dame) V. Strachan
2000	

Defence

1947	Sir H. Wilson Smith
1948	Sir H. Parker
1956	Sir R. Powell
1960	Sir E. Playfair
1961	Sir R. Scott
1964	Sir H. Hardman
1966	Sir J. Dunnett
1974	Sir M. Cary
1976	Sir F. Cooper
1983	(Sir) C. Whitmore
1988	Sir M. Quinlan
1993	Sir C. France
1995	R. Mottram
1998	K. Tebbit

Defence (Procurement)

(Chief Executive)

1971	(Sir) D. Rayner
1972	Sir M. Cary
1974	(Sir) G. Leitch
1975	(Sir) C. Cornford

1980	(Sir) D. Cardwell
1983	D. Perry
1985	(Sir) P. Levene
1991	M. McIntosh
1996	Sir R. Walmsley

Dominions Office

1925	Sir C. Davies
1930	Sir E. Harding
1940	Sir C. Parkinson
1940–47	Sir E. Machtig

Economic Affairs

1964	Sir E. Roll
1966	(Sir) D. Allen
1968–69	Sir W. Nield

Economic Warfare

(Director-General)

1939 ⎰	Sir F. Leith-Ross
1940 ⎱	Sir F. Leith-Ross
1940	E of Drogheda
1942–45	E of Drogheda

Education (and Science 1964–92)

1900	Sir G. Kekewich
1903	Sir R. Morant
1911	Sir A. Selby-Bigge
1925	Sir A. Symonds
1931	Sir H. Pelham
1937	(Sir) M. Holmes
1945	Sir J. Maud
1952	(Sir) G. Flemming
1959	Dame M. Smieton
1967	Sir H. Andrew
1970	(Sir) W. Pile
1976	(Sir) J. Hamilton
1983	(Sir) D. Hancock
1989	(Sir) J. Caines
1992	Sir D. Holland
1994	Sir T. Lankester

(Education and Employment)

1996	(Sir) M. Bichard

Employment

(see Labour)

Energy

1974	Sir J. Rampton
1980	Sir D. Maitland
1983	Sir K. Couzens
1985	(Sir) P. Gregson
1989	G. Chipperfield
1991–92	J. Guinness

Environment (Transport and the Regions)

1970	Sir D. Serpell
1972	Sir J. Jones
1975	Sir I. Bancroft
1978	Sir J. Garlick
1981	(Sir) G. Moseley
1985	(Sir) T. Heiser
1992	(Sir) R. Wilson
1994	A. Turnbull
1998	Sir R. Mottram

Food

(Director-General)

1918	Sir C. Fielding
1919–21	F. Coller
1939	Sir H. French
1945	Sir F. Tribe
1946	Sir P. Liesching
1949	(Sir) F. Lee
1951	Sir H. Hancock
1955	*(see Agriculture, Fisheries & Food)*

Foreign Office

1894	Sir T. Sanderson (Ld)
1906	Sir C. Hardinge (Ld)
1910	Sir A. Nicolson
1916	Ld Hardinge
1920	Sir E. Crowe
1925	Sir W. Tyrrell
1928	Sir R. Lindsay
1930	Sir R. Vansittart
1938	Sir A. Cadogan
1946	Sir O. Sargent
1949	Sir W. Strang
1953	Sir I. Kirkpatrick
1957	Sir F. Hoyer Millar
1962	Sir H. Caccia
1965	Sir P. Gore-Booth

(Foreign and Commonwealth Office)

(Also, from 1968, Head of Diplomatic Service)

1969	Sir D. Greenhill
1973	Sir T. Brimelow
1975	Sir M. Palliser
1982	Sir A. Acland
1986	Sir P. Wright
1991	Sir D. Gillmore
1994	Sir J. Coles
1997	Sir J. Kerr

(Foreign Office, German Section)

1947	Sir W. Strang
1949	Sir I. Kirkpatrick
1950–51	Sir D. Gainer

Forestry Commission

(Chairman)

1920	Ld Lovat
1927	Ld Clinton
1929	Sir J. Stirling-Maxwell
1932	Sir R. Robinson (Ld)
1952	E of Radnor
1964	Earl Waldegrave
1966	L. Jenkins
1970	Ld Taylor of Gryfe
1976	J. Mackie
1979	Sir D. Montgomery
1989	(Sir) R. Johnstone
1994	Sir P. Hutchison

Fuel & Power

1942	Sir F. Tribe
1945	Sir D. Fergusson
1952	Sir J. Maud

(Power)

1957	Sir J. Maud
1958	(Sir) D. Proctor
1965	Sir M. Stevenson
1966	Sir D. Pitblado
1969	*(see Technology)*

Government Accountancy Service

1984	(Sir) A. Wilson
1989	Sir A. Hardcastle
1993	A. Likierman

Health

1919	Sir R. Morant
1920	Sir A. Robinson
1935	Sir G. Chrystal
1940	Sir J. Maude
1945	Sir W. Douglas
1951	(Sir) J. Hawton
1960	(Sir) B. Fraser
1964–68	(Sir) A. France

(Health & Social Security)

1968	Sir C. Jarrett
1970	Sir P. Rogers
1975	Sir P. Nairne
1981	Sir K. Stowe
1987	Sir C. France

(Health)

1988	Sir C. France
1992	(Sir) G. Hart
1997	C. Kelly

Home Office

1895	Sir K. Digby
1903	Sir M. Chalmers
1908	Sir E. Troup
1922	Sir J. Anderson
1932	Sir R. Scott
1938	Sir A. Maxwell
1948	Sir F. Newsam
1957	Sir C. Cunningham
1966	Sir P. Allen
1972	Sir A. Peterson
1977	(Sir) R. Armstrong
1979	Sir B. Cubbon
1988	Sir C. Whitmore
1994	(Sir) R. Wilson
1998	(Sir) D. Omand

Home Security

1939	(Sir) T. Gardiner
1939	(Sir) G. Gater
1940	Sir G. Gater
1942	Sir H. Scott
1943–45	Sir W. Brown

Housing & Local Government

(see Town & Country Planning)

1951	Sir T. Sheepshanks
1955	Dame E. Sharp
1966	Sir M. Stevenson
1970	(see *Environment*)

India

1883	Sir A. Godley
1909	Sir R. Ritchie
1912	Sir T. Holderness
1920	Sir W. Duke
1924	Sir A. Hirtzel
1930	Sir F. Stewart

(India & Burma)

1937	Sir F. Stewart
1941–47	(Sir) D. Monteath

Industry

1974	Sir A. Part
1976–83	Sir P. Carey
(see Trade and Industry)	

Information

(Director of Propaganda)

1918–19	A. Bennett

(Director-General)

1939	Sir K. Lee
1940	F. Pick
1941	Sir C. Radcliffe
1945–46	E. Bamford

(Central Office of Information)

(Director-General)

1946	Sir E. Bamford
1946	Sir R. Fraser
1954	(Sir) T. Fife Clark
1971	F. Bickerton
1974	H. James
1978	J. Groves
1982	D. Grant
1985	N. Taylor
1989	G. Devereux

(Chief Executive)

1996	A. Douglas
1998	Carol Fisher

Board of Inland Revenue

(Chairman)

1899	Sir H. Primrose
1907	(Sir) R. Chalmers
1911	Sir M. Nathan
1914	Sir E. Nott-Bower
1918	W. Fisher
1919	Sir J. Anderson
1922	Sir R. Hopkins
1927	Sir E. Gowers
1930	(Sir) J. Grigg
1934	Sir E. Forber
1938	Sir G. Canny
1942	Sir C. Gregg
1948	Sir E. Bamford
1955	Sir H. Hancock
1958	Sir A. Johnston
1968	Sir A. France
1973	(Sir) N. Price
1976	Sir W. Pile
1980	Sir L. Airey
1986	Sir A. Battishill
1997	N. Montagu

International Development

1997	(Sir) J. Vereker

Irish Office

1893	Sir D. Harrel
1902	Sir A. Macdonnell
1908	Sir J. Dougherty
1914	Sir M. Nathan
1916	Sir W. Byrne
1918	(Sir) J. Macmahon
1920–22	Sir J. Anderson

Labour

1916	(Sir) D. Shackleton
1920	Sir J. Masterton-Smith
1921	Sir H. Wilson
1930	Sir F. Moud
1935	Sir T. Phillips

(Labour & National Service)

1939	Sir T. Phillips
1944	(Sir) G. Ince
1956	Sir H. Emmerson

(Labour)

1959	Sir L. Helsby
1962	Sir J. Dunnett
1966	(Sir) D. Barnes

(Employment & Productivity)

1968	Sir D. Barnes

(Employment)

1970	Sir D. Barnes
1974	(Sir) C. Heron
1975	(Sir) K. Barnes
1983	(Sir) M. Quinlan
1988	(Sir) G. Holland
1993–95	(Sir) N. Monck

(see Education)

Land & Natural Resources

1964	F. Bishop
1965–66	Sir B. Fraser

Local Government Board

1898	(Sir) S. Provis
1910–19	(Sir) H. Monro

Secretary to the Ld Chancellor & Clerk of the Crown in Chancery

1885	(Sir) K. Mackenzie
1915	(Sir) C. Schuster
1944	(Sir) A. Napier
1954	(Sir) G. Coldstream
1968	(Sir) D. Dobson
1977	(Sir) W. Bourne
1982	(Sir) D. Oulton
1989	(Sir) T. Legg
1999	Sir H. Phillips

Materials

1951	A. Hitchman
1952	Sir J. Helmore
1953–54	Sir E. Bowyer

Munitions

1915	Sir H. Llewellyn Smith
1916	E. Phipps
1917	Sir G. Greene
1920–1 {	Sir S. Dannreuther
1920–1 {	D. Neylan

National Health Service Management Board

(Chairman)

1985	V. Paige
1986	L. Peach
1989	(Sir) D. Nichol
1994	(Sir) A. Langlands

National Heritage

1992	H. Phillips

(see Culture)

National Insurance

1944	Sir T. Phillips
1949	Sir H. Hancock
1951	Sir G. King
1953	*(see Pensions & National Insurance)*

National Service

1917	S. Fawcett
1918–19	W. Vaughan

National Statistics

(Chief Executive)

1996	T. Holt

Northern Ireland

1972	Sir W. Nield
1973	(Sir) F. Cooper
1976	(Sir) B. Cubbon
1979	Sir P. Woodfield
1984	(Sir) R. Andrew
1988	Sir J. Blelloch
1990	(Sir) J. Chilcot
1997	J. Pilling

Overseas Development

1964	Sir A. Cohen
1968	Sir G. Wilson
1970	*(see Foreign & Commonwealth Office)*
1974	(Sir) R. King
1976	(Sir) P. Preston
1982	Sir W. Ryrie
1984	Sir C. Tickell
1987	J. Caines
1989	(Sir) T. Lankester
1994–97	J. Vereker

(see International Development)

Pensions

1916	Sir M. Nathan
1919	Sir G. Chrystal
1935	Sir A. Hore
1941	(Sir) A. Cunnison
1946	Sir H. Parker
1948	Sir A. Wilson

(Pensions & National Insurance)

1953 Sir G. King
1955 Sir E. Bowyer
1965–66 Sir C. Jarrett
(see Social Security)

Post Office

1899 Sir G. Murray
1903 Sir H. Babington-Smith
1909 Sir M. Nathan
1911 Sir A. King
1914 (Sir) E. Murray

(Director-General)

1934 (Sir) D. Banks
1936 Sir T. Gardiner
1946 Sir R. Birchall
1949 (Sir) A. Little
1955 (Sir) G. Radley
1960 Sir R. German
1966–68 (Sir) J. Wall
(Deputy Chairman of Post Office Board)

Power

(see Fuel & Power)

Prices and Consumer Protection

1974–79 (Sir) K. Clucas

Privy Council

(Clerk of the Council)

1899 (Sir) A. FitzRoy
1923 Sir M. Hankey
1938 Sir R. Howorth
1942 (Sir) E. Leadbitter
1951 F. Fernau
1953 (Sir) W. Agnew
1974 (Sir) N. Leigh
1984 (Sir) G. de Deney
1992 N. Nicholls
1999 A. Galloway

Production

1942 Sir H. Self
1943 J. Woods

Property Services

1979 Sir R. Cox
1981 A. Montague
1984 Sir G. Manzie
1990 P. Brown
1991 (Sir) G. Chipperfield

Office of Public Service (and Science 1992–5)

1992 R. Mottram
1995 (Sir) R. Mountfield

Reconstruction

1943–45 N. Brook

General Register Office

(Registrar-General for England and Wales)

1880 Sir B. Henniker
1900 R. MacLeod
1902 (Sir) W. Dunbar
1909 (Sir) B. Mallet
1921 (Sir) S. Vivian
1945 (Sir) G. North
1959 E. Firth
1964 M. Reed
1972 G. Paine
1978 A. Thatcher
1986 Gillian Banks
1990 P. Wormald
1996 T. Holt

Department of Scientific and Industrial Research

(Secretary)

1916 (Sir) F. Heath
1927 H. Tizard
1929 (Sir) F. Smith
1939 (Sir) E. Appleton
1949 Sir B. Lockspeiser
1956 (Sir) H. Melville
(merged with Science Research Council 1965)

Office of the Minister for Science

1962–64 F. Turnbull

Scottish Office

1892 Sir C. Scott-Moncrieff
1902 Sir R. Macleod
1909 Sir J. Dodds
1921 Sir J. Lamb
1933 Sir J. Jeffrey
1937 J. Highton
1937 Sir H. Hamilton
1946 (Sir) D. Milne
1959 Sir W. Murie
1965 (Sir) D. Haddow
1973 (Sir) N. Morrison
1978 (Sir) W. Fraser
1988 (Sir) R. Hillhouse
1998 M. Russell
(Scottish Executive took over 1 Jul 99)

Shipping

1917 (Sir) J. Anderson
1919–20 T. Lodge
1939–41 Sir C. Hurcomb

Social Security

1966 Sir C. Jarrett
1968–88 *(see Health & Social Security)*
1988 (Sir) M. Partridge
1996 Dame A. Bowtell
1999 Dame R. Lomax

Supply

1939 Sir A. Robinson
1940 Sir G. Gater
1940 Sir W. Brown
1942 Sir W. Douglas
1945 O. Franks
1946 Sir A. Rowlands
1953 Sir J. Helmore
1956 Sir C. Musgrave
1959–59 Sir W. Strath

Technology

1964 Sir M. Dean
1966 Sir R. Clarke
1970 *(see Trade & Industry*

Town & Country Planning

1943 Sir G. Whiskard
1946 Sir T. Sheepshanks

(Local Government & Planning)

1951 Sir T. Sheepshanks
1951 *(see Housing & Local Government)*

Board of Trade

1893 Sir C. Boyle
1901 Sir F. Hopwood
1907 (Sir) H. Llewellyn Smith
1913 { Sir G. Barnes
1913 { Sir H. Llewellyn Smith
1916 { Sir H. Llewellyn Smith
1916 { (Sir) W. Marwood
1919 { Sir S. Chapman
1919 { Sir W. Marwood
1919 { Sir S. Chapman
1919 { Sir H. Payne
1920 Sir S. Chapman
1927 Sir H. Hamilton
1937 Sir W. Brown
1941 Sir A. Overton
1945 Sir J. Woods
1951 Sir F. Lee
1960 Sir R. Powell
1968 Sir A. Part

(Trade & Industry)

1970	Sir A. Part

(Trade)

1974	Sir P. Thornton
1977	(Sir) L. Pliatzky
1979	Sir K. Clucas

(Trade and Industry)

1979	Sir P. Carey
1983	{ Sir B. Hayes
1983	{ Sir A. Rawlinson
1985	Sir B. Hayes
1989	Sir P. Gregson
1996	(Sir) M. Scholar

Transport

1919	Sir F. Dunnell
1921	Sir W. Marwood
1923	Sir J. Brooke
1927	C. Hurcomb
1937	Sir L. Browett

(Director-General of War Transport)

1941	Sir C. Hurcomb

(Transport)

1946	Sir C. Hurcomb
1947	Sir G. Jenkins

(Transport & Civil Aviation)

1953	Sir G. Jenkins

(Transport)

(see also Aviation)

1959	Sir J. Dunnett
1962	Sir T. Padmore
1968	Sir D. Serpell
1970–76	*(see Environment)*
1976	(Sir) P. Baldwin
1982	(Sir) P. Lazarus
1986	(Sir) A. Bailey
1991	(Sir) P. Brown

(Dept merged with Environment 1997)

Treasury

1894	Sir F. Mowatt
1902	{ Sir F. Mowatt
1902	{ Sir E. Hamilton

1903	{ Sir E. Hamilton
1903	{ Sir G. Murray
1908	Sir G. Murray
1911	{ Sir R. Chalmers
1911	{ Sir T. Heath
1913	{ Sir J. Bradbury
1913	{ Sir T. Heath
1916	{ Sir J. Bradbury
1916	{ Sir R. Chalmers
1919	Sir W. Fisher
1939	Sir H. Wilson
1942	Sir R. Hopkins
1945	Sir E. Bridges
1956	{ Sir N. Brook
1956	{ Sir R. Makins
1959	Sir N. Brook
1960	{ Sir F. Lee
1960	{ Sir N. Brook
1962	{ W. Armstrong
1962	{ Sir L. Helsby
1963	(Sir) W. Armstrong
1968	{ Sir W. Armstrong
1968	{ Sir D. Allen
1968	Sir D. Allen
1974	(Sir) D. Wass
1983	(Sir) P. Middleton
1991	Sir T. Burns
1998	Sir A. Turnbull

Unemployment Assistance Board

(Chairman)

1934	Sir H. Betterton (Ld Rushcliffe)

(Assistance Board)

1940	Ld Rushcliffe
1941	Ld Soulbury

(National Assistance Board)

1948	G. Buchanan
1954	Sir G. Hutchinson (Ld Ilford)
1964–66	Ld Runcorn

University Grants Committee

(Chairman)

1919	Sir W. McCormick
1930	Sir W. Buchanan-Riddell
1935	Sir W. Moberly
1949	(Sir) A. Trueman
1953	(Sir) K. Murray

1968	(Sir) K. Berrill
1973	Sir F. Dainton
1978	(Sir) E. Parks
1983	Sir P. Swinnerton-Dyer

(Higher Education Funding Council)

1992	Sir R. Dearing
1993	B. Gough
1997	Sir M. Checkland

War Office

1897	Sir R. Knox
1901	Sir E. Ward
1914	Sir R. Brade
1920	Sir H. Creedy
1939	Sir J. Grigg
1942	{Sir F. Bovenschen
1942	{Sir E. Speed
1945	Sir E. Speed
1949	Sir G. Turner
1956	Sir E. Playfair
1960	(Sir) R. Way
1963	(Sir) A. Drew
1964	*(see Defence)*

Welsh Office

1964	(Sir) G. Daniel
1969	(Sir) I. Pugh
1971	(Sir) H. Evans
1980	(Sir) T. Hughes
1985	(Sir) R. Lloyd-Jones
1993	M. Scholar
1996	Rachel Lomax
1999	J. Shortridge

(office modified July 1999)

Works

1895	Sir R. Brett (Vt Esher)
1901	Sir S. McDonnell
1912	Sir L. Earle
1933	Sir P. Duff
1941	Sir G. Whiskard
1943	Sir P. Robinson
1946	Sir H. Emmerson
1956	Sir E. Muir

(Public Building & Works)

1962	Sir E. Muir
1965	(Sir) A. Part
1968	Sir M. Cary
1970	*(see Environment)*

Salary of Permanent Secretary to the Treasury

1900	£2,500
1910	£2,500
1920	£3,500
1930	£3,500
1940	£3,500
1950	£3,750
1960	£7,450
1970	£12,700
1980	£33,500
1990	£89,500
1998	£95,720–£164,110

Prime Minister's Principal Private Secretary

1900	S. McDonnell	1939	A. Rucker	1964	D. Mitchell
1902	J. Sandars	1940	E. Seal	1966	A. Halls
1905	A. Ponsonby	1941	J. Martin	1970	A. Isserlis
1908	V. Nash	1945	L. Rowan	1970	R. Armstrong
1912	M. Bonham-Carter	1947	L. Helsby	1975	K. Stowe
1916	J. Davies	1950	D. Rickett	1979	C. Whitmore
1922	(Sir) R. Waterhouse	1951	D. Pitblado	1982	R. Butler
1928	R. Vansittart	1952 {	D. Pitblado	1985	N. Wicks
1930	P. Duff	1952 {	J. Colville	1988	A. Turnbull
1933	J. Barlow	1955	D. Pitblado	1992	A. Allan
1934	H. Vincent	1956	F. Bishop	1997	J. Holmes
1937	O. Cleverly	1959	T. Bligh	1999	J. Heywood

'Chief of Staff'

1979–85	D. Wolfson
1997	J. Powell

Secretary for Public Appointments

1947	(Sir) A. Bevir	1982	(Sir) J. Catford
1956	D. Stephens	1993	(Sir) J. Holroyd
1961	J. Hewitt	2000	W. Chpman
1972	C. Peterson		

Prime Minister's Staff

In addition to an official Civil Service Principal Private Secretary, all Prime Ministers have made their own arrangements for advice and help. These cannot be consistently categorised. The following have played significant roles.

Policy Advisers

General advisers

1917–18	W. Adams
1918–21	P. Kerr
1921–22	E. Grigg
1940–45	F. Lindemann (Ld Cherwell)
1945–46	D. Jay
1946–48	W. Gorell Barnes

Head of Policy Unit

1974	B. Donoughue
1979	J. Hoskyns
1983	F. Mount
1983	J. Redwood
1985	B. Griffiths
1990	Sarah Hogg
1995	N. Blackwell
1997	D. Miliband (*acting 97–98*)

(see also Heads of Central Policy Review Staff p.301)

Specialist Advisers

1935–39	Sir H. Wilson (Industrial Relations)
1982–83	Sir A. Parsons (Foreign Policy)
1984–92	Sir P. Cradock (Foreign Policy)
1983–89	Sir A. Walters (Economics)
1983–89	Sir D. (Ld) Rayner (Efficiency)
1983–88	Sir R. Ibbs (Efficiency)
1988–92	Sir A. Fraser (Efficiency)
1992–97	Sir P. Levene (Efficiency and Competition)
1992–93	Sir R. Braithwaite (Foreign Policy)

Political Secretary/Adviser

1929–35	H. D. Usher
1929–35	Rosa Rosenberg
1957–63	J. Wyndham
1964–70	Marcia Williams
1964–68	T. Balogh
1970–74	D. Hurd

1974–74	W. Waldegrave		1955–56	W. Clark
1974–76	Marcia Williams (Lady Falkender)		1957–64	S. Evans
1976–79	T. McNally			*Press Secretary*
1979–81	R. Ryder			
1981–83	D. Howe		1964–69	T. Lloyd-Hughes
1983–87	S. Sherbourne		1969–70	J. Haines
1987–90	J. Whittingdale			*Chief Press Secretary*
1990–92	Judith Chaplin			
1992–94	J. Hill		1970–73	D. Maitland
1994–97	H. James		1973–74	W. Haydon
1997–	Sally Morgan			*Press Secretary*

Press Officers

Chief Press Liaison Officer

| 1931–44 | G. Steward |

Adviser on Public Relations

1945–47	F. Williams
1947–51	P. Jordan
1951–52	R. Bacon

| 1974–76 | J. Haines |
| 1976–79 | T. McCaffrey |

Chief Press Secretary

1979–90	B. Ingham
1990–94	G. O'Donnell
1994–96	C. Meyer
1996–97	J. Haslam
1997–	A. Campbell

Special or Political Advisers to Ministers

Many Ministers have brought in unofficial advisers and secretaries but political advisers only became established in an official way after 1974 (although in 1970–74 six or seven Conservative ministers had full-time assistants paid from party funds). During H. Wilson's 1974 ministry it was agreed that any Cabinet minister could appoint two political advisers with a tenure that lasted only as long as he or she continued in office. In 1979 Margaret Thatcher limited Cabinet ministers to one political adviser – except for the Treasury, the Home Office, the Foreign Office and the Department of the Environment. In May 1997 the incoming Labour Government agreed that each Cabinet Minister could have two Special Advisers and there was a significant increase in the number employed in the Prime Minister's Office. Two Special Advisers (A. Campbell and J. Powell) were dispensed from the restriction on Special Advisers having any authority over civil servants.

Number of Special Advisers

| Nov 1974 | 28 | | Jul 1999 | 72 (22 working in 10 Downing St.) |
| Feb 1997 | 38 (8 working in 10 Downing St.) | | | |

Size of Civil Service

Adequate statistics of the number of civil servants engaged in each branch of government activity since 1900 are not readily available. Moreover, the transfer of functions between departments makes comparisons of one year with another potentially misleading. An analysis of civil service strength for certain years is to be found in *The Organisation of British Central Government, 1914–1956*, by D. N. Chester and F. M. G. Wilson. The figures in heavy type in the following table are taken from the statement *Staffs Employed in Government Departments* which has been published annually, or more frequently, by the Treasury as a Command Paper since 1919 (with retrospective figures for 1914 included in the first issue). The figures in light type in the table are taken from the Annual Estimates presented to Parliament by the Civil Service and Revenue Departments, and the East India House Accounts. These figures are liable to slight error as they are estimates and not reports of the actual staff employed. In each case they are estimates for the year ending March 31 of the following year (e.g. under the third column headed '1 Apr 1920' the estimates are for 1920–21). The source for the 1971 figures is the departmental returns made to the Civil Service Department. The figures in this table should be used with great caution because of the considerable differences in the sources.

Number of Civil Servants

	1901	1 Aug 1914	1 Apr 1920	1 Apr 1930	1 Apr 1938	1 Apr 1950	1 Apr 1960	1 Apr 1970	1 Apr 1980	1 Apr 1990	1 Oct 1998
Total Non-industrial	n.a.	282,420	380,963	306,154	376,491	575,274	637,374	498,425	547,486	495,000	462,254
Total Industrial	n.a.	497,100	n.a.	483,100	204,400	396,900	358,900	201,660	157,417	67,000	31,919
Total Civil Service staff	n.a	779,520	n.a.	789,254	580,891	972,174	996,274	700,085	704,903	562,388	494,173
Admiralty	n.a.	4,366	13,432	7,433	10,609	30,801	30,731	f	f	f	f
War Office	n.a.	1,636	7,434	3,872	7,323	33,493	47,244	f	f	f	f
Air	–	–	2,839	1,704	4,317	24,407	27,563	f	f	f	f
Aviation Sup.	–	–	–	–	–	5,271	24,756	f	f	f	f
Defence (incl. R. Ordnance Factories)	–	–	–	–	–	–	–	128,803	118,450	141,373	44,080
Foreign O.[an]	142	187	885	730	902	6,195	5,992	12,802	11,291	9,491	5,458
Colonial Off.	109	214	256	365	438	1,286	1,211	g	–	–	–
Dominions, CRO	–	–	–	52	91	904	847	g	–	–	–
India Office	589	554	342	n.a.	539	–	–	–	–	–	–
Irish Office	559	1,007	829	–	–	–	–	i	208	194	223
Scottish Off.	159	401	517	68	n.a.	749	887	5,651	9,990	10,274	3,505
Welsh O.[h]	–	–	–	–	–	–	–	903	2,324	2,284	2,081
Treasury[bq]	120	140	291	299	344	1,396	1,322	1,012	1,044	3,135	890
Home Office	297	773	926	1,024	1,688	3,953	3,534	21,743	30,289	42,721	10,729
Agriculture	182	2,976	3,446	2,463	4,588	16,842	14,938	14,874	13,273	9,881	10,330
Education	864	2,187	1,522	1,041	1,435	3,280	2,738	4,127	2,594	2,560	4,454
Energy	–	–	–	–	–	–	–	–	1,252	1,024	–
Environment	–	–	4,142	–	–	–	–	38,806	28,177	6,074[p]	4,589
Food	–	–	–	–	–	30,785	c	–	–	–	–
(Fuel &) Power	–	–	–	–	–	6,358	1,768	k	–	–	–
Health (& Soc. Sec.)	–	a	5,820	6,711	6,771	5,893	4,993	71,811	95,923	5,422	4,770
Social Security	–	–	–	–	–	–	–	–	–	80,890	2,888
Labour (Emp.)[m]	–	4,428	17,835[d]	18,076[d]	26,934[d]	29,902	21,394	31,099[j]	48,718	48,138	–
Housing (& Local Govt.)	425	963	–	–	–	1,312	2,802	–	–	–	–
Munitions	–	–	11,440	–	–	–	–	–	–	–	–
Nat. Insurance	–	1,250	2,263	–	–	n.a.	36,323	n.a.[e]	35,539[e]	–	–
Pensions	–	1,957	24,169	6,175	3,147	10,954	–	–	–	–	–
Post Office	79,482	88,890	209,269	194,933	224,374	249,869	254,919	u	–	–	–
Supply	–	–	–	–	–	13,312	–	k	–	–	–
Bd of Trade	1,359	2,535	5,410	4,398	4,611	10,136	6,735	k	–	–	–

	1901	1 Aug 1914	1 Apr 1920	1 Apr 1930	1 Apr 1938	1 Apr 1950	1 Apr 1960	1 Apr 1970	1 Apr 1980	1 Apr 1990	1 Oct 1998
Trade & Industry	–	–	–	–	–	–	–	24,549[k]	–	11,793	4,359
Trade	–	–	–	–	–	–	–	–	7,163	–	–
Industry	–	–	–	–	–	–	–	–	8,499	–	–
Transport	–	–	876	759	2,820	**6,906**	**6,909**	[p]	12,792	15,513	–
Works	140	**679**	580	2,054	3,584	**17,573**	**10,693**	–	–	–	–
Customs & Ex.	3,792	10,256	12,602	11,659	14,669	14,236	15,338	17,949	27,232	26,864	23,045
Exchequer	230	269	269	331	369	501	532	577	–	–	–
Inland Revenue	**5,345**	**9,753**	**19,446**	**21,059**	**24,342**	**49,740**	**56,026**	69,765	78,282	66,063	49,530
Nat. Assistance	–	n.a.	n.a.	n.a.	8,105	8,516	10,509	[e]	–	–	–
H.M.S.O.	100	517	728	1,660	1,947	3,241	2,903	3,480	3,070	3,201	3,080
Civil Serv. Dpt[q]	–	–	–	–	–	–	[q]	2,070	3,210	–	–
Cabinet Office	–	–	–	–	186	393	319	565	580	1,484	1,548
C.S.O./O.N.S.[r]	–	–	–	–	–	–	–	–	[s]	999	2,890
C.P.S.[s]	–	–	–	–	–	–	–	–	–	4,710	5,568
Ld Chancellor	–	–	–	–	–	–	–	–	–	10,454	9,999
Nat.Heritage[t]	–	–	–	–	–	–	–	–	–	[t]	601

[a] Home civil servants only.

[b] Not including subordinate departments (e.g. Committee of Imperial Defence, University Grants Commission).

[c] Combined with Ministry of Agriculture and Fisheries.

[d] The functions of the Local Government Board passed to the Ministry of Health in 1919. In 1943 the Ministry of Town and Country Planning (later becoming the Ministry of Housing and Local Government) took back many of these functions from the Ministry of Health.

[e] National Insurance merged with the Ministry of Pensions, and in 1966 together with the N.A.B. became the Ministry of Social Security.

[f] In 1964 the Admiralty, War Office and Air Office were combined into the Ministry of Defence.

[g] In 1965 the Foreign Office, Commonwealth Relations Office, and attaches abroad were combined into the Diplomatic Service, whose personnel appear under Foreign Office.

[h] The Welsh Office was set up in 1964.

[i] The Northern Ireland Office was set up in 1972.

[j] In 1970 the Ministry of Housing and Local Government, Ministry of Public Building and Works and the Ministry of Transport were combined into the Department of the Environment.

[k] In 1970 the Board of Trade and the the Ministry of Technology combined into the Department of Trade and Industry. In 1974 the DTI was broken up into four Departments (Trade, Industry, Energy and Prices & Consumer Protection). Prices was absorbed back into Trade in 1979. Trade and Industry merged in 1983. Energy was re-absorbed into the DTI in 1992.

[l] In 1968 the Ministry of Social Security and the Ministry of Health combined into the Department of Health and Social Security. They were split again in 1988.

[m] The Ministry of Labour became the Department of Employment in 1968. In 1995 it was absorbed into the Dept. of Education and Employment.

[n] Staff of the Overseas Development Administration are included in the Foreign Office total throughout, although for a period after 1974 the Ministry of Overseas Development was technically a separate department.

[p] The Ministry of Transport became a separate department in 1976.

[q] The Civil Service Department was formed in 1968 by the merger of the Civil Service Commission and the pay and management side of the Treasury. It was abolished in 1981 and its functions divided between the Cabinet Office and the Treasury.

[r] The Central Statistical Office was established on 31 Jul 89.

[s] The Crown Prosecution Service was established on 20 Jul 87.

[t] The Department of National Heritage was established on 3 Jul 92. It became the Department of Culture, Media and Sport in Jul 97.

[u] The Post Office was turned into a Public Corporation in 1969.

Next Steps

In 1987 the Prime Minister commissioned a report into Civil Service reform, published in 1988 under the title *Improving Management in Government: The Next Steps* (The Ibbs Report). It proposed that many of the functions currently performed by the Civil Service could be undertaken more efficiently by semi-autonomous agencies managing themselves outside the main Civil Service structure. The programme began the same year, and was given legislative effect by the *Government Trading Act, 1990*. By 1 Jan 98, 383,290 civil servants were operating on *Next Steps* lines.

	Launched	*Wound up/sold*
Lord Chancellor's Dept		
Court Service	3 Apr 95	
HM Land Registry	2 Jul 90	
Public Record Office	1 Apr 92	
Public Trust Office	1 Jul 94	
Foreign Office		
Wilton Park	1 Sep 91	
Treasury		
Central Statistical Office	19 Nov 91	31 Mar 96
HM Customs and Excise[1]	1 Apr 91	
Inland Revenue[1]	1 Apr 92	
National Savings	1 Jul 96	
Office for National Statistics	1 Apr 96	
Paymaster	1 Apr 93	1 Apr 97
Royal Mint	2 Apr 90	
Valuation Office	30 Sep 91	
Home Office		
Fire Service College	1 Apr 92	
Forensic Science Service	1 Apr 91	
HM Prison Service (see p.344)	1 Apr 93	
UK Passport Agency	2 Apr 91	
Trade and Industry		
Accounts Services	1 Oct 91	1 Apr 95
Companies House	3 Oct 88	
Employment Tribunals	1 Apr 97	
Insolvency Service	21 Mar 90	
Govt. Chemistry Lab.	30 Oct 89	31 Mar 96
National Physical Lab.	3 Jul 90	1 Oct 95
Nat. Weights & Measures Lab.	18 Apr 89	
Patent Office	1 Mar 90	
Radiocommunications	2 Apr 90	
Warren Spring Laboratory	20 Apr 89	31 Mar 94
Environment, Transport and Regions		
Building Research	2 Apr 90	19 Mar 97
Coastguard	1 Apr 94	
Driver and Vehicle Licensing	2 Apr 90	
Driving Standards	2 Apr 90	
Highways	1 Apr 94	
Marine Safety	1 Apr 94	
Planning Inspectorate	1 Apr 92	
Ordnance Survey	1 May 90	
QEII Conference Centre	6 Jul 89	
Security Facilities Executive	15 Oct 91	

	Launched	Wound up/sold
Transport Research Laboratory	2 Apr 92	31 Mar 96
Vehicle Certification	2 Apr 90	
Vehicle Inspectorate	1 Aug 88	
Defence		
Armed Forces Personnel Admin.	1 Apr 97	
Army Base Repair Organisation	1 Apr 93	
Army Base Storage and Distribution	4 Apr 95	
Army Personnel Centre	2 Dec 96	
Army Technical Support	19 Oct 95	
Army Training & Recruiting	1 Jul 97	
Chemical & Biological Defence	1 Apr 91	1 Apr 95
Defence Accounts	1 Apr 91	1 Feb 96
Defence Analytical Services	1 Jul 92	
Defence Animal Centre	1 Jun 93	
Defence Bills	1 Jan 96	
Defence Clothing and Textiles	22 Nov 94	
Defence Codification	20 Jun 96	
Defence Dental	1 Mar 96	
Defence Estates	18 Mar 97	
Defence Medical Training	1 Apr 97	
Defence Communications	1 Apr 98	
Defence Evaluation and Research	1 Apr 95	
Defence Intelligence & Security	1 Oct 96	
Defence Operational Analysis	1 Jul 92	1 Apr 95
Defence Postal & Courier Service	1 Jul 92	
Defence Research	2 Apr 91	1 Apr 95
Defence Secondary Care	30 Apr 96	
Defence Transport and Movements	4 Apr 95	
Defence Vetting	1 Apr 97	
Disposal Sales	1 Oct 94	
Duke of York's Royal Military Sch.	1 Apr 92	
Hydrographic Office	6 Apr 90	
Joint Air Reconnaissance Intell.	19 Apr 96	
Logistic Information Systems	21 Nov 94	
Medical Supplies	1 Mar 96	
Meteorological Office	2 Apr 90	
Military Survey	2 Apr 91	
MOD Police	1 Apr 96	
Naval Aircraft Repair Org.	1 Apr 92	
Naval Bases and Supply	11 Dec 96	
Naval Manning	1 Jul 96	
Naval Recruiting and Training	1 Apr 95	
Pay and Personnel	1 Feb 96	
Queen Victoria School	1 Apr 92	
RAF Logistic Support	9 Dec 96	
RAF Maintenance Group	1 Apr 91	
RAF Personnel Management	2 Feb 97	
RAF Signals Engineering	22 Nov 94	
RAF Training Group	1 Apr 94	
Service Children's Education	24 Apr 91	
Ships Support	11 Nov 96	
Specialist Procurement Services	1 Jun 97	
Agriculture, Fisheries and Food		
ADAS	1 Apr 92	2 Apr 97
Central Science Laboratory	1 Apr 92	
Centre for Environment, Fisheries		
and Aquaculture Science	1 Apr 97	

	Launched	*Wound up/sold*
Farming and Rural Conservation	1 Apr 97	
Intervention Board	2 Apr 90	
Meat Hygiene Service	1 Apr 95	
Pesticides Safety Directorate	1 Apr 93	
Veterinary Laboratories	2 Apr 90	
Veterinary Medicines Directorate	2 Apr 90	
Culture, Media and Sport		
Historic Royal Palaces	1 Oct 89	
Royal Parks	1 Apr 93	
Wales		
Cadw: Welsh Historic Monuments	2 Apr 91	
Social Security		
Benefits	2 Apr 91	
Child Support	5 Apr 93	
Contributions	2 Apr 91	
Information Technology Services	2 Apr 90	
Resettlement	24 May 89	31 Mar 96
War Pensions	1 Apr 94	
Public Service		
Buying Agency	31 Oct 91	
Central Computer & Telecom.	1 Apr 96	
Central Office of Information	5 Apr 90	
Chessington Computer Centre	1 Apr 93	31 Jul 96
Civil Service College	6 Jun 89	
Government Car and Despatch	1 Apr 97	
HMSO	14 Dec 88	30 Sep 96
Occupational Health Service	2 Apr 90	18 Sep 96
Property Advisers to Civil Estate	1 Apr 96	
Recruitment & Assessment Services	2 Apr 91	30 Sep 96
Security Facilities Executive	15 Oct 93	
Scotland		
Fisheries Research Services	1 Apr 97	
Forest Research	1 Apr 97	
Forest Enterprise	1 Apr 96	
Historic Scotland	2 Apr 91	
Registers of Scotland	6 Apr 90	
Scottish Agricultural Science	1 Apr 92	
Scottish Court Service	3 Apr 95	
Scottish Fisheries Protection	12 Apr 91	
Scottish Office Pensions	1 Apr 93	
Scottish Prison Service	1 Apr 93	
Scottish Record Office	1 Apr 93	
Student Awards	5 Apr 94	
Northern Ireland		
Business Development Service	1 Oct 96	
Compensation	1 Apr 92	
Construction Service	1 Apr 96	
Driver and Vehicle Licensing	2 Aug 93	
Driver and Vehicle Testing	1 Apr 92	
Child Support	5 Apr 93	
Environment & Heritage Service	1 Apr 96	
Forensic Science	1 Sep 95	
Government Purchasing	1 Apr 96	

	Launched	*Wound up/sold*
Health Estates	2 Oct 95	
Industrial Research & Technology	3 Apr 95	
Land Registers	1 Apr 96	
Ordnance Survey	1 Apr 92	
Planning Service	1 Apr 96	
Prison Service	1 Apr 95	
Public Record Office	3 Apr 95	
Rate Collection	1 Apr 91	
Rivers	1 Oct 96	
Roads Service	1 Apr 96	
Social Security	1 Jul 91	
Statistics and Research	1 Apr 96	
Training and Employment	2 Apr 90	
Valuation and Lands	1 Apr 93	
Water	1 Apr 96	
Education and Employment		
Employment Service	2 Apr 90	
Teachers' Pensions	1 Apr 92	30 Sep 96
Health		
Medical Devices	29 Sep 94	
Medicines Control	11 Jul 91	
NHS Estates	1 Apr 91	
NHS Pensions	20 Nov 92	
Attorney General		
Crown Prosecution Service[1]	1 Oct 88	
Government Property Lawyers	1 Apr 93	
Serious Fraud Office[1]	1 Apr 88	
Treasury Solicitor's Department	1 Apr 96	
Overseas Development		
Natural Resources Institute	2 Apr 90	1 May 96

[1] Not strictly a Next Steps agency, but operating on Next Steps lines.

Sources: *Improving Management in Government: The Next Steps. A Report to the Prime Minister* (Ibbs Report), HMSO 1988. National Audit Office: Report by the Comptroller and Auditor General – *The Next Steps Initiative*, HMSO 1989. Public Accounts Committee, 38th Report. *The Next Steps Initiative*, HMSO 1989. *The Financing and Accountability of Next Steps Agencies* (Cm 914) 1989. *Making the most of Next Steps. A Report to the Prime Minister* (the Fraser Report), HMSO 1991. *Setting Up Next Steps – a short account of the origins, launch and implementation of the Next Steps Project in the British Civil Service*, HMSO 1991. *The Next Steps: review 1993*, HMSO 1993.

VII

ROYAL COMMISSIONS, COMMITTEES OF
INQUIRY AND TRIBUNALS

Investigatory Process

The public investigation of problems can take a number of forms – Royal Commissions, Tribunals, ad hoc departmental Committees and special parliamentary conferences or committees. This chapter does not deal with purely parliamentary bodies such as the Speaker's Conferences (on Electoral Reform – see p.258, and on Devolution see p.470) or like the Select Committees set up from time to time by the House of Commons and/or the House of Lords. But there is an attempt at an exhaustive listing of all domestic Royal Commissions and of all Tribunals of Inquiry appointed under the Tribunals of Inquiry Act, 1921. There is also an arbitrary selection from the 1,000 or so *ad hoc* and statutory Committees of Inquiry appointed since 1900. It is, however, important to remember that the decision whether to refer a problem to a Royal Commission or a Committee is not necessarily determined by the importance of the subject. Royal Commissions are listed fully here because the number is not excessive. Departmental Committees, which have been much more numerous, often deal with relatively narrow and limited matters; the selection here covers only a few which seem plainly to be as important as the average Royal Commission. No reference is made to the committees and sub-committees appointed by Royal Commissions and by standing governmental advisory bodies, though these include some reports of importance, such as the Report to the Central Advisory Council on Education by Lady Plowden's Committee on Primary Education (1967).

Advisory Committees appointed by the Government are of two basic types (apart from those which are just internal committees of Civil Servants): (a) standing committees, set up to give advice on such matters, usually within some general class of subjects, as may from time to time be referred to them or otherwise come to their attention; and (b) *ad hoc* committees, which are appointed to carry out some specific mandate and which come to an end when that mandate is discharged. These committees may be appointed directly by the Minister in his own name or indirectly in the name of the Crown. Finally, standing and *ad hoc* committees may both be appointed in two different ways: namely, by virtue of conventional or (in the case of the Crown) prerogative powers, or by virtue of authority conferred by Parliament by means of a statute.

Royal Commissions

Royal Commissions are *ad hoc* advisory committees formally appointed by the Crown by virtue of its prerogative powers. All such committees appointed since the turn of the century are listed in the table below, along with the name of their chairman, their size, the dates of their appointment and adjournment, and the Command number of their final report. There is no 'official' title for a Royal Commission, so that usage may vary slightly from the names given below. Where there were two successive chairmen for a single committee, both are listed. The size of a Royal Commission is given as of the date of its appointment; subsequent changes in membership are not shown. The date of appointment is the date on which the Royal Warrant appointing the committee was signed, and the date of adjournment is the date of signature of the last report issued (or, failing that, the date of its presentation to the House of Commons). Command numbers in the twentieth century form part of four successive series, each of which is marked by a different abbreviation of the word 'Command' as follows:

1900–18   Cd. 1 to Cd.9239
1919–56   Cmd. 1 to Cmd. 9889
1956–86   Cmnd. 1 to Cmnd.99271
1986–   Cm.1–

Title	Chairman	Size	Date appointed	Date of Report	Command number
Military and Civil Expenditure of India	Ld Welby	14	Apr 96	Aug 00	131
Local Taxation	Ld Balfour	14	Aug 96	May 01	638
University of London Act	Ld Davy	8	Aug 98	Feb 00	83
Newfoundland. Operation of Certain Treaties	Sir J. Bramston	2	Aug 98	Report not published	
Accidents to Railway Servants	Ld Hereford	14	May 99	Jan 00	41
Salmon Fisheries	E of Elgin	9	Mar 00	Jul 02	1188
Administration of the Port of London	Earl Egerton Ld Revelstoke	7	Jun 00	Jun 02	1151
South African Hospitals	Sir R. Romer	5	Jul 00	Jan 01	453
Poisoning by Arsenic (Arsenic in Beer and Other Articles of Diet)	Ld Kelvin	6	Feb 01	Nov 03	1848
University Education (Ireland)	Ld Robertson	11	Jul 01	Feb 03	1483
Tuberculosis	Sir M. Foster W. H. Power	5	Aug 01	Jun 11	5761
Coal Supplies	Ld Ailerton	15	Dec 01	Jan 05	2353
Alien Immigration	Ld James	7	Mar 02	Aug 03	1741
Physical Training (Scotland)	Ld Mansfield	9	Mar 02	Mar 03	1507
Martial Law Sentences in S. Africa	Ld Alverstone	3	Aug 02	Oct 02	136
South African War	E of Elgin	7	Sep 02	Jul 03	1789
Superannuation in the Civil Service	L. Courtney	9	Nov 02	Aug 03	1744
Locomotion and Transport in London	Sir D. Barbour	12	Feb 03	Jun 05	2597
Militia and Volunteer Forces	D of Norfolk	10	Apr 03	May 04	2061
Food Supply in Time of War	Ld Balfour of Burleigh	17	Apr 03	Aug 05	2643
Trade Disputes and Trade Combinations	A. Murray (Ld Dunedin)	5	Jun 03	Jan 06	2825
Ecclesiastical Discipline	Sir M. Hicks Beach	14	Apr 04	Jun 06	3040
The Feeble-Minded	M of Bath	10	Sep 04	–	
Churches (Scotland)	E of Elgin	3	Dec 04	Apr 05	2494
War Stores in South Africa	Sir G. Farwell	5	Jun 05	Jul 06	3127
Motor-car	Ld Selby	7	Sep 05	Jul 06	3080
Poor Laws	Ld Hamilton	18	Dec 05	Feb 09	4498
Canals and Inland Navigation of the United Kingdom	Ld Shuttleworth	15	Mar 06	Dec 09	4979
Duties of the Metropolitan Police	D. B. Jones A. Lyttelton	5	May 06	Jun 08	4156
Registration of Title	Ld Dunedin	8	May 06	Jul 10	5316
Safety in Mines	Ld Monkswell H. Cunynghame	9	Jun 06	–	–
Trinity College, Dublin	Sir E. Fry	9	Jun 06	Jan 07	311
Coast Erosion	I. Guest	13	Jul 06	reconstituted	
Congested Districts in Ireland	E of Dudley	9	Jul 06	May 08	4097
Lighthouse Administration	G. Balfour	5	Aug 06	Jan 08	3923
Vivisection	Ld Selby A. Ram	10	Sep 06	Mar 12	6114
Care and Control of the Feeble-Minded	E of Radnor	12	Nov 06	Jul 08	4202
Shipping 'Rings' or Conferences generally	A. Cohen	21	Nov 06	reconstituted	
Mines and Quarries	Ld Monkswell	9	May 07	Feb 11	5561
Church of England in Wales and Monmouthshire	Sir R. Vaughan-Williams	9	Jun 07	Nov 10	5432
Indian Decentralisation	Sir H. Primrose C. Hobhouse	6	Sep 07	Feb 09	4360

Title	Chairman	Size	Date appointed	Date of Report	Command number
Whisky and other Potable Spirits	Ld Hereford	8	Feb 08	Jul 09	4796
Coast Erosion and Afforestation	I. Guest	19	Mar 08	May 11	5708
Land Transfer Acts	Ld St Aldwyn	12	Jul 08	Jan 11	5483
Systems of Election	Ld R. Cavendish	8	Dec 08	May 10	5163
University Education in London	Ld Haldane	8	Feb 09	Mar 13	6717
Mauritius	Sir F. Swettenham	3	May 09	Apr 10	5185
Trade Relations between Canada and the West Indies	Ld Balfour	5	Aug 09	Aug 10	5369
Selection of Justices of the Peace	Ld James	16	Nov 09	Jul 10	5250
Divorce and Matrimonial Causes	Ld Gorell	14	Nov 09	Nov 12	6478
Metalliferous Mines and Quarries	Sir H. Cunynghame	9	May 10	Jun 14	7476
Public Records	Sir F. Pollock	9	Oct 10	Apr 18	367
Railways Conciliation and Arbitration Scheme of 1907	Sir D. Hamel	5	Aug 11	Oct 11	5922
Malta	Sir F. Mowatt	3	Aug 11	May 12	6090
Civil Service	Ld MacDonnell H. Smith	19	Mar 12	Nov 15	7832
The Natural Resources, Trade and Legislation of the Dominions	E. Vincent	10	Apr 12	Feb 17	8462
Public Services (India)	Ld Islington	12	Sep 12	Aug 15	8282
Housing of the Industrial Population of Scotland, rural and urban	G. Ballantyne	12	Oct 12	Sep 17	8731
Delay in the King's Bench Division	Ld St Aldwyn	11	Dec 12	Nov 13	7177
Finance and Currency (East Indies)	A. Chamberlain	10	Apr 13	Feb 14	7236
Venereal Diseases	Ld Sydenham	15	Nov 13	Feb 16	8189
Meat Export Trade of Australia	P. Street	1	Jun 14	Apr 15	7896
The circumstances connected with the Landing of Arms at Howth July 26th, 1914	Ld Shaw	3	Aug 14	Sep 14	7631
University Education in Wales	Ld Haldane	9	Apr 16	Feb 18	8991
The Rebellion in Ireland	Ld Hardinge	3	May 16	Jun 16	8729
The Arrest and subsequent treatment of Mr Francis Sheehy Skeffington, Mr Thomas Dickson, and Mr Patrick James McIntyre	Sir J. Simon	3	Aug 16	Sep 16	8376
Allegations against Sir John Jackson	A. Chamel	3	Nov 16	Mar 17	8518
Limited Proportional Representation	J. Lowther	5	Feb 18	Apr 18	9044
Decimal Coinage	Ld Emmott	20	Aug 18	Feb 20	628
Income Tax	Ld Colwyn	21	Apr 19	Mar 20	615
Agriculture	H. Peat	2	Jul 19	Dec 19	473[1]
Oxford and Cambridge Universities	H. Asquith	19	Nov 19	Mar 22	1588
The University of Dublin (Trinity College)	A. Geikie	5	Mar 20	Nov 20	1078
Fire Brigades and Fire Prevention	Sir P. Laurence	14	Jan 21	Jul 23	1945
The Importation of Store Cattle	Ld Finlay	5	May 21	Aug 21	1139
Local Government of Greater London	Vt Ullswater	8	Oct 21	Feb 23	1830
Honours	Ld Dunedin	7	Sep 22	Dec 22	1789
Local Government	E of Onslow	12	Feb 23	Nov 29	3436
Mining Subsidence	Ld Blanesburgh	13	Jun 23	Jun 27	2899
Superior Civil Services India	H. Lee	9	Jun 23	Mar 24	2128
Lunacy and Mental Disorder	H. Macmillan	10	Jul 24	Jul 26	2700
National Health Insurance	Ld Lawrence	13	Jul 24	Feb 26	596
Food Prices	Sir A. Geddes	16	Nov 24	Apr 25	2390
Indian Currency and Finance	E. Hilton Young	9	Aug 25	Jul 26	*Parl.paper*
The Coal Industry	Sir H. Samuel	4	Sep 25	Mar 26	2600
Court of Session and the Office of Sheriff Principal (Scotland)	Ld Clyde	9	Jan 26	Jan 27	2801
Agriculture in India	M of Linlithgow	10	Apr 26	Apr 28	3132

Title	Chairman	Size	Date appointed	Date of Report	Command number
Cross-River Traffic in London	Ld Lee of Fareham	6	Jul 26	Nov 26	2772
Land Drainage in England and Wales	Ld Bledisloe	11	Mar 27	Dec 27	2993
National Museums and Art Galleries	Vt d'Abernon	11	Jul 27	Jan 30	3463
London Squares	M of Londonderry	14	Aug 27	Sep 28	3196
Police Powers and Procedure	Ld Lee	8	Aug 28	Mar 29	3297
Transport	Sir A. Griffith-Boscawen	12	Aug 28	Dec 30	3751
Labour in India	J. Whitley	11	Jul 29	Mar 31	3583
Licensing (England and Wales)	Ld Amulree	19	Sep 29	May 31	3988
Civil Service	Ld Tomlin	16	Oct 29	Jul 31	3909
Licensing (Scotland)	Ld Mackay	14	Oct 29	May 31	3894
Unemployment Insurance	H. Gregory	7	Dec 30	Oct 32	4185
Malta	Ld Askwith	3	Apr 31	Jan 33	3993
Lotteries and Betting	Sir S. Rowlatt	12	Jun 32	Jun 33	4341
Newfoundland	Ld Amulree	3	Feb 33	Aug 33	4480
The University of Durham	Ld Moyne	8	Mar 34	Jan 35	4815
Tithe Rentcharge in England and Wales	J. Williams	4	Aug 34	Nov 35	5095
Despatch of Business at Common Law	Earl Peel	7	Dec 34	Jan 36	5065
Private Manufacture of and Trading in Arms	J. Bankes	7	Feb 35	Sep 36	5292
Local Government in the Tyneside Area	Sir A. Scott	5	May 35	Feb 37	5402
Merthyr Tydfil	Sir A. Lowry	2	May 35	Nov 35	5039
Safety in Coal Mines	Ld Rockley	10	Dec 35	Dec 38	5890
Palestine	Earl Peel	1	Aug 36	Jun 37	5479
The Distribution of the Industrial Population	Sir M. Barlow	13	Jul 37	Dec 39	153
Rhodesia-Nyasaland	Vt Bledisloe	1	Mar 38	Mar 39	5949
West Indies	Ld Moyne	1	Aug 38	Dec 39	6607
Workmen's Compensation	Sir H. Hetherington	15	Dec 38	Dec 44	658
Population	Vt Simon	16	Mar 44	–	
	Sir H. Henderson	14	May 46	Mar 49	7695
Equal Pay	C. Asquith	9	Oct 44	Oct 46	6937
Justices of the Peace	Ld du Parcq	16	Jun 46	May 48	7463
The Press	Sir D. Ross	17	Apr 47	Jun 49	7700
Betting, Lotteries and Gaming	H. Willink	13	Apr 49	Mar 51	8190
Capital Punishment	Sir E. Gowers	12	May 49	Sep 53	8932
Taxation of Profits and Income	Ld Cohen Ld Radcliffe	14	Jan 51	May 55	9474
University Education in Dundee	Ld Tedder	9	Mar 51	Apr 52	8514
Marriage and Divorce	Ld Morton of Henryton	18	Sep 51	Dec 55	9678
Scottish Affairs	E of Balfour	15	Jul 52	Jul 54	9212
East Africa	Sir H. Dow	8	Jan 53	May 55	9475
The Civil Service	Sir R. Priestley	12	Nov 53	Nov 55	9613
The Law Relating to Mental Illness and Mental Deficiency	Ld Percy of Newcastle	11	Feb 54	May 57	169
Common Land	Sir I. Jennings	12	Dec 55	Jul 58	462
Doctors' and Dentists' Remuneration	Sir H. Pilkington	9	Mar 57	Feb 60	939
Local Government in Greater London	Sir E. Herbert	7	Dec 57	Oct 60	1164
The Police	Sir H. Willink	15	Jan 60	Apr 62	1728
The Press	Ld Shawcross	5	Mar 61	May 62	1811
The Penal System in England and Wales	Vt Amory	16	Jul 64	(wound up May 66)	
Reform of the Trade Unions and Employers' Associations	Ld Donovan	12	Apr 65	Jun 68	3623
Medical Education	Ld Todd	16	Jun 65	Mar 68	3569
Tribunals of Inquiry	Sir C. Salmon	7	Feb 66	Nov 66	3121
The Examination of Assizes and Quarter Sessions	Ld Beeching	8	Nov 66	Sep 69	4153

Title	Chairman	Size	Date appointed	Date of Report	Command number
Local Government, England	Sir J. Maud (Ld)	11	May 66	Jun 69	4040
Local Government, Scotland	Ld Wheatley	9	May 66	Sep 69	4150
The Constitution	Ld Crowther	16	Apr 69	Oct 73	5460
	Ld Kilbrandon				
Civil Liability and Compensation	Ld Pearson	16	Mar 73	Mar 78	7054
The Press	Sir M. Finer	11	Jun 74	Jul 77	6810
	O. McGregor				
Standards of Conduct in Government	Ld Salmon	12	Jul 74	Jul 76	6526
Gambling	Vt Rothschild	10	Feb 76	Jul 78	7200
National Health Service	Sir A. Merrison	16	May 76	Jul 79	7613
Legal Services	Sir H. Benson	15	Jul 76	Oct 79	7648
Criminal Procedures	Sir C. Philips	16	Dec 77	Jan 81	8092
Criminal Justice	Ld Runciman	11	Jun 91	Jul 93	2263
Care of the aged	Sir S. Sutherland	12	Dec 97	Mar 99	4192
Reform of the House of Lords	Ld Wakeham	11	Feb 99	Jan 00	

Permanent and Operating Commissions

Certain Royal Commissions have an enduring existence:

The Royal Commission on Historical Manuscripts set up in 1869 sits under the *ex officio* Chairmanship of the Master of the Rolls. It was reconstituted with extended powers in 1959. Its task is to advise and assist in the preservation of historical manuscripts and to publish them.

The Royal Commission on Historical Monuments was set up for England in 1908 with similar bodies for Scotland (reconstituted 1948) and Wales and Monmouthshire. Their task is to maintain an inventory of Ancient Monuments.

The Royal Fine Arts Commission was set up in 1924 (reconstituted in 1933 and 1946) and the Royal Fine Art Commission for Scotland in 1927 (reconstituted 1948): their task is to inquire into questions of public amenity and artistic importance. The Royal Fine Arts Commission was replaced in 1999 by the Commission for Architecture and the Built Environment.

The Royal Commission for the Exhibition of 1851, surviving from the winding up of the affairs of the Great Exhibition, still distributes the income from surplus funds to promote scientific and artistic education. There was also the Royal Commission for the Patriotic Fund (1854–1904). In addition, there have been operating Commissions for the Paris Exhibition of 1900, the St Louis Exhibition of 1904, and for the International Exhibitions at Brussels, Rome and Turin in 1910 and 1911. Another miscellaneous group of operating Royal Commissions covered Sewage Disposal (1898–1915), Horse-Breeding (1887–1911), and Crofter Colonisation (1888–1906).

War produced another group of operating or semi-permanent Royal Commissions, Sugar Supply (1914–21), Wheat Supplies (1916–25), Paper and Paper making materials (1917–18), Defence of the Realm Losses (1915–20), Compensation for Suffering Damage by Enemy Action (1921–24), Awards to Inventors (1919–35, 1946–56) and Foreign Compensation Commission (1950–). The Royal Commission on the Distribution of Incomes, set up under Ld Diamond in 1974, had a continuing existence until 1979.

In 1994 The Committee on Standards in Public Life was set up (Chair: Ld Nolan 1994–97; Ld Neill 1997). It produced major reports Cm.2850/95; Cm.3270/96; Cm.3702/97 and Cm.4057/98 on political finance).

Other Crown Committees

The Crown has also appointed a number of other advisory committees, some of which are called 'Royal Commissions' but all of which are different from those listed above. Some of them are different because they are standing, not *ad hoc*, in nature. Two of these appointed in the nineteenth century are still in existence: the Commission on the Exhibition of 1851 (appointed in 1850) and the Historical Manuscripts Commission (appointed in 1869). In the present century there have been thirteen others appointed (see table below), of which six are still in existence. All of them were appointed by virtue of prerogative powers. Other Crown advisory committees are different from those listed above because they were appointed by virtue of statutory, not prerogative, powers. Four, all of them *ad hoc* in nature, have been appointed in this century; they dealt with Property of the Free Church of Scotland (1905–10, Cd./5060), the Election in Worcester in 1906 (1906, Cd. 3262), the Coal Industry (1919, Cmd./360), and Indian Government (1927–30, Cmd. 3568). Finally, the Government in Ireland prior to 1922 appointed a special kind of committee in the name of the Crown called a 'Vice-Regal Commission'; thirteen were appointed in this century (see table below).

Advisory Committees Appointed by the Crown since 1900
(including continuing Royal Commissions producing reports)

	Date of appointment	Date of adjournment	Report Cd.No.
Ancient and Historical Monuments and Constructions in Scotland	Feb 08	*	9404
Ancient Monuments and Constructions of Wales and Monmouthshire	Aug 08	*	8645
Ancient and Historical Monuments and Constructions in England	Oct 08	*	9351
Supply of Sugar	Aug 14	Apr 21	1300
Defence of the Realm Losses	Mar 15	Nov 20	1044
Supply of Paper	Feb 16	Feb 18	None
Supply of Wheat	Oct 16	Jul 25	2462
Awards to Inventors	Mar 19	Nov 37	5594
Compensation for Suffering and Damage by Enemy Action	Aug 21	Feb 24	2066
Fine Art	May 24	*	4832
Fine Art for Scotland	Aug 27	*	4317
Awards to Inventors	May 46	Apr 56	9744
Environmental Pollution	Feb 70	*	9149

Irish Vice-Regal Commissions

Title	Chairman	Size	Date appointed	Date of Report	Command number
Irish Inland Fisheries	S. Walker	7	Aug 99	Jan 01	448
Poor Law Reform in Ireland	W. L. Micks	3	May 03	Oct 06	3202
Trinity College, Dublin, Estates Commission	G. Fitzgibbon	3	Jun 04	Apr 05	2526
Arterial Drainage (Ireland)	A. Binnie	5	Sep 05	Feb 07	3374
Irish Railways, including Light Railways	C. Scotter	7	Jul 06	Jul 10	5247
Circumstances of the Loss of the Regalia of the Order of St. Patrick	J. Shaw	3	Jan 08	Jan 08	3936
Irish Milk Supply	P. O'Neill	9	Nov 11	Oct 13	7129
Primary Education (Ireland) System of Inspection	S. Dill	8	Jan 13	Jan 14	7235
Dublin Disturbances	D. Henry	2	Dec 13	Feb 14	7269
Primary Education (Ireland) 1918	Ld Killanin	17	Aug 18	Feb 19	60
Intermediate Education (Ireland)	T. Molony	14	Aug 18	Mar 19	66
Under Sheriffs and Bailiffs (Ireland)	T. O'Shaughnessy	5	Oct 18	May 19	190
Reorganisation and Pay of the Irish Police Forces	J. Ross	6	Oct 19	Dec 19	603
Clerk of the Crown and Peace, etc. (Ireland)	J. Wakely	7	Oct 19	Jun 20	805

Departmental Committees

Departmental Committees are *ad hoc* advisory committees appointed by Ministers by virtue of their conventional powers. As such they are the direct counterpart of Royal Commissions. In the table below are listed some of the more important Departmental Committees appointed since the turn of the century. As with Royal Commissions, there is no 'official' title for a Departmental Committee, so usage may vary slightly; where there were two successive chairmen, both are listed; and the dates of appointment and report as well as the Command number are derived in the same manner as for Royal Commissions.

A Select List of Departmental Committees 1900–

In the absence of any single official title for a Committee we have tried to select the most commonly used short title. The Command number given is that of the final report.

Title	Chairman	Date appointed	Date of Report	Command number
Compensation for Injuries to Workmen	K. Digby	Nov 03	Aug 04	208
Motor Cars	R. Hobhouse	Jan 04	Apr 04	2069
War Office	Vt Esher	Jul 03	Mar 04	2002
Income Tax	C. Ritchie	–	Jun 05	2575
Company and Commercial Law and Practice	C. Warmington	Feb 05	Jun 06	3052
Accounts of Local Authorities	W. Runciman	Jan 06	Jul 07	3614
Law of Copyright	Ld Gorell	Mar 09	Dec 09	4967
Probation of Offenders Act 1907	H. Samuel	Mar 09	Dec 09	5001
Procedure of Royal Commissions	Ld Balfour of Burleigh	Apr 09	Jun 10	5235
Railway Agreements and Amalgamations	R. Rea	Jun 09	Apr 11	5631
Alien Immigrants at the Port of London	R. Lehmann	–	Mar 11	5575
Educational Endowments	C. Trevelyan	–	Mar 11	5662

Title	Chairman	Date appointed	Date of Report	Command number
National Guarantee for the War Risks of Shipping	A. Chamberlain	–	–	7560
Local Taxation	Sir J. Kempe	Nov 12	Mar 14	7315
Retrenchment in the Public Expenditure	R. McKenna	Jul 15	Sep 15	8068
Royal Aircraft Factory	R. Burbridge	Mar 16	Jul 16	8191
Increase of Prices of Commodities since the beginning of the War	J. Robertson	Jun 16	Sep 16	8358
Summer Time	J. Wilson	Sep 16	Feb 17	8487
Commercial and Industrial Policy, Imperial Preference	Ld Balfour of Burleigh	–	Feb 17	8482
Currency and Foreign Exchanges	Ld Cunliffe	Jan 18	Dec 19	464
National Expenditure	Ld Geddes	Aug 21	Feb 22	1589
Broadcasting	Sir M. Sykes	Apr 23	Aug 23	1951
Imperial Wireless Telegraphy	Sir R. Donald	Jan 24	Feb 24	2060
National Debt and Taxation	H. Colwyn	Mar 24	Nov 26	2800
Broadcasting	Ld Crawford & Balcarres	Aug 25	Mar 26	2599
Ministers' Powers	E of Donoughmore	Oct 29	Apr 32	4060
Finance and Industry	H. Macmillan (Ld)	Nov 29	Jun 31	3897
Regional Development	H. Chelmsford	Jan 31	Mar 31	3915
National Expenditure	Sir G. May	Mar 31	Jul 31	3920
Depressed Areas	(Three Area Chairmen)	Apr 34	Nov 34	4728
Broadcasting	Vt Ullswater	Apr 35	Mar 36	5091
Parliamentary Pensions	Sir W. Fisher	Jul 35	Nov 37	5624
Compensation and Betterment	Sir A. Uthwatt	Jan 41	Sep 42	6291
Social Insurance and Allied Services	Sir W. Beveridge	Jun 41	Nov 42	6404
Training of Civil Servants	R. Assheton	Feb 43	Apr 44	6525
Public Schools and the General Education System	Ld Fleming	Jul 42	Jun 44	27-261
Company Law Amendment	Sir L. Cohen	Jun 43	Jun 45	6659
Television	Ld Hankey	Sep 43	Dec 44	N-p
Rent Control	Vt Ridley	Nov 43	Feb 45	6621
Legal Aid and Legal Advice in England and Wales	Ld Rushcliffe	May 44	May 45	6641
Gas Industry	G. Heyworth	Jun 44	Nov 45	6699
Social and Economic Research	Sir J. Clapham	Jan 45	Jun 46	6868
Care of Children	Myra Curtis	Mar 45	Aug 46	6922
National Parks (England and Wales)	Sir A. Hobhouse	Jul 45	Mar 47	7121
New Towns	Ld Reith	Oct 45	Jul 46	6876
Port Transport Industry	R. Evershed	Nov 45	Dec 45	N-p
Shops and Non-Industrial Employment	Sir E. Gowers	Jan 46	Mar 49	7664
Resale Price Maintenance	Sir G. Lloyd-Jacob	Aug 47	Mar 49	7696
Higher Civil Service Remuneration	Ld Chorley	Jan 48	Sep 48	7635
Leasehold	Ld Uthwatt Ld Jenkin	Feb 48	Jun 50	7982
Political Activities of Civil Servants	J. Masterman	Apr 48	Apr 49	7718
Intermediaries	Sir E. Herbert	Feb 49	Oct 49	7904
Broadcasting	Ld Beveridge	Jun 49	Dec 50	8116
Fuel and Power Resources	Vt Ridley	Jul 51	Jul 52	8647
Departmental Records	Sir J. Grigg	Jun 52	May 54	9163
National Health Service	C. Guillebaud	May 53	Nov 55	9663
Air Pollution	Sir H. Beaver	Jul 53	Nov 54	9322
Crichel Down	A. Clark	Nov 53	May 54	9176
Electricity Supply Industry	Sir E. Herbert	Jul 54	Dec 55	9672
Homosexual Law Reform	Sir J. Wolfenden	Aug 54	Aug 57	247
Crown Lands	Sir M. Trustram Eve	Dec 54	May 55	9843
Dock Workers' Scheme	Sir P. Devlin	Jul 55	Jun 56	9813
Administrative Tribunals and Inquiries	Sir O. Franks	Nov 55	Jul 57	218
Children and Young People	Vt Ingleby	Oct 56	Oct 60	1191
Damage and Casualties in Port Said	Sir E. Herbert	Dec 56	Dec 56	47

Title	Chairman	Date appointed	Date of Report	Command number
Working of the Monetary System	Ld Radcliffe	May 57	Jul 59	827
Interception of Communications	Sir N. Birkett	Jun 57	Sep 57	283
Preservation of Downing Street	E of Crawford	Jul 57	Mar 58	457
The Structure of the Public Library Service in England and Wales	Sir S. Roberts	Sep 57	Dec 58	660
The Youth Service in England and Wales	Ctss of Albemarle	Nov 58	Oct 59	929
Consumer Protection	J. Molony	Jun 59	Apr 62	1781
Control of Public Expenditure	Ld Plowden	Jul 59	Jun 61	1432
Company Law Committee	Ld Jenkins	Dec 59	May 62	1749
Broadcasting	Sir H. Pilkington	Jul 60	Jun 62	1753
Higher Education	Ld Robbins	Feb 61	Sep 63	2154
Major Ports of Great Britain	Vt Rochdale	Mar 61	Jul 62	1824
Security in the Public Service	Ld Radcliffe	May 61	Nov 61	1681
Economy of Northern Ireland	Sir R. Hall	May 61	Jun 62	1835
Sunday Observance	Ld Crathorne	Jul 61	Sep 64	2528
Decimal Currency	E of Halsbury	Dec 61	Jul 63	2145
Organisation of Civil Science	Sir B. Trend	Mar 62	Sep 63	2171
The Vassall Case	Sir C. Cunningham	Oct 62	Nov 62	1871
Security Service and Mr Profumo	Ld Denning	Jun 63	Sep 63	2152
Remuneration of Ministers and M.P.s	Sir G. Lawrence	Dec 63	Oct 64	2516
Social Studies	Ld Heyworth	Jun 63	Feb 65	2660
Housing in Greater London	Sir M. Holland	Aug 63	Mar 65	2605
Port Transport Industry	Ld Devlin	Oct 64	Nov 64	2523
Aircraft Industry	Ld Plowden	Dec 64	Dec 65	2853
Shipbuilding	R. Geddes	Feb 65	Feb 66	2939
Age of Majority	Sir J. Latey	Jul 65	Jun 67	3342
Local Authority Personal Social Services	F. Seebohm	Dec 65	Jul 68	3703
Death Certification and Coroners	N. Brodrick	Mar 65	Sep 71	4810
Civil Service	Ld Fulton	Feb 66	Jul 68	3638
Prison Security	Earl Mountbatten	Oct 66	Dec 66	3175
Fire Service	Sir R. Holroyd	Feb 67	May 70	4371
Shipping	Vt Rochdale	Jul 67	Feb 70	4337
Intermediate Areas	Sir J. Hunt	Sep 67	Feb 69	3998
Civil Air Transport	Sir E. Edwards	Nov 67	Apr 69	4018
Legal Education	Sir R. Ormrod	Dec 67	Jan 71	4595
Commercial Rating	D. Anderson	Aug 68	Apr 70	4366
Overseas Representation	Sir V. Duncan	Aug 68	Jun 69	4107
Consumer Credit	Ld Crowther	Sep 68	Dec 70	4596
Adoption of Children	Sir W. Houghton F. Stockdale	Jul 69	Jul 72	5107
Small Firms	J. Bolton	Jul 69	Sep 71	4811
One-Parent Families	Sir M. Finer	Nov 69	Oct 74	5629
Rent Acts	H. Francis	Oct 69	Jan 71	4609
Privacy	K. Younger	May 70	May 72	5012
Safety and Health at Work	Ld Roberts	May 70	Jun 72	5034
Defence Procurement	D. Rayner	Oct 70	Mar 71	4641
Dispersal of Government Work from London	Sir H. Hardman	Oct 70	Jun 73	5322
Lotteries	K. Witney	Jan 71	Dec 73	5506
Abuse of Social Security	Sir H. Fisher	Mar 71	Mar 73	5228
Liquor Licensing	Ld Erroll of Hale	Apr 71	Oct 72	5154
Scottish Licensing Laws	G. Clayson	Apr 71	Aug 73	5354
Official Secrets Act	Ld Franks	Apr 71	Sep 72	5104
Public Trustee Office	H. Hutton	May 71	Nov 71	4913
Contempt of Court	Ld Phillimore	Jun 71	Dec 74	5794
National Savings	Sir H. Page	Jun 71	Jun 73	5273
Brutality in Northern Ireland	Sir E. Compton	Aug 71	Nov 71	4823
Interrogation of Terrorists	Ld Parker of Waddington	Nov 71	Jan 72	4901
Probation Officers and Social Workers	J. Butterworth	Dec 71	Aug 72	5076

Title	Chairman	Date appointed	Date of Report	Command number
Psychiatric Patients	Sir C. Aarvold	Jun 72	Jan 73	5191
Mentally Abnormal Offenders	Ld Butler	Sep 72	Oct 75	6244
Legal Procedures to deal with Terrorists in Northern Ireland	Ld Diplock	Oct 72	Nov 72	5185
Handling of Complaints against Police	A. Gordon-Brown	Apr 73	Mar 74	5582
Export of Animals for Slaughter	Ld O'Brien	Jul 73	Mar 74	5566
Conduct in Local Government	Ld Redcliffe-Maud	Oct 73	May 74	5636
Broadcasting	Ld Annan	Apr 74	Mar 77	6753
Pay of Non-University Teachers	Ld Houghton	Jun 74	Jan 75	5848
Civil Liberties in Northern Ireland	Ld Gardiner	Jun 74	Jan 75	5879
Local Government Finance	F. Layfield	Jun 74	Mar 76	6543
Ministerial Memoirs	Vt Radcliffe	Apr 75	Jan 76	6386
Tape Recording Police Interrogations	W. Hyde	Apr 75	Oct 76	6630
Industrial Democracy	Ld Bullock	Dec 75	Apr 77	6706
Recruitment of Mercenaries	Ld Diplock	Feb 76	Aug 76	6569
Age of Consent	Sir G. Waller	Dec 75	Apr 81	8216
Data Protection	Sir N. Lindop	Jun 76	Dec 78	7341
Political Activities of Civil Servants	Sir A. Armitage	Aug 76	Jan 78	7057
Genetic Manipulation	Sir G. Wolstenholme	Dec 76	Sep 82	8665
Insolvency Law	Sir K. Cork	Jan 77	Jun 82	8558
Functioning of Financial Institutions	Sir H. Wilson	Jan 77	Jun 80	7937
Financing of Small Firms	Sir H. Wilson	Jan 77	Mar 78	7503
Cabinet Document Security	Ld Houghton	Jul 77	Oct 77	6677
Obscenity and Film Censorship	B. Williams	Jul 77	Nov 79	7772
Ownership of Agricultural Land	Ld Northfield	Sep 77	Jul 79	7599
Police Pay	Ld Edmund-Davies	Oct 77	Jul 78	7283
Review of the Terrorism Act	Ld Shackleton	Dec 77	Aug 78	7324
Police Interrogation in Northern Ireland	H. Bennett	Jun 78	Mar 79	7497
Public Records	Sir D. Wilson	Aug 78	Mar 81	804
U.K. Prison Service	Sir J. D. May	Nov 78	Oct 79	7673
Education of Ethnic Minority Children	A. Rampton Ld Swann	Mar 79	Feb 85	9403
Local Government in Scotland	Sir A. Stodart	Dec 79	Jan 81	8115
Postgraduate Education	Sir P. Swinnerton-Dyer	Dec 79	Apr 82	8537
University Scientific Research	Sir A. Merrison	Mar 80	Jun 82	8567
Police Complaints	Ld Plowden	Jul 80	Mar 81	8193
Brixton Disorders	Ld Scarman	Apr 81	Nov 81	8427
Civil Service Pay	Sir J. Megaw	Jun 81	Jul 82	8590
Review of 1976 Terrorism Act	Earl Jellicoe	Mar 82	Feb 83	8803
Cable Television	Ld Hunt of Tanworth	Apr 82	Oct 82	8679
Fertilisation of Human Embryos	Dame M. Warnock	Jul 82	Jul 84	9314
Falkland Islands Review	Ld Franks	Jul 82	Jan 83	8787
Protection of Military Information	Sir H. Beach	Feb 83	Dec 83	9112
Education of Children from Minority Groups	Ld Swann	Mar 83	Mar 85	9453
Crowd Safety at Football Grounds	Sir O. Popplewell	May 85	Jan 86	9710
Academic Valuation of Degree Courses	Sir N. Lindop	Apr 84	Apr 85	9501
Conduct of Local Authority Business	D. Widdecombe	Feb 85	Jun 86	9797
Financing the B.B.C.	A. Peacock	Mar 85	Jul 86	9824
Review of the Terrorism Act	Vt Colville	Jan 87	Dec 87	264
Public Health in England	Sir D. Acheson	Jan 86	Jan 88	289
Child Abuse in Cleveland	Dame E. Butler-Sloss	Jul 87	Jul 88	412
King's Cross Underground Fire	D. Fennell	Nov 87	Nov 88	499
Parole System in England & Wales	Ld Carlisle of Bucklow	Sep 87	Feb 89	532
Banking Services	R. Jack	Jan 87	Feb 88	622
War Crimes	Sir T. Hetherington	Feb 88	Jul 89	744
Clapham Junction Railway Accident	A. Hidden	Dec 88	Nov 90	820
Review of the Terrorism Acts	Vt Colville	Sep 89	Jul 90	1115
The Piper Alpha Disaster	Ld Cullen	Jul 88	Nov 90	1330

Title	Chairman	Date appointed	Date of Report	Command number
River Safety	J. Hayes	Dec 91	Jul 92	1991
Press Self-Regulation	Sir D. Calcutt	Jul 92	Jan 93	2135
Police Responsibilities and Rewards	Sir P. Sheehy	Jul 92	Jun 93	2263
Pollution from Merchant Shipping	Ld Donaldson	Jan 93	May 94	2560
Review of the Terrorism Act	J. Rowe	May 94	Feb 95	2706
Escapes from Whitemoor Prison	Sir J. Woodcock	Sep94	Dec 94	2741
Sinking of M.V. Derbyshire	Ld Donaldson	Mar 95	Dec 95	3128
Criminal Appeals and Miscarriages of Justice in Scotland	Sir S. Sutherland	Nov 94	Jun 96	3245
Dunblane School Massacre	Ld Cullen	Mar 96	Oct 96	3386
Review of Hillsborough Inquiry	Sir M. Stewart-Smith	Jun 97	Feb 98	3878
Crown Prosecution Service	Sir I. Glidewell	Jul 97	Jun 98	3960
Money in Politics	Ld Neill	Nov 97	Oct 98	4057
Electoral Systems	Ld Jenkins	Dec 97	Nov 98	4090
Murder of Stephen Lawrence	Sir W. Macpherson	Jul 97	Feb 99	4262

Enquiries Held under the Tribunals of Inquiry (Evidence) Act, 1921

Upon a resolution of both Houses of Parliament on a matter of urgent public importance a tribunal might be appointed by the Sovereign or a Secretary of State with all the powers of the High Court as regards examination of witnesses and production of documents, for the objective investigation of facts.

Title	Members of Tribunal	Year	Command number
Destruction of documents by Ministry of Munitions officials	Ld Cave Ld Inchape Sir W. Plender	1921	1340
Royal Commission on Lunacy and Mental Disorder given powers under the Act	H. Macmillan(Ch)	1924	2700
Arrest of R. Sheppard, R.A.O.C. Inquiry into conduct of Metropolitan Police	J. Rawlinson	1925	2497
Allegations made against the Chief Constable of Kilmarnock in connection with the dismissal of Constables Hill and Moore from the Burgh Police Force	W. Mackenzie	1925	2659
Conditions with regard to mining and drainage in an area around the County Borough of Doncaster	Sir H. Monro (Ch)	1926/8	–
Charges against the Chief Constable of St.Helens by the Watch Committee	C. Parry T. Walker	1928	103
Interrogation of Miss Irene Savidge by Metropolitan Police at New Scotland Yard	Sir J.E. Banks H. Lees-Smith J. Withers	1928	3147
Allegations of bribery and corruption in connection with the letting and allocation of stances and other premises under the control of the Corporation of Glasgow	Ld Anderson Sir R. Boothby J. Hunter	1933	4361
Unauthorised disclosure of information relating to the Budget	Sir J. Porter G. Simonds R. Oliver	1936	5184
The circumstances surrounding the loss of H.M. Submarine 'Thetis'	Sir J. Bucknill	1939	6190
The conduct before the Hereford Juvenile Court Justices of the proceedings against Craddock and others	Ld Goddard	1943	6485
The administration of the Newcastle upon Tyne Fire, Police and Civil Defence Services	R. Burrows	1944	6522

Title	Members of Tribunal	Year	Command number
Bribery of Ministers of the Crown or other public servants in connection with the grant of licences, etc.	Sir J. Lynskey G. Russell Vick G. Upjohn	1948	7616
Allegations of improper disclosure of information relating to the raising of the Bank Rate	Ld Parker E. Holland G. Veale	1957	350
Allegations that John Waters was assaulted on 7 December 1957 at Thurso and the action taken by Caithness Police in connection therewith	Ld Sorn Sir J.Robertson	1959	718
The circumstances in which offences under the Official Secrets Act were committed by William Vassall	Ld Radcliffe Sir J. Barry Sir E. Milner Holland	1962	2009
The disaster at Aberfan	Sir E. Davies H. Harding V. Lawrence	1967	HC553
The events on Sunday, 30th January 1972, which led to loss of life in connection with the procession in Londonderry on that day	Ld Widgery	1972	HC220/72
The circumstances leading to the cessation of trading by the Vehicle and General Insurance Co. Ltd	Sir A. James M. Kerr S. Templeman	1972	HC133
The extent to which the Crown Agents lapsed from accepted standards of commercial or professional conduct or of public administration as financiers on their own account in the years 1967–74	Sir D. Croom-Johnson Ld Allen Sir W. Slimmings	1978	HC48

Tribunals and Commissions

A large number of statutory tribunals, with jurisdiction to decide quasi-legal disputes, have been created since 1900. By 1960 there were over 2,000 tribunals within the supervisory role of the Council on Tribunals. The fifteen-member Council on Tribunals was set up under the Tribunals and Inquiries Act, 1958, following the report of the Franks Committee (Cmnd. 218/1957). Its role is purely advisory, but it has to report annually to Parliament.

The reports list the tribunals that fall within its purview and the number of cases each type of tribunal has dealt with during the past year. In the following table some categories have been merged and appeals from lower to higher tribunals are not included nor are tribunals which have had no cases to deal with. Separate Scottish tribunals are also excluded.

Category	Latest enabling legislation	Number of Tribunals	1960	1970	1980	1990	1996
Agriculture	1947	8	459	402	461	337	722
Air Transport	1960	1	–	3,537	1,002	1,754	4,279
Betting Levy	1963	1	–	196	–	97	–
Commons	1965	4	–	–	1,544	147	13
Compensation	1958	10	27	–	–	1,785	36
Data Protection	1984	1	–	–	–	–	3,052
Education	1944	*ad hoc*	1	3	–	0	64,744
Immigration	1969	59	–	991	11,344	17,241	39,794
Industry and Employment	(1964)	84	–	10,318	31,736	30,751	77,496
Land	1949	1	1,121	1,511	1,237	992	1,476
Mental Health	1959	15	1	1,114	709	7,487	12,701
Milk and Dairies	1955	8	1	2	–	–	–
Misuse of Drugs	1971	3	–	–	–	–	–

Category	Latest enabling legislation	Number of Tribunals	1960	Number of cases			
				1970	1980	1990	1996
National Assistance	1948	152	7,757	–	–	a	a
(Non-Contrib.Benefits)	1966	151	–	28,717	–	a	a
(Supplement'y Benefit)	1975	123	–	–	45,471	a	a
National Health Service	1946	204	1,235	979	1,137	2,031	n.a
National Insurance	1946	228	60,914	54,787	–	a	a
National Service	1948	83	5,954	–	–	1	–
Patents	1907	3	5,652	6,566	7,564	6,460	8,836
Pensions	1919	11	4,784	3,388	–	3,115	a
Performing Rights	1956	14	–	–	–	–	–
Rates	1968	42	–	25,513	40,400	185,000	448,000
Rents	1968	53	4,652	14,923	5,086	315	338
Rent Assessment	1977	ad hoc	–	–	9,734	16,479	11,176
Revenue	1970	654	n.a.	6,562	n.a.	n.a.	149,100
Road Traffic	1960	23	22,110	23,205	29,528	47	29,955
Social Security	1975	179	–	–	25,258	119,645[a]	188,608
Vaccine Damages	1979	6	–	–	897	16	24
Value Added Tax	1972	5	–	–	61	2,724	3,039

[a] Included under Social Security

Political Honours Scrutiny Committee

The Political Honours Scrutiny Committee was established in 1924, following scandals over the 'sale of honours'. It was to 'consider before they are submitted to the King, the names and particulars of persons recommended for appointment to any dignity or honours on account of political services ... and to report ... whether such persons ... are fit and proper persons to be recommended'. Its activities were virtually never reported but they continued after H. Wilson announced the ending of 'political honours' in 1966 and again in 1974. In 1976, following agitation over Sir H. Wilson's resignation honours list, there was a complete change of membership. It has always had three members:

1923–25	Sir E. Cecil (Ch 1923–25)	1929–38	G. Barnes	1961–76	Ld Crathorne (Ch 1971–76)
1923–23	Ld Dunedin	1934–45	M of Crewe	1962–76	Ld Rea
1923–24	Ld Mildmay	1938–52	Ld Rushcliffe	1967–76	Bness Summerskill
1923–24	Vt Ullswater	1945–49	J. Clynes	1976–92	Ld Shackleton (Ch 1976–92)
1924–25	T. Richards	1949–59	Vt Templewood (Ch 1954–59)	1976–87	Ld Carr
1925–25	J. Rawlinson	1949–61	Ld Pethick-Lawrence	1976–87	Ld Banks
1925–29	Vt Novar (Ch 1925–29)	1952–54	Ld Asquith (Ch 1952–54)	1987–92	Ld Grimond
1925–29	W. Nicholson	1954–61	Vt Thurso	1987–	Ld Pym (Ch 1992–)
1925–29	Ld Merrivale	1959–61	Ld Crookshank (Ch 1959–61)	1992–99	Ld Cledwyn
1929–34	Ld Buckmaster (Ch 1929–34)	1961–67	Ld Williams	1992–	Ld Thomson
1929–52	H. (Ld) Macmillan (Ch 1934–52)	1961–62	C. Davies	1999–	Bness Dean

Source: *Whitaker's Almanack*

VIII

JUSTICE AND LAW ENFORCEMENT

Major Criminal Justice Legislation 1900–

Poor Prisoners' Defence Act, 1903. This was the first Act which made provision for legal aid, which was limited to trials on indictment.

The Probation of Offenders Act, 1907. This extended courts' probation powers and allowed appointment of official probation officers.

The Criminal Appeal Act, 1907. This created the Court of Criminal Appeal.

The Prevention of Crime Act, 1908. This provided for 'borstal training' of young recidivists and 'preventive detention' for adult habitual criminals.

The Children Act, 1908. This created 'places of detention' (later 'Remand Homes') and Juvenile Courts; it also prohibited imprisonment of those under 14, restricted imprisonment of those from 14–17 and abolished death sentence for those under 17.

The Criminal Justice Administration Act, 1914. This required Summary Courts to give time for payment of fines.

Poor Prisoners' Defence Act, 1930. This Act provided a comprehensive system of legal aid, extending aid to preliminary inquiries and to cases heard summarily before magistrates' courts.

Summary Jurisdiction (Appeals) Act, 1933. This Act made provision for free legal aid for criminal cases, payable out of county or borough funds at the discretion of the magistrates.

The Children and Young Persons Act, 1933. This Act, which followed the 1927 Report of the Cecil Committee on the treatment of young offenders, codified and extended 'care and protection' law; it also raised the age of criminal responsibility from 7 to 8.

The Administration of Justice (Miscellaneous Provisions) Act, 1933. This abolished Grand Juries.

The Criminal Justice Act, 1948. Following the lines of a 1938 Bill abandoned through the onset of war, this extended the fining powers of higher courts; it further restricted imprisonment of juveniles and abolished distinction between penal servitude, imprisonment, etc.; it also improved law on probation, introduced corrective training and a new form of preventive detention and it provided for remand centres, attendance centres and detention centres. It also abolished the right of peers to be tried by the House of Lords.

Legal Aid and Advice Act, 1949. This introduced a new system of aid for civil cases. It provided for the establishment of a network of local committees, composed of solicitors and some barristers to grant legal aid under regulations made by the Lord Chancellor. By this Act, aid was extended to cover all proceedings in civil courts and civil proceedings in magistrates' courts, except for certain types of action (of which defamation and breach of promise were the most important).

Cost in Criminal Cases Act, 1952. This Act empowered the courts, in the case of an indictable offence, to order reasonable defence costs to be paid out of public funds, when the accused was discharged or acquitted.

The Homicide Act, 1957. This amended the law on murder, distinguishing capital and non-capital murder and introducing the defence of diminished responsibility.

The First Offenders Act, 1958. This restricted imprisonment of adults by Summary Courts.

Administration of Justice Act, 1960. This gave a greatly extended right of appeal to the House of Lords in criminal matters and reformed the law relating to habeas corpus and to contempt of court.

Legal Aid Act, 1960.   This related financial conditions for legal aid and made further provision for the remuneration of counsel and solicitors.

The Criminal Justice Act, 1961.   This provided compulsory supervision after release from detention centres and rationalised custodial sentences for 17–21 age-group.

The Children and Young Persons Act, 1963.   This raised the age of criminal responsibility from 8 to 10, and redefined the need for 'care, protection, and control'.

The Criminal Injuries Compensation Board was set up in 1964, under an ex gratia State Scheme for compensating victims of crimes of violence.

The Murder (Abolition of Death Penalty) Act, 1965.   This suspended the death penalty until 1970, and substituted a mandatory 'life' sentence. Motions for its restoration were rejected on 11 Dec 75, 19 Jul 79, 13 Jul 83, 1 Apr 87. On 16 Dec 69 Parliament voted to continue the suspension indefinitely.

Criminal Appeal Act, 1966.   This amalgamated the Court of Criminal Appeal and the Court of Appeal.

The Criminal Justice Act, 1967.   This introduced suspended sentences, a Parole Board (see p.345), a new type of sentence for recidivists and further restricted imprisonment of adults. It allowed majority verdicts (10–2) by juries.

The Theft Act, 1967.   This rationalised definitions of theft and other dishonesty.

The Criminal Law Act, 1967.   This replaced the distinction between felonies and misdemeanours, with a distinction between arrestable and non-arrestable offences.

The Children and Young Persons Act, 1969.   Redefined the circumstances in which juvenile courts could make orders dealing with children and young persons, and simplified the nature of such orders; it also provided for the raising of the minimum age of liability to prosecution (although this has not yet been implemented) and for the reorganisation of approved schools, children's homes, etc., into a system of 'community homes' controlled by local authorities.

The Courts Act, 1971.   Replaced Assizes and Quarter Sessions with a system of Crown Courts.

The Criminal Justice Act, 1972.   Provided courts with several new means of dealing with offenders, including criminal bankruptcy orders, community service orders, deferment of sentence, day centres for probationers; and further restricted the imprisonment of adults.

The Rehabilitation of Offenders Act, 1974.   This made it an offence to refer to criminal proceedings after the lapse of a certain period. This involved consequential amendments to the law of defamation.

Prevention of Terrorism (Temporary Provisions) Act, 1974.   This proscribed organisations concerned in terrorism and gave power to exclude certain persons from Great Britain in order to prevent acts of terrorism.

Criminal Jurisdiction Act, 1975.   This extended the jurisdiction of the criminal courts in Northern Ireland to allow them to try certain offences committed in the Irish Republic.

District Courts (Scotland) Act, 1975.   This set up a new system of courts of summary jurisdiction in Scotland.

Police Act, 1976.   This established a Police Complaints Board to deal with complaints from the public against members of the police.

Bail Act, 1976.   This extensively reformed the law on the granting of bail, requiring reasons to be given for refusal and creating a general presumption in favour of bail, particularly for offences not punishable with imprisonment.

Criminal Law Act, 1977.   This simplified the rules governing the distribution of cases between the Crown Court and magistrates courts, with a view to allowing many more cases to be tried summarily rather than on indictment. It also raised the level of fines which can be imposed for many types of offence.

Judicature (Northern Ireland) Act, 1978. This modernised the structure of the superior courts in Northern Ireland, notably by abolishing the separate Court of Criminal Appeal and by setting up a new Crown Court to try all cases of indictment.

Criminal Attempts Act, 1981. This replaced the common law offence of attempt with a statutory offence and modified the statutory definition of criminal conspiracy. It also implemented the recommendation by the Home Affairs Committee of the House of Commons that the offence of 'sus' be repealed; it was partially replaced by a new offence of vehicle interference.

Criminal Justice Act, 1982. This created a completely new framework of custodial offences for offenders under 21, superseding imprisonment, Borstal training and detention in detention centres. It also amended the law on suspended sentences and introduced a new scale of standard maximum fines for summary offences.

Police and Criminal Evidence Act, 1984. This derived largely from various recommendations made by the Royal Commission on Criminal Procedure, the Criminal Law Revision Committee, and Lord Scarman's Report on the Brixton disorders. It reformed the law relating to police powers to stop and search, police powers of entry, search and seizure, powers of arrest and detention, the treatment, interrogation and identification of suspects, the admissibility of evidence obtained during police questioning, and public complaints against the police.

Prosecution of Offences Act, 1985. This established an independent Crown Prosecution Service under the Director of Public Prosecutions.

Public Order Act, 1986. This abolished the Common Law offences of riot, unlawful assembly and affray and established new statutory offences relating to public order.

Criminal Justice Act, 1987. Established the Serious Fraud Office.

Criminal Justice Act, 1988. This empowered the Attorney-General to refer unduly light sentences to the Court of Appeal.

Criminal Justice Act, 1991. This set up a new structure for dealing with juvenile offenders, introduced a system of 'unit' fines related to ability to pay, and altered the rules on sentencing persistent offenders, making it harder for courts to take previous offences into account.

Criminal Justice Act, 1993. This repealed the provisions of the 1991 Act relating to unit fines and sentencing persistent offenders.

Criminal Justice Act, 1994. This lowered the age of consent below which homosexual acts are illegal from 21 to 18, and introduced a number of changes to the composition of police authorities.

Criminal Appeal Act, 1995. This established the Criminal Cases Review Commission to consider suspected miscarriages of justice and where appropriate to refer them to the Court of Appeal.

Crime and Disorder Act, 1998. This introduced measures for tackling youth crime such as Anti-social Behaviour Orders, Child Curfews, and Child Safety Orders.

Youth Justice and Criminal Evidence Act, 1999. This established a Young Offenders Panel to deal with first-time offenders, and provided for greater use of television links.

Sources: R.M.Jackson, *Enforcing the Law* (1967); N.D.Walker, *Crime and Punishment in Britain* (2nd ed., 1968); K. Smith and D.J.Keenan, *English Law* (10th ed., 1992); G.Rose, *The Struggle for Penal Reform* (1961); J. Smith and B.Hogan, *Criminal Law* (7th ed., 1992); L. Blom-Cooper and G. Drewry, *Final Appeal: The House of Lords in its Judicial Capacity* (1972); C. McCrudden, *Individual Rights in the U.K.*(1993).

Major Legislation Relating to the Administration of Civil Justice, 1900–

Industrial Courts Act, 1919. This Act provided a standing body for voluntary arbitration and inquiry in cases of industrial dispute (see p. 377).

Supreme Court of Judicature (Consolidation) Act, 1925. This is still the principal Act defining the structure, composition and jurisdiction of the High Court and the Court of Appeal.

Administration of Justice (Miscellaneous Provisions) Act, 1933. This restricted the right to jury trial in King's Bench civil proceedings.

Administration of Justice (Appeals) Act, 1934. This made it necessary to obtain leave to appeal to the House of Lords in civil matters arising in English courts.

County Courts Act, 1934. This effectively abolished jury trials in county courts and rationalised the procedure for appointing registrars.

Summary Jurisdiction (Domestic Proceedings) Act, 1937. This rationalised procedure in matrimonial, guardianship and affiliation proceedings before magistrates.

Administration of Justice (Miscellaneous Provisions) Act, 1938. This Act made important changes relating in particular to the King's Bench Division of the High Court and to Courts of Quarter Sessions.

Juries Act, 1949. This abolished special juries outside the City of London.

Justices of the Peace Act, 1949. This Act brought about the extensive revision of the functions and organisation of magistrates' courts.

County Courts Act, 1955. This fixed the general limit of county court jurisdiction at £400 (subsequently regularly raised by successive Orders in Council; abolished by the *Courts and Legal Services Act, 1990*).

County Courts Act, 1959. This consolidated existing legislation on county courts.

Judicial Pensions Act, 1959. This fixed a retiring age of 75 for the higher judiciary and revised the system of judicial pensions.

Legal Aid Act, 1964. This gave limited powers for a non-legally aided litigant to be awarded his costs out of the legal aid fund where his unsuccessful opponent is in receipt of legal aid.

Justices of the Peace Act, 1968. This abolished ex officio J.P.s and redefined the powers and functions of magistrates' clerks.

Administration of Justice Act, 1969. This increased the jurisdiction of county courts to £750 and allowed certain categories of civil case in the High Court to 'leapfrog' directly to the House of Lords.

Administration of Justice Act, 1970. This Act rearranged the jurisdictions of the three divisions of the High Court (the Probate, Divorce and Admiralty Division becoming the Family Division) and abolished imprisonment for debt.

Courts Act, 1971. This replaced Courts of Assize and Quarter Sessions by Crown Courts staffed by Recorders and circuit judges; it rationalised the location of civil and criminal courts throughout England and Wales; it made sweeping changes in the administration of courts of intermediate jurisdiction and it abolished the use of juries in civil proceedings other than defamation.

Industrial Relations Act, 1971. This established the National Industrial Relations Court (see p.379).

Legal Aid and Advice Act, 1972. This Act empowered solicitors to do up to £25 worth of work for a client without the latter first having to obtain a certificate from the Law Society.

Solicitors (Amendment) Act, 1974. This made a number of changes in the administration of the solicitors' profession and made provision for a Lay Observer to examine the Law Society's handling of complaints against solicitors. *The Solicitors (Scotland) Act, 1976,* made similar changes in Scotland.

Litigants in Person (Costs and Expenses) Act, 1975. This enabled parties successfully conducting their own cases in civil proceedings to recover their costs and expenses from the other side.

The Legal Aid Act, 1979. This extended the 'green form' legal advice and assistance scheme to cover representation in inferior courts and tribunals.

The Contempt of Court Act, 1981. This implemented with modifications the Phillimore Report on Contempt of Court (Cmnd. 5794, 1974) and harmonised the law of England and Wales with the European Court's judgment in The *Sunday Times* (Thalidomide) case, 1973.

The Supreme Court Act 1981. This consolidated and significantly updated the legislation relating to the Supreme Court, superseding the Act of 1925 (see above).

Courts and Legal Services Act, 1990. This laid down a framework to give some solicitors rights of audience in the higher courts, removed the bar on solicitors becoming High Court judges, and allowed lawyers to take on cases on a 'no win, no fee' basis. It also removed the upper limit on the jurisdiction of the County Court in most cases.

Family Law Act, 1996. This made substantial changes to the legal arrangements for divorce, removing the concept of fault in most cases. In 1999 it was announced that its main provisions would not be implemented.

Human Rights Act, 1998. This made provision for the European Convention on Human Rights to be considered in English Courts.

Access to Justice Act, 1999. This greatly extended 'no win, no fee' and solicitors' rights of audience in the higher courts. It also reorganised the provision of Legal Aid.

Sources: R.M. Jackson, *The Machinery of Justice in England* (8th edition, Ed. J.R. Spencer, 1989); D. Pannick, *Judges* (1987); J. Griffith, *The Politics of the Judiciary* (4th edition, 1991); M. Berlins and C. Dyer, *The Law Machine* (5th Ed., 2000); J. Rozenberg, *Trial of Strength* (1997); D. Robertson, *Judicial Discretion and the House of Lords* (1998).

Cases of Political Significance

The number of lawsuits that have had major domestic political implications is not great. Most of the celebrated ones have involved trade unions and are listed on pp.380–2. Successful election petitions are listed on p.262. Although European Court of Human Rights rulings are listed more fully on pp.510–11, two of the most significant are included here. But these cases also seem to have left a significant mark on the political scene.

Bowles v. Bank of England [1913] 1 Ch.57 (Ch.D.). Collecting new taxes in advance of the Finance Act violates the Bill of Rights. This case led to the passage of the *Provisional Collection of Taxes Act, 1913.*

Viscountess Rhondda's Claim [1922] A.C. 339. The *Sex Disqualification (Removal) Act, 1919* did not entitle a peeress in her own right to sit in the House of Lords.

Vauxhall Estates Ltd v. Liverpool Corporation [1932] 1 K.B.733. Parliament cannot bind its successors as to the subject matter of legislation.

Liversidge v. Anderson [1942] A.C. 206 (H.L.). A Court of law may not inquire into whether a Minister has 'reasonable grounds' for exercising a statutory discretion.

Duncan v. Cammell Laird & Co. Ltd. [1942] A.C. 624 (H.L.). The Crown may withhold documents or refuse questioning if a minister certifies that the answer would be injurious to the public interest.

R. v. Tronoh Mines Ltd. [1952] I All E.R., 697. Election expenditure has to be declared only if it is specifically directed to secure the election of a particular candidate.

MacCormick v. Lord Advocate ('The Royal Numeral Case') [1953] S.L. T. 225. A Scottish case laying down that the unlimited sovereignty of Parliament does not apply to Scotland.

Re Parliamentary Privilege Act, 1770 [1958] A. C. 331 (P. C.) (Strauss Case). Not every communication between an M.P. and a Minister is protected by parliamentary privilege.

Costa v. Enel [1964] CML Rep 425. Community law prevails over all existing inconsistent national law since 'the member States have restricted their sovereign rights, albeit within limited spheres'.

Burmah Oil Co. v. the Lord Advocate [1965] A.C. 75 (H.L.). Government held liable to compensate firm ordered to destroy its property to impede the advance of the enemy in wartime. (Reversed by the *War Damage Act, 1965*.)

Conway v. Rimmer [1968] A.C. 910 (H.L.). This judgment supersedes and amplifies *Liversidge v. Anderson* (above). The courts have a residuary power to inspect documents privately to determine whether the public interest in suppressing them outweighs the interests of parties, and of the public in the unfettered administration of justice.

Padfield v. Minister of Agriculture [1968] A.C. 997 (H.L.). Where a statute confers a discretion on a minister it is beyond his power to exercise it in such a way as to frustrate the policy of Parliament, as interpreted by the court.

John v. Rees [1969] 2 W.L.R. 1294. Chairman may not adjourn meeting without consent of majority present, majority entitled to carry on and elect a new Chairman; Constituency Labour Parties not allowed to disaffiliate from the national Labour Party; a group of members may be suspended by the National Executive Committee only if natural justice is complied with by giving them an opportunity to put their case; all persons entitled to attend a meeting must be summoned or the meeting is improperly constituted and hence invalid. (The case concerned D. Donnelly and the Pembroke Constituency Labour Party.)

Anisminic Ltd. v. Foreign Compensation Commission [1969] 2 A. C. 147 (H.L.). A clause in a statute ousting the jurisdiction of the court to review administrative decisions will not be recognised and such decisions are a nullity ab initio.

The Hauptzollamt Hamburg Case [1970] CMLR 141. If Community law occupies a certain field in a matter within Community competence, the European Court of Justice does not recognise the right of Parliaments to pass any law on the matter, unless to implement this law.

McWhirter v. A.G. [1972] CMLR 882. The court will review the scope, but not the exercise, of the Crown's prerogative.

Attorney-General v. Jonathan Cape Ltd. [1976] Q.B. 752 (The Crossman Diaries Case). The courts have power to prevent publication of Cabinet material in circumstances where such publication would be both a breach of confidence and a threat to the maintenance of the doctrine of collective responsibility. (In this instance injunctions were refused owing to the considerable time which had elapsed since the events described in the Diaries.)

Gouriet v. Post Office Union [1977] 3 All E.R. 70 (H.L.). The Attorney-General is not obliged to bring an action to prevent a breach of the law when required to by a member of the general public, as distinct from someone materially damaged by the breach. Neither is an injunction or declaration available without the Attorney-General's consent; and he need give no reasons for his decision. (The case concerned the blocking of mail to South Africa.)

Laker Airways v. Dept. of Trade [1977] Q.B. 643. Ministerial guidance, albeit approved by Parliament, is ultra vires if it conflicts with express policy objectives contained in an Act. (The case concerned the proposal for 'Skytrain' cheap flights to America.)

Sec. of State for Education v. Tameside Met B/C [1977] A. C. 1014 (H.L.). Where a statute gives a minister certain powers if he is satisfied that a local authority is acting unreasonably; he may exercise them only if no reasonable authority would have done what was done, and never simply because he disagrees with the local authority's policy. (This case concerned the Tameside council's response to the Government's policy on comprehensive schools.)

Lewis v. Heffer [1978] T.L.R. 25 Jan 1978. In confirming a series of High Court judgements, arising from disputes in the Newham North-East Labour Party, the Court of

Appeal ruled that the National Executive Committee of the Labour Party had the power to suspend the constituency party and, in general, argued that the courts should only be used as a very last resort in factional party controversies.

Mead v. Haringey [1979] All E.R. 1016 A.C. The Court of Appeal held that it was arguable that a local authority might be in breach of its statutory duty to provide for children's education when it failed to do so by reason of the industrial action of School caretakers.

Duport Steels Ltd. v. Sirs [1980] 1 All E.R. 529. In the course of a pay dispute with the British Steel Corporation, the trade unions involved took secondary industrial action against private steel firms in the hope of causing a total shutdown of the industry. The Court of Appeal granted injunctions to the private steel companies, but the House of Lords reversed the decision, holding that the secondary action was 'in furtherance of a trade dispute' within the meaning of the *Trade Union and Labour Relations Act, 1974*. The Thatcher Government subsequently reversed the decision by legislation (see p.380).

Williams v. Home Office [1981] 1 All E.R. 151. Following the principles laid down in *Conway v. Rimmer* (above), the judge ordered the disclosure of internal Home Office documents relating to experimental control units, in an action brought against the department by a prisoner.

Harman v. Home Office [1982] 2 All E.R. 151. A solicitor was given confidential policy documents by way of discovery in the course of a civil action brought against the Home Office, and undertook not to disclose them outside the course of the proceedings. The documents were read out in open court and the solicitor then showed them to a journalist. The House of Lords affirmed, by a 3:2 majority, the lower courts' finding that this amounted to contempt of court.

Norwich City Council v. Secretary of State for the Environment [1982] 1 All E.R. 737. The Court of Appeal upheld the exercise of default powers by a minister against a local authority in circumstances where the minister adjudged the authority to have been dilatory in fulfilling statutory obligations to sell council houses to tenants.

O'Reilly v. Mackman [1982] 3 All E.R. 1182 (H.L.). There is a fundamental distinction between private law and public law proceedings which cannot be evaded by seeking a private law remedy against a public authority in circumstances where a public law remedy is appropriate.

Bromley London Borough Council v. GLC [1983] A.C. 768 (H.L.). The GLC 'Fares Fair' case. The Council acted ultra vires the *Transport (London) Act, 1969*, and in breach of its fiduciary duty towards ratepayers by its decision to cut fares by 25%.

Pickwell v. Camden Borough Council [1983] 1 All E.R. 602. A local authority, responding to a strike by its employees, agreed a pay settlement that turned out to be more generous than the settlement agreed nationally. The Queen's Bench Divisional Court denied the district auditor's claim that the action of the council was ultra vires.

Air Canada v. Secretary of State for Trade [1983] 1 All E.R. 910. Action brought by foreign airlines disputing increases in fees at Heathrow Airport. The House of Lords declined to order disclosure of ministerial documents on the grounds that the plaintiffs had failed to show that the documents were likely to assist their case.

The Council of Civil Service Unions v. Minister for the Civil Service [1984] Industrial Cases Reports 1985, 15. The House of Lords decided that the 'reasonable expectations' of the Civil Service unions to be consulted before the Government banned union membership at GCHQ were overridden by considerations of national security. However, their Lordships held, contrary to the Government's contentions, that ministerial actions based on the royal prerogative could, in principle, be reviewed by the courts.

Attorney General v. Guardian Newspapers Ltd [1987] 3 All E.R. 316; Attorney General v. Guardian Newspapers (no. 2) [1988] 3 All E.R. 545. The House of Lords first upheld by a 3 –2 majority the Attorney General's efforts to prevent publication of extracts from the book *Spycatcher* on the grounds that a member of the Security Service owed a lifelong duty of confidentiality to the Crown.   In the second case they removed the ban on the grounds that the material was now in the public domain.

Brind v. Secretary of State for the Home Department [1991] 1 All E.R. 720. The House of Lords upheld the decision of the Home Secretary banning the direct broadcasting of words spoken in support of terrorist organisations (in effect banning interviews with Sinn Fein).

Barber v. Guardian Royal Exchange Insurance Group [1990] 2 All E.R. 660; E.C.J. C-262/88. The European Court of Justice ruled since occupational pensions constitute a form of pay, any unjustified discrimination in benefits paid under the scheme are illegal (with implications for different pension ages).   The ruling was modified in the case of *Neath v. Hugh Sleeper Ltd E.C.J. C-152/1991,* which ruled that actuarial factors such as women's longer life expectancy could be taken into account.

R. v. Secretary of State for Transport ex parte Factortame Ltd. (No.2) 1991 E.C.J. C-213/89. The European Court of Justice ruled in a case concerning a Spanish fishing firm that where a British Act of Parliament conflicts with European legislation the Act of Parliament is not enforceable in the courts.

Pepper v. Hart [1993] 1 AC593. The House of Lords ruled that judges are entitled to scrutinise *Hansard* to establish what Ministers had said in Parliament about the intended effect of legislation.

R. v. Secretary of State for Foreign and Commonwealth Affairs ex parte Ress-Mogg [1994] QB 552. The Government was entitled to decide to ratify the Maastricht Treaty; it did not constitute an unlawful transfer of prerogative powers.

M v. Home Office [1994] 1 AC 377. The Home Secretary can be subject to proceedings for contempt of court if a court order against him is disregarded. The case concerned the removal of an illegal alien in defiance of a court ruling; the Home Secretary had argued that contempt of court could not be applied to him.

R. v. Secretary of State for Foreign and Commonwealth Affairs ex parte World Development Movement [1995] 1 WLR 386. The Foreign Secretary was not entitled to grant financial aid to Malaysia for the building of the Pergau dam, since the scheme was economically unsound. The Foreign Secretary had argued that it was a legitimate exercise of his discretion.

R. v. Ministry of Defence ex parte Smith [1996] QB 517. The Court of Appeal ruled that the prohibition on homosexuals serving in the armed forces, though perhaps regrettable, was not unreasonable in the legal sense.

R. v. Bartle and the Commissioner of Police for the Metropolis and others ex parte Pinochet [1999] 2 All ER 97. The House of Lords ruled that the former ruler of Chile Augusto Pinochet was not entitled to diplomatic immunity in respect of extradition proceedings alleging torture of political opponents.

Reynolds v. Times Newspapers and others [1999] 1 WLR 478. The House of Lords ruled that newspapers have a defence of qualified privilege in defamation proceedings brought by politicians.

R. v. Bow Street Metropolitan Stipendiary Magistrate ex parte Pinochet (No.2) 2 WLR 272 [1999] W.L.R. 272. The House of Lords set aside an earlier ruling on the extradition of Augusto Pinochet on the grounds that Lord Hoffmann had links with Amnesty International (a party to the case) which he had not declared.

Principal Judges

Lord Chancellor
(See page 55)

Vice Chancellor

1971	Sir J. Pennycuik	1985	Sir N. Browne-Wilkinson
1974	Sir A. Plowman	1991	Sir D. Nicholls
1976	Sir R. Megarry	1994	Sir R. Scott

Master of the Rolls

1897	Sir N. Lindley (Ld)	1923	Sir E. Pollock
1900	Sir R. Webster		(Ld Hanworth)
	(Ld Alverstone)	1935	Ld Wright
1900	Sir A. Smith	1937	Sir W. Greene (Ld)
1901	Sir R. Collins	1949	Sir R. Evershed
1907	Sir H. Cozens-Hardy (Ld)	1962	Ld Denning
1918	Sir C. Eady	1982	Sir J. Donaldson (Ld)
1919	Ld Sterndale	1992	Sir T. Bingham
		1996	Ld Woolf

President of the Family Division
(until 1971 the Probate, Divorce and Admiralty Division)

1892	Sir F. Jeune	1933	Sir B. Merriman (Ld)
1905	Sir G. Barnes	1962	Sir J. Simon
1909	Sir J. Bigham	1971	Sir G. Baker
1910	Sir S. Evans	1979	Sir J. Arnold
1918	Ld Sterndale	1988	Sir S. Brown
1919	Sir H. Duke	1999	Dame E. Butler-Sloss
	(Ld Merrivale)		

Lord Chief Justice

1894	Ld Russell of Killowen	1946	Ld Goddard
1900	Ld Alverstone	1958	Ld Parker of Waddington
1913	Ld Reading (Vt) (E)	1971	Ld Widgery
1921	Ld Trevethin	1980	Ld Lane
1922	Ld Hewart	1992	Ld Taylor of Gosforth
1940	Vt Caldecote	1996	Ld Bingham

Lord Chief Justice of Ireland

1889	Ld O'Brien	1917	Sir J. Campbell
1914	R. Cherry	1918–24	T. Molony

Lord Chief Justice of Northern Ireland

1921	(Sir) D. Henry	1971	Sir R. Lowry (Ld)
1925	(Sir) W. Moore	1988	Sir B. Hutton
1937	(Sir) J. Andrews	1997	Sir R. Carswell
1951	Ld MacDermott		

Lord President of the Court of Session

1899	Ld Kinross	1947	Ld Cooper
1905	Ld Dunedin	1954	Ld Clyde
1913	Ld Strathclyde	1974	G. Emslie (Ld)
1920	Ld Clyde	1989	Ld Hope
1935	Ld Normand	1996	Ld Rodger

Lord Justice Clerk

1888	Ld Kingsburgh	1947	Ld Thomson
1915	Ld Dickson	1962	Ld Grant
1922	Ld Alness	1972	Ld Wheatley
1933	Ld Aitchison	1985	Ld Ross
1941	Ld Cooper	1996	Ld Cullen

Lords of Appeal in Ordinary

1887–1910	Ld Macnaghten	1962–1969	Ld Pearce
1894–1907	Ld Davey	1962–1965	Ld Evershed
1899–1909	Ld Robertson	1963–1971	Ld Upjohn
1899–1905	Ld Lindley	1963–1971	Ld Donovan
1905–1928	Ld Atkinson	1964–1982	Ld Wilberforce
1907–1910	Ld Collins	1965–1974	Ld Pearson
1909–1929	Ld Shaw	1968–1985	Ld Diplock
1910–1912	Ld Robson	1969–1980	Vt Dilhorne
1912–1921	Ld Moulton	1971–1977	Ld Cross of Chelsea
1913–1918	Ld Parker	1971–1977	Ld Simon of Glaisdale
1913–1930	Ld Sumner (Vt)	1971–1977	Ld Kilbrandon
1913–1932	Ld Dunedin (Vt)	1972–1980	Ld Salmon
1918–1922	Vt Cave	1974–1981	Ld Edmund-Davies
1921–1929	Ld Carson	1975–1985	Ld Fraser of Tullybelton
1923–1937	Ld Blanesburgh	1975–1982	Ld Russell of Killowen
1928–1944	Ld Atkin	1977–1996	Ld Keith of Kinkel
1929–1935	Ld Tomlin	1977–1986	Ld Scarman
1929–1946	Ld Russell of Killowen	1979–1980	Ld Lane
1929–1948	Ld Thankerton	1980–1986	Ld Roskill
1930–39 & 1941–47	Ld Macmillan	1980–1992	Ld Bridge of Harwich
1932–35 & 1937–47	Ld Wright	1981–1991	Ld Brandon of Oakbrook
1935–38 & 1939–41	Ld Maugham (Vt)	1982–1986	Ld Brightman
1935–1938	Ld Roche	1982–1994	Ld Templeman
1938–1944	Ld Romer	1985–1993	Ld Griffiths
1938–1954	Ld Porter	1985–1987	Ld Mackay of Clashfern
1944–51 & 1954–62	Ld Simonds (Vt)	1986–1993	Ld Ackner
1944–1946	Ld Goddard	1986–1998	Ld Goff of Chieveley
1946–1949	Ld Uthwatt	1986–1992	Ld Oliver of Aylmerton
1946–1949	Ld du Parcq	1988–1996	Ld Jauncey of Tullichettle
1947–1951	Ld MacDermott	1988–1994	Ld Lowry
1947–1953	Ld Normand	1991–	Ld Browne-Wilkinson
1947–1957	Ld Oaksey	1992–1997	Ld Mustill
1947–1959	Ld Morton of Henryton	1992–	Ld Slynn of Hadley
1948–1975	Ld Reid	1992–1996	Ld Woolf
1949–1950	Ld Greene	1993–1999	Ld Lloyd
1949–1964	Ld Radcliffe	1994–1998	Ld Nolan
1950–1961	Ld Tucker	1994–	Ld Nicholls of Birkenhead
1951–1954	Ld Asquith of Bishopstone	1995–	Ld Steyn
1951–1960	Ld Cohen	1995–	Ld Hoffmann
1953–1961	Ld Keith of Avonholm	1996–	Ld Hope of Craighead
1954–1960	Ld Somervell of Harrow	1996–	Ld Clyde
1957–1962	Ld Denning	1997–	Ld Hutton
1959–1963	Ld Jenkins	1997–	Ld Saville of Newdigate
1960–1973	Ld Morris of Borth-y-Gest	1998–	Ld Hobhouse
1960–1971	Ld Hodson	1998–	Ld Millett
1961–1971	Ld Guest	1999–	Ld Phillips of Worth Maltravers
1961–1964	Ld Devlin		

Any peers of Parliament as are holding or have held, high judicial office are also entitled to take part in cases before the House of Lords. Normally, a hearing is before five Law Lords.

Lords Justices of Appeal

1892–1900	Sir A. Levin Smith	1959–1970	Sir C. Harman
1894–1901	Sir J. Rigby	1960–1961	Sir P. Devlin
1897–1901	Sir R. Collins	1960–1963	Sir G. Upjohn
1897–1914	Sir R. Williams	1960–1963	Sir T. Donovan
1899–1906	Sir R. Romer	1961–1969	Sir H. Danckwerts
1900–1906	Sir J. Stirling	1961–1974	Sir W. Davies
1901–1906	Sir J. Mathew	1961–1968	Sir K. Diplock
1901–1907	Sir H. Cozens-Hardy	1962–1975	Sir C. Russell
1906–1912	Sir J. Moulton	1964–1972	Sir C. Salmon
1906–1913	Sir G. Farwell	1965–1972	Sir E. Winn
1906–1915	Sir H. Buckley	1966–1974	Sir E. Davies
1907–1915	Sir W. Kennedy	1966–1971	Sir E. Sachs
1912–1913	Sir J. Hamilton	1968–1971	Sir J. Widgery
1913–1918	Sir C. Eady	1968–1971	Sir F. Atkinson
1913–1916	Sir W. Phillimore	1968–1974	Sir H. Phillimore
1914–1919	Sir W. Pickford	1968–1973	Sir S. Karminski
1915–1927	Sir J. Bankes	1969–1983	Sir J. Megaw
1915–1926	Sir T. Warrington	1970–1983	Sir D. Buckley
1916–1937	Sir T. Scrutton	1970–1977	Sir D. Cairns
1918–1919	Sir H. Duke	1971–1978	Sir B. Stamp
1919–1928	Sir J. Atkin	1971–1985	Sir J. Stephenson
1919–1923	Sir R. Younger	1971–1980	Sir A. Orr
1923–1928	Sir C. Sargant	1971–1980	Sir E. Roskill
1926–1934	Sir P. Lawrence	1972–1986	Sir F. Lawton
1927–1938	Sir F. Greer	1973–1977	Sir L. Scarman
1928–1929	Sir J. Sankey	1973–1976	Sir A. James
1928–1929	F. Russell	1974–1983	Sir R. Ormrod
1929–1940	Sir H. Slesser	1974–1983	Sir P. Rrowne
1929–1938	Sir M. Romer	1974–1979	Sir G. Lane
1934–1935	Sir F. Maugham	1975–1980	Sir W. Goff
1934–1935	Sir A. Roche	1975–1980	Sir N. Bridge
1935–1937	Sir W. Greene	1975–1982	Sir S. Shaw
1935–1948	Sir L. Scott	1976–1984	Sir G. Waller
1937–1946	Sir F. MacKinnon	1976–1985	Sir R. Cumming-Bruce
1938–1942	Sir A. Clauson	1977–1985	Sir E. Eveleigh
1938–1945	Vt Finlay	1978–1981	Sir H. Brandon
1938–1944	Sir F. Luxmoore	1978–1982	Sir S. Templeman
1938–1944	Sir R. Goddard	1979–1982	Sir J. Donaldson
1938–1946	Sir H. du Parcq	1979–1982	Sir J. Brightman
1944–1947	Sir G. Lawrence	1980–1986	Sir D. Ackner
1944–1947	Sir F. Morton	1980–1984	Sir R. Dunn
1945–1950	Sir F. Tucker	1980–1986	Sir P. Oliver
1945–1951	Sir A. Bucknill	1980–1993	Sir T. Watkins
1946–1954	Sir D. Somervell	1980–1989	Sir P. O'Connor
1946–1951	Sir L. Cohen	1980–1985	Sir H. Griffiths
1946–1951	Sir C. Asquith	1981–1992	Sir M. Fox
1947–1948	Sir F. Wrottesley	1981–1989	Sir M. Kerr
1947–1949	Sir R. Evershed	1982–1989	Sir J. May
1948–1957	Sir I. Singleton	1982–1991	Sir C. Slade
1948–1957	Sir A. Denning	1982–1993	Sir F. Purchas
1949–1959	Sir D. Jenkins	1982–1986	Sir R. Goff
1950–1957	Sir N. Birkett	1982–1994	Sir B. Dillon
1951–1960	Sir F. Hodson	1983–1988	Sir S. Brown
1951–1960	Sir J. Morris	1983–1992	Sir R. Parker
1951–1960	Sir C. Romer	1983–1985	Sir N. Browne-Wilkinson
1954–1958	Sir H. Parker	1984–1989	Sir D. Croom-Johnson
1957–1968	Sir F. Sellers	1984–1993	Sir A. Lloyd
1957–1963	Sir B. Ormerod	1985–1992	Sir M. Mustill
1957–1962	Sir H. Pearce	1985–1996	Sir B. Neill
1958–1968	Sir H. Willmer	1985–1995	Sir I. Glidewell

Lords Justices of Appeal *(cont.)*

1985–	Sir M. Nourse	1993–	Sir D. Henry
1985–1995	Sir A. Balcombe	1994–1998	Sir M. Saville
1985–1994	Sir R. Gibson	1994–	Sir S. Thomas
1986–1991	Sir D. Nicholls	1994–	Sir A. Morritt
1986–1992	Sir T. Bingham	1995–	Sir P. Otton
1986–1992	Sir J. Stocker	1995–	Sir R. Auld
1986–1992	Sir H. Woolf	1995–	Sir M. Pill
1987–1996	Sir P. Russell	1995–	Sir W. Aldous
1988–1992	Sir P. Taylor	1995–	Sir A. Ward
1988–1999	Dame E. Butler-Sloss	1995–1999	Sir M. Hutchison
1988–1999	Sir M. Stuart-Smith	1995–	Sir K. Schiemann
1988–1998	Sir C. Staughton	1995–1999	Sir N. Phillips
1988–1995	Sir M. Mann	1995–	Sir M. Thorpe
1989–1995	Sir D. Farquharson	1996–	Sir M. Potter
1989–1997	Sir A. McCowan	1996–	Sir H. Brooke
1989–1999	Sir R. Beldam	1996–	Sir I. Judge
1990–1997	Sir A. Leggatt	1996–	Sir M. Waller
1991–1994	Sir M. Nolan	1996–	Sir J. Mummery
1991–1994	Sir R. Scott	1997–	Sir C. Mantell
1992–1995	Sir J. Steyn	1997–	Sir J. Chadwick
1992–	Sir P. Kennedy	1997–	Sir R. Walker
1992–1995	Sir L. Hoffmann	1997–	Sir R. Buxton
1992–1999	Sir D. Hirst	1997–	Sir A. May
1992–	Sir Simon Brown	1997–	Sir S. Tuckey
1992–	Sir A. Evans	1998–	Sir A. Clarke
1992–	Sir C. Rose	1999–	Sir J. Laws
1993–1997	Sir J. Waite	1999–	Sir S. Sedley
1993–	Sir J. Roch	1999–	Sir J. Mance
1993–	Sir P. Gibson	1999–	Dame B. Hale
1993–1998	Sir J. Hobhouse		

The Lord High Chancellor (President), the Lord Chief Justice, the Master of the Rolls, and the President of the Family Division serve *ex officio* on the Court of Appeal.

SOURCE: *The Law List, 1900–; Who Was Who 1900–*, and *Who's Who; Whitaker's Almanack 1900–*.

Other Legal and Law Enforcement Officials

Law Commission
Chairman

1965	Sir L. Scarman
1973	Sir S. Cooke
1978	Sir M. Kerr
1981	Sir R. Gibson
1985	Sir R. Beldam
1990	Sir P. Gibson
1993	Sir H. Brooke
1996	Dame Mary Arden
1999	Sir R. Carnworth

Police Complaints Board
Chairman

1977	Ld Plowden
1981	Sir C.Philips

(Police Complaints Authority)

1985	Sir C. Clothier
1989	F. Petre
1992	Sir L. Peach
1996	P. Moorehouse

Director of Public Prosecutions

1894	H. Cuffe (E of Desart)
1909	Sir C. Mathews
1920	Sir A. Bodkin
1930	Sir E. Atkinson
1944	Sir T. Mathew
1964	(Sir) N. Skelhorn
1978	(Sir) T. Hetherington
1987	A. Green
1992	(Dame) Barbara Mills
1998	D. Calvert-Smith

Serious Fraud Office, 1988–
Director

1988	Sir J. Wood
1990	Barbara Mills
1992	G. Staple
1997	Rosalind Wright

Monopolies and Restrictive Practices Commission
Chairman

1948	Sir A. Carter
1954	Sir D. Cairns

(Monopolies Commission)

1956	R. Levy
1965	(Sir) A. Roskill

(Monopolies and Mergers Commission)
(renamed Competition Commission, 1999)

1973	Sir A. Roskill
1975	(Sir) J. Le Quesne
1988	Sir S. Lipworth
1993	(Sir) G. Odgers
1998	D. Morris

Commissioner of Metropolitan Police

1890	Sir E. Bradford
1903	Sir E. Henry
1918	Sir N. Macready
1920	Sir W. Horwood
1928	Vt Byng
1931	Ld Trenchard
1935	Sir P. Game
1945	Sir H. Scott
1953	Sir J. Nott-Bower
1958	Sir J. Simpson

1968	Sir J. Waldron
1972	(Sir) R. Mark
1977	(Sir) D. McNee
1982	Sir K. Newman
1987	(Sir) P. Imbert
1993	(Sir) P. Condon
2000	(Sir) J. Stevens

Criminal Injuries Compensation Board 1964–
Chairman

1964	(Sir) W. Carter
1975	M. Ogden
1989	Ld Carlisle of Bucklow
1996	M. Lewer

Procurator-General and Treasury Solicitor

1894	H. Cuffe (E of Desart)
1909	(Sir) J. Mellor
1923	C. Lawrence
1926	(Sir) M. Gwyer
1934	Sir T. Barnes
1953	Sir H. Kent
1964	(Sir) H. Druitt
1971	Sir H. Ware
1975	(Sir) B. Hall
1980	Sir M. Kerry
1984	J. Bailey
1988	J. Nursaw
1992	G. Hooker
1995	G. Hooker
1997	A. Hammond

Clerk of the Crown in Chancery[1]

1885	(Sir) K. Mackenzie
1915	(Sir) C. Schuster
1944	(Sir) A. Napier
1954	(Sir) G. Coldstream
1968	(Sir) D. Dobson
1977	(Sir) W. Bourne
1982	(Sir) D. Oulton
1989	(Sir) T. Legg
1998	Sir H. Phillips

Criminal Cases Review Commission
Chairman

1997	Sir F. Crawford

[1]Full title, Permanent Secretary to the Chancellor and Clerk of the Crown in Chancery. *See also* p. 304.

Intelligence Services

MI5 (the Security Service) and MI6 (the Secret Intelligence Service) can trace their origins back to 1909, and the establishment of the Secret Service Bureau with domestic and foreign intelligence arms. In 1916 the internal arm, known as M.O. 5, was reorganised within the the Military Intelligence Directorate, and became known as MI5. The Secret Intelligence Service was given the acronym MI 1 (c) in 1916, but by the 1920s had become known as MI6. In 1989 MI5 was put on a statutory footing by the *Security Service Act*. In 1994 MI6 was put on a similar statutory footing by the *Intelligence Services Act*, which also established a joint committee of both houses to bring the intelligence services under parliamentary scrutiny for the first time.

Security Service (MI5)	Secret Intelligence Service (MI6)
Director General	*Director General*
1909 (Sir) V. Kell	1909 (Sir) M. Smith Cumming
1940 Sir D. Petrie	1923 H. Sinclair
1946 (Sir) D. White	1939 (Sir) S. Menzies
1956 (Sir) R. Hollis	1952 Sir J. Sinclair
1965 (Sir) M. Furnival Jones	1956 Sir D. White
1972 (Sir) M. Hanley	1968 (Sir) J. Rennie
1979 Sir H. Smith	1973 (Sir) M. Oldfield
1981 (Sir) J. Jones	1978 (Sir) A. Franks
1985 Sir A. Duff	1981 (Sir) C. Figurres
1988 Sir P. Walker	1985 (Sir) C. Curwen
1992 Stella Rimington	1989 (Sir) C. McColl
1996 S. Lander	1993 (Sir) D. Spedding

Sources: N. West, *A Matter of Trust: MI5 1945–72* (1983). N. West, *The Friends: Britain's Post-war Secret Intelligence Operations* (1988).

Security Commission

The Security Commission was set up by Sir A. Douglas-Home in Jan 1964. In a statement to the House of Commons (HC Deb vol 687, col 1271) he set out terms of reference: 'If so requested by the Prime Minister, to investigate and report upon the circumstances in which a breach of security is known to have occurred in the public service, and upon any related failure of departmental security arrangements or neglect of duty; and in the light of any such investigation, to advise whether any change in security arrangements is necessary or desirable.' There were minor amendments to these terms of reference in 1965 and 1969 to take account of difficulties investigating matters which were before the courts. Its role was redefined under the *Security Service Act, 1989*.

Security Commission 1964–

Chairman
1964   Sir R. Winn
1971   Ld Diplock
1982   Ld Bridge of Harwich
1985   Ld Griffiths
1992   Sir A. Lloyd (Ld)
1998   Sir M. Stuart-Smith

Judicial and Criminal Satistics

Number of Judges
(England and Wales)

Year	Lords of Appeal Lord Justices & ex officio Judges	High Court Judges	Circuit Judges
1910	12	24	57
1920	14	24	54
1930	15	26	57
1940	18	29	59
1950	20	35	60
1960	24	57	75
1970	26	68	103
1980	31	75	333
1990	40	83	420
1999	47	96	551

Sources: *Criminal Statistics, Civil Judicial Statistics*.

Volume of Civil Proceedings

Appellate Courts

	Privy Council	House of Lords	Court of Appeal	High Court
1938	107	43	574	263
1958	44	52	668	315
1968	37	52	948	776
1978	52	83	1,401	831
1988	61	90	1,645	2,151
1997	73	83	1,715	4,842

Source: *Civil Judicial Statistics.*

Civil Proceedings Commenced

	Chancery	Queen's Bench	County Court
1938	9,826		1,212,253
1958	10,071	89,284	1,300,942
1968	21,461	167,447	1,481,416
1978	13,813	151,003	1,467,545
1988	27,054	235,721	2,285,125
1997	38,360	121,446	2,208,878

Source: *Civil Judicial Statistics.*

Judicial Review

Applications for leave to apply for judicial review of administrative action

1968	87	1978	340	1988	1,229
1969	184	1979	410	1989	1,580
1970	396	1980	491	1990	2,129
1971	227	1981	533	1991	2,089
1972	180	1982	685	1992	2,439
1973	140	1983	850	1993	2,886
1974	160	1984	915	1994	3,208
1975	270	1985	1,169	1995	3,604
1976	290	1986	816	1996	3,901
1977	376	1987	1,529	1997	3,848

Source: *Civil Judicial Statistics.*

Criminal Statistics: England and Wales

Higher Courts All Ages

	Total	No. for trial Male	Female	No.found Guilty[b]	Death[j]	Custody[c]	Probation	Fine	Nom. pen.[d]	Other[a]
1900	10,149	8,928	1,219	7,975	0.3	90.5	–	1.1	8.1	2.2
1910	13,680	12,522	1,157	11,337	0.2	83.6	5.2	0.6	10.2	0.2
1920	9,130	8,141	989	7,225	0.5	76.5	8.1	0.8	13.4	0.7
1930	8,384	7,781	601	6,921	0.2	71.4	11.3	1.6	15.0	0.5
1938	10,003	9,322	681	8,612	0.3	62.4	19.2	1.3	16.0	0.8
1950	18,935	17,990	945	17,149	0.2	62.6	17.2	6.6	13.2	0.2
1960	30,591	29,462	1,129	27,830	0.1	53.8	22.5	13.8	9.3	0.6
1970	44,134	41,691	2,443	35,709	–	54.3[l]	10.7	13.9	3.5	2.7
1980	73,892	66,410	7,482	59,008	–	46.2[l]	6.2	14.6	5.7	8.6
1990	101,900	89,300	8,600	92,900	–	45.6[l]	10.4	9.4	5.2	13.2
1997	81,300	73,400	7,900	79,500	–	58.6	9.9	4.2	3.6	23.6

For notes see p.344

CRIMINAL STATISTICS

Summary Courts : Indictable Offences

	Adults[fg]		Sentences as a percentage of those found guilty				Juveniles[i]	
	No. proceeded against	No. found guilty or charge proved[b]	Custody[c]	Probation	Fine	Other[e]	No. proceeded against	No. found guilty or charge proved[b]
1900[h]	43,479	30,736	47.1	14.0	26.7	12.8	n.a.	n.a.
1910	40,434	36,094	7.5	11.3	22.1	19.1	12,275	10,786
1920	37,107	32,942	31.7	11.3	38.6	28.4	14,380	12,919
1930	43,464	38,709	25.6	21.1	28.3	25.0	12,198	11,137
1938	46,014	41,976	22.0	22.2	28.9	25.9	29,388	27,875
1950	61,701	57,102	18.5	11.9	48.8	20.8	43,823	41,910
1960	84,527	79,538	13.4	12.5	56.1	18.0	58,350	56,114
1970	227,072	201,017	8.2[m]	9.5	56.1	12.3	63,531	71,860
1980[k]	407,363	306,183	7.0[m]	7.9	59.2	9.4	98,082	89,192
1990[k]	433,000	256,200	2.8[m]	9.5	49.8	35.1	66,000	n.a.
1997	486,700	242,300	10.4	11.5	35.2	57.1	76,000	46,300

[a] Including the Central Criminal Court and the Crown Courts.

[b] Excluding those found guilty but insane or (since 1964) acquitted by reason of insanity.

[c] Including imprisonment, or committal to a reformatory, approved school, remand home, or (since 1952) detention centre, or (in the case of Assizes and Quarter Sessions) borstal training.

[d] Includes absolute and conditional discharge and binding over with recognances.

[e] Includes whipping (abolished 1948), fit person orders (introduced 1934), as well as days in prison cells, admission to mental institutions, and other miscellaneous and numerically unimportant methods of disposal.

[f] Until 1932, persons aged 16 or older were tried and sentenced as adults (although in some cases sent to establishments reserved for younger offenders, e.g. borstals). From 1933, however, 'adult' means a person aged 17 or older.

[g] Includes small numbers of juveniles tried jointly with adults.

[h] The published tables for 1900 unfortunately do not distinguish adults from juveniles, although one table shows that those found guilty include 9,450 persons under 16. Consequently the figures showing the disposal of adult offenders in 1900 include unknown numbers of juveniles. Almost certainly most of the 3,218 who were whipped in 1900 were boys.

[i] From 1908 there were in effect 'juvenile courts', although lacking many special features which were introduced later.

[j] The death penalty was in practice, confined to murder throughout this period (except for war-time executions for treason or similar offences). 'Infanticides' were excluded from 'murder' from 1922, and from 1957 murders in certain circumstances became 'non-capital': the death penalty for murder was completely suspended from 1965. A large proportion of the murderers who were sentenced to death were subsequently reprieved.

[k] Figures for 1980 and 1990 are based on indictable and summary offences as redefined by the *Criminal Law Act, 1977*, and on a new counting procedure.

[l] Not including suspended sentences: 1970–14.9; 1980–18.6; 1990–15.9.

[m] These figures do not include suspended prison sentences: 1970–9.9; 1980–6.5; 1990–2.8.

Sources: N.D. Walker in A.H. Halsey (ed.) *Trends in British Society since 1900* (2nd ed., 1988), *Criminal Statistics*.

Recorded Crime, 1900–1997

England and Wales

	Murder Other Killing	Wounding	Robbery	Burglary	Rape	Theft
1900	312	1,212	256	3,812	231	63,604
1910	291	1,294	198	6,499	146	76,044
1920	313	791	235	6,863	130	77,417
1930	300	1,443	217	11,16	89	110,159
1950	315	5,177	1,021	29,834	314	334,222
1960	282	14,142	2,014	46,591	515	537,003
1970	393	38,735	6,273	190,597	884	952,666
1980	620	95,044	15,006	294,375	1,225	1,463,469
1990	664	178,684	36,200	529,200	3,400	2,374,400
1997	666	187,347	63,100	519,300	6,600	2,165,000

Source: *Criminal Statistics*.

Traffic Offences

Highway/Motoring Offences[a]
(all courts)

	No. found guilty	As % of all found guilty of non-indictable offences
1900	2,548	0.4
1910	55,633	9.1
1920	157,875	24.9
1930	267,616	42.8
1938	475,124	60.3
1950	357,932	52.6
1960	622,551	60.1
1970	1,014,793	60.6
1980	1,309,992	74.9
1990	1,501,100	n.a.
1997	648,700	49.4

[a] From 1900 to 1938 'highway offences' have been taken to include all offences under the Highway Acts together with offences against regulations etc., dealing with stage coaches, trams, trolleybuses and so on. For 1950 they have been taken to include offences numbered 123–38, 173 and 180 in the Home Office code, and for 1960 onwards offences numbered 124, 130, 135–8, 173 and 180. The advent of fixed penalty notices in the 1980s and 90s substantially changed the basis of statistics so that comparison becomes of little value.

Prison Sentences and Prison Populations, 1901–

England and Wales

	Prisoners received under sentence[a]	Daily average prison population[b]		
		Male	Female	Total
1901	149,397	14,459	2,976	17,435
1910	179,951	19,333	2,685	22,018
1920	35,439	8,279	1,404	9,683
1930	38,832	10,561	785	11,346
1940	24,870	8,443	934	9,377
1950	33,875	19,367	1,107	20,474
1960	42,810	26,198	901	27,099
1970	62,020	38,040	988	39,028
1980	75,896	42,180	1,580	43,760
1990	67,510	44,039	1,597	45,636
1997	80,800	58,439	2,675	61,114

[a] This column excludes those sentenced by courts martial and those under sentence of death or recalled under licence; but includes sentences of penal servitude (which were abolished in 1948), borstal training and committals to detention centres from 1952. Civil prisoners are not included as they are not 'under sentence'.

[b] Figures are for daily average population of penal establishments in prisons, borstals and (from 1952) detention centres.

Source: *Annual Reports* of the Prison Commissioners (changed in 1964 to the Prison Department of the Home Office). *Prison Statistics.*

H.M. Chief Inspector of Prisons

| 1987 | (Sir) S. Tumin |
| 1995 | Sir D. Ramsbotham |

Director General of the Prison Service

1993	D. Lewis
1995	R. Tilt
1999	M. Narey

Parole Board, 1967–

Chairman

1967	Ld Hunt
1974	Sir L. Petch
1979	Ld Harris of Greenwich
1982	Ld Windlesham
1988	Vt Colville of Culross
1992	Ld Belstead
1997	Usha (Lady) Prashar

Police Force

	England & Wales		Scotland		Ireland (N.I. only from 1930)	
	No of forces	No.of Police	No.of forces	No.of Police	No of forces	No.of Police
1900	179	41,900	64	4,900	1	12,300
1910	190	49,600	63	5,600	1	11,900
1920	191	56,500	59	6,500	1	11,600
1930	183	58,000	49	6,600	1	2,800
1940	183	57,300	48	6,800	1	2,900
1950	129	62,600	33	7,200	1	2,800
1960	125	72,300	33	8,700	1	2,900
1970	47	92,700	20	11,200	1	3,800
1980	43	115,900	8	13,200	1	6,900
1990	43	125,646	8	13,981	1	8,243
1999	43	126,096	8	14,810	1	8,456

Sources: *The War against Crime in England and Wales 1959–64,* Cmnd. 2296/1964; C. Reith, *A Short History of the British Police* (1948); J.M. Hart, *The British Police* (1951); B. Whitaker, *The Police* (1965); M. Banton, *The Police and the Community* (1964); Sir F. Newsam, *The Home Office* (2nd Ed. 1955); *Royal Commission on Police Powers and Procedure,* Cmd. 3297/1929; *Royal Commission on the Police,* Cmnd. 1728/1962; G. Marshall, *Police and Government* (1965); R. Reiner, *The Politics of the Police* (2nd ed. 1992); Annual Reports of H.M. Inspectors of Constabulary for England and Wales Further information from Scottish Office and Northern Ireland Office.

IX

SOCIAL CONDITIONS

Population

U.K. POPULATION 1901–
(thousands)

1901	41,459	1921	47,123	1941	48,216	1961	52,709	1981	56,352
1902	41,893	1922	44,372	1942	48,400	1962	53,274	1982	56,306
1903	42,237	1923	44,597	1943	48,789	1963	53,553	1983	56,347
1904	42,611	1924	44,916	1944	49,016	1964	53,885	1984	56,460
1905	42,981	1925	45,060	1945	49,182	1965	54,218	1985	56,618
1906	43,361	1926	45,233	1946	49,217	1966	54,500	1986	56,763
1907	43,738	1927	45,389	1947	49,571	1967	54,800	1987	56,930
1908	44,124	1928	45,578	1948	50,065	1968	55,049	1988	57,065
1909	44,519	1929	45,672	1949	50,363	1969	55,263	1989	57,236
1910	44,916	1930	45,866	1950	50,616	1970	55,421	1990	57,411
1911	45,222	1931	46,038	1951	50,225	1971	55,515	1991	57,649
1911	45,136	1932	46,335	1952	50,430	1972	55,781	1992	57,998
1913	45,648	1933	46,520	1953	50,593	1973	55,913	1993	58,191
1914	46,048	1934	46,666	1954	50,765	1974	55,922	1994	58,295
1915	44,333	1935	46,869	1955	50,946	1975	55,900	1995	58,606
1916	43,710	1936	47,081	1956	51,184	1976	55,886	1996	58,801
1917	43,280	1937	47,289	1957	51,430	1977	55,852	1997	59,009
1918	43,116	1938	47,494	1958	51,652	1978	55,822	1998	59,237
1919	44,599	1939	47,762	1959	51,956	1979	55,881		
1920	46,472	1940	48,226	1960	52,372	1980	55,945		

Census figures for 1901, 1911, 1921, 1931, 1951, 1961, 1971, 1981 and 1991. Figures for other years are mid-year estimates. Figures for 1901–21 are inclusive of S. Ireland. Figures for 1915–20 and for 1940–50 relate to civil population only.

Sources: *Annual Reports of the Registrar-General for England and Wales, Scotland and Northern Ireland; Annual Abstract of Statistics; Monthly Digest of Statistics.*

INTERCENSAL CHANGES IN POPULATION
(thousands)

		Average Annual Change			
	Population at beginning of period	Total Increase	Excess of births over deaths	Net Civilian Migration	Other Adjustments
1901–1911	38,237	38	467	−82	
1911–1921	42,082	195	286	−92	
1921–1931	44,027	201	268	−67	
1931–1951	46,038	212	190	+22	
1951–1961	50,290	252	246	−7	+13
1961–1971	52,807	280	324	−32	−12
1971–1981	55,928	42	69	−44	+17
1981–1991	56,352	130	103	+21	+6

Census enumerated population up to 1951; mid-year estimates of home population from 1951 onwards.

Source: *Annual Abstract of Statistics.*

POPULATION OF COMPONENTS OF U.K.
(thousands)

	(Sq.km.)	1911	1931	1951	1961	1971	1981	1991	1996
Standard Regions									
North	19,349	2,815	3,038	3,137	3,250	3,296	3,104	3,109	3,091
Yorks & Humb	14,196	3,877	4,285	4,522	4,635	4,799	4,860	4,797	5,036
East Midlands	12,179	2,263	2,531	2,893	3,100	3,390	3,819	3,919	4,141
East Anglia	12,565	1,192	1,232	1,382	1,470	1,669	1,872	2,018	2,142
South East	27,408	11,744	13,539	15,127	16,271	17,230	16,796	16,794	18,120
South West	23,660	2,687	2,794	3,229	3,411	3,781	4,349	4,600	4,842
West Midlands	13,013	3,277	3,743	4,423	4,758	5,110	5,148	5,089	5,317
North West	7,993	5,796	6,197	6,447	6,567	6,743	6,414	6,147	6,410
Wales	20,763	2,421	2,593	2,599	2,664	2,731	2,792	2,812	2,921
Scotland	77,179	4,760	4,843	5,097	5,179	5,229	5,131	4,962	5,128
N. Ireland	13,570	1,251	1,280	1,371	1,425	1,536	1,482	1,578	1,663
Metropolitan counties etc									
Greater London	1,578	7,160	8,110	8,197	7,992	7,452	6,696	6,394	7,074
West Midlands	899	1,780	2,143	2,547	2,732	2,793	2,646	2,511	2,642
West Yorkshire	2,034	1,852	1,939	1,985	2,005	2,067	2,037	1,992	2,109
Greater Manch.	1,286	2,638	2,727	2,716	2,720	2,729	2,595	2,455	2,578
Merseyside	655	1,378	1,587	1,663	1,718	1,657	1,513	1,380	1,420
Tyne and Wear	540	1,105	1,201	1,201	1,244	1,212	1,143	1,090	1,127
Strathclyde	13,502	2,270	2,400	2,524	2,584	2,575	2,404	2,219	n.a.

Source: *Annual Abstract of Statistics.*

BIRTH RATES, DEATH RATES AND MARRIAGES IN THE U.K.
(per thousand population)

	Total Births per 1000 Population	Infant Mortality (under one year) per 1000 live births	Total Deaths per 1000 Population	Total Marriages per 1000 Population
1900	28.2	142.0	18.4	15.1
1910	25.0	110.0	14.0	14.3
1920	25.4	82.0	12.9	19.4
1930	16.8	67.0	11.7	15.5
1940	14.6	61.0	14.4	22.2
1950	16.2	31.2	11.8	16.1
1960	17.5	22.4	11.5	15.0
1970	16.3	18.5	11.8	17.0
1980	13.2	12.2	11.6	14.9
1990	13.9	7.9	11.1	13.1
1997	12.3	5.8	10.7	11.6

Figures for 1900, 1910 and 1920 (except for infant mortality) include Southern Ireland. Death rate in 1940 based on civil deaths and population only.

Source: *Annual Abstract of Statistics, OPCS Marriage and Divorce Statistics, Birth Statistics.*

AGE DISTRIBUTION OF THE POPULATION OF THE U.K.
(Percentages)

Age Group	1901	1911	1921[a]	1931	1939	1951	1961	1971	1981	1991
Under 10	22.2	21.0	18.2	16.1	14.1	16.0	15.1	16.6	12.6	13.0
10–19	20.3	19.1	19.0	16.8	16.3	12.9	14.9	14.6	16.3	12.6
20–29	18.3	17.3	16.2	17.1	15.6	14.2	12.7	14.3	14.1	15.4
30–39	3.9	15.1	14.5	14.5	16.0	14.5	13.7	11.6	13.8	13.9
40–49	10.5	11.4	13.1	12.9	13.1	14.8	13.5	12.3	11.3	13.4
50–59	7.3	7.9	9.6	11.1	11.3	11.9	13.2	11.9	11.7	10.6
60–69	4.7	5.1	6.0	7.3	8.5	8.9	9.4	10.6	10.2	10.1
70–79	.2	2.5	2.7	3.4	4.1	5.3	5.6	5.9	7.2	7.3
80+	0.6	0.6	0.7	0.8	1.0	1.5	1.9	2.2	2.7	3.7
Total	100.0	100.0	100.0	100.0	100.0	100.0	100.0	100.0	100.0	100.0

[a] Percentages for 1921 are for England, Wales and Scotland only.

Sources: Census figures except for 1939, which is mid-year estimate. Registrar-General for England and Wales, and Scotland, *Censuses of Population*, and the *Annual Abstract of Statistics*.

EXPECTATION OF LIFE
England and Wales
(Average future expected lifetime at birth)

Years	Male	Female	Years	Male	Female
1900–02	46	50	1960–62	68	74
1910–12	52	55	1969–71	69	75
1920–22	56	60	1978–80	70	77
1930–32	59	63	1988–90	73	79
1938	61	66	1995–97	74	80
1950–52	66	72			

Sources: *Annual Reports of Registrar-General for England and Wales*, and the *Government Actuary's Department, Annual Abstract of Statistics*.

MAIN CAUSE OF DEATH
England and Wales
(000s)

	1900	1910	1920	1930	1940	1950	1960	1970	1980	1990	1996
Total deaths	588	483	466	455	572	510	526	575	581	565	563
Due to:											
Tuberculosis	61	51	43	36	27	16	3	2	1	1	–
Cancer	27	35	44	57	69	83	96	114	131	145	140
Vascular lesions of the											
nervous system	[a]41	30	49	41	52	65	76	79	71	67	60
Heart diseases	n.a.	49	53	90	136	146	153	179	192	193	179
Pneumonia	44	40	37	28	29	18	24	43	54	27	55
Bronchitis	54	34	38	19	46	28	26	29	19	7	4
Violent causes	20	19	17	22	47[b]	19	23	23	20	18	16

[a] All diseases of the nervous system, 1900–30, cerebrovascular disease (including strokes), 1970 onwards.

[b] Including 22,000 deaths of civilians due to operations of war.

Source: *Annual Reports and Statistical Reviews of the Registrar-General for England and Wales; Annual Abstract of Statistics*.

AVERAGE AGE AT FIRST MARRIAGE
England and Wales

Year	Bachelors	Spinsters	Year	Bachelors	Spinsters
1901–05	26.9	25.4	1951–55	26.5	24.2
1911–15	27.5	25.8	1961–65	25.5	22.9
1921–25	27.5	25.6	1970	24.4	22.7
1931–35	27.4	25.5	1980	25.3	23.0
1941–45	26.8	24.6	1990	27.2	25.2
			1996	29.6	27.5

Sources: *Annual Reports of the Registrar-General for England and Wales;* figures since 1970 are from *OPCS Marriage and Divorce Statistics.*

BIRTHS OUTSIDE MARRIAGE

	% Out		In (000s)	Out (000s)	% Out
1900–02	6.4	1961	890	54	5.7
1910–12	7.4	1971	828	74	8.2
1920–22	7.2	1981	640	91	12.4
1930–32	7.2	1991	556	236	29.8
1940–42	6.6	1997	460	266	36.6
1950–52	5.0				

Source: *Annual Abstract of Statistics*

LEGAL ABORTIONS
England and Wales (residents only)

	Married	Single	Other[a]	Total
1968[b]	10,090	10,302	1,840	22,332
1969	22,979	22,287	4,563	49,829
1970	34,314	34,492	7,156	75,962
1971	41,536	44,302	8,732	94,570
1972	46,894	51,115	10,556	108,565
1973	46,766	52,899	10,903	110,568
1974	45,167	53,334	10,934	109,432
1975	43,322	52,423	10,903	106,648
1976	39,868	50,481	10,934	101,003
1977	39,445	51,604	11,188	102,237
1978	42,200	56,600	13,300	112,100
1979	42,800	61,700	14,500	119,000
1980	44,300	68,800	15,900	128,900
1981	42,400	70,000	16,100	128,600
1982	40,500	71,800	16,200	128,600
1983	38,400	73,200	15,400	127,200
1984	38,700	81,100	16,600	136,400
1985	37,700	72,200	16,200	141,100
1986	38,200	93,000	16,400	147,600
1987	38,200	100,700	17,300	156,200
1988	38,700	111,000	18,600	168,300
1989	38,100	113,000	19,300	170,500
1990	38,200	116,200	19,600	173,900
1991	37,800	110,900	18,700	167,400
1992	36,394	105,636	18,500	160,501
1993	35,408	103,784	19,700	157,846
1994	34,632	102,532	19,400	156,539
1995	33,018	102,274	19,000	154,315
1996	34,262	114,086	19,500	167,916
1997	34,181	116,425	19,500	170,145
1998	34,466	122,661	19,600	177,871

[a] Widowed, divorced, separated, or women whose marital status was unknown.
[b] The 1968 figures are from 27 Apr when the Act came into effect.

Source: *Population Trends; Abortion Statistics*

DIVORCES
(Great Britain)

The law on divorce was significantly relaxed by the *Matrimonial Causes Act*s of 1937, 1950 and 1967, and by the *Divorce Reform Act, 1969.*

	Decrees made absolute		Decrees made absolute
1910	801	1960	25,672
1920	3,747	1970	62,010
1930	3,944	1980	158,829
1940	8,396	1990	165,658
1950	32,516	1995	167,748

Source: *Annual Reports of the Registrars-General for England and Wales and Scotland. OPCS Marriage and Divorce Statistics.*

NET EMIGRATION FROM GREAT BRITAIN AND IRELAND

(Commonwealth citizens travelling by the long sea routes to non-European countries, 1900–59; all routes 1970–. Southern Ireland excluded from 1938 onwards).

	1900	1910	1920	1931	1938	1946	1950	1959	1970	1980	1990	1997
All	71,188	241,164	199,047	–39,056	–6,467	103,504	54,153	28,400	92,700	55,400	–36,000	–60,000
U.S.A.	47,978	75,021	60,067	–10,385	–1,432	45,151	8,541	4,500	4,500	11,800	13,000	2,000
Canada	7,803	115,955	94,496	–10,464	–3,974	43,414	6,464	–400	12,700	14,300	2,500 } 5,000	
Aust'lasia	6,259	34,657	28,405	–8,760	2,204	8,443	54,581	28,800	59,300	28,000	300	
S. Africa	7,417	8,314	7,844	–1,263	2,037	2,242	1,912	–800	19,400	7,600	2,700	–6,000

Sources: 1900–1950: *External Migration 1815–1950*, N.H. Carrier and J.R. Jeffrey, *Studies on Medical and Population Subjects No. 6*, General Register Office (1953); figures from 1959 on are from the *Annual Abstract of Statistics*.

PEOPLE BORN OVERSEAS[a]
Great Britain

Birthplace	1931 000s	1931 % of pop.	1951 000s	1951 % of pop.	1961 000s	1961 % of pop.	1971 000s	1971 % of pop.	1981 000s	1981 % of pop.	1991 000s	1991 % of pop.
Foreign countries[b]	347	0.8	722	1.5	842	1.6	984	1.7	1,274	2.3	1,288	2.3
Canada, Australia, New Zealand	75	0.2	99	0.2	110	0.2	136	0.4	152	0.3	177	0.3
Other Commonwealth	137	0.3	218	0.4	541	1.1	1,140	2.1	1,325	2.5	1,688	3.1
Irish Republic[c]	362	0.8	532	1.1	709	1.4	718	1.3	606	1.1	593	1.1
Total born overseas	921	2.0	1,571	3.2	2,202	4.3	2,976	5.5	3,360	6.2	3,775	6.9

[a] Persons resident in Great Britain at the time of the Census who had been born outside the United Kingdom; including United Kingdom citizens born overseas but excluding short-term visitors.
[b] Including South Africa.
[c] Including Ireland (part not stated).

Sources: *Social Trends* 1972. Census for 1981 and 1991.

NATURALISATION
Total certificates granted by the Home Department or oaths taken in period

1901–10	7,997	1931–40	15,454	1961–70	40,252
1911–20	11,293	1941–50	51,132	1971–80	28,717
1921–30	9,849	1951–60	44,977	1981–90	23,108

Sources: 1900–1950: *External Migration 1815–1950*, N.H. Carrier and J.R. Jeffrey, *Studies on Medical and Population Subjects No. 6*, General Register Office (1953); and *Whitaker's Almanack*.

COMMONWEALTH IMMIGRATION

Commonwealth immigration came under systematic control under the *Commonwealth Immigrants Act,1962*. This Act was strengthened by the *Commonwealth Immigrants Act, 1968* and largely replaced by the *Immigration Act, 1971*. The *British Nationality Act, 1981*, completely revised the definition of British nationality, introducing three classes of citizenship with the right to live in Britain largely restricted to those with a British grandparent.

MAIN SOURCES OF IMMIGRATION INTO THE UNITED KINGDOM 1956–62

Year	West Indians	Indians	Pakistanis (Bangladeshis)
1956	26,400	5,600	2,100
1957	22,500	6,000	5,200
1958	16,500	6,200	4,700
1959	20,400	2,900	900
1960	52,700	5,900	2,500
1961	61,600	23,750	25,100
1962	35,000	22,100	24,900

ACCEPTANCES FOR SETTLEMENT IN THE UNITED KINGDOM 1963–

	Foreign	Old Commonwealth	New Commonwealth	Total
1963	15,349	3,735	56,071	75,155
1964	19,211	3,060	52,840	75,111
1965	20,615	3,454	53,898	77,967
1966	18,948	4,214	48,104	71,266
1967	18,346	4,335	60,633	83,314
1968	20,093	3,761	60,620	84,474
1969	21,862	3,581	44,503	69,946
1970	20,917	4,497	37,893	63,307
1971	23,467	4,577	44,261	72,305
1972	19,681	3,989	68,519	92,189
1973	21,118	3,099	32,247	55,162
1974	26,800	3,948	42,531	68,878
1975	31,477	5,387	53,265	82,405
1976	31,464	5,967	55,013	80,745
1977	31,917	6,572	44,155	69,313
1978	34,364	7,453	30,514	72,331
1979	36,600	6,960	26,110	69,670
1980	38,410	6,900	24,610	69,920
1981	31,280	5,380	22,400	59,060
1982	26,080	5,150	22,650	53,880
1983	20,120	5,800	27,550	53,460
1984	18,720	7,440	24,800	50,950
1985	20,150	8,160	27,050	55,360
1986	17,740	6,560	22,520	46,820
1987	18,230	6,900	20,850	45,980
1988	19,100	7,380	22,800	49,280
1989	18,330	7,870	22,860	49,060
1990	20,700	6,030	25,660	52,400
1991	22,850	3,120	27,930	53,900
1992		4,100		52,570
1993		4,510		55,640
1994		4,890		55,110
1995		4,390		55,480
1996		4,490		61,730

This table covers work permit holders admitted for more than one year. Voucher holders were admitted for settlement on arrival. Work permit holders may qualify for settlement after 4 years in approved employment.

Source: *Control of Immigration: Statistics.*

COMMONWEALTH IMMIGRANTS IN THE U.K

Defined as those living in households whose head was born in the relevant area, according to the 1961, 1971, and 1981 Censuses.

Year	W. Indians	Bangladeshis Indians and Pakistanis	Australians	Others in British Territories	Total
1961	173,076	115,982[a]	23,390[a]	285,962[b]	596,755
1971	302,970	462,125	32,400	496,410[b]	1,293,905
1981	295,179	628,589	61,916	280,466	1,666,120

[a] Persons born in these countries but British by birth or descent have been deducted for 1961.
[b] The largest contributors to this total are Cypriots, New Zealanders, Maltese, Canadians and South Africans.

The 1991 Census was the first to ask respondents to categorize themselves in terms of colour; previous census questions about the birthplace of the head of household would now be less informative about race, since so many non-white people living in Britain are now second- or third-generation. This was the breakdown in 1991:

Black (Caribbean)	Black (Other)	Indian	Pakistani	Bangladeshi	Other non-white
499,964	290,763	840,255	476,555	162,835	644,678[a]

[a] Of which the largest components are 'other Asian' and Chinese.

According to the 1991 Census, 837,464 people resident in Great Britain gave their place of birth as the Irish Republic, or simply Ireland.

Source: *Census*. See also Radical Statistics Race Group, *Britain's Black Population* (2nd ed., 1987).

Race Relations Legislation

Race Relations Act, 1965, set up the Race Relations Board to receive complaints of unlawful discrimination and to investigate them.

Race Relations Act, 1968, enlarged the Race Relations Board and extended its scope. It also set up the Community Relations Commission to establish harmonious race relations.

Race Relations Act, 1976, made discrimination unlawful in employment, training, education and in the provision of goods and services and made it an offence to stir up racial hatred. It extended discrimination to include indirect discrimination and discrimination by way of victimisation. It replaced the Race Relations Board and the Community Relations Commission by the Commission for Racial Equality.

Race Relations Board 1966–77

Chairman

17 Feb 66	M. Bonham Carter
1 Jan 71	Sir R. Wilson (Acting)
1 Oct 71	Sir G. Wilson

Community Relations Commission 1968–77

Chairman

17 Feb 68	F. Cousins
1 Jan 71	M. Bonham Carter
1 Mar 77	Ld Pitt

Housing

(a) **Major Housing Acts** *(England and Wales; in most cases there were parallel Acts for Scotland.)*

Housing and Town Planning Act, 1909. This amended the law relating to the housing of the working classes, and provided for town-planning schemes. It also provided for the establishment of public health and housing committees of county councils.

Housing Acts, 1919, 1923, and 1924. These Acts provided for varying subsidies to encourage the building of new houses for the working classes. The 1923 Act made subsidies available to private owners.

Housing Act, 1930. This Act extended subsidies and provided wider powers for slum clearance.

Housing (Financial Provisions) Act, 1933. This reduced the general subsidies, but presented subsidies for slum clearance.

Housing (Financial Provisions) Act, 1938. This Act regulated subsidies to housing.

Housing Act, 1949. This Act allowed local authorities to make grants for the improvement of houses and it removed 'for the working classes' from the law covering local authorities' housing duties.

Housing (Financial Provisions) Act, 1958. This Act provided grants for improvements to private houses.

House Purchase and Housing Act, 1959. This extended grants for improvements.

Housing Act, 1961. Laid down regulations for landlords leasing houses for less than seven years to keep the structure, exterior, installations, etc., of the house in repair and proper working order.

Housing Act, 1964. Set up the Housing Corporation to assist Housing Societies to provide housing accommodation and conferred powers and duties on local authorities with regard to housing improvements.

Building Control Act, 1966. Controlled and regulated building and constructional work.

Housing Subsidies Act, 1967. Provided for financial assistance towards the provision, acquisition or improvement of dwellings and the provision of hostels.

Housing Act, 1969. Made further provision for grants by local authorities towards the cost of improvements and conversions; made provision as to houses in multiple occupation; altered the legal standard of fitness for human habitation; and amended the law relating to long tenancies.

Housing Act, 1971. Increased the amount of financial assistance available for housing subsidies in development or intermediate areas.

Housing Finance Act, 1972. Increased financial help to local authorities needing to clear slums, provided national rent rebate scheme for Council tenants and rent loans for private tenants of unfurnished accommodation, and based rent of public sector and private unfurnished accommodation on the 'fair rent' principle.

Housing Act, 1974. Extended functions of Housing Corporation, provided for the registration and giving of asistance to housing associations, introduced new powers for declaration of Housing Action Areas and made provisions for higher renovation grants.

Housing Finance (Special Provisions) Act, 1975. Prevented surcharges arising out of the *Housing Finance Act, 1972* (relating to refusal by Clay Cross Councillors to charge proper rents under the Act) and substituted other means of making up losses.

Housing Rents and Subsidies Act, 1975. Repealed provisions of *Housing Finance Act, 1972* relating to fixing of public sector rents; introduced new subsidies for local authorities and new town corporations and made certain housing associations eligible for housing association grant.

Housing (Homeless Persons) Act, 1977. Local authorities put under a duty to house homeless persons in 'priority need' unless the homelessness could be shown to be intentional.

Home Purchase Assistance and Housing Corporation Guarantee Act, 1978. Set up the 'Homeloan' scheme (to provide a reduction in the cost of house purchase for first-time purchasers).

Housing Act, 1980. Provided a new and much more flexible subsidy system; repealed the 'no-profit rule'; local authority tenants of 3 years' standing or more to have the right to buy their houses at discounts ranging from 33% to 50%.

Social Security and Housing Benefits Acts, 1982. Replaced rent rebates, rent allowances, rate rebates, and the 'rent' element in tenants' Supplementary Benefit by Housing Benefit.

Housing and Building Control Act, 1984. Maximum discount on 'right-to-buy' purchase increased to 60%; exercise of right to buy simplified and extended; new system of building control.

Housing Act, 1988. This established new forms of rented tenure, assured tenancies and assured shorthold tenancies. It provided for Housing Action Trusts in designated areas to take over run-down local authority housing, and pass on the ownership and management to new private sector landlords – subject to a ballot by local residents.

Local Government and Housing Act, 1989. This amended the rules for local government housing revenue, placed strict limits on housing improvement grants and extended the 'right-to-buy' to occupants of houses and flats designed for the elderly and disabled.

Leasehold Reform, Housing and Urban Development Act, 1993. This proposed new rights for leaseholders of flats and houses to buy the freehold of their buildings. It also established an Urban Regeneration Agency to promote the redevelopment of derelict land in cities.

Housing Act, 1996. This modified local authorities' duties to provide houses for homeless persons to prevent them from being treated more favourably than other applicants for housing.

(b) Major Rent and Mortgage Interest Restriction Acts

Increase of Rent and Mortgage Interest (Restrictions) Acts, 1915. These acts established a limit to the rent of small houses, and protected tenants from eviction.

Rent Restrictions Acts, 1919–39. These altered the exact limits on rent.

Rent and Mortgage Interest (Restriction) Act, 1939. This extended rent restriction and security of tenure to houses which had become decontrolled and to new houses.

Furnished Houses (Rent Control) Act, 1947. This Act created rent tribunals to fix the prices of furnished lettings.

Landlord and Tenant Rent Control Act, 1949. Rent tribunals were authorised to determine 'reasonable' rents, on the application of the tenants, who could also apply for the recovery of premiums. The Act applied to unfurnished houses and flats.

Housing Repairs and Rents Act, 1954. This Act authorised landlords to increase rents where sufficient repairs to their property had been carried out. Rent could also be increased to cover the increase in cost since 1939 of other services provided by the landlord.

Rent Act, 1957. This decontrolled the 1939 restriction on rents for many houses in 1958 and permitted substantial increases on controlled rents.

Protection from Eviction Act, 1964. This prevented a landlord of residential premises from recovering possession without an order of the county court. (Consolidated in *Protection from Eviction Act, 1977.*)

Rent Act, 1965. Provided for the registration of rents, and for the fixing of 'fair rents'. It introduced controls, and provided security of tenure subject to certain conditions. A landlord cannot enforce a right to possession against a tenant without a court order.

Leasehold Reform Act, 1967. Enabled tenants of houses held on long leases at low rents to acquire the freehold or an extended lease.

Rent Act, 1968. Consolidated the statute law relating to protected or statutory tenancies, rents under regulated or controlled tenancies and furnished tenancies.

Rent Act, 1974. Extended indefinite security of tenure and access to rent tribunals to furnished tenants. Landlords resident on the premises exempt from provisions of the Act. It brought most residential furnished tenancies of absentee landlords into the full protection of the Rent Acts.

Finance Act, 1974. This introduced a £25,000 ceiling on the sum on which mortgage payers could get tax relief.

Rent (Agriculture) Act, 1976. Afforded security of tenure for agricultural workers housed by their employers and imposed duties on housing authorities in respect to agricultural workers.

Housing (Homeless Persons) Act, 1977. Made local authorities more fully responsible for providing accommodation for the homeless.

Rent Act, 1977. Consolidated law relating to control and regulation of rent, security of tenure, and powers and duties of Rent Officers, Rent Assessment Committees and Rent Tribunals.

Housing Act, 1980. All remaining rent-controlled dwellings transferred to regulation. 'Shorthold' tenure introduced, with security of tenure for limited period only.

Finance Act, 1983. Raised the ceiling on mortgage interest tax relief from £25,000 to £30,000.

Housing Act, 1988. This abolished 'fair rent' assessment for future tenancies and introduced 'shorthold leases'.

Finance Act, 1993. This further restricted mortgage interest tax relief by restricting it to 20% of the interest on the first £30,000.

Finance Act, 1994. This restricted mortgage interest tax relief to 15%.

Finance Act, 1997. This restricted mortgage interest tax relief to 10%.

Permanent Dwellings Completed

Great Britain: 1919–45; United Kingdom: 1945–

	Public Sector (000s)	Private Sector (000s)	Total (000s)		Public Sector (000s)	Private Sector (000s)	Total (000s)
1919/20	–	1	1	1933/34	72	222	294
1920/21	17	23	40	1934/35	57	294	351
1921/22	110	32	142	1935/36	70	280	350
1922/23	67	45	112	1936/37	87	283	370
1923/24	20	74	94	1937/38	92	268	360
1924/25	24	120	144	1938/39	122	237	359
1925/26	50	134	184	1939/40	69	152	221
1926/27	84	151	235	1940/41	26	31	57
1927/28	120	141	261	1941/45	8	3	11
1928/29	70	119	189	(*Annual Average*) (April–May)			
1929/30	73	147	220	1945	11	12	
1930/31	64	133	197	1946	109	31	140
1931/32	79	136	215	1947	148	41	189
1932/33	68	151	219	1948	217	34	251

	Public Sector (000s)	Private Sector (000s)	Total (000s)		Public Sector (000s)	Private Sector (000s)	Total (000s)
1949	177	28	205	1973	114	191	305
1950	175	30	205	1974	134	145	280
1951	176	25	202	1975	167	155	322
1952	212	37	248	1976	170	155	325
1953	262	65	327	1977	170	144	314
1954	262	92	354	1978	136	152	289
1955	208	116	324	1979	108	144	252
1956	181	126	308	1980	110	131	240
1957	179	129	308	1981	88	119	207
1958	148	130	278	1982	54	129	183
1959	128	153	282	1983	56	153	209
1960	133	171	304	1984	55	166	221
1961	122	181	303	1985	44	163	208
1962	135	178	314	1986	39	178	216
1963	130	178	308	1987	35	191	226
1964	162	221	383	1988	35	207	242
1965	174	217	391	1989	34	187	221
1966	187	209	396	1990	35	163	198
1967	211	204	415	1991	31	153	185
1968	200	226	426	1992	17	147	164
1969	192	186	378	1993	47	146	193
1970	188	174	362	1994	68	153	211
1971	168	196	364	1995	22	156	178
1972	130	201	331	1996	30	153	183

Notes: From 1919/20 to 1944/45, the figures are combinations of England and Wales financial year figures and Scottish calendar year figures.

For 1946 onwards the figures are for the United Kingdom including Northern Ireland. 'Public sector' comprises local authorities, new towns, housing associations, and public bodies in their capacity as employers. Before 1945 the last two were included in the private sector.

Sources: *Housing and Construction Statistics*; The Department of the Environment.

Housing by Tenure
Great Britain

	Owner Occupied %	Local Authority[a] %	Private Rented etc.[b] %	Total Stock (millions)
1914	10[c]	_[d]	90	9.0
1938	25	10	65	12.7
1945	26	12	62	12.9
1951	29	18	53	13.9
1956	34	23	43	15.1
1960	42	26	32	16.2
1965	47	28	25	17.4
1970	50	30	20	18.7
1975	53	31	16	19.9
1980	55	32	13	21.0
1985	62	27	11	21.8
1990	67	22	11	22.9
1996	67	19	14	23.9

[a] Includes New Towns.

[b] Includes dwellings rented with farm and business premises, or occupied by virtue of employment.

[c] Approximate only: true figure probably lies between 8% and 15%.

[d] Included under private landlord.

Source: *Housing and Construction Statistics*

Council House Sales
(England and Wales)

Under the *Housing Act, 1980,* tenants in local authority, new town and housing association properties were given the 'Right to Buy' their homes at substantial discounts:

Year	Sales Completed	Year	Sales Completed
1980	84,000	1990	103,000
1981	100,000	1991	56,000
1982	201,000	1992	65,148
1983	137,000	1993	45,000
1984	101,000	1994	45,000
1985	90,000	1995	49,000
1986	87,000	1996	36,000
1987	99,000	1997	34,000
1988	149,000	1998	42,000
1989	162,000		

Source: *Housing and Construction Statistics.*

Social Security

Old Age Pensions Act, 1908. This granted non-contributory pensions ranging from one to five shillings a week to be paid from national funds, subject to a means test, at the age of 70, where income was under £31 p.a.

National Insurance Act, 1911 (National Health Insurance, Pt. I). This was the first part of an act providing insurance against both ill-health and unemployment. The Act covered all those between the ages of 16 and 70 who were manual workers or earning not more than £160 p.a. (This income limit was raised in 1920 and 1942.) The self-employed, non-employed, and those already provided for by other health insurance schemes were not insurable under this Act. The scheme was administered through independent units, or 'approved societies'. Local insurance committees were set up. The insurance included benefits for sickness, maternity, and medical needs. A weekly contribution was made by the insured person, his employer and the government. The basic weekly sickness benefit was 10s. for men, 7s. 6d. for women. It also set up general medical and pharmaceutical services.

Widows', Orphans' and Old Age Contributory Pensions Act, 1925. This provided for a contributory scheme, covering almost the same field as the national health insurance scheme. Pensions were payable to the widows of insured persons, and to insured persons and their wives over the age of 70. This age limit was reduced to 65 in 1928. The weekly rates were 10s. for widows, with additional allowances of 5s. for the first child and 3s. for each other child, 7s. 6d. for orphans and 10s. for old age pensioners.

Widows', Orphans' and Old Age Contributory Pensions Act, 1929. This Act provided a pension at age 55 for certain widows who could not satisfy the conditions of the 1925 Act.

Widows', Orphans' and Old Age Contributory Pensions (Voluntary Contributors) Act, 1937. This Act created a new scheme of voluntary insurance for old age, widows' and orphans' benefits open to certain persons who were not within the scope of the main scheme.

Old Age and Widows' Pensions Act, 1940. This reduced to 60 the age at which a woman who was herself insured or who was the wife of an insured man could become entitled to an old age pension. The Act also introduced supplementary pensions in cases of need for widow pensioners over the age of 60 and for old age pensioners. The Unemployment Assistance Board was renamed the Assistance Board and became responsible for payment of these supplementary pensions.

National Health Insurance, Contributory Pensions and Workmen's Compensation Act, 1941. This raised the income limit for compulsory insurance of non-manual workers for pensions purposes to £420 p.a.

Family Allowances Act, 1945. This granted a non-contributory allowance, to be paid to the mother, for each child other than the first. 1945–52 5s. per week; 1952–68 8s. per week; 1956–68 l0s. per week for third and subsequent children; 1968 15s. (75p) per week for second, £1 per week for third and subsequent children.

National Health Service Act, 1946. By this Act, hospitals were transferred from local authorities and voluntary bodies and were to be administered by the Minister through regional hospital boards, general medical and dental services through executive councils, and other health services by county and county borough councils. Health centres were to be provided by local authorities for general, mental, dental, and pharmaceutical services, but few were built. Almost all services under the Act were to be free.

National Health Service (Amendment) Act, 1949, National Health Service Acts, 1951 and 1952, and *National Health Service Contributions Acts, 1957–1958.* These made modifications in the original scheme by imposing charges for certain parts of the scheme (prescriptions, dental treatment, etc.).

National Insurance Act, 1946. This Act provided a new scheme of insurance replacing the National Health Insurance and contributory pensions schemes with effect from 5 Jul 1948. All persons over school-leaving age, except certain married women, became compulsorily insurable. In addition to provisions for unemployment (see p.378) benefits payable were retirement pension, widow's benefit, and death grant.

National Insurance Act, 1951. This Act introduced an allowance payable with widows' benefits for each dependent child in the family.

Family Allowances and National Insurance Act, 1956. Enabled allowances for dependent children to be paid in certain cases up to the age of 18; introduced new personal rate of widowed mother's allowance, reduced length of marriage condition for widow's pension, and introduced amendments to widows' pensions.

National Insurance Act, 1957. This introduced the child's special allowance for the children of divorced parents payable on the death of the father if he had been contributing towards their support and the mother had not remarried.

National Insurance Act, 1959. This introduced a state scheme of graduated pensions, requiring that both contributions and pensions should be graduated according to salary level.

Mental Health Act, 1959. The Board of Control was abolished and its functions passed to the new Mental Health Review Tribunals, local authorities, and the Minister of Health. The Act redefined the classifications of mental disorders, provided for further safeguards against improper detention, and extended the provisions for voluntary and informal treatment of patients.

Family Allowances and National Insurance Act, 1964. This increased from 18 to 19 the age limit up to which a person could be regarded as a child for the purposes of an increase of benefit or widowed mother's allowance.

Prescription Charges were ended in 1965. They were reimposed in 1968 with exemptions for some categories.

National Insurance Act, 1966. This extended the period of widow's allowance, introduced a scheme of earnings-related supplements to unemployment and sickness benefits and included a widow's supplementary allowance.

Ministry of Social Security Act, 1966. This repeated and amended much previous legislation. It provided for the abolition of the Ministry of Pensions and National Insurance and the National Assistance Board and the establishment of the Ministry of Social Security. The Act also provided for a scheme of supplementary benefits to replace the system of allowances which had previously been administered by the National Assistance Board. The benefits were paid as of right to those people whose incomes were below the levels set in the Act and not according to national insurance contribution records.

Chronically Sick and Disabled Persons Act, 1970. This placed more stringent obligations on local authorities to seek out and provide for the chronically sick and disabled.

National Insurance (Old Persons' and Widows' Pensions and Attendance Allowance) Act, 1970. Gave pensions to those of pensionable age in 1948. Reduced from 50 to 40 the qualifying age for widows' pensions.

Family Income Supplements Act, 1970. Created new benefit for families with small incomes.

Social Security Pensions Act, 1975. This provided for social security pensions and other related benefits to consist of a basic element and an additional component related to higher earnings and made various other provisions in relation to pensions. Made full National Insurance contributions obligatory for women except widows and women already on reduced rates.[1]

Child Benefits Act, 1975. Replaced family allowances with child benefit, and provided for an interim benefit for unmarried or separated parents with children.

Social Security Act, 1980. This ended discretion in supplementary benefits by introducing a detailed rule-based scheme. It also removed the obligation to uprate pensions in line with earnings.

Social Security (no 2) Act, 1980. Phased out earnings-related supplements to unemployment and sickness benefits, and brought short-term benefits into tax.

Health Services Act, 1980. Made provision for increased access to Health Service facilities by private patients and made other alterations to the law regarding private health care.

Social Security and Housing Benefits Act, 1982. Made provision for the payment of statutory sick pay by the employers and amended rent and rate rebate procedure.

Social Security Act, 1986. This transformed supplementary benefit into income support, and family income supplement into family credit. It also restructured housing benefits, widows' benefits and the State Earnings Related Pension Scheme.

Social Security Act, 1988. This removed entitlement to Income Support from unemployed 16- and 17-year olds who refused to join a Youth Training Scheme. It also put the cold weather payment scheme on a statutory footing.

Social Security Act, 1989. This removed entitlement to benefit from claimants who were unable to satisfy officials that they were genuinely seeking work, and from those who had been unemployed for three months and had turned down work on the grounds that the pay was too low.

Social Security Act, 1990. This provided greater protection and right for members of occupational pension schemes. It also restructured disability benefits, increasing the scope of attendance allowance and severe disability allowance, but restricting payments under the industrial injuries scheme and earnings-related additions to invalidity benefits.

Child Support Act, 1991. This established the Child Support Agency to ensure that absent parents paid, where possible, for the upkeep of their children.

Statutory Sick Pay Act, 1991. This reduced the proportion of statutory sick pay recoverable by employers from the government.

On 1 Dec 1993 the Social Security Secretary announced reforms of social security including a new job seekers' allowance which would replace unemployment benefit and income support from 1996. Pension ages would be equalised at 65, to be phased in between 2010 and 2020.

Statutory Sick Pay Act, 1994. This abolished the reimbursement of statutory sick pay by the government to all but the smallest employers.

[1] For further provisions see Women's Rights legislation below.

Old Age Pensions

Maximum rate for a single person

Jan 1909	5/-	Nov 1981	£29.60
Feb 1920	10/-	Nov 1982	£32.85
Oct 1946	26/-	Nov 1983	£34.05
Sep 1952	32/6	Nov 1984	£35.80
Jan 1958	50/-	Nov 1985	£38.30
Apr 1961	57/6	Jul 1986	£38.70
Mar 1963	67/6	Apr 1987	£39.50
Mar 1965	81/-	Apr 1988	£41.15
Oct 1967	90/-	Apr 1989	£43.60
Nov 1969	100/-	Apr 1990	£46.90
Sep 1971	£6.00	Apr 1991	£52.00
Oct 1972	£6.75	Apr 1992	£54.15
Oct 1973	£7.35	Apr 1993	£56.10
Jul 1974	£10.00	Apr 1994	£55.15
Apr 1975	£11.60	Apr 1995	£56.35
Nov 1975	£13.30	Apr 1996	£58.50
Nov 1976	£15.30	Apr 1997	£60.70
Nov 1977	£17.50	Apr 1998	£64.70
Nov 1978	£19.50	Apr 1999	£66.75
Nov 1979	£23.30	Apr 2000	£67.50
Nov 1980	£27.15		

In 1972 a £10 Christmas bonus for pensioners was instituted.

Sources: Sir E. Wilson and G.S. Mackay, *Old Age Pensions* (1941); *Keesing's Contemporary Archives 1931–88*, and *Keesing's UK Record 1988–; Report on Social Insurance and Allied Services* (Beveridge), Cmd. 6404/1944, Appendix B, *National Superannuation and Social Insurance*, Cmnd. 3883/1969, and the Department of Social Security.

Women's Rights

Representation of the People Act, 1918. Gave women over 30 the right to vote.

Sex Disqualification (Removal) Act 1919. Abolished disqualification by sex or marriage for entry to the professions and universities, and the exercise of any public function.

Matrimonial Causes Act, 1923. Relieved a wife petitioner of necessity of proving cruelty, desertion etc. in addition to adultery as grounds for divorce. (Further Acts in 1927 and 1950 extended grounds for divorce and codified the matrimonial law.)

Guardianship of Infants Act, 1924. Vested guardianship of infant children in the parents jointly. If parents disagreed either could apply to court, the Court's subsequent decision being guided solely by consideration of the infant's interest.

New English Law of Property, 1926. Provided that both married and single women may hold and dispose of their property, real and personal, on the same terms as a man.

Representation of the People Act, 1928. Gave women over 21 the right to vote.

Law Reform (Married Women and Tortfeasors) Act, 1935. Empowered a married woman to dispose by will of all her property as if she were single.

British Nationality of Women Act, 1948. Gave British women the right to retain British nationality on marriage to a foreigner, and ended the right of alien women to acquire automatic British nationality when marrying.

Equal Pay Act, 1970. (See p.379.)

Matrimonial Proceedings and Property Act, 1970. Empowered courts to order either spouse to make financial provision for the other spouse or a child of the family. Laid down that if either spouse had contributed money or money's worth to property during marriage, then a share in that property had been acquired.

Finance Act, 1971. Allowed husband's and wife's earnings to be taxed separately if they so applied.

Domicile and Matrimonial Proceedings Act, 1973. Allowed women to stay in the family home.

Matrimonial Causes Act, 1973. Gave effect to recommendations of the Law Commission on Matrimonial Proceedings, validity of marriage, nationality and maintenance. Gave British women married to foreigners the same right as men for their spouses to live in Britain.

Employment Protection Act, 1975. Made dismissal because of pregnancy unlawful, and made it obligatory for employers to offer a new contract when the pregnancy was over. Also made provisions for paid maternity leave.

Sex Discrimination Act, 1975. The *Equal Pay Act* of 1970 amended and included in this Act. Together they outlawed discrimination on grounds of sex in all aspects of employment, education, provision of professional services, recreational facilities, banking, insurance and credit. Established Equal Opportunities Commission (see below).

Social Security Act, 1975. Set up a special maternity allowance fund, incorporated into *Employment Protection Act, 1975,* and included income supplements for divorced women.

Social Security Pensions Act, 1975. Stipulated that pension schemes must be open on an equal basis to women doing the same or broadly similar work as men. Abolished the 'half-test' by which women had to have twenty consecutive years in employment to qualify for a full state pension.

Equal Pay (Amendment) Act, 1984. Updated legislation in line with European law on equal pay for different work of equal value.

Sex Discrimination Act, 1986. This extended the provisions of the 1975 *Sex Discrimination Act* in line with European directives, and also removed some restrictions on women's hours of work.

Finance Act, 1988. Further amended tax law to remove disadvantage for married women by introducing independent taxation for all.

Employment Act, 1989. This removed further restrictions on women's conditions of employment, including the statutory bar on working in mines.

Trade Union Reform and Employment Rights Act, 1993. Introduced much stronger employment protection for pregnant women in line with European directives.

Family Law Act, 1996. This made provision for 'no fault' divorce. The provisions on divorce were never implemented.

Homosexual Rights

Sexual Offences Act, 1967. This decriminalised sexual acts in private places between consenting males over the age of 21. The law was not brought into line in Scotland until 1981, and in Northern Ireland until 1982.

Local Government Act, 1988. Section 28 of this Act prohibited 'the teaching in any maintained school of the acceptability of homosexuality as a pretended family relationship' and banned local authorities from the intentional 'promotion of homosexuality'.

Criminal Justice and Public Order Act, 1994. This reduced the age of consent for homosexual sex to 18. An amendment to equalise the age of consent at 16 for both homosexual and heterosexual sex was defeated.

Equal Opportunities Commission, 1975–

	Chairman
Dec 75	Betty Lockwood (Lady)
May 83	Lady Platt
May 88	Joanna Foster
Jun 93	Kamlesh Bahl
Feb 99	Julie Mellor

Maternity and Child Welfare

Midwives Act, 1902. This Act sought to improve the standards of midwifery. It only became fully operative in 1910. Further Acts were passed in 1936 and 1951.

Notification of Births Act, 1908. This gave powers to local authorities to insist on compulsory notification of births.

Notification of Births Extension Act, 1915. This made notification universally compulsory.

Children Act, 1908. This Act consolidated the existing law and recognised the need for legal protection of children. It provided legislation covering negligence to children. Imprisonment of children was abolished, and remand homes were set up for children awaiting trial. This was to be only in special juvenile courts.

Education (Choice of Employment) Act, 1910. This empowered authorities to set up their own juvenile employment bureaux.

Maternity and Child Welfare Act, 1918. This empowered authorities to set up 'home help' schemes and clinics.

Children and Young Persons Act, 1933. This extended responsibility for children until the age of 17 and included a careful definition of the meaning of the need for care and protection. It established approved schools, and made detailed regulations about juvenile court procedure.

Children Act, 1948. This gave local authorities new responsibilities, with children's officers to administer the children's service (see Local Government section).

Children and Young Persons Act, 1963. This extended the power of local authorities to promote the welfare of children and dealt with children and young persons in need of supervision, ordered approved schools, employment of children and young persons (amended by *Children and Young Persons Act, 1969*).

Abortion Act, 1967. Made it legal for a registered medical practitioner to perform an abortion provided two registered practitioners are of the opinion termination is justifiable, either because continuance of the pregnancy would involve more risk to the life of the pregnant woman or injury to her physical or mental health or any existing children, than if the pregnancy were terminated, or because there would be a substantial risk that if the child were born it would be seriously physically or mentally handicapped.

Family Law Reform Act, 1969. This reduced the age of majority from 21 to 18. It also secured rights for illegitimate children.

Guardianship of Minors Act, 1971. Made some provision for equal rights for mothers and gave either spouse the right to appoint any person as guardian after his or her death.

Children Act, 1975. Gave new rights to children, foster-parents, local authorities and adoptive parents, and diminished rights of natural parents in care proceedings and adoption cases. Allowed adopted children over 18 access to information about their natural parents.

Children's Homes Act, 1982. Required children in the care of local authorities to be accommodated in registered and inspected homes.

Abortion (Amendment) Act, 1988. This reduced the time limit within which abortions had to be performed from 28 to 24 weeks.

Children Act, 1989. This put greater emphasis on the rights and wishes of children in cases of marriage break-up. It also made numerous changes to the law relating to adoption and children's homes.

Child Support Act, 1991. Established a Child Support Agency to ensure that divorced and separated parents made financial contributions to the cost of raising the family, according to a formula laid down by Parliament rather than the courts.

Rates of Child Benefit

	First Child	Each other child		First Child	Each other child
Apr 77	£1.00	£1.50	Apr 91	£8.25	£7.25
Apr 78	£2.30	£2.30	Oct 91	£9.25	£7.50
Nov 78	£3.00	£3.00	Apr 92	£9.65	£7.80
Apr 79	£4.00	£4.00	Apr 93	£10.00	£8.10
Nov 80	£4.75	£4.75	Apr 94	£10.20	£8.25
Nov 81	£5.25	£5.25	Apr 95	£10.40	£8.45
Nov 82	£5.85	£5.85	Apr 96	£10.80	£8.80
Nov 83	£6.50	£6.50	Apr 97	£11.05	£9.00
Nov 84	£6.85	£6.85	Apr 98	£11.45	£9.30
Nov 85	£7.00	£7.00	Apr 99	£14.60	£9.60
Jul 86	£7.10	£7.10	Apr 2000	£15.00	£10.00
Apr 87	£7.25	£7.25			

Education

Education Act, 1902. This abolished school boards, gave powers to local authorities to provide secondary education, and made provisions for rate aid to voluntary schools (see Local Government section).

Education (Provision of Meals) Act, 1906. By this Act cheap school meals for children attending public elementary schools were given statutory recognition. Local authorities were to use voluntary organisations, contributing only to the cost of administration. In 1914 half the cost of the meals was provided by the Exchequer.

Education (Administrative Provisions) Act, 1907. This provided for medical inspection for elementary schools. In 1912 the Board of Education made grants to Local Education Authorities to make the treatment of children possible.

Education Act, 1918. Compulsory attendance was made universal until the age of 14. Day continuation (part-time compulsory) education was introduced for children between school-leaving age and 18. This almost disappeared under the economies proposed by Geddes but was revived in 1944.

Free milk was supplied to children in need in 1921. In 1934 it was subsidised by the Milk Marketing Board. From 1946 to 1971 it was free to all.

Education Act, 1936. Provision was made for the school-leaving age to be raised to 15 in Sep 1939 but this was not implemented. 1940–41, the school meal service was expanded and subsidised to meet war-time needs.

These provisions were continued after the war, by the *Education Act, 1944.*

Education Act, 1944. This Act changed the title of the President of the Board of Education to the Minister of Education. Primary and secondary education were divided at '11–plus', and secondary education was generally provided under this Act in three types of schools: grammar, technical, and modern. Some local authorities preferred to use their powers to amalgamate these into comprehensive schools. Provision was made for compulsory part-time education between the school-leaving age and 18 in county colleges, but this has not been implemented. The minimum school-leaving age was raised to 15 (in 1947) and provision was made for raising it to 16. Powers were granted under this Act, which led to a great expansion of technical colleges. No fees were to be charged in schools which were publicly provided or aided by grants from the local authority.

School-leaving Age. It was announced in 1964 that the school-leaving age would be raised to 16 in the educational year 1970–71. In 1968 this date was put back for four years. The change was eventually made in 1973.

Comprehensive Schools. In 1965 the Department of Education asked all local authorities to submit plans for reorganising secondary education on comprehensive lines, with a view to ending selection at 11-plus and the tripartite system. The policy of universal comprehensivisation was suspended in 1970 but revived in 1974 by Government Circular 4/74. In 1976 the Direct Grant system was phased out (119 of the 170 Direct Grant schools decided to become independent) and the *Education Act, 1976*, required Local Education Authorities to submit comprehensivisation proposals (7 had earlier refused. See the Tameside case, p.334).

Nursery Schools. In 1972 the Department of Education (Cmnd. 5174) accepted that within ten years it should provide nursery education for 90 per cent of 4-year-olds and 50 per cent of 3-year-olds.

Education Act, 1980. The Assisted Places Scheme was established to provide financial support for some students in independent education, and various other changes were made to increase parental choice and participation in the schooling of their children.

Education Reform Act, 1988. This introduced a National Curriculum to be followed by all pupils from the ages of 5 to 16. The governing bodies of all secondary schools and larger primary schools were given responsibility for their own budgets. All secondary schools as well as larger primary schools were given the right to apply for grant-maintained status – 'opting out' of local education authority control, subject to a ballot by parents. Funding of higher education was transferred from local authorities to a Polytechnics and Colleges Funding Council. The University Grants Committee was replaced by a Universities Funding Council. The Act also abolished the Inner London Education Authority, vesting most of its responsibilities with the inner London boroughs.

Education (Student Loans) Act, 1990. This introduced 'top-up' loans for students in higher education as a partial replacement for maintenance grants.

Education (Schools) Act, 1992. This compelled schools and local education authorities to cooperate with the publication of information about examination results, including 'league tables'.

Further and Higher Education Act, 1992. This transferred further education colleges and sixth form colleges out of local authority control; they were to be funded instead by a new Further Education Funding Council. The Act also set up Higher Education Funding Councils for England and Wales, replacing the Universities Funding Council and the Polytechnics and Colleges Funding Council. Polytechnics were given the right to assume the title of university.

Education Act, 1993. This established a Funding Agency for schools which had opted out of local authority control. A machinery was established for dealing with 'failing' schools. The National Curriculum Council and the Schools Examination and Assessment Council were abolished and replaced by the School Curriculum and Assessment Authority.

Education Act, 1994. This restricted the role and funding of student unions and regulated teacher training.

Teaching and Higher Education Act, 1998. This abolished entirely the system of maintenance grants for students, and replaced it with an expanded loan scheme to be repaid by graduates on an income-related basis. It also laid down that in future all but the poorest students would pay a contribution to their education fees.

Sources: *Education of the Adolescent* (Hadow) (1926); *The Primary School* (Hadow) (1931); *Secondary Education* (Spens) (1938); *The School Curriculum* (Norwood) (1943); *Education Reconstruction* (Cmd. 6458/1942–3); *Public Schools* (Fleming) (1944); *Education from 15 to 18* (Crowther) (1959); *Half our Future* (Newsom) (1963); *Higher Education* (Robbins) (Cmnd. 2154/1963); *Primary Education* (Plowden) (1967). Since 1947 the Department of Education has published an *Annual Report* and *A Guide to the Educational Structure of England and Wales*. See also J. Vaizey and J. Sheehan, *Resources for Education* (1968); A.H. Halsey, A.F. Heath and J.M. Ridge, *Origins and Destinations* (1980); M. Scott, *Net Investment in Education in the United Kingdom*, in the Oxford Review of Education 1 (6): 21–30 (1980); K. Fogelman (ed.), *Growing Up in Britain: Papers from the National Child Development Study* (1983); Chapters on Schools and Higher Education in A.H. Halsey, *Twentieth-Century British Social Trends* (2000).

Pupils in Schools

England and Wales (000s) (age 2–14)

	Public Elementary	Secondary Schools	Efficient Independent	Other Independent
1900	5,709	n.a.	n.a.	n.a.
1910	6,039	151	22	n.a.
1920	5,878	340	46	n.a.
1930	4,936	411	82	n.a.
	Primary & Secondary Maintained	Direct Grant		
1950	5,710	95	204	n.a.
1960	6,924	111	294	203
1970	7,960	143	304	110
	State Nursery and Primary	State Secondary	Special Schools	Independent Schools
1970	5,952	3,555	103	621
1980	5,260	4,546	148	619
1990	5,060	3,393	114	613
1997	5,493	3,743	116	615

Sources: G. Walford (ed.), *British Public Schools: Policy and Practice* (1984); *Annual Abstract of Statistics; Education Statistics.*

Percentage of Various Ages Receiving Full-Time Education

Great Britain 1870–1970; UK 1970–

Age	10	14	16	19
1870	4	2	1	1
1902	100	9	2	1
1938	100	38	4	2
1962	100	100	15	7
1970	100	100	20	13
1980	100	100	27	12[a]
1990	100	100	43	18[a]

[a]Figures for 1980 and 1990 cover 19 and 20 year olds and are not therefore strictly comparable.

Sources: *Report on Higher Education* (Robbins), Cmnd. 2154/1963; *Education Statistics.*

Students in Full-Time Higher Education

Great Britain

	University	Teacher Training	Further Education[a]
1900/1	20,000	5,000	–
1924/5	42,000	16,000	3,000
1938/9	50,000	13,000	6,000
1954/5	82,000	28,000	12,000
1962/3	118,000	55,000	43,000
1970/1	235,000	124,000	98,000
1980/1[b]	307,000	228,000	
1990/1[b]	370,000	378,000	
1996–7[bc]	1,195,000	860,000	

a Advanced Courses only.
b Includes N. Ireland.
c This reflects the granting of University status to Polytechnics and other institutions

Sources: *Report on Higher Education* (Robbins), Cmnd. 2154/1963; *Education Statistics.*

Expenditure on Education (U.K.)

(current prices)

	Net public current expenditure on educaton (£m)	Private expenditure on education (£m)	Current expenditure of universities (£m)	University expenditure from parliamentary Grants %
1919/20	65.1	8.4	4.4	22
1929/30	92.8	8.3	6.6	29
1939/40	107.5	10.0	8.2	30
1949/50	272.0	27.8	23.0	56
1954/5	410.6	30.9	33.9	65
1964/5	1,114.9	60.0	123.9	72
1970/1	1,644.3	n.a.	317.7	72
1980/1	12,940.8	n.a.	1381.5[a]	76
1990/1	26,677.8	n.a.	2476.0[a]	76

[a] Excluding Oxford and Cambridge college accounts.

Sources: 1919–1965 J. Vaizey and J. Sheehan, *Resources for Education* (1968); *Annual Abstract of Statistics* and *Education Statistics*.

Public Library Service

Year	Books in Stock (000s)	Book Issues (000s)	Total Expenditure (£000)
1906	4,450	26,255	286
1911	10,874	54,256	805
1924	14,784	85,668	1,398
1939	32,549	247,335	3,178
1953	56,056	359,700	11,183
1962	77,200	460,504	24,431
1971	114,472	628,000	73,436
1980/1	108,400	551,000	263,600
1989/90	129,533	476,916	528,028
1996/7	130,634	1,501,170	726,025

Source: A.H. Halsey (ed.), *Twentieth-Century British Social Trends* (2000). *Report by the Minister for the Arts on Library and Information Matters*, HC35. Annual CIPFA Reports. www.Lboro.ac.uk/departments/dis/lse

Pressure Groups

There are a large number of groups in the social field representing causes or offering voluntary services. These may seek to influence public policy by direct contact with Parliament and Government Departments or indirectly through the publication of information and research or appeals to public opinion. Some notable examples of pressure groups are listed below. They include some registered charities which have also sought to direct public funds and attention to the causes they represent (e.g. the National Council for One-Parent Families); some which were founded to bring about a change in the law (e.g. Committee for Homosexual Law Reform); some which were formed to safeguard and promote the interests of a minority racial group (e.g. the Indian Workers' Association) or of a profession or trade (e.g. the Road Haulage Association); and some whose main target has been industry rather than government (e.g. the Campaign for Real Ale). Most are financed by voluntary contributions but some receive grants from central or local

government and may, indeed, be directly involved in the implementation of public policy.
Think-tanks and political pressure groups are listed on p.184.

See *Whitaker's Almanack* for a full list of names and addresses.

Abortion and Birth Control

Workers' Birth Control Group, 1924. Together with four other bodies became National
    Birth Control Council, 1930. Changed name to National Birth Control Association
    in 1931. Changed name to Family Planning Association, 1939–
Abortion Law Reform Association, 1967–
Society for the Protection of Unborn Children, 1967–
Life, 1970–

Animal Welfare

Society for the Prevention of Cruelty to Animals, 1824. Changed name to Royal Society
    for the Prevention of Cruelty to Animals, 1840–
League Against Cruel Sports, 1924–
National Anti-vivisection Society, 1975–
Hunt Saboteurs
Royal Society for the Protection of Birds, 1889–

Constitutional Questions

Proportional Representation Society, 1885. Changed name to Electoral Reform Society,
    1958
Freedom Association, 1975–
Campaign for Press and Broadcasting Freedom, 1979–
Campaign for Freedom of Information, 1984–
Charter 88, 1988–.
Anti-Federalist League, 1991–
(See also p.231)

Consumers

Consumers' Association, 1946–
Campaign for Real Ale, 1971–
National Consumer Council, 1975–

Education

Advisory Centre for Education, 1960–
Confederation for the Advancement of State Education, 1961–

The Elderly

National Old People's Welfare Council, 1940. Changed name to Age Concern, 1971–
Help the Aged, 1961–
British Pensions and Trade Union Action Committee, 1972–

Environment

National Trust, 1895–
Council for the Protection of Rural England, 1926–
Ramblers' Association (1935)
Civic Trust, 1957–
Council for Environmental Conservation (COENCO), 1969–
Friends of the Earth, 1970–
Greenpeace, 1971–
Campaign for Lead-free Air (CLEAR), 1982–
Transport 2000
Worldwide Fund for Nature (formerly World Wildlife Fund), 1961–
Countryside Alliance, 1998–

Family Welfare

Charity Organisation Society (1869) Family Welfare Association
National Council for the Unmarried Mother and her Child, 1918. Changed name to
      National Council for One Parent Families, 1973–
National Society for the Prevention of Cruelty to Children, 1884–
National Marriage Guidance Council, (RELATE 1988) 1938–88
Gingerbread, 1970–

Health

Alcoholics Anonymous, 1947–
British and Foreign Society for Improving the Embossed Literature for the Blind, 1868.
      Changed name to British and Foreign Blind Association, 1870. Changed name to
      National Institute for the Blind, 1914. Changed name to Royal National Institute for
      the Blind, 1953–
National Bureau for Promoting the General Welfare of the Deaf, 1911. Changed name to
      the National Institute for the Deaf, 1924. Changed name to the Royal National
      Institute for the Deaf, 1961–
The Voluntary Euthanasia Society, 1935–79, 1982– (Exit, 1979–82)
National Association for Mental Health, 1946. Changed name to Mind, 1973–
National Association of Parents of Backward Children, 1946. Changed name to The
      National Society for Mentally Handicapped Children, 1955. Became National
      Society for Mentally Handicapped Children and Adults, with the short title
      MENCAP, in 1980. Became the Royal Society for Mentally Handicapped Children
      and Adults (MENCAP), 1981–.
Samaritans, 1953–
SCOPE (formerly Spastics Society 1957–)
Patients' Association, 1961–
Disablement Income Group, 1966–
Action on Smoking and Health (ASH), 1971–
Terence Higgins Trust, 1983–

Homosexuals

Committee for Homosexual Law Reform, 1967. Changed name to Campaign for
      Homosexual Equality, 1970–

Stonewall, 1989–
OutRage, 1990–

Housing

Shelter, 1966–
Crisis at Christmas, 1967. Changed name to Crisis, 1989–
Campaign for the Homeless and Rootless (CHAR), 1972–

Legal System

Howard League for Penal Reform, 1886–
Central Discharged Prisoners' Aid Society, 1924. Changed name to National Association
  of Aid to Discharged Prisoners' Societies, 1960. Changed name to National
  Association for the Care and Resettlement of Offenders, (NACRO), 1966–
National Council for Civil Liberties, 1934–. Adopted short title Liberty, 1988.
National Campaign for the Abolition of Capital Punishment, 1955–69
Justice, 1957–
National Association of Victim Support Schemes, 1979–
Amnesty International, 1961–

Morality

Lord's Day Observance Society, 1831–
The National Viewers' and Listeners' Council (Mary Whitehouse), 1964–
British Humanist Association, 1928– (formerly Ethical Association)
Keep Sunday Special, 1985–

Overseas Aid

War on Want, 1954–
Save the Children Fund, 1919–
Oxfam, 1942–
Christian Aid, 1945–

Poverty

Child Poverty Action Group, 1965–
Low Pay Unit, 1974–

Race

Indian Workers' Association, 1956–
West Indian Standing Conference, 1958–
Anti-Apartheid Movement, 1959–
Runnymede Trust, 1968–
Standing Conference of Pakistani Organisations, 1975–
Anti-Nazi League, 1992–
Anti-Racist Alliance, 1991–

Temperance

United Kingdom Alliance, 1853–

Transport

Royal Automobile Club, 1897–
The Automobile Association, 1905–
National Association of Railway Users, 1971–

Women's Rights

London Society for Women's Suffrage, 1866–1918 (now Fawcett Society)
Women's Freedom League, 1908–1961
National Federation of Women's Institutes, 1917–
Women's Social and Political Union, 1903–1918
Women's Liberation Workshop, 1969–
National Women's Aid Federation, 1975–
Women in Media, 1971–

Sources: A. Butt Philip (ed.), *Directory of Pressure Groups in the European Community* (1991). *Directory of British Associations.*

Transport and Communications

Transport by mode – as percentage of miles travelled

	Bus & Coach	Cars	Motorcycle	Cycle	All Road	Rail	Air
1952	42	27	3	11	82	18	0.1
1960	28	49	4	4	86	14	0.3
1970	15	74	1	1	91	9	0.5
1980	11	79	2	1	92	7	0.6
1990	7	85	1	1	94	6	0.7
1997	6	86	1	1	93	6	0.9

Source: *Transport Statistics.*

CURRENT VEHICLE LICENCES IN GREAT BRITAIN[a]

Year	Cars[b]	Public Transport[c]	Goods Vehicles[d]	Total
1905[f]	15,895	7,491	9,000	32,386
1910[f]	89,411	24,466	30,000	143,877
1915[f]	277,741	44,480	84,600	406,821[e]
1920[f]	474,540	74,608	101,000	650,148[e]
1925	1,151,453	113,267	259,341	1,524,061
1930	1,760,533	114,762	391,997	2,287,326
1935	1,973,945	96,419	490,663	2,581,027
1938	1,406,769	96,718	590,397	3,093,884
1940	1,701,500	88,200	542,200	2,331,900
1945	1,795,700	110,800	740,500	2,647,000
1946	2,232,279	110,704	769,747	3,112,930
1950	3,009,611	141,091	1,263,131	4,413,833
1955	4,781,741	104,664	1,581,814	6,468,219
1960	7,387,075	93,942	1,958,856	9,439,873
1965	10,623,900	96,500	2,219,500	12,939,900
1970	12,687,000	103,000	2,161,000	14,950,000
1975	15,051,000	112,000	2,337,000	17,500,000
1980	16,545,000	110,000	2,555,000	19,210,000
1985	19,406,000	120,000	1,632,000	21,157,000
1990	22,822,000	115,000	1,736,000	24,673,000
1995	23,366,000	82,000	1,936,000	25,369,000

[a] 1905–1920 – Figures at 31 Mar 1925; and 1945 at 31 Aug; 1930–38 and from 1946 during quarter ending 30 Sep.

[b] Cars, motor cycles, tricycles and pedestrian-controlled vehicles. In the figures for 1985 and 1990 Light Goods Vehicles are classified as cars.

[c] Buses, coaches, trams and taxis.

[d] Goods vehicles, haulage including agricultural vehicles, tax exempt vehicles including electric cars and government vehicles. In the figures for 1985 onwards Light Goods Vehicles are classified as cars.

[e] These figures do not include trams. In 1920 there were 14,000 trams.

[f] Figures before 1921 are estimates only, from The Motor Industry of Great Britain, 1935. They may be exaggerated.

Sources: *Census of Mechanically Propelled Vehicles* (Ministry of Transport), 1926–62 *Highway Statistics* (Ministry of Transport), 1963 onwards, *The Motor Industry of Great Britain* (Soc. of Motor Manufacturers and Traders). *Reports of the Steering Group appointed by the Ministry of Transport, Traffic in Towns* (Buchanan Report, H.M.S.O.); D. Munby and A. Watson, *Inland Transport Statistics, Great Britain 1900–1970,* vol II. *Transport Statistics.*

RAILWAYS

Great Britain

	Standard Gauge Route Miles	Train Miles (millions)	Passenger Journeys (millions)	Freight	
				Tons (millions)	Ton miles (millions)
1900	18,680	379.3	962	461.1	n.a.
1910	19,986	386.7	936	504.7	n.a
1920	20,147	355.7	2064[a]	332.2	19.2
1930	20,243	397.7	1250	304.3	17.8
1938	19,934	420.9	1237	265.7	16.7
1950	19,471	384.1	1010	281.3	22.1
1960	18,369	375.4	1037	248.5	18.6
1970	11,799	195.9	824	199.0	15.0
1980	10,964	246.4	760	145.7[bc]	10.8
1990	10,307	225.3	812	143.1[c]	10.4
1998	10,343	n.a.	846	105.4[c]	10.5

Excluding operations of London Electric Railway, London Passenger Transport Board, and London Transport throughout. Standard Gauge railways only (except 1900 and 1910).

[a] Figure for 1919 excluding free hauled traffic.

[b] Figure for 1982/3.

[c] Figures in metric tonnes.

Sources: 1930–38 *Railway Returns*; 1950– *British Railways Annual Reports*.

SHIPPING

Tonnage registered
(United Kingdom)

	Gross tons (000s)	% of world tonnage
1900	11,514	51.5
1910	16,768	45.0
1920	18,111	33.6
1930	20,322	29.9
1939	17,891	26.1
1950	18,219	21.5
1960	21,131	16.3
1970	25,825	11.0
1980	27,135	6.4
1990	5,512	1.7
1997	7,108	2.0

Steam and motor ships of 100 gross tons and over.

Source: *Lloyd's Register of Shipping* (Statistical Tables), published annually.

VOLUME OF AIR TRAFFIC

Terminal Passengers at U.K. Civil Aerodromes

1950	2,133,000
1960	10,075,000
1970	31,606,000
1980	57,822,000
1990	89,900,000
1996	130,800,000

Source: *Transport Statistics*.

VOLUME OF POSTAL TRAFFIC

Letters, postcards, parcels, registered letters (excluding football pools). Number of inland deliveries.

	millions
1903–04	4,300
1911–12	5,508
1922–23	5,638
1929–30	6,622
1935–36	6,569
1939–40	7,624
1946–47	6,601
1951–52	7,964
1956–57	8,753
1959–60	9,244
1965–66	10,461
1975–76	8,890
1983–84	10,793
1992–93	15,745[a]
1996–97	18,101[a]

[a] Excluding parcels now carried by Parcelforce, a separate company.

COST OF LETTER MAIL

(inland)

	First Class	Second Class
May 1840	1d	–
Jun 1918	$1^{1}/_{2}$d	–
Jun 1920	2d	–
May 1922	$1^{1}/_{2}$d	–
May 1940	$2^{1}/_{2}$d	–
Oct 1957	3d	–
May 1965	4d	–
Sep 1968	5d[a]	4d
Feb 1971	3p	2.5p
Sep 1973	3.5p	3p
Jun 1974	4.5p	3.5p
Mar 1975	7p	5.5p
Sep 1975	8.5p	6.5p
Jun 1977	9p	7p
Aug 1979	10p	8p
Feb 1980	12p	10p
Jan 1981	14p	11.5p
Feb 1982	15.5p	12.5p
Apr 1983	16p	12.5p
Sep 1984	17p	13p
Nov 1985	17p	12p
Oct 1986	18p	13p
Sep 1988	19p	14p
Oct 1989	20p	15p
Sep 1990	22p	17p
Sep 1991	24p	18p
Nov 1993	25p	19p
Jul 1996	26p	20p
Apr 1999	26p	19p
Apr 2000	27p	19p

[a] Two-tier postal pricing introduced.

TELEPHONES

United Kingdom

	Total number of telephones[a]	Total number of connections
1900	3,000	
1910	122,000	
1920	980,000	
1930	1,996,000	1,196,000
1940	3,339,000	2,061,000
1950	5,171,000	3,140,000
1960	7,864,000	4,784,000
1970	13,844,000	8,551,000
1980	27,870,000	17,592,000
1990	n.a.[b]	25,013,000
1999	n.a.[b]	32,626,000

[a] Including Southern Ireland, 1900–20
[b]Following deregulation, these figures ceased to be kept.

Sources: General Post Office, *Post Office Commercial Accounts*, published annually; *Annual Abstract of Statistics*; *British Telecom Annual Reports*.

MOBILE PHONES AND FAXES 1986-

Two mobile phone companies, Cellnet and Vodaphone, were given licences to establish national cellular phone networks from 1 Jan 85. Facsimile machines using standard phone lines started to be used at the same period.

Number in use at end of year

	Fax Machines (000s)	Mobile Phones (000s)
1986	86	120
1987	173	260
1988	370	500
1989	556	870
1990	750	1,157
1991	920	1,253
1992	1,065	1,396
1993	1,195	1,950
1994	1,425	3,940
1995	1,757	5,736[a]
1996	1,992	8,109[a]
1997	[b]	9,023[a]
1998	[b]	10,375[c]

[a] Figures for Mar 31 the following year.
[b] Figures not calculated after 1996
[c] Figure for Sep 30 1998.

Sources: Market Information Update; Oftel Annual Reports; British Facsimile Industry Consultative Committee. General Post Office, *Post Office Commercial Accounts*, published annually; *Annual Abstract of Statistics; British Telecom Annual Reports*.

X

EMPLOYMENT AND TRADE UNIONS

Major Employment and Trade Union Legislation

Factory and Workshop Act, 1901. This consolidated, with amendments, all previous Factory and Workshop Acts.

Unemployed Workmen Act, 1905. This established 'Distress Committees' to investigate needs and to provide employment or assistance. Funds were to be partly voluntary, and partly from the local rates.

The Trade Disputes Act, 1906, reversed the *Taff Vale* decision (see p.380) and freed trade unions from liability caused by the calling of a strike.

Labour Exchanges Act, 1909. These were established in 1909 and renamed Employment Exchanges in 1919.

National Insurance Act, 1911. This Act covered all those between the ages of 16 and 70 years, but was limited to manual workers in industries known to be subject to severe and recurrent unemployment. (The Act covered about 2.25 million people.) Within these limits it was compulsory, and financed by a triple weekly levy, from the worker, the employer, and the government. Payment of benefit continued only for a limited period, after which responsibility for the unemployed person lapsed to the Poor Law. In 1916 the Act was extended to include munitions workers.

The Trade Union Act, 1913. This reversed the Osborne judgment and laid down the conditions under which political objects could be included in the rules of a Union by its members' consent.

Industrial Courts Act, 1919. This provided for the establishment of an Industrial Court and Courts of Inquiry in connection with trade disputes, and made other provisions for the settlement of such disputes.

Unemployment Insurance Act, 1920. The scheme was extended to cover the same field as the National Health Insurance scheme, and included non-manual workers with an income of under £250 p.a. Workers in agriculture or domestic service were excluded from the insurance scheme until 1936–37. It was administered through the local employment exchanges of the Ministry of Labour. The basic unemployment benefit was 7s. in 1911, increased to 15s. in 1920. It was increased in 1921, and in 1924 was 18s. It was reduced in 1928 and 1931. Additional allowances for dependants were introduced in 1921.

Unemployment Insurance Act, 1927. By this Act the original scheme was completely revised in accordance with the recommendations of the Blanesburgh Committee Report. The new scheme was to provide unlimited benefits after the insured person had satisfied certain qualifying contribution conditions.

Trades Disputes and Trade Unions Act, 1927. This made a sympathetic strike or a lockout designed to coerce the government illegal; it also severed the connection between civil service organisations and other unions; and it imposed new restrictions on the unions' political activities and their conduct of trade disputes. The political levy could only be raised from workers who 'contracted in'.

Local Government Act, 1929. This Act abolished the Poor Law Guardians, and their responsibilities passed to county councils and county borough councils, who were so far as possible to administer the specialised branches through separate committees.

Poor Law Act, 1930. By this Act Poor Law was renamed Public Assistance. The existing law was consolidated.

Unemployment Insurance Act, 1930. This made qualification easier for transitional benefit, and abolished the requirement that the unemployed receiving benefits should be 'genuinely seeking work'. Transitional benefits were made to claimants in need of assistance, but unable to fulfil the usual qualifying conditions. Responsibility for the long-term unemployed was placed directly on the Exchequer in 1931, though receipt of benefit was made subject to a 'means test'. Dependants' benefits were increased.

Unemployment Act, 1934. An amended scheme was introduced distinguishing between 'unemployed benefit' paid from the Fund (at the basic rate of 17s. a week) for a limited period to those satisfying contribution conditions, and 'unemployment assistance' which was paid, subject to a 'means test', to those still needing assistance after exhausting their title to benefit, or those who were not entitled. These long-term unemployed were paid directly by the Exchequer through the newly created Unemployment Assistance Board (known as Assistance Board from 1940 and from 1948 until 1966 as National Assistance Board). In 1937 juveniles between the ages of 14 and 16 were brought into the scheme for medical benefits only.

Unemployment Insurance (Agriculture) Act, 1936. A separate insurance scheme was set up for agricultural workers, granting lower rates of benefit than the general scheme. In 1937, the benefits of voluntary insurance for widows, orphans, etc. (see *Contributory Pensions Act, 1925*), were extended to those with small incomes, without the qualifications of insurable employment essential to insurance under the main scheme. For the first time married women could become voluntary contributors for pensions.

Control of Employment Act, 1939. This gave the government wide powers for the organisation of labour in war-time. Its aim was to make the best use of labour and to direct it to the most vital work.

Determination of Needs Act, 1941. This abolished the household 'means test'.

National Insurance (Industrial Injuries) Act, 1946. This covered all those in insurable employment against injuries and industrial diseases arising from their employment. It was financed by contributions from the insured person, his employer, and the government.

National Insurance Act, 1946. This Act covered all contributors between school-leaving age and pensionable age for benefits for unemployment, sickness, maternity, retirement, widows' pensions, guardians' allowances, and death grants. The self-employed and non-employed were entitled to fewer benefits. The basic weekly rate for unemployment benefit was raised to 26s. The national insurance scheme was amended by Acts in 1949, 1951, 1953, 1954, 1955, 1956, 1957, 1959, 1960, 1961, 1964, 1965, 1967, 1969, 1971, and 1973 (for rates, see p.385).

The Trade Unions Act, 1946. This repealed *The Trades Disputes and Trade Unions Act, 1927.*

National Assistance Act, 1948. This Act repealed all the Poor Law still in existence and it established a comprehensive scheme to be financed from government funds, to cover all the arrangements for assistance then in force. Provision was also made for those not qualified for benefits under national insurance schemes, or where the benefits were insufficient.

Local Employment Act, 1960. This made provision for promoting employment in areas of persistent or threatened unemployment.

Payment of Wages Act, 1960. This removed certain restrictions on methods of payment of wages and permitted them to be paid otherwise than in cash by payment into a banking account in the name of the employee, by Postal Order, by Money Order or by Cheque.

The Contracts of Employment Act, 1963, laid down the notice required to be given by an employer to terminate the contract of a person who had been continuously employed for 26 weeks or more (reduced to 13 weeks in 1974), the length of notice to be given varying according to the length of continuous employment.

Offices, Shops and Railway Premises Act, 1963, contained sweeping provisions relating to the health, safety, and welfare of employees, fire precautions, accidents and other matters in connection with office, shop and railway premises.

Industrial Training Act, 1964, gave power to establish an industrial training board for the training of persons over compulsory school age for employment in any activities of industry or commerce.

Trade Disputes Act, 1965, reversed the *Rookes v. Barnard* case (see p.381) and disallowed actions for tort or reparation being brought in respect of some kinds of activities in the conduct of industrial disputes (see p.381).

Redundancy Payments Act, 1965, obliged employers in certain industries to make payment to redundant workers and set up a Redundancy Fund to which employers had to contribute.

Equal Pay Act, 1970, made provision for the application to all workers of the principle of equal remuneration for men and women for work of equal value and required that terms and conditions of employment applicable to one sex should not be in any respect less favourable than those applicable to the other.

Industrial Relations Act, 1971, established new legal rights for the individual worker, mainly in relation to trade union activity but also in protection from unfair dismissal, information about the terms of employment, and long duration of notice. Most of these rights were preserved and expanded in the *Trade Unions and Labour Relations Acts of 1974* and *1975*. It also introduced fundamental and wide ranging changes in the legal framework of industrial relations. It repealed the *Trade Union Acts, 1871* and *1876*, and the *Trade Disputes Acts, 1906* and *1965*. Its provisions established new legal rights for the individual mainly in relation to trade union membership and activity, protection from unfair dismissal, information about his employment, and improved terms of notice. The Act introduced a new concept of 'unfair industrial practice'. It established a National Industrial Relations Court which, together with the industrial tribunals, was required to maintain these standards and rights by hearing complaints of unfair industrial practice and determining rights and liabilities. The Act also provided for a new system of registration and restricted legal immunities to registered trade unions; new methods of settling disputes over trade union recognition to be administered by a Commission on Industrial Relations; and new powers to be exercised by the Secretary of State for Employment to deal with emergency situations (i.e. the 'cooling off period' and ballots of membership).

Employment and Training Act, 1973, extended provisions for public authorities to provide work or training for unemployed persons.

Health and Safety at Work Act, 1974, provided a comprehensive system of law to deal with health and safety at work and established a Health and Safety Commission and Executive.

Trade Unions and Labour Relations Act, 1974, repealed the *Industrial Relations Act, 1971*, except for the provisions on unfair dismissal. The Act abolished the National Industrial Relations Court and the Commission on Industrial Relations.

Employment Protection Act, 1975, amended the law relating to workers and employers and provided redress against arbitrary dismissal. It extended the scope of redundancy payments and guaranteed suspension pay to those whose work was interrupted for external causes. It also provided for the establishment of the Advisory Conciliation and Arbitration Service (ACAS) as an independent statutory body and of a Central Arbitration Commission, together with a Certification Officer to take over the functions previously exercised by the Registrar of Friendly Societies in monitoring Trade Unions.

Trade Union and Labour Relations (Amendment) Act, 1975, amended the 1974 Act and provided for a charter on Freedom of the Press.

Sex Discrimination Act, 1975 (see p.362).

Race Relations Act, 1976 (see p.353).

Employment Act, 1980, provided for payment of public funds towards the costs of ballots among Trade Union members over strike action.

Employment Act, 1982, provided for compensation from public funds for employees dismissed as a result of closed shop agreements.

Trade Union Act, 1984, made legal immunity conditional on the conduct of strike ballots and made the continued existence of political funds dependent on ten-yearly votes by the membership.

Wages Act, 1986. This reduced the powers and scope of wages councils by limiting them to determining a single minimum rate, and removing young people from their jurisdiction. Unauthorized deductions from wages became a civil matter rather than a criminal offence.

Sex Discrimination Act, 1986. (See p.362)

Employment Act, 1988. This made dismissal for non-membership of a union unfair dismissal in all circumstances. It made it illegal for trade unions to discipline members for crossing picket lines or refusing to strike, even if the strike had been approved by a ballot. It gave members of trade unions the right to prevent union funds from being used for unlawful purposes.

Employment Act, 1989. This removed restrictions on the hours and other employment terms of 16- and 17-year olds. It abolished some restrictions on women's employment, such as the ban on working in mines. The Training Commission, which had replaced the Manpower Services Commission, was abolished.

Employment Act, 1990. This banned the pre-entry closed shop, and made it unlawful to refuse employment to someone for belonging or not belonging to a union. Trade unions lost their immunity from civil damages claims for all forms of secondary action.

Trade Union Reform and Employment Rights Act, 1993. This introduced restrictions on deduction of union subscriptions from wages, compelled unions to publish fuller accounts, tightened rules on strike ballots, abolished wages councils, and gave workers the right to join any union regardless of whether it was organised in their workplace.

National Minimum Wage Act, 1998. Established a National Minimum Wage with a regulatory and enforcement framework, and gave statutory authority for the Low Pay Commission.

Employment Relations Act, 1999. Established procedures for statutory trade union recognition, a right to unpaid parental leave and a shorter, one-year qualifying period for unfair dismissal.

Major Trade Union Litigation

Taff Vale Railway Co. v. Amalgamated Society of Railway Servants [1901] A.C. 426 (H.L.). A trade union, registered under the *Trade Union Acts, 1871* and *1876,* may be sued in its registered name. Lord Halsbury said, 'If the legislature has created a thing which can own property, which can employ servants, or which can inflict injury, it must be taken, I think, to have impliedly given the power to make it suable in a court of law, for injuries purposely done by its authority and procurement.'

Amalgamated Society of Railway Servants v. Osborne, [1910] A.C. 87 (H.L.).

There is nothing in the Trade Union Acts from which it can reasonably be inferred that trade unions as defined by Parliament were meant to have the power of collecting and administering funds for political purposes. Exercise of such powers is ultra vires and illegal.

Bonsor v. Musicians' Union, [1956] A.C. 104 (H.L.). A member of a registered trade union wrongfully expelled from it was entitled to maintain an action for damages for breach of contract against the union in its registered name.

Rookes v. Barnard, [1964] A.C. 1129 Threats to strike in breach of a contractual agreement for the purpose of injuring a third party were unlawful and were, even if done in furtherance of a trade dispute, not protected by the *Trade Disputes Act, 1906.*

Stratford v. Lindley, [1964] 3 All E.R. 102 Strike action not taken in pursuance of a trade dispute about terms of employment with the plaintiff's firm was not prima facie protected by the *Trade Disputes Act of 1906.*

1971–4 Between 1971 and 1974 there were a series of confrontations under the terms of the *Industrial Relations Act.* The T.U.C. in Sep 1971 instructed all unions not to register under the Act and in Sep 1972 the 32 which had registered were suspended and 20 of them were expelled in Sep 1973. In Apr 1972 the T.G.W.U. was fined £55,000 for contempt of the N.I.R.C. (though the fine was quashed by the Court of Appeal in Jun 1972). In Dec 1972 the A.U.E.W. refused to pay £50,000 in the *Goad* case (over the individual rights of a union member). In Oct 1973 £75,000 of seized A.U.E.W. assets were used to pay a further £47,000 N.I.R.C. contempt fine in the *Con-Mech* case. In May 1974 a further seizure of A.U.E.W. assets was ordered to pay £47,000 compensation to Con-Mech (the money was then paid by an anonymous donor). On 17 Apr 1972 the N.I.R.C. ordered a 14-day cooling off period in a national railway dispute and on 13 May 1972 ordered a ballot which produced an 85% vote in favour of a railway strike. On 21 Jul 1972 the N.I.R.C. committed five docker shop stewards to prison over the blacking of London container depots. They were released on 26 Jul. On 6 Aug 1974 the *Industrial Relations Act* was repealed.

Gouriet v. Post Office Union, [1977] 3 All E.R. (H.L.) An attempt to enjoin the Post Office Union from blacking mail to South Africa was frustrated because the Attorney-General refused his fiat to bring the case on the ground that the plaintiff was not directly involved (see p.334).

Grunwick Processing Laboratories Ltd. v. Advisory Conciliation and Arbitration Service, [1977] T.L.R. 14 Dec 77 The House of Lords ruled that an A.C.A.S. recommendation on union recognition was void because A.C.A.S. had not ascertained the opinions of two-thirds of the work-force involved (this was due to the non-cooperation of the firm's management).

B.B.C. v. Hearn, [1977] I.R.L.R. 273; Beaverbrook Newspapers v. Keys, [1978], I.R.L.R. 34; Star Sea Transport v. Slater, [1978] I.R.L.R. 507; McShane v. Express Newspapers, [1979] I.R.L.R. 79; United Biscuits v. Fall [1979] I.R.L.R. 110; Associated Newspaper Group v. Wade [1979] I.R.L.R. 201. The decisions in each of these cases reduced the area of legal immunity for actions taken in furtherance of an industrial dispute.

Thomas et al. v. Haringey [1979] The Court of Appeal held that it was arguable that a local authority might be in breach of its duty to provide education when it failed to do so by reason of industrial action by school caretakers.

Messenger Newspaper Group Ltd v. NGA [1982] Industrial Relations Law Reports 1984, 397. The Court of Appeal endorsed the powers of sequestrators seeking to secure control of union funds when the union had been fined for contempt for its actions in seeking to enforce a closed shop.

Mercury Communications Ltd v. Scott Garer (Industrial Cases Reports) 1984, 74). The Court of Appeal ruled that it was possible under the *Employment Act 1982* to secure an interlocutory injunction against union actions that were not 'wholly or mainly' related to an industrial dispute.

Dimbleby & Sons Ltd. v. National Union of Journalists (Industrial Cases Reports 1984, 386). The House of Lords endorsed the granting of an interlocutory injunction preventing a union from instructing its members to break contracts of employment in pursuits of a trade dispute that, under the *Employment Act 1980,* was excluded from protection.

Barretts and Baird (Wholesale) Ltd v. IPCS [1987] IRLR 3.   Not only are union members liable in damages to their employer for breach of their employment contract, but the same breach of contract may give rise to further liabilities based on its 'unlawful' character.

Boxfoldia Ltd v. NGA [1988] ICR 752.   Although members may authorize their union to decide on official industrial action, it does not follow that the union is authorised to act as their agent in terminating their employment contracts.

Associated British Ports v. TGWU [1989] IRLR 305, 318 CA.   The Court issued an injunction against industrial action on the grounds that the union had no immunity against tort liability for inducing workers to breach their statutory duty with intent to injure. The judgment was subsequently reversed by the House of Lords on other grounds.

Dimskal Shipping Sa v. ITWF [1991] 3WLR 875 HL.   Industrial action could be ruled unlawful secondary action even if it took place in another country (in this case Sweden) under whose law it was legal, according to the commercial law principle of 'economic duress'.

Associated Newspapers Ltd v Wilson and *Associated British Ports v Palmer and others [1995] IRLR 258.*   The House of Lords held that it was not unlawful to refuse to pay financial benefits to those who refused to forsake collective bargaining and sign individual contracts.

SOURCES. – Lord Wedderburn of Charlton, *The Worker and the Law* (3rd Ed., 1986). W.E.J. McCarthy (ed.), *Trade Unions* (2nd Ed., 1985). W.E.J. McCarthy, *Legal Intervention in Industrial Relations* (1992).

National Industrial Relations Court 1971–4

President

1971	Sir J. Donaldson

Commission on Industrial Relations 1971–4

Chairman

1969	G. Woodcock

(Made a Statutory Body, 1 Nov 71)

1971	(Sir) L. Neal

(Advisory) Conciliation and Arbitration Service (A.C.A.S.)[1] 1974–

Chairman

1974	J. Mortimer
1981	(Sir) P. Lowry
1987	(Sir) D. Smith
1993	J. Hougham

[1] The Conciliation and Arbitration Service was established within the Department of Employment in 1974. It was made an independent statutory body by the *Employment Protection Act, 1975.*

Low Pay Commission 1997–

Chairman

1997	G. Bain

Earnings and Hours Worked

United Kingdom

| Year | Average Weekly Earnings (£) | | | | Average Weekly Hours | | | |
| | Manual workers | | Non-manual workers | | Manual workers | | Non-manual workers | |
	Men aged 21 & over	Women aged 18 & over	Men aged 21 & over	Women aged 18 & over	Men aged 21 & over	Women aged 18 & over	Men aged 21 & over	Women aged 18 & over
1924	2.8	1.4			n.a.	n.a.		
1935	3.2	1.6			n.a.	n.a.		
1938	3.5	1.6			47.7	43.5		
1940	4.5	1.9			n.a.	n.a.		
1941	5.0	2.2			n.a.	n.a.		
1942	5.6	2.7			n.a.	n.a.		
1943	6.1	3.1			52.9	45.9		
1944	6.2	3.2			51.2	44.6		
1945	6.1	3.2			49.7	3.3		
1946	6.0	3.3			47.6	42.5		
1947	6.4	3.5			46.6	41.4		
1948	6.9	3.7			46.7	41.4		
1949	7.1	3.9			46.8	41.5		
1950	7.5	4.1			47.6	41.8		
1951	8.3	4.5			47.8	41.3		
1952	8.9	1.8			47.7	41.7		
1953	9.5	5.1			47.9	41.8		
1954	10.2	5.4			48.5	41.8		
1955	11.1	5.8			48.9	41.6		
1956	11.9	6.2			48.5	41.3		
1957	12.6	6.5			48.2	41.0		
1958	12.8	6.7			47.7	41.0		
1959	13.6	7.0	18.0	9.7	48.5	41.4		
1960	14.5	7.4	19.1	10.2	48.0	40.5		
1961	15.3	7.7	20.0	10.7	47.4	39.7		
1962	15.9	8.0	21.1	11.3	47.0	39.4		
1963	16.7	8.4	22.3	12.0	47.6	39.7		
1964	18.1	9.0	23.5	12.6	47.7	39.4		
1965	19.6	9.6	25.5	13.7	47.0	38.7		
1966	20.3	10.1	26.7	14.2	46.0	38.1		
1967	21.4	10.6	27.9	14.9	46.2	38.2		
1968	23.0	11.3	29.8	15.8	46.4	38.3		
1969	24.8	12.1	32.1	17.0	46.5	38.1		
1970	26.7	13.3	35.1	17.7	45.9	38.6	39.0	36.9
1971	29.4	15.3	39.1	19.8	45.0	38.4	38.7	36.9
1972	32.8	17.1	43.5	22.2	46.0	39.9	38.7	36.8
1973	38.1	19.7	48.1	24.7	46.7	39.9	38.8	36.8
1974	43.6	23.6	54.4	28.6	46.5	39.8	38.8	36.8
1975	55.7	32.1	68.4	39.6	45.5	39.4	38.7	36.6
1976	65.1	39.4	81.6	48.8	45.3	39.3	38.5	36.5
1977	71.5	43.7	88.9	53.8	45.7	39.4	38.7	36.7
1978	80.7	49.4	100.7	59.1	46.0	39.6	38.7	36.7
1979	93.0	55.2	113.0	66.0	46.2	39.6	38.8	36.7
1980	111.7	68.0	141.3	82.7	45.4	39.6	38.7	36.7

| | Average Weekly Earnings (£) | | | | Average Weekly Hours | | | |
| | Manual workers | | Non-manual workers | | Manual workers | | Non-manual workers | |
Year	Men aged 21 & over	Women aged 18 & over	Men aged 21 & over	Women aged 18 & over	Men aged 21 & over	Women aged 18 & over	Men aged 21 & over	Women aged 18 & over
1981	121.9	74.5	163.1	96.7	44.2	39.4	38.4	36.5
1982	133.8	80.1	178.9	104.9	44.3	39.3	38.2	36.5
1983	143.6	87.9	94.9	115.1	43.9	39.3	38.4	36.5
1984	152.7	93.5	109.0	124.3	44.3	39.4	38.5	36.5
1985	163.6	101.3	225.0	133.8	44.5	39.5	38.6	36.6
1986	174.4	107.5	244.9	145.7	44.5	39.5	38.6	36.7
1987	185.5	115.3	265.9	157.2	44.6	39.7	38.7	36.8
1988	200.6	123.6	294.1	175.5	45.0	39.8	38.7	36.9
1989	217.8	134.9	323.6	195.0	45.3	39.9	38.8	36.9
1990	239.5	148.4	346.4	214.3	45.4	40.0	38.9	36.9
1991	253.1	159.2	375.7	236.8	44.4	39.7	38.7	36.8
1992	268.3	170.1	400.4	256.5	44.5	39.8	38.6	36.8
1993	274.3	177.1	418.2	268.7	44.3	39.8	38.6	36.9
1994	280.7	181.9	428.2	278.4	44.7	40.1	38.9	37.0
1995	291.3	188.1	443.3	288.1	45.2	40.2	39.0	37.0
1996	301.3	195.2	464.5	302.4	44.8	40.2	39.1	37.1
1997	314.3	201.1	483.5	317.8	45.1	40.2	39.1	37.1

The figures to 1969 cover manufacturing industry and some non-manufacturing industries and services, but exclude coal mining, dock labour, railways, agriculture, shipping, distributive trades, catering, entertainments and domestic service.   In 1940–5, the figures are for July but otherwise up to 1969 they are for October. The figures to 1969 come from the *Ministry of Labour Gazette British Labour Statistics: Historical Abstract 1886–1968*. From 1970 the figures come from the New Earnings Survey of a sample of all employees in Great Britain and are not therefore strictly comparable with those for pre-1970. They relate to April in each year.

Sources: *British Labour Statistics: Historical Abstract 1886–1968; Department of Employment Gazette: New Earnings Survey.*

Size of Labour Force

Great Britain
(to nearest 000)

Year	Total	Male	Female
1901	16,312	11,548	4,763
1911	18,354	12,930	5,424
1921	19,357	13,636	5,701
1931	21,055	14,790	6,265
1939	19,750	14,656	5,094
1960	24,436	16,239	8,197
1970	24,721	15,977	8,743
1980	26,198	15,637	10,561
1990	28,189	16,031	12,158
1998	28,423	15,796	12,628

1901, 1911, and 1921 figures cover persons aged 10 years and over.
1931 and 1939 figures cover persons aged 14 years and over.
1951, 1960 and 1970 figures cover persons aged 15 years and over.
1980 onwards figures cover persons 16 and over.

Rates of Unemployment Benefit

(other than agricultural)

	Men over 18	Women over 18		Men over 18	Women over 18
15 Jan 13	7/-	Nil	20 Nov 75		£11.10
25 Dec 19	11/-	Nil	18 Nov 76		£12.90
8 Nov 20	15/-	12/-	17 Nov 77		£14.70
3 Mar 21	20/-	16/-	16 Nov 78		£15.75
30 Jun 21	15/-	12/-	15 Nov 79		£18.50
14 Aug 24	18/-	15/-	27 Nov 80		£20.65
8 Oct 31	15/3	13/6	26 Nov 81		£22.50
26 Jul 34	17/-	15/-	25 Nov 82		£25.00
1 Aug 40	20/-	18/-	24 Nov 83		£27.05
2 Nov 44	24/-	22/-	26 Nov 84		£28.45
3 Jun 48	26/-	26/-	28 Nov 85		£30.45
24 Jul 52	32/6	26/-	31 Jul 86		£30.80
19 May 55	40/-	26/-	9 Apr 87		£31.45
6 Feb 58		50/-	14 Apr 88		£32.75
6 Apr 61		57/6	10 Apr 89		£34.70
7 Mar 63		67/6	9 Apr 90		£37.35
28 Jan 65		80/-	11 Apr 91		£41.40
30 Oct 67		90/-	9 Apr 92		£43.10
6 Nov 69		£5 10/-	5 Apr 93		£44.65
23 Sep 71		£6.00	11 Apr 94		£45.45
20 Oct 72		£6.75	13 Apr 95		£46.45
4 Oct 73		£7.35	9 Apr 96		£48.25
22 Jul 74		£8.60	7 Apr 97		£49.15
7 Apr 75		£9.80	5 Apr 98		£50.35
			5 Apr 99		£51.40
			10 Apr 00		£52.20

After 6 Oct 66 flat rate unemployment benefit was supplemented by earnings related benefit. From 7 Oct 96 Unemployment Benefit was replaced by Jobseekers' Allowance, only payable at the full rate to claimants aged 25 or over.

Source: Department of Health and Social Security. Department of Social Security. *Annual Abstract of Statistics*.

Industrial Analysis of the Occupied Population 1911–1981

Great Britain
(000s)

	1911	1921	1931	1951	1961	1971	1981
Total Working Population[a]	18,351	19,369	21,074	22,610	24,014	25,021	26,697
Total Out of Employment	n.a.	n.a.	2,524	476	676	1,289	2,176
Total in Employment	n.a.	n.a.	18,550	22,013	23,501	24,615	24,323
Agriculture & Fishing	1,493	1,373	1,180	1,126	855	635	352
Mining & Quarrying	1,308	1,469	1,040	841	722	391	336
Manufacturing Industries	6,147	6,723	5,981	7,902	8,383	8,136	5,974
Building & Contracting	950	826	970	1,404	1,600	1,669	1,117
Gas, Electricity & Water	117	180	224	358	377	362	338
Transport & Communications	1,260	1,359	1,430	1,705	1,673	1,564	1,422
Distributive Trades	n.a.	n.a.	2,697	2,742	3,189	3,016	2,715
Insurance, Banking & Finance[b]	n.a.	328	388	489	722	952	1,295
Public Administration:							
National (inc. Defence)	452	480	368	1,036	798	812	589
Local	555	457	541	602	629	760	931
Professional, Scientific	n.a.	868	1,018	1,536	2,120	2,901	3,649
Miscellaneous Services	n.a.	n.a.	2,713	2,393	2,270	2,534	2,522[c]
(of which domestic service)	n.a.	(1,390)	(1,509)	(499)	(362)	(239)	(n.a.)

The Table shows only the changes in the general pattern of industry over the period. The figures are based on the Census of Population figures published by the Registrar-General. The figures for 1911 and 1921 are not completely comparable with those for the later years due to changes in classification and the inclusion of the unemployed who are excluded in the analysis from 1931 onwards. From 1981 a new system of classification was introduced which was no longer compatible with previous figures:

[a] 1911, 12 and over; 1921, 1931, 14 and over; 1951 on, 15 and over.
[b] Including Business Services.
[c] Not Including private domestic service.

Sources: *Department of Employment Gazette, Annual Abstract of Statistics.*

Employees in employment by industry, 1975–1998

Great Britain
(000s)
Figures for June of each year

	1975	1980	1985	1990	1993	1998
Agriculture, Forestry, Fishing	388	352	321	277	255	252
Coal, Oil, Gas extraction	356	355	273	157	103	44
Gas, Electricity, Water supply	361	361	309	284	247	211
Metals, Mechanical Engineering[a]	4,159	3,867	2,840	2,646	2,156	1,839
Chemicals and man-made fibres	432	420	339	325	293	249
Food, drink, tobacco	731	705	575	524	459	464
Textiles, leather, clothing	875	716	550	477	401	321
Timber, rubber, plastics, furniture	602	554	473	540	438	439
Paper, printing, publishing	553	538	477	481	443	471
Construction	1,207	1,206	994	1,060	807	1,066
Wholesale, Retail, Hotels, Catering	3,906	4,204	4,213	4,756	4,452	5,204
Transport, Post, Telecommunications	1,480	1,464	1,308	1,361	1,248	1,376
Banking, Insurance, Finance	1,468	1,669	2,039	2,701	2,577	b
Public Administration	1,937	1,925	1,862	1,942	1,823	b
Education	1,534	1,586	1,557	1,735	1,806	1,822
Health	1,112	1,214	1,489	1,664	,713	1,551

[a] SIC 1980 Classifications 21–24, 31–37
[b] Impossible to derive compatible figures due to changes in classification.

Source: *Department of Employment Gazette.*

Trades Union Congresses 1900–

Date	Place	President	General secretary	No. of Delegates	Members represented (000s)
3–8 Sep 00	Huddersfield	W. Pickles	S. Woods	386	1,250
2–7 Sep 01	Swansea	C. Bowerman	–	407	1,200
1–6 Sep 02	London	W. Steadman	–	485	1,400
6–11 Sep 03	Leicester	W. Hornidge	–	460	1,500
5–10 Sep 04	Leeds	R. Bell	–	453	1,423
4–9 Sep 05	Hanley	J. Sexton	W. Steadman	457	1,541
3–8 Sep 06	Liverpool	D. Cummings	–	491	1,555
2–7 Sep 07	Bath	A. Gill	–	521	1,700
7–12 Sep 08	Nottingham	D. Shackleton	–	522	1,777
6–11 Sep 09	Ipswich	–	–	598	1,705
12–17 Sep 10	Sheffield	J. Haslam	–	505	1,648
4–9 Sep 11	Newcastle	W. Mullin	C. Bowerman	523	1,662
2–7 Sep 12	Newport	W. Thorne	–	495	2,002
1–6 Sep 13	Manchester	W. Davis	–	560	2,232
6–11 Sep 15	Bristol	J. Seddon	–	610	2,682
4–9 Sep 16	Birmingham	H. Gosling	–	673	2,851
3–8 Sep 17	Blackpool	J. Hill	–	697	3,082
2–7 Sep 18	Derby	J. Ogden	–	881	4,532
8–13 Sep 19	Glasgow	G. Stuart-Bunning	–	851	5,284
6–11 Sep 20	Portsmouth	J. Thomas	–	955	6,505
5–10 Sep 21	Cardiff	E. Poulton	–	810	6,418
4–9 Sep 22	Southport	R. Walker	–	723	5,129
3–8 Sep 23	Plymouth	J. Williams	F. Bramley	702	4,369
1–6 Sep 24	Hull	A. Purcell	–	724	4,328
7–12 Sep 25	Scarborough	A. Swales	–	727	4,351
6–11 Sep 26	Bournemouth	A. Pugh	W. Citrine	696	4,366
5–10 Sep 27	Edinburgh	G. Hicks	–	646	4,164
3–8 Sep 28	Swansea	B. Turner	–	621	3,875
2–6 Sep 29	Belfast	B. Tillett	–	592	3,673
1–5 Sep 30	Nottingham	J. Beard	–	606	3,744
7–11 Sep 31	Bristol	A. Hayday	–	589	3,719
5–9 Sep 32	Newcastle	J. Bromley	–	578	3,613
4–8 Sep 33	Brighton	A. Walkden	–	566	3,368
3–7 Sep 34	Weymouth	A. Conley	–	575	3,295
2–6 Sep 35	Margate	W. Kean	Sir W. Citrine	575	3,389
7–11 Sep 36	Plymouth	A. Findlay	–	603	3,615
6–10 Sep 37	Norwich	E. Bevin	–	623	4,009
5–9 Sep 38	Blackpool	H. Elvin	–	650	4,461
4–5 Sep 39	Bridlington	J. Hallsworth	–	490	4,669
7–9 Oct 40	Southport	W. Holmes	–	667	4,867
1–4 Sep 41	Edinburgh	G. Gibson	–	683	5,079
7–11 Sep 42	Blackpool	F. Wolstencroft	–	717	5,433
6–10 Sep 43	Southport	Anne Loughlin	–	760	6,024
16–20 Oct 44	Blackpool	E. Edwards	–	730	6,642
10–14 Sep 45	Blackpool	–	–	762	6,576
21–25 Oct 46	Brighton	C. Dukes	V. Tewson	794	6,671
1–5 Sep 47	Southport	G. Thomson	–	837	7,540
6–10 Sep 48	Margate	Florence Hancock	–	859	7,791
5–9 Sep 49	Bridlington	Sir W. Lawther	–	890	7,937
4–8 Sep 50	Brighton	H. Bullock	Sir V. Tewson	913	7,883

Date	Place	President	General secretary	No. of Delegates	Members represented (000s)
3–7 Sep 51	Blackpool	A. Roberts	–	927	7,828
1–5 Sep 52	Margate	A. Deakin	–	943	8,020
7–11 Sep 53	Douglas	T. O'Brien	–	954	8,088
6–10 Sep 54	Brighton	J. Tanner	–	974	8,094
5–9 Sep 55	Southport	C. Geddes	–	984	8,107
3–7 Sep 56	Brighton	W. Beard	–	1,000	8,264
2–6 Sep 57	Blackpool	Sir T. Williamson	–	995	8,305
1–5 Sep 58	Bournemouth	T. Yates	–	993	8,337
7–11 Sep 59	Blackpool	R. Willis	–	1,017	8,176
5–9 Sep 60	Douglas	C. Bartlett	G. Woodcock	996	8,128
4–8 Sep 61	Portsmouth	E. Hill	–	984	8,299
3–7 Sep 62	Blackpool	A. Godwin	–	989	8,313
2–6 Sep 63	Brighton	F. Hayday	–	975	8,315
7–11 Sep 64	Blackpool	G. Lowthian	–	997	8,326
6–10 Sep 65	Brighton	H. Collison	–	1,013	8,771
5–9 Sep 66	Blackpool	J. O'Hagan	–	1,048	8,868
4–8 Sep 67	Brighton	Sir H. Douglass	–	1,059	8,787
2–6 Sep 68	Blackpool	Ld Wright	–	1,051	8,726
1–5 Sep 69	Portsmouth	J. Newton	–	1,034	8,875
7–11 Sep 70	Brighton	Sir S. Greene	V. Feather	1,064	9,402
6–10 Sep 71	Blackpool	Ld Cooper	–	1,064	10,002
4–8 Sep 72	Brighton	G. Smith	–	1,018	9,895
3–7 Sep 73	Blackpool	J. Crawford	–	991	10,001
2–6 Sep 74	Brighton	Ld Allen	L. Murray	1,032	10,002
1–5 Sep 75	Blackpool	Marie Patterson	–	1,030	10,364
6–10 Sep 76	Brighton	C. Plant	–	1,114	11,036
5–9 Sep 77	Blackpool	Marie Patterson	–	1,148	11,516
4–8 Sep 78	Brighton	D. Basnett	–	1,172	11,865
3–7 Sep 79	Blackpool	T. Jackson	–	1,200	12,128
1–5 Sep 80	Brighton	T. Parry	–	1,203	12,173
7–11 Sep 81	Blackpool	A. Fisher	–	1,188	11,601
6–10 Sep 82	Brighton	A. Sapper	–	1,163	11,006
5–9 Sep 83	Blackpool	F. Chapple	–	1,155	10,810
3–7 Sep 84	Brighton	R. Buckton	N. Willis	1,121	10,082
2–6 Sep 85	Blackpool	J. Eccles	–	1,124	9,855
1–5 Sep 86	Brighton	K. Gill	–	1,091	9,586
7–11 Sep 87	Blackpool	F. Jarvis	–	1,065	9,243
5–9 Sep 88	Bournemouth	C. Jenkins	–	1,052	9,127
4–8 Sep 89	Blackpool	A. Christopher	–	1,006	8,652
3–7 Sep 90	Blackpool	Anne Maddocks	–	985	8,405
2–6 Sep 91	Glasgow	A. Smith	–	937	8,193
7–11 Sep 92	Blackpool	R. Bickerstaffe	–	892	7,762
6–10 Sep 93	Brighton	A. Tuffin	J. Monks	874	7,303
5–9 Sep 94	Blackpool	J. Knapp	–	878	7,298
4–8 Sep 95	Brighton	L. Mills	–	828	6,895
2–6 Sep 96	Blackpool	Margaret Prosser	–	821	6,790
1–5 Sep 97	Brighton	A Dubbins	–	827	6,795
7–11 Sep 98	Blackpool	J. Edmonds	–	811	6,639
13–16 Sep 99	Brighton	Ld McKenzie	–	809	6,799

Source: *Trades Union Congress Reports, 1900–*.

The Largest Unions

(Unions which, at some time, have had over 200,000 members)[a]

Amalgamated Engineering and Electrical Union 1920 (1992)

Amalgamated Society of Engineers (founded 1851) merged with other unions to form the Amalgamated Engineering Union (AEU) in 1920. In 1968 the AEU merged with the Amalgamated Union of Foundry Workers (AEF) which in 1970 merged with the Construction Engineering Workers and the Draughtsmen and Allied Technicians Association, taking the title the Amalgamated Union of Engineering Workers. Merged in 1992 with EETPU and took its present title.

	President		*Gen. Sec.*
1920	J. Brownlie	1920	T. Mann
1930	W. Hutchinson	1921	A. Smethurst
1933	J. Little	1933	F. Smith
1939	J. Tanner	1943	B. Gardner
1954	R. Openshaw	1957	C. Hallett
1956	(Sir) W. Carron (Ld)	1964	J. Conway
1967	H. Scanlon	1976	(Sir) J. Boyd
1978	T. Duffy	1982	G. Laird
1986	W. Jordan	1994	P. Gallagher
1995	D. Hall	1996	(Sir) K. Jackson
1996	*(office abolished)*		

Amalgamated Weavers' Association 1884–1974

An association of many small local unions in the Cotton Trade. In 1974 it merged with the National Union of Textile and Allied Workers to form the Amalgamated Textile Workers Union.

	Secretary
1907	J. Cross
1925	J. Parker
1929	(Sir) A. Naesmith
1953	L. Wright (Ld)
1969	H. Kershaw
1972	F. Hague

Manufacturing, Science, Finance (MSF) 1917 (1988)

National Foremen's Association became Association of Supervisory Staff, Executives and Technicians (ASSET) in 1941. Became Association of Scientific, Technical and Managerial Staffs (ASTMS) in 1968 when it merged with the Association of Scientific Workers (founded in 1918 as National Union of Scientific Workers and became AScW in 1925). NFA joined TUC in 1919; AScW in 1942. Merged with TASS in 1988 to become MSF.

	Secretary
1917	H. Reid (NFA)
1939	T. Agar (NFA)
1945	W. Bretherton (ASSET)
1946	H. Knight (ASSET)
1960	C. Jenkins (ASSET)
1968	{ J. Dutton
	{ C. Jenkins
1970	C. Jenkins
1988	{ C. Jenkins
	{ K. Gill
1989	K. Gill
1992	R. Lyons

[a] Not including the Royal College of Nursing.

Communication Workers Union (CWU) 1920 (1995)

Postal Telegraph Clerks' Association and U.K. Postal Clerks' Association merged in 1914 to form Postal and Telegraph Clerks' Association. This merged in 1920 with Fawcett Association and other unions to form UPW. Name changed to Union of Communication Workers in 1980. (Legally banned from membership of TUC 1927–1946). In 1995 UCW merged with the National Communications Union (NCU – until 1975 the POEU), which represented telecommunications engineers, to form CWU.

Secretary

1920	J. Bowen	1993	A. Johnson
1936	T. Hodgson	1995	{ A. Johnson
1944	C. Geddes		{ T. Young
1957	R. Smith	1997	{ D. Hodgson
1966	T. Jackson		{ T. Young
1982	A. Tuffin	1998	D. Hodgson

Confederation of Health Service Employees (COHSE) 1946–1992

Formed by a merger of various small hospital unions. Merged with NUPE and NALGO to form UNISON in 1992.

Secretary

1946	G. Gibson	1969	F. Lynch
1948	C. Comer	1974	A. Spanswick
1953	J. Waite	1983	D. Williams
1959	W. Jepson	1987	H. MacKenzie
1967	A. Akers		

Electrical, Electronics, Telecommunications and Plumbing Union (EETPU) 1889–1992

Originally Electrical Trades Union. In 1968 following mergers it became the Electrical, Electronic and Telecommunications Union – Plumbing Trades Union and then the Electrical, Electronics, Telecommunications and Plumbing Union. Expelled from TUC in 1988. Merged with AUEW 1992; EEPTU wing readmitted to TUC 1993.

President/General Secretary

1907	J. Ball	1963	(Sir) L. Cannon
1931	E. Bussey	1971	F. Chapple
1940	H. Bolton	1984	E. Hammond
1944	F. Foulkes	1992	P. Gallagher

General Municipal Boilermakers and Allied Trades Union (GMB) 1924

National Union of General Workers (founded 1889 as the National Union of Gasworkers and General Labourers of G.B. and Ireland), National Amalgamated Union of Labour (founded 1889 as Tyneside and General Labourers' Union), and Municipal Employees' Association (founded 1894). Became National Union of General and Municipal Workers in 1924. Changed name to General and Municipal Workers Union for popular use in 1965. Merged with Amalgamated Society of Boilermakers, Shipwrights, Blacksmiths and Structural Workers to form GMB in 1982.

Secretary

1924	W. Thorne	1962	J. (Ld) Cooper
1934	C. Dukes	1972	D. Basnett
1946	(Sir) T. Williamson	1986	J. Edmonds

Graphical, Paper and Media Union (GPMU), 1847 (1991)

Established by amalgamation of the National Union of Bookbinders and Machine Rulers and the National Union of Printing and Paper Workers as the National Union of Printing Bookbinding and Paper Workers (NUPBPW). In 1968 merged with the National Society of Operative Printers (NATSOPA) to form SOGAT. In 1971 the merger was dissolved but NUPBPW section kept name of SOGAT. Merged with National Graphical Association in 1991 to form GPMU.

Secretary

1921	T. Newland	1974	W. Keys
1938	E. Spackman	1985	Brenda Dean
1946	V. Flynn	1991	A. Dubbins
1947	W. Morrison		
1959	T. Smith (1968–71 jointly with R. Briginshaw)		

National and Local Government Officers' Association, 1905–1993

National Association of Local Government Officers. 1930 amalgamated with National Poor Law Officers' Association and in 1963 with the British Gas Staffs Association. 1952 changed name to National and Local Government Officers' Association (joined TUC 1965). Merged with COHSE and NUPE to form UNISON in 1993.

General Secretary

1905	F. Ginn	1957	W. Anderson
1909	L. Hill	1973	G. Drain
1943	J. Simonds	1983	J. Daly
1945	H. Corser (Acting)	1990–3	A. Jinkinson
1946	J. Warren		

National Union of Mineworkers (NUM), 1889 (1945)

Formed as the Miners' Federation of G.B., amalgamated with specialist unions, and renamed NUM in 1945.

President		*Secretary*	
1912	R. Smillie	1920	F. Hodges
1921	H. Smith	1924	A. Cook
1929	T. Richards	1932	E. Edwards
1931	E. Edwards	1946	A. Homer
1932	P. Lee	1959	W. Paynter
1934	J. Jones	1969	L. Daly
1938	W. Lawther	1984	P. Heathfield
1954	W. Jones	1992	*(vacant)*
1960	S. Ford		
1971	J. Gormley		
1982	A. Scargill		

National Union of Public Employees (NUPE) 1888 (1928)-1993

Formed as London County Council Protection Association; in 1894 became Municipal Employees Association; in 1920 the MEA and the National Union of Corporation Workers jointly affiliated to the TUC but in 1924 MEA was absorbed by NUGMW. The National Union of Corporation Workers became NUPE in 1928. Merged with COHSE and NALGO to form UNISON in 1993.

Secretary

1926	J. Wills	1968	A. Fisher
1934	B. Roberts	1982–93	R. Bickerstaffe
1962	S. Hill		

National Union of Rail, Maritime, and Transport workers (RMT) 1913 (1989)

The National Union of Railwaymen was formed in 1913 from the merger of the Amalgamated Society of Railway Servants the General Railway Workers' Union, and others. In 1989 the NUR merged with the National Union of Seamen and took its present title.

Secretary

1920	J. Thomas and C. Cramp	1948	J. Figgins
1931	C. Cramp	1953	J. Campbell
1933	(Acting Secretary)	1958	(Sir) S. (Ld) Greene
1934	J. Marchbank	1975	S. Weighell
1943	J. Benstead	1982	J. Knapp

National Union of Teachers (NUT) 1870

Originally National Union of Elementary Teachers (till 1890). Affiliated to TUC in 1970.

Secretary

1892	(Sir) J. Yoxall	1970	(Sir) E. Britton
1924	F. Goldstone	1975	F. Jarvis
1931	(Sir) F. Mander	1989	D. McAvoy
1947	(Sir) R. Gould		

Public and Commercial Services Union (PCS) 1902 (1998)

Assistant Clerks Association became Clerical Officers Association in 1919 and Civil Service Clerical Association in 1922. Changed name to CPSA in 1969 (not in TUC 1927–1946). Merged with Public Services, Tax and Commerce Union (PTC) in 1998 to form PCS.

Secretary

1916	W. Brown	1982	A. Kendall
1942	L. White	1987	J. Ellis
1955	G. Green	1992	B. Reamsbottom
1963	L. Wines	1998	{ B. Reamsbottom
1967	W. Kendall		{ J. Sheldon
1976	K. Thomas		

Transport and General Workers Union 1922

Dock, Wharf, Riverside and General Workers' Union, National Union of Dock Labourers and other dockers' unions, United Vehicle Workers, National Union of Vehicle Workers and others. 1928 amalgamated with the Workers' Union.

Secretary

1921	E. Bevin	1966	F. Cousins
1940	A. Deakin *(Acting till 1946)*	1969	J. Jones
1955	A. Tiffin	1977	M. Evans
1956	F. Cousins	1985	R. Todd
1964	H. Nicholas *(Acting)*	1992	B. Morris

Union of Construction, Allied Trades and Technicians (UCATT), 1860 (1971)-

Amalgamated Society of Carpenters and Joiners became, in 1921 after mergers, Amalgamated Society of Woodworkers (ASW). ASW merged in 1971 with the Amalgamated Union of Building Trade Workers (formed 1921), the Amalgamated Society of Painters and Decorators and the Association of Building Technicians.

Secretary

1919	A. Cameron	1978	L. Wood
1925	F. Wolstencroft	1985	A. Williamss
1949	J. MacDermott	1992	G. Brumwell
1959	(Sir) G. Smith		

UNISON 1993

See above entries for COHSE, NALGO and NUPE.

	General Secretary
1993	A. Jinkinson
1996	R. Bickerstaffe

Union of Shop, Distributive and Allied Workers (USDAW) 1921 (1946)

Cooperative Employees, and Warehouse and General Workers amalgamated in 1921 to form the National Union of Distributive and Allied Workers. 1946 fusion with National Amalgamated Union of Shop Assistants, Warehousemen and Clerks.

Secretary

1921	J. Hallsworth and W. Robinson	1962	A. (Ld) Allen
1924	(Sir) J. Hallsworth	1979	W. Whately
1947	*(Acting Secretary)*	1986	G. Davies
1949	(Sir) A. Birch	1997	W. Connor

Source: *Trades Union Congress Reports, 1920–.*

THE LARGEST UNIONS

Membership

The Eight Largest Unions (in 1960)
(to nearest 000) (at 31 December)

Year	AUEW	ETU	NALGO	(NU)GMW	NUM	NUR	T&GWU	USDAW
1920	407	57	36	–	900	458	–	–
1921	357	46	36	–	800	341	300	100
1922	256	31	33	–	750	327	300	90
1923	246	26	33	–	750	327	300	90
1924	206	28	34	327	800	327	300	93
1925	205	29	37	320	800	327	300	95
1926	162	29	40	300	800	327	300	94
1927	146	26	44	278	725	327	300	100
1928	151	26	46	258	600	313	286	109
1929	155	29	49	261	600	310	389	115
1930	154	31	61	258	600	321	384	119
1931	146	31	65	240	600	310	390	121
1932	136	31	68	220	500	285	390	127
1933	135	31	73	230	500	272	370	131
1934	146	34	79	252	500	291	403	134
1935	164	40	86	280	500	306	460	145
1936	248	48	93	340	518	338	523	158
1937	299	58	101	405	538	365	611	172
1938	334	64	106	417	584	367	635	183
1939	376	70	114	430	589	350	648	194
1940	454	80	111	441	589	362	650	223
1941	550	97	113	548	580	376	680	234
1942	645	113	121	721	599	394	806	254
1943	825	124	127	726	603	406	1,089	268
1944	811	132	133	661	605	404	1,017	272
1945	704	133	134	605	533	410	975	275
1946	723	162	146	795	538	414	1,230	374
1947	742	170	171	824	572	448	1,264	343
1948	743	182	176	816	611	455	1,271	342
1949	714	188	189	805	609	421	1,253	340
1950	716	192	197	785	602	392	1,242	343
1951	756	198	212	809	613	396	1,285	348
1952	796	203	222	808	641	397	1,277	346
1953	810	212	225	790	669	378	1,259	339
1954	823	216	230	787	675	372	1,240	344
1955	854	223	236	805	675	368	1,278	347
1956	860	228	243	808	674	369	1,264	349
1957	900	239	247	804	681	371	1,244	352
1958	888	230	252	775	674	355	1,225	353
1959	908	233	263	769	639	334	1,241	351
1960	973	243	274	769	586	334	1,302	355
1961	982	253	285	786	545	317	1,318	351
1962	986	257	295	781	529	311	1,331	356
1963	981	272	226	782	501	283	1,374	355
1964	1,011	282	338	785	479	264	1,426	352
1965	1,049	293	349	796	446	255	1,444	349

Year	AUEW	ETU	NALGO	(NU)GMW	NUM	NUR	T&GWU	USDAW
1966	1,055	293	361	793	413	220	1,428	336
1967	1,107	352	367	782	380	218	1,451	321
1968	1,136	365	373	798	344	199	1,476	311
1969	1,195	392	397	804	297	191	1,532	316
1970	1,295	421	440	853	279	198	1,629	330
1971	1,284	420	464	842	276	194	1,643	319
1972	1,340	417	498	848	271	184	1,747	325
1973	1,173	420	518	864	261	174	1,785	326
1974	1,211	414	542	884	255	173	1,857	353
1975	1,429	420	625	881	262	180	1,856	377
1976	1,412	420	683	916	260	180	1,930	413
1977	1,423	420	709	945	258	180	2,023	441
1978	1,484	420	729	965	255	180	2,073	462
1979	1,499	420	753	967	253	180	2,086	470
1980	1,381	405	782	916	257	170	1,887	450
1981	1,290	395	796	865	250	160	1,696	438
1982	1,238	380	784	940	245	150	1,633	417
1983	1,220	365	780	875	208	143	1,547	403
1984	1,221	355	766	847	200	136	1,491	392
1985	975	348	752	840	135	130	1,434	385
1986	858	336	750	814	105	125	1,378	382
1987	815	330	759	803	91	118	1,349	387
1988	794	330	755	864	77	110	1,313	397
1989	742	360	751	823	59	123	1,271	376
1990	702	367	744	933	53	118	1,224	362
1991	702	357	760	860	44	110	1,127	341
1992	884	–	1,487	831	31	105	1,037	316
1993	835	–	1,458	835	18	86	949	299
1994	781	–	1,369	790	11	68	919	283
1995	726	–	1,355	740	11	59	897	283
1996	725	–	1,375	718	10	60	885	290
1997	720	–	1,300	710	5	56	881	293
1998	718	–	1,272	712	5	56	882	303

Source: *Trades Union Congress Reports, 1920–*.

Other Unions Which Have Exceeded 200,000 Members

	ASTMS (MSF)	CPSA	COHSE	NUPE	NUT	SOGAT	UCATT	UCW
1950	12	134	53	175	192	124	197	149
1960	25	140	54	200	225	158	192	166
1970	221	185	90	373	311	192	221	209
1980	491	224	213	692	249	206	348	203
1990	653	123	203	579	169	166	207	201
1998	416	254	–	–	194	203	112	238

The Amalgamated Weavers' Association had 219,000 members in 1920. It fell to 89,000 by 1940.

Source: *Trades Union Congress Reports, 1920–*.

Income, Expenditure and Funds of Registered Trade Unions

(in shillings per member) 1910–1970

Year	Income from Members	Expenditure					
		Benefits			Other		
		Dispute benefit	Unemployment benefit	Other Welfare benefits	Working expenses	Political Funds	Total
1910	27.8	5.3	6.8	11.1	–	8.1	59.3
1920	32.4	9.3	4.5	5.1	0.5	17.2	45.8
1930	37.6	1.6	9.7	12.1	0.5	16.6	62.0
1940	36.0	0.2	3.0	10.4	0.4	14.8	92.2
1950	39.6	0.6	0.4	10.4	1.1	22.8	156.4
1960	58.8	1.1	0.4	15.5	1.2	34.9	211.6
1970	104.9	8.6	0.6	25.9	3.7	72.4	322.6

Sources: A. Flanders, *Trade Unions* (1967); *Department of Employment Gazette; Annual Reports of the Certification Officer.*

Income and Expenditure of Registered Trade Unions 1980–1995

Year	Total Income £m	Benefits to Members £m	Administration £m	Political Funds income £m
1980	230.7	33.9	195.1	5.0
1990	462.7	65.8	489.2	15.6
1995	548.5	78.0	575.5	15.7

Source: *Annual Reports of the Certification Officer.*

Density of Union Membership in Total Labour Force (%)

United Kingdom

1901	12.6		1961	43.1
1911	17.7		1970	47.7
1920	45.2		1974	49.6
1933	22.6		1981	43.7
1938	29.5		1991	34.3
1951	44.1			

Sources: G.S. Bain, *The Growth of White Collar Unionism* (1970); G.S. Bain and R. Price, 'Union Growth and Employment Trends in the U.K. 1964–70', *British Journal of Industrial Relations* (1972), pp.366–81 and 'Union Growth Revisited 1948–70', *British Journal of Industrial Relations* (1976), pp.339–55; *Annual Reports of the Certification Officer.*

Major Industrial Disputes

(strikes and lockouts in which more than 500,000 working days were lost)

Dispute Began		Industrial group	Area	Numbers affected (000s)	Working days lost (000s)[a]
1900	Apr	Potters	N. Staffs.	20	640
	Nov	Quarrymen	Bethesda	3	505
1902	Jul	Miners	UK	103	872
1906	Oct	Shipyard workers	Clyde	15	592
1908	Feb	Shipyard workers	Humber, Barrow, Birkenhead, Clyde, E. Scotland	35	1,719
	Feb	Engineers	N.E. Coast	11	1,706
	Sep	Cotton operatives	Lancs., Cheshire, Derby	120	4,830
1909	Jul	Miners	S. Wales and Mon.	55	660
1910	Jan	Miners	Durham	85	1,280
	Jan	Miners	Northumberland	30	1,080
	Apr	Miners	Rhondda	13	2,985
	Jun	Cotton operatives	Lancs. and Chesh.	102	600
	Sep	Shipyard workers	N.E. and Scotland	35	2,851
1911	Jun	Seamen and dockers	U.K.	120	1,020
	Aug	Dockers and carters	London	22	500
	Aug	Railwaymen	U.K.	145	500
	Dec	Cotton weavers	N.E. Lancs.	160	2,954
1912	Feb	Miners	U.K.	1,000	30,800
	Feb	Jute workers	Dundee	28	726
	May	Dockers and carters	Port of London and Medway	100	2,700
1913	Jan	Cab drivers	London	11	637
	Apr	Tube and metal workers	S. Staffs. and N. Worcs.	50	1,400
	Aug	Transport workers	Dublin	20	1,900
1914	Jan	Builders	London	20	2,500
	Feb	Miners	Yorks.	150	2,654
1915	Jul	Miners	S. Wales	232	1,400
1916	Mar	Jute workers	Dundee	30	500
1917	May	Engineers	U.K.	160	2,880
1918	May	Miners	S. Wales and Mon.	40	760
	Dec	Cotton spinners	Lancs. and Chesh.	100	900
1919	Jan	Miners	Yorks.	150	1,950
	Jan	Shipyard workers	N.E. Coast	40	820
	Mar	Miners	Various districts	100	600
	Jun	Cotton operatives	Lancs. and adjoining counties	450	7,500
	Jul	Miners	Yorks.	150	4,050
	Sep	Ironfounders	England, Wales, and Ireland	50	6,800
	Sep	Railwaymen	U.K.	500	3,850
1920	Sep	Cotton operatives	Oldham area	400	620
	Oct	Miners	U.K.	1,100	16,000
	Dec	Shipyard carpenters	U.K.	10	2,200
1921	Apr	Miners	U.K.	10	2,200
	Jul	Builders	U.K.	100	2,970
1925	Jul	Wool textile workers	W. Yorks, Lancs.	165	3,105
1926	May	Miners	U.K.	1,050	145,200
	May	General Strike	U.K.	1,580[b]	15,000[b]
1928	May	Cotton weavers	Nelson	17	600
1929	Jul	Cotton operatives	Lancs. and adjoining counties	388	6,596
1930	Apr	Wool textile workers	W. Yorks, Lancs.	120	3,258
1931	Jan	Cotton weavers	Lancs. and adjoining counties	145	3,290
	Jan	Miners	S. Wales, Mon.	150	2,030
1932	Aug	Cotton weavers	Lancs., Yorks.	148	4,524
	Oct	Cotton spinners	Lancs. and adjoining counties	130	760
1937	May	Busmen	London	24	565
1944	Mar	Miners	Wales and Mon.	100	550
	Mar	Miners	Yorkshire	120	1,000

Dispute Began		Industrial group	Area	Numbers affected (000s)	Working days lost (000s)[a]
1945	Sep	Dockers	Birkenhead, Hull, Manchester, Liverpool, London	50	1,100
1953	Dec	Engineers and Shipyard workers	U.K.	1,070	1,070
1954	Sep	Dockers and sympathy strikes	Port of London	45	726
1955	May	Dockers	English ports	21	673
	May	Railwaymen	U.K.	70	865
1957	Mar	Engineers	U.K.	615	4,000
	Mar	Shipyard workers	U.K.	165	2,150
	Jul	Busmen	Provinces	100	770
1958	Apr	Dockers, transport and market workers	London	24	515
	May	Busmen	Greater London	49	1,604
1959	Jun	Printing workers	U.K.	120	3,500
1962	Feb	Engineering & Shipbuilding	U.K.	1,750	1,750
	Mar	Engineering & Shipbuilding	U.K.	1,750	1,750
1966	May	Shipping	U.K.	30	850
1968	May	Engineering	U.K.	1,500	1,500
1969	Feb	Motor Vehicles	Various areas	38	561
	Oct	Miners	Various areas	121	979
1970	Jul	Dockers	U.K.	42	502
	Sep	Local authority workers	England and Wales	134	1,216
	Oct	Miners	Various	99	1,050
1971	Jan	Motor vehicles	Various areas	42	1,909
	Jan	Post Office workers	U.K.	180	6,229
1972	Jan	Miners	U.K.	309	10,726
	Jun	Construction	England and Wales	120	2,904
	Jun	Construction	Scotland	36	933
	Jul	Dockers	U.K.	35	548
1974	Feb	Miners	U.K.	250	5,567
1977	Nov	Firemen	U.K.	30	1,250
1978	Oct	Motor Vehicles (Ford)	U.K.	56	2,529
	Dec	Printworkers	London	3	592
1979	Jan	Lorry drivers	U.K.	85	950
	Jan	Public employees	U.K.	1,500	3,239
	Feb	Civil servants	U.K.	279	508
	Jul	Television staff	U.K.	12	600
	Aug	Engineers	U.K.	1,500	16,000
1980	Jan	Steelworkers	U.K.	151	8,800
1981	Mar	Civil servants	U.K.	318	867
1982	Jan	Railway footplatemen	U.K.	59	814
	Apr	Health service	U.K.	180	781
	May	All workers	U.K.	948	672
1983	Jan	Water workers	England, Wales, N. Ireland	35	766
1984	Mar	Miners	U.K.	130	26,100
1985	Feb	Teachers	England & Wales	168	772
1987	Jan	Engineers	Various U.K.	113	1,471
	Apr	Civil servants	Various U.K.	14	624
1988	Jun	Shipbuilding	Cumbria	13	754
	Sep	Postmen	U.K.	119	1,036
1989	Jul	Local authority white collar	G.B.	350	2,004
	Oct	Engineers	Various G.B.	9	611
1996	Jun	Postal workers	Various G.B.	115	789

[a] Where figures for working days lost have not been given in the Gazettes, they have been estimated.
[b] Excluding miners.

Sources: *The Board of Trade Labour Gazette*, (1900–17); *The Ministry of Labour Gazette* (1918–68); *Employment and Productivity Gazette* (1968–70); *Department of Employment Gazette* (1970–97); *Labour Market Trends* (1997–).

Emergency Powers

Under the *Emergency Powers Act, 1920*, the government may proclaim a State of Emergency if the essentials of life of the country are threatened. The Act then empowers the government to make regulations by Order-in-Council which have the full force of law. All the occasions on which States of Emergency have been proclaimed under the Act have been associated with strikes.

31 Mar 21	Coal
26 Mar 24	London Transport[a]
2 May 26	General Strike
29 Jun 48	Docks
11 Jul 49	Docks
31 May 55	Rail
23 May 66	Seamen
16 Jul 70	Docks
12 Dec 70	Electricity
9 Feb 72	Coal
3 Aug 72	Docks
13 Nov 73	Coal and Electricity (also Middle East oil crisis)

[a] It is doubtful whether this proclamation was ever made.

Unemployment, Industrial Disputes and Trade Union Statistics

	Unemployment[b]		Industrial Disputes[c]						
	Maximum (000s)	Minimum (000s)	Working Days Lost[d] (000s)	No.of Stoppages beginning in year[e]	Total Workers involved[d] (000s)	Total No. of Unions	No. of Union Members (000s)	No.of Unions affiliated to TUC	No.of Members of Unions affiliated to TUC (000s)
1900			3,088	633	185	1,325	1,911	184	1,250
1901			4,130	631	179	1,323	2,022	191	1,200
1902			3,438	432	255	1,322	2,025	198	1,400
1903			2,320	380	116	1,297	2,013	204	1,500
1904			1,464	346	87	1,285	1,994	212	1,423
1905			2,368	349	92	1,256	1,967	205	1,541
1906			3,019	479	218	1,244	1,997	226	1,555
1907			2,148	585	146	1,282	2,210	236	1,700
1908			10,785	389	293	1,283	2,513	214	1,777
1909			2,687	422	297	1,268	2,485	219	1,705
1910			9,867	521	514	1,260	2,477	212	1,648
1911			10,155	872	952	1,269	2,565		
1912			40,890	834	1,462	1,290	3,139	202	1,662
1913			9,804	1,459	664	1,252	3,416	201	2,002
1914			9,878	972	447	1,269	4,135	207	2,232
1915			2,953	672	448	1,260	4,145	215	2,682
1916			2,446	532	276	1,229	4,359	227	2,851
1917			5,647	730	872	1,225	4,644	235	3,082
1918			5,875	1,165	1,116	1,241	5,499	262	4,532
1919			34,969	1,352	2,591	1,264	6,533	266	5,284
1920			26,568	1,607	1,932	1,360	7,926	215	6,505
1921	2,038[a]		85,872	763	1,801	1,384	8,348	213	6,418

	Unemployment[b]		Industrial Disputes[c]						No.of
	Maximum (000s)	Minimum (000s)	Working Days Lost[d] (000s)	No.of Stoppages beginning in year[e]	Total Workers involved[d] (000s)	Total No. of Unions	No. of Union Members (000s)	No.of Unions affiliated to TUC	Members of Unions affiliated to TUC (000s)
1922	2,015 Jan	1,443 Oct	19,850	576	552	1,275	6,633	206	5,129
1923	1,525 Jan	1,229 Dec	10,672	628	405	1,232	5,625	194	4,369
1924	1,374 Jan	1,087 Jun	8,424	710	613	1,192	5,429	203	4,328
1925	1,443 Aug	1,243 Dec	7,952	603	441	1,194	5,544	205	4,351
1926	1,432 Dec	1,094 Apr	162,233	323	2,734	1,176	5,506	207	4,366
1927	1,451 Jan	1,059 May	1,174	308	108	1,164	5,219	204	4,164
1928	1,375 Aug	1,127 Mar	1,388	302	124	1,159	4,919	196	3,875
1929	1,466 Jan	1,164 Jun	8,287	431	533	1,142	4,866	202	3,673
1930	2,500 Dec	1,520 Jan	4,399	422	307	1,133	4,858	210	3,744
1931	2,880 Sep	2,578 May	6,983	420	490	1,121	4,842	210	3,719
1932	2,955 Jan	2,309 Nov	6,488	389	379	1,108	4,624	209	3,613
1933	2,407 Jan	1,858 Dec	1,072	357	136	1,081	4,444	208	3,368
1934	2,295 Jan	2,080 Sep	959	471	134	1,081	4,392	210	3,295
1935	2,333 Jan	1,888 Dec	1,955	553	271	1,063	4,590	211	3,389
1936	2,169 Jan	1,640 Aug	1,829	818	316	1,049	4,867	214	3,615
1937	1,739 Jan	1,373 Sep	3,413	1,129	597	1,036	5,295	214	4,009
1938	1,912 Dec	1,818 Apr	1,334	875	274	1,032	5,842	216	4,461
1939	2,032 Jan	1,230 Aug	1,356	940	337	1,024	6,053	217	4,669
1940	1,471 Jan	683 Dec	940	922	299	1,019	6,298	223	4,867
1941	653 Jan	151 Dec	1,079	1,251	360	1,004	6,613	223	5,079
1942	162 Jan	100 Dec	1,527	1,303	456	996	7,165	232	5,433
1943	104 Jan	–	1,808	1,785	557	991	7,867	230	6,024
1944	84 Jan	–	3,714	2,194	821	987	8,174	190	6,642
1945	111 Jan	–	2,835	2,293	531	963	8,087	191	6,576
1946	408 Jan	360 Jan	2,158	2,205	526	781	7,875	192	6,671
1947	1,916 Feb	262 Sep	2,433	1,721	620	757	8,803	187	7,540
1948	359 Dec	299 Jun	1,944	1,759	424	734	9,145	188	7,791
1949	413 Jan	274 Jul	1,807	1,426	433	735	9,319	187	7,937
1950	404 Jan	297 Jul	1,389	1,339	302	726	9,274	186	7,937
1951	367 Jan	210 Jul	1,694	1,719	379	732	9,289	186	7,828
1952	468 Apr	379 Jan	1,792	1,714	415	735	9,535	183	8,020
1953	452 Feb	273 Jul	2,184	1,746	370	719	9,583	183	8,088
1954	387 Feb	220 Jul	2,457	1,989	448	717	9,523	184	8,094
1955	298 Jan	185 Jul	3,781	2,419	659	703	9,556	183	8,107
1956	297 Dec	223 Jun	2,083	2,648	507	694	9,726	186	8,264
1957	383 Jan	244 Jul	8,412	2,859	1,356	685	9,829	185	8,305
1958	536 Nov	395 Jan	3,462	2,629	523	675	9,639	185	8,337
1959	621 Jan	395 Jul	5,270	2,093	645	668	9,623	186	8,176
1960	461 Jan	292 Jul	3,024	2,832	817	664	9,835	184	8,128
1961	419 Jan	259 Jul	3,046	2,686	771	646	9,897	183	8,299
1962	566 Dec	397 Jun	5,795	2,449	4,420	626	8,887	182	8,313
1963	878 Feb	449 Jul	1,755	2,068	591	607	9,934	176	8,315
1964	501 Jan	318 Jul	2,277	2,524	871	598	10,079	175	8,326
1965	376 Jan	276 Jun	2,925	2,354	871	630	10,325	172	8,771
1966	564 Dec	261 Jun	2,398	1,937	530	622	10,261	170	8,868
1967	603 Feb	497 Jul	2,787	2,116	734	603	10,110	169	8,787

	Unemployment[b]		Industrial Disputes[c]			Total No. of Unions	No. of Union Members (000s)	No.of Unions affiliated to TUC	No.of Members of Unions affiliated to TUC (000s)
	Maximum (000s)	Minimum (000s)	Working Days Lost[d] (000s)	No.of Stoppages beginning in year[e]	Total Workers involved[d] (000s)				
1968	631 Jan	515 Jul	4,690	2,378	2,255	584	10,193	160	8,726
1969	595 Jan	499 Jun	6,846	3,116	1,654	563	10,472	155	8,875
1970	628 Jan	547 Jun	10,980	3,906	1,793	540	11,179	150	9,402
1971	868 Dec	655 Jan	13,551	2,228	1,776	523	11,128	142	10,002
1972[f]	929 Jan	745 Dec	23,909	2,497	1,722	503	11,353	132	9,895
1973	785 Jan	486 Dec	7,197	2,873	1,513	513	11,449	126	10,001
1974	628 Aug	515 Jun	14,750	2,922	1,622	498	11,756	109	10,002
1975	1,152 Dec	738 Jan	6,012	2,282	789	488	12,184	111	10,364
1976	1,440 Aug	1,220 Jun	3,284	2,016	882	462	12,376	113	11,036
1977	1,567 Aug	1,286 May	9,985	2,627	1,143	485	12,719	112	11,516
1978	1,608 Aug	1,364 Dec	9,306	2,349	939	485		112	11,865
1979	1,464 Jul	1,299 May	29,474	4,583	2,080	462	13,112	112	12,128
1980	2,244 Dec	1,471 Jan	11,964	830	1,330	453	13,289	109	12,173
1981	2,772 Oct	2,271 Jan	4,266	1,499	1,338	438	12,947	108	11,601
1982	3,097 Dec	2,770 Jun	5,313	2,101	1,528	414	12,106	105	11,006
1983	3,225 Jan	2,984 Jun	3,754	571	1,352	408	11,593	102	10,810
1984	3,284 Sep	3,030 Jun	27,135	1,221	1,464	394	11,236	98	10,082
1985	3,346 Sep	3,179 Jun	6,402	903	791	375	10,994	91	9,855
1986	3,408 Jan	3,216 Nov	1,920	1,074	720	370	10,821	88	9,586
1987	3,297 Jan	2,686 Nov	3,546	1,016	887	335	10,539	87	9,243
1988	2,722 Jan	2,047 Dec	3,702	781	790	330	10,475	83	9,127
1989	2,074 Jan	1,612 Nov	4,128	701	727	315	10,376	78	8,652
1990	1,850 Dec	1,556 Jun	1,903	630	298	309	10,158	78	8,405
1991	2,552 Dec	1,960 Jan	761	369	176	287	9,947	74	8,193
1992	2,983 Dec	2,674 Jan	528	240	148	275	9,585	72	7,762
1993	3,062 Jan	2,679 Nov	649	211	385	268	9,048	69	7,303
1994	2,887 Jan	2,417 Dec	278	203	107	254	8,700	68	7,298
1995	2,503 Jan	2,196 Nov	415	232	174	243	8,278	67	6,895
1996	2,311 Jan	1,868 Dec	1,303	230	364	238	8,089	73	6,790
1997	1,908 Jan	1,388 Nov	235	206	130	75	6,757		
1998	1,479 Jan	1,310 Dec		159	91				

[a] Figures for December available only.

[b] 1900–20, unemployment figures for certain skilled trade unions available in Ministry of Labour Gazettes. Figures are given as percentages. No comparable figures of total unemployed are available before 1921. Figures for insured workers registered as unemployed. Agricultural workers, insurable in 1936, are included from that date. Numerous changes in coverage throughout.

[c] Disputes involving less than 10 work people and those lasting less than one day are omitted, except where aggregate duration exceeded 100 working days.

[d] S. Ireland included from 1900–1907.

[e] Workers involved directly and indirectly. 'Indirectly' involved means those unable to work at establishments where disputes occurred, though not themselves parties to the dispute.

[f] After the passage of the *Industrial Relations Act, 1971*, many trade unions ceased to be registered and as a result many trade union statistics for the following four years are non-existent or non-comparable.

Sources: *Annual Abstract of Statistics, Ministry of Labour Gazette, Employment Gazette, Abstract of Labour Statistics. Trades Union Congress Reports.*

Bibliography: H.A. Clegg, *The Changing System of Industrial Relations in Great Britain* (1979); G.S. Bain (ed.), *Industrial Relations in Britain* (1983); H. Pelling, *A History of British Trade Unionism* (5th Ed., 1992); H.A. Clegg et al., *A History of British Trade Unions since 1889* (1985); Lord Wedderburn, *The Worker and the Law* (4th Ed., 1994); N. Selwyn, *The Law of Employment* (8th Ed., 1993); Hepple and Fredman, *Labour Law and Industrial Relations in Great Britain* (2nd Ed., 1992); K. Coates and T. Topham, *Trade Unions in Britain* (3rd Ed., 1988); R. Hyman, *Strikes* (4th Ed., 1989); *Trade Unions and the Labour Party: Final Report of the Review Group on Links between the Trade Unions and the Labour Party* (1993).

XI

THE ECONOMY

Some Landmarks in the British Economy

1 Aug 14	War emergency measures, including temporary increase in Bank Rate to 10%.
Dec 16	Exchange rate pegged at $4.77 to £.
15 Aug 18	Report of Cunliffe Committee on Currency and Foreign Exchanges (Cd. 9182) recommended eventual return to an effective gold standard at pre-war par value.
20 Mar 19	Withdrawal of official peg from sterling-dollar exchange; exchange rates allowed to fluctuate.
Jan 21	Post-war trade slump. Unemployment exceeded 1 million (it remained above that level until 1939).
28 Apr 25	Return to fixed gold parity, at pre-1914 level ($4.86 = £1). Britain now on gold bullion standard.
3 May 26	General Strike.
23 Jun 31	Report of Macmillan Committee on Finance and Industry (Cmd. 3897).
24 Jul 31	Report of May Committee on National Expenditure (Cmd. 3920), recommended big cuts in Government expenditure.
21 Sep 31	Gold Standard suspended; sterling on fluctuating rate.
29 Feb 32	Import Duties Act set up Import Duties Advisory Council.
25 Apr 32	Exchange Equalisation Fund established to smooth variations in exchange rates.
30 Jun 32	Bank rate reduced to 2% and held at this level until 1939.
21 Aug 32	Ottawa Agreements on Imperial Preference.
21 Dec 33	Agricultural Marketing Act authorised quota controls on agricultural imports.
21 Dec 34	Special Areas (Development and Improvement) Act recognised problems of distressed areas.
3 Feb 36	Publication of J. M. Keynes, *General Theory of Employment, Interest and Money.*
12 Oct 36	Tripartite Agreement between Britain, France, and the U.S.A. to promote greater exchange stability by inter-Treasury Cooperation.
4 Sep 39	War emergency measures including imposition of exchange control with formal definition of the Sterling Area. Exchange rate fixed at $4.03 = £1.
21 Aug 41	Start of Lend-Lease.
22 Jul 44	Bretton Woods agreement leading to establishment of International Monetary Fund. (27 Dec 1945).
26 Aug 44	White Paper on Employment Policy (Cmd. 6527) accepted Government responsibility for 'maintenance of a high and stable level of employment'.
21 Aug 45	End of Lend-Lease followed by U.S. and Canadian loans to Britain.
1 Jan 46	Nationalisation of Bank of England.
Feb 47	Fuel Crisis.
5 Jun 47	Gen. Marshall's speech leading to establishment of Marshall Aid (Jul 48) and of Organisation for European Economic Co-operation (Apr 48).
15 Jul 47	Sterling made convertible. Convertibility suspended 20 Aug.
4 Oct 47	Agriculture Act put the policy of agricultural subsidy and protection on a peranent basis.
4 Feb 48	'Wage Freeze' and dividend restraint.
30 Jul 48	Monopolies and Restrictive Practices (Inquiry and Control) Act established Monopolies Commission.
18 Sep 49	Devaluation of £ from $4.03 to $2.80.
13 Dec 50	Marshall Aid suspended as no longer necessary.
7 Nov 51	Bank rate increase from 2% to 2.5% signalled the revival of use of monetary policy. Import liberalisation rescinded to check record dollar drain.
25 Oct 55	Autumn budget following balance-of-payments crisis.
2 Aug 56	Restrictive Trade Practices Act established Restrictive Trade Practices Court.
11 Dec 56	Stand-by credits arranged following post-Suez balance-of-payments crisis.
12 Aug 57	Council on Prices Productivity and Incomes ('Three Wise Men') set up. (Disbanded 1961).
19 Sep 57	Bank rate raised to 7% to meet sterling crisis.
27 Dec 57	Convertibility announced for non-resident sterling on current account.
20 Aug 59	Report of Radcliffe Committee on the working of the monetary system (Cmnd. 827).
20 Nov 59	European Free Trade Association Treaty signed.
4 Dec 60	O.E.E.C. reconstituted and broadened to include U.S.A. and Canada and retitled O.E.C.D.
20 Jul 61	Plowden Report on Control of Public Expenditure.
25 Jul 61	'Pay Pause' measures of S. Lloyd following balance-of-payments crisis. Establishment of National Economic Development Council.
10 Aug 61	Britain applied to join European Economic Community (negotiations terminated Jan 63).

16 Jul 64	Resale Prices Act greatly limited resale price maintenance.
26 Oct 64	New Government met balance-of-payments deficit by imposing 15% import surcharge (reduced to 10% in Apr 65 and ended Nov 66).
18 Mar 65	Establishment of Prices and Incomes Board.
5 Aug 65	Monopolies and Mergers Act extended 1948 Monopolies Act to cover services as well as goods.
13 Sep 65	Publication of first National Economic Plan (Cmnd. 2764).
25 Jan 66	Industrial Reorganisation Corporation established to encourage 'concentration and rationalisation and to promote the greater efficiency and international competitiveness of British Industry'. (Cmnd. 2889.)
6 Mar 66	Announcement that Decimal Currency would be adopted in 1971.
20 Jul 66	Sterling crisis led to Bank rate 7%, tax increases, credit restraints, and prices and incomes standstill (Cmnd. 3073).
12 Aug 66	Prices and Incomes Act became law (Part IV activated 6 Oct 66).
7 Mar 67	First landing of North Sea Gas.
11 May 67	Britain applied (for second time) to join European Economic Community. (De Gaulle gives second veto 27 Nov 67).
18 Nov 67	Devaluation of £ from $2.80 to $2.40. Bank Rate 8%.
19 Jan 68	Major cuts in Government expenditure announced, followed by drastically deflationary Budget 19 Mar.
17 Mar 68	Two-tier Bond system announced by World Central Banks.
30 Mar 68	Agreement on Special Drawing Rights in International Monetary Fund.
27 Oct 70	Expenditure cuts of £330m. announced, together with tax cuts.
15 Feb 71	Changeover to decimal currency.
30 Mar 71	Budget announced switch from surtax to graduated tax and to adopt Value Added Tax in 1973.
15 Aug 71	U.S.A. ended dollar-gold convertibility and, thereby, the Bretton Woods era.
23 Aug 71	£ floated.
19 Dec 71	General currency realignment under the Smithsonian agreement.
18 Feb 72	Wilberforce Court of Enquiry (Cmnd. 4903) ended six-week miners' strike with 22% pay increase recommendation.
26 Sep 72	Anti-inflation programme announced including pay and prices freezes and establishment of Prices Commission and Pay Board.
1 Jan 73	Britain joined European Economic Community.
4 Mar 73	European currencies floated against £.
1 Apr 73	Value Added Tax supplanted other excise duties and Selective Employment Tax.
6 Oct 73	Outbreak of Middle East War followed by short term cut in Middle East oil supplies and quadrupling of world oil prices.
8 Oct 73	Announcement of 'Phase 3' anti-inflation proposals.
13 Dec 73	Announcement of 3-day week for industry, starting in January, to cope with miners' overtime ban since 12 Nov.
11 Feb 74	Complete mine stoppage until 11 Mar. 3-day week ended 8 Mar.
31 Dec 74	End of year during which retail prices rose by 19% and wage rates by 29% while total industrial production fell by 3% (each figure a post-war record).
30 Jan 75	Financial Times Index of leading shares prices touched 252 having been at 146 on 9 Jan 75 and at 339 on 28 Feb 74.
5 Jun 75	Referendum on continued British membership of the EEC. 67% to 33% voted to stay in Community.
18 Jun 75	First landing of North Sea Oil.
11 Jul 75	Government published White Paper, *The Attack on Inflation*, which introduced a universal pay rise limit of £6 per week from 1 Aug 75. (In the year up to June 1975 earnings for manual workers had risen by 33.3%.)
12 Aug 75	Monthly retail price index showed a 26.9% increase in a year – a post-war record.
20 Nov 75	Announcement that cash limits will be applied to most public expenditure in the financial year 1976/7.
19 Feb 76	Public expenditure White Paper published, showing cuts in spending of £1.0 billion in 1977/8 and £2.4 billion in 1978/9 compared with previous plans.
2 Mar 76	Sterling fell below $2 for first time.
6 Apr 76	In Budget £1.3 billion tax cuts are announced but made dependent on agreement by the T.U.C to a new low pay norm in Stage 2. 4.5% pay formula agreed on 5 May and endorsed at special T.U.C. meeting on 16 Jun.
22 Jul 76	Announcement of further £1,000m. cut in public expenditure in 1977/8.
29 Sep 76	Government approached IMF for a $3.9 billion stand-by credit.
7 Oct 76	Minimum Lending Rate increased to 15%.

28 Oct 76	Sterling closes at $1.5675 – its lowest ever.
15 Dec 76	Cuts in public expenditure of £1,000m. in 1977/8 and £1,500m. in 1978/9 are announced as part of the agreement with the IMF.
11 Aug 77	Unemployment reaches peak of 1,635,800.
7 Sep 77	T.U.C. supports 12-month rule for Stage 3. Government continues to seek voluntary 10% limit on earnings increases
4 Jan 78	U.K. official reserves rise to $20.6 billion – the highest ever.
5 Jan 78	U.S. Treasury announces it will intervene in foreign exchange markets to halt decline in dollar.
17 Feb 78	Inflation (year on year) falls below 10% for first time since 1973.
12 Mar 79	European Monetary system starts.
12 Jun 79	New Conservative Government's budget cuts income tax from 33% to 30% and raises VAT from 8% to 15%.
24 Oct 79	Abolition of exchange controls.
15 Nov 79	Minimum lending rate touches 17%.
26 Mar 80	Announcement of Medium Term Financial Strategy (MTFS).
Jun 80	Britain becomes net exporter of oil.
2 Jun 80	Agreement on reduction of Britain's EEC budget contribution.
21 Nov 80	Youth Opportunities Programme doubled.
Oct 80	£ reaches peak exchange with $ (2.41).
Jan 81	Bottom of worst post-war slump for Britain.
20 Aug 81	Minimum lending rate abolished.
27 Jul 82	Hire purchase controls abolished.
9 Sep 82	Unemployment reaches three million.
13 Mar 84	Beginning of miners' strike.
26 Jun 84	Fontainebleau summit agrees permanent settlement of Britain's EEC contribution.
28 Nov 84	Government sells 33% of British Telecom.
3 Dec 84	British Telecom Shares (sold in Nov) gain 45% premium in first Stock Exchange dealings.
19 Dec 84	Hong Kong Agreement for 1997 handover.
18 Jan 85	FT Index breaks 1000 for the first time.
4 Mar 85	End of year-long miners' strike (26.1m. days lost).
7 Mar 85	£ touches bottom level of $1.05.
10 Mar 86	Budget lowers basic income tax to 29%.
27 Oct 86	'Big Bang' revolutionises stock exchange mechanics.
17 Feb 86	Margaret Thatcher signs Single European Act.
Jan 87	Guinness scandal leads to top City prosecutions.
5 Feb 87	Wapping strike ends and transforms newspaper finances.
17 Mar 87	Budget lowers basic income tax to 27%.
19 Oct 87	'Black Monday' collapse in stock market.
27 Nov 87	£ reaches $1.88, a five year high.
11 Mar 88	Budget reduces basic income tax to 25%; top rate to 40%.
26 Nov 88	Worst ever trade deficit announced.
29 Oct 89	Lawson resigns as Chancellor. Major succeeds.
1 Apr 90	Start of poll tax.
Apr 90	Unemployment begins strong upward rise.
2 Aug 90	Invasion of Kuwait starts 6 month Gulf War.
8 Oct 90	United Kingdom joins Exchange Rate Mechanism at £1 = 2.95DM.
1 Nov 90	Sir G. Howe resigns.
28 Nov 90	J. Major becomes Prime Minister with N. Lamont as Chancellor.
28 Feb 91	End of Gulf War.
17 Mar 91	End of poll tax announced.
11 Dec 91	Maastricht agreement signed with U.K. opt-outs.
25 Dec 91	Yeltsin succeeds Gorbachev in Russia.
10 Mar 92	Budget announces ending of April Budgets.
9 Apr 92	Conservatives win General Election with low tax promises.
17 Jun 92	Chancellor announces abolition of NEDC.
16 Sep 92	'Black Wednesday': Britain leaves Exchange Rate Mechanism. By Oct 1 £1 = 2.48DM.
12 Nov 92	Chancellor predicts a £37bn. Public Sector Borrowing requirement for next year.
16 Mar 93	Last Spring Budget imposes V.A.T. on fuel.
23 Apr 93	After 8 negative Quarters recession officially ends.
27 May 93	K. Clarke replaces N. Lamont as Chancellor.
23 Jul 93	Maastricht treaty finally approved by Parliament.
29 Nov 93	House of Commons votes for Sunday shopping.

30 Nov 93	First unified Budget involves expenditure cuts and higher taxes.
15 Dec 93	GATT changes (Uruguay Round) approved by 117 countries.
1 Apr 94	End of British Rail.
5 May 94	Channel Tunnel opened.
8 Jun 94	Dept. of Employment figures show union penetration down to 31%.
21 Jul 94	Blair takes over as Labour leader.
6 Nov 94	Blair addresses CBI.
28 Nov 94	Norway rejects EU membership.
30 Nov 94	Budget cuts public expenditure.
1 Jan 95	Austria, Finland and Sweden join EU.
2 Feb 95	Bank rate up to 6.75%.
26 Feb 95	Barings' Bank bankrupted by Far East speculation.
26 Mar 95	Schengen agreement on open frontiers in much of EU.
5 May 95	Clarke overrules Bank Governor on bank rate rise.
30 Sep 95	Euro-Summit agrees 1999 date for European Monetary Union.
16 Nov 95	Budget includes tax cuts.
21 Mar 96	EU ban on British beef exports.
20 Oct 96	Bank rate up to 6%.
26 Nov 96	Budget takes 1p. off income tax.
18 Dec 96	Unemployment falls below 2m.
20 Jan 97	Shadow Chancellor promises no Labour income tax increases.
24 Feb 97	Halifax Building Society votes to become a Bank.
1 May 97	Labour wins election. Brown becomes Chancellor.
6 May 97	Control over interest rates transferred to Bank of England Monetary Policy Committee.
2 Jun 97	Monetary policy committee named.
12 Jun 97	Brown confirms Bank's responsibility for a $2^1/2$% inflation target.
1 Sep 97	Hong Kong Market slump foreshadows Far Eastern slump.
20 Oct 97	Brown indicates likelihood of UK joining EMU.
6 Nov 97	Interest Rates peak at 7.25%.
25 Nov 97	Last November Budget includes 1% income tax cut.
16 Mar 98	EU ban on British beef exports partially lifted.
16 May 98	G8 summit in Birmingham.
11 Jun 98	Chancellor announces public-private partnership initiative with 51% of Air Traffic Control, the Tote, the Royal Mint and the Commonwealth Development Corporation made available for private ownership.
14 Jul 98	Publication of Public Expenditure Review includes an extra £21bn for Health and £19bn for Education.
1 Jan 99	EMU starts with 11 EU countries switching to Euro currency.
27 Apr 99	First quarter GDP figures reveal Britain has narrowly avoided recession.
7 May 99	Decision to sell half Britain's gold reserves announced.
10 Jun 99	Interest rates bottom at 5%.
1 Aug 99	UK beef exports permitted.

Sources of Government Economic Advice

The Treasury and, from 1964–69, the Department of Economic Affairs have provided governments with their main official guidance (see p.306 for Permanent Secretaries). In addition, under the Cabinet Office or the Treasury, there have been the following official economic advisers.

Economic Section of the Cabinet Office (1941–53)

Director

1941	J. Jewkes	1946	J. Meade
1941	L. Robbins	1947	R. Hall

Economic Adviser to the Government (1953–64)

1953	(Sir) R. Hall	1961	A. Cairncross

Head of Government Economic Service (1964–)

1964	(Sir) A. Cairncross	1976	Sir A. Atkinson
1969	Sir D. MacDougall	1980	(Sir) T. Burns
1973	Sir K. Berrill	1991	(Sir) A. Budd
1974	Sir B. Hopkin	1997	G. O'Donnell

Outside the Civil Service there have been the following official bodies:

Bank of England (1696)

Governor

1899	S. Gladstone	1944	Ld Catto
1901	(Sir) A. Prevost	1949	C. Cobbold (Ld)
1903	S. Morley	1964	E of Cromer
1905	A. Wallace	1966	(Sir) L.O'Brien (Ld)
1908	R. Johnston	1971	G. Richardson (Ld)
1913	W. Cunliffe (Ld)	1983	R. Leigh-Pemberton
1918	Sir B. Cokayne		(Ld Kingsdown)
	(Ld Cullen of Ashbourne) 1993		E. George
1920	M. Norman (Ld)		

Economic Advisory Council (1930–39)

(No full meeting of this body was held after the first year, but until 1939 its Standing Committee on Economic Information was active under Sir J. Stamp (Ld).)

Import Duties Advisory Council (1932–39)

Chairman
1932   Sir F. May (Ld)

Economic Planning Board (1947–62)

Chairman
1947–53 Sir E. Plowden

(After 1953, when some of its functions were merged with the Economic Section of the Treasury, the Permanent Secretary of the Treasury was made *ex officio* Chairman of the Board of outside advisers.)

National Economic Development Council (1961–92)

Director-General of National Economic Development Office

1962	Sir R. Shone	1973	(Sir) R. McIntosh
1966	(Sir) F. Catherwood	1983	J. Cassels
1966	Sir F. Figgures	1988	W. Eltis

Council on Pay, Productivity and Incomes (1957–61)

Chairman

1957	Ld Cohen	1960	Ld Heyworth

National Incomes Commission (1961–64)

Chairman
1962   Sir G. Lawrence

Prices and Incomes Board (1965–70)

Chairman
1965   A. Jones

Prices Commission (1973–79)

Chairman

1973   Sir A. Cockfield   1976   C. Williams

Pay Board (1973–74)

Chairman

1973   Sir F. Figgures

Industrial Adviser to the Government (1974–75)

1974   Sir D. Ryder (Ld)

Commission on Pay Comparability (1979–80)

Chairman

1979   H. Clegg

(See also Monopolies Commission, p.448; Royal Commissions and Committees of Inquiry, pp.315–19; Central Policy Review Staff, p.301.)

Economic Interest Groups

Industrial and Commercial Organisations

Federation of British Industry (1916–1965)

President

1916	F. Docker	1930	Sir J. Lithgow	1945	Sir C. Ballieu
1917	Sir R. Vassar-Smith	1931	Sir A. Duckham	1947	Sir F. Bain
1918	Sir V. Gaillard	1932	Sir G. Beharrell	1949	Sir R. Sinclair
1919	Sir P. Rylands	1933	Sir G. Macdonough	1951	Sir A. Forbes
1921	O. Armstrong	1934	Ld H. Scott	1953	Sir H. Pilkington
1923	Sir E. Geddes	1935	Sir F. Joseph	1955	Sir G. Hayman
1925	V. Willey	1936	Ld Hirst	1957	Sir H. Beaver
1927	Sir M. Muspratt	1937	(Sir) P. Bennett	1959	Sir W. MacFadzean
1928	Ld Ebbisham	1940	Ld D. Gordon	1961	Sir C. Harrison
1929	L. Lee	1943	Sir G. Nelson	1963	Sir P. Runge

Director

1916	R. Nugent	1919	(Sir) R. Nugent	1946	(Sir) N. Kipping
1917	E. Hill	1932	(Sir) G. Locock		

Confederation of British Industry (1965–)

Formed by a merger of the Federation of British Industries (FBI) (founded 1916), the National Association of British manufacturers (1915) and the British Employers Confederation (1919). It held its first Annual Conference at Brighton 13–15 Nov 77.

President

1965	Sir M. Laing	1976	Vt Watkinson	1988	Sir T. Holdsworth
1966	Sir S. Brown	1978	Sir J. Greenborough	1990	Sir B. Corby
1968	Sir A. Norman	1980	Sir R. Pennock	1992	Sir M. Angus
1970	Sir J. Partridge	1982	Sir C. Fraser	1994	Sir B. Nicholson
1972	Sir M. Clapham	1984	Sir J. Cleminson	1996	Sir C. Marshall
1974	Sir R. Bateman	1986	D. Nickson	1998	Sir C. Thornton

Director-General

1965	J. Davies	1980	Sir T. Beckett	1995	A. Turner
1969	(Sir) C. Adamson	1987	(Sir) J. Bannam	2000	D. Jones
1976	(Sir) J. Methven	1992	H. Davies		

Economic Pressure Groups

Adam Smith Institute (1977)
Aims of Industry (1942)
Association of British Chambers of Commerce (1860)
British Institute of Management (1947)
Building Societies Association (1860)
Free Trade League (1873)
National Chamber of Trade (1897)
National Farmers' Union (1908)
Tariff Reform League (1903)
Trades Union Congress (1868) (see p.387)
Institute of Directors (1903)
Child Poverty Action Group (1968)
National Federation of Small Business (1974)
Low Pay Unit (1974)

Consumer Organisations

(a) **Official**

Consumer Council (1963–1970). Director 1963: (Dame) E. Ackroyd.
Office of Fair Trading (1973–). Director General: 1973 J. Methven; 1976 (Sir) G. Borrie; 1992 J. Bridgeman.
National Consumer Council (1975–). Chair: 1975 Ld Young of Dartington; 1977 M. Shanks; 1984 M. Montague; 1987 Sally Oppenheim-Barnes; 1989 Lady Wilcox; 1996 D. Hatch. Director: 1992 Ruth Evans; 1999 Anna Bradley.

In 1972 Sir G. Howe was appointed Minister for Trade and Consumer Affairs in the Department of Trade and Industry, but with a seat in the Cabinet.

In 1974 the Department of Prices and Consumer Protection was established (Secretaries of State: 1974, Mrs S. Williams; 1976, R. Hattersley), but in 1979 it was absorbed into the Department of Trade.

(b) **Unofficial**

Consumers' Association (1956–)

Select Statistics

NATIONAL INCOME, TAXES AND PRICES

	Net National Income (at factor cost)[a] (£m) 1	Income Tax (Standard rate in £) 2	Amount Retained of Bachelor's £10,000 earned income after Income Tax and Surtax 3	Wholesale PriceIndex Number (1963 = 100) 4	Retail PriceIndex Number (1963 = 100) 5	Purchasing Power of £ (1900 = £1) 6	Real gross domestic product per head (1963 = 100) 7
1900	1,750	8d.	9,667	22	19	20/–	53
1901	1,727	1/–	9,500	21	19	19/9	54
1902	1,740	1/2	9,417	21	19	19/7	54
1903	1,717	1/3	9,375	21	19	19/4	52
1904	1,704	11d.	9,542	22	19	19/1	52
1905	1,776	1/–	9,500	21	19	19/4	53
1906	1,874	1/–	9,500	22	19	19/4	53
1907	1,966	1/–	9,500	23	20	18/8	53
1908	1,875	1/–	9,500	23	20	18/4	49
1909	1,907	1/–	9,500	23	20	18/4	51
1910	1,984	1/2	9,242	24	20	18/1	52
1911	2,076	1/2	9,242	24	21	17/1	53
1912	2,181	1/2	9,242	25	21	17/3	53
1913	2,265	1/2	9,242	26	21	17/3	54
1914	2,209	1/2	9,242	26	21	17/5	54
1915	(2,591)	1/8	8,669	31	26	14/2	–
1916	(3,064)	3/–	7,721	41	30	11/1	–
1917	(3,631)	5/–	6,721	53	37	9/1	–
1918	(4,372)	5/–	6,721	59	42	8/7	–
1919	(5,461)	6/–	5,813	66	46	8/1	–
1920	5,664	6/–	5,813	79	52	7/–	–
1921	4,460	6/–	5,672	50	47	7/8	48
1922	3,856	6/–	5,672	41	38	9/6	48
1923	3,844	5/–	6,150	41	37	10/–	49
1924	3,919	4/6	6,389	43	37	9/11	49
1925	3,980	4/6	6,389	41	37	9/11	54
1926	3,914	4/–	6,968	38	36	10/1	50
1927	4,145	4/–	6,968	36	35	10/5	54
1928	4,154	4/–	6,968	36	35	10/6	56
1929	4,178	4/–	6,968	35	35	10/7	57
1930	3,957	4/–	6,968	30	33	11/–	56
1931	3,666	4/6	6,487	27	31	11/10	52
1932	3,568	5/–	6,103	26	30	12/1	52
1933	3,728	5/–	6,103	26	30	12/5	52
1934	3,881	5/–	6,103	27	30	12/4	56
1935	4,109	4/6	6,340	27	30	12/2	59
1936	4,388	4/6	6,341	29	31	11/10	60
1937	4,616	4/9	6,222	33	32	11/4	63
1938	4,671	5/–	6,103	30	33	11/2	65
1939	5,037	5/6	5,867	31	34	10/10	–

[a] Changes in sources at 1914 and 1947.

	Net National Income (at factor cost)ᵃ (£m) 1	Income Tax (Standard rate in £) 2	Amount Retained of Bachelor's £10,000 earned income after Income Tax and Surtax 3	Wholesale PriceIndex Number (1963 = 100) 4	Retail PriceIndex Number (1963 = 100) 5	Purchasing Power of £ (1900 = £1) 6	Real gross domestic product per head (1963 = 100) 7
1940	5,980	7/–	4,965	42	38	8/11	–
1941	6,941	8/6	3,921	47	42	8/–	–
1942	7,664	10/–	3,138	48	45	7/5	–
1943	8,171	10/–	3,138	50	47	7/2	–
1944	8,366	10/–	3,138	51	47	7/–	–
1945	8,340	10/–	3,138	53	49	6/10	–
1946	7,974	10/–	3,138	58	51	6/7	–
1947	8,587	9/–	3,637	67	54	6/2	–
1948	9,669	9/–	3,501	63	57	5/9	72
1949	10,240	9/–	3,587	66	59	5/7	73
1950	10,784	9/–	3,587	71	61	5/5	75
1951	11,857	9/–	3,598	80	67	5/–	78
1952	12,763	9/6	3,361	84	73	4/8	78
1953	13,766	9/6	3,411	84	75	4/8	81
1954	14,573	9/–	3,646	83	76	4/7	84
1955	15,511	9/–	3,646	86	80	4/5	86
1956	16,861	8/6	3,873	89	84	4/2	87
1957	17,863	8/6	3,873	92	87	4/1	89
1958	18,615	8/6	4,341	93	90	4/–	88
1959	19,559	8/6	4,341	93	90	4/–	90
1960	20,809	7/9	4,648	94	91	3/11	94
1961	22,268	7/9	4,648	97	94	3/10	97
1962	23,267	7/9	4,648	99	98	3/8	97
1963	24,810	7/9	4,648	100	100	3/7	100
1964	26,953	7/9	4,845	103	103	3/6	105
1965	28,807	8/3	5,922	107	108	3/5	107
1966	30,423	8/3	5,922	110	112	3/3	108
1967	32,037	8/3	5,715	111	115	3/2	111
1968	34,177	8/3	5,715	115	121	3/–	114
1969	36,056	8/3	5,715	120	127	2/10	116
1970	39,567	7/9	5,715	128	135	2/8	118
1971	44,674	38.75%	6,188	140	148	12.5p	121
1972	49,984	38.75%	6,141	147	159	11.5p	122
1973	58,588	30%	6,377	158	173	10.5p	130
1974	67,379	33%	6,088	195	201	9p	129
1975	83,958	35%	5,930	242	250	7.5p	127
1976	99,504	35%	5,966	281	291	6.5p	132
1977	111,285	34%	6,580	335	337	5.5p	134
1978	128,001	33%	7,013	365	365	5p	138
1979	146,586	30%	7,387	–	414	4.5p	141
1980	167,042	30%	7,413	–	488	3.5p	138
1981	181,179	30%	7,413	–	546	3.5p	137
1982	206,192	30%	7,470	–	593	3p	139

ᵃ Changes in sources at 1914 and 1947.

	Net National Income (at factor cost)[a] (£m) 1	Income Tax (Standard rate in £) 2	Amount Retained of Bachelor's £10,000 earned income after Income Tax and Surtax 3	Wholesale PriceIndex Number (1963 = 100) 4	Retail PriceIndex Number (1963 = 100) 5	Purchasing Power of £ (1900 = £1) 6	Real gross domestic product per head (1963 = 100) 7
1983	227,905	30%	7,536	–	620	3p	143
1984	246,239	30%	7,602	–	651	3p	146
1985	268,315	30%	7,661	–	691	3p	152
1986	287,809	29%	7,777	–	714	3p	158
1987	316,271	27%	7,955	–	744	2.5p	165
1988	353,229	25%	8,151	–	781	2.5p	173
1989	388,467	25%	8,196	–	841	2.5p	177
1990	419,316	25%	8,251	–	921	2p	178
1991	433,047	25%	8,324	–	975	2p	173
1992	458,771	25%	8,461	–	1015	2p	171
1993	485,112	25%	8,486	–	1031	2p	174
1994	521,504	25%	8,511	–	1056	1.5p	182
1995	542,996	25%	8,541	–	1093	1.5p	186
1996	575,196	24%	8,660	–	1119	1.5p	190
1997		23%	8,753	–	1149	1.5p	196
1998		23%				1.5p	

[a] Changes in sources at 1914 and 1947.

Sources:
1. 1990–14, C.H.Feinstein, 'Income and Investment in the U.K. 1856–1914', *Economic Journal*, June 1961. 1914–46, A.R.Prest, 'National Income of the U.K. 1870–1946', *Economic Journal*, March 1948. 1947 to 1985, *National Income and Expenditure* Annual Blue Books, renamed since 1985 *United Kingdom National Accounts* Annual Blue Books.
2. and 3. *Reports of the Commissioners for Inland Revenue* and *Inland Revenue Statistics*.
4. and 5. *The British Economy: Key Statistics 1900–1970* and *Annual Abstract of Statistics*.
6. 1900–14 based on unofficial price index compiled by G.H.Wood, in W.T.Layton and G.Crowther, *An Introduction to the Study of Prices* (1938); 1914–38 based on Ministry of Labour *Cost of Living Index (Min. of Labour Gazette)*; 1938 onwards based on figures in the *Annual Abstract of Statistics*.
7. Based on *The British Economy: Key Statistics 1900–1970* and *Economic Trends*.

PRODUCTION AND INTEREST RATES

	Index Number of Industrial Production (1963 = 100)	Steel[a] Production (000s)	Car Production (000s)	Coal[b] Production (000s)	Raw Cotton Consumption[c] (m.lbs)	Agriculture[d] Output (1963 = 100)	Employment (000s)	Price of 2.5% Consols (Ave for year)	Bank Rate % (Max and Min for year)	
	1	2	3	4	5	6	7	8	9	
1900	27	4,900	–	225	1,737	52	2,243	99.6	6	3
1901	27	4,900	–	219	1,569	52	–	94.3	5	3
1902	28	4,910	–	227	1,633	53	–	94.4	4	3
1903	28	5,030	–	230	1,617	52	–	90.8	4	3
1904	28	5,030	–	232	1,486	52	–	88.3	4	3
1905	28	5,810	–	236	1,813	54	–	89.8	3	2.5
1906	29	6,460	–	251	1,855	54	–	88.3	6	3.5
1907	30	6,520	–	268	1,985	53	–	84.1	7	4
1908	28	5,290	–	262	1,917	53	–	86.0	7	2.5
1909	29	5,880	–	264	1,824	55	–	83.9	5	2.5
1910	29	6,370	–	264	1,632	56	–	81.1	5	3
1911	30	6,460	–	272	1,892	54	2,205	79.3	4	3.5
1912	31	6,800	–	260	2,142	55	–	76.2	5	3
1913	33	7,664	–	287	2,178	56	–	73.6	5	4.5
1914	31	7,835	–	266	2,077	54	–	74.8	10	3
1915	–	8,550	–	253	1,931	–	–	65.5	5	5
1916	–	8,992	–	256	1,972	–	–	58.0	6	5
1917	–	9,717	–	249	1,800	–	–	54.7	6	5
1918	–	9,539	–	228	1,499	–	–	56.9	5	5
1919	30	7,894	–	230	1,526	51	–	54.1	6	5
1920	33	9,067	–	230	1,726	49	1,553	47.0	7	6
1921	27	3,703	–	163	1,066	50	1,488	48.0	7	5
1922	31	5,801	–	250	1,409	50	1,453	56.5	5	3
1923	33	8,482	71	276	1,362	52	1,415	58.0	4	3
1924	36	8,201	117	267	1,369	50	1,423	57.0	4	
1925	38	7,385	132	243	1,609	53	1,420	56.3	5	4
1926	36	3,596	154	126	1,509	55	1,407	55.0	5	5
1927	41	9,097	165	251	1,557	55	1,389	54.8	5	4.5
1928	40	8,520	165	238	1,520	58	1,380	55.9	4.5	4.5
1929	42	9,636	182	258	1,498	58	1,372	54.3	6	4.5
1930	40	7,326	170	244	1,272	60	1,340	55.8	5	3
1931	38	5,203	159	220	985	54	1,312	56.9	6	2.5
1932	37	5,261	171	209	1,257	57	1,300	66.8	6	2
1933	46	7,024	221	207	1,177	62	1,296	73.7	2	2
1934	44	8,850	257	221	1,322	62	1,279	80.6	2	2
1935	47	9,859	338	222	1,261	60	1,260	86.6	2	2
1936	52	11,785	354	228	1,366	60	1,232	85.1	2	2
1937	55	12,984	390	240	1,431	59	1,213	76.3	2	2
1938	53	10,398	341	227	1,109	58	1,180	74.1	2	2
1939	–	13,221	305	231	1,317	–	1,168	67.2	4	2
1940	–	12,975	2	224	1,389	–	1,128	73.5	2	2
1941	–	12,312	5	206	965	–	1,177	80.0	2	2

[a] Great Britain only.

[b] Including S. Ireland, 1900–21 inclusive.

[c] From 1958 a revised bale weight was used in calculations.

[d] Including forestry and fishing. From 1978 onwards the figures include only employees and not the farmers themselves.

	Index Number of Industrial Production (1963 = 100) 1	Steel[a] Production (000s) 2	Car Production (000s) 3	Coal[b] Production (000s) 4	Raw Cotton Consumption[c] (m.lbs) 5	Agriculture[d] Output (1963 = 100) 6	Agriculture[d] Employment (000s) 7	Price of 2.5% Consols (Ave for year) 8	Bank Rate % (Max and Min for year) 9	
1942	–	12,942	5	205	939	–	1,192	82.6	2	2
1943	–	13,031	2	199	885	–	1,235	80.7	2	2
1944	–	12,142	2	193	804	–	1,226	79.6	2	2
1945	–	11,824	17	183	717	–	1,207	85.5	2	2
1946	55	12,695	219	190	813	65	1,240	96.3	2	2
1947	58	12,725	287	197	815	62	1,231	90.7	2	2
1948	62	14,877	335	209	977	67	1,274	78.0	2	2
1949	66	15,553	412	215	979	72	1,274	75.9	2	2
1950	70	16,293	523	216	1,017	73	1,258	70.5	2	2
1951	72	15,639	476	223	1,024	75	1,232	66.1	2.5	2
1952	71	16,418	448	227	686	77	1,203	59.1	4	2.5
1953	75	17,609	595	224	831	79	1,177	61.3	4	3.5
1954	79	18,520	769	224	892	81	1,164	66.6	3.5	3
1955	83	19,791	898	222	778	80	1,155	60.0	4.5	3
1956	83	20,659	708	222	714	84	1,121	52.8	5.5	4.5
1957	85	21,699	861	224	744	86	1,111	50.2	7	5.5
1958	84	19,566	1052	216	628	84	1,091	50.2	7	4
1959	88	20,186	1190	206	623	87	1,044	51.8	4	4
1960	95	24,305	1353	194	599	93	1,017	46.1	6	4
1961	96	22,086	1004	192	536	93	985	46.1	7	5
1962	97	20,491	1249	199	473	96	951	40.7	6	4.5
1963	100	22,520	1607	197	483	100	929	44.8	4.5	4
1964	108	26,230	1868	195	508	104	890	41.5	7	4
1965	112	27,006	1722	187	492	107	846	39.0	7	6
1966	114	24,315	1604	175	454	106	814	36.7	7	6
1967	115	23,895	1552	175	384	110	789	37.4	8	5.5
1968	122	25,862	1816	167	382	109	757	33.8	8	7
1969	125	26,422	1717	153	376	110	727	28.2	8	7
1970	125	27,868	1641	145	366	116	707	27.3	7.5	7
1971	126	23,792	1742	147	316	123	–	27.6	7	5
1972	128	24,921	1941	120	291	126	709	27.5	9	5
1973	138	26,228	1747	130	278	130	713	23.2	13	7.5
1974	133	22,072	1534	109	245	131	681	16.8	13	11.5
1975	126	19,879	1268	127	218	119	664	17.1	11.75	9.75
1976	129	21,922	1333	122	249	110	660	17.6	15	9
1977	134	20,088	1304	120	212	130	658	20.4	14.25	5
1978	139	19,989	1223	122	184	138	366	21.0	12.5	6.5
1979	144	21,125	1070	121	192	137	350	22.1	17	12
1980	135	11,077	924	128	138	151	345	21.1	17	14
1981	128	15,573	955	125	101	152	334	19.3	16	12
1982	131	13,705	888	122	101	167	331	21.4	14.5	9
1983	134	14,986	1045	116	101	159	326	24.5	11	9
1984	135	15,121	909	50	99	190	320	24.7	12	8.5

[a] Great Britain only.
[b] Including S. Ireland, 1900–21 inclusive.
[c] From 1958 a revised bale weight was used in calculations.
[d] Including forestry and fishing. From 1978 onwards the figures include only employees and not the farmers themselves.

	Index Number of Industrial Production (1963 = 100) 1	Steel[a] Production (000s) 2	Car Production (000s) 3	Coal[b] Production (000s) 4	Raw Cotton Consumption[c] (m.lbs) 5	Agriculture[d]		Price of 2.5% Consols (Ave for year) 8	Bank Rate % (Max and Min for year) 9	
						Output (1963 = 100) 6	Employment (000s) 7			
1985	142	15,722	1048	91	99	180	321	24.8	14	9.5
1986	145	14,725	1019	105	105	180	310	26.4	12.5	10
1987	150	17,414	1143	102	114	175	302	27.7	11	8.5
1988	155	18,950	1227	102	94	172	293	27.4	13	7.5
1989	156	18,740	1299	99	83	182	280	27.1	15	13
1990	155	17,841	1296	92	67	188	277	23.1	15	14
1991	151	16,474	1237	93	45	195	268	25.1	14	10.5
1992	151	16,212	1291	84	31	202	260	27.3	12	7
1993	155	16,625	1376	68	13	186	255	31.1	7	5.5
1994	163	17,286	1467	49	–	185	243	29.9	6.25	5.25
1995	166	17,604	1532	53	–	183	241	29.8	6.75	6.25
1996	168	17,992	1686	50	–	179	238	30.6	6.5	5.75
1997	169	18,489	1698	48	–	–	235	34.9	7.25	6
1998	170	17,318	1748	41	–	–	–	43.3	7.5	6.25
1999	168	–	–	–	–	–	–	52.9	6.25	5.25

[a] Great Britain only.

[b] Including S. Ireland, 1900–21 inclusive.

[c] From 1958 a revised bale weight was used in calculations.

[d] Including forestry and fishing. From 1978 onwards the figures include only employees and not the farmers themselves.

Sources:

1. *The British Economy, Key Statistics 1900–1970* and *Annual Abstract of Statistics*.

2. British Iron and Steel Federation, *Annual Abstract of Statistics*.

3. B. R. Mitchell, *British Historical Statistics* (1988). *Annual Abstract of Statistics*.

4. Department of Trade and Industry, *Annual Abstract of Statistics*.

5. R. Robson, *The Cotton Industry in Britain* (1957), p.332. *Annual Abstract of Statistics*.

6 and 7. *The British Economy, Key Statistics 1900–1970* and *Annual Abstract of Statistics*. 1972 onwards *Economic Trends*.

8 and 9. Bank of England and *Annual Abstract of Statistics*.

INTERNATIONAL TRADE FIGURES

	Net Balance of Payments Current account[a] (£m)	Imports and Exports of the U.K.			Volume Indices		Foreign Exchange Rates			
		Terms of Trade Index[b] (1963 = 100)	Imports cif[c] (£m)	Exports of UK[c] Products (m)	Re-exports f.o.b (m)	Imports[d]	Exports	USA ($)	France (Francs)	Germany (Marks)	Japan (Yen)
	1	2	3	4	5	6	7	8	9	10	
1900		72	523	291	63	48	44	4.84	25.1	20.4	
1901		71	522	280	68	49	44	4.85	25.2	20.4	
1902		69	528	283	66	51	47	4.85	25.2	20.5	
1903		67	543	291	70	51	48	4.85	25.1	20.4	
1904		69	551	301	70	52	49	4.85	25.2	20.4	
1905		68	565	330	78	53	54	4.85	25.2	20.5	
1906		68	608	376	85	54	58	4.82	25.1	20.5	
1907		68	646	426	92	55	63	4.84	25.1	20.5	
1908		69	593	377	80	53	58	4.85	25.1	20.4	
1909		65	625	378	91	54	60	4.86	25.2	20.4	
1910		65	678	430	104	56	65	4.84	25.2	20.4	
1911		67	680	454	103	57	68	4.84	25.3	20.4	
1912		66	745	487	112	61	72	4.85	25.2	20.5	
1913	237	69	769	525	110	64	75	4.83	25.2	20.4	
1914		–	697	431	95	–	–	4.87	25.2	20.5	
1915		–	852	385	99	–	–	4.77	26.3	–	
1916		–	949	506	98	–	–	4.76	28.2	–	
1917		–	1,064	527	70	–	–	4.76	27.4	–	
1918		–	1,316	501	31	–	–	4.76	27.2	–	
1919	–128	79	1,626	799	165	56	41	4.60	29.7	–	
1920	235	86	1,933	1,334	223	56	53	3.97	47.9	145	
1921	119	87	1,086	703	107	47	37	3.73	46.7	268	
1922	173	90	1,003	720	104	54	51	4.41	52.8	1,654	
1923	169	89	1,096	767	119	59	56	4.58	75.2 720,000		
1924	72	86	1,277	801	140	66	57	4.33	81.8	18 bn.	
1925	46	85	1,321	773	154	69	56	4.86	106.1	20.4	
1926	–15	87	1,241	653	125	70	50	4.87	167.5	20.4	
1927	82	86	1,218	709	123	72	58	4.85	124.0	20.5	
1928	123	82	1,196	724	120	69	60	4.87	124.2	20.4	
1929	103	85	1,221	729	110	73	61	4.84	124.0	20.4	
1930	28	92	1,044	571	87	71	50	4.86	123.7	20.4	
1931	–104	102	861	391	64	72	38	4.86	124.2	20.5	
1932	–51	102	702	365	51	63	38	3.58	91.1	15.0	
1933	–	104	675	368	49	63	39	4.30	86.2	14.3	
1934	–77	103	731	396	51	66	41	5.04	76.6	13.3	
1935	32	100	756	426	55	67	45	4.94	74.5	12.2	
1936	–18	99	848	441	61	72	45	5.01	75.7	12.4	
1937	–56	93	1,028	521	75	76	49	4.94	120	12.3	
1938	–70	102	920	471	62	72	43	4.95	178	12.3	
1939	–250	99	886	440	46	69	40	4.68	177	11.7	

[a] Changes in sources and methods in 1924.

[b] Export price index as a percentage of import price index. A fall indicates an adverse price movement.

[c] 1900–22 inclusive, S.Ireland is included. From 1923 direct foreign trade of S.Ireland is excluded, and imports and exports include trade of Great Britain and N.Ireland with S.Ireland. There are small changes in coverage from time to time.

[d] 1900–23 inclusive, including S. Ireland.

	Net Balance of Payments Current account[a] (£m)	Imports and Exports of the U.K.				Volume Indices		Foreign Exchange Rates			
		Terms of Trade Index[b] (1963 = 100)	Imports cif[c] (£m)	Exports of UK[c] Products (m)	Reexports f.o.b (m)	Imports[d]	Exports	USA ($)	France (Francs)	Germany (Marks)	Japan (Yen)
	1	2	3	4	5	6	7	8	9	10	
1940	−804	85	1,152	411	26	61	31	4.03	177	−	
1941	−816	93	1,145	365	13	50	21	4.03	−	−	
1942	−663	94	997	271	5	47	16	4.03	−	−	
1943	−680	94	1,234	234	6	50	12	4.03	−	−	
1944	−659	100	1,309	266	16	54	13	4.03	−	−	
1945	−875	94	1,104	399	51	44	20	4.03	203.8		
1946	−230	95	1,298	912	50	49	43	4.03	480.0		
1947	−381	88	1,798	1,142	59	55	47	4.03	480.0		
1948	26	85	2,075	1,578	61	57	60	4.03	f	−	
1949	−1	86	2,279	1,789	58	61	66	e	g	−	
1950	307	80	2,609	2,174	85	61	75	2.80	980.0	−	
1951	−369	73	3,905	2,582	127	69	74	2.80	979.7		
1952	163	80	3,456	2,567	142	63	69	2.79	981.5	West Germany only	
1953	145	87	3,328	2,558	103	68	71	2.81	982.8	11.7	
1954	117	87	3,359	2,650	98	69	74	2.81	981.6	11.7	
1955	−155	84	3,861	2,877	116	76	80	2.79	978.1	11.7	
1956	208	86	3,862	3,143	144	75	84	2.80	982.7	11.7	
1957	233	87	4,044	3,295	130	78	86	2.79	h	11.7	
1958	346	95	3,748	3,176	141	79	83	2.81	i	11.7	
1959	158	97	3,983	3,330	131	84	86	2.81	13.77[j]	11.7	
1960	−244	97	4,557	3,536	141	94	90	2.81	13.77	11.7	
1961	27	99	4,398	3,682	158	93	93	2.80	13.74	11.17	
1962	130	101	4,492	3,792	158	96	95	2.81	13.76	11.22	
1963	129	100	4,820	4,080	154	100	100	2.80	13.72	11.16	
1964	−358	99	5,696	4,412	153	111	103	2.79	13.68	11.10	
1965	−45	101	5,751	4,724	173	111	108	2.80	13.70	11.17	
1966	109	103	5,949	5,047	194	114	112	2.79	13.72	11.17	
1967	−294	104	6,437	5,029	185	123	111	2.79[k]	13.68[l]	11.10[m]	
1968	−286	101	7,897	6,182	220	136	126	2.39	11.86	9.56	
1969	463	101	8,315	7,039	259	138	140	2.39	12.43[n]	9.38	
1970	731	103	9,051	7,741	323	144	143	2.40	13.24	8.74	
1971	1,090	104	9,799	9,071		153	154	2.44	13.47	8.61	864[o]

[a] Changes in sources and methods in 1924.

[b] Export price index as a percentage of import price index. A fall indicates an adverse price movement.

[c] 1900–22 inclusive, S.Ireland is included. From 1923 direct foreign trade of S.Ireland is excluded, and imports and exports include trade of Great Britain and N.Ireland with S.Ireland. There are small changes in coverage from time to time.

[d] 1900–23 inclusive, including S. Ireland.

[e] 4.03 to 19 Sep, 2.80 thereafter.

[f] 480 to 25 Jan, 864 from 26 Jan to 17 Oct, 1,062 thereafter.

[g] 1,062 to 26 Apr, 1,097 from 27 Apr to 20 Sep, 980 thereafter.

[h] 984.9 to 19 Aug, 1,117.1 thereafter.

[i] 1,775.5 to 24 Dec, 13,74 from 29 Dec (in units of 100 francs).

[j] In units of 100 francs (100 francs = 1 New Franc).

[k] 2.79 to 18 Nov, 2.40 thereafter.

[l] 13.68 to 18 Nov, 11.88 thereafter.

[m] 11.10 to 18 Nov, 9.50 thereafter.

[n] 11.86 to 11 Aug, 13.31 thereafter.

[o] 864 to 13 Aug, 811 to 17 Dec, 803 therafter.

	Net Balance of Payments	Imports and Exports of the U.K.			Volume Indices		Foreign Exchange Rates			
	Current account[a]	Terms of Trade Index[b]	Imports cif[c]	Exports of UK[c] Products	Reexports f.o.b	Imports[d]	Exports	USA ($)	France (Francs)	Germany (Marks)	Japan (Yen)
	(£m)	(1963 = 100)	(£m)	(m)	(m)						
	1	2	3	4	5	6	7	8	9	10	
1972	135	106	11,073	9,602		171	154	2.50	12.61	7.97	794[p]
1973	−979	93	15,724	12,087		195	175	2.45	10.90	6.54	665
1974	−3,278	81	23,139	16,309		196	187	2.34	11.25	6.05	683
1975	−1,523	87	24,046	19,607		179	180	2.22	9.50	5.45	658
1976	−846	85	31,084	25,277		190	197	1.80	8.61	4.55	535
1977	53	87	36,219	31,990		193	213	1.75	8.57	4.05	468
1978	1,162	92	39,533	35,330		202	218	1.92	8.65	3.85	403
1979	−525	96	46,925	40,637		224	229	2.12	9.03	3.89	466
1980	3,629	100	49,773	47,364		212	231	2.33	9.83	4.23	526
1981	7,221	100	51,169	50,998		204	229	2.03	10.94	4.56	445
1982	4,034	99	56,978	55,558		213	234	1.75	11.48	4.24	435
1983	3,336	98	66,101	60,684		233	236	1.52	11.55	3.87	360
1984	1,473	97	78,967	70,488		259	255	1.34	11.64	3.79	317
1985	2,888	97	85,027	78,392		268	273	1.30	11.55	3.78	307
1986	−2,265	92	82,614	72,997		287	284	1.47	10.16	3.18	247
1987	−5,583	93	91,229	79,531		309	301	1.64	9.84	2.94	237
1988	−17,537	94	102,264	80,711		351	308	1.78	10.60	3.12	228
1989	−23,491	94	117,335	92,611		380	326	1.64	10.45	3.08	226
1990	−19,513	95	121,020	102,313		380	346	1.79	9.69	2.88	257
1991	−8,374	95	114,162	103,939		360	350	1.77	9.95	2.93	238
1992	−10,082	97	120,913	107,863		383	358	1.77	9.32	2.75	224
1993	−19,618	99	135,358	122,039		399	371	1.50	8.51	2.48	167
1994	−1,458	98	146,351	135,260		416	409	1.53	8.49	2.48	156
1995	−3,745	95	165,449	153,725		440	448	1.58	7.87	2.26	148
1996	−600	96	180,489	167,403		479	483	1.56	7.99	2.35	170
1997	6,303	97	183,590	171,798		523	522	1.64	9.56	2.84	198
1998	1,474	97						1.66	9.77	2.91	217

[a] Changes in sources and methods in 1924.

[b] Export price index as a percentage of import price index. A fall indicates an adverse price movement.

[c] 1900–22 inclusive, S.Ireland is included. From 1923 direct foreign trade of S.Ireland is excluded, and imports and exports include trade of Great Britain and N.Ireland with S.Ireland. There are small changes in coverage from time to time.

[d] 1900–23 inclusive, including S. Ireland.

[e] 4.03 to 19 Sep, 2.80 thereafter.

[f] 480 to 25 Jan, 864 from 26 Jan to 17 Oct, 1,062 thereafter.

[g] 1,062 to 26 Apr, 1,097 from 27 Apr to 20 Sep, 980 thereafter.

[h] 984.9 to 19 Aug, 1,117.1 thereafter.

[i] 1,775.5 to 24 Dec, 13,74 from 29 Dec (in units of 100 francs).

[j] In units of 100 francs (100 francs = 1 New Franc).

[k] 2.79 to 18 Nov, 2.40 thereafter.

[l] 13.68 to 18 Nov, 11.88 thereafter.

[m] 11.10 to 18 Nov, 9.50 thereafter.

[n] 11.86 to 11 Aug, 13.31 thereafter.

[o] 864 to 13 Aug, 811 to 17 Dec, 803 therafter.

[p] 794 to 23 Jun, 713 thereafter.

Sources:

1. *Key Statistics* and *Balance of Payments Pink Books*.

2. *The British Economy, Key Statistics 1900–1970*.

3, 4 and 5. *Trade and Navigation Accounts of the UK*, Board of Trade, annually. From 1965, *Overseas Trade Accounts of the UK*.

6 and 7. *The British Economy, Key Statistics 1900–1970. Annual Abstract of Statistics*.

8, 9 and 10. 1900–1939, *The Economist*, figures for the end of June; 1940–1970 *Annual Abstract of Statistics*. 1970– *Financial Statistics*.

CENTRAL GOVERNMENT REVENUE

	Total Central Government Revenue[a] (£m) 1	Income Tax[b] (£m) 2	Main Sources of Revenue					
			Surtax (£m) 3	Profits (Corporation) Tax (£m) 4	Customs & Excise (£m) 5	Death Duties (£m) 6	Capital Gains Tax (£m) 7	Capital Transfer (Inheritance) Tax (£m) 8
1900	140	28	–	–	65	17		
1901	153	35	–	–	68	19		
1902	161	39	–	–	72	18		
1903	151	31	–	–	71	17		
1904	153	31	–	–	72	17		
1905	154	31	–	–	70	17		
1906	155	31	–	–	69	19		
1907	157	31	–	–	68	19		
1908	152	34	–	–	63	18		
1909	132	13	–	–	61	22		
1910	204	60	3	–	73	25		
1911	185	42	3	–	72	25		
1912	189	41	4	–	71	25		
1913	198	44	3	–	85	27		
1914	227	59	10	–	81	28		
1915	337	112	17	–	121	31		
1916	573	186	19	140	127	31		
1917	707	216	23	220	110	32		
1918	889	256	36	285	162	30		
1919	1,340	317	42	290	283	41		
1920	1,426	339	55	220	334	48		
1921	1,125	337	62	48	324	52		
1922	914	315	64	21	280	57		
1923	837	269	61	23	268	58		
1924	799	274	63	19	234	59		
1925	812	259	69	14	238	61		
1926	806	235	66	8	240	67		
1927	843	251	61	2	251	77		
1928	836	238	56	2	253	81		
1929	815	238	56	2	247	80		
1930	858	256	68	3	245	83		
1931	851	287	77	2	256	65		
1932	827	252	61	2	288	77		
1933	809	229	53	2	286	85		
1934	805	229	51	2	290	81		
1935	845	238	51	1	303	88		
1936	897	257	54	1	321	88		
1937	949	298	57	1	335	89		
1938	1,006	336	63	22	340	77		

[a] Total national revenue includes ordinary and self-balancing revenue. Figures relate to year ending 31 Mar the following year.
[b] 1900–1910 'Income Tax' includes Property and Income Tax. 1910 figure includes arrears for 1909.

	Total Central Government Revenue[a] (£m) 1	Income Tax[b] (£m) 2	Main Sources of Revenue						
			Profits Surtax (Corporation) Tax (£m) 3	(£m) 4	Customs & Excise (£m) 5	Death Duties (£m) 6	Capital Gains Tax[d] (£m) 7	Capital Transfer (Inheritance) Tax (£m) 8	General Govt. Receipts as % of GDP 9
1939	1,132	390	70	27	400	78			
1940	1,495	524	76	96	529	81			
1941	2,175	770	75	269	704	91			
1942	2,922	1,007	75	378	885	93			
1943	3,149	1,184	76	500	1,043	100			
1944	3,355	1,317	74	510	1,076	111			
1945	3,401	1,361	69	466	1,111	120			
1946	3,623	1,156	76	357	1,184	148			
1947	4,011	1,189	91	289	1,421	172			
1948	1,168	1,368	98	279	1,557	177			
1949	4,098	1,438	115	297	1,520	190			
1950	4,157	1,404	121	268	1,630	185			
1951	4,629	1,669	130	315	1,752	183			
1952	4,654	1,736	131	376	1,764	152			
1953	4,606	1,731	132	188	1,764	165			
1954	4,987	1,893	135	173	1,872	188			
1955	5,160	1,943	139	193	2,014	176			
1956	5,462	2,114	158	195	2,101	169			
1957	5,679	2,208	157	251	2,149	171			
1958	5,850	2,322	167	274	2,191	187			
1959	6,016	2,243	181	261	2,282	227			
1960	6,344	2,433	189	263	2,390	236			
1961	6,644	2,727	224	335	2,595	262	–	–	
1962	6,794	2,818	184	383	2,668	270	–	–	
1963	6,890	2,745	177	390	2,766	310	–	–	
1964	8,157	3,088	184	423	3,174	297	–	–	
1965	9,144	3,678	203	438	3,401	292	–	–	
1966	10,219	3,246	242	1,118[c]	3,536	301	7	–	
1967	11,177	3,826	239	1,253[c]	3,721	330	15	–	
1968	13,363	4,337	225	1,354[c]	4,601	382	47	–	
1969	15,266	4,900	255	1,689	4,933	365	127	–	
1970	15,843	5,728	248	1,591	4,709	357	139	–	40.3
1971	16,932	6,449	348	1,560	5,325	451	156	–	39.9
1972	17,178	6,475	341	1,533	5,744	459	208	–	37.9
1973	18,226	7,136	307	2,263	6,220	412	324	–	38.5
1974	23,570	10,239	186	2,851	7,407	338	380	–	40.5
1975	29,417	15,054	109	1,998	9,176	212[d]	387	118[d]	40.2
1976	33,778	17,013	62	2,655	10,900	124[d]	323	260[d]	41.0
1977	38,773	17,420	30	3,343	12,284	87[d]	340	310[d]	39.7
1978	43,088	18,748	15	3,940	13,835	46[d]	353	317[d]	38.7

[a] Total national revenue includes ordinary and self-balancing revenue. Figures relate to year ending 31 Mar the following year.
[b] 1900–1910 'Income Tax' includes Property and Income Tax. 1910 figure includes arrears for 1909.
[c] Corporation tax replaced Profits Tax and Income Tax on Companies from 1966. Some Profits Tax is included in the figures for subsequent tax years (negligible by 1968).
[d] Capital Transfer Tax began to replace Estate Duty in 1975. It was renamed Inheritance Tax in 1986.

	Total Central Government Revenue[a] (£m) 1	Income Tax[b] (£m) 2	Surtax (£m) 3	Profits (Corporation) Tax (£m) 4	Customs & Excise (£m) 5	Death Duties (£m) 6	Capital Gains Tax[d] (£m) 7	Capital Transfer (Inheritance) Tax (£m) 8	General Govt. Receipts as % of GDP 9
1979	54,331	20,599	11	4,646	18,032	32[d]	431	404[d]	38.8
1980	66,213	24,295	5	4,645	22,095	27[d]	508	423[d]	40.7
1981	76,754	28,725	4	4,926	25,248	17[d]	525	480[d]	43.7
1982	83,270	30,474	2	5,564	27,895	12[d]	632	499[d]	43.7
1983	88,364	31,306	2	6,011	31,435	9[d]	671	571[d]	42.9
1984	95,194	32,063	1	7,124	33,883	6[d]	694	652[d]	43.4
1985	104,193	33,965	–	9,485	37,770	8[d]	855	846[d]	42.3
1986	110,867	39,283	–	12,647	40,259	–	971	939[d]	41.4
1987	122,969	40,040	–	14,510	44,736	–	1,230	1,053	41.1
1988	133,593	43,268	–	17,303	49,566	–	2,172	1,068	40.3
1989	144,926	46,546	–	22,430	52,190	–	2,002	1,171	40.1
1990	162,366	53,739	–	22,062	55,336	–	1,892	1,315	39.3
1991	171,475	57,417	–	19,346	61,827	–	1,359	1,263	38.3
1992	173,041	57,570	–	16,184	63,398	–	1,073	1,227	36.7
1993	170,059	57,363[e]	–	15,284	66,885	–	788	1,268	35.9
1994	191,272	62,701	–	17,657	71,342	–		1,438	36.9
1995	201,093	67,725	–	22,755	76,363	–		1,441	38.0
1996	210,432	68,593	–	26,984	81,252	–		1,621	38.1
1997	225,451	70,381	–	30,394	87,271	–		1,601	39.3
1998	247,320	86,639			31,236	92,866	–	1,793	39.6

[a] Total national revenue includes ordinary and self-balancing revenue. Figures relate to year ending 31 Mar the following year.

[b] 1900–1910 'Income Tax' includes Property and Income Tax. 1910 figure includes arrears for 1909.

[c] Corporation tax replaced Profits Tax and Income Tax on Companies from 1966. Some Profits Tax is included in the figures for subsequent tax years (negligible by 1968).

[d] Capital Transfer Tax began to replace Estate Duty in 1975. It was renamed Inheritance Tax in 1986.

[e] Capital Gains Tax revenue included in Income Tax total from 1993.

Source: *Annual Abstract of Statistics* and *Financial Statistics*.

GOVERNMENT EXPENDITURE AND TARIFFS

	Main Heads of Expenditure			Specimen Tariffs			
	Defence (£m) 1	Health, Labour and Insurance[a] (£m) 2	Pensions[b] (£m) 3	Sugar[c] (per cwt) s.d. 4	Tea[c] (per lb.) s.d. 5	Excise Duty on Beer[d] (per barrel of 36 gallons) s.d. 6	National Debt[e] (£m) 7
1900	121	–	–	–	6	6/9	628–9
1901	124	–	–	4/2	6	7/9	689–5
1902	101	–	–	4/2	6	7/9	745–0
1903	72	–	–	4/2	6	7/9	770–8
1904	66	–	–	4/2	8	7/9	762–6
1905	62	–	–	4/2	6	7/9	755–1
1906	59	–	–	4/2	5	7/9	743.3
1907	58	–	–	4/2	5	7/9	724.5
1908	59	–	–	1/10	5	7/9	709.0
1909	63	–	–	1/10	5	7/9	702.7
1910	67	–	–	1/10	5	7/9	713.2
1911	70	–	–	1/10	5	7/9	685.2
1912	72	–	–	1/10	5	7/9	668.3
1913	77	14	1	1/10	5	7/9	656.5
1914	437	14	1	1/10	5	7/9	649.8
1915	1,424	14	1	1/10	8	23/–	1,105.0
1916	2,007	14	1	14/–	1/–	24/–	2,133
1917	2,436	14	1	14/–	1/–	25/–	4,011
1918	2,238	15	1	25/8	1/–	50/–	5,871
1919	692	74	100	25/8	1/–	70/–	7,434
1920	292	73	110	25/8	1/–	100/–	7,828
1921	189	73	96	25/8	1/–	100/–	7,574
1922	111	61	83	25/8	8	100/–	7,654
1923	105	59	72	25/8	8	100/–	7,742
1924	114	65	71	11/8	4	100/–	7,641
1925	119	65	70	11/8	4	100/–	7,597
1926	116	75	65	11/8	4	100/–	7,558
1927	117	73	62	11/8	4	100/–	7,554
1928	113	76	59	11/8	4	100/–	7,527
1929	113	86	56	11/8	–	100/–	7,500
1930	110	108	55	11/8	–	103/–	7,469
1931	107	121	52	11/8	–	103/–	7,413
1932	103	155	49	11/8	4	134/–	7,433
1933	107	151	49	11/8	4	24/–	7,643
1934	113	151	47	11/8	4	24/–	7,822

[a] 1900–13, the system of classification prevents entries comparable with those for later years. 1949–53, figures cover Housing, Local Government, Health, Labour, National Insurance and National Assistance. From 1954 figures cover Health, Housing and Local Government.

[b] 1900–13, the system of classification prevents entries comparable with those for later years. Before 1954, 'Pensions' equivalent to 'non-effective' charges. 1954 onwards figures cover Pensions, National Insurance and National Assistance.

[c] Full Customs duty given. In many cases preferential rates apply to Commonwealth trade. Sugar: exceeding 98° of polarisation.

[d] 1900–32 beer of 1,055° specific gravity. 1933–49 beer of 1,027° specific gravity.

[e] Debt of U.K. Exchequer, debt created by N. Ireland Exchequer excluded. Bonds tendered for death duties and held by National Debt Commissioners excluded from 1920. External debt arising out of 1914–1918 war, excluded from 1935, when it was £1,035.5m at 31 Mar.

	Main Heads of Expenditure			Specimen Tariffs		Excise Duty	
	Defence (£m) 1	Health, Labour and Insurance[a] (£m) 2	Pensions[b] (£m) 3	Sugar[c] (per cwt) s.d. 4	Tea[c] (per lb.) s.d. 5	on Beer[d] (per barrel of 36 gallons) s.d. 6	National Debt[e] (£m) 7
1935	136	162	46	11/8	4	24/–	6,763
1936	186	162	45	11/8	6	24/–	6,759
1937	197	162	44	11/8	6	24/–	6,764
1938	254	166	43	11/8	8	24/–	6,993
1939	626	167	42	11/8	8	24/–	7,130
1940	3,220	165	41	23/4	8	90/–	7,899
1941	4,085	170	41	23/4	8	90/–	10,366
1942	4,840	186	40	23/4	8	118/1	13,041
1943	4,950	199	39	23/4	8	138/4	15,822
1944	5,125	208	40	23/4	8	140/7	18,562
1945	4,410	219	42	23/4	8	140/7	21,365
1946	1,653	334	97	23/4	8	140/7	23,636
1947	854	380	91	23/4	8	140/7	25,630
1948	753	598	96	23/4	8	178/10	25,620
1949	741	806	97	11/8	2	157/10	25,167
1950	777	835	94	11/8	2	155/4	25,802
1951	1,110	810	91	11/8	2	155/4	25,921
1952	1,404	884	100	11/8	2	155/4	25,890
1953	1,365	903	97	11/8	2	155/4	26,051
1954	1,436	619	419	11/8	2	155/4	26,583
1955	1,405	652	433	11/8	2	155/4	26,933
1956	1,525	750	463	11/8	2	155/4	27,038
1957	1,430	782	490	11/8	2	155/4	27,007
1958	1,468	794	575	11/8	2	155/4	27,232
1959	1,475	1,209	610	11/8	2	111/9	27,376
1960	1,596	1,384	634	11/8	2	111/9	27,732
1961	1,689	1,417	659	11/8[f]	2	111/9	28,251
1962	1,767	1,549	705	–	2	123/–	28,674
1963	1,792	1,716	772	–	2[g]	123/–	29,847
1964	1,909	1,897	792	–	–	147/–	30,226
1965	2,055	–[h]	–[h]	–	–	171/–	30,440
1966	2,145	–	–	–	–	171/–	31,340
1967	2,274	–	–	–	–	188/8	31,935
1968	2,232	–	–	–	–	188/8	34,193
1969	2,204	–	–	–	–	207/6	33,982

[a] 1900–13, the system of classification prevents entries comparable with those for later years. 1949–53, figures cover Housing, Local Government, Health, Labour, National Insurance and National Assistance. From 1954 figures cover Health, Housing and Local Government.

[b] 1900–13, the system of classification prevents entries comparable with those for later years. Before 1954, 'Pensions' equivalent to 'non-effective' charges. 1954 onwards figures cover Pensions, National Insurance and National Assistance.

[c] Full Customs duty given. In many cases preferential rates apply to Commonwealth trade. Sugar: exceeding 98° of polarisation.

[d] 1900–32 beer of 1,055° specific gravity. 1933–49 beer of 1,027° specific gravity.

[e] Debt of U.K. Exchequer, debt created by N. Ireland Exchequer excluded. Bonds tendered for death duties and held by National Debt Commissioners excluded from 1920. External debt arising out of 1914–1918 war, excluded from 1935, when it was £1,035.5m at 31 Mar.

[f] April 1962; excise duty on sugar was repealed.

[g] June 1963 tariffs on tea ceased to be direct revenue and became chargeable under the Import Duties Act, 1958.

[h] From 1965 onwards figures no longer collected in this form.

| | Main Heads of Expenditure | | | Specimen Tariffs | | | |
	Defence (£m) 1	Health, Labour and Insurance[a] (£m) 2	Pensions[b] (£m) 3	Sugar[c] (per cwt) s.d. 4	Tea[c] (per lb.) s.d. 5	Excise Duty on Beer[d] (per barrel of 36 gallons) s.d. 6	National Debt[e] (£m) 7
1970	2,493	–	–	–	–	207/6	33,079
1971	2,799	–	–	–	–	£1.37	33,441
1972	3,083	–	–	–	–	£10.37	35,839
1973	3,495	–	–	–	–	£6.90[i]	36,910
1974	4,228	–	–	–	–	£9.36[i]	40,124
1975	5,458	–	–	–	–	£13.68[i]	45,925
1976	6,282	–	–	–	–	£15.84[i]	56,581
1977	6,965	–	–	–	–	£17.42[i]	67,165
1978	7,701[j]	–	–	–	–	£17.42[i]	79,179
1979	9,431	–	–	–	–	£21.35	86,884
1980	11,759	–	–	–	–	£29.45	95,314
1981	12,968	–	–	–	–	£33.37	113,036
1982	14,288	–	–	–	–	£33.37	118,390
1983	15,592	–	–	–	–	£35.33	127,727
1984	16,851	–	–	–	–	£39.26	142,885
1985	17,857	–	–	–	–	£42.20	158,127
1986	18,163	–	–	–	–	£42.20	171,456
1987	18,856	–	–	–	–	£42.20	185,796
1988	19,072	–	–	–	–	£44.17	197,441
1989	20,755	–	–	–	–	£44.17	197,232
1990	22,298	–	–	–	–	£47.60	192,553
1991	24,562	–	–	–	–	£52.01	198,698
1992	23,762	–	–	–	–	£54.38	214,528
1993	23,424	–	–	–	–	£57.07	249,127
1994	22,519	–	–	–	–		307,307
1995	21,517	–	–	–	–		349,535
1996	22,341	–	–	–	–		391,171
1997	21,840	–	–	–	–		419,909

[a] 1900–13, the system of classification prevents entries comparable with those for later years. 1949–53, figures cover Housing, Local Government, Health, Labour, National Insurance and National Assistance. From 1954 figures cover Health, Housing and Local Government.

[b] 1900–13, the system of classification prevents entries comparable with those for later years. Before 1954, 'Pensions' equivalent to 'non-effective' charges. 1954 onwards figures cover Pensions, National Insurance and National Assistance.

[c] Full Customs duty given. In many cases preferential rates apply to Commonwealth trade. Sugar: exceeding 98° of polarisation.

[d] 1900–32 beer of 1,055° specific gravity. 1933–49 beer of 1,027° specific gravity.

[e] Debt of U.K. Exchequer, debt created by N. Ireland Exchequer excluded. Bonds tendered for death duties and held by National Debt Commissioners excluded from 1920. External debt arising out of 1914–1918 war, excluded from 1935, when it was £1,035.5m at 31 Mar.

[f] April 1962; excise duty on sugar was repealed.

[g] June 1963 tariffs on tea ceased to be direct revenue and became chargeable under the Import Duties Act, 1958.

[h] From 1965 onwards figures no longer collected in this form.

i Subject to VAT at standard rate from 1 Apr 73.

j From 1978, Defence figures cover expenditure in the year ending in April the following year.

Sources:
1. *Annual Abstract of Statistics*. From 1970 *Financial Statistics*.
2 and 3. *Annual Abstract of Statistics. Central Statistical Office.*
4 and 5. *Customs Tariff of the U.K. (Annual Reports of Commissioners for Customs and Excise).*
6. *Reports of Commissioners for Customs and Excise.*
7. *Finance Accounts of the U.K.*, from 1969 *Consolidated Fund and National Loans Fund Accounts* and *Financial Statistics*.

PERCENTAGE SHARES IN NET NATIONAL INCOME
(BASED ON CURRENT PRICES)
United Kingdom (percentages)

Year	Wages	Salaries	Income from self-employment	Private companies	Gross Trading Profits of: Public corporations	Rent
1900	39.0	10.6		34.6		12.1
1910	41.4	9.1		36.4		12.5
1921	43.6	17.9	13.4	5.7	0.5	5.8
1930	39.4	21.1	14.8	11.3	1.2	8.5
1938	40.8	21.9	13.4	14.3	1.4	9.3
1950	44.8	25.5	12.8	19.6	3.0	4.9
1960	42.8	29.2	9.5	17.7	3.4	5.9
1970	68.6		8.3	12.0	3.5	7.5
1980	68.5		9.0	13.8	3.1	7.1
1990	65.2		12.7	13.5	0.8	8.1

Sources: *National Income and Expenditure*; Blue Books.

SELECTED ITEMS OF CONSUMER EXPENDITURE AS
PERCENTAGES OF TOTAL CONSUMER EXPENDITURE
United Kingdom

Year	Food	Alcohol	Tobacco	Durables	Cars	Clothing
1900	27.3	20.8	3.7	2.5	0.0	10.0
1910	28.7	16.0	4.0	2.5	0.1	10.1
1921	29.9	12.4	6.0	3.4	0.2	9.4
1930	30.2	8.4	5.7	4.7	0.8	9.8
1938	29.0	7.2	6.3	4.7	1.2	9.3
1950	31.1	6.2	6.6	4.0	0.7	9.8
1960	24.9	5.9	7.0	4.8	2.7	9.6
1970	20.3	7.4	5.5	4.3	3.1	8.5
1980	16.7	7.3	3.5	5.1	4.6	7.2
1990	12.0	6.2	2.5	4.5	5.5	6.0
1998	10.3	8.0		4.4	5.4	6.1

INCOME DISTRIBUTION AFTER TAX
United Kingdom
(tax units–000's)

Year	£50–£250	£250–£500	£500–£750	£750–£1000	£1000–£2000	£2000–£6000	£6000–£10000	£10000+
1938	n.a.	1,940	375	132	142	66	7	0
1949	13,040	10,140	2,020	442	368	90	0	0
1959	6,200	7,440	6,630	3,880	2,052	295	3	0
1967	2,338	5,90	5,418	4,822	8,298	954[a]	63[b]	0
1972/3	7,465			4,164	11,138	5,474	101	9
1978/8	1,446				7,580	16,709	2,988	353
1990/1	6,350						7,840	12,101
1996/7	5,122						7,920	14,256

[a] £2000–£5000
[b] £5,000–£10,000

Source: *National Income and Expenditure* Blue Books. *Inland Revenue Statistics.*

DISTRIBUTION OF PERSONAL WEALTH AMONG ADULT[c] POPULATION

Percent of total wealth owned by top groups

Wealth Group	1911–3[a]	1924–30[a]	1936[a]	1951–6[a]	1960[b]	1970[b]	1980[b]	1990[b]	1995[b]
Top 1%	65.5	59.5	56.0	42.0	37.6	29.6	19	18	19
Top 5%	86.0	82.5	81.0	56.7	63.6	54.4	36	35	38
Top 10%	90.0	89.5	88.0	79.8	76.1	70.1	50	47	50
Top 20%	–	96.0	94.0	89.0	–	–	–	–	–
Top 25%	–	–	–	–	93.2	92.9	73	71	73

[a] England and Wales.
[b] Great Britain.
[c] Over 21, 1911–56 Over 18 1960–.

Sources: H. Lydall and D. Tipping 'The Distribution of Personal Wealth in Britain', *Bulletin of the Oxford University Institute of Statistics* (1961); Inland Revenue Statistics (1978).

OUTPUT PER MAN 1900–1970
(1913=100)

	U.K.	U.S.	France	Germany	Italy	Sweden
1900	98.1	79.8	90.0	85.5	77.3	70.1
1913	100.0	100.0	100.0	100.0	100.0	100.0
1929	121.6	126.7	135.6	96.5	126.3	101.6
1938	143.6	136.0	125.7	122.4	145.2	127.5
1950	159.4	177.1	146.1	124.1	153.2	171.1
1960	193.1	217.3	215.8	207.5	229.4	223.6
1970	247.6	271.8	352.8	321.2	418.2	315.1
1970 (U.K.= 100.0)	100.0	251	146	142	100	166

Source: Adapted from A. Maddison, *Economic Growth in the West* (1964) and updated with OECD material.

INDUSTRIAL OUTPUT OF THE U.K.
(Census of Production figures)

	Value of Production (Gross Output) (£m.)
1907[a]	1,765
1924	3,747[b]
1930	3,371[b]
1935	3,543[b]
1948[c]	12,961
1951	18,733
	—[d]
1958	26,980
1963	34,467
1968	48,216
1973	68,472[e]
1982	212,640[e]
1990	380,790
1994	495,992

[a] Including firms in the Irish Republic.
[b] Firms employing more than 10 persons only.
[c] Great Britain only.
[d] Prior to 1951 classified according to the 1948 edition of the standard Industrial Classification; for 1958 and 1963 according to the 1958 edition; for 1968 and 1973 the 1968 edition; for 1982 and 1990 the 1980 edition; and for 1994 the 1990 edition.
[e] Excludes construction.

Source: *Annual Abstract of Statistics*.

SURTAX, 1909–1972

Year of Change	Level for Paying Surtax £	Maximum Rate Payable		£
1909	5,000	6d.	on amount in excess of	3,000
1914	3,000	1/9$^1/_2$	"	"	8,000
1915	3,000	3/6	"	"	10,000
1918	2,500	4/6	"	"	10,000
1920	2,000	6/-	"	"	30,000
1929	2,000	7/6	"	"	50,000
1930	2,000	8/3	"	"	50,000
1938	2,000	9/6	"	"	30,000
1939	2,000	9/6	"	"	20,000
1946	2,000	10/6	"	"	20,000
1951	2,000	10/-	"	"	15,000
1961	2,000[a]	10/-	"	"	15,000
1969	2,500	50%	"	"	15,000
1971	3,000	50%	"	"	15,000

[a] In 1961 special reliefs introduced for earned incomes made the threshold effectiively £5000.
In 1973 the system of personal income tax and surtax was replaced by a single graduated tax. Therefore surtax ceased to be charged after 1972–3.

Source: *Annual Reports of Commissioners of Inland Revenue.*

CAPITAL TRANSFER TAX

Following the abolition of Estate Duty in 1974, a Capital Transfer Tax of 45% became payable on property transferred from a £100,000 estate on death or within three years preceding death. The maximum rate of Capital Transfer Tax reached 75% for an estate over £2m. However, from 1984 the top brackets were abolished, leaving the highest rate at 60% on estates over £285,000. In 1986 Capital Transfer Tax was renamed Inheritance Tax.

CONSUMER CREDIT 1947–

Hire Purchase and other instalment credit (Finance Houses, Durable Goods, Shops and Department Stores) – total outstanding business at end of period (£m.).

1947	68	1965	1,196	1983	18,933
1948	105	1966	1,104	1984	22,307
1949	128	1967	1,058	1985	26,112
1950	167	1968	1,089	1986	30,548
1951	208	1969	1,063	1987	36,566
1952	241	1970	1,127	1988	42,839
1953	276	1971	1,377	1989	48,384
1954	384	1972	1,769	1990	52,522
1955	461	1973	2,151	1991	53,449
1956	376	1974	1,944	1992	52,593
1957	448	1975	1,892	1993	52,334
1958	556	1976	2,163	1994	57,068
1959	849	1977	4,184	1995	68,205
1960	935	1978	5,499	1996	77,494
1961	934	1979	6,901	1997	88,100
1962	887	1980	7,844	1998	101,928
1963	959	1981	13,403		
1964	1,115	1982	16,030		

From 1981 figures include all consumer credit companies licensed to take deposits, both in monetary and retail sectors.
The basis of calculations is different after 1977. The figures jump in 1983 with the inclusion of bank loans.

Sources: *Key Statistics 1900–1970; Annual Abstract of Statistics 1970–; Economic Trends 1977–*

BUDGET DATES

1900	5	Mar	1935	15	Apr	1967	11	Apr
1901	1	Apr	1936	21	Apr	1968	19	Mar
1902	14	Apr	1937	20	Apr	1969	15	Apr
1903	23	Apr	1938	26	Apr	1970	14	Apr
1904	19	Apr	1939	25	Apr	1971	30	Mar
1905	10	Apr		27	Sep	1972	21	Apr
1906	30	Apr	1940	23	Apr	1973	7	Mar
1907	18	Apr		23	Jul	1974	26	Mar
1908	7	May	1941	7	Apr		12	Nov
1909	29	Apr	1942	14	Apr	1975	15	Apr
1910	30	Jun	1943	12	Apr	1976	6	Apr
1911	16	May	1944	25	Apr	1977	29	Mar
1912	2	Apr	1945	24	Apr	1978	11	Apr
1913	22	Apr		23	Oct	1979	3	Apr
1914	4	May	1946	9	Apr		12	Jun
	17	Nov	1947	15	Apr	1980	26	Mar
1915	4	May		12	Oct	1981	10	Mar
	21	Sep	1948	6	Apr	1982	9	Mar
1916	4	Apr	1949	6	Apr	1983	15	Mar
1917	3	May	1950	18	Apr	1984	13	Mar
1918	22	Apr	1951	10	Apr	1985	19	Mar
1919	3	Apr	1952	11	Apr	1986	18	Mar
1920	19	Apr	1953	14	Apr	1987	17	Mar
1921	25	Apr	1954	6	Apr	1988	15	Mar
1922	1	May	1955	19	Apr	1989	14	Mar
1923	17	Apr		26	Oct	1990	20	Mar
1924	29	Apr	1956	17	Apr	1991	19	Mar
1925	28	Apr	1957	9	Apr	1992	10	Mar
1926	26	Apr	1958	15	Apr	1993	16	Mar
1927	11	Apr	1959	7	Apr	1993	30	Nov
1928	24	Apr	1960	4	Apr	1994	29	Nov
1929	15	Apr	1961	17	Apr	1995	28	Nov
1930	14	Apr	1962	8	Apr	1996	26	Nov
1931	27	Apr	1963	3	Apr	1997	3	Jul
	10	Sep	1964	14	Apr	1998	17	Mar
1932	19	Apr		11	Nov	1999	9	Mar
1933	25	Apr	1965	6	Apr			
1934	17	Apr	1966	5	May			

Occasionally *ad hoc* statements by the Chancellor of the Exchequer on revised fiscal and economic arrangements have been referred to by the media as 'Budgets', although not so regarded by the Treasury. Such statements or 'mini-Budgets' occurred on 22 Jul 74, 12 Nov 74, 11 Jul 75, 19 Feb 76, 22 Jul 76, 15 Dec 76, 15 Jul 77, 26 Oct 77, 8 Jun 78, and 15 Nov 80.

In 1982 the forecast required under the *Industry Act 1975* for decisions on public expenditure plans and proposed changes to National Insurance contributions were brought together in one 'Autumn Statement'. These took place on the following dates:

1982	8	Nov	1988	8	Nov
1983	17	Nov	1989	15	Nov
1984	11	Nov	1990	8	Nov
1985	12	Nov	1991	6	Nov
1986	6	Nov	1992	12	Nov
1987	3	Nov			

The Chancellor announced in his 1992 Budget that as from November 1993, the Budget and the Autumn Statement would be brought together and announced on the same day, in late November or early December. In the course of his 1997 Budget, the Chancellor announced that from 1998 the Budget would revert to the Spring, with a Pre-Budget Report published in November each year. These were given on 25 Nov 97, 3 Nov 98 and 9 Nov 99.

XII

THE PUBLIC SECTOR

Economic activity by the state – other than the core activity undertaken by the Civil Service – takes a range of forms which defy easy categorisation. Whereas a public corporation (or a limited company in which the state is a majority shareholder) can clearly be classified as being within the public sector, there have often been grey areas resulting from minority government shareholdings, 'golden shares', and changing accounting rules over the raising of private capital.

Public corporations, defined as public trading bodies which have a substantial degree of financial independence of the public authority which created them, include not only the major nationalised industries, but a number of other bodies listed on pages 447–9. For practical purposes 'nationalised industries' can be defined as public corporations whose assets are in public ownership, whose boards are appointed by a Secretary of State, whose employees are not civil servants, which are engaged in trading activities, and which derive the greater part of their revenue directly from customers.

Main Landmarks in Nationalisation

1908   **The Port of London Authority** was set up in 1909 under the *Port of London Act, 1908* (but it only followed the pattern of the Mersey Docks and Harbour Board, set up in 1874).

1914   The Government acquired a majority shareholding in **The Anglo-Persian Oil Company**, with the intention of safeguarding the supply of fuel for the Admiralty.

1926   **The Central Electricity Board** was set up by the *Electricity (Supply) Act,1926*, to control generation by purchasing all electricity output.

1926   **The British Broadcasting Corporation** was granted its first charter as a public corporation.

1933   **The London Passenger Transport Board** was established.

1943   **The North of Scotland Hydro-Electricity Board** was established.

1946   **The Bank of England** was taken into public ownership.

1946   **The coal industry** was nationalised by the *Coal Industry Nationalisation Act,1946*, which set up the National Coal Board.

1946   **Civil aviation** was reorganised by the *Civil Aviation Act, 1946*. This covered the British Overseas Airways Corporation (set up in 1939), and two new corporations, British European Airways and British South American Airways. B.S.A.A. was merged with B.O.A.C. in 1949. B.O.A.C. and B.E.A. were merged into British Airways in 1972–74.

1947   **Electricity** was fully nationalised by the *Electricity Act, 1947*, which set up the British Electricity Authority. The *Electricity Act, 1957*, set up the Electricity Council and the Central Electricity Generating Board. The twelve area boards remained financially autonomous.

1948   **Railways, Canals** (and some other transport) were nationalised by the *Transport Act,1947*. The British Transport Commission was established, and the Docks and Inland Waterways, Hotels, Railways, London Transport, Road Haulage, and Road Passenger Transport were administered by six executive boards. The *Transport Act, 1953*, denationalised Road Haulage. The *Transport Act, 1962*, reorganised nationalised transport undertakings and provided for the establishment of separate Boards for Railways, London Transport, Docks and Waterways, and for a Transport Holding Company, as successors to the British Transport Commission.

1948   **Gas** was nationalised by the *Gas Act, 1948*, which established twelve Area Gas Boards and the Gas Council. The *Gas Act, 1972*, established the British Gas Corporation which replaced the Gas Council and Area Boards.

1949   **Iron and steel** were nationalised by the *Iron and Steel Act, 1949*, and the Iron and Steel Corporation of Great Britain was established. The vesting date of the Act was 15 Feb 51. *The Iron and Steel Act, 1953*, denationalised the industry, and set up the Iron and Steel Board. In 1967 the *Iron and Steel Act* renationalised the industry, as from 28 Jul 67.

1954   **The U.K. Atomic Energy Authority** was established by the *Atomic Energy Authority Act, 1954*.

1969   **The Post Office** ceased to be a Government Department and became a public corporation.

429

1971–73 **Hiving-off.** The Conservative Government began to hive-off some concerns of nationalised industries. In 1971–72 some B.O.A.C. routes were allotted to British Caledonian. In 1973 Thomas Cook's travel agency and the Carlisle state breweries (which was nationalised in 1916) were sold to the private sector.

1971 **Rolls-Royce Ltd** was established following the company's bankruptcy. The shares were vested in the National Enterprise Board in February 1976.

1975 **British Leyland.** The majority of shares were acquired by the Government and later vested in the National Enterprise Board.

1975 **The National Enterprise Board** established by the *Industry Act, 1975.*

1976 **British National Oil Corporation** was established by the *Petroleum and Submarines Pipelines Act, 1975.*

1977 **British Aerospace and British Shipbuilders** were established by the *Aircraft and Shipbuilding Industries Act, 1977.* In June 1977 the Labour Government sold off 17% of the shares in British Petroleum, leaving it with a 51% stake.

Privatisation

In May 1979 the Conservatives came to power pledged to 'roll back the frontiers of the state', although the objective of systematically selling off state-owned assets was not at that stage clearly spelled out. Below is a list of the main privatisations since 1979, and the proceeds; it does not include sales by public corporations which retained the proceeds themselves, such as BR's sale of Sealink in 1984.

	Assets sold	Net proceeds £m
Nov 1979	5% of British Petroleum	276
Dec 1979	25% of ICL Computers	37
	Suez Finance Company shares	22
	Miscellaneous (mainly land and property)	42
Total revenue for 1979/80 from privatisation		**377**
Jun 1980	100% of Fairey (NEB subsidiary)	22
Jul 1980	50% of Ferranti (NEB subsidiary)	55
Feb 1981	49% of British Aerospace	43
	North Sea Oil licences	195
	Miscellaneous (mainly property assets)	90
Total revenue for 1980/81 from privatisation		**405**
Oct 1981	49% of Cable and Wireless	182
Feb 1982	100% of Amersham International	64
Feb 1982	100% of National Freight Corporation	5
Feb 1982	24% of British Sugar	44
	NEB subsidiaries	
	New Towns	73
	Oil stockpiles	50
	Miscellaneous	74
Total revenue for 1981/82 from privatisation		**494**
Nov 1982	51% of Britoil (first cash call)	334
Feb 1983	52% of Associated British Ports	46
	Oil stockpiles	33
	Miscellaneous	42
Total revenue for 1982/83 from privatisation		**455**

	Assets sold	Net proceeds £m
Apr 1983	Britoil (second cash call)	293
Sep 1983	7% of British Petroleum	543
Dec 1983	25% of Cable and Wireless	263
Mar 1984	Scott Lithgow shipyard	12
	Miscellaneous	31
Total revenue for 1983/84 from privatisation		**1,132**
Apr 1984	48% of Associated British Ports	51
Jun 1984	Enterprise Oil	384
Nov 1984	British Telecom (first instalment)	1,358
	British Telecom (loan stock)	44
	NEB subsidiaries	168
	Forestry Commission land and miscellaneous	55
Total revenue for 1984/85 from privatisation		**2,060**
May 1985	British Aerospace	347
Jun 1985	British Telecom (second instalment)	1,246
Aug 1985	Britoil	426
Dec 1985	Cable and Wireless	577
	British Telecom (loan stock)	61
	NEB subsidiaries	30
	Land and buildings	18
Total revenue for 1985/86 from privatisation		**2,706**
Apr 1986	British Telecom (third instalment)	1,081
Dec 1986	British Gas (first instalment)	1,820
Feb 1987	British Airways (first instalment)	435
	British Gas (redemption of debt)	750
	British Telecom (loan stock)	53
	British Telecom (preference shares)	250
	NEB subsidiaries	34
	Wytch Farm	18
	Miscellaneous	16
Total revenue for 1986/87 from privatisation		**4,458**
Apr 1987	Royal Ordnance	186
May 1987	Rolls-Royce	1,029
Jun 1987	British Gas (second instalment)	1,758
Jul 1987	BAA	534
Aug 1987	British Airways (second instalment)	419
Aug 1987	Plant Breeding Institute	65
Oct 1987	British Petroleum (first instalment)	863
	British Telecom (loan stock)	23
	British Telecom (preference shares)	250
	Miscellaneous	12
Total revenue for 1987/88 from privatisation		**5,140**
Apr 1988	British Gas (third instalment)	1,555
May 1988	BAA	689
Aug 1988	British Petroleum (second instalment)	3,030
Dec 1988	British Steel	1,138
Mar 1989	General Practice Finance Corporation	67
(May 1987)	Rolls-Royce	3
	British Gas (redemption of debt)	250
	British Telecom (loan stock)	85
	British Telecom (preference shares)	250
	Miscellaneous	2
Total revenue for 1988/89 from privatisation		**7,069**

	Assets sold	Net proceeds £m
Aug 1988	Rover Group	150
Apr 1989	British Petroleum (third instalment)	1,363
Jun 1989	Short Brothers	30
Dec 1989	Water companies (first instalment)	423
	British Gas (mainly redemption of debt)	804
	British Steel	1,289
	British Telecom (loan stock)	92
	Harland and Wolff	8
	Water companies (debt redemption)	73
	Miscellaneous	−13
Total revenue for 1989/90 from privatisation		**4,219**
Jul 1990	British Gas (sale of shares)	150
Jul 1990	Water companies (second instalment)	1,487
Dec 1990	Electricity shares (England & Wales)	3,134
	British Gas (redemption of debt)	350
	British Telecom (loan stock)	100
	Wytch Farm	130
	Miscellaneous	−6
Total revenue for 1990/91 from privatisation		**5,346**
Jun 1991	Electricity shares (Scotland)	1,112
Jul 1991	Water companies (sale of shares)	1,483
Oct 1991	National Transcommunications	70
Dec 1991	British Telecom (first instalment)	1,666
Dec 1991	Insurance Services Group	12
Mar 1992	British Technology Group	24
	British Telecom (loan stock)	106
	Electricity shares (England and Wales)	2,329
	Redemption of Electricity debt	1,106
	Miscellaneous	15
Total revenue for 1991/92 from privatisation		**7,923**
	British Gas (redemption of debt)	350
Jun 1992	British Telecom (second instalment)	3,544
Aug 1992	Electricity shares (England and Wales)	1,465
	British Telecom (Loan stock)	113
	Electricity shares (Scotland)	907
	Redemption of Electricity debt	110
	Privatised companies' debt	1,337
	Northern Ireland Electricity	350
	Miscellaneous	−62
Total revenue for 1992/93 from privatisation		**8,114**
	British Telecom (third instalment)	3,773
	British Telecom (loan stock)	124
	Electricity shares (Scotland)	703
	Redemption of Electricity debt	−154
	Northern Ireland Electricity	218
	Miscellaneous	−32
Total revenue for 1993/94 from privatisation		**4,632**
	British Coal	811
	British Telecom (third instalment)	1,519
	British Telecom (loan stock)	130
	Electricity shares (England and Wales)	1,724
	Redemption of Electricity debt	−361

Assets sold	Net proceeds £m
Northern Ireland Electricity	187
Privatised companies' debt	1,617
Miscellaneous	21
Total revenue for 1994/5 from privatisation	**5,648**
British Telecom (loan stock)	130
Electricity shares (England and Wales)	1,029–
Privatised companies' debt	517
Residual Share sales	750
Total revenue for 1995/6 from privatisation	**2,426**
AEA Technology	215
British Coal	111
British Telecom (loan stock)	140
Electricity shares (England and Wales)	796
Nuclear industry (shares)	525
Nuclear industry (redemption of debt)	160
Privatised companies' debt	663
Railtrack (shares)	910
Railtrack (redemption of debt)	282
Residual Share Sales	560
Miscellaneous	138
Total revenue for 1996/7 from privatisation	**4,500**

Sources: R. Vernon (ed.), *The Promise of Privatisation* (1988). J. Vickers and G. Yarrow, *Privatisation: an Economic analysis* (1988). Also *Public Expenditure Statistical Analyses*, HM Treasury.

Nationalised Industries

Air

British Overseas Airways Corporation (BOAC) 1939–74

	Responsible Minister		*Chairman*
1939	Sec. of State for Air	26 May 43	Vt Knollys
1944	Min. for Civil Aviation	1 Jul 47	Sir H. Hartley
1951	Min. for Transport and Civil	1 Jul 49	Sir M. Thomas
	Aviation	1 May 56	(Sir) G. d'Erlanger
1959	Min. of Civil Aviation	29 Jul 60	Sir M Slattery
1964	Min. of Aviation	1 Jan 64	Sir G. Guthrie
1968	Min. of State at Board of Trade	1 Jan 69	(Sir) C. Hardie
1970	Min. of Aviation at the Dept of	1 Jan 71	K. Granville
	Trade and Industry	1 Sep 72	J. Stainton
1971	Min. for Aerospace (and Shipping 1972) at the Dept of Trade and Industry		
1974	Sec. of State for Trade		

Established under the *Air Corporations Act, 1939*, as successor to Imperial Airways. In 1946 became one of the three corporations set up under the *Civil Aviation Act, 1946*, to provide passenger and cargo flights to all parts of the world, other than Europe and Latin America. Under the *Civil Aviation Act, 1971*, merged with BEA in April 1974 to form British Airways.

British European Airways Corporation (BEA), 1946–74

	Responsible Minister		*Chairman*
1946	Min. for Civil Aviation	1 Aug 46	Sir H. Hartley
1951	Min. of Transport and Civil Aviation	1 Apr 47	G. d'Erlanger
1959	Min. of Aviation	14 Mar 49	Ld Douglas
1968	Min. of State at the Board of Trade	3 May 56	(Sir) A. Milward
1970	Min. of Aviation Supply	1 Jan 71	H. Marking
1971	Min. for Aerospace (and Shipping 1972) at the Dept of Trade and Industry	1 Sep 72	P. Lawton
1974	Sec. of State for Trade		

Established under the *Civil Aviation Act, 1946*, to take over European, domestic and some North African flights. In April 1974, under the *Civil Aviation Act, 1971*, merged with BOAC to form British Airways.

British South American Airways Corporation (BSAA) 1946–49

	Responsible Minister		*Chairman*
1946	Min. for Civil Aviation	1 Aug 46	J. Booth
		1 May 49	Sir M. Thomas

Established under the *Civil Aviation Act, 1946*, to take over Central and South American routes from BOAC. Merged with BOAC 1949.

British Airways, 1974–87

	Responsible Minister		*Chairman*
		7 Oct 71	D. Nicolson
1972	Min. for Aerospace and Shipping at the Dept. of Trade and Industry	1 Jul 76	Sir F. McFadzean
		1 Jul 79	Sir R. Stainton
1974	Sec. of State for Trade	3 Jan 81	J. (Ld) King
1983	Sec. of State for Transport		

Established under the *Civil Aviation Act, 1971*, to take overall responsiblility for the activities of BEA and BOAC from 1 Apr 72. Became fully operational from 1 Apr 74. Became Limited Company in 1983. Sold by share issue in 1987.

British Airports Authority, 1966–87 (BAA plc, 1986–7)

	Responsible Minister		*Chairman*
1966	Min. of Aviation	3 Jun 65	(Sir) P. Masefield
1968	Min. of State at the Board of Trade	9 Jan 72	N. Foulkes
1970	Min of Aviation Supply at the Dept of Trade and Industry	1 Mar 77	(Sir) N. Payne
1971	Min. for Aerospace (and Shipping 1972) at the Dept of Trade and Industry		
1974	Sec. of State for Trade		
1983	Sec. of State for Transport		

Established under the *Airports Authority Act, 1965*, to run Gatwick, Heathrow and Stansted, and since 1971 Edinburgh Turnhouse airports. Aberdeen and Glasgow were acquired in 1975. Became BAA plc under *Airports Act, 1986*. Sold by public share issue Jul 87.

British Aerospace 1977–81

	Responsible Minister		Chairman
1977	Sec. of State for Industry	22 Mar 77	Ld Beswick
1983	Sec of State for Trade and Industry	22 Mar 80	(Sir) A. Pearce

Established under the *Aircraft and Shipbuilding Act, 1977*, to promote the efficient and economical design, development, production, sale, repair and maintenance of civil and military aircraft, of guided weapons and of space vehicles. Became a public limited company under the *British Aerospace Act, 1980*. In 1981 51% of shares were sold to the private sector and employees. The remaining shares in government hands were sold in 1985.

Fuel and Power

British Electricity Authority 1947–55, (Central Electricity Authority 1955–57)

	Responsible Minister		Chairman
1947	Min. of Fuel and Power	15 Aug 47–31 Dec 57	Ld Citrine
1957	Min. of Power		

Established under the *Electricity Act, 1947*, to be responsible for generation and main transmission throughout Great Britain excluding the North of Scotland. There were 14 Area Boards responsible for distribution. Under *Electricity Reorganisation (Scotland) Act, 1954*, two of these Area Boards (S.E. Scotland and S.W. Scotland) merged and took over generation in their areas from British Electricity Authority which was now renamed Central Electricity Authority.

Electricity Council, 1957–90

	Responsible Minister		Chairman
1957	Min. of Power	1 Sep 57	Sir H. Self
1969	Min. of Technology	1 Sep 59	(Sir) R. King
1970	Sec. of State for Trade and Industry	1 Jan 66	Sir R. Edwards
1974	Sec. of State for Energy	1 Nov 68	Sir N. Elliott
		1 Apr 72	Sir P. Menzies
		1 Apr 77	(Sir) F. Tombs
		1 Jan 81	(Sir) A. Bunch
		1 Apr 83	(Sir) P. Jones

Established under the *Electricity Act, 1957*, to co-ordinate development of the industry. Consisted of 14 statutory corporations: the Electricity Council, the CEGB and 12 Area Electricity Boards. The Council was wound up in 1990, when the CEGB was broken up in anticipation of electricity privatisation.

Central Electricity Generating Board (CEGB), 1957–90

	Responsible Minister		Chairman
1957	Min. of Power	1 Sep 57	Sir C. Hinton
1969	Min. of Technology	1 Jan 65	(Sir) S. Brown
1970	See. of State for Trade and Industry	1 Jul 72	A. Hawkins
1974	Sec. of State for Energy	9 May 77	G. England
		9 May 82	*(office vacant)*
		1 Jul 82	Sir W. (Ld) Marshall
		18 Dec 89	*(office vacant)*

Established under the *Electricity Act, 1957*, to own and operate the power stations and the National Grid, and to provide electricity in bulk to the 12 Area Boards. Under the *Electricity Act, 1989*, the CEGB was broken up into four companies – National Power, PowerGen, National Grid and Nuclear Electric, with effect from 1 Apr 90.

North of Scotland Hydro-Electricity Board 1943–90 (Scottish HydroElectric, 1990–91)

	Responsible Minister		*Chairman*
1943	Secretary of State for Scotland	1 Sep 43	E of Airlie
		1 Apr 46	T. Johnston
		1 Jul 59	Ld Strathclyde
		1 Sep 69	T. Fraser
		30 Apr 73	Sir D. Haddow
		1 Jan 79	Ld Greenhill
		1 Jan 84	M. Joughin

Established under the *Hydro-Electric Development (Scotland) Act, 1943*, to supply electricity and to develop water power in the Highlands and Islands. In 1947 became responsible for all public generation and distribution of electricity in the North of Scotland. Under *Electricity Act, 1989*, name changed to Scottish HydroElectric, in Apr 1990, in preparation for privatisation which took place in Jun 91.

South of Scotland Electricity Board, 1955–90 (Scottish Power, 1990–91)

	Responsible Minister		*Chairman*
1955	Secretary of State for Scotland	1 Dec 54	(Sir) J. Pickles
		20 Feb 62	N. Elliot
		1 Apr 67	C. Allan
		1 Jan 74	F. Tombs
		1 Apr 77	D. Berridge
		22 Mar 82	(Sir) D. Miller

Established under the *Electricity Reorganisation (Scotland) Act, 1954*, to generate and distribute electricity throughout south of Scotland. Became Scottish Power in Apr 90 under *Electricity Act, 1989*, and lost responsibility for nuclear power stations in Scotland. Sold by public share offer Jun 91.

National Coal Board (NCB), 1946–87; British Coal, 1987–97

	Responsible Minister		*Chairman*
1946	Min. of Fuel and Power	15 Jul 46	Ld Hyndley (Vt)
1956	Min. of Power	1 Aug 51	Sir H. Houldsworth
1969	Min. of Technology	1 Feb 56	(Sir) J. Bowman
1970	Sec. of State for Trade and Industry	1 Feb 61	A. Robens (Ld)
1974	Sec. of State For Energy	3 Jul 71	(Sir) D. Ezra
1992	Pres. of Board of Trade	3 Jul 82	(Sir) N. Siddall
		1 Sep 83	I. MacGregor
		1 Sep 86	Sir R. Haslam
		1 Jan 91	N. Clarke
		1 Jul 97	P. Hutchinson

Established under the *Coal Industry Nationalisation Act, 1946*, to own and run the coal industry and certain ancillary activities. Changed name to British Coal under the *Coal Industry Act, 1987*. Most functions transferred to the Coal Authority under *Coal Industry Act, 1994*. On 31 Dec 97 the Corporation disposed of its remaining property and staff, although the shell company still exists.

Gas Council and Boards, 1948–73

	Responsible Minister		*Chairman*
1948	Min. of Fuel and Power	23 Nov 48	Sir E. Sylvester
1957	Min. of Power	1 Jan 52	(Sir) H. Smith
1969	Min. of Technology	1 Jan 60	Sir H. Jones
1970	Sec. of State For Trade and Industry	1 Jan 72	A. Hetherington

Established by the *Gas Act, 1948*, to co-ordinate 12 Area Gas Boards which were set up to manufacture and retail town gas. The Gas Council was responsible for the purchase and distribution of natural gas. Under the *Gas Act, 1972*, it was replaced by British Gas Corporation.

British Gas, 1973–86

	Responsible Minister		Chairman
1973	Sec of State For Trade and Industry	1 Jan 73	(Sir) A. Hetherington
1974	Sec. of State for Energy	1 Jul 76	(Sir) D. Rooke

Established under the *Gas Act, 1972*, to take over responsibilities of Gas Council and Area Gas Boards. In 1984 British Gas offshore oil interests were hived off to form Enterprise Oil. Became a public limited company under *Gas Act, 1986*, and sold by public share offer in Dec 86.

United Kingdom Atomic Energy Authority (UKAEA) 1954–

	Responsible Minister		Chairman
1954	Ld President	1 Aug 54	Sir E. Plowden (Ld)
1956	Prime Minister	1 Jan 60	Sir R. Makins
1959	Min. of Science	10 Feb 64	Sir W. Penney (Ld)
1963	Ld President	16 Oct 67	(Sir) J. Hill
1964	Min. of Technology	7 Jul 81	Sir W. Marshall
1970	Sec. of State For Trade and Industry	1 Oct 82	Sir P. Hirsch
1974	Sec. of State for Energy	1 Oct 84	A. Allen
1992	President of the Board of Trade	1 Jan 87	J. Collier
		1 Jul 90	J. Maltby
		1 Jul 93	Sir A. Cleaver
		12 Mar 96	Sir K. Eaton

Established under the *Atomic Energy Authority Act, 1954*, to be responsible for the development of nuclear energy and its applications. In May 1989 a commercial arm, AEA Technology, was established, which was privatised in 1996.

British National Oil Corporation (BNOC), 1976–82

	Responsible Minister		Chairman
1976	Sec. of State for Energy	1 Jan 76	Ld Kearton

Established under the *Petroleum and Submarines Pipelines Act, 1975*, to search for and get, move, store and treat, buy, sell, and deal in petroleum. In Nov 1982 the government sold its majority shareholding to the private sector.

British Nuclear Fuels, 1971–

	Responsible Minister		Chairman
1971	Sec. of State for Trade and Industry	1 Apr 71	(Sir) J. Hill
1974	Sec. of State for Energy	1 Apr 83	C. Allday
1992	Pres. of Board of Trade	1 Apr 86	(Sir) C. Harding
		1 Jul 92	J. Guinness

Established under the *Atomic Energy Act, 1971*, from the former production group of the UK Atomic Energy Authority, taking over responsibility for the production, enrichment and reprocessing of nuclear fuel. Became a public limited company in 1984, with the Government the sole shareholder.

Nuclear Electric, 1990–96

	Responsible Minister		Chairman
1990	Sec. of State for Energy	1 Jan 90	J. Collier
1992	President of the Board of Trade		

Established by the CEGB to take over the running of the nuclear power stations following the decision to exclude nuclear power stations from privatisation. In Dec 95 Nuclear Electric became an operational subsidiary of a holding company, British Energy, which was floated on the stock exchange on 15 Jul 96.

Scottish Nuclear, 1990–96

	Responsible Minister		Chairman
1990	Sec. of State for Scotland	1 Apr 90	J. Hann

Took over the running of Scottish nuclear power stations from the South of Scotland Electricity Board as the electricity industry was prepared for privatisation under the *Electricity Act, 1989*. In Dec 95 Scottish Nuclear became an operational subsidiary of a holding company, British Energy, which was floated on the stock exchange on 15 Jul 96.

PowerGen, 1990–91

	Responsible Minister		Chairman
1990	Sec. of State for Energy	1 Apr 90	R. Malpas
		16 Nov 90	Sir G. Day

Formed when the CEGB was broken up prior to privatisation, with 39% of non-nuclear generating capacity. The Government sold 60% of the shares in February 1991.

National Power, 1990–91

	Responsible minister		Chairman
1990	Sec. of State for Energy	1 Apr 90	Ld Marshall
		5 Jul 90	Sir T. Holdsworth

Formed when the CEGB was broken up prior to privatisation, with 61% of non-nuclear generating capacity. The Government sold 60% of the shares in February 1991.

Magnox Electric, 1996–98

	Responsible Minister		Chairman
1992	President of the Board of Trade	1 Apr 96	M. Baker

Magnox Electric was formed to run the Magnox power stations when the rest of Nuclear Electric was prepared for privatisation as part of British Energy. It was absorbed into BNFL in Jan 98.

Transport

London Passenger Transport Board (LPTB), 1933–47

	Responsible Minister		Chairman
1933	Min. of Transport	1933	Ld Ashfield
1941	Min. of War Transport		
1946	Min. of Transport		

Established under the *London Passenger Transport Act, 1933*, to take over railway, tramway, bus and coach undertakings within the London area. Under the *Transport Act, 1947*, responsibilities transferred to the British Transport Commission operating through a London Transport Executive.

London Transport Board, 1963–70

	Responsible Minister		Chairman
1963	Min. of Transport	1 Jan 63	(Sir) A. Valentine
		1 Apr 65	(Sir) M. Holmes

Established under the *Transport Act, 1962*, to replace part of the British Transport Commission, to provide an adequate and properly co-ordinated system of passenger transport for the London area. Under the *Transport (London) Act, 1969*, responsibilities transferred to the Greater London Council.

London Regional Transport (LRT), 1984–

Responsible Minister		Chairman	
1984	Sec. of State for Transport	29 Jun 84	(Sir) K. Bright
		13 Mar 89	(Sir) W. Newton
		15 Sep 94	P. Ford
		23 Apr 98	B. Appleton

Established under the *London Regional Transport Act, 1984*, to take over responsibility for transport in London from the GLC.

British Transport Commission (BTC), 1947–62

Responsible Minister		Chairman	
1947	Min. of Transport	8 Sep 47	Sir C. Hurcomb (Ld)
1953	Min. of Transport and Civil Aviation	15 Sep 53	Sir B. Robertson
1959	Min. of Transport	1 Jun 61	R. Beeching (Ld)

Chairman of Executives of BTC

Docks and Inland Waterways Executive
1947–53	Sir R. Hill

Hotels Executive
1948–51	Ld Inman *(part-time from 1950)*
1951–53	Sir H. Methven *(part-time)*

Railway Executive
1947–51	Sir E. Missenden
1951–53	J. Elliot

Road Haulage Executive
1948–53	G. Russell

London Transport Executive
1947–53	Ld Latham
1953–59	(Sir) J. Elliot
1959–62	A. Valentine

Road Passenger Service
1948–52	G. Cardwell

Established under the *Transport Act, 1947*, to provide an integrated system of transport facilities (excluding air). The separate executives were wound up in 1953 (except for the London Transport Executive). The *Transport Act, 1962*, transferred the whole of the BTC to new separate corporations.

British Railways Board (BR), 1963–

Responsible Minister		Chairman	
1962	Min. of Transport	1 Jan 63	R. Beeching (Ld)
1970	Sec. of State for the Environment	1 Jun 65	(Sir) S. Raymond
1976	Sec. of State for Transport	1 Jan 68	(Sir) H. Johnson
		13 Sep 71	(Sir) R. Marsh
		12 Sep 76	(Sir) P. Parker
		12 Sep 83	(Sir) R. (Robert) Reid
		1 Apr 90	(Sir) R. (Bob) Reid
		1 Apr 95	J. Welsby
		1 Apr 99	Sir A. Morton

Established services. The *Railways Act, 1993*, laid down a framework for removing almost all operational functions to Railtrack, the train operating companies and the regulators. It continued to exist principally to manage a property portfolio. In Jan 98 it became known for most purposes as Rail Property Ltd. The Government announced in Jul 98 that the residual functions of the British Railways Board would be transferred to a Strategic Rail Authority. On 24 Feb 99 the Government announced that the Chairman of the British Railways Board would in due course become Chairman of the Strategic Rail Authority.

British Transport Docks Board, 1963–84

Responsible Minister			*Chairman*
1962	Min. of Transport	3 Dec 62	Sir A. Kirby
1970	Sec. of State for the Environment	15 Jun 67	S. Finnis
1976	Sec. of State for Transport	6 Aug 69	R. Wills
		25 Sep 69	C. Cory (acting)
		19 Jan 70	Sir C. Doye
		1 May 71	Sir H. Browne
		1 May 82	K. Stuart

Established under the *Transport Act, 1962*, to administer publicly owned ports throughout the country. Under *Docks and Harbours Act, 1966*, became licensing authority for all but three ports. Sold off in 1983 and 1984 under the *Tranport Act, 1981*, to form Associated British Ports.

British Waterways Board, 1963–

Responsible Minister			*Chairman*
1963	Min. of Transport	1 Jan 63	F. Arney
1970	Sec. of State for the Environment	1 Jul 63	Sir J. Hawton
		1 Jul 68	Sir F. Price
		1 Jul 84	Sir L. Young
		1 Jul 87	A. Robertson *(acting)*
		22 Oct 87	D. Ingman
		1 Nov 93	*(office vacant)*
		1 Apr 94	B. Henderson

Established under the *Transport Act, 1962*, to take over inland waterways from the BTC. The *Transport Act, 1968*, extended its powers particularly in regard to recreation and amenities.

National Bus Company, 1968–91

Responsible Minister			*Chairman*
1968	Min. of Transport	28 Nov 68	A. Todd
1970	Sec. of State for the Environment	1 Jan 72	F. Wood
1976	Sec. of State for Transport	1 Jan 79	Ld Shepherd
		1 Jan 85	R. Brook
		8 Apr 86	R. Lund
		1 Apr 88	Sir P. Harrup

Established under the *Transport Act, 1968*, to take over responsibility for state-owned bus companies and bus manufacturing interests from the Transport Holding Company. Broken up and sold off following *Transport Act, 1985*. Formally wound up in Apr 91.

National Freight Corporation, 1968–82

Responsible Minister			*Chairman*
1968	Min. of Transport	1 Jan 69	Sir R. Wilson
1970	Sec. of State for the Environment	1 Jan 71	(Sir) D. Pettit
1976	Sec. of State For Transport	1 Jan 79	Sir R. Lawrence

Established under the *Transport Act, 1968*, to take over road haulage and shipping interests of the Transport Holding Company. Shipping interests terminated in 1971. Sold to the National Freight Consortium in 1982.

Scottish Transport Group, 1968–

	Responsible Minister		Chairman
1968	Secretary of State for Scotland	18 Nov 68	(Sir) P. Thomas
		1 Jan 78	A. Donnet (Ld)
		1 Jan 81	W. Stevenson
		1 Jan 87	I. Irwin

Established under the *Transport Act, 1968*, to control various transport activities in Scotland, including road passenger, insurance, tourism and shipping. Under the *Transport (Scotland) Act, 1989*, the Scottish Office announced a programme to dispose of STG's assets. This was largely complete by 1991, although the Group still formally exists.

Transport Holding Company, 1962–72

	Responsible Minister		Chairman
1962	Min. of Transport	15 Nov 62	Sir P. Warter
1970	Sec. of State for the Environment	15 Nov 67	Sir R. Wilson
		1 Jan 71	L. Whyte

Established by the *Transport Act, 1962*, to take over all BTC investments not given to British Rail, London Transport, Docks or Waterways Boards. The *Transport Act, 1968*, transferred its road interests to the National Freight Corporation and the National Bus Company. Its residual interests (Thomas Cook, Lunn-Poly, etc.) were sold 1970–72.

Miscellaneous

Iron and Steel Corporation, 1950–53

	Responsible Minister		Chairman
1950	Min. of Supply	2 Oct 50	S. Hardie
		25 Feb 52	Sir J. Green

Established under the *Iron and Steel Act, 1949*, to take over 298 companies in the iron and steel industries. Wound up by the *Iron and Steel Act, 1953*.

British Steel Corporation, 1968–88

	Responsible Minister		Chairman
1967	Min. of Power	28 Jul 67	Ld Melchett
1969	Min. of Technology	18 Jun 73	(Sir) M. Finniston
1970	Sec. of State For Trade and Industry	10 Sep 76	Sir C. Villiers
1974	Sec. of State for Industry	1 Jul 80	I. MacGregor
1983	Sec. of State for Trade and Industry	1 Sep 83	(Sir) R. Haslam
		1 Apr 86	(Sir) R. Scholey

Established under the *Iron and Steel Act, 1967*, to take over the management of the major part of the steel industry. Sold by public share issue in Dec 1988 after becoming a public limited company under the terms of the *British Steel Act, 1988*.

Cable and Wireless Ltd, 1947–81

Responsible Minister		*Chairman*	
1947	Postmaster-General	1 Jan 47	Sir A. Augwin
1969	Min. of Posts and	1 Apr 51	(Sir) L. Nicholls
	Telecommunications	1 Feb 56	Sir G. Ince
1970	Sec. of State for Trade and Industry	1 Jan 62	Sir J. Macpherson
1974	Sec. of State for Industry	1 Nov 67	D. McMillan
1983	Sec. of State for Trade and Industry	1 Mar 72	H. Lillicrap
		1 Nov 76	E. Short (Ld Glenamara)
		15 Oct 80	(Sir) E. Sharp

Under the *Cable and Wireless Act, 1946*, the Government acquired all those shares of Cable and Wireless Ltd. not already in its possession. The company's U.K. assets were integrated into the Post Office and it continued to own and operate telecommunications services outside the U.K. In 1981 the Government sold the majority of its shares; the remainder were sold in 1983 and 1985.

Post Office Corporation, 1970–

Responsible Minister		*Chairman*	
1970	Min. of Posts and	1 Oct 69	Vt Hall
	Telecommunications	22 Apr 71	(Sir) W. Ryland
1974	Sec. of State for Industry	31 Oct 77	Sir W. Barlow
1983	Sec. of State for Trade and Industry	1 Sep 80	Sir H. Chilver
		1 Oct 81	(Sir) R. Dearing
		1 Oct 87	Sir B. Nicholson
		1 Jan 93	(Sir) M. Heron
		16 Mar 98	N. Bain

Established under the *Post Office Act, 1969,* to take over from the office of the Postmaster General responsibility for postal services, Giro and remittance services and telecommunications throughout the U.K. In March 1974 all broadcasting functions transferred to Home Office supervision. In 1981 all telecommunications services were transferred to British Telecom.

British Telecom, 1981–84

Responsible Minister		*Chairman*	
1981	Sec. of State for Industry	27 Jul 81	Sir G. Jefferson
1983	Sec. of State for Trade and Industry		

Established under the *British Telecommunications Act, 1981*, to take over the telecommunication functions of the Post Office prior to privatisation. 50.2% of shares were sold in Nov 1984; the government eventually sold its last 22% stake in the company in Jul 1993.

British Shipbuilders, 1977–90

Responsible Minister		*Chairman*	
1977	Sec. of State for Industry	1 Jul 77	Sir A. Griffin
1983	Sec. of State for Trade and Industry	1 Jul 80	(Sir) R. Atkinson
		1 Sep 83	G. Day
		1 May 86	P. Hares
		1 May 88	J. Lister
		4 Sep 89	C. Campbell

Established under the *Aircraft and Shipbuilding Industries Act, 1977*, to promote the efficient and economical design, development, production, sale, repair and maintenance of ships. Broken up from 1984. The last yard was sold in 1990, although the company was never formally wound up.

British Technology Group, 1981–92

Responsible Minister		*Chairman*
1981	Sec. of State for Industry	20 Jul 81	Sir F. Wood
1983	Sec. of State for Trade and Industry	1 Nov 83	C. Barker

Established in 1981 as an umbrella organisation for the National Enterprise Board and the National Research Development Corporation, which retained separate legal identities until merged by the *British Technology Group Act, 1991*. It acted as a holding company for shares in high technology firms and had a brief to develop the potential of inventions made within the public sector. The group was sold to a consortium of investors in March 1992.

Rolls Royce Ltd, 1971–87

Responsible Minister		*Chairman*
1971	Min. For Aerospace at the Dept. of	22 May 71	Ld Cole
	Trade and Industry	5 Oct 72	Sir K. Keith (Ld)
1974	Sec. of State for Industry	22 Jan 80	Ld McFadzean
1983	Sec. of State for Trade	31 Mar 83	Sir W. Duncan
		13 Nov 84	Sir A. Hall *(acting)*
		31 Jan 85	Sir F. Tombs

Established in Feb 1971 under the *Companies Act, 1960*, with the Government as the sole shareholder to ensure the continuance of those activities of Rolls-Royce Ltd which are essential to national defence and to air forces and airlines all over the world. Shares vested in N.E.B. from 1 Feb 76 to 12 Aug 80. The Government sold its shares in 1987.

BL (British Leyland), 1975–86; Rover Group, 1986–8

Responsible Minister		*Chairman*
1975	Sec. of State for Industry	30 Oct 75	Sir R. Edwards
1983	Sec. of State For Trade and Industry	14 Apr 76	Sir R. Dobson
		1 Nov 77	(Sir) M. Edwardes
		8 Nov 82	Sir A. Bide
		1 May 86	(Sir) G. Day

Majority of shareholdings were purchased in 1975, using *Companies Act, 1960*, following financial problems. Shares vested in NEB from 30 Oct 75 to 31 Mar 81. Sold to British Aerospace, Aug 88.

Nationalised Industries: Assets and Employees, 1950–90

| | 1950 | | 1960 | | 1970 | | 1980 | | 1990 | |
	Net Assets (£m.)	Total Employed (000s)	Net Assets (£m.)	Total Employed (000s)	Net Assets (£m.)	Total Employed (000s)	Net Assets (£m.)	Total Employed (000s)	Net Assets (£m.)	Total Employed (000s)
BOAC	42	16	132	21	251	23	–	–	–	–
BEA	6	7	58	13	116	25	–	–	–	–
British Airways	–	–	–	–	–	–	880	57	–	–
British Airports Authority	–	–	–	–	73	4	748	7	–	–
British Aerospace	–	–	–	–	–	–	992	78	–	–
British Electricity Board, Electricity Council, CEGB, Area Boards	686	161	1,948	189	4,921	197	7,179	159	31,741[a]	130
NSHEB	53	3	197	3	267	4	610	4	2,203	4
SSEB	–	–	153	13	418	15	828	14	827	10
Gas industry	269	132	585	127	1,658	119	2,576	104	–	–
National Coal Board	337	749	910	631	666	356	2,128	294	5,868	85
UKAEA	–	–	488	39	256	30	98	14	134	11
BNOC	–	–	–	–	–	–	1,000	2	–	–
Brit.Trans. Comm.	1,226	889	1,828	729	–	–	–	–	–	–
British Rail	–	–	–	–	850	273	1,230	238	2,108	134
National Bus Company	–	–	–	–	93	84	214	51	–	–
National Freight Company	–	–	–	–	116	65	74	31	–	–
British Transport Docks	–	–	–	–	123	11	166	11	–	–
I.&S.C./British Steel	492	292	–	–	1,222	250	2,056	121	–	–
Post Office Corporation	–	–	–	–	2,521	407	7,342	423	2,360	211
Cable and Wireless	38	13	46	10	70	10	248	12	–	–
British Shipbuilders	–	–	–	–	–	–	88	70	–	–

[a] The last available figures for the Electricity industry are 1989.

External Financing Requirements of Nationalised Industries

(excluding central government grants generally available to private sector)
(£billions. Year ending Apr.)

Year	BA	Coal	Gas	BR	Ship[b]	Steel	BT	Elec	LRT	PO	Water	Total
1977	–	0.4	–0.1	0.6	–	1.0	–	0.3	–	0.2	–	2.7
1978	0.1	0.3	–0.2	0.6	–	0.8	–	0.3	–	–	–	2.0
1979	0.1	0.6	–0.4	0.6	0.1	0.8	–0.1	–0.1	–	–	0.3	2.3
1980	0.2	0.7	–0.4	0.7	0.2	0.6	0.3	0.3	–	–	0.3	3.0
1981	0.3	0.8	–0.4	0.8	0.2	1.1	–0.1	0.2	–	–	0.3	3.2
1982	0.2	1.2	–	1.0	0.1	0.8	0.2	–0.1	–	–	0.3	3.6
1983	–	1.0	–0.2	0.8	0.1	0.6	–0.3	–0.1	–	–0.1	0.3	2.1
1984	–0.2	1.2	–	0.8	0.3	0.3	–0.2	–0.3	–	–0.1	0.4	2.3
1985	–0.3	1.7	–0.2	1.0	0.2	0.5	–0.3	0.8	–	–	0.3	3.9
1986	–0.2	0.4	–0.2	0.9	–	0.4	–	–0.3	0.3	–0.1	0.2	1.7
1987	–0.1	0.9	–0.7	0.8	0.2	–	–	–1.2	0.3	–0.1	0.1	0.3
1988	–	0.9	–	0.5	0.1	–0.3	–	–1.1	0.2	–0.1	–	0.2
1989	–	0.8	–	0.4	0.1	–0.4	–	–1.7	0.2	–0.1	–	–0.5
1990	–	1.3	–	0.7	–	–	–	–1.4	0.3	–	–	1.0
1991	–	0.9	–	1.1	–	–	–	–0.3	0.5	–	–	2.3
1992	–	0.6	–	1.5	–	–	–	–0.1	0.6	–0.1	–	3.8
1993	–	0.8	–	2.1	–	–	–	–0.3	0.9	–0.1	–	4.4
1994	–	1.4	–	1.5	–	–	–	–	0.7	–0.2	–	3.6
1995	–	0.7	–	–0.4	–	–	–	–	0.8	–0.2	–	1.0
1996	–	–	–	–1.6	–	–	–	–	0.9	–0.2	–	–0.4
1997	–	–	–	1.0	–	–	–	–	1.0	–0.3	–	–0.5
1998	–	–	–	0.1	–	–	–	–	0.7	–0.3	–	0.7

Regulators of Privatised Industries

As utilities and public services were sold off into the private sector in the 1980s and 1990s, a number of regulating authorities were established with varying remits – all intended to protect the public interest.

Office of Gas Supply (OFGAS), 1986–

Director General

1 Aug 86	(Sir) J. McKinnon
1 Nov 93	Clare Spottiswoode
1 Nov 98	C. McCarthy

Established under the *Gas Act, 1986*. In 1998 the Government announced its intention to merge the Gas and Electricity regulators in 1999.

Office of Electricity Regulation (OFFER), 1990–

Director General of Electricity Supply

1 Sep 89	S. Littlechild
1 Jan 99	C. McCarthy

Established under the *Electricity Act, 1989*. In 1998 the Government announced its intention to merge the Gas and Electricity regulators in 1999.

Office of Telecommunications (OFTEL), 1984–

Director General

1 Aug 84	(Sir) B. Carsberg
13 Jun 92	W. Wigglesworth
1 Apr 93	D. Cruikshank
1 Apr 98	D. Edmonds

Established under the *Telecommunications Act 1984*.

Office of Water Services (OFWAT), 1989–

Director General

1 Aug 89	I. Byatt

Established under the *Water Act, 1989*.

Office of Passenger Rail Franchising (OPRAF), 1993–

Franchising Director

9 Nov 93	R. Salmon
1 Oct 96	J. O'Brien
1 May 99	M. Grant

Established under the *Railways Act, 1993*. It is responsible for letting the 25 passenger train franchises operating on the national railway network in Great Britain. It monitors and manages those franchises with a brief to protect passengers' interests, and encourage fresh investment in the railway.

Office of the Rail Regulator (ORR), 1993–

Rail Regulator

1 Dec 93	J. Swift
1 Dec 98	C. Bolt *(acting)*
5 Jul 99	T. Winsor

Established under the *Railways Act, 1993* to oversee the issue, modification and enforcement of licences to operate trains, networks, stations and light maintenance depots; the enforcement of domestic competition law in connection with the provision of railway services; the approval of agreements for access by operators of railway assets to track, stations and light maintenance depots; and consumer protection and promotion of passengers' interests.

Office of Electricity Regulation in Northern Ireland (OFFER-NI), 1992–6
Office for the Regulation of Electricity and Gas, (OFREG), 1996–

Director General

| 1 Apr 92 | G. Horton |
| 1 Dec 95 | D. McIldoon |

Established in 1992 to regulate the provision of electricity in Northern Ireland in 1992. Took over responsibility for gas when it became available in Northern Ireland. D. McIlhoon formally appointed Director General of Gas Supply 10 Jun 96.

Coal Authority, 1994–

Chairman

| 1 Oct 94 | Sir D. White |

Established in 1992 the *Coal Industry Act, 1994* to take over the residual functions of British Coal, including ownership of unmined reserves and settling subsidence claims not covered by coal mining companies.

Inquiries into Nationalised Industries

The nationalised industries were frequently the subject of a number of Government inquiries into different aspects of their organisation and performance. Later examples include *Report of the Post Office Review Committee*, July 1977 (Cmnd 6850), and *The Structure of the Electricity Supply Industry in England and Wales*, January 1976 (Cmnd 6388). In addition, the National Economic Development Office in June 1975 were invited to undertake a wide-ranging inquiry into the role of nationalised industries in the economy and 'the way in which they are to be controlled in future'. Their report published in 1976, together with an appendix volume and seven background papers, add up to the most comprehensive analysis of the industries' post-war performance.

Between 1965 and 1970 the National Board for Prices and Incomes produced reports which, while primarily concerned with prices and wages, considered the efficiency of the industries. From 1967–70 all major price increase proposals by the nationalised industries were referred to the National Board for Prices and Incomes.

The Select Committee on Nationalised Industries (1956–79) also published regular reports.

Central Government Trading Bodies

Some central government trading bodies have raised revenue through the sales of goods and services, but have not been organised as public corporations:

Export Credits Guarantee Department 1975–
Forestry Commission 1918–
Her Majesty's Stationery Office (HMSO) 1786–[a]
Horserace Totalisator Board 1963–
National Savings Bank 1969–
Land Authority for Wales 1975–
Royal Mint 11th cent, reorganised 1870–[a]
Royal Ordnance Factories (sold to British Aerospace 1987)
Crown Estate Commission 1762, reorganised 1961–
Land Registry 1862–[a]
National Audit Office 1983–

[a] Became an agency under the Government's Next Steps programme. Privatised in Oct 1996.

Other Quasi-governmental Organisations

The dividing line between nationalised industries and other quasi-autonomous national government organisations (quangos) is by no means a clear one. Many of the organisations listed below enjoy similar legal status to the public corporations listed above – the main difference in many cases being one of size. Most official and academic studies indicate that there are between 250 and 350 central non-Departmental bodies of a permanent nature in the U.K. The categories set out below do not purport to represent a comprehensive list, but do include some of the more notable examples. For a comprehensive list of agencies operating under the Government's Next Steps programme, see pp.311–14.

1.   Those which act as agencies for the spending of government money

Regional Health Authorities
University Grants Committee 1919–89
Universities Funding Council 1989–93
Polytechnics and Colleges Funding Council 1989–93
Higher Education Funding Councils 1993–
Manpower Services Commission 1974–88
Sports Council 1972–
Agricultural (and Food) Research Council 1931–
HS Hospital Trusts 1991–
Medical Research Council 1920–
Natural Environment Research Council 1965–
Arts Council 1946–
National Film Finance Corporation 1949–84
National Research Development Corporation 1967–91 *(see above entry for British Technology Group)*
National Enterprise Board 1975–91 *(see above entry for British Technology Group)*
Housing Corporation 1964–
Social Science Research Council 1965–83
Economic and Social Research Council 1983–
British Council 1934–
British Film Commission, 1992–
Legal Aid Board, 1989–

2. *Quasi-judicial and prosecuting bodies*

Prices and Incomes Board 1965–70
Monopolies Commission 1956–73
Monopolies and Mergers Commission 1973– (renamed Competition Commission 1999)
Price Commission 1973–79
Criminal Injuries Compensation Board 1964–
General and Special Commissioners of Income Tax
Parole Board 1967–
Mental Health Act Commission 1983–
Police Complaints Authority 1984–
Serious Fraud Office 1987–
Crown Prosecution Service 1986–

3. *Bodies with statutory powers of regulation and licensing*

H.M. Land Registry 1925–[a]
Charity Commission 1853–
Independent Broadcasting Authority 1954–1990 (see p.549)
Independent Television Commission 1991–
Radio Authority 1991–
Civil Aviation Authority 1971–
Office of Fair Trading 1973–
Commission for Local Authority Accounts in Scotland 1975–
Audit Commission 1983–
Office of the Data Protection Registrar 1984–
Broadcasting Standards Council 1988–96
National Rivers Authority 1989–

4. *Statutory advisory or consultative bodies nominated wholly or in part by Ministers*

Gaming Board for Great Britain 1968–
Metrication Board 1969–80
Consumer Councils of the Nationalised Industries
Health and Safety Commission and Executive 1974–
Law Commission 1965–
Industrial Reorganisation Corporation 1966–70
Countryside Commission 1968–
Equal Opportunities Commission 1975–
Commission for Racial Equality 1977–
Advisory, Conciliation and Arbitration Service 1975–

5. *Executive agencies administering specific activities*

National Dock Labour Board 1947–89
Covent Garden Market Authority 1961–
Northern Ireland Electricity 1973–92
Northern Ireland Transport Holding Company 1968–
National Ports Council 1964–81
Regional Water Authorities (until 1991)

[a] Now an agency under the Government's Next Steps programme.

6.   Development agencies

New Town Development Corporations and Commission (see pp.478–9)
Scottish Development Agency 1975–91
Scottish Enterprise 1991–
Welsh Development Agency 1976–
Highlands and Islands Development Board 1965–91
Highlands and Islands Enterprise 1991–
Colonial Development Corporation 1948–63
Commonwealth Development Corporation 1963–
Development Commission (for Rural England) 1909–88
Rural Development Commission 1988–
Urban Development Corporations

Policy for Nationalised Industries

Four important White Papers on the control of Nationalised Industries have been issued
since the war. They are:

Nationalised Industries: Financial and Economic Obligations (Cmnd 1337/61)
Nationalised Industries: A Review of Economic and Financial Objectives (Cmnd 3437/67)
Ministerial Control of Nationalised Industries (Cmnd 4027, 1969)
The Nationalised Industries (Cmnd 7131, 1978)

In addition a series of White Papers have been published on both Fuel Policy (1965, 1967)
and Transport Policy (1952, 1966, 1977) which have had an important impact on the operation of the nationalised industries in these sectors.

Sources: For an analysis of the statutory provisions of the nationalised industries, see D.N.Chester, *The Nationalised Industries*
(1951). Other studies of the nationalised industries include: Action Society Trust, *Twelve Studies on Nationalised Industries*
(1950–3); H.A.Clegg and T.E.Chester, *The Future of Nationalisation* (1953); D.Coombes, *The Member of Parliament and the
Administration: The case of the Select Committee on Nationalised Industries* (1966); M. Rees, *The Public Sector in the Mixed
Economy* (1973); R. Kelf-Cohen, *British Nationalisation 1945–73* (1973); R.Pryke, *The Nationalised Industries: Policy and
Performance since 1968* (1981); R. Vernon (ed.), *The Promise of Privatisation* (1988); J. Vickers and G. Yarrow, *Privatisation:
an Economic Analysis* (1988). Also *Public Expenditure Statistical Analyses*, HM Treasury.

XIII

ROYALTY

British Kings and Queens, 1900–

	Accession	Coronation	Died	Age	Reigned
Victoria	20 Jun 1837	28 Jun 1838	22 Jan 1901	81	63 yrs
Edward VII	22 Jan 1901	9 Aug 1902	6 May 1910	68	9 yrs
George V	6 May 1910	22 Jun 1911	20 Jan 1936	70	25 yrs
Edward VIII	20 Jan 1936	–	(Abdicated)	–	325 days
George VI	11 Dec 1936	12 May 1937	6 Feb 1952	56	15 yrs
Elizabeth II	6 Feb 1952	2 Jun 1953	–	–	–

Use of Royal Power

Throughout this century great efforts have been made to avoid involving the Crown in politics. But there have been a few occasions when, unavoidably or deliberately, the Sovereign has been involved in decision making. No list of such occasions can be very satisfactory. It may omit times when in private audience the Sovereign expressed strong views to the Prime Minister. It may include times when, despite all the formality of consultation, the Sovereign had no real opportunity of affecting the outcome. The following list of incidents is compiled primarily from Sir Ivor Jennings, *Cabinet Government*; Sir Harold Nicolson, *King George V*; Sir J. W. Wheeler-Bennett, *King George VI*; F. Hardie, *The Political Influence of the Monarchy 1868–1952*; *The Royal Encyclopaedia* (ed. R. Allison) and V. Bogdanor, *The Monarchy and the Constitution* (1995).

1903	Edward VII's visit to France, on his own initiative; prelude to Entente Cordiale of 1904.
Dec 1909	Edward VII's refusal to promise to create peers until after a second general election, if necessary to pass the Parliament Act.
Jul 1910	George V's sponsorship of the Constitutional Conference.
Nov 1910	George V's secret pledge to create peers, if necessary to pass the Parliament Act.
Jul 1914	George V's sponsorship of Buckingham Palace Home Rule Conference.
1915	Buckingham Palace conference on conscription.
Dec 1916	Buckingham Palace Conference on choice of Prime Minister following H. Asquith's resignation.
1917	Relinquishment of German titles. Proclamation of dynasty of Windsor.
Mar 1917	George V's support for General Haig, when in danger of being dismissed.
May 1923	George V's choice of S. Baldwin rather than Curzon as Prime Minister.
Jan 1924	George V's request to R. MacDonald to form first Labour Government.
Oct 1924	George V's agreement to dissolution.
May 1926	George V blocks government proposal during General Strike to embargo trade union funds.
Aug 1931	George V's invitation to R MacDonald to form National Government.
Oct 1931	George V agrees to General Election.
Dec 1936	Edward VIII's decision to abdicate.
May 1940	George VI's invitation to W. Churchill to form Coalition Government.
Jun 1944	George VI's veto on W. Churchill's plan to accompany troops on D-Day invasion.
Jul 1945	George VI's suggestion on switching appointment of Bevin and Dalton (a disputed allegation).
Jan 1957	Elizabeth II's summons of H. Macmillan as Prime Minister.
Oct 1963	Elizabeth II's invitation to E of Home to form a Government.
Nov 1965	Elizabeth II's award of G.C.V.O. to Governor of Rhodesia.
May 1977	Elizabeth II's Silver Jubilee Speech to Parliament stressing her Coronation oath as Queen of the United Kingdom.
Jul 1986	Elizabeth II's reference to her role as head of the Commonwealth, interpreted as a reproach to the Prime Minister, Margaret Thatcher, over the issue of sanctions on South Africa.

Regency Acts, 1937 and 1953

These Acts provide that if the Sovereign is under 18 years of age, the royal functions shall be exercised by a Regent appointed under the provisions of the Acts. (Formerly the appointment of a Regent was *ad hoc*.) The Regent may not give assent to Bills altering the succession to the throne or repealing the Acts securing the Scottish Church.

The Acts provide for Counsellors of State to be appointed during the Monarch's absence from the U.K., or infirmity; and empower certain high officials of the state to declare that 'the Sovereign is by infirmity of mind or body incapable for the time being of performing the royal function'.

The Royal Family

Children of Queen Victoria

1. H.R.H. Princess Victoria (Princess Royal). Born 21 Nov 1840, married H.R.H. Prince Frederick of Prussia (1858), afterwards Kaiser Frederick III, died 5 Aug 1901.
2. **H.M. King Edward VII.** Born 9 Nov 1841, married H.R.H. Princess Alexandra (eldest daughter of King Christian IX of Denmark), 10 Mar 1863, succeeded to the throne 22 Jan 1901, crowned at Westminster Abbey 9 Aug 1902, died 6 May 1910 (for children, see below).
3. H.R.H. Princess Alice. Born 25 Apr 1843, married H.R.H. Prince Louis (1862), afterwards Grand Duke of Hesse, died 14 Dec 1878.
4. H.R.H. Prince Alfred, D of Edinburgh. Born 6 Aug 1844, married Marie Alexandrovna (1874) only daughter of Alexander II, Emperor of Russia. Succeeded as D of Saxe-Coburg and Gotha 22 Aug 1893, died 30 Jul 1900.
5. H.R.H. Princess Helena. Born 25 May 1846, married H.R.H. Prince Christian of Schleswig-Holstein (1866), died 9 Jun 1923.
6. H.R.H. Princess Louise. Born 18 Mar 1848, married M of Lorne (1871), afterwards 9th D of Argyll, died 3 Dec 1939.
7. H.R.H. Prince Arthur, D of Connaught. Born 1 May 1850, married H.R.H. Princess Louisa of Prussia (1879), died 16 Jan 1942.
8. H.R.H. Prince Leopold, D of Albany. Born 7 Apr 1853, married H.R.H. Princess Helena of Waldeck (1882), died 28 Mar 1884.
9. H.R.H. Princess Beatrice. Born 14 Apr 1857, married H.R.H. Prince Henry of Battenberg (1885), died 26 Oct 1944.

Children of Edward VII

1. H.R.H. Prince Albert, D of Clarence and Avondale (1891). Born 8 Jan 1864, died 14 Jan 1892.
2. **H.M. King George V.** H.R.H. Prince George, D of York (1893), Prince of Wales (1901–1910). Born 3 Jun 1865, married (6 Jul 1893) H.R.H. Princess Mary of Teck (Queen Mary, died 24 Mar 1953), succeeded to the throne 6 May 1910, crowned at Westminster Abbey 22 Jun 1911, assumed by Royal Proclamation (17 Jun 1917) the name of Windsor for his House and family, died 20 Jan 1936 (for children, see below).
3. H.R.H. Princess Louise (Princess Royal). Born 20 Feb 1867, married to 1st D of Fife (1889), died 4 Jan 1931. Children: (i) H.H. Princess Alexandra, Duchess of Fife. Born 17 May 1891, married H.R.H. Prince Arthur of Connaught (1913), died 26 Feb 1959.

Child: Alastair, D of Connaught, born 9 Aug 1914, died 26 Apr 1943. (ii) H.H. Princess Maud. Born 3 Apr 1893, married to 11th E of Southesk (1923), died 14 Dec 1945. Child: D of Fife, born 23 Sep 1929, married (1956) Hon. Caroline Dewar.

4. H.R.H. Princess Victoria. Born 6 Jul 1868, died 2 Dec 1935.
5. H.R.H. Princess Maud. Born 26 Nov 1869, married H.R.H. Prince Charles of Denmark (1896), afterwards King Haakon VII of Norway, died 20 Nov 1938. Child: H.M. Olaf V, King of Norway. Born 2 Jul 1903, married (1929) H.R.H. Princess Marthe of Sweden. Died 17 Jan 1991. Children: (i) H.R.H. Princess Ragnhild, born 9 Jun 1930, married (1953) to E. Lorentzen. (ii) H.R.H. Princess Astrid, born 12 Feb 1932. (iii) H.M. Harald V, King of Norway, born 21 Feb 1937, married (1968) Miss S. Haraldsen. Children: (i) H.R.H. Princess Martha Louise, born 22 Sep 1971. (ii) H.R.H. Prince Haakon Magnus, Crown Prince of Norway, born 20 Jul 1973.

Children of George V

1. H.R.H. Prince Edward, D of Windsor (1936), Prince of Wales (1910–36). Born 23 Jun 1894, succeeded to the throne as King Edward VIII on 20 Jan 1936, abdicated 11 Dec 1936. Married Mrs W. Simpson on 3 Jun 1937. Died 28 May 1972.
2. **H.M. King George VI.** H.R.H. Prince Albert, D of York (1920). Born 14 Dec 1895, married Lady Elizabeth Bowes-Lyon, daughter of 14th E of Strathmore and Kinghorne on 26 Apr 1923, succeeded to the throne on 11 Dec 1936, crowned at Westminster Abbey 12 May 1937, died 6 Feb 1952 (for children, see below).
3. H.R.H. Princess Victoria (Princess Royal). Born 25 Apr 1897, married (1922) to 6th E of Harewood, died 28 Mar 1965. Children: (i) George, 7th E of Harewood. Born 7 Feb 1923, married (1949) Marion, daughter of E. Stein. Divorced, 7 Jul 1967. Children: David, Vt Lascelles, born 21 Oct 1950; J. Lascelles, born 5 Oct 1953; R. Lascelles, born 14 Feb 1955, married (1967) Patricia Tuckwell; M. Lascelles, born 5 Jul 1964. (ii) G. Lascelles, born 21 Aug 1924, married (1952) Miss A. Dowding. Children: H. Lascelles, born 19 May 1953; M. Lascelles, born 9 Feb 1962. Divorced July 1978. Married Mrs E. Colvin 1978. Died 27 Feb 1998.
4. H.R.H. Prince Henry, D of Gloucester (1928). Born 31 Mar 1900, married (1935) Lady A. Montagu-Douglas-Scott, daughter of 7th D of Buccleuch, died 10 Jun 1974. Children: (i) H.R.H. Prince William, born 18 Dec 1941, died 28 Aug 1972. (ii) H.R.H. Prince Richard, D of Gloucester, born 26 Aug 1944, married (1972) Birgit Van Deurs. Children: Alexander, Earl of Ulster, born 28 Oct 1974. Lady Davina Windsor, born 19 Nov 1977. Lady Rose Windsor, born 1 Mar 1980.
5. H.R.H. Prince George, D of Kent (1934). Born 20 Dec 1902, married (1934) H.R.H. Princess Marina of Greece and Denmark, killed on active service 25 Aug 1942. Children: (i) H.R.H. Prince Edward, D of Kent, born 9 Oct 1935, married (1961) Katherine, daughter of Sir W. Worsley. Children: (a) George, E of St Andrews, born 26 Jun 1962, married (1988) Sylvana Tomaselli. Children: Edward, Lord Downpatrick, born 2 Dec 1988; Lady Marina Windsor, born 13 Sep 1992; (b) Lady Helen Windsor, born 28 April 1964, married (1992) Timothy Taylor; Lord Nicholas Windsor, born 25 Jul 1970. (ii) H.R.H. Princess Alexandra, born 25 Dec 1936, married (1963) Hon. (Sir) Angus Ogilvy. Children: James Ogilvy, born 29 Feb 1964, married (1988) Julia Rawlinson; Marina Ogilvy, born 31 Jul 1966, married (1990) Paul Mowatt. Child: Zenouska Mowatt, born 26 May 1990. (iii) H.R.H. Prince Michael, born 4 July 1942, married (1978) Baroness Marie-Christine von Reibnitz. Children: Lord Frederick Windsor, born 6 Apr 1979; Lady Gabriella Windsor, born 23 Apr 1981.
6. H.R.H. Prince John. Born 12 Jul 1905, died 18 Jan 1919.

Children of George VI

1. **H.M. Queen Elizabeth II.** Born 21 Apr 1926, married to Philip, D of Edinburgh on 20 Nov 1947, succeeded to the throne 6 Feb 1952, crowned at Westminster Abbey 2 Jun 1953. Children: (i) H.R.H. Prince Charles, Prince of Wales (26 Jun 1958), D of Cornwall, born 14 Nov 1948, married Lady Diana Spencer 29 Jul 1981. Children: Prince William Arthur Philip Louis, born 21 Jun 1982; Prince Henry Charles Albert David, born 15 Sep 1984. Separated 9 Dec 1992. Divorced 15 Jul 1996. (Princess Diana died 30 Aug 1997) (ii) H.R.H. Princess Anne, the Princess Royal (13 Jun 1987), born 15 Aug 1950, married Mark Phillips 14 Nov 1973. Divorced 23 Apr 1992. Children: Peter Mark Andrew Phillips, born 15 Nov 1977; Zara Anne Elizabeth Phillips, born 15 May 1981. Married Timothy Lawrence 12 Dec 1992. (iii) H.R.H. Prince Andrew, Duke of York (23 Jul 1986), born 19 Feb 1960, married Sarah Ferguson 23 Jul 1986. Divorced 1996. Children: Princess Beatrice of York, born 8 Aug 1988; Princess Eugenie of York, born 23 Mar 1990. (iv) Prince Edward, E of Wessex born 10 Mar 1964, married 19 June 1999 Sophie Rhys-Jones.
2. H.R.H. Princess Margaret. Born 21 Aug 1930, married on 6 May 1960 to Antony Armstrong-Jones (created E of Snowdon, 1961). Divorced 24 May 1978. Children: (i) David, Vt Linley, born 3 Nov 1961, married Serena Stanhope 2 Oct 1993. (ii) Lady Sarah Armstrong-Jones, born 1 May 1964, married Daniel Chatto 14 Jul 1994. Children: Samuel born 29 Jul 1996; Arthur born 5 Feb 1999.

Private Secretaries to the Sovereign

1895–1901	Sir A. Bigge (Ld Stamfordham)	1953–72	Sir M. Adeane
1901–13	Sir F. Knollys (Ld 1902) (Vt 1911)[1]	1972–77	Sir M. Charteris
1910–31	Sir A. Bigge (Ld Stamfordham 1911)[1]	1977–86	Sir P. Moore
1931–36	Sir C. Wigram (Ld)	1986–90	Sir W. Heseltine
1936–43	Sir A. Hardinge	1990–99	Sir R. Fellowes
1943–52	Sir A. Lascelles	1999–	Sir R. Janvrin

[1] Ld Stamfordham and Ld Knollys were joint private secretaries 1910–13 to King George V.

Lord Chamberlains

1898	E of Hopetoun	1938	6th E of Clarendon
1900	5th E of Clarendon	1952	E of Scarborough
1905	Vt Althorp (Earl Spencer)	1963	Ld Cobbold
1912	Ld Sandhurst (Vt)	1971	Ld Maclean
1921	D of Atholl	1984	E of Airlie
1922	E of Cromer	1998	Ld Camoys

Poets Laureate

1896	A. Austin	1971	Sir J. Betjeman
1913	R. Bridges	1984	E. Hughes
1930	J. Masefield	1999	A. Motion
1968	C. Day Lewis		

Civil List of the Crown

The annuities payable to the Sovereign and Members of the Royal Family are known as the Civil List, which is granted by Parliament upon the recommendation of a Select Committee. Specific sums are allocated to named members of the Royal Family. In 1981 the Queen undertook to bear the cost of the Civil List vote to three of her cousins (the Duke of Kent, the Duke of Gloucester and Princess Alexandra), by refunding to the Exchequer an equivalent sum. In 1990 it was agreed that a fixed sum would be paid each year up to 2000. On 11 Feb 93 the Prime Minister announced that from 6 Apr 93 the Queen would refund the Civil List payments to all other members of her family except the Queen Mother, the Duke of Edinburgh and herself. At the same time he announced that the Queen's personal income from investments and other sources would henceforth be taxed, along with such revenues from the Privy Purse and the Duchy of Cornwall as were to be used for personal purposes.

Year	Privy Purse	Total Voted	Total retained by Sovereign
1900	£60,000	£385,000	
1901	£110,000	£470,000	
1931[a]	£97,000	£420,000	
1938	£110,000	£410,000	
1952	£60,000	£475,000	
1972	_[b]	£980,000	
1975	–	£1,400,000	
1976	–	£1,614,575	
1977	–	£1,905,000	
1978	–	£2,394,962	
1979	–	£2,609,200	
1980	–	£3,527,550	
1981	–	£4,249,200	£3,964,200
1982	–	£4,612,883	£4,308,183
1983	–	£4,833,900	£4,515,600
1984	–	£5,017,000	£4,686,000
1985	–	£5,180,000	£4,838,000
1986	–	£5,387,300	£5,031,700
1987	–	£5,661,200	£5,289,500
1988	–	£5,922,300	£5,535,700
1989	–	£6,195,300	£5,795,200
1990	–	£6,762,000	£6,327,000
1991	–	£10,420,000	£9,790,000
1993–2000	–	£10,420,000	£8,900,000

[a] By command of the King the Civil List was reduced by £50,000 p.a. as from 1 Oct 1931, in view of the national economic situation.
[b] In 1972 the Privy Purse, as a separate head, was abolished.

Source: V. Bogdanor, *The Monarchy and the Constitution* (1995).

XIV

THE BRITISH ISLES

Scotland

Under the *Treaty of Union, 1707*, Scotland preserved her independent legal and judicial systems. Scotland developed arrangements for education and local government which have never been assimilated to those of England and Wales. The established (Presbyterian) Church was also recognised by the Union settlement. After the abolition of the post of Secretary of State for Scotland in 1746, until the date of the establishment of the Secretaryship for Scotland in 1885. This office became a full Secretaryship of State in 1926; Scotland had been controlled into the nineteenth century by a 'Manager', then the Lord Advocate acting through the Home Secretary, and, for a short period from 1881, by an Under-Secretary at the Home Office with responsibility for Scottish Affairs, as well as by the developing system of Boards.

The continued existence of the Boards was criticised as anachronistic, maintaining a system of patronage and lacking direct responsibility to Parliament in practice, if not in theory (see Reports of the Royal Commission on the Civil Service in 1914[1] and the Haldane Committee on the Machinery of Government in 1918[2]). Under the *Reorganisation of Offices (Scotland) Act, 1928*, the Boards of Agriculture and Health for Scotland became Departments statutorily defined as independent of, though in reality responsible to, the Scottish Secretary of State.

This constitutional peculiarity disappeared along with the remaining Boards after a general review of the Scottish administration by the Gilmour Committee[3] which led to the *Reorganisation of Offices (Scotland) Act, 1939*. This Act brought into being four Departments of the Scottish Office: Agriculture, Education, Health, and Home Affairs, each with their permanent head and with a Permanent Under Secretary of State over them. Further responsibilities were allocated to the Scottish Office during and after the Second World War such as the Crown Estates in 1943 and Forestry in 1945. Following the Report of the Royal Commission on Scottish Affairs,[4] published in 1954, there were further transfers to the Scottish Departments such as the responsibility for roads, bridges and ferries, Justices of the Peace, animal health, and the duties of the defunct Ministry of Food. Functions withdrawn from the Scottish Office have been fewer; roads were lost to the Ministry of Transport in 1911, though regained in 1956, but the most notable function transferred from the Scottish Office was that of pensions and national insurance in 1948. In 1962 the Scottish Development Department was created and the Scottish Economic Planning Department was established in 1973. A Scottish Development Agency, responsible to the Scottish Office, was set up in 1975. By 1977 most 'United Kingdom' Departments had regional offices in Scotland. Over the period from 1885, the Scottish Office has gained additional Ministers including Under-Secretaries in 1919, 1940, and 1952. A Minister of State was added to assist the Secretary of State in 1952. By 1983 the Scottish Office was organised into five Departments: the Department of Agriculture and Fisheries for Scotland, the Scottish Development Department, the Scottish Economic Planning Department, the Scottish Education Department, and the Scottish Home and Health Department. The office's headquarters in Edinburgh was complemented by a liaison office in Dover House, Whitehall. In 1995 the Departments were reorganised as Agriculture, Environment and Fisheries; Development; Education and Industry; Health; Home. From 1999 these departments came under the aegis of the devolved Scottish executive.

[1] Cmd.7338/1914. [2] Cmnd. 9320/1918. [3] Cmnd. 5563/1936–37. [4] Cmnd. 9212/1953–4.

Scotland has always had its own separate legal and judicial systems, its bar, its established church, and its heraldic authority, Lord Lyon King-at-Arms. A Scottish Grand Committee was established by the House of Commons on an experimental basis in 1894/5 and then from 1907 had a continued existence. Scottish Standing Committees dealing with peculiarly Scottish legislation were created in 1957 and 1962, and a Select Committee on Scottish Affairs was established in 1969 (see p.209), although it went into abeyance in 1972, but in 1979 the Select Committee on Scottish Affairs was reconstituted (see p.221) and, except for 1987–92 lasted until 1999. After the passage of the *Scotland Act, 1978*, a referendum was held on 1 Mar 1979 to ascertain the electorate's views on the provisions for legislative devolution contained in the Act. In the referendum 1,230,937 voted 'Yes' and 1,153,502 voted 'No' but as the 'Yes' majority represented 32.9% of the registered electorate, failing to overcome the 40% provision of the enactment, an Order to Repeal the *Scotland Act, 1978*, was successfully moved on 20 Jun 1979, following the General Election of 3 May.

After its election in May 1997, the Labour Government moved quickly to fulfil its devolution promises. On 11 Sep 1997, a 60.2% turnout, Scotland voted 74.3% for the establishment of a Scottish Parliament and 63.5% for it to have limited taxing powers. The *Scotland Act, 1998*, gave the Scottish Parliament power in most fields; but it reserved authority to the United Kingdom Parliament on a number of matters including the Constitution, social security, economic and monetary policy, aspects of trade and industry (including inward investment), consumer protection, employment (including minimum wage and equal opportunities), broadcasting, abortion, energy, defence, and foreign affairs.

The Parliament is composed of 129 members, 73 elected first-past-the-post in the Westminster constituencies and 56 (7 in each of eight regions) under the additional member system of proportional representation. The first election took place on 6 May 1999 and the Parliament met in Edinburgh on 13 May. D. Dewar (Lab.) was chosen by the Scottish Parliament as the first First Minister of Scotland. J. Wallace (Lib.Dem.) was chosen as his Deputy. D. Dewar was sworn in by the Queen on 17 May 99. The Queen opened the new Parliament on 1 Jul 1999.

The Scottish Executive
(assumed power on 1 Jul 1999)

First Minister D. Dewar (Lab)
Deputy First Minister and Min. for Justice J. Wallace (Lib.D.)
Deputy Min. for Justice A. Mackay (Lab)
Minister for Enterprise H. McLeish (Lab)
Deputy Min. for Enterprise N. Stephen (Lib. D.)
Deputy Min. for Highlands and Islands A. Morrison (Lab)
Min. For Children and Education S. Galbraith (Lab)
Deputy Min. for Culture and Education P. Peacock (Lab)
Deputy Min. for Culture and Sport Rhona Brankin (Lab)
Min. for Finance J. McConnell (Lab)
Min. for Health Susan Deakin (Lab)
Deputy Min. for Community Care I. Gray (Lab)
Min. for Rural Affairs R. Finnie (Lib.D.)
Deputy Min. for Rural Affairs J. Home Robertson (Lab)
Min. for Communities Wendy Alexander (Lab)
Deputy Min. for Communities Jackie Baillie (Lab)
Deputy Min. for Local Government F. McAveety (Lab)
Min. for Transport and the Environment Sarah Boyack (Lab)
Min. for Parliament T. McCabe (Lab)
Deputy Min. for Parliament I. Smith (Lib.D.)
Lord Advocate Lord Hardie (Lab)
Solicitor-General C. Boyd (Lab)

Scottish Parliament Election 6 May 1999

On 6 May 1999 the new Scottish Parliament was chosen. Each elector had two votes. 73 members were chosen directly, first-past-the-post, from the existing Westminster constituencies; 56 were elected on top-up lists from the eight Euro-constituencies.

	Con.	Lab.	Lib. D.	SNP	Other
Top-up seats	18	3	5	28	2
Direct seats	–	53	12	7	1
Total seats	18	56	17	35	3
Top-up vote	15.5%	34.0%	12.6%	27.6%	10.3%
Direct vote	15.6%	38.8%	14.2%	28.7%	2.1%

Turnout – Top-up 57.2%; Direct 58.9%

Sources: Sir D. Milne.*The Scottish Office (1957)*; G. Pryde, *Central and Local Government in Scotland Since 1707* (1960); H. Hanham, *Scottish Nationalism* (1969); J.G.Kellas, *The Scottish Political System* (4th ed 1989); G. Pottinger, *The Secretaries of State for Scotland* (1979); M. Keating and A. Midwinter, *The Government of Scotland* (1983); A. Midwinter et al., *Politics and Public Policy in Scotland* (1991); M. Linklater and x. Denniston (eds.) *Anatomy of Scotland* (1992); A. Marr, *The Battle for Scotland* (1992); See also *The Scottish Government Year Book (1977–1991)* which was replaced by the *Scottish Quarterly* (1992–) and then by Scottish Affairs (1992–). The latest sources include A. Brown, G. McCrone and L. Paterson, *Politics and Society in Scotland* (2nd ed. 1998) and *Scotland's Parliament* (Cm 3658/1997) B. Taylor and K. Thompson,*Scotland and Wales: Nations Again?* (1999).

See also Govermental Reports: (Gilmour) *Scottish Administration* (Cmd 5563/1937; (Balfour) *Royal Commission on Scottish Affairs,* (Cmnd.9212/1954)*;* (Wheatley) *Royal Commission on Local Governmernt in Scotland,* (Cmnd. 4150/1969); (Kilbrandon) *Royal Commission on the Constitution,* Cmnd. 5460–1/1973.

Wales

From Plantagenet times the administration of Wales was London-centred. The only significant devolution of administrative responsibility from Westminster to Wales has taken place since 1950, and this to a much more limited extent than in Scotland. In 1907 a Welsh Department of the Board of Education (until 1999 part of the Department of Education) was established. A Welsh Board of Health was set up in 1919, but was only to exercise such powers in Wales as the Minister thought fit. A Welsh Office in the Ministry of Housing and Local Government was also established. In 1951 a Minister for Welsh Affairs was appointed, holding the office jointly with the Home Office from 1951 to 1957. From 1957 to 1964 the Minister for Welsh Affairs was also the Minister of Housing and Local Government. A second parliamentary secretary was appointed at the Home Office from 1951 to 1957 to be responsible for Welsh Affairs; in 1957 a Minister of State for Welsh Affairs was appointed and in 1964 a Welsh Office was established with a Secretary of State for Wales. Since 1964 in many detailed ways, powers have been devolved from Whitehall to the Welsh Office in Cardiff. In 1960 a Welsh Grand Committee analogous to the Scottish Grand Committee was appointed by the House of Commons to consider all Bills and other parliamentary business relating exclusively to Wales. In 1979 a Select Committee on Welsh Affairs was appointed (see p.221).

Welsh national or separatist feeling has, however, expressed itself in forces other than the movement for home rule or devolution. The most important aspects of this have been the campaigns on such matters as the Church, education, land, temperance reform and the Welsh language. The 1881 *Welsh Sunday Closing Act* and the 1889 *Intermediate Education (Wales) Act* were the beginning of separate legislation for Wales. In 1961, 1968, 1975 and 1982 referendums were held throughout Wales on Sunday opening of licensed premises. The *Elections (Welsh Forms) Act 1964,* provided for the use of Welsh on election forms and following the recommendations of the Hughes Parry committee, the

Welsh Language Act, 1967, paved the way for the removal of restrictions on the use of the Welsh language in official documents and in the administration of justice in Wales; the *Welsh Language Act, 1993,* extended the provisions of the 1967 Act. The *Education Reform Act, 1988* and the *Education Act, 1992* provided opportunities for the development of a Welsh ethos in education (Curriculum Cymreig) and the use of Welsh in the 15–18 age group was estimated at 25 per cent in 1999.

In 1901, 50 per cent of the population spoke Welsh; in 1931 the figure was 37 per cent; in 1951, 29 per cent; in 1961, 26 per cent; in 1971, 21 per cent; in 1981, 19 per cent and in 1991, 19 per cent. A Welsh language television channel was established in 1982.

In 1978 the *Wales Act* provided for the establishment of a devolved Welsh Assembly in Cardiff, subject to a referendum. In the referendum on 1 Mar 1979, 243,048 (11.9 per cent or 20.2 per cent of valid votes) voted 'yes', 956,330 (46.9 per cent or 79.8 per cent of valid votes) voted 'no' and 41.2 percent did not vote; the highest 'yes' vote (34.5 per cent) was in Gwynedd and the lowest (12.1 per cent) was in Gwent.

Following its election victory in May 1997, the Labour Party moved swiftly to implement its promise of a Welsh Assembly. In a Referendum on 18 Sep 1997, on a 50.1% turnout Wales voted by 50.3% to 49.7% in favour of a Welsh Assembly. The *Government of Wales Act, 1998* provided for a National Assembly (Cynulliad) for Wales. The Assembly has limited political functions and, unlike the Scottish Parliament, has no tax-raising powers. It is composed of sixty members, 40 elected first-past-the-post in the Westminster constituencies and 20 (4 in each of five regions) under the additional member system of proportional representation. The first election took place on 6 May 1999 and the Assembly met on 13 May in Cardiff.

Welsh Cabinet
(assumed power 1 Jul 1999)

First Secretary of Wales A. Michael
Economic Development R. Morgan
Education Rosemary Butler
Health and Social Services Jane Hutt
Agriculture Christine Gwyther
Environment P. Law
Trefnydd Manager A. Davies

Welsh Assembly Election 6 May 1999

On 6 May 1999 the new Welsh Assembly was chosen. Each elector had two votes. 40 members were chosen directly, first-past-the-post, from the existing Westminster constituencies; 20 were elected on top-up lists from the eight Euro-constituencies.

	Con.	Lab.	Lib. D.	PC	Other
Top-up seats	8	1	3	8	–
Direct seats	1	27	3	9	–
Total seats	9	28	6	17	–
Top-up vote	16.5%	35.5%	12.5%	30.6%	4.9%
Direct vote	15.8%	37.6%	13.5%	28.4%	4.7%

Turnout: Top-up –46.1%; Direct 46.3%

Sources: J. Davies, *A History of Wales* (1993); K. Morgan, *Wales in British Politics 1868–1922*(3rd. ed. 1980); K. Morgan, *Rebirth of a Nation: Wales 1880–1980* (1981); D. Foulkes et al (eds.), *The Welsh Veto: The Wales Act 1978 and the Referendum* (1983); D. Balsom and M. Burch, *A Political and Electoral Handbook for Wales; 1959–1979* (1980). B. Taylor and K. Thompson, *Scotland and Wales: Nations Again?* (1999).

Ireland 1900–1922

From 1900 to 1921 the Lord-Lieutenant of Ireland was responsible for the administration of Irish affairs, with an office in Dublin. His Chief Secretary was a member of the House of Commons, and assisted him in carrying on the parliamentary business of the department, for which he was the responsible minister. At the same time there were several departments in Dublin, working under the presidency of the Chief Secretary: the Department of Agriculture and Technical Instruction, the Irish Congested Districts Board, and the Local Government Board for Ireland. There were three boards of education commissioners, all of whom were appointed by the Lord-Lieutenant or the Government, and there was the Irish Land Commission. The Irish Public Works Board was controlled by the Treasury in London, and not by the Irish Government. There was scarcely any further devolution of administrative authority to Ireland between 1900 and 1922.

The Irish Office remained in existence until 1924 after the partition of Ireland, though the posts of Chief Secretary and Lord-Lieutenant lapsed in 1922, with the recognition of the Irish Free State. The functions previously exercised by the Irish Office became the responsibility of the Home Office (for Northern Ireland) and the Colonial Office handled relations with the Free State (in 1937 renamed Eire). When Ireland became a republic in 1949, the Commonwealth Relations Office continued to be the department responsible for relations with her. In 1966 this responsibility was transferred to the Commonwealth Affairs Office (since 1968 the Foreign and Commonwealth Office).

	Lord-Lieutenant of Ireland 1900–22		Chief Secretary for Ireland 1900–22
1895	Ld Cadogan	1900	G. Balfour
8 Aug 02	E of Dudley	7 Nov 00	G. Wyndham
3 Feb 06	E of Aberdeen	12 Mar 05	W. Long
19 Feb 15	Ld Wimborne	10 Dec 05	J. Bryce
12 May 18	Vt French	23 Jan 07	A. Birrell
2 May 21	Vt FitzAlan	31 Jul 16	(Sir) H. Duke
	(Office in cabinet only	5 May 18	E. Shortt
	Jun 95–8 Aug 02 and	10 Jan 19	I. Macpherson
	28 Oct 19–2 Apr 21)	2 Apr 20	S. H. Greenwood
			(Irish Office wound up 1922)

(See p.61 for Lord Chancellors of Ireland and Irish Law Officers.)

Northern Ireland 1922–1972

The Northern Ireland Parliament was created by the *Government of Ireland Act 1920*. The powers of the Crown were exercised by the Governor, appointed by the Crown. Provision was made in the Act for the continued representation of Northern Ireland constituencies in the House of Commons of the United Kingdom. The constitutional position of Northern Ireland was thus unique in that it was part of the United Kingdom and sent representatives to the United Kingdom Parliament but was subject in most internal matters to the jurisdiction of a Parliament and Government of its own. The *Government of Ireland Act* conferred on that Parliament extensive powers for the regulation of the affairs of Northern

Ireland, but excluded a number of specified matters from its jurisdiction. In respect of these excluded matters executive power remained with the United Kingdom Government, and only the United Kingdom Parliament could legislate. Consequently Northern Ireland was subject to two jurisdictions, and although most of Northern Ireland's public services were administered by Ministers who were members of the Northern Ireland Government, there were some public services, such as, for example, the Post Office services, the Customs and Excise service and the Inland Revenue service, for which Ministers of the United Kingdom Government were responsible.

In respect of all matters on which the Northern Ireland Parliament was empowered to make laws, executive powers were exercisable by the Government of Northern Ireland. At the head of this Government was the Governor appointed by the Crown who formally summoned, prorogued and dissolved the Parliament, appointed the members of the Privy Council, and appointed Ministers to administer such Government departments as the Northern Ireland Parliament might establish. The departments were the Prime Minister's Department, the Ministry of Finance, the Ministry of Home Affairs, the Ministry of Development, the Ministry of Education, the Ministry of Agriculture, the Ministry of Commerce and the Ministry of Health and Social Services. The Ministers in charge of these eight departments (together with the Minister in the Senate, the Minister of State in the Ministry of Development and the Minister who was Leader of the House) formed an Executive Committee of the Privy Council which aided and advised the Governor in the exercise of his executive powers.

The Parliament of Northern Ireland consisted of a Senate and a House of Commons. The House of Commons had 52 members. Proportional Representation was used in the elections of 1921 and 1925 but after 1929, except for 4 members for Queen's University, Belfast, they were chosen directly by single-member constituencies. In 1969 the University constituency was abolished and four new territorial seats were created. The Senate had 26 members, 24 being elected by the House of Commons by proportional representation, and two being ex officio, the Lord Mayor of Belfast and the Mayor of Londonderry. The main differences between the Northern Ireland law relating to elections to the Northern Ireland Parliament and the United Kingdom law relating to elections to the United Kingdom Parliament were that, after 1950, Northern Ireland law retained the University seats (until 1965) and the 'business premises' qualification for a vote (until 1968). It also required qualified electors either to have been born in Northern Ireland or to have been resident in the U.K. for seven years and to possess the requisite residence, business premises or service qualification. The Parliament of Northern Ireland could legislate on all matters except certain fields that were permanently excepted by the 1920 Act, such as the succession to the Crown, the making of peace or war, the armed forces of the Crown, the making of treaties, honours, naturalisation and aliens, and certain functions that were reserved such as postal and telegraph services, the Supreme Court and the important forms of taxation. It was also prohibited from making laws which would interfere with religious freedom or might discriminate against any religious body and, until 1961, from taking property without compensation. All United Kingdom bills applied to Northern Ireland unless there was express provision to the contrary. In general, legislation at Stormont followed very closely legislation in Westminster. The revenue of the Government of Northern Ireland was derived partly from taxes imposed by the United Kingdom Parliament (known as 'reserved' taxes) and partly from taxes imposed by the Northern Ireland Parliament (known as 'transferred taxes'). The powers of the Northern Ireland Parliament were similar to those of the United Kingdom Parliament as regards the appropriation of revenue. The Treasury was responsible for financial relations with Northern Ireland, and other departments were concerned with trade, commerce, and employment, but the Home Office retained the major responsibility for Northern Ireland.

Governors of Northern Ireland 1922–73		**Prime Ministers of Northern Ireland 1921–72**	
11 Dec 22	D of Abercorn	7 Jun 21	Sir J. Craig
7 Sep 45	Earl Granville		(1927 *Vt Craigavon*)
1 Dec 52	Ld Wakehurst	26 Nov 40	J. Andrews
1 Dec 64	Ld Erskine	6 May 43	Sir B. Brooke
2 Dec 68	Ld Grey		(*1952 Vt*
	(*office abolished 19 Jul 73*)		*Brookeborough*)
		25 Mar 63	T. O'Neill
		1 May 69	J. Chichester-Clark
		23 Mar 71	B. Faulkner
		(*office suspended 30 Mar 72*)	

Members of Northern Ireland Cabinet 1921–72

Minister of Finance

1921	H Pollock	1956	G. Hanna	1968	W. Long
1937	J. M. Andrews	1956	T. O'Neill	1969	R. Porter
	(*also PM 1940–1*)	1963	J. L. Andrews	1970	J. Chichester-Clark *(PM)*
1941	J. Barbour	1964	I. Neill	1971	B. Faulkner *(PM)*
1943	J. Sinclair	1965	H. Kirk		
1953	W. Maginess	1966	W. Craig		

Minister of State (Finance)

1971	J. Brooke

Minister of Home Affairs

1921	(Sir) D. Bates	1956	T. O'Neill	1965	W. Morgan
1943	W. Lowry	1956	W. Topping	1969	R. Porter
1944	J. Warnock	1959	B. Faulkner	1969	W. Fitzsimmons
1949	W. Maginess	1963	W. Craig		
1953	G. Hanna	1964	R. McConnell		

Minister of Health (and Local Government)

1944	W. Grant	1964	W. Craig	1966	W. Fitzsimmons
1949	Dame D. Parker	(*1965 became Minister of*		1968	I. Neill
1957	J. L. Andrews	*Development*)		1969	W. Long
1961	W. Morgan	1965	W. Craig	1969	B. Faulkner
				1971	R. Bradford

Minister of Education

1921	M of Londonderry	1950	H. Midgely	1966	W. Long
1926	Vt Charlemont	1957	W. May	1969	P. O'Neill
1937	J. Robb	1962	I. Neill	1969	W. Long
1943	R. Corkey	1964	H. Kirk		
1944	S. Hall-Thompson	1965	W. Fitzsimmons		

Minister of Public Security

1940	J. MacDermott	1941	W. Grant	1943	H. Midgely

Minister of Labour (and National Insurance 1949)

1921	J. M. Andrews	1945	W. Maginess	1962	H. Kirk
1938	J. Gordon	1949	W. McCleery	1964	W. Morgan
1943	W. Grant	1949	H. Midgely		*(1965 became Minister*
1944	H. Midgely	1950	I. Neill		*of Health and Social*
					Services)

Minister of Agriculture (and Commerce 1921–5)

1921	(Sir) E. Archdale	1943	R. Moore	1969	P. O'Neill
1933	Sir B. Brooke	1960	H. West	1971	H. West
1941	Ld Glentoran *(1st)*	1967	J. Chichester-Clark		

Minister of Commerce

1925	J. Barbour	1949	W. Maginess	1963	B. Faulkner
1941	Sir B. Brooke	1949	W. McCleery	1969	R. Bradford
	(also PM 43–5)	1953	Ld Glentoran (2nd)	1971	R. Bailie
1945	Sir R. Nugent	1961	J.L. Andrews		

Minister without Portfolio

1944–44	Sir R.Nugent	1966–67	J. Chichester-Clark	1969–71	J. Dobson

Minister in the Senate

1949	Sir R. Nugent	1951	A. Gordon	1964	J. L. Andrews
1950	*(office vacant)*	1961	Ld Glentoran (2nd)		

Minister of State (PM's Office)

1971	G. Newe

Minister of Community Relations

1970	R. Simpson	1971	D. Bleakley	1971	B. McIvor

Minister of State (Development)

1966	B. McConnell	1969	N. Minford

Minister of State (Home Affairs)

1971	J. Taylor

General Elections of Northern Ireland 1921–69

	Unionist	Ind. Unionist	Lib.	Lab	Nat	S.Fein Repub. Abstentionist	Ir.Lab. Rep.Lab. Soc.Rep. Ind. Lab.	Ind.& Other
24 May 21	40	–	–	–	6	6	–	–
28 Apr 25	32	4	–	3	10	2	–	1
22 May 29	37	3	–	1	11	–	–	–
30 Nov 33	36	2	–	2	9	2	–	1
9 Feb 38	39	3	3	1	8	–	1	–
14 Jun 45	33	2	–	2	9	–	3	3
10 Feb 49	37	2	–	–	9	–	2	2
22 Oct 53	38	1	–	–	7	2	3	1
20 Mar 58	37	–	–	4	8	–	2	1
31 May 62	34	–	1	4	9	–	3	1
25 Nov 65	36	–	1	2	9	–	2	2
24 Feb 69	36	3	–	2	6	–	2	3

Northern Ireland 1972–

After sectarian troubles and terrorist activities which from 1969 onwards cost several hundred lives and led to the sending of substantial British military forces, the British Government on 30 Mar 72 passed the *Northern Ireland (Temporary Provisions) Act*. This Act suspended Stormont and transferred all the functions of the Government and Parliament of Northern Ireland to a new Secretary of State for Northern Ireland, acting by Order-in-Council, for one year (extended in Mar 1973 for a further twelve months).

Secretary of State for Northern Ireland

24 Mar 72	W. Whitelaw	11 Sep 84	D. Hurd
2 Dec 73	F. Pym	3 Sep 85	T. King
5 Mar 74	M. Rees	24 Jul 89	P. Brooke
10 Sep 76	R. Mason	11 Apr 92	Sir P. Mayhew
5 May 79	H. Atkins	2 May 97	Mo Mowlam
14 Sep 81	J. Prior	11 Oct 99	P. Mandelson

On 8 Mar 73 on a 58.1% poll, the electors of Northern Ireland voted, 591,820 for the province to remain part of the U.K. and 6,463 for it to be joined with the Republic of Ireland. Following a White Paper (Cmnd.5259 published on 2 Mar 73) the *Northern Ireland Constitution Act, 1973* was passed; this abolished the office of Governor and the Northern Ireland Privy Council; vested the executive power in the Crown, exercisable by the Secretary of State; provided for a complex system of power-sharing in a new Assembly (to be elected by single Transferable Vote proportional representation from multi-member constituencies) with an Executive to be appointed by the Secretary of State after consulting with the parties, and also authorised any department in Northern Ireland 'to consult' or 'enter into agreements with any authority of the Republic of Ireland in respect of any transferred matter'. Local elections were held on 30 May 1973 for 26 district councils (using proportional representation) in place of the old local government bodies. On June 28 1973 the 78-member Assembly was elected; its composition was 22 Ulster Unionist (B. Faulkner), 13 other Unionist (12 anti-White Paper), 15 Loyalist Coalition (7 Vanguard (W. Craig), 8 Democratic Unionist (I. Paisley), 3 Alliance (O. Napier), 1 Northern Ireland Labour Party (D. Bleakley), and 19 Social Democratic and Labour Party (G. Fitt).

The election was followed by prolonged negotiations over the formation of a Northern Ireland Executive, which was finally agreed in December. The Executive which took over on 1 Jan 1974 consisted of 6 Ulster Unionists accepting the Leadership of B. Faulkner, the Chief Executive, 4 Soc. DLP members under G. Fitt, the Deputy Chief Executive, and 1 Alliance Party member. Opposition to the Sunningdale agreement of Dec 1973 (which provided, among other things, for the establishment of a Council of Ireland) led to Mr Faulkner's repudiation by the Unionist Party. In May 1974 a strike of Protestant workers forced the ending of the Northern Ireland Executive and the return to direct rule from Westminster.

On 1 May 75 elections were held for a Northern Ireland constitutional Convention. 46 of the 78 seats went to the Ulster Unionists (H. West), 5 to the Unionist Party of Northern Ireland (B. Faulkner) and one to an Independent Loyalist; there were 8 Alliance members, 1 from the Northern Ireland Labour Party and 17 from the Social Democratic and Labour Party. The Convention discussions proved abortive.

On 7 Nov 75 it submitted a majority (42–31) draft final report to the Secretary of State, and then adjourned. It reconvened 3 Feb 76, at the request of the Secretary of State, to reconsider the report. The Convention was finally dissolved by Order in Council on 6 Mar 76 because, as reported in the House of Commons on 5 Mar (H.C. Deb. 906 c. 1715–1727), the debates and resolutions in the Convention had made it plain that there was no prospect of agreement between the parties and that no further progress could be made.

The *Northern Ireland Act 1982*, again attempted to restore devolved institutions to the province. On 25 Oct 1979, the Secretary of State, H. Atkins, had announced that the new Conservative Government favoured devolution in Northern Ireland. In Nov 1979 a White Paper was published, *The Government of Northern Ireland: A Working Paper for a Conference* (Cmnd. 7763), setting out principles to be observed in the transfer of power, and issues for discussion at a round-table conference. The conference held between Jan and Mar 1980 failed to reach agreement. A further White Paper, *The Government of Northern Ireland – Proposals for Further Dicussion* (Cmnd. 7950), published in Jul 1980, put forward further proposals for discussion.

In Feb 1982, J. Prior, the new Secretary of State, held further discussions with the Northern Ireland parties, and in Apr 1982, a third White Paper, *Northern Ireland – A Framework for Devolution* (Cmnd. 8451), was published, proposing a scheme of 'rolling devolution' given legislative effect by the *Northern Ireland Act* which was placed on the statute book on 23 Jul 1982. This provided for the election of a Northern Ireland Assembly whose functions would initially be limited to scrutiny, deliberation and advice, pending cross-community agreement on the transfer of certain legislative powers.

The election for the Assembly was held on 20 Oct 1982, and of the 78 seats, 26 went to the Official Unionists, 21 to the Democratic Unionists, 14 to the SDLP, 10 to Alliance, 5 to Sinn Fein, 1 to a Popular Unionist and 1 to an Independent Unionist. However, Sinn Fein and the SDLP refused to take their seats in the Assembly, while on 21 Nov 83 most of the Official Unionists withdrew after some murders in Armagh.

The SDLP took part in a New Ireland Forum with the leaders of the three main parties in Ireland – Fine Gael, Fianna Fail and the Labour Party – which met for the first time on 30 May 1983 in Dublin, and produced a report on 2 May 84 advocating fresh approaches.

On 15 Nov 1985 an Anglo-Irish Agreement was signed at Hillsborough. Article 1 restated the British Government's commmitment to Northern Ireland remaining part of the United Kingdom as long as that was the wish of the majority of the population. Article 2 provided for regular inter-governmental conferences. The 15 Unionist M.P.s resigned their seats in protest against the Agreement; 14 of them were returned in the subsequent by-elections.

On 26 Mar 1991 the UK Government announced a basis ('the three strands') on which peace talks should proceed. After some meetings the initiative came to a halt in Jul 1991.

Renewed talks in Mar–Nov 92 again ended in failure. In the following year there were increased contacts between the London and Dublin governments which resulted in the Downing Street Declaration of 15 Dec 93 offering talks about reform to all parties that would renounce violence.

A cease-fire was announced by the IRA on 31 Aug 1994 and by the Loyalist para-military organisations on 13 Oct 1994. An international body on the decommissioning of para-military weapons was appointed by the Government under the former US Senator, George Mitchell; it published its report on 20 Jan 1996, setting out principles of non-violence under which settlement talks could begin. However, the IRA ended its cease-fire on 9 Feb 1996 with a bomb at Canary Wharf. On 30 May 1996 elections took place for a Northern Ireland Forum, from which those participating in multi-party talks were to be drawn. On 16 May 1997 the newly elected Labour Government approved contacts between officials and Sinn Fein. The IRA renewed its cease-fire on 20 Jul 1997 and on 9 Sep 1997 the IRA accepted the Mitchell principles for the talks.

The talks climaxed with the 'Good Friday Agreement' of 10 Apr 1998 supported by almost all parties except I. Paisley's Democratic Unionist Party. The Agreement stated that the status of N.Ireland could only be changed with the consent of its people and committed the Irish Government to formally withdrawing its Constitutional claim to sovereignty over the whole of the island. It provided for a 108 seat parliament to be elected by proportional representation. Executive functions were to be taken over by ministers and committees, allocated according to party strength. A North-South Ministerial Council was to develop cooperation between Belfast and Dublin. Prisoners were in time to be released and para-military weapons decommissioned.

On 22 May 1998 the Agreement was endorsed by 71 per cent of the electorate on an 80% turnout. On 25 Jun 1998 Assembly elections returned 28 Official Unionists, 24 SDLP, 20 Democratic Unionists, 18 Sinn Fein, 6 Alliance, 5 UK Unionists, 3 Independent Unionists, 2 Progressive Unionists and 2 Women's Coalition.

On 1 Jul 98 the Assembly met for the first time and elected the Ulster Unionist David Trimble as First Minister, and Seamus Mallon of the SDLP as Deputy First Minister. However, arguments over decommissioning delayed the establishment of the new Executive. In September 1999 Senator Mitchell was brought back to break the deadlock and by November it was agreed that the Executive would be established on the understanding that decommissioning would follow soon afterwards. On 29 Nov 99 the parties in the Assembly nominated 10 Ministers to the Executive. On 2 Dec 99 powers were devolved to the Assembly and the Executive, bringing an end to Direct Rule from Westminster. The British and Irish governments signed a new agreement setting up new British-Irish and North-South institutions and the Irish Taoiseach signed a declaration ending the Constitutional territorial claim over Northern Ireland. On 2 Dec 99, the IRA announced the appointment of an interlocutor to the Independent International Commision on Decommissioning. The new North-South Council held its first meeting on 13 Dec 99 and the new Council of the Isles held its first meeting on 17 Dec 99.

(See p.523 for Army activities.)

Sources: N. Mansergh, *The Government of Northern Ireland* (1936); T. Wilson (ed.) *Ireland under Home Rule* (1955); R. Lawrence, *The Government of Northern Ireland* (1965); M. Wallace, *Northern Ireland: 50 years of Self-Government (1971)*; R. Rose, *Governing without Consensus: an Irish Perspective* (1971); S. Elliott, *Northern Ireland Parliamentary Election Results 1921–72* (1973); A. Maltby, *The Government of Northern Ireland 1922–1972: a Catalogue and Breviate of Parliamentary Papers* (1974); P. Bew et al., *Northern Ireland 1921–1996* (1996); P. Buckland, *A History of Northern Ireland* (1981); W.D. Flackes and S. Elliott (eds) *Northern Ireland: A Political Directory 1968–93* (1994); J. McGarry and B. O'Leary (eds) *The Future of Northern Ireland* (1990) and *The Politics of Antagonism* (1993); M. Cunningham *The Constitution of Northern Ireland* (1989); D. Keogh and M. Haltzel (eds) *Northern Ireland and the Politics of Reconciliation* (1993); P. O'Malley, *The Uncivil Wars* (1983); J. Whyte, *Interpreting Northern Ireland* (1990); D. McKittrick, *The Search for Peace in Northern Ireland* (1994).

The Channel Islands

The Channel Islands which were originally part of the Duchy of Normandy have been associated with England since 1066. They have their own legislative assemblies, systems of local administration, fiscal systems, and courts of law. The Islanders have general responsibility for the regulation of their local affairs subject to the prerogative of the Crown over appointment to the chief posts in the local administrations and the necessity of Royal Assent to legislative measures passed by the insular assemblies. Most of the laws by which they are governed emanate from their representative assemblies and although they cannot be regarded as local authorities most of their public services are provided by these assemblies in the same way as local government services are provided and administered in Great Britain.

The Channel lslands are divided into 2 Bailiwicks, one comprising Jersey and the other, Alderney, Sark, and Guernsey with its dependants, Herm and Jethou. Each Bailiwick has a Lieutenant-Governor appointed by the Crown for a period of 5 years, through whom all official communications between the U.K. Government and the Islands pass, and in whom certain executive functions are vested. A Bailiff, also appointed by the Crown, presides over the local legislatures, the States, and over the sittings of the Royal Court. Since 1948 all members of the States who have the right to vote are elected directly or indirectly by the electorate. The Islands have their own Courts of Law, but there remains leave to appeal to the Judicial Committee of the Privy Council.

The Island Assemblies may initiate legislation but they must then petition the Sovereign in Council to give these measures force of law. Acts of the U.K. Parliament do not apply to the Channel Islands unless by express provision or necessary application. As a general rule Parliament refrains from legislating on matters with which these assemblies can deal unless for some special reason a U.K. act must be preferred to local legislation.

The public revenues of the Islands are raised by duties on imported goods, by income taxes and other taxes. Proposals made by the States for raising revenue require authorisation by Order in Council but responsibility for determining how the revenue shall be spent is, in practice, left to the States. Immunity from taxation for Crown purposes has been a privilege of the Islanders since the time of Edward VI.

Source: *Report of the Commission on the Constitution* (Cmnd.5460–1/1973).

Jersey

Lieutenant-Governor

1895	(Sir) E. Hopton	1929	Ld Ruthven	1963	Sir M. Villiers
1900	H. Abadie	1934	(Sir) H. Martelli	1969	Sir J. Davis
1904	H. Gough	1939	R. Harrison	1974	Sir D. Fitzpatrick
1910	(Sir) A. Rochfort	1940	(*office vacant*)	1979	Sir P. Whiteley
1916	Sir A. Wilson	1945	Sir A. Grassett	1985	Sir W. Pillar
1920	Sir D. Smith	1953	Sir R. Nicholson	1990	Sir J. Sutton
1924	Sir F. Bingham	1958	Sir G. Erskine	1995	Sir M. Wilkes

Bailiff

1899	(Sir) W. Venables-Vernon	1935	(Sir) (Ld) A. Coutanche	1973	(Sir) F. Ereaut
1931	C. Malet de Carteret	1961	C. Harrison	1988	(Sir) P. Crill
		1962	(Sir) R. le Masurier	1995	(Sir) P. Bailhache

Guernsey

Lieutenant-Governor

1899	M. Savard	1929	E. Willis	1964	Sir C. Coleman
1903	B. Campbell	1934	(Sir) E. Broadbent	1969	Sir C. Mills
1908	R. Auld	1939	J. Minshull-Ford	1974	Sir J. Martin
1911	Sir E. Hamilton	1940	*(Office Vacant)*	1980	Sir P. Le Cheminant
1914	Sir R. Hart	1945	Sir P. Neame	1985	Sir A. Boswell
1918	Sir F. Kiggell	1953	Sir T. Elmhirst	1990	Sir M. Wilkins
1920	Sir J. Capper	1958	Sir G. Robson	1994	Sir J. Coward
1925	Sir C. Sackville-West (Ld Sackville)				

Bailiff

1895	(Sir) T. Carey	1929	A. Bell	1973	(Sir) J. Loveridge
1902	W. Carey	1935	(Sir) V. Carey	1982	(Sir) C. Frossard
1915	(Sir) E. Chepnell Ozanne	1946	(Sir) A . Sherwill	1992	(Sir) G. Dorey
1922	Sir H. de Sausmarez	1960	(Sir) W. Arnold	1999	de V. Carey

The Isle of Man

This island was successively under the rule of Norway, of Scotland, of the Stanley family and of the Dukes of Atholl before it became a Crown Dependency in 1765. For over 1000 years the internal affairs of the island have been regulated by the Tynwald, which has evolved from the Lord of Man's Council composed of his chief officials and other persons of importance and the House of Keys. The latter comprises 24 representatives elected by all over the age of 18 who have resided in the island for 6 months. The consent of both the Legislative Council and the Keys is requisite for any Act of Tynwald except when in two successive sessions of a Parliament the Keys pass the same Bill, or an essentially similar one, which is once rejected by the Council. In that case the Bill is deemed to have been passed by the Council. All legislation by Tynwald depends for its validity on confirmation by Royal Assent granted by the Lieutenant-Governor or, in certain rare cases, in the form of orders made by the Queen in Council.

Most of the public services are provided by Tynwald and administered by Boards of Tynwald, but the Lieutenant-Governor is still the executive authority for certain services, including the administration of justice. In 1866, Tynwald was granted certain financial powers which had been removed from it in 1765. This process continued through the following decades until by Tynwald's *Isle of Man Contribution Act 1958* the Treasury's control over the Island's finance was removed enabling the Tynwald to regulate its own finances and customs, although under the Act, the Island continues to make an annual contribution to the Exchequer for defence and common services. There is a statutory body of members of Tynwald known as the Executive Council, the duty of which is to consider and advise the Lieutenant-Governor upon all matters of principle, policy and legislation.

Source: *Report of the Commission on the Constitution* (Cmnd.5460–1/1973); D. Kermode, *Devolution at Work: A Case Study of the Isle of Man* (1979).

Lieutenant-Governor

1899	Ld Henniker	1945	Sir G. Bromet	1980	Sir N. Cecil
1902	Ld Raglan	1952	Sir A. Dundas	1985	(Sir) L. New
1919	(Sir) W. Fry	1959	Sir R. Garvey	1990	Sir L. Jones
1926	Sir C. Hill	1966	Sir P. Stallard	1995	Sir T. Daunt
1933	Sir M. Butler	1973	Sir J. Paul		
1937	W. Leveson-Gower (Earl Granville)				

Devolution

Main Landmarks

1906–14	Scottish Home Rule Bills given First or Second Readings 6 times in House of Commons, though never reaching Committee Stage.
1912	First draft of *Government of Ireland Bill* proposed that all Bills referring exclusively to England, Scotland, or Ireland should be dealt with by national Grand Committees. This was to be a prelude to full legislative devolution but was abandoned to avoid overloading the *Government of Ireland Bill*.
4 Jun 19	Resolution in favour of devolution carried by 187 to 34.
12 May 20	Speaker's Conference reported (Cmd 692/1920) in favour of either full legislative devolution or devolution to Grand Committees.
7 Jun 21	Devolved powers transferred to Northern Ireland government at Stormont under Government of Ireland Act 1920.
12 Apr 45	First Scottish Nationalist M.P. elected (defeated 5 Jul 45).
1949–51	Scottish Covenant attracts 1,100,000 signatures in Scotland.
1950	Parliament for Wales Campaign.
14 Jul 66	First Plaid Cymru M.P. elected.
2 Nov 67	S.N.P. win Hamilton by-election.
9 May 68	E. Heath in Declaration of Perth proposes directly elected Scottish Assembly. (Endorsed by Douglas-Home Committee 1970).
11 Jun 69	Royal Commission on Local Government (Redcliffe-Maud, Cmnd 4040/1969) envisages eight provincial Councils for England (not directly elected).
15 Apr 69	Committee on the Constitution set up under Ld Crowther (Lord Kilbrandon from 1970).
30 Mar 72	Suspension of Stormont.
18 Jul 73	Northern Ireland Constitution Act provides for a power-sharing Executive.
31 Oct 73	Kilbrandon Commission report (Cmnd 5460/1973) rejects separatism or federation but unanimously favours directly elected Scottish Assembly and approves devolution in general.
1 Jan 74	Power-sharing Executive established in Northern Ireland.
28 Feb 74	General Election results in 7 S.N.P. and 2 Plaid Cymru M.P.s. It also returned 11 (out of 12) Ulster M.P.s opposed to power-sharing.
28 May 74	Power-sharing Executive resigns, following strike (see p.466).
3 Jun 74	Privy Council Office publishes discussion document, Devolution in the U.K.
17 Jul 74	*Northern Ireland Act* confirms suspension of Northern Ireland Executive.
17 Sep 74	Government announces decision to set up elected assemblies (Cmnd 5732/1974).
10 Oct 74	General Election results in 11 S.N.P. M.P.s (with 30% of Scottish vote) and 3 Plaid Cymru M.P.s.
27 Nov 75	Government outlines detailed proposals in *Our Changing Democracy* (Cmnd 6348/1975, modified by Cmnd 6585/1976).
16–19 Jan 76	Four-day debate on devolution in House of Commons.
9 Dec 76	Consultative document published, *Devolution – the English Dimension*.
16 Dec 76	Second Reading of *Scotland and Wales Bill* carried 292–247.
22 Feb 77	Government fails (312–283) to secure guillotine on *Scotland and Wales Bill*.
5 Mar 77	Abortive all-party talks on devolution started.
16 Jun 77	*Scotland and Wales Bill* 1976 withdrawn by government.
14 Nov 77	Second Reading of *Scotland Bill* carried 307–263.
15 Nov 77	Second Reading of *Wales Bill* carried 295–264.
23 Nov 77	House of Commons rejects Proportional Representation for Scottish Assembly Elections 290–107.
25 Jan 78	Amendments setting referendum condition (40% of electorate voting 'Yes') carried against Government (confirmed 298–243 15 Feb 78).
22 Feb 78	*Scotland Bill* gets Third Reading, 297–257.
31 Jul 78	*Scotland Bill* and *Wales Bill* receive Royal Assent.
1 Mar 79	Scotland votes 'yes' in Referendum (33% to 31% with 36% not voting); Wales votes 'no' (12% to 47% with 41% not voting).
28 Jun 79	Parliament passes resolution nullifying *Scotland Act, 1978*.
5 Jul 79	Parliament passes resolution nullifying *Wales Act, 1978*.
5 Apr 82	Government outlines new Northern Ireland proposals in Northern Ireland – *A Framework for Devolution* (Cmnd. 8451).
26 Oct 82	Northern Ireland Assembly elected (see p. 466).

2 May 84	Irish forum proposals published in Dublin.
Nov 86	Anglo-Irish Agreement.
30 Mar 89	First meeting of Scottish Convention on interparty discussion forum, boycotted by the Conservatives and the Nationalists.
10 Dec 93	Downing Street Declaration on Northern Ireland.
May 94	Reorganisation of Welsh local government.
May 94	Reorganisation of Scottish local government.
1 May 97	Labour win General Election with a commitment to Scottish and Welsh devolution.
11 Sep 97	Scottish Referendum.
18 Sep 97	Welsh Referendum.
Apr 98	Good Friday Agreement.
22 May 98	Good Friday Agreement endorsed by Referendum.
1 Apr 98	Government of Wales Act gets Royal Assent.
19 Nov 98	Scotland Act gets Royal Assent.
6 May 99	First Election to Scottish Parliament.
6 May 99	First Election to Welsh Assembly.
22 May 99	D. Dewar becomes First Minister of Scotland.
1 Jul 99	Welsh Assembly installed.
3 Dec 99	Northern Ireland Executive takes office.

Sources: Wan-Hsuan Chiao, *Devolution in Great Britain* (1926): J. Mackintosh, *The Devolution of Power* (1968); J.Banks, *Federal Britain* (1973); A. Birch, *Political Integration in the British Isles* (1977); K. Wright *The People say Yes: the Making of Scotland's Parliament* (1997); V. Bogdanor, *Devolution in the United Kingdom* (1999); see also the White Papers listed in the chronology above.

XV

LOCAL GOVERNMENT

Structure

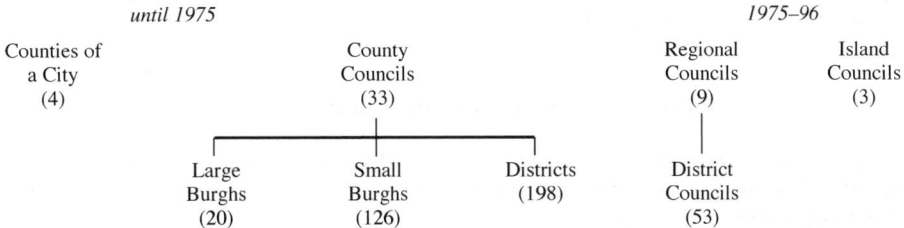

London

until 1965	since 1965
until 1965	*since 1965*
London County Council	Greater London Council
Metropolitan Boroughs (28)	Greater London Boroughs (32)

Rest of England & Wales

until 1974

County Boroughs (83)   County Councils (58)

Non-County Boroughs (270)   Urban Districts (535)   Rural Districts (471)

1974–1986

Metropolitan County Councils (6)

Metropolitan District Councils (36)

1974–1995

County Councils (47)

District Councils (333)

Metropolitan County Councils were abolished in 1986 and the Metropolitan Districts became single purpose authorities.
In 1995 Welsh County Councils were abolished and the principality was divided into 22 single purpose authorities.
Between 1995 and 1997 45 English districts were converted into single-purpose unitary authorities but all the 35 English Counties (except the Isle of Wight) shared power with the 333 non-metropolitan districts.

Scotland

until 1975

Counties of a City (4)

County Councils (33)

Large Burghs (20)   Small Burghs (126)   Districts (198)

1975–96

Regional Councils (9)   Island Councils (3)

District Councils (53)

In 1996 the Regional Councils were abolished. Local government fell to 29 Unitary Authorities and 3 Island Councils.

Number of Councils in England & Wales[a]

	County Councils inc. London	County Boroughs[b]	Non-County Boroughs	Urban District Councils	Rural District Councils	London Boroughs & City of London
1900	62	67	250	800	663	29
1910	62	75	249	812	657	29
1920	62	82	246	799	649	29
1930	62	83	300	780	638	29
1940	61	83	256	581	476	29
1950	61	83	309	572	475	29
1960	62	83	319	564	473	29
1973	58	83	270	535	471	33
		Met. Boroughs	Unitary Auts.	District Councils	Welsh Councils	
1974	47	36	–	333	–	33
1998	34	36	47	238	22	33

[a] This table does not include parish councils. No exact figures for their numbers are available. In 1900 there were about 8,000. In 1920 about 7,000 and in 1966 about 7,700. Following the 1974 reorganisation of local government a number of the local authorities that had been abolished applied for parish council status.
[b] The figures in this column are deceptively constant. In the 1960s a few County Boroughs disappeared through local government amalgamation while a few more Non-County Boroughs were promoted to county status.

Local Government Finance – England and Wales

Year (ending 31 Mar)	Total Receipts from Rates (£000s)	Assessable Values of all Rateable Property (£000s)	Average Rates collected per £ Assessable Value	Government Grants[b] (£000s)	Total Expenditure (£000s)
1900	40,734	175,623	4s.11d.	12,249	100,862
1910	63,261	15,310	6s. 2d.	20,915	166,105
1920	105,590	220,714	9s. 6d.	48,263	289,353
1930	156,312	284,937	11s. 6d.	107,828	423,655
1940	200,567	318,834	12s. 7d.	181,900	578,798[c]
1950	280,195	325,262	17s. 3d.	294,358	849,099[c]
1960	646,608	687,618	18s. 1d.	705,590	1,865,718[c]
1965	988,054	2,099,034	9s. 6d.[a]	1,102,989	2,902,829[c]
1970	1,515,184	2,440,500	12s. 4d.[a]	1,954,931	5,405,264[c]
1975	2,927,262	6,659,700	43.95p.[d]	5,651,767	12,253,941[c]
1980	6,122,518	7,441,233	100.03p.	11,845,505	18,688,038
1985	11,792,986	7,822,200	n.a.	17,165,363	17,165,363
1990	23,591m.	32,916,000	n.a.	1,785m.	48,030m.
1995	23,052m.	33,912,000	n.a.	1,984m.	51,646m.

[a] This spectacular fall was partly due to the de-rating of industry and partly to the general revaluation on 1 Apr 93.
[b] Consisting partly of grants-in-aid and partly of receipts from the Local Taxation Account and from the local Taxation Licence Duties, not including capital receipts.
[c] Expenditure other than loans for capital works, including the repayment of loans by various local authorities to the L.C.C. Consolidated Loans Fund.
[d] A revised system of returns after 1969 may invalidate comparisons with earlier years. In 1973 a general revaluation of rateable values may account for the sharp changes shown here.

Source: *Annual Abstract of Statistics.*

Major Legislation Affecting Local Government

Education Act, 1902. This transferred the responsibility for education from school boards and school attendance committees to county councils, county borough councils, and some of the larger county districts.

Housing Acts. A series of acts from 1919 onwards provided for the building of houses by local authorities with varying rates of subsidy from the Exchequer and from the rates.

Local Government Act, 1929. This abolished the guardians of the poor, and transferred their responsibilities for poor law and registration to county councils and county borough councils. It also re-organised the system of grants-in-aid, creating the general grant, partly as compensation for the complete de-rating of agriculture and the de-rating of industry to 25%.

Town and Country Planning Act, 1932. This established a general system of planning control which could be adopted by second tier local authorities.

Local Government Act, 1933. This was a codifying Act covering the structure and constitution of local authorities of all sorts, but making no fundamental change in the law.

Local Government (Boundary Commission) Act, 1945. This provided for the establishment of a Local Government Boundary Commission, which was later abolished by the *Local Government Boundary Commission (Dissolution) Act, 1949.* (But see *Local Government Boundary Commission Act, 1958.*)

New Towns Act, 1946. This provided for the establishment of new towns to be built by development corporations appointed by the Ministry, and was succeeded by further Acts which were consolidated in the *New Towns Act, 1965.*

National Health Service Act, 1946. This transferred local authority hospitals to the Ministry of Health. It made counties and county boroughs responsible for ambulance service, maternity and child welfare, health visiting, home helps, prevention of illness and after-care, etc.

Town and Country Planning Act, 1947. This applied planning control to the whole country, transferred responsibility to county councils and county borough councils, and introduced development charges balanced by a compensation fund of £300m. Development charges and the £300m. fund were abolished by the *Town and Country Planning Act, 1953.*

Children Act, 1948. After the Curtis Committee Report, this Act made counties and county boroughs responsible for all children without proper homes.

National Assistance Act, 1948. This repealed the existing poor law. It made counties and county boroughs responsible for accommodation of the aged and those temporarily homeless, also for welfare services for the blind, deaf, dumb, etc. Financial assistance and residual responsibilities were passed to the National Assistance Board.

Local Government Act, 1948. This replaced the block grant by the Exchequer Equalisation grant. It transferred responsibility for valuation from local authorities to Inland Revenue and it provided for revaluation: small houses being valued on pre-war building costs, other houses by reference to pre-war rents.

Local Government Act, 1958. This abolished most percentage grants and the Exchequer Equalisation grant, substituting a general grant and a rate deficiency grant.

Local Government Boundary Commission Act, 1958. This set up local boundary commissions, producing a number of reports before being wound up in 1966. The main recommendations put into effect were in the Black Country and Teesside.

Town and Country Planning Act, 1959. This Act altered the basis of compensation for compulsory acquisition.

Public Bodies (Admission to Meetings) Act, 1960. This extended the rights of members of the public and press to be admitted to local authority meetings. There have since been extended to meetings of Regional Water Authorities, Regional Health Authorities and Community Councils.

Rating and Valuation Act, 1961. This Act ended the de-rating of industrial and freight-transport property, empowered the Minister to reduce by order the rateable value of dwellings in valuation lists, offered 50% relief from rates on property occupied by charities, and introduced a new method of rating statutory water undertakings. Industry and Commerce re-rated to 100% values.

Town and Country Planning Act, 1962. This consolidated enactments for England and Wales from 1944 onwards and incorporated planning sections of other Acts.

Local Authorities (Land) Act, 1963. This introduced a new 'positive planning' power for local authorities to acquire land by agreement in advance of requirements, and powers to develop their land and to make advances to promote developments by others on land released by them.

London Government Act, 1963. This Act replaced the old LCC with a Greater London Council which covered, in addition to the old LCC area, almost all of Middlesex and some suburban portions of Surrey, Kent, Essex, and Hertfordshire. All the existing 85 local authorities in the GLC area were merged into 32 new boroughs (the City of London alone preserved its complete independence). The first GLC election took place on 9 Apr 64, two, three or four councillors being chosen en bloc from each of the 32 boroughs. The GLC formally took over from the LCC on 1 Apr 65.

Local Government (Financial Provision) Act, 1963. This extended the powers of local authorities to defray expenses incurred by their members and officers, and to contribute to other local authorities and to bodies having activities connected with local government, and made further provision with respect to borrowing by local authorities, the management of local authority debt, the application by local authorities of capital funds, renewal and repair funds, unexpected balances of loans, and capital money received by way of financial adjustment.

Housing Act, 1964. This set up a new Housing Corporation to assist Housing Associations, conferred new compulsory powers on local authorities to secure improvement of houses, amended the improvement grant system and strengthened the powers of local authorities in dealing with houses in multi-occupation.

Rating Act, 1966. This conferred on rateable occupiers of dwellings the right to pay rates in monthly instalments and provided for the granting of rebates in respect of such rates.

Town and Country Planning Act, 1968. This introduced a fundamental change in the land-use planning system in the direction of greater flexibility and speed of action and a greater degree of public participation. The development plan was replaced by the 'structure, action area' and 'local' plans.

Local Authority Social Services Act, 1970. This required counties and county boroughs to combine, under one social services department, the child care, personal health, and welfare services.

Local Government Act, 1972. This was the first full-scale reorganisation of the local government structure of England and Wales since 1889. It abolished the existing system entirely (outside Greater London) and replaced it with a top tier of metropolitan counties in the six conurbations and 47 non-metropolitan counties in the rest of the country. The new second tier comprised 36 metropolitan districts within the areas of the metropolitan counties and 333 districts in the rest of the country.

Local Government Act, 1974. This provided for a Commissioner for Local Administration (an Ombudsman) to be established (see p.477).

Lotteries Act, 1975. This gave power to local authorities to conduct lotteries under certain restricted conditions.

Inner Urban Areas Act, 1978. This provided for designated urban districts to lend money for land acquisition or for works on land within their areas. Other powers are exercisable in declared 'improvement areas' and by 'partnership' authorities (to make loans for site preparation, grants for industrial and commercial rents, and for small firms' interest payments).

Local Government, Planning Act, 1980. This complex and diverse Act relaxed certain Ministerial controls on authorities and required them to publish reports and information about the performance of their functions (as prescribed by the Secretary of State). It brought the operations of direct labour organisations under control to secure more regulated working, separate accounting, open tendering and prescribed rates of return. It extended arrangements for the payment of rates by instalments and added rate rebates for the disabled. It provided for registers of under-used land owned by public authorities in designated areas. The Act also provided for a new control system for local authority capital expenditure – giving expenditure allocations a switching of resources between authorities and between financial years. A new system for the distribution of rate support grant – with a single block grant in place of the previous 'needs' and 'resources' elements – was a major change.

Local Government Finance Act, 1982. This provided for the abolition of supplementary rates and precepts and required them to be levied for complete financial years. By amendment of the 1980 Act it provided expressly for adjustments in block grant payable to an authority to be made by reference to central government guidance. This was designed to encourage reductions in expenditure on account of general economic conditions. The Act also established the Audit Commission for Local Authorities in England and Wales – which will appoint the auditors (whether from the private sector or from the Commission). The Commission is also responsible for studies of the economy, efficiency and effectiveness of local services (and the impact on them of statutory provisions and Ministerial initiatives). It is appointed by the Secretary of State, who may direct it in the discharge of its functions.

Local Authority (Expenditure Powers) Act, 1983. This was intended to facilitate the aid which local authorities could give to industry – in particular to top up expenditure by the 'free two pence' powers in s.137 of the *Local Government Act, 1972.*

Rates Act, 1984. This allowed for rate limitation – 'rate capping' – by a selection scheme or by one of general limitation. It also required authorities to consult industrial and commercial ratepayers before reaching decisions on expenditure and its financing and to provide additional information to ratepayers.

Local Government Act, 1985. This abolished the Greater London Council and the six Metropolitan County Councils and distributed their functions and responsibilities among their component boroughs and some joint authorities.

Local Government Finance Act, 1988 This replaced the domestic rates with a community charge (or 'poll tax'). Non-domestic rates were nationalised and the systems of grant reformed. Changes were to take effect in 1990.

Education Reform Act, 1988. This transferred control of polytechnics from local to central government as well as allowing schools to opt out of local authority control and introducing the national curriculum.

Local Goverment Act, 1989. This required local authorities to expose their provision of services to compulsory competitive tender.

Local Government Act, 1992. This abolished the poll tax and replaced it with a 'council tax'. It provided for a structural reorganisation of local government in Scotland, Wales and the non-metroplitan areas of England.

Local Government (Scotland) Act, 1994 This replaced the 9 Regional Council and 53 districts in Mainland Scotland with 29 Unitary Authorities.

Local Government (Wales) Act, 1994. This replaced the 12 Counties and 37 Districts in Wales with 22 Unitary Authorities.

Local Government Act, 1998.

(See also Housing, pp.354–8.)

Local Authority Interest Groups

The interests of the local authorities have been represented by two main kinds of groups. First, there are the associations of each tier of local authorities. Most powerful amongst these have been the Association of Municipal Corporations (1873–1974) and the County Councils Association (1889–1974). They were replaced in 1974 by the Association of Metropolitan Authorities and the Association of County Councils; a new Association of District Councils was also formed. In 1997 these organisations merged into a single Local Government Association; there is a separate Convention of Scottish Local Government Authorities. In addition, there are associations representing each of the professions in local government services. Examples would be the Institute of Municipal Engineers (1873) and the Institute of Municipal Treasurers and Accountants (1885), renamed in 1973 the Chartered Institute of Public Finance and Accountancy. All kinds of municipal employees are represented by the National and Local Government Officers Association (1905), the National Union of Public Employees (1886) and other Unions. In 1993 NALGO and NUPE combined to form UNISON.

Many pressure groups which have focused on Local Authorities are listed on pp. 367–71.

Commission for Local Government in England

Chairman

1974	Lady Serota
1982	(Sir) D. Yardley
1994	E. Osmotherly

Commission for Local Government in Wales
Chairman

1974	D. Jones-Williams	1991	E. Moseley
1979	A. Jones		

Commission for Local Government in Scotland
Chairman

1975	R. Moore	1982	E. Gillett
1978	J. Russell	1986	R. Peggie

New Towns

The *New Town Act, 1946*, with subsequent amendments as consolidated in the *New Towns Act, 1965*, provided for New Towns to be built by development corporations appointed by the Minister. The *New Towns Act, 1959*, set up a Commission for the New Towns to take over responsibility for New Towns as soon as the development corporations' purposes were substantially achieved. The *New Towns (Amendment) Act, 1976*, provided for the transfer in April 1978 to local authorities of certain of the New Towns Commission's housing and related assets. In May 1999 the New Towns Commission merged with the Urban Regeneration Authority to form English Partnerships (Chair: Sir A. Cockshaw).

New Towns	Development Corporation Formed	Handed over to Commission	Area (acres)	1951	Population (000s) 1961	1971	1981
Aycliffe[a], Durham	1947	1988	2,508	0.6	12	24	26
Basildon, Essex	1949	1986	7,818	24	54	85	100
Bracknell, Berks.	1949	1982	3,303	5	20	34	48
Central Lancs.	1970	1986	35,225			252	47
Corby, Northants.	1950	1980	4,296	15	36	48	48
Crawley, Sussex	1947	1962	6,047	10	54	68	76
Cwmbran[a], Gwent	1949	1988	3,157	13	30	46	45
Harlow, Essex	1947	1980	6,395	5	53	71	79
Hatfield, Herts.	1948	1966	2,340	9	20	26	25
Hemel Hempstead, Herts	1947	1962	5,910	21	55	70	81
Milton Keynes, Bucks.	1967	1992	22,000			46	97
Northampton	1968	1985	19,966			148	162
Peterborough	1968	1988	15,940			87	121
Peterlee[a], Durham	1948	1988	2,799	0.2	14	22	23
Redditch, Worcs.	1964	1995	7,200			38	64
{ Runcorn, Cheshire	1964	1989	7,234			36 }	
{ Warrington (Merged 1981)	1968	1989	19,000			125 }	198
Skelmersdale, Lancs.	1962	1985	4,100			27	41
Stevenage, Herts.	1946	1980	6,256	7	42	68	74
Telford, Salop.	1963	1991	10,243			80	104
Warrington (see Runcorn)							
Washington, Durham	1964	1986	5,300			25	52
Welwyn, Herts.	1948	1966	4,317	19	35	44	42
Cumbernauld, Dunbarton	1956		7,788		5	32	51
East Kilbride, Lanarks.	1947		10,250	6	32	64	76
Glenrothes, Fife	1948		5,760	2	13	27	38
Irvine, Ayrshire	1966		16,000			42	60
Livingston, W. Lothian	1962		6,868			14	39

In 1973 Stonehouse, Lanarks., was designated a New Town, but its status was cancelled in 1977. In 1967 Newtown, Powys, was designated a New Town, but in 1977 its status was cancelled and it fell under the Development Board for Rural Wales.
[a] These development corporations were wound up in 1988.
Sources: F.J. Osborn and J. Whittick, *The New Towns* (1963). See also *Annual Reports* of the New Towns and of the Commission for New Towns.

New Towns Commission 1961–99

Chairman

1961	Sir D. Anderson	1971	(Sir) D. Pilcher	1982	Sir N. Shields
1964	Sir M. Wells	1978	C. Macpherson	1995	Sir A. Cockshaw

Local Government Elections

After the Second World War the results of Local Government Elections became increasingly accepted as barometers to the national political mood. They could be misleading. The custom of fighting under national party labels spread only gradually and sporadically. The fact that, under the triennial system, only a third of the seats on borough and district councils were fought each year caused much confusion (a party might claim a great trend in its favour because it was gaining compared to three years before, even though it was losing compared to the previous year). Moreover the results were very patchily reported and no altogether satisfactory statistics are available. However, the results in the boroughs of England and Wales (excluding London), both county and non-county, provided some pointer to the national mood (even though the smaller non-county boroughs introduced a very distorting element). Between 3,300 and 3,500 seats used to be fought each year, usually on a party basis; after 1964 the number of seats at risk was between 3,000 and 3,200 owing to the merging of councils under the London Government Act. After 1946 the outcome of these borough contests was fairly accurately reported, although it was not until 1965 that the first really detailed analyses of the voting figures appear (see *The Economist* for the Saturday nine days after the elections each year since 1965).

Borough Council Election Results 1949–72

	Conservative and Conservative-supported Independent	Independent without Conservative Support	Labour	Liberal	Total	Labour % of vote (County Boroughs only)	Turnout % (County Boroughs only)
1947	1,892	359	776	97	3,124	41.7	52.6
1949	1,749	426	1,091	79	3,345	43.2	52.2
1950	1,610	510	1,132	72	3,324	46.2	45.5
1951	1,893	548	883	79	3,403	n.a.	44.4
1952	1,138	488	1,718	53	3,397	55.4	49.9
1953	1,571	447	1,448	60	3,562	52.0	45.2
1954	1,498	511	1,438	74	3,521	49.2	42.8
1955	1,604	514	1,470	56	3,644	47.6	43.8
1956	1,358	454	1,614	72	3,498	51.1	37.6
1957	1,292	435	1,642	89	3,458	50.0	40.0
1958	1,307	460	1,705	118	3,590	49.3	40.3
1959	1,545	441	1,399	103	3,488	45.5	41.0
1960	1,750	449	1,137	130	3,466	40.0	35.4
1961	1,453	470	1,387	196	3,506	43.3	40.6
1962	995	465	1,571	454	3,485	42.4	40.2
1963	973	524	1,733	255	3,485	46.0	41.3
1964	967	474	1,494	149	3,084	47.0	40.5
1965	1,140	476	1,027	154	2,797	38.3	37.7
1966	1,107	467	1,259	151	2,984	43.1	35.6
1967	1,690	466	846	148	3,150	36.4	40.3
1968	2,184	436	450	152	3,222	29.8	35.8
1969	1,972	453	542	168	3,135	33.1	35.6
1970	1,382	406	1,207	133	3,128	44.0	37.6
1971	823	391	1,848	128	3,180	55.7	39.2
1972	890	375	1,643	155	3,063	52.6	36.7

Party Control in Major Cities 1945–

Party politics in many cities goes back to the first half of the nineteenth century but, although in most sizeable towns (practically all over 50,000) councillors have worn political labels throughout this century, in only a few larger councils did a majority of councillors of one party mean that that party exercised control. Labour successes after the first World War introduced a more organised form of party politics into some councils. After the Second World War, the local government franchise was extended to practically the same basis as that for parliamentary elections (it had hitherto been confined to ratepayers) and, with sweeping Labour successes in the 1945 municipal elections and an organised Conservative counter-attack in the succeeding years, party politics extended their hold to most urban authorities, including practically all those with more than 20,000 inhabitants. Here is the record since 1945 of the party control in cities which in 1972 had more than 200,000 inhabitants: 'Citizen' in Bristol, 'Ratepayers' in Southampton and 'Progressive' (also called 'Moderate') in Scottish cities and Newcastle refer to local anti-Socialist, Conservative-supported parties. For England and Wales the 1974 entries refer to the district councils elected in 1973 (in some cases on enlarged boundaries).

Belfast
> 1945– Unionist.

Birmingham
> 1945 No clear majority.[1] 1946–47 Labour. 1947–49 No majority. 1949–52 Conservative. 1952–66 Labour. 1966–72 Conservative. 1972–75 Labour. 1975–76 No clear majority. 1976–79 Conservative. 1979–80 No clear majority. 1980–82 Labour. 1982–84 Conservative. 1984– Labour.

Bradford
> 1945–51 Labour. 1951–52 No clear majority. 1952–59 Labour. 1959–61 No clear majority. 1961–62 Conservative and National Liberal. 1962–63 No clear majority. 1963–67 Labour. 1967–72 Conservative. 1972–74 Labour. 1974–80 Conservative. 1980–82 Labour. 1982–86 No clear majority. 1986–88 Labour. 1988–90 Conservative. 1990– Labour.

Bristol
> 1945–49 Labour. 1949–51 No clear majority. 1951–52 Citizen. 1953–60 Labour. 1960–63 Citizen. 1963–67 Labour. 1967–72 Citizen. 1972–83 Labour. 1983–86 No clear majority. 1986– Labour.

Cardiff
> 1945–58 anti-Labour coalition. 1958–61 Labour. 1961–63 No clear majority. 1963–66 Labour. 1967–74 Conservative. 1974–76 Labour. 1976–79 Conservative. 1973–83 Labour. 1983–87 Conservative. 1987–91 No clear majority. 1991– Labour.

Coventry
> 1945–67 Labour. 1967–72 Conservative. 1972–75 Labour. 1975–79 Conservative. 1979– Labour.

Edinburgh
> 1945–62 Progressive. 1962–65 No clear majority. 1965–71 Progressive[2]. 1971–77 No clear majority. 1977–84 Conservative. 1984–92 Labour. 1992– No clear majority. 1996– Labour

Glasgow
> 1945–47 Labour. 1947–50 No clear majority. 1950–52 Progressive. 1952–68 Labour. 1968–69 No clear majority. 1969–70 Progressive. 1970–77 Labour. 1977–80 No clear majority. 1980– Labour.

Leeds
> 1945–51 Labour. 1951–53 Conservative. 1953–67 Labour. 1967–72 Conservative. 1972–74 Labour. 1974–76 No clear majority. 1976–79 Conservative. 1979–80 No clear majority. 1980– Labour.

Leicester
> 1945–49 Labour. 1949–52 Conservative. 1952–61 Labour. 1961–62 Conservative. 1962–63 No clear majority. 1963–66 Labour. 1966–67 No clear majority. 1967–72 Conservative. 1972–76 Labour. 1976–79 Conservative. 1979– Labour.

---

[1] 'No clear majority' is shown wherever no party had a clear overall majority of seats; frequently a party holding half the seats was able to exercise some control in this situation with the aid of the mayoral vote and in other cases a party exercised control in alliance with a minor group.

[2] The position in Edinburgh and Glasgow is complicated by two *ex officio* councillors who make clear definition of overall majority difficult.

Liverpool

1945–54 Conservative. 1954–55 Conservative with Protestant support. 1955–61 Labour. 1961–63 Conservative. 1963–67 Labour. 1967–72 Conservative. 1972–74 Labour. 1974–83 No clear majority (Liberal largest party 1974–76. Labour 1976–83). 1983–92 Labour. 1992–98 No clear majority. 1998– Liberal Democrat.

Manchester

1945–47 Labour. 1947–49 No clear majority. 1949–52 Conservative. 1952–53 No clear majority. 1953–67 Labour. 1967–71 Conservative. 1971– Labour.

Newcastle

1945–49 Labour. 1949–58 Progressive. 1958–67 Labour. 1967–74 Conservative. 1974–Labour.

Nottingham

1945–50 Labour. 1950–51 No clear majority. 1951–52 Conservative. 1952–53 No clear majority. 1953–60 Labour. 1960–61 No clear majority. 1961–63 Conservative. 1963–67 Labour. 1967–72 Conservative. 1972–76 Labour. 1976–79 Conservative. 1979–87 Labour. 1987–89 Conservative. 1989–91 No clear majority. 1991– Labour.

Plymouth

1945–53 Conservative. 1953–59 Labour. 1959–63 Conservative. 1963–66 Labour. 1966–91 Conservative. 1991– Labour.

Portsmouth

1949–64 Conservative. 1964–65 Labour. 1965–90 Conservative. 1990– No clear majority. 1995– Labour.

Sheffield

1945–68 Labour. 1968–69 Conservative. 1969–99 Labour. 1999– Liberal Democrat.

Southampton

1945–50 Labour. 1950–54 Ratepayers. 1954–61 Labour. 1961–62 Conservative. 1962–67 Labour. 1967–72 Conservative. 1973–76 Labour. 1976–84 Conservative. 1984–87 Labour. 1987–88 No clear majority; 1988– Labour.

Stoke on Trent

1945–70 Labour. 1970–71 Conservative. 1971– Labour.

Sunderland

1945–68 Labour. 1968–72 Conservative. 1972– Labour.

Teesside (created 1967, abolished 1974)

1967–72 Conservative. 1972–74 Labour.

Wolverhampton

1945–49 Labour. 1949–52 Conservative and allies. 1952–67 Labour. 1967–72 Conservative. 1972–78 Labour. 1978–79 No clear control. 1979–87 Labour. 1987–88 No clear majority. 1988–92 Labour. 1992–94 No clear majority. 1994– Labour.

Local Government Elections 1973–

| | Party Control | | | | Seats | | | | |
	Con.	Lab.	Lib.	No Clear Control	Con.	Lab.	Lib/Al.	Other	Nat. or Ind.
Metropolitan Counties[1]									
12 Apr 73	–	6	–	–	141	402	49	9	–
5 May 77	4	2	–	–	360	213	19	8	–
7 May 81	–	6	–	–	122	425	50	3	–
Other Counties									
(England and Wales)									
12 Apr 73	18	11	–	18	1484	1397	210	513	18
5 May 77	36	3	–	8	2524	641	71	445	37
7 May 81	19	14	–	13	1560	1376	340	371	23
2 May 85	10	9	12	7	1370	1269	640	360	21
4 May 89	17	13	1	7	1456	1297	458	273	25
6 May 93	1	14	32	9	966	1389	867	237	41
(England only)									
1 May 97	9	8	2	15	873	745	495	90	–

[1]Not including GLC.

	Party Control				Seats				
	Con.	Lab.	Lib.	No Clear Control	Con.	Lab.	Lib./Al.	Other	Nat. or Ind.
Metropolitan Districts									
10 May 73	5	26	–	5	716	1566	183	48	–
7 May 75[2]	9	22	–	5	919	1361	173	58	–
6 May 76[2]	15	18	–	3	1088	1199	151	75	–
4 May 78[2,4]	18	14	–	4	1169	1127	124	82	–
3 May 79[2,4]	11	18	–	7	986	1317	116	87	–
1 May 80	6	27	–	3	770	1548	133	75	–
6 May 81	7	24	–	5	751	1457	222	42	–
5 May 83	7	24	–	5	745	1481	213	39	–
3 May 84	5	25	–	6	690	1523	228	40	–
1 May 86	1	27	–	8	560	1663	228	30	–
7 May 87	1	27	–	8	552	1632	271	26	–
5 May 88	2	28	–	6	537	1656	268	20	–
3 May 90	2	31	–	3	505	1721	238	17	–
2 May 91	1	32	–	3	460	1748	244	29	–
7 May 92	1	24	–	11	556	1612	273	40	–
6 May 94	1	23	–	12	519	1581	338	43	–
5 May 95	–	30	–	6	382	1738	324	37	–
3 May 96	–	32	–	4	196	1877	355	53	
7 May 98	–	31	1	4	230	1815	382	54	–
6 May 99	–	29	3	4	295	1682	449	55	–
Other Districts (England)									
7 Jun 73	86	73	–	137					
6 May 76	176	29	–	91					
4 May 78[3]	176	30	–	90					
3 May 79[3, 4]	166	49	–	81					
1 May 80	148	53	3	82					
6 May 82	139	59	2	96					
5 May 83	145	55	3	93					
3 May 84	140	53	3	100					
8 May 86	123	64	5	104					
7 May 87	123	56	9	108					
5 May 88	128	58	8	102					
3 May 90	116	65	5	110					
2 May 91	72	78	20	126					
7 May 92	76	74	21	125					
6 May 94	65	70	30	125					
5 May 95	8	111	45	124					
3 May 96	9	117	50	111					
7 May 98	12	112	37	123					
6 May 99	62	89	21	112					
Other districts (Wales)[5]									
7 Jun 73	1	19	–	17					
6 May 76	4	9	–	24					
3 May 79[4]	2	16	–	17					
5 May 83	3	14	–	20					
7 May 87	2	18	–	17					
2 May 91	–	20	–	17					
Welsh Unitary Authorities									
5 May 95	–	14	–	8	42	726	79	113	312

[2] From 1975 onwards one-third of Metropolitan District Councillors came up for re-election in each year, except those in which there are no county elections. The seats are the totals for both continuing and newly elected councillors.

[3] 44 of the 316 non-metropolitan districts in England opted that after 1976 one-third of their councillors would retire at a time. 1978 saw the first such elections.

[4] The 1979 elections took place simultaneously with the General Election.

[5] A few Welsh authorities before 1995 had annual elections which are not reported here.

	Party Control				Seats				
	Con.	Lab.	Lib.	No Clear Control	Con.	Lab.	Lib./Al.	Other	Nat. or Ind.
Scottish Regions									
9 May 74	1	2	–	6	115	171	11	18	19
2 May 78	2	4	–	3	135	174	7	96	17
6 May 82	2	3	–	4	119	186	25	88	23
8 May 86	–	4	–	5	65	223	40	81	36
3 May 90	–	4	–	5	52	233	40	78	42
6 May 94	–	4	–	5	31	220	62	73	67
Scottish Districts									
9 May 74	5	17	–	31	241	428	17	335	62
3 May 77	8	5	–	40	277	299	31	335	170
1 May 80	6	24	–	23	229	494	40	307	54
3 May 84	4	25	1	23	189	545	78	278	59
5 May 88	3	24	2	24	162	553	84	242	113
7 May 92	4	19	2	28	204	468	94	392	150
Scottish Unitary Authorities									
4 Apr 95	–	20	–	12	82	613	123	181	160
6 May 99	–	15	–	17	108	550	156	205	203

Sources: D. Clark, *Battle for the Counties* (1977); and the series by J. Bochel and D. Denver, *The Scottish Local Government Elections* (1974, 1977, 1980, 1984); *The Scottish Regional Elections* (1978, 1982).

Metropolitan Counties 1973–1981

	Councillors				% of vote			
	Con.	Lab.	Lib.	Other	Con.	Lab.	Lib.	Other
2 Apr 1973								
Greater Manchester	24	69	13	–	38.7	45.1	14.9	1.3
Merseyside	26	53	19	1	33.7	41.3	22.0	3.0
South Yorkshire	13	82	1	4	25.5	55.8	11.3	7.4
Tyne & Wear	27	74	1	2	36.3	55.7	4.6	3.4
West Midlands	27	73	4	–	48.3	42.5	7.7	1.5
West Yorkshire	25	51	11	1	37.3	44.8	14.6	3.3
Greater London	32	58	2	–	38.0	47.4	12.5	2.1
5 May 1977								
Greater Manchester	82	23	–	1	56.6	34.6	7.5	1.9
Merseyside	67	26	6	–	47.7	32.0	19.1	1.2
South Yorkshire	31	62	2	5	39.7	44.7	6.3	9.4
Tyne & Wear	44	54	4	2	49.4	40.7	6.4	3.4
West Midlands	82	18	3	1	56.5	31.7	4.1	6.1
West Yorkshire	54	30	4	–	50.3	35.4	10.3	4.1
Greater London	64	28	–	–	52.6	32.9	7.8	6.3
7 May 1981								
Greater Manchester	19	78	9	–	30.6	49.8	18.0	1.7
Merseyside	27	56	15	–	29.3	45.6	24.2	1.0
South Yorkshire	14	82	3	1	25.8	58.2	12.8	3.2
Tyne & Wear	23	72	7	2	29.4	55.9	12.2	2.5
West Midlands	25	74	5	–	36.0	50.3	9.8	3.9
West Yorkshire	14	63	11	–	30.2	47.5	21.0	1.3
Greater London	41	50	1	–	39.4	41.4	15.0	4.2

Party Representation on the London County Council, 1898–1964

| Year | Councillors (elected) | | | | | Aldermen | | | | | |
	Pr.	MRM	Lab.	Ind.	Total	Pr.	MRM	Lab.	Ind.	Total	Majority
1898	84	34	–	–	118	13	6	–	–	137	Pr.
1901	87	31	–	–	118	14	5	–	–	137	Pr.
1904	83	35	–	–	118	15	4	–	–	137	Pr.
1907	38	79	–	1	118	9	10	–	–	137	MRM
1910	55	60	3	–	118	2	15	–	2	137	MRM
1913	50	67	1	–	118	3	14	–	2	137	MRM
1919	40	68	15	1	124	6	12	2	–	144	MRM
1922	25	82	17	–	124	5	12	3	–	144	MRM
1925	6	83	35	–	124	3	13	4	–	144	MRM
1928	5	77	42	–	124	1	12	6	1	144	MRM
1931	6	83	35	–	124	–	13	6	1	144	MRM
1934	–	55	69	–	124	–	9	11	–	144	Lab.
1937	–	49	75	–	124	–	8	12	–	144	Lab.
	Lib.	Con.	Lab.	Comm.		Lib.	Con.	Lab.	Comm.		
1946	2	30	90	2	124	–	6	14	–	144	Lab.
1949	1	64	64	–	129	–	5	16	–	150[a]	Lab.
1952	–	37	92	–	129	–	6	15	–	150	Lab.
1955	–	52	74	–	126	–	8	13	–	147	Lab.
1958	–	25	101	–	126	–	7	14	–	147	Lab.
1961	–	42	84	–	126	–	7	14	–	147	Lab.

[a] Plus Chairman, an outsider and a Labour nominee.

PR	Progressives (Lib.)	Ind.	Independent
MRM	Municipal Reform Moderates (Con.)	Comm.	Communist
Lab.	Labour	Lib.	Liberal

Sources: Sir G. Gibbon and R.W. Bell, *History of the London County Council, 1889–1939* (1939); *General Election of County Councillors* (published after each election by the L.C.C.), 1919–61.

Greater London Council, 1964–1981

| | Councillors | | | Aldermen | | |
	Con.	Lab.	Lib.	Con.	Lab.	Lib.
1964	36	64	–	5	11	–
1967	82	18	–	10	6	–
1970	65	35	–	11	5	–
1973	32	58	2	6	9	–
1977	64	28	–	*(Aldermen abolished)*		
1981	41	50	–			
1986[a]						

[a] From 1964 to 1986 the Inner London Education Authority (ILEA) covering the former LCC area, was a special committee of the GLC, made up of all its members in the Inner London Area. Following the abolition of the GLC, ILEA members were directly elected on 8 May 1986; Labour won 45 seats, the Conservatives 11 and the Alliance 2. ILEA was abolished on 1 April 1990.

Control and Representation in London Boroughs, 1964–

	Control				Councillors			
	Con.	Lab.	Lib.	No clear Control	Con.	Lab.	Lib./ Alln.	Other
1964	9	20	–	3	668	1,112	13	66
1968	27	4	–	1	1,441	350	10	57
1971	10	21	–	1	601	1,221	9	32
1974	13	18	–	1	713	1,090	27	37
1978	17	14	–	1	960	882	30	36
1982	17	12	–	3	984	781	124	25
1986	11	15	–	4	685	957	249	23
1990	12	14	3	3	731	925	229	29
1994	5	17	3	7	518	1045	323	31
1998	4	18	2	8	538	1050	301	28

London Referendum

On 7 May 98, on a 34 per cent turnout electors in the Greater London Area voted 72 per cent–28 per cent in favour of the Government's proposals for a Greater London Authority with a directly elected Mayor and the Council. The first election was to be on 5 May 00.

Sources: J. Redlich and F. Hirst (ed.B. Keith-Lucas) *The History of Local Government in England* (1958); *Report of the Royal Commission on Local Taxation* (1901); *Report of the Royal Commission on the Poor Law* (1909); *Report of the Royal Commission on the Poor Law* (1925); *Social Insurance and Allied Services* (Beveridge Report) (1942); *Report of the Committee on Care of Children* (Curtis Report) (1946); *Local Goverment Functions of County Councils and District Councils* (Cmnd 161/1957) *Local Government Finance* Cmnd (209/1957); *Report of the Royal Commission on Local Government in Greater London* (Cmnd 1164/1960); *Report of the Royal Commission on Local Goverment in England* (Redcliffe-Maud Report);(Cmnd 4040/1969); P.Richards, *The Reformed Local Government System* (1973); J. Stewart and G. Stoker, *The Future of Local Government* (1989); T.Travers, *The Politics of Local Government Finance* (1987); T. Byrne, *Local Government* (5th ed. 1990); D. Butler et al., *Failure in British Government: the Politics of the Poll Tax* (1994); C. Rallings and M. Thrasher, *The Local Elections Handbook* (annually from 1985); C. Rallings and M. Thrasher (eds), *Local Elections in Britain* (1993) gives summary election results for all local authorities in Great Britain 1973–1992.

XVI

THE COMMONWEALTH

Main Territories under British Rule since 1900

Commonwealth Status Jan 2000		Original entry to British rule and Status (1900)	Changes of Status
	Aden	Colony (1839) and adjacent Protectorate	Acceded to South Arabian Federation 1963. Became People's Republic of South Yemen 1967.
Dependency	Anguilla	See St. Kitts	Became separate Dependency 1980.
Member	Antigua and Barbuda	Colony (1663)	*See* Leeward Isles.
Dependency of St Helena	Ascension	Admiralty-administered territory (1815)	Became dependency of Colony of St Helena 1922.
Member	Australia	First settled 1788, 6 self-governing colonies (1855 and later)	Federal government formed 1901. Dominion status recognised 1907.
Member	Bahamas	First settled 1646. Colony (1783)	Independence granted 1973.
Member	Bangladesh		Became East Pakistan 1947. Broke away from Pakistan 1971. Commonwealth Member 1972.
Member	Barbados	Settled 1627 Colony (1662)	Part of West Indies Federation 1958–62. Independence granted 1966.
	Basutoland	Protectorate (1871) Colony (1884)	Independence granted 1966. Now Lesotho.
	Bechuanaland	Protectorate (1885)	Independence granted 1966. Now Botswana..
Member	Belize	Formerly Br. Honduras	Independence granted 1981.
Colony	Bermuda	First settled 1609. Colony (1684)	
Member	Botswana		Formerly Bechuanaland Protectorate. Independence granted 1966 as Republic.
Dependency	British Antarctic Territory	Discovered (1819)	Became a Territory 1982. Part was devolved to Australia 1933.
	British Guiana	Ceded Colony (1814)	Independence granted 1966. Now Guyana.
	British Honduras	First settled 1638. Colony (separated from Jamaica 1884)	Changed name to Belize 1973.
Dependency	British Indian Ocean Territory	Dependencies of Mauritius or Seychelles	The Chagos Archipelago and Aldabra, Farquhar and Desroches Islands were formed into a single British Dependency in 1965.
	British North Borneo	Protectorate (1888)	Administered by Chartered Company 1882–1946. Became part of North Borneo Colony 1946. Entered Malaysian Federation as Sabah 1963.

Commonwealth Status Jan 2000		Original entry to British rule and Status (1900)	Changes of Status
Member	British Solomon Islands	Protectorate (1893)	Independence granted 1978 as Solomon Islands.
	British Somaliland	Protectorate (1887)	Independence granted 1960 when it became part of Somalia, a Republic outside the Commonwealth.
	British Togoland		Administered by Britain under League of Nations mandate 1922–46 and U.N. Trusteeship 1946–57. Merged with Ghana 1957.
Member	Brunei	Protectorate (1888)	Independence granted 1984 as indigenous Monarchy.
	Burma	Indian Province (1852)	Separated from India 1937. Independence granted in 1948 when it became a Republic outside the Commonwealth.
	Cameroons (British)		Administered as part of Nigeria under League of Nations mandate 1922. Northern Cameroons incorporated in Nigeria 1961. Southern Cameroons joined Cameroun Republic, outside the Commonwealth.
Member	Canada	Ceded Colonies from 1714 onwards. Self-governing Federation (1867)	Dominion status recognised 1907.
	Cape of Good Hope	Ceded Colony (1814)	Dominion status recognised 1907. Province of Union of South Africa.
Dependency	Cayman, Turks and Caicos	Ceded (1670) Dependencies of Jamaica (1848)	Separate dependencies under Colonial Office following Jamaican Independence 1962.
Member	Ceylon	Ceded Colony	Independence granted 1948. Became Republic and changed name to Sri Lanka 1972.
	Christmas Island	Annexed (1888)	Part of Straits Settlements 1900 by incorporation with Singapore. Separate Colony Jan 1958. Transferred to Australia Oct 1958.
	Cocos-Keeling Islands	Annexed (1857)	Part of Straits Settlement 1903. Incorporated in Singapore Colony 1946. Transferred to Australia 1958.
Ass. State of N.Z.	Cook Islands	Protectorate (1888)	Annexed 1900. Administered by New Zealand since 1901.
Member	Cyprus	British administered territory (1878)	Annexed by Britain 1914. Colony 1925. Independence granted as a Republic 1960.
Member	Dominica	Colony (1763)	Part of Leeward Islands till 1940. Separate Colony 1940. Associated State 1967. Independent Republic 1978.
	East African Protectorate	Protectorate (1895)	Became a Colony and protectorate of Kenya 1920. See Kenya.
	Egypt	Occupied by British 1882	British Protectorate 1914–22.

Commonwealth Status Jan 2000		Original entry to British rule and Status (1900)	Changes of Status
	Eire	(see Ireland)	
Dependency	Falkland Islands	Colony (1833)	Invaded by Argentina, then recaptured 1982.
Member	Fiji	Colony (1874)	Independence granted 1970. Republic and out of Commonwealth 1987. Readmitted 1997.
Member	Gambia	Settlement began 1618. Colony (1843) and adjacent Protectorate (1888)	Independence granted 1965. Republic 1970.
Member	Ghana		Formerly Gold Coast. Independence granted 1957. Republic 1960.
Dependency	Gibraltar	Ceded Colony (1713)	
Member	Gilbert and Ellice Islands	Protectorate (1892)	Colony 1915. Ellice Islands separated 1975. See Tuvalu. Independence granted to Gilbert Islands as Republic 1979 with name of Kiribati.
	Gold Coast	Settlement began 1750. Colony (1821 and 1874)	Independence granted 1957. Now Ghana.
Member	Grenada	Ceded Colony (1763)	Part of Leeward Isles 1871–1974. Independence granted 1974.
Member	Guyana		Formerly British Guiana. Independence granted 1966. Republic 1970.
	Hong Kong	Ceded Colony (1843)	Kowloon ceded to Britain in 1860. New Territories leased to Britain for 99 years in 1898. 1997 reversion to China agreed 1984. Reverted 1997.
Member	India	Settlement began 1601. Indian Empire (1876)	Independence granted 1947. Republic 1950.
	Iraq		Administered by Britain under League of Nations Mandate 1922–32.
	Ireland	Union with Great Britain (1801)	26 counties became Irish Free State 1922 with Dominion Status. 1937 Constitution asserted Sovereign Independence. Became Republic of Ireland (Eire) outside Commonwealth in 1949.
Member	Jamaica	Colony (seized 1655 and ceded 1670)	Part of West Indies Federation 1958–62. Independence granted 1962.
Member	Kenya		Formerly East African Protectorate. Colony and Protectorate of Kenya (1920). Independence granted 1963. Republic 1964.
Member	Kiribati		Formerly Gilbert Islands. Independence granted as Republic 1979.
	Labuan	Colony (1848) governed by North Borneo Company (1890)	Administered by Straits Settlement 1907. Became separate Straits Settlement 1912. Part of North Borneo (1946;) now Sabah 1963.

Commonwealth Status Jan 2000		Original entry to British rule and Status (1900)	Changes of Status
	Lagos	Colony (1861)	Amalgamated with protectorate of Southern Nigeria 1906.
	Leeward Isles	Colonies federated (1871)	Federated Colony dissolved 1956. (Antigua, Montserrat, St Kitts-Nevis and, until 1940, Dominica and Virgin Is.) Part of West Indies Federation (except for Virgin Is.) 1958–62. See separate entries.
Member	Lesotho		Formerly Basutoland Colony. Independence granted 1966 with indigenous monarch.
Member	Malawi		Formerly Nyasaland. Part of Federation of Rhodesia and Nyasaland 1953–63. Independence granted 1964. Republic 1966.
	Malay States	9 Protectorates, 4 of which were federated	
	Malaya		Formerly Malay States (federated and unfederated) and Straits Settlements. Independence granted in 1957 as elective monarchy. Merged in Malaysia Federation 1963.
Member	Malaysia		Formed in 1963 by a federation of Malaya, Singapore, Sabah (North Borneo), and Sarawak; Singapore seceded in 1965. An indigenous elective monarchy.
Member	Maldives	Protectorate (1887)	Independence granted 1965. Republic 1980.
Member	Malta	Ceded Colony (1814)	Independence granted 1964. Republic 1974.
Member	Mauritius	Ceded Colony (1814)	Independence granted 1968.
Dependency	Montserrat	First settled (1642) as Colony	See Leeward Isles. Separately administered since 1962.
Member	Namibia	South African mandate (1920)	Formerly German S.W. Africa. Independent Republic 1990.
	Natal	Colony (1843)	Province of South Africa 1910.
Member	Nauru		Administered by Australia under League of Nations mandate 1920–47 and under U.N. Trusteeship 1947–68. Independent Republic 1968.
	New Guinea		Administered by Australia under League of Nations mandate 1921–46 and under U.N. Trusteeship since 1946. United with Papua 1946 as Papua-New Guinea.
Member	New Hebrides		Administered as Anglo-French condominium 1906. Independence granted as Republic of Vanuatu 1980.
Member	New Zealand	Colony (1840)	Dominion status recognised 1907.
	Newfoundland	Settlement began 1623. Self-governing Colony (1855)	Dominion Under Commission government 1933–1949. Acceded to Canada 1949.

Commonwealth Status Jan 2000		Original entry to British rule and Status (1900)	Changes of Status
Member	Nigeria	Protectorates	Colony of Lagos joined Southern Nigeria 1906. Protectorates of Northern and Southern Nigeria joined 1914. Independence granted 1960. Republic 1963. Suspended from Commonwealth 1995–9.
	Norfolk Island	Settled 1788. Under New South Wales (1896)	Became dependency of Australian Government 1914.
	North Borneo		Colony created in 1946 mainly from British North Borneo. Entered Malaysian Federation as Sabah 1963.
	Northern Rhodesia	Chartered Company territory (1889)	Administered by British South Africa Company. Became Protectorate 1924. Part of Federation of Rhodesia and Nyasaland.1953–63. Independence granted 1964. Now Zambia.
	Nyasaland	Protectorate (1891)	Part of Federation of Rhodesia and Nyasaland 1953–63. Independence granted 1964. Now Malawi.
	Orange Free State	Colony (1902)	Province of Union of South Africa 1910.
	Pakistan	Part of Indian Empire	Independence granted 1947. Republic 1950. Left Commonwealth 1972. Rejoined 1989. Suspended 1999.
	Palestine		Administered by Britain under League of Nations mandate 1922–48. Achieved Independence as State of Israel 1948.
	Papua	Protectorate (1884) Colony (1888)	Administered by Australia since 1906 since 1906. United with New Guinea 1946.
Member	Papua-New Guinea		Papua and New Guinea were united under Australian Trusteeship 1946. Independence granted 1975.
Dependency	Pitcairn Islands	Settled 1790 Colony (1898)	
Member	Rhodesia		Formerly Southern Rhodesia. Part of Federation of Rhodesia and Nyasaland 1953–63. Resumed status as a self-governing colony with name of Rhodesia 1964. Unilateral declaration of independence 1965. Granted independence as Zimbabwe 1980.
	Rhodesia and Nyasaland		Federation of Northern Rhodesia, Nyasaland, and Southern Rhodesia established in 1953 and dissolved in 1963.
	Sabah		Formerly North Borneo. Part of Malaysian Federation since 1963.
Member	St Christopher (St Kitts) and Nevis	Colony (1625)	See Leeward Isles.
Colony	St Helena	Administered by E.India C. 1673 Colony (1834)	Ascension 1922 and Tristan da Cunha 1938 are its dependencies.

Commonwealth Status Jan 2000		Original entry to British rule and Status (1900)	Changes of Status
Member	St Lucia	Ceded Colony (1814)	(*See* Windward Isles) Independence granted 1979.
Member	St. Vincent and the Grenadines	Ceded Colony(1763)	*See* Windward Isles.
	Sarawak	Protectorate (1888)	Ceded to Britain in 1946 as Colony. Part of Malaysian Federation since 1963.
Member	Seychelles	Dependency of Mauritius (1810)	Separate Colony 1903. Independence granted 1976. Republic 1976.
Member	Sierra Leone	Colony (1808) Protectorate (1896)	Independence granted 1961. Republic 1971. Suspended from Commonwealth 1997–99.
Member	Singapore	Under Indian government 1824.	Separate Colony 1946. Part of Malaysian Federation 1963–65. Seceded to form Republic 1965.
Member	Solomon Is.	Protectorate (1893)	Formerly British Solomon Islands. Independence granted 1978.
Member	South Africa		Union of South Africa formed 1910 from the Colonies of Cape of Good Hope, Natal, Orange Free State and Transvaal. Dominion status 1910. Became Republic 1961 and left the Commonwealth. Readmitted 1994.
	South Arabia		Federation formed in 1959 from 6 states or sheikhdoms. A further 16 subsequently acceded together with (1963) the Colony of Aden. Became Republic of South Yemen 1967.
	South-West Africa		Administered by South Africa under League of Nations mandate 1920–46 and under U.N. Trusteeship since 1946. Unilaterally incorporated in South Africa 1949. Became independent as Namibia 1990.
	South Yemen		Formerly Aden Protectorate.
	Southern Rhodesia	Chartered Company (1889)	Administered by British South Africa Company. Self-governing Colony 1923. Part of Federation of Rhodesia and Nyasaland 1953–63. Rhodesia 1963–80. Now Zimbabwe.
Member	Sri Lanka	Formerly Ceylon	Independence granted 1948. Became Republic and changed name 1972.
	Straits Settlements (Singapore, Penang, Malacca)	Colonies (1867)	Part of Straits Settlements. Malacca, Labuan added 1912. Labuan and Penang joined Malay States 1948. Singapore joined Malaysian Federation 1963 but seceded 1965.
	Sudan	Condominium with Egypt (1899)	Independence granted 1956 when it became a Republic outside the Commonwealth.
Member	Swaziland	British Protectorate 1903	Independence granted 1968. Indigenous monarchy.

Commonwealth Status Jan 2000		Original entry to British rule and Status (1900)	Changes of Status
	Tanganyika		Administered by Britain under League of Nations mandate 1920–46 and under U.N. Trusteeship 1946–61. Independence granted 1961. Republic 1962. Merged with Zanzibar to form Tanzania 1964.
Member	Tanzania		Formed by merging Tanganyika and Zanzibar 1964.
Dependency of N.Z.	Tokelau	Protectorate (1877)	Annexed by U.K. 1916. Administration transferred to New Zealand 1925.
Member	Tonga	Protectorate (1900)	Independence granted under indigenous monarchy 1970.
	Transjordan		Administered by Britain under League of Nations mandate 1922–28. Full independence recognised 1946. Now Jordan.
	Transvaal	Annexed 1902	Responsible Government 1906. Province of Union South Africa 1910.
Member	Trinidad and Tobago	Ceded (1802 and 1814). Colony 1814 (combined 1889)	Part of West Indies Federation. Independence granted 1962.
	Tristan da Cunha	British settlement (1815) Evacuated 1961–63	Dependency of Colony of St Helena 1938.
Dependency	Turks and Caicos Islands	Annexed 1766 Dependency of Jamaica (1873)	Dependency under Colonial Office following Jamaican independence 1962.
Member	Tuvalu	Protectorate (1892)	Formerly Ellice Islands. Part of Gilbert and Ellice Islands. Separated 1975. Independence granted 1978.
Member	Uganda	Protectorate (1894)	Independence granted 1962. Sovereign State 1963.
Member	Vanuatu		Formerly New Hebrides. Administered as Anglo-French condominium 1906. Independence granted as Republic of Vanuatu 1980.
Dependency	Virgin Islands West Indies Federation	Colonies (1666)	*See* Leeward Isles. Independence was granted in 1958 to a Federation of the colonies of Jamaica, Trinidad and Tobago, Barbados, the Leeward Isles (except for the Virgin Isles) and the Windward Isles. The Federation broke up in 1962 when Jamaica and Trinidad and Tobago became independent. Some common institutions were continued by the other members of the Federation.
Member	Western Samoa		Administered by New Zealand under League of Nations mandate 1920–46 and under U.N. Trusteeship 1946–62. Independent Republic 1962. Full Commonwealth member 1970.

Commonwealth Status Jan 2000		Original entry to British rule and Status (1900)	Changes of Status
Members	Windward Isles	Colonies (1763 and 1814, federated 1885)	The colonies Grenada, Dominica, St Lucia, and St Vincent. Part of West Indies Federation 1958–62. Attained Associated Statehood 1967. Independence granted to Grenada 1974; Dominica 1978; St Lucia 1979; St Vincent 1979.
Member	Zambia		Formerly Northern Rhodesia. Part of Federation of Rhodesia and Nyasaland 1953–63. Independence granted as Republic 1964.
	Zanzibar	Protected State (1890)	Independence granted 1963. Republic 1964. Merged with Tanganyika as Tanzania 1964.
Member	Zimbabwe	Chartered Company (1889)	Formerly Rhodesia. Independence granted as Republic 1980.

Independent Self-Governing Members of the Commonwealth

United Kingdom
1856 New Zealand
1867 Canada[1]
1901 Australia[1]
1909–61, 1994–   South Africa[1]
1907–33   Newfoundland[1][2]
1922–49   Ireland (Eire)
1947 India[3] *(Republic 1950)*
1947–72,1989–99 Pakistan *(Republic 1956)*
1948 Ceylon (Sri Lanka 1972) *(Republic 1972)*
1953–63   Federation of Rhodesia and Nyasaland[4]
1957 Ghana *(Republic 1960)*
1957 Malaya (Malaysia 1963) *(Elective Monarchy)*
1958–62[5]   West Indies Federation
1960–95,1999–   Nigeria *(Republic 1963)*
1961 Cyprus *(Republic 1960)*
1961–1997[6] Sierra Leone *(Republic 1971)* 1999–
1961 Tanganyika (Tanzania 1965) *(Republic 1962)*
1962 Jamaica
1962 Trinidad and Tobago *(Republic 1976)*
1962 Uganda *(Republic 1963)*
1963–1964 Zanzibar (See Tanzania)
1963 Kenya *(Republic 1964)*
1964 Zambia *(Republic 1964)*
1964 Malta *(Republic 1974)*
1964 Malawi *(Republic 1966)*
1965 The Gambia *(Republic 1970)*
1965 Singapore *(Republic 1965)*
1966 Botswana *(Republic 1966)*
1966 Lesotho *(Indigenous Monarchy)*

1966 Guyana *(Republic 1970)*
1966 Barbados
1968 Nauru *(Republic 1968)*
1968 Swaziland *(Indigenous Monarchy)*
1968 Mauritius *(Republic 1992)*
1970–87, 1997–   Fiji *(Republic 1987)*
1970 Tonga *(Indigenous Monarchy)*
1970 Western Samoa *(Indigenous Monarchy)*
1972 Bangladesh *(Republic 1972)*
1973 Bahamas
1974 Grenada
1975 Papua-New Guinea
1976 Seychelles *(Republic 1976)*
1978 Dominica
1978 Solomon Islands
1978 Tuvalu
1979 St Lucia
1979 Kiribati *(Republic 1979)*
1979 St Vincent and the Grenadines
1980 Vanuatu *(Republic 1980)*
1980 Zimbabwe *(Republic 1980)*
1981 Antigua and Barbuda
1981 Belize
1982 Maldive Islands *(Republic 1982)*[7]
1983 St Christopher and Nevis
1984 Brunei *(Indigenous Monarchy)*
1990 Namibia *(Republic 1990)*
1995 Mozambique *(Independent Republic)*[8]
1995 Cameroon *(Independent Republic)*

See p.495 for notes to above table.

[1] These were recognised as having 'Dominion Status' 1907.

[2] From 1933 to 1949 Newfoundland was governed by a U.K. Commission of Government. In 1949 Newfoundland joined Canada as the tenth Province.

[3] Indian representatives were invited to attend Imperial Conferences and Prime Ministers' Meetings 1917–47.

[4] Although the Central African Federation, set up in 1953, and composed of N. Rhodesia, S. Rhodesia and Nyasaland, was not a fully independent member of the Commonwealth, her Prime Ministers were invited to Prime Ministers' Meetings 1955–62 and the Prime Minister of Rhodesia was invited 1962–65.

[5] Barbados, Jamaica, Trinidad and Tobago, the Leeward and Windward Islands all formed the West Indies Federation between 1958 and 1962.

[6] Following a coup, Sierra Leone's membership was suspended in 1997.

[7] Special Membership, 1982. Full member 1985.

[8] Special Membership.

Commonwealth Prime Ministers' Meetings, 1900–1970

(All took place in London)

30 Jun–11 Aug 02	Colonial Conference
15 Apr–9 May 07	Colonial Conference
23 May–20 Jun 11	Imperial Conference
Mar–May 17	Imperial War Conference
Jun–Aug 18	Imperial War Conference
1 Oct– 8 Nov 23	Imperial Conference
19 Oct–23 Nov 26	Imperial Conference
1 Oct–14 Nov 30	Imperial Conference
14 May–15 Jun 37	Imperial Conference
1–16 May 44	Commonwealth Prime Ministers' Meeting
23 Apr–23 May 46	Commonwealth Prime Ministers' Meeting
11–22 Oct 48	Commonwealth Prime Ministers' Meeting
21–28 Apr 49	Commonwealth Prime Ministers' Meeting
4–12 Jan 51	Commonwealth Prime Ministers' Meeting
3–9 Jun 53	Commonwealth Prime Ministers' Meeting
31 Jan–8 Feb 55	Commonwealth Prime Ministers' Meeting
27 Jun–6 Jul 56	Commonwealth Prime Ministers' Meeting
26 Jun–5 Jul 57	Commonwealth Prime Ministers' Meeting
3–13 May 60	Commonwealth Prime Ministers' Meeting
8–17 Mar 61	Commonwealth Prime Ministers' Meeting
10–19 Sep 62	Commonwealth Prime Ministers' Meeting
8–13 Jul 64	Commonwealth Prime Ministers' Meeting
17–25 Jan 65	Commonwealth Prime Ministers' Meeting
6–15 Sep 66	Commonwealth Prime Ministers' Meeting
7–15 Jan 69	Commonwealth Prime Ministers' Meeting

Commonwealth Heads of Government Meetings 1971–

14–22 Jan 71	Commonwealth Heads of Government Meeting (Singapore)
2–10 Aug 73	Commonwealth Heads of Government Meeting (Ottawa)
29 Apr–6 May 75	Commonwealth Heads of Government Meeting (Kingston)
8–15 Jun 77	Commonwealth Heads of Government Meeting (London)
1–10 Aug 79	Commonwealth Heads of Government Meeting (Lusaka)
30 Sep–7 Oct 81	Commonwealth Heads of Government Meeting (Melbourne)
23–29 Nov 83	Commonwealth Heads of Government Meeting (New Delhi)
16–22 Oct 85	Commonwealth Heads of Government Meeting (Nassau)
13–17 Oct 87	Commonwealth Heads of Government Meeting (Vancouver)
18–24 Oct 89	Commonwealth Heads of Government Meeting (Kuala Lumpur)
16–22 Oct 91	Commonwealth Heads of Government Meeting (Harare)
21–25 Oct 93	Commonwealth Heads of Government Meeting (Nicosia)
10–13 Nov 95	Commonwealth Heads of Government Meeting (Auckland)
24–27 Oct 97	Commonwealth Heads of Government Meeting (Edinburgh)
12–15 Nov 99	Commonwealth Heads of Government Meeting (Durban)

Certain other meetings of comparable status have been held

20 Jun–5 Aug 21	Conference of Prime Ministers and Representatives of the United Kingdom, the Dominions and India, London.
21 Jul–20 Aug 32	Imperial Economic Conference, Ottawa.
4–13 Apr 45	British Commonwealth Meeting, London
27 Nov–11 Dec 52	Commonwealth Economic Conference, London.
11–12 Jan 66	Commonwealth Prime Ministers' Conference on Rhodesia, Lagos.

Sources: *Commonwealth Relations Office List 1951*, pp. 56–58; *Annual Register 1900–*; *Keesing's Archives 1931–*.

Commonwealth Secretariat

As a result of the Commonwealth Prime Ministers' Meeting of Jul 1964 a Commonwealth Secretariat was established in London with its own civil servants seconded from Commonwealth Governments.

Secretary-General

Aug 65	A. Smith (Canada)
Jul 75	(Sir) S. Ramphal (Guiana)
Jul 90	E. Anyaoku (Nigeria)
Apr 00	D. McKinnon (New Zealand)

Viceroys and Governors-General

Antigua and Barbuda 1981–

1 Nov 81	Sir W. Jacobs
1 Jun 93	(Sir) J. Carlisle

Australia 1901–

1 Jan 01	E of Hopetoun	8 Oct 25	Ld Stonehaven	22 Sep 65	Ld Casey
9 Jan 03	Ld Tennyson	22 Jan 31	Sir I.Isaacs	30 Apr 69	Sir P. Hasluck
21 Jan 04	Ld Northcote	23 Jan 36	Ld Gowrie	11 Jul 74	Sir J. Kerr
9 Sep 08	E of Dudley	30 Jan 45	D of Gloucester	8 Dec 77	Sir Z. Cowan
31 Jun 11	Ld Denman	11 Mar 47	Sir W. McKell	29 Jul 82	Sir N. Stephen
18 May 14	Sir R. Munro-Ferguson	8 May 53	Sir W. Slim	16 Feb 89	W. Hayden
6 Oct 20	Ld Forster	2 Feb 60	Vt Dunrossil	16 Feb 96	Sir W. Deane
		3 Aug 61	Vt de L'Isle		

Bahamas 1973–

10 Jul 73	Sir J. Paul	24 Sep 79	Sir G. Cash	1 Mar 91	Sir H.Taylor
1 Aug 73	Sir M. Butler	26 Jun 88	Sir H. Taylor	2 Jan 92	Sir C. Darling
22 Jan 76	Sir G. Cash *(acting)*		*(acting)*	22 Feb 95	Sir O. Turnquest

Barbados 1966–

30 Nov 66	Sir J. Stow	23 Jan 79	Sir G. Cash (acting)	1 Jun 96	Sir C. Husbands
15 May 67	Sir W. Scott	24 Feb 84	Sir H. Springer		
17 Nov 76	Sir D. Ward	6 Jun 90	Dame N. Barrow		

Belize 1981–

21 Sep 81	Dame M. Gordon
17 Nov 93	Sir C. Young

Canada 1900–

1898	E of Minto	2 Nov 35	Ld Tweedsmuir	22 Jan 79	E. Schreyer
10 Dec 04	Earl Grey	21 Jun 40	E of Athlone	14 May 84	Jeanne Sauve
13 Oct 11	D of Connaught	12 Apr 46	Vt Alexander	29 Jan 90	R. Hnatyshin
11 Nov 16	D of Devonshire	28 Feb 52	V. Massey	22 Nov 95	R. LeBlanc
11 Aug 21	Ld Byng	15 Sep 59	G. Vanier	7 Oct 99	Adrienne Clarkson
2 Oct 26	Vt Willingdon	4 Apr 67	R. Michener		
4 Apr 31	E of Bessborough	14 Jan 74	J. Leger		

Ceylon 1948–71

4 Feb 48	Sir H. Moore	17 Jul 54	Sir O. Goonetilleke	*22 May 72*	*Declared Republic*
6 Jul 49	Ld Soulbury	2 Mar 62	W. Gopallawa		*(Sri Lanka)*

Fiji 1970–1986

10 Oct 70	Sir R. Foster
13 Jan 73	Sir G. Cakobau
12 Feb 83	Sir P. Ganilau
7 Oct 87	*Declared Republic*

The Gambia 1965–70

18 Feb 65	Sir F. Singhateh
24 Apr 70	*Declared Republic*

Ghana 1957–60

6 Mar 57	E of Listowel
1 Jul 60	*Declared Republic*

Grenada 1974–

7 Feb 74	(Sir) L. de Gale
30 Sep 78	Sir P. Scoon
6 Aug 92	Sir R. Palmer
8 Aug 96	Sir D. Williams

Guyana 1966–70

26 May 66	Sir R. Luyt
16 Dec 66	Sir D. Rose
23 Feb 70	*Declared Republic*

Viceroys of India 1900–47

1899	Ld Curzon	10 Apr 25	E of Lytton	18 Apr 36	M of Linlithgow
30 Apr 04	Ld Ampthill		*(officiating)*	25 Jun 38	Ld Brabourne
	(officiating)	3 Apr 26	Ld Irwin		*(officiating)*
13 Dec 04	Ld Curzon	29 Jun 29	Vt Goschen	25 Oct 38	M of Linlithgow
18 Nov 05	E of Minto		*(officiating)*	20 Oct 43	Vt Wavell
23 Nov 10	Ld Hardinge	24 Oct 29	Ld Irwin	24 Mar 47	Vt Mountbatten
4 Apr 16	Ld Chelmsford	18 Apr 31	E of Willingdon		(Earl)
2 Apr 21	E of Reading	16 May 34	Sir G. Stanley		
			(officiating)		

Dominion of India 1947–50

Governors-General

15 Aug 47	Earl Mountbatten
21 Jun 48	C. Rajagopalachari
26 Jan 50	*Declared Republic*

Ireland 1922–37

6 Dec 22	T. Healy
15 Dec 27	J. McNeill
30 Nov 32	D. O'Buachalla
29 Dec 37	*Declared Republic*

Jamaica 1962–

6 Aug 62	Sir C.Campbell
27 Jun 73	(Sir) F. Glasspole
1 Aug 91	(Sir) H.Cooke

Kenya 1963–64

12 Dec 63	M. Macdonald
12 Dec 64	*Declared Republic*

Malawi 1964–66

6 Jul 64	Sir G. Jones
6 Jul 66	*Declared Republic*

Malta 1964–74

21 Sep 64	Sir M. Dorman
5 Jul 71	Sir A. Mamo
13 Dec 74	*Declared Republic*

Mauritius 1968–1992

1 Sep 68	Sir A. Williams
27 Dec 72	Sir R. Osman
19 Nov 77	Sir W. Garrioch *(acting)*
Mar 78	(Sir) D. Burrenchobay
27 Dec 83	Sir S. Ramgoolam
17 Jan 86	Sir V. Ringadoo
22 Mar 92	*Declared Republic*

New Zealand 1900

(Governors)

1897	E of Ranfurly
20 Jun 04	Ld Plunkett
22 Jun 10	Ld Islington
19 Dec 12	E of Liverpool

(Governors-General)

28 Jun 17	E of Liverpool	16 Jun 46	Ld Freyberg	26 Oct 77	Sir K. Holyoake
27 Sep 20	Earl Jellicoe	1 Dec 52	Sir C. Norrie (Ld)	26 Oct 80	(Sir) D. Beattie
13 Dec 24	Sir C. Fergusson	3 Sep 57	Vt Cobham	10 Sep 85	Sir P. Reeves
18 Mar 30	Ld Bledisloe	9 Nov 62	Sir B. Fergusson	20 Nov 90	Dame K. Tizard
12 Apr 35	Vt Galway	19 Oct 67	Sir A. Porritt	21 Mar 95	Sir M. Boys
21 Feb 41	Ld Newall	26 Sep 72	Sir D. Blundell		

Nigeria 1960–63

1 Oct 60	N. Azikwe
1 Oct 63	*Declared Republic*

Dominion of Pakistan 1947–56

15 Aug 47	M. Jinnah
14 Sep 48	Khwaja Nazimuddin
19 Oct 51	Ghulam Mohammed
6 Oct 55	Iskander Mirza
23 Mar 56	*Declared Republic*

Papua-New Guinea 1975–

15 Sep 75	Sir J. Guise	28 Feb 89	Sir I. Kilage	14 Nov 97	(Sir) S. Atopare
1 Mar 76	Sir T. Lokoloko	12 Dec 90	(Sir) V. Eri		
28 Feb 83	Sir K. Dibela	12 Nov 91	(Sir W) Korowi		

Federation of Rhodesia and Nyasaland 1957–63

8 Oct 57	E of Dalhousie
31 Dec 63	*Federation dissolved*

St Christopher and Nevis 1983

19 Sep 83	Sir C. Arrindell
1 Jan 96	Sir C. Sebastian

St Lucia 1979–

22 Feb 79	B. Williams	13 Dec 82	Sir A. Lewis	21 Feb 92	(Sir) S. James
	(acting)	16 May 87	Sir V. Floissac	1 Jun 96	G. Mallet
21 Feb 80	B.Williams		*(acting)*	17 Sep 97	P. Louisy

St Vincent and the Grenadines 1979–

27 Oct 79	Sir S. Gun-Munro
1 Mar 85	Sir J. Eustace
20 Sep 90	(Sir) D. Jack
15 Oct 96	Sir C. Antrobus

Sierra Leone 1961–71

27 Apr 61	Sir H. Lightfoot-Boston

(In Mar 67 the Constitution was suspended)

7 Apr 68	B. Tejan-Sie *(acting)*
19 Apr 71	*Declared Republic*

Solomon Islands 1978–

7 Jul 78	(Sir) B. Devesi
7 Jul 88	Sir G. Lepping
26 Jun 94	Sir M. Pitakaka
99	J. Lapli

South Africa 1910–61

31 May 10	Vt Gladstone	21 Jan 24	E of Athlone	1 Jan 46	G.van Zyl
8 Sep 14	Vt Buxton	26 Jan 31	E of Clarendon	1 Jan 51	E. Jansen
20 Nov 20	Prince Arthur of Connaught	5 Apr 37	Sir P. Duncan	25 Nov 59	C. Swart

The Union of South Africa became an independent republic outside the British Commonwealth on 31 May 61.

Tanganyika 1961–62

9 Dec 61	Sir R. Turnbull
9 Dec 62	*Declared Republic*

Trinidad and Tobago 1962–76

31 Aug 62	Sir S. Hochoy
31 Jan 73	Sir E. Clarke
1 Aug 76	*Declared Republic*

Tuvalu 1978–

1 Oct 78	(Sir) P. Teo
1 Feb 86	Sir T. Leupena
1 Oct 90	(Sir) T. Lauti
28 Nov 93	(Sir) T. Sione
26 Jun 94	Sir T. Manuella
Jun 98	Sir T. Puapua

Uganda 1962–63

9 Oct 62	Sir F. Crawford
9 Oct 63	*Declared Republic*

West Indies 1957–62

10 May 57	Ld Hailes
Feb 62	*Federation dissolved*

Sources: C. Cook and J. Paxton, *Commonwealth Political Facts* (1979); *Statesman's Year-Book* (1900–) (1979).

XVII

INTERNATIONAL RELATIONS

Major Treaties and Documents Subscribed to by Britain since 1900[1]

30 Jan 02	Anglo-Japanese Alliance
8 Apr 04	Anglo-French Entente
31 Aug 07	Anglo-Russian Entente
18 Mar 15	Anglo-Russian Agreement over Constantinople
25 Apr 15	Treaty of London (Italy)
16 May 16	Sykes-Picot Agreement (Middle East)
31 Oct 17	Balfour Declaration (Palestine)
28 Jun 19	Treaty of Versailles (Germany) and League of Nations Covenant[2]
10 Sep 19	Treaty of St Germain (Austria)
27 Nov 19	Treaty of Neuilly (Bulgaria)
9 Feb 20	Spitzbergen Treaty (status and sovereignty of Spitzbergen Archipelago)
4 Jun 20	Treaty of Trianon (Hungary)
10 Aug 20	Treaty of Sèvres (Turkey)
6 Dec 21	Articles of Agreement for an Irish Peace
13 Dec 21	Washington Four Power Treaty (Pacific)
6 Feb 22	Washington Nine Power Treaty (China)
6 Feb 22	Washington Five Power Treaty (Naval)
23 Aug 23	Treaty of Lausanne (Middle East and the Straits)
17 Jun 25	Geneva Protocol on the use of Asphyxiating and Poisonous Gases
15 Oct 25	Locarno Pact
27 Aug 28	General Pact for the Renunciation of War (Briand-Kellogg)
22 Apr 30	London Naval Treaty
18 Jun 35	Anglo-German Naval Agreement
25 Mar 36	London Naval Treaty
20 Jul 36	Montreux Agreement (Straits)
7 Aug 36	Non-Intervention Agreement (Spain)
26 Aug 36	Anglo-Egyptian Treaty
29 Sep 38	Munich Agreement
31 Mar 39	Franco-British Guarantee to Poland
13 Apr 39	British Guarantee to Roumania and Greece
12 May 39	British Guarantee to Turkey
25 Aug 39	Anglo-Polish Agreement of Mutual Assistance
14 Aug 41	Atlantic Charter
23 Feb 42	Anglo-American Aid Mutual Agreement (Lend-Lease 'Master Agreement')
26 May 42	Anglo-Soviet Treaty
22 Jul 44	Bretton Woods Agreement (International Finance)
7 Dec 44	Chicago Convention on International Civil Aviation
11 Feb 45	Yalta Agreement
26 Jun 45	United Nations Charter[3]
2 Aug 45	Potsdam Agreement
16 Oct 45	Institution of the Food and Agriculture Organisation
6 Dec 45	Anglo-American Financial Agreement
9 Feb 47	Peace Treaties with Italy, Hungary, Roumania, Bulgaria, and Finland
17 Mar 48	Brussels Treaty Organisation
16 Apr 48	Organisation for European Economic Co-operation
6 Jul 48	Economic Co-operation Agreement (Marshall Aid)
4 Apr 49	North Atlantic Treaty Organisation (NATO)

[1] See also the section on the Commonwealth (pp.487–500) and on Britain and Europe (pp.505–15).

[2] The *International Labour Organisation* (I.L.O.) was created by the Treaty of Versailles, as a semi-autonomous organisation in association with the League of Nations. On 16 Dec 20 a statute was drawn up for the establishment of the *Permanent Court of International Justice* at The Hague. The Hague Court had its preliminary session on 30 Jan 22. It was dissolved by resolution of the League Assembly in Apr 1946.

[3] The Charter made provision for the continuance of the *International Court of Justice* at The Hague. The I.L.O. continued to function as one of the specialised agencies of the United Nations. (Among other subsidiary organisations were F.A.O., U.N.E.S.C.O., W.H.O., I.M.F., etc. See *The Statesman's Year-Book* for a brief summary of the organisations and their member countries).

5 May 49	Council of Europe
12 Aug 49	Red Cross Convention on the protection of civilians in war-time
4 Nov 50	Convention for the protection of Human Rights and Fundamental Freedom (U.N. Declaration on Human Rights)
28 Nov 50	Colombo Plan (South and South-East Asia)
8 Sep 51	Treaty of Peace with Japan
20 Jul 54	Geneva Conventions on Indo-China
8 Sep 54	South-East Asia Defence Treaty (SEATO)
3 Oct 54	London Nine Power Agreement (European security and integration)
23 Oct 54	Western European Union (formerly Brussels Treaty Organisation)
21 Dec 54	European Coal and Steel Community (Britain made an agreement of association). Community formed on 18 Apr 51
4 Apr 55	Special agreement whereby Britain joined the Baghdad Pact (defence). (Pact signed 24 Feb 55).
5 May 55	Bonn/Paris Conventions terminating the Occupation Regime in West Germany
15 May 55	Austrian State Treaty (occupation ended and declaration of neutrality)
29 Jul 57	International Atomic Energy Agency
29 Apr 58	Law of the Sea Convention (Continental Shelf)
4 Feb 59	European Atomic Energy Community (Euratom). Britain made an agreement of association. (Euratom formed 1 Jan 58)
21 Aug 59	Central Treaty Organisation (Cento). Formerly the Baghdad Pact
20 Nov 59	European Free Trade Association
31 May 59	Antarctic Treaty
14 Dec 60	Organisation for Economic Co-operation and Development (formerly Organisation for European Economic Co-operation)
18 Apr 61	Vienna Convention on Diplomatic Relations
30 Sep 62	Convention on the High Seas
6 Apr 63	Polaris Sales Agreement with the U.S.A.
5 Aug 63	Test-ban Treaty
30 Aug 63	European Space Research Organisation
9 Mar 64	European Fisheries Convention
20 Aug 64	INTELSAT agreement (interim arrangements for a global commercial communications satellite system)
27 Jan 67	Outer Space Treaty
25 Aug 67	'Hotline' Agreement with U.S.S.R.
22 Apr 68	Agreement on the Rescue and Return of Astronauts and Space Vehicles
1 Jul 68	Nuclear Non-Proliferation Treaty
13 Aug 70	Ratification by U.K. of The Hague Convention on the Pacific Settlement of International Disputes (originally signed 29 Jul 1889)
11 Feb 71	Treaty on prohibition of weapons of mass destruction on sea-bed
20 Aug 71	Revised INTELSAT Agreement and INTELSAT operating Agreement
3 Sep 71	Quadripartite Agreement on Berlin
22 Jan 72	Treaty of Accession to European Economic Community and European Atomic Energy Community
10 Apr 72	Convention on the Prohibition of the Development, Production and Stockpiling of Bacteriological (Biological) and Toxic Weapons
9 Nov 72	Quadripartite Declaration on the entry of the Federal Republic of Germany and the German Democratic Republic into the U.N.
28 Feb 75	Lome Convention (E.E.C. with 46 African, Caribbean and Pacific Territories)
1 Aug 75	Final Act of Conference on Security and Co-operation in Europe (Helsinki Conference)
20 May 76	International (U.N.) Covenants on Economic and Social Rights and on Civil and Political Rights
18 May 77	Convention on the Prohibition of military or any other hostile use of environmental modification techniques
21 Dec 79	Lancaster House agreement between Britain and the leaders of the main parties in Zimbabwe-Rhodesia
19 Dec 84	Hong Kong treaty between Britain and China signed in Peking
17 Feb 86	Single European Act
7 Feb 92	Maastricht Treaty on European Union (ratified 2 Aug 93)
14 Jun 94	Sulphur Emissions Protocol
15 Apr 94	Agreement establishing World Trade Organisation (GATT Uruguay Round)
2 Apr 97	Amsterdam Treaty on European Union
16 Dec 97	NATO expansion protocol
10 Apr 98	British-Irish Agreement on N. Ireland (Good Friday Agreement)

League of Nations, 1919–1946

Britain was a founder member of the League of Nations. Between 1919 and 1922 the British Government conducted its relations with the League through its cabinet secretariat. After 1922 the Foreign Office was responsible for British representation at the League. A member of the Government was generally deputed to act as British representative at meetings of the League. No permanent national delegation stayed at Geneva. A. Eden was the only Minister appointed officially for League of Nations Affairs (7 Jun–22 Dec 35). Vt Cranborne was Parliamentary Under-Secretary at the Foreign Office with special responsibility for League of Nations Affairs from 6 Aug 35 until 20 Feb 38. The League was formally dissolved in 1946 although in practice it ceased to meet during the war.

United Nations, 1946–

Britain was one of the original signatories of the Charter of the United Nations. Since 1946 the British Government has had a permanent representative at the United Nations in New York. In addition, a Minister of State at the Foreign Office has usually been given special responsibility for United Nations affairs (see p.515). From 1964 to 1970 the permanent representative was a Minister of State at the Foreign Office.

Foreign Affairs Pressure Groups

The League of Nations Union (1920–45) and the United Nations Association (1945–) have provided nationwide forums for the discussion of foreign affairs. Other bodies concerned with the country's international involvements include the Royal Institute of International Affairs (Chatham House) (1920), the European Movement (1949), Amnesty International (1960) and the Campaign for Nuclear Disarmament (1958).

British Ambassadors to Leading Powers and International Organisations, 1900–

Austria-Hungary (–1914)

1896	Sir H. Rumbold	1 Nov 08	Sir F. Cartwright	12 Aug 14	*War declared by U.K.*
9 Sep 00	Sir F. Plunkett	1 Nov 13	Sir M. de Bunsen		*on Austria-Hungary*
7 May 05	Sir W. Goschen				

France

1896	Sir E. Monson	1 Nov 39	Sir R. Campbell	13 Nov 72	Sir E. Tomkins
1 Jan 05	Sir F. Bertie (Ld)	24 Jun 40	*Diplomatic*	8 Dec 75	Sir N. Henderson
19 Apr 18	E of Derby		*mission withdrawn*	20 Apr 79	Sir R. Hibbert
27 Nov 20	Ld Hardinge of	23 Oct 44	A. Duff Cooper	4 Mar 82	Sir J. Fretwell
	Penhurst	9 Jan 48	Sir O. Harvey	22 Jun 87	Sir E. Fergusson
31 Dec 22	M of Crewe	13 Apr 54	Sir G. Jebb	29 Jun 93	Sir C. Mallaby
30 Jul 28	Sir W. Tyrrell (Ld)	11 Apr 60	Sir P. Dixon	10 Jul 96	Sir M. Jay
17 Apr 34	Sir G. Clerk	11 Feb 65	Sir P. Reilly		
24 Apr 37	Sir E. Phipps	17 Sep 68	(Sir) C. Soames		

Germany

				(Ambassadors to (West) Germany)	
1895	Sir F. Lascelles	*(Military Governors)*		5 May 55	Sir F. Hoyer Millar
1 Nov 08	Sir W. Goschen	1945	Sir B. Montgomery	7 Feb 57	Sir C. Steel
4 Aug 14	*War declared by U.K. on Germany*	1946	Sir S. Douglas	15 Feb 63	Sir F. Roberts
		1947	Sir B. Robertson	15 May 68	Sir R. Jackling
10 Jan 20	Ld Kilmarnock *(ch. d'aff.)*			25 Jul 72	Sir N. Henderson
29 Jun 20	Ld D'Abernon	*(British High Commissioners)*		30 Sep 75	Sir O. Wright
12 Oct 26	Sir R. Lindsay	17 Mar 49	Sir B. Robertson	17 Mar 81	Sir J. Taylor
1 Aug 28	Sir H. Rumbold	24 Jun 50	Sir I. Kirkpatrick	1 Sep 84	Sir J. Bullard
2 Aug 33	Sir E. Phipps	29 Sep 53	Sir F. Hoyer Millar	20 Mar 88	Sir C. Mallaby
29 Apr 37	Sir N. Henderson			17 Jan 93	(Sir) N. Broomfield
3 Sep 39	*War declared by U.K. on Germany*			Mar 97	Sir C. Meyer
				31 Dec 97	(Sir) P. Lever

Italy

1898	Sir P. Currie (Ld)	11 Jun 40	*War declared by Italy on G.B.*	17 Dec 66	Sir E. Shuckburgh
17 Jan 03	Sir F. Bertie			16 Sep 69	Sir P. Hancock
1 Jan 05	Sir E. Egerton	5 Apr 44	Sir N. Charles	14 Oct 76	Sir A. Campbell
1 Dec 08	Sir J. Rennell Rodd	*(1944, High Commissioner, 1945,*		12 Jul 79	Sir R. Arculus
21 Oct 19	Sir G. Buchanan	*Representative of H.M.*		1 Mar 83	Ld Bridges
25 Nov 21	Sir R. Graham	*Government with the personal*		3 Dec 87	Sir D. Thomas
26 Oct 33	Sir E. Drummond (E of Perth)	*rank of Ambassador)*		14 Nov 89	Sir S. Egerton
		9 Oct 47	Sir V. Mallet	5 Jul 92	Sir P. Fairweather
1 May 39	Sir P. Loraine	12 Nov 53	Sir A. Clarke	10 Jul 96	(Sir) T. Richardson
		19 Sep 62	Sir J. Ward		

Russia (U.S.S.R.)

1898	Sir C. Scott	24 Oct 33	Vt Chilston	27 Aug 65	Sir G. Harrison
28 Apr 04	Sir C. Hardinge (Ld)	19 Jan 39	Sir W. Seeds	3 Oct 68	Sir D. Wilson
10 Feb 06	Sir A. Nicolson	12 Jun 40	Sir S. Cripps	9 Sep 71	Sir J. Killick
23 Nov 10	Sir G. Buchanan	4 Feb 42	Sir A. Kerr (Ld Inverchapel)	13 Nov 73	Sir T. Garvey
1917	*Diplomatic mission withdrawn*			18 Jan 76	(Sir) H. Smith
		17 May 46	Sir M. Peterson	1 Apr 78	(Sir) C. Keeble
1 Feb 24	Sir R. Hodgson *(ch. d'aff.)*	22 Jun 49	Sir D. Kelly	16 Sep 82	Sir I. Sutherland
		18 Oct 51	Sir A. Gascoigne	18 Jul 85	Sir B. Cartledge
3 Jun 27	*Suspension of diplomatic relations*	1 Oct 53	Sir W. Hayter	23 May 88	Sir R. Braithwaite
		19 Feb 57	Sir P. Reilly	3 Jun 92	Sir B. Fall
		29 Apr 60	Sir F. Roberts	12 Jul 95	Sir A. Wood
7 Dec 29	Sir E. Ovey	27 Nov 62	Sir H. Trevelyan	12 Jan 00	(Sir) R. Line

Turkey

1898	Sir N. O'Conor	*(Ambassador)*		7 Mar 63	Sir W. Allen
1 Apr 08	Sir G. Barclay	12 Nov 26	Sir G. Clerk	16 Mar 67	Sir R. Allen
	(Min.plen.ad.int.)	16 Dec 33	Sir P. Loraine	8 Feb 73	Sir H. Phillips
1 Jul 08	Sir G. Lowther	25 Feb 39	Sir H. Knatchbull-Hugessen	15 Jun 77	Sir D. Dodson
10 Oct 13	Sir L. Mallet			30 Jan 80	Sir P. Laurence
5 Nov 14	*War declared by U.K. on Turkey*	29 Sep 44	Sir M. Peterson	28 Feb 83	(Sir) M. Russell
		10 May 46	Sir D. Kelly	1 Nov 86	(Sir) T. Dault
1 Nov 20	Sir H. Rumbold	20 Apr 49	Sir N. Charles	23 Oct 92	J. Goulden
2 Feb 24	(Sir) R. Lindsay	6 Dec 51	Sir K. Helm	23 Mar 95	Sir K. Prendergast
(H.M. Representative)		13 Jan 54	Sir J. Bowker	28 Mar 97	(Sir) D. Logan
1 Mar 25	Sir R. Lindsay	15 Nov 58	Sir B. Burrows		

U.S.A.

1893	Sir J. Pauncefote	29 Aug 39	M of Lothian	4 Jan 71	E of Cromer
	(Ld)	24 Jan 41	Vt Halifax (E of)	3 Mar 74	Sir P. Ramsbotham
4 Jun 02	(Sir) M. Herbert	23 May 46	Ld Inverchapel	21 Jul 77	P. Jay
23 Oct 03	Sir M. Durand	22 May 48	Sir O. Franks	9 Jul 79	Sir N. Henderson
3 Feb 07	J. Bryce	31 Dec 52	Sir R. Makins	2 Sep 82	Sir O. Wright
19 Apr 13	Sir A. Spring-Rice	2 Nov 56	Sir H. Caccia	28 Aug 86	Sir A. Acland
1 Jan 18	E of Reading	18 Oct 61	Sir W. Ormsby-	20 Aug 91	Sir R. Renwick
25 Mar 20	Sir A. Geddes		Gore (Ld Harlech)	15 Aug 95	Sir J. Kerr
2 Feb 24	Sir E. Howard	6 Apr 65	Sir P. Dean	31 Oct 97	Sir C. Meyer
11 Mar 30	Sir R. Lindsay	21 Feb 69	J. Freeman		

North Atlantic Council

18 Aug 53	Sir C. Steel	15 Nov 66	Sir B. Burrows	15 Feb 82	Sir J. Graham
7 Feb 57	Sir F. Roberts	17 Apr 70	Sir E. Peck	30 Aug 86	(Sir) M. Alexander
24 Oct 60	Sir P. Mason	17 Oct 75	Sir J. Killick	25 Jan 91	(Sir) J. Weston
7 Jan 63	Sir E. Shuckburgh	18 Sep 79	Sir C. Rose	1 Apr 95	P. Goulden

The United Nations

1 Feb 46	Sir A. Cadogan	4 Sep 70	Sir C. Crowe	29 May 87	Sir C. Tickell
27 Jun 50	Sir G. Jebb	May 73	Sir D. Maitland	7 Sep 90	Sir D. Hannay
13 Mar 54	Sir P. Dixon	Jun 74	I. Richard	15 Jul 95	Sir J. Weston
7 Sep 60	Sir P. Dean	9 Sep 79	Sir A. Parsons	8 Aug 98	Sir J. Greenstock
Nov 64	Ld Caradon	17 Aug 82	Sir J. Thomson		

Sources: *United Nations Year-books, 1946–*; *Foreign Office List 1953–66*; *Diplomatic Service List 1967–*.

Among the major works on international relations since 1900 are: A.J.P. Taylor, *Struggle for Mastery in Europe, 1848–1918* (1954); C.R.M.F. Crutwell, *A History of the Great War, 1914–18* (1936); E.H. Carr, *International Relations between the Two World Wars* (1947); E.H. Carr, *Twenty years' Crisis* (1947); G.F. Hudson, *The Far East in World Politics* (1939); W.M. Joran, *Great Britain, France and the German Problem, 1919–39* (1943); A.J.P. Taylor, *Origins of the Second World War* (1961); J.W. Wheeler-Bennett, *Munich: Prologue to Tragedy* (1948); A. Wolfers, *Britain and France between the two wars* (1940); Sir L. Woodward, *British Foreign Policy in the Second World War* (1962); W. McNeill, *America, Britain and Russia: Their Co-operation and Conflict 1941–46* (1953); F.S. Northedge, *The Troubled Giant, Britain among the Great Powers 1916–39* (1974); J. Frankel, *British Foreign Policy 1945–73* (1975); W. Wallace, *The Foreign Policy Process in Britain* (1976).
  Among the main works on Britain and international organisations are: F.P. Walters, *History of the League of Nations* (2 vols. 1951); G.L. Goodwin, *Britain and the United Nations* (1957); and A.H. Robertson, *European Institutions* (1966).
  The Royal Institute of International Affairs has published the *Survey of Internal Affairs* annually since 1920. Since 1915 the texts of major public documents have been printed in the *Annual Register*. For reference only, see *The Statesman's Year-Book*, and the *Year Book of International Organisations, 1951–*.

XVIII

BRITAIN AND EUROPE

A Chronology of Events

17 Mar 48	Treaty signed establishing Western European Union
7 May 48	Churchill's speech at Hague Congress leads to formation of European Movement
5 May 49	Council of Europe established at Strasbourg
9 May 50	Schuman Plan launched leading to establishment of European Coal and Steel Community
30 Aug 54	Final abandonment of Pleven Plan for European Defence Community
2 Jun 55	Messina meeting at which Economic Community negotiations began (British observer withdrawn Nov 55)
25 Mar 57	Treaty of Rome signed by the Six establishes E.E.C. and Euratom
20 Nov 59	EFTA established following failure to agree with E.E.C. on free-trade area
31 Jul 61	Conservative Government initiates negotiations to join E.E.C.
14 Jan 62	E.E.C. agrees Common Agricultural Policy
14 Jan 63	General de Gaulle vetoes British entry
29 Jan 66	'Luxembourg Compromise' preserves veto on issues of 'vital national interest'.
1 Jan 67	Merger treaty comes into effect creating common institutions for the European communities (E.C.S.C., E.E.C. and Euratom.
2 May 67	Labour Government announces intention to apply, following winter exploratory talks
27 Nov 67	General de Gaulle delivers second veto
1 Dec 69	Hague E.C. summit agrees in principle to open negotiations for British entry
8 Jun 70	E.C. invites Britain to apply and negotiations start on 30 Jun
7 Jul 71	White Paper (Cmnd 4715) sets out agreement reached on almost all major points
28 Oct 71	Parliament endorses (by 356 to 244) decision in principle to join on the terms negotiated
22 Jan 72	Treaty of Accession signed
17 Oct 72	Royal Assent to European Communities Act
1 Jan 73	Britain becomes member of E.C.
1 Apr 74	'Renegotiation' of British membership opened at Brussels
11 Mar 75	'Renegotiation' concluded at Dublin meeting of E.C. Heads of Government
9 Apr 75	Parliament endorses (by 396 to 170) 'renegotiation'
5 Jun 75	Britain votes 67.2% 'Yes' in Referendum on continued E.C. membership
7 Jul 75	Labour party delegates take seats in European Parliament for first time
29 Jun 76	Foreign ministers agree to start negotiations with Greece
13 Jul 76	Heads of Governments agree to 410 seat Parliament with direct elections in 1978
6 Jan 77	R. Jenkins becomes first British President of Commission
7 Jul 77	House of Commons gives Second Reading to European Elections Bill 394–147. Vote repeated in new session Nov 77, 381–98
13 Dec 77	Proportional representation for European elections defeated 319–222
31 Dec 77	Transitional period for U.K. ends
7 Apr 78	Copenhagen summit decides on Jun 79 for first Direct Elections to European Parliament
5 May 78	Royal Assent to European Elections Bill
6 Dec 78	Brussels summit approves European Monetary System (commenced 12 Mar 79) but Britain does not participate
4 May 79	Conservatives under Mrs Thatcher win U.K. general election
7 Jun 79	60 Con; 17 Lab; 4 Other U.K. members elected to European Parliament
2 Dec 79	Dublin summit: Mrs Thatcher asks for budgetary abatement
14 Dec 79	European Parliament rejects the Community budget for spending too much on agriculture and not enough on the Regional and Social funds
18 May 80	E.C. states impose economic sanctions against Iran in support of the United States
30 May 80	Agreement is reached among E.C. foreign ministers in dispute over Britain's budget contribution (Britain gets $^2/_3$ rebate for three years). The Commission is asked to report on long-term reform (the Mandate)
6 Jan 81	Greece enters the Community. New Commission takes office under Gaston Thorn
27 Nov 81	London summit of E.C. leaders fails to reach agreement on the Commission's Mandate report. Britain's hopes of getting a long-term solution to her budget problems fade
2 Apr 82	Argentina invades the Falklands. The E.E.C. states swiftly back Britain in a programme of economic sanctions against Argentina

18 May 82	The British veto over farm price increases is overruled in the Agriculture Council, but France states that Luxembourg Compromise still stands
24 Dec 82	European Parliament rejects supplementary budgets containing British and West German rebates
9 Jun 83	Mrs Thatcher's Government returned with an increased majority
3 Oct 83	Labour makes withdrawal 'an option' rather than a certainty should Labour Government be returned
20 Dec 83	The European Parliament freezes British and West German rebates again after the failure of the Athens summit to come to a long-term solution to the budget problem
14 Jun 84	Second direct elections to the European Parliament. Conservatives lose 15 seats: Con. 45, Lab. 32, SNP 1
14 Jun 84	Commission publishes Cockfield White Paper on completing Single Market by 31 Dec 92
29 Jun 84	At Milan Summit U.K., Danish and Portugese veto overrridden on calling an intergovernmental conference to reform treaties
26 Jun 84	British Budget settlement agreed at Fontainebleau
6 Jan 85	New Commission takes office under Jacques Delors
3 Dec 85	Luxembourg summit agrees Single European Act
1 Jan 86	Spain and Portugal join Community
11 Jun 87	Mrs Thatcher wins third U.K. election
1 Jul 87	Single European Act comes into force
20 Sep 88	Mrs Thatcher criticises further European integration in Bruges speech
6 Jan 89	Second Delors Commission takes office
15 Jun 89	Third direct elections to the European Parliament. Conservatives lose 13 seats: Con.32, Lab. 45, SNP 1
9 Nov 89	Fall of Berlin Wall
8 Dec 89	Intergovernmental Conference convened for December 1991. 11 states adopt Social Charter
3 Oct 90	German Unification takes place
8 Oct 90	Britain joins Exchange Rate Mechanism at 2.95Dm to £
28 Oct 90	Rome Summit leaves Mrs Thatcher isolated on monetary union, provoking Sir G. Howe to resign from U.K. cabinet
28 Nov 90	J. Major replaces Margaret Thatcher as PM
10 Dec 91	Maastricht Summit endorses IGC proposals
9 Apr 92	Conservatives win fourth successive U.K.election
2 Jun 92	Danish referendum narrowly rejects Maastricht Treaty
16 Sep 92	'Black Wednesday'. U.K. takes sterling from Exchange Rate Mechanism
20 Sep 92	French referendum narrowly endorses Maastricht Treaty
4 Nov 92	Commons vote 319–316 for further consideration of Maastricht Bill
6 Jan 93	Third Delors Commission takes office
17 May 93	Second Danish referendum endorses Maastricht Treaty
22 Jul 93	U.K. Government position on Social Chapter rejected by Commons, 324–316; wins vote of confidence next day 339–299
1 Nov 93	Maastricht Treaty comes into force
29 Mar 94	U.K. Cabinet accepts Ioannina compromise on blocking votes
9 Jun 94	Fourth direct elections to the European Parliament. Con. MEPs cut from 32 to 18. Lab. get 62 Lib.Dems. 2 and SNP 2
25 Jun 94	U.K. vetoes Dehaene as Commission President
15 Jul 94	Santer chosen as Commission President
28 Nov 94	Norwegian referendum rejects EU membership
1 Jan 95	Austria, Finland and Sweden join EU
18 Jan 95	European Parliament confirms Santer 418–103
26 Mar 95	Seven States accept Schengen Agreement on open borders
26 May 96	U.K. Government threatens non-cooperation after EU failure to lift ban on British beef
22 Jun 96	Compromise on beef agreed at Florence Summit
16 Jul 96	Council invites Czechoslovakia, Estonia, Hungary, Poland and Slovenia to apply for membership
1 May 97	All British parties fight general election with a commitment to a Referendum before joining monetary union. Labour wins landslide victory
Jun 97	U.K. signs Social Protocol endorsing Social Chapter
20 Oct 97	Brown indicates no constitutional objection to joining EMU
9 Nov 98	Human Rights Bill enacted, giving effect to E.C.H.R. rights in U.K. law
13 Dec 98	Luxembourg Summit lifts ban on U.K. beef exports
1 Jan 99	EMU starts for 11 countries
14 Jan 99	Santer Commission narrowly survives censure over allegations of fraud and mismanagement
15 Jan 99	European Elections Act provides for PR
15 Mar 99	Santer Commission resigns en masse

1 May 99	Amsterdam Treaty enters into force
5 May 99	Prodi approved to replace Santer as President of Commission
10 Jun 99	Fifth Direct Elections. MEPs: Con. 36; Lab. 29; Lib.Dem.10; Others 12.
15 Sep 99	Prodi Commission takes office.

Summits 1973–

Meetings of European Heads of Government occurred quite frequently but on an ad hoc basis until 1975. Since 1975 there has always been at least one 'European Council' during each member state's six-month Presidency of the Council of Ministers. The following summits have taken place since the United Kingdom joined the Community in 1973.

14–15 Dec 73	Copenhagen	17–19 Jun 83	Stuttgart	11–12 Dec 92	*Edinburgh
9–10 Dec 74	Paris	4– 6 Dec 83	Athens	20–22 Jun 93	Copenhagen
10–11 Mar 75	Dublin	19–20 Mar 84	Brussels	29 Oct 93	Brussels
1– 2 Dec 75	Rome	14–17 Jun 84	Fontainebleau	10–11 Dec 93	Brussels
13–15 Jun 76	Brussels	3– 4 Dec 84	Dublin	24–25 Jun 94	Corfu
29–30 Nov 76	The Hague	29–30 Mar 85	Brussels	15 Jul 94	Brussels
25–26 Mar 77	Rome	28–29 Jun 85	Milan	9–10 Dec 94	Essen
29–30 Jun 77	*London	2– 3 Dec 85	Luxembourg	26–27 Jun 95	Cannes
5– 6 Dec 78	Brussels	26–27 Jun 86	The Hague	22–23 Sep 95	Majorca
7– 8 Apr 78	Copenhagen	5– 6 Dec 86	*London	15–16 Dec 95	Madrid
4– 5 Dec 78	Brussels	23–24 Jun 87	Brussels	29 Mar 96	Turin
12–13 Mar 79	Paris	4– 5 Dec 87	Copenhagen	21–22 Jun 96	Florence
21–22 Jun 79	Strasbourg	27–28 Jun 88	Hanover	5 Oct 96	Dublin
29–30 Nov 79	Dublin	2– 3 Dec 88	Rhodes	13–14 Dec 96	Dublin
27–28 Apr 80	Luxembourg	26–27 Jun 89	Madrid	16–17 Jun 97	Amsterdam
12–13 Jun 80	Venice	8– 9 Dec 89	Strasbourg	20–21 Nov 97	Luxembourg
1– 2 Dec 80	Luxembourg	28 Apr 90	Dublin I	12–13 Dec 97	Luxembourg
23–24 Mar 81	Maastricht	25–26 Jun 90	Dublin II	12 Mar 98	*London
29–30 Jun 81	Luxembourg	27–28 Oct 90	Rome I	26 May 98	Brussels[1]
26–27 Nov 81	*London	14–15 Dec 90	Rome II	16–17 Jun 98	*Cardiff
29–30 Mar 82	Brussels	28–29 Jun 91	Luxembourg	11–12 Dec 98	Vienna
28–29 Jun 82	Brussels	9–10 Dec 91	Maastricht	3–4 Jun 99	Cologne
3– 4 Dec 82	Copenhagen	26–27 Jun 92	Lisbon	15–16 Oct 98	Tampera
21–23 Mar 83	Brussels	16 Oct 92	*Birmingham	10–11 Dec 99	Helsinki

[1]Special European Council
*UK Presidency

European Organisations with British Membership

Western European Union (W.E.U.), 1948–

The U.K., France, the Netherlands, Belgium and Luxembourg signed a 50-year treaty in Brussels, 17 Mar 48, for collaboration in economic, cultural and social matters and for collective self-defence. Western European Union's defence functions were formally transferred to NATO 20 Dec 50. In 1954 Italy and West Germany were invited to join and W.E.U. was formally inaugurated 6 May 55. Its social and cultural functions were transferred to the Council of Europe 1 Jul 60 but the W.E.U. Council continued to hold regular consultative meetings.

European Free Trade Association (EFTA), 1960–72

After failure to agree on a Free Trade Area with the European Economic Community in 1959 Britain joined with Austria, Denmark, Norway, Portugal, Sweden and Switzerland in EFTA under the Stockholm Convention, 20 Nov 59 signed in May 1960. Iceland joined

EFTA 27 Mar 70 and Finland became an Associate on 27 Mar 61. All inter-EFTA tariffs were removed by 31 Dec 66, three years earlier than planned. Britain and Denmark left EFTA 1 Jan 73 on joining the Common Market but on 27 Jul 72 the remaining EFTA countries had signed Free Trade Agreements with the E.E.C. and by 1 Jul 77 there was a complete free trade area between E.E.C. and EFTA.

Council of Europe, 1949–

Following the 1948 Congress of Europe at The Hague, the Council of Europe came into being in May 1949. Its founder members were Belgium, Denmark, France, Ireland, Italy, Luxembourg, the Netherlands, Norway, Sweden and the U.K. Turkey and Greece joined later in 1949, Iceland in 1950, West Germany in 1951, Austria in 1956, Cyprus in 1961, Switzerland in 1963 and Malta in 1965. It is run by a Committee of Ministers and a Consultative Assembly. The Council of Europe aims to foster European co-operation in every field and about 80 Conventions have been concluded, ranging from extradition rules to equivalence of degrees. One of its main achievements was the European Convention on Human Rights signed in 1950 (with violations examinable by the European Court of Human Rights set up in 1959).

European Court of Human Rights, 1959–

Britain has been involved in a number of cases brought under the European Convention of Human Rights, established by the Council of Europe in 1950 and agreed to by Britain although not given effect to in British law until the *Human Rights Act 1998*, which comes into effect on 2 Oct 2000. In the following cases some or all of the complainant's argument has been found proved against the British authorities.

21 Feb 75	Golder (Prisoner: Access to a solicitor)
18 Jan 78	Ireland (Internment and interrogation in N. Ireland)
25 Apr 78	Tyrer (Isle of Man: corporal punishment)
26 Apr 79	*Sunday Times* (Press freedom: Contempt of Court in Thalidomide case)
13 Aug 81	Young, James and Webster (Closed shop)
22 Oct 81	Dudgeon (Homosexuality in N. Ireland)
5 Nov 81	X (Review of mental patient's detention)
25 Feb 82	Campbell and Cosans (Corporal punishment in schools)
25 Mar 83	Silver and others (Censorship of prisoners' correspondence)
28 Jun 84	Campbell and Fell (Prison visitors: conduct of disciplinary proceedings)
2 Aug 84	Malone (Telephone tapping)
28 May 85	Abdulaziz, Cabales & Balkanadali (Sex discrimination in immigration law)
24 Nov 86	Gillow (Residence rules in Guernsey)
2 Mar 87	Weeks (Re-detention of prisoner released on licence)
8 Jul 87	O., H., W., B. & R. (Access to children in local authority care)
27 Apr 88	Boyle and Rice (Prisoners' letters and visits)
29 Nov 88	Brogan and others (Length of detention under terrorism law)
7 Jul 89	Gaskin (Access to personal records)
7 Jul 89	Soering (Extradition to USA on murder charge)
28 Mar 90	Granger (Legal aid for prisoner's appeal)
30 Aug 90	Fox, Campbell & Hartley (Detention in N. Ireland)
30 Aug 90	McCallum (Prisoner's letters)
25 Oct 90	Thynne, Wilson & Gunnell (Discretionary life sentences)
26 Nov 91	*Observer* & others, *Guardian* & others (*Spycatcher*)
26 Nov 91	*Sunday Times* (No 2) (*Spycatcher*)
25 Mar 92	Campbell (Censorship of prisoner's correspondence with solicitor)
10 Jun 96	Benham (Fair trial of poll-tax non-payer)
26 Oct 93	Darnell (Medical discipline – length of proceedings)
24 Feb 95	McMichael (Access to documents in adoption case)
13 Jul 95	Tolstoy Miloslavsky (Guarantee of plaintiffs' costs)

27 Sep 95	McCann (Costs of Gibraltar IRA shooting case)
23 Oct 95	Boner (Unfair denial of legal aid)
21 Feb 96	Singh (Release on parole; access to lawyer)
15 Nov 96	Chahal (Unfair attempt at extradition to India)
17 Dec 96	Saunders (Use of unfairly obtained evidence)
2 May 97	'D' (Enforcement of extradition)
25 Jun 97	Halford (Telephone tapping by police in sex discrimination dispute)
19 Feb 98	Bowman (Non-candidate's right to spend money in an election)
1 Jul 98	Tinnelly et al. (Access to documents in N.I. contracts case)
23 Nov 98	McLeod (disproportionate force by police in repossession case)
23 Sep 98	'A' (Corporal punishment of boy by stepfather)
23 Sep 98	Steel et al. (Police detention of animal rights protesters)
18 Feb 99	Matthews (Gibraltarians right to vote in European elections)
22 Jul 99	Scarth (Entitlement to a public hearing in an arbitration case)
27 Sep 99	Smith and Ford (Right of homosexuals to serve in armed forces)
27 Sep 99	Lustig-Prem and Beckett (Right of homosexuals to serve in armed forces)
12 Oct 99	Perks and others (Arrest for non-payment of poll-tax)
25 Nov 99	Hashman and Harrup (Binding over of hunt saboteurs)
16 Dec 99	T.; and V. (Fair trial of a child)
16 Dec 99	Taylor (Equal age for granting fuel allowances)

In all but one of the above cases found against it the British Government took measures to comply with the Convention. The exception was the Brogan case in 1988, when the Government derogated from the Convention but in 1999 the relevant Clause in the Anti-Terrorism Act was repealed.

The European Communities, 1973–

The E.E.C. was established on 1 Jan 1958 (under the treaty of Rome 25 Mar 1957) with France, Germany, Italy, Belgium, Holland and Luxembourg as members. Britain, Denmark and Ireland joined on 1 Jan 1973. Greece joined on 6 Jan 1982. Spain and Portugal joined on 1 Jan 86. In 1993, when the Maastricht Treaty came into effect, the Community formally became known as the European Union.

The European Commission (currently comprised of seventeen members, two from each of the larger nations and one each from the smaller ones) initiates all Community laws and is responsible for ensuring that they are put into operation. The laws themselves are primarily made by the Council of Ministers on which the national Minister responsible for the subject under discussion sits. Decisions are sometimes taken unanimously but in certain areas can be made by a weighted majority. Since the Single European Act and the Maastricht Treaty the European Parliament has had an increased share of law-making power in certain areas. The European Court of Justice has the final say on any dispute relating to the implementation of EU laws. Committees and Sub-committees of the House of Commons and the House of Lords scrutinise the work of the European institutions.

The fundamental policies of the European Union stemming from the Treaty of Rome have been the creation of a customs union and its transformation into a single market, the common external trade policy and the common agricultural policy. However, an increasing number of other policy areas have been developed at European level including regional and social funds, environmental policy, scientific research and development programmes and the move to create economic and monetary union in Europe. The Maastricht Treaty added two other areas of activity to run alongside the main work carried out under the Treaty of Rome. These are a common foreign and security policy and co-operation in justice and law enforcement.

Net UK payments to European Community institutions[a] (£m.)

	Gross	Abatement	Refund	Receipts	From CAP	Net Contribution
1973	181	0	0	76	63	105
1974	179	0	0	149	112	30
1975	341	0	0	396	342	−55
1976	463	0	0	295	207	168
1977	737	0	0	368	181	369
1978	1,348	0	0	526	329	822
1979	1,606	0	0	658	371	948
1980	1,767	0	98	964	550	705
1981	2,174	0	693	1,084	683	397
1982	2,862	0	1,019	1,240	791	603
1983	2,976	0	807	1,521	1,082	648
1984	3,201	0	528	2,017	1,353	656
1985	3,555	166	61	1,483	1,151	1,845
1986	4,493	1,701	0	2,216	1,385	576
1987	5,203	1,153	0	1,569	1,379	1,705
1988	4,507	1,595	0	1,569	1,379	1,343
1989	5,587	1,156	0	2,116	1,315	2,315
1990	6,355	1,697	0	2,184	1,496	2,474
1991	5,805	2,497	0	2,766	1,761	542
1992	6,737	1,881	0	2,823	1,813	2,033
1993	7,982	2,540	0	3,291	2,257	2,151
1994	7,188	1,726	0	3,254	2,297	2,208
1995	8,890	1,208	0	3,665	2,441	4,017
1996	9,133	2,412	–	4,373	2,929	2,348
1997	7,991	1,733	–	4,661	3,226	1,597
1998	10,090	1,378	–	4,115	2,964	4,597
1999	10,023	3,171	–	4,365	2,670	2,486

[a] These figures are on a 'payments' basis – that is, they show the net payments actually made during UK financial years, regardless of the Community budget to which they relate or from which they are financed.

Sources: HC Research Paper 97/137; HC Deb 11 Jul 83 col.256w.; ONS data base; Cm.3700/1997 H.M. Treasury European Community Finances (Annual Statements on EC Budget).

European Coal and Steel Community (E.C.S.C.), 1973–

E.C.S.C. was established 10 Apr 52 (following Paris Treaty 18 Apr 51) with France, West Germany, Italy and the Benelux countries as members.
Britain, Denmark and Ireland joined on 1 Jan 73. The other members of the EU joined on joining the EU. E.C.S.C. is due to expire in 2002.

European Atomic Energy Community (Euratom), 1973–

Euratom was established 1 Jan 58 for E.E.C. members to cooperate in the peaceful uses of atomic energy. Britain joined 1 Jan 73 on joining the E.E.C.

European Parliament, 1973–

Under the Treaty of Rome, each member country's Parliament nominated delegates from its own members to serve in a European Parliament which meets monthly in Strasbourg or Luxembourg. Its main functions have been advisory and supervisory. It has to be consulted on the Community Budget and it can, by a two-thirds majority, dismiss the Commissioners en bloc. After the enlargement of the Community in 1973 it had 198 members. The U.K. was entitled to send 36 members but, in the absence of Labour representation, it at first sent only 22 (18 Conservatives, 2 Liberal, 1 Scottish National Party and 1 Independent). After the 1975 Referendum a Labour delegation was selected and until 1979 there were 18 Labour, 16 Conservative, 1 Liberal and 1 Scottish National representative. (26 were M.P:s and 10 peers.)

On 7–10 Jun 1979, on 15–18 Jun 1984, and on 15–18 Jun 89, Community-wide elections took place for a directly elected Parliament which expanded by stages from 410 members to 518 members.

The 1986 Single European Act first granted the Parliament a positive, if limited, role in the European Commission's legislative process.

Following the implementation of the Maastricht Treaty in 1993, the Parliament gained important new legislative powers ('co-decision'). The Parliament also gained the power to vote in and vote out the Commission.

In 1991 it was decided to expand the Parliament to 567 members. The U.K. delegation rose from 81 to 87 at the 9–12 Jun 94 elections. Following the 1995 enlargement the Parliament was expanded to 826 members and this number was elected on 10–13 Jun 99. From 1979 to 1994 British MEPs were elected from single-member constituencies. Following the *European Parliamentary Elections Act 1999*, a system of regional list proportional representation was adopted, with the 9 regions of England returning between four and eleven members each, Scotland eight and Wales five. From 1979 onwards Northern Ireland returned three members using the Single Transferable Vote system.

Leaders of the British Party Delegations

Conservative		*Labour*	
Jan 73	(Sir) P. Kirk	Jul 75	M. Stewart
Feb 77	G. Rippon	Nov 76	J. Prescott
Jun 79	(Sir) J. Scott-Hopkins	Jun 79	Barbara Castle
Jun 82	Sir H.(Ld) Plumb	Jun 85	A. Lomas
Apr 87	(Sir) C. Prout	Jun 87	D. Martin
Jun 94	Ld Plumb	Jun 88	B. Seal
Jan 97	T. Spencer	Jun 90	G. Ford
Sep 97	E. McMillan-Scott	Jun 93	Pauline Green
		Jun 94	W. David
		Jul 98	A. Donnelly
		Jan 00	S. Murphy

Source; M. Westlake *Britain's Emerging Euro-Elite (1994)*

Referendum on E.E.C. Membership
(Thursday 5 Jun 1975)

'Do you think that the United Kingdom should stay in the European Community (the Common Market)?'

	Total electorate[1]	Total votes[2]	% turnout[1]	% 'yes'	Highest 'yes'	Lowest 'yes'
England	33,339,959	21,722,222	64.6	68.7	76.3	62.9
Wales	2,015,766	1,345,545	66.7	64.8	74.3	56.9
Scotland	3,698,462	2,286,676	61.7	58.4	72.3	29.5
N. Ireland[2]	1,032,490	498,751	47.4	52.1	52.1	52.1
U. K.[1]	40,086,677	29,453,194	64.5	64.5	76.3	29.5

[1] Service votes are only in the total votes and in the 'Yes' percentages.
[2] The votes were counted on a county basis except in Northern Ireland which was treated as a single unit. In 66 of the 68 counties there was a 'yes' majority. (Shetland voted 56.3% 'No' and Western Isles 70.5% 'No').

(For 1979 and 1997 referendums in Scotland and Wales see pp.458–60)

Direct Elections to European Parliament

	% Turnout	% votes					Seats					
		Con.	Lab.	Lib.	Nat.	Oth.	Con.	Lab.	Lib.	Nat.	UKIP	Green
1979 Thu., 7 Jun. (G.B. had 78 single member seats)												
England	31.3	53.4	32.6	13.2	–	0.8	54	12	–	–		
Wales	34.4	36.6	41.5	9.6	11.7	0.6	1	3	–	–		
Scotland	33.7	33.7	33.0	13.9	9.4	–	5	2	–	1		
G.B.	32.1	50.6	33.1	13.1	2.5	0.7	60	17	–	1		
N.Ireland*	55.7	–	–	0.2	99.8	–	–	–	–	3		
U.K.	32.7	48.4	31.6	12.6	2.5	4.9	60	17	–	3		

Electorate 41,152,763 Votes cast 13,446,083

	% Turnout	Con.	Lab.	Lib.	Nat.	Oth.	Con.	Lab.	Lib.	Nat.	UKIP	Green
1984 Thu., 7 Jun. (G.B. had 78 single member seats)												
England	31.6	43.1	35.0	20.4	–	1.5	42	24	–	–		
Wales	39.7	25.4	44.5	17.4	12.2	0.5		1	3	–		
Scotland	33.0	25.7	40.7	15.6	17.8	0.2	2	5	–	1		
G.B.	31.8	40.8	36.5	19.5	2.5	0.8	45	32	–	1		
N.Ireland*	63.5	–	–	–	100.0	–	–	–	–	3		
U.K.	32.6	39.9	36.0	19.1	2.4	5.6	45	32	–	4		

Electorate 42,493,274 Votes cast 13,998,274

	% Turnout	Con.	Lab.	Lib.	Nat.	Oth.	Con.	Lab.	Lib.	Nat.	UKIP	Green
1989 Thu., 15 Jun. (G.B. had 78 single member seats)												
England	35.8	37.2	39.2	6.7	–	16.9	32	34	–	–		
Wales	41.1	23.1	49.7	3.2	12.2	13.0	–	4	–	–		
Scotland	40.8	20.5	40.8	4.4	26.9	7.3	–	7	–	1		
G.B.	35.9	34.7	40.1	6.4	–	19.0	32	45	–	1		
N.Ireland*	48.4	–	–	–	100.0	–	–	–	–	3		
U.K.	36.8	33.5	38.7	6.2	3.2	18.4	32	45	–	4		

Electorate 43,037,821 Votes cast 15,893,403

	% Turnout	Con.	Lab.	Lib.	Nat.	Oth.	Con.	Lab.	Lib.	Nat.	UKIP	Green
1994 Thu., 9 Jun. (G.B. had 84 single member seats)												
England	35.5	30.5	43.5	18.4	–	7.6	18	51	2	–		
Wales	38.2	14.6	55.9	8.7	17.1	3.7	–	5	–	–		
Scotland	43.1	14.5	42.5	7.2	32.6	1.6	–	6	–	2		
G.B.	36.2	27.9	44.2	16.7	4.3	6.9	18	62	2	2		
N.Ireland*	48.7	–	–	–	100.0	–	–	–	–	3		
U.K.	36.8	26.9	42.6	16.1	4.1	10.2	18	62	–	5		

Electorate 43,037,821 Votes cast 15,749,417

	% Turnout	Con.	Lab.	Lib.	Nat.	Oth.	Con.	Lab.	Lib.	Nat.	UKIP	Green
1999 Thu., 10 Jun. (G.B. elected 84 M.E.P.s from proportional representation from 11 regions)												
England	23.0	38.5	21.5	13.3	–	16.7	33	24	9	–	3	2
Wales	28.3	22.8	31.9	8.2	29.6	7.5	1	2	–	2	–	–
Scotland	24.8	19.8	28.7	9.8	27.2	14.5	2	3	1	2	–	–
G.B.	23.1	35.8	28.0	12.7	4.6	18.9	36	29	10	4	3	2
N.Ireland*	57.7	–	–	–	100.0	–	–	–	–	3	–	–
U.K.	24.1	34.8	27.0	12.1	4.3	21.8	36	29	10	7	3	2

Electorate 44,495,741 Votes cast 10,681,080

*N. Ireland used the Single Transferable Vote system of proportional representation.

European Court of Justice, 1973–

This was established under the Treaty of Rome to adjudicate on disputes arising out of the application of the Community treaties. Its regulations are enforceable on all member countries. After 1973 it had 9 judges and 4 advocates-general. With the accession of Spain, Portugal and Greece the Court grew to 12 Judges. It has become increasingly important as the powers of the Community have widened. It has ruled against Britain on a number of occasions.

British Member of the European Court

1 Jan 73	Ld Mackenzie-Stuart
1 Jan 88	Sir G. Slynn
1 Jan 92	D. Edward

British Members of European Commission

1 Jan 73	Sir C. Soames	1 Jan 81	I. Richard	1 Jan 93	B. Millan
1 Jan 73	G. Thomson	1 Jan 85	Ld Cockfield	1 Jan 95	N. Kinnock
1 Jan 77	R. Jenkins	1 Jan 85	S. Clinton Davies	15 Sep 99	N. Kinnock
	(President)	1 Jan 89	Sir L.Brittan	15 Sep 99	C. Patten
1 Jan 77	C. Tugendhat	1 Jan 89	B. Millan		
1 Jan 81	C. Tugendhat	1 Jan 93	Sir L.Brittan		

British Ambassadors to the European Communities (1960–72)

17 Jul 60	Sir A. Tandy	7 Apr 65	Sir J.Marjoribanks	Oct 72	(Sir) M. Palliser
18 Apr 63	Sir C. O'Neill	30 May 71	*post vacant*		

Ministers with special E.E.C. Responsibilities
(Cabinet Ministers)

19 Sep 57–14 Oct 59	R. Maudling	28 Jul 70– 5 Nov 72	G. Rippon
27 Jul 60–20 Oct 63	E. Heath	5 Nov 72– 4 Mar 74	J. Davies
7 Jan 67–29 Aug 67	G. Thomson	5 May 79–11 Sep 81	Sir I. Gilmour
19 Jun 70–25 Jul 70	A. Barber	11 Sep 81–5 Apr 82	H. Atkins

(Ministers of State at the Foreign Office)

Mar 74–Aug 76	R. Hattersley	Jul 90–May 93	T. Garel-Jones
Aug 76–Feb 77	D. Owen	May 93–Jul 94	D. Heathcoat-Amory
Feb 77–May 79	F. Judd	Jul 94–May 97	D. Davis
May 79–Jun 83	D. Hurd	May 97–Jul 98	D. Henderson
Jun 83–Jan 86	M. Rifkind	Jul 98–Jul 99	Joyce Quin
Jan 86–Jul 89	Lynda Chalker	Jul 99–Oct 99	G. Hoon
Jul 89–Jul 90	F. Maude	Oct 99–	K. Vag

Permanent British Representative to the European Communities/Union

18 Oct 71	(Sir) M. Palliser	5 May 79	(Sir) M. Butler	2 Sep 90	(Sir) J. Kerr
1 Jul 75	Sir D Maitland	14 Oct 85	(Sir) D. Alexander	28 Aug 95	(Sir) S. Wall

Sources: M.Camps, *Britain and the European Communities, 1955–63* (1964); D.Butler and U.Kitzinger, *The 1975 Referendum* (1976); D.Butler and D.Marquand, *European Elections and British Politics* (1980); D.Butler and P.Jowett, *Party Strategies in Britain: A Study of the 1984 European Elections* (1985), D. Butler and M. Westlake, *British Politics and European Elections 1994.*(1995); D. Butler and M. Westlake, *British Politics and European Elections 1999* (2000); T. Bainbridge and A. Teasdale, *The Penguin Companion to European Union* (2nd ed.1998); S. George, *An Awkward Partner* (3rd ed.1998); H. Young, *This Blessed Plot: Britain and Europe* (1988). See also *The Times Guides to the European Parliament* (1979, 1984, 1989 and 1994).

XIX

ARMED FORCES

Service Chiefs

Royal Navy

First Naval Lord

1899	Ld W. Kerr

First Sea Lord

1904	Sir J. Fisher (Ld)
1910	Sir A. Wilson
1911	Sir F. Bridgeman
1912	Prince Louis of Battenberg
1914	Ld Fisher
1915	Sir H. Jackson
1916	Sir J. Jellicoe
1917	Sir R. Wemyss
1919	Earl Beatty
1927	Sir C. Madden
1930	Sir F. Field
1933	Sir E. Chatfield (Ld)
1938	Sir R. Backhouse
1939	Sir D. Pound
1943	Sir A. Cunningham(Ld)
1946	Sir J. Cunningham
1948	Ld Fraser of North Cape
1951	Sir R. McGrigor
1955	Earl Mountbatten
1959	Sir C. Lambe
1960	Sir C. John
1964	Sir D. Luce
1966	Sir V. Begg
1968	Sir M. Le Fanu
1970	Sir P. Hill-Norton
1971	Sir M. Pollock
1974	Sir E. Ashmore
1977	Sir T. Lewin
1979	Sir H. Leach
1982	Sir J. Fieldhouse
1985	Sir W. Staveley
1989	Sir J. Oswald
1993	Sir B. Bathurst
1995	Sir J. Slater
1998	Sir M. Boyce

Army

Commander in Chief

1895	Vt Wolseley
1900	Ld Roberts (Earl)

Chief of General Staff

1904	Sir N. Lyttelton
1908	Sir W. Nicholson

Chief of Imperial General Staff

1909	Sir W. Nicholson
1912	Sir J. French
1914	Sir C. Douglas
1914	Sir J. Wolfe-Murray
1915	Sir A. Murray
1915	Sir W. Robertson
1918	Sir H. Wilson
1922	E of Cavan
1926	Sir G. Milne
1933	Sir A. Montgomery-Massingberd
1936	Sir C. Deverell
1937	Vt Gort
1939	Sir E. Ironside
1940	Sir J. Dill
1941	Sir A. Brooke (Ld Alanbrooke)
1946	Vt Montgomery
1948	Sir W. Slim
1952	Sir J. Harding
1955	Sir G. Templer
1958	Sir F. Festing
1963	Sir R. Hull

Chief of General Staff

1964	Sir R. Hull
1965	Sir J. Cassels
1968	Sir G. Baker
1971	Sir M. Carver
1973	Sir P. Hunt
1976	Sir R. Gibbs
1979	Sir E. Bramall
1982	Sir J. Stanier
1985	Sir N. Bagnall
1988	Sir J. Chapple
1992	Sir P. Inge
1994	Sir C. Guthrie
1997	Sir R. Wheeler
2000	R. Walker

Royal Air Force

Chief of Air Staff

1918	Sir H. Trenchard
1918	Sir F. Sykes
1919	Sir H. Trenchard
1930	Sir J. Salmond
1933	Sir G. Salmond
1933	Sir E. Ellington
1937	Sir C. Newall
1940	Sir C. Portal
1946	Sir A. Tedder (Ld)
1950	Sir J. Slessor
1953	Sir W. Dickson[1]
1956	Sir D. Boyle
1960	Sir T. Pike
1964	Sir C. Elworthy
1968	Sir J. Grandy
1971	Sir D. Spotswood
1973	Sir A. Humphrey
1976	Sir N. Cameron
1977	Sir M. Beetham
1982	Sir K. Williamson
1985	Sir D. Craig
1988	Sir P. Harding
1992	Sir M. Graydon
1997	Sir R. Johns
2000	P. Squire

Defence Staff

Chief of Defence Staff[1]

1958	Sir W. Dickson
1959	Earl Mountbatten
1965	Sir R. Hull
1967	Sir C. Elworthy
1971	Sir P. Hill-Norton
1973	Sir M. Carver
1976	Sir A. Humphrey
1977	Sir E. Ashmore
1979	Sir T. Lewin
1982	Sir E. Bramall
1985	Sir J. Fieldhouse
1988	Sir D. Craig
1991	Sir R. Vincent
1993	Sir P. Harding
1994	Sir P. Inge
1997	Sir C. Guthrie

[1]Before the post of Chief of the Defence Staff was established in 1958, Sir W. Dickson acted as Chairman of the Chief of Staffs Committee (1955–58).

Defence Organisation

Committee of Imperial Defence, (C.I.D.),1904–1946

The committee was first established in 1902 on a temporary basis to advise the Prime Minister, as a result of British experience in the Boer War, of the need for planning and co-ordination of the Empire's defence forces. The C.I.D. was established permanently in 1904, as a small flexible advisory committee to the Prime Minister. Members were usually cabinet ministers concerned with defence, military leaders, and key civil servants. The Dominions also had representatives sitting on the committee occasionally. The Prime Minister was the chairman of the committee, which had no executive power, but exercised considerable influence. A secretariat was set up to assist the C.I.D., which was later adopted by the cabinet itself. During the First World War the C.I.D. was suspended. Its functions between 1914 and 1919 were taken over by the War Council (Nov 1914), the Dardanelles Committee (May 1915), the War Committee (Nov 1916), and finally the War Cabinet (Dec 1916–Nov 1919). The C.I.D. resumed plenary sessions in 1922. In the 1930s the membership of the C.I.D. rose from about 11 to 18, and the committee became unwieldy. This led to the establishment of a Minister for the Co-ordination of Defence (1936–40), who was without a department, but worked through the Committee Secretariat. On the outbreak of the Second World War the C.I.D. was again suspended, and its responsibilities taken over by the War Cabinet. In 1946 the decision to make the suspension permanent was published in a White Paper on the C.I.D. (Cmd. 6923).

Secretaries to the C.I.D. 1904–1946

1904	G. Clarke
1907	Sir C. Ottley
1912	(Sir) M. Hankey[1]
1938	(Sir) H. Ismay (Ld)

Ministry of Defence. The C.I.D. was replaced by a cabinet defence committee, with executive power, and the Ministry of Defence was set up as a regular department on 1 Jan 47. It existed as an administrative body, responsible for liaison between the Service Ministries and co-ordination of defence policy until 31 Mar 64. On 1 Apr 64 the complete reorganisation of the three Service Departments (Admiralty, War Office and Air Ministry) under the Secretary of State for Defence took place. A Defence Council was also established under the Secretary of State to exercise the powers of command and administrative control previously exercised by the separate Service councils, which became subordinate to it. Further reorganisation on 6 Jan 67 reduced the status of the administrative heads of the three Services from Ministers to Under-Secretaries of State, while creating two new posts: Minister of Defence (Administration) and Minister of Defence (Equipment). In June 1970 further reorganisation of these two posts later reduced them to that of a single Minister of State for Defence. In May 1981 a major reorganisation abolished the three Service Under-Secretaries of State and divided the Ministry of Defence between a Minister of State and Under-Secretary of State for Defence Procurement, and a Minister of State and Under-Secretary of State for Armed Forces. The present membership of the Defence Council consists of the Secretary of State for Defence, the two Ministers of State and their Parliamentary Under-Secretaries, the Chiefs of Defence, Naval, General and Air Staffs, the Chief of Personnel and Logistics, the Chief Scientific Adviser, the Chief Executive of the Procurement Executive and the Permanent Under-Secretary of State.

---

[1]Sir M. Hankey (later Ld Hankey) became joint Secretary to the C.I.D. and the Cabinet in 1916, and in 1923 he was also appointed clerk to the Privy Council.

Defence Pressure Groups

Pressure on the Service Departments and the Cabinet about the nature and scale of forces and armaments has always been informal. But arguments for the expansion of particular services have been sustained by the Navy League (founded 1895) and the Air League (1909). More recently the Institute of Strategic Studies (1958) and the Royal United Services Institute (1834) have provided an influential forum for the discussion of defence questions. See also the Foreign Affairs pressure groups listed on p.503.

Total Forces Serving[a] (Year ending 31 March) (000s)

	1900	1910	1920	1930	1940[b]	1950[b]	1960	1970	1980	1990	1997
Army	661	522	435	333	1,688	360	252	174	159	153	113
Royal Navy[c]	98	128	133	97	282	135	93	86	64	63	45
R.A.F.	–	–	28	33	303	193	158	113	90	90	57
Total	759	650	596	463	2,273[d]	688	503	373	313	306	215

[a]Men locally enlisted abroad are excluded, except that the figures for the army include those whose documents are held in the UK.
[b]Including Women's Auxiliaries. The figures for the war years include a number of casualties that had not been reported on the date to which the figures relate. They also include men and women locally enlisted.
[c]The Navy figure includes Royal Marines.
[d]The total strength of the armed forces reached its peak in 1945 with 5,098,100 men and women serving.

Total Expenditure on Defence[a] (year ending 31 March) 1900–1960 (£000s)

	1900	1910	1920	1930	1940	1950	1960
Army	43.6	27.2	395.0	40.5	81.9	291.8	428.2
Navy	26.0	35.8	156.5	55.8	69.4	186.8	364.6
Air Force	–	–	52.5	16.8	66.6	201.6	485.1
Total[b]	69.8	63.0	604.0	113.1	626.4	740.7	1475.7

[a]The figures refer to the Exchequer of the UK and include Northern Ireland only to the extent that services, taxes, etc. are reserved to the UK Parliament.
[b]The discrepancies between the service votes and the totals are due to the expenditures of the Ministries of Defence and Civil Aviation (1950 and 1960), and the Army Ordnance Factories.
[c]Including votes of credit of £408.5m. Defence expenditure reached its wartime peak in 1944–5 at £5,125m.

Sources: *Annual Abstract of Statistics. The Army Navy and Air Estimates* giving the full figures were published annually as government white papers up to 31 Mar 64.

Total Expenditure on Defence 1970– (year ending 31 March) 1970– (£000s)

	1970	1980	1990	1997
Armed Forces Personnel	1,009	3,912	8,099	8,761
Equipment	822	3,640	8,536	9,499
Other (land, stores etc)	435	1,625	4,120	4,090
Total	1,264	9,177	20,655	22,350

Conscription

After a long controversy about conscription, H. Asquith announced the introduction of the first Military Service Bill on 5 Jan 1916. Compulsory military service lapsed in 1919.

It was first introduced in peacetime on 26 April 1939. The period of service was to have been six months but war intervened. Conscription was extended to women from Dec 1941 until 1947 but few women were called up after Nov 1944. The National Service Act, 1947, provided for the continuation of military service after the war. The period of service was twelve months. It was increased to eighteen months in Dec 1948, and to two years in Sep 1950. A government White Paper published on 5 Apr 1957 announced a progressive reduction in the national service intake. No men were to be called up after the end of 1960, so that by the end of 1963 there were no national servicemen left in the forces. (This was slightly modified by the Army Reserves Bill, introduced in 1962.)

Rationing

The first national rationing scheme in this country came into operation on 31 Dec 1917, with the rationing of sugar. This was followed in Jul 1918 by national schemes for meat, lard, bacon, ham, butter and margarine. The abolition of rationing began on 28 Jul 1918 and was completed on 29 Nov 1920. Butter and meat rations were most severely restricted in Apr–May 1918 and sugar in 1919. There was much controversy during the course of World War I over the form that rationing should take. National rationing was preceded by local schemes and even after Jul 1918 rationing was, in many cases, wider in extent locally than nationally. The characteristic feature of the World War I scheme was the tie to the retailer of each customer.

When World War II broke out in Sep 1939, prearranged plans for commodity control were at once put into effect. Rationing was introduced on 8 Jan 1940 when bacon, butter, and sugar were put under control and extended during the following two years to meat, tea, margarine, lard, jam, marmalade, cheese, eggs, and milk. In Dec 1941 the 'points' system was introduced to ration such items as tinned meat and biscuits; from Jul 1942 sweets and chocolate were rationed under a system of 'personal points'. During the war animal feedstuffs, fertilisers, farm machinery, petrol, domestic coal, clothing and textiles were also rationed. Rationing was at its most stringent, however, in the immediate post-war years. In Jul 1946, bread rationing, which in 1939 the Minister of Food had described as 'the last resort of a starving nation', was introduced for the first time ever and this was followed in Nov 1947 by the rationing of potatoes. In Dec 1947 the distribution of nearly all important foods was controlled with the exception of some fresh fruit and vegetables, fish and coffee; the bacon, butter, meat and fats rations were at their lowest ebbs and the basic petrol ration had been suspended altogether. The gradual abolition of rationing began in Apr 1948; it was not completed until the abolition of butter rationing in May 1954, of meat rationing in July 1954 and of coal rationing in 1958. During the Suez crisis of 1956, petrol rationing was re-introduced. It lasted from 17 Dec 1956 to 14 May 1957.

Principal Military Operations

Boer War, 1899–1902

Following the rejection by the British Government of the Boer ultimatum, the Transvaal and Orange Free State declared war on Britain in October 1899. Major operations against the Boers ended in the summer of 1900, but guerrilla warfare continued. Peace was finally concluded at Vereeniging on 31 May 1902.

Casualties and Costs

1. Total Engaged	2. Killed[a]	Percentage Col. 2 to Col.1	Cost (£m)
448,000	22,000	4.9	217

[a](killed includes dying of wounds or as prisoners of war)

First World War, 1914–1918

4 Aug 14	Britain declares war on Germany	6 Apr 17	U.S.A. enters War
12 Aug 14	Britain declares war on Austria-Hungary	4 Oct 17	End of Battle of Passchendaele
		20 Nov 17	Tanks used successfully at Cambrai
23 Aug 14	Retreat from Mons begins	21 Nov 17	Russia asks for peace
12 Oct 14	First Battle of Ypres	9 Dec 17	Jerusalem captured by British
20 Jan 15	First Zeppelin Raid on Britain	21 Mar 18	German Somme offensive
22 Apr 15	Second Battle of Ypres	15 Jul 18	Last German offensive
25 Apr 15	Gallipoli landing	11 Sep 18	Allies break Hindenburg Line
6 Sep 15	Bulgaria joins Central Powers	2 Oct 18	British capture Damascus
25 Sep 15	British attack at Loos	30 Oct 18	Turkey signs Armistice
8 Jan 16	Evacuation of Gallipoli completed	3 Nov 18	Austria-Hungary signs Armistice
31 May 16	Battle of Jutland	11 Nov 18	Germany signs Armistice
1 Jul 16	Battle of the Somme	28 Jun 19	Treaty of Versailles
27 Mar 17	Turks defeated at Gaza		

Casualties and Costs
(Empire figures)

1. Total Engaged	2. Killed[a]	Percentage Col. 2 to Col.1	Cost (£m)
9,669,000	947,000	9.8	3,810

[a] killed includes dying of wounds or as prisoners of war

Intervention in Russia, 1918–1919

British troops landed at Murmansk and Archangel in June and August of 1918. Troops also entered the Transcaucasus in August 1918. The withdrawal of troops from the Transcaucasus was completed by 5 Apr 1919; and from Murmansk and Archangel by 28 Sep 1919.

Second World War, 1939–1945

1 Sep 39	Germany invades Poland	22 Jun 41	Germany invades Russia
3 Sep 39	Britain and France declare war	16 Jul 41	British occupy Syria
17 Sep 39	Russia invades Poland	18 Nov 41	Second British Libyan offensive
30 Nov 39	Russia invades Finland	7 Dec 41	Japan attacks Pearl Harbour
9 Apr 40	Germany invades Denmark and Norway	8 Dec 41	U.S. and Britain declare war on Japan
10 May 40	Germany invades Holland and Belgium	9 Dec 41	British relieve Tobruk
		11 Dec 41	Germany and Italy declare war on U.S. and vice versa
4 Jun 40	Dunkirk evacuation complete		
22 Jun 40	France capitulates	15 Feb 42	Japanese take Singapore
10 Jul 40	Italy declares war on Britain	21 Jan 42	German offensive in Libya
15 Sep 40	Climax of Battle of Britain	30 Jun 42	German army held at El Alamein
20 Nov 40	Hungary joins axis powers	19 Aug 42	Dieppe raid
7 Feb 41	British reach Benghazi	23 Oct 42	British attack at El Alamein
1 Mar 41	Bulgaria joins axis powers	23 Jan 43	British enter Tripoli
27 May 41	Bismarck sunk	12 May 43	Axis surrenders N. Africa
29 May 41	German N. Africa offensive halted	10 Jul 43	Allies invade Sicily

3 Sep 43	Allies invade Italy	16 Dec 44	German Ardennes offensive
22 Jan 44	Allied landing at Anzio	22 Mar 45	Rhine crossing
4 Jun 44	Allies take Rome	8 May 45	VE day, final German surrender
6 Jun 44	D-day landing in Normandy	6 Aug 45	Atomic bomb on Hiroshima
13 Jun 44	V1 Bombardment begins	9 Aug 45	Second atomic bomb on Nagasaki
25 Aug 44	Allies enter Paris	14 Aug 45	VJ Day Hostilities end
17 Sep 44	Arnhem assault	2 Sep 45	Final Japanese surrender signed

Costs and Casualties
(Great Britain)

1. *Total engaged*	2. *Killed*[a]	*Percentage* Col.2 to Col.1	*Cost* (£m)
5,896,000	265,000	4.5	34,423

[a] killed includes dying of wounds or as prisoners of war

Korean War 1950–1953

Britain declared her support for the United States' action in Korea on 28 Jun 50, following the invasion of South Korea by North Korean troops, and the call for a cease fire by an emergency session of the United Nations Security Council. The intervention of Chinese troops fighting with the North Koreans was confirmed on 6 Nov 50. An armistice was signed between the United Nations and the Communist forces on 27 Jul 53. British casualties in the Korean war were 749 killed (H.C. Deb., 1952–53, Vol. 518, Cols. 221–222). The total expenditure incurred by Britain was about £50m. (H.C. Deb.,1952–53, Vol. 517, Col. 1218).

Suez, 1956

Following the Egyptian nationalisation of the Suez Canal on 26 Jul 56, tension grew in the Middle East. The Israeli army attacked the Egyptians on 29 Oct 56 in the Sinai peninsula. The rejection of a British and French ultimatum by Egypt resulted in a combined British and French attack on Egypt on 1 Nov 56. Operations were halted at midnight on 6–7 Nov 56. On 26 Jan 61 full diplomatic relations were resumed between Britain and Egypt. British casualties were 21 men killed (H.C. Deb., 1956–57, Vol. 561, Col. 36). The military expenditure incurred was about £30m. (H.C. Deb., 1956–57, Vol.575, Col. 51).

Northern Ireland, 1969–

On 14 Aug 69 the Government of Northern Ireland informed the U.K. Government that as a result of the severe rioting in Londonderry it had no alternative but to ask for the assistance of the troops at present stationed in Northern Ireland to prevent a breakdown in law and order. British troops moved into Londonderry that day, and into Belfast on 15 Aug 69. On 19 Aug 69 G.O.C. Northern Ireland assumed overall responsibility for security in the Province. The Provisional IRA declared a ceasefire on 31 Aug 94. They resumed their activity on 9 Feb 96. A second IRA ceasefire came into effect on 20 Jul 97.

| | Regular Army | | Casualties UDR/RIR[b] | | RUC | | Civil |
	Strength[a]	Deaths	Strength	Deaths	Strength	Deaths	deaths
1969	7,495	0	–	–	3,044	1	11
1970	7,170	0	4,008	0	3,808	2	21
1971	13,762	43	6,786	5	4,086	11	104
1972	16,661	103	9,074	24	4,257	17	305
1973	15,342	58	7,982	8	4,391	13	158
1974	14,067	28	7,795	7	4,565	15	151
1975	13,913	14	7,861	6	4,902	11	205
1976	13,672	14	7,769	1	55,253	23	222
1977	13,632	15	7,843	1	45,692	14	55
1978	13,600	14	7,862	7	6,110	10	40
1979	13,000	38	7,623	10	6,642	14	37
1980	11,900	8	7,373	8	6,935	9	41
1981	11,600	10	7,479	13	7,334	21	36
1982	10,900	21	7,111	7	7,718	12	45
1983	10,200	5	6,925	10	8,003	19	44
1984	10,000	9	6,468	10	8,127	9	36
1985	9,700	2	6,494	4	8,259	23	25
1986	10,500	4	6,408	8	8,234	12	37
1987	11,400	3	6,531	8	8,236	16	66
1988	11,200	21	6,393	12	8,227	6	54
1989	11,200	12	6,230	2	8,259	9	39
1990	11,500	7	6,043	8	8,243	12	49
1991	11,200	6	6,276	8	8,217	6	75
1992	12,600	5	6,000	2	8,478	3	76
1993	12,500	6	5,600	2	8,464	6	70
1994	11,600	1	5,398	2	8,493	3	56
1995	9,900	0	5,255	0	8,415	1	8
1996	10,500	11	4,966	1	8,423	0	14
1997	8,485	1	4,792	4	8,456	4	17
1998		1	4,768	0		1	53
1999							7

[a]Figure for Regular Army strength is at 31 Dec up until 1982; 1 Jul thereafter. It does not include any UDR or Royal Irish Regiment personnel.
[b]The Ulster Defence Regiment was formed on 1 Apr 70. The figures include permanent, part-time, male and female members. On 1 Jul 92 the UDR merged with the Royal Irish Rangers to form the Royal Irish Regiment. The figures from 1994 onwards are the regular strength at 1 Apr.

Sources: Ministry of Defence and Northern Ireland Office.

Falklands, 1982

On 2 Apr 1982 Argentine forces landed on the Falklands and took over the Islands and South Georgia. An expeditionary force was despatched and on 25 Apr South Georgia was recaptured. British forces landed on West Falkland on 20 May and by 14 Jun Port Stanley was recaptured and all the Argentine forces surrendered. The British forces under Rear-Admiral J. Woodward lost six ships and twenty aircraft. The total British casualties were 254 killed and 777 wounded. The cost of the operation from Apr to Jun was estimated at £350m.

Gulf, 1990–91

On 2 Aug 1990, Iraqi Armed Forces invaded and occupied Kuwait. The same day the Security Council of the United Nations passed Resolution 660 demanding unconditional Iraqi withdrawal. US, British and other forces were deployed in Saudi Arabia and the Persian Gulf. On 29 Nov 1990 the UN Security Council authorised the use of 'all necessary means' to free Kuwait if the Iraqis failed to withdraw by 15 Jan 1991 (Resolution 678). On 16 Jan 1991 American, British and other allied planes began an aerial bombardment of Iraq. On 24 Feb 1991 Allied ground forces crossed the Iraqi and Kuwaiti borders from Saudi Arabia. On 26 Feb 1991 Kuwait City fell to Allied troops and on 28 Feb 1991 Allied and Iraqi forces agreed a ceasefire. British forces under Sir P. de la Billiere lost 24 killed and 43 wounded. The total cost was estimated at £2,094 million, although contributions from allies who took no military part in operations amounted to £2,023 million.

Yugoslavia, 1993–

In 1991 a series of conflicts started as Yugoslavia broke up into six constituent republics. In 1993 British troops were deployed in Bosnia-Herzegovina as part of UN peace-keeping forces. Following the rejection by the Yugoslav Government of a NATO ultimatum to remove forces from the mainly Albanian province of Kosovo, NATO air forces, including the RAF, started bombing targets in Yugoslavia on 25 Mar 1999. No British aircraft were lost. The bombing ceased on 10 Jun 1999 when Yugoslav forces agreed to withdraw. NATO forces, with British troops as the largest single contingent, entered Kosovo on 12 Jun 1999.

Sources: Whitaker's Almanack; First Report on the Defence Estimates by House of Commons Select Committee on Defence, (H.C.1991–2/478).

Major War Commanders

World War I

Allenby, E. 1st Vt (1919). 1861–1936
    Field-Marshal. C-in-C Egyptian Expeditionary Force 1917–19.
Beatty, D. 1st E (1919). 1871–1936
    Admiral of the Fleet. Commanded Grand Fleet 1916–19.
Fisher, J. 1st Ld (1909). 1841–1920
    Admiral of the Fleet. 1st Sea Lord 1914–15.
French, J. 1st E of Ypres (1922). 1852–1925
    Field-Marshal. C-in-C British Expeditionary force in France 1914–15. C-in-C Home forces 1916.
Haig, D. 1st E (1919). 1861–1928
    Field-Marshal. Commanding 1st Army 1914–15. C-in-C Expeditionary Forces in France and Flanders 1915–19.
Hamilton, I. Sir (1915). 1853–1947
    General. C-in-C Mediterranean Expeditionary Force 1915.
Jellicoe, J. 1st E (1925). 1859–1935
    Admiral of the Fleet. Commanded Grand Fleet 1914–16.
Plumer, H. 1st Vt (1929). 1857–1932
    Field-Marshal. General Officer Commanding Italian Expeditionary Force 1917–18. 2nd Army British Expeditionary Force 1918–19.
Robertson, W. Sir. 1st Bt (1919). 1860–1933
    Field-Marshal. Chief of Imperial General Staff 1915–18. C-in-C Eastern Command 1918. Great Britain 1918–19. B.A.O.R. 1919–20.
Trenchard, H. 1st Vt (1936). 1873–1956
    Marshal of the RAF. Assistant Commandant Central Flying School 1913–14. G.O.C. Royal Flying Corps in the Field 1915–17. Chief of Air Staff 1918. Commanded Independent Force 1918. Chief of Air Staff 1919–29.

Wilson, H. Sir. 1st Bt (1919). 1864–1922
Field-Marshal. Assistant Chief of General Staff to Ld French 1914. Commanded 1st Army Corps 1915–16. Eastern Command 1917. British Military Representative Versailles 1917. Chief of Imperial General Staff 1918–22.

World War II

Alanbrooke, 1st Ld (1945). 1st Vt (1946). 1883–1963. Sir A. Brooke.
Field-Marshal. G.O.C.-in-C Southern Command 1939 and 1940. C of Second Army Corps B.E.F. 1939–40. C-in-C Home Forces 1940–41. Chief of Imperial General Staff 1941–46.
Alexander, H. 1st E (1952). 1891–1969
Field-Marshal. C-in-C Middle East 1942–43. C-in-C North Africa 1943. C-in-C Allied Armies in Italy 1943–44. Supreme Allied Commander Mediterranean Theatre 1944–45.
Auchinleck, C. Sir. 1884–1981
Field-Marshal. C-in-C India 1941 and 1943–47. C-in-C Middle East 1941–42.
Cunningham, A. 1st Vt of Hyndhope (1946). 1883–1962
Admiral of the Fleet. Ld Commissioner of the Admiralty and Deputy Chief of Naval Staff 1938–39. C-in-C Mediterranean 1939–42. Naval C-in-C Expeditionary Force North Africa 1942. C-in-C Mediterranean 1943. 1st Sea Ld and Chief of Naval Staff 1943–46.
Dill, J. Sir. 1881–1944
Field-Marshal. Commanded 1st Corps in France 1939–40. Chief of Imperial General Staff 1940. British Representative on Combined Chief of Staffs' Committee in U.S. 1941.
Douglas, W. 1st Ld (1948). 1893–1969
Marshal of the RAF. C-in-C Fighter Command 1940–43. Air Officer C-in-C Middle East 1943–44. Air Officer C-in-C Coastal Command 1944–45. Air C-in-C British Air Forces of Occupation in Germany 1945–46.
Dowding, H. 1st Ld (1943). 1882–1970
Air Chief Marshal. Air Officer C-in-C Fighter Command 1936–1940.
Fraser, B. 1st Ld (1946). 1888–1981
C-in-C Home Fleet 1943–44. C-in-C Eastern Fleet 1944–45.
Gort, J. 6th Vt (Ireland) (1902). 1st Vt (U.K.) (1945) 1886–1946
Field-Marshal. C-in-C British Expeditionary Force 1939–40. Commanded B.E.F. in withdrawal towards Dunkirk 1940.
Harris, A. Sir. 1st Bt (1953). 1892–1984.
Marshal of the RAF. Air Officer C-in-C Bomber Command 1942–45.
Ironside, W. 1st Ld (1941). 1880–1959
Field-Marshal. C.I.G.S. 1939–40. C-in-C Home Forces 1940.
Leigh-Mallory, T. Sir. 1892–1944
Air Chief Marshal. Air Officer C-in-C Fighter Command 1942. Air C-in-C Allied Expeditionary Force 1943–44. Lost while flying to take up appointment as Allied Air C-in-C South-East Asia.
Montgomery, B. 1st Vt of Alamein (1946). 1887–1976
Field-Marshal. Commander 8th Army 1942 in N. Africa, Sicily and Italy. C-in-C British Group of Allied Armies N. France 1944. British Commander Allied Expeditionary Forces in Europe 1944–46.

Mountbatten, Ld L. 1st E (1947). 1900–1979
Admiral of the Fleet. Chief of Combined Operations 1942–43. Supreme Allied Commander S.E. Asia 1943–46.

Newall, C. 1st Ld (1946). 1886–1963
Marshal of the RAF. Chief of Air Staff 1937–40. Governor-General and C-in-C New Zealand 1941–46.

Park, K. Sir. 1892–1975
Air Chief Marshal. Air Officer Commanding RAF Malta 1942–43. Air Officer C-in-C 1944. Allied Air C-in-C South-East Asia Command 1945–6.

Peirse, R. Sir. 1892–1970
Air Chief Marshal. Air Officer C-in-C Bomber Command 1940–42. Air Officer C-in-C India 1942–43. Allied Air C-in-C South-East Asia Command 1943–44.

Percival, A. 1887–1966
Lieutenant-General. G.O.C. Malaya 1941–42.

Portal, C. 1st Vt (1946). 1893–1971
Marshal of the RAF. Air Officer C-in-C Bomber Command 1940. Chief of the Air Staff 1940–45.

Pound, D. Sir. 1877–1943
Admiral of the Fleet. C-in-C Mediterranean 1936–39. 1st Sea Lord 1939–43.

Ramsay, B. Sir. 1883–1945
Admiral. Flag Officer commanding Dover 1939–42. Naval Commander Eastern Task Force Mediterranean 1943.

Ritchie, N. Sir. 1897–1984
General. Commander of 8th Army, Libya, 1941–42.

Slessor, J. Sir. 1897–1979
Marshal of the RAF. Air Officer C-in-C Coastal Command 1943–44. C-in-C RAF Mediterranean and Middle East 1944–45.

Slim, W. 1st Vt (1960). 1891–1970
Field-Marshal. C-in-C Allied Land Forces S.E. Asia 1945–46.

Tedder, A. 1st Ld (1946). 1890–1967
Marshal of the RAF. Air Officer C-in-C Middle East 1941–43. Air C-in-C Mediterranean Air Command 1943. Deputy Supreme Commander under Gen. Eisenhower 1943–45.

Wavell, A. 1st E (1947). 1883–1950
Field-Marshal. Formed Middle East Command 1939. C-in-C India 1941. Supreme Commander S.W. Pacific 1941–43.

Wilson, H. 1st Ld (1946). 1881–1964
Field-Marshal. C-in-C Egypt 1939–41. C-in-C Greece 1941. C-in-C Persia-Iraq Command 1942–43. C-in-C Middle East 1943. Supreme Commander Mediterranean Theatre 1944.

XX

THE PRESS[1]

National Daily Newspapers

(British Gazette), 5–13 May 1926
Proprietors: His Majesty's Stationery Office. Printed at offices of *Morning Post*.
Policy: Strong opposition to the General Strike.
Editor: W. Churchill.

(British Worker), 5–17 May 1926
Proprietors: TUC printed at offices of *Daily Herald*
Policy: Support for General Strike.
Editor: H. Fyfe

(Daily Chronicle), 1869–1930
Proprietors: E. Lloyd, 1871–1918. Frank Lloyd and family trading as United Newspapers Ltd. Lloyd family parted with their interest in 1918. Bought by D. Lloyd George and associates 1918. Sold to Sir T. Catto and Sir D. Yule, 1926. Bought by Inveresk Paper Co., 1928. Sold and incorporated with *Daily News* as the *News Chronicle*, 1930.
Policy: Liberal.
Editor: W. Fisher, 1899. R. Donald, 1902. E. Perris, 1918–30.

(Daily Citizen), 1912–Jan 1915
Proprietors: Labour Newspapers Ltd.
Policy: Official Labour.
Editor: F. Dilnot, 1912–15.

Daily Express, 1900
Proprietors: A. Pearson, Daily Express (1900) Ltd. Acquired by London Express Newspaper Ltd, 1915. Ld Beaverbrook assumed control in 1916. In 1954 he relinquished it to Beaverbrook Newspapers Ltd and transferred controlling shares to the Beaverbrook Foundations. In 1977 Beaverbrook Newspapers were taken over by Trafalgar House property group (Chairman: V. (Ld) Matthews). In 1985 Express Newspapers were taken over by United Newspapers (Chairman: D. (Ld) Stevens). In 1996 Ld Stevens' United Newspapers merged with Ld Hollick's MAI Group to form United News and Media with Ld Stevens as Chairman and Ld Hollick as Chief Executive. In 1999 Sir R. Hempel succeeded Ld Stevens as Chairman.
Policy: Independent conservative.
Editors: A. Pearson, 1900. R. Blumenfeld, 1902. B. Baxter, 1929. A. Christiansen, 1933. E. Pickering, 1957. R. Wood, 1962. R. Edwards, 1964. D. Marks, 1965. I. MacColl, 1971. A. Burnet, 1974. R. Wright, 1977. D. Jameson, 1977. A. Firth, 1980. C. Ward, 1981. Sir L. Lamb, 1983. (Sir) N. Lloyd 1986. R. Addis, 1995. Rosie Boycott, 1998.

(Daily Graphic), 1890–1926. 1946–52
Proprietors: Founded by W. L. Thomas. Owned by H. Baines & Co. Amalgamated with *Daily Sketch* in 1926 (Kemsley Newspapers). Appeared as *Daily Sketch and Daily Graphic* 1926–46, as *Daily Graphic* 1946–52, then as *Daily Sketch*.
Policy: Independent conservative.
Editors: H. Hall, 1891. H. White, 1907. W. Ackland, 1909. A. Hutchinson, 1912. A. Netting, 1917. H. Lawton, 1919. E. Tebbutt, 1923. H. Heywood, 1925–26. A. Thornton, 1946. N. Hamilton, 1947. H. Clapp, 1948–52 (see *Daily Sketch*).

(Daily Herald), 1912–1964
Proprietors: Daily Herald Printing and Publishing Society in association with Odhams Press Ltd. Formed Daily Herald (1929) Ltd (Chairman: Ld Southwood). 49% of shares held by T.U.C., 51% by Odhams Press. 1960 new agreement between Odhams Press and T.U.C. 1961 Daily Mirror Newspapers Ltd take over Odhams Press. T.U.C. sign agreement for the paper to be published by the Mirror Group (International Publishing Corporation). 1964 T.U.C. sold their 49% holding to I.P.C. 1964, replaced by the *Sun*.

---

[1]The policies of national newspapers in the twentieth century have inevitably fluctuated. Policy should be taken only as a general indication of the nature of the paper. In very few cases have newspapers been the official organ of a political party.

     Policy: Radical Labour 1912–22. General support to Labour Movement, 1922–23, 1960–. Official Labour 1923–60.

    Editors: W. Seed, 1912. S. Jones, 1912. R. Kenny, 1912. C. Lapworth, 1913. G. Lansbury, 1913. H. Fyfe, 1923. W. Mellor, 1926. W. Stevenson, 1931. F. Williams, 1937. P. Cudlipp, 1940. S. Elliott, 1953. D. Machray, 1957. J. Beavan, 1960. S. Jacobson, 1962–64. (Issued as a weekly paper during 1st World War, launched again as a daily in 1919.)

Daily Mail, 1896

    Proprietors: A. Harmsworth (Vt Northcliffe), Associated Newspapers Ltd (Chairman: 1st (1922), 2nd (1932), 3rd (1971), 4th (1998) Vts Rothermere).

    Policy: Independent. Right-wing Conservative.

    Editors: T. Marlowe, 1899. W. Fish, 1926. O. Pulvermacher, 1929. W. McWhirter, 1930. W. Warden, 1931. A. Cranfield, 1935. R. Prew, 1939. S. Horniblow, 1944. F. Owen, 1947. G. Schofield, 1950. A. Wareham, 1955. W. Hardcastle, 1959. M. Randall, 1963. A. Brittenden, 1966. (Sir) D. English, 1971. P. Dacre, 1992.

Daily Mirror, 1903

    Proprietors: A. Harmsworth, Sir H. Harmsworth (Vt Rothermere), 1914. Pictorial Newspaper (1910) Co. Daily Mirror Newspapers Ltd. 1961, bought by International Publishing Corporation (Chairman: C. King. H. Cudlipp, 1968). Control acquired by Reed International 1970 (Chairman: (Sir) D. Ryder). (Sir) A. Jarratt, 1974). Control of Mirror Group Newspapers acquired by Maxwell Foundation 1984 (Chairman: R. Maxwell; I. Maxwell 1991). Control acquired by creditor banks, 1992. Mirror Group Newspapers merged with Trinity 1999.

    Policy: Independent. Since 1940s Labour-supporting.

    Editors: Mary Howarth, 1903. H. Fyfe, 1904. A. Kinealy, 1907. E. Mynn, 1915. A. Campbell, 1919. L. Brownlee, 1931. C. Thomas, 1934. S. Bolam, 1948. J. Nener, 1953. L. Howard, 1960. A. Miles, 1971. M. Christiansen, 1974. M. Molloy, 1975. R. Stott, 1985. R. Greenslade, 1990. R. Stott, 1991. D. Banks, 1992. C. Myler, 1994. P. Morgan, 1995.

(Daily News), 1846–1930

    Proprietors: Daily News Ltd, 1901 (Chairman: G. Cadbury, 1901–11). Amalgamated with *Morning Leader,* as *Daily News and Leader,* 1912. Amalgamated with *Westminster Gazette*, 1928. Amalgamated with *Daily Chronicle,* 1930. Continued as *News Chronicle* (see below).

    Policy: Liberal.

    Editors: E. Cook, 1896. R. Lehmann, 1901. A. Gardiner, 1902. S. Hodgson, 1920–30.

(Daily Paper), 1904 (32 issues only)

    Proprietor: W. Stead.

    Policy: 'A paper for the abnormally scrupulous'.

    Editor: W. Stead.

(Daily Sketch), 1908–1971

    Proprietors: E. Hulton and Co. Ltd. Daily Mirror Newspapers Ltd. and Sunday Pictorial Newspapers (1920) Ltd. Bought by the Berry brothers, 1926, and merged with the *Daily Graphic*. Name changed to *Daily Graphic,* 1946–52. Subsidiary of Allied Newspapers Ltd. Kemsley Newspapers Ltd. Bought by Associated Newspapers Ltd, 1952. Renamed *Daily Sketch,* 1953. Merged with *Daily Mail,* 1971.

    Policy: Independent Conservative.

    Editors: J. Heddle, 1909. W. Robinson, 1914. H. Lane, 1919. H. Gates, 1922. H. Lane, 1923. A. Curthoys, 1928. A. Sinclair, 1936. S. Carroll, 1939. L. Berry, 1942. A. Thornton and M. Watts, 1943. A. Thornton, 1944. N. Hamilton, 1947. H. Clapp, 1948. H. Gunn, 1953. C. Valdar, 1959. H. French, 1962. D. English, 1969–71.

Daily Sport, 1992 (previously three times a week)

    Proprietors: Sport Newspapers Ltd (Chairman D. Sullivan).

    Policy: Independent.

    Editor: P. Grimsditch, 1992. W. Robertson, 1992. W. Carson, 1993. J. McGowan, 1993.

Daily Star, 1978

    Proprietors: Beaverbrook Newspapers (Chairman: V. Matthews). At first printed in Manchester and distributed only in North. Acquired by United Newspapers (Ld Stevens) in 1985.

    Policy: Independent.

    Editor: P. Grimsditch, 1978. L. Turner, 1982. M. Gabbert, 1987. B. Hitchen, 1987. P. Walker, 1994. P. Hill, 1998.

Daily Telegraph, 1855

Proprietors:	Ld Burnham and family. Sold to Sir W. Berry (Vt Camrose), Sir G. Berry (Vt Kemsley) and Sir E. Iliffe (Ld) in 1928. Absorbed *Morning Post*, as *Daily Telegraph and Morning Post* in 1937. Vt Camrose acquired Vt Kemsley's and Ld Iliffe's interests in 1937. M. Berry (Ld Hartwell) succeeded him as Editor-in-Chief in 1968. Acquired by C. Black, 1987.
Policy:	Conservative.
Editors:	(Sir) J. le Sage, 1885. F. Miller, 1923. A. Watson, 1924. (Sir) C. Coote, 1950. M. Green, 1964. W. Deedes, 1974. M. Hastings, 1986. C. Moore, 1996.

(Daily Worker), 1930–1966

Proprietors:	Daily Worker Cooperative Society Ltd. Descendant of the *Sunday Worker*, 1925–30. Publication suppressed 1941–42. Changed name to *Morning Star,* 1966.
Policy:	Communist.
Editors:	W. Rust, 1930. J. Shields, 1932. I. Cox. 1935. R. Palme Dutt, 1936. W. Rust, 1939. J. Campbell, 1949. G. Matthews, 1959–1966.

(Financial News), 1884–1945

Proprietors:	Financial News Ltd, 1898 (H. Marks). Incorporated with the *Financial Times* in 1945.
Policy:	Finance, independent.
Editors:	H. Marks, 1884. Dr Ellis, 1916. H. O'Neill, 1921. W. Dorman and W. Lang, 1921. Sir L. Worthington-Evans, 1924. Sir E. Young, 1925. O. Hobson, 1929. M. Green, 1934. H. Parkinson, 1938–45.

Financial Times, 1888

Proprietors:	Financial Times Ltd. Incorporated *Financier and Bullionist*. Incorporated the *Financial News* in 1945. Controlling interest held by Pearson plc since 1957.
Policy:	Finance, independent.
Editors:	W. Lawson. A. Murray, 1901. C. Palmer, 1909. D. Hunter, 1924. A. Chisholm, 1938. A. Cole, 1940. H. Parkinson, 1945. (Sir) G. Newton, 1950. F. Fisher, 1973. (Sir) G. Owen, 1981. R. Lambert, 1991.

Independent, 1986

Proprietors:	Newspaper Publishing Co. Ltd. Control was acquired by Mirror Group Newspapers in 1998.
Policy:	Independent.
Editors:	A. Whittam-Smith, 1986. I. Hargreaves, 1994. A. Marr, 1996. Rosie Boycott, 1998. A. Marr, 1998. S. Kelner, 1998.

(Manchester) Guardian, 1821

Proprietors:	The Manchester Guardian & Evening News Ltd. Renamed *Guardian*, 1959. The Scott Trust.
Policy:	Independent liberal.
Editors:	C. P. Scott, 1872. E. Scott, 1929. W. Crozier, 1932. A. Wadsworth, 1944. A. Hetherington, 1956. P. Preston 1975. A. Rusbridger, 1995.

(Majority), 1906 (10–14 Jul only)

Proprietors:	Majority Ltd.
Policy:	'The organ of all who work for wage or salary'.

(Morning Herald), 1892–1900

Proprietors:	Morning Newspaper Co. Became *London Morning* in 1898, and *Morning Herald* in 1899. Merged with *Daily Express* in 1900.
Policy:	Independent.
Editor:	D. Murray, 1892–1900.

(Morning Leader), 1892–1912

Proprietors:	Colman family of Norwich. Merged with *Daily News,* as *Daily News and Leader* in 1912 (see *Daily News*).
Policy:	Liberal.
Editor:	E. Parke, 1892–1912.

(Morning Post), 1772–1937

Proprietors:	Sir A. Borthwick (Ld Glenesk), 1876–1908. Lady Bathurst, 1908–24. Absorbed in *Daily Telegraph* in 1937 (Vt Camrose).

Policy: Conservative.
Editors: J. Dunn, 1897. S. Wilkinson, 1905. F. Warr, 1905. H. Gwynne, 1911–37.

(Morning Standard), 1857–1917
Proprietors: Bought from Johnston family by A. Pearson, 1904. Sold to J. Dalziel (Ld) in 1910.
Policy: From 1904 supporter of tariff reform.
Editors: W. Mudford, 1874. G. Curtis, 1900. H. Gwynne, 1904. H. White, 1911–17.

Morning Star, 1966
Proprietors: Morning Star Co-operative Society. Successor to the *Daily Worker*.
Policy: Communist.
Editor: G. Matthews, 1966. T. Chater, 1974. J. Haylett, 1995.

(New Daily), 1960–1966
Proprietors: The British Newspaper Trust Ltd. Sponsored by the People's League for the Defence of Freedom, the Free Press Society, and the Anti-Socialist Front.
Policy: 'The only daily newspaper in Great Britain independent of combines and trade unions'.
Editor: E. Martell, 1960–66.

(News Chronicle), 1930–60
Proprietors: Amalgamation of *Daily News and Leader* and *Daily Chronicle* in 1930 (Cadbury family). Bought by Associated Newspapers Ltd in 1960, and merged with *Daily Mail*.
Policy: Liberal.
Editors: T. Clarke, 1930. A. Vallance, 1933. G. Barry, 1936. R. Cruikshank, 1948. M. Curtis, 1954. N. Cursley, 1957.

(Post), 1988 (10 Nov – 17 Dec only)
Proprietors: Messenger Group Newspapers (E. Shah).
Policy: Independent.
Editor: L. Turner.

(Recorder), 27 Oct 1953–17 May 1954
Proprietors: The Recorder Ltd. (Managing Director: E. Martell). A weekly suburban newspaper 1870–1939, continued as a weekly after 1954.
Policy: Independent. 'Keynote: pride in Britain and the British Empire.'
Editor: W. Brittain, 1953–4.

Sun, 1964
Proprietors: International Publishing Corporation (Chairman: C. King. H. Cudlipp, 1968). 1969 News International Ltd (R. Murdoch).
Policy: Labour. Independent since 1969.
Editors: S. Jacobson, 1964. R. Dinsdale, 1965. A. Lamb, 1969. B. Shrimsley, 1972. (Sir) L. Lamb, 1975. K. McKenzie, 1981. S. Higgins, 1994. D. Yelland, 1998.

The Times, 1785[1]
Proprietors: Founded as the Daily Universal Register, became The Times in 1788. Owned by the Walter family, 1785–1908. Bought by Ld Northcliffe in 1908. Owned by J. Astor and J. Walter in 1922. 7 Aug 24, Times Association formed (comprising Lord Chief Justice, Warden of All Souls, Oxford, President of the Royal Society, President of the Institute of Chartered Accountants and Governor of the Bank of England). 21 Dec 66, Monopolies Commission approved common ownership of *The Times* and the *Sunday Times* by the Thomson Organisation. Times Newspapers Ltd formed. President: G. Astor (Ld). Chairman: Sir W. Haley. 1967 K. Thomson (Ld). Acquired by News International, 1981 (Chairman: R. Murdoch).
Policy: Independent conservative.
Editors: G. Buckle, 1884. G. Dawson, 1912. H. Steed, 1919. G. Dawson, 1922. R. Barrington-Ward, 1941. W. Casey, 1948. Sir W. Haley, 1952. W. Rees-Mogg, 1967. H. Evans, 1981. C. Douglas-Home, 1983. C. Wilson, 1985. S. Jenkins, 1990. P. Stothard, 1992.

(Today), 1986–95
Proprietors: Messenger Group (E. Shah). Bought by Lonrho, 1986. Bought by News International (Chairman: R Murdoch) 1987.

---

[1] *The Times* suspended publication from 1 Dec 78 to 12 Nov 79.

Policy: Independent.
Editors: B. MacArthur 1986. D. Montgomery, 1987. M. Dunn, 1991. R.Stott, 1993–5.

(Tribune), 1906–1908
Proprietors: F. Thomasson.
Policy: Liberal.
Editors: W. Hill and S. Pryor, 1906.

(Westminster Gazette), 1921–1928 issued as a morning paper.
(See *Evening Papers*).

National Sunday Newspapers

(excluding all those not published in London)

((Illustrated) Sunday Herald), 1915–1927
Proprietors: Sir E. Hulton. Renamed *Illustrated Sunday Herald*. Bought by Berry family in 1926 and renamed *Sunday Graphic* in 1927 (see below).
Policy: Independent conservative.
Editors: J. E. Williams, 1915. T. Hill, 1926–27.

Independent on Sunday, 1990
Proprietors: Newspaper Publishing Co. Ltd. Control was acquired by Mirror Group Newspapers in 1998.
Policy: Independent.
Editor: A. Whittam Smith, 1990. I. Jack, 1992. P. Wilby, 1995. Rosie Boycott, 1996. Kim Fletcher, 1998.

Mail on Sunday, 1982
Proprietors: Associated Newspapers Ltd (Chairman: Vt Rothermere).
Policy: Independent Conservative.
Editors: B. Shrimsley, 1982. Sir D. English, 1982. S. Steven, 1982. J. Holborow, 1992. P. Wright, 1998.

(National News), 1917–1918
Proprietors: Odhams Press Ltd.
Policy: Independent.
Editor: A. de Beck, 1917–18.

News of the World, 1843
Proprietors: News of the World Ltd. (Sir) G. Riddell (Ld), 1903–34. The Carr family 1934–69. 1969 News International Ltd (R. Murdoch).
Policy: Independent conservative.
Editors: Sir E. Carr, 1891. D. Davies, 1941. R. Skelton, 1946. A. Waters, 1947. R. Cudlipp, 1953. S. Somerfield, 1959. C. Lear, 1970. P. Stephens, 1974. B. Shrimsley, 1975. K. Donlan, 1980. B. Askew, 1981. D. Jameson, 1981. N. Lloyd, 1984. D. Montgomery, 1985. Wendy Henry, 1987. Patsy Chapman, 1988. P. Morgan, 1994. P. Hall, 1995.

(News on Sunday), 1987 (Apr-Nov only).
Proprietors: News on Sunday Ltd (Chairman: N. Horsley; shares held largely by local authority pension funds and trade unions, notably TGWU). Acquired by Growfar Ltd (owned by O. Oyston) Jun 1987.
Policy: Left-wing.
Editors: K. Sutton, D. Jones, B. Whitaker, W. Nutting.

Observer, 1791
Proprietors: F. Beer. Bought by Ld Northcliffe in 1905. Bought by W. Astor (Vt) in 1911. Sold to Atlantic Richfield, 1976. 10 shares to remain with Observer Trustees. Sold to Lonrho, 1980 (Chairman: R. Rowland). Taken over by Guardian and Evening News Group, 1993.
Policy: Conservative. Independent since 1942.
Editors: F. Beer, 1894. A. Harrison, 1905. J. Garvin, 1908. I. Brown, 1942. D. Astor, 1948. D. Trelford, 1976. J. Fenby, 1993. A. Jaspan, 1995. W. Hutton, 1996. R. Alton, 1998.

People, 1881
Proprietors: W. Madge and Sir G. Armstrong. Sir W. Madge, 1914–22. M. L. Publishing Co. Ltd. The People Ltd. Odhams Press. 1961 amalgamated with International Publishing Corporation

(Chairman: C. King. H. Cudlipp, 1968). Control acquired by Reed International 1970 (Chairman: (Sir) D. Ryder. A. Jarratt, 1974). Control acquired by R. Maxwell, 1984. I. Maxwell, 1991. Control acquired by creditor banks, 1992.

Policy: Independent.
Editors: J. Hatton. J. Sansome 1913. H. Swaffer, 1924. H. Ainsworth, 1925. S. Campbell, 1958. R. Edwards, 1966. G. Pinnington, 1972. R. Stott, 1984. E. Burrington, 1985. J. Blake, 1988. Wendy Henry, 1989. R. Stott, 1990. W. Haggerty, 1991. Bridget Rowe, 1992. L. Gould, 1996. B. Parsons, 1997. N. Wallis, 1998.

(Reynolds News), 1850–1967

Proprietors: Originally Reynold's Weekly Newspaper, and later Reynold's Illustrated News. Owned by J. Dicks and family since 1879. J. Dalziel (Ld) appointed business manager in 1907. He became the sole proprietor in 1914. Bought by the National Co-operative Press Ltd. Incorporated the *Sunday Citizen*. 1962. Changed name to *Sunday Citizen and Reynolds News*.
Policy: Support for the Labour and Co-operative movements.
Editors: W. Thompson, 1894. J. Dalziel, 1907. J. Crawley, 1920. S. Elliott, 1929. (Sir) W. Richardson, 1941–67.

(Sunday Correspondent), 1989–90

Proprietors: Sunday Publishing Co. plc
Policy: Independent
Editors: P. Cole, 1989. J. Bryant 1990.

(Sunday Citizen), 1962–1967. (See above, *Reynolds News*)

(Sunday Dispatch), 1801–1961

Proprietors: Sir G. Newnes (1900). Originally the *Weekly Dispatch* until 1928. Bought by the Harmsworth family. Vt Northcliffe, Vt Rothermere from 1928. Associated Newspapers Ltd. Absorbed by the *Sunday Express* in 1961.
Policy: Independent conservative.
Editors: M. Cotton, H. Swaffer, 1915. B. Falk, 1919. W. McWhirter, 1930. H. Lane, 1933. W. Brittain, 1934. C. Brooks, 1936. C. Eade, 1938. H. Gunn, 1959–61.

Sunday Express, 1918

Proprietors: Sunday Express Ltd. (Ld Beaverbrook; From 1954 Beaverbrook Newspapers Ltd.) Taken over by Trafalgar House property group, 1977. Chairman: V. (Ld) Matthews. Acquired by United Newspapers, 1985 (Chairman: D. (Ld) Stevens). In 1996 Ld Stevens' United Newspapers merged with Ld Hollick's MAI Group to form United News and Media with Ld Stevens as Chairman and Ld Hollick as Chief Executive. In 1999 Sir R. Hempel succeeded Ld Stevens as Chairman.
Policy: Independent conservative.
Editors: J. Douglas, 1920. J. Gordon, 1928. (Sir) J. Junor, 1954. R. Esser, 1986. R. Morgan, 1989. Eve Pollard, 1991. B. Hitchen, 1994. R. Addis, 1995. Amanda Platell, 1998. Rosie Boycott, 1999.

(Sunday Graphic (and Sunday News)), 1915–60

Proprietors: Sir E. Hulton. Originally called the *Sunday Herald*, renamed the *Illustrated Sunday Herald*. Bought by the Berry family in 1926, and renamed the *Sunday Graphic* in 1927. Daily Graphic and Sunday Graphic Ltd, a subsidiary of Vt Kemsley's newspapers. Incorporated the *Sunday News* in 1931. Bought by R. Thomson in 1959. Ceased publication in 1960.
Policy: Independent.
Editors: T. Hill, 1927. A.Sinclair, 1931. R. Simpson, 1935. M. Watts, 1947. N. Hamilton, 1947. L. Lang, 1948. A. Josey, 1949. B. Horniblow, 1950. P. Brownrigg, 1952. M. Randell, 1953. G. McKenzie, 1953. A. Hall, 1958. R. Anderson, 1959. A. Ewart, 1960.

(Sunday Illustrated), 1921–23

Proprietor: H. Bottomley.
Policy: Independent.
Editor: H. Bottomley.

(Sunday (Illustrated) News), 1842–1931

Proprietors: Originally *Lloyd's Sunday News*. Sunday News Ltd. United Newspapers Ltd (W. Harrison). Merged with the *Sunday Graphic* in 1931.

Policy:		Independent liberal.
Editors:		T. Catling. W. Robinson, 1919. E. Perris, 1924. E. Wallace, 1929–31.

Sunday Mirror, 1963
Proprietors:		International Publishing Corporation (Chairman: C. King, 1963. H. Cudlipp, 1968) Control acquired by Reed International 1970 (Chairman: (Sir) D. Ryder. 1974, A. Jarratt). Bought by R. Maxwell, 1984. I. Maxwell, 1991. Control acquired by creditor banks, 1992.
Policy:		Independent.
Editor:		M. Christiansen, 1963. R. Edwards, 1972. M. Molloy, 1986. Eve Pollard, 1988. Bridget Rowe, 1991. C. Myler, 1992. Tessa Hilton, 1994. P. Connew, 1996. J. Cassidy, 1996. Amanda Platell, 1996. Bridget Rowe, 1997. B. Parsons, 1998. C. Myler, 1998.

(Sunday Pictorial), 1915–1963
Proprietors:		The Harmsworth family. Taken over by Vt Rothermere in 1922. Sunday Pictorial Newspapers (1920) Ltd. 1961 absorbed by International Publishing Corporation (Cecil King). 1963, became *Sunday Mirror (see above)*.
Policy:		Independent.
Editors:		F. Sanderson, 1915. W. McWhirter, 1921. D. Grant, 1924. W. McWhirter, 1928. D. Grant, 1929. H. Cudlipp, 1938. R. Campall, 1940. H. Cudlipp, 1946. P. Zec, 1949. H. Cudlipp, 1952. C. Valdar, 1953. L. Howard, 1959. R. Payne, 1960.

((Sunday) Referee), 1877–1939
Proprietors:		Printed by the Daily News Ltd. Owned by I. Ostrer. Incorporated in the *Sunday Chronicle* in 1939 (which was published in Manchester and ceased independent publication in 1955).
Policy:		Conservative.
Editors:		R. Butler. (Sir) R. Donald, 1922. A. Laber, 1924. M. Joulden, 1933.

(Sunday Special), 1897–1904
Proprietor:		H. Schmidt.

Sunday Sport, 1986
Proprietor:		Sport Newspapers Ltd (D. Sullivan).
Policy:		Independent.
Editors:		P. Grimsditch, 1986. M. Gabbert, 1987. D. Robertson, 1987. I. Pollock, 1990. G. Thompson, 1993. D. Mohan, 1993. J. Wise, 1995. M. Harris, 1997.

Sunday Telegraph, 1961
Proprietors:		The Sunday Telegraph Ltd (M. Berry (Ld Hartwell)). Bought by C. Black 1987.
Policy:		Independent conservative.
Editor:		D. McLachlan, 1961. B. Roberts, 1966. J. Thompson, 1976. P. Worsthorne, 1986. T. Grove, 1989. C. Moore, 1992. D. Lawson, 1995.

Sunday Times, 1822
Proprietors:		Mrs. F. Beer. Bought by H. Schmidt. Amalgamated with the *Sunday Special* in 1904. Bought by the Berry family in 1915. Bought by R. Thomson (Ld) in 1959 (Thomson Allied Newspapers). Times Newspapers Ltd, formed in 1967 to run *The Times* and *Sunday Times*. Control acquired by News International, 1981 (Chairman: R. Murdoch).
Policy:		Independent conservative.
Editors:		L. Rees, 1901. W. Hadley, 1932. H. Hodson, 1950. C. D. Hamilton, 1961. H. Evans, 1967. F. Giles, 1981. A. Neil, 1983. J. Witherow, 1994.

(Sunday Today), 1986–7
Proprietors:		Messenger Group Newspapers (E. Shah). Control acquired by Lonrho, 1986. Bought by News International (Chairman R. Murdoch) 1987.
Policy:		Independent.
Editor:		B. MacArthur.

(Sunday Worker), 1925–30
Proprietors:		The Communist Party through nominees. Published daily as the *Daily Worker* from 1930.
Policy:		Communist.
Editors:		W. Paul, 1925. W. Holmes, 1927.

London Evening Newspapers

(Evening Echo and Chronicle), 22 Mar-4 May 1915
Proprietor: E. Lloyd. Merged with Star.
Policy: Liberal.

(Echo), 1868–1905
Proprietors: Consolidated Newspapers. F. Pethick-Lawrence in control, 1901–05.
Policy: Radical, progressive.
Editors: W. Crook, 1898. T. Meech, 1900. P. Alden, 1901. F. Pethick-Lawrence, 1901–5.

(Evening News), 1881–1980, 1987 (Mar-Oct only).
Proprietors: A. Harmsworth (Evening News Ltd), 1894. Associated Newspapers Ltd, 1905. Merged with
                  Evening Standard, 1980. Briefly re-launched by Assocated Newspapers in 1987.
Policy: Conservative.
Editors: W. Evans, 1896. C. Beattie, 1922. F. Fitzhugh, 1924. G. Schofield, 1943. J. Marshall, 1950.
                  R. Willis, 1954. J. Gold, 1967. D. Boddie, 1973. L. Kirby, 1974–80. J. Lees, 1987.

Evening (New) Standard, 1827
Proprietors: Bought by A. Pearson from Johnston family in 1904. Absorbed *St James Gazette* in 1905. (Sir)
                  D. Dalziel (Ld)[1], 1910. Hulton and Co. 1915–23. Incorporated with *Pall Mall Gazette* and
                  Globe, 1923. Bought by Ld Beaverbrook in 1923. In 1954 he relinquished it to Beaverbrook
                  Newspapers Ltd and transferred controlling shares to the Beaverbrook Foundations. In 1977
                  Beaverbrook Newspapers were taken over by Trafalgar House property group. Chairman: V.
                  Matthews. Sold to Associated Newspapers, 1980 (Chairman: Vt Rothermere) and merged with
                  Evening News as *(New) Standard*. Reverted to name *Evening Standard* in 1987.
Policy: Independent conservative.
Editors: S. Pryor, 1897. W. Woodward, 1906. J. Kilpatrick, 1912. D. Sutherland, 1914. A. Mann, 1916.
                  D. Phillips, 1920. E. Thompson, 1923. G. Gilliat, 1928. P. Cudlipp, 1933. R. Thompson, 1938.
                  F. Owen, 1939. M. Foot, 1942. S. Elliott, 1943. H. Gunn, 1944. P. Elland, 1950. C. Wintour,
                  1959. S. Jenkins, 1977. C. Wintour, 1978. L. Kirkby, 1980. J. Lees, 1986. P. Dacre, 1991. S.
                  Steven, 1992. M. Hastings, 1996.

(Evening Times), 1910–1911
Proprietors: London Evening Newspaper Co. (J. Morrison, Sir S. Scott, J. Cowley).
Policy: Conservative.
Editors: C. Watney, E. Wallace.

(Globe), 1803–1921
Proprietors: (Sir) G. Armstrong, 1871–1907. H. Harmsworth, 1907–11. W. Madge, 1912–14. Absorbed by
                  Pall Mall Gazette in 1921, incorporated with *Evening Standard* in 1923.
Policy: Conservative.
Editors: Sir G. Armstrong, 1895. P. Ogle, 1907. J. Harrison, 1908. C. Palmer, 1912. W. Peacock,
                  1915–21.

(London Daily News), 1987 (Feb-Jul only)
Proprietors: Mirror Group Newspapers (Chairman: R. Maxwell).
Policy: Independent Labour-leaning.
Editor: M. Linklater.

(Pall Mall Gazette), 1865–1923
Proprietors: W. Astor (Ld), 1892. Sir H. Dalziel, 1917. Sir J. Leigh, 1923. Incorporated with *Evening
                  Standard* in 1923.
Policy: Conservative.
Editors: Sir D. Straight, 1896. F. Higginbottom, 1909. J. Garvin, 1912. D. Sutherland, 1915–23.

(St James's Gazette), 1880–1905
Proprietors: E. Steinkopff, 1888. W. Dallas Ross, A. Pearson, 1903. Amalgamated with *Evening Standard*
                  in 1905.
Policy: Conservative.
Editors: H. Chisholm, 1897. R. McNeill, 1900. G. Fiennes, 1903. S. Pryor, 1904–5.

---

[1] Later Lord Dalziel of Wooler, not to be confused with Ld Dalziel of Kirkcaldy who was proprietor of Reynolds News,
1914–20.

(**Star**), 1887–1960

Proprietors:	Star Newspaper Co. Owned by Daily News Ltd. Bought by Associated Newspapers Ltd, and incorporated in *Evening News*, 1960.
Policy:	Liberal.
Editors:	E. Parke, 1891. J. Douglas, 1908. W. Pope, 1920. E. Chattaway, 1930. R. Cruikshank, 1936. A. Cranfield, 1941. R. McCarthy, 1957–60.

(**Sun**), 1893–1906

Proprietors:	T. P. O'Connor. H. Bottomley, 1900. Sir G. Armstrong and W. Madge, 1904–6.
Policy:	Literary, non-political.
Editors:	T. P. O'Connor. T. Dahle.

(**Westminster Gazette**), 1893–1928

Proprietors:	Sir G. Newnes, 1893. Liberal Syndicate (Chairman: Sir A. Mond), 1908–15. A. Pearson, 1915–28. Last issue as evening paper 5 Nov 21. First issue as morning paper 7 Nov 21. Incorporated with *Daily News* in 1928.
Policy:	Liberal.
Editors:	J. Spender, 1896. J. Hobman, 1921–28.

National Newspapers Printing in More than One City 1900–1985[1]

	London	Manchester	Glasgow
Daily Chronicle	1869–1930	1925–1930[2]	–
Daily Express	1900–	1927–	1928–1974
Daily Herald (Sun)	1912–	1930–1969	–
Daily Mail	1896–	1900–	1946–1966[3]
Daily Mirror[4]	1903–	1955–	–
Daily News	1846–1930	1921–1924	–
Daily Star	1978–	1978–	–
Daily Sketch (Graphic)	1911–1971	1908–1953	–
Daily Telegraph	1955–	1940–	–
News Chronicle	1930–1960	1930–1960	–
(Manchester) Guardian	1961–	1821–	–
News of the World	1843–	1941–	–
Sunday Dispatch	1801–1961	1930–1961	–
Sunday Express	1918–	1927–	1927–1974
Sunday Graphic	1915–1960	1932–1952[5]	–
Sun.Pictorial/Sun.Mirror	1955–	1955–	–
(Sunday) People	1881–	1930–	–
Sunday Times	1822–	1940–1964	–
Sunday Chronicle	1939–1955	1885–1955	–

[1] From the mid 1980s new technology made printing in many different centres the norm rather than the exception.

[2] The *Daily Chronicle* was printed in Leeds, not Manchester, 1925–30.

[3] The Scottish *Daily Mail* was printed in Edinburgh, not Glasgow, 1946–66.

[4] The *Daily Mirror* was also printed in Belfast, 1966–71.

[5] The Manchester printing of the *Sunday Graphic* was suspended from 1936–50.

Partisan Tendencies and Circulations of National Daily Newspapers in British General Elections, 1945–92

Circulation (millions) & Party support

Newspaper	1945	1950	1951	1955	1959	1964	1966	1970	Feb 1974	Oct 1974	1979	1983	1987	1992	1997
D.Express	3.3 Con	4.1 Con	4.2 Con	4.0 Con	4.1 Con	4.2 Con	4.0 Con	3.6 Con	3.2 Con	3.1 Con	2.5 Con	1.9 Con	1.7 Con	1.5 Con	1.2 Con
D.Herald/Sun[1]	1.9 Lab	2.0 Lab	2.0 Lab	1.8 Lab	1.5 Lab	1.3* Lab	1.2 Lab	1.5 Lab	3.3 Con	3.5 All-Pty Coal.	3.9 Con	4.2 Con	4.0 Con	3.6 Con	3.9 Lab
D.Mail	1.7 Con	2.2 Con	2.3 Con	2.1 Con	2.1 Con	2.4 Con	2.4 Con	1.9 Con	1.8 Con	1.7 Con-Lib Coal.	2.0 Con	1.8 Con	1.8 Con	1.7 Con	2.1 Con
D.Mirror	2.4 Lab	4.6 Lab	4.5 Lab	4.7 Lab	4.5 Lab	5.1 Lab	5.1 Lab	4.7 Lab	4.2 Lab	4.2 Lab	3.8 Lab	3.3 Lab	3.1 Lab	2.9 Lab	2.8 Lab
D Sketch/ D.Graphic[2]	0.9 Con	1.0 Con	0.8 Con	0.8 Con	1.0 Con	1.2 Con	0.8 Con	0.8 Con	0.8	–	–	–	–	–	–
D Telegraph	0.8 Con	1.0 Con	1.0 Con	1.1 Con	1.2 Con	1.3 Con	1.4 Con	1.4 Con	1.4 Con	1.4 Con	1.4 Con	1.3 Con	1.1 Con	1.0 Con	1.1 Con
(Manchester) Guardian[3]	0.1 Lib	0.1 Lib	0.2 Lib/Con	0.2 Lib/Con	0.3 Lab/Lib	0.3 Lab	0.3 Lab/Lib	0.4 Lab/Lib	0.4 Party Balance	0.4 More Lib	0.3 Lab	0.4 All	0.5 /Lab	0.4 Lab/LibD	0.4 Lab/LibD
Independent	–	–	–	–	–	–	–	–	–	–	–	–	0.3 None	0.4 None	0.3 Lab
News Chronicle[4]	1.5 Lib	1.5 Lib	1.5 Lib	1.3 Lib	1.2 Lib	–	–	–	–	–	–	–	–	–	–
The Times	0.2 Lab	0.3 Con	0.2 Con	0.2 Con	0.3 Con	0.3 Con/Lib	0.3 Con/Lib	0.4 Con/Lib	0.3 Con/Lib	0.3 C/L Coal.	–	0.3 Con	0.4 Con	0.4 Con	0.8 Con
Today	–	–	–	–	–	–	–	–	–	–	–	–	0.3 Coal	0.5 Con	–
Daily Star	–	–	–	–	–	–	–	–	–	–	n.a. Neut	1.3 Con	1.3 Con	0.8 Neut	0.3 Lab

PARTISANSHIP IN ELECTIONS

	1945	1950	1951	1955	1959	1964	1966	1970	Feb 1974	Oct 1974	1979	1983	1987	1992	1997
Total circulation (000s)	12799	16632	16623	16224	16067	15679	15419	14642	14633	14573	13789[5]	14527	14824	13380	
Total Conservative circulation	6713 (52%)	8333 (50%)	8599+ (52%)	8487+ (52%)	8715 (54%)	9016 (57%)	8538 (55%)	8133+ (55%)	10441+ (71%)	6898+ (47%)	9731 (71%)	11260+ (78%)	10914+ (74%)	8728[5] (64%)	5233 (39%)
Total Conservative vote	9578 (40%)	12503 (43%)	13718 (48%)	13312 (50%)	13750 (49%)	12001 (43%)	11418 (42%)	13145 (46%)	11872 (38%)	10465 (36%)	13698 (44%)	13012 (42%)	13763 (42%)	14093 (42%)	960 (31%)
Total Labour circulation	4454 (35%)	6633 (40%)	6517 (39%)	6484 (40%)	6145+ (38%)	6663 (42%)	6608+ (43%)	6509+ (44%)	4557 (31%)	4572+ (31%)	4058 (29%)	3267 (22%)	3924+ (26%)	3,332+ (25%)	8147 (61%)
Total Labour vote	11633 (48%)	13267 (46%)	13949 (49%)	12405 (46%)	12216 (44%)	12206 (44%)	13065 (48%)	12178 (43%)	11646 (37%)	11457 (39%)	11532 (37%)	8457 (28%)	10030 (31%)	11560 (34%)	13518 (43%)
Total Liberal circulation	1632 (13%)	1666 (10%)	1646+ (10%)	1409+ (9%)	1390+ (9%)	–	556+ (4%)	705+ (5%)	716+ (5%)	2432+ (17%)	–	417 (3%)	307+ (2%)	429+ (3%)	–
Total Liberal vote	2197 (9%)	2622 (9%)	731 (2%)	722 (3%)	1639 (6%)	3093 (11%)	2327 (8%)	2117 (7%)	6059 (19%)	5347 (18%)	4314 (14%)	7781 (25%)	7341 (23%)	5999 (18%)	5243 (17%)

[1] Name changed to the *Sun* in 1964.
[2] Named *Daily Graphic*, 1946–52.
[3] '*Manchester*' dropped from title in 1959.
[4] Ceased publication in 1960.
[5] Not including the *Daily Star*.
* Figure uncertain due to relaunching at that time.
+ Including paper(s) with divided support, but omits the *Sun* in October 1974.

Source of circulation figures: 1945, 1950: Nuffield election studies; thereafter, Audit Bureau of Circulation, excepting *The Daily Telegraph* figures for 1951, 1955, 1959 (London Press Exchange). Circulation figures are for the period of the year in which the election was held.

Circulations of National Newspapers, 1910–

National Daily Newspapers
(to nearest 000)

	1910	1930	1939	1951	1960	1965	1970	1980	1990	1998[j]
D.Express	400	1,603[b]	2,486	4,193	4,130	3,981	3,607	2,325	1,585	1,134
D. Herald/Sun	–	750[b]	2,000	2,071	1,467	1,274	1,509	3,837	3,855	3,698
D.Mail	900	1,968	1,510[d]	2,245	2,084	2,464	1,917	1,985	1,708	2,343
D.Mirror[h]	630	1,071	1,367[d]	4,567	4,545	4,957[i]	4,697	3,651	3,083	2,351
D.News	320	900	–	–	–	–	–	–	–	–
D.Sketch	750[a]	1,013	850[d]	777	1,152	844	806	–	–	–
D.Star	–	–	–	–	–	–	–	1,033	833	566
D.Telegraph	230	222[c]	640[d]	976[e]	1,155[e]	1,351	1,402	1,456	1,076	1,062
D.Worker/M Star	–	n.a.	100[d]	115	73[f]	–	–	34	26	5
Guardian	40	47	51	140	190	270	303	375	424	393
Independent	–	–	–	–	–	–	–	–	411	222
M.Leader	250	–	–	–	–	–	–	–	–	–
M.Post	n.a.	119	–	–	–	–	–	–	–	–
N.Chron.[g]	800[a]	967	1,317	1,583	1,206	–	–	–	–	–
Times	45	187	213	254	255	258	402	316	420	760
Today	–	–	–	–	–	–	–	–	540	–

Unless otherwise stated the figures are taken from *T.B.Browne's Advertiser's ABC*, 1910–40, and figures after 1950 are from the Audit Bureau of Circulation.

[a] Circulation figure for 1915, *T.B.Browne*.
[b] P.E.P.: *Report on the British Press* (1938) gives 1,082 for 1930.
[c] From the P.E.P. Report.
[d] From the P.E.P. Report. Figure for 1938.
[e] *Daily Telegraph* audited circulation figures.
[f] ABC circulation in 1956. Latest available figure.
[g] 1910 and 1930 figures are for *Daily Chronicle*.
[h] This does not include circulation of *Daily Record* (Glasgow) acquired by Daily Mirror in 1955.
[i] For a period in 1964 the *Daily Mirror* became the only daily newspaper ever to top 5m. circulation.
[j] The 1998 figures are the average for the six months to the end of October.

Circulation of National Sunday Newspapers
(000s)

	1900	1910	1930	1937	1951	1960	1965	1970	1980	1990	1998[c]
Independent on S.	–	–	–	–	–	–	–	–	–	352	255
Lloyd's Weekly	1250	1250	1450[b]	–	–	–	–	–	–	–	–
News of the World	400	1500	3250[b]	3850	8407	6664	6176	6215	4472	5056	4243
Observer	60	n.a.	201	208	450	738	829	848	1018	551	401
Mail on Sunday	–	–	–	–	–	–	–	–	–	1903	2279
People	n.a.	n.a.	2535	3406	5181	5468	5538	5242	3856	2566	1734
Reynolds News	2000[a]	2000[a]	420	426	712	329	236	–	–	–	–
Sunday Dispatch	n.a.	n.a.	1197	741	2631	1520	–	–	–	–	–
Sunday Express	–	–	958[b]	1350	3178	3706	4187	4281	3100	1664	1046
Sunday Graphic	–	–	1100[b]	651	1121	890	–	–	–	–	–
Sunday Mirror	–	–	–	–	–	–	5022	4885	3856	2894	2007
Sunday Pictorial	–	–	1883	1345	5170	5461	–	–	–	–	–
Sunday Referee	n.a.	n.a.	73	342	–	–	–	–	–	–	–
Sunday Sport	–	–	–	–	–	–	–	–	–	407	342
Sunday Telegraph	–	–	–	–	–	–	662	756	1032	594	833
Sunday Times	n.a.	n.a.	153	270	529	1001	1290	1464	1419	1165	1346

Unless otherwise stated, these figures are taken from *T.B.Browne's Advertiser's ABC*, 1900–30; the figures for 1937 are from the *Report of the Royal Commission on the Press*, 1947–49 (Cmd. 7700 and 7690/1949). From 1951, Audit Bureau of Circulation.

[a] These figures should be treated with caution. They are from an advertisement in *T.B.Browne's Advertiser's ABC* for 1901 and 1911.
[b] From *Sell's World Press*.
[c] The 1998 figures are the average for the six months to the end of October.

London Evening Newspapers
(000s)

	1905	1910	1930	1939	1951	1960	1965	1970	1980	1990	1998
News	300	300	667	822	1752	1153	1238	1017	–	–	–
E. Standard	n.a.	160	n.a.	390	862	586	680	550	608	502	478
Star	250	327	744	503	1228	744	–	–	–	–	–

All circulation figures for evening newspapers exclude Sporting Editions. 1905–39 figures from *T.B.Browne's Advertiser's ABC*; from 1951 figures are from the Audit Bureau of Circulation, published in the *Newspaper Press Directory*. Information on the circulation of other evening papers is not available.

Provincial Morning Daily Newspapers, 1900–

Sporting newspapers and publications such as the *Hull Shipping Gazette* and the *Hartlepool Daily Shipping List* have been omitted. Bold type indicates newspapers still being published on 1 Jan 2000.

ABERDEEN – *Aberdeen Daily Journal* (1746). Merged with *Aberdeen Free Press* Nov 1922 and became **Aberdeen Press and Journal**.

BATH – *Bath Daily Argus* (1870). Merged with local evening paper, *Bath Daily Chronicle*, in Jan 1900.

BEDFORD – *Bedford Daily Circular* (1903). Merged with *Bedford Record* July 1939.

BELFAST – **Belfast News-Letter** (1737).
> *Northern Whig* (1824). Changed name to *Northern Whig and Belfast Post* Jun 1919. Ceased publication 1963.
> *Irish Daily Telegraph* (1904). Merged with local evening paper, *Belfast Telegraph*, Apr 1952.
> **Irish News and Belfast Morning News** (1881).

BIRMINGHAM – *Daily Argus* (1891). Merged with local evening paper, *Birmingham Evening Dispatch*, Jan 1902.
> *Birmingham Daily Post* (1857). Changed name to *Birmingham Post* May 1918. Became *Birmingham Post and Gazette* Nov 1956. Changed name to **Birmingham Post** 1973.
> *Birmingham Daily Gazette* (1862). Merged with *Midland Express* and changed name to *Birmingham Gazette and Express* 1904. Merged with *Birmingham Post* Nov 1956.

BRADFORD – *Bradford Observer* (1834). Changed name to *Yorkshire Daily Observer* Nov 1901. Changed name to *Yorkshire Observer* Jan 1909. Merged with local evening paper, *The Telegraph and Argus*, Nov 1956.

BRIGHTON – *Morning Argus* (1896). Ceased publication as morning paper May 1926.[1]
> *Sussex Daily News* (1868). Merged with *Evening Argus* Mar 1956.

BRISTOL – *Bristol Western Daily Press* (1858). Changed name to **Western Daily Press** 1928.
> *Bristol Mercury* (1790). Changed name to *Bristol Daily Mercury* Dec 1901. Ceased publication Nov 1909.
> *Bristol Times and Mirror* (1713). Merged with *Western Daily Press* 1932.

CARDIFF – *South Wales Daily News* (1872). Changed name to *South Wales News* Apr 1928. Merged with *Western Mail* Aug 1928.
> **Western Mail** (1869).
> *Cardiff Journal of Commerce* (1904). Changed name to *Cardiff and South Wales Journal of Commerce* July 1914. Changed name to *South Wales Journal of Commerce* June 1918. Ceased publication Apr 1935.

CROYDON – *Surrey Morning Echo* (1908). Ceased publication Jan 1910.

DARLINGTON – *North Star* (1881). Merged with *Newcastle Daily Journal* 1926.
> **Northern Echo** (1870).

DUNDEE – *Dundee Advertiser* (1861). Merged with *Courier and Argus* 1926 and became *Dundee Advertiser and Courier*.
> *Courier and Argus* (1861). Merged with the daily edition of *Dundee Advertiser* 1926 and became *Dundee Advertiser and Courier*.
> *Dundee Advertiser and Courier* (1926). Changed name to **Courier and Advertiser** 1926.

EDINBURGH – **Scotsman** (1817).

EXETER – *Devon and Exeter Daily Gazette* (1772). Merged with *Western Morning News* Mar 1932.
> *Western Times* (1827). Became weekly paper 1922.

GLASGOW – **(Glasgow) Herald** (1783).
> *North British Daily Mail* (1847). Became *Glasgow Daily Mail* 1901. Merged with *Glasgow Record* 1901.
> *Daily Record* (1895). Incorporated *Glasgow Daily Mail* 1901 and became *Daily Record and Daily Mail*.
>> Changed name to *Daily Record and Mail* 1902.
>> Changed name to **Daily Record** 1954.

[1] Localised editions of the Argus were published in Battle, Chichester, Eastbourne, East Grinstead, Hastings, Horsham, Hove, Lewes, Littlehampton, Rye, Tunbridge Wells, and Worthing. Those still publishing in 1926 were merged with the Brighton Morning Argus into the evening Argus.

GLASGOW (cont...)
> *Bulletin* (1915). Became *Bulletin and Scots Pictorial* Jan 1924. Ceased publication July 1960.
> *Scottish Daily News* (Apr 75). Workers' Cooperative, using *Scottish Daily Express* plant. Ceased publication Nov 1975.

HUDDERSFIELD – *Huddersfield Daily Chronicle* (1871).[2] Ceased publication Dec 1915.

HULL – *Daily Mail* (1787). Became an evening paper 1902.
> *Eastern Morning News* (1861). Ceased publication Nov 1929.

IPSWICH – **East Anglian Daily Times** (1874).

LEAMINGTON – **Leamington, Warwick, Kenilworth and District Morning News** (1896). Originally *Leamington, Warwick, Kenilworth and District Daily Circular*. Changed name and started morning publication in 1919.

LEEDS – *Leeds Mercury* (1718). Changed name to *Leeds and Yorkshire Mercury* Oct 1901–Nov 1907. Merged with *Yorkshire Post* Nov 1939.
> **Yorkshire Post** (1754).

LEICESTER – *Leicester Daily Post* (1872). Ceased publication Mar 1921.

LIVERPOOL – *Liverpool Courier* (1808). Changed name to *Liverpool Daily Courier* Sep 1922. Changed name to *Daily Courier* Oct 1922. Ceased publication Dec 1929.
> *Liverpool Mercury* (1811). Merged with *Liverpool Daily Post* Nov 1904.
> **Liverpool Daily Post** (1855).
> **Journal of Commerce** (1861).

MANCHESTER – *Manchester Courier* (1825). Ceased publication Jan 1916.
> *Daily Dispatch* (1900). Merged with *News Chronicle* Nov 1955.
> (Manchester) **Guardian** (1821). (*See under National Daily Newspapers.*)
> *Manchester Journal of Commerce*. Ceased publication 1911.
> *Telegraphic News*. Ceased publication 1901.
> *Daily Citizen* (1912). Ceased publication June 1915.
> *Daily Sketch* (1909). Ceased publication Apr 1911.

NEWCASTLE – *Illustrated Chronicle* (1910). Ceased publication June 1925.
> *Newcastle Daily Chronicle* (1858). Merged with *North Mail* Mar 1923.
> *Newcastle Daily Journal* (1832). Became *Newcastle Journal and North Mail* Sep 1939. Changed name to **Journal** Jul 1958.
> *North Mail* (1901). Incorporated *Newcastle Daily Chronicle* Mar 1923 and became *North Mail and Newcastle Daily Chronicle*. Merged with *Newcastle Journal* in Sep 1939.
> *Newcastle Morning Mail* (1898). Changed name to *Morning Mail* Feb 1901. Ceased publication Aug 1901.

NEWPORT – *South Wales Daily News* (1872). Changed name to *South Wales News* 1928. Merged with *Western Mail* 1928.

NORWICH – **Eastern Daily Press** (1870).
> *Norfolk Daily Standard* (1855). Became an evening paper in 1900.

NOTTINGHAM – *Nottingham Daily Express* (1860). Changed name to *Nottingham Journal and Express* Apr 1918. Changed name to *Nottingham Journal* 1921. Merged with *Nottingham Guardian* Sep 1953 to become *Nottingham Guardian Journal*. Ceased publication Jan 1973.
> *Nottingham Daily Guardian* (1861). Changed name to *Nottingham Guardian* Oct 1905. Merged with *Nottingham Journal* Sep 1953.

OXFORD – *Oxford Morning Echo* (1860). Ceased publication Jan 1900.

PLYMOUTH – *Western Daily Mercury* (1860). Merged with *Western Morning News* Jan 1921.
> **Western Morning News** (1860).

PORTSMOUTH – *Southern Daily Mail* (1884). Ceased publication 1905.

SHIELDS – *Shields Morning Mail* (1889). Ceased publication Feb 1901.

SHEFFIELD – *Yorkshire Early Bird* (1899). Became morning paper in 1929. Changed named to *Early Bird* Mar 1938. Merged with local evening paper, *Chronicle Midday*, May 1950.
> *Sheffield Daily Telegraph* (1855). Changed name to *Sheffield Telegraph* Jun 1934; to *Sheffield Telegraph and Daily Independent* Oct 38–May 39; to *Telegraph and Independent* Jun–Jul 42; to *Sheffield Telegraph* Jul 42–Sep 65; to *Sheffield Morning Telegraph* Sep 65. Closed 1987.
> *Sheffield and Rotherham Independent* (1819). Changed name to *Sheffield Independent* Jan 1901. Changed name to *Sheffield Daily Independent* Feb 01 – Oct 09. Changed name to *Daily Independent* June 1922. Amalgamated with *Sheffield Telegraph* Oct 1938.

SWANSEA – *Swansea Gazette*. Changed name to *Swansea Daily Shipping Register* 1900. Ceased publication 1918.

YORK – *Yorkshire Herald* (1790). Became weekly 1936.
> *Aberdeen Free Press* (1853). Merged with *Aberdeen Daily Journal* Nov 1922.

[2]Not published on Saturdays.

Source: *Willing's Press Guide 1900–*; the catalogue of the British Museum Newspaper Library at Colindale.

Main Political Weeklies

Economist, The, 1843
Proprietors: The Economist Newspaper Limited. (Since 1928 50% of shares held by Financial Newspaper Proprietors Limited, later Financial News Ltd.)
Policy: Independent.
Editors: E. Johnstone, 1883. F. Hurst, 1907. H. Withers, 1916. W. Layton, 1922. G. Crowther, 1938. D. Tyerman, 1956. A. Burnet, 1965. A.Knight, 1974. R. Pennant-Rea, 1986. B. Emmott, 1993.

(Nation), 1907
Proprietors: The Nation. 1931 Amalgamated with the *New Statesman*.
Policy: Independent radical.
Editors: H. Massingham, 1907. H. Henderson, 1923. H. Wright, 1930–1931.

New Statesman (and Society), 1913
Proprietors: Statesman Publishing Company. 1931 Amalgamated with the Nation, The Statesman and Nation Publishing Company. Merged with *New Society* in 1988 and adopted full title *New Statesman and Society*.
Policy: Independent radical.
Editors: C. Sharp, 1913. K. Martin, 1931. J. Freeman, 1961. P. Johnson, 1965. R. Crossman, 1970. A. Howard, 1973. B. Page, 1978, H. Stephenson, 1982. J. Lloyd, 1986. S. Weir, 1988. S. Platt, 1991. I. Hargreaves, 1996. P. Wilby, 1998.

The Spectator, 1828
Proprietors: The Spectator Limited since 1898. J. St. L. Strachey, 1898. (Sir) E. Wrench, 1925. I. Gilmour, 1954. H. Creighton, 1967. H. Keswick,1975. A. Clough, 1981.
Policy: Independent conservative.
Editors: J. St. L. Strachey, 1897. (Sir) Evelyn Wrench, 1925. W. Harris, 1932.W.Taplin,1953.I.Gilmour, 1954. B.Inglis, 1959. I.Hamilton, 1962. I. Macleod, 1963. N. Lawson, 1966. G. Gale, 1970. H. Creighton, 1973. A. Chancellor, 1975. C. Moore, 1984. D. Lawson, 1989. F. Johnson, 1995. B. Johnson, 1999.

(Time and Tide), 1920
Proprietors: Lady Rhondda, 1920–1958. L. Skevington, 1958. T. Beaumont, 1960. W. Brittain, 1962. Time and Tide Ltd, 1977. Re-named Time and Tide Business News 1977 and published fortnightly. From 1978 published monthly.
Policy: Independent.
Editors: Lady Rhondda, 1920. A. Lejeune, 1957. L. Skevington, 1958. J. Thompson, 1960. W. Brittain, 1962. I. Lyon, 1977.

Tribune, 1937
Proprietors: Tribune Publications, Ltd.
Policy: Left-wing.
Editors: W. Mellor, 1937. J. Hartshorn, 1938. R. Postgate, 1940. A. Bevan, 1942. J. Kimche, 1945. M. Foot, 1948. R. Edwards, 1952. M. Foot, 1956. R. Clements, 1959. C. Mullin, 1982. N. Williamson, 1984. P. Kelly, 1986. P. Anderson, 1990. M. Seddon, 1993.

The Press Council, 1953–1990

Chairman

(General Council of the Press)	*(The Press Council)*
1953 W. Astor (Ld)	1963 Ld Devlin
1955 Sir L. Andrews	1969 Ld Pearce
1959 G. Murray	1974 Ld Shawcross
	1978 (Sir) P. Neill
	1983 Sir Z. Cowen
	1989 L. Blom-Cooper

The General Council of the Press was formed in 1953 in response to a recommendation of the Royal Commission on the Press (Cmd. 7700). It consisted of 15 editorial representatives and 10 managerial representatives. Its objects were to preserve the freedom of the press, to review any developments likely to restrict the supply of information of public interest and importance, to encourage training of journalists and technical research and to study developments in the press tending towards greater concentration or monopoly.

In 1963 it was reorganised to bring in lay members and the title was changed to the Press Council. The objects of the Council were extended to include considering complaints about the conduct of the press or the conduct of persons and organisations towards the press, and publishing relevant statistical material.

In 1977 the Press Council accepted the recommendation of the Royal Commission on the Press that in addition to its independent lay Chairman, it should consist of equal numbers of press and lay members. From 1978 to 1990, the composition was 12 representatives from newspaper and magazine management, 4 from the National Union of Journalists, 2 from the Institute of Journalists, 18 lay representatives, 8 non-voting consultative members and a lay Chairman. Lay members were appointed by an independent body, the Press Council Appointments Commission. The NUJ representatives withdrew from the Council in 1980, and only returned in May 1990, seven months before the Council was wound up.

Press Complaints Commission 1991–

Chairman

| 1991 | Ld McGregor of Durris |
| 1995 | Ld Wakeham |

The Press Complaints Commission was established by the newspaper industry to take over from the Press Council following the report of the Committee on Privacy and Related Matters chaired by Sir D. Calcutt, published in Jul 1990 (Cm 1102). It is responsible for adjudicating on complaints of unfair treatment, maintaining high professional standards and implementing a code of practice drafted by editors. Seven of its members are editors of national and local newspapers and magazines; nine, including the Chairman, are drawn from other fields. In 1995 the Government endorsed self regulation of the press under the Press Complaints Commission in its White Paper *Privacy and Media Intrusion*. It endorsed a code of practice drafted by editors. Seven of its members are editors of national and local newspapers and magazines while nine, including the Chairman are drawn from other fields.

Sources: *The Cambridge Bibliography of English Literature,* Vol.III pp.797–8, lists all press directories, pp. 798–846 lists all newspapers and magazines. *The History of The Times,* Pt II, pp.1130–36 gives a chart of the metropolitan morning and evening press from 1884–1947. There are several press directories which cover all or part of the period: *T.B.Browne's Advertiser's ABC,* 1900–1932; *Sell's Dictionary of the World's Press, 1900–1921* (including a *Who's Who* of notabilities of the British Press in 1914–21 editions); *Mitchell's Newspaper Press Directory* (became *Benn's* in 1946), 1900–61; *Willing's Press Guide, 1900–.* PEP: *Report on the British Press* (1938); *Report of the Royal Commission on the Press* (Cmd. 7700 of 1949, Minutes of Evidence, Cmd. 7317 of 1948); *Report of the Royal Commission on the Press* (Cmnd. 1811 of 1962); N.Kaldor and R.Silverman, *A Statistical Analysis of Advertising Expenditure and of the Revenue of the Press* (1948); A.P.Wadsworth, 'Newspaper Circulations' (in *Proceedings of the Manchester Statistical Society* 1954). J.L.Hammond, *C.P.Scott of the Manchester Guardian* (1934); J.W.Robertson Scott, *The Life and Death of a Newspaper (The Pall Mall Gazette)*(1952); A.Gollin, *The Observer and J.L.Garvin* (1960); S.Jenkins, *The Market for Glory: Fleet Street Ownership in the Twentieth Century* (1986); F.Williams, *Dangerous Estate* (1957); C.Seymour-Ure, *Politics, the Press and the Public* (1968); C.Seymour-Ure, *The Political Impact of the Mass Media* (1974); C.Seymour-Ure, *The British Press and Broadcasting since 1945* (1991); J.Whale, *The Politics of the Media* (1977); J.Tunstall and M.Palmer, *Media Moguls* (1991); Press Council Annual Reports, *The Press and the People*; H.P.Levy, *The Press Council* (1967). *Hutton Readership Surveys,* J.W.Hobson and Harry Henry, came out annually between 1947 and 1955. See also *Royal Commission on the Press* (Cmnd. 6810) and companion papers Cmnd. 6811–16; R.Harris, *Gotcha: The Media, The Government and the Falklands Crisis* (1983); D.McQuail, *Review of Sociological Writing on the Press* (1976): C. Seymour-Ure, Oliver Boyd Barrett and Jeremy Tunstall, *Studies on the Press* (1977); J. Tunstall, *The Media in Britain* (1983); S.Jenkins, *Newspapers* (1980); R.Snoddy, *The Good, the Bad, and the Unacceptable* (1993).

XXI

BROADCASTING

The British Broadcasting Corporation

The British Broadcasting Company Ltd was formed by some 200 manufacturers and share-holders on 18 Oct 22, registered on 15 Dec 22, and received its licence on 18 Jan 23. A system of paid licences for owners of radio receivers was started in 1922. London, Manchester, Birmingham, and Newcastle stations began to operate in November and December, 1922. This was followed by the establishment of the *British Broadcasting Corporation* under Royal Charter (20 Dec 26), which came into operation on 1 Jan 27. It was to be a public service body 'acting in the national interest' and financed by licence fees paid by all owners of radio receivers. (A formal agreement with the Postmaster-General had been drawn up on 9 Nov 26.) Under the royal charter the B.B.C. was granted a licence for ten years and was to be directed by a board of governors nominated by the government. The charter was renewed and modified 1 Jan 37, 1 Jan 47, 1 Jul 52, 30 Jul 64. It was extended until 31 July 1979 in 1976 (Cmnd. 6581). In Jul 1979 it was extended for a further period until 31 Jul 1981, when it was replaced by a new charter (Cmnd 8313) to last until 31 Dec 1996. On 6 Jul 94 the National Heritage Secretary P.Brooke announced in the White Paper 'The Future of the BBC – Serving the Nation, Competing Worldwide' (Cm. 2621) that the Charter would be renewed for another ten years until 2006, and that the licence fee would remain the basis of BBC funding for at least the next five years. In Oct 98 the Secretary of State for Culture, Media and Sport C.Smith announced a review of the role and funding of the B.B.C., but confirmed that the licence fee would continue until 2006.

British Broadcasting Company, 1923–1926

Chairman: Ld Gainford

Managing Director: (Sir) J. Reith
(initially **General Manager**)

Board members: G. Isaacs *(Marconi)*, Sir W. Noble *(General Electric)*, B. Binyon *(Radio Communication Co.)*, H. Pease *(Western Electric)*, A. McKinstry *(Metropolitan Vickers)*, W. Burnham *(Burndept)*, J. Gray *(British Thomson-Houston Co.)*, Sir W. Bull *(M.P.)*.

British Broadcasting Corporation, 1927–

Board of Governors

	Chairmen		*Vice-Chairman*
1 Jan 27	E of Clarendon	1 Jan 27	Ld Gainford
2 Jun 30	J. Whitley	1 Jan 33	R. Norman
28 Mar 35	Vt Bridgeman	25 Oct 35	H. Brown
3 Oct 35	R. Norman	8 Jun 37	C. Millis
19 Apr 39	Sir A. Powell	1 Jan 47	Marchioness of Reading
1 Jan 47	Ld Inman	7 Jan 51	Ld Tedder
9 Jun 47	Vt Simon	1 Jul 54	Sir P. Morris
1 Aug 52	Sir A. Cadogan	1 Jul 60	Sir J. Duff
1 Dec 57	Sir A. fforde	19 Sep 65	Ld Fulton
1 Feb 64	Sir J. Duff *(acting)*	11 Jun 66	R. Lusty
14 May 64	Ld Normanbrook	31 Jul 67	Ld Fulton
1 Sep 67	Ld Hill of Luton	1 Jan 68	R. Lusty
1 Jan 73	Sir M. Swann	15 Feb 68	Ld Fulton
1 Aug 80	G. Howard (Ld)	12 Nov 70	Lady Plowden
1 Aug 83	S. Young	26 Jun 75	M. Bonham Carter
29 Aug 86	*(vacant)*	1 Aug 81	Sir W. Rees-Mogg
6 Nov 86	M. Hussey	1 Aug 86	Ld Barnett
1 Apr 96	Sir C. Bland	1 Aug 93	Ld Cocks
		1 Aug 98	Lady Young of Old Scone

Governors

1927–31	Sir G.Nairne		1968–71	Sir R. Bellenger
1927–32	M. Rendall		1968–72	P. Wilson
1927–32	Mrs P. Snowden (Vtess)		1968–73	T. Jackson
1932–36	H. Brown		1968–71	Sir L. Constantine (Ld)
1933–35	Vt Bridgeman		1968–73	Dame M. Green
1933–37	Mary Hamilton		1969–71	Sir H. Greene
1935–39	Lady Bridgeman		1971–76	R. Allan (Ld)
1935–39	H.Fisher		1972–79	R. Fuller
1937–39	Sir I. Fraser		1972–76	T. Morgan
1937–39	J. Mallon		1972–80	G. Howard
1938–39	Margery Fry		1973–76	V. Feather (Ld)
(From 1939–41 the Board was reduced to two			1973–78	Sir D. Greenhill (Ld)
members, the Chairman and Deputy Chairman)			1974–81	Stella Clarke
1941–46	Lady V. Bonham-Carter		1976–81	P. Chappell
1941–46	Sir I. Fraser		1976–82	Ld Allen
1941–46	J. Mallon		1977–82	Lady Serota
1941–46	A. Mann		1978–85	Sir J. Johnston
1941–46	H. Nicolson		1979–84	C. Longuet-Higgins
1946–49	Barbara Ward		1981–83	P. Moons
1946–49	G. Lloyd		1981–83	S. Young
1946–49	Sir R. Peck		1981–88	Jocelyn Barrow
1946–50	E. Whitfield		1982–87	Daphne Park
1946–50	Marchioness of Reading		1982–87	Sir J. Boyd
1947–52	J. Adamson		1983–88	M. McAlpine
1950–54	Ld Tedder		1984–89	Lady Parkes
1950–52	Ld Clydesmuir		1985–87	E of Harewood
1951–52	F. Williams		1985–90	Sir C. Keeble
1950–56	Barbara Wootton		1988–93	J. Roberts
1952–54	Sir P. Morris		1988–98	B. Jordan
1951–55	C. Stedeford		1988–93	(Lady) P. D. James
1952–56	Lady Rhys Williams		1988–93	K. Oates
1954–59	Ld Rochdale		1990–95	Jane Glover
1955–60	Sir E. Benthall		1990–95	Shawhar Sadeque
1956–61	Thelma Cazalet-Keir		1990–98	Ld N. Gordon-Lennox
1956–62	Dame F. Hancock		1993–98	Margaret Spurr
1959–60	Sir J. Duff		1994–99	Janet Cohen
1960–62	E of Halsbury		1995–	Sir D. Scholey
1960–65	R. Lusty		1995–	R. Eyre
1961–66	G. Cooke		1995–	A. White
1962–68	Dame A. Godwin		1998–	Dame P. Neville-Jones
1962–67	Sir A. Clarke		1998–	R. Sondhi
1966–67	Ld Fulton		1998–	T. Young
1966–68	J. Trower		1999–	Heather Rabbatts
1967–73	Sir R. Murray			

Governors appointed to represent national interests

	N. Ireland		*Scotland*		*Wales*
1952	Sir H. Mulholland	1952	Ld Clydesmuir	1952	Ld Macdonald
1958	J. McKee	1955	T. Johnston	1960	Mrs R. Jones
1962	Sir P. Pim	1956	E of Balfour	1965	G. Williams
1968	Ld Dunleath	1960	Sir D. Milne	1971	G. Hughes
1973	W. O'Hara	1965	Lady Baird	1979	A. Roberts
1978	Lady Faulkner	1971	Lady Avonside	1986	J. Parry
1985	J. Kincade	1976	A. Thompson	1992	G. Jones
1991	Sir K. Bloomfield	1979	(Sir) R. Young	1996	R. Jones
1999	F. Monds	1984	W. Peat		
		1989	Sir G. Hills		
		1994	N. Drummond		
		1999	Sir R. Smith		

Director-General

1 Jan 27	Sir J. Reith	17 Jul 52	B. Nicholls	1 Aug 82	A. Milne
1 Oct 38	F.Ogilvie		*(acting)*	29 Jan 87	*(vacant)*
1 Jan 42	Sir C. Graves	1 Dec 52	Sir I. Jacob	26 Feb 87	(Sir) M. Checkland
	& R. Foot	31 Dec 59	(Sir) H. Greene	23 Dec 92	(Sir) (Ld) J. Birt
24 Jun 43	R. Foot	1 Apr 68	(Sir) C. Curran	31 Jan 00	G. Dyke
31 Mar 44	(Sir) W. Haley	1 Oct 77	(Sir) I. Trethowan		

B.B.C. Radio

The B.B.C. originally offered one basic radio service, known as the National Programme, together with variant Regional Services. In 1939 these services were all replaced by a single Home Service; the Forces Programme, providing a lighter alternative, began in 1940. In 1945 Regional Home Services, as variants of the Home Service, were restarted, and the Light Programme replaced the Forces Programme. In 1946 the Third Programme was introduced to provide a second alternative service. Very high frequency (VHF) transmissions began in 1955, in order to improve the quality and coverage of the existing services. In 1964 the Music Programme was added, using the Third Programme wavelengths in the daytime, and in 1967 a fourth network came into being to provide a pop music service replacing the offshore 'pirate' stations; this was called Radio 1, and the existing national services were renamed Radio 2 (Light Programme), Radio 3 (Third and Music Programmes) and Radio 4 (Home Service).

In 1970 the radio networks were reorganised as 'generic' services following publication of the B.B.C.'s proposals in *Broadcasting in the Seventies*, and the English regional radio services were then gradually wound down, though the regional centres continued to provide programmes for the networks. The regional radio broadcasts in the three National Regions started to develop as autonomous services with the opening of Radio Ulster in 1975. In 1978 there was a major reorganisation of the radio frequencies used for the national networks, and Radio 4 became available throughout the United Kingdom on the long-wave band. This enabled the national services – Radio Scotland, Radio Wales, Radio Cymru (Welsh language, on VHF only) and Radio Ulster – to become fully independent of Radio 4. Regular network services of sports programming were carried on Radio 2 and, for cricket, on Radio 3. Radios 3 and 4 carried Open University programmes on their VHF-FM bands and Radio 4 also carried Schools and Continuing Education output. In 1978 also the B.B.C. began regular broadcasting on radio of recorded material from Parliamentary proceedings (see p.188). On 27 Aug 90 a fifth network, Radio 5, began broadcasting using medium wave frequencies to carry youth and education programmes, and take over sports broadcasting from Radio 2. In Mar 1994 Radio 5 was relaunched as Radio 5 Live, a news and sport network. Test Match Special was broadcast on Radio 4's long wave frequency.

B.B.C. Local Radio

The B.B.C. first began a limited experiment in Local Radio in 1967. The following stations broadcast in England and the Channel Islands.

Radio Berkshire	1992–96	Radio Derby	1971
Radio Bristol	1970	Radio Devon	1983
Radio Cambridgeshire	1982	Dorset FM	1993–96
Radio Cleveland (formerly Radio Teesside)	1970	Radio Durham	1968–72
Radio Cornwall	1983	Radio Essex	1986
Radio Cumbria (formerly Radio Carlisle)	1975	Radio Furness	1982
CWR (Coventry & Warwickshire Radio)	1990–95	Radio Gloucestershire	1988

GLR (formerly Radio London)	1970	Radio Shropshire	1985
GMR (formerly Radio Manchester)	1970	Radio Solent	1970
Radio Guernsey	1982	Somerset Sound	1988
Radio Hereford & Worcester	1989	Southern Counties Radio	
Radio Humberside	1971	(formerly Radio Surrey and Radio Sussex)	1994
Radio Jersey	1982	Radio Stoke	1968
Radio Kent (formerly Radio Medway)	1970	Radio Suffolk	1990
Radio Lancashire (formerly Radio Blackburn)	1971	Radio Surrey	1991–94
Radio Leeds	1968	Radio Sussex (formerly Radio Brighton)	1968–94
Radio Leicester	1967	Three Counties Radio	
Radio Lincolnshire	1980	(formerly Radio Bedfordshire)	1985
Radio Merseyside	1967	Radio WM (formerly Radio Birmingham)	1970
Radio Newcastle	1971	Wiltshire Sound	1989
Radio Norfolk	1980	Radio York	1983
Radio Northampton	1982		
Radio Nottingham	1968		
Radio Oxford	1970–96		
Radio Sheffield	1967		

BBC Television

On 2 Nov 1936 the first scheduled public service television was started from Alexandra Palace. The service was suspended from September 1939 until June 1946. The first stations outside London, in the Midlands and the North, began transmitting in 1949 and 1951 respectively. By 1966, with more than 100 transmitting stations, BBC Television in balck and white was within the range of more than 99 per cent of the population of the United Kingdom. In April 1964 a second BBC Channel was opened in the London area. In 1967 it began broadcasting in colour; by this time it was available to more than two-thirds of the population of the U.K. In 1969 colour transmissions were started on BBC1. BBC1 began breakfast-time broadcasting in 1983. In Nov 1997 BBC News 24 was launched – a news service initially available only on cable. In Sep 1998 BBC Parliament, providing live coverage of parliamentary proceedings, went on air (it succeeded a previous private venture, the Parliamentary Channel). Also in Sep 1998, the BBC launched BBC Choice, an entertainment channel available only on digital broadcasting systems. All of these were funded by the licence fee.

World Service television (BBC World) began broadcasting in Mar 1991, using local transmitters and satellites to reach a large audience initially principally in south and southeast Asia. It is self-financing, and the BBC has become increasingly involved through its commercial arm BBC Worldwide in channels financed by advertising and subscription and aimed primarily at overseas audiences. BBC Prime (an entertainment channel) went on air in 1996, and BBC America in Mar 1998. In 1997 six channels were launched as a joint venture with the American cable television channel Flextech.

Broadcast Receiving Licences and BBC Expenditure

Since 1922 the BBC has been financed mainly by the issue of licences. In 1939–45 all licence revenue went to the Government and the BBC was financed by an annual grant-in-aid. The external services have continued to be financed in this way. Except for 1950–51 the Treasury retained part of the licence fee every year until 1961.

The cost of the Licence

Year	Sound only	Sound/black & white	Colour
1922	10s	–	–
1946	£1	£2	–
1954	£1	£3	–
1957	£1	£4	–
1965	£1 5s	£5	–
1968	£1 5s	£5	£10
1969	£1 5s	£6	£11
1971	–	£7	£12
1975	–	£8	£18
1977	–	£9	£21
1978	–	£10	£25
1979	–	£12	£34
1981	–	£15	£46
1985	–	£18	£58
1988	–	£21	£62.50
1989	–	£22	£66
1990	–	£24	£71
1991	–	£25.50	£77
1992	–	£26.50	£80
1993	–	£27.50	£83
1994	–	£28	£84.50
1995	–	£28.50	£86.50
1996	–	£30	£89.50
1997	–	£30.50	£91.50
1998	–	£32.50	£97.50
1999	–	£33.50	£101

	Total Licences issued 000s	Sound only 000s	Sound & Monochrome TV 000s	Colour TV 000s	Expenditure on revenue account £000s	
1925	1,654	1,654	–	–	–	
1927	2,270	2,264	–	–	902	
1930	3,092	3,076	–	–	1,224	
1935	7,012	6,970	–	–	2,473	
1940	8,951	8,898	–	–	4,350	
1945	9,710	9,663	–	–	9,001	
					Home	External
1947	10,778	10,713	15	–	7,273	3,878
1950	12,219	11,819	344	–	9,579	4,471
1955	13,980	9,414	4,504	–	17,964	5,093
1960	15,005	4,480	10,470	–	30,560	6,408
1965	16,047	2,759	13,253	–	55,642	8,499
1970	18,184	2,279	15,609	273	81,134	10,565
1975	17,701	–	10,120	7,580	152,771	19,625
1980	18,285	–	5,383	12,902	363,400	40,100
1985	18,716	–	2,896	15,820	808,700	83,900
1990	19,645	–	1,681	17,964	1,261,900	132,500
1995	21,700	–	600	20,500	1,756,500	189,900
1997	22,300	–	400	21,300	2,044,300	184,600

The difference between the total and other licences column is explained by the issue of free licences to the blind.
The expenditure figures from 1940 onwards are for the year ending the following 31 Mar. The figures from 1947 onwards are for operational expenditure only.

SOURCE:- *BBC Annual Report & Accounts. Annual Abstract of Statistics.*

Independent Broadcasting

The Independent Television Authority was set up by the Postmaster-General under section 1 (3) of the *Television Act, 1954,* on 4 Aug 1954 for a period of ten years. The Authority was to licence programme contracting companies and to regulate their output. The whole of the finance of Independent Television was to depend on advertising revenue though the Act specifically prohibited the 'sponsoring' of programmes by advertisers. The first Independent Television programmes were transmitted on 22 Sep 1955. The ITA became the Independent Broadcasting Authority (IBA) in 1973, reflecting the introduction of Independent Local Radio, and the Independent Television Commission (ITC) in 1991, when the Radio Authority was established. The ITC licenses and regulates all commercial television services, terrestrial, cable and satellite, teletext, television advertising and sponsorship, and programme output. The following Acts have been passed significantly affecting Independent Broadcasting:

Television Act, 1963. This extended the life of the I.T.A. until 1976.

Television Act, 1964. This consolidated the *Television Acts of 1954 and 1963* and increased the I.T.A.'s power over programmes and advertising.

Sound Broadcasting Act, 1972. This Act renamed the I.T.A. the Independent Broadcasting Authority and extended its functions to include the provision of local commercial sound broadcasting services.

Independent Broadcasting Authority Act, 1973. This consolidated the *Television Act, 1964* and the *Sound Broadcasting Act, 1972.*

Independent Broadcasting Authority Act, 1974. This Act made provision for 'additional payments' to be made by television programme contractors to the I.B.A.

Independent Broadcasting Authority Act (No 2), 1974. This extended the I.B.A.'s life until July 1979.

Independent Broadcasting Authority Act, 1978. This further extended the I.B.A. until the end of 1981.

Independent Broadcasting Authority Act, 1979. This Act gave the I.B.A. responsibility for establishing transmitters for a fourth television channel.

Broadcasting Act, 1980. This Act extended the life of the I.B.A. until 1996. It laid down the operating condition of the fourth television channel, which was to be separately established in Wales by the Welsh Fourth Channel Authority, and also established a Broadcasting Complaints Commission.

Broadcasting Act, 1981. This consolidated the *Independent Broadcasting Authority Acts, 1973, 1974, and 1978,* and the *Broadcasting Act, 1980.*

Cable and Broadcasting Act, 1984. This made provision for the establishment of a Cable Authority to provide cable programmes and amended the *Broadcasting Act, 1981,* to provide for the establishment of a Satellite Broadcasting Board.

Broadcasting Act, 1987. This extended the period of the contracts between the IBA and the ITV companies, now expiring on 31 Dec 1992, to give more time for the consideration of a new licensing system.

Broadcasting Act, 1990. This replaced the Independent Broadcasting Authority and the Cable Authority with the Independent Television Commission and the Radio Authority, and laid down new procedures for licensing and regulating commercially funded television services. The most important consequence was that subject to meeting a quality threshold, regional TV licences would be awarded to the highest bidder.

Broadcasting Act, 1996. This amended and replaced certain elements of the 1990 Act, and established a regime for the introduction of digital terrestrial television. It also liberalised rules on media ownership, and merged the Broadcasting Standards Council with the Broadcasting Complaints Commission.

Independent Television Authority 1954–1972
and Independent Broadcasting Authority 1972–90

	Chairman		*Director-General*
31 Mar 55	Sir K. Clark	1 Oct 54	Sir R. Fraser
8 Nov 57	Sir I. Kirkpatrick	15 Oct 70	(Sir) B. Young
6 Nov 62	Sir J. Carmichael (acting)	31 Oct 82	J. Whitney
1 Jul 63	Ld Hill of Luton	1 Apr 89	Shirley Littler (Lady)
1 Sep 67	Ld Aylestone		
1 Apr 75	Lady Plowden		
1 Jan 81	Ld Thomson of Monifieth		
1 Jan 89	(Sir) G. Russell		

Independent Television Commission, 1991–

	Chairman		*Chief Executive*
1 Jan 91	Sir G. Russell	1 Jan 91	D. Glencross
1 Jan 97	Sir R. Biggam	5 Mar 95	P. Rogers

Radio Authority, 1991–

	Chairman		*Chief Executive*
1 Jan 91	Ld Chalfont	1 Jan 91	P. Baldwin
1 Jan 95	Sir P. Gibbings	1 Jul 95	T. Stoller

Channel 3 – ITV Programme Contracting Companies

The following programme companies have held ITV franchises in the UK. In 1964 all were re-appointed to provide programmes until July 1968. On 11 June 1967 new contractors were announced to operate from 30 July 1968 to 29 July 1974. In 1972 the Authority made plain its intention to renew the existing contracts with the programme companies for two years from 31 July 1974, subject to satisfactory performance and subject to review of rentals and areas. A further reallocation of contracts was announced on 28 Dec 1980, and took effect in Jan 1982. The *Broadcasting Act, 1990*, laid down a new procedure under which the newly established Independent Television Commission awarded licences to the highest bidder, subject to programme proposals meeting a quality threshold, and the proposals being considered financially sustainable. In 1992 Yorkshire Television merged with Tyne Tees, although they retained separate identities on air. In Nov 1993 the Government announced a limited relaxation of the ITV ownership rules, enabling one ITV company to hold two large regional licences, except in London. A number of proposed mergers were subsequently announced.

On air	*Off air*	*Company*	*Franchise Areas*
22 Sep 55	29 Jul 68	Ass. Rediffusion	London (weekday)
24 Sep 55	28 Jul 68	Associated (ATV)	London (weekend)
17 Feb 56	31 Dec 81	Associated (ATV)	Midlands (weekday)
18 Feb 56	28 Jul 68	ABC	Midlands (weekend)
3 May 56 –		Granada	N.W.England (weekday)
5 May 56	28 Jul 68	ABC	N.W.England (weekend)
31 Aug 57 –		Scottish (STV)	Central Scotland
14 Jan 58	3 Mar 68	TWW	Wales & W. England
30 Aug 58	31 Dec 81	Southern	South of England
15 Jan 59 –		Tyne-Tees	N.E.England

On air	Off air	Company	Franchise Areas
27 Oct 59 –		Anglia	East of England
31 Oct 59 –		Ulster	Northern Ireland
29 Apr 61	11 Aug 81	Westward	S.W. England
1 Sep 61 –		Border	The Borders
30 Sep 61 –		Grampian	N.E. of Scotland
1 Sep 62 –		Channel	Channel Islands
14 Sep 62	26 Jan 64	Wales (W & N)	West & North Wales
4 Mar 68 –		Harlech (HTV)	Wales & W. England
29 Jul 68 –		Yorkshire	Yorkshire
30 Jul 68	31 Dec 92	Thames	London (weekday)
2 Aug 68 –		London Weekend (LWT)	London (weekend)
12 Aug 81	31 Dec 92	TSW	S. W. England
1 Jan 81	31 Dec 92	TVS	South of England
1 Jan 81 –		Central	Midlands
1 Feb 83	31 Dec 92	TV-am	(breakfast)
1 Jan 93 –		Carlton	London (weekday)
1 Jan 93 –		GMTV	(breakfast)
1 Jan 93 –		Meridian	South of England
1 Jan 93 –		Westcountry	S. W. England

The ITV Network Centre

Founded in 1993, following the 1990 *Broadcasting Act*, the Network Centre is an organisation responsible for commissioning new programmes for the network, either from independent production companies or from ITV companies. As well as commissioning all networked programmes, the Centre is also responsible for preparing the network's programme schedule, although ultimate control over scheduling rests with the companies themselves. The programme budget in 1997 was £800m. A further £200m was spent by the companies on regional programmes.

Chief Executive

Jul 92–Oct 95   A. Quinn

Network Director

Oct 92–Oct 97   M. Plantin

Chief Executive

Oct 97–   R. Eyre

Note: Due to restructuring, M. Plantin took control of the centre on A. Quinn's retirement in 1995. R. Eyre took full control on M. Plantin's departure.

Channel Four

The fourth television channel in the UK is provided by Channel Four Television Corporation in England, Scotland and Northern Ireland, and in Wales by S4C.

The Channel 4 Television Company was established as a subsidiary of the IBA under the *Broadcasting Act, 1980.* It went on air on 2 Nov 82. It became an independent corporation as a result of the *Broadcasting Act, 1990,* selling its own advertising airtime from 1 Jan 93.

Chairman

1981	E. Dell
1987	Sir R. Attenborough
1992	Sir M. Bishop
1997	V. Treves

S4C

The S4C Authority, Sianel Pedwar Cymru, the regulatory body for the fourth channel in Wales, was also established under the *Broadcasting Act, 1980*. S4C began transmission on 1 Nov 1982.

Chairman

1981	Sir G. Daniel	1992	I. P. Edwards
1986	J. Davies	1998	Elan Stephens

Channel 5

The licence to provide the fifth channel was awarded to Channel Five Broadcasting in Oct 95. Like the Channel 3 licences, it was awarded by competitive tender for a ten year term from the start of the service which commenced on 30 Mar 97. Before the commencement of the service, Channel 5 Broadcasting was required to make arrangements to retune domestic video equipment to eliminate interference where those devices were affected by its transmissions. Around six million homes were affected. Channel 5 is regulated by the ITC.

	Chairman		*Chief Executive*
1997	G. Dyke	1997	D. Elstein
1999	R. Sautter		

Finances of Independent Broadcasting, 1955–90

(£ 000s)

Year	ITV revenue	ILR Revenue	ITA/IBA/ITC	Govt. Levy
1955			55	–
1956	13,024	–	500	–
1957	31,986	–	1,702	–
1958	48,671	–	2,284	–
1959	58,359	–	2,871	–
1960	76,960	–	3,757	–
1961	93,276	–	4,213	–
1962	99,794	–	4,693	–
1963	62,931	–	5,464	–
1964	74,433	–	5,623	–
1965	82,840	–	7,246	8,350
1966	85,825	–	8,381	21,186
1967	91,776	–	8,697	22,855
1968	98,759	–	8,697	24,811
1969	97,540	–	7,556	25,779
1970	94,742	–	6,936	26,102
1971	108,634	–	7,793	24,811
1972	134,221	–	11,248	10,839
1973	160,831	–	13,054	18,243
1974	149,245	–	13,641	22,763
1975	176,532	8,535	14,897	19,163
1976	230,807	14,700	15,614	22,162
1977	299,887	23,100	17,876	47,878
1978	363,005	29,845	21,304	65,388
1979	346,796	44,587	22,317	70,018
1980	529,311	44,858	24,443	45,380
1981	611,223	50,824	30,243	55,495
1982	697,170	60,748	36,441	59,110
1983	824,417	70,800	53,769	38,673
1984	912,265	75,700	58,253	28,321
1985	982,603	72,100	62,595	41,409
1986	1,183,000	79,006	65,331	22,090
1987	1,325,871	99,400	68,052	76,225
1988	1,508,400	125,000	71,531	87,553
1989	1,613,537	145,000	74,919	100,139
1990	1,613,672	143,400	74,759	108,298

Source: B. MacDonald, *Broadcasting in the United Kingdom – a guide to information sources* (2nd ed., 1993).

Finances of Independent Television, 1991–

Net Advertising Revenue (£m.)

	ITV	C4	S4C	TVam/GMTV	Total	Levy/Tender payment
1991	1,344	250	3.5	74	1,672	114
1992	1,411	242	3	75	1,731	69
1993	1,400	328	4	64	1,796	369
1994	1,501	391	6	74	1,972	381
1995	1,585	446	8	80	2,119	397
1996	1,658	489	8	77	2,256	412
1997	1,682	510	9	71	2,272	423

Sponsorship of terrestrial television has risen from £9 million in 1992 to £31 million in 1997.

Note: Exchequer levy ceased in 1992. Tender payments, which are the price paid to the Treasury for Channel 3, Channel 5, teletext and cable licences, are made up of two parts: percentage of qualifying revenue, set by the ITC, and the cash bid each company made for their licence, index linked and payable annually.

Source: *ITC Annual Report and Accounts, 1992–*.

Cable Television

There were experiments with cable television as early as the 1950s, when localised relay operators offered wired television in areas of poor reception. In 1972 community cable television services were established in Greenwich, Bristol, Swindon, Sheffield and Wellingborough, but most turned out not to be financially viable. In 1983 a Government White Paper took up the recommendations of the Hunt Committee and proposed granting interim licences for new cable services providing new programming material, financed by private enterprise. This was the basis of the *Cable and Broadcasting Act, 1984,* which established the Cable Authority as the regulatory body. Under the *Broadcasting Act, 1990,* the ITC took over these functions with effect from 1 Jan 1991. There are restrictions on ownership of cable operators which bar existing terrestrial TV companies or political or religious organisations from gaining control.

Cable Authority, 1984–90

	Chairman		*Director-General*
1984	R. Burton	1984	J. Davey

Cable Television in Britain since 1986

	Homes Passed	Homes Connected	Penetration (%)
1986	994,822	143,850	14.5
1987	1,251,353	207,938	16.6
1988	1,415,778	263,645	18.8
1989	1,513,557	287,887	19.0
1990	1,707,228	347,410	20.3
1991	2,096,194	429,577	20.5
1992	2,431,050	552,105	22.7
1993	3,273,310	658,884	20.1
1994	4,178,910	871,409	20.9
1995	5,562,513	1,185,553	21.3
1996	7,587,380	1,618,956	21.3
1997	9,856,004	2,158,409	21.9
1998	11,742,370	2,652,199	22.5

Note: This includes Narrowband and Broadband cable.
Source: JICCAR, ITC.

Satellite Television

The origins of direct broadcasting by satellite can be traced back to the first live television transmissions by the Telstar satellite on 11 Jul 62. But the development of a service direct into people's homes was hampered by the limitations of the technology and the large capital cost.

Chronology of development of Direct Broadcast by Satellite

Nov 82	Home Office accepts Part Report's findings on satellite system technology.
Jul 84	BBC and ITV companies are joined by other companies in 'Club of 21' to plan for DBS services.
Jun 85	Satellite Broadcasting Board tells Government the consortium cannot proceed, due to prohibitive cost of using British-made satellite stipulated by Government.
Jul 85	S.B.B. wound up after less than a year.
Apr 86	I.B.A. advertises for 15 year contract for DBS on system of contractor's choice.
Dec 86	British Satellite Broadcasting wins contract, proposing to transmit from the Marcopolo high-power satellite using the latest D-MAC transmission technology and 'squarial' home dish aerials. Major shareholders include Anglia, Granada and Pearson.
Jun 88	R. Murdoch announces plans for Sky Television on Astra satellite.
Feb 89	Sky Television begins transmission.
Apr 90	B.S.B. begins DBS transmissions.
Nov 90	B.S.B. and Sky announce merger to form British Sky Broadcasting (BSkyB).

Digital Television

The legislative framework for digital television was set out in the *Broadcasting Act 1996*, enabling the ITC to license and regulate commercial digital services. Digital signals allow far more information to be transmitted, meaning better reception, more channels, easier encryption, and the potential for interactive services such as home shopping and home banking. Analogue television will eventually be phased out, although no date has been set for discontinuing it. In Jun 97, the ITC awarded British Digital Broadcasting plc, now called OnDigital, 3 terrestrial broadcasting licences. It began broadcasting on 15 Nov 98. The ITC also awarded licences to ITV, Channel 4, SDN (S4C digital service), and Channel 5.

On 1 Oct 98 BSkyB launched Digital Satellite Broadcasting. Digital cable followed in 1999.

Channel Share of Viewing
(based on all transmission hours for all areas receiving TV)

	BBC1	BBC2	ITV	C4	Others		BBC1	BBC2	ITV	C4	Others
1956[a]	39		61			1970	48	4	48		
1957	32		68			1971	45	7	48		
1958	35		65			1972	47	7	46		
1959	35		65			1973	43	8	49		
1960	37		63			1974	45	7	48		
1961	38		62			1975	46	8	46		
1962	47		53			1976	49	8	43		
1963	48		52			1977	45	8	47		
1964	45		55			1978	45	8	47		
1965	45		55			1979	46	11	43		
1966	49		51			1980	46	11	43		
1967	49		51			-----					
1968[b]	54		46			1981[c]	39	11	50		
1969	47	4	49			1982	38	12	50		

[a]Figures from April 1996 onwards when ITV started transmission
[b]Figures from April 1969 onwards when Channel 2 started transmission
[c]Figures from July 1981 onwards when BARB took over

	BBC1	BBC2	ITV	C4	Others		BBC1	BBC2	ITV	C4	Others
1983	37	11	48	4		1991	35	10	42	10	4
1984	36	19	48	5		1992	34	10	41	11	5
1985	35	11	47	7		1993	33	10	40	11	6
1986	36	11	45	8		1994	32	11	37	11	9
1987	37	12	43	8		1995	32	11	37	11	9
1988	38	11	42	9		1996	33	12	35	11	10
1989	39	11	42	9		1997	31	12	33	11	15
1990	38	10	43	9		1998	30	11	32	10	17

Source: JICTAR (to 1980); BARB (From July 1981)

Independent Local Radio

Under the *Sound Broadcasting Act, 1972*, the IBA (from 1991 the Radio Authority) were given the responsibility for issuing licences to independent local radio stations. They also regulated programme and advertising output. The first stations to go on air were Capital Radio and LBC in London in Oct 73. The first outside London was Radio Clyde in Glasgow in Dec 73. By early 99 there were 170 ILR stations in England, 25 in Scotland, 9 in Wales and 6 in Northern Ireland.

Independent National Radio

The Radio Authority has licensed the following national radio stations, using frequencies given up by the BBC. They are

7 Sep 92	Classic FM
30 Apr 93	Virgin 1215
14 Feb 95	Talk Radio

Independent Radio News (IRN) has since October 1973 provided a news service, available to all the independent local radio stations.

Broadcasting Complaints Commission 1981–96

This was established under the *Broadcasting Act, 1980* (amended by the *Broadcasting Act, 1981,* and the *Cable and Broadcasting Act, 1984*, and replaced by the *Broadcasting Act, 1990*) to consider and adjudicate on complaints of unfair treatment or invasion of privacy by BBC, ITC or Radio Authority licensed services. Its findings are published in the *Radio Times*, *TV Times* etc. where appropriate, or broadcast on air.

Chairman

1981	Lady Pike
1985	Sir T. Skyrme
1987	Lady Anglesey
1992	Brigid Wells
1992	P. Pilkington
1996	Jane Leighton

Broadcasting Standards Council 1988–96

This was established by the Home Secretary in 1988, and put on a statutory footing by the *Broadcasting Act, 1990*, to consider standards in portrayal of sex and violence, and matters of taste and decency on TV, radio and video.

Chairman

1988	Sir W. (Ld) Rees-Mogg
1993	Lady Howe

Broadcasting Standards Commission 1997–

This was established by the *Broadcasting Act, 1996*, to take over the work of the Broadcasting Complaints Commission and the Broadcasting Standards Council.

Chairman

1997	Lady Howe
1999	Lord Holme

Inquiries into Broadcasting

Chairman	Set up	Reported	Cd.No.	Cost
Sir F. Sykes	Apr 23	Aug 23	951	£320
E of Crawford	Aug 25	Mar 26	2599	£106
Ld Selsdon	May 34	Jan 35	4793	£965
Vt Ullswater	Apr 35	Feb 36	5091	£564
Ld Hankey	Sep 43	Mar 45	Non-parl.	–
Ld Beveridge	Jun 49	Jan 51	8116	£15,415
Sir H. Pilkington	Jul 60	Jun 62	1753	£45,450
Ld Annan	Apr 74	Mar 77	6753	£315,000
Ld Hunt of Tanworth	Apr 82	Oct 82	8679	£47,388
Sir A. Part	Jul 82	Nov 82	8751	£34,625
A. Peacock	May 85	Jul 86	9824	£268,761
J. Sadler	Feb 89	Mar 91	1436	£215,000
G. Davies	Nov 98	Aug 99		

Sources: A. Briggs, *The BBC: The First Fifty Years* (1985); A. Briggs, *The History of Broadcasting in the United Kingdom* (5 vols, 1961–95); J. Cain, *The BBC: 70 Years of Broadcasting* (1992); A. Davidson, *Under the Hammer: The Inside Story of the 1991 ITV Franchise Battle* (1992); B. Henry, *British Television Advertising: The First Thirty Years* (1986); B. MacDonald, *Broadcasting in the United Kingdom: A Guide to Information Sources* (1993); N. Reville, *Broadcasting: A Guide to the New Law* (1991); B. Sendall, *Independent Television in Britain* (vols. 1 & 2, 1982 & 1983); J. Potter, *Independent Television in Britain* (vols. 3 & 4, 1989 & 1990); P. Bonner with L. Aston, *Independent Television in Britain* (vol. 5, 1998).

XXII

RELIGION

Church Membership Statistics

Extreme caution should be observed in making use of church membership statistics, as no entirely reliable sources exist giving information about membership or attendance. The last reasonably authoritative figures of religious affiliations in Britain were taken from the 1851 census, though even then there was no compulsion to answer the questions on religion. Since then no census has included questions on religious affiliation. Strictly comparable figures are impossible to obtain for church membership and church attendance since 1900. Indeed, there are at least three equally sustainable measures of affiliation to churches. First, there is the community to which a person considers themself belonging; thus someone who never goes to church, who is asked when they go into hospital: 'What is your religion?' may reply they are 'C of E' or 'Catholic'. Secondly, there is membership as defined by the individual groups. Anglicans can join their parish Electoral Roll if they are over 16 and live within the parish, whereas Baptists teach the importance of adult baptism, and Pentecostalists the necessity to speak in tongues. These membership statistics are not therefore strictly comparable. Finally, and most restrictively, there is regular weekly church attendance.

The *UK Christian Handbook* publishes regular figures for the first two, community and membership, updated every two years. As for churchgoing, extensive church censuses have been undertaken in England in 1979 and 1989, Wales in 1982 and Scotland in 1984 and 1994. The 1989 English Church Census report was published under the title *'Christian' England*, and gave details of churchgoing by denomination, county, type of area and so on.

Christianity by Numbers published by MARC Europe in 1989 gives a bibliography of books with church data on subjects like church growth, church leadership, and the unreached, as well as listing the various denominational yearbooks and comparable works for Europe and further afield. Similar material is now collected and published by the Christian Research Association. Earlier information on statistical sources for religion is given in Volume XX, *'Religion' Reviews of UK Statistical Sources*, published jointly by the ESRC and the Royal Statistical Society.

More general works on religion in Britain in the twentieth century are: R. B. Braithwaite, *The State of Religious Belief* (1927); E. O. James, *History of Christianity in England* (1949); R. Lloyd, *The Church of England in the Twentieth Century* (2 vols, 1948–50); G. Spinks (ed.), *Religion in Britain since 1900* (1952); R. F. Wearmouth, *The Social and Political Influence of Methodism in the Twentieth Century* (1957); J. Highet, *The Scottish Churches* (1960); R. Currie (ed.), *Churches and Churchgoers* (1977). Maps on the strength of religion in Britain are given in *The Reader's Digest Atlas of Britain* (1965), and in John D. Gay, *The Geography of Religion in England* (1971).

The most convenient summary of facts and statistics is to be found in P. Brierley's chapter in A. H. Halsey (ed.), *Twentieth-Century British Social Trends* (2000).

THE CHURCH OF ENGLAND

Principal degrees of membership for the Provinces of Canterbury and York.
(Totals for 43 dioceses[a])

Year	Home pop. of the two provinces 000s	Estimated baptised membership		Estimated confirmed membership		Membership of parochial electoral rolls	
		000s[d]	Per 1000 home pop.	000s[d]	Per 1000 pop.13+[e]	000s	Per 1000 adults[i]
1901	30,673[b]	n.a.		n.a.		n.a.	
1911	33,807[b]	n.a.		n.a.		n.a.	
1921	35,390[b]	22,000	622	8,100	301	3,537[f]	140
1931	37,511[b]	23,800	634	9,000	302	3,686	145
1941	39,173[c]	24,900	636	9,200	294	3,423[g]	120
1951	41,330[b]	25,800	624	9,400	284	2,923[h]	95
1960	43,296	27,323	631	9,792	281	2,862	89
1970	46,429	27,736	597	9,514	205	2,559	73
1980	46,660[j]	27,113	581	8,700	185	1,815	52
1990	48,208[j]	26,855	557	n.a.	n.a.	1,540[k]	42
1996	48,935	25,000	511	n.a.	n.a.	1,290[k]	35

[a] In 1910 there were 15,864 parochial churches. In 1966 there were 17,755.

[b] Enumerated in the Registrar-General's censuses of ecclesiastical areas.

[c] Estimates based on the Registrar-General's annual estimates of population at 30th June.

[d] Calculated by the Statistical Unit of the Central Board of Finance of the Church of England by reference to the age composition of the home population, born and resident in the two provinces, and to the respective rates of infant baptisms at Anglican fonts per 1,000 live births, and to the respective rates of Anglican confirmations per 1,000 males and females living at age 15 years (it is not possible to include in these estimates baptised and confirmed Anglicans who were born abroad but are now resident in the two provinces).

[e] In the Church of England very few boys and girls are confirmed before the age of 13 years.

[fgh] Figures for 1924, 1940, and 1953 respectively.

[i] 1957 was the first year that persons of 17 years and over were included in the electoral rolls. In previous years the minimum age was 18 years.

[j] Population figures for 1980 and 1990 are based on the census figure the following year.

[k] Membership of parochial electoral rolls is revised downwards as a result of a review every six years; the 1990 and 1996 figures followed such reviews. The percentage is calculated as a proportion of the civil electoral register for England.

Sources: *Facts and Figures about the Church of England*, Nos. 1–3. Edited by R.F.Neuss, published by the Church Information Office (1966). *UK Christian Handbook*. The Statistical Unit, Central Board of Finance of the Church of England.

Archbishops and leading Bishops of the five principal Dioceses in the Church of England
(These are the only Sees automatically represented in the House of Lords)

Archbishops of Canterbury		*Archbishops of York*	
1896	F. Temple (Frederick Cantuar:)	1891	W. Maclagan (William Ebor:)
1903	R. Davidson (Randall Cantuar:)	1909	C. Lang (Cosmo Ebor:)
1928	C. Lang (Cosmo Cantuar:)	1929	W. Temple (William Ebor:)
1942	W. Temple (William Cantuar:)	1942	C. Garbett (Cyril Ebor:)
1945	G. Fisher (Geoffrey Cantuar:)	1956	A. Ramsey (Michael Ebor:)
1961	A. Ramsey (Michael Cantuar:)	1961	F. Coggan (Donald Ebor:)
1974	F. Coggan (Donald Cantuar:)	1974	S. Blanch (Stuart Ebor:)
1980	R. Runcie (Robert Cantuar:)	1983	J. Habgood (John Ebor:)
1991	G. Carey (George Cantuar:)	1995	D. Hope (David Ebor:)

Bishops of London

1897	M. Creighton (Mandell Londin:)
1901	A. Winnington-Ingram
	(A. F. Londin:)
1939	G. Fisher (Geoffrey Londin:)
1945	J. Wand (William Londin:)
1956	H. Campbell (Henry Londin:)
1961	R. Stopford (Robert Londin:)
1973	G. Ellison (Gerald Londin:)
1981	G. Leonard (Graham Londin:)
1991	D. Hope (David Londin:)
1995	R. Chartres (Richard Londin:)

Bishop of Durham

1890	B. Westcott (B. F. Dunelm:)
1901	H. Moule (Handley Dunelm:)
1920	H. Henson (Herbert Dunelm:)
1939	A. Williams (Alwyn Dunelm:)
1952	A. Ramsey (Michael Dunelm:)
1956	M. Harland (Maurice Dunelm:)
1966	I. Ramsey (Ian Dunelm:)
1973	J. Habgood (John Dunelm:)
1984	D. Jenkins (David Dunelm:)
1994	M. Turnbull (Michael Dunelm:)

Bishops of Winchester

1895	R. Davidson (Randall Winton:)
1903	H. Ryle (Herbert E. Winton:)
1911	E. Talbot (Edward Stuart Winton:)
1924	F. Woods (Theodore Winton:)
1932	C. Garbett (Cyril Winton:)
1942	M. Haigh (Mervyn Winton:)
1952	A. Williams (Alwyn Winton:)
1961	S. Allison (Falkner Winton:)
1974	J. Taylor (John Winton:)
1985	C. James (Colin Winton:)
1995	M. Scott-Joynt (Michael Winton:)

THE CHURCH IN WALES

The Church in Wales was disestablished from 31 March 1920

Year	Parochial Easter Day Communicants Estimated No. (000s)	No. of Churches
1920	160,000	1,755
1930	151,000	1,774
1940	175,000	1,766
1950	168,000	n.a.
1960	183,000	1,783
1970	155,000	1,720
1980	132,000	1,675
1990	108,000	1,142
1998	96,000	

Source: HMSO *Social Trends*; *Whitaker's Almanack*; *UK Christian Handbook*; and the Secretary, the Representative Body of the Church in Wales.

EPISCOPAL CHURCH IN SCOTLAND

Year	Permanent Members 000s	No. of Church Buildings
1900	116	354
1910	142	404
1920	144	416
1930	134	415
1940	124	404
1950	109	397
1960	97	369
1970	86	341
1980	71	311
1990	58	310
1998	54	320

Sources: *The Year Book for the Episcopal Church in Scotland; Whitaker's Almanack; The Statesman's Year-Book; UK Christian Handbook.*

BAPTIST UNION
British Isles

Year	Members 000s	No. of Places of Worship
1900	366	2,579
1910	419	2,889
1920	405	2,866
1930	406	2,965
1940	382	3,044
1950	338	3,110
1960	318	3,053
1970	293	3,657
1980	240	3,344
1993	232	3,627
1998	202	2,942

These are statistics actually received from churches; no estimates are made for churches omitting to return figures. Figures cover the Baptist Union of Great Britain, the Baptist Unions of Wales, Scotland and Ireland, the Grace Baptist Assembly, Gospel Standard Strict Baptists and other Baptist Churches.

Sources: *The Baptist Handbook, 1900– .; Whitaker's Almanack.; The UK Christian Handbook.*

CONGREGATIONAL UNION
United Kingdom[a]

Year	Members 000s	No. of Places of Worship
1900	436	4,607[b]
1910	494	4,721
1930	490	3,556
1939	459	3,435
1950	387	3,173
1959	212	2,984
1965	198	2,799
1971	165	2,266

On 5 Oct 72 the Congregational Union merged with the Presbyterian Church of England to form the United Reformed Church.

[a] 1900 and 1910 figures for British Isles.
[b] Figure for 1901.

Source: *The Congregational Year Book, 1900–1972.*

PRESBYTERIAN CHURCH
England

Year	Members (000s)
1900	76
1911	87
1922	84
1930	84
1940	82
1950	82
1960	71
1965	70
1971	57

On 5 Oct 72 the Presbyterian Church in England merged with the Congregational Union to form the United Reformed Church.

Sources: 1900 and 1911, *The Official Handbook of of the Presbyterian Church of England;* 1922–72, *The Statesman's Year-Book.*

UNITED REFORMED CHURCH

	Members 000s	No. of Church Buildings
1973	192	2,139
1980	147	1,936
1990	120	1,813
1997	97	1,739

METHODIST CHURCH[a]
Great Britain and Ireland

	Members 000s	No.of Church Buildings
1900	794	9,037
1910	868	n.a.
1920	826	9,013
1930	868	9,070
1940	830	n.a.
1950	772	n.a.
1960	766	n.a.
1970	642	9,972
1980	531	8,492
1990	468	7,591
1995	398	6,907

[a] These are aggregate figures for all the major branches of Methodism. The Methodist Church was formed in 1932 by a union of the Wesleyan, Primitive and United Methodist Churches. The United Methodists were themselves formed by the union of three separate bodies in 1907.

Sources: *Minutes of the Methodist Conference, 1900–*; HMSO *Social Trends*; *Whitaker's Almanack*; *UK Christian Handbook.*

THE CHURCH OF SCOTLAND[a]
(Presbyterian)

Year	Total Communicants On Rolls	No. of Places of Worship
1900	662,000	n.a.
1910	714,000	1,703
1920	739,000	1,704
1930	1,271,000	2,795
1940	1,278,000	2,507
1951	1,271,000	2,348
1960	1,248,000	2,212
1970	1,154,000	2,088
1980	954,000	1,936
1990	787,000	1,813
1996	680,000	1,603

[a] In 1929 the United Free Church of Scotland rejoined the Church of Scotland, which accounts for the jump in figures.

Source: *The Church of Scotland Year Book; Whitaker's Almanack; UK Christian Handbook.*

THE ROMAN CATHOLIC CHURCH
Great Britain

Year	Estimated Catholic Population (000s)	Catholic Baptisms (000s)	No. of Public Churches and Chapels
1900	2,466	n.a.	1,536
1910	2,661	n.a.	1,773
1920	2,922	n.a.	1,408
1930	3,212	66	1,564
1940	3,471	70	1,802
1950	3,970	92	1,971
1960	4,845	123	3,204
1970	5,419	108	n.a.
1980	5,539	76	4,132
1990	5,624	80	4,297
1996	4,860	79	4,185

Sources: Census reports quoted in *The Statesman's Year-Book, 1900–. UK Christian Handbook.*

Roman Catholic Archbishops of Westminster

1892	H. Vaughan (Cardinal, 1893)
1903	F. Lourne (Cardinal, 1911)
1935	A. Hinsley (Cardinal, 1937)
1943	B. Griffin (Cardinal, 1946)
1956	W. Godfrey (Cardinal, 1958)
1963	J. Heenan (Cardinal, 1965)
1976	B. Hume (Cardinal, 1976)
1999	*(vacant)*

Source: *The Catholic Directory, 1900–.*

NORTHERN IRELAND
Religious Affiliations (000s)

Year	Roman Catholic	Presbyterian	Church of Ireland	Methodist	Other Denomination
1901	430	397	317	44	48
1911	430	395	327	46	50
1926	442	393	339	50	52
1937	428	391	345	55	58
1951	471	410	353	67	63
1961	498	413	345	72	71
1971	478	406	334	71	88
1981	415	340	281	59	113
1991	606	337	279	60	122

The figures for 1971, 1981 and 1991 are affected by much higher numbers giving 'no religion', or leaving the relevant questions blank. The totals in these categories rose from around 20,000 to 143,000 in 1971, 275,000 in 1981, and 174,000 in 1991.

Source: *Census reports.*

OTHER CHRISTIAN DENOMINATIONS

Data on the smaller denominations is of very uneven quality. However, some recent figures are worth recording.

Assemblies of God	75,000	(1998)		
Elim Pentecostal Church	68,500	(1998)		
Greek Orthodox	260,000	(1992)		
Jehovah's Witnesses	55,876	(1969)	130,000	(1998)
Mormons	180,000	(1998)		
(Plymouth) Brethren	81,000	(1992)		
Presbyterian Church of Wales	49,765	(1998)		
Salvation Army	65,168	(1998)		
Scientologists	80,000	(1992)		
Seventh-Day Adventists	19,145	(1998)		
Society of Friends (Quakers)	18,072	(1992)		
Unitarians	7,000	(1998)		
Welsh Independents	39,174	(1998)		

The Church of Christ, Scientist, does not publish estimates of its membership, but in 1991 it had 215 branch churches in the United Kingdom.

Sources: *Whitaker's Almanack; UK Christian Handbook.*

THE JEWISH COMMUNITY[a]
Great Britain

	Est. No.of Jews (000s)	Approx. No.of Synagogues
1900	160	80[d]
1910	243	200[d]
1920	287	200[d]
1929[b]	297	300[c]
1940	385[c]	200[c]
1950	450	240[c]
1960	450	240[c]
1970	450	240[c]
1980	410	321
1990	326	330
1998	285	365

a Statistics for 1900 for GB and Ireland, 1910 for British Isles, 1920 for UK, 1929 for GB, 1940 onwards for UK.
b No Jewish statistics available 1930–34.
c Including about 35,000 refugees.
d From *Whitaker's Almanack.*

Sources: *Whitaker's Almanack; the Statesman's Year-Book; the UK Christian Handbook.*

BUDDHISTS

	Members	Priests	Buildings
1970	6,000	38	8
1980	17,000	210	50
1990	28,000	350	105

HINDUS

	Members	Priests	Buildings
1970	50,000	80	60
1980	120,000	120	125
1990	140,000	150	140

MUSLIMS

	Members	Priests	Buildings
1970	204,000	1,000	75
1980	306,000	1,540	193
1990	505,000	2,500	350

SIKHS

	Members	Priests	Buildings
1970	75,000	100	
1980	150,000	140	105
1990	250,000	180	149

Marriages by Manner of Solemnisation
England and Wales

	1901	1911	1919	1934	1952	1962	1974	1980	1990	1995
Total (000s)	259	275	369	342	349	348	384	370	331	283
	%	%	%	%	%	%	%	%	%	%
C. of E.	66.6	61.1	59.7	53.5	49.6	47.4	35.8	33.3	34.8	29.6
R.C.	4.1	4.4	5.2	6.5	9.4	12.3	8.8	7.7	6.8	5.4
Jewish	0.7	0.7	0.5	0.7	0.5	0.4	0.4	0.3	0.3	0.3
Baptist			1.9	1.8	1.5	1.7	1.2	1.2	1.1	1.0
Cong.[a]	17.8	13.0	2.3	2.1	2.0	1.9	1.6	2.0	2.3	2.0
Methodist			5.6	5.3	4.8	4.9	4.1	4.5	5.1	4.5
Other Rel.			1.6	1.8	1.6	1.8	1.6	1.5	2.2	2.4
All Rel.	84.2	79.1	76.9	71.6	69.4	70.4	53.5	50.4	52.6	45.1
Secular	15.8	20.9	23.1	28.4	30.6	29.6	46.5	49.6	47.4	54.9
	100	100	100	100	100	100	100	100	100	100

[a] The Congregationalist figures since 1973 include United Reformed Church.

Source: *Annual Reports of the Registrar-General.*

BIBLIOGRAPHICAL NOTE

This book does not attempt to provide an extensive bibliography of works on British politics since 1900. We list below some attempts at comprehensive listings in various periods or fields. The main sources of factual data used in compiling this book are mentioned separately in the appropriate sections. There are, however, some works of reference of such major importance and reliability that it seems useful to collect them together here as a help or reminder to those involved in research.

This book originated before the advent of microfiches, CD-Roms and the Internet. Much of the material which could then only be found between hard covers is now available in machine-readable form. As the 1990s advanced, more and more newspaper and government publications appeared on the Internet, together with search-engines that have greatly facilitated the recovery of information. The broadsheet newspapers are available from 1988 onwards on CD-Rom and from the mid-1990s on the Internet. These can be difficult to use and some find the electronic *Telegraph* to be more user-friendly. Computerised Library Catalogues enable scholars to pursue research through increasingly sophisticated subject indexes. At the conclusion of this note a list of some of the most useful Internet sites available in 1999 is provided.

Many of the most useful sources of reference are Stationery Office publications. Summaries, guides, and short-cuts to these publications are provided in the *Stationery Office: Catalogue of Government Publications* (annually), the Sectional *Lists of Government Publications*, published by the Stationery Office for individual departments, the *List of Cabinet Papers 1880–1916* (P.R.O. handbooks), the *General Index to Parliamentary Papers, 1900–1949* (H.M.S.O.), the three volumes by P. and G. Ford, *Breviate of Parliamentary Papers* (1900–16, 1917–39, 1940–54), and C. Hughes, *The British Statute Book* (1957). An H.M.S.O. *Guide to Official Statistics* has been published biennially since 1976. J. G. Olle, *An Introduction to British Government Publications (1974)*, although dated, is still useful. Chadwyck-Healey have now published on CD-Rom and microfiche all government papers since 1986, together with a comprehensive catalogue.

For reference to day-to-day political events the *Official Index to The Times (1906–)* is the most complete guide, before 1906 *Palmer's Index to The Times* exists but it is difficult to use and by no means complete. *Keesing's Contemporary Archives* (1931–86), *Keesing's Record of World Events* (1987–), *and Keesing's Record of U.K. Events* (1988–97) give a concise summary of news reported in the national press, though they were not published in their present fuller form until 1937. Brief chronologies of the year's major events (including some very minor ones) are printed in the *Annual Register* (since 1954 the *Annual Register of World Events*), which also covers them in greater detail in the main text of the book. The Foreign Office have published an annual *Survey of World Affairs* since 1967. Fuller chronologies and narratives are available in the annual volumes *Contemporary Britain* published by the Institute of Contemporary British History since 1990. Briefer summaries of the year's events are to be found in *Whitaker's Almanack*.

For biographical details of leading figures in British politics since 1900 the main sources are the *Dictionary of National Biography* (1901–11 and in decennial or quinquennial volumes ever since, as well as *Missing Persons*), the *Concise Dictionary of National Biography*, 1901–70, *Who Was Who* (1897–1915, 1916–28, 1929–40, 1941–50, 1951–60, 1961–70, 1971–80, 1981–90, and 1991–95; there is a separate index volume for 1900–1990) and *Who's Who*, for those still alive. As supplements to these, for lesser-known figures in the Labour and Co-operative movement there is the *Labour Who's Who*, 1924 and 1927 (The Labour Publishing Company), the *Herald Book of Labour Members*

(1923, with a supplement in 1924, ed. S. Bracher), and the nine-volume *Dictionary of Labour Biography* (eds J. Bellamy and J. Saville).

Appointments are recorded in many official sources. The major annual publications are: the *Imperial Calendar and Civil Service List* (replaced in 1973 by two works, *Civil Service Year Book* and *Diplomatic List*), *H.M. Ministers and Heads of Public Departments* (published 1946–77, from four to six times a year and, after 1973, renamed *H.M. Ministers and Senior Staff in Public Departments* and now published annually, and the *London Gazette*, where appointments are announced officially, which appears about once a fortnight. Since 1978 the House of Commons has published a *Weekly Information Bulletin*. Official appointments are also recorded in the annual Lists of the Foreign Office, the Colonial Office, and the Commonwealth Relations Office, the *Army, Navy and Air Force Lists*, the *Law Lists*, and the *Annual Estimates* of the civil, revenue, and service departments.

There are handbooks on Parliament, giving the names of M.P.s, details of procedure and officials: *Dod's Parliamentary Companion* and *Vacher's Parliamentary Companion*. Up to 1931 Debrett's *Illustrated House of Commons and the Judicial Bench* is particularly useful. Valuable sources of reference for the House of Commons are the *House of Commons* published by the *Pall Mall Gazette* in 1906, 1910 and 1911. Since 1885 *The Times* has published a work after each General Election (1922–4 excepted) from 1885 to 1970 as *The (New) House of Commons* and since 1970 as *The Times Guide to the House of Commons*. M. Stenton and S. Lees with their *Who's Who of British Members of Parliament* (Volumes 2–4 cover 1886 to 1979) offer the most compact single source of M.P.s' biographies. Other biographical information can be found in Burke's *Dictionary of the Landed Gentry*, L. G. Pine, *The New Extinct Peerage, 1884–1971* (1972), the *Directory of Directors*, the *(International) Authors' and Writers' Who's Who*, and other directories or registers devoted to the members of particular professions, or to the alumni of particular schools and universities. C. Hazlehurst, *A Guide to the Papers of British Cabinet Ministers 1900–64* (1975) can lead to much recherché material. Over the years A. Roth has produced many volumes of *Parliamentary Profiles*.

The annual almanacks are also an extremely useful source of information. Amongst these the most notable are: the *Constitutional Year Book* (published annually until 1939), *Whitaker's Almanack*, *The Statesman's Year-Book*, the *Yearbook of International Organisations*, the *United Nations Yearbook*, and *Britain: An Official Handbook* (published with varying titles by the Central Office of Information). Another valuable source is *Councils, Committees, and Boards* (10th ed. 1998).

The major sources for British statistics are quoted in notes to the tables throughout the book. The most readily available is the official *Annual Abstract of Statistics*. This appears both annually, and in a form covering ten-year periods since 1945. The *Monthly Digest of Statistics* is also very helpful. The Censuses of Population, Industry and Production, though infrequent, provide the firmest figures in their area – much of the information in annual publications is only estimated. The reports of the major revenue departments, the Commissioners for Customs and Excise, the Commissioners for Inland Revenue, and the Registrars-General for England and Wales and for Scotland, are major sources of statistical information; so are the reports of the other government Departments, and especially the *Gazette* produced until 1995 by the Ministry of Labour and its successor ministries (until 1917 this was the Board of Trade *Labour Gazette*); it was succeeded by *Labour Market Trends* in 1995. There is also the annual *Abstract of Labour Statistics*. Other major sources of information are the monthly *Financial Staistics,* the London and Cambridge Economic Service published about three times a year in *The Times' Review of Industry*, B. R. Mitchell and P. Deane *British Historical Statistics* (2nd ed.1988); and C. Feinstein, *National Income, Expenditure and Output of the UK 1865–1945* (1972). Many of the

Feinstein time-series are continued in the annual Blue Books on *National Income and Expenditure* (1969–). Much statistical information is presented in A. H. Halsey, *Twentieth-Century British Social Trends* (2000).

A useful guide to works on British politics is the subject index of the British Library which covers the period up to 1975. Bibliographical references can be checked through the *British National Bibliography* and the *Cumulative Book Index*; there is also the *London Bibliography of the Social Sciences* (published from 1931 to 1989 and then absorbed into the *International Bibliography of the Social Sciences* (published annually since 1953). For information on many aspects of British politics the *Encyclopaedia Britannica* or *Chambers Encyclopaedia* may give a lead. Weekly Journals, especially *The Economist* (which is indexed), may provide much additional information. Apart from *The Times*, the national dailies were not indexed for the pre-electronic age, which makes reference a slow process. But some newspaper libraries have their own index system and may be of help.

The learned journals with most material on British politics are the *Political Quarterly* (1930–); *Parliamentary Affairs* (1947–); *Public Administration* (1923–85) and *Public Policy and Administration* (1986–); *Political Studies* (1953–); *British Journal of Political Science* (1971–); *The Table* (the Journal of the Commonwealth Parliamentary Association, 1931); *Government and Opposition* (1965–); the *Journal of Contemporary History* (1966–);*Contemporary British History* (1986–); and *Twentieth Century British History (1990–)*. *International Political Science Abstracts,* published annually since 1951, gives a classified abstract of journal articles and so does the *British Humanities Index* (1962–).

K. Robbins, *Bibliography of British History 1914–89* (1996) comes nearest to providing a single bibliography for this century. For the early years, a valuable guide is H. J. Hanham, *Bibliography of British History 1851–1914* (1976). The most comprehensive work is P. Catterall's *British History 1945–87: an Annotated Bibliography* (1994). Other bibliographies include R.U. Goehlert & F. S. Martin, *The Parliament of Great Britain: a Bibliography* (1983); J. Fletcher & N. Cooper, *Government* (Br. Council Bibliographical Section 1994); and I. Budge et al., *The New British Politics* (1998) which contains an annotated bibliography. An extensive bibliography is available for 1918–39 in C. L. Mowat's *Britain between the Wars* (1955), supplemented by his *British History since 1926: A Select Bibliography* (The Historical Association, 1960). Another critical bibliography is supplied by A. J. P. Taylor in *English History 1914–45* (1966). See also R. M. Punnett, *British Government and Politics* (1971). Other bibliographies include J. Palmer, *Government and Parliament in Britain: A Bibliography* (1964, The Hansard Society). Helpful bibliographies are to be found in A. F. Havinghurst, *Modern England 1901–70* (1976), B. Stevenson, *Reader's Guide to Great Britain* (1977), and J. Westergaard, A. Weyman and P. Wiles, *Modern British Society: a Bibliography* (1977).

British Politics: Internet Resources

This list is far from exhaustive, but most of the sites below have links to other relevant sites. One problem with information available on the Internet is that sites are continually appearing or disappearing, whilst the addresses of others are liable to alter. Publications such as *Whitaker's Almanack* and *Official UK* carry current Internet addresses for Government Departments and for Parliament. J. White, *Politico's Guide to Politics on the Internet* (1999) contains reviews of some 100 political Internet sites and a listing of more than 3,000 others. All of the Internet addresses that follow are correct as of 17 December 1999.

News

Electronic Telegraph: <URL: http://www.telegraph.co.uk>
Daily Telegraph Comment: <URL: http://www.dailytelegraph.co.uk>
The Economist: <URL: http://www.economist.com>
The Express: <URL: http://www.express.co.uk>
The Guardian and The Observer: <URL: http://www.guardian.co.uk>
Financial Times: <URL: http://www.ft.com>
The Independent: <URL: http://www.independent.co.uk>
The Mirror: <URL: http://www.mirror.co.uk>
The Scotsman: <URL: http://www.scotsman.com>
The Times and The Sunday Times: <URL: http://www.the-times.co.uk>
Palmer's Index to The Times and Palmer's Full Text Online: <URL: http://history.chadwyck.co.uk>

BBC News Online: <URL: http://news.bbc.co.uk>
Sky News: <URL: http://www.skynews.co.uk>

Television

BBC: <URL: http://www.bbc.co.uk>
Channel 4: <URL: http://www.channel4.com>
Channel 5: <URL: http://www.channel5.co.uk>
CNN: <URL: http://www.cnn.com>
ITV: <URL: http://www.itv.co.uk>
Sky TV:<URL: http://www.sky.co.uk>

Political Parties

Conservative Party: <URL: http://www.conservative-party.org.uk>
Labour Party: <URL: http://www.labour.org.uk>
Liberal Democratic Party: <URL: http://www.libdems.org.uk>

Plaid Cymru: <URL: http://www.plaidcymru.org>
Scottish Conservative Party: <URL: http://www.scottish.tory.org.uk>
Scottish Labour Party: <URL: http://www.scottish.labour.co.uk>
Scottish Liberal Democrats: <URL: http://www.scotlibdems.org.uk>
Scottish Nationalist Party: <URL: http://www.snp.org.uk>

Alliance Party:<http://www.allianceparty.org>
DUP: <URL: http://www.dup.org.uk>
SDLP: <URL: http://www.indigo.ie/sdlp>
Sinn Fein <URL: http://www.sinnfein.ie>
UUP: <URL: http://www.uup.org>

Government Departments and Agencies

Government Information Service: <URL: http://www.open.gov.uk>
Official UK – Guide to Government Websites: <URL: http://www.officialuk.co.uk>
Directory of UK Government on the Web: <URL: http://www.tagish.co.uk/tagish/links/offices.htm>
Central Office of Information (Government press releases): <URL: http://www.coi.gov.uk>

The British Monarchy: <URL: http://www.royal.gov.uk>
No. 10 Downing Street: <URL: http://www.number-10.gov.uk>
Benefits Agency (Dept of Social Security): <URL: http://www.dss.gov.uk/ba/index.htm>
The Cabinet Office: <URL: http://www.cabinet-office.gov.uk>
Child Support Agency (Dept of Social Security): <URL: http://www.dss.gov.uk/csa/index.htm>
Competiton Commission: <URL: http://www.mmc.gov.uk>
Crown Prosecution Service <URL: http://www.cps.gov.uk>
Dept for Culture, Media and Sport <URL: http://www.culture.gov.uk>
Dept for Education and Employment: <URL: http://www.dfee.gov.uk>
Dept of the Environment, Transport and the Regions: <URL: http://www.detr.gov.uk>
Dept of Health: <URL: http://www.doh.gov.uk/dhhome.htm>
Dept for International Development: <URL: http://www.dfid.gov.uk>
Dept of Social Security: <URL: http://www.dss.gov.uk>
Dept of Trade and Industry: <URL: http://www.dti.gov.uk>
Foreign and Commonwealth Office: <URL: http://www.fco.gov.uk>
HM Treasury: <URL: http://www.hm-treasury.gov.uk>
The Home Office: <URL: http://www.homeoffice.gov.uk>
The Lord Chancellor's Dept: <URL: http://www.open.gov.uk/lcd>
Millennium Experience, Greenwich: <URL: http://www.dome2000.co.uk/sniff/flash.htm>
Ministry of Agriculture, Fisheries and Food: <URL: http://www.maff.gov.uk>
Ministry of Defence: <URL: http://www.mod.uk>
The National Audit Office: <URL: http://www.open.gov.uk/nao>
National Insurance Contributions (Inland Revenue): <URL: http://www.inlandrevenue.gov.uk>
Office of National Statistics: <URL: http://www.ons.gov.uk/ons_f.htm>
Public Record Office: <URL: http://www.pro.gov.uk>
The Women's Unit: <URL: http://www.womens-unit.gov.uk>

The Northern Ireland Executive: <URL: http://www.northernireland.gov.uk>
The Northern Ireland Office: <URL: http://www.nio.gov.uk>
The Scottish Executive: <URL: http://www.scotland.gov.uk>

Parliament

Parliament: <URL: http://www.parliament.uk>
Hansard – House of Commons: <URL: http://www.publications.parliament.uk/pa/cm/cmpubns.htm>
Hansard – House of Lords: <URL: http://www.publications.parliament.uk/pa/ld/ldhansrd.htm>
House of Commons Research Papers: <URL: http://www.parliament.uk/commons/lib/research/rpintro.htm>
Bills Before Parliament: <URL: http://www.publications.parliament.uk/pa/pabills.htm>
Acts of Parliament and Other Legislation: <URL: http://www.legislation.hmso.gov.uk>

Hansard Society: <URL: http://www.hansard-society.org.uk>
Hansard Society Democracy Forum: <URL: http://www.democracyforum.org.uk>

The Stationery Office: <URL: http://www.tsonline.co.uk/>
UK Official Documents: <URL: http://www.official-documents.co.uk>

National Assembly for Wales: <URL: http://www.wales.gov.uk>
The Northern Ireland Assembly: <URL: http://www.ni-assembly.gov.uk>
The Scottish Parliament: <URL: http://www.scottish.parliament.uk>
Local Government Information Unit <URL: http://www.lgiu.gov.uk>

Other British Politics Resources

British Election Manifestos since 1945: <URL: http://www.psr.keele.ac.uk/area/uk/man.htm>
Cartoons Archive – University of Kent: <URL: http://library.ukc.ac.uk/cartoons>
Institute of Historical Research: <URL: http://www.ihrinfo.ac.uk>
International Bibliography of the Social Sciences: <URL: http://www.bids.ac.uk>
Keele University – UK Politics Resources:<URL: http://www.psr.keele.ac.uk/area/uk.htm>
Social Science Information Gateway: <URL: http://sosig.esrc.bris.ac.uk>

Encyclopaedia Britannica: <URL: http://www.britannica.com>

International Organisations

The Commonwealth Secretariat: <URL: http://www.thecommonwealth.org>
European Parliament: <URL: http://www.europarl.eu.int>
NATO: <URL: http://www.nato.int>
United Nations: <URL: http://www.un.org>
World Bank: <URL: http://www.worldbank.org>

INDEX